Kerrie Meyler,
Cameron Fuller,
John Joyner

With Andy Dominey

System Center Operations Manager 2007

UNLEASHED

SAMS | 800 East 96th Street, Indianapolis, Indiana 46240 USA

System Center Operations Manager 2007 Unleashed

ISBN-13: 978-0-672-32955-5
ISBN-10: 0-672-32955-7

Library of Congress Cataloging-in-Publication Data:

Meyler, Kerrie.
  System center operations manager 2007 unleashed / Kerrie Meyler, Cameron Fuller, John Joyner ; with Andy Dominey.
      p. cm.
  Includes bibliographical references and index.
  ISBN 0-672-32955-7 (alk. paper)
  1. Electronic data processing—Management. 2. Computer systems—Evaluation. 3. Computer networks—Management. 4. Microsoft Windows server. I. Fuller, Cameron. II. Joyner, John. III. Dominey, Andy. IV. Title.
   QA76.9.M3M59 2008
   005.4'476—dc22

                                 2008000571

Printed in the United States on America

First Printing February 2008

Trademarks

All terms mentioned in this book that are known to be trademarks or service marks have been appropriately capitalized. Sams Publishing cannot attest to the accuracy of this information. Use of a term in this book should not be regarded as affecting the validity of any trademark or service mark.

Warning and Disclaimer

Every effort has been made to make this book as complete and as accurate as possible, but no warranty or fitness is implied. The information provided is on an "as is" basis. The authors and the publisher shall have neither liability nor responsibility to any person or entity with respect to any loss or damages arising from the information contained in this book or from the use of the CD or programs accompanying it.

Bulk Sales

Sams Publishing offers excellent discounts on this book when ordered in quantity for bulk purchases or special sales. For more information, please contact

   U.S. Corporate and Government Sales

   1-800-382-3419

   corpsales@pearsontechgroup.com

For sales outside of the U.S., please contact

   International Sales

   international@pearsoned.com

Editor-in-Chief
Karen Gettman

Executive Editor
Neil Rowe

Development Editor
Mark Renfrow

Managing Editor
Gina Kanouse

Senior Project Editor
Lori Lyons

Copy Editor
Bart Reed

Indexer
Cheryl Lenser

Proofreader
Lisa Stumpf

Technical Editors
Kevin Saye,
Brett Bennett

Publishing Coordinator
Cindy Teeters

Multimedia Developer
Dan Scherf

Book Designer
Gary Adair

Composition
Jake McFarland

Manufacturing Buyer
Dan Uhrig

Safari
BOOKS ONLINE
ENABLED

The Safari® Enabled icon on the cover of your favorite technology book means the book is available through Safari Bookshelf. When you buy this book, you get free access to the online edition for 45 days. Safari Bookshelf is an electronic reference library that lets you easily search thousands of technical books, find code samples, download chapters, and access technical information whenever and wherever you need it.

To gain 45-day Safari Enabled access to this book:

▶ Go to http://www.samspublishing.com/safarienabled
▶ Complete the brief registration form
▶ Enter the coupon code XELV-7D4M-5ES2-RXM6-HBNE

If you have difficulty registering on Safari Bookshelf or accessing the online edition, please e-mail customer-service@safaribooksonline.com.

Contents at a Glance

Table of Contents

Part IV   Administering Operations Manager 2007

About the Authors

Kerrie Meyler, MA, BA, MCT, MCSE, CNA, MOM MVP, is an independent consultant and trainer with more than 15 years of Information Technology experience. A previous Senior Technology Specialist at Microsoft, she focused on infrastructure and management solutions, presenting at numerous product launches. Kerrie was also a Management Insider, presented at internal Microsoft conferences, and received company recognition and awards, including a SPAR MGS award. Kerrie presented on Operations Manager 2007 and gave several podcasts at TechEd 2007. As an MCT, she worked with Microsoft Learning on Microsoft Official Curriculum (MOC) for several courses, and did the "beta teach" for course 2250, "Implementing Microsoft Operations Manager 2000." More recently, Kerrie participated in the alpha walkthrough for Certification Exam 70-400, "Configuring Microsoft System Center Operations Manager 2007." She also participated in defining the domain objectives for Certification Exam 70-402, "IT Operations and Service Management." Kerrie is the lead author of *Microsoft Operations Manager 2005 Unleashed*, and was awarded the MOM MVP award just as this book was being completed.

Cameron Fuller, BS, MCSE, MOM MVP, is a Managing Consultant for Catapult Systems, an IT consulting company and Microsoft Gold Certified Partner with numerous competencies, including Advanced Infrastructure and Network Infrastructure Solutions. He focuses on management solutions, and serves as the Microsoft Operations Management Champion for Catapult. Cameron's 15 years of infrastructure experience include work in the retail, education, healthcare, distribution, transportation, and energy industries. Cameron continually focuses on improving his existing business and technical skill sets through hands-on experience and leveraging certifications, including MCSE (since NT 3.51), MCSA, A+, Linux+, Server+, and CCSA. Cameron is also a public speaker, presenting on Operations Manager 2007 at TechEd 2007, co-presenting with Microsoft on MOM 2005 at TechEd 2005, and the MOM 2005 product launches in Dallas and Tulsa. He is the co-author of *Microsoft Operations Manager 2005 Unleashed*.

John Joyner, LCDR USN-R, BS, MCSE, MOM MVP, is a presenter and inventor in the systems management space. A senior architect at ClearPointe—a leader and pioneer in the Managed Services Provider (MSP) industry—he has been using Microsoft systems management technologies to deliver SLA-based guarantees of application performance in multitenant environments since 2001. John received his B.S. in Business Administration on a U.S. Navy scholarship. As a Navy computer scientist, he deployed Microsoft Mail to the battlefield for NATO in the former Yugoslavia in 1995, and then took Exchange 4.0 afloat in 1996 for the first Internet-connected aircraft carrier battle group deployment in history. John retired a Lieutenant Commander from the Navy in 1998 and has worked for ClearPointe since then. He has provided consulting services on behalf of Microsoft to design some of the world's largest Operations Manager deployments. John speaks Italian and Dutch, and visits his daughter in Amsterdam as often as possible. John is a contributing author of *Microsoft Operations Manager 2005 Unleashed*, and was recently selected as a MOM MVP.

Contributor

Andy Dominey, MCSE, MOM MVP, has been in the IT industry for 8 years. He started out as a field service and support engineer and worked his way up to systems administrator, responsible for MOM, Active Directory, Exchange, web hosting, SAN technology, and clustering for an Exchange hosting provider based in the United Kingdom. He is currently working as a Senior Consultant for 1E, a Windows-management firm based in the United Kingdom. Andy has a number of large-scale MOM and OpsMgr deployments to his credit and is an avid evangelist for the product. He was also awarded the Microsoft Most Valuable Professional (MVP) award for MOM for the past 3 years. Andy authored *Microsoft Operations Manager 2005 Field Guide (Expert's Voice)*.

Dedication

We dedicate this book to the children in our thoughts as we labored over "the book."

To Ethan: When you smile, the room and the world light up. Thank you for constantly reminding me of the innocence and wonder of a child.

—Kerrie

To my children, Gavin and Alyssa: Alyssa, thank you for constantly giving me reasons to smile. Gavin, thank you for reminding me how marvelous the world is. Thank you both for who you are and for who you will become.

—Cameron

To my daughter, Ava: Knowledge and riches are nothing without love, and I love you. This fine book was great to work on, but Ava, you mean the world to me!

—John

Acknowledgments

Writing a book is an all-encompassing and time-consuming project, and this book meets that description in every way. *System Center Operations Manager 2007 Unleashed* would not be what it is without the support and assistance of numerous individuals.

We would like to extend our deep thanks and appreciation to those who assisted with this project. This includes (in alphabetical order by last name) Dan Anderson, Mike Baiano, Neale Brown, Ed Carnes, Walter Chomak, Bernie Chouinard, Drew Davis, Maarten Goet and the Techlog forum, Tony Greco, Tarek Ismail, Trevor Langston, Stan Liebowitz, Brendon McCaulley, Jack Meltzer, Robert Mouton, Kendra Thorpe, and Pete Zerger and his System Center forum.

Thank you as well to Erik McCarty, Judith Adams, and Chris Zeppa of Parker College for contributing scripts to disable and delete Active Directory user and computer objects and send email notifications to administrators. A huge thanks also to all the MOM MVPs for their continued contributions to the Operations Manager community—and we can't forget Justin Incarnato of Microsoft, for all he does to make the MOM MVP community work!

We would also like to thank Cameron's and John's employers, Catapult Systems and ClearPointe, respectively, for their support while we were writing this book. Additional thanks are due to our reviewers: Kevin Saye and Brett Bennett; the Microsoft MOM Team, including (alphabetically) Joseph Chan, Justin Incarnato, Ian Jirka, Dale Koetke, Lorenzo Rizzi, Thomas Theiner, and Boris Yanushpolsky; and to the Sams publishing team, including Neil Rowe, Curt Johnson, Lori Lyons, and Jake McFarland. A special thanks to Andy Dominey for helping as a contributing author, and Pete Zerger for providing valuable troubleshooting assistance.

To all of you—this book would not be what it is without your help!

We Want to Hear from You!

As the reader of this book, *you* are our most important critic and commentator. We value your opinion and want to know what we're doing right, what we could do better, what areas you'd like to see us publish in, and any other words of wisdom you're willing to pass our way.

You can email or write me directly to let me know what you did or didn't like about this book—as well as what we can do to make our books stronger.

Please note that I cannot help you with technical problems related to the topic of this book, and that due to the high volume of mail I receive, I might not be able to reply to every message.

When you write, please be sure to include this book's title and author as well as your name and phone or email address. I will carefully review your comments and share them with the author and editors who worked on the book.

Email: feedback@samspublishing.com.

Mail: Neil Rowe
Executive Editor
Sams Publishing
800 East 96th Street
Indianapolis, IN 46240 USA

Reader Services

Visit our website and register this book at informit.com/register for convenient access to any updates, downloads, or errata that might be available for this book.

Introduction

The process of operations management is a combination of people, procedures, and tools—all three are necessary, and the absence of one component can put an entire enterprise solution at risk. At a more granular level, operations management is about correlating what may appear to be seemingly unrelated events and data across machines to determine what information is significant to your operational environment versus what is not.

With System Center Operations Manager 2007, Microsoft continues its commitment to providing a solid monitoring and management product. Although Microsoft licensed NetIQ's Operation Manager technology in 2000, not until Operations Manager 2007 did Microsoft put its finishing touches on reengineering the product. Now in its third major release, the software formerly known as "MOM," or Microsoft Operations Manager, has been rewritten and rebranded into Microsoft's System Center product line. Operations Manager 2007 concentrates on end-to-end application monitoring, moving beyond its previous server monitoring focus.

Operations Manager 2007 monitors the health of an application, defined and measured by the health of the various pieces that make up that application. In today's environment, applications are no longer monolithic, so monitoring health typically includes network devices and the various pieces of a distributed application. Monitoring at the component level means that if a database used by an application has a problem, Operations Manager knows which application is affected.

Operations Manager 2007 also brings to the plate the capability to manage security and audit data, client machines, and common desktop applications, and collect and report on user application errors. Rather than being evolutionary in its changes as are most version updates to an application, Operations Manager 2007 is truly revolutionary in its approach to monitoring when compared to its MOM 2005 predecessor.

Successfully implementing Operations Manager requires planning, design, and a thorough understanding of how to utilize its many capabilities. This complete guide for using Operations Manager 2007 from the authors of *Microsoft Operations Manager 2005 Unleashed* gives system administrators the information they need to know about Operations Manager 2007 and what it can do for their operations—from an overview of why operations management is important, to planning, installing, and implementing Operations Manager 2007.

Microsoft System Center Operations Manager 2007 Unleashed provides a comprehensive guide to this newest version of Microsoft's premier management product.

As always, we do have a disclaimer: Resources and management packs related to the product continue to change rapidly. Sometimes it seemed that even before we finished a chapter, the information was changing. This has been particularly challenging because Microsoft is close to releasing its first service pack for Operations Manager 2007 as we complete this book. We have done our best to present the information as it relates to both the released version and the service pack, even as that continues to take shape. The information in the book is current as of the time it was written, and the authors have done their best to keep up with the constant barrage of changing management packs, utilities, URLs, and Knowledge Base articles.

Part I: Operations Management Overview and Concepts

Part I of this book introduces the reader to Operations Manager 2007 (OpsMgr), outlining its features and functionality and comparing and contrasting it to MOM 2005.

- ▶ Chapter 1, "Operations Management Basics," discusses the concepts behind operations management and Microsoft's management approach, and introduces Microsoft's management suite of products. An overview of ITIL and MOF (and an alphabet soup of other acronyms) is included, along with a discussion of how the different MOF quadrants relate to Operations Manager.

- ▶ Chapter 2, "What's New," appropriately tells you just that. You will find there is an incredible amount of new functionality in this version! We also cover the history of Operations Manager and compare OpsMgr 2007 with MOM 2005 and System Center Essentials 2007.

- ▶ Chapter 3, "Looking Inside OpsMgr," discusses the Operations Manager components, its processing flow and architecture, and how management packs work.

Part II: Planning and Installation

Before diving into OpsMgr's setup program, it is best to take a step back to map out the requirements for your management environment and plan your server topology.

- ▶ Chapter 4, "Planning Your Operations Manager Deployment," discusses the steps required for successfully planning an Operations Manager installation. We also introduce the OpsMgr databases sizing spreadsheet and discuss the logic behind the sizing calculations.

- ▶ Chapter 5, "Planning Complex Configurations," addresses advanced implementations of OpsMgr. We also discuss planning for redundancy and designing large and more interesting environments.

- ▶ In Chapter 6, "Installing Operations Manager 2007," we discuss hardware and software requirements before going through the steps to install the various server components in a management group.

- ▶ Chapter 7, "Migrating to Operations Manager 2007," discusses the required steps to migrate from an existing MOM 2005 environment to OpsMgr 2007. Note that the process is a migration, not an upgrade. If you have MOM 2005, you will want to read this chapter—because not everything can be migrated.

Part III: Moving Toward Application-Centered Management

With OpsMgr 2007 installed, how does one start using it? Part III moves beyond setup to post-installation activities and potential adjustments to your initial configuration.

- ▶ Chapter 8, "Configuring and Using Operations Manager 2007," discusses what you need to know to get started with OpsMgr. We provide an overview of the Operations console and a drilldown into its functionality.

- ▶ Chapter 9, "Installing and Configuring Agents," goes through the details of computer discovery, the different techniques for implementing agents, and potential problems related to agent installation.

- ▶ Chapter 10, "Complex Configurations," discusses various management server and management group configurations, and presents suggestions for implementing redundant components.

- ▶ In Chapter 11, "Securing Operations Manager 2007," we discuss role-based security, Run As Profiles and Accounts, required accounts, and mutual authentication, as well as when you need and how to install certificates. We also discuss security for the ACS component, an optional but highly recommended part of your OpsMgr implementation.

Part IV: Administering Operations Manager 2007

All applications require administration, and OpsMgr is no exception.

- ▶ Chapter 12, "Backup and Recovery," discusses the components required for a complete backup and recovery plan, and the steps for designing a disaster recovery plan.

- ▶ Chapter 13, "Administering Management Packs," covers the components of a management pack, how to troubleshoot, deploy, and manage management packs, and the details of converting, importing, and exporting management packs into your OpsMgr environment.

- ▶ Chapter 14, "Monitoring with Operations Manager," discusses the different monitors and rule types in Operations Manager and their functionality. It also covers creating alerts, overrides, resolution states, notification workflow, and approaches for tuning monitors and rules.

Part V: Service-Oriented Monitoring

In this section of the book we get into what Operations Manager 2007 is really about—using it to ease the pain of monitoring and managing your environment, from end-to-end. We discuss using OpsMgr to manage different aspects of your environment.

- ▶ Chapter 15, "Monitoring Audit Collection Services," focuses on auditing and security monitoring concerns. Audit Collection Services is a new component with OpsMgr 2007 that is a valuable addition to your monitoring toolkit.

- ▶ In Chapter 16, "Client Monitoring," we discuss new capabilities in OpsMgr for client monitoring. We also cover managing crash errors using the new Agentless Exception Monitoring functionality.

- ▶ Chapter 17, "Monitoring Network Devices," shows how to use Simple Network Management Protocol (SNMP) with OpsMgr and discusses monitoring hardware and network devices.

- ▶ Chapter 18, "Using Synthetic Transactions," talks about simulating connections into applications to verify their performance.

- ▶ Chapter 19, "Managing a Distributed Environment," discusses OpsMgr's capability to monitor the various pieces and components that make up the distributed applications commonly used in today's multisystem computing environment.

These chapters talk about the issues faced by administrators in each of these areas, and they show how Operations Manager 2007 helps to monitor operational issues and maintain application health and stability.

Part VI: Beyond Operations Manager

In this section we look at extending one's use of Operations Manager 2007 with connectors, third-party management packs, and customization. We also look at Microsoft's direction for operations management.

▶ Chapter 20, "Automatically Adapting Your Environment," begins the last part of the book by looking at how you can use Operations Manager 2007 to automatically adapt your environment as changes occur.

▶ Chapter 21, "Reading for the Service Provider: Remote Operations Manager," talks about utilizing OpsMgr 2007 in conjunction with System Center Essentials 2007 in Microsoft's hybrid product designed for use by service providers.

▶ In Chapter 22, "Interoperability," we cover connecting to other management groups, the role of product connectors in communicating with other management systems and third-party enterprise consoles, and integration between OpsMgr 2007 and other System Center components. This chapter also discusses management packs that monitor hardware, other operating systems, and network components.

▶ Chapter 23, "Developing Management Packs and Reports," discusses the process of customizing OpsMgr using management packs and reports. Although XML plays a big part in this, we also discuss other tools, including the part the Authoring and Operations consoles play in developing management packs.

Appendixes

This book contains six appendixes:

▶ Appendix A, "OpsMgr by Example: Configuring and Tuning Management Packs," is a compilation of articles from the *OpsMgr by Example* series published in our Operations Manager blog (http://ops-mgr.spaces.live.com).

▶ Appendix B, "Performance Counters," discusses the performance counters specific to Operations Manager.

▶ Appendix C, "Registry Settings," discusses some of the more significant Registry settings used by Operations Manager 2007.

▶ Appendix D, "Active Directory and Exchange 2003 Management Pack Parameters," lists parameters for shared scripts in the Active Directory (AD) and Exchange 2003 management packs.

▶ Appendix E, "Reference URLs," provides references and descriptions for many URLs helpful for OpsMgr administrators. These are also included on the CD as live links.

▶ Appendix F, "On the CD," discusses the utilities on the CD accompanying this book.

Conventions Used in This Book

Here's a quick look at a few book elements designed to help you get the most out of this book:

Text that you are supposed to type is styled in bold type, as in the following examples:

> In the Properties dialog, enter **Agent View** in the Name field.
>
> Open the Operations Manager command shell and enter the following command:
>
> **C:\DumpMPContents.ps1 –mpDisplayName:'*<management pack name>*'**

When a line of code is too long to fit on only one line of this book, it is broken at a convenient place and continued to the next line. The continuation of the line is preceded by a code continuation character (➡). You should type a line of code that has this character as one long line without breaking it.

NOTE

For Extra Information

The Note box presents asides that give you more information about the current topic. These tidbits provide extra insights that give you a better understanding of the task. In many cases, they refer you to other sections of the book for more information.

TIP

Quick Ideas

Tips point out quick ways to get the job done, or good ideas or techniques.

CAUTION

Important Information

Cautions contain warnings or significant material about potential pitfalls, including information critical to the proper functioning of your system.

About the CD

This book includes a CD containing scripts, utilities, and examples referred to throughout the book. It also includes live links from Appendix E to save you the trouble of having to type in what sometimes are lengthy and strange-looking URLs. The Operations Manager 2007 Resource Kit (Wave 1) is also on the CD.

Who Should Read This Book

This book is targeted towards systems professionals who want to be proactive in managing their operational environments. This book is targeted toward systems professionals who want to be proactive in managing their operational environments. These individuals are responsible for the operational health of the operating system and the subsystems running within it. This book should be a useful tool for system administrators regardless of the size of their organization or the industry in which it resides. By providing insight into Operation Manager's many capabilities, discussing tools to help with a successful implementation, and sharing real-world experiences, we hope to enable a more widespread understanding and use of System Center Operations Manager.

PART I

Operations Management Overview and Concepts

IN THIS PART

Operations Management Basics

W elcome to System Center Operations Manager 2007— Microsoft's revolutionary, completely revamped product for managing servers and applications in the Windows environment. System Center Operations Manager (OpsMgr) is a management tool that consolidates information about Windows servers and non-Windows devices, providing end-to-end monitoring of your applications and services, and centralized administration. Operations Manager gives you the resources you need to get and stay in control of your Windows environment and helps with managing, tuning, and securing Windows Server and Windows-based applications. For example, Operations Manager includes the following capabilities:

▶ **End-to-end service monitoring**—Using the Distributed Application Designer, OpsMgr provides a new design surface to define relationships between components and assemble them together, giving you proactive management of your IT services.

▶ **Best of breed for Windows**—OpsMgr reduces your time for problem resolution. Microsoft's management packs include Microsoft expertise for Windows applications, servers, and clients.

▶ **Increased efficiency and control**—Operations Manager 2007 simplifies managing your Information Technology (IT) environment and improves its time-to-value. Microsoft's newest version of its flagship management tool includes role-based security, a self-monitoring infrastructure, and improved scalability.

This chapter introduces System Center Operations Manager 2007. Various abbreviations for the product include SCOM, OM, Operations Manager, and OpsMgr; throughout this book, we use Microsoft's preferred nomenclature of Operations Manager and OpsMgr. Operations Manager 2007, now in its third major release, is Microsoft's software solution for facilitating server operations management. OpsMgr 2007 is Microsoft's latest version of the product, with numerous portions completely rewritten and re-architected. The software contains many improvements over the previous version, including a focus on health with increased scalability, enhanced security, and service-oriented monitoring capabilities, such as application monitoring, synthetic transactions, and client and network device monitoring.

This chapter also discusses the concepts behind operations management and examines Microsoft's management approach and Dynamic Systems Initiative (DSI). We provide an overview and comparison of two methodologies for approaching operations management: the Information Technology Infrastructure Library (ITIL) standard and the Microsoft Operations Framework (MOF). We discuss ISO 20000, and how Microsoft's Infrastructure Optimization Model relates to MOF. These discussions are important because of OpsMgr's alignment with model-based monitoring. Additionally, we discuss the operations management basics of managing system health.

Ten Reasons to Use Operations Manager

So, why use Operations Manager? You may be thinking that the features Microsoft talks about sound "cool" but also are wondering why you need Operations Manager, given that new systems seldom are approved just because they are "cool." Although this book will go over the features and benefits of Operations Manager 2007, it helps to have a few short answers here that quickly bring the point home.

Let's look at ten compelling reasons why you might want to use Operations Manager:

1. The bulk of your department's budget goes towards maintaining current systems and services, rather than using the bucks to hire people to manage those assets or develop new systems.

2. You realize system monitoring would be much easier if you had a single view of the health of your environment, including the applications and services running in production.

3. You feel stuck in the IT version of the movie *Groundhog Day*—you solve the same problems over and over again every day in exactly the same way, except unlike in the movie, you and your systems can really die. Plus, this is not a particularly efficient way to maintain operations.

4. You don't have enough internal manpower (or brainpower) to solve problems as they come up, and consultants aren't cheap.

5. You find out there are problems when users (or upper management) start calling you. Although this mechanism is actually quite effective in getting your attention, it is somewhat stress inducing and definitely not proactive.

6. You realize that even though your servers are humming along just fine, you have no idea how your client applications are actually performing against what is running on those servers. This makes it tough to know whether latency issues exist.

7. Complying with regulations such as Sarbanes-Oxley takes up all the time you once had to do your real job.

8. You would be more productive if you weren't monitoring your production environment all day...and night. And during lunch and vacation.

9. Your production environment is so diverse and widespread that when a problem arises, you don't even know where to start looking.

10. You don't have the time to write down all the troubleshooting information that is in your brain, and your boss is concerned you might be hit by a truck (or want to take that vacation). This probably is not the best way to run a production environment.

Although these ten points contain some humor and a bit of satire, if any of these themes resonate with you, you really owe it to yourself to investigate OpsMgr 2007. These painful points are common to almost all users of Microsoft technologies, and System Center Operations Manager resolves them to a great degree.

However, the biggest reasons of all for using OpsMgr are confidence and *peace of mind*. Deploying Operations Manager allows you to relax; you can be secure in the knowledge that with OpsMgr watching your back, your systems will be in good shape.

The Problem with Today's Systems

Microsoft describes OpsMgr 2007 as a software solution that can meet the need for end-to-end service monitoring in an enterprise Information Technology environment. What exactly does this mean? Operations Manager provides an easy-to-use monitoring environment, is able to watch thousands of event and performance monitors across systems and applications, and provides a single view of the health of your operations environment.

These capabilities are significant because today's IT systems are prone to a number of problems from the perspective of operations management, including the following:

▶ Isolation

▶ Lack of notification

▶ Lack of historical information

▶ Not enough expertise

▶ Lack of methodology

▶ Missing information and notifications

▶ False alarms

This list should not be surprising because these problems manifest themselves in all IT shops with varying degrees of severity. In fact, Forrester Research estimates that 82% of larger shops are pursuing service management, and 67% are planning to increase Windows management. Let's look at what the issues are.

Why Do Systems Go Down?

We can start with examining reasons why systems go down. Figure 1.1 illustrates widely recognized reasons for outages, and the following list describes these reasons:

► **Software errors**—Software is responsible for somewhat less than half the errors. These errors include software coding errors, software integration errors, data corruption, and such.

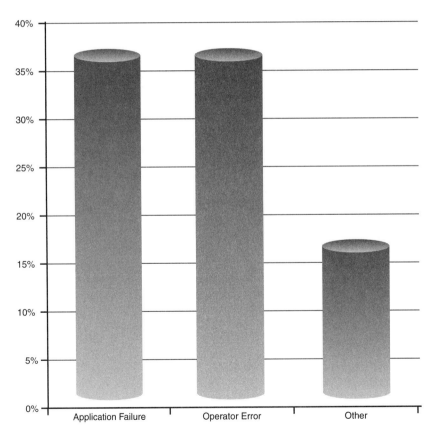

FIGURE 1.1   Causes of system outages.

- ▶ **User errors**—Users and operators cause a little less than half the errors. This includes incorrectly configured systems, missed warning messages that turn into errors, accidents, unplugged power cords, and so on.

- ▶ **Other**—This last category is relatively small. Causes of errors here include disk crashes, power outages, viruses, natural disasters, and so on.

As Figure 1.1 demonstrates, the vast majority of failures are from software-level errors and user errors. It is surprising to note that hardware failures account for the smallest percentage of problems, which is a tribute to modern systems such as Redundant Array of Independent Disks (RAID), clustering, and other mechanisms deployed to provide server and application redundancy.

The numbers show that to reduce system downtime, you need to attack the software and user error components of the equation, which are where you will get the most "bang for the buck."

No System Is an Island

Microsoft Windows Server and the applications that run on it, such as Microsoft Exchange and Microsoft SQL Server, expose a wealth of information with event logs, performance counters, and application-specific logs. However, this data is isolated and typically server-centric, making it difficult to determine where the problem really is. To get a handle on our operations, we need to take actions to prevent the situation shown in Figure 1.2, where applications and system components are isolated islands of information.

FIGURE 1.2   Multiple islands of information.

We can find isolated information in a number of locations:

▶ **Event logs**—Events are generated by the Windows operating system, components, and applications. The logs include errors, warnings, information, and security auditing events. Event logs are stored locally on each server.

▶ **Log files**—File-based logs contain information related to system and software component installations, and they can include ongoing information related to the status of an application. For example, a web server maintains log files listing every request made to the server, and Microsoft SQL Server maintains a series of log files capturing events related to its operation. Operations Manager uses log files as well.

▶ **Performance counters**—The Windows operating system and multiple applications expose detailed performance information through performance counters. The data includes processor utilization, memory utilization, network statistics, disk free space, and thousands of other pieces of operational information.

▶ **Windows Management Instrumentation (WMI)**—WMI provides access to an incredible amount of information, ranging from high-level status of services to detailed hardware information.

▶ **Expertise**—Consultants, engineers, and subject matter experts have information locked up in their heads or written down on whiteboards and paper napkins. This is as much an island of information as the statistics and data stored on any computer.

Although system information is captured through event logs, performance counters, file-based logs, and experiences, it is typically lost over time. Most logs roll over, are erased to clear space, or are eventually overwritten. Even if the information is not ultimately lost or forgotten, it typically is not reviewed regularly by systems or operations personnel.

Additionally, most application information is server-centric, typically stored on the server, and specific to the server where the application resides. There is no built-in, systemwide, cross-system view of critical information or system health.

Having islands of information, where operational data is stranded on any given island, makes it difficult to get to needed information in a timely or effective manner.

Lack of Notification

In your typical unmanaged IT environment, often no one knows when noteworthy events occur. Going to each server and reviewing its event logs regularly is a massive undertaking for the typical system administrator. Although the event logs capture a tremendous amount of information, they will eventually roll over and be overwritten without being looked at; that information is lost.

You may be familiar with an old philosophical saying: If a tree falls in a forest and no one is around to hear it, does it make a sound?

Here's the operations management equivalent: If an event is logged on a system and no one knows, does logging it make a difference?

The answer to this question is definitely "no"; if no one knows, the event may as well not be logged. This loss of information can affect the long-term health of the system—if you knew about its occurrence you could avert potential outages.

As an example, there was a situation where an Exchange server at a large manufacturing organization was receiving 1018 errors in the Application Event log for several months, but the administrators never checked the logs to catch it. Error 1018 indicates an Exchange database problem; it is a severe error requiring immediate action. The server eventually crashed and the backups were unusable—the backed up databases were corrupt. Restoring the mail system necessitated an expensive disaster recovery scenario using outside consultants, resulting in the loss of critical messaging data and the jobs of the staff held responsible.

In the end, information is only informative if you are aware of it, and it is only as good as what you do with it. To put this another way, most IT shops have many trees falling without someone hearing them...until it is too late.

Lack of Historical Information

Sometimes you may capture information about a system problem, but are not able to look back in time to see whether this is an isolated instance or part of a recurring pattern. An incident can be a one-time blip or can indicate an underlying issue; without a historical context, it is difficult to understand the significance of any particular incident. This is especially true with performance data.

Let's say an IT shop brings in a technical consultant to review a system's performance problems. To prove there is a problem, the in-house IT staff points out that users are complaining about performance and the memory and CPU are only 50% utilized. By itself, this does not tell us anything. It could be that memory and the CPU are normally 65% utilized and the problem is really a network utilization problem, which in turn reduces the load on the other resources. A historical context could provide useful information.

As a technical expert, the consultant would develop a hypothesis and test it, which will take time and cost money. Rather than trying to solve the problem, many IT shops just throw more hardware at it—only to find that this does not necessarily improve performance. With historical records, they would see that system utilization actually dropped at the same time users started complaining, and they could look elsewhere to find the network problems. Ideally, you would have historical information for troubleshooting and detecting trends.

Lack of Expertise

Do you lack the in-house expertise needed to diagnose some of the messages or trends appearing on your Windows servers and server-based applications? Do you pay an arm and a leg to call in consultants, only to find that the messages are actually not all that severe? On the other hand, do you ignore messages you don't think are significant only to later discover that they are important?

If the expertise you need is not available when you need it, you can miss diagnostic opportunities or incur higher operational costs. Missed diagnostics opportunities can translate to system outages and ultimately higher operational expenses if emergency measures are required to resolve problems.

Lack of Methodology

Many IT organizations still "fly by the seat of their pants" when it comes to identifying and resolving problems. Using standard procedures and a methodology helps minimize risk and solve issues faster.

A *methodology* is a body of practices, procedures, and rules used by those who work in a discipline or engage in an inquiry. It can also refer to a set of working methods. We can look at a methodology as a structured process that defines the who, what, where, when, and why of your operations, and the procedures to use when defining problems, solutions, and courses of action.

Consistently using a methodology gives you the tools to help measure or compare where you are to where you were. A methodology also includes identifying and using standards, policies, and rules of operation.

With IT's continually increased role in running successful business operations, having a structured and standard way to define IT operations can increase your business decision-makers' confidence that IT is a significant and ongoing business concern. In addition, that increased level of confidence may translate to higher job satisfaction for you.

Missing Information

Sometimes you detect problems by what did not occur, rather than by what actually happened. A good example of this is data backups. Regardless of whether the backup is successful or fails, it generates an event and some type of notification.

However, what happens when the backup doesn't fail or succeed, but just doesn't happen? If you are not looking closely at your event logs, you will likely not discover this fact until later. We know a case of a large educational institution doing backups that missed one server during an initial configuration. Eventually the server crashed and they attempted to restore to an earlier point, only then discovering there were no backups. Even though all their backup jobs were configured to generate success notices and notify of failures, that particular server was not generating these notifications and was missed—with severe consequences impacting management, faculty, staff, and students.

Sometimes when you do not receive a notification or event, it is a signal to take action. The bottom line is you need to be able to test whether something has failed to happen.

False Alarms

Even when you are notified of events, it may be difficult to tell whether you actually have a problem. Windows Server and the services and applications running under it are good about generating errors, warnings, and informational messages. The challenge is that there is so much information that it can be difficult to tell which of these thousands of messages are normal operating events, rather than errors that require remedial action.

False alarms are typically due to a lack of knowledge or inadequate filtering. Sometimes a benign message may look ominous to the untrained eye. One example would be event 11 from w32time in the System Event log, which is a warning indicating an unreachable Network Time Protocol (NTP) server. This actually is a normal occurrence and is not a problem (although several of these errors may indicate a problem that needs action).

What It's All About

The issues described so far generally occur in an unmanaged environment. By "unmanaged," we mean an environment that is not using a disciplined approach for managing its operational information. By not correlating operational data across systems, being aware of potential issues, maintaining a history of past performance and problems, and so on, IT shops open themselves up to putting out fires that could be prevented by using a more systematic approach to operations management (see Figure 1.3). We will cover these issues in the next section.

FIGURE 1.3   Fighting fires.

Operations Management Defined

Operations management is a not something achieved at a point in time. Instead, it is a process aimed at improving the reliability and availability of computer applications and services though addressing the problems discussed in the previous sections of this chapter. It consists of the care and feeding of an IT asset, as well as managing, maintaining, and supporting the needs and events (including dependencies) of an operation.

Operations management bliss is not attained merely by running a setup program to install a "management application." The process of operations management is a combination of people, procedures, and tools—all three are necessary, and the absence of one component can put an entire enterprise solution at risk. At a more granular level, operations management is about correlating what may appear to be seemingly unrelated events and data across machines to determine what information is significant to your operational environment versus what is not.

Operations management is also about managing the ongoing activities that Information Technology personnel perform on various IT components with the goal of improving the performance of one's business organization. It results in higher reliability, greater availability, better asset allocation, and a more predictable IT environment.

How does operations management accomplish this? As IT operations grow in size and impact, it quickly becomes apparent that effectively managing complex production environments requires the use of standardized methodologies and approaches to manage servers. Once a business relies on IT to maintain daily operations, having a disciplined and informative methodology is necessary to help ensure IT is supporting the organization's business goals and objectives. These goals typically include reducing costs, increasing productivity, and providing information security.

Reducing costs and increasing productivity is important because, in addition to taking up a significant part of the IT budget, the business impact of failed systems or performance degradation can be devastating to the entire enterprise, resulting in increased operational costs, decreased quality of service, and lost revenue and profit. Time, after all, is money! Information security is also imperative because the price tag of compromised systems and data recovery from security exposures can be large, and those costs continue to rise each year.

The Cost of Downtime

Let's consider a simplified example of the impact of temporarily disrupting an e-commerce site normally available 24×7. The site generates an average of $4,000 per hour in revenue from customer orders, for an annual value in sales revenue of $35,040,000. If the website were unavailable for 6 hours due to a security vulnerability, the directly attributable losses for the outage would be $24,000.

This number is only an average cost; most e-commerce sites generate revenue at a wide range of rates based on the time of day, date of week, time of year, marketing campaigns, and so on. Typically the outage occurs during peak times when the system is already stressed, thus greatly increasing the cost of that 6-hour loss.

Other costs are incurred from an outage as well. Some customers may decide to find alternative vendors, resulting in a permanent loss of users and making the revenue loss even greater than the direct loss of sales. The company may decide to spend additional money on advertising to counter the ill will created when customers could not reach the site. The costs from our sample 6-hour outage can therefore be far higher than the simple hourly proportion of time applied to an average revenue stream.

Another case in point would be a large-sized credit card–processing card company that estimates it would stand to lose nearly $400,000 in direct revenue if it experienced a 1-hour operational outage affecting its ability to process credit card transactions. This number assumes an estimated cost of just over $1.00 per missed transaction, and does not include the inevitable decline in revenues due to a loss of confidence from clients if such an outage were to happen.

These are not just theoretical cases. We can look at what happened on Black Friday in 2006. This is the day after Thanksgiving in the United States and is the busiest day of the year in the retail sector. On that particular Black Friday, the websites for two very large U.S. retailers (Wal-Mart and Macy's) were unavailable starting around 4:00 a.m. for approximately 10 hours, presumably from overload. Although it is possible that potential customers tried the sites at a later time, it is also possible that they took their business to competitors.

As part of an operations management plan, any company with more than nontrivial IT requirements stands to benefit by using software tools to automate tasks such as managing server networks, tracking desktop systems, and enforcing security policies. Microsoft software addresses this area through two key products—System Center Configuration Manager (ConfigMgr, formerly known as Systems Management Server or SMS) and System Center Operations Manager (in earlier releases known as MOM or Microsoft Operations Manager).

Configuration Manager is Microsoft's product for change and configuration management on the Microsoft Windows platform. It reduces the operational costs of managing and deploying software, enabling organizations to distribute relevant software and updates to users in a quick and cost-effective manner. OpsMgr provides you with knowledge to reduce the complexity of managing your IT infrastructure environment and lower your operational costs. Keep in mind, however, that ConfigMgr and OpsMgr are merely tools; they enable you to meet objectives incorporating software for automating the process.

Microsoft's Management Approach

Microsoft utilizes a multipronged approach to management. This strategy includes the following areas:

▶ Continuing to making Windows easier to manage by providing core management infrastructure and capabilities in the Windows platform itself, thus allowing business and management application developers to improve their infrastructures and capabilities. Microsoft believes that improving the manageability of solutions built on Windows Server System will be a key driver in shaping the future of Windows management.

▶ Building complete management solutions on this infrastructure, either through making them available in the operating system or by using management products such as Configuration Manager, Operations Manager, and other components of the System Center family.

▶ Integrating infrastructure and management by exposing services and interfaces that applications can utilize.

▶ Supporting a standard Web Services specification for system management. WS-Management is a specification of a SOAP-based protocol, based on Web Services, used to manage servers, devices, and applications (SOAP stands for Simple Object Access Protocol). The intent is to provide a universal language that all types of devices can use to share data about themselves, which in turn makes them more easily managed. Support for WS-Management is included with Windows Vista and Windows Server 2008, and it is leveraged by OpsMgr.

▶ Using an Infrastructure Optimization (IO) Model as a framework for aligning IT with business needs. We discuss the IO Model further in the "Optimizing Your Infrastructure" section of this chapter. The IO Model describes your IT infrastructure in terms of cost, security risk, and operational agility.

▶ Taking model-based management (used with the Dynamic Systems Initiative, discussed in the next section) to implement synthetic transaction technology. Operations Manager 2007 delivers a service-based monitoring set of scenarios, enabling you to define models of services to deliver to end users.

Microsoft's Dynamic Systems Initiative (DSI)

A large percentage of IT departments' budgets and resources typically focus on mundane maintenance tasks such as applying software patches or monitoring the health of a network, without leaving the staff with the time or energy to focus on more exhilarating (and more productive) strategic initiatives.

The Dynamic Systems Initiative, or DSI, is a Microsoft and industry strategy intended to enhance the Windows platform, delivering a coordinated set of solutions that simplify and automate how businesses design, deploy, and operate their distributed systems. Using DSI helps IT and developers create operationally aware platforms. By designing systems that are more manageable and automating operations, organizations can reduce costs and proactively address their priorities.

DSI is about building software that enables knowledge of an IT system to be created, modified, transferred, and operated on throughout the life cycle of that system. It is a commitment from Microsoft and its partners to help IT teams capture and use knowledge to design systems that are more manageable and to automate operations, which reduces costs and gives organizations additional time to focus proactively on what is most important. By innovating across applications, development tools, the platform, and management solutions, DSI will result in

- ▶ Increased productivity and reduced costs across all aspects of IT

- ▶ Increased responsiveness to changing business needs

- ▶ Reduced time and effort required to develop, deploy, and manage applications

Microsoft is positioning DSI as the connector of the entire system life cycle.

Microsoft Product Integration

DSI focuses on automating data-center operational jobs and reducing associated labor though self-managing systems. We can look at several examples where Microsoft products and tools integrate with DSI:

- ▶ Operations Manager uses the application knowledge captured in management packs to simplify identifying issues and their root causes, facilitating resolution and restoring services or preventing potential outages, and providing intelligent management at the system level. OpsMgr 2007 is a key component of DSI.

- ▶ Visual Studio is a model-based development tool that initially leveraged the System Definition Model (SDM) and now uses Service Modeling Language (SML), enabling operations managers and application architects to collaborate early in the development phase and ensure systems are defined with operational requirements in mind.

- ▶ Windows Server Update Services (WSUS) enables greater and more efficient administrative control through modeling technology that enables downstream systems to construct accurate models representing their current state, available updates, and installed software.

> **NOTE**
>
> **What's in an Acronym? Moving from SDM to SML**
>
> Microsoft originally used SDM as its standard schema with DSI but has since imple-
> mented SML, an industrywide published specification used in heterogeneous environ-
> ments. Using SML helps DSI adoption by incorporating a standard that Microsoft's
> partners can understand and apply across mixed platforms. We discuss SML in the
> "Using Service Modeling Language" section of this chapter.

DSI focuses on automating data-center operational jobs and reducing associated labor though self-managing systems. Can management software be made clever enough to know when a particular system or application has a problem and then dynamically take actions to avoid that? Consider the scenario where, without operator intervention, a management system starts an additional web server because the existing web farm is over-loaded from traffic. Rather than being far-fetched, this particular capability is available with Microsoft Application Center 2000 and more recently with Virtual Server 2005; DSI aims to extend this type of self-healing and self-management to other operations.

In support of DSI, Microsoft has invested heavily in three major areas:

- **Systems designed for operations**—Microsoft is delivering development and author-ing tools—such as Visual Studio—that enable businesses to capture and edit system knowledge and facilitate collaboration among business users, project managers, architects, developers, testers, and operations staff. Additionally, Microsoft servers and many third-party applications will be enabled to capture information necessary to dramatically improve deployment and management.

- **An operationally aware platform**—The core Windows operating system and its related technologies are critical when solving everyday operational challenges. This requires the operating system services to be designed for manageability. Additionally, the operating system and server products must provide rich instrumentation and hardware resource virtualization support.

- **Intelligent management tools**—The third and most critical piece in DSI contains the management tools for leveraging the operational knowledge captured in the sys-tem, providing end-to-end automation of system deployment.

Microsoft's Solutions for Systems Management

End-to-end automation could include updating, monitoring and change/configuration, and rich reporting services. Microsoft's System Center is a family of system management products and solutions that focus on providing you with the knowledge and tools to manage your IT infrastructure. The intent of System Center is to integrate systems management tools and technologies, thus helping to ease operations, reduce troubleshooting time, and improve planning capabilities.

Why DSI Is Important

The philosophy behind DSI is threefold:

- ▸ That Microsoft products be patched in a simplified and uniform way

- ▸ That Microsoft server applications are optimized for management, to take advantage of Operations Manager 2007

- ▸ That developers have tools (in Visual Studio) to design applications in a way that makes them easier for administrators to manage after those applications are in production

With DSI, Microsoft utilizes a nontraditional approach to systems management. DSI employs an application development standpoint, rather than a more customary operations perspective that concentrates on automating task-based processes. Remember from the "Microsoft's Dynamic Systems Initiative (DSI)" section that DSI is about building software that enables knowledge of an IT system to be created, modified, transferred, and used throughout the life cycle of a system. DSI's core principles—knowledge, models, and the life cycle—are key in addressing the challenges of complexity and manageability faced by IT organizations. By capturing knowledge and incorporating health models, DSI can facilitate troubleshooting and maintenance.

Using Service Modeling Language

Central to DSI is the XML-based (Extensible Markup Language) schema called Service Modeling Language (SML). SML can be utilized in architecting software and hardware components and creating definitions of distributed systems. Businesses can use SML to take an entire system and generate a blueprint of that system. The blueprint defines system elements and captures data pertinent to development, deployment, and operations—making that model relevant across the entire IT life cycle. SML is a core technology around which we will see many future DSI components and products developed.

IT Infrastructure Library (ITIL) and Microsoft Operations Framework (MOF)

ITIL is widely accepted as an international standard of best practices for operations management, and Microsoft has used it as the basis for the MOF, its own operations framework. Warning: Discussions of ITIL and MOF can be dry; proceed at your own risk!

What Is ITIL?

As part of Microsoft's management approach, the company relied on an international standards-setting body as its basis for developing an operational framework. The British Office of Government Commerce (OGC), provides best practices advice and guidance on using Information Technology in service management and operations. The OGC also publishes the IT Infrastructure Library, known as ITIL.

ITIL provides a cohesive set of best practices for IT Service Management (ITSM). These best practices include a series of books giving direction and guidance on provisioning quality IT services and facilities needed to support Information Technology. The documents are maintained by the OGC and supported by publications, qualifications, and an international users group.

Started in the 1980s, ITIL is under constant development by a consortium of industry IT leaders. The ITIL covers a number of areas and is primarily focused on ITSM; its IT Infrastructure Library is considered to be the most consistent and comprehensive documentation of best practices for IT Service Management worldwide.

Think of ITSM as a top-down business-driven approach to managing Information Technology. It specifically addresses the strategic business value generated by IT and the need to deliver high-quality IT services to one's business organization. ITSM itself has two main components:

▶ Service Support

▶ Service Delivery

A New Version of ITIL

ITIL has recently undergone a refresh, and the core books for version 3 (ITIL v3) were published on June 30, 2007. The major difference between v3 and its v2 predecessor is that v3 has adopted an integrated service life cycle approach to IT Service Management, as opposed to organizing itself around the concepts of IT Service Delivery and Support.

ITIL v2 was a more targeted product, explicitly designed to bridge the gap between technology and business, with a strong process focus on effective service delivery. The ITIL v3 refresh encapsulates what is in v2 and updates the terminology. The v3 documents recognize the new service management challenges brought about by advancements in technology, such as virtualization and outsourcing, as well as emerging challenges for service providers.

The framework has been repositioned from its previous emphasis on the process life cycle and alignment of IT to an emphasis on "the business" (that is, to managing the life cycle of the services provided by IT and the importance of creating business value rather than just the execution of processes). As an example, it is a publicly stated aim of the refresh to include more references to Return on Investment (ROI).

There are five core volumes of ITIL v3:

> ▶ **Service Strategy**—This volume identifies market opportunities for which services could be developed to meet a requirement on the part of internal or external customers. Key areas here are Service Portfolio Management and Financial Management.

> ▶ **Service Design**—This volume focuses on the activities that take place to develop the strategy into a design document that addresses all aspects of the proposed service and the processes intended to support it. Key areas of this volume are Availability Management, Capacity Management, Continuity Management, and Security Management.

> ▶ **Service Transition**—This volume centers on implementing the output of service design activities and creating a production service (or modifying an existing service). There is some overlap between Service Transition and Service Operation, the next volume. Key areas of the Service Transition volume are Change Management, Release Management, Configuration Management, and Service Knowledge Management.

> ▶ **Service Operation**—This volume involves the activities required to operate the services and maintain their functionality as defined in Service Level Agreements (SLAs) with one's customers. Key areas here are Incident Management, Problem Management, and Request Fulfillment.

> ▶ **Continual Service Improvement**—This volume focuses on the ability to deliver continual improvement to the quality of the services that the IT organization delivers to the business. Key areas include Service Reporting, Service Measurement, and Service Level Management.

ITIL v3 really is a repackaging of what was in v2, with an additional layer of abstraction.

ITSM is designed to focus on the people, processes, and technology issues faced by IT, which is analogous to the focus of operations management.

ITIL describes at a high level "what you must do" and why, but does not describe how you are to do it. A driving force behind its development was the recognition that organizations are increasingly dependent on IT for satisfying their corporate aims and meeting their business needs, which increases the requirement for high-quality IT services. Many large IT shops realized that the road to a customer-centric service organization runs along an ITIL framework.

ITIL also specifies keeping measurements or metrics. Measurements can include statistics such as the number and severity of service outages, along with the amount of time it takes to restore service. You can use metrics to quantify to management how you are doing.

This information can be particularly useful for justifying resources during the next budget process!

What Is MOF?

ITIL is generally accepted as the "best practices" for the industry. Being technology-agnostic, it is a foundation that can be adopted and adapted to meet the specific needs of various IT organizations. Microsoft chose ITIL as the foundation for its operations framework, such that the Microsoft Operations Framework (MOF) gives prescriptive guidance in operating Microsoft technologies in conformance with the descriptive guidance in ITIL. MOF is a set of publications providing both descriptive (what to do and why) and prescriptive (how to do) guidance on IT service management.

The key focus in developing MOF was providing a framework specifically geared toward managing Microsoft technologies. Microsoft created the first version of the MOF in 1999. MOF is designed to complement Microsoft's previously existing Microsoft Solutions Framework (MSF) used for solution and application development. Together, the combined frameworks provide guidance throughout the IT life cycle, as shown in Figure 1.4.

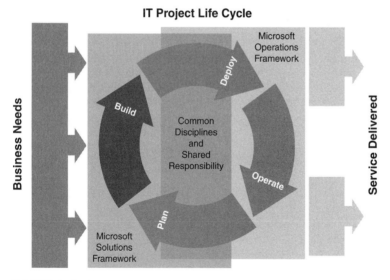

FIGURE 1.4   The IT life cycle and Microsoft frameworks.

Using MSF for OpsMgr Deployments

Microsoft uses MOF to describe IT operations and uses Operations Manager as a tool to implement that framework. However, Operations Manager 2007 is also an application and, as such, is best deployed using a disciplined approach. A suggested methodology for deployment would be using principles from the MSF, which we discuss in Chapter 4, "Planning Your Operations Manager Deployment."

At its core, the MOF is a collection of best practices, principles, and models. It provides direction to achieve reliability, availability, supportability, and manageability of mission-critical production systems, focusing on solutions and services using Microsoft products and technologies. MOF extends ITIL by including guidance and best practices derived from the experience of Microsoft's internal operations groups, partners, and customers worldwide. MOF aligns with and builds on the IT service management practices documented within ITIL, thus enhancing the supportability built on Microsoft's products and technologies.

MOF uses a process model that describes Microsoft's approach to IT operations and the service management life cycle. The model organizes the core ITIL processes of service support and service delivery, and it includes additional MOF processes in the four quadrants of the MOF process model, as illustrated in Figure 1.5.

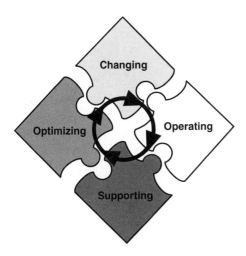

FIGURE 1.5   The MOF process model.

It is important to note that the activities pictured in the quadrants illustrated in Figure 1.5 are not necessarily sequential. These activities can occur simultaneously within an IT organization. Each quadrant has a specific focus and tasks, and within each quadrant are policies, procedures, standards, and best practices that support specific operations management–focused tasks.

Operations Manager 2007 management packs can be configured to support operations management tasks in different quadrants of the MOF Process Model. Let's look briefly at each of these quadrants and see how we can use OpsMgr to support MOF:

▶ **Changing**—This quadrant represents instances where new service solutions, technologies, systems, applications, hardware, and processes have been introduced.

As you add new components to your environment, you should investigate whether a Microsoft or third-party management pack is available to monitor a particular application, system, or hardware solution. (If a management pack is not available, you can define your own, building a model to describe the "vital signs" and monitoring attributes of that application.)

▶ **Operating**—This quadrant concentrates on performing day-to-day tasks efficiently and effectively.

OpsMgr includes operational tasks that you can initiate from the Operations console. These tasks are made available with various management packs, and you may add your own as well.

▶ **Supporting**—This quadrant represents the resolution of incidents, problems, and inquiries, preferably in a timely manner.

OpsMgr is all about monitoring daily operations. Management packs provide the capability, for knowledgeable users, to interpret and act on information gathered from each monitored component to resolve any difficulties.

▶ **Optimizing**—This quadrant focuses on minimizing costs while optimizing performance, capacity, and availability in the delivery of IT services.

OpsMgr's reporting and monitoring capabilities can help you increase efficiency and gain greater control over your IT environment. Integrating and extending problem reporting and operations monitoring to client systems help lower your client support costs, while availability reporting allows both IT operations and management to get the information needed to quickly identify and resolve issues that affect service levels.

Service Level Agreements and Operating Level Agreements (OLAs) are tools many organizations use in defining accepted levels of operation and ability. Operations Manager includes the ability to specify SLAs using Alert Resolution States. Additional information regarding the MOF Process Model is available at http://go.microsoft.com/fwlink/?LinkId=50015.

MOF Does Not Replace ITIL

Microsoft believes that ITIL is the leading body of knowledge of best practices; for that reason, it uses ITIL as the foundation for MOF. Rather than replacing ITIL, MOF complements it and is similar to ITIL in several ways:

- ▶ MOF (with MSF) spans the entire IT life cycle.

- ▶ Both MOF and ITIL are based on best practices for IT management, drawing on the expertise of practitioners worldwide.

- ▶ The MOF body of knowledge is applicable across the business community—from small businesses to large enterprises. MOF also is not limited to those using the Microsoft platform in a homogenous environment.

- ▶ As is the case with ITIL, MOF has expanded to be more than just a documentation set. In fact, MOF is now intertwined with Operations Manager 2007!

Additionally, Microsoft and its partners provide a variety of resources to support MOF principles and guidance, including self-assessments, IT management tools that incorporate MOF terminology and features, training programs and certification, and consulting services.

ISO 20000

You can think of ITIL and ITSM as providing a pathway for IT to rethink the ways in which it contributes to the business. The processes represented by ITIL and ITSM have evolved into the standard known as ISO 20000, which is the first international standard for IT Service Management.

ISO 20000 was first published in December 2005. It was developed to reflect best-practice guidance contained within ITIL. The standard also supports other IT Service Management frameworks and approaches, including MOF. ISO 20000 consists of two major areas:

- ▶ Part 1 promotes adopting an integrated process approach to deliver managed services effectively that meets business and customer requirements.

- ▶ Part 2 is a "code of practice" describing the best practices for service management within the scope of ISO 20000-1.

These two areas—what to do and how to do it—have similarities to the approach taken by the MOF.

Optimizing Your Infrastructure

According to Microsoft, analysts estimate that over 70% of the typical IT budget is spent on infrastructure—managing servers, operating systems, storage, and networking. Add to that the challenge of refreshing and managing desktop and mobile devices, and there's not much left over for anything else. Microsoft describes an Infrastructure Optimization

Model that categorizes the state of one's IT infrastructure, describing the impacts on cost, security risks, and the ability to respond to changes. Using the model shown in Figure 1.6, you can identify where your organization is, and where you want to be:

▶ **Basic**—Reactionary, with much time spent fighting fires

▶ **Standardized**—Gaining control

▶ **Rationalized**—Enabling the business

▶ **Dynamic**—Being a strategic asset

Although most organizations are somewhere between the basic and standardized levels in this model, typically one would prefer to be a strategic asset rather than fighting fires. Once you know where you are in the model, you can use best practices from ITIL and guidance from MOF to develop a plan to progress to a higher level. The IO Model describes the technologies and steps organizations can take to move forward, whereas the MOF explains the people and processes required to improve that infrastructure. Similar to ITSM, the IO Model is a combination of people, processes, and technology.

More information about Infrastructure Optimization is available at http://www.microsoft. com/technet/infrastructure.

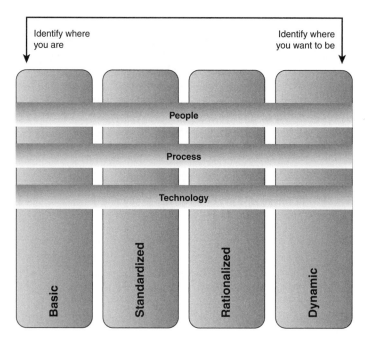

FIGURE 1.6   The Infrastructure Optimization Model.

About the IO Model

Not all IT shops will want or need to be dynamic. Some will choose, for all the right business reasons, to be less than dynamic! The IO model has a three-part goal:

▶ Communicate that there are levels

▶ Target the desired levels

▶ Provide reference on how to get to the desired levels

Realize that Infrastructure Optimization can be per application or per function, rather than a single ranking for the entire IT department.

Items that factor into an IT organization's adoption of the IO model include cost, ability, whether the organization fits into the business model as a cost center versus an asset, along with a commitment to move from being reactive to proactive.

From Fighting Fires to Gaining Control

At the Basic level, your infrastructure is hard to control and expensive to manage. Processes are manual, IT policies and standards are either nonexistent or not enforced, and you don't have the tools and resources (or time and energy) to determine the overall health of your applications and IT services. Not only are your desktop and server management costs out of control, but you are in reactive mode when it comes to security threats. In addition, you tend to use manual rather than automated methods for applying software deployments and patches.

Does this sound familiar? If you can gain control of your environment, you may be more effective at work! Here are some steps to consider:

▶ Develop standards, policies, and controls.

▶ Alleviate security risks by developing a security approach throughout your IT organization.

▶ Adopt best practices, such as those found in ITIL, and operational guidance found in the MOF.

▶ Build IT to become a strategic asset.

If you can achieve operational nirvana, this will go a long way toward your job satisfaction and IT becoming a constructive part of your business.

From Gaining Control to Enabling the Business

A Standardized infrastructure introduces control by using standards and policies to manage desktops and servers. These standards control how you introduce machines into your network. As an example, using Directory Services will manage resources, security policies, and access to resources. Shops in a Standardized state realize the value of basic standards and some policies, but still tend to be reactive. Although you now have a managed IT infrastructure and are inventorying your hardware and software assets and starting to manage licenses, your patches, software deployments, and desktop services are not yet automated. Security-wise, the perimeter is now under control, although internal security may still be a bit loose.

To move from a Standardized state to the Rationalized level, you will need to gain more control over your infrastructure and implement proactive policies and procedures. You might also begin to look at implementing service management. At this stage, IT can also move more toward becoming a business asset and ally, rather than a burden.

From Enabling the Business to Becoming a Strategic Asset

At the Rationalized level, you have achieved firm control of desktop and service management costs. Processes and policies are in place and beginning to play a large role in supporting and expanding the business. Security is now proactive, and you are responding to threats and challenges in a rapid and controlled manner.

Using technologies such as zero-touch deployment helps you to minimize costs, deployment time, and technical challenges for system and software rollouts. Because your inventory is now under control, you have minimized the number of images to manage, and desktop management is now "low touch." You also are purchasing only the software licenses and new computers the business requires, giving you a handle on costs. Security is now proactive with policies and control in place for desktops, servers, firewalls, and extranets.

Mission Accomplished: IT as a Strategic Asset

At the Dynamic level, your infrastructure is helping run the business efficiently and stay ahead of competitors. Your costs are now fully controlled. You have also achieved integration between users and data, desktops and servers, and the different departments and functions throughout your organization.

Your Information Technology processes are automated and often incorporated into the technology itself, allowing IT to be aligned and managed according to business needs. New technology investments are able to yield specific, rapid, and measurable business benefits. Measurement is good—it helps you justify the next round of investments!

Using self-provisioning software and quarantine-like systems to ensure patch management and compliance with security policies allows you to automate your processes, which in turn improves reliability, lowers costs, and increases your service levels. Welcome to IT nirvana!

Managing System Health

ITIL and MOF are utilized to define management approaches, and the IO Model prescribes actions to become a strategic asset. However, the day-to-day operations, strategies, and solutions in today's world are at a different level of granularity. Typically, computing environments consist of distributed systems where work is performed utilizing dispersed servers—because distributed computing often requires using numerous machines that may be in multiple locations. Having an overall management strategy is necessary for preventing chaos and gaining control, but daily management of production server environments also requires being thoroughly aware of the operational health and security of those systems—are they performing the tasks they are meant to, are they the focus of a hacker, or are they even reachable across the network?

Operations management, in addition to introducing an alphabet soup of acronyms of management concepts, is concerned with monitoring your servers to ensure they maintain a required level of performance. Looking specifically at the Windows platform, Microsoft provides a number of basic monitoring utilities with the Windows Server product. These tools incorporate core event monitoring, performance monitoring, and management components such as the Event Viewer and Performance/System Monitor.

However, as mentioned in "The Problem with Today's Systems," understanding the significance of the information that is available with such utilities can be daunting, particularly with a large number of servers and a complex environment. Although these basic tools are included with Windows Server, they provide a view of the trees without the ability to see the entire forest. In other words, they give a detailed view of a single server and do not scale or give easy diagnoses of information to resolve problems that occur across multiple systems.

Because these utilities only provide raw data, effectively using that data requires personnel with the knowledge to select, understand, filter, and interpret and correlate the information. These tools typically only show pieces and parts of the overall picture, and additional data may be required from different sources.

The information spewing from these systems consists of thousands of events and other types of operational data that can be captured from a single server, which brings to mind the phrase "drinking water from a fire hose," as shown in Figure 1.7. You are inundated with a gushing stream of facts and figures coming at you with tremendous built-up pressure. Making sense of all that data, or "taming the fire hose," is a challenge facing IT shops of all sizes, and one that OpsMgr is designed to address.

Unlike scenes in the movie *The Matrix*, numbers are not just pouring vertically down the screen—and you don't need the ability to jump from roof to roof or dodge bullets to be able to decipher them. You merely need the tools and products available to mere mortals.

FIGURE 1.7   Drinking water from a fire hose.

Fixing the Monitoring Problem: Operations Manager 2007

System Center Operations Manager 2007 is Microsoft's software tool for solving operation management problems and is a key component in Microsoft's management strategy and System Center. Operations Manager is a comprehensive operations management solution, using an agent-based centralized management model to localize data collection while centralizing collected data and agent configuration information. As discussed at the beginning of this chapter, OpsMgr 2007 provides the following benefits:

▶ **End-to-end service management**—This is the capacity to integrate application, client, server, and synthetic transaction monitoring into a single end-to-end solution. Service-oriented views and availability reporting allow your operations team and IT management to get the information they need to quickly identify and resolve issues that impact service levels. You get end-to-end management without the day-to-day drama.

▶ **Best of breed for Windows**—OpsMgr includes expertise from Microsoft's Server, Client, and Application teams to provide you with prescriptive knowledge and auto-mated inline tasks that improve monitoring, troubleshooting, and problem resolu-tion for over 60 Microsoft applications and Windows Server components. Operations

Manager also includes problem management and troubleshooting of client computers to accelerate identifying and resolving end-user issues.

▶ **Increased efficiency and control of your IT environment**—OpsMgr automates routine and redundant tasks, providing intelligent reporting and monitoring that can help increase efficiency and control of your environment. It builds on the Windows PowerShell and includes a Software Development Kit (SDK) for secure scripted automation across an Operations Manager environment. Its scalability can support organizations with tens of thousands of managed servers and hundreds of thousands of managed clients, using multiple management servers and connected management groups for a consolidated view of your entire enterprise. By introducing self-tuning thresholds that learn and adjust behavior, OpsMgr can help minimize false alarms.

Agents operate under sophisticated sets of rules, collected in management packs. These management packs, which are models based on the SML schema, allow the rules to be targeted to just the systems that need them. Operations Manager 2007 utilizes SML to monitor not just servers, but also logical services. Using this service-centric view, OpsMgr can understand service and application structures as well as monitor the overall health of services and applications by viewing the state of any object. Problems identified by these rules can be acted on by operational and systems personnel; the results collected by this process can be analyzed and published using OpsMgr's reporting capabilities.

To put Operations Manager's capabilities in a clearer context, we will discuss key technical features as they relate to the issues identified earlier in "The Problem with Today's Systems" section of this chapter.

Connecting Systems

OpsMgr 2007 solves the isolated systems problem with end-to-end monitoring and collecting information from your different islands of information. It monitors event logs, performance monitor counters, application programming interfaces, WMI information, and network devices, locally gathering the data from each monitored object, centrally storing it, and taking action as appropriate. OpsMgr also provides a centralized console to monitor the operational status of your entire network. Figure 1.8 shows the health state of computers in a monitored organization. The view shows that there is currently a problem area on the Quicksilver computer, and if we scroll right in the Computers view in the Operations console, we would see that the affected area is within the IIS subsystem.

Using this view enables us to see which systems and components are healthy and which are not. Health is based on rolling up information from each monitored object.

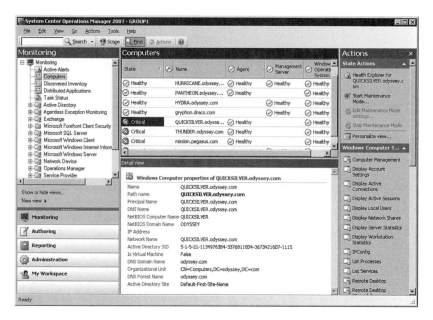

FIGURE 1.8   Viewing computer health in the Operations Manager console.

Distributed Management

The job of collecting and handling data is managed by each monitored computer, which distributes the work of collecting and handling information. Distributed management includes the following advantages over centralized management:

▶ Local information collection (scales outward and enables a smaller footprint at the central management server)

▶ Increased fault tolerance

▶ Reduced network impact

▶ Better response times

With a distributed model, information is collected, buffered, and processed locally. A distributed model also enables fault tolerance and flexibility for network outages. If the network is unavailable, the local agents still collect information and respond to alerts. This model also reduces the impact of data collection on the network by forwarding only information that needs forwarding. The agent on the local system compresses the data stream for an even smaller footprint to send to its primary management server. This model dramatically reduces response time.

1

The Role of the Agent

The key to connecting information is the intelligent agent. Operations Manager deploys an agent to monitored servers, distributing the workload, information gathering, and intelligence. (OpsMgr 2007 also incorporates client monitoring as well as agentless monitoring of a limited number of systems.) The agent enables a monitored system to forward only the information deemed important, rather than everything. It also allows the monitored system to continue to collect operations data when communications with the central console is disrupted. If the designated management server is unavailable, the data is automatically sent to an alternate management server. In the event of a total network outage, the data is forwarded when communications are reestablished.

Using a distributed model, the agent collects information locally. A centralized management server ultimately receives the information, gathering data from all the "islands" and storing it in a common database. This database is centrally located and stored on a SQL Server system, allowing OpsMgr to correlate and respond to networkwide events, such as an attempt to breach security on several systems at once. Operations Manager monitors continuously, ensuring nothing is missed.

The agents process rules, which specify what data to collect and what to do about it. Rules can filter information and aggregate and consolidate the collected information. These model-based rules are really the core functionality of OpsMgr and are covered in detail in Chapter 14, "Monitoring with Operations Manager." Rules are components of management packs, which are applied as a unit to the systems utilizing the specified components. Management packs also contain monitors, which represent the state of individual components of a system. We discuss using some of the more interesting management packs in Chapters 16 through 19.

Eliminating Islands of Information

Using centralized data storage also addresses our islands of information issue by enabling consolidated views and reports of the many different "islands" across multiple servers. As an example, an administrator can generate a report that compares error events, CPU performance, the length of message queues, and network interface performance on Exchange servers in different parts of the network at the same time. Without Operations Manager, providing this information would require multiple interfaces and tools. Having a holistic view of the information allows the system to respond to complex conditions where several events taken independently would not constitute a problem, but taken together demand immediate action.

Throughout this book, we use a fictitious company named the Odyssey Company to illustrate many of our examples. Odyssey has 750 servers spread throughout two locations. For instance, let's say Odyssey has a network load-balanced farm using four web servers to provide Web Services. By using a web farm, the failure of any one system does not jeopardize the overall service. Arguably, that is the purpose for having load-balanced servers. However, the failure of two or three of these web servers would constitute a critical condition requiring immediate attention. OpsMgr can detect the difference and generate an error alert if any individual server fails, yet create a critical alert if two or more servers fail.

Operations Notification: Errors and Availability

If you right-click a system in the Results pane shown in Figure 1.8, you can open the alert, diagram, event, performance, and state views associated with this object. You can also open the Health Explorer here from the Actions pane. The Health Explorer is displayed in Figure 1.9. You can see how OpsMgr shows the various monitored components, known as *monitors*, and the rollup for those monitors.

At a glance, this shows that although the Web Components on Quicksilver are experiencing issues, other components on the server are available and functioning properly. Each object is shown as healthy, in an error state, or not yet monitored. Using the Health Explorer, you can quickly isolate the target area. You can even customize the view to see which applications are impacted by the affected monitor.

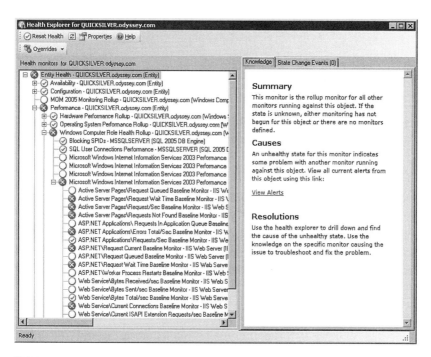

FIGURE 1.9   The Operations Manager Health Explorer.

Operations Manager 2007 resolves the notification problem by automatically detecting and responding to changes in state, generating alerts processed using its notification workflow engine. As it collects information, responses to conditions and changes in state can be triggered at each collection point in the OpsMgr architecture. The local agent processes data and analyzes it using the business logic in OpsMgr's rules, making a decision whether to pass the information to a central management server.

Microsoft designed the entire process to incorporate the best of all possible worlds. Agents on the monitored servers collect and initially process the information; this reduces the load placed on the management server because information is centrally acted on only as necessary.

The design also allows the local agents to continue to respond to alerts even when communication with the management server is disrupted. Preprocessing keeps the traffic flow from the agents lean and the database storage footprint light. Even so, an administrator would prefer to not be notified about all the myriad data collected by Operations Manager 2007. Accordingly, OpsMgr detects changes in state and incorporates self-tuning thresholds to be selective about the alerts it raises.

Using the Health Explorer shown in Figure 1.9, you can view the alerts related to a given monitor. You can also use the Active Alerts pane in the Operations console to look at all outstanding alerts. Figure 1.10 shows that currently four alerts are Warnings and 11 are Critical alerts.

You can also highlight any particular alert in the Active Alerts pane to view the detail behind that alert. In Figure 1.11, you can see what a specific error is on the Pantheon server, including the cause of the error and potential actions for resolution.

You can also click the Alert Rule link in the Alert Details pane in Figure 1.11 to bring up the specific rule behind that alert. Notice in Figure 1.12 that the information is broken into six areas or tabs:

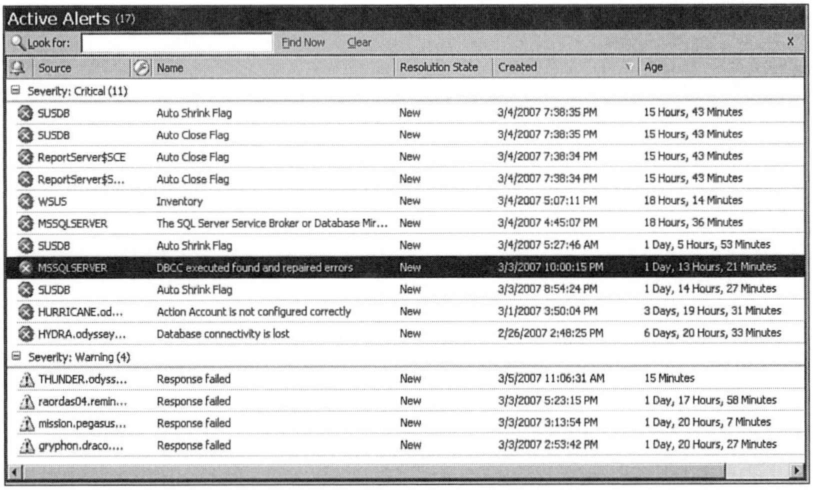

FIGURE 1.10   The Active Alerts pane in the Operations console.

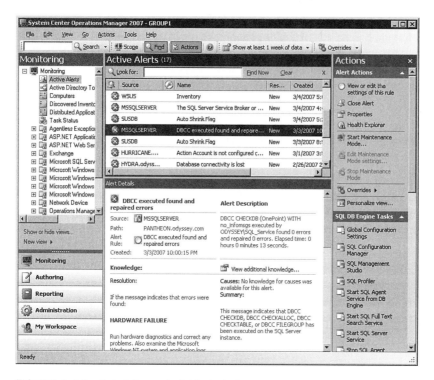

FIGURE 1.11   Detail for an individual alert.

▶ **General**—This tab provides general information, including the management pack and the name of the rule.

▶ **Product Knowledge**—Provides information collected by the vendor (in this case, Microsoft) about the conditions related to the alert, including causes and potential resolutions.

▶ **Company Knowledge**—In this area you can add information specific to this condition at your particular organization.

▶ **History**—History about this particular alert; you can add comments that will be added to the alert history.

▶ **Alert Context**—Displays in XML format information regarding the event behind the alert.

▶ **Custom Fields**—Up to ten custom fields are available to add information regarding the alert.

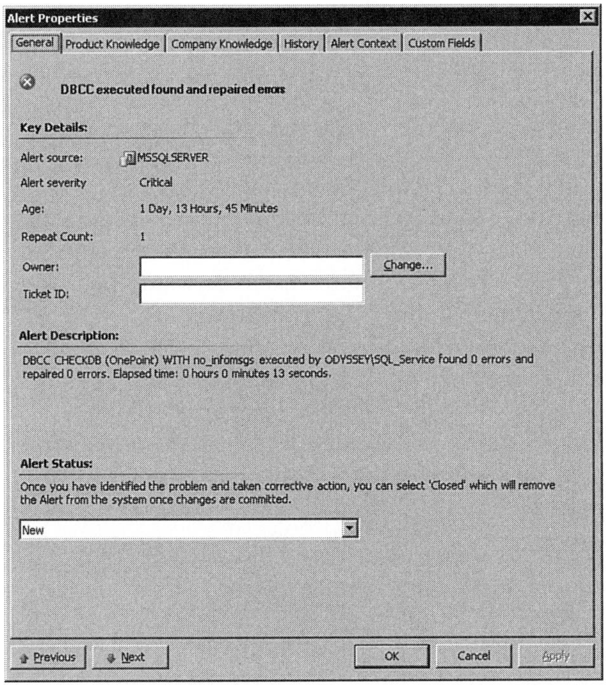

FIGURE 1.12   Alert description.

In addition to generating alerts, Operations Manager can send notifications based on the severity or age of a particular alert. Using the notification workflow engine, you can define subscriptions where alerts are sent to targeted recipients in a variety of ways:

▶ Via a network message, email message, instant message, or short message service (text messaging).

▶ By generating a Simple Network Management Protocol (SNMP) trap via a command piped to an external SNMP generator to integrate with another management system.

▶ By launching a script for complex processing. This ensures that even when alerts are generated, they do not intrusively notify you unless necessary.

Using the Operations console, Operations Manager allows you to view the state of your organization as a whole or to drill down into detail about any particular alert.

Security Policy Notification: Enforcement and Auditing

A big problem in IT is the distributed nature of security in Microsoft applications. Many administrators have local administrative access to servers, allowing them to modify things such as system and security logs. An unscrupulous administrator can use this access to circumvent security policies, ostensibly with the purpose of getting the job done. This is a gaping hole in any organization trying to maintain tight security. You need to know if there are security changes.

Operations Manager's new Audit Collection Services (ACS) Component can help you manage the security of your IT environment by collecting security events from managed computers for analysis. ACS helps facilitate the separation of security personnel from other IT job functions. It collects significant security events and can warn appropriate security personnel of violations of security policy. The local agent immediately forwards security log information to the Audit Collection database, moving it outside the control of the local administrator. Even if an administrator attempts to cover his tracks by clearing the Security Event log, ACS has sequestered the information. If a local administrator attempts to circumvent the process by shutting down the agent, the central console detects that and can generate an appropriate alert. You can use ACS to address regulatory compliance requirements such those legislated by the Sarbanes-Oxley Act. The product comes with reports out of the box. Figure 1.13 displays the Audit Collection Services data flow.

With security information safely and centrally stored, the security officer can generate reports and analyze the data to look for potential security problems.

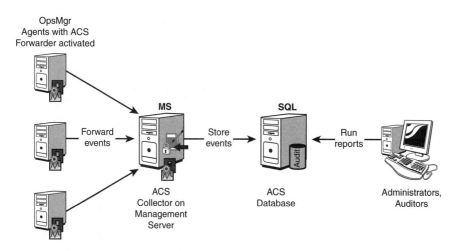

FIGURE 1.13   How information flows in ACS.

Historical Information

OpsMgr lets you view the information it gathers quickly and effectively. It is all well and fine that information is collected, but it is for naught if the information is not easily accessible. Operations Manager presents information in ways to make it easy to view, print, or publish.

Data collected includes availability, health, and performance statistics—invaluable information for analyzing what your servers and services are doing over the long term. To help review and understand the long-term trends and conditions of your servers and applications, OpsMgr generates reports both automatically and in an ad hoc fashion, including an easy-to-use graphical report designer that's part of the Operations Manager 2007 console. The reporting capabilities allow you to generate sophisticated reports complete with titles, numeric information, text information, graphs, and charts.

Using Views

In Figure 1.14, the Hydra computer shows some spikes in performance around midnight on 3/2/2007, which are the largest spikes captured in the graphs. This particular view actually displays several performance counters: percent processor time, processor queue length, and context switches. Using views gives you immediate access to information as it is collected, and you can adjust the view of that information quickly, perhaps to compare it with another system or examine other performance aspects, as we are in this particular view.

However, the display in Figure 1.14 does not tell us if what we see is normal performance for the computer because it only shows a 24-hour period.

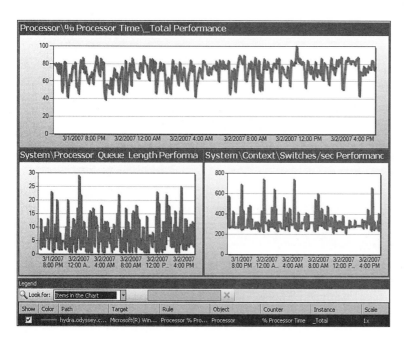

FIGURE 1.14 CPU performance analysis view.

TIP

Self-Tuning Thresholds

OpsMgr 2007 introduces *self-tuning thresholds*, which serve to monitor performance counters and set upper and lower thresholds based on historical activity. The system generates an alert only when activity exceeds these normal limits.

Reporting

We can also visually put the CPU utilization spike in context by seeing what a longer-term CPU utilization looks like for that system. Views, such as the one displayed in Figure 1.14, give us a quick look at the data. We can access the long-term view of historical data using the Reporting Component. The Performance Top Objects report shown in Figure 1.15 shows performance for Hydra and several other systems, but includes a range of what Operations Manager has determined is normal activity for the week and a standard deviation.

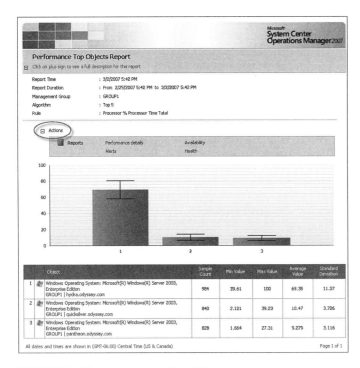

FIGURE 1.15   Performance Top Objects report.

You may notice an Actions section circled in the middle of the report that allows you to open other reports of interest. For example, selecting Performance details opens a Performance Detail report for Hydra, displayed in Figure 1.16. This report gives a graphic drilldown on the minimum, maximum, and average values for the week, along with the standard deviation, which is the degree of variation for those numbers. You can expand the Actions section on this report as well to see additional reports or views. With just a few mouse clicks, we now know that the average processor utilization is about 70%. Knowing what is normal can be half the battle when troubleshooting!

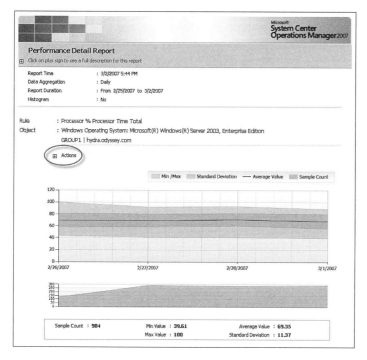

FIGURE 1.16   Performance Detail report for the Hydra computer.

Reports are static once generated, whereas views are interactive and will update as the underlying data changes. Reports can be exported as XML, saved in CSV, TIF, Excel, or PDF format, or published as HTML (MHTML) files using the Web Archive option. The HTML option is particularly powerful because it allows you to generate reports to publish for general viewing. The only requirement is having a browser and access to the web page, which allows IT to schedule reports showing routine stats, uptime, and so on, easily and effectively. You can email reports in PDF format to specified recipients. We discuss reporting capabilities in detail in Chapter 8, "Configuring and Using Operations Manager 2007," and report development in Chapter 23, "Developing Management Packs and Reports."

You can generate historical reports of what has happened over any period the data is collected for use with long-term trending and capacity planning. As we just discussed in the "Using Views" section, you can also look at the information as it is collected in real time for a snapshot view of what is happening within your organization, drilling down into detailed specifics as needed.

Access to a long-term view of information can help you detect trends and patterns otherwise hidden in a snapshot view. Recall our previous example, in the "Lack of Historical Information" section of this chapter, where the IT staff called out that CPU utilization was at 50%. Using Operations Manager, we can look at the historical information and see this was actually a normal condition. Using the same process, we can detect increases in network utilization and diagnose the problem appropriately. With OpsMgr at work, the IT staff might not even need outside consulting services!

As you might suspect, the amount of data collected from all these information sources can be quite massive. To handle this flood of data, Operations Manager uses the Microsoft SQL Server 2005 database platform for centralized storage of data, collecting and storing the reporting data in a separate database from the operational information. The Operations database is used for viewing current and historical data, performance statistics, and availability data. A data warehouse separately maintains data used for reports. Storing historical data separately allows OpsMgr to respond quickly to operational situations while enabling access to historical information in the data warehouse. This capability is invaluable for a system administrator trying to understand what his servers, services, and applications are really doing.

TIP

A New Type of Data Warehouse

With OpsMgr 2007, data transfer to the data warehouse is near real time; as operational information is collected from the monitored systems, it is also aggregated and written to the data warehouse, available with virtually no latency, and accessible for long-term usage.

As an example, Operations Manager can produce system and service availability reports to help keep the organization in line with its SLAs. These reports can be invaluable for managers proving the value of IT initiatives or driving home the need for IT improvements. Figure 1.17 shows a 7-day availability report. The Operations console Reporting function generated this report as a PDF file, without requiring use of any additional software. Within the console, you can schedule reports to be automatically generated. These reports can then be emailed or posted to a file share. The report output can be in the following formats: an Adobe Acrobat PDF, Excel, CSV comma delimited, TIF image, Web Archive, and XML file with report data.

Expertise

As soon as OpsMgr is installed, it begins to use its built-in expertise. Management packs, models containing a comprehensive set of predefined rules that form an expert system, focus on the health of your systems and will alert you to significant events, suppress unimportant data, and correlate seemly unimportant information to identify potential underlying problems. Rather than simply collecting a ton of information for the administrator to sort out, OpsMgr uses its knowledge to decide what is important, what's not, and will escalate as needed. When it determines a downgraded change in state has occurred, OpsMgr alerts appropriate personnel that you identify. Before escalating to a live person, Operations Manager can automatically respond to various situations, such as restarting stopped services. These actions are accomplished with management packs, which are collections of objects including monitors, rules, alerts, tasks, and reports.

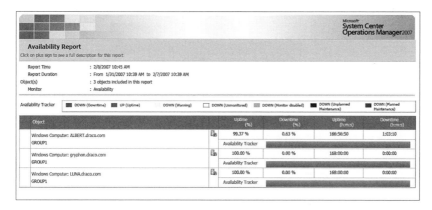

FIGURE 1.17   Availability report.

Management packs contain the knowledge, in essence the gray matter, from Microsoft's best people. These include the product support teams, developers, and vast resources of TechNet, Microsoft's technical database. This expertise is enhanced with the local expertise within your organization. Knowledge is added as alerts are generated, troubleshooting is performed, and problems are resolved, thereby enhancing the system. Similar to a human expert, OpsMgr improves its skills and capabilities over time. OpsMgr looks for changes in the state of an object. After alerting the appropriate personnel, it assists in resolving the problem by providing detailed knowledge including historical performance and event information, suggestions for fixes, direct links to tasks to resolve the problem, and pointers for where to research further.

As shown earlier in the Alert Details pane in the lower part of Figure 1.11, the highlighted alert contains concrete and specific guidance on what it means, the possible causes, possible resolutions, and where to get additional information if needed. In some cases the Alert Details pane does not show the entire contents of the knowledge for a particular alert, so we duplicate the full text of the Product Knowledge tab in the following sidebar. While in the console, you could click the View additional knowledge link in the Alert Details pane in Figure 1.11 to launch the alert properties window with the product knowledge text in it.

Alert Properties—Product Knowledge

Summary

This message indicates that DBCC CHECKDB, DBCC CHECKALLOC, DBCC CHECK-TABLE, or DBCC FILEGROUP has been executed on the SQL Server instance.

This message is never returned to the calling application; it is only written to the SQL Server error log and to the application event viewer. It is written to those logs even if the WITH NO_INFOMSGS option is used, as that option only controls what is returned to the calling application.

Resolutions

If the message indicates that errors were found:

Hardware Failure

Run hardware diagnostics and correct any problems. Also examine the Microsoft Windows NT system and application logs and the SQL Server error log to see if the error occurred as a result of a hardware failure. Fix any hardware-related problems.

If you have persistent data inconsistency problems, try to swap out different hardware components to isolate the problem. Check that your system does not have write caching enabled on the disk controller. If you suspect this to be the case, contact your hardware vendor.

Finally, you might find it beneficial to switch to a completely new hardware system, including reformatting the disk drives and reinstalling the operating system.

Restore from Backup

If the problem is not hardware related and a known clean backup is available. Restore the database from the backup.

DBCC CHECKDB

If no clean backup is available, execute DBCC CHECKDB without a repair clause to determine the extent of the corruption. DBCC CHECKDB will recommend a repair clause to use. Then, execute DBCC CHECKDB with the appropriate repair clause to repair the corruption.

Caution: If you are unsure what effect DBCC CHECKDB with a repair clause has on your data, contact your primary support provider before executing this statement.

If running DBCC CHECKDB with one of the repair clauses does not correct the problem, contact your primary support provider.

External Knowledge Sources

http://go.microsoft.com/fwlink/?linkid=54994&ProdName=Microsoft%20SQL%20Server&ProdVer=9.0.1399.0&EvtSrc=MSSQLSERVER&EvtID=8957

As issues are resolved, OpsMgr learns over time and builds that experience into its knowledge repository. If the situation recurs, OpsMgr is ready to provide the knowledge of what happened before and how it was resolved.

Using a Methodology

Operations Manager 2007 includes monitors and rules in management packs that keep tabs on your services and applications. OpsMgr focuses on the health of an application. Management packs are containers that include what we call *service models*, these use the SMLs discussed earlier in the "Microsoft's Dynamic Systems Initiative" section of this chapter and are formal definitions of types of objects. OpsMgr captures knowledge through models, putting knowledge in a structure the software can act on.

Management packs describe what we call *classes*. We don't see classes anywhere in the Operations console, and that is by design. Classes are a concept, we can describe things about them. A class is a type of object. A database is an object, and it has common types of properties, regardless of the server it runs on. Properties give us a common way to describe a database—it has a name, an owner, and other assorted attributes.

We can describe what makes up a database, and we can describe a relationship between other objects. A Microsoft SQL database has to run on a SQL Server—so it has to have some type of relationship with the SQL Server. The SQL Server runs on a Windows computer—so it has some relationship with the Windows computer. These relationships come into play when building management packs.

As an example, let's say we want to monitor a particular SQL database. We can define a relationship between that particular database instance and associate that database with its SQL Server engine, which is its parent object. If there is a fault condition on the database, it reports up to the parent. This changes the SQL Database Engine state in the OpsMgr console, and the information flows up to the computer, which is the parent for the SQL Server, and its state. State is the focal monitoring point. In Operations Manager 2007, changes in state trigger alerts; when the alert is resolved, the state changes to healthy. Using the Distributed Application Designer, we can also define a relationship between the database and applications that use it.

By incorporating models and methods for monitoring in its management packs, OpsMgr uses a structured approach to determine if there are situations requiring attention.

Catching Missed Information

OpsMgr continually monitors, helping ensure there are no missed events. The system also understands that certain events should take place and can generate an alert if those events do not occur. A special type of rule checks for a condition to occur within a defined time frame, such as every day between midnight and 5:00 a.m. If the specified condition does not occur within that time frame, that information is caught and an alert is generated, thus helping you to catch and take action on problems such as missed backups—one of the more useful items to check for in terms of a job not executing. Still, OpsMgr needs to be told to watch for the event; it is not quite smart enough to do what you're thinking or to catch what it isn't looking for.

Reducing False Alarms

OpsMgr uses its built-in knowledge and self-tuning capability to correlate different types of information and changes in state, ensuring that it alerts only when needed, typically reducing the number of alerts to a fraction of the underlying data. This capability reduces the flood of information typical management systems generate, allowing you to focus on what is important to keep your system up with optimal performance.

Operations Manager does all this easily and automatically. OpsMgr can automatically scan the network and install agents without any administrative intervention (although this is not turned on by default). You can even establish an Active Directory Organizational Unit (OU) managed by Operations Manager; OpsMgr uses that information to determine the management group an agent belongs to and the management server with which the agent will communicate. Updated rules and management packs are distributed automatically, helping you deploy your management infrastructure quickly and effectively. With its central console, OpsMgr allows you to implement a consistent systems monitoring and alerting policy to all your systems. Agents perform monitoring and apply the specific business logic and models for each monitored computer, automatically updating each system with the appropriate logic. Operations Manager also automatically removes business logic rules from the distributed systems, once the specified conditions no longer apply.

OpsMgr is scalable to all sizes of organizations, performing well even as it scales. The same product and basic architecture can be used to support medium, large, and enterprise-sized organizations with their varied requirements:

▶ It works well for medium-sized organizations, where you would have a single AD forest and between 30 and 500 servers to monitor. If you are planning to manage less than 200 Windows-based computers, you can install everything on a single box that is appropriately sized and configured (or separate the SQL components for improved performance).

▶ It works for large organizations, where fault tolerance and performance might be critical factors in the requirements. In this case, OpsMgr supports redundant and load-balanced components to ensure that it can monitor up to 2500 systems with no loss of performance or service.

▶ It also works well for enterprise organizations, where fault tolerance, performance, and organizational divides must be bridged. OpsMgr supports communication between an infinite number of connected management groups, capable of using a hierarchical architecture to handle a large organization's requirements, in addition to its redundant and load-balancing needs. Moreover, while scaling, Operations Manager still provides the cohesive view needed for a centralized management model.

TIP

Monitoring for Small-Sized Organizations

The smallest-sized organizations can use System Center Essentials, which uses a simplified version of the OpsMgr engine and supports up to 30 monitored servers. More information is found in the "System Center Essentials" section of this chapter.

Operations can be monitored through a console or a web interface. The console has views into the collected information—be it state, events, diagrams, alerts, or performance. You can also view reports. You can even view the status of your IT systems in a graphical diagram view that rapidly shows you the status of all systems, as in Figure 1.18, which shows the current Active Directory status. The highest-level state is shown in the state of the group, found at the top-left side of Figure 1.18. In this particular example, the highest-level state is Healthy, immediately letting us know that directory services are functioning properly in our Odyssey.com domain. We can also drill down into more detailed status of any particular component that has a plus sign (+) next to the diagram, indicating the view can be expanded.

Operations Manager 2007 can be deployed from medium to enterprise-sized organizations. Its flexibility also allows you to start small, managing a specific group of servers or a department. Once you are comfortable with the management platform, you can then scale it up to the rest of your organization.

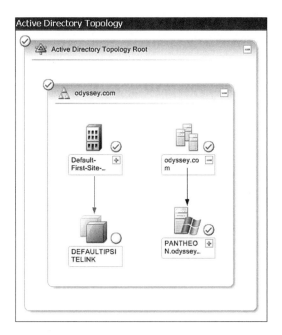

FIGURE 1.18   Active Directory Topology diagram view.

With OpsMgr handling your monitoring needs, you as an operations manager can relax (somewhat!) knowing that you will be alerted when there is a problem and have help in resolving it. It is like having your own IT genie on the job 24×7! But it won't take your job, not if you read this book.

Microsoft System Center

Beginning with MOM 2005, Operations Manager has been aligned with System Center. System Center is an umbrella or brand name for Microsoft's Systems Management family of products, and as such will have new products and components added over time. System Center is not a single integrated product; it represents a means to integrate system management tools and technologies to help you with systems operations, troubleshooting, and planning.

Different from the releases of Microsoft Office (another Microsoft product family), System Center is being released in "waves." The first wave included SMS 2003, MOM 2005, and System Center Data Protection Manager 2006; the 2006 additions included System Center Reporting Manager 2006 and System Center Capacity Planner 2006. The second wave includes Operations Manager 2007, Configuration Manager 2007, System Center Essentials 2007, System Center Service Manager, Virtual Machine Manager 2007, and new releases of Data Protection Manager and System Center Capacity Planner. (Most of these products are available as we are finalizing this book, with the exception of Capacity Planner and Service Manager.) And if that's not enough, there are already discussions of a third wave.

Microsoft System Center products share the following DSI-based characteristics:

- ▶ Ease of use and deployment
- ▶ Based on industry and customer knowledge
- ▶ Scalability (both up to the largest enterprises and down to the smallest organizations)

Reporting and Trend Analysis

The data gathered by Operations Manager 2007 is collected in a self-maintaining data warehouse, enabling numerous reports to be viewable using the Operations console. OpsMgr 2007 reports are now interactive and can launch other reports, console views, and tasks. Reports can also be exported to a Report Server file share; using the Web Archive format retains links. You can configure OpsMgr to schedule and email reports, enabling users to open these reports without accessing the Operations console. Approximately 150 reports are available out of the box. Reporting in MOM 2005 used the System Center Reporting Manager product released with the first wave. With the second wave, the Reporting Manager capability is moving under the to-be-released System Center Service Manager product and is no longer a separate product.

NOTE

OpsMgr Reporting and SRS

The OpsMgr reporting function uses the Microsoft SQL Server Reporting Services engine; if you know the GUID of an OpsMgr report, you can view it within the SRS Reporting web console.

Change and Configuration Management

Microsoft rebranded its SMS v4 product as System Center Configuration Manager (ConfigMgr), Microsoft's renamed and revamped systems management solution for change and configuration management. Like OpsMgr, the product is completely rewritten. Microsoft focuses Configuration Manager on addressing simplicity, deployment, security, and configuration. Features in ConfigMgr 2007 include the following:

▶ Network Access Protection (NAP), a policy enforcement platform, is built in to the Microsoft Windows Vista and Windows Server 2008 operating systems. NAP helps protect network assets by enforcing compliance with system health requirements, including enforcement across most common network access scenarios. This technology extends the Quarantine Access Control solution, previously only applicable in Microsoft Virtual Private Network (VPN) scenarios, to wired and wireless computers on the local area network (LAN), including clients using Dynamic Host Configuration Protocol (DHCP) for Transmission Control Protocol/Internet Protocol (TCP/IP) address assignment.

▶ Operating system deployment with the Windows Imaging (.wim) file format used with Windows Vista, is a technology based on the Operating System Deployment (OSD) Feature Pack available with SMS 2003 (note the OSD piece is also completely rewritten).

▶ A simplified user interface (UI), including enhanced multiple selection and drag-and-drop operations, is based on version 3 of the Microsoft Management Console (MMC).

▶ Software updates no longer use the legacy SMS software distribution components (packages, programs, and advertisements) when distributing software updates to clients. ConfigMgr now creates software update packages using simpler native technologies and uses WSUS 3.0 for software distribution.

▶ Maintenance windows, based on computer collections, are rules applied to a collection of clients that prevent those systems from executing programs in packages, running the Software Updates Component, and launching any Operating System Deployments except during the time specified in the window. (Other client actions such as policy refresh, inventory, package downloads, and desired configuration monitoring can still occur.)

▶ For software distribution, branch distribution points allow small office locations to host software packages on workstation computers without requiring the equivalent of an SMS secondary site. Package transfers to the branch distribution points trickle across the corporate wide area network (WAN) or VPN according to bandwidth-controlled settings using the Background Intelligent Transfer Service (BITS).

System Center Essentials

System Center Essentials, also called *Essentials*, is a System Center application for the small to medium-sized business that combines the monitoring features of OpsMgr with the inventory and software distribution functionality found in ConfigMgr. The monitoring function takes the form of a simplified OpsMgr 2007 engine that can use OpsMgr 2007 management packs, and the software distribution function is performed by the WSUS version 3.0 engine. Essentials is a wraparound shell and user interface for these functionalities in a small business network, including the essential features for monitoring, managing, and reporting as well as change and configuration management.

Using Essentials, you can centrally manage Windows-based servers and PCs, as well as network devices, by performing the following tasks:

▶ Monitor the health of computers and network devices and view summary reports of computer health.

▶ Centrally distribute software updates, track installation progress, and troubleshoot problems using the update management feature.

▶ Centrally deploy software, track progress, and troubleshoot problems with the software deployment feature.

▶ Collect and examine computer hardware and software inventory using the inventory feature.

Essentials provides a small subset of OpsMgr 2007 functionality when it comes to monitoring and managing infrastructures. The flip side of this reduced functionality is that Essentials greatly simplifies many functions compared to its OpsMgr 2007 counterparts. For example, by default the Discovery Wizard in Essentials automatically searches for both Windows computers and SNMP-based network devices in the Essentials server's domain and local subnet—without requiring the user to enter any networking information.

Customization and connectivity options for Essentials are limited, however. An Essentials deployment includes a single management server; all managed devices must be in the same Active Directory forest. Reporting functionality is included, but it is not as robust as that included with Operations Manager 2007.

Essentials also limits the number of managed objects per deployment to 30 Windows server-based computers and 500 Windows non-server-based computers. There is no limit to the number of network devices. Chapter 2, "What's New," includes a full feature comparison of the differences between OpsMgr and Essentials 2007.

Service Manager: A Self-Service Desk

Using System Center Service Manager implements a single point of contact for all service requests, knowledge, and workflow. The Service Manager (previously code named "Service Desk") incorporates processes such as incident, problem, change, and asset management. Just as OpsMgr is master of the MOF Operating quadrant, Service Manager will be an anchor for the MOF Supporting quadrant. Figure 1.19 illustrates the mapping between the quadrants of the MOF Process Model and System Center Components.

The Service Manager is Microsoft's new help desk product and fills a gap in Operations Manager: What do we do when OpsMgr detects a condition that requires human intervention and tracking for resolution? Until Service Manager, the answer was to create a ticket or incident in one's help desk application. Now, within the System Center framework, OpsMgr can hand off incident management to Service Manager.

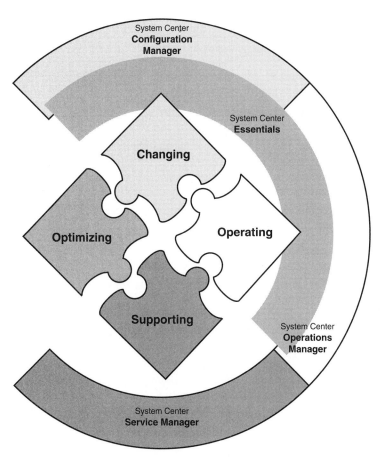

FIGURE 1.19   MOF quadrants and System Center applications.

Design goals of Service Manager include the following:

▶ Utilizing Microsoft technologies that people already use or are familiar with; for example, Service Manager uses the SharePoint and InfoPath products for web portal and knowledge base functions.

▶ Incorporating Self-Service Portal technologies to help organizations reduce support costs, including providing the administrator with a view into the overall performance of the IT environment using reports and dashboards.

▶ Ready-to-use process-automated workflows based on the Microsoft Operations Framework using DSI models.

▶ A Service Manager Solution Pack framework, similar to the Operations Manager Management Packs to enable customers and partners to develop additional custom functionality for the Service Manager.

▶ A Configuration Management Database (CMDB) based on SML and XML schema. Microsoft is positioning the CMDB as the foundation of its asset and change-management capability.

Supported scenarios include the following Service Management Functions (SMFs) and capabilities from the MOF Operating and Supporting quadrants:

▶ **Incident management**—Creating incident records based on information in management tools

▶ **Problem management**—Identifying problems by searching common incidents

▶ **Asset management**—Tracking movement and ownership of hardware assets

▶ **Change management**—Reviewing and approving change requests

▶ **Self-Service Portal**—Resolving an issue without calling the help desk

Service Manager utilizes a Winforms console, which has an appearance similar to Outlook and Operations Manager. It uses the OpsMgr agent, and the console will have the ability to run OpsMgr tasks. Service Manager brings the "designed for operations" moniker full circle by providing a means to feed production and user data back into the development process using Visual Studio.

Protecting Data

System Center's Data Protection Manager (DPM) 2007 is a disk-based backup product for continuous data protection supporting servers running Windows 2003 Service Pack (SP) 1 and above. (The DPM Server itself must have SP 2, and x64-bit Windows Server is recommended.) DPM provides byte-level backup as changes occur, utilizing Microsoft's Virtual Disk Service and Shadow Copy technologies.

Microsoft describes DPM 2007 as a "best of breed" product, adding support for tape media. The Enterprise Edition offers native protection for Windows applications such as Microsoft SQL Server, Exchange, SharePoint Portal Server, and Virtual Server, plus bare metal. This means that in addition to selecting file shares, you can back up SQL Server databases and Exchange Server storage groups. Via online snapshots, disk-based recovery can maintain backup points to a 15-minute window.

Capacity Planning

System Center Capacity Planner is designed to provide tools and guidance to determine an optimal architecture for successful deployments, while also incorporating hardware and architecture "what-if" analyses for future planning. The Capacity Planner assists with planning deployments of Operations Manager and Exchange Server.

In conjunction with the second "wave" of System Center, the newest version of Capacity Planner will include OpsMgr 2007 support for ACS; modeling gateway servers; backup servers for the Operations database, RMS, and data warehouse; 64-bit hardware support; database sizing recommendations and support for background loads; trusted and untrusted agents; and an enhanced predeployment wizard. Planning is expected to be more granular to include different branch configurations and be component based.

Capacity Planner will only support OpsMgr 2007 installations running Operations Manager SP 1.

The Capacity Planner creates models with information on topology, hardware, software, and usage profiles. It also allows you to run iterative simulations on the models for performance information. Capacity Planner ties into the DSI strategy by identifying when systems deviate from a defined performance model, providing guidance to correct those variations.

Virtual Machine Management

System Center Virtual Machine Manager is a standalone server application, providing centralized management of your Windows Virtual machines. It currently supports Virtual Server 2005 R2, and Windows Server virtualization will be supported with the Microsoft Windows Server 2008 operating system.

Virtual Machine Manager enables increased physical server utilization, centralized management of a virtual infrastructure, and rapid provisioning of new virtual machines by system administrators and users via a self-service portal.

The Value Proposition of Operations Manager

The value of Operations Manager lies in three areas:

▶ Increasing the quality of service that IT departments deliver to their business units

▶ Reducing the operational cost to deliver that service

▶ Delivering a best-of-breed tool for Windows Management

As a management tool monitoring system health, Operations Manager is designed as a best-of-breed monitoring solution for the Windows Server platform, providing enterprise scale and operations management. By incorporating a rich application and service monitoring environment using its management packs, OpsMgr provides a high level of automation.

As an enterprise-ready solution, OpsMgr provides redundant support and high availability with an open architecture—a requirement for computing enterprises that encompass multiple environments that include non-Microsoft platforms. Operations Manager is extensible, so it can integrate with other computing environments including third-party management suites such as Tivoli's TEC, HP OpenView, and the HP Network Mode Manager.

Operations Manager 2007 can monitor, manage, and secure a wide range of resources, including computers, applications, server farms, e-commerce sites, network devices, and corporate servers. It supports networked systems scaling up to thousands of computers on the network. OpsMgr can continuously monitor user actions, application software, servers, and desktop computers running Microsoft Windows 2000 and later versions.

The goal for the IT manager considering OpsMgr is to lower the cost of deploying and managing Windows solutions. This goal includes the "time to resolution"—or how rapidly the IT manager can get an understanding of what is happening in the operating environment and then automatically (or as quickly as possible) achieve a resolution. Operations Manager 2007 (when correctly tuned) is positioned to help you tame the fire hose (as shown in Figure 1.20) and control the deluge of system and operational information pouring at you from across your operating environment. It is a key component of DSI.

FIGURE 1.20   Taming the fire hose.

Out of the box, Operations Manager 2007 hits the ground running by supporting key applications such as SQL Server, Microsoft Exchange, and Active Directory. What's more, Microsoft has announced management packs for the second quarter of 2008 that will include support for all the Windows Server 2008 roles. OpsMgr's model-based management packs include monitors, rules, alerts, tasks, best-practice knowledge, reports, and templates, requiring little or no configuration or setup for the majority of applications. Its Distributed Application Designer provides the flexibility to design your own management packs with a Visio-like interface that generates the rules behind the scenes.

OpsMgr's huge body of expertise solves one of the major obstacles that many enterprise management solutions encountered prior to the availability of Microsoft's product. Most of the big framework management platforms, such as Unicenter TNG, HP OpenView, and Tivoli TEC, provide an infrastructure that has the potential to do great things, and they are sold based on that potential. After a company has spent mucho dollars to deploy the infrastructure, the hard work of configuring the product begins. Sometimes, due to the difficulty of configuration, the plug is pulled on these framework products, which leaves a bad taste in the mouth of the company after apparently wasting its money.

OpsMgr completely changes the paradigm by shipping the product with the vast majority of the configuration done for you. This instant return on investment provides a huge win when the system starts detecting operational problems, alerting the appropriate personnel, resolving issues, and providing extensive reports with little or no IT effort.

Summary

This chapter introduced you to operations management. You learned that operations management is a process to enhance the supportability of a production environment. The chapter illustrated how Operations Manager can solve a horde of problems. System Center Operations Manager 2007 works to eliminate the isolated islands of information in your shop, notifies you of problems, and maintains a historical database of what happened and how issues were resolved.

We discussed ITIL, which is an international set of best practices for IT Service Management. ITIL describes at a high level what should be accomplished, although not actually how to accomplish it. In furtherance of that process, Microsoft chose ITIL as the foundation for its own operations framework. With the MOF, Microsoft provides both descriptive (what to do and why) as well as prescriptive (how to do it) guidance for IT service management.

Microsoft's management approach, which encompasses MOF and also DSI, is a strategy or blueprint intended to automate data center operations. Microsoft's investment in DSI includes building systems designed for operations, developing an operationally aware platform, and establishing a commitment to intelligent management software.

Operations Manager is a tool for managing the Windows platform to increase the quality of service IT delivers while reducing the operational cost of delivering that service. Together with ConfigMgr and the other System Center products, OpsMgr is a crucial player in Microsoft's approach to system management.

Management software is a key element in Microsoft's strategy to convince corporate customers that Redmond is serious about proactive management of Windows systems. As we step through the different areas of this book, you'll become aware of just how powerful Operations Manager is, and how serious Microsoft is about operations management.

CHAPTER 2

What's New

When picking up a book about a new software release, one usually finds a chapter or section of material discussing "what's new." This material typically covers what has changed in the latest, greatest, and most wonderful release of the product. However, so many things have changed between Microsoft Operations Manager (MOM) 2005 and System Center Operations Manager (OpsMgr) 2007, we gave serious consideration to calling this chapter "What's *Not* New," or perhaps "What Stayed the Same!"

This state of affairs occurs because the newest version of Operations Manager is truly a revamped product. In its third major release by Microsoft, the product team totally rewrote its guts. Database names are different, Registry keys are renamed, consoles continue to evolve, and most importantly, the product approaches operations management in a totally different way.

Now that you've had an introduction to the concepts behind operations management and the capabilities of Operations Manager 2007, we are ready to focus on the differences in various versions of Microsoft's flagship management product. We will look at what has changed between MOM 2005 and OpsMgr 2007, including changes in approach, changes to component functionality, changes in terminology, changes to consoles, changes to the reporting feature, and differences in scalability with the new version. Although we discussed similar topics in *Microsoft Operations Manager 2005 Unleashed* as we looked at the differences between MOM 2000 and MOM 2005, those changes were evolutionary in nature; the changes between MOM 2005 and OpsMgr 2007 are far more revolutionary. We will also take a look at OpsMgr's smaller brother, System

Center Essentials (or just Essentials for short), discussing its capabilities and the differences between Essentials and the full version of OpsMgr 2007.

The History of Operations Manager

First, let's spend a moment on a brief history of Microsoft's presence in the server monitoring marketplace. Microsoft began including server health and monitoring functionality with Microsoft Application Center 2000, Systems Management Server 2.0, and BackOffice Server 2000. The monitoring capability enabled a system administrator to have a centralized view of information pertaining to functional health, performance, and the Event log data of the servers used within that specific application server environment.

> **NOTE**
>
> **A Free Utility**
>
> If you have ever tried looking through the Windows NT Event log files for security or application issues? It can be an overwhelming task—particularly if you have thousands, or tens of thousands, of servers. Indeed, this is the reason software such as Operations Manager was developed.
>
> Not to be confused with the extended capabilities of Operations Manager, a free utility called EventCombMT.exe is available from Microsoft. EventComb parses multiple Event logs across the network and organizes the information into a single location. EventComb started as a command-line tool and was less than an overwhelming success. Microsoft has since added a GUI. You can find EventComb at http://www.microsoft.com/downloads. Search on "Security Guide Scripts Download" in the keyword field to download secops.exe, which includes EventCombMT.exe.

Operations Manager was originally based on technology developed by Mission Critical Software for its OnePoint Operations Manager product, licensed by Microsoft in 2000 from NetIQ shortly after that company acquired Mission Critical. Microsoft's first release of the management software addressed scalability and performance issues, along with significant improvements to management packs for Microsoft applications software. With an oft-stated goal of making the Windows Server platform more manageable, Microsoft positioned MOM 2000 as an enterprise monitoring solution, including comprehensive event management, monitoring and alerting, reporting, a built-in knowledge base, and trend analysis capabilities.

During the MOM 2000 life cycle, a single service pack was released. MOM 2000 Service Pack (SP) 1 included globalization, clustered support for the MOM database on failovers, a number of performance improvements to the event management infrastructure, enhancements to most of its management packs with particular emphasis on those for Microsoft

Exchange Server and Active Directory monitoring, and several new management packs. Continuing development of the product, Microsoft began work in 2003 on the next version of MOM.

Some Acquisition Trivia

A question typically asked in every major software development project is whether to build the application in house or buy it from others. In October 2000, Microsoft and NetIQ Corporation announced a technology licensing agreement and partnership in operations management, where Microsoft licensed NetIQ's Operations Manager technology—newly acquired by NetIQ with its recent merger with Mission Critical Software—for managing the Windows 2000 environment and later versions of Windows. The agreement between Microsoft and NetIQ also included a 3-year technology partnership to jointly develop management software for Windows 2000 and other servers.

For those of you who are really into factoids, Mission Critical Software also was responsible for the technology that became the basis of Microsoft's Active Directory Migration Tool (ADMT). Stephen Kangas, Vice President of Strategic Alliances at Mission Critical Software prior to its merger with NetIQ, was behind the technology license and development agreement pertaining to ADMT and also facilitated the Microsoft/NetIQ Operations Manager licensing agreement. Stephen later retired from NetIQ Corporation.

Microsoft Operations Manager 2005 was released in August 2004 with an improved user interface, additional management packs, enhanced reporting, and improved performance and scalability. Microsoft next released MOM 2005 SP 1 in July 2005 with support for Windows 2003 SP 1 and SQL Server 2000 SP 4. SP 1 was also a prerequisite for the MOM 2005 support of the SQL Server 2005 engine after that product's release later that year. Development for the next version, initially code-named "MOM V3," also commenced in 2005. In 2006, Microsoft officially announced the upcoming version as System Center Operations Manager 2007. Work on Operations Manager 2007 was completed in March 2007, and OpsMgr 2007 SP 1's release is anticipated in early 2008.

Figure 2.1 illustrates Operations Manager's life cycle.

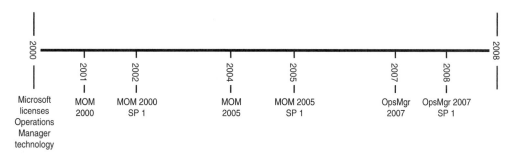

FIGURE 2.1   Operations Manager development timeline.

OpsMgr 2007 SP 1: What's Planned?

With the normal disclaimer that until it is released nothing is cast in concrete, the OpsMgr 2007 Service Pack 1 improvements are expected to

▶ Address bugs and hotfixes, including fixes to Setup, the OpsMgr core, management packs, reporting, the Operations console, and the Web console.

▶ Improve product deployability and supportability.

▶ Improve performance and usability (alerts, overrides, search performance)

▶ Support SNMP v1

▶ Incorporate fixes to ACS and AEM

To keep track of the list of fixes (more than 20 at the time of the Release Candidate) incorporated into the service pack, see http://support.microsoft.com/kb/944443. SystemCenterForum also discusses changes in SP 1 at http://www.systemcenterforum. org/features-in-sp1-rc-for-operations-manager-2007-you-need-to-know-about-part-1/. These changes include:

▶ **Web console enhancements**—My Reports is now exposed in the Web console.

▶ **Export to Visio**—This functionality, previously available in MOM 2005, returns, allowing easy export of diagrams.

▶ **Removing instances where discovery is disabled**—The ability to easily remove discovery data was an enormous gap in the OpsMgr RTM (Released to Manufacturing version). The sealed MP concept prevented the removal of instances from monitoring (such as a test Active Directory domain controller) once the instance was discovered (without digging way into the SDK). A new PowerShell cmdlet, `Remove-DisabledMonitoringObject`, has been introduced to allow removal of instances for which discovery is disabled.

▶ **ACS forwarder on management and gateway servers**—You can now also enable the ACS forwarder on management servers and gateway servers, allowing collection of Security Event log data for these roles as well.

▶ **Improved console performance**—The query performance used to retrieve alert info and other data has been improved dramatically to enhance the user experience in the Operations Console UI. Hopefully this means the end of what some call the "Green Bar Watchers Club."

▶ **Performance data filtering in ceb Console**—The Web console provided improved filtering capabilities for performance data when working in Performance views, with filtering options similar to what you see in the Operations console.

Although the Release Candidate should be feature complete, there is no guarantee everything included in the RC will make the released version of the service pack.

Questions will arise regarding compatibility between the RTM and SP code. This will be a moving target for quite a while. One question already is *Can I use my RTM Operations console to access a SP 1 management group?* The answer is yes, but ... If you don't disable version checking in the Registry, you will get an error telling you that "You have attempted to connect to a server which is incompatible with your Operations Console." To disable version checking, perform the following steps (Thanks to the folks at Techlog.nl for documenting this!):

1. Open the Registry Editor (Start -> Run -> **REGEDIT**)
2. Navigate to HKEY_CURRENT_USER\SOFTWARE\Microsoft\Microsoft Operations Manager\3.0\Console.
3. Create a new key called **ManagementGroupSessionManager**.
4. Under this key, create a DWORD Value named **DisableVersionCheck**.
5. Set the Value data to **1**.

One other thing: Since this is HKCU, it only applies to that user and that computer—so you have to change the registry for every system that has the RTM Operations console installed. A script can help with this task; just include it with login processing for those people with access to the console.

Introducing Operations Manager 2007

What's so different and new about Operations Manager 2007? To start, the name of the product itself indicates OpsMgr has had a facelift. Less noticeable, at least until you start looking into the product, is that its approach towards monitoring has completely shifted. We discuss these changes in the following sections.

What's in a Name?

One of the first differences you may notice between the versions of Operations Manager is the evolution of the product name. Versions 2000 and 2005 were known as *MOM*, an acronym built using the company name "Microsoft" + "Operations Manager." Version 2007 has a System Center branding, making the complete product name "System Center Operations Manager." (This is not to say you may not find some "MOM shrapnel" or remnants in utility names or elsewhere.) The purpose of the branding ostensibly is to align Operations Manager with the System Center umbrella of products. Although this may be the official name, we have noted some effort within Microsoft to avoid using the umbrella moniker or any associated acronyms, and simply call the software *Operations Manager*, thus developing a following for the product itself regardless of where it is in Microsoft's lineup. There does continue to be a dichotomy, though. You can note this in Microsoft's System Center Pack Catalog, located at http://go.microsoft.com/fwlink/ ?LinkId=71124. The search function on the page includes the ability to specify the product version; the associated dropdown box displayed in Figure 2.2 includes the ability to search on all three versions of Operations Manager, but distinguishes between the older versions and the newer System Center branded software.

The Change in Focus

More than just a name change, Operations Manager's focus in monitoring has also evolved. OpsMgr 2007 provides best-of-breed end-to-end service management for the Microsoft Windows platform, helping you increase efficiency and achieve greater control over your Information Technology (IT) environment. Operations Manager can manage

thousands of event and performance monitors across operating systems and applications
to provide a single view of the health of your IT environment. This focus on viewing a
service's *health* is key for responding to things that may affect the normal running of business and ultimately cost an organization money. This differs from earlier versions of
Operations Manager that concentrated on monitoring events and generating alerts.
OpsMgr 2007 is all about monitoring health. It moves away from monitoring only individual servers and applications to holistically monitoring server and client environments.

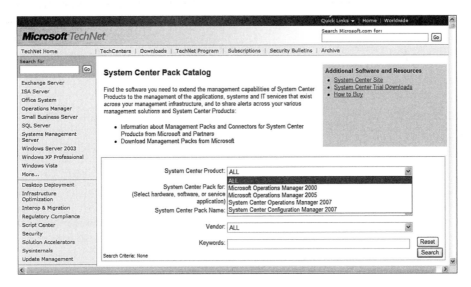

FIGURE 2.2   Operations Manager versions displayed in the System Center Pack Catalog.

Operations Manager 2007 builds on its predecessors by adding key features and functionality requested by customers. System administrators told Microsoft they wanted to
monitor more than just individual servers; they wanted it to be easier to find computers
and applications needing to be monitored, and they wanted more detailed troubleshooting and best practice knowledge. The market for management solutions also had an
impact in designing Operations Manager 2007. More enterprises are implementing
Service Level Management, and more companies are finding a need to monitor their
ever-expanding network of Microsoft Windows–based systems.

Operations Manager 2005 versus Operations Manager 2007

Operations Manager 2007 is far-reaching in its changes from its predecessor, MOM 2005. Not only is there the change in focus discussed in the previous section, but scalability is enhanced, security is revamped, the structure and functionality of management packs has changed, and major alterations were made to the user interface as well as in reporting capabilities. Additionally, Microsoft has reworded some of the terminology and redesigned roles; therefore, if you were an Operations Manager 2005 administrator, you'll find it useful to understand these changes as part of planning your transition to OpsMgr 2007.

Terminology Changes

Several terms have changed between MOM 2005 and OpsMgr 2007. This section gives you an overview of these changes, and Table 2.1 recaps these terms.

TABLE 2.1   Terminology Equivalents and Changes

Operations Manager 2005 Term	Operations Manager 2007 Term
MOM service	Health service
Alert severity	Health state
Alert-generating rule	Monitor
Performance rule	Performance collection rule
Computer group	Computer group class, installation class
Data Access Server	Part of SDK service functionality
First installed Management Server	Root Management Server
Tasks	Console and agent tasks

Health Service
The OpsMgr Health service monitors the health of the computer it is installed on; it optionally can be configured to monitor the health of other computers with agentless monitoring. The Health service is on management servers and all computers running the Operations Manager agent.

Health State
Operations Manager 2007 monitors health and looks for changes in state. The health state is the status of any monitored object. Available health states are Success (green), Warning (yellow), and Error (red).

Monitor

OpsMgr 2007 uses *monitors* to evaluate conditions that occur in monitored objects. A monitor can assess the values of a performance counter, the existence of an event, the occurrence of data in a log file, the status of a Windows service, or the occurrence of a Simple Network Management Protocol (SNMP) trap. Based on its assessment, the monitor determines the health state (status) of a target and the alerts generated. See the "Monitoring Engine" section later in this chapter for more information on how monitors work.

Performance Collection Rule

Performance rules have been renamed *performance collection rules*, which collect performance-based numeric data. Information collected by these rules displays in a performance view for those objects. A sample view is displayed in Figure 2.3.

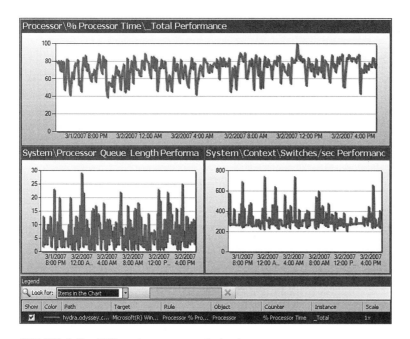

FIGURE 2.3   CPU performance analysis view.

Computer Group Class and Installation Class

Computer groups in Operations Manager 2005 are used to group computers with similar characteristics. Rule groups then target groups of rules to these computers.

Operations Manager 2007 monitors individual services and applications rather than computer objects. This approach allows Operations Manager 2007 to monitor the physical server separately from the software installed on the computer. When a computer group is converted from Operations Manager 2005 to Operations Manager 2007, two object types are created. The *computer group class* is for the physical computer, and the *installation class* applies to software. Computer groups are often used for targeting overrides.

SDK Service

In MOM 2005, the Data Access Server (DAS) is a Component Object Model Plus (COM+) application running on the management server and managing access to the Operational database. The DAS provides a communication interface between the Operational database and other components.

The OpsMgr SDK service is many things (which we discuss in detail in Chapter 3, "Looking Inside OpsMgr"), but similar to the DAS, data flowing to and from the database is transported via the SDK service.

Root Management Server

The *Root Management Server* (RMS) is a new server component and maintains the topology data for the entire management group. The console user interface comes from the RMS, which is also responsible for importing management packs. We discuss the RMS in more detail in the "Server Components" section of this chapter.

Console and Agent Tasks

In MOM 2005, a task automated a management process. OpsMgr 2007 has several new types of tasks, such as diagnostic and recovery tasks that diagnose and repair problems, respectively. The MOM 2005 task, which could be initiated from the console or on the agent, is now known as a console task or an agent task.

Functionality Changes

OpsMgr 2007 introduces an incredible amount of new functionality and a new approach to monitoring. In this section, we discuss some of the more significant changes.

Model-based Management

Operations Manager 2007 uses model-based management, where an IT environment is defined as a *model*. Models allow for more granular discovery of service components and present the ability to monitor not only the servers but also the entire end-to-end service as a unique object. Once it's defined, you can monitor an end-to-end service just like any other device.

Knowledge is captured through models. Models put knowledge in a structure that software can act on, and they define the health of complex IT services and systems—including their structure, constraints, and policies. OpsMgr 2007 models are defined natively and represented in eXtensible Markup Language (XML). By defining the IT environment as models, Operations Manager can better understand the relationships between the distributed applications and components that make up your IT services.

Service-Oriented Monitoring

Earlier versions of Operations Manager focused on monitoring individual server health, not taking into account the distributed nature of many enterprise applications and services. OpsMgr 2007 introduces service modeling, which allows distributed applications to be represented as a service. The software includes a graphical Distributed Application Designer, making the task of defining service models easier. With the Designer, you can diagram the flow of your critical distributed applications and set interdependencies for each object. Any object that OpsMgr manages can be included in a service model; you can represent and monitor applications, hardware, and networking components.

As an example, let's consider a classic three-tiered business application with two front-end web services, a middle logic tier, and a backend database. Using the Distributed Application Designer displayed in Figure 2.4, you can quickly and easily describe monitoring requirements for this application that correspond to how it was architected. The Designer allows you to create your tiers and drag and drop each component object into the correct tier. This creates a distributed view, from which you can be alerted on every aspect of your application, minimizing resolution time for other affected systems. Now that is cool!

This end-to-end service modeling enables proactive monitoring of IT service health, end-user perspective modeling, new service-oriented views, dashboards, reports, and templates. Using the Designer will accelerate third-party management pack development for infrastructure and other types of applications.

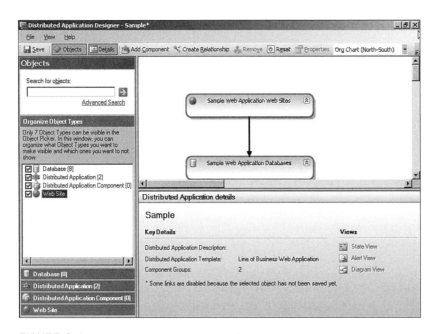

FIGURE 2.4   The Distributed Application Designer.

Agentless Exception Monitoring

Operations Manager 2007 introduces Agentless Exception Monitoring (AEM). AEM captures, aggregates, and reports on application crashes—commonly known as Dr. Watson errors—throughout your enterprise, giving you a view of which applications and systems are suffering the most crashes.

Using Group Policy, AEM redirects Watson clients to a designated management server and allows OpsMgr to monitor client crash and hang data as part of enterprise health. Alerts are generated based on aggregated crash trends, and reports display top crashes and trends across the organization.

Consoles

Operations Manager 2005 had three consoles:

▶ An Administrator console for making configuration changes, which used Microsoft Management Console (MMC) technology.

▶ An Operator console for managing alerts, events, and performance.

▶ A Reporting console for defining and publishing reports. This was actually the SQL Reporting Services (SRS) Report Manager console.

Operations Manager 2007 consolidates these three functions into one console (which is similar to the approach in MOM 2000, which combined the Administrator and Operator consoles). Whereas MOM 2005 supported a limit of 15 active Operator consoles in a single management group, there is no theoretical limit to the number of active Operations consoles with OpsMgr 2007, with 50 simultaneous consoles tested.

The OpsMgr 2007 Operations console, displayed in Figure 2.5, does not use the MMC interface, but like the MOM 2005 Operator console it has a similar look and feel to Microsoft Outlook. The console includes a toolbar, a Navigation pane and navigation buttons on the left side, the Results pane and Details pane in the center, and the Actions pane on the right side. Selecting options such as overrides, search, the Health Explorer, or Reporting launches new windows to support those operations. There are also a number of views in the Monitoring and Authoring spaces. Further information about using the Operations console can be found in Chapter 8, "Configuring and Using Operations Manager 2007."

Web-based Monitoring   Both versions of Operations Manager include a Web console. Whereas the MOM 2005 Web console used port 1272 by default, the OpsMgr 2007 Web console, displayed in Figure 2.6, uses port 51908. The Web console provides similar functionality to the full console for operational monitoring.

Command-line Interface   PowerShell support, included with Exchange 2007 and Windows Server 2008, is also available using the Command Shell, which is an instance of PowerShell customized with OpsMgr extensions. Using PowerShell, an administrator can make configuration changes, view alerts, run tasks, deploy agents, and so on. The primary advantages of using PowerShell over the Operations console is that it supports scripting, thus allowing an administrator to perform most of the work that can be done in the Operations and Web consoles in a batch mode.

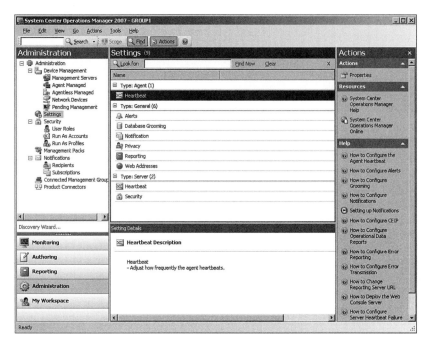

FIGURE 2.5   The OpsMgr 2007 Operations console.

FIGURE 2.6   The OpsMgr 2007 Web console.

Securing the Console   Role-based security allows limiting the privileges that users have for various aspects of Operations Manager, giving OpsMgr 2007 administrators granular control over what is visible and restricting user access to only those features they are authorized to use. SQL database administrators can only see SQL information; Exchange admins can just see Exchange information; and so on.

TIP

How Far Does Security Reach?

Role-based security is not limited to the Operations console; it encompasses any SDK client or application that uses the OpsMgr class libraries to connect to the SDK service. SDK clients include the Operations console, Web console, Operations Manager Command Shell, and other customized applications.

New with Service Pack 1: the Authoring Console   The Authoring console, planned for release with OpsMgr 2007 Service Pack 1, will provide new functionality for writing management packs without the requirement to use XML. We discuss the Authoring console in Chapter 23, "Developing Management Packs and Reports."

Health Explorer

The Health Explorer is a window in Operations Manager where you can view and then take action on alerts, state changes, and other significant issues. You access the Health Explorer from the Actions pane in the Operations console after selecting an object, alert, or event in the Results pane.

Health Explorer organizes information into several categories:

▶ Availability

▶ Configuration

▶ Performance

▶ Security

Within each category, all monitors and rules defined for a particular selected object will display. When the Explorer first opens, all monitors in a failed (red) state are expanded by default. If a monitor is a rollup monitor so that it contains other monitors (as in the example in Figure 2.7), those monitors are shown in a hierarchical layout displaying monitoring data for all services and applications dependent on the one that failed. This particular example shows that the MonitoringHost Private Bytes Threshold is in an error state. Hierarchically, this threshold is under the Performance category. You can see the rollup through the different monitors in the hierarchy, with the topmost monitor reflecting the state of health of the worst object.

FIGURE 2.7   The Health Explorer.

A New Command Shell
The Command Shell in OpsMgr 2007 uses Windows PowerShell technology, providing a command-line environment administrators can use to automate administration. Using the Command Shell, you can use the `get-momcommand` cmdlet to get a list of Operations Manager 2007 cmdlets and the `get-Help` cmdlet to display help for each cmdlet.

WS-Management Support
OpsMgr 2007 supports the Web Services for Management (WS-Management) industry-standard management protocol. WS-Management identifies core Web service specifications and usage requirements to enable management using Web services. By providing a common way for systems to access and exchange management information, WS-Management addresses the cost and complexity of IT management.

SNMPv2 Support
MOM 2005 only supported SNMP trap monitoring. Operations Manager 2007 supports the full SNMPv2 stack (and SP 1 adds support for SNMPv1), including polling and trap monitoring. OpsMgr is now able to not only receive traps but also use SNMP to discover network devices such as routers, print servers, and computers not running Windows, even if the device or operating system is not being monitored with a management pack. You can also create your own monitors and rules using SNMP to monitor network devices or other operating systems. SNMP-based monitors and rules can collect data from SNMP events or traps, generate alerts, or change the health state of the monitored object.

Role-Based Security

MOM 2005 had limited security options: a user could be a MOM Administrator, a MOM Author, or MOM User. These were local security groups residing on each management server. Members of these groups had access to the entire Operator console, but actions were limited based on group membership. MOM Administrators and Authors also could access the Administrator console.

OpsMgr 2007 uses role-based security. Operations such as resolving alerts, executing console tasks, overriding monitors, creating user roles, viewing alerts, viewing events, and so on, have been grouped into profiles. A *role* is a combination of a profile (capabilities) and a scope (the breadth of data and objects one is able to access), as illustrated in Figure 2.8. Active Directory (AD) security groups typically are assigned to roles, with individual user accounts assigned to those security groups.

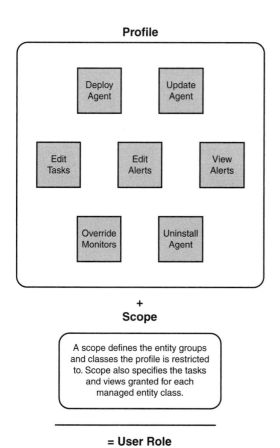

FIGURE 2.8   A role is associated with a profile and a scope.

Role-based security eliminates the need of using multiple management groups solely to control scope between different types of users looking at data. As an example, many MOM 2005 implementations used a separate management group for security monitoring. Administrators are now able to define user roles that have access to only specific systems, views, and tasks within the console. This gives you the capability to grant access to a user who needs to manage events and performance for a select group of computers, such as mail servers or database servers. The user cannot see any other systems in the console and is unable to execute tasks other than those approved for that particular role.

This role-based security is in effect for the Operations console, Web console, command line, and any other SDK-level interfaces. Roles created during setup include the following:

- **Operations Manager Administrator**—This role has full privileges to Operations Manager. The role initially includes the local Administrators group (BUILTIN\Administrators) or the OM Admins global group if specified during setup.

- **Operations Manager Advanced Operators**—Gives access to limited tweaking of the monitoring configuration and Operators privileges, described later. Members can override the configuration of rules and monitor specific targets or groups of targets within a configured scope.

- **Operations Manager Authors**—This role includes a set of privileges allowing authoring of the monitoring configuration. Members have the ability to create, edit, and delete monitoring configurations (tasks, rules, monitors, and views) with a configured scope.

  Authors are often given Advanced Operator privileges.

- **Operations Manager Operators**—Includes a set of privileges to give access to alerts, views, and tasks.

- **Operations Manager Read-Only Operators**—Gives read-only access to alerts and views.

- **Operations Manager Report Operators**—this role is designed for users who need to access reports.

- **Operations Manager Report Security Administrators**—Includes a set of privileges designed to enable integrating SRS security with Operations Manager, giving Operations Manager Administrators the ability to control access to reports.

A user can belong to multiple roles; the resultant scope is the union of all roles the user belongs to.

Run As Profiles and Run As Accounts

Run As Profiles and Run As Accounts are used to specify users with the necessary privileges to run rules, tasks, and monitors. Keep the following points in mind:

- Using a *Run As Profile* associates an identity with a module so that it can run as that identity. The default account for the Run As Profile is the Agent Action account. A management pack author can use a Run As Profile to associate a different identity with a module. You can override the account associated with a Run As Profile on a per-computer basis.

▶ A *Run As Account* is an identity that you can associate with a Run As Profile. Using Run As Accounts alleviates the need for users to have administrator access. A Run As Account is an Operations Manager object that maps to an AD user account. Multiple Run As Accounts can be associated with a Run As Profile.

Run As Accounts are stored on the RMS and accessed by the SDK service, which we describe in the next section.

New Windows Services
OpsMgr 2007 runs three services on the RMS:

▶ **Health service (HealthService)**—Monitors computer health. This service is renamed from the MOM service in MOM 2005. The Health service runs on management servers and agent-managed computers.

▶ **Config service (OMCFG)**—Sends updates from the RMS to other management servers and agents in that management group. It manages the relationships and topology of the OpsMgr environment.

▶ **SDK service (OMSDK)**—The SDK service can be considered the core service in OpsMgr. If the SDK service isn't running, you cannot connect to the Operations console, because this service allows client applications to access OpsMgr data and functionality. The SDK service is responsible for importing and storing management packs in the Operations database, and it writes operational data (events, state changes, and performance counters) into the Operations database.

There is also the Operations Manager Audit Forwarding service, which sends events to a collector for storage in the Audit Collection Services (ACS) database. ACS is introduced in the "Audit Collection" section of this chapter.

Active Directory Integration
OpsMgr 2007 uses Active Directory for security, discovery, and agent management. Here are some key points:

▶ During setup, you can designate the OM Admins global group as Operations Manager Administrators, rather than using the default BUILTIN\Administrators group.

▶ The OpsMgr Discovery Wizard makes great use of OpsMgr's integration with Active Directory, using standard Lightweight Directory Access Protocol (LDAP) queries to find devices in the directory to manage. Administrators can customize these LDAP queries.

▶ The MOMADAdmin.exe support tool integrates agent management with Active Directory. MOMADAdmin creates an OpsMgr container, which is an AD Organizational Unit (OU) with subcontainers for each management group in your domain. The subcontainers include service connection point objects; agents query these objects to get configuration information that identifies the management groups and management servers the agents connect to and are managed by. To view these containers, you must select the option View Advanced Features in the Active Directory Users and Computers snap-in.

The MOMADAdmin tool does not extend the Active Directory schema.

▶ An agent can be included in an operating system image. When the image is deployed, the agent queries AD to find and register with the appropriate management server.

As an example, let's say you add the Operations Manager agent to your SQL Server 2005 image and configure the agent to get its management group information using AD. When you bring up a new SQL Server 2005 Server built with that image, it is already configured for management by the specified management group, and it will download the applicable management packs.

Databases

You can now specify database names during OpsMgr installation! The name of the Operational database, where monitoring and configuration information is stored, has changed from the previous hard-coded name of OnePoint. The default database name is *OperationsManager*, but you are able to specify a unique name. Specifying the database name allows you to house multiple Operational databases on a single SQL Server 2005 database server.

You also can specify a name for the Reporting database/data warehouse, which has a default name of *OperationsManagerDW*. The data warehouse can be on the same database server as the Operations database or on a different one (for performance reasons, we recommend they be separate), and unlike MOM 2005 Reporting, it natively supports multiple management groups.

Sharing Hardware Between Releases   Using unique database names enables you to do a side-by-side migration from MOM 2005 and its OnePoint database using the same hardware, although there are some considerations with the Reporting Database Server Component:

▶ MOM 2005 Reporting and the OpsMgr 2007 data warehouse do not share code structures, so they will not be "colliding."

▶ Placing two "data warehouses" on the same server could be risky since they could be competing for the same resources (CPU, memory), so using a single server is not recommended with a medium or high load. Chapter 7, "Migrating to Operations Manager 2007," provides in-depth information regarding the migration process.

Installing Databases from the Command Line   You do not have to run the Operations
Manager setup program to install the Operations and Reporting databases—you can just
run the appropriate .msi file standalone from the command line.

- ▶ The Operations database setup can run remotely (and silently) from the intended
  management server.

- ▶ A single script can deploy the Reporting Server and Reporting data warehouse database.

- ▶ When using SQL Server clustering, you do not have to install the database on every
  node of a cluster—just run it on the active cluster only.

Database Maintenance   Earlier versions of Operations Manager included SQL jobs that
performed various types of database maintenance. This approach changes with Operations
Manager 2007, which uses management pack rules to execute the database maintenance
stored procedures. Grooming information, as before, is a Global Setting (in the Operations
console under Administration -> Settings -> Database Grooming).

Registry Key Changes

One of the less visible areas of change in Operations Manager 2007 is Microsoft's removal
of evidence pointing to the product's Mission Critical Software predecessor. We previously
mentioned in the "Databases" section of this chapter that the Operational database no
longer uses Mission Critical Software's hard-coded name of OnePoint. Microsoft also
revamps the Registry structure in this version, renaming the keys under
HKEY_LOCAL_MACHINE\SOFTWARE\Microsoft from *OnePoint* to *Microsoft Operations Manager*.

Server Components

Operations Manager 2007 adds several new server components. MOM 2005 had four
server components (Management Server, Database Server, Data Warehouse Server, and the
Reporting Server). OpsMgr 2007 adds a number of new components, including the Root
Management Server and Gateway Server components.

- ▶ **Root Management Server**—By default, this server is the first management server
  installed in a management group. The RMS supports failover clustering and manages
  role-based security, extensibility, and analysis of the distributed health models
  defined in the OpsMgr infrastructure. Two Windows services run only on the RMS:
  the Config service and the SDK service. You can think of the RMS in some sense as
  analogous to a Flexible Single Master Operations (FSMO) role; it performs unique
  functions in the management group.

  Only members of the Operations Manager Administrators user role can connect to
  the RMS.

▶ **Gateway Server**—MOM 2005 included the option to use mutual authentication for secure communications between the management server and agent. OpsMgr 2007 requires mutual authentication. The dilemma here is that if an agent belongs to an untrusted domain, is outside the corporate firewall, in a demilitarized zone (DMZ), or in a workgroup, it is not able to communicate with a management server if mutual authentication is required.

The gateway server uses certificates to communicate with those agents without compromising OpsMgr's secure communication channel. You can think of this server as a proxy server; it aggregates communications from agents and forwards them to a management server inside the firewall. The gateway server belongs to the management group, but it does not have direct access to the Operations database, Data Warehouse database, or RMS. In a sense, it is a stripped-down management server. Using a gateway server allows the Operations Manager Discovery Wizard to discover target computers across one-way trusted domains, in untrusted domains, and in workgroups. (In a workgroup environment, certificates are required between agents and the gateway server.) Because all communication flows through the gateway, you only need one open port (TCP 5723) on your firewall. You will read more about the gateway server in Chapter 10, "Complex Configurations."

NOTE

What, More Components?

Operations Manager 2007 also includes new components for Audit Collection Services, which is introduced in the "Audit Collection" section later in this chapter.

High Availability

The RMS supports Microsoft Clustering Services (MSCS) on Windows Server 2003. The database servers, which use the Microsoft SQL Services 2005 engine, support active/passive database clustering. Further availability enhancements include:

▶ Active/Passive: Operations, data warehouse, and ACS databases can be on the same active node of the cluster.

▶ Active/Active: Operations database can be on one active node with the data warehouse database on the other active node.

▶ Active/Active: Data warehouse database can be on one active node with the ACS database on the other active node.

▶ Active/Active: Operations database can be on one active node with the ACS database on the other active node.

▶ Active/Passive: Operations database and the Root Management Server can be on the same active node.

You can deploy management servers and gateway servers in pairs for failover purposes. OpsMgr 2007 supports fully automated agent failover for management servers; if a management server fails, the agents communicating with it will automatically fail over to another management server in that management group. Chapter 5, "Planning Complex Configurations," includes more information regarding high availability.

Self-Tuning Thresholds
A large part of MOM 2005 customization consisted of tuning performance thresholds for each installation's unique environment. OpsMgr 2007 is more intuitive and supports self-tuning thresholds, which monitor a performance counter and set an upper and lower threshold based on historical activity within a particular business cycle. If performance exceeds these limits, the system generates an alert.

Agents
Agent deployment options now include using Active Directory, Systems Management Server/System Center Configuration Manager, or the Operations Manager Command Shell (a PowerShell instance). Agent support includes a couple of new areas: embedded devices and Windows Vista. Like most of Operations Manager 2007, the agent code has been totally rewritten.

Maintenance Mode
MOM 2005 included the capability to place monitored servers in maintenance mode, suppressing any alerts related to those servers during planned maintenance. OpsMgr 2007's granularity allows you to apply maintenance mode to an object at any level in the hierarchy. As an example, an individual database on a SQL Server can be in maintenance mode while the rest of the server is not. This functionality gives you a much more accurate picture of the health of your environment.

Notifications
Operations Manager has always supported notification using email or a pager. Improvements to notification in OpsMgr 2007 include adding instant messaging, Session Initiation Protocol (SIP), Simple Message Service (SMS) support, and support for redundant Simple Mail Transfer Protocol (SMTP) servers. Users can configure notifications individually, selecting the notification method they prefer.

Monitoring Engine
Microsoft has made numerous improvements to the OpsMgr 2007 monitoring engine. The new engine uses a modular and more extensible design. The monitoring engine is the same on the management server, agent, and RMS. The new design allows for workflow isolation, with increased efficiency and more reliable monitoring. You can read more about the monitoring engine in Chapter 3.

The way OpsMgr monitors has also changed. To demonstrate the difference in monitoring between MOM 2005 and OpsMgr 2007, let's step through the following comparison, illustrated in Figure 2.9.

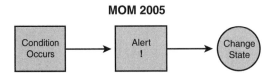

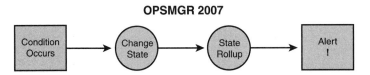

FIGURE 2.9   Monitoring changes between MOM 2005 and OpsMgr 2007.

Operations Manager 2005:

▶ Watches for a condition

▶ Raises an alert

▶ Creates a state change from the alert

Operations Manager 2007:

▶ Watches for a condition

▶ Changes state

▶ Rolls up state as required

▶ Optionally generates an alert or notification

Operations Manager 2007 also refers to "monitors." A *monitor* is a state machine, which monitors some aspect of an application. A monitor can be in one state at any time. Monitors have a limited number of operational states (currently three—Success, Warning, and Error). Each operational state maps to a health state. Monitors can optionally define alerting conditions.

How do monitors differ from rules?

▶ A monitor consists of a monitor type, made up of data sources, condition detection modules, and write actions; rules are defined directly from individual modules and do not have an intermediate "type."

▸ Monitors can only produce state change information, whereas rules cannot produce state information at all (that is, monitors are the only thing that can affect the state of an instance).

▸ Monitors exist in a hierarchy for every instance in the system. Rules are single work-flows that act independently of one another.

Data sources for monitors include events, performance counters, Windows Management Instrumentation (WMI) information, log files, SNMP traps, WS-Management information, scripts, Object Linking and Embedding Database (OLEDB) data, LDAP data, syslog information, and so on. These data sources sound quite similar to the data sources used with management packs in Operations Manager 2005; but using monitors enables a more granular level of monitoring.

This new architecture sets a foundation for increased monitoring capabilities and extensibility.

Client Monitoring

In Operations Manager 2007, you can define synthetic transactions and deploy them to *watcher nodes*, which are client computers designated to run these transactions. These synthetic transactions execute and perform a sequence of steps defined in the transaction. Transactions are monitored for success or failure, performance, and duration.

Client monitoring is important because although a service may be running and available to the servers that support it, there is no guarantee that service is available to clients. Using synthetic transactions allows you to have visibility not only into service health but also into the end user's experience.

There are multiple aspects to client monitoring, which we discuss in Chapter 16, "Client Monitoring."

Connector Framework

Operations Manager includes a software development kit (SDK) and a connector framework, enabling developers to build custom management packs or product connectors for OpsMgr 2007. You can extend these components to monitor non-Microsoft software and operating systems, hardware, and network devices. The connector framework enables easy integration of OpsMgr with other management technologies.

Connectors differ conceptually from management packs. Management packs are a vehicle for capturing knowledge associated with managing a particular component, which can roll up multiple components that describe an end-to-end service. Connectors are typically conduits for passing information between different management tools such as those from HP, Tivoli, and CA. You may also see connectors created for EMC Smarts and service desk solutions such as Remedy.

Connecting Management Groups

MOM 2005 supported a three-level hierarchy of tiered management groups, connected with the MOM-to-MOM Connector (part of the Connector Framework or MCF), which transmitted alert and discovery information between the management groups.

Operations Manager 2007 no longer uses the MOM-to-MOM Connector. Instead, you can implement *connected management groups*. Using connected management groups gives you a single console view, enabling you to view and edit alerts and other monitoring data from multiple management groups from the local management group. You can also initiate tasks from the local management group to run on managed objects of a connected group. There is no limit on the number of connected management groups.

Audit Collection

New with Operations Manager 2007, ACS provides a secure and efficient way to gather Windows Security logs from systems and consolidate them for analysis and reporting.

Security events from monitored computers are stored in an Audit database. You can install the database on the same database server as the Operations database, although for security reasons Microsoft recommends they be separate. Deploying ACS involves ACS forwarders, the ACS collector, and the ACS database. The ACS agent is included in the OpsMgr agent deployment.

Microsoft gives the following numbers for ACS capacity:

- ▶ 150 domain controllers (DCs) to one collector
- ▶ 3000 Windows servers to one collector
- ▶ 10,000 agents monitoring workstations to a single collector
- ▶ 65 simultaneous consoles

NOTE

ACS Maintenance and SQL Server 2005 Editions

Although ACS supports both SQL Server 2005 Standard and Enterprise Edition, the version you select affects ACS behavior during its daily database maintenance window. SQL Server 2005 Standard Edition cannot perform online indexing, so it will not insert security events into the ACS database during this time. Inserts do take place with Enterprise Edition.

Refer to Chapter 15, "Monitoring Audit Control Services," for more information about ACS.

How Does the Data Flow?

Perhaps one way to show how much has changed between OpsMgr 2007 and Microsoft's earlier versions is by looking at the following two figures. Figure 2.10 shows the differences in data flow between MOM 2000 and MOM 2005.

MOM 2000 DATA FLOW

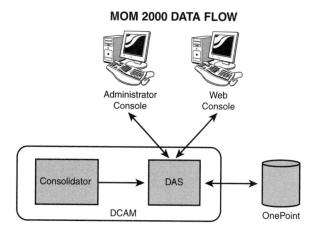

MOM 2005 DATA FLOW

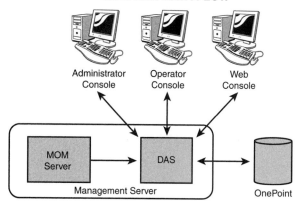

FIGURE 2.10   Data flow in earlier versions of Microsoft Operations Manager.

These are fairly simplistic drawings compared with Figure 2.11, which shows data flow between major OpsMgr 2007 components (for simplicity, the Web console and ACS are not included in Figure 2.11). In OpsMgr 2007, the RMS is at the center of the hub, because it is the only component that has direct communication with the user interface and the Reporting server. OpsMgr designs need to take into consideration the unique responsibilities of the RMS, which we discuss in Chapter 4, "Planning Your Operations Manager Deployment."

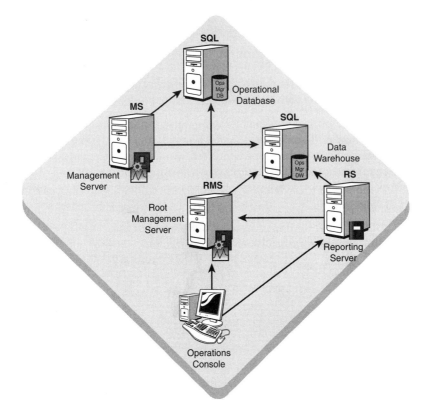

FIGURE 2.11   Operations Manager 2007 data flow.

What's New in Reporting

Similar to MOM 2005, OpsMgr uses the Microsoft SQL Server Reporting Component, also known as Reporting Services (SRS), as its reporting engine, although OpsMgr 2007 does not use the SRS user interface. SRS 2005 includes many enhancements to the SRS included with Microsoft SQL Server 2000 and used in MOM 2005, including easier authoring and publishing.

A New Look to the Reporting Console

Microsoft has integrated reporting with OpsMgr security and incorporated reporting functionality into the Operations console. As mentioned in the "Consoles" section of this chapter, you no longer use the SQL Server Report Manager web interface to view reports. The OpsMgr 2007 console includes an intuitive and easy-to-use graphical report designer—it is no longer necessary to be an SRS/Visual Studio expert to author reports!

Reporting also has several new controls to create sophisticated reports and dashboards, and Microsoft's management packs already include many of the more common reports. Designing reports is discussed in Chapter 23.

Just In Time Reports
Unlike MOM 2005 Reporting, a Data Transformation Services (DTS) job is not necessary to transfer operational data to the Data Warehouse database. The agent sends data directly to the data warehouse. This means that reporting data is now available with virtually no latency. Nor is user maintenance required on the database warehouse used to store reporting data; it automatically grooms, partitions, and optimizes itself. The data is preaggregated, summarized, and indexed; reports covering long periods of time display quickly.

Object-Oriented Reporting
Operations Manager 2007 uses object-oriented monitoring, collecting data against objects. This object-oriented approach also applies to reporting. As an example, performance reports look at a performance rule and an object when generating a report. In MOM 2005, the Processor - %Processor Time - _Total report collected data against a computer, which you found using its NetBIOS name. OpsMgr 2007 collects this information against an object—in this case Windows Operating System. The report finds data when it searches for objects that are of type Windows Operating System. You would search for objects that contain "Server 2003," then look for those objects that are of type "Windows Operating System." Performance reports use performance collection data, differing from some other reports such as the generic Availability report, which is based on state data and looks at entity health. The Reporting console includes knowledge showing which objects to search for to get data.

Not Your MOM's Management Packs

The heart of Operations Manager is its management packs, which are collections of events, alerts, and performance counters for a specific application or product feature set. Management packs (MPs) in OpsMgr 2007 use eXtensible Markup Language, supporting Microsoft's move to model-based management and making management packs more "extensible."

Sealed Management Packs
Management packs shipped from Microsoft and other vendors are now sealed, versioned, and signed with a certificate. After a management pack is imported into Operations Manager 2007, it immediately starts to monitor objects based on default configurations and thresholds. You can customize these default settings using either overrides or by creating your own monitoring objects such as monitors, rules, and tasks.

Because vendor MPs are sealed, any customizations you create are saved to a separate unsealed MP, by default, to the *Default Management Pack*. This ensures that when a new version of a sealed MP becomes available, the management pack is replaced without overlaying your customizations. Sealed MPs also make it easy to delete a management pack if you no longer need it, and the operation of removing a management pack is part of the Operations console.

New Formats

Operations Manager 2000 and 2005 management packs used a proprietary .akm format. Using XML makes it easier to develop management packs supporting OpsMgr's new model-based architecture.

You can convert your MOM 2005 management packs to the new format using a two-step process:

1. The MP2XML utility in the MOM 2005 Resource Kit converts the MOM 2005 MP from .akm file format to MOM 2005 .xml file format.

2. The OpsMgr 2007 MPConvert support tool converts the MOM 2005 .xml file to the OpsMgr 2007 .xml file format.

Alternatively, you can use the Migration Wizard, discussed in Chapter 7.

The following MOM 2005 MP objects cannot be converted to the 2007 format:

▶ Operator

▶ Report

▶ Console scope

Templates

OpsMgr 2007 includes monitoring templates, making it quick and easy to create management packs with the Add Monitoring Authoring Wizard in the Operations console.

Applying Updates

MOM 2005 did not immediately deploy management pack updates to agents. Changes to the agents occurred on a scheduled basis, or you could force changes immediately by specifying the Commit Configuration Changes option. Updates occur as needed in OpsMgr 2007, making the Commit Configurations Changes option unnecessary.

The Default Management Pack

The Default MP is imported during the installation process. By default, any new management pack objects you create are saved to Default, although you can specify a different location (which is recommended). In addition, if you create an override to customize a setting in a sealed management pack, the override is saved to the Default MP, by default.

Summarizing the Changes: A Table Is Worth a Thousand Words

You may have heard the expression that "a picture is worth a thousand words." Sometimes a comparison table can also be worth a thousand words. Perhaps we can best summarize the scope of changes using Table 2.2, which shows the differences in features between Operations Manager 2007 and its predecessor, MOM 2005.

TABLE 2.2   Enhancements in Operations Manager 2007

Feature	MOM 2005	Operations Manager 2007
Service-Oriented Monitoring		X
Synthetic Transactions	X	X (enhanced)
Model-based architecture		X
Monitoring templates		X
WS-Management support		X
SNMPv1 support	X	Added with SP 1, enhanced
SNMPv2 support	X	X (enhanced)
Client Monitoring		X
Audit Collection		X
Native XML management packs		X
Reporting	X	X (enhanced)
Self-Tuning Thresholds		X
Server components	X	X (enhanced)
High Availability	X	X (enhanced)
Monitoring Engine	X	X (enhanced)
Notifications	X	X (enhanced)
Connector Framework	X	X (enhanced)
Consolidated Console		X
Role-based security		X
Active Directory integration		X
Windows PowerShell command console		X

Changes in Capacity

With the most recent version of Operations Manager, Microsoft has increased capacity in several areas to extend the product's monitoring capabilities. Table 2.3 compares MOM 2000, MOM 2000 Service Pack 1 (SP 1), MOM 2005, MOM 2005 SP 1, and OpsMgr 2007's management features. The terminology utilizes Operations Manager 2007 nomenclatures.

TABLE 2.3   Comparison of Operations Manager Capabilities Across Versions

Feature	MOM 2000	MOM 2000 SP 1	MOM 2005	MOM 2005 SP 1	OpsMgr 2007
Managed computers in a management group	1000	2000	3500	4000	5000
Managed computers per management server	700	1000	1200	2000	2000
Management servers per management group	4	10	10	10	No defined limit
Source management groups forwarding to a destination management group	6	10	10	10	n/a
Agents per gateway server	n/a	n/a	n/a	n/a	200 recom-mended

No capacity increases for OpsMgr 2007 Service Pack 1 have been announced at the time of the SP 1 Release Candidate.

Prerequisites

In Table 2.4, we compare the basic hardware and software requirements for the different versions of Operations Manager. The hardware requirements are considerably beefed up for the newest version. (The hardware and software requirements do not change with OpsMgr 2007 SP 1.)

The Prerequisite Checker is an invaluable part of the installation process, letting you know exactly what deficiencies you have before starting your installation. We describe requirements for OpsMgr 2007 in detail in Chapter 6, "Installing Operations Manager 2007."

TIP

Eval Version of Operations Manager 2007 Available

You can download a 180-day evaluation copy of OpsMgr 2007 at http://www.microsoft.com/technet/prodtechnol/eval/scom/default.mspx.

TABLE 2.4   Comparison of Minimum Requirements Across Versions

Component	MOM 2000	MOM 2000 SP 1	MOM 2005	MOM 2005 SP 1	OpsMgr 2007
Processor	Pentium-compatible 550MHz or higher.	Pentium-compatible 550MHz or higher.	Pentium-compatible 550MHz or higher.	Pentium-compatible 550MHz or higher.	Pentium-compatible 1.8GHz or higher.
Memory	512MB of RAM.	512MB of RAM.	1GB of RAM if all components are on a single server; otherwise 512MB.	1GB of RAM if all components are on a single server; otherwise 512MB.	1GB of RAM suggested for each component.
Hard disk	1GB plus 5GB for OnePoint.	1GB plus 5GB for OnePoint.	1GB plus 5GB for OnePoint. 200GB for MOM Reporting.	1GB plus 5GB for OnePoint. 200GB for MOM Reporting.	5GB plus 10GB for Operations database. 20GB for Data Warehouse database and Audit database.
Operating System	Windows 2000 Server Family, SP 2 or later.	Windows 2000 Server Family, SP 2 or later.	Windows 2000 Server Family, SP 4 or later, or Windows Server 2003 Family.	Windows Server 2003 Family, SP 1 or later.	Windows Server 2003 Family, SP 1 or later.
Database Server	SQL Server 2000 and Access 2000 or later for reporting.	SQL Server 2000 and Access 2000 or later for reporting.	SQL Server 2000, SP 3.0a or later, and SQL Server 2000 Reporting Services for reporting.	SQL Server 2000, SP 3.0a or later, SQL Server 2005, and SQL Server 2000 Reporting Services with SP 1 for reporting (or the SQL Server 2005 Reporting Services component)	SQL Server 2005 (with SQL_Latin1_General_CP1_CS_AS collation) for Operations and Audit Collection databases. Reporting Services Component with SP 1 for Reporting Server and Reporting Data Warehouse.

Operations Manager versus System Center Essentials

System Center Essentials 2007 (Essentials) is a new product in the System Center family. Essentials is designed specifically for IT professionals in small and midsize businesses who face challenges similar to those of large enterprises—troubleshooting end-user problems, automating management tasks, managing multiple systems, and diagnosing and resolving problems.

Like larger environments, many small and midsize organizations use a multitude of tools to manage their IT environments; these tools tend to focus on individual areas of monitoring rather than being a comprehensive set of management tools. Tools that are easy to use often are narrow in scope and limited in functionality, whereas tools that are more functional may be overkill, are complex, and are difficult to learn—particularly for organizations with smaller IT departments. To address this need for small to medium-sized businesses, Microsoft developed Essentials 2007, which replaces MOM 2005 Workgroup Edition.

Unlike MOM 2005 Workgroup Edition, Essentials is not just a stripped-down version of Operations Manager. Microsoft spent a considerable amount of time talking to small and midsize companies with IT organizations of one or two people. Essentials, the result of this research, integrates operations management and configuration management capabilities into one central console.

In addition to a monitoring console that looks similar to the OpsMgr 2007 Operations console, Essentials can assess, configure, and distribute Microsoft and third-party software updates using the System Center Update Packager (SCUP) and WSUS 3.0; manage software and hardware inventory using over 30 attributes; and deploy software to targeted groups and computers. Although this sounds similar to that available with Configuration Manager (ConfigMgr) 2007, Essentials is limited to monitoring 30 Windows servers and 500 Windows non-server-based computers. Essentials can also monitor an unlimited number of network devices using SNMP.

Table 2.5 compares the functionality between OpsMgr 2007 and Essentials 2007.

Now let's look at the other Microsoft product Essentials shares features with. Table 2.6 compares the functionality between System Management Server/Configuration Manager 2007 and Essentials 2007.

Microsoft has a 30-day evaluation version of System Center Essentials available as a virtual machine. You can download it from http://www.microsoft.com/downloads/details.aspx?FamilyID=27342759-e9d6-4073-918c-e9dff77d0206&DisplayLang=en (this URL is also available as a live link in Appendix E, "Reference URLs"). The image enables you to try Essentials 2007 on up to 10 servers and 50 clients.

TABLE 2.5   Features Available in Operations Manager 2007 and System Center
Essentials 2007

Features	OpsMgr	Essentials	Comments
Management packs	X	X	
Monitor servers, clients, and services	X	X	
Management pack authoring	X	X	Essentials has a basic interface; the OpsMgr interface is more sophisticated.
Role-based security	X		Essentials does not include a facility for role-based administration.
Multiple management servers in domain	X	X	All monitored systems must be in the same Active Directory forest.
Reporting	X	X (basic)	Essentials does not include a data warehouse or fixed grooming schedule (only a maximum of 37 days of report data can be stored); the Operations and Reporting databases are on the same server, and Report authoring is not supported.
Fault tolerance support	X		Essentials does not support database clustering of the Operations or Reporting database or clustering the Essentials management server.
Connector framework	X		
ACS	X		
AD Integration	X	X	AD integration with Essentials consists of pushing Group Policy Objects (GPOs) and creating AD security groups.
PowerShell Integration	X		
Web console	X		

TABLE 2.6   Features Available in ConfigMgr 2007 and System Center Essentials 2007

Features	ConfigMgr	Essentials	Comments
Update management	X	X	
Software distribution	X	X	
Hardware and software inventory	X	X	Essentials captures approximately 30 hardware and software attributes.
Operating System deployment	X		
Mobile device management	X		
Desired configuration management	X		
Branch office support	X	X (basic)	Essentials does not include site servers.
Network Access Protection (NAP) support	X		
Wake on Local Area Network (LAN)	X		

Summary

In this chapter, we discussed the differences between MOM 2005 and OpsMgr 2007. We covered changes in terminology, functionality, capacity, and prerequisites. We also introduced System Center Essentials 2007 and compared its features with Operations Manager 2007. Essentials 2007 is the upgrade from MOM 2005 Workgroup Edition for smaller IT shops, although its functionality is very different.

The next chapter talks about how Operations Manager works; it includes an architectural overview and discussion of the workflow engine in OpsMgr 2007.

# CHAPTER 3

Looking Inside OpsMgr

▶ Architectural Overview

▶ Windows Services

▶ Communications

▶ How Does OpsMgr Do It?

▶ Presentation Layer

Microsoft System Center Operations Manager 2007 (OpsMgr) is a monitoring and operations management system, implemented using one or more computers that perform their assigned roles as components of a management group. The components cooperate over several secure communication channels to achieve management information workflow and present information to operators and administrators. The most important data collected is the health of the managed objects; this health status is arrived at via models that affect the tactical placement of software probes called *monitors*.

This chapter endeavors to make these terms and relationships clear so that the job of deploying and supporting OpsMgr 2007 becomes easier and more effective. Those readers tempted to skip this chapter covering OpsMgr internals, definitions, and concepts are probably asking themselves, "What practical use can I expect to get from reading this chapter?" Some administrators avoid looking under the hood deliberately, and that's totally OK. For those individuals, we do recommend reading at least the "Management Group Defined" section of this chapter.

So, for those OpsMgr administrators who yearn to know exactly what is going on behind the scenes, this chapter is for you. We want you to understand the lingo and reasoning used by the software developers of Operations Manager. In doing so, we hope that more advanced material about OpsMgr will make sense more quickly to you, the OpsMgr administrator, when reading this book, using the product, or interacting with fellow professionals in the Microsoft systems management community.

Architectural Overview

This chapter looks at OpsMgr design and internals at two levels:

▶ **The macro level**—We'll look at the computer roles that comprise a management group.

▶ **The micro level**—We'll examine the objects that constitute a management pack, in particular its workflow and presentation of data to the operator.

As an OpsMgr administrator, you have no influence over server component characteristics—these are hard-coded features of the Operations Manager software and hardware architecture. On the other hand, administrators can enjoy almost complete flexibility regarding the manner in which management packs are utilized.

OpsMgr administrators of the smallest environments—administrators who will run all applicable OpsMgr components on a single server and manage only computers and devices on their local area network (LAN)—generally are less concerned about this section on OpsMgr architecture. In that small-scale scenario of the "all-in-one" management group server, there is much less to be concerned about with architectural considerations of the various OpsMgr computer roles (components) as long as you stay below capacity thresholds for that single server and its network segment. In this simplest OpsMgr environment, the only OpsMgr components not resident on the single server are the OpsMgr agents running on the managed computers on the network.

However, many OpsMgr administrators will need to distribute multiple components across different servers, deploying OpsMgr roles across multiple computers. Even OpsMgr 2007 deployments on small business networks may include an Audit Collection Services (ACS) Component to centralize security event auditing, or an OpsMgr Gateway Server Component to monitor service delivery at a branch office where there is no Virtual Private Network (VPN) connectivity. Deploying the feature sets added when installing these additional roles, by definition, adds one or more physical management servers to the management group and requires an understanding of Operations Manager 2007 management group architecture. Chapter 4, "Planning Your Operations Manager Deployment," and Chapter 5, "Planning Complex Configurations," provide information on hardware specifications and sizing server configurations.

Management Group Defined

A *management group* is an instance of the Microsoft end-to-end service management solution named Operations Manager 2007. Organizations may host several management groups (instances of OpsMgr on their networks) if appropriate for their business needs. Likewise, any managed computer or device can participate in one or more instances (management groups) of OpsMgr if appropriate. Most organizations of all sizes deploy a single management group, which is analogous to a single Active Directory (AD) forest or a single Exchange organization. Most organizations, including some very large ones, have their business needs met with just one AD forest and one Exchange organization.

Figure 3.1 illustrates a default, single management group in an organization, and contrasts that with a more complex implementation one might encounter in a large organization. In the simple all-in-one example on the left in Figure 3.1, all OpsMgr components are installed on one server, which is the only OpsMgr server in the single management group serving the managed computers (agents) in the organization. Several hundred computers can be managed with an all-in-one deployment of OpsMgr 2007.

In the complex large organization scenario on the right-hand portion of Figure 3.1, a single computer agent is reporting simultaneously to two management groups (known as a *multihomed* agent), while one of those management groups, through its Root Management Server (RMS), participates with several connected management groups. This creates an architecture capable of servicing tens of thousands of widely distributed computers.

3

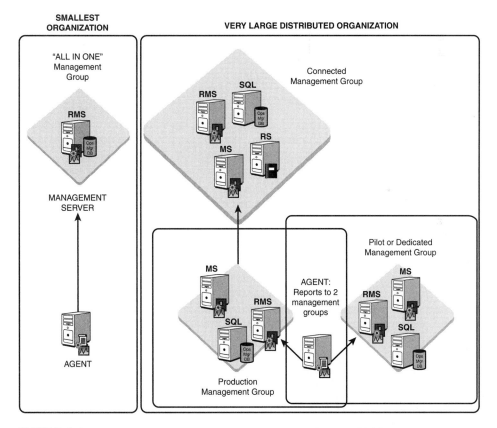

FIGURE 3.1   Contrasting the smallest with a very large OpsMgr 2007 deployment model.

You will seldom need multiple management groups to get the most out of OpsMgr 2007 since the product's design provides full functionality to all but the largest of organizations while still using a single management group. For the very large organization (over 10,000 computers or over 100 remote sites), deploying several OpsMgr 2007 management groups can distribute the workload. Connecting these management groups enables you to query multiple management groups from the same Operations console.

Both having more than one production instance of OpsMgr in your organization and having a computer or device report status to more than one management group are advanced configurations to accomplish particular business goals. We describe these situations in Chapter 10, "Complex Configurations."

TIP

Management Group Names

A management group name is a unique alphanumeric name specified by the administrator when installing the Operations Database Server Component. The management group name cannot be changed after installation, so it is a good idea to select a name that is easy to remember and makes sense given the organization's geographic or administrative needs.

When creating a management group, remember that the name is case-sensitive.

Server Components

Here are a dozen possible computer components, or roles, that can be deployed in an OpsMgr 2007 management group. Focusing now on what components constitute a single OpsMgr 2007 management group, let's begin with describing the core, or basic, server components. The core components are those that an OpsMgr 2007 deployment must include to have minimum functionality. These basic components (displayed in Figure 3.2) are installed in every management group, including the all-in-one server OpsMgr environment.

▶ **Operations Database Server Component**—The heart of the management group is the Operations database. The Operations database contains operational data about managed objects, the configuration store of what objects are managed, and all customizations to the OpsMgr environment. The Operations database is the central repository and processing point for all data in a management group. When you install an OpsMgr 2007 management group on multiple computer systems, the first thing to take place is installing the Operations database on an existing SQL 2005 database server running Service Pack (SP) 1 or later. The Operations Database Server Component can be clustered in high-availability environments.

▶ **Root Management Server Component**—The first management server installed in a management group is the Root Management Server Component. Like all OpsMgr 2007 management servers, the RMS sends configuration information to managed computers and receives data from agents. The RMS alone runs some distinctive services that the entire management group depends on, and like the Operations Database Server Component, the RMS Component can be clustered. The RMS requires that the Operations database be available and accessible. The function of

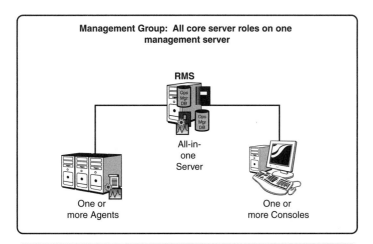

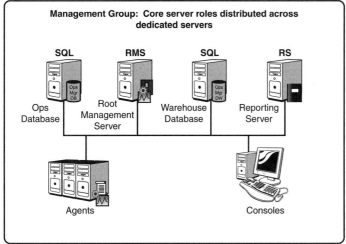

FIGURE 3.2   OpsMgr 2007 core components combined in one server, and distributed across dedicated servers.

the entire management group also depends on the RMS; in high-availability environments you should consider clustering both the Operations database and the RMS components.

▶ **Agent Component**—The Agent Component is used to monitor servers and clients. This is a Windows service that runs on managed servers and client computers. You might create an all-in-one server management group whose only purpose is monitoring network devices such as routers or switches; in that case, no agents need to be deployed. However, for most OpsMgr setups, the deployment of core management group components is not complete until one or more computers are selected for management and the Agent Component is installed. As we mentioned previously in the "Management Group Defined" section of this chapter, an OpsMgr 2007 agent can participate in more than one management group simultaneously.

▶ **Console Component**—The OpsMgr 2007 console is the only application needed to interact with the management group, and it is used by both operators and administrators. Operations Manager 2007 implements role-based security to ensure an optimized experience for all users. There is also a web-based console with a subset of the regular console functions.

Each console connects directly to the RMS, even if additional management servers have been deployed in the management group. This dependence makes RMS availability critical to perform almost every function in OpsMgr 2007. The first time a user opens the Operations console, there is a prompt to enter the name of the RMS, unless the user accessing the console is at a management server. After connecting, the console stores that server name, as well as the management group name, in the Connect to Server dialog box shown in Figure 3.3.

FIGURE 3.3   The Connect to Server dialog box stores the name of the RMS and associated management group.

The four components listed here are mandatory components and required for any OpsMgr management group to function. In addition, there are two core components related to reporting that most OpsMgr administrators will install regardless of their environment size:

▶ **Reporting Data Warehouse Server Component**—A long-term data store is created with the Reporting Data Warehouse Server Component. The data warehouse stores aggregated historical performance and availability data beyond the few hours or days of data available in the Operations database. Without a data warehouse, an OpsMgr management group will only present information based on the real-time and very recent data captured in the Operations database, which is aggressively groomed of historical data. The Reporting Data Warehouse Server Component can be hosted on a clustered SQL Server backend.

▶ **Reporting Server Component**—This component adds the reporting function to an OpsMgr management group and is required for the Reporting Data Warehouse Server Component. The Reporting Server is installed on a server running SQL Reporting Services 2005 SP 1 or later. Because of the integration between the Operations console and the Reporting Server, it is transparent to the user that the data for the reports is coming from the Reporting Server and not the Operations database or the RMS. This differs from the Microsoft Operations Manager (MOM) 2005 Reporting implementation.

You can install the Reporting Data Warehouse Server and Reporting Server Components on the same Windows server, although in large and high-availability environments, these two components typically run on dedicated servers.

Finally, there are six optional components in an OpsMgr management group. Computers are deployed with these components as needed or desired to increase the monitoring capacity, or to add further features to the management group:

▶ **Management Server Component**—This component refers to additional management servers installed after the RMS is installed. The primary reasons to deploy additional OpsMgr 2007 management servers are to enable agent failover and to manage a larger number of objects. There are specific procedures to promote a management server to the RMS Role in a disaster-recovery scenario, which we discuss in Chapter 12, "Backup and Recovery." You would also install an additional management server to host the Audit Collector Component, described later in this list, because that component requires installation on an existing OpsMgr management server that is not the RMS.

▶ **Audit Database Server Component**—SQL Server 2005 is required for the Audit Database Server Component when adding the Audit Collection Services feature to the management group. Security events from managed computers are stored in this database and are used in generating reports. The Audit Database Server can be a clustered service for high availability. Reports on security events are generated from the Audit database.

▶ **Audit Collector Component**—This server function collects events from the audit collection–enabled agents. The Audit Collector Component is added to an existing OpsMgr management server. Audit collection is enabled on OpsMgr agents by running a task in the OpsMgr console. Each collector needs its own individual Audit Database Server. The Audit database can be located on the same computer as the ACS Collector, but for optimal performance, each of these components should be installed on a dedicated server.

▶ **Web Console Server Component**—Any OpsMgr management server running the Internet Information Services (IIS) web server service can optionally host a web-based version of the OpsMgr console. Functionally similar to using a thin client much like Outlook Web Access (OWA), operators can view topology diagrams and performance charts and run tasks made available to them appropriate for their role. The Web Console Server might be a management server dedicated to hosting this role in an organization that makes heavy use of the Web console.

▶ **Gateway Server Component**—A communications conduit to monitoring agents in untrusted domains (or on remote networks without routed network connectivity), this server resides in an external environment and uses certificates to secure communication back to the other roles in the management group. A gateway server can also host the Audit Collector Component.

▶ **Client Monitoring Server Component**—The Client Monitoring Configuration Wizard is used to configure the Client Monitoring Server Component on one or more management servers in a management group. The Agentless Exception Monitoring (AEM) Client Component is activated by a Group Policy Object (GPO) applied to client computers. An important note is that the management server and AEM clients must be in the same domain or fully trusted domains.

Figure 3.4 illustrates a management group with all components on distributed servers, and with many high-availability features deployed. This large-enterprise management group could provide end-to-end service monitoring of many thousands of objects with a high degree of reliability.

Sharing Resources Between Management Groups

We have discussed how the OpsMgr agent on a managed computer can be a member of more than one management group. There are other ways to leverage hardware across multiple management groups, particularly at the database server layer. Because the Operations database can be assigned any user-selectable name during installation, and because the Data Warehouse database natively supports multiple management groups, a single SQL 2005 server can provide database backend services to multiple management groups, which need not be aware of each other.

This feature lets organizations with more than one management group consolidate OpsMgr database duties to a single SQL Server, or more likely a highly available clustered SQL Server configuration. This significantly reduces the incremental cost of adding another management group in an organization.

Windows Services

Computers running OpsMgr components also host particular Windows services in specific configurations depending on their function(s). The presence of the OpsMgr Health service is universal to all Windows computers participating in an Operations Manager 2007 management group. The next sections describe the Health service as well as the other four services that exist in a management group with Audit Collection Services deployed.

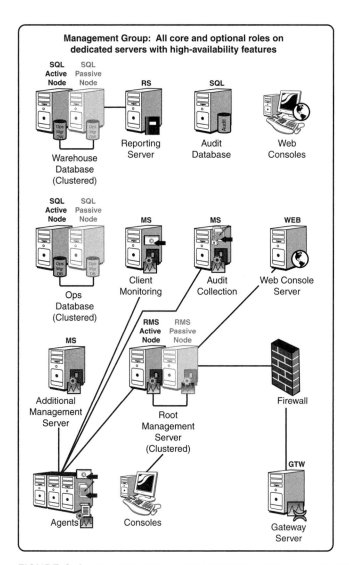

FIGURE 3.4   All basic and optional OpsMgr server roles deployed on dedicated servers.

OpsMgr Health Service

The Health service provides a general execution environment for monitoring modules. Such modules form different workflows, enabling end-to-end monitoring scenarios.

Health Service Implementations

There are actually two flavors of the Health service:

▶ The first implementation, the Agent Health service, runs on monitored Windows computers. The service executes tasks, collects performance data, and performs other functions on the managed computer. The Agent Health service continues to run, collecting data and performing tasks, even when disconnected from a management server. Data and events accumulate in a disk-based queue, and they are reported when the connection to the management server is restored.

▶ The other implementation of the Health service runs on a management server. The functionality of the Health service running on a management server varies depending on the setup of the management group and the management packs installed.

Installing new or additional management packs extends the Health service running on both types of computers (agent-managed computers and management servers). Another important feature of the Health service is that it provides credential management services to other OpsMgr processes, supporting execution of modules running as different users.

Security

A public/private key pair, used for secure communications, is created on each instance of the Health service (RMS, Management Server, Gateway Server, and agent). This key pair can be regenerated at any time. The public key is published at the following times:

▶ During startup

▶ When the key expires

▶ During a failure to decrypt a message

▶ Upon request by the SDK (discussed in the next section) to republish the key

If the key is not successfully published, the SDK may post errors. The agent key may also drop "key mismatch" events. Because OpsMgr is self-healing, the agent republishes the key or the SDK re-requests the key if there is a problem. When the key is close to expiring, the Health service restarts itself, regenerating the key. If you think the key has been compromised, remove it and restart the Health service to generate a new key.

OpsMgr SDK Service

The OpsMgr SDK service is found in the services list of all management servers. However, the service is disabled unless the server is also the RMS. This service and the OpsMgr Config service, described next, are both found only on management servers. All data flowing to and from the Operations database is transported via the OpsMgr SDK service running on the RMS.

The SDK service is responsible for providing access for the OpsMgr console to the Operations database, viewing the current state of a monitored object, importing management packs to the database, storing management packs in the database, and storing management group configuration information in the database. The SDK service also handles the following functions:

- ▶ Writing event data to the database

- ▶ Writing state-change data to the database

- ▶ Writing performance counter data to the database

In addition, the SDK service owns a symmetric encryption key for the management group that accesses the Run As Account information, which is stored in the Operations database. We introduced Run As Accounts in Chapter 2, "What's New."

The encryption key information is stored in the Registry. If you lose this key, you will have to clear out and reset the Run-as accounts. The management group key is also required if you are promoting a management server to become your new RMS and want to keep your Run As Accounts. You can back up and restore this key using a Microsoft-provided key backup tool. This process is further discussed in Chapter 10.

OpsMgr Config Service

Similar to the OpsMgr SDK service described earlier, the OpsMgr Config service will also be found installed on all management servers, but disabled unless the server is also the RMS. The OpsMgr Config service manages the relationships and the topology of the OpsMgr 2007 environment.

The OpsMgr Config service is responsible for providing the monitoring configuration to each agent's Health service, which may include sensitive information. The service acts as an intermediary for delivering sensitive information in an encrypted format from the Operations database to the target Health service on a monitored agent.

OpsMgr Audit Forwarding Service

This service sends events to an ACS collector server for storage in a SQL Server database. The Audit Forwarding service is found on each Windows computer in an OpsMgr management group. By default, the service needed for an agent to be an ACS forwarder is installed but not enabled when the OpsMgr agent is installed. After you install the ACS collector and database, you can then remotely enable this service on multiple agents through the Operations console by running the Enable Audit Collection task.

OpsMgr Audit Collection Service

The Audit Collection service is responsible for receiving audit events over the network and writing them to the Audit database. This service is found running on management servers that also have the ACS Audit Collector Service Component Installed. The service and the Audit database are created during setup of the ACS service on the selected management server(s).

Communications

Operations Manager 2007 uses a variety of communications methods that are optimized for security and efficiency. Communication with the three OpsMgr database backend components—the Operations database (DB), the Data Warehouse DB, and the Audit Collection Services DB—is always via standard SQL client/server protocols, specifically OLE DB (Object Linking and Embedding Database).

Between agents, as well as management and gateway servers, the primary Transmission Control Protocol (TCP) port used by OpsMgr is 5723, which is the only outbound firewall hole needed to manage a computer in a minimal configuration (after the agent is installed or preinstalled). Additional outbound ports are used when enabling ACS and AEM. A complete list of communications protocols and default ports used in an OpsMgr management group is provided in Table 3.1.

The logic in Table 3.1 is diagrammed in Figure 3.5. A quick study of the communication paths verifies the criticality of the RMS in an OpsMgr 2007 management group. The RMS is clearly the communications nexus for the monitoring organization, with most features of OpsMgr unavailable if the RMS is down or inaccessible. Of course, the RMS depends completely on its connection to the Operations database to function.

In effect, both the RMS and the Operations database need to be continuously available to provide uninterrupted continuity of management functions. That makes clustering the Ops DB and the RMS top considerations when seeking to architect a highly available management solution for the enterprise. For computers managed via the Gateway Server Component, additional gateway servers can be deployed to the same remote domain or site, providing failover coverage to one another.

The diagram in Figure 3.5 does not illustrate the need for RPC/DCOM communication between a management server and a managed computer in order to push the agent to a managed computer. Details on this, as well as how to configure the Windows Firewall on a managed computer to perform "push" installation of the agent from a management server, are covered in Chapter 9, "Installing and Configuring Agents."

TABLE 3.1   Communication Paths and Ports

From Component	To Component	Bidirectional	TCP Port
Root Management Server (RMS) or Management Server (MS)	Operational Database (Ops DB) and Data Warehouse Database (DW DB)	No	OLE DB 1433 (SQL); in a cluster the second node requires a unique port number.
RMS	MS or Gateway Server	Yes	5723.
Operations console	RMS	No	5723.
Agent	RMS, MS, or Gateway	No	5723.
Reporting Server, Web Console Server	RMS	No	5724.
Connector Framework Source	RMS	No	51905.
Agentless Exception Monitoring (AEM) Client	AEM file share on RMS or MS	No	SMB 445, 51906.
Software Quality Metrics (SQM) Client	SQM Endpoint	No	51907.
Web console	Web Console Server	No	HTTP 51908.
Audit Collection Services (ACS) Agent	ACS Collector	Yes	59109.
ACS Collector	ACS DB	No	OLE DB 1433 (SQL).
Reporting Server	DW DB	No	OLE DB 1433 (SQL); in a cluster the second node requires a unique port number.
Operations console	Reporting Server	No	HTTP 80.

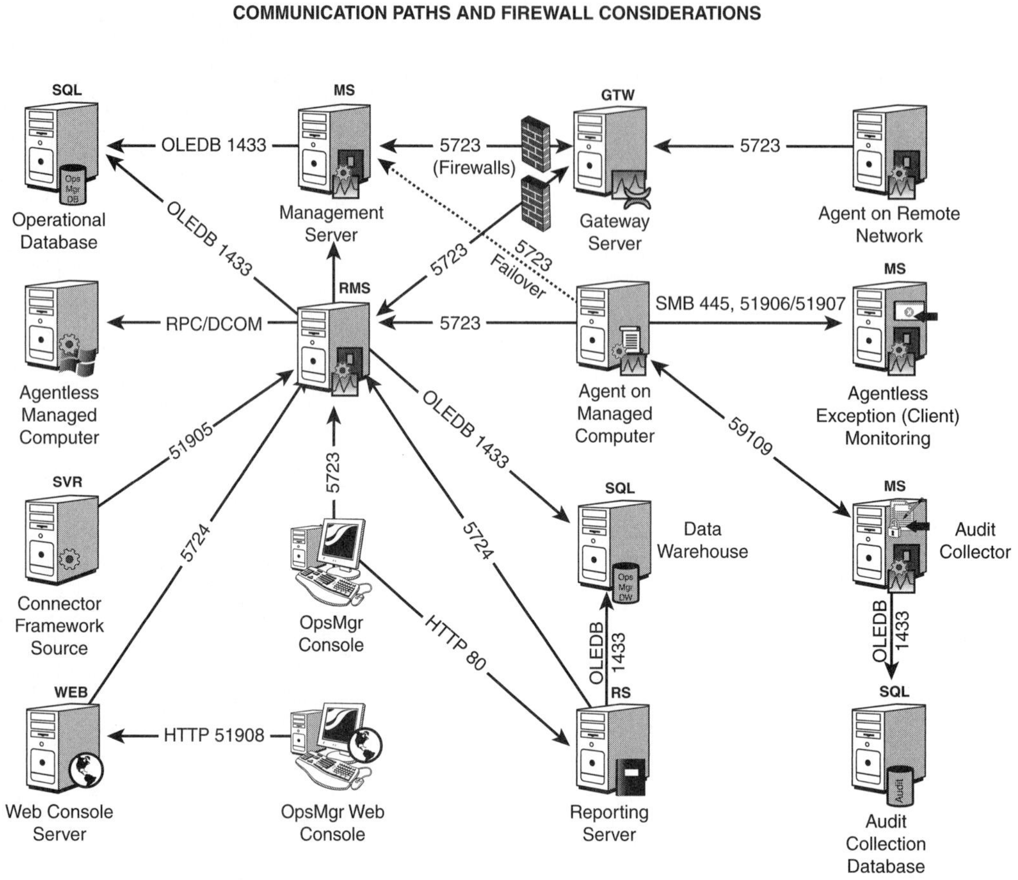

COMMUNICATION PATHS AND FIREWALL CONSIDERATIONS

FIGURE 3.5   Communication channels between computers in a management group.

How Does OpsMgr Do It?

So far in this chapter, we have covered what a management group is, and how the components, or computer roles, of a management group communicate with one another—the macro view. Now we shift our focus to the micro view of the management pack—the computer and device management work the whole OpsMgr infrastructure was deployed for. The management group is the framework within which management packs do that work.

Operations Manager 2007 is a product established on the concept of model-based management. The abstraction of services into *models* is needed to describe and act on physical entities such as routers, and logical entities such as distributed applications, using software tools that by definition exist in cyberspace. Using models is a way to transform human knowledge and experience into something machines can operate with. In OpsMgr, service models live inside management packs. The management pack author or vendor encapsulates service health knowledge into the redistributable management pack.

Having a solid, accurate model of an object's health lets OpsMgr 2007 present information to the operator in the most immediately useful way. As you will see, the models underpin both the OpsMgr 2007 application, with a workflow framework, and the OpsMgr 2007 operator, with augmented and accelerated decision making.

Operations Manager 2007 introduces an architecture that sets the foundation for a new, broader spectrum of monitoring capabilities and extensibility than has ever been available before using Microsoft management technologies. OpsMgr 2007 fundamental concepts include service and health modeling (we will explain and differentiate between those terms). We'll briefly cover the schema of a management pack so that you understand how a service model is distilled into actionable components such as monitors and tasks. In addition, we will illustrate how monitors are the intersection between the models, and how health information progresses inside the OpsMgr workflow engine to its presentation in the OpsMgr console.

Service Modeling

One can capture knowledge through models! Service modeling in Operations Manager 2007 is rooted in the well-known Service Modeling Language (SML) used by Microsoft developers in the .NET development environment. SML is an extensible language, built for describing the cooperating systems found not just inside the computer, but also inside an entire datacenter. SML provides a way to think about computer systems, operating systems, application-hosting systems, and application systems—as well as how they interact and are combined, connected, deployed, and managed. SML is used to create models of complex IT services and systems.

A software engineer authoring in Visual Studio Team Edition for Software Architects uses SML to define how an application interacts with various layers of the datacenter, such as the hardware layer, where the servers and routers live, and the operating system layer, which is "hosted" by the hardware layer. The SML concept of one layer hosting another is used in OpsMgr service modeling when relationships are defined between objects managed by OpsMgr, such as a hard drive that hosts a website.

OpsMgr 2007 operates on a class-based structure. When the monitoring infrastructure discovers an "object" (or entity), it assigns a set of logical classes to the object. These classes serve as descriptors for the managed object. The SML for a managed object is imported into OpsMgr using the vehicle of the management pack. Specifically, the management pack adds the formal definitions of "types of objects" (or classes), their properties, and the relationship between objects in the management group. Relationships usually take the form of a dependence on another object, or of a container of another object.

Without management packs and the knowledge they deliver, any OpsMgr group is just a big empty brain. You can compare a management group to the brain, which is a physical structure; in contrast, management packs are analogous to the memories and ideas that live in that brain. Useful thoughts are crafted in the brain based on knowledge and experience. Useful workflow in a management group is made possible by management packs.

We can continue to use a biological metaphor to explain the way management packs convert human knowledge and experience into actionable machine workflows. In the medical profession, a very precise lexicon exists to describe objects in the body. If you think of the parts of your body, you realize the many classes, properties, and relationships that exist. Here are some examples to get you thinking this way:

▶ You have a sensory organ "class" that include "objects" such as your eyes, ears, tongue, nose, and skin.

▶ Many objects in your body need to be described along with a property or qualifier, such as "left" or "right," or "proximal" or "distal" to distinguish the particular body part (object).

▶ Every object in the body has one or more relationships with other objects, such as the hand "depending" on the arm, or arteries that "contain" blood.

Classes, objects, and relationships are how OpsMgr recognizes an object, understands what the object is, and how to work with the object. Just as we more precisely describe a particular body part by adding the descriptor "left" to the object "hand," OpsMgr describes objects using a hierarchical system of descriptors that are increasingly specific.

Now you will see this SML layer concept in action as we describe a particular object, a website running on a managed Windows server. See the diagram in Figure 3.6, starting in the upper-left portion of the description, the *Entity*. This is another word for "object" in OpsMgr, and it's like a placeholder for the object's root.

Proceeding down and to the right in the hierarchy, or "tree," depicted in Figure 3.6, we add descriptors to successively narrow, or focus, the description of the particular managed object. As depicted, the Windows Computer Role is a subordinate descriptor to Computer Role. Likewise, the Internet Information Services (IIS) service is a particular Windows Computer Role in OpsMgr, and the monitored website is a particular feature of the IIS service.

Also illustrated in Figure 3.6 are relationships between objects, such as the Windows Operating System (OS) hosting the IIS service, and a particular disk drive hosting the monitored website—which is the object of interest in this description.

The ability of management packs to define relationships between objects, using such terms as "reference," "using," "hosting," and "containing," is critical to technological innovations found in OpsMgr over previous Microsoft management technologies. OpsMgr features such as monitoring distributed applications with containment relationships, diagrammatic cross-platform fault identification, and maintenance mode on individual computer components are possible via SML and its layered approach to describing objects.

DESCRIBING OBJECT TYPES IN OPERATIONS MANAGER 2007

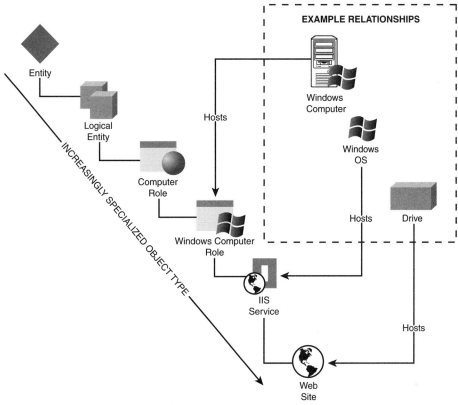

FIGURE 3.6   Describing an object using the System Modeling Language.

Management pack authors include the ability to discern both objects and relationships between objects in the discovery process. Objects and relationships are discovered with probes that examine computer registries using Windows Management Instrumentation (WMI) queries, scripts, database queries (OLE DB), the Lightweight Directory Access Protocol (LDAP), and custom or "managed" code.

We're going to dive right into an advanced view of the Authoring space to highlight the importance of the process to discover both objects and their relationships in order to understand how OpsMgr works. In Figure 3.7, observe the OpsMgr Authoring space, focused on the Object Discoveries branch of the Management Pack Objects section. In the upper portion of the center pane, notice we have expanded three discovered type classes:

- ▶ Windows Server 2003 Disk Partition
- ▶ Windows Server 2003 Logical Disk
- ▶ Windows Server 2003 Physical Disk

Arrows on the left in Figure 3.7 point to object discovery rules (distributed in the Windows Server 2003 Base OS management pack) that discover disk partitions, logical disks, and physical disk attributes using WMI queries. In the lower (Details) portion of the center pane, we can see the actual WMI query strings used when discovering Windows logical disks (in this case looking for attributes such as what file system is in use and whether the volume is compressed).

Of course, disk partitions as well as logical and physical disks are highly interrelated object classes. Physical disks can contain multiple disk partitions, which in turn may contain multiple logical disks. Logical disks can span multiple disk partitions and physical disks.

Notice in Figure 3.7 that the target column of the discovery rules for a particular object type such as "Windows Server 2003 Disk Partition" identifies the object type that hosts the discovered type. For example, the Windows Server 2003 Operating System (OS) hosts Windows disk partitions; therefore, the Discover Windows Disk Partitions object discovery rule targets the Windows Server 2003 OS object type (or class).

Relationship discovery rules operate in addition to object discovery rules. Object discovery rules use WMI or other probes to locate managed objects and populate the Operations database with actionable object attributes. This enables relationship discovery rules to look at object properties for particular discovered attributes that indicate a dependence, hosting, or containing relationship.

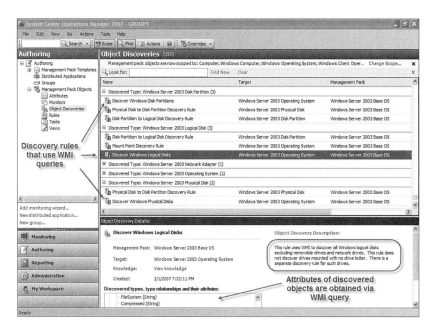

FIGURE 3.7   Probes such as WMI and Registry key queries discover object attributes.

After the Windows Server 2003 Base OS management pack discovers various disk objects, it also discovers the relationships between these classes of disk objects using separate relationship discovery rules. See the relationship discovery rules called out in Figure 3.8. The four relationship discovery rules in this example identify the relationships between physical disks and disk partitions, and between disk partitions and logical disks.

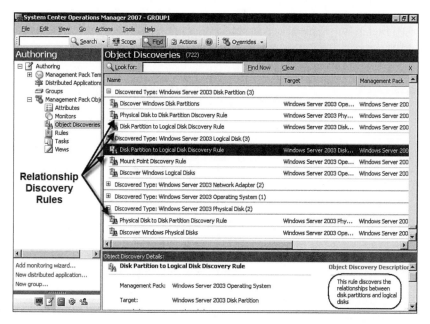

FIGURE 3.8   Both object and relationship discovery rules are associated with most object types, or "classes."

Health Models

After object and relationship discovery is complete, the Operations database is populated with the object's descriptive data (its attributes). Now OpsMgr can begin performing the primary work of the management pack, managing the state of the object's health model.

Every class, or object type, has a health model. The status, or health, of even the simplest managed object is represented by a health model. A *model* is a collection of monitors. We will be covering monitors in detail later in the "Monitors" section of this chapter. As we add monitors, we enrich the health model.

Monitors are arranged in a tree structure that is as deep or as shallow as required. The status of the health model represents the current state of the object. The Health Explorer shows a live view of an object's health model. The Health Explorer tool can be launched against any managed object from all views in the Monitoring pane of the console.

A key monitoring concept in OpsMgr 2007 is the *rollup*. We first heard this term from Microsoft early in OpsMgr development, used to describe the way health status "bubbles up" from lower levels in the health model hierarchy, or tree, to higher-level monitors. The top-level monitor in a health model, located at the root Entity object layer, is the rollup, which represents the overall health state of the object.

We return to the Service Modeling Language layer-based method of classifying objects introduced along with the concept of service modeling. Figure 3.9 diagrams (on the left side) the tree-like class hierarchy of the IIS service on a Windows computer. Notice the unit monitors located at the lower right of the diagram inline with the IIS service. Monitors in

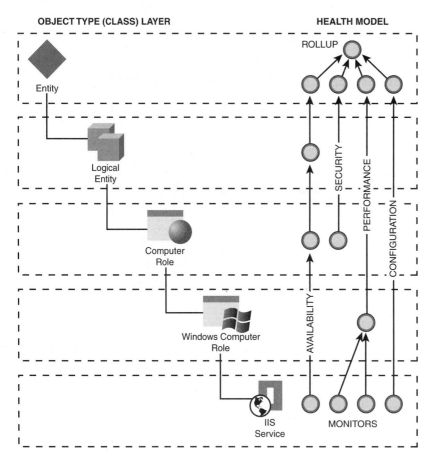

FIGURE 3.9   The layers of SML allow for tactical placement of hierarchical monitors.

each of the four basic categories (Availability, Security, Performance, and Configuration) are represented by round "pearl" shapes.

Lower-layer monitor status is propagated by the health model up to monitors in successively higher layers. For any given health model, monitors are not necessarily located at every layer, or within every monitor category. The management pack author determines what monitors are targeted against what object classes.

Finally, notice in Figure 3.9 the uppermost, triangular arrangement of four monitors rolling up into the health state for the managed object. The rollup occurs at the entity level; this is a universal feature of OpsMgr object health models. The second-level monitors that roll up into the top-level state monitor are called *aggregate monitors*.

State-based Management

Another key theme in OpsMgr is the employment of *state-based management*, in contrast to previous versions of Operations Manager that were alert-based. An alert-based management system watches for a condition, raises an alert, and optionally changes the state of the object due to the generation of the alert.

The point of the Health Explorer is to illustrate the state of a managed object's health, not to present a list of new or unacknowledged alerts that require operator evaluation. MOM 2005 administrators already know the difficulty in rapidly correlating and triaging a laundry list of alerts in order to answer the question, "What do we need to do to fix the problem?"

The OpsMgr implementation of state-based management applies the following workflow sequence:

1. A unit monitor watches for a condition.
2. When the unit monitor detects the condition, it changes the state of the unit monitor.
3. Unit monitor states are rolled up as required to higher-level aggregate monitors in the object's health model.
4. Rules optionally generate an alert or initiate a notification event.

Management Pack Schema

A management pack is an eXtensible Markup Language (XML) document that provides the structure to monitor specific software or hardware. A sealed managed pack is a read-only, encrypted version of the XML document. This XML document contains the definitions of the different components in software or hardware and the information needed by an administrator who must operate that application, device, or service efficiently.

We will take a quick look at the schema of the management pack so that you can appreciate how tightly management pack construction is aligned with the health model of an object. A high-level view of the management pack schema is diagrammed in Figure 3.10. From the management pack root, moving right, there are eight major sections: Manifest, TypeDefinitions, Monitoring, Templates, PresentationTypes, Presentation, Reporting, and LanguagePacks.

Only the Manifest section is mandatory, and that section is expanded in the upper-right portion of Figure 3.10. The Manifest section defines the identity and version of the management pack as well as all other management packs it is dependent on. The Identity, Name, and References sections are common and included in every management pack. Any management packs referenced must be sealed, and they must be imported to the OpsMgr management group before the management pack can be imported.

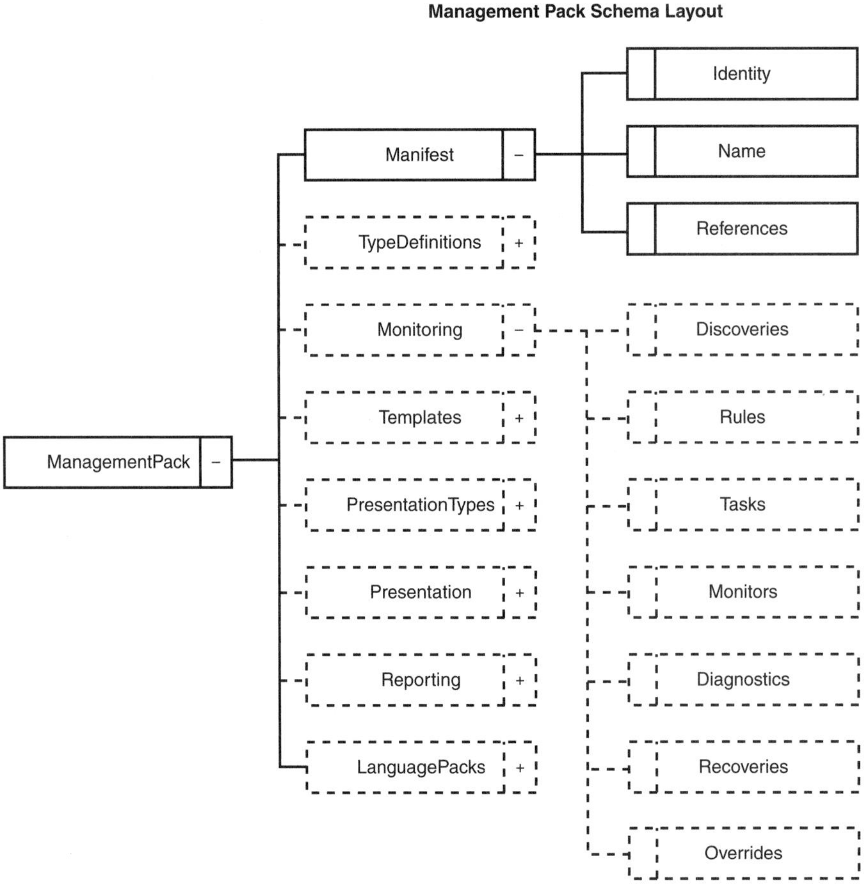

FIGURE 3.10   Management pack schema, with the Manifest and Monitoring sections expanded.

The other major schema section that is expanded in Figure 3.10, Monitoring, is where most of the action takes place in OpsMgr, and this chapter also is mainly about the sections you see contained there. The following list summarizes the purpose of each section of the Monitoring schema:

▶ **Discoveries**—A *discovery* is a workflow that discovers one or more objects of a particular type. A discovery can discover objects of multiple types at one time. As introduced previously in the "Service Modeling" section of this chapter, there are both object discovery and relationship discovery rules.

▶ **Rules**—A *rule* is a generic workflow that can do many different things. As an example, it could collect a data item, alert on a specific condition, or run a scheduled task at some specified frequency. Rules do not set state at all; they are primarily used to collect data to present in the console or in reports and to generate alerts.

▶ **Tasks**—A *task* is a workflow that is executed on demand and is usually initiated by a user of the OpsMgr console. Tasks are not loaded by OpsMgr until required. There are also agent-initiated tasks, where the agent opens up a TCP/IP connection with the server, initiating the communication. After the connection is established, it is a two-way communication channel.

▶ **Monitors**—A *monitor* is a state machine and ultimately contributes to the state of some type of object that is being monitored by OpsMgr. There are three monitor types: aggregate (internal rollup), dependency (external rollup), and unit monitors. The unit monitor is the simplest monitor, one that simply detects a condition, changes its state, and propagates that state to parent monitors in the health model that roll up the status as appropriate. We cover monitors in more detail in the next section of this chapter.

▶ **Diagnostics**—A *diagnostic* is an on-demand workflow that is attached to a specific monitor. The diagnostic workflow is initiated automatically either when a monitor enters a particular state or upon demand by a user when the monitor is in a particular state. Multiple diagnostics can be attached to a monitor if required. A diagnostic does not change the application state.

▶ **Recoveries**—A *recovery* is an on-demand workflow that is attached to a specific monitor or a specific diagnostic. The recovery workflow is initiated automatically when a monitor enters a particular state or when a diagnostic has run, or upon demand by an operator. Multiple recoveries can be attached to a monitor if required. A recovery changes the application state in some way; hopefully it fixes any problems the monitor detected!

▶ **Overrides**—Overrides are used to change monitoring behavior in some way. Many types of overrides are available, including overrides of specific monitoring features such as discovery, diagnostics, and recoveries. Normally the OpsMgr administrator or operator sets overrides based on his specific, local environment. However, in some cases, a management pack vendor may recommend creating overrides in particular scenarios as a best practice.

Monitors

It all starts with monitors in Operations Manager 2007. We have mentioned that a health model is a collection of monitors. If you were to author a management pack, you would probably start with creating unit monitors. Unit monitors would detect conditions you determine are essential to assess some aspect of the health of the application, device, or service needing to be managed.

Monitors provide the basic function of monitoring in OpsMgr. You can think of each monitor as a *state machine*, a self-contained machine that sets the state of a component based on conditional changes. A monitor can be in only one state at any given time, and there are a finite number of operational states.

A monitor can check for a single event or a wide range of events that represent many different problems. The goal of monitor design is to ensure that each unhealthy state of a monitor indicates a well-defined problem that has known diagnostic and recovery steps.

Using a single monitor to cover a large number of separate problems is not recommended, because it provides less value. We mentioned in the lead-in to the "Health Models" section of this chapter that adding monitors to a health model increases the richness of an object's monitoring experience. The enhancement of an object's health model with many monitors adds fidelity to the health state of the object. More monitors in a health model also means more relationship connection points for other managed objects that host, contain, depend on, or reference that object.

We pointed out the "pearl" icon used to represent a monitor in health model diagrams. An empty pearl icon represents a generic or a non-operational monitor. Figure 3.11 is a chart showing the default monitor icon images and their corresponding operational state.

A functioning monitor displays exactly one of the primary state icons: green/success, yellow/warning, or red/critical. A newly created or nonfunctional monitor will show the blank pearl icon. The gray maintenance mode "wrench" icon appears in all monitoring views inline with the object that was placed in maintenance mode. The final type of state icon you will encounter is the grayed state icon, which indicates that the managed object is out of contact. For example, this could reference a managed notebook computer that is off the network at the moment.

To be clear, there are three kinds of monitors that management pack authors can create: aggregate rollup monitors, dependency rollup monitors, and unit monitors. In the next sections we will describe each of these monitor types.

Aggregate Rollup Monitors

Let's return to the Figure 3.9 view of the layers of the SML, which permits tactical placement of interrelated monitors. On the right, notice the monitors are classified in categories, essentially four vertical columns that are connected by a rollup to the top-level entity health status. Microsoft selected these four categories during OpsMgr development as a framework to aggregate the health of any managed object.

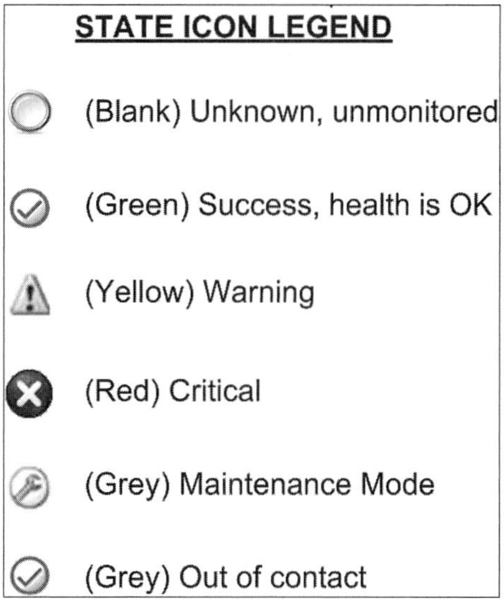

STATE ICON LEGEND

(Blank) Unknown, unmonitored

(Green) Success, health is OK

(Yellow) Warning

(Red) Critical

(Grey) Maintenance Mode

(Grey) Out of contact

FIGURE 3.11   These state icons are encountered in the Operations console.

The four standard types of aggregate monitors in a state monitor are detailed in the following list:

▶ **Availability Health**—Examples include checking that services are running, that modules within the OpsMgr health service are loaded, and basic node up/down tracking.

▶ **Performance Health**—Examples include thresholds for available memory, processor utilization, and network response time.

▶ **Security Health**—Monitors related to security that are not included in the other aggregate monitors.

▶ **Configuration Health**—Examples include confirming the Windows activation state and that IIS logging is enabled and functioning.

Dependency Rollup Monitors

The second category of monitor is the dependency rollup. Such a monitor rolls up health states from targets linked to one another by either a hosting or a membership relationship. Dependency rollup monitors function similarly to aggregate rollup monitors, but are located at intermediate layers of the SML hierarchy.

In Figure 3.9, notice again the unit monitors for the IIS service located in the lower right. There are two unit monitors of the performance type at the IIS Service level that merge at the Windows Computer Role level. The merge point represents one or more dependency rollup monitor(s) targeted at the Windows Computer Role.

Earlier in the "Service Modeling" section of this chapter, we explored how objects such as disk partitions, logical disks, and physical disks have numerous relationships. Figure 3.12 shows a sample dependency rollup monitor involving disk systems created in the OpsMgr authoring space.

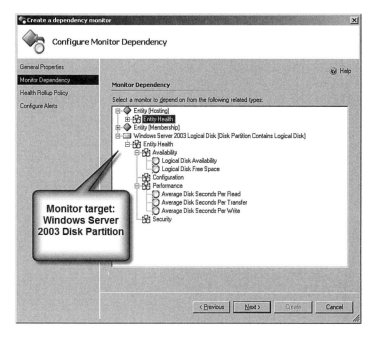

FIGURE 3.12   Creating a dependency rollup monitor when the target is a disk partition.

The monitor created in Figure 3.12 is targeted against the Windows Server 2003 Disk Partition class. OpsMgr knows that disk partitions contain logical disks, so when you create a new dependency rollup monitor targeting the Windows Server 2003 Disk Partition class, OpsMgr offers existing monitors to select from for the Windows Server 2003 Logical Disk class.

We can also expand the example of the "merged" IIS service performance unit monitors in Figure 3.9. If we were creating that dependency rollup monitor in the authoring space, we would have selected the Windows Computer Role as the target of our monitor. The Create a Dependency Monitor Wizard would provide us with a list of dependent objects to select from that includes those IIS service performance monitors.

Unit Monitors

A unit monitor allows management pack authors to define a list of states and how to detect those states. A simple unit monitor is a Basic Service Monitor. This monitor raises state changes when a Windows service stops running. More complex unit monitors run scripts, examine text logs, and perform Simple Network Management Protocol (SNMP) queries. A unit monitor is deployed, or targeted, at a class of objects when it is authored.

TIP

Target the Agent to Deploy a Monitor to All Computers

Targeting a monitor at the Agent object class deploys the monitor to all managed computers. Use the Agent target like an "All Computers" group for monitors, but also use it sparingly. It is an OpsMgr best practice to deploy the minimum set of appropriate monitors to a managed computer.

When creating monitors and envisioning operational states, Microsoft advises OpsMgr administrators and management pack authors to do so without initially regarding actual implementation of those monitors. The reasoning is that OpsMgr not only provides many monitor types by default for common scenarios, but makes it possible to build different workflows to meet any monitoring requirement. Basically, the management pack architect is encouraged to think "outside the box" and describe in plain ideas how an application's health can be assessed. After that, you can look to the many tools OpsMgr provides to instrument the application accordingly.

Figure 3.13 presents a montage screenshot that includes all possible types of unit monitors available in the authoring space of the OpsMgr console. These are the tools used to architect the instrumentation of the health model.

Over 50 unit monitor types are available to place as software instrumentation in the SML framework. Remember that unit monitors roll up into the aggregate monitors (Availability, Performance, Security, and Configuration), sometimes via dependency rollup monitors. The goal of monitor design is to ensure that each unhealthy state of a monitor indicates a well-defined problem that has known diagnostic and recovery steps. Table 3.2 provides some explanation of the unit monitor types found in the menu in Figure 3.13.

To conclude this section on monitors, we're going to put it all together by overlaying the SML and the health model for a live service monitor. Figure 3.14 is a fully expanded view of the health model of the OpsMgr Health service itself running on a management server.

Beginning at the lowest level of the object description tree, we see the MonitoringHost Private Bytes Threshold unit monitor on the computer Hurricane. Five unit monitors are shown in the lowest row that roll up into the Health Service Performance monitor. These unit monitors are labeled with the abbreviations Svc Handle, Svc Priv, Mon Handle, Mon Priv, and Send Queue in Figure 3.14. The MonitoringHost Private Bytes Threshold (abbreviated Mon Priv) unit monitor is in a critical state.

TABLE 3.2   Unit Monitor Types

Monitor type	Description
Average Threshold	Average value over a number of samples.
Consecutive Samples over Threshold	Value that remains over or below a threshold for a consecutive number of minutes.
Delta Threshold	Change in value.
Simple Threshold	Single threshold.
Double Threshold	Two thresholds (monitors whether values are between a given pair of thresholds).
Event Reset	A clearing condition occurs and resets the state automatically.
Manual Reset	Event based; wait for operator to clear.
Timer Reset	Event based; automatically clear after certain time.
Basic Service Monitor	Uses WMI to check the state of the specified Windows service. The monitor will be unhealthy when the service is not running or has not been set to start automatically.
Two State Monitor	Monitor has two states: Healthy and Unhealthy.
Three State Monitor	Monitor has three states: Healthy, Warning, and Unhealthy.

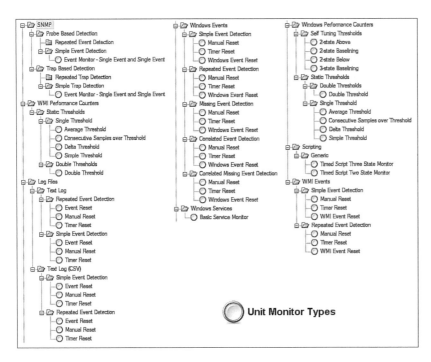

FIGURE 3.13   The complete menu of types of unit monitors that can be created.

We can follow the propagation of this unit monitor state up the health model. The OpsMgr Health service is an application component of Windows Local Application Health Rollup. The Health Service is in a critical state due to the critical state of the MonitoringHost Private Bytes Threshold (abbreviated Mon Priv) unit monitor. Progressing upward, the application state is rolled up along with the hardware, OS, and computer states to the performance component of the object.

The critical state is propagated to the application component of the performance monitor. Finally at the top of the health model, an aggregate monitor rolls up the performance, availability, security, and configuration monitors. The root entity, which is the server Hurricane itself, indicates the aggregated health state, which is critical.

Figure 3.15 shows the Health Explorer for the computer in the state illustrated in Figure 3.14. If you noticed the critical state of the computer in the Monitoring pane of the Operations console, you would probably open the Health Explorer for the computer, which allows you to understand quickly what is wrong. By comparing the structure of the Health Explorer in Figure 3.15 with the SDK and health model layers presented in Figure 3.14, you can match up the same critical health icons in the health model and the Health Explorer.

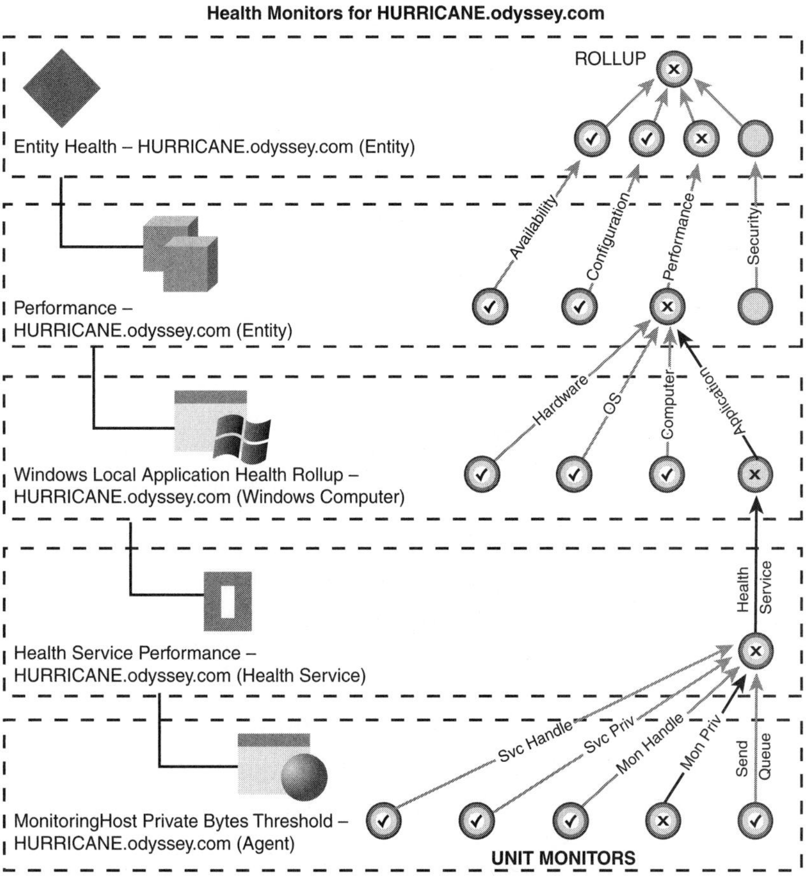

FIGURE 3.14   Expanded view of the health model for the OpsMgr Health Service.

FIGURE 3.15   Health Explorer screenshot of the health model detailed in Figure 3.14.

Workflow

It is accurate to describe Operations Manager 2007 at its core as being a giant workflow engine. In fact, monitoring in OpsMgr is based around the concept of workflows. An Operations Manager agent and server will run many workflows simultaneously in order to discover and monitor applications, devices, and services.

Module Types

Module types are the building blocks of Operations Manager workflows. Workflows are defined in management packs and then distributed to managed computers. Workflows can do many things, including collecting information and storing data in the Operations database or data warehouse, running timed scripts, creating alerts, and running on-demand tasks. Workflows are defined using modules, and modules are defined to be of a particular type known as a *module type*. Four different module types can be defined: data source, probe action, condition detection, and write action. Figure 3.16 illustrates these module types.

In the "Architectural Overview" section of this chapter, we compared the management group and management pack to macro and micro views that answer the question "How does OpsMgr do it"? In this section, we are going sub-micro! At the programmatic level, these are the terms and data flow structures used internally by the OpsMgr services:

▶ **Data Source**—A data source module type generates data using some form of instrumentation or some timed trigger action. As an example, a data source may provide events from a specific Windows event log or it could poll Windows performance counters every 10 minutes for a specific performance counter. A data source takes no input data and provides one output data stream. Data sources do not change the state of any object.

▶ **Probe Action**—A probe action module type uses some input data to provide some output data. A probe action will interrogate a monitored entity in some way, but it should not affect system state in any way. An example would be running a script that queries WMI to get some data. A probe action is often used in conjunction with a data source to run some action on a timed basis. The probe action module type may or may not use the input data item to affect the behavior. In other words, when triggered, a probe action generates output from external sources. Probe actions have one input stream and one output stream. Like data source modules, probe action modules do not change the state of objects.

▶ **Condition Detection**—A condition detection module type filters the incoming data in some way. Examples of filter types include a simple filter on the input data, consolidation of like data items, correlation between multiple inputs, and averaging performance data. A condition detection module type can take one or more input data streams and provides a single output data steam. Condition detection modules do not use any external source and do not change object state.

▶ **Write Action**—A write action module type takes a single input data stream and uses this in conjunction with some configuration to affect system state in some way. This change could be in the monitored system or in Operations Manager itself. As an example, the action may be to run a script that writes data into the Operations database, or one that generates an alert. A write action may or may not output data. This data cannot be passed to any other module because the write action is the last module in a workflow. However, the data may be sent to the Operations database. A sample action is running a command that outputs data, such as a command line that returns a report of success or errors. This data may be useful to the operator who executes the command, and it is returned to the Operations console and stored as task output.

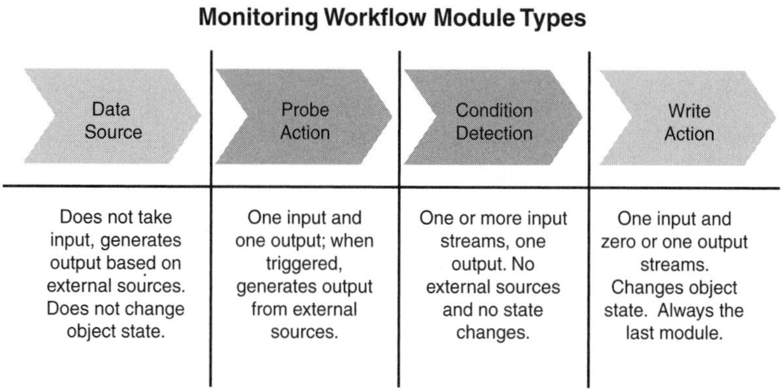

Monitoring Workflow Module Types

Data Source	Probe Action	Condition Detection	Write Action
Does not take input, generates output based on external sources. Does not change object state.	One input and one output; when triggered, generates output from external sources.	One or more input streams, one output. No external sources and no state changes.	One input and zero or one output streams. Changes object state. Always the last module.

FIGURE 3.16   Workflow in OpsMgr is performed through four specific module types.

> **TIP**
>
> **Probe Actions Can Cause Unintended State Changes**
>
> Changes to object states should only occur in response to write action modules. Take note that Operations Manager cannot determine if a probe action is being used to change an object's state in some way. For example, if you run a script that is part of a probe action module type, you could be changing object state in some way in your script. It is up to the management pack author to adhere to the module type definition guidance. If you are changing system state, you should use a write action module type instead.

"Cook Down"

Cook down is an important concept in management pack authoring. The Operations Manager agent or server is running many hundreds or even thousands of workflows at any given time. Each workflow that is loaded takes some system resource. Obviously the less system resources we take up for monitoring, the better.

The management pack author can do a lot to reduce the impact of monitoring on the system. One way is to ensure that workflows are not targeted too generically. We mentioned this already in this chapter, in the section on "Unit Monitors." For example, if you have a rule that is only applicable to servers running Microsoft ISA Server 2006, don't target the rule at all Windows servers; instead, you should target it at the appropriate ISA Server class.

Cook down is not about targeting; it is a principle whereby in most modules the Operations Manager Health service will try to minimize the number of instances in memory. This is accomplished by considering the configuration of modules. Usually, if the Health service sees two modules with the same configuration in different workflows that have the same configuration, it will only execute a single module and feed the output to all the workflows that defined the module. This is an efficiency you should be aware of, particularly if you will be authoring scripts for use by OpsMgr.

Here is a simple example of two rules that will "cook down":

- ▶ **Rule 1**—Collect an event from the application log where Event ID =11724 and Event Source = MsiInstaller (application removal completed).

- ▶ **Rule 2**—Collect an event from the application log where Event ID =1005 and Event Source = MsiInstaller (system requires a restart to complete or continue application configuration).

Operations Manager sees that the event log provider data source (application log events) is configured the same for both rules. Only one instance of the module will run. The two MsiInstaller event ID rules, or expression filters, will take input data from the output of the same module. A large number of expression filters can be handled by one condition detection module. In the case of the event log provider example, there will normally be only one module executing for each log being monitored (unless you are running the module under different credentials for different workflows).

Cook down becomes particularly important when writing scripts to be run by OpsMgr, especially when there are scripts running against multiple instances of an object type on the same Health service. If you do not think about cook down, you could end up running many scripts when you could actually run a single script by thinking about configuration and targeting.

Data Types

We have discussed module types and how they are used by OpsMgr internally to achieve workflow. Obviously, OpsMgr must pass data between modules. The format of this data varies depending on the module that output the data. As an example, a data source that reads from the event log will output a different type of data than a module that reads from a text-based log file. Some module types expect a certain type of data. A threshold module type expects performance data and the module type that writes data to the Operations Manager database expects event data. Therefore, it is necessary for Operations Manager to define and use different data types.

Data types are defined in management packs. However, this definition is merely a pointer to a code implementation of the data type. Operations Manager 2007 does not support extension of the data types provided out of the box.

Data types follow an inheritance model in a manner similar to class definitions, introduced in the "Service Modeling" section of this chapter. Whereas the class hierarchy starts with a base class called System.Entity, the data type hierarchy starts with a data type called System.BaseData. All data types eventually inherit from the base data type. Examples of data types in the System.BaseData class include Microsoft.Windows.RegistryData (for a probe action module that examines Registry values) and System.CommandOutput (for write action modules that return useful command-line output).

When a module type is defined it must, where applicable, specify the input and output data types that it accepts and provides. These must be valid data types defined in the same management pack or a referenced management pack. When a module is used in a workflow, the data types that the module type accepts and provides must be compatible with the other modules in the workflow.

Presentation Layer

This chapter has dived into progressively more detailed descriptions of how OpsMgr works at the management group, management pack, and workflow levels. Now we will come up for some air and finish with a discussion of the presentation layer in OpsMgr. This is the part of OpsMgr that you see with your eyes and will work with on a continuous and routine basis.

As with any user-level application (as opposed to an application designed only to be run in the background by machines as a Windows service) the presentation layer in OpsMgr is responsible for delivering and formatting relevant and interesting information to the user or operator. The main interface for Operations Manager 2007 is the Operations console. For doing monitoring work away from the office, Microsoft provides a web-based console with a subset of the full console's functionally, optimized for monitoring functions. Finally, there is the command-line PowerShell for text-based interaction with OpsMgr.

OpsMgr can deliver management information to users with a variety of external notification techniques, such as email and instant messaging. Examples of those notifications and how they are configured are discussed in detail in Chapter 8, "Configuring and Using Operations Manager 2007." However, OpsMgr cannot be administered and run only through notifications.

Operations Console

Unless you are using the Web console from a remote location, or running PowerShell for specialized work, all interaction between operations personnel and the Operations Manager 2007 application will occur using the Operations console. The console is not a Microsoft Management Console (MMC) snap-in, but a standalone application installed on management servers and optionally installed on any supported Windows computer.

The Operations console is composed of several panes, as shown in Figure 3.17, each of which serves a particular purpose. We will be covering the OpsMgr features accessed in the various console panes in detail in Chapter 8.

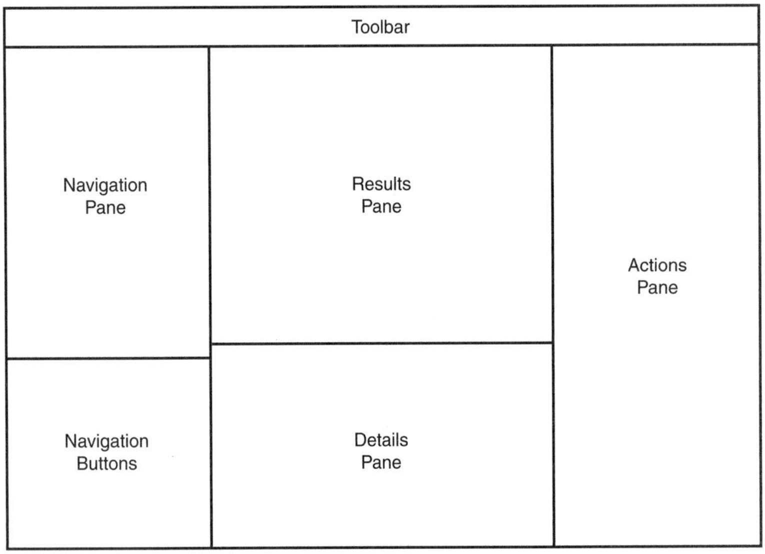

FIGURE 3.17   Layout of the Operations console.

As you can see in Figure 3.17, the OpsMgr console shares some features with the popular Microsoft Office Outlook application, such as the Navigation pane and navigation buttons. The Actions pane shares the look of another contemporary Microsoft application, Exchange 2007 (which also features PowerShell as an integrated component). The navigation buttons in the lower-left corner are a key feature of the console. They provide a rapid, intuitive way to shift between management tasks without firing up other consoles or applications. Here is a quick rundown on those navigation buttons:

▶ **Monitoring Pane**—Displays several different types of views that enable operators to analyze monitoring results within the managed environment(s). This is where most users of OpsMgr will spend their time because the Monitoring pane is where the action is!

Views of alerts, events, object states, performance, diagrams, tasks, and dashboards exist here. When reporting is installed, the lower portion of the Actions pane provides context-aware reports for the objects in the Results pane.

▶ **Authoring Pane**—Enables creation of additional monitoring objects to customize or supplement the default monitoring settings provided in management packs. New customized management packs can be created using several templates provided with OpsMgr. Custom groups used to target rules are created here. Only administrators and advanced operators have access to this pane.

▶ **Reporting Pane**—If OpsMgr reporting is installed in the management group, this pane displays a report library with the reports included in management packs, and it enables editing of customized reports. Only administrators and report operators have access to this pane. This navigation button is not present if reporting is not installed.

The report library contains generic reports, such as Alert Logging Latency and Most Common Events reports. Reports launched from the Reporting pane have no prespecified context, and operators must manually specify the context for the report in the parameter header before running the report. Reporting is discussed in more detail in Chapter 8.

▶ **Administration Pane**—Enables editing of high-level Operations Manager settings that affect the entire management group. It also enables viewing and configuring individual management servers and managed objects. The critical Security roles, Run As Accounts, and Run As Profiles are managed here. All work related to adding and deleting agent-managed computers, agentless managed computers, and network devices is performed in this pane. Only administrators have access to this pane.

▶ **My Workspace Pane**—Enables creation and storage of console customizations for later reuse. Although OpsMgr administrators can modify the main views and add new views using the Administration pane, there are many occasions where the operator has her own ideas or requirements for monitoring. The My Workspace pane is a personal area where console users can make new customized views to their heart's content and not impact other system users. Users can also store possibly complex search criteria here, saving lots of time on each future occasion when those searches are used.

> **TIP**
>
> **Turn the Navigation Button Area into a Toolbar**
>
> The navigation button area of the Operations console provides a quick way to change the functionality of the Results, Details, and Action panes in the console. However, the default navigation buttons encroach on the more useful Navigation pane above them and occupy almost 10% of the console area. You can recover that space by dragging the grouping bar above the top navigation button downward. This collapses the larger navigation buttons into much smaller icons that resemble a standard toolbar.

The center portion of the console, where the Results and Details panes are located, is particularly reconfigurable and divides into as many as nine separate panes in some console views. The Operations console also uses multiple windows, which open like pop-ups, and can be closed without affecting the main console. For example, when Operations Manager features such as override, search, Health Explorer, and Security are being used, new windows open to support the selected operation.

The Find, Search, and Scope buttons in the Operations console make it easier for users to manage data. The Scope and Search controls are located at the top of the console in the toolbar area, and the Find filter is found at the top of the Results pane. Because OpsMgr can manage many thousands of objects, these filtering functions are a critical usability feature in large environments.

Web Console

Borrowing again from the success of the Outlook interface, which is a very well received, almost identical web interface to Outlook Web Access, Microsoft delivered a Web console for OpsMgr. The Operations Manager 2007 Web console is really a triumph of web interface design and execution. It mimics many features of the Monitoring and My Workspace portions of the full Operations console.

An ActiveX control is downloaded to the user's web browser on his first visit to the Web console from any given computer. If the Web console is installed on a management server, additional notification and access features become available to the management group. Specifically, there is a mobile access feature for smart phones and Personal Digital Assistants (PDAs) with network or Internet access, along with a Really Simple Syndication (RSS) version 2.0 feature that allows operators to set up RSS subscriptions to OpsMgr alerts.

PowerShell

PowerShell provides a means to interact with the OpsMgr application without any graphical interface. Much of the work that can be done in the Operations and Web consoles can also be done using PowerShell. PowerShell is particularly useful in a variety of specialized situations. Compared to the immensely usable OpsMgr console, it is an adjustment to work with the command line of PowerShell, particularly at first. However, just having the opportunity to view and set data in the Operations database programmatically using the command line is a fantastic addition to the administrator's toolkit.

We will close this section with an example of the functionality and presentation of PowerShell compared to the OpsMgr console. We created a custom user role in the Security -> User Roles node of the OpsMgr Administration pane, named Partner Staff Acme. In Figure 3.18, you can see the properties of that user role, in a window launched from the console.

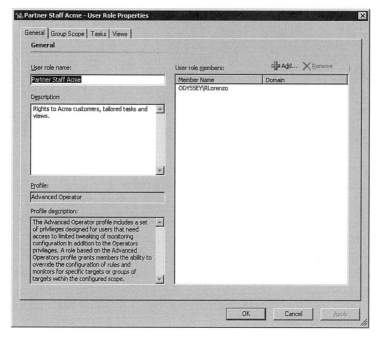

FIGURE 3.18   Properties of a custom user role, viewed with the OpsMgr console.

To access the Properties window in Figure 3.18, you simply right-click the user role in the OpsMgr console and select Properties. Notice that there is one user, RLorenzo, who is a member of that role in the ODYSSEY domain. Now we will use PowerShell to access the same information.

In Figure 3.19, notice the command window with the output of the PowerShell cmdlet get-UserRole. You can see the same information, such as the description of the role and the membership for RLorenzo. However, to achieve that output, you have to know the GUID (Globally Unique Identifier), a code name that is a long set of alphanumeric characters associated with the Partner Staff Acme user role. To learn the GUID of that role, you first have to use PowerShell to list the GUIDs for all the created and installed user roles. Of course, you also have to learn the syntax of the cmdlet. So there is a learning curve, and a rather brutal interface involved. For the true scripter, however, PowerShell could become the presentation layer of choice in some situations, and it adds the ability to perform OpsMgr actions in batch mode.

FIGURE 3.19   Properties of the custom user role shown in Figure 3.18, now viewed with PowerShell.

Summary

This chapter promised a look inside OpsMgr from the macro and micro perspectives. We described first how OpsMgr components are deployed on a single server to a small organization, or across many servers for the large enterprise. We also closely examined the communication channels used between components. We next covered how management packs encapsulate and distribute knowledge about objects and classes of objects, including relationships between objects. Then we looked even deeper at the workflows occurring between modules in a management pack. Finally, we discussed how the Operations console, Web console, and PowerShell present useful management information to the operator and administrator.

With this information, you are ready for the next two chapters, where we discuss designing an OpsMgr 2007 implementation.

PART II

Planning and Installation

IN THIS PART

CHAPTER 4

Planning Your Operations Manager Deployment

As you have read in earlier chapters of this book, Operations Manager (OpsMgr) 2007 is definitely a new product compared to Microsoft Operations Manager (MOM) 2005. However, one thing that has not changed is the requirement for effectively planning your deployment before rushing the product into production.

Proper planning of your OpsMgr deployment is key to its success. Just like implementing any other application or technical product, the time spent preparing for your installation is often more important than the time spent actually deploying the product! The majority of technical product deployments that fail do so due to ineffective planning.

Too often for Information Technology (IT) organizations, the thought process is to deploy new products as quickly as possible, but this approach frequently results in not gaining full benefit from those tools. We refer to this as the RSA approach: Ready, Shoot, Aim. Using RSA results in technology deployments not architected correctly, which then require changes, or potentially a complete redeployment to resolve issues identified after the fact. Our recommended technique is RAS:

▶ **Ready**—Are you ready to deploy Operations Manager? Assess your environment to better understand it and where OpsMgr is required.

▶ **Aim**—What is the target you are trying to hit? Based on your assessment, create a design and execute both a proof of concept and a pilot project.

▶ **Shoot**—Implement the solution you designed!

Creating a single high-level planning document is essential because Operations Manager affects all IT operations throughout the enterprise. Many projects fail due to missed expectations, finger pointing, or the "not invented here" syndrome, which occurs when some IT staff members have stakes in preexisting or competitive solutions. You can avoid these types of problems ahead of time by developing a comprehensive plan and getting the backing from the appropriate sponsors within your organization.

A properly planned environment helps answer questions such as the number of OpsMgr management servers you will have, how many management groups to use, the management packs you will deploy, and so forth.

Proper technical deployments require usage of a disciplined approach to implement the solution. Microsoft's recommended approach for IT deployments is the Microsoft Solutions Framework (MSF). MSF consists of four stages:

- ▶ **Envisioning**—Development of the vision and scope information.
- ▶ **Planning**—Development of the design specification and master project plan.
- ▶ **Developing**—Development and optimization of the solution.
- ▶ **Deployment & Stabilization**—Product rollout and completion.

Additional information on MSF is available at http://www.microsoft.com/technet/solutionaccelerators/msf. For purposes of deploying Operations Manager 2007, we have adapted MSF to a slightly different format. The stages of deployment we recommend and discuss in this chapter include

- ▶ **Assessment**—Similar to the Envisioning stage.
- ▶ **Design & Planning**—Roughly correlates to the Planning & Developing stages of MSF.
- ▶ **Proof of Concept, Pilot, Implementation, Maintenance**—These stages follow steps similar to the Deployment & Stabilization stages.

The specific stages we will discuss in this chapter include Assessment, Design, Planning, Proof of Concept, Pilot, Implementation, and Maintenance.

NOTE

Using Both MSF and MOF

Chapter 1, "Operations Management Basics," discussed Operations Manager 2007's alignment with the Microsoft Operations Framework (MOF) as an operational framework. Using MOF is an approach to monitoring, which is independent from using a deployment methodology such as the MSF when planning an OpsMgr deployment.

Assessment

The first step in designing and deploying an Operations Manager 2007 solution is to understand the current environment. A detailed assessment gathers information from a variety of sources, resulting in a document that you can easily review and update. This process ensures there is a complete understanding of the existing environment. Although the concept of an assessment document is very common within consulting organizations as part of the process of implementing new technologies, we recommend also using this approach for projects internal to an organization.

The principles underlying the importance of assessments is summed up well by Stephen R. Covey's Habit #5, "Seek first to understand, then to be understood," in *The 7 Habits of Highly Effective People* (Simon & Schuster, 1989). From the perspective of an Operations Manager assessment, this means you should fully understand the environment before designing a solution to monitor it.

A variety of sources is used to gather information for an assessment document, including the following:

- **Current monitoring solutions**—These products may include server, network, or hardware monitoring products (including earlier versions of Operations Manager such as MOM 2005 and MOM 2000). You will want to gather information regarding the following areas:

  - What products are monitoring the production environment

  - What servers the product is running on

  - What devices and applications are being monitored

  - Who the users of the product are

  - What the product is doing well

  - What the product is currently not doing well

  Options for existing monitoring solutions include integration with Operations Manager, replacement by Operations Manager, and no impact by Operations Manager.

  Understanding any current monitoring solutions and what functionality they provide is critical to developing a solid understanding of the environment itself.

- **MOM 2005 upgrade/replacement**—This is applicable in environments currently using Operations Manager 2005. An in-depth analysis of what functionality MOM 2005 provides is critical to presenting an Operations Manager 2007 design that can effectively replace and enhance the existing functionality.

- **Current Service Level Agreements**—A Service Level Agreement (SLA) is a formal written agreement designed to provide the level of support expected (in this case, the SLA is from the IT organization to the business itself). For example, the SLA for web servers may be 99.9% uptime during business hours. Some organizations have official SLAs, whereas others have unofficial SLAs.

Unofficial SLAs actually are the most common type in the industry. An example of an unofficial SLA might be that email cannot go offline during business hours at all. You should document both the existence and nonexistence of SLAs as part of your assessment to take full advantage of Operations Manager's capability to increase system uptime.

▶ **Administrative model**—Organizations are either centralized, decentralized, or a combination of the two. The current administrative model and plans for the administrative model help determine where OpsMgr server components may best be located within the organization.

▶ **Integration**—You can integrate Operations Manager 2007 with a variety of solutions, including help desk/problem management solutions and existing monitoring solutions. Some of the available connectors provide integration from OpsMgr to products such as BMC Remedy, HP OpenView, and Tivoli TEC. Chapter 22, "Interoperability," discusses the various connectors that are available for Operations Manager 2007.

If OpsMgr needs to integrate with other existing solutions, you should gather details including the name, version, and type of integration required.

▶ **Service dependencies**—New functionality provided within Operations Manager 2007 makes it even more important to be aware of any services on which OpsMgr may have dependencies. These include but are not limited to local area network (LAN)/wide area network (WAN) connections and speeds, routers, switches, firewalls, Domain Name Server (DNS), Active Directory, instant messaging, and Exchange. A solid understanding of these services and the ability to document them will improve the design and planning for your Operations Manager 2007 deployment.

▶ **Functionality requirements**—You will also use the assessment to gather information specific to the functionality required by an OpsMgr environment. You will want to determine what servers Operations Manager will monitor (what domain or workgroup they are in), what applications on these servers need to be monitored, and how long to retain alerts.

While gathering information for your functionality requirements, concentrate on the applications OpsMgr will be managing. As we discussed in Chapter 2, "What's New," OpsMgr's focus centers on modeling applications and identifying their dependencies. Identifying these applications and mapping out their dependencies will provide information important to your Operations Manager 2007 design.

▶ **Business and technical requirements**—What technical and financial benefits does OpsMgr need to bring to the organization? The business and technical requirements you gather are critical because they will determine the design you create. For example, if high server availability is a central requirement, this will significantly impact your Operations Manager design (which we discuss in Chapter 5, "Planning Complex Configurations"). It is also important to determine what optional components are required for your Operations Manager monitoring, audit collection, and reporting environments. Identify, prioritize, and document your requirements; you can then discuss and revise them until you finalize your requirements.

Gather the information you collect into a single document, called an *assessment document*. This document should be reviewed and discussed by the most appropriate personnel within your organization who are capable of validating that all the information contained is correct and comprehensive. These reviews often result in, and generally should result in, revisions to the document; do not expect that a centrally written document will get everything right from the get-go. Examine the content of the document, particularly the business and technical requirements, to validate they are correct and properly prioritized. After reaching agreement on the document content, move the project to the next step: designing your OpsMgr solution.

Design

The assessment document you created in the previous stage now provides the required information to design your new Operations Manager 2007 environment. As with other technology projects, a best practice approach is to keep the design simple and as straightforward as possible.

Do not add complexity just because the solution is cool; instead, add complexity to the design only to meet an important business requirement! For example, it is best not to create a SQL cluster for OpsMgr reporting functionality unless it is determined that there is a business requirement for high availability with OpsMgr Reporting. Business requirements are critical because they drive your Operations Manager design. Rely on your business requirements to determine the correct answer whenever there is a question as to how you should be designing your environment.

The starting point for designing an Operations Manager environment is the management group.

Management Groups

As introduced earlier in this book, an Operations Manager management group consists of the Operations database, Root Management Server (RMS), Operations Manager consoles (Operations, Web, Authoring), optional components (additional management servers, reporting servers, data warehouse servers, Audit Collection Services, database servers, gateway servers), and up to 5000 managed computers. Start with one management group and add more only if more than one is necessary. For most cases, a single management group is the simplest configuration to implement, support, and maintain.

> **NOTE**
>
> **The OpsMgr Authoring Console**
>
> The Authoring console will be available with Operations Manager 2007 Service Pack (SP) 1. We will discuss it in more detail in Chapter 23, "Developing Management Packs and Reports."

Exceeding Management Group Support Limits

One reason to add an additional management group is if you need to monitor more than the 5000 managed computers supported in a single management group. The type of servers monitored directly affects the 5000 managed computers limit; there is nothing magical or hard-coded about this number. For example, monitoring many Exchange backend servers has a far more dramatic impact on a management server's performance than if you were monitoring the same number of Windows XP or Vista workstations.

If the load on the management servers is excessive (servers are reporting excessive OpsMgr queue errors or high CPU, memory, disk, or network utilization), consider adding another management group to split the load.

Separating Administrative Control

Another common reason for establishing multiple management groups is separating control of computer systems between multiple support teams. In MOM 2005, this was often the rationale used to split the security monitoring functionality from the application/operating system monitoring functionality. For most organizations, the new Audit Collection Services (ACS) functionality introduced in Chapter 2 should remove the need to split out security events into a separate management group.

However, let's look at an example where the Application support team is responsible for all application servers, and the Web Technologies team is responsible for all web servers, and each group configures the management packs that apply to the servers it supports.

With a single Operations Manager 2007 management group, each group may be configuring the same management packs. In our scenario, the Application support team and Web Technologies team are both responsible for supporting Internet Information Services (IIS) web servers. If these servers are within the same management group, the rules in the management packs are applicable to each of the two support groups. If either team changes the rules within the IIS management pack, it may impact the functionality required by the other team.

Although there are ways to minimize this impact using techniques such as overrides, in some situations you will want to implement multiple management groups. This typically occurs when multiple support groups are supporting the same management packs. In a multiple management group solution, each set of servers has its own management group and can have the rules customized as required for the particular support organization.

Security Model

Historically, multiple management groups were required due to limitations with the MOM security model. MOM 2005 provided very limited granularity in what level of security was available to users who had permission to work within the Administrator console. If a user had access to update rules in the Administrator console, she could not be restricted to specific rule groups or specific functions. OpsMgr 2007's role-based user security removes the need to create multiple management groups to provide this level of security.

A *role* in Operations Manager 2007 consists of a profile and a scope. A *profile*, such as the Operations Manager Administrator or Operations Manager Operator, defines the actions one can perform; the *scope* defines the objects against which one can perform those actions. What this means is roles limit the access users have.

Although previous versions of Operations Manager often required multiple management groups to separate different groups from performing actions outside their area of responsibility, using roles limits who is able to monitor and respond to alerts generated by different management packs—and can eliminate the need to partition management groups for security purposes. (We discuss security in more detail in Chapter 11, "Securing Operations Manager 2007.")

As an example, a MOM 2005 organization with one support group for operating systems and a second support group for applications would require multiple management groups for each group to maintain and customize its own rules and not affect the other support group. This is not necessary in OpsMgr 2007 because you can define different user roles for the personnel within each organization.

Dedicated ACS Management Group

Although ACS does not require a separate management group to function, splitting this functionality into its own management group may be required to meet your company's security requirements. Splitting into a separate management group may be required if your company mandate states that the ACS functionality be administered by a separate group of individuals. For more information on ACS, see Chapter 15, "Monitoring Audit Collection Services."

Production and Test Environments

We recommend creating a separate test environment for Operations Manager so you can test and tune management packs before deploying them into the production environment. This approach minimizes the changes on production systems and allows for a large amount of testing because it will not affect the functionality of your production systems.

Geographic Locations

Physical location is also a factor when considering multiple management groups. If many servers exist at a single location with localized management personnel, it may be practical to create a management group at that location. Let's look at a situation where a company—Odyssey—based in Plano has 500 servers that will be monitored by Operations Manager; an additional location in Carrollton has 250 servers that also will be monitored. Each location has local IT personnel responsible for managing its own systems. In this situation, maintaining separate management groups at each location is a good approach.

NOTE

Management Group Naming Conventions

When you are naming your management groups, the following characters cannot be used:

( ) ^ ~ : ; . ! ? ", ' ` @ # % \ / * + = $ | & [ ] <>{}

Management groups also cannot have a leading or trailing space in their name. To avoid confusion, we recommend creating management group names that are unique within your organization. Remember that the management group name is case sensitive.

Network Environment

If you have a server location with either minimal bandwidth or an unstable network connection, consider adding a management group locally to reduce WAN traffic. The data transmitted between the agent and a management server (or gateway server) is both encrypted and compressed. The compression ratio ranges from 4:1 to 6:1, approximately. We have found that an average client will use 3Kbps of network traffic between itself and the management server. We typically recommend installing a management server at network sites that have between 30 and 100 local systems. Operations Manager can support approximately 30 agent-managed computers on a 128KB network connection (agent-managed systems use less bandwidth than agentless-managed systems).

Table 4.1 lists the minimum network connectivity speeds between the various OpsMgr components.

TABLE 4.1   Network Connectivity Requirements

OpsMgr Component 1	OpsMgr Component 2	Network Connectivity
RMS/Management Server	Agent	64Kbps
RMS/Management Server	Agentless	1024Kbps
RMS/Management Server	Operations database	256Kbps
RMS	Operations Console	768Kbps
RMS	Management Server	64Kbps
RMS/Management Server	Data Warehouse	768Kbps
RMS	Reporting Server	256Kbps
Management Server	Gateway Server	64Kbps
Web Console Server	Web Console	128Kbps
Reporting Data Warehouse	Reporting Server	1024Kbps
Console	Reporting Server	768Kbps
Audit Collector	Audit Database	768Kbps

The Microsoft View on Network Bandwidth Utilization

Satya Vel's article "Network Bandwidth Utilization for the Various OpsMgr 2007 Roles" (http://blogs.technet.com/momteam/archive/2007/10/22/network-bandwidth-utilization-for-the-various-opsmgr-2007-roles.aspx) includes a good discussion on bandwidth utilization by the various OpsMgr components. There are three major areas of discussion, which we summarize here:

▶ **Agent communication to the RMS, management servers, and gateway servers**—The amount of data sent by the agent depends on the management packs installed on each agent, the type of activity generated, how those management packs are tuned, and conditions in your environment. The good news is the data between the agents and the management server/gateway server is compressed. Satya's tests determined about 200Kbps sent for 200 agents in an environment with the AD, Basic Windows Base OS, DNS, and OpsMgr management packs.

Gateway servers are basically proxy agents that send data from multiple agents to a management server. Satya has noted bandwidth utilization of about 22Kbps received by gateway servers from agents.

▶ **RMS and management server communication to the operational and data warehouse databases**—In OpsMgr 2007, management servers write directly to the operational database and the data warehouse. (This differs from MOM 2005, where the operational database populated the reporting database using a nightly DTS, or Data Transformation Services, job.) Data sent from the management servers to the databases is not compressed.

The best practice here is to place your management servers close to your databases with fast network links between them. It is better for agents to report to a remote management server (compressed data) than have management servers in remote locations writing to the OpsMgr databases (uncompressed data) over slower links.

▶ **Audit Collection Systems (forwarder to collector)**—Security events are sent in near real time, rather than being batched together. If there is a loss of network connectivity, the forwarder re-sends all security events not yet confirmed as written to the Audit database by the collector. The forwarder heartbeats the collector every 45 seconds to try to re-send the data. If three heartbeats are missed, the collector drops the connection and the forwarder (if it is alive) automatically reinitiates it.

Security events sent from the agent to the collector are typically less than 100 bytes, and the event in the database is less than .05KB. Typical CPU and memory utilization used by the agent is generally less than 1%, with memory overhead approximately 4MB to 6MB.

Installed Languages

You must install each server in your management group providing Operations Manager components using the same language. As an example, you cannot install the RMS using the English version of Operations Manager 2007 and deploy the Operations console in a different language, such as Spanish or German. If these components must be available in different languages, you must deploy additional management groups to provide this functionality.

Further Thoughts on Additional Management Groups

As part of your migration planning, let's examine two of the factors that required multiple management groups in earlier versions of Operations Manager:

▶ **Security boundaries**—Gateway servers can also influence the number of management groups. A gateway server acts as a consolidation point for communications between agents and management servers on opposite sides of a Kerberos trust boundary. In earlier versions of Operations Manager, one might implement additional management groups when there was a trust boundary. This is no longer necessary because OpsMgr 2007 agents communicate with a gateway server, which communicates with the management servers.

▶ **Processing power**—OpsMgr 2007 comes with an overall increase in the scalability of its components. If processing requirements in the past needed an additional management group to handle the load of alerts and events, this may no longer be the case.

These changes may affect your OpsMgr 2007 management group design.

Multiple Management Group Architectures

Implementing multiple management groups introduces two architectures for management groups:

▶ **Connected management groups**—If you are familiar with MOM 2005, multitiered architectures exist when there are multiple management groups with one or more management groups reporting information to another management group. OpsMgr 2007 replaces this type of functionality with the connected management group. A *connected management group* provides the capability for the user interface in one management group to query data from another management group. The major difference between a multitiered environment and a connected management group is that data only exists in one location; connected management groups do not forward alert information between them.

For example, let's take our Odyssey company, which has locations in Plano and Carrollton. For Odyssey, the administrators in the Carrollton location need the autonomy to manage their own systems and Operations Manager environment. The Plano location needs to manage its own servers and also needs to be aware of the alerts occurring within the Carrollton location. In this situation (illustrated in

Figure 4.1), we can configure the Carrollton management group as a connected management group to the Plano management group.

▶ **Multihomed architectures**—A multihomed architecture exists when a system belongs to multiple management groups, reporting information to each management group.

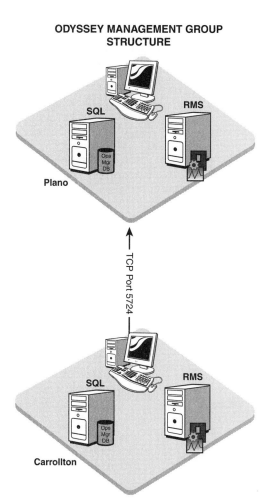

FIGURE 4.1   Connected management group.

For example, Eclipse (Odyssey's sister company) has a single location based in Frisco. Eclipse also has multiple support teams organized by function. The Operating Systems management team is responsible for monitoring the health of all server operating systems within Eclipse, and the Application management team oversees the business critical applications. Each team has its own OpsMgr management group for monitoring servers. In this scenario, a single server running Windows 2003 and IIS is configured as "multihomed" and reports information to both the Operating Systems management group and the Application management group (see Figure 4.2 for details).

Another example of where multihoming architectures are useful is testing or prototyping Operations Manager management groups. Using multihomed architectures, you can continue to report to your production MOM management group while also reporting to a new or preproduction management group. This allows testing of the new management group without affecting your existing production monitoring.

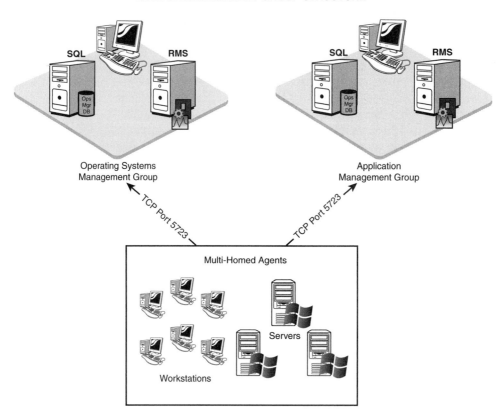

FIGURE 4.2   Multihomed architecture.

Operations Manager Server Components

The number of management groups you have directly impacts the number and location of your OpsMgr servers. The server components in a management group include at a minimum a Root Management Server (RMS), an Operations Database Server, and

Operations consoles. Various additional server components are also available within Operations Manager 2007 depending on your business requirements.

Optional server components within a management group include additional Management Servers, Reporting Servers, Data Warehouse Servers, ACS Database Servers, and Gateway Servers. In this section, we will discuss the following components and the hardware and software required for those components:

- ▶ Root Management Server
- ▶ Management Servers
- ▶ Gateway Servers
- ▶ Operations Database Servers
- ▶ Reporting Servers
- ▶ Data Warehouse Servers
- ▶ ACS Database Servers
- ▶ ACS Collector
- ▶ ACS Forwarder
- ▶ Operations console
- ▶ Web Console Servers
- ▶ Operations Manager agents

These server components are all part of a management group as discussed in Chapter 3, "Looking Inside OpsMgr."

In a small environment, you can install the required server components on a single server with sufficient hardware resources. As with management groups, it is best to keep things simple by keeping the number of Operations Manager servers as low as possible while still meeting your business requirements.

With the new components in Operations Manager 2007, the hardware requirements vary depending on the role each server component provides. We will break down each of the different server components and discuss both their minimum and large-environment hardware requirements.

Root Management Server

The Root Management Server (RMS) Component is the first management server installed. This server provides specific functionality (such as communication with the gateway servers, connected management groups, and password key storage) that we discussed in Chapter 3. It also serves as a management server; as a reminder, management servers provide communication between the OpsMgr agents and the Operations database.

The RMS can run on a single server, or it can run on a cluster. Table 4.2 describes minimum hardware requirements for the RMS; Table 4.3 shows the recommended requirements for larger environments. We recommend clustering if your business requirements for OpsMgr include high-availability and redundancy capabilities. See Chapter 5 for details on supported redundancy options for each OpsMgr component.

TABLE 4.2   Root Management Server Minimum Hardware Requirements

Hardware	Requirement
Processor	1.8GHz Pentium
RAM	1GB
Disk	10GB space
CD-ROM	Needed
Display adapter	Super VGA
Monitor	800×600 resolution
Mouse	Needed
Network	10Mbps
Operating system	Windows 2003 Server SP1 32 bit or 64 bit

TABLE 4.3   Suggested Root Management Server Hardware Requirements for Large Environments

Hardware	Requirement
Processor	Two Dual-Core processors
RAM	8GB
Disk	10GB Space
CD-ROM	Needed
Display adapter	Super VGA
Monitor	800×600 resolution
Mouse	Needed
Network	100Mbps
Operating system	Windows 2003 Server SP1 64 bit

Management Servers

Additional management servers (MS) within the management group can provide increased scalability and redundancy for the Operations Manager solution. The minimum hardware requirements and large-scale hardware recommendations match those of the RMS.

The number of management servers required depends on the business requirements identified during the Assessment stage:

- ▶ If redundancy is a requirement, you will need at least two management servers per management group. Each management server can handle up to 2000 agent-managed computers. With MOM 2005, there was a limit of 10 agentless managed systems per management server. With Operations Manager 2007, there is no documented limit of agentless monitored systems per management server, but each additional agentless monitored system increases the processing overhead on the management server. For details on agentless monitoring, see Chapter 9, "Installing and Configuring Agents."

  If a management group in your organization needs to monitor more than 2000 computers, install multiple management servers in the management group. If you need to monitor agentless systems, start out with a maximum of 10 agentless managed systems and then track the performance of the system as you increase the number of agentless systems monitored (as an example, from 10 to 20). In addition, a good practice is to split the load of the agentless monitoring between management servers in the environment.

- ▶ Each management group must have at least one management server (the RMS) in that management group.

Using a sample design of 1000 monitored computers for the purposes of our discussion, we would plan for multiple management servers to provide redundancy. Each management server needs to support one-half the load during normal operation and the full load during failover situations. Although the management server does not store any major amounts of data, it does rely on the processor, memory, and network throughput of the system to perform effectively.

When you design for redundancy, plan for each server to have the capacity to handle not only the agents it is responsible for but also the agents it will be responsible for in a failover situation. For example, with a two–management server configuration, if either management server fails, the second needs to have sufficient resources to handle the entire agent load.

The location of your management servers also depends on the business requirements identified during the Assessment stage:

- ▶ Management servers should be separate from the Operations database in anything but a single-server OpsMgr management group configuration. In a single-server configuration, one server encompasses all the applicable Operations Manager components, including the RMS and the Operations database.

▶ Management servers should be within the same network segment where there are large numbers of systems to monitor with Operations Manager.

▶ If the RMS and Operations database are on the same server, we recommend monitoring no more than 200 agents on that server because it can degrade the performance of your OpsMgr solution. If you will be monitoring more than 200 agents, you should split these components onto multiple servers, or use an existing SQL Server (even a SQL cluster!) for the Operations database, thus lowering your hardware cost and increasing scalability. We discuss clustering in Chapter 5.

TIP

Using Existing SQL Systems for the OpsMgr Databases

The question arises about leveraging an existing SQL Server database server by using it for the OpsMgr databases. Using existing hardware can lower hardware costs and increase scalability.

As a rule, we do not recommend this because there are high processing requirements on both the Operations and Data Warehouse databases, and they perform better if they have their own server. However, in small environments or if you want to add a significant amount of memory to an existing system (or if you have a lot of available processing and memory resources), you may consider installing the OpsMgr databases on an existing SQL system.

Gateway Servers

Install gateway servers in untrusted domains or workgroups to provide a point of communication for servers in untrusted domains or workgroups. Gateway servers enable systems not in a trusted domain to communicate with a management server. The large-environment hardware recommendations (shown in Table 4.4) vary from those of management servers by the number of processors, required amount of memory, and operations system recommendations. Redundancy is available by deploying multiple gateway servers, which is the same approach used with management servers.

Operations Database

The Operations Database Component stores all the configuration data for the management group and all data generated by the systems in the management group. We previously discussed this server component and all other components in Chapter 3.

Place the Operations database on either a single server or a cluster; we recommend clustering if your business requirements for OpsMgr include high-availability and redundancy capabilities. Each management group must have an Operations database. The Operations database (by default named *OperationsManager*) is critical to the operation of your management group—if it is not running, the entire management group has very limited functionality. When the Operations database is down, agents are still monitoring issues, but the database cannot receive that information. In addition, consoles do not function and eventually the queues on the agent and the management server will completely fill.

TABLE 4.4   Suggested Gateway Server Hardware Requirements for Large Environments

Hardware	Requirement
Processor	One Dual-Core processor
RAM	2GB to 4GB
Disk	10GB space
CD-ROM	Needed
Display adapter	Super VGA
Monitor	800×600 resolution
Mouse	Needed
Network	100Mbps
Operating system	Windows 2003 Server SP1 32 bit or 64 bit

As a rule of thumb, the more memory you give SQL Server, the better it performs. Using an Active/Passive clustering configuration provides redundancy for this server component; the Operations database does not currently support Active/Active clustering. See Chapter 10, "Complex Configurations," for details on supported cluster configurations.

We recommend that you not install the Operations database with the RMS in anything but a single-server Operations Manager configuration. Although this server component can coexist with other database server components, this is not a recommended configuration because it may also cause contention for resources, resulting in a negative impact on your OpsMgr environment.

Disk configuration and file placement strongly affects database server performance. Configuring all the OpsMgr database server components with the fastest disks available will significantly improve the performance of your management group. We provide additional information on this topic, including recommended Redundant Arrays of Inexpensive Disks (RAID) configurations, in Chapter 10.

Tables 4.5 and 4.6 discuss database hardware requirements.

NOTE

Measuring Database Server Performance

The time it takes Operations Manager to detect a problem and notify an administrator is a key performance metric; this makes alert latency the best measure of performance of the OpsMgr system. If there is a delay in receiving this information, the problem could go undetected. Because of the criticality of this measure, OpsMgr SLAs tend to focus on alert latency.

TABLE 4.5   Operations Database Minimum Hardware Requirements

Hardware	Requirement
Processor	1.8GHz Pentium
RAM	1GB
Disk	20GB space
CD-ROM	Needed
Display adapter	Super VGA
Monitor	800×600 Resolution
Mouse	Needed
Network	10Mbps
Operating system	Windows 2003 Server SP1 32 bit or 64 bit

TABLE 4.6   Suggested Operations Database Hardware Requirements for Large Environments

Hardware	Requirement
Processor	Two Dual-Core processors
RAM	8GB
Disk	100GB space, spread across dedicated drives for the operating system, data, and transaction logs
CD-ROM	Needed
Display adapter	Super VGA
Monitor	800×600 resolution
Mouse	Needed
Network	100Mbps
Operating system	Windows 2003 Server SP1 64 bit

Reporting Servers

The Reporting Server Component uses SQL 2005 Reporting Services to provide web-based reports for Operations Manager. The Web Reporting Server Component typically runs on a single server. This server is running SQL 2005 with Reporting Services, so its hardware requirements match those discussed previously for the Operations Database Server Component. Redundancy is available for the Reporting servers by using web farms or Network Load Balancing (NLB), but there are issues associated with keeping the reports in sync. Chapter 5 includes information on redundant configurations.

Data Warehouse Servers

The OpsMgr agent data goes through the management server and writes to the data warehouse, which provides long-term data storage for Operations Manager. This data provides daily performance information gathering and longer-term trending reports.

The Data Warehouse server hosts the Data Warehouse database (by default named *OperationsManagerDW*) that OpsMgr uses for reporting. The Data Warehouse Component typically runs on a single server but can run on a cluster if high availability and redundancy are required for reports.

For reasons similar to the requirements for the operational database, this server should not exist on the same system hosting RMS.

The hardware requirements for Data Warehouse database servers match those of Operations database servers, with the added requirement being additional storage for the database and log files on the server.

ACS Database Servers

Audit Collection Services provides a method to collect records generated by an audit policy and to store them in a database. This centralizes the information, which you can filter and analyze using the reporting tools in Microsoft SQL Server 2005. The ACS Database Server Component provides the repository where the audit information is stored. The hardware requirements for ACS database servers match those of the Operations database servers, with a requirement of additional storage for the database and log files on the server.

ACS Forwarder

The ACS Forwarder Component uses the Operations Manager Audit Forwarding service, which is not enabled by default. After the service is enabled, the ACS Collector Component captures all security events (which are also saved to the local Windows NT Security Event log). Because this component is included within the OpsMgr agent, the hardware requirements mirror those of the agent. Chapter 6, "Installing Operations Manager 2007," discusses hardware requirements for OpsMgr.

ACS Collector

The forwarders send information to the ACS Collector Component. The collector receives the events, processes them, and sends them to the ACS database. The hardware requirements for the collector mirror those of the RMS. Currently there are no options available to provide a high-availability solution for the ACS Collector Component.

Operations Console

As we discussed in Chapter 2, the Operations console provides a single user interface for Operations Manager. All management servers, including the RMS, should install this console. You can also install the console on desktop systems running Windows XP or Vista. Installing these consoles on another system removes some of the load from the management server. Desktop access to the consoles also simplifies day-to-day administration.

The number of consoles a management group supports is an important design specification. As the number of consoles active in a management group grows, the database load also grows. This load accelerates as the number of managed computers increases because consoles, either operator or web-based, increase the number of database queries on both the Operations Database Server and the Data Warehouse Server Components. From a performance perspective, it is best to run the Operations consoles from administrator workstations rather than from servers running the OpsMgr components. Running the Operations console on the RMS increases memory and processor utilization, which in turn will slow down OpsMgr.

The hardware requirements for this component match those of the Gateway Server Component.

Web Console Server

The Web Console Server Component runs IIS and provides a web-based version of the Operations console. The hardware requirements for this server match those of the Gateway Server Component. You can configure redundancy for the Web Console Server Component by installing multiple Web Console Servers and leveraging Network Load Balancing (NLB) or other load-balancing solutions.

Operations Manager Agents

There are no Operations Manager–specific hardware requirements for systems running the OpsMgr agent. The hardware requirements are those of the minimum hardware requirements for the operating system itself.

TIP

Processor Performance with OpsMgr Server Components

Multi-core 64-bit-capable processors provide your best performance option for the various Operations Manager server components.

Operations Manager Server Software Requirements

Operations Manager 2007 supports a variety of operating systems and requires additional software as installation prerequisites. We discuss these in the following sections.

Operating Systems

Operating system requirements for the OpsMgr components vary somewhat because the various components have different operating system requirements. Table 4.7 through Table 4.10 list the various operating systems and their suitability for the Operations Manager server components. Tables 4.7, 4.8, and 4.9 show the supported operating systems for each of the different server components. Table 4.7 shows management server components, Table 4.8 shows database server components, 4.9 shows ACS–related server components, and 4.10 shows the console and agent components.

TABLE 4.7   Management Server Component Operating System Support

Operating System	Root Management Server	Management Server	Gateway Server	MS with Agentless Exception Monitoring File Share
Microsoft Windows Server 2003, Standard Edition SP1 X86 and X64	X	X	X	X
Microsoft Windows Server 2003, Enterprise Edition SP1 X86 and X64	X	X	X	X
Microsoft Windows Server 2003, Datacenter Edition SP1 X86 and X64	X	X		
Microsoft Windows XP Professional X86 and X64				
Vista Ultimate X86 and X64				
Vista Business X86 and X64				
Vista Enterprise X86 and X64				

TABLE 4.8   Database Server Component Operating System Support

Operating System	Operations Database	Reporting Server	Data Warehouse
Microsoft Windows Server 2003, Standard Edition SP1 X86, X64, and IA64	X	X	X
Microsoft Windows Server 2003, Enterprise Edition SP1 X86, X64, and IA64	X	X	X
Microsoft Windows Server 2003, Datacenter Edition SP1 X86 X64, and IA64	X	X	X
Microsoft Windows XP Professional X86 and X64			

TABLE 4.8   Continued

Operating System	Operations Database	Reporting Server	Data Warehouse
Vista Ultimate X86 and X64			
Vista Business X86 and X64			
Vista Enterprise X86 and X64			

TABLE 4.9   Audit Collection Server Component Operating System Support

Operating System	ACS Database Server	ACS Collector
Microsoft Windows Server 2003, Standard Edition SP1 X86 and X64	X	X
Microsoft Windows Server 2003, Enterprise Edition SP1 X86 and X64	X	X
Microsoft Windows Server 2003, Datacenter Edition SP1 X86 and X64	X	
Microsoft Windows XP Professional X86 and X64		
Vista Ultimate X86 and X64		
Vista Business X86 and X64		
Vista Enterprise X86 and X64		

TABLE 4.10   Console and Agent Operating System Support

Operating System	Operations Console	Web Console	Agent
Microsoft Windows Server 2003, Standard Edition SP1 X86 and X64	X	X	X
Microsoft Windows Server 2003, Enterprise Edition SP1 X86 and X64	X	X	X
Microsoft Windows Server 2003, Datacenter Edition SP1 X86 and X64	X		X
Microsoft Windows Server 2003, Professional Edition SP2 X86 and X64			X
Microsoft Windows Server 2003, Standard Edition SP1 IA64			X
Microsoft Windows Server 2003, Enterprise Edition SP1 IA64			X

TABLE 4.10   Continued

Operating System	Operations Console	Web Console	Agent
Microsoft Windows Server 2003, Datacenter Edition SP 1 IA64			X
Microsoft Windows Server 2003, Professional Edition SP 2 IA64			X
Microsoft Windows XP Professional X86 and X64	X		X
Vista Ultimate X86 and X64	X		X
Vista Business X86 and X64	X		X
Vista Enterprise X86 and X64	X		X
Microsoft Windows Server 2000 SP4			X
Microsoft Windows 2000 Professional SP4			X

The edition of the operating system chosen for each of the server components should correspond with the hardware that will be available for that component. As an example, the Windows Server 2003 Standard Edition supports up to four processors and 4GB of memory. If you purchase hardware to scale beyond that, use Windows Server 2003 Enterprise Edition instead (or use the X64 version of Windows Server 2003 Standard Edition).

Planning for Licensing

Part of your decision regarding server placement should include evaluating licensing options for Operations Manager 2007. Each device managed by the server software requires an Operations Management License (OML), whether you are monitoring it directly or indirectly. (An example of indirect monitoring would be a network device such as a switch or router.) There are two types of OMLs:

▶ **Client OML**—Devices running client operating systems require client license OMLs.

▶ **Server OML**—Devices running server operating systems require management license OMLs.

To determine licensing costs, it is important to understand that there are also two different levels of OMLs available:

▶ **Standard OML**—Provides monitoring for basic operating system workloads

▶ **Enterprise OML**—Provides monitoring for all operating system utilities, service workloads, and any other applications on that particular device

If you plan to monitor servers that run on virtual server technology, an OML is only required for the physical server. This must be an enterprise OML.

Table 4.11 lists the products associated with the standard and enterprise OML levels. (This list is complete as of mid–2007.)

TABLE 4.11   Levels of Management Licenses and Products

License Type	Monitoring Capability
Standard OML	System Resource Manager
	Password Change Notification
	Baseline Security Analyzer
	Reliability and Availability Services
	Print Server
	Distributed File System (DFS)
	File Replication Service (FRS)
	Network File System (NFS)
	File Transfer Protocol (FTP)
	Windows SharePoint Services
	Distributed Naming Service (DNS)
	Dynamic Host Configuration Protocol (DHCP)
	Windows Internet Naming Service (WINS)
	Windows Operating System 2000/2003 Operating System Management Pack
Enterprise OML	BizTalk Server 2006
	Internet Security and Accelerator (ISA) Server 2006
	Microsoft Exchange Server 2003/2007 Management Pack
	Microsoft SharePoint Portal Server (SPS) 2003 Management Pack
	Microsoft SQL Server 2000/2005 Management Pack
	Microsoft Windows Server 2000/2003 Active Directory Management Pack
	Microsoft Windows Server Internet Information (IIS) 2000/2003 Management Pack
	Operations Manager 2007 Servers (other than the server OML required for each management server)
	Office SharePoint Server 2007
	Virtual Server 2005
	Windows Group Policy 2003 Management Pack

You need to acquire an OpsMgr 2007 license for each Operations Manager server (RMS, management servers, and gateway servers; OpsMgr 2007 licenses for the Operations database, Reporting database, or other components are not required) as well as OMLs for managed devices as discussed earlier in this section.

When placing the Database Server Component separate from the Management Server Component, consider the following licensing aspects:

- No Client Access Licenses (CALs) are required when you are licensing SQL Server on a per-processor basis.

- CALs are required for each managed device when you are licensing SQL Server per user.

- If the SQL Server is licensed using the System Center Operations Manager 2007 with the SQL 2005 Technologies license, no CALs are required. The SQL license in this case is restricted to supporting only the OpsMgr application and databases. No other applications or databases can use that instance of SQL Server.

TIP

Licensing for SNMP Devices

An OML is only required to manage network infrastructure devices if the device provides firewall, load balancing, or other workload services. OMLs are not required to manage network infrastructure devices such as switches, hubs, routers, bridges, or modems.

There has been a lot of confusion concerning what licensing is required to use the AEM functionality of Operations Manager. Using AEM requires a client license for each system from which AEM will collect crash information. So if you want to use AEM in your environment and you have 2000 workstations that you want to use AEM on, 2000 client OMLs are required. The exceptions to this license model include the following:

- When the client device is also licensed for the Microsoft Desktop Optimization Pack for Software Assurance (MDOP for short), an OML is not required to use AEM on the device. The MDOP offering we are concerned with here is System Center Desktop Error Monitoring, or DEM for short. Either an OML or MDOP allows the device to use AEM.

- Corporate Error Reporting (CER) was previously a Software Assurance (SA) benefit that was part of DEM. Customers with Software Assurance on Windows Client, Office, or Server products were entitled to use CER. Customers with Software Assurance on preexisting agreements can use DEM for the remainder of their agreement. After the current agreement expires, they will either need to purchase an OML or MDOP (DEM) if they want to continue to use AEM.

▶ You do not need to purchase a client OML in addition to a standard or enterprise OML. As an example, if you have a Windows server (which has a standard OML), it is not necessary to purchase a client OML for this system to monitor it with AEM.

As an example of how this would work, let's look at how we would license Operations Manager 2007 for the Eclipse Company. Eclipse is a 1000-user corporation with one major office. The company has decided to deploy one management group with a single management server. Eclipse is interested in monitoring 100 servers, which includes 30 servers requiring monitoring with domain controller, Exchange, SharePoint, or SQL functionality.

From a licensing perspective, Eclipse will be purchasing the following:

▶ One server OML (one for each OpsMgr management server)

▶ Thirty enterprise client OMLs (one for each Active Directory, Exchange, SharePoint, or SQL Server system)

▶ Seventy standard client OMLs (for the remaining servers covered by the Enterprise Client OML licenses)

To help estimate costs, Microsoft has provided a pricing guide for Operations Manager 2007, available at http://www.microsoft.com/systemcenter/opsmgr/howtobuy/default. mspx. This guide lists the following prices for the components we just discussed:

▶ Operations Manager Server 2007: $573 U.S.

▶ Operations Manager Server 2007 with SQL Server Technology: $1,307 U.S.

▶ Enterprise OML: $426 U.S.

▶ Standard OML: $155 U.S.

▶ Client OML: $32 U.S.

For our licensing example, our estimate would be

▶ Operations Manager Server 2007: 1 × $573 = $573

▶ Enterprise OML: 30 × $426 = $12,780

▶ Standard OML: 70 × $155 = $10,850

The total estimate for Operations Manager licensing in this configuration is $24,203. Note, however, that this figure is a ballpark estimate only. Your specific licensing costs may be higher or lower based on the license agreement your organization has as well as your specific server configuration.

For more details on Operations Manager 2007 licensing, see the Microsoft Volume Licensing Brief, which is available for download at http://go.microsoft.com/fwlink/ ?LinkId=87480. Updates to the list of basic workloads are available at http://www. microsoft.com/systemcenter/opsmgr/howtobuy/opsmgrstdoml.mspx.

Additional Software Requirements

Table 4.12 shows the additional software requirements for each of the different Operations Manager database–related components.

TABLE 4.12   Additional Software Requirements

Server Component	RMS, MS, Gateway Server	Operations Database, Reporting Data Warehouse	Audit Collection Database	Reporting Server	Ops Console	Web Server Console
Microsoft SQL Server 2005 SP1 Standard		X				
Microsoft SQL Server 2005 Enterprise		X	X			
Microsoft SQL Server Reporting Services with SP1				X		
.NET Framework 2.0	X				X	X
.NET Framework 3.0	X			X	X	X
Microsoft Core XML Services (MSXML) 6.0	X					
Windows PowerShell					X	
Office Word 2003 (for .NET programmability support)					X	
Internet Information Services 6.0						X
ASP.NET 2.0						X

Additional Design Factors

You have a variety of other factors to consider when designing your operations management environment. These include the servers monitored by OpsMgr, distributed applications, management packs, security, user notifications, and agent deployment considerations. We discuss these in the following sections.

Monitored Servers

As part of the assessment phase, you should have collected a list of servers to monitor with Operations Manager. As part of the design, you have identified each server and, based on its location, determined the management server it will use. You can now use your management group design to match the servers and their applications with an appropriate management group and management server.

User Applications

As we discussed in Chapter 2, distributed applications have taken on a much more important role within OpsMgr. Categorize the applications identified in the Assessment phase to determine whether you can model them as distributed applications. You should also compare this list with the available management packs on the System Center Pack Catalog website (http://go.microsoft.com/fwlink/?linkid=71124).

Management Packs

Your design should also include the management packs you plan to deploy, based on the applications and servers identified during the assessment phase. As you are identifying management packs for deployment, it is important to remember that certain management packs have logical dependencies on others. As an example, the Exchange management pack is logically dependent on the Active Directory management pack, which in turn is logically dependent on the DNS management pack. To monitor Exchange, you should plan to deploy each of those management packs.

You can import MOM 2005 management packs into Operations Manager 2007 after converting them to the new OpsMgr 2007 format. Converted management packs do not have the full functionality of management packs designed for Operations Manager 2007; they do not become model-based as part of the conversion process. Converted management packs also do not include reports because Microsoft rewrote the reporting structure in OpsMgr 2007.

Security

Operations Manager 2007 utilizes multiple service accounts to help increase security by utilizing lower privileged security accounts. Chapter 11 discusses how to secure your OpsMgr environment. Identifying these accounts and their required permissions is necessary for an effective Operations Manager design. OpsMgr uses several accounts that are typically Domain User accounts:

> ▶ **SDK and Config Service account**—Provides a data access layer between the agents, consoles, and database. This account distributes configuration information to agents

- **Management Server Action account**—Gathers operational data from providers, runs responses, and performs actions such as installing and uninstalling agents on managed computers

- **Agent Action account**—Gathers information and runs responses on the managed computer

- **Agent Installation account**—Used when prompted for an account with administrator privileges to install agents on the managed computer(s)

- **Notification Action account**—Creates and sends notifications

- **Data Reader account**—Executes queries against the OpsMgr Data Warehouse database

- **Data Warehouse Write account**—Assigned permissions to write to the Data Warehouse database and read from the Operations database

User Notifications

Operations Manager's functionality includes the ability to notify users or groups as issues arise within your environment. For design purposes, you should document who needs to receive notifications and what circumstances necessitate notification. OpsMgr can notify via email, instant messaging, Short Message Service (SMS), or command scripts. Notifications go to recipients, configured within Operations Manager. As an example, if your organization has a team that supports email, the team will most likely want notifications if issues occur within the Exchange environment. (In this particular instance because the team is supporting email, it would be advisable to provide multiple Exchange servers that can send the notification or use other available notification methods in the event that Exchange is down.)

Reporting

Operations Manager 2007 includes a robust reporting solution. With the reporting components installed, OpsMgr directly writes relevant information from the management server to the Data Warehouse database. This is a significant change from MOM 2005, which uses a DTS package to move data from the OnePoint database and transfers that information into the SystemCenterReporting database. Writing data directly into the reporting database enables near real-time reporting. It also decreases the space required within the database because only specific information is written, versus shipping all information over a certain age into the Data Warehouse database.

Agent Deployment

Monitored systems will have agents deployed to them. Deployment can be manual, automatic from the Operations console, or through automated distribution methods such as Active Directory, Microsoft Systems Management Server, and the recently released System Center Configuration Manager. For small to mid-sized organizations, we recommend deploying agents from the Operations console because it is the quickest and most supportable approach. For larger organizations, we recommend Systems Management Server/Configuration Manager or Active Directory deployment. Manual agent deployment is most often required when the system is behind a firewall, when there is a need to limit bandwidth available on the connection to the management server, or if a highly secure server configuration is required. Chapter 9 provides more detail on this topic. For the purposes of the Design stage, it is important to identify the specific approach you plan for distributing the agent.

System Center Capacity Planner 2007

Microsoft's System Center Capacity Planner (SCCP), shown in Figure 4.3, can provide you with the answers you need to design your OpsMgr environment. The System Center Capacity Planner, designed to architect your Operations Manager solution, provides the ability to create "what-if" analysis, such as "What-if I add another 100 servers for monitoring by OpsMgr?"

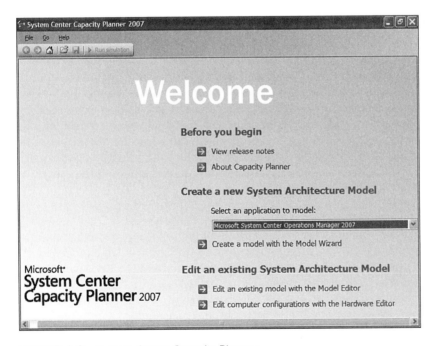

FIGURE 4.3   System Center Capacity Planner.

You can use the System Center Capacity Planner to provide a starting point for your OpsMgr 2007 design because it can provide you with answers needed for an effective design of your environment. According to discussions during the beta of the SCCP, we expect database-sizing estimates to be included within the released version of the SCCP. We recommend using database-sizing estimates from the SCCP as the final authority for sizing once that capability is available.

In the next few sections, we will provide sample designs for a single-server configuration, dual-server configuration, and finally a mid-to-enterprise-sized configuration.

Designing a Single-Server Monitoring Configuration with System Center Essentials

You can create single-server configurations either using Microsoft System Center Essentials or Microsoft Operations Manager 2007, depending on the business requirements identified for your organization.

Microsoft System Center Essentials (or just Essentials) is designed to provide core operations management capabilities for small to medium-sized businesses. System Center Essentials combines the monitoring functionality of Operations Manager 2007 with the patch management functionality of Windows Software Update Services (WSUS) 3.0. However, Essentials is a different product that has specific restrictions on its functionality, including the following:

- ▶ Although System Center Essentials can run in a multiserver configuration (with the RMS and database server on separate computers), all monitored systems must be in the same Active Directory forest.

- ▶ There is no fault tolerance support (clustering) for the database server or management server.

- ▶ Essentials does not include a data warehouse or fixed grooming schedule, and report authoring is not available.

- ▶ No role-based security.

- ▶ No Web console, support for ACS, or PowerShell integration.

- ▶ Essentials can only monitor a total of 30 servers (31 including itself), and up to 500 non-server operating systems. Essentials can monitor an unlimited number of network devices.

Single-Server Requirements with Essentials

Because the Essentials components typically are on a single server, the design process is greatly simplified. Figure 4.4 shows an example of this configuration. System Center Essentials is always a single–management server implementation; the only supported alternative option for Essentials puts the SQL database component on a second server when managing between 250 and 531 computers (remember, only 30 of those can be running a server operating system!).

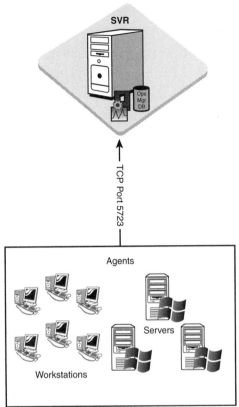

**SYSTEM CENTER ESSENTIALS
CONFIGURATION**

SVR

Ops
Mgr
DB

TCP Port 5723

Agents

Servers

Workstations

FIGURE 4.4   System Center Essentials single-server configuration.

A single-server configuration is the simplest Operations Manager design. Assuming an average level of activity, your server should be two dual-core processors or higher with 4GB of memory to achieve optimal results (shown in Table 4.13). The goal is to avoid taxing your processor by having a sustained CPU utilization rate of more than 75%. Consequently, a configuration of less than 30 managed nodes using the proper hardware should not exceed this threshold. Ensure that the tests you perform include any management packs you might add to Essentials because management packs can easily add 25% to your server CPU utilization.

To provide sufficient server storage, we recommend approximately 250GB of disk storage available on the Essentials Server. Table 4.14 lists various methods for configuring drive space.

TABLE 4.13 System Center Essentials Hardware Recommendations

Hardware	Requirement
Processor	Two Dual-Core processors
RAM	4GB
Disk	250GB space that's spread across dedicated drives for the operating system, data, and transaction logs
CD-ROM	Needed
Display adapter	Super VGA
Monitor	800×600 resolution
Mouse	Needed
Network	100Mbps
Operating system	Windows 2003 Server SP1 64 bit

TABLE 4.14 Single-Server Drive Configuration

Drive Size	Number of Drives	Configuration	Usable Space
36GB	8	RAID5	252GB
72GB	5	RAID5	288GB
146GB	3	RAID5	292GB
300GB	2	RAID1	300GB

We recommend always placing the database on a disk array separate from the operating system; combining them can cause I/O saturation. Essentials also works best on a 100Mb (or 1Gb) network and connected to a switch (preferably on the backbone with other production servers).

Server Components for Essentials
In the single-server configuration, the server runs all components of the typical Essentials installation, including the management and database components.

Single-Server Configuration Using Operations Manager 2007

You can also design Operations Manager to run in a single-server configuration. This is a good option when you need to monitor more than 30 servers but less than 100 servers or when there are requirements to monitor more than 500 non-server operating systems.

Single-Server Requirements with OpsMgr

As with many other technical systems, using the simplest configuration meeting your needs works the best and causes the fewest problems. This is also true of OpsMgr; many smaller-sized organizations can design a solution composed of a single Operations Manager server that encompasses all required components. Certain conditions must exist in your infrastructure to make optimal use of a single-server OpsMgr installation. If the following conditions are present, this type of design scenario may be right for your organization:

▸ Monitoring less than 100 servers but more than 30 servers (see the "System Center Essentials" section of the chapter for less than 30 servers).

▸ The number and type of management packs directly affect the hardware requirements for the OpsMgr solution. A general recommendation for a single-server configuration is not to deploy more than a dozen management packs and to make sure that they are fully tuned.

▸ Maintaining one year or less of stored data.

Generally, a single Operations Manager server configuration works for smaller to medium-sized organizations and particularly those who prefer to deploy Operations Manager to smaller, phased groups of servers. Another advantage of Operations Manager's architecture is its flexibility concerning changes in design scope. You can add more component servers to a configuration later without the worry of major reconfiguration.

Figure 4.5 shows the single-server configuration with all the components on one server.

Server Components for OpsMgr

In the single-server configuration, the server runs components of a typical Operations Manager installation, including the management and database components.

Designing a Two-Server Monitoring Configuration

Sometimes the scalability Microsoft builds into its products makes it challenging to determine how to deploy a multiple-server solution. We will cut through that and show you where you can deploy a relatively simple Operations Manager solution.

Operations Manager can scale from the smallest office to the largest, worldwide enterprises. Consequently, you must make decisions as to the size and placement of the OpsMgr servers. As part of the design process, an organization must decide between implementing a single server or a deployment using multiple servers. Understanding the criteria defining each design scenario aids in selecting a suitable match.

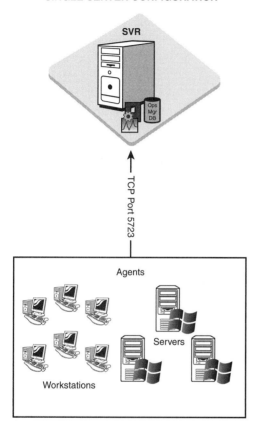

**OPERATIONS MANAGER 2007
SINGLE SERVER CONFIGURATION**

FIGURE 4.5   Ops Mgr single-server configuration.

Two-Server Requirements

Figure 4.6 shows the two-server configuration with the OpsMgr components split between two servers (one to provide management server functionality, one to provide database functionality).

Using the SCCP to design the Operations Manager solution (using 200 servers to be monitored), we can identify the recommended hardware for the environment, as shown in Figure 4.7, which illustrates a two-server configuration splitting the OpsMgr components.

Assuming an average level of activity, your servers should be two dual-core processors or higher with 4GB of memory to achieve optimal results (as shown in Table 4.15). The goal is to avoid taxing your processor by having a sustained CPU utilization rate of more than 75%. Consequently, a configuration of fewer than 100 managed nodes should not exceed this threshold if you use the proper hardware. Remember to test with any management packs that you might add to OpsMgr because management packs can easily add 25% to your server CPU utilization.

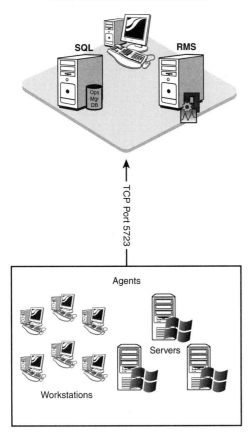

OPERATIONS MANAGER 2007
TWO SERVER CONFIGURATION

FIGURE 4.6   OpsMgr two-server configuration.

Now let's apply some numbers to this. We will use a standard growth rate of 5MB per managed computer per day for the Operational database (discussed in the "Operations Database Sizing" section), and 3MB per managed computer per day on the Data Warehouse database (see the "Data Warehouse Sizing" section of this chapter). The total space for the year of stored data is 100 agents * 3MB/day * 365 days, which equals 109,500MB, or approximately 100GB. The Operational database stores data for 7 days by default, which translates to 100 agents * 5MB/day * 7 days, which equals 3500MB, or approximately 4GB. The Operational database no longer has the 30GB sizing restriction that existed with MOM 2005, but it is still prudent to allocate adequate space for it to grow to that size or greater. Approximating once again, we arrive at 250GB total space required. Table 4.16 lists a variety of drive sizes, the RAID configuration, and the usable space. This table assumes that the number of drives includes the parity drive in the RAID, but not an online hot spare.

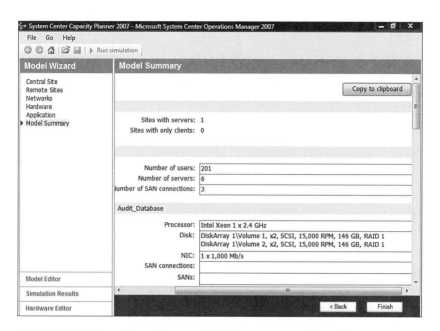

FIGURE 4.7   Operations Manager SCCP two-server configuration.

TABLE 4.15   Operations Manager Two-Server Hardware Recommendations

Hardware	Requirement
Processor	Two Dual-Core processors
RAM	4GB
Disk	Management Server: 10GB space
	Database Server: 150GB spread across dedicated drives for the operating system, data, and transaction logs.
CD-ROM	Needed
Display adapter	Super VGA
Monitor	800×600 resolution
Mouse	Needed
Network	100Mbps
Operating system	Windows 2003 Server SP1 64 bit

TABLE 4.16   OpsMgr Database Server Drive Configuration

Drive Size	Number of Drives	Configuration	Usable Space
36GB	8	RAID5	252GB
72GB	5	RAID5	288GB
146GB	3	RAID5	292GB
300GB	2	RAID1	300GB

You should always place the database on a disk array separate from the operating system because combining them can cause I/O saturation. OpsMgr also works best on a 100Mb (or 1Gb) network, connected to a switch (preferably on the backbone with other production servers).

Server Components

In the two-server configuration, the two servers split the components of the typical Operations Manager installation, based on function. The first server provides management server functionality, and the second provides all database functionality. See Chapter 6 for the specific steps for installing a two-server configuration.

Designing Multiple Management Server Monitoring Configurations

Although it is often simpler to install a single Operations Manager management server to manage your server infrastructure, it may become necessary to deploy multiple management servers if you require the following functionality:

▶ Monitoring more than 200 servers.

▶ Collecting and reporting on more than a month or two of data.

▶ Adding redundancy to your monitoring environment.

▶ Monitoring computers across a WAN or firewall using the Gateway Server Component.

▶ Providing centralized auditing capabilities for your environment using the Audit Collection Services functionality.

▶ Segmenting the operational database to another server. (We discuss this in the "Designing a Two-Server Monitoring Configuration" section of this chapter.)

In multiple-server configurations, you will split the OpsMgr components onto different physical servers. These components, introduced earlier in the "Design" section of this chapter, include the following:

▶ Root Management Server

▶ Management Servers

▶ Gateway Servers

- Operations Database Servers

- Reporting Servers

- Data Warehouse Servers

- ACS Database servers

- ACS Collector

- ACS Forwarder

- Operations console

- Web Console Servers

- Operations Manager agents

You can have more than one server configured for each of these server roles, depending on your particular requirements.

Multiple-Server Requirements

It is generally a good practice to include high levels of redundancy with any mission-critical server, such as the RMS, Operations consoles, and database servers. We recommend you include as many redundant components as feasible into your server hardware design and choose enterprise-level servers whenever possible.

Disk space for the Operations database server is always a consideration. As with any database, it can consume vast quantities of drive space if left unchecked. Although Microsoft has removed the historical limit of 30GB on the Operations database, we still recommend that you limit the size of the Operations database to maximize performance and to minimize backup timeframes. The disk drive storing the Operations database should have at least slightly more than double the total size of the database in free space to support operations such as backups and restores, as well as in case of emergency growth of the Operations database. In addition, backups of the entire database on a regular basis are a must. We discuss backups in detail in Chapter 12, "Backup and Recovery."

You can configure the Data Warehouse server in a manner similar to the Operations database server, but the Data Warehouse database requires a much larger storage capacity. Whereas the Operations database typically stores data for a period of days, the Data Warehouse database typically stores the data for a year. This data can grow rapidly; we discuss this in the "Designing OpsMgr Sizing and Capacity" section later in this chapter.

Placement of the Management Servers

For optimal performance, place management servers close to their database servers or to the agents they manage. However, several key factors can play a role in determining where the servers will reside:

- **Maximum bandwidth between components**—OpsMgr servers should have fast communication between all components in the same management group to maximize the performance of the system. The management server needs to be able to upload data quickly to the Operations database. This usually means T1 speed or better, depending on the number of agents the management server is supporting.

▶ **Redundancy**—Adding management servers increases the failover capability of OpsMgr and helps to maintain a specific level of uptime. Depending on your organization's needs, you can build additional servers into your design as appropriate.

▶ **Scalability**—If a need exists to expand the OpsMgr environment significantly or increase the number of monitored servers with short notice, you can establish additional OpsMgr management servers to take up the slack.

In most cases, you can centralize the management servers in close proximity with the Operations database and allow the agents to communicate with the management servers over any slow links that might exist.

As a rule, for multiple-server OpsMgr configurations, you should have at least two management servers for redundancy.

Using Multiple Management Groups

As defined in Chapter 3, Operations Manager management groups are composed of a single SQL Server operational database, a unique name, the RMS, and optional components such as additional management servers. Each management group uses its own Operations database and maintains its own separate configuration. As an example, two management groups can have the same management pack (MP) installed but different overrides configured within the MP. OpsMgr 2007 allows multiple management groups to write to a single Data Warehouse database (unlike MOM 2005, where the reporting environment could only have one management group report directly to the Reporting database).

It is important to note that you can configure agents to report to multiple management groups and connect management groups to each other. This increases the flexibility of the system and allows for the creation of multiple management groups based on your organization's needs. There are five major reasons for dividing your organization into separate management groups:

▶ **Geographic or bandwidth-limited regions**—Similar in approach to Windows 2003 sites or Exchange 2003 routing groups, you can establish Operations Manager management groups in segregated network subnets to reduce network bandwidth consumption. We do not recommend spanning management groups across slow WAN links because this can lead to link saturation (and really upset your company's network team). Aligning management groups on geographic or bandwidth criteria is always a good idea.

The size of the remote office has to justify creating a new management group. As an example, a site with fewer than 10 servers typically does not warrant its own management group. The downside to this is a potential delay in notification of critical events.

▶ **Functional or application-level control**—This is a useful feature of Operations Manager, enabling management of a single agent by multiple management groups. The agent keeps the rules it gets from each of the management groups completely separated and can even communicate over separate ports to the different management groups.

▶ **Political or business function divisions**—Although not as common a solution as bandwidth-based management groups, OpsMgr management group boundaries can be aligned with political boundaries. This would normally only occur if there was a particular need to segregate specific monitored servers to separate zones of influence. For example, the Finance group can monitor its servers in its own management group to lessen the security exposure those servers receive.

▶ **Very large numbers of agents**—In a nutshell, if your management group membership approaches the maximum number of monitored servers, it is wise to segment the number of agents into multiple management groups to improve network performance. This is appropriate when the number of managed computers approaches 5000 or when the database size increases to a level that decreases performance or the database cannot effectively be backed up and restored. In MOM 2005, the maximum supported database size was 30GB (including 40% free space for indexing). In OpsMgr 2007, there is no supported size limit, but the best-practice approach is to keep it less than 40GB, or even 30GB if you are able to do so. We have heard of transient issues when the Operations database is greater than 40GB.

▶ **Preparing for mergers**—Organizations expecting company mergers or with a history of mergers can use multiple management groups. Using multiple management groups enables quick integration of multiple OpsMgr environments.

Let's illustrate this point using the bandwidth-limited criteria. If your organization is composed of multiple locations separated by slow WAN links, it is best to separate each location not connected by a high-speed link into a separate management group and set up connected management groups.

Another example of using multiple management groups is when IT support operations functionally is divided into multiple support groups. Let's take an example where there is a platform group (managing the Windows operating system) and a messaging group (managing the Exchange application). In this instance, two management groups might be deployed (a platform management group and a messaging management group). The separate management groups would allow both the platform group and the messaging group to have complete administrative control over their own management infrastructures. The two groups would jointly operate the agent on the monitored computers.

The Operations Database—Placement and Issues

Keeping in mind that each management group has a separate database, you should note that, as opposed to management servers, a management group has only one Operations database. Consequently, keep the following factors in mind when placing and configuring each SQL Server installation:

▶ **Network bandwidth**—As with the other OpsMgr components, it is essential to place the Operations database on a well-connected, resilient network that can communicate freely with the management server. Slow network performance can significantly affect the capability of OpsMgr to respond to network conditions.

▶ **Hardware redundancy**—Most enterprise server hardware contains contingencies for hardware failures. Redundant fans, RAID mirror sets, dual power supplies, and the like will all help to ensure the availability and integrity of the system. SQL Server databases need this level of protection because critical online systems require immediate failover for accessibility.

If you have high-availability requirements, you should cluster and/or replicate the database to provide redundancy and failover capabilities.

▶ **Backups**—Although some people consider high availability to be a replacement for backups, setting up your OpsMgr environment for hardware redundancy can be an expensive proposition. You should establish a backup schedule for all databases used by Operations Manager as well as the system databases used by SQL Server. We discuss backups in Chapter 12.

▶ **SQL Server licensing**—Because SQL Server is a separate licensing component from Microsoft, each computer that accesses the database must have its own Client Access License (CAL), unless you are using per-processor licensing for the SQL Server. As we discussed in the "Planning for Licensing" section of this chapter, if you use System Center Operations Manager 2007 with the SQL 2005 Technologies license, no CALs are required. However, remember that no other databases or applications can use that instance of SQL Server.

Licensing can be an important cost factor. Database clustering requires SQL Server Enterprise Edition.

With MOM 2005, the Operations database server transferred data to the reporting database on a daily basis using a DTS package. In OpsMgr 2007, writes occur directly from the management server to the Data Warehouse database rather than using a daily scheduled DTS package. In OpsMgr 2007, solid network connectivity should exist between the Operations database server and the Data Warehouse database server.

Designing OpsMgr Sizing and Capacity

Although Operations Manager 2007 contains multiple mechanisms that allow it to scale to large environments, design limitations may apply depending on your specific environment. The number of agents you deploy and the amount of data you want to collect directly impact capacity limitations and the size of your database. A better understanding of exactly what OpsMgr's limitations are can help to better define which design to utilize.

Data Flows in OpsMgr

Data flow in OpsMgr 2007 is an important design consideration. A typical Operations Manager environment has a large quantity of data flowing from a relatively small percentage of sources within the IT environment. The data flows are latency sensitive, due to needing alerts and notifications in a short timeframe (measured in seconds).

We have found that agent traffic varies depending on the management packs you deploy, ranging from about 1.2Kbps to 3Kbps travelling from the agent to the management server. For our calculations, we use the following formula:

> 3Kbps * <number of agents> = total traffic (in Kbps)

The data flowing from each agent is not that great when considered individually. However, when looked at in aggregate for a large number of servers, the load can be significant, as illustrated in Table 4.17, which shows the estimated minimum bandwidth for just the Windows operating system base management pack. Using Table 4.17, you can see that the need for multiple 100Mbps or Gigabit network cards becomes important above the 500-agent mark.

You can adjust the data flow in two ways:

▶ How often the agents upload their data

▶ How much data you upload

TABLE 4.17   Management Server Aggregate Bandwidth for Agents

Agents	Total Kbps	Utilization of a 100Mbps NIC
1	0.50	0%
5	2.50	0%
10	5.00	1%
100	50.00	5%
500	250.00	25%
1000	500.00	50%

When considering how to adjust the setting for low-bandwidth agents, you can tune the heartbeat and data upload times. However, this will *not* reduce the overall volume of information. You will be uploading more information at less frequent intervals, but it will be the same quantity of data. To reduce the data volume, you need to adjust the rules to collect less data. As an example, adjusting the sample interval of a performance counter from 15 minutes to 30 minutes will reduce the volume of data by half.

CAUTION

Don't Over-tune Those Performance Counters

Performance counters have the most impact on network traffic and the size of the Operations database. Be very careful if you change a performance interval to gather data more often.

Limitations, Provisos, and Restrictions

Management servers, management groups, and collections of management groups have some inherent limitations. In some cases, these are hard limits that cannot be technically broken; others are supportability limits that should not be broken. Microsoft tests and supports its products but sets limits on the scale of the systems that reflect the limits of the testing and support. Table 4.18 summarizes the capacity limitations for OpsMgr components. Although OpsMgr includes implicit design components that allow it to scale to large groups of managed nodes, there are some maximum levels that could limit the size of management groups.

TABLE 4.18   Limitations Summary as of Operations Manager 2007

Area	Limitation Description	Limit
Management Group	Maximum agents per management group	5000
	Maximum agentless computers per management group	No limits defined
	Maximum management servers per management group	No limits defined
	Maximum consoles per management group	Unlimited
Management Server	Maximum agents per management server	2000
	Maximum agentless computers per management server	10
Agent	Maximum management servers per agent	4
Database	Maximum size of operations database	None
	Maximum size of reporting database	None

We have grouped Table 4.18 by the type of limitation. Even though there is a stated limit, in a given environment the limit might not be practical. As an example, the maximum number of agents supported by a management server is 2000. However, a single management server is unlikely to be capable of supporting 2000 Exchange servers due to the particularly heavy load these agents place on it.

Many of these capacity limitations are actually supportability limitations rather than hard technical limitations. For example, monitoring the 5001st agent will not generate an error or alert. Exceeding the limitations does not immediately cause the system to fail but rather starts to affect the performance, latency, and throughput of the OpsMgr infrastructure. For this reason, Microsoft imposes these limitations from a supportability perspective; the Operations Manager 2007 product may not function properly if you exceed those limits.

Doing the Math

Because each management group can support up to a maximum of 5000 agents and there is no restriction on the number of connected management groups, this effectively means that there are no documented scalability limits on OpsMgr 2007. This is an excellent functional increase from MOM 2005, where you could support a maximum of 44,000 managed computers in a single cohesive MOM 2005 infrastructure.

In the next two sections, we will evaluate database sizing, which has also changed significantly since MOM 2005.

Operations Database Sizing

Sizing the Operations Manager 2007 database can be a complex endeavor. You have to take several factors into account and use a complex formula to calculate database size. We suggest purchasing a large quantity of disk space for your OpsMgr database so that the database can increase in size over time if it is required. If space limitations are an issue, you can reduce the size of the database through decreasing the data retention period on the database. By doing some simple math, we can estimate the size of the OpsMgr database.

From reviewing the Operations database, we determined that a fresh installation of OpsMgr 2007 with a 1500MB database size used a total of 510MB of the total database and log size. We reviewed all the tables in the Operations database and tracked what tables increase over time. Through this trending, we determined that the tables related to alerts, alert history, events, state changes, and performance counters increased over time and were related to the number of agents and the retention period for the database. We found that data increases in the Operations database at an average rate of 5MB/day per agent. From this exercise, we determined the following formula to estimate the size of the Operations database:

(5MB/day × Number of Agents × Retention Days) + 510MB = Operations Database

As an example, at 5MB/day for 10 agents with a default retention period of 7 days, the database should have approximately 860MB of space used in the database.

With a growth rate of 5MB/day per agent, the size of the database is determined by the number of days the data is in the Operations database—that is, the grooming interval. Table 4.19 highlights in bold the default grooming interval of 7 days.

As you can see from Table 4.19, using the default grooming interval of 7 days, the Operations database will use approximately 35GB of space for 1000 agents.

TABLE 4.19   Operations Database Sizes in MB for Various Grooming Intervals and Agents

Grooming Interval (days)	3000 Agents	2000 Agents	1000 Agents	500 Agents	100 Agents	50 Agents	10 Agents
1	15,510	10,510	5510	3010	1010	760	560
2	30,510	20,510	10,510	5510	1510	1010	610
3	45,510	30,510	15,510	8010	2010	1260	660
4	60,510	40,510	20,510	10,510	2510	1510	710
5	75,510	50,510	25,510	13,010	3010	1760	760
6	90,510	60,510	30,510	15,510	3510	2010	810
7	105,510	70,510	35,510	18,010	4010	2260	860
8	120,510	80,510	40,510	20,510	4510	2510	910
9	135,510	90,510	45,510	23,010	5010	2760	960
10	150,510	100,510	50,510	25,510	5510	3010	1010

Figure 4.8 charts the growth of the Operations database for ease of reference. The series lines for each of the agent counts plot the projected size of the Operations database for grooming intervals, varying from 1 to 10 days. You can see the projected growth of the operations database as the grooming interval is increased and as the number of agents increases.

It is important to note there is a third factor we are unable to build into this type of an estimate: management packs. Although a correlation exists between an increased number of management packs and a larger Operations database, the database size depends on not only the actual number of rules in the management pack, but also what those rules do. A single rule could gather the entire Application Event log and record it in the database, in contrast with another rule that only writes to the database when a specific error condition occurred. To consider this factor in the database sizing, we gathered metrics from varying environments with a variety of management packs to identify a growth range covering the majority of deployments. To trend your environment effectively, it is important to conduct appropriate testing and monitor the growth rates of your own installation over time; your growth rate may vary from the estimates we have developed.

Figure 4.9 gives a clear view of how the Operations database is using the data. If you need to limit the growth of your Operations database, remember that performance measurements contain the bulk of the data within this database. Tuning the frequency with which performance measurements are gathered is a good target for reducing database growth.

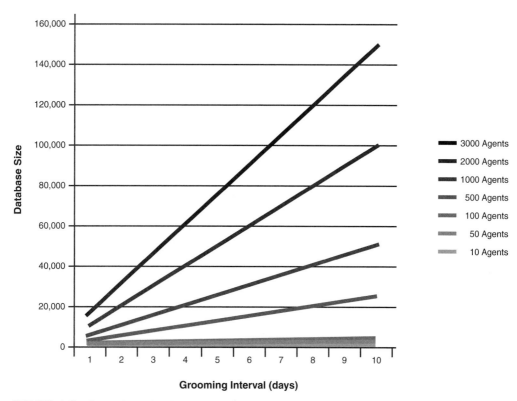

FIGURE 4.8   Operations database size chart.

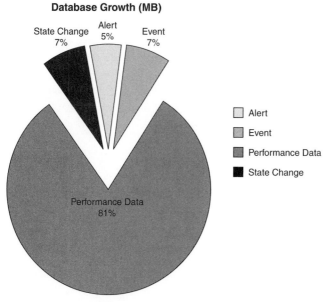

FIGURE 4.9   Operations database data distribution chart.

Real World—Microsoft on Operations Database Sizing

The following information was taken from the Microsoft OpsMgr newsgroups related to sizing the Operations database, and is based on an experience with the Microsoft IT (MSIT) implementation:

Sizing for the Ops DB is highly variable depending on which Management Packs are installed and what grooming policy is configured. ...some "worst case scenario" numbers derived from an MSIT Management Group that manages 3000 servers and has all of the out-of-the-box MPs deployed along with 18 custom MPs and a 4-day retention policy (with the exception of performance signature data which is retained for just 2 days). In this case, MSIT allocated 60 GB for the Ops DB, of which they actually use about 35 GB. Performance data accounts for about 75% of the total storage requirement with about 55% being used to store sampled performance data (which is retained for 4 days) and another 20% being used for performance signature data (which is retained for 2 days). After performance data, collected events and monitor state change events account for the next largest category of storage used in the Ops DB with each accounting for about 10% of the total storage requirements. Alerts account for about 1% of the storage requirement. The remainder of the storage used is divided among a large number of tables with no other individual tables or data type accounting for any significant percentage of storage. With over 85% of total storage requirements being derived from the above operational data I wouldn't spend much time doing detailed calculations of storage requirements for other data types. Unless you have unusual data retention requirements, the recommendation is to use something similar to the MSIT storage allocation, which will give you plenty of room for growth and some flexibility in adjusting data retention.

With regards to SQL log file storage requirements, the operational requirements are fairly trivial, but you will want to allocate quite a bit more storage than required for day-to-day operations in order to cover the occasional need to delete Management Packs. MSIT uses 16 GB for transaction logs in their 3000-server MG. Under normal operations they rarely use more than a few hundred MB of this space (even while using the full recovery model with 15-minute log dumps), but much more is required on the rare occasions when large MPs need to be deleted. A significant amount of data can be deleted in a single SQL transaction when large MPs are deleted. MSIT has used up to 12 GB of log space while deleting some MPs. I would recommend that you allocate a similar amount of storage to avoid any problems with full transaction logs when deleting MPs.

Data Warehouse Sizing

The Data Warehouse database is the long-term data repository for Operations Manager 2007. In MOM 2005, the size of the Reporting database was closely tied to the size of the Operations database—a DTS package tied the two databases together by transferring data from one database to the other. With OpsMgr 2007, this approach has changed.

Management pack objects write data directly to the Data Warehouse database. OpsMgr aggregates rule and performance data for reporting, rather than storing and reporting on raw data. This approach has the potential to provide much longer-term reports for a larger number of agents and to use a smaller Data Warehouse database.

This has interesting results in providing effective sizing estimates for the data warehouse. To determine this, we took the same approach as we did with the Operations database and applied it to the Data Warehouse database.

In reviewing the Data Warehouse database, we found that a fresh installation of Reporting for OpsMgr 2007 with a 1500MB database used a total of 570MB of the total database and log size. We reviewed all the tables in the Data Warehouse database and tracked which ones increase over time.

As with the Operations database, we found that the same data was growing over time: alerts, alert history, events, state changes, and performance counters. The number of agents and the retention period also affect the amount of the increase. We found that data increases in this database at an average rate of 3MB/day per agent. From our exercise, we have determined the following formula to estimate the size of the Data Warehouse database:

$$(3MB/day \times Number\ of\ Agents \times Retention\ Days) + 570\ MB = Data\ Warehouse\ size$$

As an example, at 3MB/day for 10 agents with a retention period of 30 days, the database should have approximately 1470MB of space used. The Data Warehouse database is set to autogrow, so it will automatically increase in size to accommodate the additional data.

Table 4.20 shows the Data Warehouse database size for various grooming intervals and agent counts.

TABLE 4.20   Data Warehouse Database Sizes in MB for Various Grooming Intervals and Agents

Retention Period	3000 Agents	2000 Agents	1000 Agents	500 Agents	100 Agents	50 Agents	10 Agents
1 Month	270,570	180,570	90,570	45,570	9570	5070	1470
2 Month	540,570	360,570	180,570	90,570	18,570	9570	2370
1 Qtr	810,570	540,570	270,570	135,570	27,570	14,070	3270
2 Qtr	1,620,570	1,080,570	540,570	270,570	54,570	27,570	5970
3 Qtr	2,430,570	1,620,570	810,570	405,570	81,570	41,070	8670
1 Yr	3,285,570	2,190,570	1,095,570	548,070	110,070	55,320	11,520
5 Qtr	4,095,570	2,730,570	1,365,570	683,070	137,070	68,820	14,220
6 Qtr	4,905,570	3,270,570	1,635,570	818,070	164,070	82,320	16,920
7 Qtr	5,715,570	3,810,570	1,905,570	953,070	191,070	95,820	19,620
2 Yr	6,570,570	4,380,570	2,190,570	1,095,570	219,570	110,070	22,470

As you can see from Table 4.20, with large numbers of agents and a long retention period, this database can quickly go beyond the 1TB or 2TB level; therefore, it is good news that no documented size limits exist on the Data Warehouse database! Figure 4.10 displays a graph showing the impact to the size of the Data Warehouse database depending on the number of agents and how long the data is retained.

When estimating the size of the data warehouse, it is important to consider the amount of data collected daily and how long you intend to keep that data in the data warehouse, because this will directly affect your storage requirements. Your proof of concept (POC) should provide good figures for projecting the size of your Data Warehouse database.

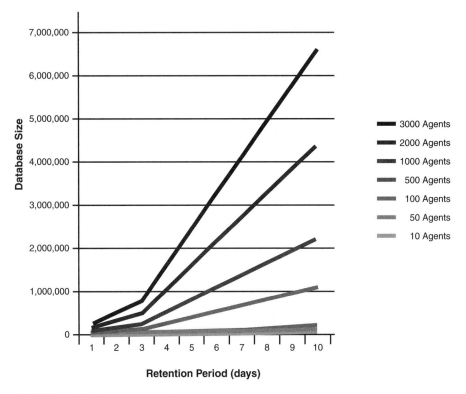

FIGURE 4.10   Reporting database size chart.

Real World—Microsoft on Data Warehouse Sizing

The following was taken from the Microsoft OpsMgr newsgroups related to sizing of the OpsMgr Data Warehouse:

Data warehouse storage requirements can vary considerably depending on the data retention requirements so we would need more information in order to make any estimates. As with the Ops DB, the single largest factor in DW size is the amount of perf data that will be retained. Since the DW will automatically aggregate performance data on an hourly and daily basis you can dramatically lower storage requirements by grooming out raw perf data aggressively and relying on the aggregated data for long-term trending.

If limiting the amount of data collected is not an option, there are several potential solutions for managing this volume of data:

▶ **Extract the data to reports**—One approach to resolve this issue is to generate monthly reports of the data and to archive the reports. This provides a method to summarize the information and retain it for long durations of time. Using this approach limits your flexibility because you cannot generate new reports from the data.

▶ **Reduce the time interval**—Although keeping data for a year might be nice, it may be sufficient to have only a quarter or so of reporting database data online to generate reports. If that horizon is sufficient and keeps the database size to where you need it to be, it is an easy solution.

▶ **Create archive snapshots**—Another approach to provide long-term access to reports is to create a snapshot of the database on a regular basis. You can archive and restore these database backups to a temporary database when needed. This technique is further discussed in Chapter 12.

You can implement these potential workarounds to the problem of database volume individually or together. For example, you might create quarterly archive snapshots to review the historical data up to 1 year old and use archived monthly reports to view historical data up to 5 years old.

TIP

Databases Sizing Spreadsheet

The CD accompanying this book includes a databases sizing spreadsheet. The spreadsheet allows you to calculate approximate sizes for the Operations database, Data Warehouse database, and ACS database. The calculations use the sizing information presented in this book.

Management Group Scalability

As your OpsMgr environment increases to large amounts of managed nodes, Operations Manager responds with the capability to scale to those groups. By using multiple management groups, multiple management servers, and event forwarding, you can make almost any project a real possibility.

If you plan to monitor over 100 nodes, consider adding multiple management servers in your management group (as shown in Figure 4.11). After the first two management servers, we recommend adding an additional management server for every increase of 250 to 500 nodes.

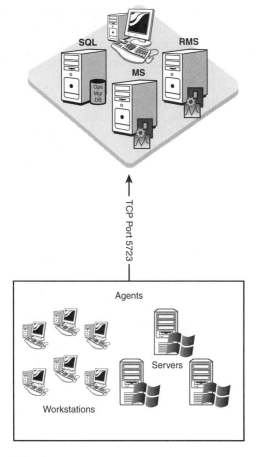

**OPERATIONS MANAGER 2007
THREE SERVER CONFIGURATION**

FIGURE 4.11   Multiple management servers in a management group.

Multiple Management Groups

Expanding your implementation to use multiple management groups, as previously defined, can take place at the designer's discretion, although implementing multiple management groups generally takes place to segregate different geographic areas with slow WAN links from each other. If the link speeds to remote managed nodes are under 256Kbps, we recommend either creating a new management group or greatly throttling the amount of information collected from remote agents. Determining whether to create a new management group or simply to throttle the events sent will depend on the amount of remote servers. It does not make sense to create a new management group if you have only two small sites with four servers each to monitor.

If, however, you have distributed your remote servers around various offices and they have better connections to each other than to your primary management group, it may be wise to create a new management group. This would typically be the case if you were to create management groups based on continent, for example. Figure 4.12 shows a world-wide OpsMgr 2007 infrastructure with regional management groups (North America, Europe, and Asia-Pacific). The global management group connects to each of the regional management groups to review their alerts.

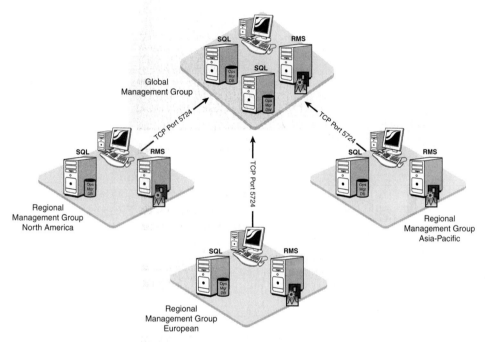

FIGURE 4.12   Management groups by geographic region.

In this configuration, each region can operate the management groups semi-autonomously, yet still allow a global view of the environment worldwide using a global console.

Through creating and manipulating management groups and management servers, your OpsMgr environment can scale from a handful of monitored servers to large numbers of nodes worldwide. This scalability helps establish Operations Manager as an enterprise monitoring solution.

Tying It All Together

To complete the design piece of this stage, each of the aspects discussed needs to be documented, discussed, revised, and agreed upon ("DDRA" for short). Following this process identifies potential issues with the design before testing it as a proof of concept. It also facilitates communication with other members of your organization and helps drive acceptance of Operations Manager within your company.

Planning

After determining your Operations Manager design, the next step is to plan for the remaining phases, which include Proof of Concept, Pilot, and Implementation. These phases have the same goals: limiting potential risk to your production environment and avoiding "alert overload" for your organization.

> **NOTE**
>
> **Defining Risk**
>
> Any time a production environment changes, there is a risk that the change can cause a problem within the environment.

It is important to try to avoid alert overload, which refers not to a technical hardware constraint but to an attention constraint on the part of the people involved with monitoring OpsMgr, who can only handle a limited number of alerts. Alert overload occurs when the number of alerts generated causes the human receivers of these alerts to ignore the errors (or actively oppose using the tool providing the notifications). You don't want to cry wolf unless there really is a good chance a wolf is at the door. Avoiding risk of alert overload can positively impact the likelihood of a successful OpsMgr deployment. Your planning document should include details on your Proof of Concept, Pilot, and Implementation phases.

Proof of Concept Planning

A proof of concept should emulate the production hardware as closely as possible. Use production hardware for the OpsMgr solution if it is available because that will most closely emulate your production environment. Isolate your POC network configuration from the production environment to allow full testing of servers without affecting their production equivalents. The planning phase identifies what needs testing as part of the POC—base testing on your business requirements.

For example, the following steps may comprise a high-level POC plan for a single-server Operations Manager 2007 configuration:

- ▶ Creating an isolated network for POC testing.
- ▶ Installing the domain controllers.
- ▶ Installing the application servers that will be monitored by OpsMgr.
- ▶ Installing the OpsMgr server(s). (Install Windows 2003 SP 1 and SQL Server 2005 SP 1 or greater.)

- Creating any required OpsMgr service accounts and confirming rights to service accounts.

- Installing the Data Warehouse Server and Root Management Server Components.

- Installing the OpsMgr reporting components.

- Discovering and installing OpsMgr agents.

- Installing management packs.

- Configuring management packs.

- Configuring recipients and notifications.

- Configuring the Operations Manager Web console and OpsMgr web reports.

- Executing tests defined for the OpsMgr environment.

The actual content of your POC plan will vary depending on your environment, but it is important to plan what steps will occur during POC. This helps you avoid a "mad scramble" of installing systems without a plan, which you can leverage both in the POC stage and in the Pilot stage.

Pilot Planning

A pilot deployment moves the OpsMgr solution that you have created into a production environment. A pilot is by its nature limited in scope. In planning your pilot, you should consider how to limit either the number of servers you will be monitoring or the number of management packs you will deploy, or potentially both. Pilot planning should detail what servers you are deploying OpsMgr to, what servers it will monitor, and the management packs you will utilize. Because the pilot occurs in the production environment, you should be deploying your production OpsMgr hardware.

Implementation Planning

The Implementation phase takes the pilot configuration you created and rolls it to a full production deployment. The order in which you will add servers and management packs should be included as part of your implementation plan.

Proof of Concept

The purpose of a proof of concept is to take the design that you have created, build it, and "kick the tires." Production is not a POC environment; when you are in a production environment you are past the Proof of Concept stage, and any errors you encounter have much larger costs than if you had caught them in the POC.

TIP

Setting Up a POC

Virtual server environments make it much easier to create an isolated proof of concept environment.

A POC environment is also a great opportunity to try out a variety of management packs and see how they perform and what information they can provide. If possible, retain your POC environment even after moving on to later phases of your OpsMgr deployment. This provides an infrastructure to test additional management packs, management pack updates, and service packs in a non-business-critical environment.

POC Challenges

It can be difficult to emulate a full production environment within the confines of a POC. A primary reason is the hardware used in the POC environment because production-level hardware is not typically accessible. Should the type of hardware used within the POC not reflect the level of hardware in production, you may be unable to assess the speed or full functionality of your solution.

There are also some inherent challenges in any POC environment. How does one effectively scale for production? For example, if you are monitoring logon and logoff events, how do you generate enough events to successfully monitor them? From our perspective, two options are available:

▶ Using scripts to generate sample events that can provide a large amount of event data.

▶ Using a *POC exclusion*, which is a document describing items that you could not effectively test within the POC environment. You can use this document during the Pilot phase to determine additional testing that needs to occur as part of the pilot.

Another complexity of POC environments is they often are isolated from the production network, removing potential interaction between the two environments. Network isolation removes the risk of inadvertently affecting production, but also adds complications because production network resources are not available (file shares, patching mechanisms, and so on). If your POC testing is in an isolated environment, you will want to establish a separate Internet connection to be able to patch systems and access non-POC resources.

Establishing an Effective POC

With the challenges inherent within the POC environment, how do you determine what to focus on during your POC? We suggest focusing on two major concepts: basic design validation and complexities within your specific environment.

To validate your design, test the design and determine whether there are inherent issues. This process requires deploying your design and testing OpsMgr's basic functionality including alerts, events, notifications, and functionality using the OpsMgr consoles. Part of basic design validation testing should also include tuning alerts and documenting your processes. If you are running in an isolated environment, you will also need a domain controller, DNS, and a mail server for email notification. Basic design validation should only require a small percentage of time within your POC.

Spend the majority of the POC time testing the complexities specific to your design or environment. Let's say your design includes Tivoli or OpenView integration. This represents a complexity to test during the POC; you should deploy the other management software within your POC. Although this sounds like a lot of difficulty, how would you know how the two systems will interact without any testing? The only other option is testing within the production environment, which we obviously do not recommend! (Before you decide to test in production, ask yourself how your boss would respond if your testing caused an outage in your production environment. We doubt he or she would be impressed with your testing methodology.)

Other examples of potential complexities are connected management groups or multi-homed environments, highly redundant configurations, third-party management packs, and any requirements to create custom management packs. Your focus during POC testing should directly relate to the business requirements identified for your OpsMgr solution.

POC testing provides a safe method to effectively assess your design and make updates as required based on the results of your tests. Do not be surprised if your design changes based on the results of your POC tests.

Using POC environments also gives you the ability to configure production systems as multihomed, reporting to both production and POC management groups. Utilizing a subsection of types of production systems can provide strong insights for how Operations Manager will function in your production environment. This gives you a method to test changes to management packs, which you can then export and import into production.

Pilot

During the Pilot phase, you deploy your production hardware with Operations Manager 2007 and integrate it into your production environment with a limited scope. In the Pilot phase, you are installing your production OpsMgr hardware and implementing the architecture you have designed.

Although you are deploying your production environment design, you will limit the number of servers to which you are deploying OpsMgr agent, or limit the number of management packs used. The Pilot phase provides a timeframe to identify how various management packs respond to the production systems you are monitoring. Out of the box, Operations Manager will provide a limited number of alerts, but additional changes are often required to "tune" it to your particular environment. Initial tuning of OpsMgr may occur now, but is also limited in scope. During the Pilot phase, you should test any POC exclusions identified within the actual production environment.

During the Pilot phase, track the amount of data gathered in the operations database to determine whether your OpsMgr database has sufficient space on a per-server basis. You can check the amount of free space available on the operations database using Microsoft's SQL Server Management Studio. The Operations console also provides tracking for both database free space and log free space. To access this functionality, use the menu command Monitoring -> Microsoft SQL Server -> Databases -> Database Free Space and Transaction Log Free Space.

TIP

Tracking MOM Database Size and Growth

The SQL Database Space Report provides the ability to track the percentage of free space for trending purposes. This report is included within the SQL management pack.

Implementation

The Implementation phase moves from pilot into full production deployment. Two major methods are generally used for deploying Operations Manager 2007 during the Implementation phase:

▶ **Phased deployment**—Using this approach, you will add in servers and management packs over time, allowing dedicated time for each server or management pack to tune alerts and events.

The phased deployment approach takes a significant amount of time, but you will have the benefit of thoroughly understanding each management pack and the effect it has on the servers in your environment. Using a phased approach can also minimize risk.

▶ **Bulk deployment**—The second approach is a bulk deployment of Operations Manager, which limits the notifications to the individual or group doing the OpsMgr deployment.

If you have deployed all servers and all management packs and your notification groups are thoroughly populated, the resulting flood of alerts may annoy the recipients in the notification groups, and they may just ignore the alerts. The benefit of a bulk deployment with limited notification is that you can deploy the entire OpsMgr environment quickly.

With either deployment approach, time is required to tune Operations Manager for your specific environment. Tuning within OpsMgr is the process of fixing the problems about which OpsMgr is alerting, overriding the alerts for specific servers, or filtering those alerts.

> **TIP**
>
> **Tuning Management Packs**
>
> Chapter 13, "Administering Management Packs," covers the basic approaches of tuning. Specific steps involved in implementing each management pack include utilizing the processes discussed in that chapter.

Maintenance

Now that you have implemented Operations Manager, you are finished, right? Not exactly. OpsMgr is a monitoring product and requires maintenance to keep it working effectively within your environment.

Although you can design OpsMgr to provide responses to common error situations, operators and technical specialists should regularly monitor your management system. Part of regular maintenance for Operations Manager involves responding to and addressing alerts, responding to the notifications it provides, and monitoring the Operations console to respond to events and alerts that occur. The tasks included with the various management packs can provide an efficient manner to perform common maintenance tasks.

Like other systems, your OpsMgr server environment will require maintenance through deployments of software patches, service packs, antivirus updates, backups, and other regularly scheduled maintenance.

Another part of the Maintenance phase is maintaining management packs within OpsMgr. Management packs constantly change. Microsoft updates existing management packs as it identifies new features or bug fixes. Microsoft, third-party vendors, and other Operations Manager administrators create new management packs, and you can download these from the Internet. As part of the Maintenance phase, you need to consider additions, updates, or the removal of management packs.

Agents in OpsMgr also require maintenance. As you add new servers to your environment, deploy OpsMgr agents to monitor them. Likewise, as servers become obsolete, you should uninstall their agents. Agent software requires updates as you apply service packs to the management server.

In summary, within the Maintenance phase it is important to monitor, maintain, and update your OpsMgr infrastructure. Operations Manager environments are constantly evolving because the infrastructures they support are continually changing.

Sample Designs

This chapter contains a lot of guidance and information, which can be a bit overwhelming to absorb and translate into a design. However, many OpsMgr implementations fit into the same general guidelines. Taking a closer look at a sample organization and its Operations Manager environment design can give you some clues into your own organization's design.

We will look at three sample designs to get an idea of how the process works through using System Center Capacity Planner 2007.

Single-Server OpsMgr Design

Eclipse is a 1000-user corporation headquartered in Frisco. A single Windows 2003 domain, eclipse.com, is set up and configured across the enterprise. Company headquarters has 100 Windows Server 2003 servers performing roles as file servers, DHCP servers, Active Directory domain controllers, DNS servers, SQL 2000 and 2005 database servers, and Exchange 2003 messaging servers.

Due to a recent spate of system failures and subsequent downtime, which could have been prevented with better systems management, Eclipse's IT group looked at Operations Manager 2007 as a solution for providing much-needed systems management for its server environment.

Because Eclipse will be monitoring approximately 100 servers, IT decided to deploy a single management group consisting of an OpsMgr server running all OpsMgr components. The server chosen is a dual-processor P4 2.4GHz server with 2GB of RAM and redundant hardware options.

Eclipse created a single management group for all its servers, and it distributed OpsMgr 2007 agents throughout the server infrastructure. In addition, Eclipse deployed and configured the default management packs for the Base OS, DNS, DHCP, Active Directory, Exchange, and SQL Server.

Figure 4.13 shows the final design.

Eclipse's OpsMgr administrator feels that the company can easily scale its Operations Manager implementation to higher numbers of servers if it wants because the hardware can accommodate increased numbers of users. Eclipse is mildly concerned with the single point of failure of its single OpsMgr server, but has decided that it is most cost-effective to deploy a simple single-server management group.

Eclipse evaluated the Operations database retention and decided to use a retention period of four days to keep the Operations database size down to approximately 3GB, per Table 4.19. It wants to retain its reporting data for a total of one year, which referring back to Table 4.20 would require approximately 110GB of storage.

Table 4.21 summarizes the design points and decisions.

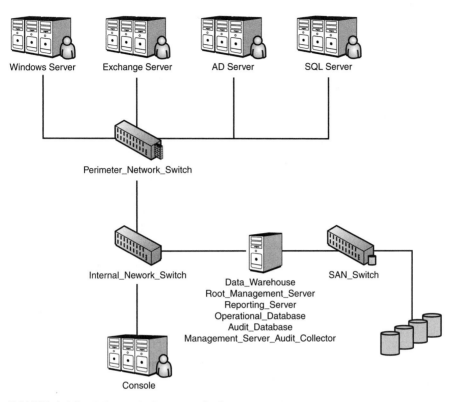

FIGURE 4.13   Eclipse single-server design.

TABLE 4.21   Eclipse Single-Server OpsMgr Design Summary

Design Point	Decision
Monitored computers	100
Management group	1
Management group name(s)	GROUP1
Management server(s)	1
Operations database retention	4 days
Estimated Operations database size	3GB
Data Warehouse database retention	1 year
Estimated Data Warehouse database size	110GB

Single-Management Group Design

After using OpsMgr for some amount of time, the Eclipse Corporation decides it needs redundancy and better performance for Operations Manager. The company also goes through a round of acquisitions, which increases the number of managed computers to 500 servers. Eclipse re-evaluated their Operations database retention, deciding the default period of seven days better meets their requirements, giving in a database size of 18GB per Table 4.19. Eclipse still wants to retain its operations data for a total of one year, which requires approximately 550GB of storage when increasing the number of servers to 500 and based on the information in Table 4.20.

The option chosen is a single OpsMgr management group named GROUP1 with a five-server design, including an Operations database server, a Reporting server, a Data Warehouse server, a RMS, and an additional management server. The servers chosen are all dual-processor P4 2.4GHz servers with 2GB of RAM and redundant hardware options. Figure 4.14 shows the diagram.

For the storage requirements, the Operations Database Server Component uses a dual-channel controller with a mirrored set of 72GB drives for the OS/logs and a RAID5 set of three 72GB drives for the database. The Reporting/Data Warehouse Server Component uses a dual-channel controller with a mirrored set of 72GB drives for the OS/logs and an external array with a total capacity of 2TB.

The dual–management server configuration allows Eclipse to assign 250 of its managed computers to each of the management servers. In the event of a failover, either management server could handle the load of 500 total agents. This gives Eclipse the fault tolerance it needs.

In the event of a database server outage, the management servers and agents will buffer the operations data. The datacenter stocks standard spare parts and servers to be able to restore operations within 4 hours. The data warehouse will take longer to bring back to full operations, but this database is less mission-critical because its only impact is on report generation capabilities.

Table 4.22 summarizes the design points and decisions.

Multiple-Management Group Design

Odyssey is a large, 2000-user corporation with two major offices in Plano and Carrollton. The Plano office hosts 500 servers, and the Carrollton location hosts 250. Most of the servers are Windows Server 2003 machines, but a minority is composed of Novell NetWare, Linux, and Windows 2000 machines. Odyssey utilizes a single-domain Windows 2003 Active Directory.

Odyssey needs to deploy a robust server management system to increase its uptime levels and improve productivity across the enterprise. It chose Operations Manager 2007 to accomplish this task.

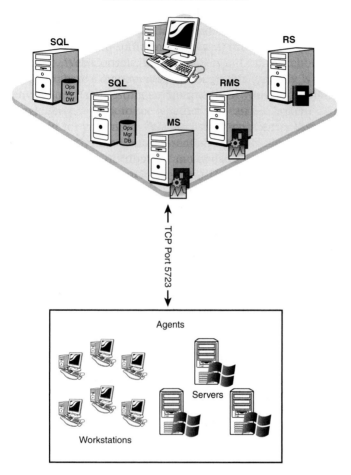

FIGURE 4.14   Eclipse multiserver design.

TABLE 4.22   Eclipse Single Management Group OpsMgr Design Summary

Design Point	Decision
Monitored computers	500
Management group	1
Management group name(s)	GROUP1
Management Server(s)	4
Operations database retention	7 days
Estimated Operations database size	18GB
Data Warehouse database retention	1 year
Estimated Data Warehouse database size	550GB

The early design sessions indicated that two management groups for OpsMgr are required, one for each geographical location. This is due to the independent nature of the two locations. Connected management groups could then be set up between the management groups.

The Plano management group will manage up to 500 servers, and the Carrollton location will manage up to 250 servers. A connected management group (discussed in the "Multiple Management Group Architectures" section of this chapter) is used to integrate the two management groups, and both management groups use a single data warehouse in the Plano management group.

For the storage requirements, the combined database and reporting server uses a dual-channel controller with a mirrored set of 72GB drives for the OS/logs and a RAID5 set of eight 72GB drives for the databases. The total storage for the databases is approximately 500GB.

Odyssey makes extensive use of the Microsoft-provided management packs and purchases add-on management packs from third-party vendors to manage its disparate operating systems and application environments.

This design allows the organization to have a corporate view of all alerts within the entire company but still allows the regions to have full operational control over their servers and utilize the Operations Manager 2007 features to ensure uptime. The strategic placement of components allows for server consolidation and redundancy where needed.

Table 4.23 summarizes the design points and decisions.

TABLE 4.23   Odyssey Multiple Management Group Design Summary

Design Point	Decision
Monitored computers	750
Management groups	2
Management group name(s)	Plano Carrollton
Management Server(s)	4
Operations database retention	7 days
Estimated Operations database size	11GB, 6GB
Data Warehouse database retention	1 year
Estimated Data Warehouse database size	825GB (550 GB + 275 GB)

Summary

This chapter explained why it is important to develop a plan before implementing OpsMgr into your environment. We discussed assessment and design as a part of that plan, as well as some of the technical design considerations for the various components of an OpsMgr infrastructure. We also discussed the planning phases needed for an effective deployment of Operations Manager 2007 in your organization and looked at some sample designs. The next chapter discusses planning complex OpsMgr configurations.

4

Planning Complex Configurations

This chapter discusses details to consider when you plan more complex configurations of Operations Manager 2007. Complexity in this context refers to a variety of concepts, including the following:

▶ Adding components

▶ Multihomed configurations

▶ Connected management groups

▶ Multiple domains

▶ Active Directory integration

▶ Impact of component faults in OpsMgr 2007

▶ Highly available configurations

As part of planning complex configurations for OpsMgr 2007, remember the Assessment, Design, Planning, Proof of Concept (POC), Pilot, Implementation, and Maintenance stages. You should follow these stages, introduced in Chapter 4, "Planning Your Operations Manager Deployment," when planning your OpsMgr implementation.

Planning for Additional Components

An Operations Manager 2007 deployment includes several components that are required for any installation. These components include the Root Management Server (RMS), Operations Database Server, Operations Console, and the

Operations Manager Agents. For some organizations, these components may provide all the functionality required. However, a variety of additional components are available (introduced in Chapter 4) that can be used and should be considered part of your planning process. You should identify the requirements to use any or all of these components during the Assessment stage, in which you gather functional, business, and technical requirements for the OpsMgr design.

The business requirements we want to achieve with these additional functions include the following:

▶ Reporting and Trending

▶ Audit Collection

▶ Large Numbers of OpsMgr Agents

▶ Agents in Workgroups or DMZs

▶ Client Crash Monitoring

▶ Web-based Administration

We will review each of these concepts and discuss any planning-specific aspects of how to deploy them into an Operations Manager 2007 solution.

Reporting and Trending

With OpsMgr 2007, reporting is more closely integrated than it was with the Microsoft Operations Manager (MOM) 2005 product. Data now flows directly from the management server to the Operations database and the Data Warehouse database (if installed). It is important to understand that reporting is an optional component, and is not required. Once you install the reporting component, data begins to flow to the Data Warehouse database.

Although Operations Manager 2007 can function without the reporting features, there is a very limited subset of situations where this would be the recommended design. We can think of several examples:

▶ A nonproduction OpsMgr environment, used as a testing environment.

▶ An environment where server monitoring hardware is severely constrained that cannot effectively provide the additional functionality.

▶ An environment that does not function proactively or think it is important to understand utilization or historic trends.

   If you remember the basic stage of the Infrastructure Optimization (IO) model discussed in Chapter 1, "Operations Management Basics," there are customers who choose to stay in the basic stage and install only what they need. Those organizations may not consider reporting to be necessary functionality.

Although all these are potential cases where you might not deploy OpsMgr reporting capabilities; reporting is a core piece of functionality for the vast majority of OpsMgr deployments.

The OpsMgr 2007 reporting components provide both short-term reporting of data and long-term reporting of data (known as *trending*). Figure 5.1 shows an example of short-term reporting of data using information from the Operations database, which shows system uptime for agents in the environment. (Looks like we did a reboot on the Juggernaut server recently!)

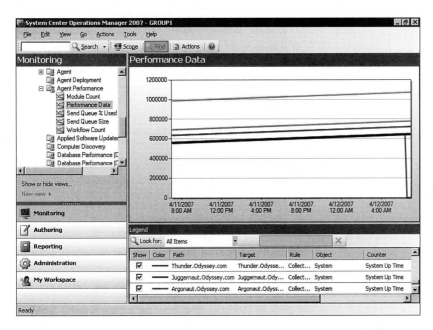

FIGURE 5.1   Agent system uptime.

By changing the default interval that OpsMgr uses to report data (performed in the Actions pane by clicking the Select Time Range button), we can also provide trending information within the Operations console. Figure 5.2 shows the number of SQL connections occurring on multiple SQL servers over a 1-week period.

The Reporting Server Component and Data Warehouse Server Component provide the Operations Manager 2007 reporting functionality for that information stored outside of the Operations database. These two components often run on the same physical system, but you can split them onto different systems. When planning to implement reporting within Operations Manager, you have the following items to consider:

▶ **What hardware will be necessary?** In Chapter 4, we discussed recommended hardware for these components and provided methods to estimate sizing for the Data Warehouse database.

▶ **Is high availability required?** With MOM 2005, it was common to have a highly available Operational environment (multiple management servers, clustered Operations database), but to not provide highly available reporting functionality. This was due to the nature of how MOM 2005 transferred data on a scheduled basis to its reporting database.

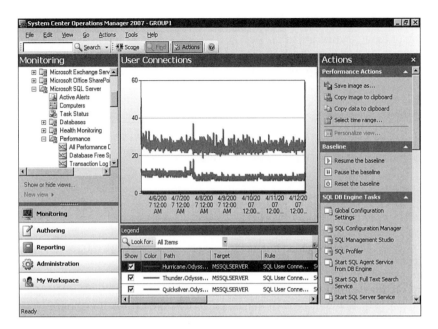

FIGURE 5.2   SQL user connections.

OpsMgr 2007 writes data directly to the data warehouse from the management server (this differs from MOM 2005, where data was moved using a DTS transaction). Because Operations Manager manages the data differently, we can now provide more real-time information for reporting.

With data now written in near real time (instead of batched nightly via DTS) to a data warehouse, the need to have a highly available Data Warehouse database becomes more important than it was in MOM 2005. We will review high availability options for all components within the "Planning for Highly Available Configurations" section of this chapter.

As a rule, we recommend that you deploy both the Reporting Server Component and the Data Warehouse Server Component in your environment unless there is a specific reason not to deploy them.

Audit Collection

Audit Collection Services (ACS) provides a way to gather Windows Security logs and consolidate them to provide analysis and reporting. From a planning perspective, it is important to understand that there are actually three components required for ACS to function:

- ▶ **ACS Database Server**—The centralized database repository for security information gathered from the servers in your environment.

- ▶ **ACS Forwarder**—This is a service deployed with the OpsMgr agent but not enabled by default.

▶ **ACS Collector**—Receives information from the ACS forwarders. The collector receives the events, processes them, and sends them to the ACS database server.

If ACS is a requirement for your OpsMgr environment, it should be one of the areas to focus on when working on the Proof of Concept (POC) stage. During the POC stage, you should determine design factors such as resource impacts on the OpsMgr agents and the ACS collector. The POC stage also provides a good starting point to identify sizing requirements for your ACS database. Additionally, the POC stage is an excellent time to determine any network impacts resulting from gathering security information from your OpsMgr agents.

Each of the three ACS components needs to be included in the OpsMgr design. The ACS collector and ACS database server both need to have sufficient hardware (see Chapter 4 for details on this). The number of forwarders that can report to a single collector varies depending on several items:

▶ The number of events the audit policy generates.

▶ The role of the computer that the forwarder is monitoring. (As an example, domain controllers will most likely create more events than member servers do.)

▶ The hardware specifications of the ACS collector server.

You can install multiple ACS collectors and multiple ACS database servers, but each ACS collector will report to its own ACS database server. Chapter 15, "Monitoring Audit Collection Services," provides recommendations around sizing for the ACS database, including a discussion on how to estimate database size based on projected loading scenarios.

Comparing ACS to Vista/Windows Server 2008 Event Forwarding

New functionality included with Windows Vista is *event forwarding*. Event forwarding allows you to collect events from multiple systems (Windows Vista or Windows Server 2008) and send (forward) them to another machine. Microsoft added this functionality (combined with moving away from text-based log files) to allow administrators to manage events from computers anywhere on the network. At first glance, this would appear to be able to do exactly what ACS does! However, there are significant differences:

▶ When gathering security event information, ACS uses a compression algorithm so that the information collected will have minimal impact on the network connection between the two systems.

▶ After gathering the data, ACS stores it in a SQL Server database that you can use to provide reports based on the collected information.

Overall, ACS provides a more robust solution to both collect and report on the information that is gathered.

The decision to deploy ACS as part of OpsMgr 2007 really depends on the requirements of your particular organization. Although the addition of ACS to the OpsMgr 2007 environment increases the complexity of the design, it also brings some significant functionality benefits, which should be seriously considered.

Large Number of OpsMgr Agents

With a single-management group design, if the requirements identified during the Assessment phase indicate that you will monitor more than 2000 agents or that redundancy is necessary, you will want to deploy additional management servers.

The first item to consider when adding multiple management servers is identifying the hardware requirements for those additional management servers. See Chapter 4 for recommended hardware specifications for the Management Server Component.

The next thing to consider is how you will distribute the agent load in your environment. Assign each management server a maximum of one-half of the agents it will be responsible for monitoring. As an example, in an environment where OpsMgr will be monitoring 4000 servers, the RMS would be primary for 2000 of the servers and secondary for the other 2000 servers. The additional management server would be primary for the second set of monitored servers, and secondary for the first set of agents. Figure 5.3 illustrates this example.

The ability to use multiple management servers in a management group increases the scalability Operations Manager can provide for your environment, and it increases the redundancy options available for your OpsMgr solution. The "Planning for Highly Available Configurations" section of this chapter provides further discussions on redundancy for all of the OpsMgr components.

Agents in Workgroups or DMZs

Operations Manager 2007 introduced the Gateway Server Component to provide the ability to monitor agents within untrusted domains or workgroups. MOM 2005 recommends, but does not require, using mutual authentication between the management server and the agent.

Mutual authentication is now required in Operations Manager 2007. Using the Gateway Server Component makes this viable in a DMZ, untrusted domains, and workgroup environments. This component gathers communications from the agents and forwards them to a management server on the other side of the firewall using port 5723.

To effectively plan to monitor agents with a gateway server, you need to provide hardware for that server (see Chapter 4 for hardware recommendations on this component) and consider the additional design impacts on OpsMgr. If you have a gateway server, it needs to report to a management server. We recommend that the specified management server handle only gateway server communication; because of load issues, we do not recommend that agents report directly to the same management server as a gateway server. However, you can configure multiple gateway servers to report to a single management server.

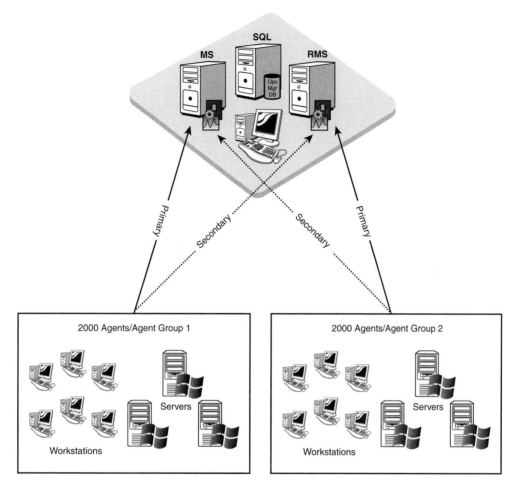

FIGURE 5.3   Management server agent distribution.

From a design perspective, be sure to plan for additional hardware for those management servers your gateway servers will report to. Figure 5.4 shows an example of an architecture using gateway servers.

The ability to monitor agents within workgroups, untrusted domains, or a DMZ in a secure manner is an important feature to consider when designing your OpsMgr solution. Chapter 10, "Complex Configurations," discusses gateway server implementation and configuration, and Chapter 11, "Securing Operations Manager 2007," discusses using certificates to communicate with workgroups, untrusted domains, and DMZs.

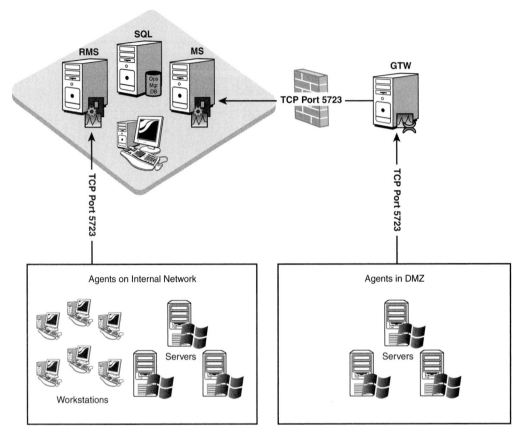

FIGURE 5.4   Gateway server architecture.

NOTE

Reduced Traffic when Deploying Agents with a Gateway Server Configuration

If you are deploying agents and going through a gateway server to the other domain, know that although the RMS sends the command to deploy the agents to the gateway server, the gateway server does the actual agent deployment. This means there is minimal traffic on the link between the RMS and the gateway server.

Client Crash Monitoring

Operations Manager 2007 adds functionality that captures, aggregates, and reports on application crashes (Dr. Watson errors). This functionality uses the OpsMgr 2007 feature called Agentless Exception Monitoring (AEM).

From a planning perspective, if there is a requirement to deploy AEM, there needs to be a plan that provides a server that stores the crash information and deploys a group policy to redirect the errors to the AEM server.

Clients running Windows 2000 or Windows XP use SMB (Server Message Block Protocol) to write crash information to a folder that you specify. Windows Vista clients use HTTP to send crash information. From a planning viewpoint, the server you will use must be identified and have sufficient space to store crash information. (Crash information can range from very small up to 8GB.)

The initial reaction to gathering Dr. Watson crash information and analyzing it is often a question of, why bother? The application crashes; the user restarts it. What's the big deal? The big deal here is that every crash affects end-user productivity and has an effect on the bottom line for a company. By collecting this information, identifying patterns, and working to resolve them, an organization can take a large step forward to becoming more proactive in situations affecting the end users in the organization, which in turn affects the productivity of that organization. An example of how we can use the data collected by AEM is shown in Figure 5.5, where we display a sample AEM report showing the top applications crashing over time.

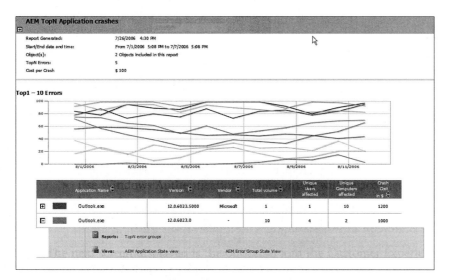

FIGURE 5.5   Agentless Exception Monitoring report.

NOTE

Collecting Crash Information for Server Applications

You also want to consider the case of server application crashes. In most organizations, if there were a major outage in a mission-critical application, nontechnical executives will be aware of the situation and will typically ask two questions: "What happened? And how are we going to prevent it in the future?" Collecting the information helps you answer "what happened," and working with support staff will help you answer "how to prevent it in the future."

Web-based Administration

The Web Console Server provides a web-based version of the Operations console. This console provides monitoring-only functionality, not the full functionality available within the Operations console. The Web console does not provide Administration, Authoring, or Reporting functionality.

Adding this component means that the various management servers providing web-based administration must have IIS installed and sufficient resources to provide the additional functionality. The Web console uses port 51908, so there may also need to be port exceptions made if this functionality is required outside the local area network (LAN).

From a planning point of view, the Web console is most likely installed on the RMS and any other management servers in your environment. This component is often used to provide access to OpsMgr for users who are either monitoring OpsMgr (helpdesk, or peripheral users of OpsMgr) or will not be using the Operations console regularly.

Figure 5.6 shows a sample architecture where each of the optional functions for OpsMgr is integrated, including reporting and trending, ACS, multiple management servers, servers in the DMZ, AEM, and Web console functionality. The graphic shows each component running on a separate server, but you can combine them in certain situations. Chapter 6, "Installing Operations Manager 2007," discusses in detail how to deploy these configurations.

For quick reference, Table 5.1 shows each of the different Operations Manager components and whether they can coexist on the same machine with other components (an "X" indicates that the two specific components can coexist on the same system).

As we have discussed, a variety of additional components are available that provide additional functionality in Operations Manager 2007. Properly planning for their deployment will go a long way toward developing a solid OpsMgr architecture that meets the requirements of your organization.

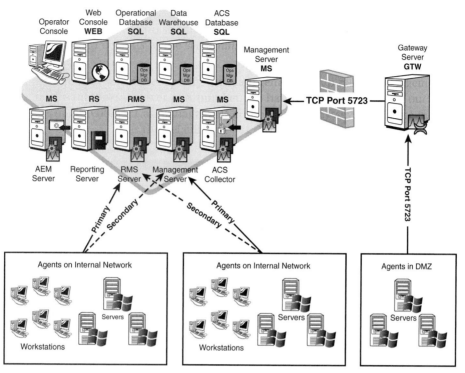

FIGURE 5.6   Operations Manager with all optional components.

TABLE 5.1   Operations Manager Components Coexistence

	RMS	Management Server	Gateway	Operations Database	Reporting	Data Warehouse	ACS Database	ACS Collector	ACS Forwarder	Operations Console	Web Console	AEM Server	Agent
RMS	X			X	X	X	X	X		X	X	X	1
Management Server		X		X	X	X	X	X		X	X	X	X
Gateway			X					X					X
Operations Database	X	X		X	X	X	X	X	X	X	X	X	X
Reporting	X	X		X	X	X	X	X	X	X	X	X	X
Data Warehouse	X	X		X	X	X	X	X	X	X	X	X	X
ACS Database	X	X		X	X	X	X	X	X	X	X	X	X
ACS Collector	X	X	X	X	X	X	X	X	X	X	X	X	X
ACS Forwarder				X	X	X	X	X	X	X	X	X	X

TABLE 5.1   Continued

	RMS	Management Server	Gateway	Operations Database	Reporting	Data Warehouse	ACS Database	ACS Collector	ACS Forwarder	Operations Console	Web Console	AEM Server	Agent
Operations Console	X	X		X	X	X	X	X	X	X	X	X	X
Web Console	X	X		X	X	X	X	X	X	X	X	X	X
AEM Server	X	X		X	X	X	X	X	X	X	X	X	X
Agent	1	X	X	X	X	X	X	X	X	X	X	X	X

¹*True except in clustered configurations*

Planning a Multihomed Deployment

Chapter 4 discussed the concepts of multihomed architectures and considerations for deploying multihoming. Examples when multihomed architectures may be appropriate include the following:

▶ Providing horizontal support silos (one group focusing on applications, another on services)

▶ Transitioning to OpsMgr 2007 from MOM 2005

▶ Testing or pre-production environments

By definition, a *multihomed* architecture is based on the concept of an agent reporting to two management groups; if we're considering multihoming, we must plan for a multiple-management group configuration. Deploying multiple management groups increases the number of servers required to provide the OpsMgr functionality.

Another item to consider when planning a multihomed deployment is the impact on the agent. Although Microsoft officially supports up to four management groups for multihoming (it may work beyond that, but Microsoft supports four), each additional management group an agent reports to increases the load on the client. This increase is because the agent is sandboxed (it keeps a separate area of memory) for each management group to which it is multihomed.

Testing multihomed architectures should focus on determining the resource impacts on the client as well as validating that rules from each management group do not impact each other.

Planning a Connected Management Group Deployment

As we discussed in Chapter 4, connected management groups in OpsMgr 2007 have replaced the functionality referred to as *tiering* in MOM 2005.

There are a number of reasons for using a connected management group design when you have multiple management groups:

▶ The number of agents to monitor exceeds supported limits.

▶ You need total separation of administration control to match geographic locations or to address bandwidth limits in your network environment.

▶ There is a requirement to facilitate communication between two OpsMgr environments in the case of a merger of two organizations.

Unlike MOM 2005 tiering, connected management groups do not forward alerts between management groups. This greatly simplifies the planning requirements for this type of a configuration. Because alerts are not forwarded, there is no increase in the volume of data sent from a lower-level management group (which was the case with MOM 2005).

From a planning perspective, here are the important items to remember

▶ This is a multiple-management group design.

▶ Each management group must be designed and have the hardware necessary to provide its required functions.

> **TIP**
>
> **What Can Be Seen in a Connected Management Group**
>
> When you open the Operations console and connect to another management group, you can see the alert information and can perform tasks on the connected management group. You cannot see performance data or state data for the connected management group.

From a networking perspective, a connected management group connects to the SDK service on the RMS in the other management group. When connected to the Operations console, your console is communicating with the RMS in the management group you connected to, which in turn talks to the RMS of the connected management group.

Figure 5.7 shows the communication between these connected management groups.

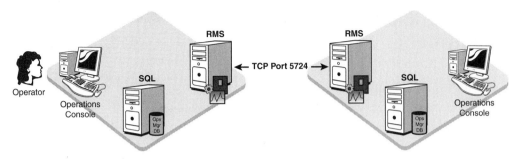

FIGURE 5.7   Connected management group communication.

Communication occurs via TCP port number 5724, so any firewall configurations must have this port open between the RMS in the first management group and the RMS in the second management group.

During the POC phase, you should spend time validating the ability to access alert information, performing tasks from each of the connected management groups, and validating communication between each of these environments.

In summary, connected management groups provide a simple method to bring together multiple management groups in OpsMgr 2007. If you plan your management groups properly, the amount of additional planning required to support connected management groups is minimal.

Planning for Multiple Domains

When planning to deploy Operations Manager 2007 in a multiple-domain environment, you have two primary areas to focus on:

▶ Providing secure authentication for all agents being monitored

▶ Identifying the accounts to use to perform functions in each of the domains

As we discuss in the "Agents in Workgroups or DMZs" section of this chapter, OpsMgr 2007 requires mutual authentication. Mutual authentication, in turn, depends on either Kerberos or certificate authentication.

Kerberos authentication is available within a domain, within a multidomain configuration where a two-way trust exists, or across a cross-forest trust. Figure 5.8 shows these authentication scenarios.

You can use certificates to provide mutual authentication for environments that cannot use Kerberos authentication, such as a DMZ, untrusted domains, and workgroup scenarios, which we discuss in the "Agents in Workgroups or DMZs" section of this chapter.

Kerberos Within a Domain

Odyssey.com

Kerberos in Multiple Domains with 2-Way Trusts

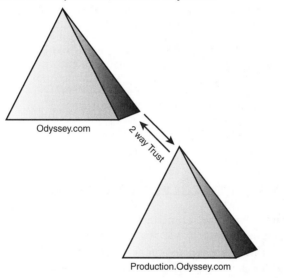

Odyssey.com

2 way Trust

Production.Odyssey.com

Kerberos in Multiple Domains with a Cross-Forest Trust

Cross-Forest Trust

Odyssey.com   Eclipse.com

FIGURE 5.8   Kerberos and mutual authentication scenarios.

> **TIP**
>
> **Communications Across Trust Boundaries**
>
> Chapter 11 discusses the gateway server and using certificates for mutual authentication.

The other concept to remember when planning for multiple domains is that each domain requires implementing security accounts with the necessary access rights. Keep the following points in mind:

- You will need an account with permissions to deploy agents to each system you will monitor. This often translates to a user account that is a member of the Local Administrators group on all systems or is a Domain Admin.

- You will also need accounts to perform the functions the management packs execute (as an example, the Active Directory management pack will need rights to perform specific checks on information within Active Directory).

To summarize, deploying OpsMgr into an environment with multiple domains requires mutual authentication and user accounts with access rights to perform the actions required in each domain that has monitored agents.

Planning Active Directory Integration

As part of planning your OpsMgr environment, you will want to determine what approach to use for deploying agents. In MOM 2005, the recommended method to deploy agents used the MOM user interface. This approach placed the console in the software distribution business, rather than embracing existing technologies to deploy the agent. OpsMgr 2007 includes multiple approaches to agent deployment. Methods include an enhanced push of the agent from the Operations console, manual installation, deployment via Systems Management Server/Configuration Manager, and automated configuration through Active Directory integration.

Active Directory Integration provides a method to auto-assign those agents to management servers. Assignment is dynamic, based on the configuration you define within the Operations console. If you have a medium to large-sized enterprise environment, we strongly suggest considering Active Directory integration as a primary deployment technique.

Requirements and prerequisites for using Active Directory integration include the following:

- You must configure AD integration in every domain that has agents.

- Each domain must be at the Windows 2000 Native or Windows Server 2003 functional mode.

▶ Run the MOMADAdmin tool to prepare each domain. This tool makes changes within Active Directory to create the required container, folder, and objects, and to assign the appropriate security rights. To run the tool, you must be a domain administrator with .NET Framework 2.0 installed on the system the tool will run on. Active Directory integration does not require any schema extensions.

In Chapter 9, "Installing and Configuring Agents," we review each of the available options for deploying the OpsMgr agent. In this chapter, we are focusing specifically on the planning aspects necessary for setting up Active Directory integration in your OpsMgr environment.

Planning How to Connect Operations Manager

The out-of-the box functionality that comes with Operations Manager 2007 includes strong management capabilities for Microsoft-based products. However, most organizations are heterogeneous and require monitoring functionality beyond what is available with a Microsoft-specific solution. Using product connectors, the OpsMgr Software Development Kit (SDK), and PowerShell can help address expanding functionality beyond a Microsoft-specific environment:

▶ Product connectors exist to connect OpsMgr to third-party products such as management solutions or helpdesk solutions.

▶ The OpsMgr SDK is a .NET library for developers to use when programming integration with OpsMgr 2007.

▶ The Command Shell is a customized instance of PowerShell and provides an extremely powerful command shell interface to Operations Manager.

Product Connectors

Depending on the requirements identified for your Operations Manager solution, you may need to integrate OpsMgr with other systems. Examples of this often include integrating with other management products or a trouble ticketing system.

As part of integrating with a trouble ticketing system, specific OpsMgr-generated alerts will create tickets within the ticketing system. As the status of the OpsMgr Alert changes, the status of the trouble ticket updates as well. Finally, if the ticket closes out in the trouble ticketing system, the alert is also resolved in OpsMgr.

Product connectors can be either unidirectional or bidirectional. Unidirectional connectors only forward alerts from OpsMgr to another product. Bidirectional connectors forward alerts from OpsMgr to another product and keep the products synchronized, as illustrated in the example of the trouble ticketing system.

Based on the deployment stages we discussed in Chapter 4 (Assessment, Design, Planning, POC, Pilot, Implementation, and Maintenance) there are multiple points where you would need to consider product connectors during your OpsMgr planning:

▶ Consider product connectors during the Assessment phase, and determine if there is a business requirement for their deployment. If a particular product connector is necessary, also assess the specifics of the connection—including which connector is required, the server OpsMgr will communicate with, the product and version of the product OpsMgr will connect to, and whether alerts will be forwarded in one or both directions. Integrate this information into the design document to describe how to implement the product connector.

▶ The Planning stage is where the majority of the work takes place related to deploying the product connector. The tasks that occur during the POC, Pilot, and Implementation steps are also determined in the Planning stage. To deploy a product connector effectively, we recommend you also deploy it as part of your POC environment. In the case of a product connector, this requires that a server in the POC environment run the third-party management solution. We suggest testing the product connector during a POC rather than first trying to incorporate it into a production environment!

▶ Tasks during the POC include downloading, installing, configuring, and documenting the process for the product connector. After the product connector is functional, test the connector to verify that alerts are forwarding between OpsMgr and the third-party management tool. You will want to stress-test the connector to determine how many alerts it can forward in a given period of time and to see if it can handle the load expected in the production environment.

▶ Finally, during the Pilot stage, use the document you created that describes the process used in the POC. This document should provide the steps needed to configure the connector in the pilot environment.

There are times when OpsMgr cannot match the business requirements without having to extend its functionality. To address this, Microsoft has provided both the Operations Manager SDK and the Command Shell.

Operations Manager SDK

Before we discuss the Operations Manager SDK, we want to avoid any confusion on the topic by clarifying the difference between the Operations Manager SDK and the Operations Manager SDK service:

▶ The Operations Manager SDK provides the ability to extend the capabilities of Operations Manager 2007.

▶ The Operations Manager SDK service (OpsMgr SDK service) primarily provides connectivity to database resources (see Chapter 3, "Looking Inside OpsMgr," for details on the OpsMgr SDK service).

If the SDK needs to be part of your OpsMgr solution, identify this requirement during the Assessment stage. As an example, if your OpsMgr requirements include a custom solution (such as a custom management console), you should identify the SDK as a potential tool. During the Assessment phase, identify in detail as much as possible regarding SDK requirements to provide effective information for the design. During the Design stage, these custom requirements should be included as part of the design document.

Actually creating the customized solution should occur during the POC stage. Within the POC, you can create and test the solution without potential impact to a production environment. Evaluate and update the solution during the POC phase to validate that it effectively meets your business requirements. You should deploy the custom solution into the production environment as part of the Pilot stage and roll it into full production during the Implementation phase.

Command Shell

As you evaluate how to meet the requirements identified for your OpsMgr solution, consider the Command Shell as a potential tool. The Operations Manager Command Shell is a customized instance of Windows PowerShell functionality that is available within Operations Manager. The Command Shell is extremely powerful and can perform multiple tasks, including tasks not available within the Operations Manager User Interface (UI). To provide effective information for your design, during the Assessment phase you will want to identify and specify as much information as possible regarding Command Shell requirements. These custom requirements for Command Shell would also be included within the design document.

You can use the Command Shell to do things that are difficult within the UI, such as enabling proxying on your Exchange servers, creating new management group connections, discovering Windows computers, and importing and exporting management packs. An excellent resource for information on Command Shell is available at http://blogs. msdn.com/scshell/.

As with the SDK, any customized solutions you identify should be created during the POC so they can be tested without affecting production systems. Deploy the customized solution during the Pilot phase and roll it into full production during the Implementation phase.

Planning for Highly Available Configurations

To ensure a highly available OpsMgr 2007 configuration, you should assess each of its components to determine the best method to make it highly available for your environment. We will review each of the components, discuss the impacts of an outage of each component, review high availability solutions for the component, and provide a recommended approach to provide high availability.

The requirement for a highly available configuration should be identified during the Assessment stage and integrated into the OpsMgr design document. Test these available configurations in POC, deploy them as part of the Pilot stage, and finally roll them into full production.

It is important to note that while high availability may be a business requirement, it may not apply to all components. As an example, if the need is to provide a high-availability solution on the monitoring aspects of OpsMgr only, you may not need to provide high availability for the ACS components of OpsMgr. In addition, high-availability requirements will only apply to those components you deploy in your particular OpsMgr configuration.

Root Management Server

As we previously discussed in Chapter 4, the RMS is the first management server installed. The RMS performs specific functions within the OpsMgr environment. At first glance, the role that this system provides seems similar in concept to that of an Active Directory FSMO (Flexible Single Master Operations) role. However, Active Directory can often function for some time without available FSMO roles. The impacts of an outage on the RMS are more apparent and include the following:

▶ You cannot open the Operations console (as shown in Figure 5.9). However, OpsMgr itself is still functioning, and information is still being gathered and stored in the Operations and Data Warehouse databases.

▶ Communication with gateway servers is interrupted.

▶ Connected management groups will not function because they connect via the RMS servers in each management group.

▶ The RMS may be providing management server functionality to agents that will need to be able to fail over to another management server in the management group to continue monitoring.

Based on the impacts to your OpsMgr installation when the RMS is not available, we strongly recommend providing a form of redundancy for this component.

A single redundancy option is available that provides automated failover of the RMS services: clustering. Microsoft supports an Active/Passive RMS cluster configuration that provides failover of the RMS service (as a generic resource type) to the passive node of the cluster. This capability offers a method for providing redundancy on this role to address situations such as patch management or temporary system outages. In the base version of OpsMgr 2007, if you do not initially install your environment with a clustered RMS, the only way to make the RMS clustered is by reinstalling Operations Manager 2007. It currently appears that this will change with OpsMgr Service Pack (SP) 1, and Microsoft will support that particular functionality approximately a month after releasing SP 1.

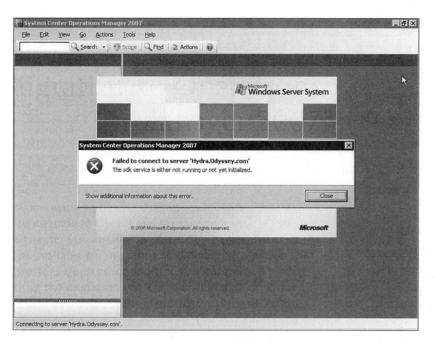

FIGURE 5.9   Root Management Server or OpsMgr SDK service unavailable.

TIP

Monitoring RMS Clustered Nodes

Prior to SP 1, you cannot install an agent on the RMS clustered nodes. These nodes must be configured as agentless managed.

A nonautomated method for addressing the loss of RMS functionality is to promote another management server to become the RMS. The ManagementServerConfigTool utility, located on the Operations Manager installation media in the \SupportTools directory, provides this functionality. The tool provides the ability to promote a management server to an RMS using the PromoteRMS option. Using this tool involves exporting the key from the RMS, importing it on a designated management server, promoting that management server to the RMS role, restarting services on the original RMS, and reconnecting to the console. We describe this procedure in detail in Chapter 12, "Backup and Recovery."

> **NOTE**
>
> **RMS Promotion Issues**
>
> The original released version of Operations Manager 2007 has an issue in promoting a management server to the RMS role. The issue is that data warehouse processing does not move correctly to the new RMS. The only workaround available prior to SP 1 is to continue to run the SDK service on the machine that was the previous RMS.

The recommended approach for providing a high-availability solution for the RMS is to deploy it on an Active/Passive cluster. Moving the RMS role to another management server is a manual (and not a trivial) process.

Management Servers

The Management Server Component provides redundancy and increased scalability for Operations Manager. The approach for providing redundancy for management servers is to have multiple servers, such that you can split the agent load if there is a server failure. The impact of a single management server failing is minor if other management servers are available to handle the load. Management servers (other than the RMS) do not support other redundancy approaches such as clustering and load balancing.

Gateway servers can be configured to use secondary management servers should their primary management server fail (we do not recommend using the RMS as a secondary management server).

In summary, the recommended approach for redundant management servers is to install sufficient management servers to distribute the agent load among them without exceeding the recommended limit of 2000 agents per management server.

Gateway Servers

The gateway server functionality provides a secure method for monitoring agents in untrusted domains or workgroups. Similar to the Management Server Component, redundancy is available by deploying multiple gateway servers.

If a gateway server is offline, the agents in the remote domain or workgroup will be unable to provide information to OpsMgr until a gateway server is available. Agents will queue up the data until the gateway server is available again, but if an agent queue fills up, data will be lost.

The gateway servers themselves can be configured to fail over to multiple management servers using the Command Shell Set-ManagedServer-GatewayManagementServer command.

To summarize, the recommended approach for redundancy is to install enough gateway servers to distribute the load of agents in the DMZ or workgroup and to not exceed the recommended limit of 200 agents per gateway server (see the Operations Manager 2007 Performance and Scalability White Paper at http://technet.microsoft.com/en-us/library/ bb735308.aspx). You should also configure the gateway server to fail over to multiple different management servers.

Reporting Servers

The Reporting Server Component uses SQL 2005 Reporting Services to provide web-based reports for Operations Manager. MOM 2005 reporting servers could be highly available by installing multiple servers into a web farm or through using a load-balancing solution (such as Microsoft Network Load Balancing, or NLB).

In OpsMgr 2007, the reporting server integrates directly with the Operations console, introducing another level of complexity into the equation. If you try to access the Reports space while the server is unavailable, an error message is generated about a failure loading the reporting hierarchy (shown in Figure 5.10). To avoid this type of message, it would be better to provide a more highly available reporting solution. You can configure the reporting server settings in the Operations console by navigating to Administration -> Settings -> Reporting.

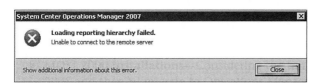

FIGURE 5.10   Reporting server unavailable.

Although it is not optimal or supported, you can access reports from outside the Operations console with a web browser at http://<servername>/reports. As long as reports are accessible outside of the Operations console, we can deploy multiple reporting servers and use NLB to provide redundancy. The major issue with this is keeping the reports synchronized between the various reporting servers; Chapter 10 discusses the available options.

There are currently no officially supported options to provide high availability for the Reporting Server Component in Operations Manager 2007.

Operations Database Servers

The Operations Database Component can be a single point of failure for the management group. If the management server loses connectivity to the Operations database, the management server buffers the data from the agents it manages. The size of this queue is 100MB by default. If the buffer fills, the management server stops taking data from agents until it reconnects with the database. Once the connection with the database is reestablished, the management server uploads the buffered information and resumes accepting data from its agents. If the Operations console is opened while the Operations database is down, no message is generated, but the Operations console hangs or "gets stuck" on loading, as shown in Figure 5.11.

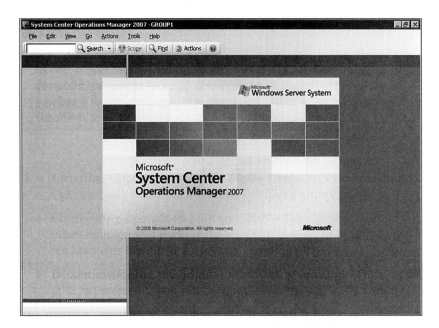

FIGURE 5.11   Application hang due to the Operations database being unavailable.

The recommended method that provides a high-availability solution for the Operations Database Component is clustering. Microsoft supports an Active/Passive Operations database using SQL Server clustering, providing database failover to the passive node of the cluster. Database clustering provides the ability to maintain the functionality of the Operations database in situations such as patch management and temporary outages.

Data Warehouse Servers

The Data Warehouse Component provides the long-term repository for Operations Manager 2007, similar to the Reporting Component used with MOM 2005. The impact of an outage is much more visible than it was in MOM 2005:

▶ If the MOM 2005 Reporting database was down, you could not pull up reports and could not transfer data from the Operations database to the Reporting database. Data transfer was a nightly job.

▶ In OpsMgr 2007, the Data Warehouse Component is part of the Operations console and written to in real time. This makes the impact of a failure much more apparent.

If you select the Reporting button in the Operations console while the database is down, a message appears (displayed in Figure 5.12) stating that the loading of the reporting hierarchy failed. To reconnect, close and reopen the Operations console after the data warehouse is back online.

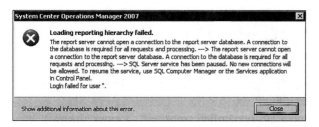

FIGURE 5.12   Data warehouse down.

The recommended method that provides a high-availability solution for the Data Warehouse Component is clustering. Microsoft supports an Active/Passive Operations database (SQL Server clustering), which provides failover of the database to the passive node of the cluster.

ACS Database Servers

The ACS Database Server Component provides the central repository for audit information gathered by Operations Manager. If the ACS database is unavailable, information continues to gather in the ACS collector's queue. The size of the ACS collector queue is configurable through Registry settings. See Appendix C, "Registry Settings," for details on Operations Manager Registry settings.

As the ACS collector queue fills, it will begin to stop accepting new connections from the forwarders and eventually disconnect additional forwarders. This leaves the forwarders holding the data until the ACS collector is available again.

The only currently supported method to provide a high-availability solution for the ACS Database Component is clustering. Microsoft supports using an Active/Passive ACS database (SQL Server clustering) providing database failover to the passive node of the cluster.

ACS Collector

The ACS Collector Component gathers events from the ACS forwarders, processes them, and sends the data to the ACS database. If a collector is down, it cannot take events from its forwarders or send them to the database. The agents (forwarders) do not have queues for ACS forwarding, because the Windows NT Security Event log provides that functionality. Several options are available for redundancy on the ACS Collector Component, although Microsoft does not support these:

> ▶ Establish a backup ACS collector server. At first, this seems like the logical approach, but the problem is that you cannot have two collectors reporting to the same ACS database. Because each collector writes to a different ACS database, using a backup

during a collector outage means security events are sent to a different database server during that outage. An additional ACS database server would also be required to provide this type of functionality.

▶ Provide redundancy for the collector with a cold standby collector. This computer is configured as a collector where the service is not running. This can be a cold server configured to report to the same ACS database server at the same time. To activate the server, you would turn on the service and copy over the AcsConfig.xml file (which controls the state of all the forwarders). This option provides a method to avoid adding a redundant ACS database server to provide high availability for the ACS Collector Server Component.

▶ Cluster the collector as a generic cluster service. The problem here is that this is not a supported configuration.

Overall, none of the options available for redundancy on the ACS collector server are optimal. Our recommended approach for providing redundancy on this component is to use a cold standby collector.

Agentless Exception Monitoring Share

OpsMgr's capability to capture, aggregate, and report on application crashes requires an AEM share and a communications port for the Vista clients. If these are unavailable, clients will not be able to report crash data.

There are currently no supported (or recommended) methods to provide high availability for this file share. Chapter 10 discusses potential approaches to provide redundancy for the AEM functionality.

Operations Console

The Operations console is the primary interface to access your Operations Manager environment. Loss of the console prevents performing any of the major actions available within the console, such as monitoring, authoring, reporting, and administration.

You can achieve high availability for the Operations console by installing multiple consoles. Install an Operations console on each management server (including the RMS) and on your OpsMgr administrators' workstations.

Web Console Servers

The Web console provides monitoring capabilities for OpsMgr for systems without an installed Operations console. Helpdesk personnel and subject matter experts (SMEs) will typically use the Web console. These groups require monitoring functionality only for their particular areas of focus.

During the time the Web Console Component is unavailable, the impact would be the inability for anyone to access this console. You can mitigate the impact of losing the Web console by installing the Operations console for primary Operations Manager users.

The recommended method for providing a highly available Web console solution is by installing multiple Web console servers and leveraging Network Load Balancing (NLB) or other load-balancing solutions. Using a load-balanced configuration, the Web console is accessible even if one of the Web console servers is unavailable.

Operations Manager Agents and ACS Forwarder

The last major components to discuss from a high-availability perspective are the agent itself and the ACS forwarder functionality, which is configurable with the agent. A nonfunctioning agent is unable to report information to the management servers, which in turn makes it unable to provide any current information for the Operations console.

Redundancy on the agent itself should not be required, because the agent's function is only to report information to the management servers. You can obtain high availability for the agent by configuring multiple management servers for the agent to report to.

However, the forwarder functionality has additional complexities when it comes to highly available configurations. If a forwarder is assigned to a collector that is unavailable, the forwarder cannot send its information and will rely on the Security Event log to store the information, which is sent to the ACS collector when it becomes available. You can define multiple collectors by changing the Registry settings on the forwarder. The change is at `HKLM\SOFTWARE\Policies\Microsoft\AdtAgent\Parameters`, within the `AdtServers` value. List each available collector in this key, with a hard return entered after each entry. To fail the forwarder back to the original collector, stop the service on the new collector so that the agent will fail itself back over to the original machine.

OpsMgr and Virtualization

A commonly asked question is whether one can "virtualize" the various Operations Manager 2007 components. There are two short answers for this: yes and no. Before delving into how to answer this for your environment, let's review the benefits to virtualization:

▶ Virtualization can reduce IT costs by consolidating multiple server operating systems onto a single physical server. Using a single server reduces the hardware costs and the space required to store your servers (thus decreasing the datacenter costs such as power and air conditioning).

▶ You can move virtual machines between different physical hardware easily, and it can be easier to back out changes made to the operating system than with a physical machine. For more details on the concepts and products available for virtualization, see Chapter 20, "Automatically Adapting Your Environment."

You will also want to consider your organization's policy regarding server virtualization. We include the following sidebar as an example of a virtualization policy.

A Sample Virtualization Policy

Virtualization should be considered as the recommended solution unless one of the following situations is true:

▶ The application is highly disk intensive and is a production system. Examples of this include applications such as Microsoft SQL Server and Exchange. Virtualization can be used on highly intensive applications in a nonproduction environment.

▶ The application in question is distributed and it is a best-practice approach to have at least one physical system running the application. A prime example of this is Active Directory, where at least one domain controller should be a physical machine.

▶ Applications have specific hardware requirements not supported within guest operating systems (either for functionality or for licensing), such as Host Bus Adapters (HBAs), parallel port connections, or USB port connections.

Virtualization for production servers should only occur on production-level host systems. The addition of a single production server as a guest operating system effectively makes the host operating system have to comply with production-level SLAs.

From an Operations Manager 2007 supportability perspective, Microsoft officially supports virtualization of the Operations Database Component, Data Warehouse Component, RMS, Management Server Component, Reporting Server Component, Gateway Server Component, and agents on virtual machines running Virtual Server 2005.

As you consider virtualization of these components, it is important to think about any limitations in the virtualization product. As an example, Virtual Server 2005 R2 is currently limited to a single processor and 3.6GB of memory. A single processor cannot effectively take advantage of multithreaded applications. Both of these restrictions may represent bottlenecks to the Operations Manager 2007 components. Both VMWare and updates to the Microsoft virtualization functionality should address these limitations (the Microsoft virtualization functionality is scheduled for release approximately 6 months after the release of Windows Server 2008).

Smaller environments, such as those with fewer than 100 agents, or lab/testing environments will make good candidates for virtualization. The smaller environments are not as likely to push the limits of the virtualized operating systems, and for the lab and testing environments performance does not generally have to be optimal.

Finally, when considering whether to use virtualization technologies, do not forget System Center Virtual Machine Manager (SCVMM), combined with Operations Manager 2007. The Virtual Machine Manager can identify likely candidates for virtualization and assist with the Physical-to-Virtual (PtoV) conversion of these systems. We discuss SCVMM more in Chapter 20.

Our own recommendation is that you *not* virtualize any of the database components of Operations Manager 2007 (Operations database, Data Warehouse database, and ACS database) because these are disk intensive and may also be processor intensive. A good document on SQL 2005 virtualization is available for download at http://download. microsoft.com/download/a/c/d/acd8e043-d69b-4f09-bc9e-4168b65aaa71/ SQLVirtualization.doc. (We include this link in Appendix E, "Reference URLs," for your convenience.) We also do not recommend virtualization of the Root Management Server Component, because this component is memory and processor intensive.

Some components we do recommend as candidates for virtualization include the following:

▶ **Gateway Server**—The gateway server is a good candidate for virtualization because it is not a very intensive OpsMgr component. As with other components, you should monitor it for bottleneck conditions. If the server is bottlenecked, consider the addition of another gateway server to split the load between the systems.

▶ **Management Server**—Management servers can be virtualized to provide failover capabilities for agents without adding additional hardware. The number of agents reporting to the management server should be determined by how much of a load can be sustained before the server starts to bottleneck. The number of agents reporting to the management server will vary depending on the performance of the host hardware and the type of agents being monitored, but will most likely be less than 2000 agents.

▶ **Reporting Server**—The SQL Server 2005 Reporting Server Component is an intensive application, but because it provides reporting functionality (which may not require the highest levels of performance given that reports can be scheduled), it may make a good candidate for virtualization.

▶ **Agents**—If your agents are virtualized, OpsMgr can monitor them, so that doesn't need to be a concern.

Determining whether you should virtualize any of the servers in your OpsMgr environment ultimately depends on the virtualization policy you have in place and the business requirements for your Operations Manager 2007 environment.

Summary

This chapter discussed the planning considerations when working with optional components and complex Operations Manager 2007 configurations.

With all of the different components available within Operations Manager 2007, it can be extremely complex or impossible to provide an OpsMgr configuration that is fully redundant and highly available. The good news is that for most organizations, highly available configurations are not required for all of the OpsMgr components. Chapter 10 moves from planning to detailed discussions of the steps involved in deploying complex configurations.

The next chapter discusses steps to implement OpsMgr, including optional components discussed in this chapter.

# CHAPTER 6

Installing Operations Manager 2007

This chapter discusses the procedures to install a new Operations Manager 2007 (OpsMgr) environment on the Windows 2003 operating system. The discussion will focus on prerequisites for installation and the installation steps required for each of the Operations Manager components discussed in Chapter 4, "Planning Your Operations Manager Deployment," and Chapter 5, "Planning Complex Configurations." We will also review two scenarios (single-server and multiple-server configurations) for an OpsMgr configuration and discuss potential troubleshooting areas. This chapter provides the information for a successful installation of each of the components of an OpsMgr configuration. We discuss more complex implementations, including multilocation deployments, connected management groups, multihomed deployments, and redundant configurations, in Chapter 10, "Complex Configurations."

By this point in the book, you should be very familiar with the concepts of how to plan for your deployment of Operations Manager 2007 (if you still have questions, go back and read Chapters 4 and 5). As a reminder, the specific stages we introduced in Chapter 4 included Assessment, Design, Planning, Proof of Concept, Pilot, Implementation, and Maintenance. This installation chapter should be applicable both during the Proof of Concept and Pilot phases of your OpsMgr deployment.

Planning Your Installation

Before actually running the setup program, you need to determine what your Operations Manager environment will look like. As part of the planning discussion in Chapters 4 and 5, you should have considered the following questions:

▶ Which server will run the Root Management Server (RMS)?

▶ Which server will host the Operations database?

▶ Will you be installing the Reporting Component? Which system will host the data warehouse?

▶ Will you be using Audit Collection Services and/or Agentless Exception Monitoring?

▶ Is redundancy for your OpsMgr solution a business requirement?

▶ What operating systems are running on the computers you want to manage?

▶ How many devices will you want to manage and where are they located? What type of activities do these systems perform?

Prior to your installation, be sure you have completed the discovery in the planning chapters of this book. To assist as a quick reference, we have developed a pre-installation checklist for your use. The checklist includes the major components you will be installing and information you will need to have ready prior to beginning the installation.

TIP

On the CD

The Operations Manager 2007 pre-installation checklist, OpsMgr Pre-installation Checklist.xls, is included with the CD for this book.

Installation Prerequisites

The specific prerequisites for the installation of your OpsMgr environment depend on the component you will be installing. Microsoft designed Operations Manager 2007 to be simple to install, with most of the OpsMgr components installed through wizards launched from the System Center Operations Manager 2007 Setup (SetupOM.exe).

Install from SetupOM.exe

We recommend installation using the SetupOM executable rather than running the individual executables that install the components shown on the wizard itself. The wizard correctly identifies which version of the executable to run for your environment (amd64, ia64, or i386) and enables logging. The programs run by SetupOM.exe include the following:

▶ Check Prerequisites:

  preqreq/*<path>*/prereqviewer.exe

▶ Install Operations Manager 2007:

  server/*<path>*/MOM.msi

▶ Install Operations Manager 2007 Agent:

  agent/*<path>*/MOMAgent.msi

▶ Install Operations Manager 2007 Reporting:

  server/*<path>*/Reporting2007.msi

▶ Install Audit Collection Server:

  ACS/*<path>*/AdtSetup.exe

▶ Install MOM 2005 to OpsMgr 2007 Migration Tool:

  Support Tools/*<path>*/MomMigration.msi

The *<path>* variable refers to the folder containing the bits for the amd64 or i386 hardware platform. The Agent and the Migration tool can also be installed on ia64 hardware.

Table 6.1 includes the complete list of all the command-line parameters for OpsMgr 2007 components, including Audit Collection. You can use the syntax shown in Table 6.1 from the command line to install the various components, or with System Center Configuration Manager to automate deploying the OpsMgr components.

One of the huge benefits to the installation approach implemented with OpsMgr is that it is very easy to identify and resolve any missing prerequisites for your installation. As shown in Figure 6.1, installation options include the following components:

▶ Operations Manager 2007

▶ Operations Manager 2007 Agent

▶ Operations Manager 2007 Reporting

▶ Audit Collection Server

▶ MOM 2005 to OpsMgr 2007 Migration tool

We will review each of these options (except for the OpsMgr 2007 Migration tool, which we discuss in Chapter 7, "Migrating to Operations Manager 2007") discuss their prerequisites and the installation process itself.

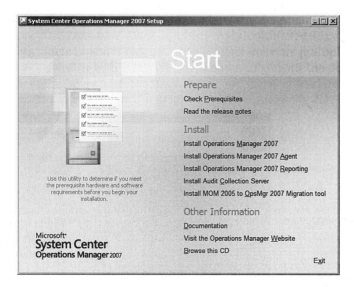

FIGURE 6.1   Setup splash screen for OpsMgr.

There are a number of prerequisites either common to all OpsMgr components or that you should address prior to implementing OpsMgr. These prerequisites include server hardware, domain requirements, required Windows accounts, and the order for installing OpsMgr components.

You should have identified the hardware required for the Operations Manager components during the Design phase. We presented recommended hardware specifications in Chapter 4.

Windows Domain Prerequisites

You must install Operations Manager 2007 in a Windows Server domain environment, but the servers it manages do not necessarily need to be in that (or any) domain. The Windows domain functional level must be Windows 2000 Native, Windows Server 2003 Interim, or Windows Server 2003; prior to installing OpsMgr, you need to raise the domain to at least one of these functional levels if it is not already. Although Operations Manager 2007 does not make any schema changes, it can create containers within Active Directory based on your agent deployment strategy. Microsoft does not recommend installing OpsMgr components on a domain controller; this generates a warning message when you check the OpsMgr prerequisites.

TABLE 6.1   OpsMgr Command Line Parameters for Installation

Component	Command
Agent — MOMAgent.msi	msiexec.exe /I \\path\Directory\MOMAgent.msi /qn /l*v \logs\MOMAgent_install.log USE_SETTINGS_FROM_AD=0 MANAGEMENT_GROUP=<Management Group Name> MANAGEMENT_SERVER_DNS=<Management Server DNSName> ACTIONS_USE_COMPUTER_ACCOUNT=0 ACTIONSUSER=<Action Account> ACTIONSDOMAIN=<Domain> ACTIONSPASSWORD=<Password>
Typical — MOM.msi msiexec.exe /i	msiexec.exe /I \\path\Directory\MOM.msi /qn /l*v \logs\ MOMTypical_install.log ADDLOCAL=ALL USE_SETTINGS_ FROM_AD=0 MANAGEMENT_GROUP=<Management Group Name> MANAGEMENT_SERVER_DNS=<Management Server DNSName> SQLSVR_INSTANCE=<ServerName\Instance> ADMIN_ROLE_GROUP= "Domain/Account" ACTIONS_USE_ COMPUTER_ACCOUNT=0 ACTIONSUSER=<Action Account> ACTIONSDOMAIN=<Domain> ACTIONSPASSWORD=<Password> SDK_USE_COMPUTER_ACCOUNT=0 SDK_ACCOUNT= <SDK Account> SDK_DOMAIN=<Domain> SDK_PASSWORD= <Password>
Database — MOM.msi msiexec.exe /i	msiexec.exe /i \\path\Directory\MOM.msi /qn /l*v \logs\ MOMDB_install.log ADDLOCAL=MOMDB USE_SETTINGS_ FROM_AD=0 MANAGEMENT_GROUP=<Management Group Name> SQLSVR_INSTANCE=<ServerName\Instance> DB_SIZE=500 ADMIN_ROLE_GROUP=<AD Security Group Name> DATA_DIR=<SQL data files folder> LOG_DIR= <SQL log files folder>
Server — MOM.msi	msiexec.exe /i \\path\Directory\MOM.msi<file:///\\path\ Directory\MOM.msi> /qn /l*v \logs\MOMServer_install.log ADDLOCAL=MOMServer USE_SETTINGS_FROM_AD=0 MANAGEMENT_GROUP=<Management Group Name> MOM_ DB_SERVER=<ServerName\Instance> ACTIONS_USE_ COMPUTER_ACCOUNT=0 ACTIONSUSER=<Action Account> ACTIONSDOMAIN=<Domain> ACTIONSPASSWORD=<Password> SDK_USE_COMPUTER_ACCOUNT=0 SDK_ACCOUNT=<SDK Account> SDK_DOMAIN=<Domain> SDK_PASSWORD= <Password>
Console — MOM.msi	msiexec.exe /i \\path\Directory\MOM.msi /qn /l*v \logs\ MOMUI_install.log ADDLOCAL=MOMUI USE_SETTINGS_ FROM_AD=0 MANAGEMENT_GROUP=<Management Group Name> ROOT_MANAGEMENT_SERVER_DNS=<RMS DNSName>

TABLE 6.1   Continued

Component	Command
Web Console — MOM.msi	msiexec.exe /i *path**Directory*\MOM.msi /qn /l*v \logs\ MOMUI_install.log ADDLOCAL=MOMWebConsole WEB_ CONSOLE_AUTH_TYPE=0 ROOT_MANAGEMENT_SERVER_DNS= *\<RMS NetbiosName>* ("0" is windows auth and "1" is Forms auth)
Data Warehouse — Reporting2007	msiexec.exe /i *path**Directory*\Reporting2007.msi /qn / l*v "D:\LOGS\REPORTING_INSTALL.LOG" ADDLOCAL= "MOMREPORTINGDB" SQLSVR_INSTANCE="*\<ServerName\ Instance>*" MOMREPORTINGDBNAME="*SCOMDW*" DB_SIZE= "*1000*"
Reporting Server — Reporting2007.msi	msiexec.exe /i *path**Directory*\Reporting2007.msi /qn / l*v "D:\LOGS\REPORTING_INSTALL.LOG" ADDLOCAL= "MOMREPORTING" SQLSVR_INSTANCE="*\<ServerName\ Instance>*" MOMREPORTINGDBNAME="*\<SCOMDW>*" MGSERVER=*\<Management Server Name>* PREREQ_ COMPLETED="1" REPORT_SERVER_FULL_HTTP_PATH="http:// %COMPUTERNAME%:80/*ReportServer$Instance*<http:// %25computername%25/*ReportServer$Instance>*" DATAREADER_USER=*\<Data Reader Account>* DATAREADER_ PASSWORD=*\<Password>* DATAREADER_DOMAIN=*\<Domain>* DBWRITEACTIONSUSER=*\<DBWrite Action Account>* DBWRITEACTIONSPASSWORD=*\<Password>* DBWRITEACTIONSDOMAIN=*\<Domain>*
Gateway Server — MOMGateway.msi	msiexec /i *path**Directory*\MOMGateway.msi /qn / l*v *D*:\GATEWAY_SERVER_INSTALL_1.LOG ADDLOCAL= MOMGateway,MOMNonRootServer SECURE_PORT=5723 MANAGEMENT_GROUP=*\<Management Group Name>* MANAGEMENT_SERVER_DNS=*\<Management Server Name>* IS_ROOT_HEALTH_SERVER=0 ROOT_MANAGEMENT_SERVER_ AD=*\<RMS_Name>* ROOT_MANAGEMENT_SERVER_DNS= *\<RMS_Name>* ROOT_MANAGEMENT_SERVER_PORT=5723 ACTIONS_USE_COMPUTER_ACCOUNT=0 ACTIONSUSER= *\<Action Account>* ACTIONSDOMAIN=*\<Domain>* ACTIONSPASSWORD=*\<Password>*
Audit Collection Server — AdtSetup.exe	*path**Directory*\AdtSetup.exe /i /s /p:*ACSInstallParameters.xml* The ACSInstallParameters.xml file contains your settings.

Syntax for these commands is also available at http://blogs.technet.com/momteam/archive/2007/ 12/05/opsmgr-2007-command-line-parameter-complete-list.aspx.

Security Accounts

Prior to starting the installation process, you should also create the Windows security accounts required for installation. Table 6.2 lists the required security accounts as well as the account name used for each within this book.

TABLE 6.2   OpsMgr Required Security Accounts

Required Service Account	Name Used in This Book
Management Server Action account	OM_MSAA
Agent Action account	OM_AAA
Gateway Action account	OM_GWAA
Data Warehouse Write account	OM_DWWA
Data Reader account	OM_DRA
Software Development Kit and Configuration Service account	OM_SDK

We discuss details on these accounts, including the required security permissions, in Chapter 11, "Securing Operations Manager 2007."

Software Requirements

Obtain all the software required to deploy Operations Manager prior to installing the components.

> **TIP**
>
> **Installation Prerequisites**
>
> As a rule, go for "green" on your prerequisites for the OpsMgr components. To install OpsMgr, you have to fix the critical issues (red). OpsMgr will install if there are warnings (yellow). However, the installation will not be a recommended configuration and can result in a solution that may not perform optimally.

The prerequisite software varies depending on what component you installed, but the full list of software to have available during the installation includes the following:

- ▶ Operations Manager 2007.

- ▶ Windows Server 2003 Standard or Enterprise Edition.

- ▶ Windows Server 2003 Service Pack 1 or 2.

- ▶ Microsoft SQL 2005 Standard or Enterprise Edition.

- ▶ Microsoft SQL 2005 Service Pack 1 or 2.

▶ .NET Framework 3.0.

   The X86 version is available for download at
   http://go.microsoft.com/fwlink/?LinkId=74965.

   You can download the X64 version at
   http://go.microsoft.com/fwlink/?LinkId=74966.

▶ Windows PowerShell (available for download at http://www.microsoft.com/win-
   dowsserver2003/technologies/management/powershell/download.mspx).

TIP

Service Packs Approach

In general, although service packs address bug fixes, they also tend to introduce new
sets of features and issues. This is true for operating systems and monitored applications as well as OpsMgr itself. Always thoroughly test service packs before introducing
them into a production environment.

Order of Installation

Although the recommended order for installation depends on the components you are
installing, there are certain components that you cannot install before others. As an
example, the first management server installed is always the RMS, and you cannot install
the RMS before installing the Operations database.

The following list is a recommended order for installation, which focuses on getting the
core components installed first (including all components required to manage agents,
such as the RMS, Management Server[s], Audit Collection Server[s], and Gateway
Server[s]), followed by optional components and, finally, the deployment of OpsMgr
agents. The components are as follows:

▶ Operations Database Server

▶ Root Management Server, Operations Console, and Web Console Server

▶ Management Servers

▶ Reporting Server and Data Warehouse Server

▶ ACS Database Server and ACS Collector Server

▶ Gateway Servers

▶ Agentless Exception Monitoring

▶ Operations Manager Agents

▶ ACS Forwarder

Single-Server Operations Manager Installation

You can install almost all the Operations Manager 2007 components on a single system. A single server (with sufficient hardware) can run the RMS, Operations Database, Operations Console, Web Console, Reporting Server, Data Warehouse Database, ACS Collector, and ACS Database Components—although this typically is not recommended, except for small environments or testing environments. If you are installing all the components on a single server, check to see whether you can use System Center Essentials, which may be a better fit for your needs. We discuss System Center Essentials and selection criteria in Chapter 4. (System Center Essentials also includes configuration management capabilities, such as software distribution and updates, and limited software and hardware inventory capacities for small environments.) There are three steps when performing the single-server installation:

▶ The first step of the installation process involves running the Install Operations Manager 2007 option and choosing all the components available. This installs the Operations database, RMS, Operations console, and Web console.

▶ The next step of the process is to run the Install Operations Manager 2007 Reporting option and then choose all the components available. This installs the Reporting Server and Data Warehouse Server Components.

▶ The third step is to install the ACS-related components by using the Install Audit Collection Server option. This installs the ACS Collector and ACS Database Server Components.

These are also the steps performed when installing the OpsMgr components onto multiple servers. We discuss the details of how to install these components within the next sections of this chapter.

Multiple-Server Operations Manager Installation

For our example, we will show the process for installing a multiple-server Operations Manager configuration. You can install each of these components (roles) individually, but we will gather them by function for our example. Table 6.3 lists the servers we are using in our fictitious organization (Odyssey) and their roles.

Figure 6.2 displays the server configuration we are installing, for reference throughout this chapter.

You can install the majority of the OpsMgr components from the setup screen. These include the Operational Database, Management Server (and Root Management Server), Operations Console/PowerShell, Web Console, Reporting Server, and the Data Warehouse Server Components. The only components not installed from the setup screen are the Gateway Server (discussed in Chapter 10) and Client Monitoring functionality, which we introduce in Chapter 16, "Client Monitoring."

TABLE 6.3   OpsMgr Servers in and Roles

Server	Operations Manager Role
Thunder	Operations Database Server
Hydra	Root Management Server, Operations Console, Web Console Server
Quicksilver	Reporting Server and Data Warehouse Server
Hurricane	ACS Collector Server
Fireball	ACS Database Server
Ambassador	Gateway Server
Hydra	Agentless Exception Monitoring, Client Monitoring

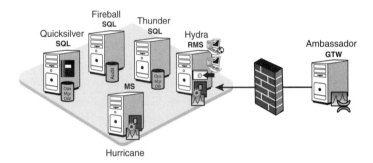

FIGURE 6.2   Multiple-server Operations Manager 2007 configuration.

Operations Database Server

For production systems monitoring more than 100 servers, we recommend a dedicated server for the Operations database. Figure 6.3 shows the prerequisites for installing the Operations Database Component, which include the following items:

▶ 2048MB of memory. This is recommended but not required; the prerequisite checker warns if the hardware on which you are running the prerequisite checker has less than 2048MB of memory.

▶ Windows Server 2003 Service Pack 1 or Service Pack 2.

▶ SQL Server 2005 and then SQL Server 2005 Service Pack 1 (or Service Pack 2). When installing SQL Server 2005, check the option to install the Workstation components, Books Online, and development tools. Also, be sure to reboot your database server after completing the installation of any SQL Server 2005 Service Pack.

Operations Manager 2007 does not support using SQL Server 2000 to provide database functionality for any of the Operations Manager components (Operational Database, Data Warehouse, or ACS Database).

FIGURE 6.3   Prerequisite report for Operations database installation.

TIP

Identifying SQL Server Versions

KB article 321185 describes the process of identifying the installed SQL Server Service Pack version and edition of SQL Server. This is available at the Microsoft support website at http://support.microsoft.com/kb/321185.

Now we will walk through the installation itself. The following steps are performed on the computer that will be hosting the Operational database:

1. After addressing prerequisite requirements, the installation process goes through a standard System Center Operations Manager 2007 Setup Wizard. The first screen shown is a typical welcome to the wizard screen, which you move past by clicking Next.

2. The next screen displays the End-User License Agreement, which has to be accepted (check the I accept the terms in the license agreement option) and click Next to continue.

3. On the Product Registration screen, you need to enter the user name, organization, and 25-digit CD key, which is on the back of the CD case. (If your organization has a volume licensing agreement with Microsoft, this key is available on the Microsoft Volume License website.) Click Next to continue with the wizard.

4. The next screen is where you identify what OpsMgr components you will be installing. When installing the Operations database on a separate database server, this screen is where you choose only the Database Component and uncheck all the other components. Figure 6.4 shows the configuration to have the Database Component installed but none of the other components (displayed with a red X on them).

After you select the Database Component, the installation program automatically (re)runs the prerequisite checker to validate that the system has all required prerequisites installed. In our example, the checker passed with warnings due to the amount of memory available on the system selected for the Operations Database Server (shown in Figure 6.5). You can click on View Log to view information in the report.

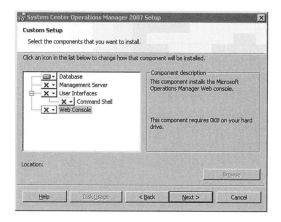

FIGURE 6.4   Custom Setup screen for the Operations database.

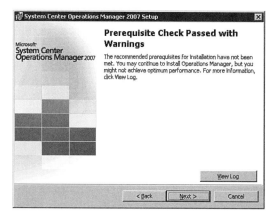

FIGURE 6.5   Prerequisite check passed with warnings.

5. On the next screen of the wizard, you need to specify the management group name for your Operations Manager 2007 environment. This name is case-sensitive. The management group name should be unique (if you have existing Operations Manager 2007 or MOM 2005 environments) and easy to identify.

For our environment, we are using the management group name GROUP1, as shown in Figure 6.6. Note that once it's specified, you cannot change the management group name without reinstalling the management group!

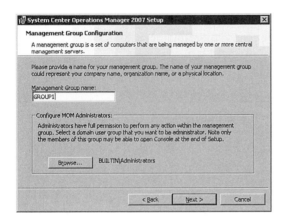

FIGURE 6.6   Management group configuration.

6. Next, identify the SQL Server database instance that the Operations database will run in. Because our environment is running SQL with a single (default) instance, the wizard defaults to the name of the server, as shown in Figure 6.7.

If you are installing to a SQL server instance, the syntax would be the servername\instance. For example, for our Thunder server having a named instance of Instance2, the syntax would be Thunder\Instance2.

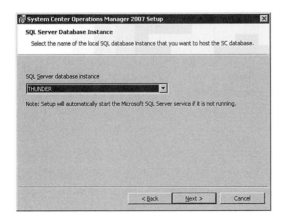

FIGURE 6.7   SQL Server instance.

TIP

Different Service Names with SQL Server Instances

The service names for Microsoft SQL Server services are different if you have installed named instances of SQL Server—the format would be MSSQL$*<instance>* and SQLAgent$*<instance>*.

7. After we identify the instance into which the Operations database will install, the next configuration screen sets the database and log file options. As shown in Figure 6.8, this screen allows us to specify the name of the database, the database size, and the location of the data files (set on the Advanced tab).

NOTE

Database Size Estimates

Chapter 4 discusses approaches to providing estimated sizes for the Operations and Data Warehouse databases. Microsoft also has the System Center Capacity Planner 2007 tool, which will provide sizing information for OpsMgr and is available at no cost. Note that the version released in late 2007 does not yet provide sizing information or the capability to model the OpsMgr environment. Microsoft says OpsMgr support will be available in an "out of band" release.

Information on the current version of System Center Capacity Planner is available at http://www.microsoft.com/systemcenter/sccp/default.mspx.

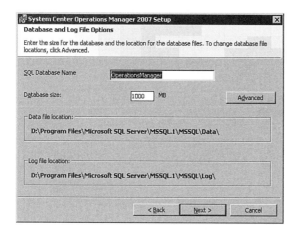

FIGURE 6.8   Operations database and log file options.

8. The next screen of the wizard asks whether you want to send error reports to Microsoft. The default configuration on this is not checked, but you can check it and select one of the suboptions:

▶ Automatically send error reports to Microsoft.

▶ Prompt the user for approval before sending the error reports to Microsoft.

We have chosen the option to send error reports to Microsoft automatically, as shown in Figure 6.9.

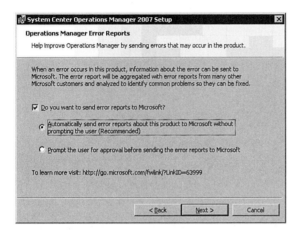

FIGURE 6.9   Operations Manager Error Reports screen.

Real World—Sending Error Reports to Microsoft

Most administrators we work with tend not to send the error reports to Microsoft and are not aware of any benefits to sending the reports, because it is not really known if anyone is doing anything with this information. What happens behind the scenes is that Microsoft uses the information, generating reports off the summarized data so it can identify errors commonly occurring in the field. Microsoft then prioritizes errors to work on based on those that are causing the most issues.

We have met the person responsible for working with this information, and we can state with confidence that the data is actually used to a positive benefit. Sending in your error reports is constructive, and as a result it is highly recommended. You can also change this configuration after installation. In the Operations console, navigate to Administration -> Settings -> Privacy -> Operational Data Reports and then check the option to send operational data reports to Microsoft. (The Operational Data Reports are described in Chapter 16.)

9. On the next screen, you specify if you want to use Microsoft Update to keep the system up to date with various security and other updates. If you do not currently have a method of providing patch management to the servers in your environment and you have configured your server to have access to the Internet, you should check the option to use Microsoft Update, as shown in Figure 6.10.

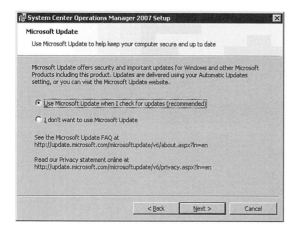

FIGURE 6.10   Microsoft Update specification and configuration.

10. After the Microsoft Update screen, the next screen indicates that Operations
Manager is ready to install. Click Install to continue with the installation process.
Once the installation is completed, the wizard finishes and displays the Completing
the System Center Operations Manager 2007 Setup Wizard screen (see Figure 6.11.)

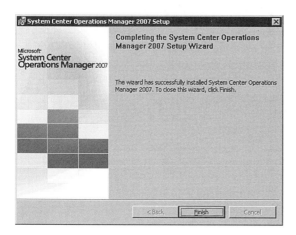

FIGURE 6.11   Wizard screen to finish the installation.

Closing this screen completes the installation of the Operations Database
Component. If you want to validate that the installation was successful, you can use
the Microsoft SQL Server Management Studio to validate that the Operations
database was created correctly.

Root Management Server and Consoles

Now that we have installed the Operations database, we can install the RMS. You can install the Root Management Server Component without either the Operations console or Web console. For most environments, we recommend installing multiple components on this server, including the RMS, Operations Console/PowerShell, and the Web Console components for consistency with the other management servers in your environment. Use the RMS for the Operations Web consoles only when consoles on other computers are unavailable, because the RMS functionality is very resource intensive. The prerequisites for these components include the following (which we display in Figure 6.12):

▶ 2048MB of memory.

▶ Windows Server 2003 Service Pack 1 or 2.

▶ ASP.NET 2.0.

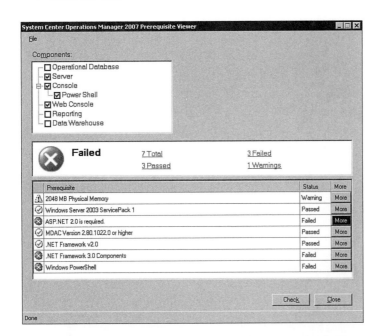

FIGURE 6.12   Prerequisite errors on Root Management Server installation.

Real World—ASP.NET 2.0 Prerequisite Failure

Even after you install ASP.NET through the Add or Remove Programs Control Panel applet -> Add/Remove Windows Components -> Application Server (checking the ASP.NET and Internet Information Services options), the Operations Manager prerequisite checker may still fail, stating that ASP.NET 2.0 is required but not enabled. This failure occurs if you installed Internet Information Services (IIS) *after* you installed the .NET Framework 2.0. Take the following approaches to try to resolve this:

▶ Open a command prompt and navigate to the *%windir%*\microsoft.net\ framework\v2.0.50727 folder (the 64-bit platform version has the same name but is located under *%windir%*\microsoft.net\framework64\v2.0.50727). Within this folder, type the command `aspnet_regiis -i`.

▶ If the prerequisite checker still fails on the ASP.NET prerequisite, open Internet Information Services -> Web Service Extensions. For the ASP.NET v2.0.50727 option, set it to Allowed (if it is not already).

▶ If the prerequisite checker continues to fail, do a Start -> Run `IISReset` to reset the website.

Sometimes you just need to close the prerequisite checker and reopen it to get it to clear out the error.

▶ MDAC 2.80.1022.0 or higher.

▶ Active Directory (AD) must be available; the installation process communicates with AD to verify service account information.

▶ .NET Framework v2.0.

▶ .NET Framework 3.0 components. If you did not download these components prior to this point of the installation process, you can click the More information button (highlighted in Figure 6.12), which provides the URL to download the framework components.

▶ Windows PowerShell. We recommend installing PowerShell if you are installing the Operations console. If you did not download PowerShell prior to this point of the installation process, you can click the More information button, which provides the URL to download PowerShell.

▶ If you will be editing management pack knowledge information in the Operations console, you must install Microsoft Office Word 2003 (or higher) with the .NET Programmability feature and Microsoft Visual Studio 2005 Tools for the Microsoft Office System. The Visual Studio 2005 Tools are available for download at http://go.microsoft.com/fwlink/?LinkId=74969.

Microsoft.interop.security.azroles.dll Not Registered in the Global Assembly Cache

The Operations Manager 2007 prerequisite checker may return an error that the Microsoft.interop.security.azroles.dll is not registered in the global assembly cache. This problem occurs when the DLL is no longer registered after you install a Windows Server service pack. If you are running with Windows Server 2003 Service Pack 1, apply the hotfix available at http://support.microsoft.com/kb/915786. For Service Pack 2, perform the following steps to re-register the assembly.

1. From a CMD prompt on the system drive, type the following:

   CD *%windir%*\Microsoft.NET\AuthMan\1.2

2. Execute the following command:

azrlreg register Microsoft.interop.security.azroles.dll

The azrlreg utility is not present with Windows Server 2003 Service Pack 1, only on SP 2. This problem is known to affect Windows Server 2003 SP 2 slipstream builds only and not SP 1–to–SP 2 upgrades.

Thank you to Clive Eastwood for finding this and documenting it at http://blogs. technet.com/cliveeastwood. This information is now published as a KB article, available at http://support.microsoft.com/kb/937292.

After all prerequisites have been addressed, the process to install the RMS and Operations Console can begin. Installing these components is very similar to the steps performed when we installed the Operations database in the "Operations Database Server" section of this chapter. Perform these steps:

1. The OpsMgr Setup Wizard displays the startup screen; you will accept the license agreement and proceed to the product registration screen. After these screens, select the components you will install. These components are shown in Figure 6.13 and include all the components available (Management Server, User Interfaces, Command Shell, Web Console), except for the Database Component, which you have previously installed.

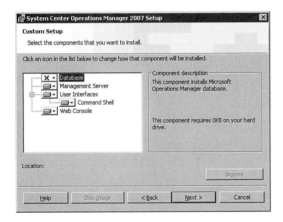

FIGURE 6.13   Custom installation for all components except for the Operations Database Component.

2. After you've chosen these components, the prerequisite checker runs. You then need to specify the database server, name, and port that contains the Operations database. For our environment, we are using the Thunder server with the OperationsManager database on port 1433. Enter the FQDN (Fully Qualified Domain Name) of the server to avoid any potential name resolution errors, as we show in Figure 6.14. OperationsManager is the default name for the Operational database.

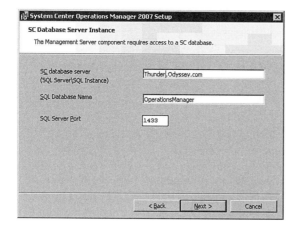

FIGURE 6.14   Database server instance.

3. The next screen prompts you to identify a Management Server Action Account. As we discuss earlier in the "Security Accounts" section of this chapter, you should have already identified and configured each of these accounts prior to this step in the installation process. The account needs at least the following privileges:

   ▶ Member of the Users group

   ▶ Read access to the Windows Event logs

   ▶ Member of the Performance Monitor Users group

   ▶ Manage Auditing and Security Log permission

   ▶ Allow Log on Locally permission

   We are using the OM_MSAA account in the Odyssey domain, as displayed in Figure 6.15.

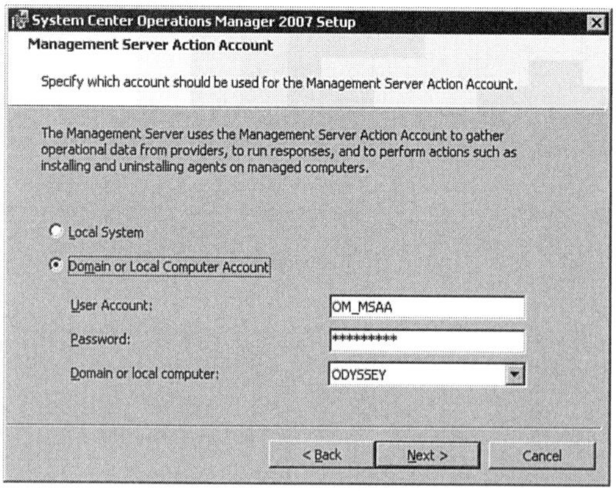

FIGURE 6.15   Specifying the Management Server Action Account to use.

4. Next, we specify the SDK and Config Service Account, which we would also have previously identified. We are using the OM_SDK account, as shown in Figure 6.16. This account should have Local Administrator privileges. If your management group has the RMS and Operational database installed on the same server, you can also use Local System, although you may have issues during the Reporting Component setup.

TIP

Using a Domain Account for the SDK and Config Service Account

If you choose the Local System option on this screen, it will cause installation issues during installation of the reporting components. Using a domain account (as shown in Figure 6.16) will avoid the issue, which we discuss in the "Troubleshooting Tips" section of this chapter.

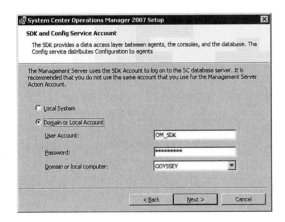

FIGURE 6.16   Specifying the SDK and Config Service Account to use.

5. After the SDK account is configured, the next step is to specify the type of authentication to use for the Web console (shown in Figure 6.17). The options available are Windows Authentication and Forms Authentication.

   ▶ Use Windows Authentication if the console will be accessed only via an intranet.

   ▶ Choose Forms Authentication if the console will be accessed over the Internet.

6. The next screen displayed is the option to join the Customer Experience Improvement Program, shown in Figure 6.18. If you choose to select this option, information about OpsMgr 2007 usage is collected and forwarded to Microsoft. If you do not choose the option, usage data is not sent to Microsoft.

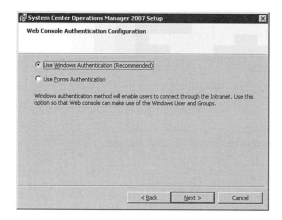

FIGURE 6.17   Choosing the Web console authentication.

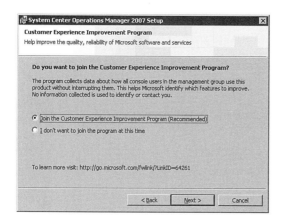

FIGURE 6.18   Customer Experience Improvement Program.

7. Next, the Microsoft Update option is configured (which we discussed in the "Operations Database Server" section of the chapter), and installation is ready to begin. After the installation is complete, there is a default action to start the console, shown in Figure 6.19. The wizard also strongly recommends that you run the Secure Storage Backup tool to export the RMS key.

   Refer to Chapter 12 for more information on how to use the Secure Storage Backup tool.

After the wizard completes, you now have a functional Operations Manager 2007 environment! After you launch the Operations console (shown in Figure 6.20), the next steps include configuring computers and devices to manage and importing management packs. We discuss these steps in detail in Chapter 8, "Configuring and Using Operations Manager 2007."

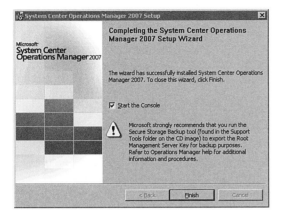

FIGURE 6.19   Completing the Setup Wizard.

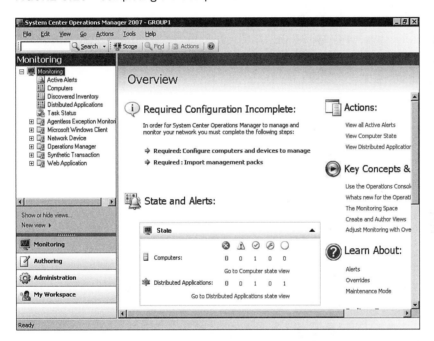

FIGURE 6.20   Operations console after installation.

NOTE

Backing Up the RMS Key

The release of OpsMgr 2007 Service Pack 1 adds a new backup wizard to the end of the RMS setup that walks through the process of backing up the RMS encryption key. Prior to of the service pack, the key was backed up only using a command-line tool, and many organizations did not realize how important this process was for disaster recovery situations. For further information on the RMS key and its importance, refer to Chapter 12.

If you want to validate the installation was successful, open the Operations console and verify that information displays within the console.

Now that we have installed the two core components for Operations Manager 2007, we will next discuss the steps required to install other OpsMgr components.

Management Server

You can install additional management servers after installing the RMS. For redundancy and load-balancing purposes, we recommend deploying additional management servers and consoles. If your environment only requires installation of a management server without the consoles, the prerequisites are decreased to include only the following:

▶ Windows Server 2003 Service Pack 1 or 2.

▶ MDAC 2.80.1022.0 or higher.

▶ Active Directory must be available; the installation process communicates with AD to verify service account information.

▶ .NET Framework v2.0.

▶ .NET Framework 3.0 components.

The installation process for just the management server (without the consoles) includes a subset of the steps required in the "Root Management Server and Consoles" section, earlier in this chapter.

To verify that a particular management server installation was successful, open the Operations console, navigate to Administration -> Device Management -> Management Servers, and validate that the new management server is in the list.

TIP

Installing the Consoles Later

You can always add the Operations console and Web console at a later point in time. If you re-run the OpsMgr installation program, it will display any previously installed components on that particular server as enabled. To install these new components, select the items to install but do not deselect any previously installed items; otherwise, those components will be removed from the server!

If you are running the original version of OpsMgr 2007 and install secondary management servers after installing reporting, by default the secondary management servers will not be able to write data warehouse data because the required profiles are not created by the setup process. The symptom will be alerts that say the second management server cannot write to the data warehouse using the Management Server Action account (although this may be the same Action account used on the RMS).

Service Pack 1 resolves this issue. If you are using the original release of OpsMgr 2007, perform the following steps to resolve the problem:

1. Log on as an OpsMgr administrator and open the Operations console.
2. Navigate to Administration -> Security -> Run As Profiles.
3. In the list of Run As Profiles, select the Data Warehouse account. Right-click and choose Properties; then select the Run As Accounts tab.
4. See if the new management server name is in the list. If it is not, click New.... In the Matching Computers list, click the name of the management server. Be sure the Run As Account specified is the Data Warehouse Action account.

    This workaround was identified by Satya Vel, a Program Manager on the MOM team, and is written up at http://blogs.technet.com/momteam/archive/2007/08/29/if-you-install-opsmgr-2007-reporting-and-then-install-secondary-ms-then-it-will-not-be-able-to-write-dw-data-as-profiles-are-not-created.aspx

Reporting

In our example, we will install both reporting components (the Data Warehouse and Reporting Server Components) on a single server. To check the prerequisites, we chose the Check Prerequisites option and selected both the Data Warehouse and Reporting Server options.

TIP

OpsMgr Reporting Server on a Domain Controller

The installation of the Reporting components on a domain controller was not initially supported when Operations Manager 2007 was released (per the Operations Manager help file). Microsoft has updated its support statement, which is available at http://support.microsoft.com/default.aspx/kb/942862.

The prerequisites to install the Reporting components include the following items:

▶ Windows Server 2003 Service Pack 1 or 2.

▶ SQL Server 2005 and then SQL Server 2005 Service Pack 1 (or 2). When installing SQL Server 2005, check the option to install the Reporting Services and the Workstation components, Books Online, and development tools. Also, be sure to reboot after the installation of any SQL Server 2005 Service Pack is completed.

▶ The SQL Server service must be in automatic startup (except for clusters where it can be in manual startup, which we discuss in Chapter 10).

▶ Microsoft SQL Server 2005 Reporting Services Service Pack 1 or 2.

▶ Active Directory must be available; the installation process communicates with AD to verify service account information.

▶ ASP.NET 2.0.

▶ KB918222 for SQL 2005. A warning message will display if this hotfix is not already installed on the system.

▶ You must turn off the Windows Firewall or configure it for the Reporting components. The Reporting Server Component needs to be able to communicate through the default TCP (Transmission Control Portocol) ports 80, OLEDB 1433, and 5724.

TIP

Windows Firewall and Group Policy

Just because there is a group policy installed to disable the firewall does not mean that the firewall is actually disabled. We've seen situations where the group policy was configured to disable the firewall. The firewall configuration was grayed out, and it did not look like it was running. However, the actual service was still running on the system! In this situation, we had to stop the service and disable it to install the OpsMgr component.

▶ .NET Framework v2.0.

▶ .NET Framework 3.0 components.

Validating SQL Reporting Services Is Working Correctly

Prior to installing the OpsMgr Reporting components, validate that SQL Reporting Services (SRS) is working correctly. You can do this by browsing to both http://localhost/reports and http://localhost/ReportServer from the SRS server. Next, verify you do not have an SSL certificate installed on the default website of the server (if you need to, do that later!).

If there are still issues with the SRS installation, the Operations Manager 2007 installation media includes a utility in the Support Tools folder named ResetSRS.exe. This utility was used extensively during the OpsMgr 2007 beta test cycles. The syntax is ResetSRS.exe MSSQLSERVER. Theoretically, this utility is for resetting SRS after you removed a prior OpsMgr or Essentials installation. The Operations Manager 2007 Deployment Guide (available at http://www.microsoft.com/technet/opsmgr/2007/library/proddocs.mspx) contains additional information about the ResetSRS utility.

After running ResetSRS.exe, your last step is to modify the SRS configuration. Click Start -> Microsoft SQL Server 2005 -> Configuration Tools, and then select Reporting Services Configuration. On the left side of the screen, select Web Service Identify, and on the right side click Apply.

These steps restore the SRS installation to its original pre-Operations Manager 2007 Reporting Server Component state.

To install the Reporting components, perform the following steps.

1. Choose the option to Install Operations Manager 2007 Reporting from the setup screen. The wizard displays the starting screen, the license agreement, product registration, and the custom setup screen. At Custom Setup, choose the Data Warehouse and Reporting Server Components, as displayed in Figure 6.21.

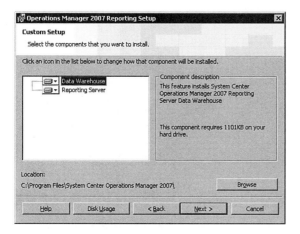

FIGURE 6.21   Custom installation for all reporting components.

2. The prerequisites for the components are checked, and you must specify the name of the Root Management Server. In our example, the Root Management Server is named Hydra.Odyssey.com (shown in Figure 6.22), which we fully qualify as we do when we installed the RMS component.

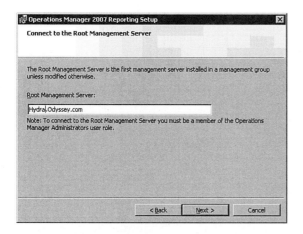

FIGURE 6.22   Connect to the Root Management Server.

3. At the next screen, specify the SQL Server database instance to connect to. For our case, we are connecting to the default database instance of Quicksilver, as displayed in the dropdown box in Figure 6.23.

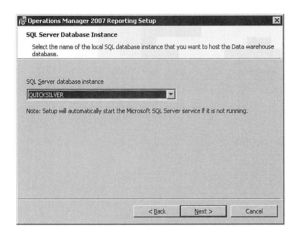

FIGURE 6.23   Specify the Reporting SQL Server.

4. On the Database and Log File Options screen, we specify the name of the Reporting database, its size, and the locations for the data and log files (see Figure 6.24). The default name for the Data Warehouse database is OperationsManagerDW.

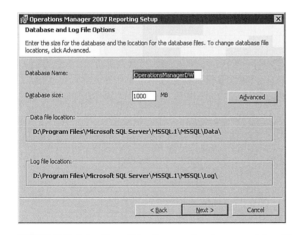

FIGURE 6.24   Data Warehouse database and log file options.

5. Now that we have determined which SQL Server Reporting Services Server to use and its configuration, we need to identify the instance to use, as shown in Figure 6.25. Note the warning in Figure 6.25 that Operations Manager role-based security will supersede (integrate) the security of the specified Reporting Services instance.

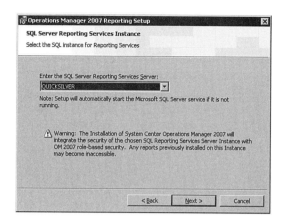

FIGURE 6.25   Specify the Reporting SQL Server instance.

6. On the next screen, we specify the Data Warehouse Write Account. This account will write to the data warehouse, as shown in Figure 6.26. The account should be a domain user account.

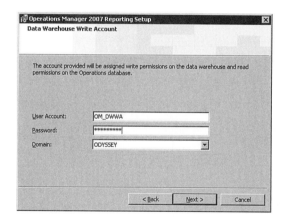

FIGURE 6.26   Data Warehouse Write Account.

7. The last account we specify is the Data Reader Account, as seen in Figure 6.27. This can be a domain user account.

8. The final installation screens include the configuration for operational data reports, Microsoft Update (discussed in the "Operations Database Server" section), and then the installation is completed.

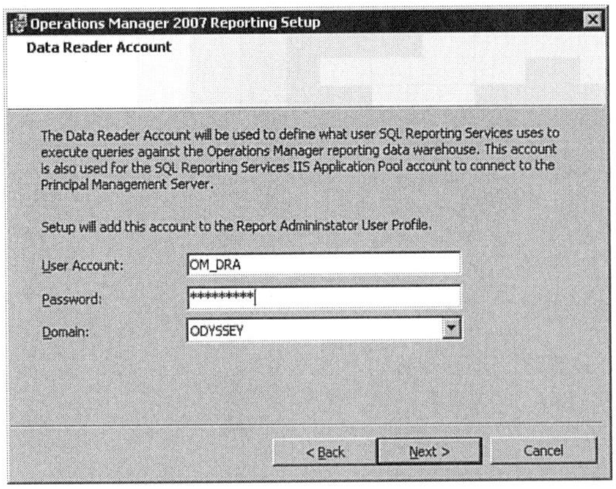

FIGURE 6.27   Data Reader Account.

TIP

No Reports?

If you have opened Operations Console -> Reporting and there are no reports listed, the issue might be you have not installed the OpsMgr agent.

When installing reporting components on a separate server, reports will *not* appear until the OpsMgr agent is deployed to the Reporting server and/or Data Warehouse server.

To validate that the reports have installed correctly, open the Operations console and navigate to Reporting -> Microsoft ODR Report Library and double-click any of the reports available (Management Group, Management Packs, Most Common Alerts). If this report displays successfully, the reporting functionality within Operations Manager 2007 is working correctly.

Audit Collection Services

The prerequisites for installing ACS include the following:

▸ A functional OpsMgr 2007 environment, which as a minimum includes the RMS and the Operations database.

▸ We recommend an additional management server to run the ACS collector. We will be using a new server named Hurricane.

▸ SQL Server 2005 needs to be installed and configured on a system that will host the ACS database. Our SQL Server system for ACS is on Fireball.

To install Audit Collection Services, perform the following steps:

1. Install the ACS components by choosing the Install Audit Collection Server option from the setup screen. This installation needs to run on a management server, not on the server that will host the ACS database. When the installation process runs, the first screen is a Welcome to the Audit Collection Services Collector Setup Wizard screen. After the welcome screen, the license agreement screen displays, and then the database installation options start with the choice to either create a new database or use an existing database, as shown in Figure 6.28.

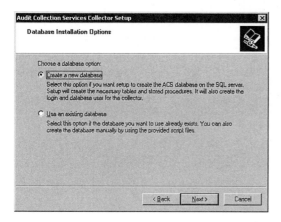

FIGURE 6.28   Database installation options.

2. The next screen specifies the data source name (DSN) to use to communicate with the ACS database. The default is OpsMgrAC, as shown in Figure 6.29.

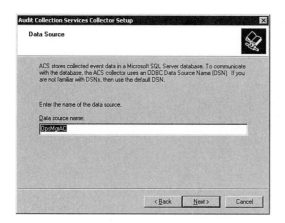

FIGURE 6.29   Data source name for ACS.

3. The Database screen provides you with two options regarding the location of the database server:

   ▶ If the collector will be providing the ACS database functionality, you can connect to a database server running locally.

   ▶ If the server is remote (as it is with our example), the remote option is chosen and the name of the remote server is required.

   The instance and database name are also specified on this screen, with the defaults for these two fields set to blank for the instance and OperationsManagerAC for the database name, respectively. For our example, we are installing to a remote database server named Fireball (identified using its Fully Qualified Domain Name) and will take the defaults for the instance and database name, as shown in Figure 6.30.

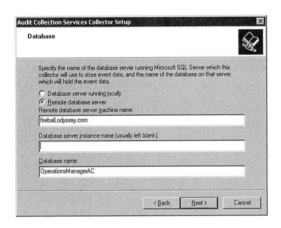

FIGURE 6.30   Connecting to a remote database server for ACS.

4. Next, we specify the type of database authentication to use. The two options available are Windows Authentication and SQL Authentication. We recommend using the Windows Authentication option unless the collector and database server are not in the same or trusting domains. Figure 6.31 shows the options available for authentication to the ACS database.

5. Next, specify where the ACS database and log file information will be stored on the SQL Server system. As a standard for increased database performance, the database and log files should be on different drives, and the drives should have sufficient space available. If the nondefault location is chosen (as we show in Figure 6.32), the directories need to be manually created.

6. Now, we specify the event retention information, which defaults to performing daily maintenance at 2:00 a.m. and retaining data for 14 days, as we see in Figure 6.33.

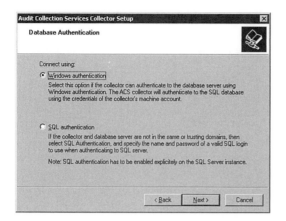

FIGURE 6.31   Database Authentication screen.

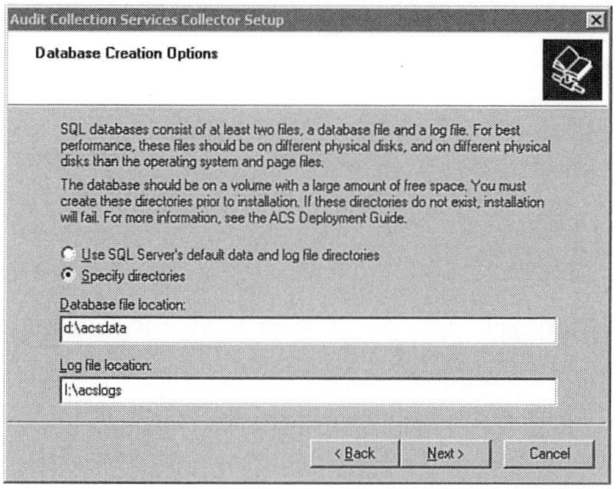

FIGURE 6.32   Database Creation Options screen.

Audit Collection Services Collector Setup

Event Retention Schedule

Audit Collection performs database maintenance on a daily basis. Database performance will be impacted during the maintenance window.

Local hour of day to perform daily database maintenance:

`02:00 AM`

Number of days an event is retained in database:

`14`

< Back   Next >   Cancel

FIGURE 6.33   Event Retention Schedule screen.

7. Two options are available for how the timestamp information will be stored in the ACS database: Local and Universal Coordinated Time (UTC). The Local option is the default and is recommended, unless there are multiple ACS databases or you are very familiar with UTC. We have chosen to go with the default setting, Local, as shown in Figure 6.34.

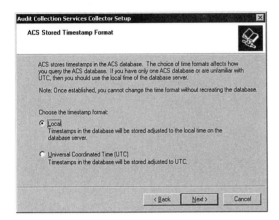

FIGURE 6.34   ACS Stored Timestamp Format screen.

8. The remaining screens show a summary of the configuration, connecting to the ACS database server to create the database, and displaying a screen to notify when the setup has finished. Start the Operations Manager Audit Collection service to verify that ACS is properly installed.

After installing ACS, you will need to add the ACS reports to Operations Manager 2007. Chapter 15, "Monitoring Audit Collection Services," discusses details on this process.

Gateway Server

The prerequisites for the installation of the Gateway Server Component include the following items:

▶ Windows Server 2003 Service Pack 1 or 2.

▶ Microsoft Core XML Services (MSXML) 6.0, also known as the *MSXML 6.0 Parser*, is required prior to installing the gateway server. The XML Services are installed as part of the OpsMgr agent installation (see Chapter 9) or can be separately downloaded and installed from http://go.microsoft.com/fwlink/?LinkId=76343.

Unlike the other Operations Manager components, you do not install the Gateway Server Component using the setup screen for OpsMgr. You will install this component by running the MOMGateway.msi file from the \gateway\<*path*> folder on the Operations Manager 2007 installation media (the path will be either i386 or amd64, depending on your hardware platform). Perform the following steps:

1. The first screen displayed is the Welcome to the System Center Operations Manager Gateway Setup Wizard screen. The next screen identifies where to install the gateway files, which defaults to the *%ProgramFiles%*\System Center Operations Manager 2007 folder.

2. On the next screen, we specify the management group name, management server, and management server port number. We have configured these for our sample environment (GROUP1 as management group, Hydra.Odyssey.com as the management server, and 5723 as the default port), as shown in Figure 6.35.

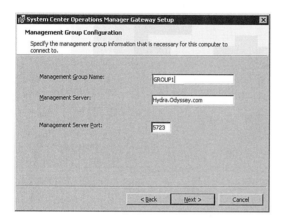

FIGURE 6.35   Management Group Configuration screen for the gateway server.

CAUTION

Changing the Default Port

You can change the default port number of 5723, but Microsoft only supports this when done during setup.

3. Next, we need to identify what account to use for the Gateway Action Account. The options available are Local System and a domain or local account. This account needs the permissions to be able to install and uninstall agents and to manage the computers. For our example, shown in Figure 6.36, we are using the OM_GWAA account within the domain that the gateway is a member of.

4. The remainder of the installation includes the Microsoft Update screen, a summary screen, and a wizard completion screen.

You must approve the Gateway Server Component after its installation. You will approve this component on the management server that the gateway was configured to communicate with. Follow these steps:

1. Copy the Microsoft.EnterpriseManagement.GatewayApprovalTool from the \SupportTools folder on the Operations Manager 2007 installation media to the *%ProgramFiles%*\System Center Operations Manager 2007 folder.

2. After copying the program, open a command prompt (cmd.exe) to that folder and run the program with the required options.

Chapter 10 discusses additional information on the approval process.

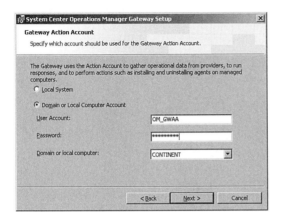

FIGURE 6.36   Gateway Action Account screen.

Agentless Exception Monitoring

There is not really an actual installation process required to install a server to provide Agentless Exception Monitoring (AEM) functionality. However, there are prerequisites that need to be in place to activate this functionality, which include the following:

▶ A functional RMS and/or management server

▶ At least 2GB of available free space

▶ No existing share named "AEM" on the specified system

To use AEM, you need to activate one of the management servers in the environment to provide the AEM capability. Active the server using the Operations console on the Administration tab under Device Management -> Management Servers. Right-click the management server and choose Configure Client Monitoring. This starts a wizard that enables the client monitoring functionality on this server. Here are the steps to follow:

1. The wizard starts with an introduction page, which introduces each of the steps that will occur, including CEIP (Client Experience Improvement Program) Forwarding, Error Collection, Error Forwarding, Create File Share, Task Status, and Client Settings.

2. On the CEIP Forwarding screen of the wizard, we configure the Customer Experience Improvement Program. You can configure how CEIP collects data in several ways:

   ▶ Continue to send data directly to Microsoft.

   ▶ Use the selected Management Server to collect and forward the data to Microsoft.

If you select the second option, you can specify whether you want to use the Secure Sockets Layer (SSL) protocol, whether you use Windows Authentication, and the specific port number (which defaults to 51907), as shown in Figure 6.37.

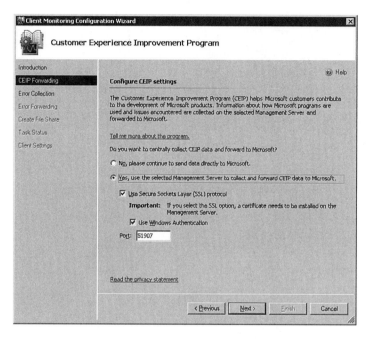

FIGURE 6.37   Customer Experience Improvement Program screen.

3. On the Error Collection settings screen, specify the following:

   ▶ The location of the file share path (which needs to have at least 2GB of free disk space)

   ▶ Whether error reports will be gathered for Windows Vista-based computers and, if so, what port to use (defaults to 51906)

   ▶ Whether you will use SSL and Windows Authentication for the Vista clients

   ▶ The organization name displayed in messages displayed on the local client

   In our example, we have created a file share path of D:\AEM and have enabled all the Windows Vista configurations for the organization name of Odyssey, as shown in Figure 6.38.

4. Figure 6.39 shows the next step of the wizard, where you configure forwarding to send either basic or detailed information to Microsoft.

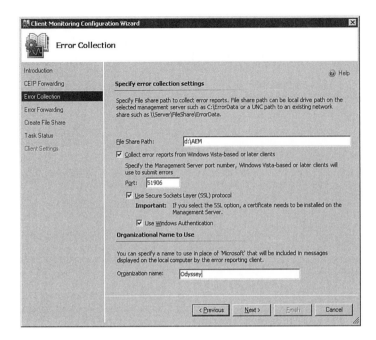

FIGURE 6.38   Error collection settings.

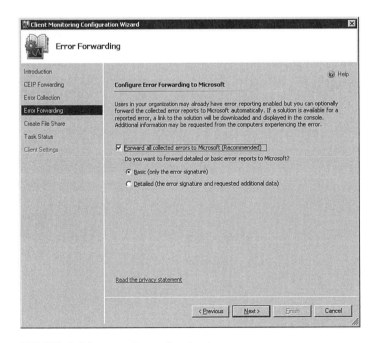

FIGURE 6.39   Error forwarding Settings.

5. Finally, we need to specify which account will provide the credentials required to create the share on the system. The default configuration is to use the Action Account (see Figure 6.40), but another account can be specified.

Once each of these configurations is complete, the wizard configures the system and displays a tasks status screen indicating that the task completed successfully. Finally, the client settings screen indicates the location of the Administrative template (the .adm file used by Group Policy to set the configuration required on the clients to report errors to the new location).

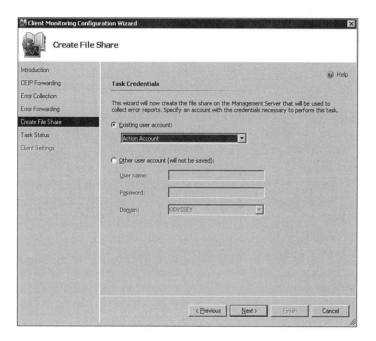

FIGURE 6.40   Create the file share and specify credentials.

Removing OpsMgr

If you need to remove Operations Manager from your environment, the recommended process is by reversing the order in which you installed the components. As a sample deployment, we have an RMS named Hydra, a operational database server named Thunder, and a reporting server named Quicksilver. These systems are monitoring systems in the environment that have locally deployed agents and agentless monitored systems. We installed these systems in the following order:

- ▶ Operations database
- ▶ RMS
- ▶ Reporting server and Data Warehouse server
- ▶ Agents and agentless monitoring

You would remove Operations Manager by reversing this process: agentless monitoring, agents, Reporting and Data Warehouse server, RMS, and then the Operations database.

To remove OpsMgr from this configuration, we would first uninstall the agentless monitored systems (Operations Console under Administration -> Device Management -> Agentless Managed) and then uninstall the agent monitored systems (Operations Console under Administration -> Device Management -> Agent Managed).

After successfully uninstalling the agents, we can uninstall the Reporting Server/Data Warehouse Server Components through Control Panel -> Add/Remove Programs. The RMS is uninstalled next with Add/Remove Programs. Finally, you can uninstall the Operations database through Add/Remove Programs. Use the SQL Server 2005 tools to archive or delete the databases from SQL Server, and use your regular Windows utilities to remove them from the file system.

Operations Manager Cleanup Tool

If components do not uninstall correctly through Add/Remove Programs, a command-line tool is available to remove the components of Operations Manager. The CleanMom tool is available for download at http://technet.microsoft.com/en-us/opsmgr/bb625978.aspx as part of the Operations Manager 2007 Resource Kit.

CleanMom removes components only on the computer you run it on, using command-line switches to enable the actions listed in Table 6.4.

In addition to removing the components listed in Table 6.4, CleanMom removes the associated services, Registry keys, and installation directories and files.

There are two versions of CleanMom. Use CleanMom.exe on 32-bit systems and CleanMom64 for 64-bit systems. Additional documentation is available in the zip file that includes the tool.

TABLE 6.4   CleanMom Switches and Actions

Command-line Switch	Description
/CleanAgents	Removes all agent components from that computer
/CleanServers	Removes all server components from that computer
/c	Creates an .xml file listing the installed components
/a	Selectively removes components listed in the .xml file previously created using the /c switch

Troubleshooting Tips

The prerequisite checker and the straightforward approach to installing Operations Manager 2007 will help to avoid many installation issues. However, you may encounter some common problems that which should be pointed out when installing Operations Manager.

Table 6.5 describes some of the potential errors that might occur when installing Operations Manager. You can use the Knowledge Base article number to get additional information in the Microsoft knowledge database at http://support.microsoft.com.

TABLE 6.5   Potential Installation Errors and Their Resolutions

Process Erroring	Error Message	Potential Cause	KB Article #
2007 Install	When you try to install Microsoft System Center Operations Manager 2007 or you try to install Microsoft System Center Essentials 2007, the Setup Welcome page appears to be empty.	Configure Internet Options Security to allow Active Scripting on this website.	932812
2007 Install	SDK service on the RMS may consume more than 2GB of memory.	The SDK service data source module does not limit the number of data items that are processed at one time. The module tries to read all pending data items from the database and process the items in a batch. The MonitoringHost.exe process may stop unexpectedly in response to an unhandled exception if too many data items have to be processed. A hotfix is available: see KB 943706. Apply the hotfix to all management and gateway servers. This is fixed in Service Pack 1.	943706
2007 Install	Prerequisite checking fails, stating you must install Service Pack 1 for SQL Server 2005 although the Service Pack is already installed.	This can occur on a 64-bit Windows Server 2003 SP 1 computer if you have installed SQL Server 2005 (32 bit) SP 1. Use the CreateDBWizard tool to create the database before starting the installation. Please note the requirements for running this tool in KB 938997.	944346

TABLE 6.5   Continued

Process Erroring	Error Message	Potential Cause	KB Article #
2007 ACS Install	Event ID: 4668 and the Audit Collection Services does not start.	Activate the Audit Collection Service. Clear the Read-only attribute on the AcsConfig.xml file and restart the service.	932812
2007 ACS Install	The Audit Collection service does not start and SPN issues are occurring.	The NETWORK SERVICE account does not have permission to write the SPN (service principal name) information to Active Directory. Create a temporary domain admin account and give it permission to run as a service on the server where this service is failing. Change the Audit Collection service to run using this new account and start the service. Once the SPNs are written, the service can be changed back to NETWORK SERVICE and restarted.	936579
2007 Reporting Install	Message during reporting installation "The wizard was interrupted before Operations Manager 2007 could be installed." This also logs a return value 3 in the reporting installation log file MOMReporting(*N*).log. This log file is incremented for each installation attempt and is stored in the user's *%temp%* folder. To verify that the error is due to query timeout, search for the following text: "SetPropertiesToManagementServerActionAndSDKAccountCA error."	This occurs if you attempt to use the Local System account to install reporting. The installation process queries Active Directory for the computer account associated with the RMS. In a large domain, the query may time out. This can be resolved through using a domain account for the OpsMgr SDK Service. After the installation is complete, you can configure the OpsMgr SDK Service to use the Local System account (documented in KB 936220). This is fixed in Service Pack 1.	936219
2007 Reporting Install	OpsMgr 2007 Reporting fails because the SDK service does not have appropriate permissions.	You installed a domain environment with the Permissions compatible only with Windows 2000 or Windows Server 2003 operating systems option, and the SDK service account does not have read access to the `tokenGroupsGlobalAndUniversal` attribute.	938627

TABLE 6.5   Continued

Process Erroring	Error Message	Potential Cause	KB Article #
2007 Reporting Install	You cannot install the Reporting feature in a disjointed namespace environment.	The primary DNS suffix of the computer does not match the FQDN of the domain in which the computer resides. A hotfix is available (see http://support.microsoft.com/kb/936481 for additional information). This is fixed in Service Pack 1.	936481
2007 Reporting Install	Reporting does not install, Error 26204, Error -2147217900: failed to execute SQL string, error detail: Incorrect syntax near the keyword 'with'. ... previous statement must be terminated with a semicolon.	Reporting installation fails when the DB name contains special characters. This problem may occur when there is a "-" in the reporting database name (example: OPSMGR-Reporting). This is a special character.	944347

Summary

This chapter discussed the steps involved in deploying a multiple-server Operations Manager 2007 configuration. In the next chapter, we discuss the process to migrate an existing MOM 2005 environment to Operations Manager 2007.

CHAPTER 7

Migrating to Operations Manager 2007

If you are using Microsoft Operations Manager (MOM) and plan to upgrade to Operations Manager (OpsMgr) 2007, this is the chapter you are looking for. This chapter discusses the options available for migrating to Operations Manager 2007 and provides troubleshooting tips you'll want to be aware of during the migration process. We will talk first about what you need to know for planning for your migration.

Planning Your Migration

Before starting the migration process, you will need to plan your OpsMgr 2007 implementation. As discussed in Chapter 4, "Planning Your Operations Manager Deployment," prior to migrating to OpsMgr 2007 you should assess, design, plan, and test the process within a proof of concept (POC) environment.

Part of your assessment should include identifying the servers that currently provide MOM services. The specific server configuration used by your organization will determine which steps are required for your migration and the complexity of the migration. If you installed all MOM components on a single server or single management group, the migration is far simpler than if there are multiple management groups. If you are not familiar with the details of your current MOM 2005 environment, *do not pass Go.* Return to Chapter 4!

The first major concept to be aware of when migrating to Operations Manager 2007 is that there is no upgrade process. Although it would be great to be able to put in the installation media and click "upgrade," that is not viable with OpsMgr 2007 due to the significant changes that have occurred since MOM 2005. You can approach a migration to OpsMgr 2007 in three different ways:

▶ Starting clean

▶ Same hardware

▶ New hardware

The approach you will take will vary, depending on the current state of your monitoring environment and the hardware in place for that environment. For a quick reference on the information needed prior to the installation or migration of OpsMgr, see the pre-installation checklist (OpsMgr Pre-installation Checklist.xls) introduced in Chapter 6, "Installing Operations Manager 2007," and included on the CD for this book.

Starting Clean

One option for implementing Operations Manager 2007 is to start clean and install OpsMgr as if it was a new installation. This approach includes the following activities:

▶ Install Operations Manager as a new installation (see Chapter 6 for installation details).

▶ Configure your installation to provide the required functionality.

▶ Once Operations Manager 2007 meets the requirements of the organization, decommission the original monitoring product.

The starting clean option does not provide a migration path but may be the best solution in certain cases. To explain this better, we need first to discuss the supported migration options for OpsMgr 2007:

▶ **MOM 2000 SP 1—MOM 2005 SP 1—OpsMgr 2007**

If you are currently on MOM 2000, you can upgrade to MOM 2005 SP 1 (see *Microsoft Operations Manager 2005 Unleashed* for details on migrating from MOM 2000 to MOM 2005). After completing that upgrade, you can then migrate to OpsMgr 2007.

▶ **MOM 2005 Workgroup—MOM 2005—OpsMgr 2007**

The supported upgrade path is to upgrade to the full version of MOM 2005 and then migrate to OpsMgr 2007.

▶ **OpsMgr 2007 RC2—OpsMgr 2007**

If you were involved in the beta process for Operations Manager, you can update Release Candidate 2 (RC2) to OpsMgr 2007.

▶ **Evaluation OpsMgr 2007—OpsMgr 2007**

If you have a Select CD image, you can upgrade the evaluation version of OpsMgr 2007 to the full release version.

TIP

Upgrading the Evaluation Version to the Full Volume Licensed Edition

You can upgrade the 180-day evaluation version of Operations Manager 2007 (available at http://www.microsoft.com/technet/prodtechnol/eval/opsmgr/default.mspx) without reinstalling the product. The Microsoft Volume License (MVLS) website, located at https://licensing.microsoft.com, provides license keys and downloadable media for Microsoft Volume License customers.

The Volume License version of the Operations Manager 2007 installation media includes LicensingWizard.msi in the \SupportTools folder. This wizard provides the capability to convert the evaluation version of OpsMgr 2007 to the full version.

This information is documented at http://support.microsoft.com/kb/937826.

Here are some situations where it may make more sense to start clean and install OpsMgr as a new installation:

▶ **MOM 2000 installations**—Considering the time required for upgrading to MOM 2005 and then to migrate to Operations Manager 2007, it may make more sense to use the clean start approach.

▶ **MOM 2005 Workgroup installations**—Similar to a MOM 2000 installation, it may make more sense to start clean in this situation, considering the time required to upgrade to MOM 2005 and then to migrate to Operations Manager 2007.

▶ **Non-MOM installations**—If the current monitoring product is not a previous version of Microsoft Operations Manager, we recommend you start clean.

▶ **Abandoned MOM 2005 installations**—If the current installation of MOM 2005 is abandoned or no longer in use, there is minimal investment in what was previously installed.

The starting clean approach includes planning, installing, configuring, and decommissioning steps:

▶ **Planning Operations Manager 2007**—Read Chapter 4 and Chapter 5, "Planning Complex Configurations," for information on the planning process for Operations Manager 2007 deployments. These chapters apply regardless of what approach you will take for installing or migrating to OpsMgr 2007; focus on identifying the current monitoring solution and the functionality that it provides.

TIP

Documenting Your MOM 2005 Environment

As part of your migration to Operations Manager 2007 from MOM 2005, you should document the current MOM 2005 environment during the Assessment phase. Enhansoft provides a tool to assist with documentation, available from its website at http://www.enhansoft.com/ under Downloads -> MOM Documentation Script.

▶ **Installing Operations Manager 2007**—Chapter 6 discusses the process to install OpsMgr 2007, including the various available components.

▶ **Configuring Operations Manager 2007**—The OpsMgr solution will need the appropriate management packs installed and will need to be configured to meet the requirements identified during the planning phase.

▶ **Decommissioning the original monitoring solution**—Once OpsMgr 2007 has met your requirements, you can decommission the original solution.

The primary issue with the starting clean approach is that it does not automate converting your current monitoring solution to OpsMgr 2007. By comparison, Table 7.1 shows the items converted during either a same hardware or new hardware approach.

TABLE 7.1   MOM 2005 Management Pack Components with OpsMgr 2007 Converted Equivalents

MOM 2005	OpsMgr 2007
Alert severity	Health state
Rule monitor	Alert-generating rules
Rule	Non-state-generating rules
Collection rule	Performance rule
Computer group	Computer Group class
Installation class	Two discovery rules generated during conversion
Class (used for state monitoring)	Class
Rule	Rule or monitor
Script	Module type
Task	Task
Notification group	Notification rules
Knowledge	Knowledge article
Topology	View

With that long of a list in Table 7.1, it looks like about everything converts, right? Well, not exactly. The migration does not convert the following items:

▸ **Reports**—With OpsMgr 2007, the Data Warehouse and the reporting functionality are completely rewritten.

▸ **Operators**—You must manually re-create operators as part of the migration.

▸ **Console scopes**—You must define console scopes as part of the migration.

To perform these conversions, we will review the other options available for migrating to Operations Manager 2007. These are the same hardware and new hardware approaches, which we review in the following sections of this chapter.

Same Hardware

If you have decided not to use the starting clean approach for your migration, the next consideration is whether to use the same hardware or new hardware for your migration to Operations Manager 2007.

The migration process enables you to share the hardware used by your current MOM 2005 environment with the new Operations Manager 2007 environment. You can install the OpsMgr agent on the those systems currently running the MOM 2005 agent, resulting in a new OpsMgr 2007 agent reporting to the OpsMgr 2007 environment, while the original MOM 2005 agent continues to report to the original MOM 2005 environment. We refer to sharing hardware between MOM 2005 and OpsMgr 2007 as the *same hardware approach*. Figure 7.1 shows a simple two-server configuration running on MOM 2005 before the same hardware migration is started.

This configuration displays a single management server monitoring the agents in the environment with an additional server providing database and reporting functionality.

When you're considering what migration approach to take, the first question to ask is whether the hardware current provides the MOM 2005 functionality is sufficient to run both OpsMgr 2007 and MOM 2005. To provide the Operations database functionality in this configuration, the recommended hardware specifications will vary based on the number of monitored agents:

▸ **100–500 agents**—Dual-processor, 2GB memory, and two-drive RAID0+1 disk subsystem

▸ **500–750 agents**—Dual-processor, 4GB memory, and four-drive RAID0+1 disk subsystem

▸ **1000 agents**—Dual-processor, 4GB memory, and eight-drive RAID0+1 disk subsystem

The first OpsMgr 2007 management server you install will be the Root Management Server (RMS). The recommended hardware for this component is a dual-processor system with 4GB of memory and a two-drive RAID1 disk subsystem.

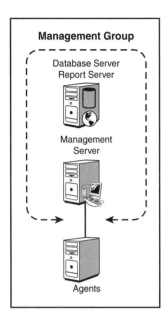

FIGURE 7.1   Single MOM 2005 management group.

When considering performing a same hardware migration, if any of the following items are true, you should seriously consider a new hardware migration (discussed in the "New Hardware" section of this chapter) instead:

▶ **Current hardware insufficient**—If the current hardware installed for MOM 2005 does not meet the hardware specifications mentioned in this chapter or Chapter 4, there will be a negative impact on OpsMgr performance both during and after the migration.

▶ **Change of design**—With the new components of OpsMgr 2007, you may want to consider a new design. Using a same hardware approach, the same design exists after the migration is complete. As an example, if your current MOM 2005 environment has a single nonclustered management server (which is a common configuration in small organizations), you cannot use the same hardware to provide a high-availability solution such as a clustered RMS.

▶ **Shared SQL Server**—If the server providing database functionality is shared with other applications, this may represent an issue for a same hardware approach. The OpsMgr 2007 operational database requires at least SQL 2005 Service Pack 1.

▶ **MOM 2005 Reporting impacted**—As part of the upgrade process to Operations Manager 2007, there are significant changes made to the reporting functionality. *Once you install the reporting components for OpsMgr 2007 on the MOM 2005 reporting environment, the reports for MOM 2005 are no longer accessible.*

▶ **64-bit systems**—OpsMgr 2007 supports 64-bit Windows operating systems and benefits from the performance of running in a 64-bit OS. If the current hardware running MOM 2005 is 64 bit but the operating system is not, you will be unable to take advantage of the 64-bit platform unless you use the new hardware approach.

Figure 7.2 shows what the configuration would look like when performing a same hardware migration for the management group configuration, previously displayed in Figure 7.1.

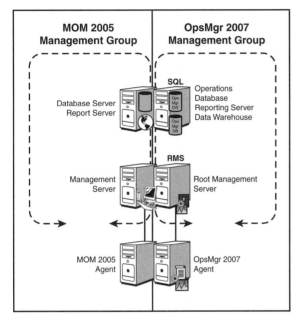

FIGURE 7.2   Same hardware migration approach.

TIP

Always Back Up!

The one time you do not have a backup is the one time you will need the backup. This is our MOM/OpsMgr version of Murphy's Law.

The good news is that both migration approaches use the same steps; they vary only on what servers you actually perform the installation. We will review using the same hardware approach in a case study later in this chapter.

We next discuss the new hardware approach and the steps required to perform it, because you can also use these steps with the same hardware approach.

New Hardware

If new hardware is available for the migration to Operations Manager 2007, from the component perspective the installation will mirror those discussed in Chapter 6.

If we take our example shown in Figure 7.1 and perform a new hardware migration on it, Figure 7.3 is the result.

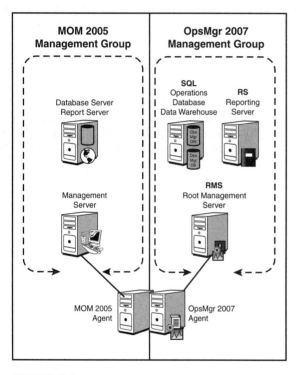

FIGURE 7.3   New hardware migration approach.

In a new hardware migration (as well as the scenario previously discussed in the "Same Hardware" section), the OpsMgr agent is installed on the systems currently running the MOM 2005 agent. The MOM 2005 agent reports to the MOM 2005 environment, and the OpsMgr 2007 agent reports to the OpsMgr 2007 environment.

> **TIP**
>
> **Issues with 64-Bit Domain Controllers in Migrations from MOM 2005 to OpsMgr 2007**
>
> There is an issue if you are monitoring 64-bit domain controllers with both MOM 2005 and OpsMgr 2007 while using the Active Directory Management Pack. This is due to a conflict between the Active Directory Helper Object (OOMADS) between the two agents.
>
> To work around this issue, exclude each 64-bit domain controller from monitoring by MOM 2005 and uninstall OOMADS 1.0.3 (the version used by the MOM 2005 agent) from the 64-bit domain controllers. Then install the new version of OOMADS on the domain controller. OOMADS is located on the OpsMgr CD within the HelperObjects/<version> directory.

Comparing the New Hardware and Same Hardware Approaches

The primary negative for using the new hardware approach is the requirement to purchase additional hardware to provide OpsMgr functionality (hardware specifications should be determined based on the information in Chapter 4). Additional negatives with this approach include requirements for more rack space, backup power, and increased management for supporting the additional servers.

Many organizations purchased hardware designed for the growth required for their MOM 2005 solution. As a result, the hardware is often insufficient to run both solutions on the same physical systems.

In the "Same Hardware" section of this chapter, we explained the reasons why you should or should not use the same hardware as part of the migration process. In general, it results in a better migration experience when you use the new hardware migration approach versus the same hardware migration. With the new hardware approach, the installation gains the benefits of a clean installation of the operating system (including the benefits of a 64-bit platform if one is chosen) and will not have to share resources between the two applications.

Although you must acquire extra hardware for the new hardware approach, it does not necessarily mean that additional hardware will be required once the project is complete. Let's take an example where your current MOM 2005 solution is running in a two-server configuration (a management server and a SQL Server system running the reporting and database components) and the hardware is relatively new. You install new hardware for the OpsMgr 2007 solution, and the agents are reporting to both environments. Once the OpsMgr 2007 solution provides the required functionality, you can shut down the MOM 2005 solution. After you decommission MOM 2005, the server(s) providing that solution will now be available for use elsewhere in your organization.

Hybrid Approach

The same hardware and new hardware approaches are just that: approaches. They are not strict in their interpretation that you can only do a same hardware approach or a new hardware approach. Your environment may require a hybrid of the two approaches. As an example, we can look at an organization with a MOM 2005 environment that has a single management server as well as a combined database and reporting server. Due to performance issues in this configuration, the goal is to split out some of the functionality that the combined database and reporting server is providing.

Figure 7.4 displays the resultant hybrid migration. This migration uses a same hardware approach for the management server and part of the database requirements. However, it introduces new hardware into the design to enable separating the OpsMgr 2007 Reporting Server and Data Warehouse Server Components.

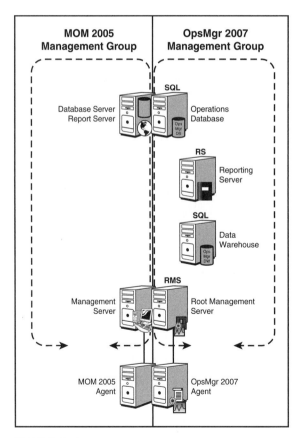

FIGURE 7.4   Hybrid migration approach.

Using a hybrid method, combining both the same hardware and new hardware approaches, provides a much more diverse approach to deploying the OpsMgr solution, and you should consider it if there is a requirement to use at least some of the original hardware from the MOM 2005 solution.

Swing Server Approach

One other concept to think about when migrating to OpsMgr 2007 is the *swing server approach*. You will often see this approach in Exchange migrations, where a new server is deployed running the new version of Exchange and then users are migrated to the new server. Once the old server is no longer required, it is rebuilt using the new version of Exchange; users are then migrated back to the original server. The swing server provides a method to use temporary hardware in a migration, which allows you to use the original system hardware for the new solution.

With OpsMgr 2007, you can apply some of the swing server concepts, but the migration will be far more complex than any other migration approaches discussed in this chapter. This is not a recommended migration approach, but we include it for consideration as an approach that may be available later in the product cycle for OpsMgr 2007. The high-level approach to this type of a migration would include the following tasks:

1. Back up the current MOM 2005 environment.
2. Install the RMS on new hardware.
3. Install the Operations database on new hardware.
4. Install the Data Warehouse database on new hardware.
5. Install the Reporting Server Component on new hardware.
6. Install the OpsMgr agent on the servers you will be monitoring.
7. Validate functionality of the new OpsMgr 2007 solution.
8. Configure OpsMgr to meet the identified requirements.
9. Uninstall the MOM 2005 environment, including agents.
10. Reinstall the operating system on the original MOM 2005 management server, database server, and reporting server machines.
11. Install the OpsMgr 2007 management server on the original MOM 2005 management server hardware.
12. Install SQL Server 2005 and configure it with database and/or reporting functionality.
13. Move the RMS from the new hardware back to the original management server hardware.
14. Move the database and reporting functionality.
15. Decommission all new hardware provided for the migration.

> **TIP**
>
> **Moving the Database and Reporting Functionality**
>
> While initially there was no method to move the Operations and Data Warehouse databases to other servers, we have investigated these processes and documented the procedures for moving both these databases.
>
> An article on how to move the Operations database is available at http://ops-mgr. spaces.live.com/blog/cns!3D3B8489FCAA9B51!177.entry. Microsoft has since updated the Backup and Recovery guide (available at http://technet.microsoft.com/en-us/opsmgr/bb498235.aspx) to include a process to move the Operations database.
>
> We also have written an article on how to move the data warehouse, which is available at http://ops-mgr.spaces.live.com/Blog/cns!3D3B8489FCAA9B51!235.entry. (Links to both these articles are available as live links in Appendix E, "Reference URLs," and these processes are also discussed in Chapter 12, "Backup and Recovery.")
>
> Microsoft has also updated their Backup and Recovery guide to include the steps to move the data warehouse.

We have discussed a variety of approaches to migration within this chapter, including starting clean, same hardware, new hardware, hybrid, and swing server. In the next section of this chapter, we will review the same and new hardware approaches as examples of migrations.

Case Studies

To understand the actual migration process in more depth, we will go through two case studies on how to approach the migration. These examples will focus on the two primary methods to migrate to OpsMgr 2007: same hardware and new hardware.

Same Hardware Migration for Eclipse

The Eclipse Company deployed MOM 2005 in a single management group using a single-server configuration. Eclipse monitors 100 servers with MOM 2005 and wants to be able to use the same hardware to monitor its environment with OpsMgr 2007. Eclipse has accepted that once the migration process is complete, the reporting information from the MOM 2005 environment will no longer be accessible online. Therefore, Eclipse has generated a backup of the database and the reports so it can re-create the reporting system if that is required later.

See Chapter 4 for information on planning a migration such as this one. This section assumes that you performed an effective assessment, planning, and design prior to installing OpsMgr 2007.

The first step in the Eclipse migration was to deploy OpsMgr 2007 on the same server where MOM 2005 was already functional. The company identified a unique name (GROUP2) for the new management group. The deployment involved installing the Operations Manager 2007 RMS, Operations Console, Operations Database Server, and the Reporting and Data Warehouse Components (for details on installing these components, see Chapter 6). Eclipse deployed agents using the Operations console and validated the functionality of the OpsMgr solution.

Next, Eclipse installed the MOM 2005 to OpsMgr 2007 Migration Tool. You can find this tool on the System Center Operations Manager 2007 installation media. Run the setup program (SetupOM.exe) and select the option Install MOM 2005 to Operations Manager 2007 Migration Tool. This option requires that both the MOM 2005 SP 1 user interface and the OpsMgr 2007 user interface exist on the same system.

Security Requirements to Migrate Management Packs

The following permissions are required for migrating management packs from MOM 2005 to OpsMgr 2007:

▶ Local Administrator rights on the MOM 2005 management server.

▶ Member of the OpsMgr 2007 Administrators group.

▶ Both management groups must be in the same domain, or there must be at least a one-way trust between the domains.

Running the Migration Tool

The actual installation of the migration component has no wizard screens; there is only a confirmation message that the setup succeeded. The installation creates a program called the Migration Tool, available on the Start menu within the System Center Operations Manager 2007 folder. To run the Migration Tool, perform the following steps:

1. The Migration Tool invokes the System Center Operations Manager Migration Wizard, which is displayed in Figure 7.5.

   This wizard provides management pack migration from a MOM 2005 management group or the file system. Use the file system approach in a two-stage migration, where you gather the information from the MOM 2005 management group and store it on the file system for later integration with OpsMgr 2007.

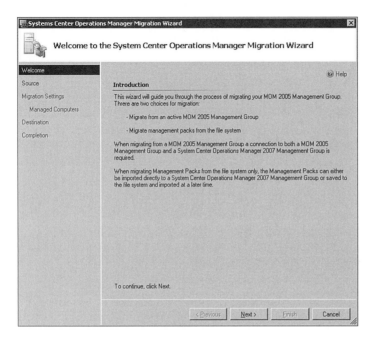

FIGURE 7.5   Welcome to the System Center Operations Manager Migration Wizard screen.

2. On the next screen of the wizard, we specify management server name, as shown in Figure 7.6. For the Eclipse environment, the management server is named MOM.

3. The next step is to configure the settings for whether the wizard will migrate managed computers and management packs, as well as what specific management packs to migrate. These choices are shown in Figure 7.7.

On this screen we specify whether we going to migrate computers and management packs. "Migrating" computers is quite benign; this option generates a file of the computers that we can later use for installing agents, so it is highly recommended to check the option.

Deciding which management packs to migrate is a little more complex to determine. Figure 7.7 shows all the management packs installed in the MOM 2005 environment, including those that were custom developed.

Our recommendation is to take the list and uncheck those that have corresponding management packs listed on Microsoft's System Center Pack Catalog site as Operations Manager 2007 management packs (http://go.microsoft.com/fwlink/?LinkId=71124). Mark the check box of any custom management packs required in OpsMgr 2007 so the wizard will attempt migration.

On our first attempt with this wizard, we chose to migrate the DHCP Server, DNS Server, and Print Server management packs (which were not available as OpsMgr

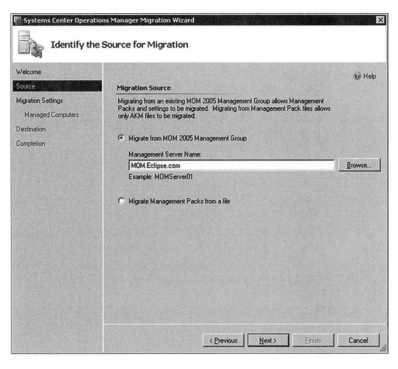

FIGURE 7.6   Specifying the migration source.

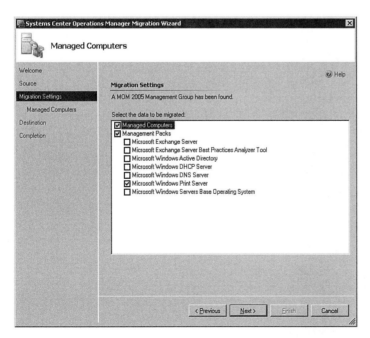

FIGURE 7.7   Configuring the settings for the wizard.

2007 management packs at that time). Although the wizard completed successfully, it was unable to actually migrate the DHCP and DNS management packs. If you cannot successfully convert your MOM 2005 management packs with the Migration Wizard, you may want to try using the MP2XML and MPConvert utilities, which we discuss in Chapter 13.

Another Method to Convert Management Packs

There is another technique for converting MOM 2005 management packs to OpsMgr 2007 management packs, although the technique is no longer officially supported by Microsoft. Here are the four steps for this method:

1. Export the management pack from the MOM 2005 Administrator console or locate the original AKM file.

2. Use the MP2XML utility (available as part of the MOM 2005 resource kit at http://www.microsoft.com/technet/opsmgr/2005/downloads/tools/reskit.mspx) to convert the AKM file to an XML file.

3. Use the MPConvert utility from the Operations Manager 2007 installation media to convert the MOM2K5 XML file into an OpsMgr XML file.

4. Import the OpsMgr XML version of the management pack into Operations Manager 2007.

You can also read about this process at http://technet.microsoft.com/en-us/library/ bb309603.aspx. Syntax for these tools is available at http://technet.microsoft.com/ en-us/library/bb309532.aspx. We also discuss this further in Chapter 13, "Administering Management Packs."

---

4. For our example in Figure 7.7, we have left only the Managed Computers and Microsoft Windows Print Server management pack options checked. Because we chose the Managed Computers check box, the next screen requests the location to save the managed computer export file, as shown in Figure 7.8.

   This file contains the names of the servers currently managed by the MOM 2005 management group. The file itself is a text file with each server's fully qualified name (FQDN) on a separate line within the file. In our example, we stored this at the top of the C:\ drive in a file named called c:\export.txt.

5. Because we are doing a same hardware migration, the server name is the same name as on the wizard source screen. For our example in Figure 7.9, where we specify the managed destination, the server is MOM.Eclipse.com.

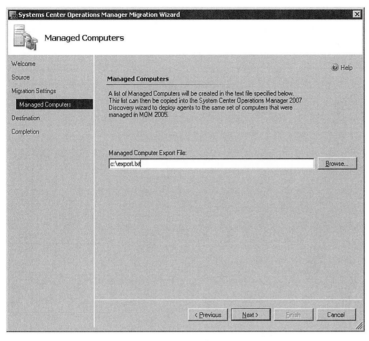

FIGURE 7.8   Specifying where the managed computer export file is created.

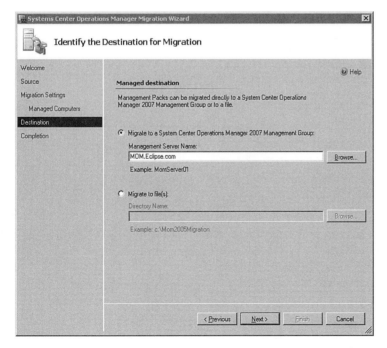

FIGURE 7.9   Specifying the migration destination.

6. The last step runs the migration and displays the status for actions specified. For our Eclipse migration, we successfully performed both the export and migration of the Microsoft Windows Print Server management pack (see Figure 7.10).

Performing this process integrated the Print Server management pack with the Operations Manager 2007 environment and generated an exported file listing the computers managed by MOM 2005.

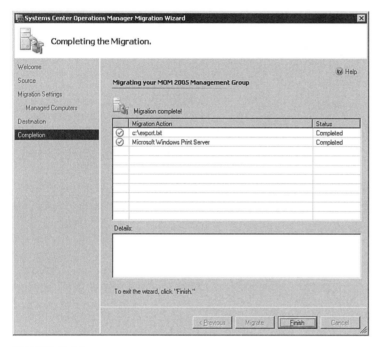

FIGURE 7.10   Completing the Migration Wizard.

Installing OpsMgr 2007 Agents

The next step is to take the exported file and install the agents on OpsMgr 2007 using this file. Run the Discovery Wizard in the Operations console. In the Administration node, navigate to Discovery Wizard -> Advanced Discovery and then choose the option Browse for, or type-in computer names (see Figure 7.11).

You can now deploy these systems using the Discovery Wizard, which will integrate the new agents with OpsMgr 2007 while they continue to be managed by MOM 2005. To deploy to the systems that were exported, copy and paste the contents of the exported file into the Discovery Wizard into the Browse for box shown in Figure 7.11. For more detail on the Discovery Wizard, see Chapter 9, "Installing and Configuring Agents."

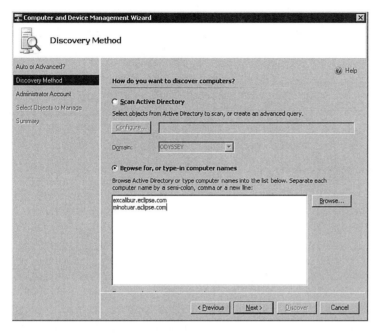

FIGURE 7.11   Discover the agents using the export file from the Migration Wizard.

Summarizing the Eclipse Migration

For the Eclipse Company, the following list summarizes the same hardware implementation as it occurred during the migration:

▶ Assessed the current MOM 2005 environment.

  We identified one management group, one management server, and one database/reporting server.

▶ Identified requirements for OpsMgr 2007.

▶ Performed a backup of the current MOM 2005 environment.

▶ Downloaded all prerequisites identified by the two different systems.

  The original management server will now be an RMS, Operations console, and Web console in addition to the original functions. The first server required installing .NET Framework 2.0, PowerShell, and .NET Framework 3.0.

▶ The original database server/reporting server is now the Operations database, Reporting server, and data warehouse, in addition to its the original functions.

  This server required SQL 2005 SP 1, KB918222 (both SQL and Reporting components), and .NET framework 3.0.

▶ Validated the functionality of the original MOM 2005 environment.

- SMS 2003 also uses the database server; we validated that SMS 2003 was still functional after installing the OpsMgr prerequisites.

- Determined the current name for the management group in MOM 2005 (Eclipse).

- Used GROUP2 as the new management group name for OpsMgr 2007.

- Created service accounts, including OM_MSAA, OM_SDK, OM_DWWA, and OM_DRA.

- Installed the OpsMgr operational database on the original database server.

- Installed the RMS, Operations console, and Web console on the original management server.

- Validated the functionality of the reporting services on the original database server.

- Installed the Reporting components on the original database server.

- Validated functionality of both the OpsMgr and MOM installations.

- Installed the Migration Wizard and ran the wizard.

- The domain controllers immediately showed up as discovered.

- Pushed the agent to a subset of the servers using the list exported from the wizard.

- Identified issues with agent deployment. One issue was a Windows 2003 server without Service Pack 1 installed.

- Validated the functionality of the MOM 2005 Operator console.

- Validated the functionality of the OpsMgr 2007 Operations console.

The result from the same hardware approach was a two-server configuration running both MOM 2005 and OpsMgr 2007, displayed earlier in Figure 7.2. This process provided the foundation required for meeting the business requirements identified for the solution; once those matched, the original MOM 2005 environment could be decommissioned.

Decommissioning MOM 2005

Once the MOM 2005 environment is no longer required, you can decommission it by uninstalling the components. The recommended order for uninstalling components is as follows:

1. Active Directory Helper Object (OOMADS)
2. MOM 2005 agents
3. MOM 2005 Reporting server
4. MOM 2005 Web console
5. MOM management server(s)
6. MOM console(s)
7. MOM Operational database
8. MOM data warehouse

New Hardware Migration for Eclipse

The second possible approach for migrating the Eclipse company was to perform a new hardware migration. After evaluating this approach, it was determined to be the approach that would provide the best long-term functionality for the company. Two primary reasons were identified for taking this approach rather than the same hardware approach:

▶ The ability to provide a 64-bit platform for the OpsMgr solution

▶ The opportunity to split out the Reporting server functionality from the Data Warehouse and Operations Database server

The original recommended configuration had also included the split of the data warehouse and Operational database to separate servers, but due to software and hardware costs, the decision was to keep these components together and to split them in the future if there were performance bottlenecks.

The first step in the Eclipse new hardware migration was installing the servers required for Operations Manager 2007. The company identified a unique name (GROUP2) for the new management group. Based on the business requirements for the OpsMgr 2007 product, the design included three servers:

▶ RMS

▶ Operations database and Data Warehouse server

▶ Reporting server

After installing these servers and bringing the new OpsMgr 2007 environment online, the next step of Eclipse's new hardware migration was deploying the Operations Manager 2007 console on the MOM 2005 management server. The reverse approach could also have been taken (installing the MOM 2005 console on the OpsMgr 2007 RMS), but because the goal is to obsolete the MOM 2005 environment, the decision was made to not install any MOM 2005 components on the permanent OpsMgr 2007 equipment.

After the current MOM 2005 management server was configured with the required OpsMgr 2007 components, the Migration Wizard was ready to install. As with the same hardware migration, this is available from the System Center Operations Manager 2007 Setup (SetupOM.exe) screen by selecting the Install MOM 2005 to Operations Manager 2007 Migration Tool. Then you can run the Migration Tool from the Start menu.

The following summarizes the Eclipse company's new hardware implementation as it occurred during the migration:

▶ Assessed the current MOM 2005 environment.

The assessment identified one management group, one management server, and one Database/Reporting server.

▶ Identified the requirements for OpsMgr 2007.

▶ Downloaded all prerequisites identified by all three systems.

▶ Determined the current name for the MOM 2005 management group (Eclipse).

▶ Used GROUP2 as the new management group name for OpsMgr 2007.

▶ Created service accounts, including OM_MSAA, OM_SDK, OM_DWWA, and OM_DRA.

▶ Backed up the current MOM 2005 environment.

▶ Installed the OpsMgr Operations database on the new database server.

▶ Installed the RMS, Operations Console, and Web Operations Console Components on the new RMS.

▶ Installed the Data Warehouse Components on the new database server.

▶ Installed the Reporting Components on the new reporting server.

▶ Validated the functionality of the OpsMgr and MOM installations.

▶ Installed the Migration Wizard on the MOM 2005 management server and ran the wizard.

Using the wizard required installation of the OpsMgr 2007 user interfaces, which also required installation of the MSXML 6.0 parser and .NET Framework 3.0. Figure 7.12 is an example of the Migration Wizard running, displaying MOM 2005 custom-developed management packs.

▶ The domain controllers in the environment immediately showed up as discovered .

▶ Pushed the agent to a subset of the servers exported from the wizard.

▶ Identified issues with agent deployment. One issue was a Windows 2003 server that did not have Service Pack 1 installed.

▶ Validated the functionality of the MOM 2005 Operator console.

▶ Validated the functionality of the OpsMgr 2007 Operations console.

The result of using the new hardware approach was the previous two-server configuration running MOM 2005 and a new three-server configuration running OpsMgr 2007, previously displayed in Figure 7.3. This process provided the foundation needed for the business requirements identified for the solution; after those requirements were met, the original MOM 2005 environment could be decommissioned.

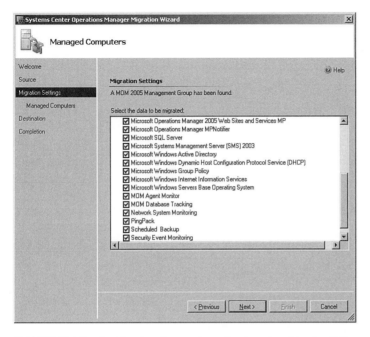

FIGURE 7.12   Configuring the settings for the wizard in the Eclipse new hardware migration.

Troubleshooting Tips

Because there is no upgrade path to OpsMgr 2007, with only a migration path from MOM 2005 to OpsMgr 2007, the troubleshooting process is greatly simplified. Currently no documented errors are associated with the migration from MOM 2005 to OpsMgr 2007 on the Microsoft knowledge base at http://support.microsoft.com. Here are the best tips related to providing the cleanest migration to OpsMgr 2007 from MOM 2005:

▶ Back up your current environment prior to starting any installation.

▶ Plan what you want your OpsMgr 2007 environment to look like (see Chapters 4 and 5).

▶ Understand what MOM 2005 is performing in the environment so you can replicate that functionality in OpsMgr 2007. Plan to have sufficient time available to replicate all required functionality prior to decommissioning the MOM 2005 environment.

▶ Be careful when choosing a same hardware approach. Remember that installing the OpsMgr 2007 Reporting Component causes the existing MOM 2005 reporting environment to be unavailable, as shown in the error displayed in Figure 7.13.

▶ Be aware of the details of the installation steps for each of the components you will use in your design (see Chapter 6).

▶ Make an educated decision on whether to start clean or use one of the hardware approaches (same hardware or new hardware) based on the content of this chapter.

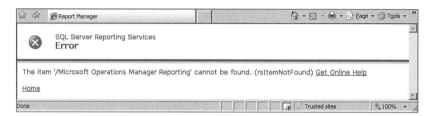

FIGURE 7.13   Error when installing the OpsMgr 2007 Reporting Component on the MOM 2005 reporting server.

Summary

This chapter discussed three different options available for migrating to Operations Manager 2007 and presented case study examples for the same hardware and new hardware migration approaches. In the next chapter, we discuss how to configure and use Operations Manager 2007.

PART III

Moving Toward Application-Centered Management

IN THIS PART

Configuring and Using Operations Manager 2007

This chapter discusses tasks to perform after installing Microsoft System Center Operations Manager (OpsMgr). As we begin this chapter, we assume you have previously installed the PowerShell Command Shell and the core server-side components of OpsMgr on one or more servers. The core components we will refer to are listed here:

▶ The OpsMgr operational database

▶ The Root Management Server (RMS)

▶ Reporting components, including the Data Warehouse database

▶ The Web Console Server

After a default installation of OpsMgr with reporting, all these components are installed and will function at a baseline level.

If the core OpsMgr components are not installed, you may want to first read Chapter 6, "Installing Operations Manager 2007," to step through a fresh install, or Chapter 7, "Migrating to Operations Manager 2007," if you are migrating from Microsoft Operations Manager (MOM) 2005.

If you are familiar with any version of Operations Manager, you most likely will approach this chapter to become acclimated to the new System Center-based release of Microsoft's server-monitoring software and its user interfaces. In this case, we suggest you read Chapter 2, "What's New," as an introduction. Chapter 2 describes the differences between Operations Manager 2007 and MOM 2005, as well as the different functionality in Operations Manager 2007 versus System Center Essentials 2007. If you are entirely new to Microsoft management products, focus instead on this chapter to familiarize yourself with Operations Manager 2007.

This chapter discusses basic configuration and administration of Operations Manager 2007, beginning with several mandatory post-installation tasks. You will learn about the functions and components of the Operations console, and how to install the console on remote machines. We step through wizards in the console to install agents and management packs. We also discuss Operations Manager security groups and their utilization in the Operations console, maintenance for the Operations database, and Operations Manager Reporting administration. In several sections of this chapter, we will also demonstrate how to perform tasks using PowerShell as an alternative to, or in preference to, the console.

Mandatory Minimum Configuration Activities

After you successfully install the core management group components, two major configuration activities must take place before Operations Manager can start working for you. These actions are to import management packs and to discover objects to manage. We will walk you through these activities after we confirm the basic health of the management group.

Confirming Management Group Health

Before you import management packs and discover objects to manage, we recommend a waiting period of about 24 hours after initial installation of the core components. This is particularly the case when you have distributed OpsMgr components across two or more computers, or when you need to wait to allow domain Group Policy-based Windows Firewall exceptions to propagate. Many interconnected components must cooperate to establish a management group; some workflows occur only periodically, and there is a lag between when you add an object and when the data for that object is available for the first time in the various reporting views. To let all the initial workflows progress completely and identify any problems, let the new management group components "percolate" for a business day or two before continuing. If you are in a hurry, you can also restart the OpsMgr-related services to kick-start this process.

Your Initial Configuration

After installing the core OpsMgr components, you will have a Root Management Server, Operations and Data Warehouse databases, a Reporting Server Component, and at least one Operations console. We begin our discussion with such a baseline management group configuration, which has just been deployed across three servers and has been running for a few days. If your deployments are more complex (for example, if you are clustering the RMS or deploying redundant management servers or gateway servers), we recommend you build out and validate the core components before implementing additional components. Figure 8.1 shows our sample management group, with server names listed, to help you follow the validation steps we will be performing.

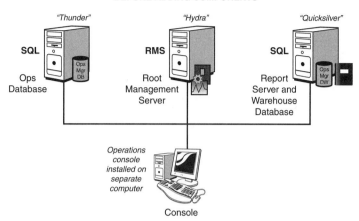

FIGURE 8.1   Core management group components to verify before building out.

Loading the Operations Console

We are going to "kick the tires" a little to make sure we have a stable foundation before moving forward with bringing this management group into a monitoring environment. Start with verifying that all instances of the console are closed; then open a new instance of the Operations console. (After you install the Reporting Component, this is necessary to make the Reporting features appear in the console.) Even better, we recommend installing the Operations console on an administrator workstation and performing all tests and production work using Operations consoles not installed on management servers.

TIP

Where to Run the Operations Console

We do not recommend running the Operations console on the RMS desktop or using a Remote Desktop Protocol (RDP) session to the RMS during the tests. It is not a good practice to run the Operations console on the RMS itself—you want to dedicate all RMS resources for the critical OpsMgr services it hosts.

In addition, using the Operations console from a computer other than the RMS tests several important communication channels between components in the management group. We will get a more complete checkup of OpsMgr's health using a separate Operations console installed on a workstation or uninvolved server. For validation purposes, the computer running the console should be a member of the domain and on the same network segment as the Root Management Server and Reporting components.

Procedures for installing the Operations console on separate computers appear later in the "Deploying and Using the Operations Console" section of this chapter.

After connecting the console to the RMS, and possibly authenticating with the domain, we will expect to see a screen similar to Figure 8.2. This is the initial view of the Operations console, in a new management group with the Reporting Component installed. The first view of the Operations console displayed is the Administration Overview page, also seen when the root of the Administration hierarchy is selected in the Navigation pane on the left side of the console.

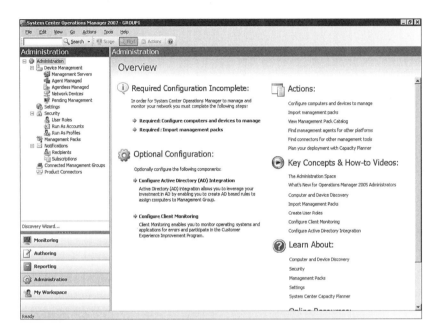

FIGURE 8.2   The Administration Overview page after initial management group installation.

The Administration Overview page shown in Figure 8.2 includes an information element that will go away once mandatory initial configuration procedures are complete; this is the Required Configuration Incomplete banner with the comment:

In order for System Center Operations Manager to manage and monitor your network, you must complete the following steps.

The two steps listed are:

▶ Configure computers and devices to manage

▶ Import management packs

These two steps are just links to the same-named tasks on the right side of the Administration Overview page in the Actions section of the page.

We will perform these mandatory configuration activities after we check out the health of the core management group components. Begin by clicking the Monitoring navigation button. The Operations console reconfigures to display its default view of the Monitoring pane. Figure 8.3 shows the Monitoring Overview page, displayed when you select the root of the Monitoring hierarchy in the Navigation pane on the left side of the console.

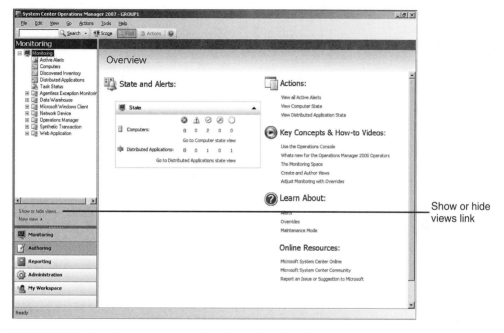

Show or hide views link

FIGURE 8.3   The Operations console's Monitoring Overview page after initial installation.

The distinctive feature of the Monitoring Overview page is its dashboard-style chart of the quantity of computers and distributed applications in the Critical, Warning, Success, Maintenance Mode, and Unknown states. We expect to see a small number of computers at this point, because we have not added any objects to manage! The only managed computers in the new management group so far are the management server and the system running the operational database.

Global Views

On the left side of the console, below the root of the Monitoring hierarchy in the Navigation pane in the upper corner, are seven view folders and the five default global views:

- ▶ Active Alerts
- ▶ Computers
- ▶ Discovered Inventory
- ▶ Distributed Applications
- ▶ Task Status

Global views are views located immediately under the root of the Monitoring hierarchy. You can create new, custom global views under the Monitoring hierarchy root, as well as new view folders and hierarchies of folders. Notice the Show or hide views... link at the bottom of the Navigation pane. Clicking this link pops up the Show or Hide Views control shown in Figure 8.4.

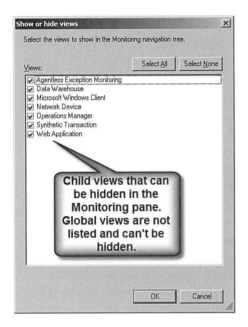

FIGURE 8.4   The visibility of individual view folders can be toggled on or off in the Operations console.

As you can see in Figure 8.4, you cannot toggle on or off the visibility of the global views—these views are always visible to those users who have permission to access them. The Show or Hide Views dialog box only applies to child view folders. The user role associated with the user running the console individually controls access to every view; this includes global views as well as each view in each child view folder. (We discuss user roles in detail in Chapter 11, "Securing Operations Manager 2007.") Whereas users only see the views they have rights to, they can choose which child view folders to display in their console.

Selecting to look at just some of the view folders is useful when the organization has a large number of management packs installed and/or has created custom views; in these cases, an operator can hide the view folders that are not involved in performing their job. The three most important global views are the Active Alerts, Computers, and Distributed Applications views. You will access these views frequently when using OpsMgr. The Actions area on the top of the right side of the Monitoring Overview page includes shortcuts to these views. (The Go to Computers State view and Go to Distributed Applications State view links in the dashboard area are also shortcuts to the same views.)

Don't Overdo the Number of Global Views You Create!

Because the operator cannot hide global views, OpsMgr administrators should avoid creating so many custom global views that the list of child view folders is pushed out of the Navigation pane.

We are going to check out the health of our new management group using the distributed applications monitor for the management group, created during installation of the OpsMgr 2007 product. The Monitoring Overview dashboard indicates that two distributed applications are monitored: One is in the success state and one is in the unknown state. To investigate further, we can click one of the convenience links to the Distributed Applications state view on the Monitoring Overview page, or navigate directly to the Distributed Applications state global view in the Navigation pane.

In a default installation of OpsMgr 2007, two objects are listed in the Distributed Applications state global view. Because of our dashboard view, we expect one to be in the unknown state, and the other we hope is in a success state. The distributed application in the unknown state is clarified in the state view to be in a "Not monitored" status, and it's identified as "A connector used by MOM components to insert discovery data, please create your own connector do not use this connector" (partially displayed in Figure 8.5). This object is "MOM shrapnel," and we are going to ignore it. However, we do have to get used to seeing that particular distributed application in a perpetually "Not monitored" state.

Distributed Application Health Explorer

The other object listed in the Distributed Applications state global view is valid and important to us—this is the Operations Manager Management Group distributed application. Figure 8.5 shows us navigating to the Distributed Applications state view, right-clicking the Operations Manager Management Group distributed application, and expanding the context-sensitive menu choices available for selection. Our cursor is over the command to invoke the Health Explorer for Operations Manager Management Group.

This distributed application object represents the health of our management group and is a convenient and centralized vehicle to oversee the end-to-end monitoring capabilities of OpsMgr.

Tools for Reviewing Distributed Application Health

The best OpsMgr tools for reviewing the health of distributed applications are the Health Explorer and the Diagram view.

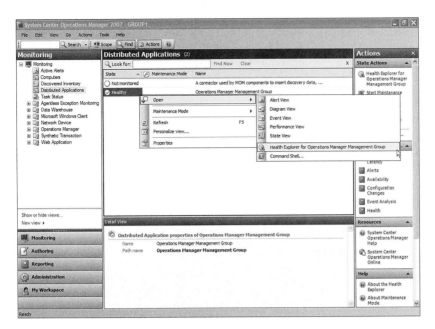

FIGURE 8.5   Right-clicking the distributed application object presents menu choices.

The Health Explorer for a distributed application clearly shows that data from multiple managed objects is included in the health model for that application. Figure 8.6 shows the Health Explorer for the Operations Manager management group. The Health Explorer opens in its own window. In this figure, we expanded some paths in the health model to verify that monitors in the success state exist for multiple components of our management group.

Notice in Figure 8.6 that availability data of various services and features is included from both the OpsMgr Operations Database Component (on Thunder in our environment) and the OpsMgr Root Management Server Component (Hydra). The availability monitor for the management group appears as a rollup of the availability state from several perspectives. The Thunder computer (database server) is hosting the watching processes for agent group availability, whereas Hydra (RMS) is reporting on availability of the SDK service.

Agents connect to the RMS, but the Health Explorer shows that the computer hosting the Operations Database Component watches this process. Likewise, the SDK service connects to the operational database, but the RMS watches this process. At first glance, these monitoring perspectives seem contrary; that is, one might expect to monitor the database from the database component. In fact, the concept of externally watching a process from a separate component is a chief design feature and strength of the OpsMgr 2007 architecture.

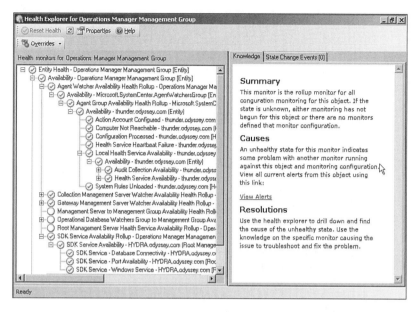

FIGURE 8.6   The Health Explorer for a distributed application includes monitors from multiple managed objects.

With the health model showing success indicators for the Operations Manager Management Group, we can close the Health Explorer. Returning to the distributed application menu choices displayed in Figure 8.5, we will select the Diagram view to continue our validation of a successful installation of OpsMgr 2007. The Diagram view opens in its own window, similar to the Health Explorer. When we select a view by right-clicking an object and that view opens in its own window, we are said to be *pivoting* to that view.

Distributed Application Diagram View

Figure 8.7 shows the Diagram view of the Operations Manager Management Group after pivoting from the Distributed Applications global view to the Diagram view. We observe a simplified presentation of the health model, specifically calling out dependencies and relationships between the managed objects that constitute the management group.

Notice in Figure 8.7 the object icons with the eyeglasses element. When you see those eyeglasses in a Diagram view, it means the object is a *watcher node* for one or more other objects. Follow the connection arrows in the Diagram view to discover the dependencies and relationships between objects and their watcher nodes.

8

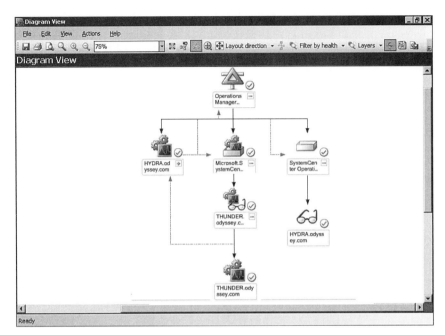

FIGURE 8.7 Components and watchers in the Diagram view of the OpsMgr distributed application.

Just as we validated in the Health Explorer (refer to Figure 8.6), we observe in the Diagram view in Figure 8.7 that Thunder, which hosts our Operations Database Component, is watching the availability of the agent group. Notice how the highlighted object, the Health Service Watcher Group, has an arrow pointing down to the Thunder Health Service Watcher. Similarly, notice the desk tray icon to the right of the highlighted object. This desk tray icon represents the Operations Database Watchers Group, and the arrow to the Hydra watcher icon below that indicates that Hydra is the watcher node for the health of the operational database.

For a large, complex distributed application, the Diagram view is the best way (or perhaps the only way) to visually diagnose cross-platform interdependencies. The Diagram view makes clear what objects are watching what other objects. This is invaluable to enable you to rule out that an alert of a failed distributed application is not simply a failure of a watcher node process.

Another unusual icon you might notice in Figure 8.7 is the top-level (or rollup object) triangle laid over a T-shaped intersection of pipes. This icon represents a distributed application in OpsMgr Diagram views. We can select this rollup object in our Diagram view and read useful high-level information about the distributed application in the Details pane. Figure 8.8 shows the management group details when you select the rollup object in the Diagram view.

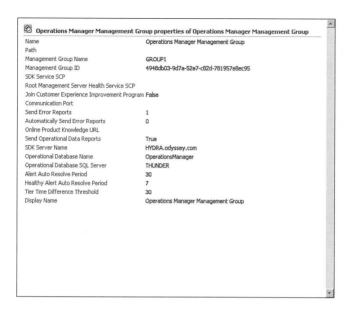

FIGURE 8.8   High-level management group properties in the distributed application Diagram view.

Distributed Application PowerShell Integration

Closing the Diagram view, we return once more to the Distributed Applications global view in the Monitoring pane, shown previously in Figure 8.5. Now we want to test our PowerShell installation and integration with OpsMgr. Right-clicking again the distributed application Operations Manager Management Group, we will select Open -> Command Shell... to launch PowerShell in the OpsMgr group context. We type in the cmdlet **get-State** and observe the reply in Figure 8.9.

Notice in Figure 8.9 the prompt line after the line Connecting to Operations Manager Management Server 'HYDRA.odyssey.com'. From the prompt line, we confirm that the PowerShell (PS) context is

```
Monitoring:\HYDRA.odyssey.com\Microsoft.SystemCenter.ManagementGroup
```

This context represents the rollup monitor of the distributed application—the same triangle-and-pipes object we reviewed the properties of in Figure 8.8. The response from PowerShell to the get-State cmdlet returns the health state and some descriptive details related to the shell's context. We are looking for the response line HealthState: Success. This is the command-line equivalent to the green check mark of the Success state in the Operations console!

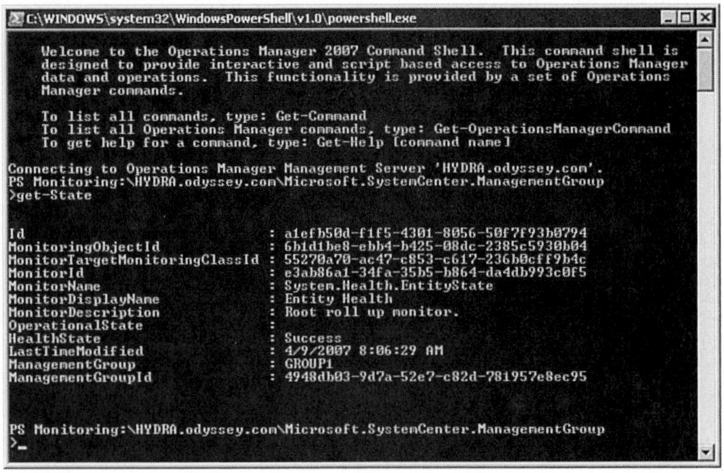

FIGURE 8.9   Validating the health of the management group using PowerShell.

Distributed Application Performance View

Another functionality we want to validate is graphing performance counters in the Operations console. After closing the PowerShell window, we right-click once again the distributed application Operations Manager Management Group and pivot to the Performance view by selecting Open -> Performance View. A new Performance window will open with an initially empty Results area and rows of counters to select for display in the Details area. The empty Results pane will have neither a units nor a time scale, and there will be a reminder that we need to select some counters to see data on the graph.

In Figure 8.10, we sorted the list of counters by the type of counter; then we scrolled down to locate the System Up Time counters. Because there are counters from two managed computers forming part of the Operations Manager distributed application, we notice two System Up Time counters—one for each computer. We tick the check boxes for those counters in the Show column and immediately see the graph populated with linear data; units appear on the left scale and time on the lower scale (see Figure 8.10).

Our test of the console's graphical performance counter display function is successful, as shown in Figure 8.10. In the instance of System Up Time performance counters, the units on the left scale are seconds. The chart correctly reflects that both computers were restarted about 5:00 p.m. the previous day, so their chart lines, although of different colors, are almost superimposed on one another. The counters increment steadily to the right as the quantity of seconds of uptime accumulates. Now that we have confirmed that rendering of performance graphs is functional, we want to unselect the check boxes in the Show column to clear the charted results pane and restore the view to its defaults. Then we can close the Performance window.

These checks verify the Operations Manager distributed application is healthy. There are just a few more items to check before we are ready to import management packs and discover objects to manage. We need to look at any unresolved alerts in the management group, and we want to validate that the Reporting Component is installed correctly and working.

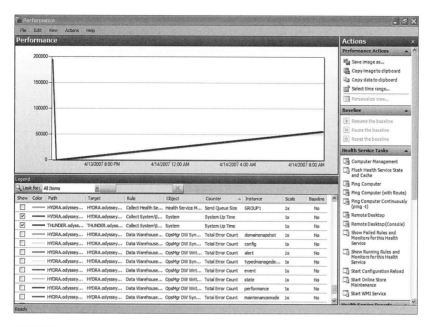

FIGURE 8.10   Confirming that we can view performance data in the Operations console.

Active Alerts

To view alerts, we need to change our focus to the Active Alerts global view. The quickest way to do this is to click directly the Active Alerts view immediately under the root of the Monitoring hierarchy in the Navigation pane on the left. Or, if you prefer, you can return via the Monitoring Overview page by clicking the root of the Monitoring hierarchy. Then in the Monitoring Overview page, click the View All Active Alerts shortcut in the Actions area on the right.

Because we have not imported any application or operating system management packs, we will only observe alerts created by the base Operations Manager management pack. These alerts will relate to the health of the management group itself, and we will want to resolve any critical alerts before proceeding. Figure 8.11 shows our initial view of the active alerts in our new management group.

It is normal for there to be just a few alerts here, which we hope were transitory and coincide with installing the management group components. It's certainly possible for certain OpsMgr components to raise alerts during the installation of other components and then not properly auto-resolve—we call this a *transitory alert* because such events occurred during atypical conditions and are not expected to reoccur during normal operation of the management group.

Alerts we do not expect to reoccur can be resolved. These would include alerts with a low alert repeat count, or an alert where a reasonable interval of time has passed without that alert reoccurring. You can check the age and repeat count for an alert by right-clicking the alert and selecting Properties, which brings up a dialog box similar to the one shown in Figure 8.12.

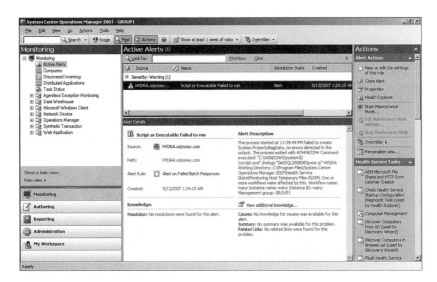

FIGURE 8.11   Active Alerts view will display problems with the management group.

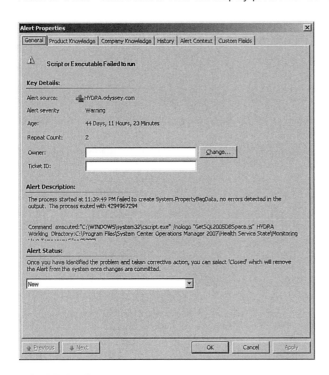

FIGURE 8.12   Alert properties assist with the evaluation of the alert relevance.

This figure shows the General tab of an alert, involving a monitoring script failure, after we selected to view alert properties. In this case, we have a Warning alert, which is less serious than a Critical alert. The alert has only occurred twice, and not in the past 5 days.

Reading the alert description tells us the script failed, reporting that the specified domain does not exist or cannot be contacted. This could have been due to temporary connectivity issues, or because domain controllers or DNS servers were being restarted. It is safe in this case to close this alert; if it reoccurs, we can escalate our investigation. We close the alert by changing the alert status from New to Closed and clicking the OK button.

On the other hand, if there are many alerts, particularly if they do not appear to be transitory, these need to be resolved before going further. In particular, you should not import management packs or add additional managed objects if there are critical alerts that you cannot resolve or perhaps do not understand.

Techniques for Resolving Alerts

Here are some tips on getting past critical alerts:

▶ Locate and investigate monitors in the Warning (yellow) and Error (red) states in the Health Explorer of the computer that was the source of the alert. (Open the Health Explorer by right-clicking the alert and selecting Open -> Health Explorer.) If there are unhealthy monitors, they may correlate with the alert you are researching. Check out the Context pane of the State Change Events tab for possible additional clues to the root cause.

▶ Read all the text in the alert properties. (Right-click the alert and select Properties.) In particular, carefully review the Alert Description field on the General tab and the Description field on the Alert Context tab.

▶ Right-click the alert and pivot to the Event view (select Open -> Event View). Sort the events by the Level column and then locate the events with the Error and Warning event levels. Events may correlate with the alert you are investigating and provide insight to its resolution.

▶ Review the complete Event logs of the computer that is the source of the alert. Do this via an RDP session to the computer or by remotely connecting your computer's Event Viewer to that computer. Look for clues in the usual System and Application logs (or other applicable Event logs based on the computer's role in the domain). If your local or domain security policy enables logging for security events, there may be security-related clues to the problem found in the Security Event log.

▶ Examine the Operations Manager Event log on the involved computers. You will find the Operations Manager Event log on any computer with an installed OpsMgr component, including the Agent and Operations Console components. Figure 8.13 shows the location of the Operations Manager log in the Event Viewers for the Windows 2003 and Windows XP operating systems and for the Windows Vista operating system. Notice in the Vista Event Viewer that the Operations Manager log is located in the Applications and Services Logs group. You may not understand the meaning of every event in the Operations Manager log, but Warning and Critical events found there may help you make progress on resolving your issue.

▶ Make sure to restart all the involved systems, including the Operational Database and RMS components. Review each system's Event logs after restarting.

8

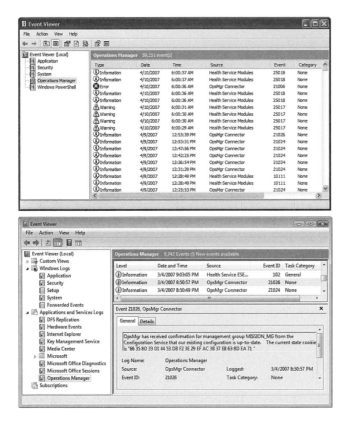

FIGURE 8.13   The Operations Manager Event log on Windows 2003 and XP (above) and Vista (below).

▶ Invest a couple of hours in viewing the TechNet Support webcast "Troubleshooting Microsoft Operations Manager Top Issues," found online at http://support.microsoft.com/kb/828936. A PowerPoint presentation is also available at that location for offline download if you want to skim the troubleshooting topics without watching the entire webcast.

▶ Review the resources available at http://www.microsoft.com/technet/community/en-us/mom/default.mspx. Resources include blogs, links to newsgroups, top product support issues, and other online venues to assist you. You can also use your preferred general-purpose search engines such as Google, Yahoo!, and MSN Live.

▶ Install a temporary management group on a second set or subset of computers and attempt to replicate or isolate the issue occurring in the first management group.

▶ Attempt a Repair installation from the OpsMgr 2007 setup media on some or all of the components of the management group.

▶ Uninstall and perform a clean setup of the management group components (basically, start over). If the same issues persist after a complete uninstall and reinstall of all OpsMgr components, reattempt installation but modify the setup environment. Examples of elements to alternate during reinstallation include using different or rebuilt Windows servers for management group components, modifying the proposed architecture to reallocate components in a different manner, and using different options for running the services. For example, in subsequent setup attempts, you can vary running the SDK service on the RMS as Local System, Network Service, or as a named user account.

Although some of these later tips may require a significant time investment, the goal is for you to end up with a management group installation that functions properly.

Reporting Function

The last feature to validate for our new management group is the reporting function. This is particularly important to test when the Reporting Server and/or Data Warehouse Server components are on distributed servers. Because the Reporting Component installation uses a separate setup procedure than the one shared by most of the other core management group components, issues may come up with a distributed installation.

Because the reporting function in the OpsMgr console also depends on the IIS services of the Reporting Server component, you will want to test that the dependency is working properly. It is best to wait at least 24 hours after installing the reporting function before running a report in the Operations console.

To check out the reporting feature, we will return to the Operations Manager Distributed Application view. Click the Distributed Applications view in the Monitoring hierarchy in the Navigation pane on the left side of the Operators console.

Reports are views that you cannot pivot to in the Monitoring space by right-clicking an object. Although we are now at the same view shown in Figure 8.5 (the Distributed Applications State view), we see that Reports and Reporting are not options on the context-sensitive menu. To view the reports involving an object, select the object in the Results pane that you want the report on using a single left-click. Then in the Actions pane on the right, a collection of context-relevant reports appears to select from, as shown in Figure 8.14.

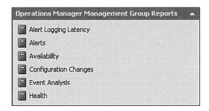

FIGURE 8.14   Reporting actions available in the context of the management group distributed application.

We are going to select the Health report to validate that the management group has been in a healthy state for at least the last 24 hours. The Health Report Setup and Run window appears; we show the top part of that window in Figure 8.15.

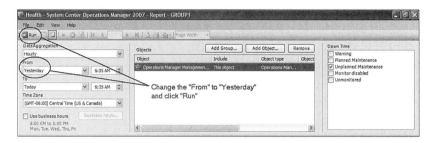

FIGURE 8.15   Change at least the start date of the report to get any data.

When the report window opens, the period of the report setup defaults to start and end times equal to the current date and time; so if you run the report without changing the time period, there would never be any data in it. We change the From (or start) date of the report from Today to Yesterday, creating a 24-hour interval to sample for the report. Click the Run button, and the report results appear shortly in the report window, as shown in Figure 8.16.

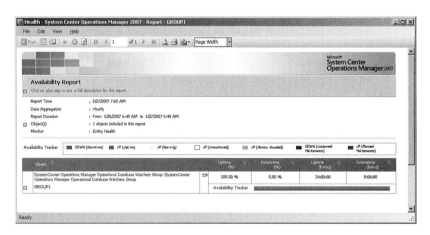

FIGURE 8.16   Availability report on the 24-hour health of the OpsMgr management group.

What we hope to see in the Availability Report shown in Figure 8.16 is 100% in the Uptime (%) column and 24:00:00 in the Uptime (h:mm:ss) column. This indicates that the health status of the management group was "success" for the 24-hour period of the report. We can drill down into each hour of the previous day by clicking the Availability Tracker link at the bottom of the Uptime column. This action generates an Availability Time report like the one shown in Figure 8.17, confirming the uptime of the management group for each of the preceding 24 hours.

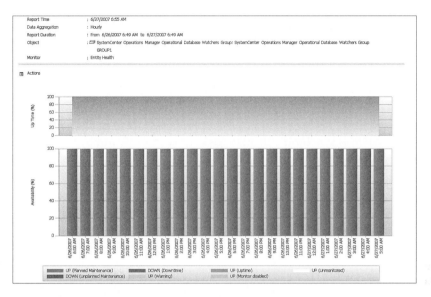

Report Time	: 6/27/2007 6:55 AM
Data Aggregation	: Hourly
Report Duration	: From 6/26/2007 6:49 AM to 6/27/2007 6:49 AM
Object	: SystemCenter Operations Manager Operational Database Watchers Group: SystemCenter Operations Manager Operational Database Watchers Group GROUP1
Monitor	: Entity Health

FIGURE 8.17   The Availability Time report validates the OpsMgr distributed application's health for each hour of the day.

If the reporting windows contain data and appear similar to those shown in Figures 8.16 and 8.17, consider your OpsMgr management group baseline installation complete and successful; you are ready to proceed with build-out activities such as importing management packs and discovering objects to manage. If your reports did not contain data or they did not render correctly in the Operations console, we recommend you troubleshoot and repair the reporting function before proceeding.

TIP

The Importance of Validating Before Going Further

When you import management packs, you also want accompanying reports to import correctly into your management group. If there is a problem with OpsMgr reporting functions, even before importing management packs, the reporting features of the management packs may not import or work correctly.

General data warehouse troubleshooting guidelines include the following:

▶ All error information is contained in the errors posted in the Operations Manager Event log, under the Data Warehouse category. Examine the log for errors. If you suspect the Error log has wrapped, restart the OpsMgr Health service to freshen up errors on that box. The data warehouse does not report errors after their first occurrance, unless there was a recovery in between; restarting the service causes the data warehouse to forget it had already reported the error.

▶ Verify that the synchronization process is working. Check the contents of the ManagementPack table in the Data Warehouse database. This table normally has a list of the management packs installed in your management group (if you have more than one management group in your data warehouse, also check the ManagementGroupManagementPackVersion table). If the ManagementPack table is empty, check the Operations Manager Event log for errors concerning synchronization.

▶ Check that your system is synchronizing Managed Entity information by viewing the contents of the ManagedEntityStage and ManagedEntity tables. If these tables do not have data, check the Event log for errors.

▶ Verify that the SQL Services Reporting (SRS) component has all reports deployed by opening http://*<reportserver>*/Reports. See whether you have management pack folders that contain a Guid.mp file in them and whether the System Center Data Warehouse Report Library Management Packs reports are deployed.

SQL Reporting 2005 May Fill Up Your System Drive

We have heard of instances where the C:\ drive begins filling up after SQL 2005 Reporting Services is installed. Check the size of your log file folder at *%ProgramFiles%*\Microsoft SQL Server\MSSQL.x\Reporting Services\Logfiles\. If it seems larger than is optimal, you can change the location of the log files using Notepad. Perform the following steps:

1. Using Notepad, open *%ProgramFiles%*\Microsoft SQL Server\MSSQL.x\Reporting Services\ReportServer\Bin\ReportingServicesService.exe.config. Be sure to make a backup copy of this file before proceeding.

2. Add the following code to the <RStrace> section:

   <add name="*FileName*" value="*ReportServer_*" />

   <add name= "*Directory*" value= "*YourPath*" />

   This location should be on a drive with extra space to accommodate this growth.

3. Using Notepad, open *%ProgramFiles%*\Microsoft SQL Server\MSSQL.x\Reporting Services\ReportServer\Web.config. Once again, be sure to make a backup copy of this file before proceeding.

4. Add the code listed in step 2 to the Web.config file.

5. Using Notepad, open *%ProgramFiles%*\Microsoft SQL Server\MSSQL.x\Reporting Services\ReportManager\Web.config. Again, be sure to make a backup copy of this file before proceeding.

6. Add the code listed in step 2 to the Web.config file.

7. For the new log file folder, set the same permissions as there were on the old log file folder.

8. Restart the ReportServer service.

Thanks to Walter Eikenboom for documenting these steps at http://weblogwally. spaces.live.com/Blog/cns!A913F865098E0556!165.entry.

Integrating Management Packs

After stepping through the management group installation validation procedures outlined throughout in this chapter, we now have a solid foundation on which to build our production management solution. Congratulations on getting this far, and we hope your understanding of some basic OpsMgr functionality is already enhanced! Now we are ready to import management packs into our new management group.

Management Packs Installed with Setup

The installation process automatically imports a number of management pack libraries. These libraries provide a foundation of object types on which other management packs depend, and they contain basic settings used by OpsMgr for the minimum functionality to manage the OpsMgr application itself, such as the management pack for Operations Manager 2007. To see the list of default libraries and management packs, navigate to the Management Pack node of the Administration workspace as displayed in Figure 8.18. (We turned off the Actions pane in this screenshot, normally on the right side of the Operations console, to allow you to read more of the Description column in the list of management packs.)

Just to the right of the Management Packs heading in the Details pane of Figure 8.18 you can see the quantity (40). These are the management packs automatically imported in a new management group with the reporting component installed. Notice the listing of the Default Management Pack, which does not have a Yes in the Sealed column. The Default Management Pack is where new, custom management pack objects such as monitors, alerts, and rules are stored. In addition, overrides to customize default settings in a sealed management pack are saved to the Default Management Pack, by default.

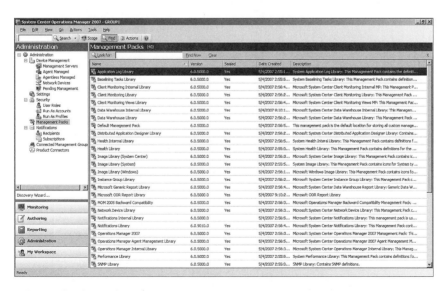

FIGURE 8.18   List of management pack libraries installed with OpsMgr 2007 Released to Manufacturing (RTM) version.

Source files for currently installed management packs are located on each management server at *%ProgramFiles%*\System Center Operations Manager 2007\Health Service State\Management Packs. Do not import from this folder when performing future management pack import operations because these management packs are already part of your OpsMgr environment.

You must import other management packs into the OpsMgr management group to monitor specific applications. These management packs fall into several categories:

▶ Management packs designed for OpsMgr 2007. These are included with the OpsMgr software distribution (that is, on the OpsMgr 2007 installation media in the \ManagementPacks folder). The OpsMgr 2007 RTM software distribution includes 41 additional management packs, listed in Table 8.1.

TABLE 8.1   Management Packs Included with the OpsMgr 2007 Installation Media[1]

Software/Product	Related Management Pack(s)
Exchange	Exchange.Server.2003.Discovery
	Exchange.Server.2003.Monitoring
	Exchange Server Library
Information Worker	InformationWorker.CommonLibrary
	InformationWorker.Office.2003
	InformationWorker.Office.2007
	InformationWorker.Office.XP
	InformationWorker.Windows.Explorer
	InformationWorker.Windows.Internet Explorer
	InformationWorker.Windows.MediaPlayer
	InformationWorker.Windows.Outlook ExpressandMail
	InformationWorker.Windows.WindowsAndMSNMessenger
SharePoint	SharePointPortalServer.2003
	SharePointPortalServer.Library
SQL Server	SQLServer.2000.Discovery
	SQLServer.2000.Monitoring
	SQLServer.2005.Discovery
	SQLServer.2005.Monitoring
	SQLServer.Library
System Center ASP.NET	SystemCenter.ASPNET20.2007

TABLE 8.1   Continued

Software/Product	Related Management Pack(s)
Windows Client	Windows.Client.2000
	Windows.Client.BusinessCritical (XML)
	Windows.Client.Library
	Windows.Client.XP
Windows Server Internet Information Services	Windows.InternetInformationServices.2000
	Windows.InternetInformationServices.2003
	Windows.InternetInformationServices.CommonLibrary
Windows Server	Windows.Server.2000
	Windows.Server.2003
	Windows.Server.Library
Windows Server Active Directory	Windows.Server.AD.2000.Discovery
	Windows.Server.AD.2000.Monitoring
	Windows.Server.AD.2003.Discovery
	Windows.Server.AD.2003.Monitoring
	Windows.Server.AD.ClientMonitoring
	Windows.Server.AD.Library
Windows Server Terminal Services	Windows.Server.TerminalService.2000
	Windows.Server.TerminalService.2003
Windows SharePoint Services	Windows.SharePointServices.2003
	Windows.SharePointServices.Library

[1]*"Microsoft" prefix omitted from each MP name in Table 8.1 for clarity.*

▶ Management packs designed for OpsMgr 2007, available from Microsoft and other vendors. Check the online System Center Pack Catalog at http://go.microsoft.com/fwlink/?linkid=71124.

▶ Management packs converted from MOM 2005 format. These would include management packs that do not have an OpsMgr 2007 version available yet.

▶ Custom OpsMgr 2007 and converted custom MOM 2005 management packs that you or a technology partner authored for specific situations.

Selecting Management Packs

It is a best practice to import only the management packs required to meet your monitoring and management goals. Specifically, it is a poor practice to import "every management pack you can find." Each imported management pack incrementally increases the overhead load of the management group. Too many unused or unnecessary management packs can clutter the Operations console to the point that you miss indications of issues with the applications you do need to monitor.

In the next section, we will import some of the additional operating system and application management packs provided by Microsoft on the installation media. You might ask, "Why not import all of them?" Although you certainly may do that, we recommend you carefully review the list of management packs in Table 8.1 and import only those you will use in your environment.

Importing Management Packs

You can use the Operations console or PowerShell to import management packs. Using the console provides visual feedback on the progress and status of the import operation, whereas using PowerShell offers opportunities for automating and error-proofing the import process. We will import some management packs using the console and then import some with PowerShell to demonstrate both methods. Perform the following steps:

1. Log on to the computer running the Operations console using a user account that is a member of the OpsMgr Administrators security group.

2. Navigate to the Administration pane, returning to the view shown in Figure 8.2 at the beginning of this chapter. Either click the Import management packs link in the Actions area of the Administration Overview or right-click the Management Packs node in the Navigation pane and select Import Management Packs....

3. The wizard prompts you for the location of the management packs to import. To import some or all of the management packs distributed with the OpsMgr setup media and listed in Table 8.1, navigate to the OpsMgr CD or software distribution folder and then to the \ManagementPacks child folder. You will see the list of sealed management packs with .mp file extensions (and one unsealed management pack with the .xml file extension), as displayed in Figure 8.19.

CAUTION

Use the Most Current Version of Any Management Pack

Check the System Center Pack Catalog for more current versions of any of the management packs included on the installation media. You will definitely want to install the updated version of the Operations Manager management pack. The update includes bug fixes, several enhancements, and updates content for some of the rules and monitors. You can download the updated version from the System Pack Catalog.

FIGURE 8.19   Selecting management packs to import from the OpsMgr installation media.

4. To demonstrate some features of the import process, we will initially (and incorrectly) select only the Microsoft.SQLServer.2005.Monitoring.mp file. Choosing that file and clicking the Open button returns the error message shown in Figure 8.20.

There is a red "X" error symbol in the column to the left of the management pack name. In the Details section of the error message in Figure 8.20, we can read that the SQL 2005 Monitoring management pack depends on the SQL 2005 Discovery management pack and the SQL Server Library management pack. Because the SQL Server 2005 Monitoring MP is dependent on these two management packs, we cannot import the SQL 2005 Monitoring management pack without importing those required management packs as well.

Options in the Import Management Packs Dialog Box

Several options are available in the Import Management Packs dialog box shown in Figure 8.20:

▶ **Properties button**—This allows you to get more information about the dependencies of a particular management pack.

▶ **Add button**—Use this to search for and select other (required) management packs.

▶ **Remove button**—Use this to delete management packs from the list to import, in case you change your mind or cannot locate the prerequisite management packs at this time.

Using the Add button in the Import Management Packs dialog box, we will include the required SQL 2005 management packs, as well as select the necessary management packs to monitor SQL 2000, Windows 2003 Server, and Terminal Services and IIS on Windows 2003, for a total of 11 management packs.

8

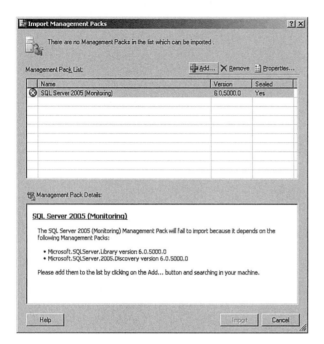

FIGURE 8.20   Management packs may have dependencies on other management packs.

We recommend that you extend your management group initially with a subset of the available management packs—import only management packs for applications you know you will be actively monitoring. Although we will be monitoring Exchange and Active Directory, we will wait and import those management packs later, after confirming that this first, smaller group of management packs imports properly and begins working correctly.

5. After adding these management packs to the list to be imported, we confirm that a large green check mark appears in the leftmost column, next to each management pack. The check mark indicates you have already installed the prerequisites for each management pack or they are in the list you just built. Clicking the Import button begins the process of importing each management pack in alphabetical order as it appears in the display, and we can observe the progress of the import job.

As each management pack is successfully imported, the large green check mark to the left of the management pack name changes to a smaller green check mark inside a green circle. Figure 8.21 confirms the successful import of the selected packs.

After the selected management packs have been imported, our new management group is ready to begin monitoring the SQL 2000 and SQL 2005 database server applications, the Windows 2003 operating system, and the IIS and Terminal Services features of Windows 2003. Before these management packs were imported, the only monitored application was Operations Manager 2007 itself! The discovery rules contained in the management packs immediately go to work, detecting which monitored computers the new management packs apply to, and deploying appropriate monitors and rules to those computers.

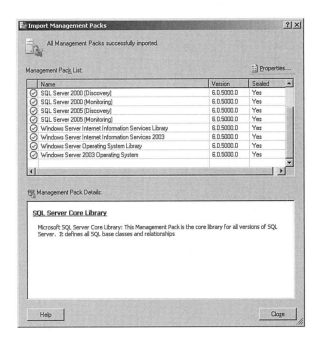

FIGURE 8.21   Confirmation of successful import of several management packs.

Next, we will import some management packs using the PowerShell command shell. We will add monitoring support for Microsoft Information Worker applications and the Windows Client operating systems to our new management group by importing the applicable management packs. We could import the management packs with PowerShell one at a time using the `install-ManagementPack` cmdlet. Perform the following steps:

1. Figure 8.22 shows the PowerShell output to the command `get-Help install-ManagementPack`.
   As you can see in Figure 8.22, the `get-Help` cmdlet provides us with the correct basic syntax to use the `install-ManagementPack` cmdlet. Notice in the Remarks section of the output that you can get even more help and details by adding the `-detailed` or `-full` switch to the `getHelp` cmdlet line; this is true for most PowerShell cmdlets.

2. Rather than running the `install-ManagementPack` cmdlet each time for the dozen management packs we want to import, we will perform a batch import. To do this, we can create a PowerShell script and run the script inside a PowerShell instance. The script in this case is just a collection of `install-ManagementPack` cmdlets, one on each line of the script. Figure 8.23 shows Notepad open to the ImportMP.ps1 PowerShell script we created to import the Information Worker and Windows Client management packs.

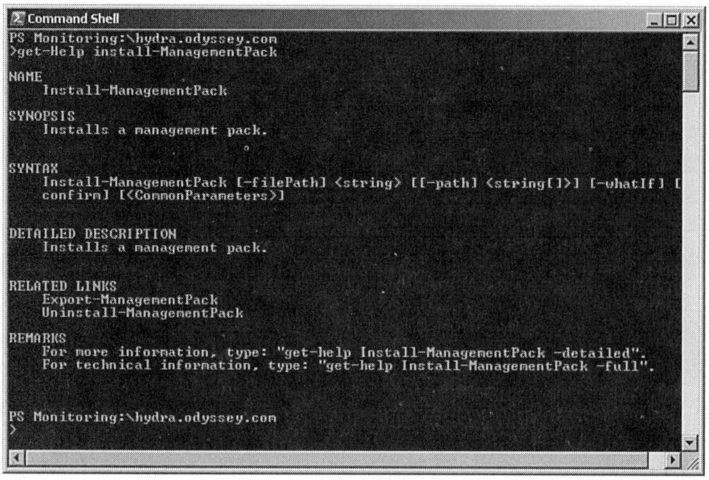

FIGURE 8.22   Syntax for the `install-ManagementPack` cmdlet.

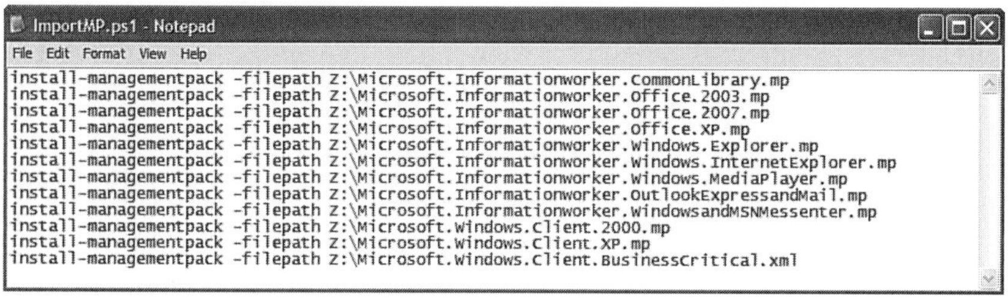

FIGURE 8.23   A PowerShell script to import a dozen management packs at one time.

3. Our script is a text file that contains an `install-ManagementPack` cmdlet line for each management pack. To run the script shown in Figure 8.23 (saved as Z:\ImportMP.ps1), we open a PowerShell instance (Start -> Program Files -> System Center Operations Manager 2007 -> Command Shell) and type **Z:\ImportMP.ps1** at the PowerShell prompt.

Unlike the Operations console when we import management packs, using PowerShell does not provide feedback during the import process. If the import completes successfully without errors, you return to the PowerShell prompt without any status notifications. If errors occur during the import, PowerShell provides feedback with some details on the error(s) when the script completes.

Management pack dependencies are something to watch out for when using PowerShell to import management packs. Whereas the Operations console validates dependencies and will not proceed with management pack import if there is a problem, PowerShell batch operations fail unexpectedly when dependent management packs are not previously installed. It is a good idea to use the Operations console's Import Management Pack feature to investigate management packs for their dependencies before creating a

PowerShell script for bulk import. Then ensure your PowerShell script lists the management pack import cmdlets in a sequence that considers any dependencies.

TIP

Client Business-Critical Operating Systems

All the management packs distributed on the OpsMgr 2007 installation media are in the sealed .mp file format, except the Client Business Critical Operating System management pack, which is in unsealed .xml format. This management pack discovers and manages business-critical Windows client operating systems. This management pack has a dependency on the Windows 2000 Client OS Management Pack, as well as a dependency for the Windows XP Client OS Management Pack. Even if you are only going to manage business-critical Windows XP desktops, you also need to import the Windows 2000 Client OS Management Pack.

Now we will perform two quick checks to verify that the imported management packs are installed correctly and working. We will exit the Operations console and start it up again after the import operations, to make sure our console loads the new management pack elements.

You will recall that after completing our initial installation of OpsMgr 2007 with the reporting component, 40 management packs were installed in our management group. We observed the count of the number of installed management packs in the results pane header shown in Figure 8.18. We know we added 11 management packs using the Operations console and 12 with our PowerShell script (for 23 total additional management packs imported). Now, when we return to the list of installed management packs in the Administration space, we confirm with pleasure that there are 63 (40 + 23) management packs installed in our management group.

You can note in Figure 8.3, earlier in this chapter, that prior to any management packs being imported, seven child folders of views were present below the global views in the Navigation pane. After importing these 23 management packs, we expect some new views to be available in the Monitoring space. As a final check, we will navigate to the Monitoring space and open a view added by one of the newly imported management packs.

Figure 8.24 shows the Monitoring space after the additional management packs have successfully been imported. In the Navigation pane, we observe 11 view folders, four of which are new: Microsoft SQL Server, Microsoft Windows Internet Information Services, Microsoft Windows Server, and Microsoft Windows Terminal Services. The imported management packs added these folders of views, as well as new views in the Microsoft Windows Client folder.

To verify we are getting the correct functionality of the Operations console after importing the new management packs, we can open one of the new view folders shown in Figure 8.24. The Windows Server State view in the Microsoft Windows Server view folder correctly shows that the operating systems of the two OpsMgr core component servers are in a Healthy state.

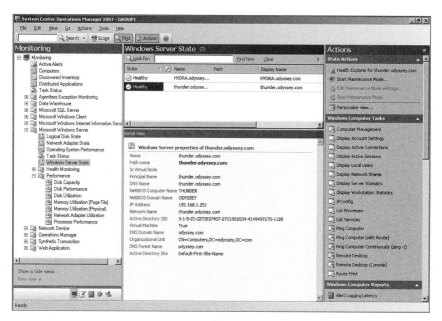

FIGURE 8.24   Verifying the functionality of the newly imported Windows 2003 Server management pack.

Before You Put the Installation Media Away...

Some important items appear on the software distribution media for Operations Manager 2007. In addition to the application and operating system management packs available for import, there are a number of utilities you may need during your initial deployment and later as you maintain and extend your OpsMgr management group(s). The management packs to be imported are in the \ManagementPacks folder on the CD, and the utilities are in the \SupportTools folder. Utilities include those needed to cluster the core management group components such as the RMS, and to convert MOM 2005 management packs to OpsMgr 2007 format. The \ReportModels and \Gateway folders are also required to implement some management group features. Because you may need to access software on the OpsMgr CD from time to time, it is a good idea to copy the whole CD or other installation media to a folder on a file server for quick access in the future. Microsoft's default name for an OpsMgr 2007 installation media folder is SystemCenterOperationsManager.

Discover Objects to Manage

Our carefully deployed OpsMgr management group is now prepared to start doing work! That means identifying the objects we want to manage with OpsMgr, determining a method to bring those objects into a managed state, and making it all happen.

Operations Manager 2007 can manage computers and network devices. A computer is a Windows computer running one of the following operating systems: Windows 2000, Windows 2003, Windows XP, or Windows Vista. A network device is any computer or appliance that responds to Simple Network Management Protocol (SNMP) queries, such as a router, switch, print server, or even a computer running a non-Windows operating system such as Unix or Linux.

Computers can be monitored using the Operations Manager Agent Component (agent-managed) or with agentless monitoring. Because we are just doing the simple stuff in this chapter, we will illustrate a simple agent-managed deployment. See Chapter 9, "Installing and Configuring Agents," for a full description of the different ways to deploy and use agents and network devices in your OpsMgr environment.

The simplest method for discovering objects is invoking the Computer and Device Management Wizard in the Administration space of the Operations console. Launch the wizard by right-clicking any node in the Navigation pane of the Administration space and selecting the Discovery Wizard option. You can also launch the wizard by clicking the Configure computers and devices to manage link in the Actions area of the Administration Overview page.

> **NOTE**
>
> **Configuring the Windows Firewall**
>
> For any computer running the Windows Firewall, which includes Windows Server 2003 with Service Pack 1 or later, Windows XP with Service Pack 2 or later, and Windows Vista, you must modify the default configuration prior to installing agents to be sure that TCP ports 135 and 445 permit communications. We discuss this process in Chapter 11.

Let's walk through the process of running the Discovery Wizard and bringing a computer into management. Perform the following steps:

1. After clicking Next through the introductory screen, your first decision to make is whether you will use an automatic or an advanced discovery method to locate prospective managed computers.

   Selecting automatic computer discovery results in the wizard scanning all computers in the domain, quick and simple. Skip to step 3 in this procedure if you selected automatic computer discovery.

   Choosing advanced discovery lets you select the computer or device type, choose the Management Server to perform the scan, and verify that you can contact the discovered computers.

2. If you selected advanced discovery type, the wizard next asks if you want to scan Active Directory for objects, browse for computer names, or type in computer names.

Scanning Active Directory (AD) requires that you specify the AD domain name and construct a query. Select or type the appropriate domain name in the domain field and then click the Configure button to bring up the Find Computer dialog box. You can type in a wildcard search string for the computer name field, including "*" to scan for all computer names. Clicking the Advanced tab lets you construct a multi-line If query using the following fields: computer name, managed by, description, operating system (OS), and OS version.

If you are browsing for or typing in computer names, click the Browse button to bring up the domain object picker. Here, you can type any computer name or Fully Qualified Domain Name (FQDN), as well as use the picker to browse the AD and change or narrow the scope of the selection search.

3. Specify the administrator account the Discovery Wizard will use for installing agents. The Management Server Action Account performs computer discovery, and agent installations typically use this account.

4. Click the Discover button and the wizard uses the discovery type and method you selected to return a list of computers matching the discovery criteria and not yet managed by that OpsMgr management group (see Figure 8.25).

FIGURE 8.25   Confirming which discovered computers will be added to agent management.

5. On the Discovery Results page of the wizard, shown in Figure 8.25, select one, several, or all of the discovered computers and then click Next. (We are selecting one computer, Quicksilver, which is the Reporting and Data Warehouse Database Component in our management group.)

6. A summary screen displays your choices. On the summary page, you can also change the default installation path for the agent (*%ProgramFiles%*\System Center Operations Manager 2007) and specify credentials for the agent to use when performing actions. This is the Agent Action Account, which is typically Local System. We recommend you accept the default installation path and use the default Local System for the Agent Action Account unless you have clear indications to use the other options.

7. The Agent Management Task Status window opens and allows you to track the progress of the agent installation. You can close the status window at any time without interrupting the agent installation tasks. The Management Server Action Account remotely connects and starts the computer's MOMAgentInstaller service, which in turns starts the Windows Installer service. The System Center Operations Manager 2007 Agent installation now completes, and the OpsMgr Health Service starts.

8. If the task status window is open, you will receive a Success indicator and notice that the agent installation completed. The complete install process takes less than 1 minute for a single computer on the local network segment. Within 5 minutes after the agent installation task is complete, the computer name will appear in the Operations console views as an agent-managed computer.

Deploying and Using the Operations Console

A useful feature of the Operations Manager 2007 architecture is the modular nature of the Operations console application. Although the console must minimally exist on the RMS, we do not recommend your monitoring operations staff exclusively utilize the console on the RMS or RDP sessions to the RMS to employ the console. Install the Operations console on workstations or access it using Terminal Server solutions, connecting to a server other than the RMS.

The console communicates with other components of the management group to render the data and views observed in the console. Install the console on whatever computers or virtual desktop solution your operations staff will use for monitoring duties. The console is completely dependent on network-level connectivity to the RMS and the Reporting server to function.

Although the console successfully operates against a management group when connected by a low-bandwidth connection such as a Virtual Private Network (VPN), its performance and responsiveness significantly decreases. The Operations console should optimally run on a computer in the same local area network (LAN) as the RMS and Reporting servers, or connect by private, routed networks that operate at 10Mbps or faster, such as 100Mbps or Gigabit Ethernet speed (recommended).

Workstations used by Network Operations Center (NOC) engineers responsible for system uptime are good choices for installing the Operations console. In a smaller environment, the system administrator's desktop works great!

If the administrator or NOC engineer workstations are not co-located with the OpsMgr core servers and if a LAN-speed connection between the sites is not possible, consider installing the Operations console on one or more Terminal Servers licensed in Application Server mode. Locate the Terminal Server(s) in the datacenter where the OpsMgr core servers reside, and the NOC engineers can run the Operations console on virtual desktops wherever they might be. The network bandwidth consumed by the Terminal Services protocol, RDP, is much less than the bandwidth of the Operations console when communicating with the RMS.

Installation Requirements

You can install the Operations console on any computer that meets the following minimum prerequisites:

▶ 1GB physical memory minimum to install (2GB memory recommended).

▶ One of these operating systems (or later): Windows 2003 Service Pack 1, Windows XP Service Pack 2, or Windows Vista.

▶ .NET Framework 2.0 and .NET Framework 3.0 components

▶ Windows PowerShell.

▶ Microsoft Visual Studio 2005 Tools for Office Second Edition Runtime (VSTO 2005 SE) and Microsoft Office Word 2003 or Word 2007. (These are optional to edit company knowledge.)

The Operations console application files installed on the local disk of the computer will total about 150MB, placed in the *%ProgramFiles%*\System Center Operations Manager 2007 folder by default. Here is a step-by-step list of actions related to getting the Operations console running on a computer:

1. Run the SetupOM.exe application located in the root of the OpsMgr installation media.

2. At the splash screen, select to Install Operations Manager 2007 as if you were going to install another management server or a new management group.

3. When presented with the Custom Setup dialog box, change the install action to This component will not be available for the Database, Management Server, and Web Console items, leaving only the User Interfaces and Command Shell items selected. Figure 8.26 displays the setup options to install only the Operations console as part of Custom Setup.

4. If the computer you are installing the console on does not meet all necessary prerequisites, you will see a Prerequisite Check Passed with Warnings or a Prerequisite Check Failed notice. These notification dialog boxes include View Log buttons that

display details for prerequisites not met. For example, Figure 8.27 lists the prerequisites for installing the Operations console and notes a warning that the computer we are installing the console on has less than the recommended 2048MB (2GB) of physical memory.

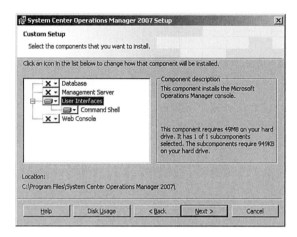

FIGURE 8.26   The correct setup selections to install only the Operations console.

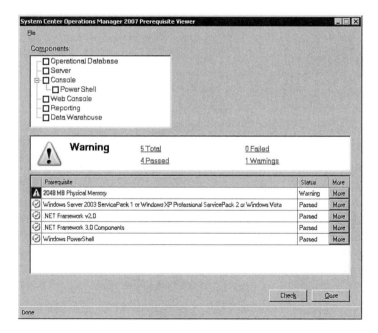

FIGURE 8.27   Prerequisite Viewer to install the Operations console only.

Connecting to the Console

Upon completing a successful installation, the default action is to open the Operations console for the first time on that computer. Here are some points to keep in mind:

▶ The first time you open the Operations console on a computer that is not an OpsMgr management server, you will see a Connect to Server dialog box, and you must enter the name of the OpsMgr management group and the name of the RMS for that management group. The console connects to the RMS and attempts to authenticate the user logged on at the computer where the console is running. (You saw the Connect to Server applet previously in Chapter 3, "Looking Inside OpsMgr.")

▶ If the RMS is not in the same Active Directory domain as the computer running the console, the Enter Credentials dialog box appears, as shown in Figure 8.28. Remember to add domain user accounts that are not members of the OpsMgr Administrators group to appropriate OpsMgr user roles before connecting to a management group. Add user accounts or groups to roles prior to using the Operations console's Administration space or equivalent PowerShell commands.

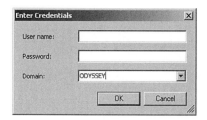

FIGURE 8.28   Enter domain credentials authorized to access the Operations console.

Connecting to the RMS

The console's Connect to Server applet remembers the identity of the RMS first connected to, and it will not prompt you again for the name of a management group. By default, the console connects to the RMS it last connected to. To change the focus of the Operations console to another management group, select the Tools -> Connect... item from the console's main menu bar. This invokes the Connect to Server applet, where you can enter the information for another OpsMgr management group. Connecting to another management group adds an entry to the Registered Servers list remembered by the Connect to Server applet, and it changes the default connection to the last management group selected.

Entering Credentials in Untrusted Domains

The Enter Credentials dialog box does not remember domain user logon information, and it only displays the local computer and the domains it is a member of as choices in the Domain drop-down selection list. The console will prompt for user credentials authorized to access the Operations console in the domain where the OpsMgr RMS is located. When accessing OpsMgr management groups in domains that do not trust the domain where the Operations console is located, you must manually supply appropriate user credentials and domain names on each use of the console.

Maximum Number of Console Sessions

There is no theoretical upper limit on the number of Operations consoles installed in a single management group. Install the console wherever it makes work more convenient and efficient for the operations staff. However, each console that is open creates several network connections and causes the RMS to open a connection to the operational database on behalf of the console. This means that consoles are not inconsequential in terms of their impact on the network and the OpsMgr management group.

Microsoft suggests that you not plan for more than 30 simultaneous Operations console sessions in one management group. We recommend you close any console sessions when not in active use.

Editing Company Knowledge

If you installed Microsoft Office Word 2003 or Word 2007 as well as the Microsoft Visual Studio 2005 Tools for Office Second Edition (VSTO 2005 SE) redistributable package on the computer where the console is running, you will be able to edit the company knowledge associated with a rule. Without the software installed, an operator will simply have read-only access to view company knowledge.

TIP

Visual Studio Tools for Office (VSTO) Second Edition

VSTO 2005 Second Edition is the fully backward compatible replacement for the Visual Studio Tools for Office runtime that was available with VSTO 2005. It contains updates that allow applications authored using VSTO 2005 (such as the OpsMgr 2007 Company Knowledge function) to run with either Office 2003 or Office 2007 installed. Microsoft has withdrawn the original VSTO 2005 for download.

Console Errors

Errors may occur when using the console, and OpsMgr provides a way to learn more about console errors that occur and share the details of the errors with other staff and support personnel. When an error occurs, the user receives a notice like that in the top portion of Figure 8.29. This is an abbreviated statement of the error, which may not provide much useful information. Clicking the item Show additional information about this error expands the notice window and includes the text of the error, shown in the lower portion of Figure 8.29.

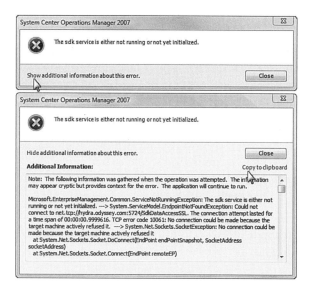

FIGURE 8.29   Operations console error message with the additional information hidden and exposed.

The additional information (exposed in the lower portion of Figure 8.29) includes a header warning that the information may appear cryptic. As an example, the additional information might include a complete server stack trace and be pretty lengthy. In this case, there is some useful information in the details, specifically that the RMS the console is trying to connect to actively refused the connection.

Notice also in the lower portion of Figure 8.29 (the expanded version of the error notification window) that there is a Copy to clipboard item below the Close button. This saves time and increases accuracy when communicating about errors with others. When you select this item, details about the error, exposed in the additional information view, are copied to the clipboard as text, ready to paste into an email or trouble log. The heading about the information appearing cryptic is replaced with a date/time stamp and the name of the OpsMgr product and version, displayed in Figure 8.30.

Running the Console Without Trusted Authentication

Another potential issue exists if you invoke the Operations console in a user context without trusted authentication between the core components of the management group and the user running the console. This issue appears when PowerShell launches against an object in the Operations console (for example, by right-clicking the object and selecting Open -> Command Shell). Although the user provides credentials when starting the Operations console, those credentials are not passed to PowerShell when it is invoked from the console.

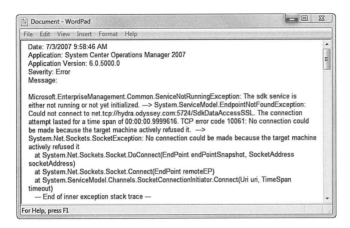

FIGURE 8.30   The additional error information in the clipboard after selecting Copy to clipboard.

As an example, if you check the health state of the OpsMgr Management Group distributed application using PowerShell (as we did in Figure 8.9 in the "Confirming Management Group Health" section of this chapter) without a domain trust in place, you now receive another credentials prompt like that shown in Figure 8.31.

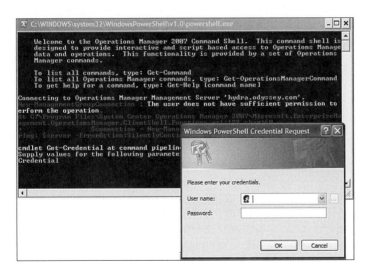

FIGURE 8.31   Launching PowerShell from the Operations console prompts for credential.

The Windows PowerShell Credential Request box remembers the domain name and user combinations of previous connections in the drop-down list, but there is no option to save the associated passwords. So, similar to the manual credential entry needed to start the Operations console without trust authentication, a manual credential entry is required on each launch of PowerShell in that untrusted environment.

In this case, we specifically mean that the user account logged in to the Windows desktop session (where the Operations console is running) must match a domain user account included in an authorized user role in the OpsMgr management group. Passthrough authentication does not work in this instance. If the user does not log on to the local computer with a matching domain account, there will be frequent prompts for credentials!

Console Configuration Data

The Operations console stores configuration data locally and in the Operations database. Customizations to the My Workspace portion of the console are stored in the database, and they follow the user from console to console, similar to a Windows roaming profile. This feature lets a user leverage the time spent creating favorite views and saved searches across all consoles in a management group. Most other console settings are locally stored in the user Registry key HKEY_CURRENT_USER\SOFTWARE\Microsoft\Microsoft Operations Manager\3.0\ (and will apply only to the user on that computer).

For example, you can increase the number of computers that can be selected at once when executing the same task against multiple targets. The default is 10, and in some scenarios you might want to select 20, or even 50 computers at once for task execution. Modify the DWORD value at HKCU\SOFTWARE\Microsoft\Microsoft Operations Manager\3.0\ Console\TaskSelectedObjectsLimit.

Other console settings saved in the current logged on user's Registry key (only affecting the console for that user on that computer) include the following:

▶ Connection history with the names of management groups the console has connected to.

▶ Show or Hide Views selections.

▶ Whether the console is in a window or full screen, and if it's in a window, what the size and position of the window is.

▶ What the last navigation pane the console was open to when it was closed.

The next time that user uses the console on that computer, it reopens with the same settings. The console always reopens with its focus on the root of the hierarchy of the selected navigation pane, such as the Monitoring Overview if the Monitoring pane was in use, or the Administration Overview if the Administration space was open the last time you used the console.

Whatever child monitoring views were expanded during the last console use are also remembered. Therefore, although the console will always open to the root of the navigation hierarchy, if you have a carefully selected set of view folders that you keep open, the console saves you time by remembering those settings. The console also remembers what performance counters you have previously selected in particular performance views—another major timesaver!

Drilldown: OpsMgr 2007 Operations Console

Much of this book provides you with detailed assistance in the setup and configuration of the numerous features of OpsMgr 2007. How you actually use the Operations Manager application to accomplish your organizational objectives is where your creativity and experience comes in. You build on a solid understanding of what OpsMgr can do, and you add the deep "insider" knowledge of your organization's technology processes.

There is no one right way to use OpsMgr; in fact, a strength of a product with such a broad feature set is that you have a lot of latitude in how to operate it and still get great value from it. We assume that prior to deploying Operations Manager 2007, you had in mind general answers to such questions as the following:

▶ **What do I want to monitor?** You might consider servers, desktops, and mobile computers, network devices such as routers, and applications such as third-party websites that users depend on to perform the organization's work. The small business owner might want to monitor "everything," whereas the large enterprise might deploy OpsMgr just to monitor some portions of their infrastructure.

▶ **How can I measure success?** In a small environment, it could be that if your boss is happy with his or her use of the network, you're doing fine. As OpsMgr deployments get bigger, the measure of success often becomes the percentage of application uptime, with "5-9's" or 99.999% application availability considered the highest service level to contract for in a Service Level Agreement (SLA).

▶ **How am I going to interact with OpsMgr?** Depending on how you deployed your management group, and what your success measurements are, envision various levels of constant, daily, or periodic use of the Operations console. In larger environments, team solutions for cooperatively configuring and using the Operations console are called for.

In this last part of the chapter, we focus on the Operations console, highlighting features of the various panes, wizards, and dialog boxes that we think are of value when using OpsMgr 2007. We will approach some suggested configurations of features from the perspectives of both the small system administrator and the enterprise management professional.

Managing Operations with the Console

The Operations console has five major navigation panes, which are also called *spaces*. Table 8.2 lists these panes and gives a brief description of each pane.

We will discuss each of these console areas in the following sections.

TABLE 8.2   Navigation Panes in the Operations Console

Navigation Pane	Description
Monitoring	Displays different types of views that enable analyzing your monitoring needs.
Authoring	Lets you to create additional monitoring objects to customize or supplement the default monitoring settings provided with management packs.
Administration	Enables editing Operations Manager settings that affect the management group. Also allows you to view and configure individual management servers and managed objects.
Reporting	Displays reports included in installed management packs and enables editing customized reports.
My Workspace	Enables creating and storing console customizations for later reuse.

Monitoring

The Monitoring space displays different aspects of monitoring data, enabling you, through tracking and resolving issues, to quickly find and analyze the monitoring results within your environment. The Monitoring pane's goal, when there are no problems, is to validate the continuing successful function of the OpsMgr instrumentation. When there is an issue with an object you are managing, the Monitoring pane's purpose is to clearly present a statement of the problem (and even propose to take suggested repair actions), or make it as easy and quick as possible for you to locate the root cause and achieve resolution.

You can start using the Operations console to monitor your environment "out of the box" (that is, with the default views in their default configurations). However, you can get a lot more value from OpsMgr by customizing the look and feel of the Operations console to match the business and technological aspects of your organization. The most effective use of the Monitoring space is a combination of configuration decisions involving these features:

▶ Personalizing the global views and other default views

▶ Creating new global views and views in child view folders

▶ Creating new child view folders or hierarchies of view folders

▶ Creating new tasks, specific for your environment, that automate actions related to the object(s) selected in console views

In a team-managed setting, it is important for all participants to collaborate on, and have input to, modifications that affect everyone. In addition, it is critical to communicate what features have been customized or added, because people cannot use new features they do not know about. We will walk though some real-world examples of using these techniques to make the Operations console more useful.

To start, we will personalize the properties of the Computers global view. We navigate there by clicking the Computers node in the Navigation pane of the Monitoring space. When we see the names of our managed computers in the Results pane, we select the Personalize view action from the Actions pane on the right side of the console. You can also access Personalize view from a context-sensitive menu by right-clicking the header (or any row) of the Results pane, or by selecting View -> Personalize view from the OpsMgr window menu. Figure 8.32 shows that, by default, only the Maintenance Mode and Name columns are displayed.

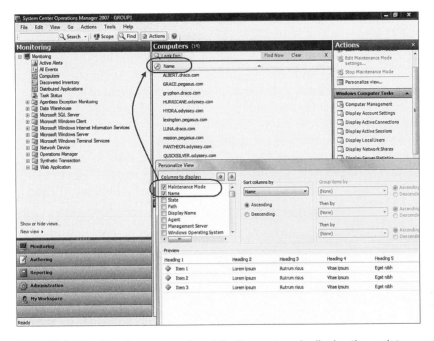

FIGURE 8.32   The Computers view defaults are to only display the maintenance mode status and the name.

The blank slate listing of alphabetically sorted names of managed computers and their management mode status really invites customizing to match your monitoring interests. The default view does not even include the health state of the computer! We will select to display additional information: the columns for State, NetBIOS Domain Name, and Virtual Machine. We'll also select to sort by NetBIOS Domain Name. Figure 8.33 shows the results pane of the Computer view after we've added those columns.

The Computers view with just these few changes, shown in Figure 8.33, has a lot more useful information.

We elected to view the domain name and the virtual server status because those are important considerations for our organization, particularly because we have computers in multiple domains. An administrator in a single large domain might add columns such as

Active Directory Site and Organizational Unit instead. Adding columns to the display lets you quickly sort and group computers by that attribute. In our case, we want to be able also to sort by State, bringing the critical computers to the top, and then view what domain they are in and whether or not they are virtual servers.

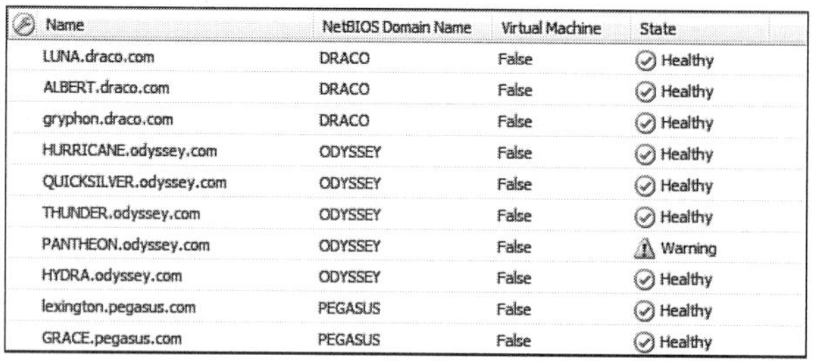

Name	NetBIOS Domain Name	Virtual Machine	State
LUNA.draco.com	DRACO	False	⊘ Healthy
ALBERT.draco.com	DRACO	False	⊘ Healthy
gryphon.draco.com	DRACO	False	⊘ Healthy
HURRICANE.odyssey.com	ODYSSEY	False	⊘ Healthy
QUICKSILVER.odyssey.com	ODYSSEY	False	⊘ Healthy
THUNDER.odyssey.com	ODYSSEY	False	⊘ Healthy
PANTHEON.odyssey.com	ODYSSEY	False	⚠ Warning
HYDRA.odyssey.com	ODYSSEY	False	⊘ Healthy
lexington.pegasus.com	PEGASUS	False	⊘ Healthy
GRACE.pegasus.com	PEGASUS	False	⊘ Healthy

FIGURE 8.33   The Computers view personalized to display additional columns of interest.

Web Page and Dashboard Views

Operations Manager 2007 includes a simple but invaluable feature to embed any relevant web content right in the Operations console. We will demonstrate this by creating a global view using the Web Page view type. We right-click the Monitoring space and select New -> Web Page View. In the simple setup dialog box, we enter the information shown in Figure 8.34 to link to the online System Center Pack Catalog at Microsoft's website.

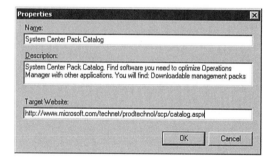

FIGURE 8.34   Creating a Web Page view that links to the System Center Pack Catalog.

After we create the Web Page view with the settings shown in Figure 8.34, we find a new custom global view named "System Center Pack Catalog" in the Operations console. Clicking this view opens the website at Microsoft in the Results pane, as shown in Figure 8.35. You can image the many possibilities for integrating the OpsMgr console with your intranet, partner extranets, vendor support sites, and other network management applications.

The Web Page view is added to your OpsMgr monitoring toolkit along with the other views we have seen, such as the Alert, Event, State, Performance, and Diagram views. You can combine any of these view types to create custom, functional *dashboards* that intermingle the content of any view in the management group. In a fashion similar to how OpsMgr's distributed applications allow you to combine monitoring of disparate objects into a single entity, dashboard views enable you to merge visual instrumentation elements from anywhere in your OpsMgr monitoring space into one view.

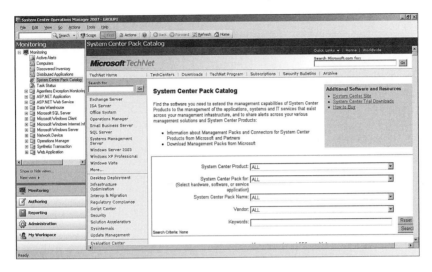

FIGURE 8.35   Web page view pulls relevant web-based content right into the Operations console.

Management packs add many dashboard views to the console; as an example, all the performance and health monitoring views in the Windows Server management pack are dashboard views. Next, we will create a dashboard view that combines several other types of views. Perform the following steps:

1. Right-click the Monitoring space and select New -> Dashboard View. Figure 8.36 shows the Properties page that appears to configure the new view.

   We are going to create a new dashboard view with four embedded views. You can create new dashboard views with between two and nine embedded views, and a variety of arrangements for each, based on the possible geometry of the selected quantity of embedded views.

2. Select the quadrant view (four equal sections) and save the view with the name **Management Group Hardware**. We are going to add embedded views that focus on the health of the hardware in our management group.

3. Immediately after saving the new dashboard view, navigate to that view to see the layout design we selected (in this case, the four quadrants). Also, notice the Click to add a view link in the center of each empty embedded view. Clicking that link pops up a Select View list, where you can pick any type of existing view in your management group to appear in the dashboard embedded view.

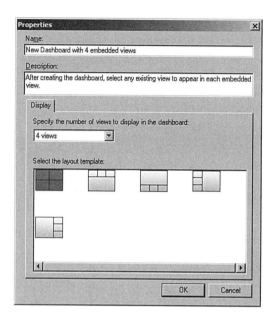

FIGURE 8.36   Selecting the number of embedded views to display when creating a new dashboard view.

In our Management Group Hardware dashboard view, shown in Figure 8.37, we have added four different kinds of views. We have a State view in the upper left, a Performance view in the lower left, a Diagram view in the lower right, and in the upper right, a Web Page view.

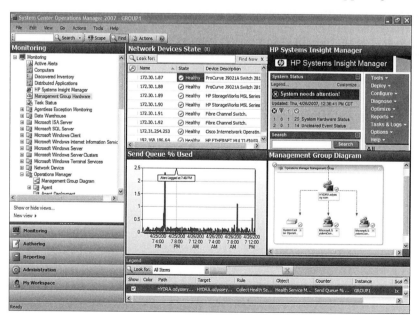

FIGURE 8.37   Dashboard view focusing on hardware, integrating an external web-based management application.

In the embedded Web Page view, we have extended our OpsMgr console view to include a live view into a dashboard from another management application, the web-based HP Systems Insight Manager. After you have added the desired embedded views to your dashboard, you can later swap out an embedded view by right-clicking its header and selecting Remove View.

Maintenance Mode

Access to the maintenance mode status (the wrench icon) appears throughout the OpsMgr monitoring space. This makes it easy to quickly view or update the maintenance mode state for an object. Maintenance mode enables you to avoid alerts or errors that might occur when a monitored object, such as a computer or distributed application, goes offline for maintenance. In a small environment with just a single administrator, this feature might not get used that often. However, in a large environment, maintenance mode is a key mechanism to permit team collaboration.

Figure 8.38 shows the Diagram view of a distributed application created to monitor an enterprise backup solution. The diagram illustrates a backup media server, passing through a pair of network switches, connecting to a pair of tape libraries. The Tape Libraries entity is a distributed application component we created that includes the two physical tape libraries as contained objects. We placed the parent entity in maintenance mode and selected to propagate those settings to contained objects, because the repair work we will be doing affects both tape libraries equally. Notice the wrench icon present, the empty unmonitored circle (rather than a check mark) next to the Tape Library component, and the contained tape library objects.

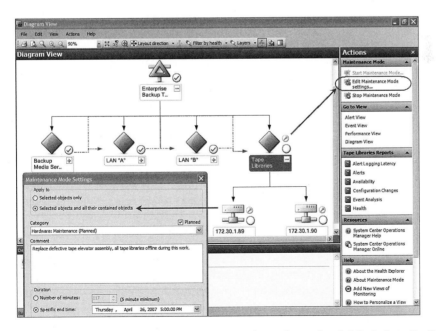

FIGURE 8.38   Viewing the maintenance mode settings of a distributed application.

We noted in the Duration field of the maintenance mode settings that we expect the work to be complete at 5:00 p.m. At that time, all three objects (the Tape Libraries entity and the contained tape library objects) will come back out of maintenance mode, and monitoring will resume on all components. OpsMgr 2007 polls maintenance mode settings only once every 5 minutes, so there can be a delay in an object's scheduled removal from maintenance mode.

TIP

Automating the Maintenance Mode Process

We wrote a management pack for MOM 2005 that you could use to put a system into maintenance mode. For OpsMgr 2007, Boris Yanushpolsky of the MOM team provides a PowerShell script that puts a system into maintenance mode. The script uses parameters including the computer name (FQDN), number of hours to be in maintenance mode, and a comment. The script also puts the instances of the HealthService and HealthServiceWatcher associated with the computer object into maintenance mode, to prevent an alert that the management server is not getting heartbeats from that agent.

The script is available at http://blogs.msdn.com/boris_yanushpolsky/archive/2007/07/25/putting-a-computer-into-maintenance-mode.aspx. There is also a script to take the computer out of maintenance mode at http://blogs.msdn.com/boris_yanushpolsky/archive/2007/08/30/stoping-maintenance-mode.aspx.

For your convenience, we include these scripts (maintenance mode.ps1 and stop maintenance mode.ps1) with the CD accompanying this book.

Clive Eastwood has written a command line tool to put OpsMgr agents into maintenance mode, similar to what Boris does in PowerShell. You can read about this approach at http://blogs.technet.com/cliveeastwood/archive/2007/09/18/agentmma-command-line-tool-to-place-opsmgr-agents-into-maintenance-mode.aspx.

Andrzej Lipka of Microsoft Consulting Services (MCS) enhances this using the PsExec tool from SysInternals. PsExec (see http://technet.microsoft.com/en-us/sysinternals/bb897553.aspx) lets you execute processes on other systems. Andrzej describes how to put the two together at http://blogs.technet.com/alipka/archive/2007/12/20/opsmgr-2007-putting-computers-in-maintenance-mode-remotely.aspx. We include these URLs as live links in Appendix E.

By default, the Operations console can only put 50 objects into maintenance at any one time. To adjust the amount of objects that can be selected and put into maintenance, modify the following Registry value: HKCU\SOFTWARE\Microsoft\Microsoft Operations Manager\3.0\Console\ConsoleUserSettings\MaxItemsForMaintenanceMode.

Health Explorer

The Health Explorer is a very important feature in OpsMgr 2007. It is so useful in assessing the true operational state of an object that we nominate it as the "top tool" on the OpsMgr workbench! Earlier in this book, in Chapter 3, we explained how the Health Explorer is bound to the Service Modeling Language (SML) used by OpsMgr management pack developers that architect health models. When you have an object's Health Explorer open, you are really looking into the brain of that monitor, with lots of accessory tools available to help you explore further.

When you see an object in the Operations console that is not healthy, the quickest way to answer the question "What's wrong?" (and even possibly to fix what's wrong) is to right-click the object and select Open -> Health Explorer. In our management group, the computer Gryphon is in a critical state, so we open that object's Health Explorer in Figure 8.39.

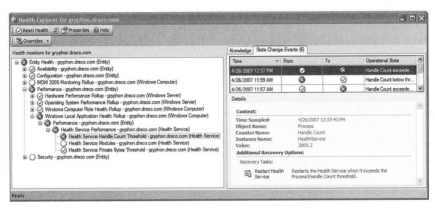

FIGURE 8.39   The Health Explorer for an object can offer recovery tasks to fix the problem.

As we walk down the health model of Gryphon in the Health Explorer shown in Figure 8.39, we see the problem is in the computer's performance, specifically that the threshold for a handle count was exceeded. This indicates a possible problem with memory on the computer.

The Health Explorer exposes and provides access to many other features of OpsMgr. For example, the upper portion of the Explorer has controls to reset the health state, view the detailed properties of a monitor, and apply an override for any selected monitor. Using the Overrides control, you can also view any other managed objects in your OpsMgr management group that have overrides for that monitor.

On the State Change Events tab on the right side of the Health Explorer, you can always see a chronological history of state change events for that object, as well as the context for the event that caused the state to be changed. Additionally, if the management pack author has included them, you may find suggested recovery tasks available to run in the Additional Recovery Options area. In our example in Figure 8.39, see the recovery task Restart Health Service, which you can select to run. We can infer, from the presence of this recovery task, that the management pack author's experience indicates this recovery task may fix the memory-related handle count threshold error.

Authoring

The Authoring space of the Operations console is where the OpsMgr administrator is truly unleashed. In the Authoring space, you perform actions related to management pack components, such as creating additional monitors, attributes, groups, and rules to customize or supplement the default monitoring settings. In addition to working with previously installed management packs, you can create new management packs and distributed applications based on templates. An additional function of the Authoring space is creating and modifying OpsMgr groups.

Management Pack Templates

Management pack templates and the Add Monitoring Wizard are used to create and target custom object types, enabling you to extend the management capabilities of OpsMgr 2007. To create a new management pack from a template, you can right-click the Management Pack Template node and select Add monitoring wizard. Alternatively, you click the Add monitoring wizard shortcut in the lower portion of the Navigation pane.

OpsMgr 2007 provides templates for similar object types to help make it easier to create custom objects with the Add Monitoring Wizard. Management pack templates are conceptually comparable to Microsoft Word templates, which make it easier to create similar Word document types. Operations Manager provides the following default templates:

- ▶ **OLE DB Data Source**—Generates synthetic transactions that monitor the availability of databases

- ▶ **TCP Port**—Generates synthetic transactions that monitor the availability of services

- ▶ **Web Application**—Generates monitors that verify the availability of web-based applications

- ▶ **Windows Service**—Generates monitors and rules that verify the availability of a Windows service

Distributed Applications

A distributed application service monitors the health of a distributed application that you define. It creates the monitors, rules, views, and reports necessary to monitor your distributed application and the individual components it contains. When creating a distributed application in OpsMgr 2007, you first create the service that defines the distributed application monitoring object at a high level. Next, use the Distributed Application Designer to define the individual components that are part of the distributed application you want to monitor. We cover using the Distributed Application Designer in detail in Chapter 19, "Managing a Distributed Environment."

To create a new distributed application service and invoke the Distributed Application Designer, right-click the Distributed Applications node and select Create a new distributed application. You can also click the New distributed application shortcut in the lower portion of the Navigation pane. Templates are available for the following categories of distributed applications:

- ▶ Line of Business Web Application

- ▶ Messaging (such as Microsoft Exchange)

- ▶ Terminal Services Farm

- ▶ Windows Explorer Data Source Service (Explorer clients accessing physical resources via data source directories)

- ▶ Windows Internet Explorer Service (Internet Explorer clients getting to resources using Proxy services)

Groups

Operations Manager 2007 groups can delegate authority, scope access to specific areas of the Operations console, and override the default settings of management packs. To create a new group, right-click the Groups node and select Create a New Group, or click the New group shortcut in the lower portion of the Navigation pane. This invokes the Create New Group Wizard, which walks you through these five steps:

1. **General Properties**—Assign a name and description, and select the unsealed management pack to save the new group. You can also create a new management pack for this purpose if desired.

   This is the only mandatory page of the wizard; the remaining four steps are optional. However, if you do not enter anything on one or more of the remaining steps, no objects will be members of the group.

2. **Explicit Group Membership**—Here you can choose specific objects that will be members of the group. An Add/Remove Objects button opens an Object Selection page where you can locate and select any existing object in the management group.

3. **Dynamic Members**—This is where you will normally enter information in the wizard. As a best practice, you want your groups to automatically populate with objects of the type you are interested in, rather than depend on manual population of the group using the explicit group membership step. A Create/Edit Rule button opens a Query Builder where you select the desired object class and build a formula. Discovered objects with attributes that match the formula's criteria automatically become members of the group.

4. **Subgroups**—Here you can choose subgroups to add to the group. An Add/Remove Subgroups button opens an Object Selection page where you can select any existing groups in the management group to include as subgroups.

5. **Excluded Members**—This is the opposite of step 2, the Explicit Group Membership screen. Just as in that step, an Add/Remove Objects button opens an Object Selection page where you can locate and select any existing object in the management group. Selected objects will not be members of the group, even if included by one of the other methods, such as dynamic or subgroup membership.

8

> **TIP**
>
> **What's in My Groups?**
>
> Boris Yanushpolsky has developed a PowerShell script that retrieves groups and lists the contents of each group as well as the types of objects contained in that group. Boris's utility is described at http://blogs.msdn.com/boris_yanushpolsky/archive/2007/10/27/what-s-in-my-groups.aspx. For your convenience, we include his EnumerateGroupsAndMembers.ps1 file on the CD accompanying this book.

Management Pack Objects

Use the Management Packs Objects node, in the Authoring pane of the Operations console, to create objects that define how monitoring will be performed in your management group. You can view existing attributes, monitors, object discoveries, rules, tasks, and views by clicking the appropriate leaf object under the Management Pack Objects node. You can also create new attributes, monitors, rules, and tasks from each corresponding leaf object. Here is a description of each leaf object and its purpose:

▶ **Attributes**—Displays a list of attributes for each object type in your management group. Attributes consist of either Windows Registry or Windows Management Instrumentation (WMI) queries. You can also create new attributes for use by discovery rules and dynamic group membership criteria. After you create an attribute, you can create a group whose members are only objects that have the commonality described in your attribute.

For example, if you want to monitor a set of servers that all have a common Registry value, you create an attribute based on that Registry value. To find the servers that have that Registry value, you create a group that has a dynamic inclusion rule for only those servers that have the newly created attribute and target the group only to the server object type. Operations Manager then checks the Registry of each server to see whether that Registry value exists. If it exists, the server is added as a member of the group.

Figure 8.40 shows the second and final pages of the Create Attribute Wizard. We are creating a custom attribute that checks for the existence of a Registry key on Windows 2003 computers. In this particular case, we are checking whether Windows Update is configured for automatic updating. We could use this attribute to define a group of Windows 2003 computers participating in automatic updates.

▶ **Monitors**—Displays a list of monitors sorted by object type. Monitors continually assess the condition of specified objects. Based on this assessment, a monitor can also generate alerts and change the health state of an object.

In Operations Manager 2007, you can use monitors to assess various conditions that can occur in monitored objects. For example, a monitor can assess the values of a performance counter, the existence of an event, the occurrence of data in a log file, the status of a Windows Service, or the occurrence of a Simple Network Management

Protocol (SNMP) trap. The result of this assessment determines the health state of a target and the alerts generated. The three types of monitors for these assessments are unit monitors, aggregate rollup monitors, and dependency rollup monitors. Chapter 3 explains these in detail, and Chapter 14 "Monitoring with Operations Manager," discusses how to create and use these monitors.

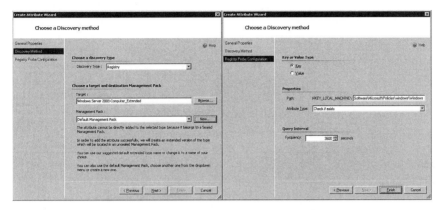

FIGURE 8.40   Creating a new attribute that checks for the existence of a Registry key.

TIP

Avoid Creating Unnecessary Attributes

There is no feature in the Operations console to delete attributes after they are created, so it is not a good idea to create attributes unless you know you are going to use them. (To remove an attribute, you must export the management pack, delete the attribute in the XML file, and reimport the management pack.)

If you create an attribute by mistake, it will have no effect on your management group; just don't associate the bogus attribute with other, valid management pack objects. You can also disable attributes by disabling the corresponding discovery rule in the Object Discoveries node.

▶ **Object Discoveries**—Displays a list of discovery objects currently in use in your management group. A discovery dynamically finds objects on your network that you want to monitor. You can right-click any of the object discoveries listed in the results pane to view its properties or to override it. You would override an object discovery if it would find objects on your network that you do not want to monitor.

You cannot create object discoveries from the Authoring pane. Because management pack developers do not know the specific objects that are in your network environment, they define only the type of objects that their management pack monitors. However, the developers also include discovery objects so that, after the management pack is imported, the object discoveries find the specific objects on your network that are of the types monitored by the management pack.

8

▶ **Rules**—Displays a list of rules sorted by object type. Rules collect data, such as event information, generated by managed objects. Use rules instead of monitors to generate alerts when the data collected from managed objects does not indicate the health state of the managed objects.

An example of a rule's functionality is the collection of a specific event from the Application Event log of Windows-based computers. The collected event is stored in the Operational and/or Data Warehouse databases of the management group, where you can analyze it in views and reports.

Rules can also be overridden or disabled. Select the rule in the Results pane, right-click it, and select Overrides -> Override the Rule (or Overrides -> Disable the Rule). An overrides summary for a particular rule is also available to select when you right-click a rule.

▶ **Tasks**—Lists the tasks that are available within your management group, sorted by object type. Tasks are predefined actions that run against a monitored object. Tasks are accessible to view, modify, or delete in the Authoring pane of the Operations console. When you create a task, you can choose to create an agent task or a console task. Agent tasks can run remotely on an agent or a management server. Console tasks can run only on the local computer. In OpsMgr 2007, a batch file or script can run as a task remotely or locally; however, if an alert or event generates the task, the task must run locally.

You can also create new tasks by running the Create a new task action. Table 8.3 lists the task types you can create.

TABLE 8.3   Tasks You Can Create

Type	Description
Command line	Runs a batch file or starts an application on an agent or management server. You can run this task locally or remotely.
Run a script	Runs a script on an agent or management server.
Alert command line	Runs a task automatically when a specified alert (or alerts) is generated. Specify the alert by using the Parameters drop-down list in the Command Line wizard page of the Create Task Wizard. This task must run locally.
Event command line	Runs a task automatically when a specified event (or events) is generated. Specify the event by using the Parameters drop-down list in the Command Line wizard page of the Create Task Wizard. This task must run locally.

▶ **Views**—Displays a list of available views in the management group. Views display a particular aspect of monitoring settings. When you select a view, a query is sent to the operational database. The results of the query are displayed in the Results pane in the Monitoring space.

You cannot create views from the Authoring space. You can only examine the properties of views in the Authoring space. Views are created in the Monitoring space, so this list of views in the Authoring space is a convenient summary.

Administration

The Administration space enables you to edit high-level OpsMgr settings that affect the security and configuration of the entire management group. You can also view and configure individual management servers and managed objects. The Administration space is only displayed when the user running the console is a member of the OpsMgr Administrators security group. The Administration space presents controls for various major OpsMgr functions that are highly sensitive to the integrity of the management group. Seven nodes appear in the Administration space, and we will drill down into each of them.

Device Management

The following five leaf objects in the Device Management node allow you to perform post-installation configuration of specific Management Servers, agent-managed computers, agentless managed computers, and network devices:

▶ **Management Servers**—Displays all the management servers installed in your management group. Select the properties of a management server to override global management server defaults such as the heartbeat failure and manual agent install settings. The RMS for the management group is identified by a Yes in the Root Management Server column. The Configure Client Monitoring action is available to begin collecting error information from managed computers. Chapter 16, "Client Monitoring," includes detailed procedures for configuring client monitoring.

▶ **Agent-Managed**—Shows all computers with installed agents. The agents are grouped under the management server that the agent reports to. Actions are provided to repair or uninstall an agent. You can also pivot to the Event, Alert, Performance, Diagram, or State view for an agent-managed computer by right-clicking the computer name and selecting Open. Select the properties of an agent-managed computer to override global heartbeat failure and security settings.

▶ **Agentless Managed**—Displays all agentless managed computers, under the proxy agent that monitors them remotely. You can change the proxy agent for a particular agentless managed computer, and delete an agentless managed computer from the management group.

▶ **Network Devices**—Displays all discovered network devices, under the proxy agent that monitors them remotely. You can also delete discovered network devices here using the Delete action.

▶ **Pending Management**—Allows you to select to approve or reject manual agent installations that are awaiting approval to join the management group. The default setting in a management group will automatically reject manually installed agents,

8

so unless you have modified that setting from Administration -> Settings -> Server -> Security menu, no computers will appear in the Pending Management node.

Configuring Agent Proxying

From the blogs, Clive Eastwood provides a small utility to configure and view agent proxying. Here are some useful tidbits on this utility:

▶ It's remoteable (you can run it over the network).

▶ You can view current agent proxy settings.

▶ You can change proxy settings for an agent in a group.

▶ You can update agents based on a flexible query expression.

The tool, with documentation, is available at http://blogs.technet.com/cliveeastwood/archive/2007/08/30/operations-manager-2007-agent-proxy-command-line-tool-proxycfg.aspx. We also include the tool (proxyCFG.zip) for your convenience on the CD accompanying this book.

Settings

Nine management group settings are exposed at this node, organized under the Agent, General, and Server headings. These are global settings because they control the behavior of the entire management group.

▶ **Agent**—The only setting here to modify is the global heartbeat interval. Agents generate heartbeats at specific intervals to ensure they are functioning properly. The default heartbeat interval is 60 seconds.

▶ **General**—You'll find six settings under this heading:

▶ **Alerts**—Here you can add new alert resolution states and modify the auto-resolution intervals. You can create up to 254 custom resolution states; it's a great idea to expand on the two built-in states (Closed and New). We suggest at least adding the new resolution states of Acknowledged and Assigned to help manage alerts. The default auto-resolve settings are used to resolve active alerts in the New state after 30 days and active alerts when the alert source is healthy after 7 days.

▶ **Database Grooming**—The OpsMgr grooming process removes unnecessary data from the database in order to maintain performance. The default setting is to purge all resolved alerts as well as all event and performance data after 7 days. Grooming is discussed in Chapter 12, "Backup and Recovery."

▶ **Notification**—Enables configuration of email, instant messaging, Short Message Service (SMS), and command-line notification channels. Later in this section, we discuss setting up notification recipients and subscriptions at the Notifications node of the Administration pane. Those notifications depend on the setup of the Notification settings here at the Settings node. Before you can configure actual notification recipients and subscriptions, you need to enable the notification channels here.

▶ **Privacy**—Provides the procedures to configure what Customer Experience Improvement Program (CEIP) information, error reports, and solution responses are transmitted and received from Microsoft. We recommend enabling at least the CEIP and operational data reporting options; these do not impact the operation of the management group or its users, and they provide anonymous data to Microsoft that helps improve the quality of the OpsMgr product.

▶ **Reporting**—This setting lets you modify the Uniform Resource Locator (URL) path to the reporting server. The default is http://<*ReportingServername*>:80/ ReportServer. You would only modify this setting if you changed the identity of the reporting server in your management group or the composition of the URL, such as enabling SSL.

▶ **Web Addresses**—If you have installed the OpsMgr Web console in your management group, you can put the URL to the Web console here. Whatever URL you enter here will appear in notifications as a link for the recipient to follow to the Web console for more information about the alert that caused the notification. A default installation of the Web console would indicate a URL setting of http://<*WebConsoleServername*>:51908/default.aspx.

TIP

Web Console Error—Requested Value UrlViewType Not Found

If you try to access a Web Page view in the Web console, you will receive a Requested Value 'UrlViewType' not found error. This occurs because the URL view type is not supported in the Web console. A hotfix is available, with additional information, at http://support.microsoft.com/kb/935898. The hotfix is incorporated into OpsMgr 2007 Service Pack 1.

▶ **Server**—The two settings here are Heartbeat and Security. We describe the security setting in the "Device Management" section of this chapter; the Security setting determines how manually installed agents are handled. These agents can be automatically rejected or accepted, or placed in the Pending Management node where an administrator must approve them.

The heartbeat setting is the number of consecutive missed heartbeats from an agent before OpsMgr initiates a loss of heartbeat alert; the default is 3. Therefore, the default settings of OpsMgr will fire an alert on a down agent after about 3 minutes, which is the server missed heartbeat setting multiplied by the agent heartbeat interval.

Using the OpsMgr Mobile Console

Yes, Virginia, there really is a way to get alerts on your mobile device. Use the URL for your Web console and add **/mobile** at the end (for example, http://<WebConsoleServername>:51908/mobile). Assuming your Web console is accessible from the Internet, you now can receive "mobile" alerts, including associated knowledge and potential response actions. After logging in with your username and password, you proceed to the Overview screen, where you get a summary of the state and alerts. You can also drill down into details. Figure 8.41 shows the Overview and Alert Details screens.

A little too close for you? Just don't take your mobile device on vacation!

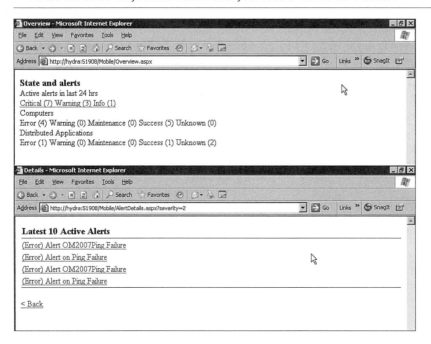

FIGURE 8.41   The Overview and Alert Details screens from the Mobile console.

Security

Chapter 11 discusses the creation and management of user roles and Run As Accounts and Profiles in detail. Here is a summary of the functions located at the Security node of the Administration pane:

▶ **User Roles**—Displays all existing user roles. You can create new user roles of the following types: Read-only Operator, Operator, Advanced Operator, and Author.

▶ **Run As Accounts**—Displays all Action accounts and Run As Accounts. You can create new Run As Accounts from the navigation menu (right-click any node in the Navigation pane of the Administration space and select Create Run As Account).

▶ **Run As Profiles**—Displays the Run As Profiles used by workflows to run under specific identities. Open the properties page for a selected Run As Profile, and on the Run As Accounts tab, you can select existing Run As Accounts to associate with that Run As Profile.

Management Packs

At the Management Pack node of the Administration space, you can view a list of all the management packs that exist in your management group—both sealed and unsealed management packs that you imported, and unsealed management packs that you created. You can create new unsealed management packs as well as import sealed and unsealed management packs from vendors and other OpsMgr community professionals. There is also an export management pack function; use this to create an unsealed management pack copy in a file system location of your selection. Exported management packs can be stored for backup purposes, imported into other management groups, and exchanged with other OpsMgr community professionals.

When you create a new management pack, a corresponding view folder is created in the Monitoring space. By viewing the properties of a management pack here, you can see the same management pack dependencies information exposed by the Import Management Pack Wizard when importing new management packs.

Notifications

OpsMgr 2007 can send a notification to operators when an alert occurs, in case the operator is not watching the Operations console at that moment. Three steps are required to enable external notification to an operator. As we noted previously in this section, when describing the Settings -> General -> Notification feature, you must create notification channels before proceeding to create recipients and subscriptions. That is the first step to enable notifications. Perform the remaining two steps here at the Notifications node of the Administration pane:

1. **Recipients**—A notification recipient defines when and from what devices OpsMgr can send notifications. When you create a new notification recipient, you select a notification channel (such as email) and associate a delivery address (such as an email address) to create the recipient. You can optionally create a schedule to indicate days and times to generate notifications.

2. **Subscriptions**—The final configuration step to enable notification services is associating a recipient with categories of alerts; this is a *subscription*. Remember that a subscriber can be an individual user account or a distribution list. When you create a subscription, it invokes the Notification Subscription Properties Wizard. The wizard guides you through the steps that create the subscription: Optionally filter notifications by user role; select the groups, classes, and alert criteria to notify subscribers about; optionally use alert aging as a notification criteria; and indicate whether modifications to the default notification messages are desired for that subscriber.

TIP

Details on Setting Up Notifications

You may want to check the Operations Manager 2007 Operations Guide for additional information about setting up and configuring notifications. We discuss the process in Chapter 14 as well.

Connected Management Groups

A connected management group provides the capability for the Operations console user interface in one management group to query data from another management group. You can add the connection information for a connected management group here. That information is the management group name, the FQDN of the RMS, and the credentials to use to connect to the other RMS. The default credentials are those of the SDK service account of the local management group.

Product Connectors

OpsMgr 2007 supports the ability to synchronize alert data with other applications, such as other management systems, using product connectors. Product connectors subscribe to alerts and forward them to other products. OpsMgr comes with one product connector installed, the MOM Internal Connector. OpsMgr components use the MOM Internal Connector to insert discovery data. You should ignore this entry in your product connector list. If you install other product connecters developed by third parties, they will appear in the product connector list. The properties page of a product connector has a subscriptions area where you would configure the connected product to receive forwarded alerts as desired.

Reporting

Reporting in OpsMgr 2007 refers to the process of storing, retrieving, and presenting historical data stored in the Data Warehouse database. You can access data from OpsMgr reporting in three main fashions:

▶ Targeted reports

▶ Generic reports

▶ Scheduled reports

All three categories of reports yield the same reporting products; what differs is the method in which the report criteria is assembled. The Reporting space in the Operations console can save reports you author, save your favorite reports, and schedule reports. We discuss the report types in the next sections of this chapter.

Targeted Reports

The most common way to use OpsMgr Reporting is the targeted report method. With this method, you access the report from the Monitoring space, select the object you want report data for, and click one of the reports displayed in the Actions area on the right side of the Monitoring space.

This launches the report view, with the object of interest prepopulating the object list in the report parameters. Figure 8.42 shows a report on the memory performance of the Hydra computer for the last week. It also shows a performance report, which is generated by selecting to view the parameters of the report (View -> Parameters from the report view).

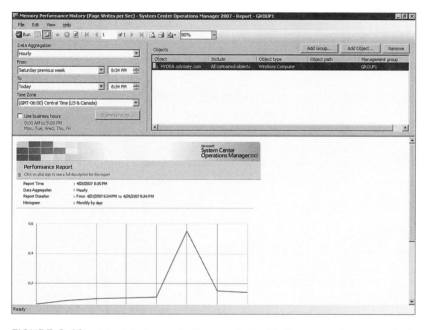

FIGURE 8.42   A targeted report after running, with the parameter pane displayed.

In Figure 8.42, the performance report graph in the lower portion is the report itself, and the parameters header in the upper portion includes the criteria used to generate the report. (For this figure, we scaled the graph to 80% of its actual size to fit it in the screenshot along with the parameters header.) We call this a *targeted report* because we invoked the reporting view in the context of the Windows Server 2003 Monitoring view with a particular computer selected. It just took a few mouse clicks to generate the report, and we did not need to know details about the report's construction, such as the fact that memory performance history is part of the Window Computer object class.

Real World—Operations Manager Report Parameters

How do you know what to use as the "object" or "group" for a report? When you open a report, you must first change parameters to specify the start date and the targeted groups or objects. Before you even run the report, review the text at the bottom (the report details section). It specifies what objects provide what information.

A quick way to determine the parameters you can use is to go to the state views and run reports from there. As an example, in the Monitoring -> Computer section, click a server. In the Actions pane you get a list of available reports for the object. Running the report from here passes the parameters to the report. As another example, in Monitoring -> Microsoft Windows Active Directory -> DC State, click a server. In the Actions pane you get a list of five Active Directory-related reports and six Windows Computer reports.

You can highlight multiple systems at the same time; the necessary parameters are passed to the report (as we did for the results shown in Figure 8.43).

If you find a report that you like, click File and save it to your Favorites so that it will be easier to locate later (these are available under Reporting -> Favorite Reports).

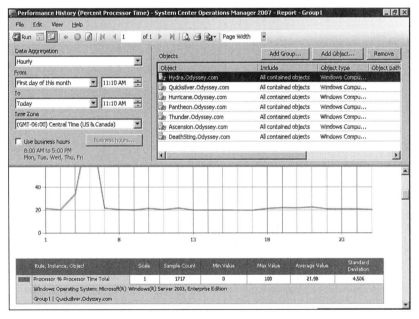

FIGURE 8.43   The Percent Processor Time report for multiple systems, initiated from the Actions pane.

Generic Reports

We can create the identical report, with a few more mouse clicks, by navigating to the Reporting space, selecting the Windows Server 2003 Operating System report library, opening the Memory Performance History report, and adding the computer object(s) to report on in the report parameters. Figure 8.44 shows the report details after selecting that report in the Reporting space.

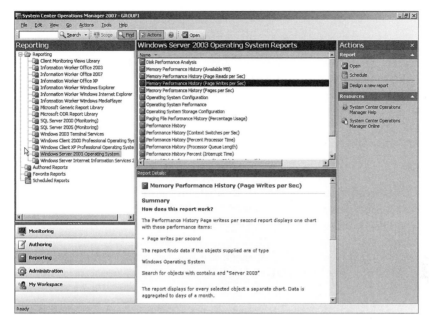

FIGURE 8.44   The Reporting space exposes available reports in the generic report library.

If you design and save a new custom report, you can locate it at the Authored Reports node of the Reporting space. Notice also in Figure 8.44 that one of the report libraries is the Generic Report Library.

Generic reports are really like templates, used to derive the targeted and context-focused reports. For example, generic reports exist for data based on alerts, availability, events, configuration changes, and performance. By opening a generic report of the type of data you want to report on, you are then free to select any criteria from across the management group to construct a custom report.

After running a targeted report or a generic report you have customized, you can export the results from the report view using the File -> Export command. Available export formats are XML, comma-delimited (CSV), graphic TIFF, Acrobat (PDF), Web archive (MHT), and Excel workbook. Another option available after you have run a report is to save that report as a "favorite report," which puts a shortcut to that report in the Favorite Reports node of the Reporting space for quick access in the future.

Scheduled Reports

You can create scheduled reports by selecting File -> Schedule from the Report window after running a report. A three-step wizard allows you to specify a delivery method, schedule, and parameter(s) for your report to automatically run and save to a file share of your selection. You can select the same file formats for scheduled reports as when exporting a targeted or generic report. A list of scheduled reports in your management group appears at the Scheduled Reports node in the Reporting space.

8

> **TIP**
>
> **Enabling the Email Option as a Delivery Method**
>
> If you don't see an option for email as a delivery method for your reports, run the Reporting Services Configuration tool on your SQL Reporting Services server. Specify the sender address and SMTP server in the email settings. Now reload the report and you should see the option for email as a delivery method.

My Workspace

The My Workspace area is a private place for you to create and store console customizations for later reuse. Many console settings, related to the configuration of the console, reside in the user area of the Registry of the computer running the Operations console. As we previously discussed in the "Console Configuration Data" section, those customizations are only available on the computer running the console you have customized. Microsoft has also provided a way to leverage the shared OpsMgr operational database to permit console operators to save some settings in the My Workspace area. Views saved in My Workspace will follow the operator from console to console, and notably are also made available when using the Web console.

> **TIP**
>
> **Tuning the Web Console Refresh Interval**
>
> If you are using the Web console as an alerting dashboard, you might want to speed up the refresh interval. The default is 5 minutes, which can be modified to any number, including 0 (which disables automatic refresh). The refresh interval is set in a text file named web.config on the local disk of the Web Console Server, in the location *%ProgramFiles%*\System Center Operations Manager 2007\Web Console. Simply locate and modify the value in the following line:
>
>   <add key="ViewAutoRefresh" value = "5" />

There are three practical uses of the My Workspace area:

- ▶ **Create shortcuts to views in the Monitoring pane**—You can have quick access to any view in the Monitoring pane by creating a shortcut to it in your Favorite Views folder. Right-click any view in the Monitoring pane and select Add to my workspace.... Give the shortcut a name and select which Favorite Views folder to save the shortcut in (or create a new folder). The shortcut view reflects changes to the source view, and vice versa. However, deleting the shortcut does not delete the source view.

- ▶ **Create My Views**—These are unique views, not links to existing views. To create a My View, right-click the Favorite Views folder in My Workspace (or a favorite views child folder you created) and select New. Then you can create any view, such as an alert view or a dashboard view, just as if you were creating it in the Monitoring space. Views created here are only visible to you, so you can create all the views you want without affecting any other users in your management group.

▶ **Access saved searches**—Search functions are available from all console views, accessed via the top menu area of the Operations console, and you can save complex search criteria in My Workspace. A toolbar-style Search button is located there, or you can select Tools, Search from the menu bar. The button is not context-sensitive; it always calls up the same blank search window for you to enter your search terms in. Perhaps more useful is the Advanced Search function, which you can select from the bottom of the Search toolbar menu or from Tools -> Advanced Search. In the Advanced Search window is an option to save your search criteria for reuse later. Figure 8.45 shows the Advanced Search window with the Save parameters to My Favorites link highlighted.

Although the euphemistic term "fishing expedition" means an investigation with little chance of success, Microsoft urges OpsMgr administrators to teach console operators "how to fish." A good fisherman makes an educated guess about where he may find the fish, and he drops a baited hook at the appropriate spot and depth. The My Workspace area is the tackle box for your operators, where each professional can store his or her assemblage of preferred tools (views and searches) for quick access every time he or she needs to "go fishing."

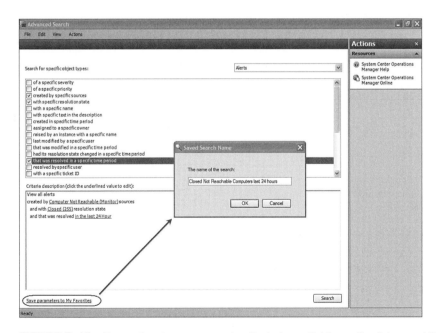

FIGURE 8.45   The option to save search criteria is available on the Advanced Search window.

Summary

We started this chapter with our core Operations Manager 2007 components just installed and in a default configuration. We walked though a testing scenario to validate that our core management group functions were working. After confirming that OpsMgr was correctly installed and functioning, we began the build-out of our management group. We imported a score of management packs, and we discussed several discovery methods to add managed objects. We had a detailed discussion on deploying and using the Operations console, and we concluded with a drilldown on each of the console's activity panes.

It is now time for an in-depth discussion of agents, which is the topic of the next chapter.

CHAPTER 9

Installing and Configuring Agents

This chapter focuses on agents and their use in System Center Operations Manager (OpsMgr) 2007. However, there is a lot more to agents in OpsMgr 2007 than just installing and configuring them. We will start with understanding the core concepts, such as how the discovery and approval processes work. We will explain the differences between agent-managed systems, agentless monitored systems, unknown states, and network devices. We will discuss different methods available for deploying and configuring the OpsMgr agent; these methods include using Active Directory Integration, Systems Management Server, the Deployment Wizard, and manual installation. We will then discuss the features, limitations, and procedures associated with agentless monitoring in OpsMgr.

Next, we will discuss the various configurations available when you are also using other management software, such as Microsoft Operations Manager (MOM 2005), or have other OpsMgr 2007 management groups. In the last part of this chapter, we will discuss managing agents and the relationship between Agentless Exception Monitoring (AEM) and agents, and we will present some troubleshooting tips associated with agents in Operations Manager 2007.

Understanding Core Concepts

Several core concepts, such as the discovery process and the approval process, are relevant to understanding how agents function within OpsMgr 2007. In addition, a monitored server can exist in one of three management states: agent-managed, agentless managed, and unmanaged.

Discovery Process

The *discovery process* identifies systems to which you can install agents or systems you can configure for agentless monitoring. This discovery process queries the Active Directory directory service for computer information matching the requirements you defined for discovery.

The Microsoft MOM team provides an excellent graphical representation of how the discovery process works. It is available at http://blogs.technet.com/momteam/archive/2007/12/10/how-does-computer-discovery-work-in-opsmgr-2007.aspx/. Figure 9.1 is based on that graphic, with the specific steps for discovery listed next.

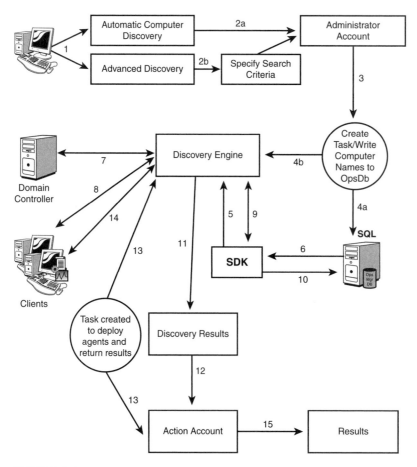

FIGURE 9.1   Computer discovery in OpsMgr 2007.

To follow along with the steps in Figure 9.1, the process for computer discovery is as follows:

1. The discovery wizard process is initiated from the Operations console.
2. Discovery can be automatic or advanced:

    a. The automatic computer discovery option is chosen, or

    b. The advanced computer discovery option is selected, and search criteria options are available to provide the computer and device type, specify the management server, and whether to verify if discovered computers can be contacted
    Additional options are to either scan Active Directory or browse for computer names.

3. The administrator specifies if the Management Server Action account or another account with administrator-level privileges will be used.
4. Two tasks are created:

    ▶ A task is created to write computer names to the Operations database

    ▶ The task is submitted to the discovery engine

5. The discovery process reads credentials from the database using the SDK.
6. The current list of computers is read from the Operations database.
7. The discovery engine contacts a Domain Controller for resources, including Active Directory computer account information.
8. If the option to verify discovered computers is checked (step 2b), each of the clients is contacted through ports 135, 137, 139, 445, and 5723.
9. Results of the computer discovery are passed to the SDK from the discovery engine.
10. The computer discovery results are written from the SDK to the Operations database.
11. The discovery engine checks for the management mode and reports the discovery results.
12. The Action account uses either the Local System or the specified domain account to create tasks to deploy the agents.
13. The tasks are created to deploy the agents and to return the results.
14. The discovery engine deploys agents and returns the results.
15. The results are gathered from deploying all of the agents and displayed at the Operations console.

The Discovery Wizard has been enhanced since MOM 2005, with capabilities for automatic discovery of all Windows-based computers, and can scan computers in a specific Organizational Unit (OU). You can discover machines residing in nontrusted domains and workgroups if you provide the computer name in the format *Domain\ComputerName* or *Workgroup\ComputerName*.

> **TIP**
>
> **Failed Discovery Same Computer Name**
>
> During an OpsMgr deployment, we found that if you have the same computer name existing in multiple domains, discovery fails on the second system if OpsMgr is already monitoring the first system. Although this is not a common scenario for servers, it is an important consideration when deploying OpsMgr into workstation configurations with multiple domains, because the same workstation name can easily exist in different domains.

Scheduling Computer Discovery

MOM 2005 included the capability to schedule computer discovery. This functionality was replaced in OpsMgr 2007 with Active Directory Integration (discussed in the "Active Directory Integration" section of this chapter), which applies the OpsMgr settings to systems with the agent deployed.

Because not all environments use Active Directory Integration, how can you schedule computer discovery in OpsMgr? You can use PowerShell with a scheduled task; an example of which is provided by Tarek Ismail at http://tarek-online.blogspot.com/2007/07/how-to-schedule-discover-and-install.html:

```
param ($OpsMgrservername,$Domainname)
#Initialize the OpsMgr Provider
Add-PSSnapin Microsoft.EnterpriseManagement.OperationsManager.Client
#Set the location to the root of the provider namespace
cd OperationsManagerMonitoring::
#create a connection to the Management Group
New-ManagementGroupConnection $OpsMgrservername
#change the path
cd $OpsMgrservername
#configure query setting
$ldap_query = new-ldapquerydiscoverycriteria -domain $Domainname
➥-ldapquery "(sAMAccountType=805306369)(name=*ABC*)"
#configure discovery setting
$windows_discovery_cfg = new-windowsdiscoveryconfiguration -ldapquery
➥$ldap_query #discoveryresults
$discovery_results = start-discovery -managementserver (get-managementserver)
➥-windowsdiscoveryconfiguration $windows_discovery_cfg
#install Agent
install-agent -managementserver (get-managementserver) -agentmanagedcomputer
➥$discovery_results.custommonitoringobjects
```

Save this script using a name such as Agentdiscoverinstall.ps1 and configure it to run periodically from the Windows scheduler on the RMS using the following syntax:

```
Powershell.exe Agentdiscoverinstall.ps1 -OpsMgrservername:
➥localhost-Domainname:<domain>
```

When this script runs, it will discover the computers that match the Lightweight Directory Access Protocol (LDAP) query defined in the script.

Approval Process

OpsMgr's default configuration rejects manually installed agents. You can change this configuration in the Administration node of the Operations console. Perform the following steps:

1. Navigate to Administration -> Settings -> Security. Right-click Security and then select Properties.

2. The General tab shows that the default configuration is Reject new manual agent installations. If your environment will use manual agent installation, check the option that says Review new manual agent installations in pending management view, as shown in Figure 9.2.

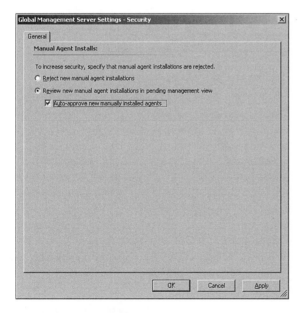

FIGURE 9.2   Configuring manual agent installs.

3. If you choose the option to review new manual agent installations, a check box is available that reads Auto-approve new manually installed agents. If you select the second option, new manual agents automatically approved.

If you do not choose the second option, manually installed agents display in the Operations console in the Administration -> Device Management -> Pending Management folder (where you can approve or reject their installation).

Agent-Managed State

An agent-managed system runs a software component called the OpsMgr *agent*, which runs as a local service on each computer it is installed on. The agent monitors the computer using management pack objects, which apply to that agent. The management server will update these objects as changes are applied to the management packs used by that management group. Updates are received by the agents at the next configuration request interval (5 minutes by default) after changes are applied. Typically, OpsMgr configurations use agent-managed systems.

Installing OpsMgr 2007 and the Reporting capability automatically imports approximately 40 management packs, listed in Table 9.1. The majority of these management packs are libraries, which provide a foundation of object types and settings that other management packs depend on. The other installed management packs monitor the health and availability of Operations Manager and the OpsMgr agent.

TABLE 9.1   Default Management Packs in OpsMgr 2007

MP Friendly Name	Internal Name	Description
Application Log Library	System.Application.Log.Library	Contains the definitions specific to application log monitoring.
Baselining Tasks Library	System.BaseliningTasks.Library	Contains definitions of baselining tasks.
Client Monitoring Internal Library	Microsoft.SystemCenter. ClientMonitoring.Internal	Contains primarily workflows for System Center Client Monitoring and CEIP features.
Client Monitoring Library	Microsoft.SystemCenter. ClientMonitoring.Library	Contains primarily various types for System Center AEM (Agentless Exception Monitoring) and CEIP features.
Client Monitoring Views Library	Microsoft.SystemCenter. ClientMonitoring.Views.Internal	Contains primarily views for System Center AEM (Agentless Error Monitoring) and CEIP features.

TABLE 9.1   Continued

MP Friendly Name	Internal Name	Description
Data Warehouse Internal Library	Microsoft.SystemCenter. DataWarehouse.Internal	Contains definitions and workflows for Operations Manager Data Warehousing features used internally.
Data Warehouse Library	Microsoft.SystemCenter. DataWarehouse.Library	Contains definitions and workflows for Operations Manager Data Warehousing features.
Default Management Pack	Microsoft.SystemCenter. OperationsManager.DefaultUser	Default location for storing all custom management pack objects such as rules, tasks, and monitors. It also stores all defined overrides and notifications.
Distributed Application Designer Library	Microsoft.SystemCenter. ServiceDesigner.Library	Contains the various Distributed Application types that show up in the Distributed Application Designer.
Health Internal Library	System.Health.Internal	Contains definitions for the System Health types that are not visible via the console user interface or the SDK client.
Health Library	System.Health.Library	Contains definitions for the core System Health types.
Image Library (System Center)	Microsoft.SystemCenter.Image. Library	Contains icons for System Center types.
Image Library (System)	System.Image.Library	Contains icons for System types.
Image Library (Windows)	Microsoft.Windows.Image.Library	Contains icons for Windows types.
Instance Group Library	Microsoft.SystemCenter.Instance Group.Library	Contains the definitions and components needed for the Group Wizard.
Microsoft Generic Report Library	Microsoft.SystemCenter. DataWarehouse.Report.Library	Generic Data Warehouse reports.

6

TABLE 9.1   Continued

MP Friendly Name	Internal Name	Description
Microsoft ODR Report Library	ODR	Microsoft ODR Report Library.
MOM 2005 Backward Compatibility	System.Mom.Backward Compatibility.Library	Contains the definitions necessary for MOM 2005 backward compatibility.
Network Device Library	Microsoft.SystemCenter. NetworkDevice.Library	Contains the definitions specific to network devices.
Notifications Internal Library	Microsoft.SystemCenter. Notifications.Internal	Used to hide notifications-related management pack objects exposed directly via the API for Operations Manager.
Notifications Library	Microsoft.SystemCenter. Notifications.Library	Contains definitions and workflows for Notifications features.
Operations Manager 2007	Microsoft.SystemCenter. OperationsManager.2007	Contains the monitoring for the System Center Operations Manager 2007.
Operations Manager Agent Management Library	Microsoft.SystemCenter. OperationsManager.AM.DR.2007	Contains the agent remediation recoveries that must be initiated by the user.
Operations Manager Internal Library	Microsoft.SystemCenter. OperationsManager.Internal	Contains internal components (views, discovery, and so on) that are specific to System Center Operations Manager.
Performance Library	System.Performance.Library	Contains definitions for core System Performance.
SNMP Library	System.Snmp.Library	Contains SNMP definitions.

TABLE 9.1   Continued

MP Friendly Name	Internal Name	Description
Synthetic Transactions Library	Microsoft.SystemCenter.Synthetic Transactions.Library	Contains the components needed to create monitored objects for lightweight Synthetic Transactions. A lightweight Synthetic Transaction is typically a single action such as "Check a specific port" or a short set of actions such as "Log in to this database and check for the existence of a table." These transactions are run from one or more agents. They remotely check a target that may or may not have a Health Service.
System Center Core Library	Microsoft.SystemCenter.Library	Contains type definitions for System Center.
System Center Core Monitoring	Microsoft.SystemCenter.2007	Contains the core monitoring for the System Center 2007 core platform and its services.
System Center Internal Library	Microsoft.SystemCenter.Internal	Contains definitions and components internal to System Center.
System Center Rule Templates	Microsoft.SystemCenter. RuleTemplates	Templates for rules.
System Center Task Templates	Microsoft.SystemCenter. TaskTemplates	Templates for tasks.
System Center UI Executed Tasks	Microsoft.SystemCenter.Internal. UI.Tasks	Contains tasks that are called and executed by the UI.
System Hardware Library	System.Hardware.Library	Contains the definitions that are specific to physical hardware.
System Library	System.Library	Root for all management packs. Contains platform independent definitions.

TABLE 9.1   Continued

MP Friendly Name	Internal Name	Description
Web Application Monitoring Library	Microsoft.SystemCenter. WebApplication.Library	Contains the components needed to monitor Web Applications and record browser sessions. Recording a browser session allows you to create a rich Synthetic Transaction to imitate exactly how users interact with the application you need to monitor.
Windows Client Operating Systems Library	Microsoft.Windows.Client.Library	This management pack is the library management pack that defines all the features and components common to all versions of Windows client operating systems.
Windows Cluster Library	Microsoft.Windows.Cluster.Library	Contains the definitions specific to Windows Clustering.
Windows Core Library	Microsoft.Windows.Library	Contains the definitions specific to the Windows platform.
Windows Service Library	Microsoft.SystemCenter. NTService.Library	Contains the definitions for monitoring a Windows Service.

As you integrate other management packs into OpsMgr 2007, additional items will be monitored depending on the functionthe server provides.

You can deploy OpsMgr 2007 agents to the following operating systems:

▶ Microsoft Windows Server 2003 SP 1 or later

▶ Microsoft Windows 2000 Server SP 4

▶ Microsoft Windows 2000 Professional SP 4

▶ Microsoft Windows XP Professional (no service pack required)

▶ Microsoft Windows Vista Business, Enterprise, and Ultimate editions

TIP

Monitoring Client Operating Systems with OpsMgr

Although you can use OpsMgr to monitor client operating systems, most organizations typically only monitor servers. An exception to this rule might be a batch-processing system that runs business-critical functions that has not been migrated to a server platform. For example, many manufacturing companies use workstation-class computers to monitor machines that produce their products.

The Windows Client/2000 XP management pack monitors Windows 2000 and XP systems. The new Windows Vista Client Monitoring management pack provides the ability to monitor the availability, configuration, and performance of Windows Vista operating systems. You can download these from the System Center Pack Catalog site at http://go.microsoft.com/fwlink/?linkid=71124. For an example of how client monitoring works in Operations Manager 2007, see Figure 9.3, which displays Windows XP and Windows Vista monitored systems within the Windows Client State view. We discuss client monitoring in Chapter 16, "Client Monitoring."

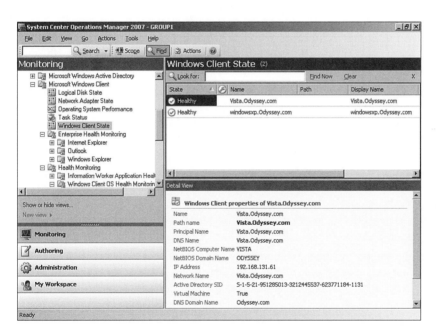

FIGURE 9.3 Windows XP and Vista systems in the Client State view.

Microsoft does not support Microsoft Windows NT 4.0 in an agent-managed configuration (or support any other operating systems that do not match the configurations listed previously). If there is a requirement to manage unsupported systems such as this, consider either agentless management or review third-party supplemental software for OpsMgr 2007.

Agentless Managed State

An agentless managed system does not run the OpsMgr agent. The Agent Component on the management server (or Root Management Server) collects data from the agentless managed computer through remote calls to that system. OpsMgr 2007 does not have a documented limit on the number of agentless managed systems that can report to a management server, but in MOM 2005 Microsoft limited support for agentless systems to 10. This limit was a supportability limit, not a physical limit (that is, 11 or more agentless systems would still function). The limit was rather a recommendation, based on the impact on the performance of the management server providing the agentless monitoring functionality.

There are restrictions to using agentless monitoring. It is not supported on several management packs and provides a reduced set of functionality for others. We discuss these topics in more detail in the "Integrating Agentless Managed Systems into OpsMgr 2007" section of this chapter.

Application owners are sometimes concerned about installing agent software onto their application servers and the potential impact on the operations of that computer. The resource load on an agent-managed computer is low and does not generally pose a problem.

Real World—OpsMgr Agent Impacts

A question often asked about the OpsMgr agent is, How large an impact does it have? Our testing, detailed in Table 9.2, indicates the following load while installing the agent (about 3 to 3 1/2 minutes).

After completing the agent installation, we compared the performance counters gathered prior to the installation to those collected after installation. The results in Table 9.3 indicate what should be the worst-case impact of the agent on the system.

If you plan to push out a large number of agents over small or congested network links, we recommend doing the deployment outside of business hours to minimize any impacts to the network environment.

TABLE 9.2   Agent Impact During Installation

Component	Impact
Processor	29%–37% increase during installation
Disk	18–19 additional pages per second
Disk storage	154MB data (*%ProgramFiles%*\System Center Operations Manager 2007)
Network	11MB data sent to the system during installation
Memory	22MB less available memory

TABLE 9.3   Agent Impact After Installation

Component	Impact
Processor	3%–4%
Disk	0.5 additional pages per second
Disk storage	156MB data (*%ProgramFiles%*\System Center Operations Manager 2007)
Network	.5–.6 MB/minute additional traffic
Memory	11MB less available memory

For some environments, any change to the configuration or installed software base may lead to complications. A good example of this is a validated system where specific testing processes must occur for any changes to the configuration, including deploying agents. (A *validated* system is one that has a strict process to validate the functionality of the system anytime software is installed on it.) In these cases, the Information Technology (IT) group responsible for server management wants to avoid even the appearance of affecting an application server, thus avoiding potential liability. If you are in this situation, you can use the agentless management mode to manage servers that might otherwise be unmanaged. As discussed earlier (in the "Agent-Managed State" section), legacy systems such as NT 4.0 or operating systems that are not current on patching are also common reasons for at least temporarily using an agentless configuration.

Agentless managed computers have a more limited set of features than do agent-based managed computers. Similar to agent-based managed computers, agentless managed computers include the following capabilities:

▶ State monitoring

▶ Heartbeat

▶ Service discovery

▶ Performance collection

▶ Script execution

▶ Event collection

However, there are some significant limitations to agentless managed systems. The primary limitation is the management packs that will not run agentless. This list includes the following:

▶ Active Directory

▶ Exchange 2003

▶ IIS

▶ SharePoint Portal Server

Agentless monitoring also increases the resource load on the management server that is monitoring the system.

Real World—OpsMgr Agentless Impacts

In the "Real World—OpsMgr Agent Impacts" sidebar, we discussed the impacts of monitoring a system with an agent. What happens when a system is without an agent—a configuration known as *agentless monitored*?

After the Discovery Wizard is used to discover the system, agentless monitoring can start immediately without the 3-to-3-1/2-minute time period while an agent is deployed. Deploying an agentless system is virtually instantaneous. Once deployed, the system goes from "Not Monitored" to "Monitored" in less than a minute.

Both while the installation was taking place and afterward, we compared performance counters gathered prior to the installation to those gathered after installation. The results in Table 9.4 discuss the impacts on the agentless monitored system, and Table 9.5 discusses the impacts on the management server monitoring that system.

Now that we have seen the impacts of monitoring a system using an agent (Tables 9.2 and 9.3) and we know the impacts of monitoring a system agentless (Tables 9.4 and 9.5), what is the impact of using one versus the other? Table 9.6 discusses the differences of the impact when a system is monitored agentless versus the impact when a system is monitored with an agent.

Given all this information the question is, When should you use agentless monitoring? We recommend using agentless monitoring in the following cases:

▶ You cannot use agent-based monitoring

▶ The computer is a Windows-based system

▶ You need to monitor more than just up/down functionality

As a best practice, be aware of the positive and negative impacts of agentless monitoring before deploying it.

TABLE 9.4   Agentless Impact on the Agentless System

Component	Impact
Processor	3.5%
Disk	No noticeable impact
Disk storage	No noticeable impact
Network	1.3MB/minute additional traffic
Memory	No noticeable impact

TABLE 9.5   Agentless Impact on the Management Server

Component	Impact
Processor	7%
Disk	No noticeable impact
Disk storage	No noticeable impact
Network	1.3MB/minute additional traffic
Memory	9MB less available memory

TABLE 9.6   Comparing Agent to Agentless Monitoring Impacts (per System Monitored)

Component	Impact
Processor	7% increase on the management server.
Disk	Decreased paging by .5 pages per second on the agentless monitored system.
Disk storage	Disk free space increased by 156MB on the agentless monitored system (because the agent is not deployed).
Network	Network traffic increased by .8 MB/minute on the agentless monitored system and 1.3MB/minute on the management server.
Memory	Decreased memory requirements by 11MB on the system being monitored agentless and a 9MB decrease in available memory on the management server.

Unknown State

Unknown systems are unmanaged systems, either identified for potential management in the future (the systems are discovered but they are not managed) or that have had the agent removed from them. OpsMgr does not collect information from unmanaged systems. Computers in an unknown state display in the right-side pane in the Operations console at the root of the Monitoring node. (In Figure 9.4, see the empty circle on the right side of the screen.)

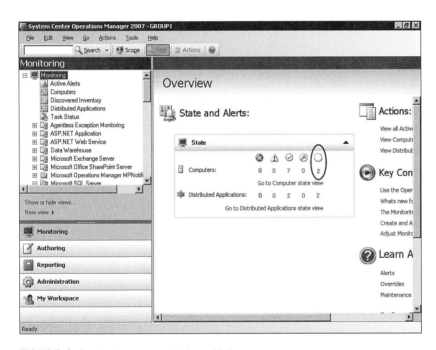

FIGURE 9.4   Devices currently in an Unknown state.

Network Devices

Operations Manager 2007 has additional functionality to provide a seamless integration for monitoring network devices. Microsoft designed the network device functionality in OpsMgr to monitor devices by providing information from the Simple Network Management Protocol (SNMP) to OpsMgr. You can view network devices through the Operations console in the Administration node, as shown in Figure 9.5. To add a network device, on the left side of the screen, right-click Device Management and start the Discovery Wizard, selecting the option for an Advanced Discovery.

Chapter 17, "Monitoring Network Devices," includes information on how to discover and use network devices with OpsMgr.

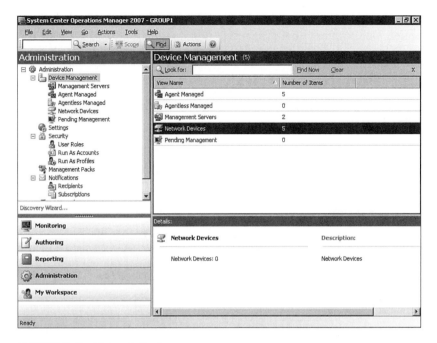

FIGURE 9.5   Network Devices.

Discovering and Deploying Agents

A number of approaches are available for deploying agents. Operations Manager 2007 continues to provide the capability available in previous versions to perform push installations from the Operations console. While the ability to deploy agents from the console is quite beneficial, it uses a proprietary approach. OpsMgr 2007 is a monitoring product; push installations to deploy the OpsMgr agent rely on OpsMgr itself for the software deployment, which was not the core focus Operations Manager was designed to perform.

TIP

Remote Agent Prerequisite Check

The OpsMgr agent, like many other software packages, has a number of required prerequisites before you can install the agent. Satya Vel of the MOM team provides information about an updated tool from the MOM 2005 Resource Kit that remotely checks these prerequisites for a group of computers. Information on this tool (MOMNetCheckCmd) and a zip file for download are available at http://blogs.technet. com/momteam/archive/2007/11/20/remote-agent-prerequisite-checker-tool-for-opsmgr-2007.aspx. (For your convenience, we provide this URL as a live link in Appendix E, "Reference URLs.")

MOMNetCheckCmd.exe is a command-line version of the MOMNetCheck tool shipped with the MOM 2005 Resource Kit.

6

Along with the functionality included in Operations Manager 2007 to deploy agents (which works extremely well for most environments), additional methods are available to discover and deploy the agent that were not available in the previous version.

You can install the agent in a variety of ways:

▶ Active Directory Integration (provides agent configuration information, but does not actually install the agent)

▶ Group Policy

▶ Systems Management Server (SMS) and Configuration Manager (ConfigMgr)

▶ Imaged systems

▶ Operations Manager Discovery Wizard

▶ Manual installation

▶ Installation from PowerShell

For small and mid-sized organizations, the recommended deployment approach is from the Operations console using the Discovery Wizard. Larger organizations may want to evaluate using Active Directory Integration coupled with other deployment methods such as SMS, Group Policy, and PowerShell. We discuss each of these techniques in the following sections.

NOTE

Active Directory Management Pack and Discovery

The Active Directory management pack (ADMP) requires enabling the proxy setting on domain controllers managed by OpsMgr. The ADMP uses this configuration to discover all the domain controllers in the environment.

This does not mean that all domain controllers have the OpsMgr agent automatically deployed to them, but it can be surprising—particularly when you are planning to phase deployment of OpsMgr agents to your domain controllers and those systems already appear in the console! Those domain controllers that are discovered but do not have the OpsMgr agent deployed are listed as "Not Monitored."

Active Directory Integration

Operations Manager 2007 adds new functionality that provides the ability to configure agents through Active Directory (AD). This takes place by publishing the OpsMgr agent configuration details to Active Directory. An OpsMgr agent performs an LDAP query to the authenticating domain controller at startup, determining the management group it belongs to and the management server with which it will communicate. Note that Active Directory Integration does not actually deploy the agent.

TIP

Active Directory Integration and Domain Functional Level

To use Active Directory Integration in OpsMgr 2007, the domain functional level needs to be either Windows 2000 or Windows 2003 Native mode.

To check the functional level of your domain, open Active Directory Users and Computers, right-click your domain, and select Properties. To change the domain functional level, right-click the domain and then select Raise Domain Functional level. You should only make this change with prior planning and within the change control windows in your environment.

Configuring Active Directory Integration

Although the AD Integration approach simplifies deploying OpsMgr 2007 agents, it increases the complexity of your OpsMgr configuration. We do not recommend AD Integration except for organizations with a very large number of agents deployed.

Three steps are involved in configuring Active Directory Integration with OpsMgr:

1. Creating Active Directory objects
2. Configuring the Operations console
3. Modifying the AD Integration Registry key

The first step is to run the MomADAdmin utility on a domain controller with an account that is a member of the Domain Admin security group. This utility is located under the \SupportTools folder in the OpsMgr installation media and creates the required Active Directory objects. The syntax to run this command is as follows:

```
MomADAdmin.exe <management group name> <OpsMgr Admins Security Group> <RMS name>
➥<AD Domain>
```

We can look at our Odyssey environment as an example. We have a single management group named GROUP1. The RMS is Hydra, and we are monitoring systems in the Odyssey.com domain.

We created a computer group named OpsMgr Admins as a global security group on the domain. This step is important because the MomADAdmin utility tool does not create the specified group; it assumes that the group already exists. To configure Active Directory Integration in our domain, we logged in to the domain controller (Pantheon) as a domain administrator and ran the following command:

```
MomADAdmin.exe GROUP1 "OpsMgr Admins" Hydra Odyssey.com
```

The MomADAdmin utility creates the Operations Manager -> (*Management Group name*) -> HealthServiceSCP container and contents in Active Directory, as shown in Figure 9.6. This container includes a security group <*Management Group Name*>_HSvcSCP_SG (for our example, this is GROUP1_HSvcSCP_SG) that is used to determine who can read the HealthServiceSCP container. In addition, the utility adds the RMS computer account to the security group the utility creates. The container also stores special objects called *service connection points*, used to publish information about desired agent settings that the agent queries at initial system startup.

TIP

How to Tell If an Agent Is Using Settings from the SCP

The Registry key HKLM\SYSTEM\CurrentControlSet\Services\HealthService\ Parameters\management groups\<*Management Group name*>\IsSourcedFromAD has a value of "1" on agent-managed machines. This indicates the agent will gather settings from the SCP (service connection point). The key is only on AD-integrated systems.

The Windows NT Operations Manager Event log on the agent-managed machine records successful access to the SCP information from the agent, with event IDs 20062 and 20013 of type Information from the event source OpsMgr Connector.

After we finish creating objects, the next step is configuring the Operations console for AD Integration. In the Operations console, navigate to Administration -> Device Management -> Management Servers.

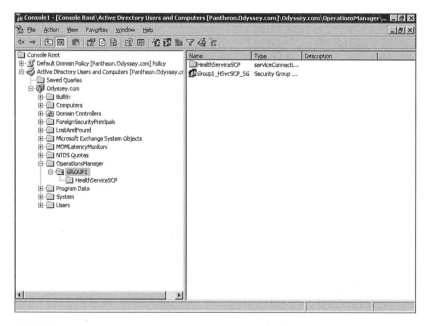

FIGURE 9.6   Operations Manager container for Active Directory Integration.

Select the management server you will configure AD integration for, right-click the management server, and choose Properties. (You can also initiate this from the Administration screen by clicking the Configure Active Directory (AD) Integration optional configuration and choosing the management server to configure.) Click Add on the Auto Agent Assignment tab. This starts the Agent Assignment and Failover Wizard. To configure agent assignment with this wizard, perform the following steps:

1. Click Next to continue on the Introduction page.

2. On the Domain screen, choose the domain to configure AD Integration on (this defaults to the domain the management server is within) and choose the account to perform the issue (which defaults to the Active Directory Based Agent Assignment account). Click Next to continue.

3. On the Inclusion Criteria screen, click Configure to define an LDAP query to target the computer accounts.

4. On the Find Computer screen, we define how to create the LDAP query. As an example, choosing the wildcard "*" will define an LDAP query that chooses all computers in the domain. Click OK to leave the Find Computers screen.
   You can create LDAP queries that are more complicated by selecting the Advanced tab and defining the criteria. The fields available include Computer name, Description, Managed By, Name, Operating System, and Operating System Version. Conditions available consist of Starts with, Ends with, Is, Is Not, Present, and Not present. Figure 9.7 shows a LDAP query defined to apply to computers that start with DAL.

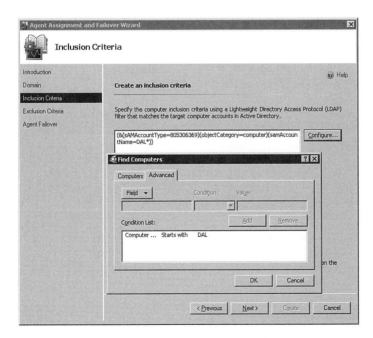

FIGURE 9.7   LDAP query to include systems that start with DAL.

5. Click Next to continue to the Exclusion Criteria screen.

6. On the Exclusion Criteria screen, specify any systems to exclude from auto-assignment. Add the Fully Qualified Domain Names (FQDNs) on this screen, delineating using a semicolon, comma, or newline. You can cut and paste text into this screen, providing a method to add large numbers of systems for exclusion. Click Next to continue.

7. The Agent Failover screen specifies how to handle agent failover. Here are the options available:

   ▶ **Automatically manage failover**—Agents will report to the other management servers in the management group.

   ▶ **Manually configure failover**—Allows you to define which management server(s) the agents should fail over to.

   We recommend using automatic failover, unless you have a requirement to fail to a specific management server in your environment. This might be when you have management servers in different physical locations and do not wish to fail over the agents to the management server in the remote location.

8. Click Create to finish the Agent Assignment and Failover Wizard.

To complete the process of activating OpsMgr integration with AD, the final step is to make a Registry change on each management server. Use the Registry editor to edit the Registry (select Start -> Run and then type **regedit**). Follow these steps:

1. Open HKEY_LOCAL_MACHINE\SYSTEM\CurrentControlSet\Services\HealthService\Parameters\ConnectorManager.

2. Right-click the EnableADIntegration key and set the value to **1**, as we show in Figure 9.8.

3. Click OK and close the Registry editor.

TIP

Active Directory Integration and Domain Controllers

You cannot configure domain controllers to use Active Directory Integration. To understand why, you need to understand how AD Integration works in more detail. To control which agents go to which management groups, an Access Control List (ACL) is used on the object. This ACL, created in Active Directory, represents the management group.

The computers allowed to join the management group have rights to read the SCP object created for the management group. When an agent using AD Integration starts up, the OpsMgr Health service (running as Local System) goes to AD, does a lookup to find what SCPs it has access to, and from that determines which management groups it should be a member of.

For a domain controller, the built-in Local System account has full access to read each of these folders for the SCP, so it would attempt to join every management group. To work around this issue, OpsMgr disables AD Integration for domain controllers.

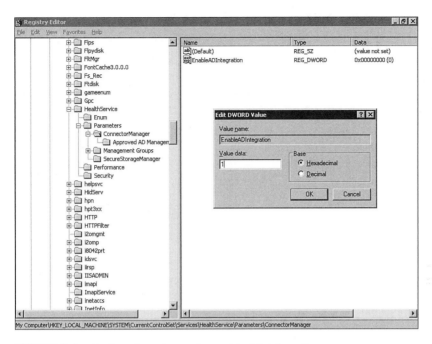

FIGURE 9.8   Registry key change to enable AD Integration.

Removing Active Directory Integration

How do we remove Active Directory Integration after configuring it? The MomADAdmin utility accepts a –d parameter, which removes this configuration. So for our configuration, to remove Active Directory Integration, we would type the following (the parameters for –d are the management group name and the domain):

```
MomADAdmin.exe –d GROUP1 Odyssey.com
```

Group Policy Deployment

Group Policy can deploy software, both through software deployment and running the installation using a startup script. Group Policy software deployment cannot run setup switches with an MSI package as part of a GPO, so using this method requires creating a transform (MST) file for the Operations Manager 2007 agent. Currently no transform files exist, so we will instead focus on how to deploy the agent through using a startup script, which requires the following steps:

1. Create a file share named **OpsMgrAgent** on a computer (we will use Hydra for our example). Copy over the agent folder structure under the new share name so that the folder structure has the \amd64, \i386, and \ia64 folders within it. Make sure that everyone in the domain has at least read-level access to the share so they can access the scripts to run the OpsMgr agent installation.

Rename the i386 folder to x86, because this is how the Processor_Architecture environment variable is defined on the i386 platform. You can also provide this share via DFS so that the files are accessible from a locally available server in the site.

2. Create a cmd file and save it in the newly shared directory. Name the file **InstallOpsMgrAgent.cmd** and include the following content (thanks to the folks at SystemCenterForum for the original version of this script from which we started our development!):

```
CD \
CD %ProgramFiles%
IF EXIST "System Center Operations Manager 2007\HealthService.exe" goto end
Net use X: \\hydra\OpsMgrAgent
X:
CD %Processor_Architecture%
Call MOMAgent.msi /qn USE_SETTINGS_FROM_AD=1
➥USE_MANUALLY_SPECIFIED_SETTINGS=0
REM *** The two lines directly above this should exist
REM *** on a single line when this script is typed.
REM ***
REM USE_SETTINGS_FROM_AD=1 SETS THE AGENT INSTALL TO
REM LOOK TO AD INTEGRATION FOR THE MANAGEMENT GROUP AND
REM SERVER CONFIGURATION
REM USE_MANUALLY_SPECIFIED_SETTINGS=0 SETS THE AGENT
REM INSTALL TO NOT REQUEST MANUAL CONFIGURATION FOR THE
REM AGENTS
C:
Net use X: /delete
:end
```

3. Use the Group Policy Management console (GPMC; Start -> All Programs –> then type **gpedit.msc**) to create a new GPO and browse to Computer Configuration -> Windows Settings -> Scripts (Startup/Shutdown). Right-click Startup and then choose Properties.

At the Startup Properties screen, click Add and browse to the file share that we created in step 1 to select the InstallOpsMgrAgent.cmd file. No script parameters are required, so click OK. Then click OK at the startup properties screen. Close out the GPMC.

Systems Management Server and System Center Configuration Manager

You can use SMS or ConfigMgr to deploy the OpsMgr 2007 agent. For the purposes of this section, we will refer to both products as SMS—this being the most familiar name to most IT professionals. The primary benefits to using these products to deploy the OpsMgr 2007 agent include the following:

▶ Strong targeting mechanisms are available through collections, including the ability to target to a group, a site, or a subnet as an example

▶ Increased reporting information on agent deployments, provided with the standard software deployment reports in SMS and ConfigMgr

The negatives to using SMS to deploy the OpsMgr 2007 agent include

▶ You must create the package and configure Active Directory Integration to provide this method to deploy the agent.

▶ You will need to define collections for whatever targeting will be required.

▶ Individual or small group agent deployments require more time than if you use the Install Wizard for deployment.

SMS uses packages that you create. These packages are deployed to collections of systems by creating an advertisement. Creating the package for OpsMgr is simple and requires only a few steps.

1. Within the SMS Administrator console, create the package from a definition file by pointing it to MOMAgent.msi. For this example, we will package the i386 version of the OpsMgr agent. Take the defaults except for the source files option, which should specify Always obtain files from a source folder, and point the folder to the path of the agent (as an example, d:\agent\i386).

2. The MSI file creates a set of installation options that are not relevant for our deployment. Delete the per-user installs and the per-system attended install because they are not required and may cause confusion.

3. Right-click the package and select Properties. On the General tab, change the properties on the per-system attended command line to:

```
MSIEXEC.exe /i MOMAgent.msi /qn /l*v MOMinstall.log
USE_MANUALLY_SPECIFIED_SETTINGS=0.
```

These parameters will install MOMAgent.msi in quiet mode. Save the MSI log file to a log named MOMinstall.log and do not provide configuration information to the client (because the agent configuration is discovered from Active Directory).

4. Change the properties on the Requirements tab to set the maximum time allowed to 10 minutes and to specify only the x86 platforms to run this agent on, as shown in Figure 9.9.

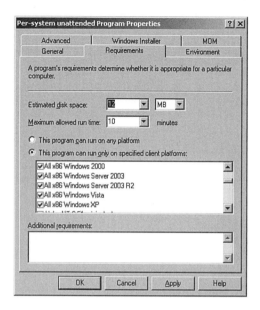

FIGURE 9.9   Configuring the per-system unattended installation in SMS.

5. After creating the package, assign it to a distribution point in your SMS environment. SMS uses distribution points to deploy software packages.

6. Create a collection that will represent the systems you want to deploy the agent to and restrict it to the particular software platform the package supports. As an example, you could create a collection for all servers in the environment that are running on the i386 platform.

7. Create an advertisement to push the agent out to a collection that will require the OpsMgr agent and make the deployment mandatory.

8. If you will be deploying agents to different platforms (such as ia64 or amd64), you will want to create separate packages for each of these platforms, which means going back through steps 1–7 for each different platform.

TIP

On the CD—the OpsMgr Agent SMS File

We have included an exported version of the package for the i386 platform on the CD for the book. To use it, create a package from the definition file and point it to the agent source directory.

Imaging

You can use various imaging technologies to install or deploy operating systems, including Norton Ghost and Systems Management Server Operating System Deployment (OSD). Imaging can deploy preconfigured operating systems that may already have applications deployed on them. Imaging provides a rapid way to install identical operating systems and software configurations on multiple systems very quickly and efficiently.

Imaged systems can integrate the OpsMgr agent as part of the image. When the system starts, it looks up its configuration in Active Directory (see the "Active Directory Integration" section earlier in this chapter), and the agent is able to report to the specified Operations Manager management server.

Integrating the OpsMgr agent into the image and using the Active Directory Integration technologies provides a deployment method that is easy to maintain after implementation. For smaller organizations that do not frequently add systems for monitoring by OpsMgr, this approach is most likely overkill.

Using the Discovery Wizard

The Operations Manager 2007 Discovery Wizard provides an easy-to-use process to discover and deploy agents for OpsMgr. The Discovery Wizard can easily scan an entire Active Directory domain for Windows-based systems, limit its scan to specific OU structures, browse for computers, or even deploy to specific systems you enter that you can cut and paste into the wizard. You have several things to consider when using the Discovery Wizard to deploy agents, including the following:

▶ Agents deployed using the Discovery Wizard do not pull their information from Active Directory, even if Active Directory Integration is in place.

▶ Agents deployed through the Discovery Wizard are defined to report to a specific management server. We define agent failover using the Agent Assignment and Failover Wizard, which we will discuss in the "Changing Agent Failover" section of this chapter.

TIP

Permitting the Audit Collection Services Driver

Installing the OpsMgr 2007 agent on a computer actually installs two services.

The primary service is the OpsMgr Health Service, which is the agent component. A second service is the Operations Manager Audit Forwarding Service, which is the agent component of the Audit Collection Services (ACS) feature of OpsMgr. This service is installed by OpsMgr during agent installation but it is not enabled.

Even if you have not installed the ACS server components into your management group, every agent-managed computer still has this service (though it is disabled). If your computer runs an antimalware application such as Microsoft Forefront Client Security, you may need to "permit" the AdtAgent.exe driver to allow it to load properly.

The Discovery Wizard first discovers the system(s); after discovery, you can choose the specific system(s) to receive the OpsMgr agent. You can see deployment successes and failures displayed within both the Deployment Wizard results and the Tasks section (Monitoring -> Tasks). We recommend using the Discovery Wizard to discover and deploy agents in all but the largest of OpsMgr environments.

MOM 2005 had a process to create discovery rules that identified what agents would report to what management server. These were auto-created with the Install/Uninstall Agents Wizard, or created manually and viewable within a Computer Discovery Rules folder in the Administrator console.

With Operations Manager 2007, the discovery process occurs as part of the Discovery Wizard, and there is no direct interaction with the discovery rules. This simplifies the process for deploying agents because the discovery rules often became complex to manage over time.

Using the wizard is the easiest method to deploy OpsMgr agents. To launch the Discovery Wizard, perform the following steps:

1. Open the Operations console -> Administration. Right-click Administration and choose the Discovery Wizard (right-clicking any item listed in the left pane provides this option).

2. On the Introduction page, click Next. You can configure this page not to appear when running on the wizard if you select the option Do not show this page again.

3. The next screen (shown in Figure 9.10) asks you to select either automatic or advanced discovery. Automatic computer discovery performs a scan for all Windows-based computers within the domain where the Root Management Server (RMS) is a member. Automatic discovery is useful in smaller organizations and is very effective when selecting large numbers of systems to which to deploy the OpsMgr agent. For most agent deployments, the preferred option will be to take the default, Advanced discovery. The following describes the Advanced discovery process:

   ▶ If you are deploying agents only to servers, select the Servers Only option from the Computer & Device Types dropdown list (available options include Servers & Clients, Servers Only, Clients Only, and Network Devices).

   ▶ If you will be deploying agents onto workstations, take the default configuration (Servers & Clients). We recommend checking the option Verify discovered computers can be contacted. This often increases the success rates of the deployment because only systems that can be communicated with on the network are listed for selection.

   ▶ If you select the Servers Only option, the option Verify discovered computers can be contacted is grayed out and checked.

   ▶ The discovery can return approximately 4000 computers if the Verify option is selected, and approximately 10,000 computers if it is not selected.

▶ Finally, select the management server the agent will communicate with from the dropdown list. Figure 9.10 shows an Advanced discovery for Servers Only using the Hydra management server; this was the most common configuration we used with the Discovery Wizard. Continue by clicking Next.

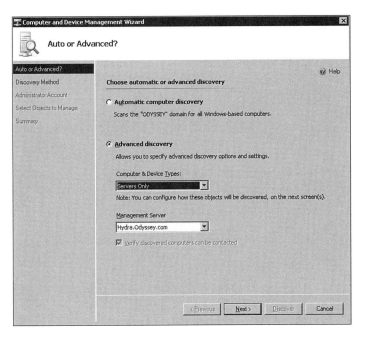

FIGURE 9.10   Automatic or Advanced configuration for the Discovery Wizard.

4. The Discovery Method page provides two options. The first option is Scan Active Directory to discover computers, the other is Browse for, or type-in computer names. The scan option searches Active Directory based on the criteria you specify. Click Configure to choose this option, which opens a Find Computers window you can use to create a custom LDAP query. Examples of this would include searching for all computers (by adding "*" to the Computer name field) or selecting all computers starting with SRV, as shown in Figure 9.11.

The Browse for or type-in computer names option includes an additional option: Browse Active Directory for computer information. Selecting the Browse... option opens a window where you can select computers by searching for computer names (or descriptions) as well as restrict your search to a specific Organizational Unit. Figure 9.12 shows a browse of Active Directory in the Computers OU for names starting with the letter T. The selected systems are then transferred to the Browse for or type-in computer names text box. Here are some points to keep in mind:

▶ The type-in option is used to receive the results from clicking the Browse button, or it can provide a location to cut and paste server names into the discovery.

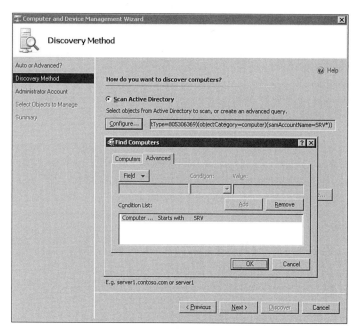

FIGURE 9.11   Using a custom LDAP query to scan Active Directory.

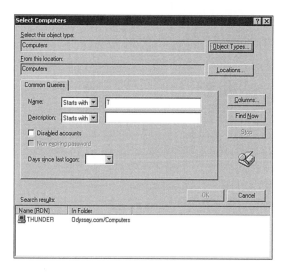

FIGURE 9.12   Browsing Active Directory with the Discovery Wizard.

▶ The cut-and-paste approach is useful when you have documented ahead of time what systems will be part of your proof of concept (POC) or pilot groups because you can cut and paste them into this field for agent deployment. This is also useful when migrating from MOM 2005 to OpsMgr 2007 because the Migration Wizard creates a managed computer export file, which you can actually paste into this screen. You can enter computer names here separated by either a semicolon, comma, or newline. This field works with either NetBIOS or Fully Qualified Domain Names.

Enter the systems you want to configure through either the scan, browse, or type-in method and click Next to continue.

5. The Administrator Account screen provides the option to choose the default account or specify another user account when installing the OpsMgr agent. The default is Use Selected Management Server Action Account (also referred to as the MSAA), as shown in Figure 9.13, which is the recommended option as long as the account has at least local administrative rights to the systems you will deploy to (Domain Admin user accounts are members of the Local Administrators group by default). Refer to Chapter 11, "Securing Operations Manager 2007," for best-practice approaches on this account. If your MSAA does not have this permission level, specify an account using the Other user account option, as shown in Figure 9.13. Click Discover to continue.

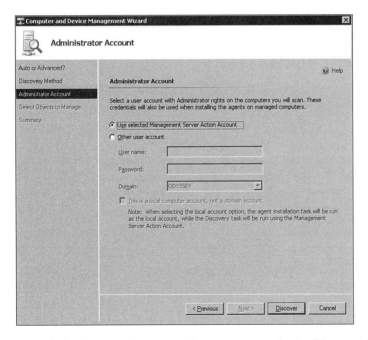

FIGURE 9.13   Specify the administrator account for the Discovery Wizard.

NOTE

Discovery Wizard Stuck on "Discovery Is in Progress"

In some circumstances, the Discovery Wizard can get stuck and not go past the stage where it displays "Discovery is in progress" (shown in Figure 9.14). Although the wizard may take several minutes to run, it should not run for several hours. One likely cause for this is that the SQL Service Broker is disabled. To determine if this is causing the situation in your environment, open the SQL Server Management Studio and execute the following query against the master database. The query assumes the default name for the Operations Manager database. If you are not using the default name, change the query appropriately.

```
SELECT is_broker_enabled FROM sys.databases WHERE name = 'OperationsManager'
```

If this query returns 0, the Broker Service is disabled. To enable the service, stop the SDK, Config, and Health services on the RMS as well as the Heath service on any secondary management server. Then execute the following statement from the query window in SQL Server Management Studio:

```
ALTER DATABASE OperationsManager

SET ENABLE_BROKER
```

Now restart the services on the RMS and the Health service on your secondary management servers. To test this, reopen the Operations console and retry the Discovery Wizard.

Microsoft documents this situation at http://support.microsoft.com/kb/941409.

With Service Pack 1, Microsoft added some instrumentation around SQL Service Broker errors by adding checks to determine if the Broker was running or not. In test environments, often there are issues where the database is too busy and SQL Server is unable to process the query to determine if the Broker is running.

---

6. The next screen (shown in Figure 9.15) provides the list of systems available for agent installation (any systems that already have the OpsMgr agent are not displayed). Select the appropriate server (or servers), validate that the Management Mode is Agent, and click Next to continue.

   You can also use this screen to install agentless systems; but for this section of the chapter, we are focusing on agent-based installations.

7. Take the defaults on the summary screen for the agent installation directory (*%ProgramFiles%*\System Center Operations Manager 2007) and for the Agent Action account to use the credentials of the Local System account. See Chapter 11 for additional information on the Agent Action account.

8. Click Finish to start installing the OpsMgr agents.

FIGURE 9.14   Discovery Wizard during "Discovery is in progress."

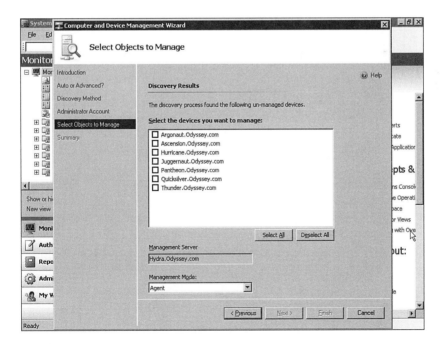

FIGURE 9.15   The Select Objects to Manage screen.

9. The status of each agent deployment displays on the Agent Management Task Status screen. The status starts at Queued, then Started, and moves to either Success or Failure. If the agent deployment failed, click the targeted computer. The task output box will show the details on why it failed. Click Close when this deployment is completed (deployments will continue even if the Agent Management Task Status screen is closed).

TIP

Trust Requirements to Deploy Agents

Agent authentication in OpsMgr requires either Kerberos or certificate-based authorization to provide mutual authentication. Use certificate-based authorization for gateway configurations where agents are in untrusted domains or workgroups. Within a forest, transitive two-way trusts are automatically created that support Kerberos. There are four other types of trusts in Windows: External, Realm, Forest, and Shortcut. Shortcut trusts improve logon time and should not apply in this scenario. Realm trusts pertain to non-Windows environments, so they should not apply when deploying agents.

Forest trusts do support Kerberos, but Realm trusts do not. So agents in domains connected to the management server's domain via an External trust will not deploy successfully unless they are deployed using a gateway server configuration.

Manual Installation

In general, manual agent installation should be the method of last resort for deploying OpsMgr agents. This deployment requires you to log in to the system that you will be installing, make configuration changes to OpsMgr, and approve the agent installation. Typically, you will use manual agent installations when specific servers are not installing the agent using the more automated methods. Take the following steps to perform a manual installation:

1. Change the default settings to Allow Manual installations within the Operations console, under Administration -> Settings -> Security -> Review new manual agent installations in the Pending Management view.

2. Log on to the server where the agent will not install and install the agent on the system. The recommend way to install the agent is by running the SetupOM.exe program on the root of the installation media and choosing the Install Operations Manager 2007 Agent option. This runs the MOMAgent.msi file for the appropriate platform and turns on logging during the installation.

3. Check the Operations console under Administration -> Device Management -> Pending Management. The manually installed system should be listed in this folder. Approve the manual installation(s).

Another Way to Manually Install

If you have issues installing with the SetupOM.exe program, you can also run MOMAgent.msi directly. To do this, map to the agents folder on the CD and run MOMAgent.msi for the platform you are using. This approach may fail due to a Microsoft Core XML Service issue. You can resolve this by downloading MSXML 6.0 from http://go.microsoft.com/fwlink/?LinkId=76343.

Installing with PowerShell

PowerShell also provides a method to deploy agents for Operations Manager 2007. Installations through PowerShell are considered manual installations and need to be approved (or your OpsMgr environment must be configured to auto-approve new manually installed agents through the Operations console -> Administration -> Settings -> Security). The following is a sample script (provided by the "PowerShell guy" and is available at http://blogs.msdn.com/scshell/archive/2007/02/09/discovering-windows-computers.aspx).

```
# ScriptName: InstallAgents.ps1
# Get the Root Management Server.
$managementServer = Get-ManagementServer -Root: $true
# Create the discovery configuration for computer2 and computer3.
➡$discoConfig = New-WindowsDiscoveryConfiguration -ComputerName: Computer1,
➡Computer2
# Discover the computers.
$discoResult = Start-Discovery -ManagementServer: $managementServer
➡-WindowsDiscoveryConfiguration: $discoConfig
# Install an agent on each computer.
Install-Agent -ManagementServer: $managementServer -AgentManagedComputer:
➡$discoResult.CustomMonitoringObjects
```

Save this script as InstallAgents.ps1. For the following example, we stored it in the D:\Scripts folder. To run the script, select Start -> Run and type the following:

```
%windir%\system32\windowsPowerShell\v1.0\PowerShell.exe
➡-noexit D:\Scripts\InstallAgents.ps1
```

Note that the command assumes you saved the script to the D:\scripts folder. The –noexit parameter stops the window from closing, which makes it possible to debug the script.

You can also run this script by opening the Command Shell (Start -> All Programs -> System Center Operations Manager 2007 -> Command Shell). To run the script from the Command Shell, change to the folder where the script is (d:, cd \, cd scripts) and then run the script by typing .**InstallAgents.ps1**.

6

Real World—OpsMgr Agent and High Processor Usage

We have seen situations where deploying the OpsMgr agent causes an increase in the processor utilization to the point that the system is no longer responsive. We have primarily seen this on servers with a single low-grade processor (mostly 1.3GHz or lower). We discuss this at the http://cameronfuller.spaces.live.com site in the "Running the OpsMgr Agent on Light Processor Hardware" article (http://cameronfuller.spaces. live.com/blog/cns!A231E4EB0417CB76!1015.entry). Others have seen this caused by using the Dell management pack with systems that have an out-of-date version of the OpenManage software. There also have been similar issues seen with servers running antivirus solutions, which required upgrading the virus software to resolve the issue (http://www.systemcenterforum.org/mcafee-85i-the-cure-for-scriptscan/).

The good news here is OpsMgr lets you know when this condition occurs pretty quickly after it occurs. We saw OpsMgr start to send alerts after deployment of the agent stating that the processor was overloaded; after investigation, we were able to determine there was a bottleneck with the systems processor.

To debug this, we stopped and disabled the OpsMgr agent and monitored the system with Performance Monitor to determine its usage levels without the OpsMgr agent. In most situations, this occurs on a server that is consistently running at more than 80%, although no one is aware of the load because the system processor is not monitored until the OpsMgr deployment!

Integrating Agentless Managed Systems into OpsMgr 2007

As discussed in the "Agentless Managed State" section of this chapter, OpsMgr 2007 provides support to monitor systems without deploying an agent. Significant limitations exist for the agentless managed state. There is no support for either the Exchange or Active Directory management packs when running in an agentless configuration. Also, strain is increased on the proxy agent, which performs the monitoring of the agentless managed system. Our recommendation is to use agentless monitoring only when an agent-managed configuration is not possible.

Deploying Agentless Monitoring

You can deploy agentless systems using the Discovery Wizard, similar to the way you deploy agent-managed systems. The wizard screens discussed in the "Using the Discovery Wizard" section of this chapter work in a similar fashion as when deploying an agent-managed system. The differences occur after the Discovery Wizard has run when choosing the devices to manage and the management mode they will use. The default on the screen is agent-managed mode, but the agentless mode is also available in the Management Mode dropdown box, as shown in Figure 9.16.

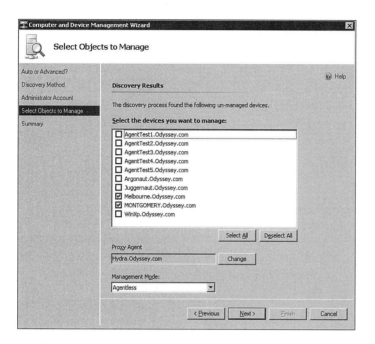

FIGURE 9.16   Discovery Wizard when deploying agentless managed systems.

When you select the agentless management mode, the screen also changes the Management Server field to Proxy Agent. This changes the available servers from the management servers in the environment to agent-deployed systems, allowing non-management servers to provide the agent proxy functionality to monitor your agentless systems. We will explain agent proxying in more detail in the next section of this chapter. Agentless managed systems display in the Administration -> Device Management -> Agentless Managed section of the Operations console, as shown in Figure 9.17.

You can remove agentless systems in the Administration -> Device Management -> Agentless Managed section of the Operations console by right-clicking the computer name, selecting Delete, and choosing Yes to stop agentless monitoring of the system.

Agent Proxying

Operations Manager 2007 supports agent proxying. When you manage an agentless managed computer, it must be assigned to a management server or agent-managed computer to provide remote (proxy) agent functionality. As we previously discussed in the "Agentless Managed State" section of this chapter, computers are managed as agentless when you either cannot or do not want to install an agent on them.

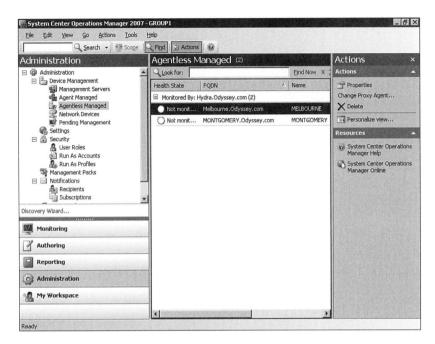

FIGURE 9.17   Agentless managed systems displayed in the Operations console.

Not all management packs work in agentless mode, and agentless management itself will not work if the agentless computer and its proxy are communicating through a firewall. Proxying is the capability for an agent to relay or forward information from other computers or network devices to the management server. Disabling agent proxying prevents spoofing by an attacker pretending to an agent, because the management server matches information sent from the agent to a known agent name before accepting the data. Agent proxying is disabled by default.

The proxy agent can be any agent-managed computer in the management group configured to be a proxy, including a management server.

Perform the following steps to configure agent proxying on an agent-managed computer:

1. In the Operations console, navigate to Administration -> Device Management -> Agent Managed.

2. Right-click the agent-managed computer you want to act as a proxy agent and select Properties. Click the Security tab, check the box labeled Allow this agent to act as a proxy and discover managed objects on other computers, and then click OK.

If you want to configure a management server as a proxy for agentless managed computers, perform the following steps:

1. Navigate to Administration -> Device Management -> Management Servers.

2. Right-click the management server you want to act as a proxy and select
   Properties. Click the Security tab, check the box labeled Allow this server to act as
   a proxy and discover managed objects on other computers, and then click OK.

You will need to perform this procedure for each agent or management server for which
you want to allow agent proxying. Enabling agent proxying allows the system to provide
information for objects that do not have an agent installed on them. One of the most
common examples for proxy agent configurations is monitoring network devices.

A number of management packs use agent proxying. For example, the Active Directory
management pack requires that you configure all agents on a domain controller to allow
proxying. For the Active Directory management pack, this setting allows the domain
controller to discover its connection object between other domain controllers from information hosted by the forest, not the domain controller itself. Other examples of management packs using agent proxying include the Exchange management pack and the
SharePoint management pack.

Real World—Management Packs Requiring "Act as a Proxy"

Quite a few management packs require you to configure them using the following
setting: Allow this agent to act as a proxy and discover managed objects on other
computers.

Our research at this point indicates the following management packs (at least) require
this configuration:

- ▶ Microsoft Windows Server 2000/2003 Active Directory
- ▶ Microsoft Exchange Server 2003
- ▶ Office SharePoint Server 2007
- ▶ Systems Management (SMS) 2003
- ▶ nWorks for VMWare ESX
- ▶ Any *clustered servers* also require this configuration

Management packs that do not appear to have this requirement include:

- ▶ Microsoft System Center Operations Manager
- ▶ Microsoft Server 2000/2003 Operating System
- ▶ Microsoft SQL Server 2000/2005
- ▶ Dell management pack
- ▶ OpsMgr 2007 MOM Backward Compatibility Update
- ▶ Windows Group Policy 2003
- ▶ Microsoft Windows Server Internet Information (IIS) 2000/2003
- ▶ Windows Print Server 2003
- ▶ Windows DHCP Server 2000/2003
- ▶ Windows Server 2000/2003 Terminal Services
- ▶ Citrix management pack
- ▶ Microsoft SharePoint Portal Server (SPS) 2003

6

▶ HP management pack

▶ Backup Exec management pack

A particular organization we worked with had 143 monitored servers, and at least 70 of them have proxying enabled—roughly half of them! These include 10 SMS servers, 44 domain controllers, 13 Exchange servers, and three SharePoint servers.

To simplify this configuration, the SystemCenterForum folks provide a script to bulk-enable agent proxying via PowerShell, available at http://www.systemcenterforum.org/enable-agent-act-as-a-proxy-in-bulk-via-powershell/.

Thanks to lots of the MOM MVPs for their help on gathering this information, including Pete Zerger, Maarten Goet, Stefan Stranger, and Andy Dominey.

Changing Agentless Managed to Agent-Managed

To change an agentless system to an agent-managed system, the process is to first delete the agentless managed system and then deploy the agent to the system. To delete an agentless managed system, follow these steps:

1. Navigate to Device Management -> Agentless Managed.
2. Right-click the agentless managed system and then choose Delete.

After deleting the agentless managed system, you can deploy an agent to the system using one of the standard methods of deploying agents discussed in the "Discovering and Deploying Agents" sections of this chapter.

CAUTION

Situations Where You Cannot Delete Agentless Managed Systems

We ran into a situation where we could not delete an agentless managed system from Operations Manager 2007. The deletion failed and generated an error in the Operations Manager Event log stating that the Data Access Layer rejected the retry on a SQLError. This event occurred with each attempt to delete the record.

The error was caused because a domain controller was configured agentless managed (it could not have an agent installed because it was running Windows 2003 without Service Pack 1), and then an agent was manually installed on the machine. To resolve this issue, we updated the row in the BaseManagedEntity table in the OperationsManager database for the agentless system that would not delete, giving IsDeleted a value of 1. Then we deleted rows from the DiscoverySourcetoTyped-ManagedEntity table for the system that would not delete, and approved the manual installation.

The system reappears as agentless in the Operations console, but now you can delete it and redeploy the agent. Additional information on this is available at our blog (see the article "Unable to delete Agentless Systems") in the June 2007 archive at http://ops-mgr.spaces.live.com/blog/cns!3D3B8489FCAA9B51!163.entry.

Systems Reporting to Multiple Management Solutions

Operations Manager 2007 supports configurations where an agent will report either to multiple OpsMgr environments or to an OpsMgr environment as well as a MOM 2005 environment.

Coexisting Agents with MOM 2005

In Chapter 7, "Migrating to Operations Manager 2007," we discuss different methods available to migrate from MOM 2005 to Operations Manager 2007. This is actually very easy to accomplish due to how the OpsMgr agent differs from the MOM 2005 agent. The MOM 2005 agent service is called "MOM," whereas the Operations Manager 2007 service is the "OpsMgr Health service." The two agents run different programs under different service names, which separates them from each other when they are on the same machine.

However, the agents perform similar tasks. Each agent collects information such as performance counters and events and runs scripts. There is potential for crosstalk between the two agents, where actions performed by the MOM 2005 agent create an event interpreted by OpsMgr 2007, and vice versa.

In some situations, the two agents may collide, but the only restriction identified at this time concerns monitoring domain controllers in a 64-bit environment. Both the MOM 2005 Active Directory management pack and the OpsMgr Active Directory management pack depend on the Active Directory Helper object, but MOM 2005 requires the 32-bit version and OpsMgr 2007 requires the 64-bit version! The Active Directory management pack guide discusses this in more detail (available for download from the OpsMgr documentation link available at http://technet.microsoft.com/en-us/opsmgr/bb498235.aspx).

Although there are some potential challenges with coexisting MOM 2005 and OpsMgr 2007 agents, with the new OpsMgr agent these should be minimal.

Multihomed Agents

Agents in Operations Manager 2007 can report to multiple management groups. These types of agents are *multihomed* agents. Multihomed agents typically are used for the following:

▶ Providing horizontal support silos

▶ Transitioning from MOM 2005 to OpsMgr

▶ Supporting test or preproduction environments

For more information on planning a multihomed environment, see Chapter 5, "Planning Complex Configurations."

In MOM 2005, there was a limit restricting a multihomed agent to a maximum of four management groups. This restriction does not exist in OpsMgr 2007 because the agent software was almost completely rewritten.

We would, however, suggest limiting the management groups to four or less, and definitely less than 30. Also, be aware that there is an increase in the memory requirements of the agent when an OpsMgr 2007 agent reports to multiple management servers.

You can deploy multihomed agents using the Discovery Wizard for each management group, or you can do so manually by running the OpsMgr Agent Setup Wizard on the managed computer.

Managing Agents

A number of tasks are associated with managing either the agents or the systems that you will monitor in your environment. The next sections describe Windows NT Event log considerations, disk performance configurations, pending actions, changing agent configurations, and removing or renaming agents.

Event Log Considerations

Event logs of a monitored system are one of Operations Manager's major data sources. If the Event log on a managed computer fills completely, event logging either stops or events are overwritten, depending on the configuration of the Windows NT Event log. A full Security log can even stop the computer from functioning! If the Event log is not able to gather information, OpsMgr cannot provide information effectively about the status of the monitored system.

CAUTION

Security Alert

If the Windows NT Security log on a managed computer fills up, the managed computer can lock up. For details on this issue, refer to knowledge base article 232564 on the Microsoft Help and Support website. This article can be located at http://support. microsoft.com/kb/232564.

The recommended log file configuration for managed systems is to increase the size to a minimum of 25 megabytes (MB) and to configure the logs to overwrite events as needed for all Event logs. The logs include the Windows NT Event logs (application, security, and system) and other Event logs (such as the Directory Service, File Replication, DNS, and Operations Manager logs).

Configuring the Event Logs

You will want to configure your Event logs such that you can capture all the events sent to the management server. Keep the following points in mind:

▶ Configure your Event logs to overwrite events as needed. This ensures that even if the Event log fills, it will continue to log new events by overwriting older ones, and prevent the logs on managed systems from filling up and stop logging event information.

▶ Caution: Setting a Security log to overwrite events as needed may result in loss of security event information. Refer to your company's security policy regarding event logging before changing this configuration.

▶ Increase the size of the log files on monitored computers to enable OpsMgr to gather Event log information successfully. If additional disk space is available, we recommend you further increase the size of the logs, especially if the system generates large amounts of data in a particular log. (This typically occurs on domain controllers or for applications that log large amounts of data.)

You can modify the log file settings for a system by clicking Start, pointing to Programs (or All Programs, depending on the version of Windows you are running), clicking Administrative Tools, and then clicking Event Viewer (or you can click Start -> Run, type **eventvwr.msc** in the Open box, and click OK). Right-click the first Event log you want to modify and then select Properties. On the General tab, modify the Maximum Log Size and Overwrite Events As Needed options. Each log must be set individually using this method.

Other Configuration Techniques

A couple other techniques are available for changing the settings for the Event logs:

▶ Using the ConfigureEventLogs utility

▶ Using a Group Policy Object (GPO)

The ConfigureEventLogs utility from the MOM 2000 Resource Kit enables you to automate the process of setting the Event log configurations based on an input file listing the server names. Microsoft does not support this tool, which is available only as part of the MOM 2000 Resource Kit, and is no longer available on the Microsoft website.

6

TIP

On the CD

As a convenience, we include the package to install the ConfigureEventLogs utility (configurelogs.exe) on the CD accompanying this book.

If you have integrated the majority of your systems with Active Directory, a more effective approach to changing these configurations might be by creating a GPO that maintains these settings. The recommended approach is to move all servers (do *not* move the domain controllers) into an Organizational Unit (OU) and apply the GPO to that OU. See Figure 9.18 for an example.

Using a Group Policy Object can save you work by automating the configuration of the application, security, and system log settings for all servers in that OU. You can apply a similar GPO to the Domain Controllers OU to change domain controller settings. Note that these GPO examples configure only the application, security, and system logs settings. You must manually modify any additional logs.

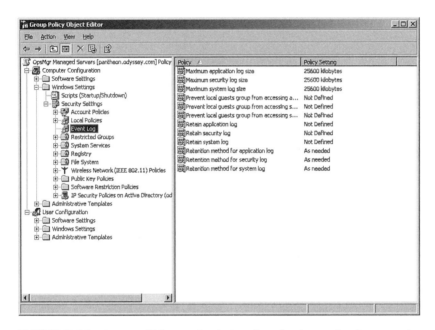

FIGURE 9.18   Sample GPO to maintain log sizes for the application, security, and system event logs.

Disk Performance Configurations

To gather disk performance information, ensure that each system with an installed OpsMgr agent has its disk performance counters activated. Activate the performance counters as necessary by using the command `diskperf -YV`; this takes effect after a reboot. In Windows 2000, the physical disk counters are on by default, but the logical disk counters are off by default. For Windows Server 2003, both the physical and logical counters are permanently enabled.

Pending Actions

By default, the global setting for Operations Manager 2007 does not accept manual agent installations. You can change this configuration by performing the following steps:

1. In the Operations console, navigate to Administration -> Settings.

2. Select the Server pane, right-click Security, and select Properties.

3. On the General tab, the default configuration is Reject new manual agent installations. You can change this to Review new agent installations in pending management view.

You can also configure this on a per–management server basis. Perform the following steps:

1. In the Operations console, navigate to Administration -> Device Management -> Management Servers.

2. Right-click the management server name and select Properties.

3. Select the Security tab, which allows you to configure the management server to override global management server settings and allow the installation of manually installed agents.

With both of these configurations, a check box is available when you select the Review new manual agent installations in pending management view setting. This check box is labeled Auto-approve new manually installed agents. If this is not checked, manually installed agents are placed into a pending actions folder for approval.

You can navigate to the Pending Management folder at Administration -> Device Management -> Pending Management. Agents that fail installation are also added to this folder, where you can re-run the agent installation process. Figure 9.19 shows an example where agents have failed installation.

FIGURE 9.19   The pending management folder with failed installs.

Agent Settings

Configure agent settings in the Operations console, under Administration -> Device Management -> Agent Managed. Right-click an agent and choose Properties. The Heartbeat tab provides a method to override the global settings for the agent's heartbeat frequency (which is 60 seconds by default).

TIP

Heartbeat Frequency

There have been discussions in the OpsMgr newsgroups about problems when the agent heartbeat frequency is set to less than the default of 60 seconds. If your environment's requirements need this to be less than 60 seconds, test it thoroughly in your environment prior to deploying the setting.

The Security tab has a check box labeled Allow this agent to act as a proxy and discover managed objects on other computers. This is an important setting if your environment will use either the Exchange management pack or the Active Directory management pack. You will need to enable this option for all domain controllers in your environment if you are using the Active Directory management pack. You will also need to check the Agent Proxy option for all Exchange servers in your environment if you are using the Exchange management pack.

Act as Proxy

Multiple third-party tools have been written to assist with checking or configuring the Act as Proxy setting, including the following:

▶ Proxy Settings (http://www.mediamax.com/opsmgr/Hosted/ProxySettings_v1.1.zip) shows all servers and their current configuration for this setting.

▶ Proxycfg by Clive Eastwood (http://home.comcast.net/~the_eastwoods/MOMDownloads/Proxycfg.zip) provides a command-line utility to configure this setting.

▶ SystemCenterForum.org provides information on how to check the settings using a PowerShell script (http://systemcenterforum.org/enable-agent-act-as-a-proxy-in-bulk-via-powershell/).

These tools are excellent examples of how the OpsMgr community has contributed to enhancing the functionality of OpsMgr!

Changing Agent Failover

You define agent failover using the Agent Assignment and Failover Wizard (Administration -> Device Management -> Management Servers). Select a management server and right-click Properties. At the Auto Agent Assignment tab, click Add to specify agent assignment settings. The Agent Assignment and Failover Wizard provides a way to define inclusion and exclusion criteria for the management servers in the management group. Figure 9.20 shows an example of how to configure failover as either automatic or manual.

FIGURE 9.20   Agent Assignment and Failover Wizard.

Which Management Server(s) Is My Agent Using?

PowerShell provides a quick way to determine what primary and failover management servers an agent is configured to use. The following commands find the primary management server for an agent:

```
$comp = get-agent | where { $_.ComputerName -eq "<Computer Name>"}
$comp.PrimaryManagementServerName |Format-List name
```

To find the failover management server the agent is using:

```
$comp = get-agent | where { $_.ComputerName -eq"<fully qualified agent name>"}
$comp.GetFailoverManagementServers() |Format-List name
```

So as an example, here's how to find the management server(s) that the Ascension server is using:

```
$comp = get-agent | where { $_.ComputerName -eq Ascension}
$comp.PrimaryManagementServerName |Format-List name
$comp.GetFailoverManagementServers() |Format-List name
```

You could change this script to use the Fully Qualified Domain Name by changing the syntax in the first line from $_ComputerName to $_Name.

You can change the failover MS for the agent via PowerShell using the following script:

```
$primaryMS = get-managementserver | where{$_.ComputerName -eq
➥"RootManagementServer"}

$secondaryMS = get-managementserver | where{$_.ComputerName –eq
➥"SecondaryManagementServer"}

$agent = get-agent | where {$_.ComputerName -eq "membersvr"}

set-managementserver -managementserver $primaryMS –agentManagedComputer

$agent -failoverServer $secondaryMS
```

PowerShell is very flexible and can be used to provide both script functionality possible in the Operations console and functionality that is not available within the Operations console.

Agent Internals

An Operations Manager agent uses a queue file to store data that needs to be sent to the management server. These queue files prevent the loss of data when a management server is not available (such as when it is rebooted to apply patches and other maintenance). If multiple management servers are configured for failover, the agent fails over to another management server.

The agent queue file is used as part of the normal communication between an agent and a management server, but it only becomes important from a sizing perspective if the agent is unable to communicate with any available management servers.

These queue files default to 15MB in size (15360KB). For most systems, this queue file size should be sufficient to hold the OpsMgr data for several hours. There may be times, however, when the size of this queue may be insufficient, such as for servers that send a large amount of data to the management server (very intensive applications such as Active Directory or Exchange), or if there will be longer periods of time when the management server will be unavailable. The size of this queue is changed on a per-agent basis from the Registry within HKLM\SYSTEM\CurrentControlSet\Services\HealthService\Parameters\ Management Groups\<Management Group Name>\MaximumQueueSizeKb.

Setting Agent Queue Size

You can change this setting in many ways. These include logging into the system and manually editing the Registry, changing via a script launched from an agent task, and changing the value using PowerShell, among others. To change this setting with an agent task, we define a script that is run as an agent task (details on this are available at http://tarek-online.blogspot.com/2007/07/how-to-change-agent-maximum-queue-size.html). The script to accomplish the task follows:

```
HKEY_CURRENT_USER = &H80000001
strComputer = "."
Set objReg = GetObject("winmgmts:\\" & strComputer &
"\root\default:StdRegProv")
strKeyPath =
"SYSTEM\CurrentControlSet\Services\HealthService\Parameters\Management
Groups\<Management Group Name>"
ValueName = "MaximumQueueSizeKb"
dwValue = 51200
objReg.SetDWORDValue HKEY_CURRENT_USER, strKeyPath, ValueName, dwValue
Set objShell = CreateObject("WScript.Shell")
objShell.Run "%COMSPEC% /c net stop healthservice",,1
objShell.Run "%COMSPEC% /c net start healthservice",,1
```

Changing this setting can also be accomplished with PowerShell, as discussed at http://weblog.stranger.nl/increase_agent_sender_queue_size_for_scom_2007. Open PowerShell on the agent where you want to change the Registry setting. We first go to the location, change the property, and then validate that the change occurred. Within PowerShell, do the following:

- ▶ Type **cd HKLM:\SYSTEM\CurrentControlSet\Services\HealthService\ Parameters\Management Groups<Management Group Name>\ MaximumQueueSizeKb**.
- ▶ Type **set-ItemProperty . -name MaximumQueueSizeKb -value "30720Kb"**.
- ▶ Check the changed setting by typing **get-ItemProperty**.

After completing your changes, restart the OpsMgr Health Service for the change to take effect.

Removing or Renaming Agents

The recommended method to remove agents involves using the Operations console. Perform the following steps:

1. Open the Operations console and navigate to Administration -> Device Management -> Agent Managed.

2. Right-click an agent and choose the Uninstall option. (Uninstall removes the agent from the system, versus the Delete option, which only deletes the agent from OpsMgr and does not actually remove the agent from the system.)

3. Selecting Uninstall launches the Uninstall Agents wizard, which prompts for credentials (the default is to use the MSAA) to uninstall the agent with.

4. Specify an account that has the permissions required (at least local administrator) to remove the agent and then click Uninstall.

You can also manually uninstall the agent on the system and then delete the agent from the Operations console.

Systems monitored by Operations Manager that have their name changed will need to have their agent removed and reinstalled. If the renamed system does not have its agent uninstalled and reinstalled, the original system name will still appear in the console, but it no longer reports information back correctly to OpsMgr.

Agentless Exception Monitoring (AEM)

An area that often causes confusion is what the relationship is between agentless monitoring and Agentless Exception Monitoring (AEM). In short, there really *isn't* a relationship between them! The issue here is that they both are called "agentless" but do different things, which can make the terminology confusing. For simplicity, remember that agentless managed systems are systems monitored by a proxy agent that performs the actual monitoring rather than deploying an agent to the system you are monitoring.

Agentless Exception Monitoring (AEM) captures aggregates and reports on application crashes (Dr. Watson errors) within the enterprise. Details on AEM are available in Chapter 16.

Troubleshooting Tips

The majority of agents will deploy from the OpsMgr 2007 console without issues. The following are some of the common failures that may occur when deploying OpsMgr agents from the Operations console and their recommended resolutions:

▶ **System is offline or cannot be contacted via RPC or Computer Browser Service is not running:** "The MOM Server failed to open service control manager on computer 123.odyssey.com. Therefore, the MOM Server cannot complete configuration of the agent on the computer. Operation: Agent Install. Install account: Odyssey\msaa Error Code: 800706BA Error Description: The RPC server is unavailable."

Solution: Bring the server online or make it able to be reached via RPC. This can occur if the Computer Browser Service is turned off or a firewall is enabled on the system where the agent is being installed.

▶ **Agent does not have the required service pack level:** "The Agent Management Operation Agent Install failed for remote computer 456.Odyssey. com. Install account: Odyssey\msaa Error Code: 80070643 Error Description: Fatal error during installation. Microsoft Installer Error Description: For more information see Windows Installer Log file 'C:\Program Files\System Center Operations Manager 2007\AgentManagement\AgentLogs\(*ServerName*)MOMAgentMgmt.log' on the Management Server." When reviewing the application log, an Event ID of 10005 is created for the source of MsiInstaller. This indicates that the system does not match the required service pack version.

Solution: Agent requires Windows 2000 SP 4 (or higher) or Windows 2003 SP 1 (or higher). Patch the server to SP 4 if it is on Windows 2000 or SP 1 if it is on Windows 2003. A temporary solution would be to monitor the system agentless until you can apply the required service pack.

▶ **Windows Installer 3.1 is required:** "The MOM Server detected that remote computer 789.Odyssey.com has older version of Windows Installer installed. Please update to Windows Installer 3.1 version. Please refer to release notes for more details. Operation: Agent Install account: Odyssey\msaa Error code: 8007064D Error Description: The installation package cannot be installed by the Windows Installer service. You must install a Windows service pack that contains a newer version of the Windows Installer service."

Solution: Apply critical updates to the system. A temporary solution would be to monitor the system agentless until you can apply the required service pack.

▶ **Needs permissions to install:** "The MOM Server failed to open service control manager on computer 789.Odyssey.com. Therefore, the MOM Server cannot complete the configuration of agent on the computer. Operation: Agent Install account: Odyssey\msaa Error Code: 80070005 Error Description: Access is denied."

Solution: Install with an account that is at least a local administrator on the system targeted for deploying the agent.

▶ **Free disk space:** "The MOM Server failed to perform specified action on computer 908.Odyssey.com. Operation: Agent Install account: Odyssey\msaa Error Code: 80070070 Error Description: There is not enough space on the disk." This failed on installation when there was less than 2048KB of free disk space. If the installation runs with more than 2048KB of free space but less than 21,998KB of free space, it will log an event on the system (application log, MsiInstaller, 11601) where you are deploying the agent, saying that at least 21,998KB of free space is required. The files for OpsMgr require at least 154MB of disk space.

Solution: Free up more disk space on the System drive for the system to which you are deploying the agent; at least 200MB should be the minimum starting point.

▶ **Requires Windows Update/Automatic Update:** "The MOM Server failed to perform specified action on computer 908.Odyssey.com. Operation: Agent Install account: Odyssey\msaa Error Code: 80070643." This problem is the result of a bug within the

6

installation code where the MSI custom action tries to register the agent for receiving updates via Microsoft Update. If the Windows Update/Automatic Update service is disabled, the agent installation will fail.

Solution: We discuss this issue in Table 9.7 with KB article number 938993.

▶ **Unknown error 0x80072971 in the Agent Management Task Status dialog box when you try to install an agent.**

Solution: See http://support.microsoft.com/kb/934760. The problem occurs if the LockFileTime.txt file is located in the following folder on the remote computer: %*windir*%\422C3AB1-32E0-4411-BF66-A84FEEFCC8E2. This file prevents concurrent agent installations from multiple management servers, and it is normally deleted after an agent is installed. If an agent installation is not currently queued, delete LocktimeFile.txt.

▶ **Unable to deploy the agent remotely.**

Solution: The C$ share does not exist, or was renamed. To resolve this either put the C$ share back or do not use the Discovery Wizard to push out the agent.

▶ **Error 25218. Failed to uninstall SDK MOF. Error Code: -2147217407.**

Solution: WMI may be corrupted. WMI can be repaired using the WMI Diagnosis Utility available at http://go.microsoft.com/fwlink/?LinkId=62562.

▶ **Error message when you try to enable AD Integration for OpsMgr 2007:** "The binary form of an ACE object is invalid." The MomADAdmin tool may create the OperationsManager directory in the Active Directory Users and Computers console, but the nested container for the management group is not created as expected. This error occurs because of an issue in .NET Framework 2.0.

Solution: See http://support.microsoft.com/kb/938992 for information about this problem. To fix the problem, install hotfix 928569 for .NET Framework 2.0. See http://support.microsoft.com/kb/928569 for details regarding this hotfix.

Port Query Utilities

Microsoft provides utilities that can test communication to TCP or UDP ports. These utilities are available at http://download.microsoft.com when you search for PortQry:

▶ PortQry v2 is a command-line utility.

▶ PortQryUI is GUI based.

These utilities can validate that the agent you are attempting to install the agent on can communicate with the management server on port 5723, or can be used to validate any port traffic requirements for OpsMgr. PortQryUI even has predefined services checks for items such as Domains and Trusts, IPSec, Networking, SQL Service, Web Service, and Exchange Server (among others). For additional information on the ports OpsMgr uses, refer to Chapter 11.

For other installation errors, review the log files on the management server and the event logs on the system to which you are pushing the agent. If those do not provide a resolution, the next step is to try a manual agent installation, which we discussed in the "Manual Installation" section of this chapter.

Table 9.7 describes some additional errors that might occur when you work with agents in OpsMgr 2007. You can use the knowledge base article number to get additional information in the Microsoft knowledge database at http://support.microsoft.com.

TABLE 9.7   Potential Processing Errors and Their Resolutions

Process Erroring	Error Message	Potential Cause	KB Article #
Computer and Device Management Wizard	Logged in the %ProgramFiles%/System Center Operations Manager 2007\AgentManagement\ Agent_NameAgentInstall.log file: CanRegisterMU: get_Services() failed. Error Code: 0x80070422.	You cannot deploy an agent using this wizard if the Automatic Updates service is disabled on the computer where you try to deploy the agent.	938993. There is also a hotfix (937456) for this issue. Fixed in SP 1.
Computer and Device Management Wizard	Discovery process does not find computers that are in your domain.	Computers are not found or appear in the queue as incomplete. The following error may also be logged to the SQL Server error log: Msg 15404, Level 16, State 19 – Could not obtain information about Windows NT group/user 'NTGROUP\ AccountName', error code 0x5. The statement has been terminated.	938994.
Computer and Device Management Wizard	Discovery Wizard may stop responding during the discovery process. You may see Event ID 11553 in the Operations Manager event log.	The SQL Server Service Broker is disabled.	941409.

TABLE 9.7   Continued

Process Erroring	Error Message	Potential Cause	KB Article #
Agent Data is not Processed	An agent running a prerelease version of SP 1 reports to management servers running the release version of System Center Operations Manager 2007. The management servers do not process the agent event data. The data is rejected as malformed data.	Service Pack 1 includes some changes to the event data types. The release version of Operations Manager 2007 considers the event data to be malformed. A hotfix is currently available: see http://support.microsoft.com/kb/941557 for further instructions.	941557. Fixed in SP 1.
Agent Removal	Some OpsMgr 2007 files and folders remain after removing the agent from a client computer.	OpsMgr 2007 does not remove helper files installed using an ASP.NET Web application template or an ASP.NET Web Service Management Pack template.	938996.
Agent Restart	The agent is unable to restart the Health Service after its monitored thresholds are breached. Event ID 6024, 6025, or 6026 appears as a warning in the event log.	The agent monitors its processes to ensure they do not consume too many system resources. If a process does consume too many resources, the agent tries to restart itself. The problem occurs if the Health Service or Monitoring Host processes are monitored on the agent with these performance counters monitored: Process\Private Bytes or Process\Handle Count.	A hotfix is available. See 939799. Fixed in SP 1.
Multihomed agent	After an OpsMgr 2007 agent sends discovery data to a management group, no rules are deployed for monitoring in later management groups.	This problem occurs if an agent reports to multiple management groups.	A hotfix is available. See 936838. Fixed in SP1.
Maintenance Mode	Heartbeats are still generated after the computer is put into maintenance mode.	Functioning as designed. To put a system into maintenance mode without receiving any alerts, the computer, Health Service, and Health Service Watcher all need to be put into maintenance mode.	942866.

Summary

This chapter discussed both agent-managed and agentless-managed configurations. We discussed how both configurations are deployed and provided some troubleshooting tips for common agent deployment failures. In the next chapter, we discuss complex configurations within Operations Manager 2007.

6

CHAPTER 10

Complex Configurations

Operations Manager (OpsMgr) 2007 can provide solutions when running on a single server or it can scale to multiple servers, depending on the specific requirements of your organization. This chapter offers insight for deploying OpsMgr in environments that require redundancy, multihoming, connected management groups, or gateway servers. The chapter also provides performance recommendations to consider when you are implementing complex configurations of OpsMgr.

Management Server Configurations

Many management server configurations incorporate a "complex" OpsMgr environment. These configurations include multilocation deployments, connected management groups, multihomed deployments, and redundant configurations. When designing Operations Manager 2007 configurations, we always ask six key questions during the Assessment phase:

▶ What devices do we need to monitor and where are they located?

▶ What functions do we need to be monitor? For example, Exchange 2003/2007, Internet Information Services (IIS), Active Directory.

▶ Is redundancy for our OpsMgr solution a business requirement?

- ▸ Is Audit Collection Services (ACS) a requirement?

- ▸ Is Agentless Exception Monitoring (AEM) a requirement?

- ▸ Is reporting a requirement? (This should be in all environments to gain the full benefits of OpsMgr.)

These questions affect how you configure your management group and the complexity of your environment.

Multilocation Deployments

To discuss multilocation deployments, we will use our fictitious company Odyssey. Odyssey's campus includes a corporate Plano location. Plano's OpsMgr implementation supports 500 servers, with the load split between two management servers named Hydra and Hornet, and a database server named Thunder. Odyssey also has a Carrollton location, with 250 servers.

A common practice is to have at least two management servers in your primary location (which typically is where the database server resides) and to split the agents between the management servers to provide load balancing and redundancy when a management server is not available.

Although only one Root Management Server (RMS) can exist in a management group, we suggest you always have at least two management servers (including the RMS) in your primary location. You should also be aware that because there is no data compression between the management server(s) and the Operational and Data Warehouse databases, these components are best placed on the same network or set up to communicate over a fast link.

Using Multiple Management Servers for Load Balancing and Redundancy

How does management server failover work with agents? If the primary management server fails, the agent finds another management server. Without AD Integration, the agent looks for the first available management server. Using AD Integration, you can define *failover partners*, which are particularly useful if you want to isolate certain management servers from agent traffic. Examples of servers you would want not collecting agent traffic include the following:

- ▸ The RMS, which is the focal point for console communication and hosts the OpsMgr SDK and Config services

- ▸ Any ACS collector(s), which are management servers but should be dedicated to collecting audit data

If you are not using AD Integration but still want to specify particular failover servers for agents, Boris Yanushpolsky of the MOM Team provides a PowerShell script that can help:

```
param($agentComputerName,$failoverManagementServerName)

$agent = get-agent ¦ where {$_.PrincipalName -eq $agentComputerName}

$primaryManagementServer  = $agent.GetPrimaryManagementServer();
```

```
if($primaryManagementServer -eq $null)

{

"Primary management server not found"

return

}

$failoverManagementServer = Get-ManagementServer ¦ where
➥{$_.PrincipalName -eq $failoverManagementServerName}

if($failoverManagementServer -eq $null)

{

"Failover management server not found"

return

}

if($failoverManagementServer.PrincipalName –eq
➥$primaryManagementServer.PrincipalName)

{

"The failover management server cannot be the same as the primary management
➥server"

return

}

$failoverServers = New-Object
System.Collections.Generic.List''1"[[Microsoft.EnterpriseManagement.
➥Administration.ManagementServer,Microsoft.EnterpriseManagement.
➥OperationsManager,Version=6.0.4900.0,Culture=neutral,
➥PublicKeyToken=9396306c2be7fcc4]]"

$failoverServers.Add($failoverManagementServer)

$agent.SetManagementServers($primaryManagementServer,$failoverServers)
```

To run this script, perform the following steps:

1. Save the script to a PS1 file (this is C:\\scripts\SpecifyFailoverServer.ps1 in our example).
2. Open the Command Shell (Start -> All Programs ->System Center Operations Manager 2007 -> Command Shell).
3. Run the script, passing the agent Fully Qualified Domain Name (FQDN) and the failover server FQDN. Here's an example (where Juggernaut is the agent-monitored server and Hornet is the failover management server in the Odyssey domain):

```
C:\scripts\SpecifyFailoverServer.ps1 -agentComputerName:'juggernaut.
➥odyssey.com'-failoverManagementServerName:'hornet.odyssey.com'
```

You can access the script and Boris' article online at http://blogs.msdn.com/boris_ yanushpolsky/archive/2007/09/11/setting-specific-failover-management-servers.aspx.

Odyssey has installed a wide area network (WAN) link between the Plano and Carrollton locations and is placing an additional management server in Carrollton, as we show in Figure 10.1. The management server (Talon) in Carrollton communicates with the database server in Plano, which contains the Operations database. Using a local management server keeps each agent in Carrollton from needing to communicate with a management server in Plano, which reduces bandwidth requirements between the agents and the management server.

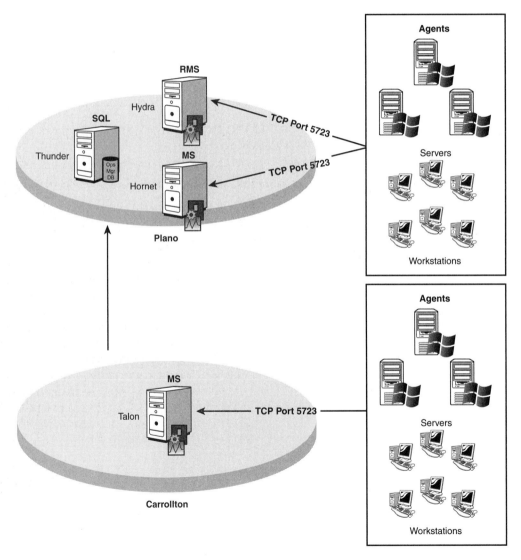

FIGURE 10.1   Management servers in Plano and Carrollton.

For multilocation deployments, we generally recommend at least one management server in each location to minimize WAN traffic and bandwidth requirements. Although the traffic between the agent and the management server is compressed, there can still be quite a bit of activity.

We can use several approaches for designing a solution for Odyssey. One implementation utilizes connected management groups, whereas the one Odyssey decided to implement uses a single management group, with a centralized database and multiple management servers to localize its server management. A potential downside of this configuration is that one of the management servers (Talon) accesses the Operations database across a WAN link. You would want to allow for this additional traffic when analyzing your WAN requirements.

Low Bandwidth Tips and Techniques

Microsoft recommends that if possible you use high-bandwidth communication links between the management server and the Operations database, between the Operations database and the OpsMgr Reporting server, and between the RMS and Operations console(s).

Several methods are available if you are using OpsMgr 2007 in a low-bandwidth environment. We will assume the management server is in one site, and the agents are in a second site. The two sites communicate over a low-bandwidth connection. There are two issues here: traffic from monitoring and traffic when installing the agent.

Because Operations Manager was designed to be an enterprise solution, Microsoft's MOM development team understood that the product would be expected to handle thousands of agents. The team designed OpsMgr such that all data going across the network between an agent and management server is not only encrypted, but also compressed. The published compression ratio ranges from 4:1 to 6:1.

You can minimize the initial impact between the two locations when using the Discovery Wizard by deploying a gateway server at the remote site. When you deploy an agent through a gateway server, the gateway server itself deploys the agent, rather than the RMS. The RMS simply issues the command to the gateway server to deploy the agent. A test (documented at http://blogs.technet.com/momteam/archive/2007/08/31/low-bandwidth-scenarios.aspx) measured the network traffic between the RMS and gateway server at about 18KB. Traffic between the gateway server and the agent was approximately 7.8MB! These figures include the initial three-way handshake and all Ethernet and TCP/IP headers. When the gateway server performs the agent installation, the network hit between the RMS and the gateway server is minimal.

10

Other techniques to reduce network traffic across a slow link would include deploying only the management packs needed for the distant site. You could implement this with a separate management group containing only the management packs you need and then use connected management groups for monitoring—which we discuss in the "Connected Management Groups" section of this chapter.

You can also adjust the heartbeat settings, both for the interval (default 60 seconds) and number of missed heartbeats allowed (3 by default). Increasing the heartbeat settings means the agent will send data less often, although there may be more data to send.

Multiple Management Groups

One way to disperse agent traffic is by placing additional management servers in various locations; an alternative is to deploy multiple management groups. Implementing multiple management groups introduces complexity, and you will want to consider this option carefully. As discussed in Chapter 4, "Planning Your Operations Manager Deployment," you should use multiple management groups in situations such as the following:

▶ You are exceeding management group support limits. (Although the number of agents is actually a function of available resources and there is no hard limit on the number, we recommend no more than 5000 managed computers in a management group.)

▶ There is a requirement to separate administrative control (application support in one group, web application support in another group).

▶ You have multiple locations with servers at each location. Multiple locations is not an absolute criterion for creating additional management groups, but it's something to consider.

▶ You have network environment restrictions (for example, minimal bandwidth or reduced network traffic requirements).

> **NOTE**
>
> **Sizing Your Management Groups**
>
> You may want take into consideration the size of your Operations database when planning your management groups. Although there technically is no limit to the size of the database, there are known issues when using a database larger than 40GB. In addition, some DBAs are unwilling to support a database larger than 100GB, which can put a serious crimp in your design if you have 6000 agents! We recommend not exceeding 40GB as a best practice, and we have heard Microsoft CSS (Customer Service and Support) recommending 30GB as a preferred maximum.

Distributing Agents

If you create a second OpsMgr management group, you must decide how to best separate agents across the two management groups. Common approaches include

- ▶ Splitting the agents geographically.

- ▶ Splitting the agents by departments. This comes into play when an IT department may have control over its group of servers but no control over a second IT department's servers.

Allow for growth in the number of agents within your management groups and do not attempt to configure more than 5000 agents (the maximum supported by Microsoft) in a single management group.

Connected Management Groups

When you have more than one management group, you can define a relationship between them. We call these *connected management groups*. When you connect management groups, you are not actually deploying new servers; rather you are defining a top-tier or local management group that will have access to the Alerts and Discovery information in a bottom-tier or connected management group. This capability allows you to use a single console to view and interact with the alerts and other monitoring data from multiple management groups. Using the Operations console, you can also execute tasks on the monitored computers of the connected management groups.

Establishing connected management groups requires that each management group is functional and able to communicate with each other using DNS name resolution. As we discussed in Chapter 4, management group names need to be unique so that they can be connected in this way.

If trust relationships are in place and the SDK service account has permissions in the connected management group, you can use the OpsMgr SDK account, which is the default configuration.

Establishing connected management groups allows you to see alerts from both the management group you originally were accessing and the alerts available through the connected management group. We discuss setting up this process in Chapter 22, "Interoperability."

Multihomed Deployments

As discussed in Chapter 5, "Planning Complex Configurations," a multihomed configuration exists when the agent on a server reports to more than one management group. Each management group has its own Operations database and management server(s). (An agent reporting to multiple management servers within a single management group is *not* multihomed.)

10

Multihoming allows you to distribute monitoring across multiple technical teams. For example, your security administrators can monitor a computer for security issues in one management group using ACS while your Exchange administrators can monitor the same system because it runs Microsoft Exchange. By installing multiple management groups and then multihoming agents, you can distribute monitoring requirements across multiple teams, thus enabling each team to use its own OpsMgr administrators and rule configurations. Because each management group has its own database, you can change rules in one group without affecting rules in another group.

A multihomed agent can report to a maximum of four management groups in a supported configuration. Each management group has its own set of processing rules and configuration information. A multihomed agent processes each set of processing rules independently, so there is no conflict in applying rules.

You deploy multihomed agents using the same mechanisms we discuss in Chapter 9, "Installing and Configuring Agents." To install a multihomed agent, just install the agent in one management group and then install it in the second management group. You can install the agent using the Discovery Wizard in the Operations console or by manual agent installation, as well as any of the other techniques discussed in Chapter 9.

Figure 10.2 shows a sample multihomed configuration with two management groups (GROUP1 and GROUP2) reporting to two different management servers.

As you can see, management servers and management groups can be implemented in a variety of ways. Evaluate these options and consider the best course of action based on your specific business requirements.

Gateway Servers

In Chapter 6, "Installing Operations Manager 2007," we discussed the process for installing a gateway server. Operations Manager 2007 requires mutual authentication between the agents and the management server, and between the gateway and the management server to which it reports. Mutual authentication increases the security of the communication model within OpsMgr by requiring the systems to authenticate.

OpsMgr supports two different methods to provide this authentication. The first method is Kerberos. You can use Kerberos authentication within the same Active Directory domain, or within domains having a two-way trust relationship with the domain with the management server. Kerberos is not available for systems in a workgroup or untrusted domain.

Operations Manager 2007 can also use x.509 certificates to provide the authentication required for mutual authentication, although there is more overhead here than with Kerberos. Gateway servers use certificate authentication to provide the mutual authentication to monitor systems that are part of a workgroup or an untrusted domain.

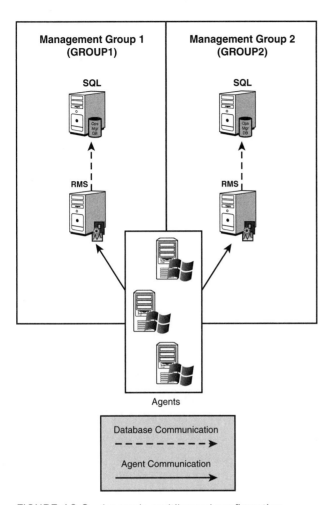

FIGURE 10.2   A sample multihomed configuration.

Figure 10.3 shows a configuration that uses both Kerberos and certificates for authentication. It includes the following components:

▶ The agents in the Active Directory domain Odyssey.com use Kerberos authentication because they are part of the same (or two-way trusted) domain.

▶ The agents in the untrusted Continent.com domain use a gateway server, which they locally communicate with from the agent using Kerberos.

▶ The gateway server communicates with the management server in the Odyssey.com domain, using certificates for authentication.

▶ The agents in a workgroup configuration each have certificates configured to communicate with the gateway server.

10

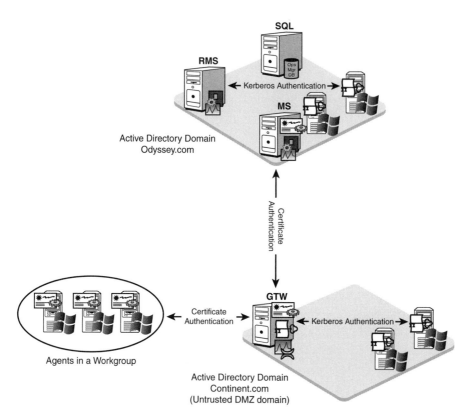

FIGURE 10.3   Authentication options within Operations Manager.

This configuration should be an uncommon one, because it uses all the major configurations available (same domain, untrusted domain, and workgroup) but shows an example of the variety of ways which these authentication methods can be used within Operations Manager 2007. You may have occasion to monitor agents in a workgroup in a DMZ that does not have its own domain.

It is also possible to monitor agents in a workgroup configuration without deploying a gateway server. This is possible by configuring certificate authentication directly from the agent to the management server. This approach is often used when there is no requirement to minimize the points of communication (using a gateway provides a single communication point from one set of agents to the management server) or when there are budget restrictions that remove the ability to add another (gateway) server.

> **NOTE**
>
> **About the Gateway Server**
>
> You will install a gateway server in an environment that does not have a trust relationship with the domain containing the RMS. A gateway server is used as a centralized point for agent communications between the agents and their management server. You will find this component in untrusted domains or workgroups.

High-level Steps

Additional steps are required on a gateway server to generate and import certificates and to approve the gateway server. At a high-level, the steps are as follows:

1. Request certificates (this will be for any computer in the agent, gateway server, and/or management server chain).
2. Import the certificates using MOMCertImport.
3. Run the Microsoft.EnterpriseManagement.GatewayApprovalTool.exe approval tool to initiate communication between the management and gateway servers.

Chapter 11, "Securing Operations Manager 2007," includes a full discussion on generating and importing certificates.

Approving the Gateway Server

After generating and importing your certificates (refer to Chapter 11), perform the following steps:

1. Copy the Microsoft.EnterpriseManagement.GatewayApprovalTool.exe approval tool from the Operations Manager installation media in the \SupportTools folder to the Operations Manager 2007 installation folder (*%ProgramFiles%*\System Center 2007 Operations Manager by default) on the management server.
2. On the management server targeted during your gateway server installation, log on using an account that is a member of the Operations Manager Administrators role.
3. Open a command prompt and navigate to the *%ProgramFiles%*\System Center Operations Manager 2007 folder or the folder to which you copied the approval tool (Microsoft.EnterpriseManagement.GatewayApprovalTool.exe).
4. At the command prompt, run
   ```
   Microsoft.EnterpriseManagement.GatewayApprovalTool.exe
   /ManagementServerName=<ManagementServerFQDN> /GatewayName=<GatewayFQDN>
   /Action=Create.
   ```
5. Successfully executing this utility returns a message that the approval of server *<GatewayFQDN>* completed successfully. (To later remove the gateway server from the management group, use the same command but change the syntax such that /Action=delete).

6. To validate that the approval occurred correctly, open the Operations console and navigate to the Administration -> Device Management -> Management Servers folder to see the gateway server in the list.

TIP

Security Considerations for the Gateway Approval Tool

The Gateway Approval Tool attempts to write data to the Operations Manager database, so you will want to ensure that the account you log in with to use the Gateway Approval Tool has write permissions to that database.

For example, you could run the Gateway Approval Tool using the same credentials you specified for the SDK and Config account.

Gateway Server Redundancy

The suggested approach for redundancy with the Gateway Server Component is installing multiple gateway servers and distributing the load of agents between the gateway servers, such that no server is monitoring more than 200 agents at any point in time. This approach provides a way for agents to report to a different gateway server if their primary server is not available.

There is an additional level at which we want to consider redundancy. Gateway servers are configured to communicate with a specific management server. To provide redundancy at this level, we need to be able to configure the gateway servers to fail over between management servers as needed.

To configure gateway server failover between management servers, log in to the management server using an account that is a member of the Administrators role for the management group and open the Command Shell (Start -> All Programs -> System Center Operations Manager -> Command Shell).

Within the Command Shell, we can define the primary management server and failover management server for the gateway server. Perform the following steps:

1. To configure gateway server failover to multiple management servers, we first must define the variables used by the Set-ManagementServer command:

```
$primaryMS = Get-ManagementServer ¦ where {your filter here}
$failoverMS = Get-ManagementServer ¦ where {your filter here}
$gatewayMS = Get-ManagementServer ¦ where {your filter here}
```

2. As an example, our environment has two management servers in the Odyssey domain named Hornet and Talon. We have a gateway server named Ambassador. The syntax to configure these filters would be:

```
$primaryMS = Get-ManagementServer ¦ where {$_.Name -eq 'Hornet.Odyssey.com' }
$failoverMS = Get-ManagementServer ¦ where {$_.Name -eq 'Talon.Odyssey.com' }
$gatewayMS = Get-ManagementServer ¦ where {$_.Name -eq
➡'Ambassador.Odyssey.com' }
```

3. After defining these variables, we can use them within the Set-ManagementServer command using the following syntax:

```
Set-ManagementServer -GatewayManagementServer: $gatewayMS -ManagementServer:
➡$primaryMS -FailoverServer: $failoverMS
```

This process configures the gateway server to have a primary management server of Hornet and a failover management server of Talon.

You can find additional information for the technologies used with the gateway server:

▶ Microsoft has provided a Certificate Services overview at http://technet2.microsoft. com/windowsserver/en/library/7d30a7ec-438f-41f8-a33a-f2e89d358b121033.mspx.

▶ The Public Key Infrastructure for Windows 2003 is available at http://www.microsoft. com/windowsserver2003/technologies/pki/default.mspx.

▶ SystemCenterForum has an excellent write-up on the gateway server and scenarios for it, available at http://systemcenterforum.org/wp-content/uploads/ OpsMgr2007_Gateway_Config_v1.2.zip.

Redundant Configurations

The "Management Server Configurations" section of this chapter listed six key questions you should consider during the Assessment phase. The third question—redundancy—is the key to determining whether or not this section of the chapter will be relevant to your environment.

If redundancy for Operations Manager is a business requirement, there are several different levels where you can apply redundant configurations. As an example, there may be a business requirement to have a highly available OpsMgr monitoring solution, but reporting may not require high availability. The key to designing a highly available OpsMgr configuration is to understand the different components and the different options available for redundancy. Table 10.1 presents a high-level overview of this.

Whereas Table 10.1 shows the current state of redundancy options available for Operations Manager 2007, we also provide "next step" theories for redundancy on those components where that is currently unsupported in a highly available configuration.

10

TABLE 10.1   Components and Redundancy Options Available

Component Name	Redundancy Option	Microsoft Supported?	Details
Root Management Server	Clustering	Yes	Active/Passive Cluster details can be found in the "Root Management Server Clustering" section of this chapter.
Root Management Server and Operations Database	Clustering	No support	Active/Passive configuration where the RMS and the Operations database are on the same node is possible, although this is not supported by Microsoft.
Root Management Server, Operations Database, and Web Console Server	Clustering	No support	Active/Passive configuration where the RMS, Operations database, and Web console server are on the same node is possible, although this is not supported by Microsoft.
Operations Database Server	Clustering	Yes	Active/Passive Cluster details can be found in the "Operations Database Clustering" section of this chapter.
Data Warehouse	Clustering	Yes	Active/Passive Cluster details can be found in the "Data Warehouse Clustering" section of this chapter.
Reporting outside of OpsMgr	No methods currently available	No support	A discussion on redundant reporting can be found in the "Reporting Installation" section of this chapter.
All-in-One database cluster	Clustering	Yes	A discussion on clustering all databases can be found in the "Complex Database Clusters" section of this chapter.
ACS Collector	No methods currently available	No support	A discussion on redundant ACS collectors can be found in the "ACS Installation" section of this chapter.

TABLE 10.1   Continued

Component Name	Redundancy Option	Microsoft Supported?	Details
Management Servers	Additional management servers	Yes	Management servers provide redundancy through providing additional management servers to fail agents to.
ACS Database Servers	Clustering	Yes	Active/Passive Cluster details can be found in the "ACS Installation" section of this chapter.
ACS Servers	No methods currently available	No support	A discussion on redundant ACS collectors can be found in the "ACS Installation" section of this chapter.
AEM Servers	No methods currently available	No support	A discussion on redundant AEM servers can be found in the "AEM Installation" section of this chapter.

High availability within Operations Manager is not an all-or-nothing situation. Many organizations may find that although they need a highly available RMS and Operations database, reporting components do not need to be highly available. Other examples of this apply for components such as ACS and AEM, which you may not be deploying in your environment or may not require redundancy.

This part of the chapter discusses how to make the various Operations Manager 2007 components redundant. We will begin with setting the prerequisites to installing high availability through discussions of common clustering concepts and processes for installing clusters. We next will discuss clustering the Operations, Data Warehouse, and ACS databases. We will discuss the Reporting database, RMS, ACS collector, and AEM server as well.

Figure 10.4 shows a fully redundant Operations Manager 2007 environment, which we will focus on how to build out throughout the chapter.

10

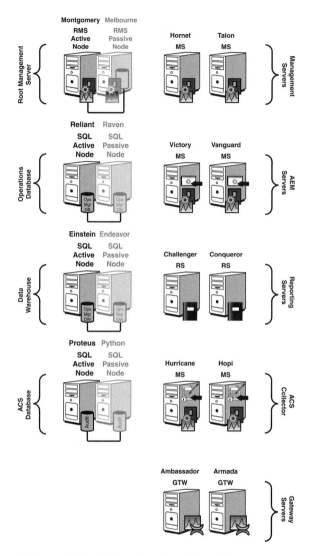

FIGURE 10.4   Redundant Operations Manager 2007 configuration.

Common Clustering Concepts

Before we delve into the specifics of how we install any of the Operations Manager 2007 components in a clustered configuration, it is important to start with a brief explanation of what a cluster is, how it works, and what is required to make it work.

A *cluster* is a group of computer systems that work together to provide either increased computing power or a platform for highly available applications. In the case of OpsMgr, the focus is not on increasing the computing power; rather, the focus is on providing a highly available application (Operations Manager).

A cluster consists of different computer systems called *nodes*. These nodes are computer systems running Windows Server operating systems (Enterprise and Datacenter edition), which are configured to be part of the cluster. Windows Server 2003 supports up to eight nodes in a server cluster. Clusters use resources that are physical or logical entities managed by the cluster. Examples of entities include IP addresses, network names, and physical disks. Each resource is owned by only by one node in the cluster at any point in time. Resources are collected together into *resource groups*, which can be moved between the nodes of the cluster. One important resource to be aware of is the quorum. The *quorum* is the resource that maintains the configuration data that is required for recovery of the cluster, including the details of changes applied to the cluster. Finally, the process of moving resources from one node to another is *failover*, and the process to move the resources back is *failback*.

Creating a Cluster

To install a cluster, you need to have multiple systems attached to a shared storage array. Installing a cluster requires at least one network adapter (per system, two recommended), two IP addresses, a cluster name, and at least one shared drive for use as the quorum drive. These components become the resources within the cluster.

The resources required in a cluster include a *cluster resource group*, which contains at a minimum the cluster IP address, cluster name, and quorum drive (shown in Figure 10.5). To share resources such as a database or the RMS, you would create a second resource group, which means defining at least one additional IP address, name, and shared drive. Use the Cluster Administrator, available under Start -> All Programs -> Administrative Tools, to create the cluster.

Prior to installing any of the Operations Manager components in a clustered configuration, you must first create the cluster and validate its functionality. You can validate the functionality of the cluster by failing resource groups from one node to the other, testing the functionality, and then failing the resource group back to the original node. Follow these steps:

1. For our cluster example shown in Figure 10.5, we start with resources running on the Melbourne server (which will host our clustered RMS). To validate the functionality of this cluster, we need to access the shared resources, which in this case are the IP Address, Network Name, and Physical Disk resources. This test involves pinging the name of the cluster (found on the parameters of the cluster name resources) from a system that is not a member of the cluster. A successful ping validates both name resolution and the IP address (found on the parameters of the IP address resource).

10

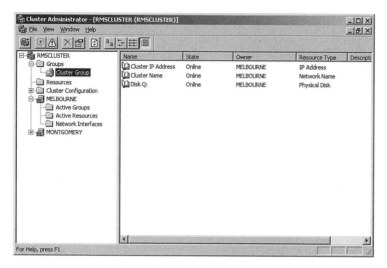

FIGURE 10.5   Default cluster configuration with minimum resources.

2. To validate the physical disk resource, we access that drive from the node that owns the resource. Opening up the Q: drive on the Melbourne server, you will get one of the following results:

   ▶ If the node owns the resource, the drive is able to read and write to the drive.

   ▶ If the node does not own the resource, a message displays stating that the device is not ready.

Testing Failover

Once we have validated the resources on the first node, we need to fail over the cluster to the second node. Right-click the resource group and choose the Move Group option. Once you have moved the resources to the other node (see Figure 10.6), perform the same process you performed on the first node. Once that test is done, fail back the resources to the original node.

If there are any failures in these tests, do not continue installing the application you will be clustering (such as the RMS or Microsoft SQL Server). Instead, focus on resolving the issues and stabilizing the cluster before starting the application installation. Do *not* install a clustered application until the cluster can successfully function on each node of the cluster and can fail over and fail back without issues.

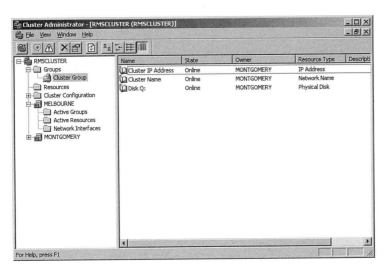

FIGURE 10.6   Cluster failover to the second node.

TIP

Installing Clusters in Virtual Server 2005 R2

You can use Microsoft Virtual Server 2005 R2 to provide a clustering environment without the extensive hardware that is typically required. With Virtual Server, you can create a cluster with a single physical node using virtual SCSI controllers to provide the shared storage for the cluster. This is an excellent method to provide both testing or demonstration environments and can also be used in production environments, depending on the hardware requirements.

An excellent write-up that provides step-by-step processes to create a virtual server cluster is available at http://www.roudybob.net/downloads/Setting-Up-A-Windows-Server-2003-Cluster-in-VS2005-Part1.pdf.

Installing a functional cluster is relevant for the OpsMgr components that use SQL Server and for the RMS component, which we will discuss in the "Root Management Server Clustering" section of this chapter.

Installing SQL Server 2005 Clusters

After installing the cluster, if you will be providing redundancy for an OpsMgr database component, your next step is to install SQL Server 2005 into your clustered configuration. You can use SQL Server 2005 clusters with the Operations Database, Data Warehouse Database, and ACS Database Components. Because installing a SQL Server 2005 cluster is very similar to a nonclustered SQL Server installation, we will focus on what the differences are and what is required to complete the installation:

▶ During the database server installation, the major change is the screen that displays what components to install in the process of installing SQL Server 2005 on a cluster. The Components to Install screen has a check box for Create a SQL Server failover cluster, which you need to select. Other items to check include the SQL Server Database Services option and the Workstation components, Books Online and development tools option (see Figure 10.7).

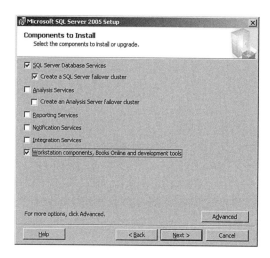

FIGURE 10.7 Installing clustered SQL components.

▶ As part of the installation, you also need to configure the Virtual Server IP address (see Figure 10.8). This address specifies the network adapter and IP address used by the SQL Server cluster.

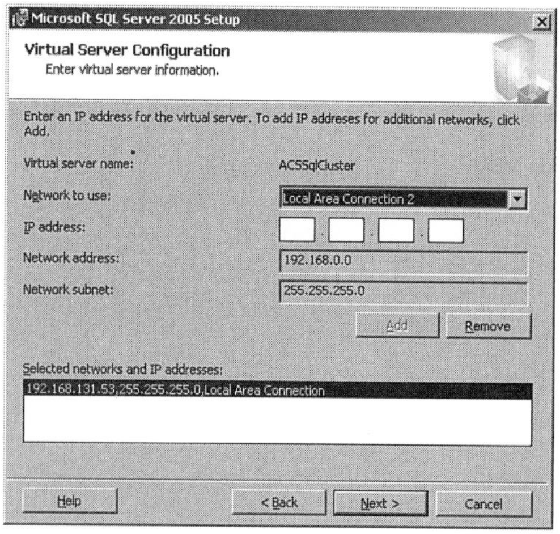

FIGURE 10.8 Configuring the SQL Virtual Server IP.

► The available cluster groups display in the Cluster Group Selection screen (see Figure 10.9). Choose the cluster group you created to use with SQL Server.

► The Cluster Node Configuration screen displays the nodes in the cluster. The available nodes display, with the node you are currently running the installation from is listed in the Required node section, and the other nodes in the cluster are listed in the Available nodes section. Highlight the additional nodes and move them to the Selected nodes section, as we have in Figure 10.10.

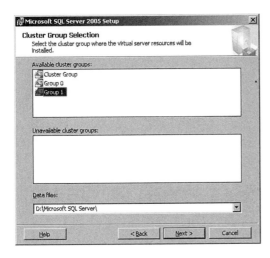

FIGURE 10.9   Choosing the SQL cluster group.

FIGURE 10.10   Choosing the SQL cluster node.

▶ There is another cluster-specific screen where you will need to specify the account to use for remote setup. This account will install the SQL Server services on each of the nodes in the cluster you specified.

▶ The final cluster-specific screen specifies the startup accounts to use for each clustered service. The installation process does not create these DomainName\ GroupName entries, so you should create them before running the setup. Figure 10.11 shows the Domain Groups for Clustered Services screen where you specify the group names.

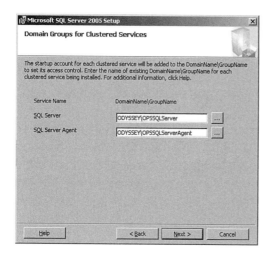

FIGURE 10.11   SQL domain groups.

The installation process actually occurs on each of the nodes at the same time (which is actually pretty cool!) and is shown in Figure 10.12.

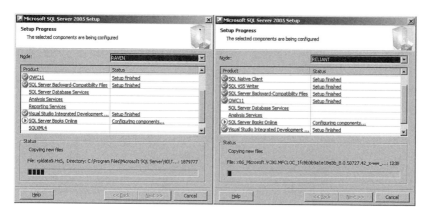

FIGURE 10.12   SQL Server simultaneously installs on two nodes.

After the SQL Server 2005 installation completes, install SQL 2005 Service Pack (SP) 1. Run the Service Pack installation in the active node in the cluster; like the SQL 2005 installation, the active node can run both SP 1 installations simultaneously. After installing SP 1, reboot each of the nodes (one at a time) before continuing with any other installation activities on the nodes.

TIP

Startup Mode for the SQL Server Service

Although the SQL Server service must be in automatic startup on nonclustered installations, the service is configured for manual startup in a clustered installation. This is a default configuration on a cluster and is set this way so that it can activate on the node on the cluster that is running SQL Server at that point in time.

Operations Database Clustering

Installing the Operations database in a clustered configuration is basically the same as the process explained in Chapter 6. The installation needs to occur on the active node of the SQL cluster. To verify the node, open the Cluster Administrator (Start -> All Programs -> Administrative Tools -> Cluster Administrator), open the connection to the SQL cluster, and make sure that all cluster resources are running on the node where you will be installing the operations database. When installing, make sure to only check the Database component (uncheck the other selections), as shown in Figure 10.13.

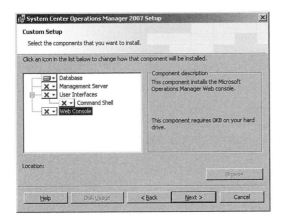

FIGURE 10.13   Installation of the Operations database only.

During the installation process, the SQL Server Database Instance screen has a check box labeled Second node of a Windows Server Cluster, as shown in Figure 10.14. This box should not be checked and can be ignored. Because no program files are installed on the cluster nodes during the database-only installation, there is no need to repeat the installation on the second node of the cluster. (We discuss sizing for the database and logs in Chapter 4.)

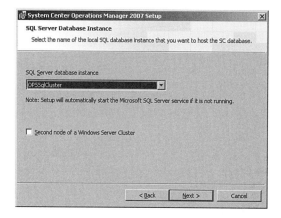

FIGURE 10.14   Specifying the SQL instance.

After completing the installation, you can verify the success of the installation by opening the SQL Server Management Studio (Start -> All Programs -> Microsoft SQL Server 2005 -> SQL Server Management Studio), connecting to the cluster, and verifying that the Operations database exists (the default database name is OperationsManager).

Redundancy Using Log Shipping

Operations Manager 2007 supports log shipping for redundancy on the Operations and Data Warehouse databases.

Log shipping is essentially the process of automating the backup of database and transaction log files on a production SQL server, then restoring them to a standby server. More than that, the key feature of log shipping is that it will automatically back up transaction logs at an interval you specify, and automatically restore them to the standby server. This essentially keeps the two SQL Server systems in sync. If the production server fails (and if you put enough effort into your log shipping setup), all you have to do is point your users to the new server and "go."

Log shipping requires that the database be set to Full Recovery mode. You can change the recovery mode using the ALTER DATABASE statement with Transact-SQL, or with SQL Server Management Studio. Select Databases -> *<database name>* and then right-click to select Properties. On the Options page, select the dropdown for Recovery model to change from Simple to Full, as displayed in Figure 10.15 for the OperationsManager database.

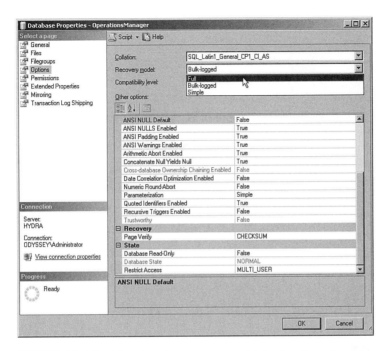

FIGURE 10.15   Changing the recovery model for the OperationsManager database.

Details on how to configure log shipping will be included in the upcoming "Operations Manager 2007 High Availability and Disaster Recovery" white paper, which when it is completed will be available at http://technet.microsoft.com/en-us/opsmgr/bb498235.aspx.

Because the ACS database already has high processing requirements, we do not recommend log shipping (or mirroring) for this database. Also, note that overhead is associated with log shipping, and clustering the Operational and data warehouse databases offers with a less resource-intensive approach.

Data Warehouse Clustering

Before installing the data warehouse, be sure to install and test the cluster (see the "Common Clustering Concepts" section earlier in this chapter) and install SQL 2005 SP 1 on the cluster, as we discuss in the "Installing SQL 2005 Clusters" section.

The actual installation process is the same when installing on a cluster as it is when installing on a single system. When you select components in the OpsMgr setup program, be sure to only choose the Data Warehouse Component (see Figure 10.16), and not the Reporting Server Component. The SQL Server Reporting feature is not cluster-aware and we do not recommend you install it on a cluster, because installing both clustered applications and nonclustered applications on a clustered system is not a recommended best practice.

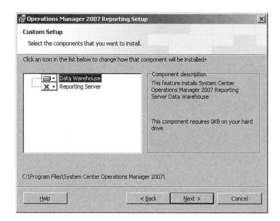

FIGURE 10.16   Installing the data warehouse without reporting components.

During the setup process, you choose the clustered instance you created when installing the SQL cluster (in the example shown in Figure 10.17, this is the Operations Database instance called OpsSqlCluster).

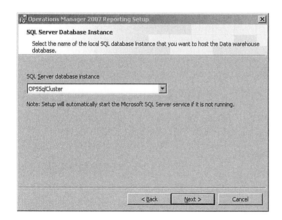

FIGURE 10.17   Specifying the database instance.

The database name defaults to OperationsManagerDW and a size of 1GB. Move the database files to shared storage, shown in Figure 10.18, where the data files are on the D: drive and the log files are on the L: drive. This database size should be set to the estimated database size based on the calculations for the data warehouse sizing, discussed in Chapter 4.

Once the database installation is complete, you should see the .mdf and .ldf files in the locations that you specified during the installation (see Figure 10.18 for the path to these files).

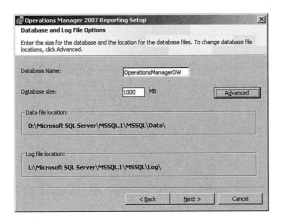

FIGURE 10.18   Specifying the location of the Data Warehouse database and log files.

ACS Installation

The ACS installation will only run from a management server. Therefore, installation prerequisites include installing a management server designated as an ACS collector, and for high availability installing a clustered SQL Server 2005 database environment for the ACS database (see the "Common Clustering Concepts" and "Installing SQL 2005 Clusters" sections for details on these processes). For detailed information on ACS (other than clustering), see Chapter 15, "Monitoring Audit Collection Services."

Installing the ACS components follows the same steps described in Chapter 6. The ACS installation process installs both the collector and the database. You can validate a successful installation of the database by accessing the server (or cluster) where you created the database and validating that the OperationsManagerAC (default name) exists.

> **NOTE**
>
> **Installing the ACS Components on Separate Servers**
>
> Although you can cluster the database, Microsoft does not support clustering the collector. The database typically is installed on the collector. If you want a redundant ACS database, you must install it separate from the collector.

The ACS Database

Consider placing the ACS database on a cluster to provide a highly available solution. Each collector reports to its own ACS database server. This means that redundancy is not available for ACS collectors by installing a second ACS collector (unlike management servers or gateway servers, which can have additional servers installed to provide redundancy).

10

The ACS Collector

To provide redundancy for the ACS collector, the best available option is installing a second collector that will work as a "cold" server. This cold server is a collector that is installed and configured to report to the ACS database server but has the ACS service (the Operations Manager Audit Collector service) disabled on the system. For our environment, the first ACS collector installed is Hurricane, and the cold backup ACS server is Hopi (as we illustrated in Figure 10.4 earlier in the chapter). Another option to provide redundancy is to install multiple pairs of ACS collectors/database servers. We discuss this approach in Chapter 15.

Using an RMS Cluster to Provide ACS Collector Redundancy

One other approach for a redundant ACS collector is installing it on the RMS cluster. Although it is not a best practice for the RMS to provide ACS collector functionality, this option provides a level of redundancy for the Collector service. You would first install the RMS cluster prior to installing the collector on the RMS cluster. Here are the steps:

1. Install the collector on each node of the RMS cluster and point to the same ACS database.

2. After configuring the servers, add the new service (Operations Manager Audit Collection service) as a generic service, similar to how you added the three other services during the RMS cluster installation.

Note that Microsoft that does not currently support installing the collector on the RMS in a clustered configuration, and no supported options are available for a high-availability solution where multiple collectors send data to the same ACS database.

Complex Database Clusters

Installing the OpsMgr Data Warehouse or Operations database only creates the database on the specified server; the installation process does not install any executable programs on the server. This is important because it increases the likelihood that these database components will be able to coexist on the same server without having issues from interaction. The ACS installation actually runs from the collector (not from the ACS database server), implying that it also does not install binary files as part of its installation process. This is important because it greatly increases the likelihood that these databases can coexist with other databases on the same server or cluster.

We have deployed multiple configurations where the Operations and Data Warehouse databases run on the same physical node and although there is an impact in terms of increased CPU, memory, disk, and network load, we have not seen any collisions caused by these databases running on the same physical server in the same SQL instance. These concepts bring two major variations on the supported cluster configurations, which would be very likely configurations to use in production deployments. Please note that Microsoft does not support either of the following two configurations at this time, but they should be viable configurations based on available information:

▶ The first configuration installs all three databases on a single server into a single SQL Server instance. The result would be one instance with the OperationsManager, OperationsManagerDW, and OperationsManagerAC databases (remember these are all default names which can be changed) in that instance. This option is now supported but not recommended by Microsoft.

Providing each of these three functions from a single server will require a more powerful hardware configuration than if these run on three separate servers. The actual configuration you would use would vary depending on the number of agents you will be monitoring and the management packs that are deployed. Best-practice approaches to this would be a configuration with high-end equipment that includes the following:

▶ At least four processors

▶ Sixteen gigabytes of memory

▶ A gigabit network adapter

▶ Dedicated drives for each of the log and database files, separated for each of the three databases

▶ A second logical configuration to draw from this is a four-node cluster in an Active/Active/Active/Passive configuration:

▶ The first node would host the Operations database in the default cluster instance.

▶ The second node would host the Data Warehouse database in a second instance.

▶ The third node would host the ACS database in a third instance.

▶ The fourth node would be available to provide high availability in case of the failure of a node in the cluster.

Installing Multiple Operational Databases on a Single SQL Server Instance

If you are going to install multiple operational databases on a single SQL Server instance, you will need to use the dbcreatewizard.exe tool. This tool requires the following files from a system that already has an OpsMgr component installed (see http://support.microsoft.com/kb/938997 for further information):

▶ %ProgramFiles%\System Center Operations Manager 2007\Microsoft.EnterpriseManagement.UI.ConsoleFramework.dll

▶ %ProgramFiles%\System Center Operations Manager 2007\Microsoft.MOM.UI.Common.dll

10

▶ *%ProgramFiles%*\System Center Operations Manager 2007\
   Microsoft.MOM.UI.Wrappers.dll

Anders Bengtsson points out (http://contoso.se/blog/?p=216) that if you have not yet installed the database—which is the first OpsMgr component installed—how can you get these files? You can copy the files from any system that has the Operations console installed. So, if necessary, install the console on a computer that you plan to use later for a management workstation.

Do not use the dbcreatewizard utility to install the Data Warehouse database. Using this tool with the Data Warehouse database creates the following problems:

▶ You cannot initialize a report when trying to generate it using a link in a view in the Operations console.

▶ Unpublished reports will not appear when you view a report in the Reporting space of the console.

These issues are further documented (with a fix!) at http://support.microsoft.com/kb/942865. The fix is incorporated into OpsMgr 2007 SP 1.

AEM Installation

OpsMgr's capability to capture, aggregate, and report on application crashes depends on the availability of the Agentless Exception Monitoring share. A Group Policy Administrative template specifies the location of this share to the ACS clients. If the AEM share is not available, crash data is not reported.

There are currently no supported (or recommended) methods to provide high availability for the AEM file share. However, using either the Windows 2003 Distributed File System (DFS) or Windows Clustering may provide a viable method of making this share available, even if one of the nodes hosting the sharing is unavailable. At this time, there are several issues with the DFS approach:

▶ The Client Monitoring Configuration Wizard does not allow using a DFS share, because the wizard itself creates the share rather than using an existing file share.

▶ Using DFS to provide redundancy may result in large amount of additional network traffic as the different DFS servers communicate crash information between them.

▶ Windows Vista clients communicate via port number 51906, so this form of high availability will not work for Vista clients, because they communicate via the port, not the share.

Clustering the server that provides the file share functionality (and running it on the RMS) may be the most viable option in the future. This method would allow both the share functionality and port 51906 functionality while providing a highly available solution.

Reporting Installation

Installing a reporting server within a highly available environment follows the same process used for new installations (which we discussed in Chapter 6).

TIP

SQL Reporting and Other OpsMgr Databases

Microsoft does not recommend installing the SQL Reporting components on a database server already providing OpsMgr functionality (such as the Operations, Data Warehouse, and ACS databases). SQL Reporting is an intensive application, and it may cause performance issues when installed on a server that is providing a role other than the SQL Server Reporting function.

However, this concern must be balanced with the reality that creating a separate SQL Reporting environment is generally overkill, especially when considering that the SQL reporting environment cannot be shared with other SQL reports due to the new security model implemented with the Operations Manager 2007 Reporting component.

We have not seen issues with these components coexisting as long as the hardware acquired for the database and reporting server is sufficient.

Note the following items of interest when installing the reporting components:

▶ When installing the prerequisites for the reporting components, remember to install IIS and ASP.NET before installing the SQL Server 2005 components (otherwise, the reporting services option is not available when you install the SQL Server components).

  During the OpsMgr installation process, specify a custom installation and only choose the Reporting Server option (see Figure 10.19).

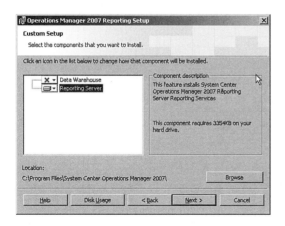

FIGURE 10.19   Installing the Reporting Server Components without the Data Warehouse Components.

▶ During the installation, there is a step where you need to enter the name of the RMS. For a highly available configuration, you need to specify the name of the RMS cluster. Figure 10.20 shows an example, where we use a RMS cluster name of OpsMgrRms.

▶ You will need to specify the name of the SQL Server Database instance (in our example, DWSQLCluster), the SQL database name (defaults to OperationsManagerDW) and the port (1433 by default), as shown in Figure 10.21. If you have multiple instances installed on the SQL Server, you will need to specify the SQL instance and the port associated with the instance on this screen.

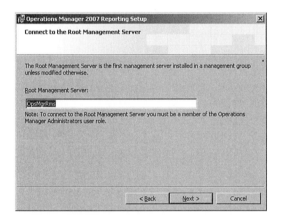

FIGURE 10.20   Connect to the Root Management Server.

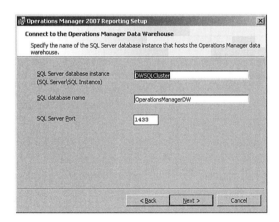

FIGURE 10.21   Connecting to the data warehouse.

When the installation completes successfully, we have a functional OpsMgr Reporting server on a single server. At this point, we have a supported configuration, but we do not have a highly available solution.

As we discuss in Chapter 4, you can establish redundancy for this component by using Network Load Balancing, although Microsoft does not support this. The trick on this is how to keep the reporting information in sync between the systems.

Our tests indicate that the first step in creating a redundant reporting configuration is installing a single Reporting server with the Data Warehouse Components on a different server (or cluster, as discussed in the "Operations Database Clustering" and "Data Warehouse Clustering" sections of this chapter). This installation places the report databases local to the system where we installed the OpsMgr reporting components.

To make the configuration redundant, manually replicate the reporting databases between the two systems, and then configure NLB on both reporting servers. Finally, change the OpsMgr configuration to use the NLB address instead of the address of the originally installed reporting server. You can change the address in the Operations console at Administration -> Settings -> Reporting.

We recommend this approach as the most likely method of providing redundancy for the Reporting Server Component at this time.

Root Management Server Clustering

The RMS is the only management server in the management group running the OpsMgr SDK and OpsMgr Config services. Clustering these services (and the RMS) can provide high availability. Installing a clustered RMS is not a simple process, because the RMS installs as a generic application using generic services.

As an example, when you installed the SQL cluster earlier in this chapter (in the "Installing SQL Server 2005 Clusters" section), the installation created the resources (such as the services) and placed them into the resource group. This is not the case for the RMS cluster. Additional steps are required during the installation process, which are not required with a more cluster-aware application such as SQL Server or Exchange.

The process to install a clustered RMS is not a short one. We recommend testing this process through a virtual configuration prior to trying it in a production environment because this is a long and complicated process.

The following are the high-level steps we will use to install the RMS Cluster.

▶ **Validate cluster prerequisites**—Install the cluster and verify it is fully functional, as discussed in the "Common Clustering Concepts" section of this chapter.

▶ **Group and resources**—Create the RMS resource group and resources (IP Address, Physical Disk, Network Name).

▶ **OpsMgr prerequisites**—Install the prerequisites on each node for the OpsMgr management server and user interface.

10

▶ **OpsMgr security**—Verify that the Operations Manager Administrators group is part of the local Administrators security group and that the Cluster service account is a member of the domain Operations Manager Administrators security group. Add the SDK and Config service accounts in the Local Administrators group on each node.

▶ **RMS and MS installations**—Perform an installation of only the management server and console options first on the primary node of the cluster and then on the secondary nodes of the cluster.

▶ **RMS cluster resources**—Create resources for the three Windows services (Health, Config, and SDK services).

▶ **Sharing the RMS key**—Create a file share and export the RMS key.

▶ **Creating the Virtual RMS**—Use the ManagementServerConfigTool to create the Virtual RMS cluster and add nodes to the cluster.

▶ **Testing the cluster**—Validate that the cluster works through the Operations console.

TIP

Redundancy for the Web Console Server Component

You could also put the Web Console Server Component on the RMS cluster as a resource to provide a redundant Web Console Server.

Group and Resources

To create the RMS resource group and resources, perform the following steps:

1. Log on to the primary node of the cluster with full administrative rights. We will refer to the first node in the cluster as the primary node of the cluster, and additional nodes of the cluster as secondary nodes.

2. Open the Cluster Administrator (Start -> All Programs -> Administrative Tools). Create a cluster group for the RMS called **RMS Group**.

   Within the cluster group, we will create resources for the IP address, physical disk, and network name, as shown in Figure 10.22.

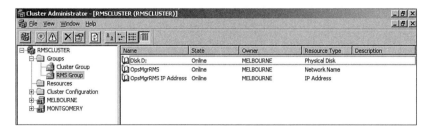

FIGURE 10.22   Creating the RMS cluster resources.

For each of the resources created, the possible owners should be all nodes in the cluster.

3. Within the RMS group, create an IP Address resource. The configuration for this resource should be as follows:

   ▶ **Possible owners**—All nodes in the cluster.

   ▶ **Resource dependencies**—None.

   ▶ **Parameters**—Publicly accessible IP address and subnet mask. Select the public network from the Network dropdown list.

4. Within the RMS group, create a Physical Disk resource. The configuration for this resource should be as follows:

   ▶ **Possible owners**—All nodes in the cluster.

   ▶ **Resource dependencies**—None.

   ▶ **Parameters**—A drive letter to the dedicated RMS disk must already exist and be available to all the nodes in the cluster.

5. Within the RMS group, create a network name resource. The configuration for this resource should be as follows:

   ▶ **Possible owners**—All nodes in the cluster.

   ▶ **Resource dependencies**—The RMS IP address resource.

   ▶ **Parameters**—A valid NetBIOS name in the Name field. Do not select the DNS Registration Must Succeed check box. Do select the Enable Kerberos Authentication check box, as shown in Figure 10.23.

6. Right-click the RMS cluster group and click Bring Online. If the group does not come online successfully, a likely cause is a previous association of the IP address or network name either in DNS or Active Directory.

OpsMgr Prerequisites

On each node of the cluster, check the prerequisites for installing the management server and user interface components, using the Check Prerequisites option from the SetupOM program on the OpsMgr installation media. These prerequisites should include Windows Server 2003 SP 1, MDAC version 2.80.1022.0 or later, .NET Framework version 2.0, and .NET Framework version 3.0 components.

You can ignore warnings from the prerequisite checker, but there is a risk of degraded performance, as shown with the example in Figure 10.24, where the system does not have enough memory available to run the RMS functionality efficiently. You must fix any failed prerequisites prior to installing the OpsMgr components.

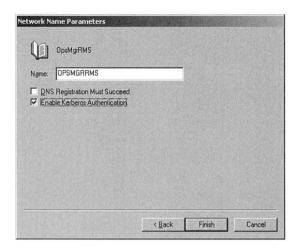

FIGURE 10.23   Configuring the RMS network name.

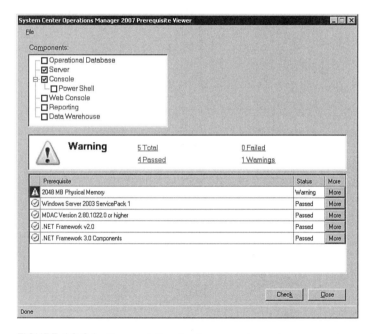

FIGURE 10.24   Prerequisites for the management server and user interface.

OpsMgr Security

For each node in the RMS cluster, add the domain Operations Manager Administrators security group into the local Administrators group (if this global group does not already exist, create a group with this name as a global security group in the domain). The cluster service account needs to be a member of the Operations Manager Administrators security group that you previously added to the local Administrators group on each node. Also, add the SDK and Config service account (OM_SDK, in our case) to the local Administrators group on each node (see Figure 10.25).

FIGURE 10.25   Security configuration required for each node in the RMS cluster.

RMS and MS Installations

Installing the RMS on a cluster is the same process used when installing a nonclustered RMS (see Chapter 6 for details). As a reminder, choose a custom installation, selecting only the Server and Console options during the installation.

For the remaining nodes in the cluster, perform the same installation process for the RMS installation again, using a custom installation and only selecting the Server and Console options.

RMS Cluster Resources

Now that we have the RMS and Management Server Components installed, log back in to the primary node of the cluster (using an account with full administrative rights). Open the Cluster Administrator. Within the RMS Group, we will be creating new services. Right-click the RMS Group and select New -> Resource. Using the New Resource Wizard, create a service with the following configuration:

- **Name**—RMS Health Service.
- **Resource type**—Generic Service.
- **Group**—RMS Group.

10

▶ **Possible owners**—All nodes in the cluster.

▶ **Resource dependencies**—The RMS Disk and RMS Network Name resources, which we previously defined in the "Group and Resources" section of this chapter.

▶ **Generic Service Parameters**—In the Service name field, enter **HealthService** (this must be exact and cannot be modified).

▶ **Startup Parameters**—Leave this blank.

▶ **Registry Replication**—Leave this blank.

Perform a similar process for the Operations Manager Config Service:

▶ **Name**—RMS Config Service.

▶ **Resource type**—Generic Service.

▶ **Group**—RMS Group.

▶ **Possible owners**—All nodes in the cluster.

▶ **Resource dependencies**—The RMS Disk and RMS Network Name resources, which we defined in the "Group and Resources" section of this chapter.

▶ **Generic Service Parameters**—On the Service name field, enter **OMCFG** (this must be exact and cannot be modified).

▶ **Startup Parameters**—Leave this blank.

▶ **Registry Replication**—Leave this blank.

Perform the same process for the Operations Manager SDK Service:

▶ **Name**—RMS SDK Service.

▶ **Resource type**—Generic Service.

▶ **Group**—RMS Group.

▶ **Possible owners**—All nodes in the cluster.

▶ **Resource dependencies**—The RMS Disk and RMS Network Name resources, which we defined in the "Group and Resources" section of this chapter.

▶ **Generic Service Parameters**—On the Service name field, enter **OMSDK** (this must be exact and cannot be modified).

▶ **Startup Parameters**—Leave this blank.

▶ **Registry Replication**—Leave this blank.

Sharing the RMS Key

To share the RMS key, we will create a file share on the network accessible from all cluster nodes and name it RMSKey. This share will provide a location for storing the RMS key. Give the account running the Cluster service full access to the file share. For security purposes, you may want to make this a hidden share—append a dollar sign ($) to the end of the share name to hide the share. Perform the following steps:

1. Log in to the primary cluster node with the account the Cluster service is running under. Move the cluster resources to the primary node of the cluster if they are not already there.

2. From the Operations Manager 2007 installation media, copy the SecureStorageBackup.exe and ManagementServerConfigTool.exe files from the \SupportTools folder to the installation folder for OpsMgr (by default %*ProgramFiles*%\System Center Operations Manager 2007).

3. Open a command prompt and `cd` to the folder where you copied the files. From the command prompt, we will make a backup of the RMS key with the following syntax:

   ```
   SecureStorageBackup.exe Backup \\<ServerName>\<ShareName>\RMSkey.bin
   ```

   For instance, the command `SecureStorageBackup.exe Backup \\Pantheon\ RMSKEY\RMSkey.bin` would back up the key to the Pantheon server in the RMSKEY share.

4. When you enter the `SecureStorageBackup` command, you must enter and confirm a password that is at least eight characters long and includes at least one symbol. Make note of this password, because it will be required not only for the process of installing the RMS cluster but also in a disaster recovery scenario.

5. Next, we need to restore the RMSKEY onto each secondary node. To do this, log in to each secondary node and copy the SecureStorageBackup file to the installation directory for the system.

6. Open a command prompt and `cd` to the folder where you copied the files. From the command prompt, we will restore the backup of the RMS key with the following syntax:

   ```
   SecureStorageBackup.exe Restore \\<ServerName>\<ShareName>\RMSkey.bin
   ```

   As an example, `SecureStorageBackup.exe Restore \\Pantheon\RMSKEY\RMSkey.bin` restores the key stored on the Pantheon server within the RMSKEY share. You will be required to enter the same password you created when you exported the RMS key from the primary node.

You have now restored the RMS key to each node of the cluster.

10

> **CAUTION**
>
> **Back Up the Operations Database**
>
> Before actually creating the RMS cluster, perform a full backup the Operations database. For details on how to backup the database, see Chapter 12, "Backup and Recovery."
>
> In the next step of this process, we will use the ManagementServerConfigTool to create the RMS cluster. Because this tool can potentially cause irrecoverable damage to the database, a backup is strongly suggested prior to continuing.

Creating the Virtual RMS

To create the virtual RMS, log back in to the primary node of the cluster and perform the following steps:

1. Open a command prompt and cd to the Operations Manager installation directory.

2. Use the ManagementServerConfigTool.exe tool to instantiate the RMS cluster group as a cluster, as follows:

   ```
   ManagementServerConfigTool.exe InstallCluster /vs:<VirtualServerNetBiosName>
   ➥/Disk:<RMS Disk resource letter>
   ```

   Figure 10.26 shows an example of using the ManagementServerConfigTool with the virtual server name of OpsMgrRms on the D: drive.

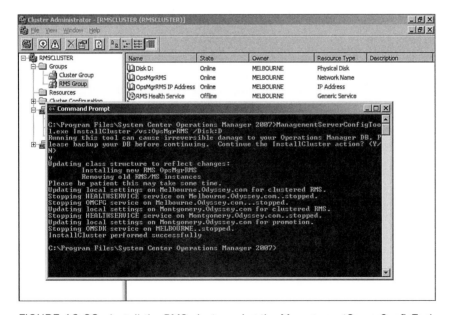

FIGURE 10.26   Install the RMS cluster using the ManagementServerConfigTool.

CAUTION

Using the SetSPN Command

Run the ManagementServerConfigTool utility using the account that is running the cluster service. If you run this under a different account, you will need to run the SetSPN utility manually.

Details on the process to create the SPN manually are included within the Operations Manager 2007 Deployment Guide, available for download at http://technet.microsoft.com/en-us/opsmgr/bb498235.aspx. SetSPN itself is available in the Windows 2000 Resource Kit at http://go.microsoft.com/fwlink/?LinkId=80094.

---

3. After the primary node has run the ManagementServerConfigTool and it has successfully completed, perform the same process on the secondary nodes as well. Log in to the secondary node, and within the cluster administrator move the RMS cluster resources to the node you are logged in to.

   As an example, if the primary node is Montgomery and the secondary node is Melbourne, we would now log in to the Melbourne server and move any cluster resources over from Montgomery onto Melbourne.

4. From the Windows Services management console, change the startup type for the OpsMgr SDK service from Disabled (the default when not the RMS) to Automatic. Then start the OpsMgr SDK service. Note that the OpsMgr SDK service must be running on the primary RMS node as well.

NOTE

Initial Startup Type for the OpsMgr SDK Service on Secondary Cluster Node

Although one might think that the service would already have its startup type set as Manual because the cluster is controlling the service, this is not the case. The first node in the cluster has the service set to Automatic because it has the RMS role. The second node initially has the startup type as Disabled; we change it to Manual here as part of establishing our RMS cluster.

---

5. Open a command prompt to the Operations Manager installation directory and run the ManagementServerConfigTool with a configuration that adds the node to the cluster:

```
ManagementServerConfigTool.exe AddRMSNode /vs:<VirtualServerNetBiosName>
➥/Disk:<RMS Disk resource letter>
```

   For the Montgomery/Melbourne example, the shared disk is D: and the VirtualServerNetBiosName is OpsMgr RMS. The sample syntax for this on the secondary node (Melbourne) would be the following:

```
ManagementServerConfigTool.exe AddRMSNode /vs:OpsMgrRms /Disk:D
```

Testing the Cluster

To test the functionality of your OpsMgr RMS cluster, open the Operations console. To log in, you will need to specify the name of the RMS cluster (in our example, it is OpsMgrRms) for the server name. In the console, navigate to Administration -> Device Management -> Management Server. You should now see the name of the RMS cluster listed as a management server. In addition, under Administration -> Device Management -> Agentless Managed, you should also see the names of the nodes in the cluster as in Figure 10.27. Notice that the cluster nodes appear as agentless managed. This should change once the Clustering management pack is available, but for now it is normal.

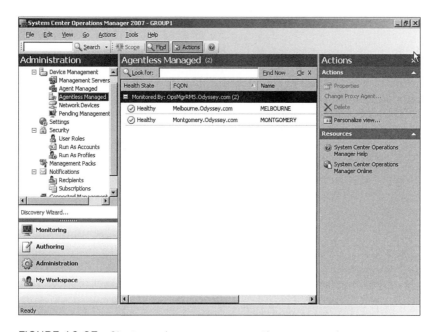

FIGURE 10.27   Cluster nodes appear as agentless managed.

You can also use the ldifde utility to verify everything is registered properly in Active Directory. Syntax would be the following:

```
Ldifde -f c:\ldifdeout.txt -t 3268 -d DC=<domain name>,DC=COM
➥-l serviceprincipalname -p subtree
```

Although the majority of the entries will register automatically during your OpsMgr installation, you may need to use SetSPN to register the virtual name of the RMS cluster. If you are registering manually, register both the NetBIOS name itself and the FQDN.

The following are SPN entries for a properly registered virtual RMS:

```
dn: CN=CLUST-RMS,CN=Computers,DC=ODYSSEY,DC=com
changetype: add
servicePrincipalName: MSOMHSvc/OPSMGRRMS
servicePrincipalName: MSOMHSvc/OPSMGRRMS.ODYSSEY.com
servicePrincipalName: MSOMHSvc/MONTGOMERY
servicePrincipalName: MSOMHSvc/MONTGOMERY.ODYSSEY.com
servicePrincipalName: MSOMHSvc/MELBOURNE
servicePrincipalName: MSOMHSvc/MELBOURNE.ODYSSEY.com
servicePrincipalName: MSClusterVirtualServer/OPSMGRRMS
servicePrincipalName: MSClusterVirtualServer/OPSMGRRMS.ODYSSEY.com
servicePrincipalName: HOST/OPSMGRRMS
servicePrincipalName: HOST/OPSMGRRMS.ODYSSEY.com
```

Here are some points to note:

▶ OPSMGRRMS is the virtual name of the RMS cluster.

▶ ODYSSEY is the domain name.

▶ MONTGOMERY and MELBOURNE are the two physical nodes in the RMS cluster.

Note that if the server is in a child domain, you will need DC entries for each level in ldifde. We have also found the following caveats:

▶ AD does not validate the service name. Be sure you type correctly!

▶ SetSPN does not return any sort of "access denied" errors if you run it with insufficient privileges.

Repromoting a Clustered RMS

Let's say your clustered RMS goes down and you need to promote another management server in your management group to become the RMS. Then, when the cluster comes back on, you want to repromote the cluster.

Unfortunately, you cannot get this to work in the OpsMgr 2007 RTM (Released to Manufacturing) code. Microsoft will be fixing this when Service Pack 1 is released. In the interim, Microsoft is making a promotion tool available that you can try in your environment. We include this tool, RMSClusterDR.zip, on the CD accompanying this book. The zip file includes an updated version of the ManagementServerConfigTool.exe utility and instructions.

Be aware that the tool is not officially supported by Microsoft. The company suggests you use it for lab testing purposes only.

Performance Considerations

When creating an Operations Manager 2007 environment, you have four primary areas to consider in providing an optimally performing configuration: memory, disk, processor, and network performance. We complete this chapter by discussing each of these aspects in the following sections.

Memory Performance

The amount of memory available to the servers in an Operations Manager 2007 environment has the most direct impact on the performance of OpsMgr. There are a variety of reasons why this is the situation:

▶ **SQL Server 2005 really likes memory**. With its default configuration, SQL Server will use as much memory as it can. We have worked in environments with fewer than 200 servers and the combined Operations and Data Warehouse SQL Server database engine was using more than 11GB on a 16GB server. In another environment we worked in, the Operations database server had a total of 4GB of memory, and all 4GB of memory were consistently in use either by SQL Server or by the Operating System.

▶ **The RMS really likes memory**. We have seen implementations with fewer than 200 agents where the RMS had 8GB of memory and consistently used more than 5GB. In another environment where there were fewer than 300 agents and the RMS had 6GB of memory, it consistently used over 4GB of memory. We used the Task Manager to gather the memory statistics discussed here on the Performance tab from Pagefile Usage. These memory statistics do not consider how much memory the System Cache was using, so the actual memory in use on the server was even higher.

▶ **The System Cache is one of the most underestimated performance boosts available within Windows**. The System Cache takes memory and uses it to store data that was accessed from the drive, and stores it in memory. While working on one client engagement, by dedicating large amounts of memory for System Cache, we were able to achieve a 500% application performance increase by using the System Cache functionality.

The current amount of memory used by the System Cache is viewable through the Task Manager. To determine how much memory you are using for the System Cache, select the Performance tab within the Task Manager. The System Cache displays within the Physical Memory section of the Task Manager, as shown in Figure 10.28. This is a server running the RMS (Windows 64-bit) with 6GB of memory installed (4.57GB in use plus just over 1GB of System Cache in use). For Operations Manager 2007, the System Cache provides benefits to the RMS by caching frequently accessed files such as those used by the OpsMgr programs that run. A great discussion on how this works is available at http://channel9.msdn.com/ShowPost.aspx?PostID=61242.

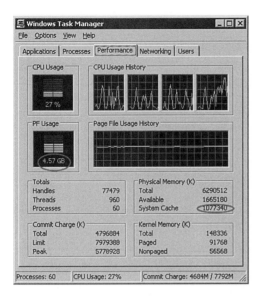

FIGURE 10.28   Task Manager on RMS.

To summarize our recommendations on memory: Go big! Particularly with 64-bit operating systems, the cost required to install systems using over 2GB of memory is not anywhere near where it was in recent years. For the RMS, go with 8GB if the cost is not prohibitive. For database servers, go with 16GB (or 32GB if that is not cost prohibitive). The more memory, the better the performance you will have with your Operations Manager environment.

Operations Manager itself will notify you when you are reaching bottlenecks with your servers that run your Operations Manager components. During one deployment, we started with an RMS on a server that had 2GB of memory, but due to messages from OpsMgr, we ended up increasing it to 6GB. On the database side, we started with a 4GB configuration but ended up upgrading it to an 8GB configuration (again due to bottlenecks identified by OpsMgr itself).

Disk Performance

Disk performance is extremely important, particularly for the database-related components used by Operations Manager. From a disk perspective, the more spindles the SQL Server has, the better it will perform. The preferred method is to configure your system using multiple drives for the operating system, SQL binaries, and the Windows page file (swap file), transaction logs, and data files:

- ▶ Use a Redundant Array of Independent Disks (RAID) 1 configuration for the operating system drive.

- ▶ Use RAID 1 or RAID 5 for SQL binaries and the swap file; these files are used as read-only.

▶ Use RAID 1 for the transaction log files.

▶ Use RAID 5 or RAID 10 for the database files.

The exception to this rule is when you are connecting your SQL Server to a Storage Array Network (SAN). In this situation, you would use the following configuration:

▶ Use RAID 1 for the operating system drive (locally stored), or boot to the SAN.

▶ Use RAID 1 or RAID 5 for SQL binaries and the swap file because they are always read from (locally stored), or store the data on the SAN.

▶ Use the SAN to store the log files on one Logical Unit Number (LUN). The personnel responsible for configuring the SAN can best determine the actual RAID configuration for the LUN.

▶ Use the SAN to store the database files on another LUN.

Remember that when it comes to performance, the more spindles you can put to a drive, the better the performance you will get from it. As an example, a RAID 10 array with four drives outperforms a RAID 10 array with two drives!

TIP

TEMPDB Placement

Configuring the SQL Server tempdb (data and log) on its own spindles boosts performance. You may want to consider this in deployments with over 1000 agents.

Processor and Network Performance

Although processor performance is important in Operations Manager, OpsMgr bottlenecks are most likely from memory or disk from a performance perspective. The same applies from a networking perspective. For high-usage environments, consider a gigabit network connection for the various OpsMgr servers to communicate with each other; but a bottleneck on the network adapter is not very likely from what we have seen.

Summary

In this chapter, we have discussed some of the more complex configurations that can exist within an Operations Manager 2007 environment. These include multihomed configurations, connected management groups, gateway servers, redundant configurations, and performance considerations. The next chapter discusses securing Operations Manager 2007.

Securing Operations Manager 2007

This chapter examines different aspects of securing Operations Manager (OpsMgr) 2007. We discuss user roles, Run As Profiles and Run As Accounts, and service accounts used by OpsMgr 2007. We also consider how security for OpsMgr works across multiple domains, how Operations Manager uses the Gateway Server Component to monitor non-trusted domains, procedures for monitoring agents in workgroups, ACS security, using OpsMgr in an environment with firewalls, and securing communications.

Role-based Security

The Operations console includes access to over 150 available operations, which fall under the following categories:

▶ **Monitoring**—These operations include opening views, resolving alerts, executing tasks, and overriding monitors.

▶ **Authoring**—Authoring includes creating and modifying management packs.

▶ **Reporting**—Reporting operations consist of using and designing reports and managing report security.

▶ **Administration**—Administrative operations include configuring security; importing, exporting, and removing management packs; changing global settings; discovering computers and devices; configuring notification; and installing agents.

As Operations Manager can monitor many types of applications potentially administered by multiple teams, using role-based security gives an administrator the ability to limit privileges that users have for various aspects of OpsMgr. User roles determine the level of functionality a user will have. Roles can also limit the scope of views and tasks that are available to each user.

Role-based security has been evolving on the Windows platform since Windows NT 3.1. You will find user roles in SQL Server and Exchange; role-based security is part of Windows Server 2003. Operations Manager 2007 uses roles to determine whether a process (an instance of an executing program) is privileged by checking the security context for a particular user or group.

Introducing Authorization Manager

When security was simple, a basic security implementation might be to authorize users to access a particular application. This usually is not enough, as you may want to define the type of access a user has within that application. Think of that as different security roles.

A simplistic mapping of roles would be to say:

> [User] has a [Role]

However, different roles often have overlapping tasks within an application, so now our mapping (or model) would be:

> [User] has [Role] is allowed to execute [Tasks] made up of [Operations]

Using this model, an application can check if a given user has permission to execute a certain operation and not worry about everything in-between.

Many packaged applications (and some written in-house) have developed their own security sub-systems to enable this concept. In Windows 2003, Microsoft gives us Authorization Manager (AzMan) to manage security subsystems.

AzMan is a Component Object Model (COM)-based Application Programming Interface (API) for managing application security. It allows you to define fine-grained operations that you can group into tasks, which you then can assign to roles. The data store for this can be an xml file or Active Directory. OpsMgr's implementation of AzMan uses an xml file named MomAuth.xml.

User roles do more than limit console access in Operations Manager. OpsMgr's role-based security also controls access to any operation that utilizes the SDK (Software Development Kit). Because nearly everything written in Operations Manager 2007 uses the SDK, this means that security at the SDK level encompasses anything that uses the OpsMgr class libraries to connect to the SDK service. As you can see in Figure 11.1, the SDK is responsible for communications between the client and the management service and accessing the Operations database, isolating the risk associated with remoting. Think of the SDK service as the gatekeeper for all access.

Figure 11.1 also shows the integration of Windows Communication Foundation (WCF) technology in SDK communications throughout Operations Manager. The initial authentication attempt uses the user's credentials and the Kerberos protocol. If Kerberos does not work, another attempt is made by using NTLM. If authentication still fails, the user is prompted to provide credentials. After authentication takes place, the data stream is encrypted as a function of either the Kerberos protocol or Secure Sockets Layer (SSL) with NTLM. Additional information about WCF is available at http://go.microsoft.com/fwlink/?LinkId=87429.

In Operations Manager, when a console is launched, it connects to the SDK service on the Root Management Server (RMS). The SDK service then connects to the Operations database. Because user roles go through the SDK, they impact not only what one can do at the console but also with PowerShell cmdlets and custom clients.

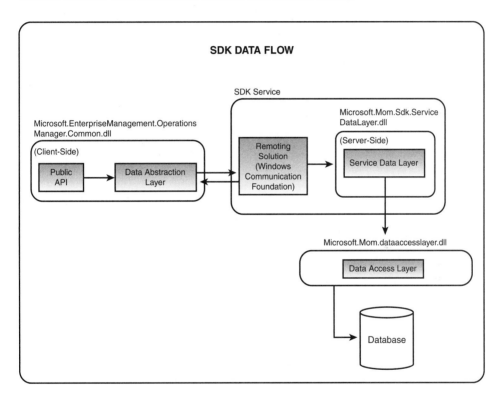

FIGURE 11.1   SDK data flow.

Active Directory Integration with Operations Manager 2007

Active Directory (AD) is integrated with Operations Manager in two ways:

▶ You can add Active Directory Users and Groups to OpsMgr user roles to control access to objects, views, and so on. Assigning AD groups to roles gives you a centralized mechanism to manage your OpsMgr security. Operations Manager 2007's role-based security encompasses all components within a management group.

▶ Active Directory is also used with OpsMgr to assign computers to a management group. We discuss this in Chapter 9, "Installing and Configuring Agents."

Roles specify the types of operations a user can perform and the scope of these operations:

```
[User] has [Role] is allowed to execute [Tasks] made up of [Operations]
```

As examples, a user role that grants authoring rights may limit its scope to a particular list of classes, whereas a user role that grants monitoring rights may limit that scope to a list of monitoring groups and views. This is diametrically different from MOM 2005, where the only way to limit a user's scope was to build a customized view as a client-side filter (which has limited results both then and now, as views do not actually limit security access) or create a separate management group—a configuration often implemented for security administrators. OpsMgr 2007 has security scoping, which directly limits access to the objects.

When discussing roles, one should also be aware of profiles and scopes:

- ▶ **Profiles**—Operations or tasks such as resolving alerts, executing tasks, overriding monitors, creating user roles, viewing alerts, viewing events, and so on, are grouped into profiles.

- ▶ **Scopes**—A scope defines the entity groups, object types, tasks, or views a profile is restricted to. Scopes do not apply to all profiles.

A role is a combination of a profile (capabilities) and a scope (the breadth of data and objects one is able to access). A *role assignment* is an association of Windows security groups and/or users to Operations Manager roles. Typically, AD security groups are assigned to roles, with individual user accounts assigned to those security groups. This again differs from MOM 2005, where each management server used local security groups to restrict access, without limiting access to scope. Role assignments also allow OpsMgr to authorize a user based on the union of his or her roles.

Table 11.1 lists the roles provided by Operations Manager out-of-the-box with their associated profiles and scope.

You may note from Table 11.1 that the built-in roles do not limit scope, meaning they have access to all groups, views, and tasks (with the exception of the Report Security Administrators). To narrow scope, you can create your own custom roles based on the Operator, Read-Only Operator, Author, and Advanced Operator profiles. There is no limit to the number of user roles you can implement.

CAUTION

Security Alert

Adding a machine account to a user role allows those services running in the Local System or Network Service context on the computer to have Software Development Kit (SDK) access.

TABLE 11.1   OpsMgr-Provided Role Definitions

Role Name	Profile Type	Profile Description	Role Scope
Operations Manager Administrators— Created at setup time, cannot be deleted, must contain one or more security groups. OpsMgr Administrators control who has access to the different areas of the console.	Administrator	The Administrator profile includes full privileges to Operations Manager, and cannot be scoped (similar to MOM Administrators in MOM 2005).	Full access to all Operations Manager data, services, administrative, and authoring tools.
Operations Manager Advanced Operators— Created at setup, is globally scoped, cannot be deleted.	Advanced Operator	Limited change access to Operations Manager configuration; ability to create overrides to rules and monitors for targets or groups of targets within the configured scope.	All groups, views, and tasks currently present and those imported in the future.
Operations Manager Authors—Created at setup time, is globally scoped, cannot be deleted.	Author	Ability to create, edit, and delete tasks, rules, monitors, and views within configured scope (similar to MOM Authors in MOM 2005). Members of the Author User profile have access to credentials for only the items they have the rights to author.	All groups, views, and tasks currently present and those imported in the future.
Operations Manager Operators—Created at setup time, is globally scoped, cannot be deleted.	Operator	Ability to interact with alerts, execute tasks, and access views according to configured scope (similar to MOM Users in MOM 2005).	All groups, views, and tasks currently present and those imported in the future.

TABLE 11.1   Continued

Role Name	Profile Type	Profile Description	Role Scope
Operations Manager Read-Only Operator— Created at setup, is globally scoped, cannot be deleted. Users who are members of the Read-Only Operator role cannot view or run any tasks. For this reason, no tasks appear in a task status view opened by a Read-Only Operator.	Read-Only Operator	Ability to view alerts and access views according to configured scope.	All groups and views currently present and those imported in the future.
Operations Manager Report Operator— Created at setup, is globally scoped. Users must be a member of the Report Operator Users role to run reports. When a report runs, it uses the OpsMgr SDK to ask what the report membership is of the user running the report. What is actually being checked is the role of the user. The OpsMgr SDK returns a GUID and the report itself has a GUID; if these match, access is allowed.	Report Operator	Grants members the ability to view reports according to configured scope.	Globally scoped.

TABLE 11.1   Continued

Role Name	Profile Type	Profile Description	Role Scope
Operations Manager Report Security Administrators— Integrates SQL Reporting Services security with OpsMgr user roles, gives Operations Manager Administrators the ability to control access to reports, and cannot be scoped. Users assigned to this role have access to all report data in the Data Warehouse database.	Report Security Administrator	Enables integration of SQL Reporting Services security with Operations Manager Roles.	No scope.

The Administrator profile is not customizable, meaning you cannot create additional user roles based on the Administrator profile, or modify the built-in Operations Manager Administrator's role. An administrator can do anything; all you can do is limit membership to this role.

By default, the Operations Manager Administrator is the only account with the right to view and act on monitoring data. All other users must first have a user role assigned in order to view or act on monitoring data.

Creating User Roles

You can add AD security groups or individual accounts to any of the predefined user roles. When creating a role, you have the option to narrow the scope of the groups, tasks, and views that it can access. If you create a user role based on either the Author or Advanced Operator profiles, those users will need access to the Operations console to perform the tasks those profiles allow.

If a user does not have the right to view a monitored object or perform an action, that object or action does not appear or it will be grayed out in the Operations console. (By contrast, the Web console is best for users with a user role based on the Operator or Read-Only Operator profiles; only the Monitoring and the My Workspace panes are available in the Web console, which is used to view monitoring data, run tasks, and resolve alerts.)

Let's step through the process of creating a new Author user role. Authors are able to create, edit, and delete tasks, rules, monitors, and views within their scope. Navigate to the Administration space in the Operations console and perform the following steps:

1. In the Administration pane, select Security. Right-click on User Roles, select New User Role, and then select the Author profile as displayed in Figure 11.2 to initiate the Create User Role Wizard.

2. In the General page of the wizard, enter a name for the User role name, and then click Add. (We typed **Odyssey_Author**.)

3. On the Select User or Groups dialog box, specify the Active Directory users or groups to add to this role and click OK.

   As a best practice, you will add groups rather than individual users to a role. On the General page, add an optional description. Figure 11.3 shows this page completed with the User role name, Description, and User role members fields populated. Click Next.

4. The Author Scope page asks you to Approve Targets. Members of this user role can create or edit monitors, rules, tasks, or views for approved targets.

   To narrow the scope, specify the option that Only targets explicitly added to the "Approved targets" grid are approved, and click the + Add icon to bring up the Scope Management Pack Objects by target(s) dialog. We will select the Agent and Windows Computer as targets (meaning that members of this role can create or edit monitors, rules, tasks, or views only for the Agent and Window Computer objects), and then click OK to return to the Author Scope pane, displayed in Figure 11.4. Click Next.

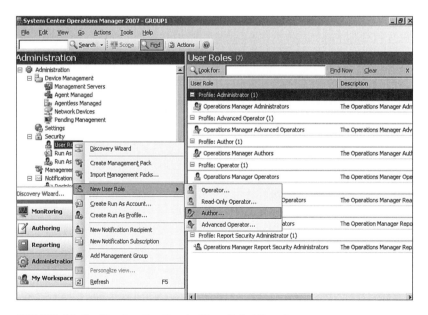

FIGURE 11.2   Starting the Create User Role Wizard.

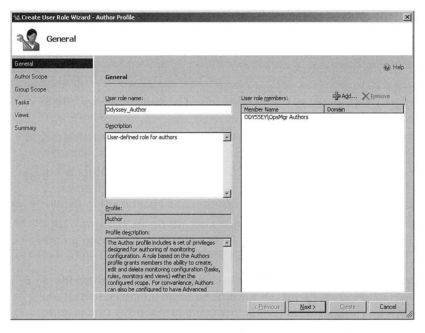

FIGURE 11.3   The General page of the Create User Role Wizard.

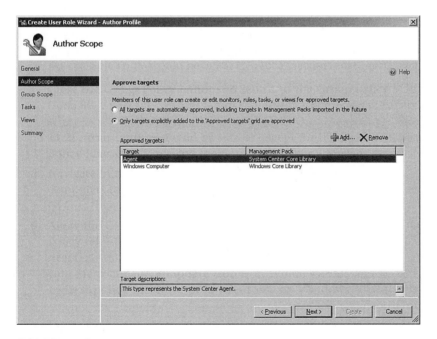

FIGURE 11.4   Defining the scope of a role.

5. The Group Scope page allows you to restrict this role to setting overrides and monitoring objects in specific computer groups. The default scope is the entire management group. For this example, we will take the default. Click Next.

6. The next two pages enable you to limit the tasks and views for members of this role.
Click Next on each page to permit all tasks and views.

7. The Summary page displays all selected properties. Click Create to create the role
and complete the wizard.

This was a fairly simple illustration of creating a role. We can further narrow the scope of
this authoring role for setting overrides, restricting access to particular computer groups,
or limiting its tasks and views. The actions you can restrict will vary based on the profile
associated with any particular role.

Groups, like other OpsMgr objects, are defined in management packs. Your Operations
Manager installation created a number of groups from the management packs (MPs)
imported during that process. If your existing groups do not contain the monitored
objects you need for a scope (you can check group membership using the
EnumerateGroupsAndMembers PowerShell script introduced in Chapter 8, "Configuring
and Using Operations Manager 2007"), create a group that does. To do this, exit the
Create User Role Wizard, switch to the Authoring space, and use the Create Group Wizard
(Authoring -> Groups, right-click on Groups to select Create a New Group, which initiates
the wizard) to create a group that better suits your needs.

How do permissions work when your user account belongs to multiple roles? Similar to
how security group privileges work with the Windows file system, the accesses given to
the roles are combined so your access is the combination of the accesses granted to all
those roles. If any one role gives you access, you will have access. One difference here
from security group permissions is there is no concept of "no access." There is no way to
"deny access" via a role.

TIP

Monitoring Security Access

Review your role memberships on a regular basis to ensure that only the necessary
user accounts and groups have access to the appropriate functionality.

We can also use PowerShell to administer roles. The next sections of this chapter look at
PowerShell cmdlets for adding a user to a user role, and creating a Report Operator role.

Adding Users to a User Role with the Get-UserRole cmdlet and SDK
Currently, there is no cmdlet for adding a user to a user role, but Boris Yanushpolsky of
Microsoft has provided the following technique to assist by combining the Get-UserRole
cmdlet with the SDK.

The following code snippet adds the \ADOperators group to the Operations Manager Operators user role:

```
$operatorsUserRole = Get-UserRole | where {$_.DisplayName
➥-eq "Operations Manager Operators"}
$operatorsUserRole.Users.Add("odyssey\AdOperators")
$operatorsUserRole.Update()
```

The next snippet removes the \ADOperators group from a user role. It is very similar; you just call the *Remove* method rather than *Add*, as follows:

```
$operatorsUserRole = Get-UserRole | where {$_.DisplayName
➥-eq "Operations Manager Operators"}
$operatorsUserRole.Users.Remove("odyssey\AdOperators")
$operatorsUserRole.Update()
```

Be sure to call the Update method (the last line of code in the snippet) on the user role object to save your changes.

This information is also available at http://blogs.msdn.com/boris_yanushpolsky/archive/2007/08/13/adding-users-to-a-user-role.aspx.

Creating a Report Operator Role

Let's say you need to create a role that only grants the users who belong to that role the ability to run Audit reports. However, the Operations console does not include the capability of creating the Report Operator role. Once again, the PowerShell Command Shell comes to the rescue! The following script is provided by Eugene Bykov of Microsoft to create an object called Test Report Operator Role:

```
$mg = (get-item .).ManagementGroup
$reportOperator = $mg.GetMonitoringProfiles() | where
➥{$_.Name -eq "ReportOperator"}
$obj = new-object
➥Microsoft.EnterpriseManagement.Monitoring.Security.MonitoringUserRole
$obj.Name = "TestReportOperatorRole"
$obj.DisplayName = "Test Report Operator Role"
$obj.Description = "Test Report Operator Role"
$obj.MonitoringProfile = $reportOperator
$mg.InsertMonitoringUserRole($obj)
```

After you execute this script, "Test Report Operator Role" appears in the console, and you will be able to add users to it.

The SystemCenterForum folks have modified Eugene's script to make it parameter-driven. The modified script accepts the parameters listed in Table 11.2.

TABLE 11.2   Parameters for the AddReportingUserRole.ps1 Script

Parameter	Explanation
rootMS	The FQDN or NetBIOS name of the RMS
roleUserName	The name user role
roleDisplayName	The display name of the role
roleDescription	The description of the role

A sample command-line execution would look like this:

```
PowerShell ./AddReportingUserRole.ps1 rootMS.server.local DBTestRole 'Test DB Role'
➥'A test role created by PowerShell'
```

The PowerShell script follows:

```
param($rootMS,$roleUserName,$roleDisplayName,$roleDescription)
#Initializing the Ops Mgr 2007 Powershell provider
    add-pssnapin "Microsoft.EnterpriseManagement.OperationsManager.Client"
    ➥-ErrorVariable errSnapin;
    set-location "OperationsManagerMonitoring::" -ErrorVariable errSnapin;
    new-managementGroupConnection -ConnectionString:$rootMS
    ➥-ErrorVariable errSnapin;
    set-location $rootMS -ErrorVariable errSnapin;
#Checks to see if it failed or succeeded in loading the provider
    if ($errSnapin.count -eq 0){
        Write-host ''nOpsMgr 2007 PSSnapin initialized!'n';
    }
    else{
        Write-host ''nOpsMgr 2007 PSSnapin failed initialize!'nPlease verify you
are running this script on a Ops Mgr 2007 Management Server";
        Write-Host;
    }
$mg = (get-item .).ManagementGroup
$reportOperator = $mg.GetMonitoringProfiles() | where
➥{$_.Name -eq "ReportOperator"}
$obj = new-object Microsoft.EnterpriseManagement.Monitoring.Security.
➥MonitoringUserRole
$obj.Name = $roleUserName
$obj.DisplayName = $roleDisplayName
$obj.Description = $roleDescription
$obj.MonitoringProfile = $reportOperator
$mg.InsertMonitoringUserRole($obj)
```

> **NOTE**
>
> **On the CD**
>
> We include Neale Browne's modified script (AddReportingUserRole.ps1) as content on the CD accompanying this book.

Troubleshooting User Roles

After user roles are created and scoped to specific tasks, the associated data is stored in *%ProgramFiles%*\System Center Operations Manager 2007\SDK Service State\MomAuth.xml. You can view the contents of this file using the AzMan.msc Microsoft Management Console (MMC) snap-in. To run AzMan (Authorization Manager), perform the following steps:

1. From Start -> Run, type **MMC**, and click OK.
2. When the MMC console comes up, click File –> Add/Remove Snap-in..., then the Add... button.
3. Select Authorization Manager and click Add, Close, and then OK.
4. In the MMC, right-click on Authorization Manager.
5. Select Open Authorization Store....
6. Browse to the MomAuth.xml file (located on the RMS at *%ProgramFiles%*\System Center Operations Manager 2007\SDK Service State) and click OK.

This process allows an administrator to browse the different rights and operations that are loaded into Authorization Manager, and is useful when rights are not working as expected. As an example, Figure 11.5 shows the mapping for the Odyssey_Author user role we just defined (see the "Creating User Roles" section of this chapter) to the AD OpsMgr Authors group.

> **TIP**
>
> **A Shortcut to AzMan**
>
> Another way to invoke Authorization Manager is Start -> Run and then type **AzMan.msc**.

Resetting the Group Assigned to the Administrators Role

During setup, you assigned a security group to the Operations Manager 2007 Administrators role (associated with the Ops Admins group in Active Directory). By default, the BUILTIN\Administrators group on the RMS in assigned to this role, and the local Administrators group is the only member of the Operations Manager Administrators role. If you plan to use the Active Directory-based agent assignment feature discussed in Chapter 9, "Installing and Configuring Agents," this role should contain a domain global or universal group.

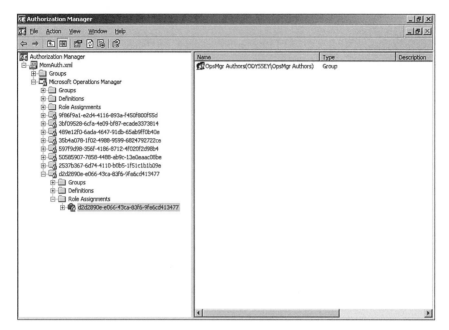

FIGURE 11.5   Using Authorization Manager to view role assignments.

If an incorrect group is configured for the Administration role, you will be unable to open the Operations console. Normally you could use the console to change the group associated with a role, but in this case you are not able to start the console! To reset this group, you will need to stop the SDK Service, edit the MOMAuth.xml file, and update the data field in the AuthorizationStore database table. The specific steps are listed next.

To stop the Operations Manager SDK Service, perform the following steps:

1. Logon to the RMS using an account with Administrator privileges.
2. Select Start -> Run.
3. In the Run dialog box, type **services.msc**, then click OK.
4. At the Services console, right-click OpsMgr SDK Service, and then click Stop.

To edit the MOMAuth.xml file, perform the following procedure. Be sure to back up the xml file before performing any edits:

1. At the Windows desktop, right-click Start -> Explore.
2. Navigate to *%ProgramFiles%*\System Center Operations Manager 2007\SDK Service State, right-click the MOMAuth.xml file, select Open With..., and then click Notepad.

3. In the MOMAuth.xml file, search for the following string:

   ```
   Description="OperationsManagerAdministrators"
   ```

   Verify that you have found the AzRole Guid tag.

4. The following SIDS are listed as members:

   ▶ S-1-5-18 (Local System)

   ▶ The SID for the Administrators group that was entered during setup

5. Replace the Administrators group SID with the desired SID (the SID for BUILTIN\Administrators is S-1-5-32-544).

6. Save the file. (In Notepad, click File, and then click Save.) Remember to make a backup of the original file first!

Next, copy MOMAuth.xml into the clipboard and replace the contents of the data field in the AuthorizationStore table in the Operations database:

1. In Notepad, select Format, and verify that Word Wrap is not enabled.

2. Select Edit, and then click Select All.

3. Select Edit, and click Copy. Close Notepad.

4. On the Windows desktop, select Start -> Programs -> Microsoft SQL Server 2005 -> SQL Server Management Studio.

5. In the Connect to Server dialog box, click Connect.

6. In the Object Explorer pane, expand Databases, right-click OperationsManager (or the name you assigned to the Operations database if different), and then click New Query.

7. In the query pane, type **update authorizationstore** and then press Enter.

8. Type **set Data = '**.

9. Paste the contents of the MOMAuth.xml file by pressing CTRL+V.

10. Type ' (single quote), and then click Execute. Figure 11.6 shows the query pane.

11. Now exit SQL Management Studio (click File, and then Exit).

Last, you need to restart the OpsMgr SDK Service:

1. If the Services console is not open, at the Windows desktop, select Start -> Run. Type **services.msc** in the Run dialog box and click OK.

2. In the Services dialog box, right-click OpsMgr SDK Service and then click Start.

3. Exit the console (File, and then click Exit).

These steps update the group assigned to the Administration role. You should now be able to open the console.

FIGURE 11.6   The SQL Query pane to update the authorization store.

TIP

Adding Groups to the Operations Manager Administrators User Role

If you try to add groups to the OpsMgr Administrators User role, you may notice that the graphical user interface will only let you search on domain groups. The BUILTIN\Administrators is a special case; it is the only local group allowed to be a member of the Operations Manager Administrators role.

Run As Profiles and Run As Accounts

Management pack components such as rules, monitors, tasks, and discoveries require credentials to run on the targeted computer. By default, these run using the Management Server Action account.

Run As Profiles

A *Run As Profile* allows a management pack author to associate an identity other than the default Action account with a particular module so that it can run using the credentials of that identity. At a minimum, the account used needs to have logon locally rights.

Run As Profiles take a Windows user account (which can be a local or domain account) and apply it to a specified profile in Operations Manager. For example, the Exchange management pack has a profile; you can assign a user to it so it will run using the credentials of that user. A Run As Account is the user account assigned to a Run As Profile. (We discuss Run As Accounts in more detail in the "Run As Accounts" section of the chapter.) Similar to Run As Accounts in Windows, privileges are elevated only while the action targeted by the Run As Profile is running.

Operations Manager automatically creates five Run As Profiles during setup:

▶ **Default Action Account**—The Operations Manager Default Action account is the default Windows account the Operations Manager processes run under. The account needs sufficient privileges to gather data from providers (modules that gather performance counter information and events). The minimum required permissions are Log On Locally, Performance Monitor Users, and a member of the Users group.

▶ **Data Warehouse Action Account**—If specified, this account will run all Data Warehouse collection and synchronization rules, rather than the regular Action account. If not overridden by the Data Warehouse SQL Authentication Action account during your OpsMgr Reporting setup, this account is also used by collection and synchronization rules to connect to the data warehouse database using Windows integrated authentication.

TIP

Bug in OpsMgr OpsMgr Code When Using the Data Warehouse Action Account

The released version of OpsMgr 2007 has a bug causing the Management Server Action account to be used as the Default Data Warehouse Action account, rather than the Data Warehouse Action account you specified. This is fixed in Service Pack 1 (SP 1).

As a workaround, you can create a Run As Account (type Simple), set the username and password to a single space, and in the same-name profile, associate this account with all your management servers, including the RMS. You will also want to verify that the Data Warehouse Action account profile is correctly associated with an account for all management servers to use as the Windows authentication account.

▶ **Data Warehouse SQL Authentication Action Account**—If specified, this login name and password is used by collection and synchronization rules to connect to the data warehouse database using SQL authentication.

▶ **Notification Action Account**—This is a Windows account used by Notification Rules. Its email address is used as the email and instant message "From" address.

▶ **Privileged Monitoring Profile**—Unlike all other profiles, this profile defaults to Local System, but it can be changed to use another privileged user if necessary. All tasks and workflows requiring system level access should use this profile; typically, this would be discovery workflows. Do not use the Privileged Monitoring Profile just to guarantee access to resources—this adds unnecessary risk to your installation.

Background on the Privileged Monitoring Profile

Near the end of the beta cycle for OpsMgr 2007, Microsoft created the Privileged Monitoring Profile. There were several reasons for this:

▶ Management Pack Authors were creating their own profiles for discovery, as discovery often requires administrator-level or other privileged rights. When there are a large number of profiles, it becomes difficult to manage the mappings, especially when the machine topology changes frequently—as every new system needs to have all the discovery mappings adjusted or it will not discover anything.

▶ Some MP Authors were using the Action account for discovery, basically ensuring the account had to be Local System.

The Privileged Monitoring Profile was created to help prevent these two scenarios.

Run As Accounts

A *Run As Account* typically maps to an Active Directory user account, although SQL credentials, forms authorization credentials, binary credentials (certificate authorization), HTTP basic authorization, HTTP digest authorization, and Simple Network Management Protocol (SNMP) community strings are also supported. The Run As Account represents an identity that can be associated with a Run As Profile. The profile maps the Run As Account to a specific computer. Rather than assigning additional rights to the Action account, using Run As Accounts and Run As Profiles provide the ability to run a task, rule, or monitor with an account that has the necessary rights.

There are also single use accounts—these are accounts that you enter to run a single task. The Operations console allows you to use the default account or a specified account. These accounts use the same infrastructure as Run As Accounts, except that the credentials are not kept. They are encrypted in memory and then discarded after use.

How Run As Accounts Help with Management Packs

Let's look at an example where using a Run As Account helps the Odyssey Company with their monitoring requirements. John is working on a custom SQL management pack that includes a task to generate database statistics. John knows that the Action account may not have sufficient rights to run this task. However, Eric, the Odyssey DBA and SQL Server Administrator, has the required access. John needs to configure the task to run with Eric's credentials.

As a Management Pack Author, one should always ask: "Am I forcing the Action account to have a higher level of privilege than necessary?" If anything requires more than the minimum level of privilege, the MP Author should create a new profile; otherwise, installations will not be able to maintain reduced Action account privileges.

John, using the Management Pack Authoring Tools, creates a Run As Profile and associates it with the task module he is including in his management pack. When the management pack containing the database statistics task is later imported into Operations Manager 2007, the Run As Profile associated with this task is included in the import and appears in the list of available Run As Profiles (under Administration -> Security -> Run As Profiles in the Operations console).

The OpsMgr administrator will use the Create Run As Account Wizard to create a Run As Account to run the task, configured with Eric's credentials. The Run As Profile's properties are then modified to add the Run As Account that the task will use. You need to explicitly define the target computer on which the Run As Account will run in the Run As Profile. (By default, all rules, monitors, and tasks on an agent run as the Action account.)

When configuring Run As Accounts, consider the rights the Action account needs and choose a user account with those privileges. Generally speaking, using a Domain Admin account is not a good choice! Using a highly privileged account ensures that all management pack features will work, but this introduces risks associated with using high-privileged accounts that have more than the required permissions to do the job, and will make your auditors unhappy.

TIP

Check Credentials When Creating Run As Accounts

The Create Run As Account Wizard does not actually verify the credentials you specify when creating the Run As Account. If you enter incorrect credentials, the account you create will not successfully run its assigned monitor, rule, or task. The Wizard does not verify the credentials—because the account might exist in another forest or individual computer's (member or workgroup computer) SAM. Since there is no check, Windows accounts are not verified either.

Of course, when OpsMgr tries to use that "bad" account, you will get an alert! As a best practice, you should verify that the account exists and its credentials are adequate before using it as a Run As Account.

You can associate multiple Run As Accounts with a single Run As Profile. This is useful in cases where you are using a Run As Profile on different machines and each machine requires different credentials. Let's say there is a task that a person has rights to run on Odyssey's Hurricane server but someone else has rights to run it on Argonaut, our Exchange front-end server. We would configure separate Run As Accounts for each server, and associate both individuals with a single Run As Profile. You would make this assignment on each computer.

Required Accounts

OpsMgr uses a number of service and action accounts on the OpsMgr server components and managed computers. The RMS requires two accounts to communicate with other Operations Manager 2007 components, as follows:

- ▶ The Management Server Action account
- ▶ The SDK and Config Service account

You must specify credentials for these two accounts when installing the RMS.

When pushing out an agent, you can provide credentials for several accounts:

- ▶ The Computer Discovery account
- ▶ The Agent Action account
- ▶ The Agent Installation account

The default is to specify the Management Server Action account; all other accounts default to using either Local System or the default Action account (the Management Server Action account).

Each management server and agent runs an instance of the OpsMgr Health service, which has an associated Health service account. The service monitors the health of the computer and potentially the health of other computers. The Health service uses Local System; this should not be changed.

If you install the Operations Manager 2007 Reporting component, you need to specify credentials for two additional accounts, as follows:

- ▶ The Data Warehouse Write Action account
- ▶ The Data Reader account

Table 11.3 lists the accounts used during installation. If you are using domain accounts and your domain Group Policy Object (GPO) allows passwords to expire, you either must change the passwords on the service accounts according to your password expiration policy, override the settings for these accounts so the passwords will not expire, or use low maintenance system accounts. Password information entered for accounts is stored, encrypted, in the Operations database.

> **TIP**
>
> **Advantages of Using Built-in Accounts**
>
> Consider using built-in accounts where it is practical. The operating system maintains these accounts, and they are not affected by password expiration policies. In addition, the passwords to these accounts are not exposed.

We discuss the accounts in Table 11.3 in the following sections.

TABLE 11.3   Service Accounts Required for OpsMgr 2007 Installation

Account Name	When Used	Used For	Use for Low Maintenance	Use for High Security
Management Server Action account	Management Server setup.	Collects data from providers, runs responses, writes to Operations database.	Local System	Domain account
SDK and Configuration Service account	Management Server setup.	Writes to Operations database, runs services.	Local System	Domain account
(Windows) Administrator account	Discovery and push agent install.	Installing agents.	Domain or local administrator account	Domain or local administrator account
Agent Action account	Discovery and push agent install, manual installations. For AD integration, this account is set to Local System, but can be modified later.	Gathers information and runs responses on managed computers.	Local System	Low-privilege domain account
Data Warehouse Write Action account	Reporting Server setup.	Writes to the Data Warehouse database.	Low-privilege domain account	Low-privilege domain account
Data Reader account	Reporting Server setup.	Query SQL Reporting Services database; also used for the SQL Reporting Services (SRS) Internet Information Services (IIS) Application Pool account to connect to the RMS.	Low-privilege domain account	Low-privilege domain account

Action Account

Every management server and agent requires an Action account.

The Action account gathers information about, and runs responses on, management servers or any computer with an installed agent. You can use the default Action account (located under Administration -> Security -> Run As Profiles), or specify a different account for the Action account. Unless an action has been associated with a Run As Profile, the credentials used to perform the action will be those defined for the Action account.

TIP

Changing the Action Account on Groups of Computers

The OpsMgr 2007 Resource Kit includes a PowerShell script that allows you to set the Action account on groups of computers with a single command. You can download the Action Account Tool directly from Microsoft's download center at http://www.microsoft.com/downloads/details.aspx?familyid=1D9A8D81-0E42-4076-88A9-8E6C08993054&displaylang=en (or go through the System Center Operations Manager 2007 Tools and Utilities page at http://go.microsoft.com/fwlink/?LinkId=94593 to access this link). The zip file includes a PowerShell script, set-ActionAccount.ps1. Using the Operations console, you can use this utility to set the Action account on multiple computers in a computer group you create, or on multiple computers using discovered inventory. Be sure to include the domain (or computer) of which the Action account is a member when you specify the account.

The Monitoring Host Process

Actions performed by the Action account or a specific Run As Account (Run As Accounts are discussed in the "Run As Accounts" section of this chapter) are run by the MonitoringHost.exe process. Each account has its own instance of MonitoringHost.exe, so there may be many MonitoringHost.exe processes running under many identities, at any given time.

The MonitoringHost.exe process manages workflows. These workflows perform actions such as the following:

▶ Monitoring and collecting Windows NT Event log data

▶ Monitoring and collecting Windows performance counter data

▶ Monitoring and collecting Windows Management Instrumentation (WMI) data

▶ Running actions such as scripts or batches

▶ Monitoring and collecting application-specific log data, such as IIS logs

▶ Running a managed code module

▶ Executing tasks, performing discovery, and other useful actions

11

Multiple Monitoring Host Instances

It is not unusual for more than one data provider, or more than one response, to run simultaneously. OpsMgr runs each provider or response in a separate MonitoringHost instance to protect other instances of MonitoringHost.exe in the event of a failure. Workflows are merged under the same identity in the same MonitoringHost, unless a workflow has specifically requested to be isolated in the workflows definition in the management pack. Typically workflows are not isolated, as creating multiple processes becomes expensive in terms of system resources.

The Management Server Action Account

The Management Server Action account is specified during your Operations Manager 2007 installation. You have the option to choose either the Local System account or a Domain or Local user account.

Each management server has its own Action account; with multiple management servers, you can specify the same Action account or use different accounts. The account is granted write access to the Operations and Data Warehouse databases. The Management Server Action account needs at least the following privileges:

▸ Member of the local Users group

▸ Read access to the Windows NT Event logs

▸ Member of the Performance Monitor Users group

▸ Granted the Allow Log on Locally permission

Using a Low-Privileged Account on the Agent

For Windows 2000 and Windows XP systems, the Agent Action account must have administrator-level rights.

In most instances, when running Windows Server 2003 and Windows Vista, you can use a low-privileged account for the Action account. This is the preferred approach, as you can use Run As Profiles for anything that requires a higher level of access. When using a low-privileged account, the account must have the following minimum privileges:

▸ Member of the local Users group

▸ Member of the local Performance Monitor Users group

▸ "Allow log on locally" permission (SetInteractiveLogonRight)

These privileges are the lowest privileges OpsMgr supports for the Action account. Other Run As Accounts can have lower privileges.

When specifying a domain account for the Action account, you may need to add privileges to the account for various management packs to function properly. Table 11.4 lists these privileges.

TABLE 11.4   Permissions Used by the Action Account

Access Type	Resource
Read	Read access to the Windows NT Event Logs.
Read	Read access to the Windows Performance Counters.
Performance Monitor Users	The Action account must be a member of the Performance Monitor Users security group.
Read	Read access to application-specific log files.
Read	If other log files or directories are monitored, the Action account must have Read access to the specific log file or directory.

The actual privileges needed for the Action account and the Run As Accounts vary depending on which management packs are running on the computer and how they are configured.

NOTE

Customizing the Action Account for Specific Management Packs

Different management packs may have different requirements for minimum privileges for the Action account, although a well-written management pack will not force the Action account to have higher privileges (with the possible exception of access to a particular logfile, and so on). Read the related management pack guide to determine the necessary privileges on the managed agent.

As an example, if the agent for which you are configuring the Action account is an Exchange server and a domain controller, you will need to combine the privileges necessary for each management pack to make sure that the Action account has the appropriate rights to support all of the management packs that apply to it. Each management pack has its own profile. Rights and privileges for each profile are added together, giving the effective rights.

There are several other caveats to using low-privileged accounts:

▶ You cannot enable Agentless Exception Monitoring (AEM) on a management server with a low-privileged Action account, although Microsoft is investigating how to address this.

▶ If a management pack will be reading an event in the Security Event log, you must assign the Action account the Manage Auditing and Security log privilege by using either a Local or a Global policy.

Note that Microsoft recommends using Audit Collection Services (ACS) for managing Security Event log data, unless that will not deliver the required functionality.

▶ If the RMS and Operations database are on separate computers and you select the option to use a Domain or Local account during installation, the Action account must be a domain account—a local user account on the RMS will not be able to access the database, and the setup process will fail.

TIP

Check Domain Policies

If you use domain accounts, password updating will have to be consistent with your organization's password policies. Otherwise, you will have to override those settings on an individual basis by either setting the passwords to not expire, or changing the passwords on the service accounts according to the schedule (or using system accounts that are not affected).

The Action Account on Windows 2000 and Windows XP Systems

On systems running Windows 2000 and Windows XP, the Action account must be a member of the local Administrators security group or run with the credentials of Local System. The Local System account has high privilege levels on the local system; it is part of the Administrators security group. On a domain controller, the Local System account privileges give it the equivalent to Domain Admin-level privileges.

The Action Account on Windows Server 2003 and Windows Vista Systems

Windows Server 2003 and Vista have additional built-in accounts. The built-in Network Service account has fewer access privileges on the system than the Local System account, but the Network Service account is still able to interact throughout the network with the credentials of the computer account.

NOTE

Why Not the Local Service Account?

For those in the know, a built-in account with lower privileges than the Local System account is the Local Service account. This has the same local privileges as the Network Service account and a smaller attack surface due to its inability to communicate outside the local computer.

However, the requirement to communicate with the management server prevents the Local Service account from being used, as it has no rights to communicate outside the local computer. The Network Service account has that right—although in OpsMgr 2007, all communication uses the Health service, which always runs as Local System. With MOM 2005, you could use the Local Service account, but at this time, that account is not supported for the OpsMgr 2007 Health service.

Changing the Credentials for the Action Account

If the Action account uses a password that expires, Operations Manager generates an alert 14 days before its expiration. Change the password in Active Directory, and then update the credentials in OpsMgr. Perform the following steps:

1. Open the Administration space in the Operations console.

2. In the Administration pane, select Administration -> Security -> Run As Accounts.

3. In the Run As Accounts pane, under Type: Action Account, right-click the account (domain\username) you want to change, and click Properties.

4. Click the Account tab in the Run As Account Properties dialog box (see Figure 11.7).

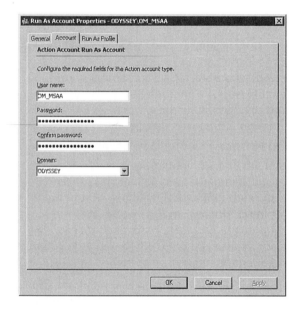

FIGURE 11.7   Run As Account user credentials.

5. Enter the user credentials for the new Action account, and click OK.

The Run As Account view provides a single spot to update all accounts.

The SDK and Config Service Account

Both the SDK service and the Config service use the SDK and Config Service account to update information in the Operations database. (Although the only management server running these services is the RMS, this does not mean the databases are only updated from the RMS, as OpsMgr uses Run As Profiles to grant appropriate rights. See the "Database Security" section in this chapter for additional information.)

11

Problems Installing OpsMgr Reporting If SDK Service Account Does Not Have Appropriate Access

You may receive an error with Event ID 26319 when you try to install the OpsMgr 2007 Reporting feature. This is because the SDK Service account does not have read access to the tokenGroupsGlobalAndUniversal attribute. The SDK service's authorization manager requires this access to determine the security groups to which a user belongs. This error occurs only if you are installing reporting in a domain environment where the Permissions compatible only with Windows 2000 or Windows 2003 Server operating systems option is enabled. To resolve the problem, perform the following steps:

1. Select Start -> Administrative Tools -> Active Directory Users and Computers.
2. From the Active Directory Users and Computers console, select Builtin, then double-click Windows Authorization Access Group.
3. Select the Members tab and add the SDK Service account to the members list.

You will also want to refer to http://support.microsoft.com/kb/938627 for updates or additional information on this error.

Credentials used for this account are assigned to the sdk_user role in the database. Note that data from managed entities written into the database may be of a security-related nature. Several options are available with this account:

▸ Run it as Local System

▸ Specify a user account

Using a local user account is not supported. Microsoft recommends the credentials assigned to this account are from a high-privileged account but not the same ones used for the Management Server Action account. The account must have Local Administrator privileges.

If you install the Operational database on a server other from the RMS and select Local System for the SDK and Configuration Service account, the computer account for the management server is assigned to the sdk_user role in the Operations database. You cannot use a local user account when the database and RMS are on separate computers.

Changing the SDK and Config Service Account to Use a Domain Account

To change the credentials for this account, perform the following steps on the RMS:

1. Ensure that the domain account is already created in Active Directory.
2. Start the Services console by clicking Start -> Run, typing **services.msc**, and then clicking OK.
3. Stop the OpsMgr SDK service and the OpsMgr Config service by right-clicking on each of them in the Details pane and selecting Stop.
4. Right-click the OpsMgr SDK service, select Properties, click the Log On tab, and click the This account option button.

5. Type a domain account name in the This account box; then type in its password in the Password box. Confirm the password and click OK.

6. Perform steps 4 and 5 for the OpsMgr Config service. Be sure to use the same account for both services!

7. Minimize the Services MMC.

8. Start SQL Server Management Studio (Start -> All Programs -> Microsoft SQL Server 2005 -> SQL Server Management Studio).

9. Connect to the server name and instance where the Operational database is installed.

10. Expand the console tree to open the Database node, right-click the Operational database, and select New Query.

11. Type and execute the following statement:

```
EXEC p_SetupCreateLogin '<Domain>\<Username>', 'sdk_users'
```

12. Now, type and execute the next statement:

```
EXEC p_SetupCreateLogin '<Domain>\<Username>', 'configsvc_users'
```

13. Finally, run this procedure for dbmodule_users:

```
EXEC p_SetupCreateLogin '<Domain>\<Username>', 'dbmodule_users'
```

14. Reopen the Services console and right-click both the OpsMgr SDK service and OpsMgr Config service to start each service.

15. You can confirm that the services started correctly by opening the Event Viewer (Start -> Run, type **Eventvwr.msc**, then OK) and checking the Operations Manager Event log for errors.

Changing the SDK and Config Service Account to Use Local System

The steps to change the SDK and Config Service account to use Local System are similar to the procedure to change it to use a domain account.

Using Local System requires the RMS and Operational database on the same server. Specifying Local System when installing OpsMgr Reporting can cause issues (return value 3). This can be resolved by using a domain account for the OpsMgr SDK service during the installation. After the installation is complete, you can configure the OpsMgr SDK service to use the Local System account. Perform the following steps:

1. Open the Services console and stop both services.

2. Now select each service, click Properties, and on the Log On tab, click the Local System account option button. Click OK.

3. Open the SQL Server Management Studio, connect to the server name and instance where the Operations database is located, select the database, and start a query.

4. Type and execute each of the following statements:

```
EXEC p_SetupCreateLogin 'NT AUTHORITY\SYSTEM', 'sdk_users'
EXEC p_SetupCreateLogin 'NT AUTHORITY\SYSTEM', 'configsvc_users'
EXEC p_SetupCreateLogin 'NT AUTHORITY\SYSTEM', 'dbmodule_users'
```

5. Return to the Services console and start the two services.

6. Check the Operations Manager Event log for any errors.

TIP

Check the Related KB Article

Check the most recent version of the Microsoft Knowledgebase article for changing credentials for the OpsMgr service accounts, at http://support.microsoft.com/kb/936220.

Computer Discovery Account

The account used for computer discovery is either the Management Server Action account or an account with administrative privileges on the targeted computer(s). If you specify a local user account rather than a domain account to limit your security exposure, the Management Server Action account will perform discovery.

Agent Installation Account

If you use discovery-based agent deployment, you are asked to specify an account with Administrator privileges. OpsMgr uses the Management Server Action account by default. As this account installs the agent on the targeted computers, it must have local Administrator rights on all the systems the agents are deployed to. If the Management Server Action account does not have Administrator rights, you must specify an account with those rights. Information for this account is not stored; it is encrypted before it is used and then discarded.

Notification Action Account

The Notification Action account is not required during setup; it is used when creating and sending notifications. This account will need to have sufficient rights for the Simple Mail Transfer Protocol (SMTP) server, instant messaging server, or Session Initiation Protocol (SIP) server that you will use for notifications.

Data Warehouse Write Action Account

OpsMgr Reporting uses the Data Warehouse Write Action account to insert and update information in the Data Warehouse database. This account writes data from the management server(s) to the data warehouse and reads data from the Operations database. The credentials used for the account are assigned to the OpsMgr Writer role in the Data Warehouse database, and the dwsynch_users role in the Operations database.

This account must be a domain account.

Data Reader Account

The Data Reader account runs and manages reports. The credentials used for the Data Reader account are assigned to the OpsMgr Reader role in the Data Warehouse database, and added to the Operations Manager Report Security Administrators user role. This account becomes the identity for the Report Server application pool in IIS. The account also must be a domain user account.

If you change the password in Active Directory for the Data Reader account, you must also change it in the Reporting Services Configuration Manager. To change the password associated with this account in the Configuration Manager, perform the following steps:

1. On the Reporting server, select Start -> All Programs -> Microsoft SQL Server 2005 -> Configuration Tools -> Reporting Services Configuration.

2. Click Connect in the Reporting Server Installation Instance Selection dialog box.

3. In the left pane of the Reporting Services Configuration Manager, select Execution Account.

4. In the Execution Account pane, enter the new password for the account (see Figure 11.8).

5. Select Apply, then click Exit to close the Reporting Services Configuration Manager.

FIGURE 11.8   Changing the password for the Reporting Server Execution account.

The Health Service Account

The OpsMgr Health service must run using the credentials of Local System. The Health service registers SPNs (Service Principal Names); using any other account results in duplicate SPNs. Agents will not be able to contact their management server when there are duplicate SPNs. Microsoft does not support running the Health service account under any credentials other than Local System.

> **NOTE**
>
> **And a SPN Is...**
>
> SPNs are used by clients to uniquely identify an instance of a service. If, as in the case of OpsMgr, you install multiple instances of a service on computers throughout an Active Directory forest, each of those instances must have a unique SPN.

The Health service process is separated from the single and multiple uses of the MonitoringHost process. This separation means if a script running on the computer stalls or fails, the functionality of the OpsMgr Service or other responses on that computer is not affected. As we discuss in Chapter 3, "Looking Inside OpsMgr," there is only one Health service, although it has two implementations:

- ▶ The Agent Health service runs on monitored computers and executes tasks, collects performance data, and so on.

- ▶ The other implementation runs on a management server.

The service's functionality is defined by the setup, binaries, and installed management packs.

Gateway Action Account

If you install a gateway server, you must provide credentials for an Action account. In reality, this is a Management Server Action account for the gateway server. As each gateway server by definition is in a different domain, each will need its own unique Action account. This account functions as a Run As Account for that domain, and allows you to monitor other servers in that external domain such as a DMZ (demilitarized zone).

The Gateway Action account can run using the credentials of Local System or a domain/local account. It is a best practice to use a low-privilege account. On systems running Windows Server 2003 and Windows Vista, be sure the account has the following privileges:

- ▶ Member of the local Users group

- ▶ Member of local Performance Monitor Users group

- ▶ Granted the Allow Log on Locally permission

Using a domain account enables the gateway server to have the permissions required to install agents and perform necessary actions.

Database Security

Operations Manager 2007 uses two SQL Server databases: the Operations database and the Data Warehouse database. OpsMgr-specific logins are added to the Master database on each database server, with corresponding users and database roles to the user databases.

ACS has a separate database and is installed separately from the other OpsMgr components. We discuss ACS in the "ACS Security" section of this chapter.

Operations Database Security

During installation, the setup process adds SQL logins for the RMS's Action account and the SDK and Config Service account. Setup then adds these logins as Operations database users and grants them the Connect permission for the database. Operations Manager Setup also creates several database roles in the Operations database:

- ▶ configsvc_users

- ▶ dbmodule_users

- ▶ dwsynch_users

- ▶ sdk_users

The RMS's Action account becomes a member of the dbmodule_users role, which is granted Execute permission for the database. The SDK and Config Service account becomes a member of the configsvc_users and sdk_users database roles. The configsvc_users role is granted the Execute database permission, and the sdk_users role is granted Execute and Subscribe query notifications permissions. The RMS's Action account, the SDK and Config Service account, and the four special database roles become members of the db_datareader and db_datawriter roles. These are default user roles, which come from the Model database.

Data Warehouse Database Security

The Reporting Setup adds SQL logins for the Data Warehouse Write Action account and Data Reader account. Setup then adds these logins as database users to the Data Warehouse database. The Operations Manager Reporting Setup also creates two database roles in the Data Warehouse database:

- ▶ OpsMgr Reader

- ▶ OpsMgr Writer

The Data Warehouse Write Action account becomes a member of the OpsMgr Writer role, and the Data Reader account becomes a member of the OpsMgr Reader role. The OpsMgr Writer is granted specific permissions to required database tables. For example, the role is granted Select and Update permissions for the AlertStage table.

Adding Management Servers to Run As Profiles

If you have multiple management servers, each server requires sufficient rights to write data to both the Operations database and the Data Warehouse database. To verify that your servers have the appropriate rights, check the following:

- ▶ Open the Run As Profile tab for the Data Warehouse SQL Server Authentication account Run As Account and verify that there is an entry for each computer that is a management server.

- ▶ Open the Run As Profile tab for the Reporting SDK SQL Server Authentication account Run As Account and verify that there is an entry for each computer that is a management server.

If there is a missing entry, perform the following steps to enter the Fully Qualified Domain Name (FQDN) for the management server(s) into the appropriate Run As Profile:

1. Logged on as an Operations Manager Administrator, click the Administration button in the Operations console.
2. Navigate to Administration -> Security -> Run As Profiles.
3. Right-click either the Data Warehouse SQL Server Authentication account or the Reporting SDK SQL Server Authentication account, and select Properties.
4. In the Run As Profiles Properties dialog box, select the Run As Accounts tab, and click New.
5. At the Run As Account menu, select the appropriate Run As Account.
6. Under Matching Computers, select the computer(s) that host an OpsMgr management server, and click OK.
7. At the Run As Profiles Properties dialog box, click OK.

Mutual Authentication

An agent and management server will use Windows (Kerberos v5) or Certificates authentication to mutually authenticate before the management server will accept data from the agent.

Because OpsMgr 2007 requires mutual authentication, the agents and management server must belong to an Active Directory domain. If these components are in separate domains, there must be a forest trust between the domains. With the trust in place, after mutual authentication occurs, the data channel between the agent and management server is encrypted. These actions take place automatically. The next sections discuss communications between the management server and agent when these components are not in domains with trust relationships.

About Mutual Authentication

Mutual authentication means that all data sent between a management server, gateway server, and the agent is signed and encrypted by default, and the components must authenticate each other before communications will occur. Mutual authentication uses the Kerberos v5 authentication protocol or certificates. Operations Manager 2007 does not support unencrypted communications.

Using mutual authentication with encryption and signing helps to mitigate a man-in-the-middle attack, since the keys are exchanged in such a manner that a person in the middle cannot intercept the communications. A man-in-the-middle attack could occur if an attacker simulates an OpsMgr agent or server component, establishing communications with the component at the other end of the conversation, with the potential to perform a harmful action on one of these components.

OpsMgr and Non-Trusted Domains

Due to DMZs and mergers (or other situations), companies may have domains that are in separate forests. Without a trust, agents in one domain cannot authenticate with a management server in the other domain. In this situation, mutual authentication takes place with certificates. Once mutual authentication occurs, data is encrypted using a public/private key pair, which we discussed in Chapter 3.

You can use the Gateway Server Component as a communication mechanism between two domains. Think of the gateway server as a proxy server; it forwards monitoring information between two environments that otherwise could not communicate between each other using Kerberos. Using a gateway server offers the following advantages:

▶ **Simplicity**—When monitoring an untrusted domain, only two certificates need to be installed and updated (on the gateway server and a management server).

▶ **Isolation**—There is no direct communication between the gateway server and the operational database server or RMS.

▶ **Certificate Support**—Standard support for Certificate Authority (CA)-issued certificates or third-party certificates. You can assign a certificate to the gateway server rather than each agent in the DMZ, which reduces the amount of configuration effort required.

In our environment, Odyssey is the domain containing the RMS and other OpsMgr server components, and our Continent domain is in our DMZ where we want to monitor agents. We will install a gateway server in the DMZ, in the Continent domain. Mutual authentication between OpsMgr components in the Odyssey domain takes place with Kerberos, and mutual authentication between the gateway server and the agents in the Continent domain uses Kerberos.

Because there is no trust between the two domains, we can install a certificate on the gateway server and the management server to provide mutual authentication and data encryption. The advantage of using a gateway is that we only need one certificate in the second domain (Continent) and one port (5723) opened through the firewall, as shown in Figure 11.9.

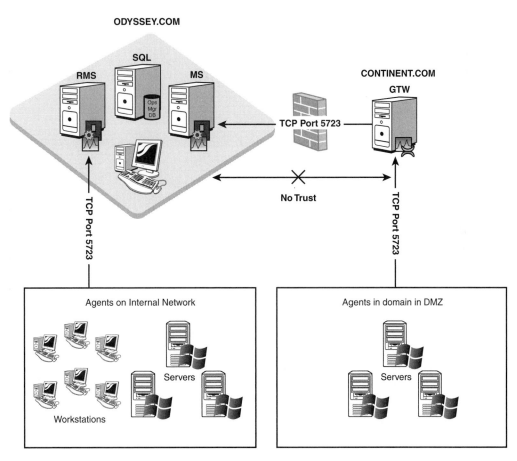

FIGURE 11.9   Using a gateway server with a DMZ and internal network.

The process of sending data from the agent in an untrusted domain to the RMS is as follows:

1. Because the gateway and the agent are in the same domain, Kerberos is used between the agent and the gateway server to encrypt the data.

2. The information is decrypted by the gateway, and then re-encrypted using certificates for the management server.

3. When the management server assigned to the gateway server receives the data, it decrypts the message.

4. When the management server communicates with the RMS, the management server re-encrypts the information using the Kerberos protocol and sends it to the RMS, where it is again decrypted.

Data sent from the RMS to the agent may include user credential information such as confirmation data and tasks. When an agent is deployed, it automatically generates a public/private key pair, sending the public key to the RMS. Anytime the RMS will send user credential information to the agent, it uses that public key for an additional layer of encryption. As we discuss in Chapter 3, the public/private key pair is generated automatically on startup, when the keys expire, or by a request from the SDK.

> **NOTE**
>
> **About Using the Gateway Server**
>
> You should use a gateway server when a firewall separates agents from management servers, if you have deployed agents and management servers in separate domains without a forest trust. You can also use a gateway server when you have a requirement to monitor agents in a workgroup.
>
> After deploying the gateway server, agents connect directly to the gateway server and the gateway server connects to the management server. With a gateway server, you only need to open one port in the firewall—for the gateway server—rather than opening a port for each agent. This improves security.
>
> In addition, when deployed in an Active Directory environment, using a gateway server reduces the number of certificates because the gateway and agent in the same Active Directory forest mutually authenticate by using the Kerberos protocol! Traffic with the management server is also reduced as the gateway server will install the agent software and collects information from the agents to send to its management server.

OpsMgr and Workgroup Support

Although agents in a workgroup environment can use a gateway server, you will need to install certificates for communication between the agents and the gateway server. These certificates are in addition to the certificate installed on the gateway itself to communicate with the management server.

As an alternative to installing a gateway server in a workgroup environment, you can configure the agents to use certificate-based authentication directly with a management server. This can be feasible when there are a small number of agents to monitor in the workgroup. The basic configuration is as follows:

▶ Ensure the management server has a copy of the trusted root CA in the computer certificate store, and that it was imported into the local computer certificate store. The subject name should match the FQDN of the management server with the private key.

▶ Run MOMCertImport.exe on the management server.

▶ Be sure the agent has a copy of the trusted root CA, and that there is a certificate with a subject name matching the NetBIOS name of the agent in the local certificate store; then run MOMCertImport.exe.

Instructions for configuring the certificate and running MOMCertImport are in the "Using a Standalone CA" and "Configuring Operations Manager 2007 to Use Certificates" sections of this chapter. There are also a number of articles available dealing with different aspects of this topic. You can find a discussion on using agents on workgroup computers at Clive Eastwood's blog at http://blogs.technet.com/cliveeastwood/archive/2007/05/02/ using-certificates-with-opsmgr07-agents-and-workgroup-computers.aspx. Duncan McAlynn has some tips on installing agents in a workgroup, at http://www.mcalynn.com/2007/08/ certificate-based-agents-are-a-no-brainer-better-think-again. Walter Eikenboom has an article that ties it all together; you can download it from http://weblog.stranger.nl/files/ DMZ_server_monitoring_with_SCOM_2007.pdf.

As pictures can be worth many words, we will illustrate the process with some screenshots, as follows:

▶ Figure 11.10 shows our workgroup computer (Gandalf-Xp64) in the workgroup, with a certificate issued by RootCA1. This figure shows the certificate listed in the personal store.

▶ Figure 11.11 illustrates the trusted root certificate, RootCA1, which we are using.

▶ In Figure 11.12, we show the certificate in the personal store for our management server (hydra.odyssey.com). Any management server communicating with the work-group computer will need to have a certificate.

▶ We can also see the certificate in Figure 11.13, which lists all the certificates in the trusted root for Hydra.

▶ Figure 11.14 is a view of the two certificates imported to the certificate server (domain controller), which is Pantheon in our case.

▶ Finally, in Figure 11.15, we see that it all comes together! Figure 11.15 displays our monitored workgroup computer, Gandalf-XP64, in the Operations console.

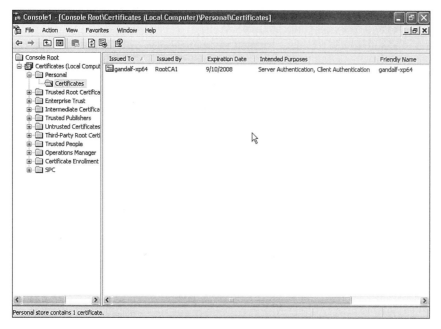

FIGURE 11.10   The personal certificate store for a workgroup computer.

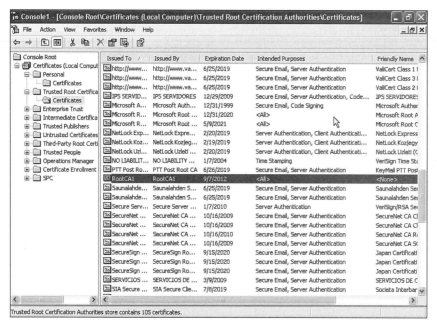

FIGURE 11.11   Trusted root certificates on the Gandalf system.

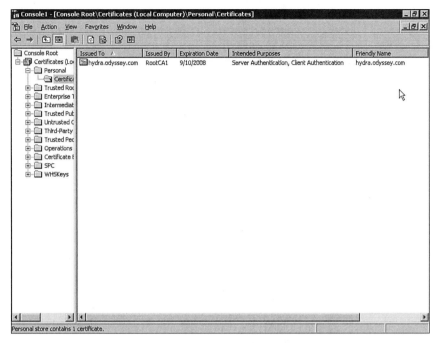

FIGURE 11.12   The personal certificate store on the management server.

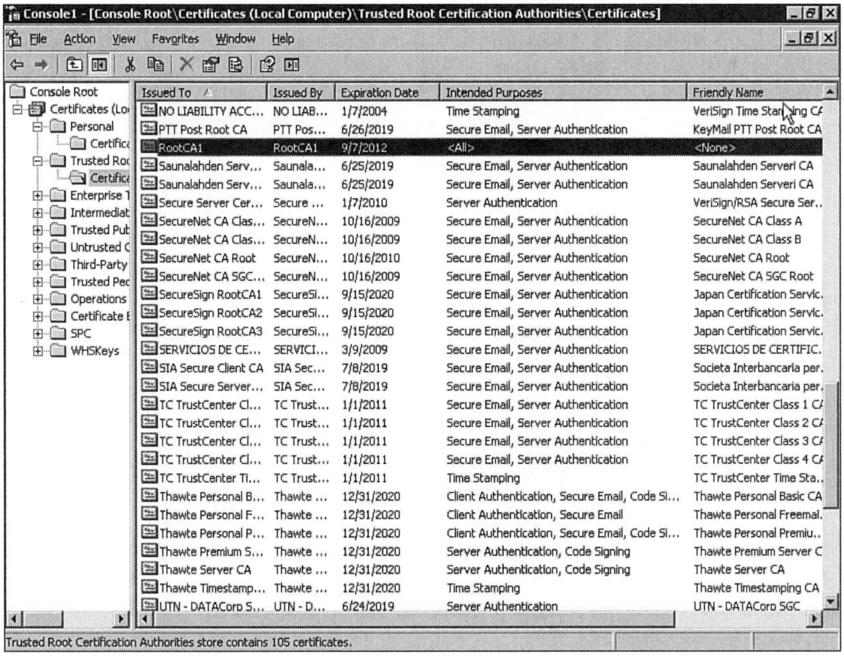

FIGURE 11.13   Trusted root certificates on the Hydra management server.

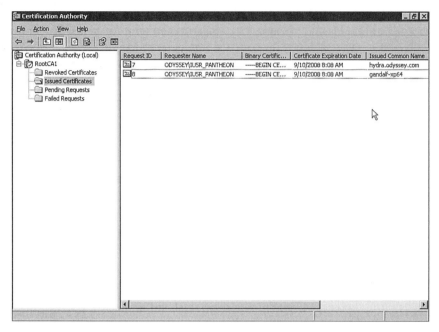

FIGURE 11.14   Certificates on the certificate server.

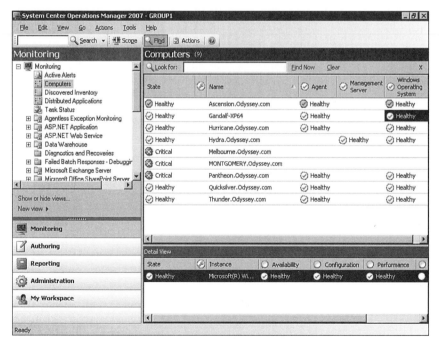

FIGURE 11.15   Viewing the workgroup computer in the management group.

TIP

Working with Manually Installed Agents

For both the untrusted domain and workgroup scenarios, agent installation and any changes to agent settings are made manually.

You will also want to deselect the Reject new manual agent installations option in the Operations console, under Administration -> Settings -> Servers -> Security. This setting does not allow newly installed manual agents to establish communications with the management server. Choose the setting to Review new manual agent installations in pending management view, and optionally to Auto-approve new manually installed agents. These settings allow the agent to establish its initial communication with the management server.

After all manually installed agents are deployed and communicating with their management server, change the setting to Reject new manual agent installations. This prevents unauthorized manually installed agents from trying to communicate with the management server.

Agent Proxying

Operations Manager 2007 supports agent proxying. When you will be managing an agentless managed computer, it must be assigned to a management server or agent-managed computer to provide remote (proxy) agent functionality. As we discuss in Chapter 9, "Installing and Configuring Agents," computers are managed as agentless when you either cannot or do not want to install an agent on them.

Not all management packs work in agentless mode, and agentless management will not work when the agentless computer and its proxy communicate through a firewall. Proxying is the capability for an agent to relay or forward information from other computers or network devices to the management server. Disabling agent proxying prevents spoofing by an attacker pretending to an agent because the management server matches information sent from the agent to a known agent name before accepting the data. Agent proxying is disabled by default.

The proxy agent can be any agent-managed computer in the management group configured to be a proxy, including a management server.

To configure agent proxying on an agent-managed computer, perform the following steps:

1. Navigate to Administration -> Device Management -> Agent Managed.
2. Right-click on the agent-managed computer you want to act as a proxy agent, and select the Security tab. Check the box to Allow this agent to act as a proxy and discover managed objects on other computers (displayed in Figure 11.16), and click OK.

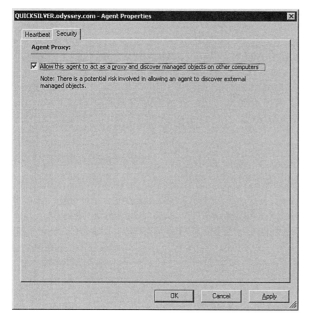

FIGURE 11.16   Configuring a proxy agent.

If you want to configure a management server as a proxy for agentless managed computers, perform the following steps:

1. Navigate to Administration -> Device Management -> Management Servers.

2. Right-click on the management server you want to act as a proxy, and select the Security tab. Check the box to Allow this server to act as a proxy and discover managed objects on other computers. Click OK.

You will need to perform this procedure for each agent or management server for which you want to allow agent proxying.

A number of management packs use agent proxying. For example, the Active Directory management pack requires agent proxying to populate its topology views. The File Replication Service (FRS) management pack also requires agent proxying for monitoring replica members.

Obtaining a Certificate

You can obtain a certificate either using an enterprise CA or a standalone CA. The process is somewhat lengthy. The next sections step through the processes for each type of certificate authority.

Once you have a certificate, you use the MOMCertImport tool to configure OpsMgr to use certificates, and then you install the certificates. We discuss these steps in the "Using MOMCertImport" section of this chapter.

Using an Enterprise CA

You can use the Certificate Services component of Windows 2000 Server and Windows Server 2003 to obtain a certificate from an enterprise certification authority (CA). The process consists of creating a certificate template, requesting a certificate, exporting the certificate, and then importing it.

Creating a Certification Template

First, perform the following steps to create a certification template:

1. On the computer hosting your enterprise CA, select Start -> Programs -> Administrative Tools -> Certification Authority.

2. In the Navigation pane, expand the CA name, right-click Certificate Template, and select Manage to open the Certificate Templates console.

3. In the Certificate Templates console, right-click IPSec (Offline request) in the results pane, then click Duplicate Template.

4. In the New Template Properties window, click on the General tab, and in the Template display name box, type a new name for this template. We are calling our template **RootCA1**.

5. At the Request Handling tab, select Allow private key to be exported, and then click CPS. At the CPS selection dialog, select a preferred cryptographic service provider, and click OK.

6. At the Extensions tab, in Extensions included in this template, click Application Policies, and click Edit.

7. At the Edit Application Policies Extension dialog, click IP security IKE Intermediate, and click Remove.

8. Now click Add, and in the Application policies list, hold down the CTRL key to multi-select items from the list. Click Client Authentication and Server Authentication, and click OK.

9. Click OK in the Edit Application Policies Extension dialog box.

10. Click the Security tab. Verify that the security group has Read and Enroll permissions, and click OK.

Requesting a Certificate from an Enterprise CA

Now you will request a certificate from an enterprise CA. Start by logging on to the computer where you will install your certificate (the gateway server or the management server), and perform the following procedure:

1. In Internet Explorer, connect to the computer hosting Certificate Servers (http://<servername>/certsrv).

2. At the Microsoft Certificate Services Welcome page, click Request a certificate. At the Request a Certificate page, click Or, submit an advanced certificate request.

3. On the Advanced Certificate Request page, click Create and submit a Request to this CA. You will also want to do the following:

   ▶ Under Certificate Template, select the name of the template you created (RootCA1).

   ▶ Under Identifying Information for Offline Template, in the name field, enter the Fully Qualified Domain Name of the computer for which you are requesting the certificate. Enter the appropriate information in the rest of the fields.

   ▶ Under Key Options, click Create a new key set. In the CSP (Certificate Service Provider) field, select the cryptographic service provider of your choice, and under Key Usage, select Both. Under Key Size, select a key size that is appropriate for your business needs. Select Automatic key container name, and verify that Mark key as exportable is selected. Clear the Export keys to file and Enable strong private key protection options. Then click Store certificate into the local computer certificate store.

   ▶ At Additional Options, under Request Format, select CMC Certificate Management). In the Hash Algorithm list, select SHA-1 (Secure Hash Algorithm-1). Clear the Save request to a file checkbox, and in the Friendly Name list, enter the FQDN ("friendly" name) of the computer you are requesting the certificate for.

   ▶ Now, click Submit. If a Potential Scripting Violation dialog box is displayed, click Yes.

   ▶ At the Certificate Issued page, click Install this certificate. If a Potential Scripting Violation dialog box is displayed, click Yes.

   ▶ On the Certificate Installed page, you will see a message that Your new certificate has been successfully installed. Close the browser.

Exporting the Certificate
The next step in the process is to export the certificate:

1. Select Start -> Run, and in the Run dialog box, type **MMC** and click OK.

2. In the File menu, select Add/Remove Snap-in.

3. In the Add/Remove Snap-in dialog box, select Add.

4. In the Add Standalone Snap-in dialog box, select Certificates, and then click OK.

5. In the Certificates snap-in box, select the Computer account. Click Next.

6. In the Select Computer dialog, select Local computer (the computer this console is running on). Click Finish.

7. In the Add Standalone Snap-in dialog box, click Close.

8. In the Add/Remove Snap-in Dialog box, click OK.

9. At the Console Root/Certificates (Local Computer) pane, navigate to Certificates (Local Computer) -> Personal -> Certificates.

10. In the Results pane, right-click the certificate you requested in the previous procedure, point to All Tasks, and click Export.

11. In the Certificate Export Wizard, click Next at the Welcome page.

12. At the Export Private Key page, select Yes, export the private key; click Next.

13. On the Export File Format page, do the following, and then click Next:

    ▶ Select Personal Information Exchange—PKCS #12 (.PFX). PKCS #12 defines a file format used to store private keys with accompanying public key certificates, protected using a password-based symmetric key.

    ▶ Clear Include all certificates in the certification path if possible.

    ▶ Select Enable strong protection (requires IE 5.0, NT 4.0 SP 4, or above).

    ▶ Clear Delete the private key if the export is successful.

14. At the Password page, type a password to protect the private key, and click Next.

15. On the File to Export page, select Browse.

16. On the Save As page, select a folder and filename for the certificate, verify that the Save as type is set to Personal Information Exchange (.pfx), and click Save.

17. On the File to Export page, ensure the path and filename are correct, press Next, and then click Finish.

Done!

Using a Standalone CA

The process differs somewhat with a standalone certificate authority. You will request the certificate, approve it, and then retrieve it. Let's start with the steps to request a certificate. This will be at the computer where you want to install the certificate (the gateway or management server):

1. Start Internet Explorer and connect to the computer running Certificate Services (http://<servername>/certsrv).

2. At the Microsoft Certificate Services Welcome page, click Request a certificate. At the Request a Certificate page, click Or, submit an advanced certificate request.

3. On the Advanced Certificate Request page, click Create and submit a Request to this CA. You will also want to do the following:

    ▶ Under identifying information, enter the FQDN of the computer for which you are requesting the certificate in the Name field.

- ▶ For the Type of Certificate Needed, click the list and select Other. Enter **1.3.6.1.5.5.7.3.1,1.3.6.1.5.5.7.3.2** for server and client authentication in the OID (object identifier) field.

- ▶ Under Key Options, click Create a new key set. In the CSP field, select the cryptographic service provider of your choice, and under Key Usage, select Both. Select 1024 for Key Size. Select Automatic key container name, and verify that Mark key as exportable is selected. Clear the Export keys to file and Enable strong private key protection options. Then click Store certificate into the local computer certificate store.

- ▶ At Additional Options, under Request Format, select CMC. In the Hash Algorithm list, select SHA-1. Clear the Save request to a file checkbox, and in the Friendly Name list, enter the FQDN of the computer for which you are requesting the certificate.

- ▶ Now, click Submit. If a Potential Scripting Violation dialog box is displayed, click Yes.

- ▶ On the Certificate Pending page, close the browser.

The next part of this process is to approve the pending certificate request. This takes place at the computer that hosts Certificate Services. If your Certificate Services is configured to auto-approve certificates, these next steps are not necessary:

1. Select Start -> Programs -> Administrative Tools -> Certification Authority.
2. At the Certification Authority console, expand the node for your Certificate Authority name, and select Pending Requests.
3. In the Results pane, right-click the request pending from your request, select All Tasks, and then select Issue.
4. Select Issued Certificates and confirm the certificate you just issued is listed. Close the console.

Now you will retrieve and import the certificate into the certificate store on the computer where you will be installing it. First, retrieve the certificate:

1. Logon to the computer that needs the certificate (the gateway server, management server, or agent if this is a workgroup).
2. In Internet Explorer, connect to the computer that hosts Certificate Services (http://*<servername>*/certsrv).
3. At the Microsoft Certificate Services Welcome page, select View the status of a pending certificate request.
4. At the View the Status of a Pending Certificate Request page, select the certificate you requested.
5. At the Certificate Issued page, select Install this certificate. Click Yes in the Potential Scripting Violation box.

11

6. At the Certificate Installed page, the message appears that Your new certificate has been successfully installed. Close Internet Explorer.

Next, export the certificate:

1. Select Start -> Run, type **MMC**, then click OK to open the Microsoft Management Console.

2. At the File menu, click Add/Remove Snap-in. At the Add-Remove Snap-in dialog box, click Add. In the Add Standalone Snap-In dialog box, select Certificates, and click Add.

3. In the Certificates snap-in dialog, select Computer account and click Next. In the Select Computer dialog box, select Local Computer (the computer this console is running on), and click Finish.

4. In the Add Standalone Snap-in dialog box, click Close, and in the Add/Remove Snap-in dialog box, click OK.

5. At the Console Root, navigate to the Certificates (Local Computer) pane -> Personal -> Certificates.

6. In the Results pane, right-click the certificate you requested, select All Tasks, and select Export.

7. Click Next at the Welcome page in the Certificate Export Wizard.

8. At the Export Private Key page, select Yes, export the private key, and click Next. Do the following at the Export File Format page:

    ▶ Select Personal Information Exchange—PKCS #12 (.PFX), and clear Include all certificates in the certification path if possible.

    ▶ Select Enable strong protection (requires IE 5.0, NT 4.0 SP 4, or above).

    ▶ Clear Delete the private key if the export is successful, and click Next.

9. At the Password page, enter a password to protect the private key. Click Next.

10. At the File to Export page, select Browse. On the Save As page, select a folder and filename for the certificate, verify that the Save as type is set to Personal Information Exchange (.pfx), and select Save. Back at the File to Export page, ensure the path and filename are correct, select Next, and then click Finish.

Configuring Operations Manager 2007 to Use Certificates

Through either of these two processes (using an Enterprise or Standalone CA), you now have a certificate! The MOMCertImport utility configures Operations Manager 2007 to use that certificate by putting the certificate's serial number in the Registry. Remember, certificates can be used as an alternative to the Kerberos protocol for mutual authentication, and typically are used in situations where there is a firewall, workgroup, or untrusted domain with agents that you want to monitor with OpsMgr. Certificates provide encryption between an agent and either a gateway server, management server, or RMS, or between a gateway server and a management server or RMS.

Using MOMCertImport

Use MOMCertImport to import certificates on all OpsMgr roles requiring certificates, including the agent. To run the utility, perform the following steps:

1. Log on to the computer with a user account that has Administrator privileges.
2. Select Start -> Run, type **cmd**, then click OK.
3. At the command prompt, navigate to the drive where the Operations Manager installation media is located.
4. Type **CD\SupportTools\<i386>** (specify the AMD64 or IA64 folder as appropriate); then press enter.
5. Type the following command; then press enter:

```
MOMCertImport <path to the PFX certificate> [/Password <password>]
```

The last part of this process is to import the CA certificate to the OpsMgr components that need to trust the certificate authority. Perform these steps on the gateway server(s), management servers(s), and any agent(s) that require certificates:

> **TIP**
>
> **Using GPOs to Simplify the Process**
>
> Consider creating a domain Group Policy Object that pushes the trusted certificate.

1. Logon to the computer that will use the certificate.
2. In Internet Explorer, connect to the computer hosting Certificate Services (http://<servername>/certsrv).
3. At the Welcome page, click Download a CA Certificate, certificate chain, or CRL.
4. At the next page, click install this CA certificate chain.
5. At the Potential Scripting Violation box, click Yes.
6. Close Internet Explorer when the CA Certificate Installation page displays.

> **Certificate Considerations**
>
> When obtaining and installing certificates to use with Operations Manager 2007, keep the following in mind:
>
> ▶ Certificates used on various OpsMgr components must be issued by the same certification authority.
> ▶ Each computer requires its own unique certificate.

- ▶ Each computer must contain the root certification authority certificate in its Trusted Root Certifications Authorities store and any intermediate certification authorities in the Intermediate Certification Authorities store.
- ▶ The subject name for the certificate must contain the DNS (Domain Name Services) FQDN of the host computer.
- ▶ Certificates need to support the following OIDs for these two extended key usage fields: server authentication and client authentication. Enter the OIDs, comma-separated:

  1.3.6.1.5.5.7.3.1

  1.3.6.1.5.5.7.3.2

- ▶ The certificate must be in PFX format and include the certificate's private key.
- ▶ You must first obtain the certificate and then use the MOMCertImport tool.

Removing Certificates Imported with MOMCertImport

Removing a certificate imported with MOMCertImport requires editing the Registry. Perform the following steps:

1. Logon to the computer with an account that is a member of the Administrators group.
2. Select Start -> Run, type **regedit**, then click OK.
3. On the Registry Editor page, navigate to HKEY_LOCAL_MACHINE\SOFTWARE\Microsoft\Microsoft Operations Manager\3.0\Machine Settings.
4. In the Results pane, right-click ChannelCertificateSerialNumber; then select Modify.
5. In the Edit binary Value dialog box, select the binary data and press Delete.

Certificate Troubleshooting Tips

If you start the OpsMgr services and receive Connector alerts with errors 20057, 21001, and 21016, you most likely are having some sort of certificate failure. Debugging steps you can take include the following:

- ▶ Validate that the gateway server can ping the RMS using the fully qualified domain name (if ping is restricted to the RMS, validate using telnet).
- ▶ Validate that the gateway server can telnet to the RMS on port 5723. Port 5724 may also be required, depending on your environment.
- ▶ Validate that the RMS can ping the gateway server by its fully qualified domain name.

Check the following for the certificates on the RMS:

▶ Validate that the certificate exists in Local Computer -> Personal -> Certificates on the RMS. Figure 11.17 displays the certificate.

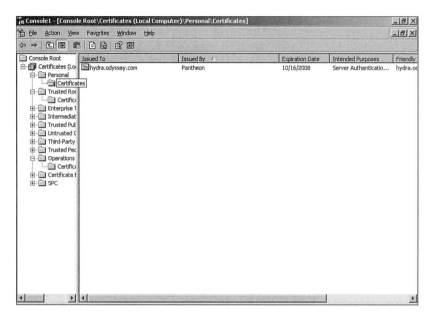

FIGURE 11.17 Certificate on the RMS under the Personal folder for hydra.odyssey.com.

▶ Validate that the root certificate exists in Local Computer -> Personal -> Trusted Root Certificates -> Certificates on the RMS (see Figure 11.18).

▶ Validate that the certificate also exists in Local Computer -> Operations Manager -> Certificates on the RMS. You can see this displayed in Figure 11.19.

Check the following areas for the certificates on the gateway server:

▶ Validate that the certificate exists in Local Computer -> Personal -> Certificates on the gateway server. See Figure 11.20 for an example of this certificate.

▶ Validate that the root certificate exists in Local Computer -> Personal -> Trusted Root Certificates -> Certificates on the gateway server (see Figure 11.21).

▶ Validate that the certificate exists in Local Computer -> Operations Manager -> Certificates on the gateway server. This is displayed in Figure 11.22.

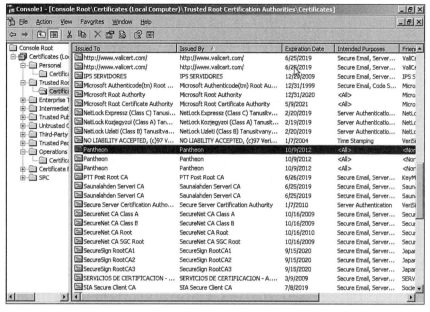

FIGURE 11.18   Certificate on the RMS under the Trusted Root.

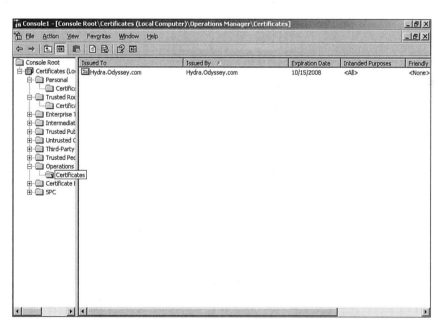

FIGURE 11.19   Viewing the certificate under the Operations Manager folder.

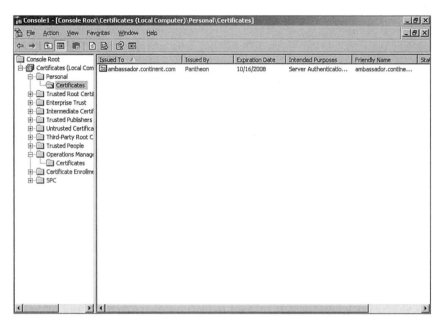

FIGURE 11.20   Certificate on the gateway server under the Personal folder for ambassador.continent.com.

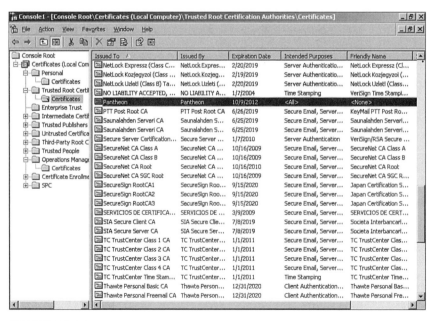

FIGURE 11.21   Certificate on the gateway server under the Trusted Root.

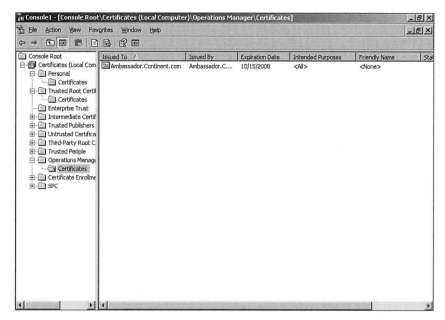

FIGURE 11.22   Viewing the certificate under the Operations Manager folder on the gateway server.

You will also want to verify Registry settings on the two computers:

▶ Validate the existence of the HKLM\SOFTWARE\Microsoft\Microsoft Operations Manager\3.0\Machine Settings\ChannelCertificateSerialNumber with the value of the certificate (from the Local Computer -> Personal -> Certificates folder within the details in the Serial number field) reversed within it on the gateway server. See Figure 11.23 for a sample of the Registry key.

▶ Validate the existence of the HKLM\SOFTWARE\Microsoft\Microsoft Operations Manager\3.0\Machine Settings\ChannelCertificateSerialNumber with the value of the certificate (from the Local Computer -> Personal -> Certificates folder within the details in the Serial number field) reversed within it on the RMS, and displayed in Figure 11.24.

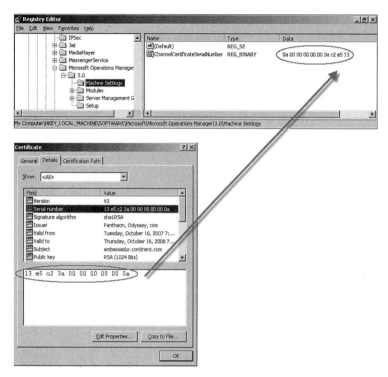

FIGURE 11.23   The certificate in the Registry on the gateway server.

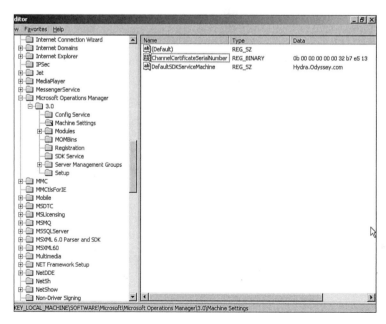

FIGURE 11.24   The certificate in the Registry on the RMS.

Configuring the Operations Console to Use SSL to Connect to a Reporting Server

Many organizations are now implementing secure websites using SSL technology. If you have SSL installed on your Reporting server, you must configure the Operations console to use SSL. Port 443 is used for secure http (https). Perform the following steps:

1. In the Operations console, select the Administration button.

2. In the Administration space, navigate to Administration -> Device Management -> Settings. Right-click on Reporting and select Properties.

3. In the General tab, under the Reporting Server Settings section, click the Reporting Server URL drop-down list and select https://.

4. Edit the URL, replacing :80 with **:443**, and click OK.

> **TIP**
>
> **Implementing SSL in IIS**
>
> KB article 299875 includes an excellent discussion of how to implement SSL in IIS. You can access this article at http://support.microsoft.com/kb/299875 or http://go.microsoft.com/fwlink/?linkId=87862.

Using the Health Service Lockdown Tool

On computers that require high security, such as a domain controller, you may want to deny certain identities access to rules, tasks, and monitors that could jeopardize the security of your service. The Health service lockdown tool (HSLockdown.exe) includes command-line options to control and limit the identities to run rules, tasks, or monitors.

The syntax is as follows:

```
HSLockdown <ManagementGroupName> /<Option>
<Option>:
/L - List accounts/groups
/A - Add an allowed account or group
/D - Add a denied account or group
/R - Remove an allowed/denied account or group
```

Accounts must either be specified in NetBIOS (domain\username) or UPN (username@fqdn.com) format.

Executing Health Service Lockdown

Run HSLockdown from the command prompt. The utility is located in the *%ProgramFiles%\System Center Operations Manager 2007* folder.

If you use the Add or Deny options, you will need to restart the OpsMgr Health service for the changes to take effect.

Unlocking the Action Account

The Health service will start but its availability state displays as Red if you used the Health Service Lockdown tool to lock out the Action account. To be able to resolve this, perform the following steps:

1. Log on as an Administrator, and select Start -> Run, type **cmd** in the Run dialog box, then click OK.

2. Navigate to the *%ProgramFiles%*\System Center Operations Manager 2007 folder.

3. Type **HSLockdown** *<Management Group>* /A *<Action account>*, and press enter.

ACS Security

ACS collects Security log events and stores these events in a central SQL Server database in near real time. After establishing a connection between an ACS forwarder and its ACS collector, the forwarder sends audit events to the database on the collector as they occur. Sending events immediately to a central repository minimizes the amount of time an attacker has to tamper with the audit log and remove evidence of the attack.

ACS can also help organizations separate the roles of the administrator and auditor. When audit events are stored on local computers, members of the local Administrators or Domain Admins group typically fulfill the auditor role. They review audit events and could possibly tamper with the Security Event log or simply overlook events that indicate they took part in an attack. However, if administrators are not auditors and do not have permissions to access the central repository, the administrator and auditor roles are separated, and unauthorized actions can be spotted.

Using ACS helps separate these roles. ACS forwarders and the ACS collector can communicate across forests, so you can collect events from computers in one forest while collecting and saving them in a different forest. With this configuration, members of the Domain Admins group in the production forest cannot hide events by using their elevated credentials to log on to the ACS forest and alter the ACS database. ACS does not completely prevent administrators from tampering with the audit trail but it minimizes the window of time for tampering. We discuss Audit Collection Services in Chapter 15, "Monitoring Audit Collection Services."

ACS System Integrity

The ACS database, created during ACS installation, is associated with the Audit Collector service, which runs on an ACS collector. Each collector requires its own database, which can be on the same computer as the ACS collector but for best performance should be on a dedicated member server. This database is separate from the Operations database. Security events that are cleared on an agent are tracked in this database, and a new table is created daily for that day's events.

ACS ensures its security in several ways:

- ▶ Requiring mutual authentication of the ACS forwarder and the collector. Before opening a connection, the forwarder authenticates to the collector and the collector authenticates to the forwarder.

- ▶ Encrypting communication between the forwarder and the collector. This ensures that the received information is not tampered with.

- ▶ Alerting an auditor if gaps are detected in the transmitted data. Each event has a sequence number expressed as a 32-bit integer. ACS remembers the sequence number and expects the next sequence number to be one greater than the current number. If the numbers are not sequential, ACS generates an alert.

- ▶ Only allowing forwarders to send information. The forwarder will not receive any information from its collector. The collector must disconnect the forwarder and allow it to reconnect before it can listen to the connector again. Although this produces some network overhead, it minimizes the possible attack surface if the collector is instructing the forwarder to do something differently.

You can use either certificates or Kerberos authentication to enable encrypted communication between forwarders and the collector. Encryption is necessary because mutual authentication is required. If the forwarders and collectors are in the same domain or domains that share a Kerberos trust, use Kerberos authentication. Use SSL/TLS (Secure Sockets Layer/Transport Layer Security) if the components are not in domains that share Kerberos trust, or if the forwarder is not in a domain.

SSL/TLS support requires that the collector and each forwarder install a certificate. Each forwarder must also have its own account in Active Directory; this can be either a computer or a user account. Computer accounts provide better security. Using SSL/TLS for mutual authentication and channel encryption requires enabling certificate support on the forwarder and a domain controller.

Installing a Certificate on an ACS Forwarder

The following steps enable certificate support on an ACS forwarder:

1. Logged on as an administrator, request or acquire a certificate that contains the object identifier (OID) 1.3.6.1.5.5.7.3.2 for the client authentication extended key usage. This certificate must have both a Subject and Issuer Name to allow one-to-one mapping to a computer account.

2. Run the MMC and add the Certificates snap-in, applying it to the local computer.

3. On the Action menu, select All tasks, then select Import.

4. Right-click the Personal folder, and select Import.

5. Use the Certificate Import Wizard to import the certificate.

6. Right-click the certificate, select All Tasks, and select Export.

7. At the Export Private Key page of the wizard, select Do not export the private key. Click Next.

8. At the Export File Format page of the Wizard, select DER encoded binary X.509 (.CER). Click Next.

9. At the File to Export page, specify the certificate name. Save the certificate to a network share or location where another computer can access it. Click Next. Review the configuration details on the Completing the Certificate Export Wizard page, and click Finish.

10. In the Services snap-in, stop the AdtAgent service if it is running.

11. Go to a command prompt (Start -> Run, type **cmd**, then click OK); run the command **AdtAgent –c**.

12. Select the certificate in the AdtAgent command-line menu.

Installing a Certificate on an ACS Collector

To enable certificate support on a collector, you must enable certificate support on a domain controller and each forwarder that will connect to the collector. The collector must be installed on a management server and belong to a domain. The following procedure enables certificate support on a collector:

1. Request or acquire a certificate containing the 1.3.6.1.5.5.7.3.1 OID for the server authentication extended key usage. This certificate must have both a Subject and Issuer Name to allow one-to-one mapping to a computer object.

2. Open the MMC, and add the Certificate snap-in to manage certificates for a local computer account.

3. Right-click the Personal folder and select Import.

4. Import the certificate using the Certificate Import Wizard.

5. Right-click on the certificate, select All Tasks, and select Export.

6. At the Export Private Key page, select Do not export the private key. Click Next.

7. At the Export File Format page of the Wizard, select DER encoded binary X.509 (CER). Click Next.

8. At the File to Export page, specify a certificate name and save the certificate to a network share or location where another computer can access it. Click Next.

9. Review the configuration details at the Completing the Certificate Export Wizard page, then click Finish.

10. In the Services snap-in, stop the AdtAgent service if it is running.

11. Go to a command prompt (Start -> Run, type **cmd**, then click OK); run the command **AdtAgent –c**.

12. Select the certificate in the AdtAgent command-line menu.

Enabling Certificate Support on a Domain Controller

Before enabling certificate support on a domain controller, verify that all forwarders and collectors have certificates installed. Then perform the following steps:

1. Open the Active Directory Users and Computers MMC snap-in.

2. At the View menu, select Advanced Features.

3. Create a unique account for the forwarder. This can be either a computer account or a user account, although Microsoft recommends using computer accounts.

4. Select the account the forwarder will use for authentication.

5. Right-click on the account; choose Name Mappings.

6. On the X.509 Certificate, click Add.

7. Locate and select the .CER file exported in the "Installing a Certificate on an ACS Forwarder" section of this chapter.

8. Check User Issuer for alternate security identify and Use Subject for alternate security identify. Click OK.

Enabling Encryption Between the ACS Database and the Collector

If the data traffic between the ACS database and the collector is over an unsecured or untrusted network, you will want to use SSL/TLS to enable encryption between these components. Be sure that an appropriate Trusted Root and Machine Certificate is installed on the SQL Server computer running the ACS database and on the collector; then perform the following steps:

1. Logon to the collector using an administrative account.

2. Select Start -> Run, type **cliconfg.exe**, then select OK. This starts the SQL Server Client Network Utility.

3. In the SQL Server Client Network Utility, select the General tab, then select Force Protocol encryption. Click OK.

4. Restart the collector.

TIP

Best Practice Recommendations for ACS Security

To create a secure ACS environment, establish a new management group for ACS and limit access to it. If that is not possible, lock down access to the database to auditors only. You will also want to lock down access to the folder structure and data sources used with reporting.

Firewall Considerations and Communications Security

In the "OpsMgr and Non-Trusted Domains" section of this chapter, we discussed using a gateway server as a proxy to communicate with a management server across a firewall. This section discusses other considerations for a firewalled environment.

Ports

Table 11.5 shows Operations Manager 2007 component interaction across a firewall. The table lists the ports used to communicate between components, which direction to open the inbound port, and if the port number can be changed.

TABLE 11.5   Ports Across a Firewall

Component A	Port/Direction	Component B	Configurable
Root Management Server	OLEDB (SQL) 1443 —>	Operations Manager Database	Yes (Setup)
Management Server	OLEDB (SQL) 1443 —>	Operations Manager Database	Yes (Setup)
Management Server	5723 —>	Root Management Server	Yes (Command-line setup)
Gateway Server	5723 —>	Root Management Server	Yes (Command-line setup)
Root Management Server	OLEDB (SQL) 1443 —>	Reporting Data Warehouse	Yes (and in a cluster, the second node requires a unique port number)
Reporting Server	5724 —>	Root Management Server	No
Operations Console	5724 —>	Root Management Server	No
Connector Framework Source	51905 —>	Root Management Server	No
Web Console Server	5724 —>	Root Management Server	No
Root Management Server (Top Tier)	5724 —>	Root Management Server (Mid-Tier)	No

TABLE 11.5   Continued

Component A	Port/Direction	Component B	Configurable
Agent	5723 —>	Root Management Server	Yes (Setup)
Agent	5723 —>	Management Server	Yes (Setup)
Agent	5723 —>	Gateway Server	Yes (Setup)
Gateway	5723 —>	Gateway Server	Yes (Setup)
Agent (ACS Forwarder)	51909 —>	Management Server ACS Collector	Yes (Registry)
AEM Data from client	SMB 445, 51906 —>	Management Server AEM File Share	Yes (AEM Wizard)
Software Quality Metrics (SQM) Data from client	51907 —>	Management Server SQM End Point	Yes (AEM Wizard)
Operations Console (Reports)	HTTP 80 —>	SQL Reporting Services	Yes
Reporting Data Warehouse	OLEDB (SQL) 1443 —>	Reporting Server	Yes (and in a cluster, the second node requires a unique port number)
Audit Collection Service (ACS) Database	OLEDB (SQL) 1443 —>	Management Server ACS Collector	Yes (and in a cluster, the second node requires a unique port number)
Web Console Browser	HTTP 51908 —>	Web Console Server	Yes (IIS Admin, Web Configuration File)

We can also illustrate this information using Figure 11.25, which you may remember from Chapter 3.

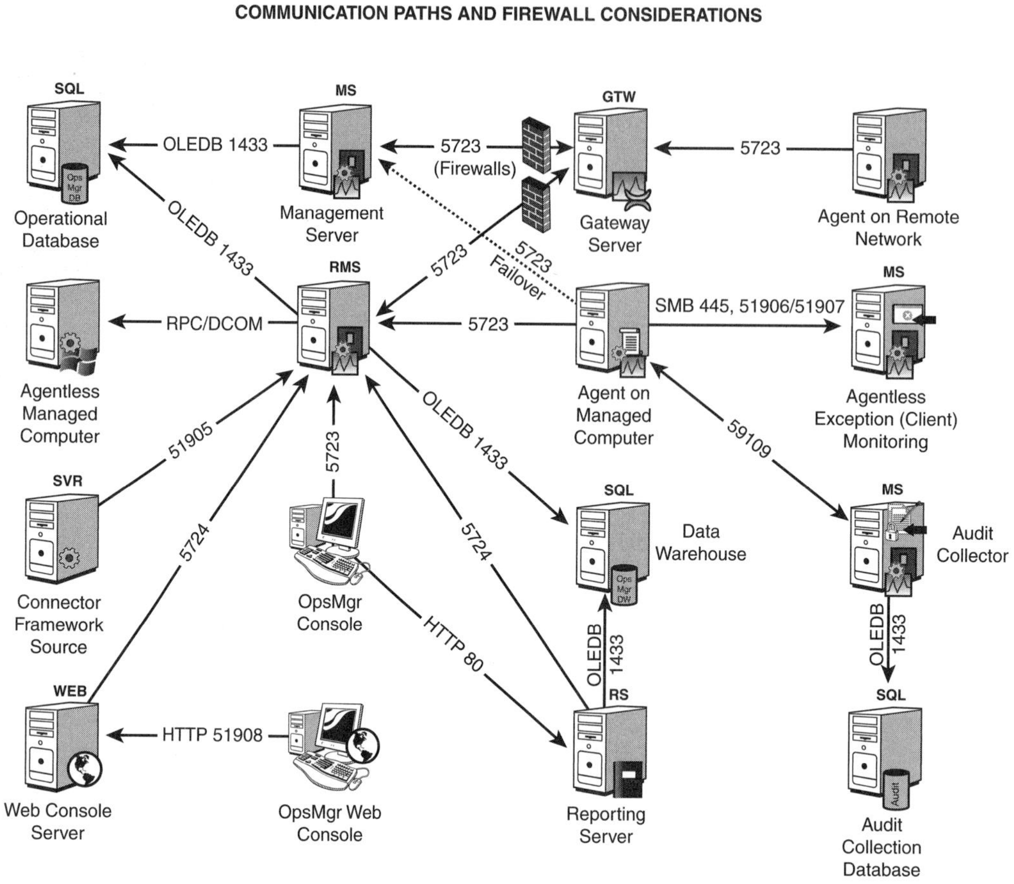

COMMUNICATION PATHS AND FIREWALL CONSIDERATIONS

FIGURE 11.25   Communication channels between computers in a management group.

Agents Across a Firewall

If you are installing agents on any computer running the Windows firewall (Windows 2003 with Service Pack 1 or later, Windows XP with Service Pack 2 or later, or Windows Vista), it is necessary to modify the default firewall configuration. This is true also for computers that will utilize the agentless managed feature of OpsMgr.

If you are certain the Windows firewall is disabled on all prospective managed computers, you do not need to perform this action. However, in many environments, the Windows firewall is deployed, particularly on managed desktop computers.

We recommend using the Group Policy Management Console (GPMC) to create and deploy an OpsMgr firewall exceptions GPO in the domain(s) where OpsMgr is going to be managing computers. Here are the steps to follow to create and deploy the GPO using the GPMC:

1. Right-click on the Group Policy Objects node and select to create a new GPO named OpsMgr Firewall Exceptions Policy.

2. Right-click on the new GPO and select Edit. The Group Policy Editor will open in its own window.

3. Navigate to the Computer Configuration -> Administrative Templates -> Network -> Network Connections -> Windows Firewall -> Domain Profile node.

4. In the setting Windows Firewall: Allow remote administration exception -> Allow unsolicited incoming messages from:, enter the Internet Protocol (IP) addresses and subnets of the primary and secondary management servers for the agent.

   If all computers are on the same subnet, you can enter the word **localsubnet**. This setting opens TCP ports 135 and 445 to permit communications using Remote Procedure Call (RPC) and Distributed Component Object Model (DCOM).

5. In the setting Windows Firewall: Allow file and printer sharing exception -> Allow unsolicited incoming messages from:, enter the IP addresses and subnets of the primary and secondary management servers for the agent in the same manner as the previous step. This setting opens TCP ports 139 and 445, and UDP ports 137 and 138 to permit network access to shared files.

6. In the setting Windows Firewall: Define port exceptions, click the Show button, then the Add button, and enter the port the agent uses to communicate with the management servers (the default is 5273): **TCP:<*IP address of RMS* >:<*subnet*>:enabled: OpsMgrAgent**.
   An example entry would be `5273:TCP:localsubnet:enabled:OpsMgrAgent`.

7. Close the Group Policy Editor and return to the Group Policy Management Console. Go to the Settings tab of the new OpsMgr Firewall Exceptions Policy and select to show all settings. Compare your GPO to the example shown in Figure 11.26. Your settings should be similar except for the localsubnet parameter; your policy may specify specific subnets or computer addresses.

8. Navigate in the GPMC to the domain and/or Organizational Unit (OU) where the computers to be managed are located. Right-click and choose to Link an Existing GPO...; then select the OpsMgr Firewall Exceptions Policy.

9. Allow the GPO to take effect on prospective managed computers. Automatic Group Policy refresh will occur within an hour on most Windows computers. To have the new GPO take effect immediately on a particular computer, either restart it, or execute the command **gpupdate /force** on Windows 2003 and XP computers or **secedit /refreshpolicy machine_policy /enforce** on Windows 2000 systems.

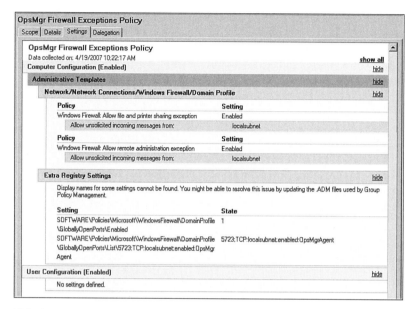

FIGURE 11.26   Setting Windows firewall exceptions to allow computers to be managed.

CAUTION

Restriction on Agentless Systems

Agentless systems are not supported on firewall systems including Microsoft ISA Server.

Configuring Internet Proxy Settings for a Management Server

You will need to configure proxy settings for a management server if it will be communicating over the Internet (for example, if you configured Client Monitoring to transmit or receive data from Microsoft). Perform the following steps:

1. In the Operations console, click on the Administration button. Navigate to Administration -> Device Management -> Management Servers, select the management server, right-click on Properties, and select the Proxy Settings tab.

2. Click on the option to Use a proxy server for communication with Microsoft and then select http:// or https:// from the drop-down list, typing the name of your proxy server in the address text box.

3. Enter the Port number, and click OK.

Summary

This chapter looked at a number of concepts new to OpsMgr 2007. We discussed user roles, Run As Profiles and Run As Accounts, and Operations Manager-required accounts. We discussed database security, mutual authentication, non-trusted domain considerations, DMZ implementations and workgroup support, obtaining certificates, and agent proxying. We concluded the chapter by looking at ACS security, firewall considerations, and communications security. Additional information on Operations Manager security is in the Operations Manager 2007 Security Guide, which you can access at the System Center Operations Manager 2007 Documentation site at http://www.microsoft.com/technet/opsmgr/2007/library/proddocs.mspx. You can also download the security guide from http://go.microsoft.com/fwlink/?linkID=64017.

The next chapter looks at backup and recovery techniques for OpsMgr 2007 and discusses disaster recovery planning.

PART IV

Administering Operations Manager 2007

IN THIS PART

Backup and Recovery

All production systems should have established backup and recovery procedures in place, and an Operations Manager (OpsMgr) infrastructure is no exception. Out-of-the-box, OpsMgr 2007 does not include a backup process. If one of the databases becomes damaged through corruption or a hardware failure and you are without its backup, you will have to reinstall that component and re-create the database. If there is damage to the Root Management Server (RMS) or Operational database, you will have to reinstall the entire management group. This creates all kinds of headaches.

Re-creating a database without the ability to restore what was previously there means that you lose all the information in the database. In the case of the Operational database, you lose all customization and operational data collected in the database. If you have installed the Reporting Component and you lose the Data Warehouse and ReportServer databases, you lose the reporting data you have accumulated in the data warehouse, plus OpsMgr report definitions and report customizations, which are stored in the ReportServer database. If you install Audit Control Services (ACS) and lose the ACS database, you have lost your security logs and audit information.

There are also critical files that you need to secure through backup. As an example, the RMS includes encryption keys. If the RMS is damaged and the encryption keys cannot be recovered, you will have to build a new management group and RMS. (Microsoft alleviates this situation somewhat with Service Pack (SP) 1, see the "Recovering from a RMS Loss" section later in this chapter.) The Reporting Server Component also has encryption keys. These types of potential data loss make it critical to create a backup and recovery plan for your OpsMgr 2007 implementation.

This chapter discusses backup and recovery strategies for Operations Manager. It also looks at a methodology for handling large report databases and requirements for disaster recovery planning.

Roles of Key OpsMgr Files and Databases

Backing up appropriate files and databases in a timely manner facilitates minimal data loss if there is a catastrophic failure in your OpsMgr infrastructure. An Operations Manager installation includes system databases, user databases, and significant files that you will want to protect from data loss.

SQL Server System and User Databases

Microsoft SQL Server *system* databases include databases established during the database engine install. These databases are integral to the functionality of the database engine, and include the master, msdb, model, and tempdb databases. Other databases, created for application-specific purposes, are *user* databases.

Operations Manager-specific user databases include the Operational database, Data Warehouse database, and ACS database. Installing the SQL Server 2005 Reporting Component (required for the data warehouse) creates two additional databases: the ReportServer and ReportServer tempdb databases.

Note that the Operations Manager 2007 setup process allows you to specify database names for the three databases it creates. This chapter will refer to the default names.

You should include the following items in your backup strategy. This includes various system and user files and databases:

▶ **The Operational database (named *OperationsManager* by default)**—This is Operation Manager's database installed for each management group, and is the most important database to back up. If you lose this database due to a hardware failure or corruption and do not have a database backup, you will have to reinstall the RMS and re-create the database, losing all rule customizations, discovery rules, and operational data collected. This database is shared among management servers within a management group, and must be backed up for every OpsMgr management group.

▶ **The Data Warehouse database (*OperationsManagerDW* by default)**—This database stores aggregated data used for reporting, which is used by SQL Reporting Services (SRS) for trend analysis and performance tracking. Based on the amount of data you are collecting and the degree of aggregation, this database may be large and thus require special handling. If you have not installed OpsMgr Reporting, your management group does not include the OperationsManagerDW, ReportServer, or ReportServerTempDB databases.

▶ **The SQL Reporting Services ReportServer database**—This database is used by the SQL Reporting Services Component. It stores the report definitions used for OpsMgr Reporting and is updated when new reports are defined or definitions of existing reports are changed.

▶ **The ReportServerTempDB database**—The only reason to back up ReportServerTempDB is to avoid having to re-create it if there is a hardware failure. If there is a hardware failure, you do not need to recover the data in the database, but you will need the table structure. If you lose ReportServerTempDB, the only way to get it back is by re-creating the SQL Reporting Services ReportServer database.

▶ **The ACS database (named *OperationsManagerAC* by default)**—This database is associated with the Audit Collector service, which runs on the ACS collector. The database uses an agent to track cleared Security Event logs, and adds a new table daily for each day's security events. If you have multiple collectors, each uses its own ACS database.

ACS typically uses its own instance of SQL Reporting Services and the SQL Reporting Services database, in which case you will also need to accommodate these items in your backup strategy. Chapter 15, "Monitoring Audit Collection Services," includes a full discussion of ACS.

▶ **The Master database**—This is a system database, recording all information used by a SQL Server instance—including database file locations, configuration settings, and security and login account information. This database should be backed up whenever there is a change to your SQL Server configuration. If you installed the Operations, Data Warehouse, Reporting, or Audit database Components on separate database servers or instances, each will have a Master database that should be backed up. This is also true for a separate database server or instance using SRS.

▶ **The Msdb database**—The Msdb database is also a SQL Server system database, containing scheduled tasks information for jobs, including regularly scheduled database backups. If you have installed the Operations, Data Warehouse, Audit database, or SRS Components on separate servers, each server will have a Msdb database that should be backed up.

▶ **Management packs and reports**—Management packs contain rules and information pertaining to how Operations Manager monitors applications, services, and devices. The management packs are stored in the Operational database, which you should back up as part of your standard procedure. We recommend separate backups of non-sealed/customized management packs because this provides the granularity to import them directly into Operations Manager if necessary and to save a self-contained copy of any rule customizations. Instances of importing management packs could include rolling back changes to an unsealed management pack or moving a customized management pack from a development to production environment.

Report templates are stored in the ReportServer database. As with management packs, we recommend separate backups of any reports you have created or customized.

▶ **IIS metabase**—Both the Web Console Server and SRS components use Internet Information Services (IIS). Most IIS settings are saved in its metabase, although several settings are in the Registry. If you are running IIS 6.0 with Windows Server 2003, the IIS metabase is automatically backed up each time the in-memory database is written to disk. The backups are saved to %*SystemRoot*%\System32\inetsrv\History.

To create your own metabase backups, see http://support.microsoft.com/kb/32477 for IIS 6.0 or http://support.microsoft.com/kb/300672 for Windows 2000 / IIS 5.0. The IIS 5.0 metabase backups, which must be performed manually, are stored at %*SystemRoot*%\system32\inetsrv\MetaBack. The IIS backup files can be saved for disaster recovery using a physical disk backup.

▶ **Custom files**—Custom files include encryption key files for the RMS and Reporting Server components. Customizations to console views are saved in the local user profile on the computer running the console. Those personalizations could be backed up with physical disk backup or a SystemState copy of the local operating system.

Establishing a Backup Schedule

In addition to identifying required files for backup, you should also establish a regular backup schedule. Tables 12.1 and 12.2 give suggested time frames for backing up significant databases and files used by Operations Manager 2007.

Establishing a daily backup schedule for those files that change regularly helps ensure any data loss affects less than 24 hours worth of data. It also makes it possible to meet your Service Level Agreements (SLAs) if you have backups of the information necessary to restore any OpsMgr components!

TABLE 12.1   OpsMgr Databases with Recommended Backup Schedule

Database	Name	Type of Data	Recommended Backup Schedule
Operations database	OperationsManager (default)	This database contains the majority of the OpsMgr configurations, settings, and the current operations data. The loss of this database would require completely reconfiguring Operations Manager and result in the loss of all operational data.	Daily
Data Warehouse database	OperationsManagerDW (default)	This database holds all the data used for reporting and can be large. The loss of this database would mean the loss of all historical operations and reporting data.	Daily or Weekly
SQL Reporting database	ReportServer	This database holds all the report definitions, as well as cached report information and snapshots. The loss of this database would mean having to reimport reports and re-create subscriptions. Minimal impact. If you have installed ACS, it will have its own reporting subsystem and instance of the ReportServer database.	Monthly
ACS database	OperationsManagerAC (default)	This database tracks Security Event logs being cleared by an agent. A new table is created daily for that day's events.	Daily
Master database	master	This database is a SQL system database and records the system information for SQL Server 2005. Back up the Master database for every SQL Server instance in your OpsMgr environment.	Daily or when changes

12

TABLE 12.1   Continued

Database	Name	Type of Data	Recommended Backup Schedule
Msdb database	msdb	This database is a SQL system database and holds information on all jobs scheduled through SQL Server. It can be found on every SQL Server instance in your OpsMgr environment. Although OpsMgr 2007 does not use this database as it schedules its maintenance internally, if you create any jobs yourself within SQL Server (backups or database maintenance, for example), you should back up the Msdb database to retain that information.	Monthly or as needed

TABLE 12.2   Significant Files with Recommended Backup Schedule

File	Type of Data	Recommended Backup Schedule
Management packs and reports (.mp and .xml files)	Source files for management packs and reports. Enable more granular restoration than entire Operations database; also used for moving management packs and reports from one management group to another.	After changes to management packs or reports
Custom files	Encryption key files, the IIS metabase, and so on.	As needed

Database Grooming

Part of maintaining the integrity of your database environment is managing data retention for your Operational and Data Warehouse databases. Data retention also affects the size of the database and the amount of data to back up, which affects your backup requirements and scheduling.

Grooming the Operational Database

The OpsMgr2007 Operations console includes the ability to modify data retention settings for the Operations database under Administration -> Settings -> General -> Database Grooming. The default setting for each of the data types is to remove or groom the data after seven days (see Figure 12.1). After the data is groomed, it is not recoverable unless it was previously backed up.

Within the Operational database, the p_partitioningandgrooming stored procedure runs automatically at midnight to perform the grooming. To run grooming manually, execute this procedure, which calls a series of other stored procedures that use your database grooming settings to perform the grooming.

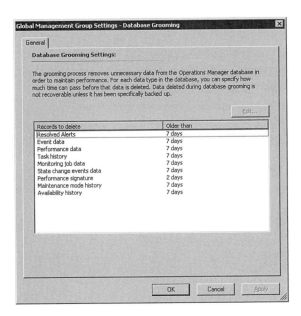

FIGURE 12.1   Operations Manager database grooming settings.

Grooming the Data Warehouse Database

The Operations console does not have a graphical interface to modify data retention settings for the data warehouse. You can groom the data warehouse settings by modifying columns in certain tables inside the OperationsManagerDW database. Data is groomed out at different intervals depending on the degree of aggregation. Data is stored by type, and the ranges for data retention vary from 10 days to 400 days by default, depending on the type of data.

Grooming Settings

Microsoft stores grooming-related settings in two areas in the MaintenanceSetting table in the Data Warehouse database:

▶ **Instance space**—Discovered objects with their properties and relationships.

▶ **Config space**—This is space that contains information about your management packs, rules they contain, overrides you have created, and so on.

Columns of interest and their default values are shown in Tables 12.3 and 12.4.

Using the default settings for the config space, a sealed management pack is removed 400 days after it was uninstalled from all management groups that are members of the data warehouse! This is also true for non-sealed management packs, but OpsMgr retains up to three old versions of a non-sealed management pack as well.

TABLE 12.3   MaintenanceSetting Table Instance Space Settings

Column	Value
LastInstanceGroomingDateTime	The last time grooming operations were performed
InstanceGroomingFrequencyMinutes	Frequency of the grooming process start in minutes (default: 480)
InstanceMaxAgeDays	Maximum age (since the day the instance was deleted) for the instance space objects (default: 400)
InstanceMaxRowsToGroom	Maximum number of objects to delete in one run (default: 5000)

TABLE 12.4   MaintenanceSetting Table Config Space Settings

Column	Value
LastConfigGroomingDateTime	The last time grooming operations were performed
ConfigGroomingFrequencyMinutes	Frequency of the grooming process start in minutes (default: 60)
ManagementPackMaxAgeDays	Maximum age for the management pack (since the day MP was uninstalled) (default: 400)
NonSealedManagementPackMaxVersion Count	Maximum number of non-sealed MP versions to preserve (independent of age) (default: 3)

Data Retention

Settings controlling data retention are located in the StandardDatasetAggregation table. You can view the grooming settings by running the following SQL query:

```
SELECT AggregationIntervalDurationMinutes, BuildAggregationStoredProcedureName,
GroomStoredProcedureName, MaxDataAgeDays, GroomingIntervalMinutes, MaxRowsToGroom
FROM StandardDatasetAggregation
```

Table 12.5 displays the default settings returned by the SQL query.

The following applies to the results shown in Table 12.5:

▶ The first column is the interval in minutes that data is aggregated. NULL is raw data, 60 is hourly, and 1440 is daily.

▶ MaxDataAgeDays is the maximum number of days data is retained. Depending on the type of data and its degree of aggregation, defaults can range from 10 to 400 days.

▶ GroomingInterval Minutes is the grooming process frequency. Performance, Alert, Event, and AEM data is groomed every 240 minutes (4 hours); State data is groomed every hour.

TABLE 12.5 Data Returned from StandardDatasetAggregation Table

AggregationInterval DurationMinutes	BuildAggregation StoredProcedureName	GroomStored ProcedureName	MaxData AgeDays	Grooming IntervalMinutes	MaxRows ToGroom
NULL	NULL	EventGroom	100	240	100000
NULL	NULL	AlertGroom	400	240	50000
NULL	NULL	StateGroom	180	60	50000
60	StateAggregate	StateGroom	400	60	50000
1440	StateAggregate	StateGroom	400	60	50000
NULL	AemAggregate	AemGroom	30	240	100000
1440	AemAggregate	AemGroom	400	240	100000
NULL	PerformanceAggregate	Performance Groom	10	240	100000
60	PerformanceAggregate	Performance Groom	400	240	100000
1440	PerformanceAggregate	Performance Groom	400	240	100000

To make sense of the grooming settings in this table, look at non-aggregated Event data, which is the first row of information in Table 12.5. We know that this pertains to Event information because of the referenced procedure name EventGroom (GroomStoredProcedureName). The information returned from the query tells us that Event data is not aggregated (AggregationIntervalDurationMinutes=NULL) and is saved for 100 days (MaxDataAgeDays). The EventGroom stored procedure grooms data (GroomStoredProcedureName), and runs every 240 minutes/4 hours (GroomingIntervalMinutes). Each time the stored procedure runs, it will groom a maximum of 100,000 rows.

You can use the following SQL code to change the grooming frequency for each type of data:

```
USE OperationsManagerDW
UPDATE StandardDatasetAggregation
SET MaxDataAgeDays = <number of days to retain data>
WHERE GroomStoredProcedureName = '<procedure name>' AND
AggregationIntervalDurationMinutes = '<aggregation interval duration>'
Go
```

Datasets

The data itself is retained by data type. Each data type is stored in a separate structure, called a *dataset*. Examples of these datasets include a performance dataset for performance data, a state dataset to monitor state transitions, an event dataset for events, and so on.

Management packs may also introduce new datasets. All datasets in existence—known today—are referred to by Microsoft as *standard datasets*. Microsoft maintains a set of tables for standard datasets that hold a description of the dataset including its data retention policies. A non-standard dataset does not have to follow the same rules; data retention settings for non-standard datasets are dataset specific.

Data retention for the standard dataset is set at the *aggregation* level, meaning that performance raw data (the samples themselves) is stored a certain number of days. The number of days may differ from the number of days the daily aggregates are stored for performance counters. These settings are stored in the StandardDatasetAggregation table, shown in Table 12.5 in the previous section.

The primary key for the StandardDatasetAggregation table is composite and consists of the database ID (from the Dataset table) and the Aggregation TypeID (from the AggregationType table). Default values will vary by dataset/aggregation type. The aggregation types, defined in the AggregationType table (which consists of the AggregationTypeID, AggregationTypeDefaultName, and AggregationTypeGuid columns), are as follows:

- ▶ **0**—Raw data
- ▶ **10**—Subhourly aggregation
- ▶ **20**—Hourly aggregations
- ▶ **30**—Daily aggregations

For performance reasons, data is not always groomed row-by-row. If the data inflow is high (typically the case for medium and large organizations for performance and event data), the Data Warehouse database uses additional tables to store data. This makes the grooming process (database row deletes) more efficient, as an entire table can be deleted rather than individual rows.

As an example, ten million performance samples are stored in the first instance of a table. After ten million records, OpsMgr creates a new table that holds the additional data and calculates a minimum and maximum date for the data in the first table. This information is stored separately in the StandardDatasetTableMap table. Grooming looks at this table to determine what data exists in each table and grooms accordingly. For OpsMgr 2007 SP 1, Microsoft has announced a ResKit tool named DWDATARP that allows you to view and set the data retention policies for all configured datasets.

The logic used by the grooming process is as follows:

▶ For a certain dataset/aggregation type combination, check to see if there is only one table in the data warehouse.

▶ If there is just one table, delete records row-by-row using the DELETE TOP SQL statement and MaxRowsToGroom parameter from the StandardDatasetAggregation Table.

▶ If there is more than one table, find the table with the oldest Maximum Date for data in it. If this date is older than the retention period, drop the entire table; otherwise, do not delete any rows.

The implication of following this process is that the data warehouse may not always be "current" on grooming. When the data in a table spans a month, some records are kept one cycle or month longer than necessary. However, the performance gains of dropping an entire table versus performing individual row deletes in SQL Server is enormous, so storing the data a little longer seems a reasonable tradeoff. Because report selection criteria includes a time period, any additional data is not visible to the user.

NOTE

How Is Grooming Actually Performed?

There are separate stored procedures to groom different types of data such as Performance, State, Alerts, Events, AEM data, and so on. The GroomStoredProcedure-Name column in Table 12.5 specifies the grooming procedures used for the data warehouse.

You can use the standarddatasetgroom stored procedure in the data warehouse database to trigger grooming to happen manually. The procedure uses a parameter, *datasetid*. This value, listed in the dataset table, represents the type of data to be acted on. Steve Rachui documents this at http://blogs.msdn.com/steverac/archive/2007/ 12/13/scom-2007-operational-and-datawarehouse-grooming.aspx. OpsMgr will call the standarddatasetmaintenance stored procedure to execute standarddatasetgroom.

As OpsMgr aggregates most of the data in the Data Warehouse database, its growth on a day-to-day basis is less than the Operational database. However, since the retention period is longer, it will grow to be considerably larger.

Data Warehouse Backup Considerations

Because the Data Warehouse database has longer data retention periods, it can grow to be quite large, although it is initially smaller than the Operational database. Large databases can present potential backup issues. A terabyte database, as an example, can take a long time to back up and restore.

One approach is to create archived or segmented versions of the Data Warehouse database, separating it by different months, quarters, or years, depending on its size and your reporting requirements. This portioning gives you granularity in backups—once a database is archived, it does not have to be backed up on a regular schedule. It also makes potential restore operations quicker.

A sophisticated backup schedule that accommodates archive databases would back up the current data warehouse (OperationsManagerDW) but retain online copies of archived versions. As you backed up each archived database when it was current, you would simply maintain those tapes in long-term storage as long as required for reporting purposes. Segmenting the reporting information allows you to reduce the volume of data backed up on a daily basis while maintaining long-term availability of the data using archived databases and long-term tape storage.

There are (of course!) several caveats to this:

▶ Adjusting the grooming settings (discussed in the "Grooming the Data Warehouse Database" section of this chapter) to groom only at the end at your designated archival period.

▶ Administrative overhead in managing the backup process at the end of each retention period. The end-of-period backup process adds complexity, which we illustrate in Figure 12.3.

▶ Tailoring your reports to run against archived data as necessary.

For purposes of illustration, consider a company monitoring 2,000 servers. For simplicity's sake, let's assume the company does not have third-party software with a SQL backup agent and uses Microsoft SQL Server's backup capability for its database backups. The company needs access to a year's worth of data. We can use the formula discussed in Chapter 4, "Planning Your Operations Manager Deployment," to determine the amount of space required for the data warehouse. Plugging these numbers into the formula

```
(3 MB/day x Number of Agents x Retention Days) + 570 MB = Data Warehouse size
```

gives a Data Warehouse database of nearly 2.2 terabytes (TB), which is too large to easily back up directly to tape. In addition, backup to a disk file requires equivalent storage on disk for the backup file, for a total of over 4TB. This is also too much storage for practical operations.

However, data for a single quarter will be just over 500 gigabytes (GB) or one-half terabyte. This amount is within the capability of the tape backup system. The company decides to break up the data warehouse into quarterly archives and accordingly sets the data warehouse grooming to groom data after each quarter (120 days). This configuration has been running for more than a year, so they have a steady state condition.

Figure 12.2 illustrates the backup process. You can see that the current data warehouse is available (OperationsManagerDW), as well as the four previous quarters of archived data (4Q2007, 3Q2007, 2Q2007, and 1Q2007). The process consists of two steps:

▶ Perform an online backup of the data warehouse to a disk file.

▶ Back up the backup disk file to tape. In the event of a disaster, the tape backup can be easily restored.

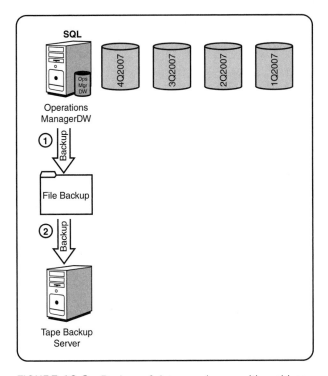

FIGURE 12.2   Backup of data warehouse with archives.

You can perform this backup process weekly, daily, or at whatever period meets your business requirements, with the procedure remaining the same. The amount of disk storage required is based on the size of the databases, which is based on the data captured by the agents. Calculating size for a 500GB database with one quarter of data, the company will need disk storage to hold five databases (5 x 500GB), plus an additional 500GB for the file backup that is archived to tape. This is a total of 3,000GB (3TB). You can contrast this figure with the original 4TB-plus storage requirement and see we have also conserved on disk storage! We also only need to back up 500GB at a time, rather than 2TB; making the backup operation more efficient.

Procedures are a bit more complex for the end-of-quarter backup process, shown in Figure 12.3. The following steps outline the process of transitioning at the end of 1Q2008:

1. First, the data warehouse is backed up to a disk file. This is an online SQL Server backup, so there is no interruption in availability.

2. Next, the backup file is copied to tape. In the event of a disaster, this tape backup can easily be restored.

3. The backup file is restored to a new SQL Server database storing data for that quarter (in this example, 1Q2008).

4. The database now outside the one-year data retention requirement (1Q2007) is deleted.

5. The tape backup of the data warehouse in Step 2 (1Q2008) is replicated for long-term tape storage.

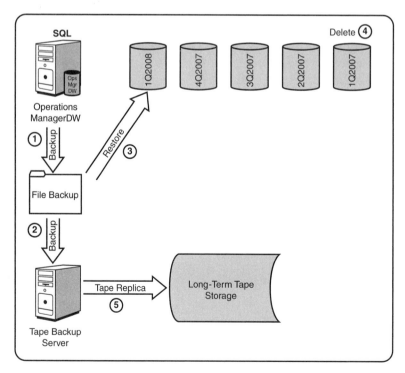

FIGURE 12.3   Quarterly backup of reporting database with archives.

These processes can be automated scripts and jobs, or you can run them manually as end-of-period procedures. The overall process is flexible and can be adjusted to support monthly archives rather than quarterly. The advantage of using monthly archives is that the backups are correspondingly shorter, but the report horizon will be shorter and only cover a single month. You could also extend this process to occur every 6 or 12 months! If it becomes necessary to query data in an archive, you could restore the archived backup as a database file and change the data source in SQL Reporting Services to point to that specific database.

This process is outside of any mechanisms designed or supported by Microsoft.

Grooming the ACS Database

Data is groomed out of the ACS database based on the data retention period specified during setup, with the default being 14 days. The ACS collector calls a SQL procedure to remove a partition that is outside of the data retention period. This procedure can be found on disk at *%SystemRoot%*\system32\Security\AdtServer\DbDeletePartition.sql. The data retention period itself is specified in the dtConfig table in the Operations-ManagerAC database.

To update the data retention period, run the following SQL query:

```
USE OperationsManagerAC
Update dtConfig
SET Value = <number of days to retain data + 1>
WHERE Id = 6
```

To retain 7 days of data, set *<Value>* = 8. Data is accumulated at approximately 7.6MB per day per workstation.

Further ACS database sizing information is available in Chapter 15.

Backing Up and Restoring the SQL Server Databases

Many Information Technology (IT) organizations have a database support group responsible for their Microsoft SQL database servers and in charge of backing up and restoring SQL Server databases. You should work with your database group to ensure that an appropriate backup and restore plan exists for your OpsMgr databases. If you do not have a group responsible for database backups, you will need to create your own backup and restore plan. This plan includes scheduling times for backups, identifying actual database files, and defining procedures for backing up and restoring those files.

Most enterprise backup implementations include a separate software module that can be installed to back up a SQL Server database while it is running. It is highly recommended that this type of backup agent be employed in your design to provide for online backups of the MOM databases.

Alternatively, you can use SQL Server's backup feature to back up the databases to (local or remote) file or local tape and then back up the resulting files during your normal backup process. This does not require a SQL backup agent and has the advantage of being very fast. The downside is that you need sufficient disk space to hold a backup the size of the entire database, which in the case of the reporting database we know can be quite large.

Database Backups

We will use SQL Server 2005's backup component to back up the Operational database, as an example of the process that you can use for the other databases used by OpsMgr 2007. SQL backups are defined using SQL Server Management Studio. For the Operational database, you should always perform a complete backup—not a differential backup—because by default, Operations Manager supports a simple recovery from a full backup only, not a forward recovery with the transaction log. By default, members of the sysadmin fixed server role and the db_owner and db_backupoperator fixed database roles have permission to back up a SQL Server database.

TIP

Types of Database Recoveries

Without getting too much into database technology, Microsoft SQL Server supports three types of recovery—full, bulk_logged, and simple. A *full* recovery uses the database and transaction log backups for full recoverability. *Bulk_logged* uses minimal transaction logging for bulk load types of operations—if a recovery is necessary, those transactions must be reapplied.

Simple, which is used by the OperationsManager, OperationsManagerDW, and OperationsManagerAC databases, recovers the database without using the transaction logs as part of the process. Using a simple recovery model, any database changes made since the previous full backup are lost. However, this model is the simplest to perform restore operations on.

(This is not to say you cannot change the recovery mode. Chapter 10, "Complex Configurations," discusses the procedures to set the Operational database to Full Recovery and configure log shipping. You can use log shipping on the Data Warehouse database as well. You may decide to implement log shipping for a high availability environment.)

Backup Steps

You should back up the Operational, Data Warehouse, and ACS databases daily. The following procedure defines a backup job for the Operational database:

1. In the left panel of SQL Server Management Studio, navigate to Databases ->
   OperationsManager. Right-click on the OperationsManager database, select Tasks,
   and then choose Backup, which brings up the Back Up Database General page
   shown in Figure 12.4.

2. The default backup type is Full, which is the backup type we will use for the
   OperationsManager database. A Full database backup backs up the entire database file,
   rather than just those changes since the previous backup.

   Under Destination, select the backup destination, which can be a disk file or tape.
   Here we will back up the OperationsManager database to disk, which is the default.

3. Select Add under Destination. The wizard provides a default location of
   %ProgramFiles%\Microsoft SQL Server\MSSQL.1\MSSQL\Backup. To enter the location and filename where the backup will be stored, click on the button with the
   ellipses (...) and name the file OperationsManager_Full_Group1.bak. In this case, we
   are using a folder named C:\Backups, rather than the default folder. Figure 12.5
   shows the location specified for the backup file.

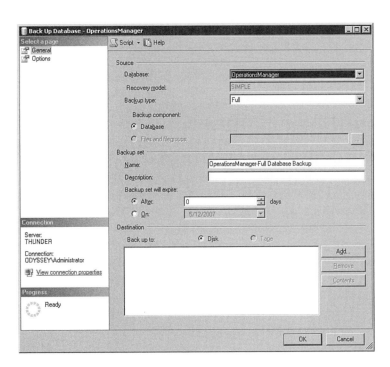

FIGURE 12.4   The SQL Server Management Studio Manager backup screen.

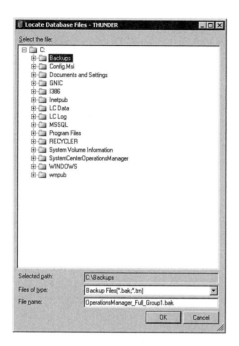

FIGURE 12.5   The backup device location screen.

TIP

Backup Naming Conventions

Because you may have more than one management group, you may want to include the management group name as part of the filename for your backup files. You may also want to include the type of backup, so that a name for the Operational database back-up might be Operational_Full_<*management group name*>.bak.

---

4. SQL Server Management Studio next displays the Select Backup Destination screen, shown in Figure 12.6.

5. After specifying the general requirements for the backup, it is time to move to the Options page shown in Figure 12.7. You must decide whether you will overwrite the file (backup set). By default, SQL Server appends the current backup to the end of the backup file if it already exists. Alternatively, you can overwrite (replace) the file. The option to truncate the transaction log is grayed out because the SQL Management Studio will not let you truncate the log when the database recovery type is defined as simple. If you want to truncate the log, you will have to add a step to do this manually.

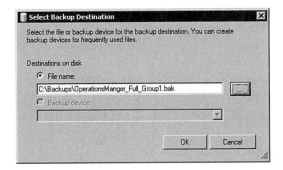

FIGURE 12.6   The Select Backup Destination screen.

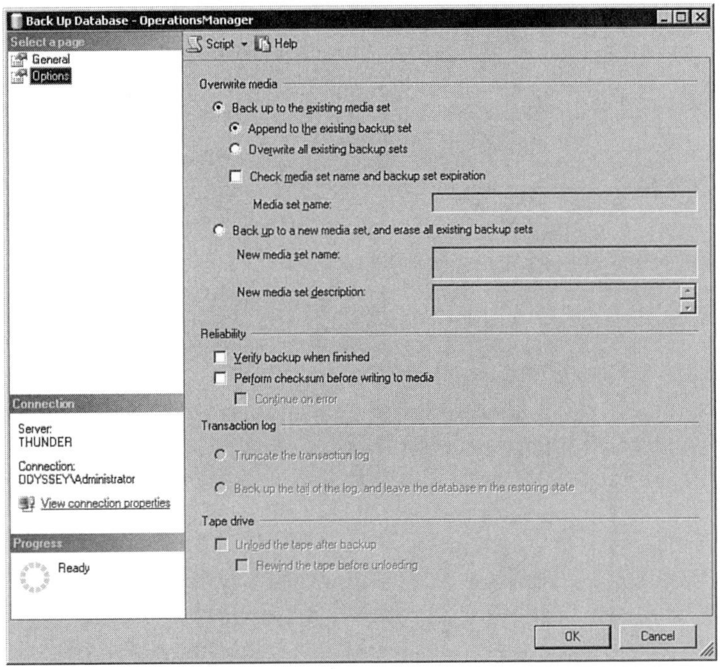

FIGURE 12.7   The backup options page.

Simple recovery is similar to truncate log on checkpoint—meaning in theory you do not need to truncate the log. In earlier versions of SQL Server, the truncate on checkpoint did not always work as advertised as part of the backup process, and the log file would eventually fill up. Some Database Administrators (DBAs) will still add a step to manually truncate the log as insurance.

6. Selecting the Script option at the top of Figure 12.7 generates Transact SQL code you can use to schedule the backup rather than having to return to SQL Management Studio each time you want to back up the database. (After the script is generated, the progress status shows that scripting completed successfully.)

7. After generating the script, select the Script menu at the top of the panel to bring up scripting options. You can select one of several listed options:

▶ Script Action to New Query Window

▶ Script Action to File

▶ Script Action to Clipboard

▶ Script Action to Job

To schedule the backup as a SQL job, select the Script Action to Job option, displayed in Figure 12.8. SQL jobs are run by the SQL Server Agent service.

8. Define the parameters of the backup job. Selecting the Script Action to Job option opens the New Job dialog. At the General page, you can change the owner and category of the job. Figure 12.9 shows the default options.

9. Select the Schedules page (see Figure 12.10) and click New to add a new schedule.

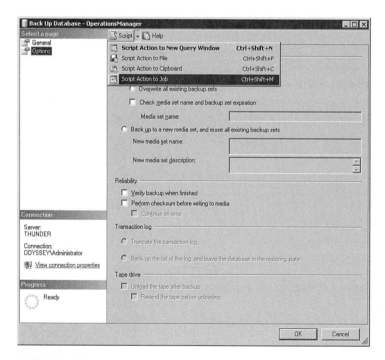

FIGURE 12.8   Create a SQL backup job.

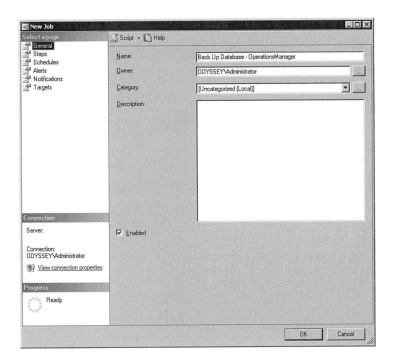

FIGURE 12.9   The New Job screen.

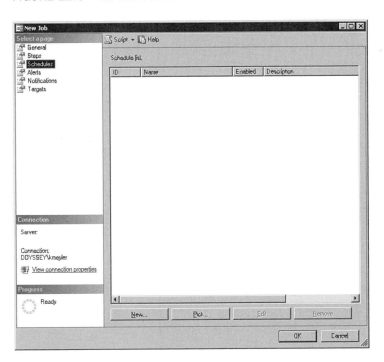

FIGURE 12.10   The New Job schedules page.

10. You can now define the details of the schedule. Figure 12.11 shows a Schedule type of Recurring with a backup frequency of daily and a start time of 3:00 AM. After completing this screen, you can also specify Notifications and Targets as part of the job properties. Click OK to save the job. The job information is saved in the Msdb database.

TIP

Scheduling Database Backups

SQL Server uses an online backup process, allowing a database backup while the database is still in use. During a backup, most operations are possible such as INSERT, UPDATE, or DELETE statements. For general processing efficiency, we recommend you perform backups during a period when you do not expect a high level of updates on the database you are backing up.

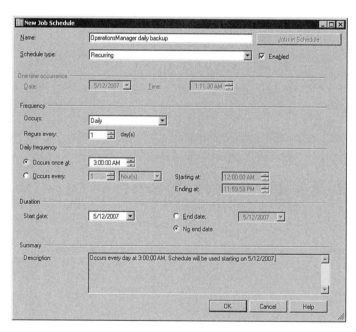

FIGURE 12.11 The new job scheduled to recur on a daily basis.

Truncating the Transaction Log

An optional step after creating the database backup step is also to truncate the transaction log.

More on Database Maintenance and Backups

Besides the fairly obvious reason for doing backups mentioned earlier—that of having a database to restore in the event of damage to the database or disk—another reason is to keep the size of the transaction log manageable, which keeps OpsMgr functional.

What is a transaction log? All updates to a SQL Server database are first written to its transaction log. The transaction log exists because SQL Server supports transaction processing. A *transaction* is a logical unit of work—all operations defined as a transaction will either succeed or fail together. For example, assume you want to move $500 from your checking account to your savings account. If the money is removed from your checking account but never deposited into savings, you have lost $500—it just disappeared! Transaction processing allows these two operations to be grouped into a single transaction, maintaining data integrity. If your deposit doesn't get to your savings account, the transaction is not "committed"—it is incomplete, and the update to your checking account is "rolled back"—and the $500 is still in your checking account.

The transaction log keeps track of every data modification performed in your database, who performed it, and when. However, if records are not eventually deleted from the transaction log, the file will fill up—or if autogrow is enabled, the file grows until it fills all available space on the disk holding the physical log files. SQL Server automatically truncates the log every time a checkpoint is processed, which occurs by executing a CHECKPOINT statement, modifying the database using the ALTER command or with SQL Management Studio, or shutting down the SQL Server instance.

Because the Operations Manager databases use a simple recovery model by default—which does not utilize the transaction log during database restores—all log records other than those at the active portion of the log can be truncated at any time, other than when running a database backup.

For those databases using the simple recovery model, SQL Server generates an automatic checkpoint. This automatic checkpoint will delete the inactive portion of the log when the log becomes 70% full (or the number of records in the transaction log reaches the number the SQL Server Database Engine estimates it can process during the time specified by the recovery interval option, whichever occurs first). You can also set a checkpoint yourself in a query to delete the inactive portion of the log using the following syntax:

```
USE OperationsManager
```

```
CHECKPOINT
```

If by some change your transaction log should fill up, don't panic. Run the following statement in a SQL query window to remove the inactive portion of the log and not log the operation:

```
DUMP TRANSACTION OperationsManaager WITH NO_LOG
```

These commands can also be run against the Data Warehouse and Auditing databases.

The Data Warehouse database has the autogrow option on by default for the data portion of the database. Do *not* set the other databases to autogrow.

Earlier versions of Microsoft SQL Server required truncating the transaction log manually when a database used the simple recovery model. (There was also a bug in SQL Server 2000 [474749] that prevented automatic checkpoints from always running as expected.) The following SQL statement initiates the truncate operation for the Operational database:

```
BACKUP LOG OperationsManager WITH TRUNCATE_ONLY
```

You can add this statement as a job step to the backup job you just created for the data-base segment. In SQL Server Management Studio, navigate to your database server, select SQL Server Agent -> Jobs, and then edit the OperationsManager backup job, adding a second step with the options shown in Figure 12.12. Be sure to change the Database drop-down box on the General page to specify the OperationsManager database.

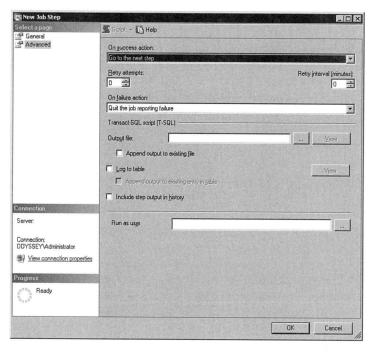

FIGURE 12.12 Truncate the transaction log as part of the backup process.

When you save the job step, you may be asked if you want to change the success action of the last step from "Go to Next Step" to "Quit with Success". Accept the changes, but then select Step 1 and change the properties of the Advanced page to change the success action to Go to the next step (see Figure 12.13).

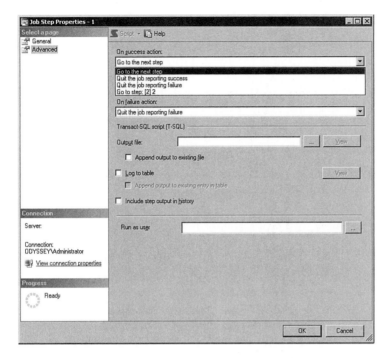

FIGURE 12.13   Change the success action for the first job step.

NOTE

Truncating the Transaction Log in SQL Server 2005

With SQL Server 2005, Microsoft is deprecating the BACKUP LOG WITH
TRUNCATE_ONLY functionality, as the log is automatically truncated with the simple
recovery model. Although this statement will still work, it will not be supported in the
next version of SQL Server.

After defining the database backup, make sure that there are procedures in place to copy
the file you create from the database backup to back up media for archival and restoration
requirements. You can use your existing nightly file backup process, adding the
OperationsManager backup file to the list of files and folders being backed up. In addition,
you should make sure that the other files mentioned earlier—such as .mp and .xml files,
encryption key files, and any custom files—are also backed up regularly as part of your
daily backup procedure.

Database Restores

If one of the Operations Manager databases becomes corrupt or a hardware issue causes you to lose a database, you will need to restore the affected database(s). We will build on the previous example where we created a backup of the Operational database using SQL Server Management Studio. For our scenario, we will assume that the Operational database is corrupt and cannot be repaired. At this point, our strategy is to restore from the latest backup.

The following procedure discusses the process of restoring the Operational database:

1. Be sure to stop the OpsMgr SDK service on the RMS to ensure that Operations Manager will not try to write data to the database. All database access goes through the SDK service.

2. Before performing a full restore for a SQL Server database, you must delete the existing version of the database. Launch SQL Server Management Studio -> Databases -> OperationsManager. Right-click on the database and select Delete. Uncheck the option to delete backup and restore history information from the database; then click OK to delete the Operational database.

3. Restore the database from the last backup. Right-click on Databases and select Restore Database. In the Source for Restore section, select From Database, and select OperationsManager from the drop-down list. This displays the Restore Database screen, as shown in Figure 12.14.

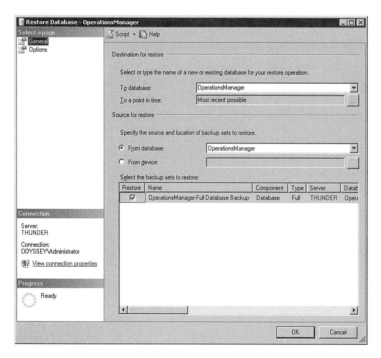

FIGURE 12.14   The Restore Database screen.

4. If you have more than one backup, verify you have selected the latest one for restore and click OK to begin the restore process. Depending on the size of your database, this may take several minutes.

> **NOTE**
>
> **Role of OpsMgr Queue Files**
>
> Remember that OpsMgr data is stored in queue files when the database is unavailable, which minimizes the chance of loss of current data not yet written to the database.

After you restore the database, restart the OpsMgr SDK service and launch the Operations console. Open the Administration node to verify it has the correct rule groups and configuration. You can also launch the Monitoring node to make sure that agents are sending heartbeats. This ensures that OpsMgr is operational.

> **TIP**
>
> **Restoring Databases Used by OpsMgr**
>
> When restoring any of your databases, be sure the database server software installed is at the corresponding service level of your database backup. As an example, you cannot install SRS without a service pack and then use a Data Warehouse database that has SQL Server 2005 Service Pack 1 or Service Pack 2 applied to it.
>
> The installation is blocked if you try to install without matching levels of maintenance.

Moving the OpsMgr Databases to a Different Server

As part of a disaster recovery scenario, or perhaps just because it is something that needs to be done, you may have a requirement to move the OpsMgr databases to a different SQL Server database server. The next sections discuss moving the OperationsManager, OperationsManagerDW, and OperationsManagerAC databases.

Moving the Operational Database

The Operational database is installed as part of your OpsMgr setup and cannot be reinstalled without reinstalling the management group. If you need to move the database to another database server, you can perform the following steps:

1. Stop all OpsMgr services on the RMS. If you have multiple management servers, stop the Health service on those machines as well.

2. Using SQL Server Management Studio, connect to the source database server and back up the OperationsManager database.

3. Connect to the destination database server and create Windows/AD SQL logins for the following OpsMgr accounts: SDK, MSAA, and DWWA.

4. Copy the OperationsManager database backup file to the destination server, and restore the database to the destination database server.

5. Using SQL Server Management Studio on the destination database server, right-click on the OpsMgr SDK login and go to Properties (Security -> Logins -> *<domain\SDK login name>* -> Properties).

6. In the properties for the Operations Manager SDK account, go to the User Mapping page and click on the OperationsManager database. Ensure that the following database roles have been assigned to the SDK account:

   ▶ Db_datareader

   ▶ Db_datawriter

   ▶ Db_ddladmin

   ▶ Db_owner

   ▶ Dbmodule_users

   ▶ Sdk_users

7. Click OK.

8. On the RMS and each of your management servers, open REGEDIT. Browse to HKLM\Software\Microsoft\Microsoft Operations Manager\3.0\Setup, and update the string called DatabaseServerName to reflect the name of the new database server.

9. Reboot the RMS and other management servers.

10. Set Enable Broker as follows:

   ▶ Open SQL Server Management Studio and connect to the database server now running the Operations database.

   ▶ Open a new Query window and type the following syntax:

   `ALTER DATABASE OperationsManager SET SINGLE_USER WITH ROLLBACK IMMEDIATE`

   ▶ Execute the query, then enter and execute the following query:

   `ALTER DATABASE OperationsManager SET ENABLE_BROKER`

   ▶ Close SQL Management Studio and reopen it, and again connect to the database server now running the Operations database.

   ▶ Open a Query window, and enter and execute the following syntax:

   `ALTER DATABASE OperationsManager SET MULTI_USER`

▶ To verify ENABLE_BROKER is set to 1, connect to the Master database and run the following query:

```
SELECT is_broker_enabled FROM sys.databases WHERE name=
➡'OperationsManager'
```

11. Restart the OpsMgr SDK and Config services on the RMS, and the OpsMgr Health service on the RMS and all management servers. You may also need to restart the SQL Server and SQL Agent services on the Operations Database Server Component.

While these steps move the Operations database, some configuration data is stored in the sys.messages system view in the Master database as part of the SetupOM process. This includes error messages specific to Operations Manager that are not tied to the Operations database.

As part of the CD content for this book, we include a script provided by Matt Goedtel of Microsoft that ensures the error messages specific to the OperationsManager database are available on the new SQL Server database instance. Run this script in the SQL Management Studio, and execute it against the Master database.

TIP

On the CD

Run the SQL script Fix_OpsMgrDB_ErrorMsgs.SQL.sql after moving the Operational database to another database server. Be sure to run it against the Master database on the new server.

Moving the Data Warehouse Database

You can take a "simpler approach" for moving the Data Warehouse database than with the Operational database. As OpsMgr Reporting is installed after the management group is created, we can be more straightforward and uninstall the OpsMgr Data Warehouse Component, install it on a different server, and then copy over the original database. However, there are several other changes to make, so it's not quite as simple as it sounds. Perform the following steps:

1. On the RMS, stop the SDK and Config services.

2. On the RMS and all other management servers, stop the Health Service. Stopping the OpsMgr services prevents updates from being posted to the databases while you are moving the data warehouse.

3. On the current Data Warehouse server, use SQL Management Studio to back up the Data Warehouse database (default name: OperationsManagerDW) to a shared folder on the server. You will want to back up the Master database as well, as a precaution.

4. On the current Data Warehouse server, uninstall the OpsMgr Data Warehouse Component. Open Control Panel -> Add/Remove Programs, select the System Center Operations Manager 2007 Reporting Server, and choose Change. In the Reporting Setup, select Modify, and then select the Data Warehouse Component to not be available. Note that this does not physically remove the data warehouse database as a SQL Server database. After removing the Data Warehouse Component from OpsMgr, delete it manually using SQL Management Studio (assuming you backed it up in step 3!).

5. On the new Data Warehouse server, install the OpsMgr Data Warehouse Component by running OMSetup.exe. Select the option to Install Operations Manager 2007 Reporting, selecting ONLY the Data Warehouse Component for installation. (Mark the Reporting Services Component to not be available on this server, as it is still installed elsewhere.)

6. On the new Data Warehouse server, copy the backup of the Data Warehouse database (step 3) to a local folder. (If the shared folder on the original server is accessible as a mapped drive from SQL Management Studio, you can skip this step.)

7. On the new Data Warehouse server, use SQL Management Studio to restore the data warehouse database backup.

   ▶ Delete the existing database first; be sure the default option to Delete backup and restore history information for databases is checked.

   ▶ Restoring the original data warehouse database is necessary to not lose the report data you have already collected for your management group.

8. On the new Data Warehouse server, create a login for the SDK account, the Data Warehouse Action account, and the Data Reader account in SQL Management Studio. Ensure the database permissions are correct for these accounts.

9. On the RMS, start the SDK service.

10. On the server running SQL Reporting Services, modify the data source. In Internet Explorer, open http://localhost/reports (add <$instancename> to the URL if using a named instance). On the Properties page, choose Show Details. The data source is named "Data Warehouse Main." Select that data source, and in the connection string, change the name of the database server from the old data warehouse server to the new data warehouse server. Click Apply to save your changes.

11. Change the name of the data warehouse server in the OpsMgr databases. Open SQL Server Management Studio to do your edits. For the OperationsManager database, go to the MT_Datawarehouse table and change the value of the MainDatabaseServerName_16781F33_F72D_033C_1DF4_65A2AFF32CA3 column (that really is the column name!) to the new data warehouse database server. For the OperationsManagerDW database, navigate to the MemberDatabase table and change the value of ServerName. Be sure to close the Management Studio when you are through, to save your changes.

12. Restart the Config and Health services on the RMS and the Health service on all management servers.

TIP

The Data Warehouse Server Name Is Stored in the OpsMgr Databases

In step 10 of the process to move the Data Warehouse database, we change the name of the data warehouse server in both the OperationManager and OperationsManagerDW database. This information is stored as metadata in the databases.

When the management group "wakes up," it needs to find its data warehouse. It looks in the OperationsManager database to find it, as the information is not stored anywhere in the Registry. However, it is possible that the data warehouse may be partitioned, consisting of multiple databases located on different servers—you may decide to store performance samples on one server, events on another, and so on, to achieve greater scalability.

The data warehouse server metabase information stored in the OperationsManager database can be considered a "master" database for the data warehouse. The system will then query the MemberDatabase table in the "master" itself, to find out where to forward particular types of data from a particular management group.

Moving the Audit Collection Database

Each ACS collector writes to its own database. This database can be installed on the Audit Collector Component or elsewhere. To move the ACS database to another database server, perform the following steps:

1. On the original ACS database server, stop the Audit Collection service. Now use SQL Server Management Studio to backup the database (OperationsManagerAC by default) to a shared folder on the server. (As always, you should also backup the associated Master database.)

2. Using SQL Server Management Studio, delete the OperationsManagerAC database. Be sure that the Delete backup and restore history information for databases and Close existing connections options are both checked.

3. On the new database server, use SQL Server Management Studio to restore the backup. You can either access the database backup from step 1 by first copying the backup file to a local drive, or map a local drive to the shared folder.

4. On the new Audit Collection database server, use SQL Server Management Studio to create a login for the ACS server. The format is *<domain\computername$>*, where *computername* is the name of the ACS server.

5. In SQL Server Management Studio, set the correct permissions for this account in the Security -> Logins folder -> Properties -> User Mapping. Check the box in the Map column that corresponds to the OperationsManagerAC database, and then select db_owner in the Database role Membership for: OperationsManagerAC list.

6. On the computer hosting the Audit Collection service, edit the Registry key HKEY_LOCAL_MACHINE\Software\ODBC\ODBC.INI\OpsMgrAC. Double-click the Server value, and set it to the name of the new ACS database server. Now start the Audit Collection service on this server.

To verify the database move was successful, use SQL Server Management Studio to check the OperationsManagerAC database for entries in the most recent dtEvent_<GUID> table. The datetime stamp should be more recent than when you restarted the Audit Collection service.

> **TIP**
>
> **Documenting Your Databases**
>
> A useful utility you may want to check out is SqlSpec by ElsaSoft. SqlSpec generates easy-to-read database documentation not only for Microsoft SQL Server but also for many other database platforms. Information is available at http://www.elsasoft.org/features.htm, and Stefan Stranger provides several examples of using it against his OperationsManager database at http://weblog.stranger.nl/documenting_your_operationsmanager_database_use_sqlspec.

Backing Up the RMS Encryption Keys

Microsoft provides the SecureStorage Backup tool (SecureStorageBackup.exe) to back up the RMS encryption keys. The syntax is as follows:

```
SecureStorageBackup.exe <Backup¦Restore> <BackupFile>
Backup      Backs up encryption keys to file specified as <BackupFile>
Restore     Restores encryption keys stored from <BackupFile>
BackupFile  Specifies file name where the keys will be backed up to and restored
            ➥from
```

Real World—Always Back Up the Encryption Keys!

If you lose your RMS and have not backed up the encryption keys, you must reinstall the RMS and your management group (Service Pack 1 incorporates some relief for this, see the "Recovering from a RMS Loss" section).

Also, be aware that after you upgrade your OpsMgr infrastructure to Service Pack 1, your previous RMS key backups will not work. An organization in Texas testing the service pack was bit by this when their RMS failed and the recovery did not work since the keys were backed up from prior to SP 1!

Microsoft plans to make it easier to backup the RMS key after your SP 1 upgrade by including a step in the upgrade wizard prompting you to do the backup at the end of the upgrade.

The SecureBackupStorage utility is located on the Operations Manager installation media in the \SupportTools folder and should be copied to the Operations Manager installation folder (*%ProgramFiles%*\System Center Operations Manager 2007).

The following procedure backs up the encryption key:

1. Log on to the RMS using an account that is a member of the Administrators group.
2. Select Start -> Run ->; then type **cmd**, and click OK.
3. At the command prompt, navigate to *%ProgramFiles%*\System Center Operations Manager 2007. The utility must be run from the OpsMgr installation directory. Remember, you must first copy this file from the installation media.

NOTE

Directory for Running the SecureStorageBackup Utility

If you do not run SecureStorageBackup.exe from the OpsMgr installation directory, you will get errors about dlls that are not registered.

4. Back up the encryption keys by typing the following:

    ```
    SecureStorageBackup Backup c:\backups\BackupKey.bin
    ```
5. You are prompted to enter a password (twice to confirm). This password is used for storage/retrieval, and must be at least eight characters.
6. The encryption key is saved to the folder and file you specify (c:\backups\BackupKey.bin, in this example). Be sure to remember the retrieval password!

To restore the encryption keys, open a command prompt and navigate to the Operations Manager installation folder (*%ProgramFiles%*\System Center Operations Manager 2007), and execute SecureStorageBackup Restore *<BackupFile>*. You will be prompted to enter the retrieval password. Using the backup key file we created, the syntax for the restore command would be as follows:

```
SecureStorageBackup Restore c:\backups\BackupKey.bin
```

You can also use the SecureStorageBackup utility to move the RMS capability to another management server, which we discuss in the next section.

Recovering from a RMS Loss

The RMS has a unique role in an OpsMgr environment. Although you can have multiple management servers accepting data from agents, only the RMS communicates directly with the OpsMgr databases. Given the importance of this role, it is not only important to back up the RMS encryption keys (see the "Backing Up the RMS Encryption Keys section"), but also to be able to transfer the RMS role to another management server if this server will be unavailable for a period of time. This section discusses the steps to restore the RMS role to another management server, as follows:

1. Confirm you have a working RMS and second management server. Figure 12.15 shows our RMS (Hydra) and a management server (DeathSting) in the Operations console.

2. Copy the SecureStorageBackup.exe and ManagementServerConfigTool.exe utilities to the Operations Manager installation folder on the RMS (*%ProgramFiles%*\System Center Operations Manager 2007). These files are available on the Operations Manager installation media in the \SupportTools folder. For our environment, the RMS is Hydra.

3. Run the SecureStorageBackup.exe tool, exporting the encryption keys file to a file share. The tool is run by opening a command prompt (Start -> Run -> and then type **cmd**), navigating to *%ProgramFiles%*\System Center Operations Manager 2007, and typing the following command:

    ```
    SecureStorageBackup Backup <BackupFile>
    ```

    where *<BackupFile>* is the shared path and filename of the backed up encryption key.

4. You are prompted to enter a password (twice to confirm). This password is used for storage/retrieval, and must be at least eight characters.

5. Be sure that the keys file is on a file share accessible from the other management server (DeathSting).

6. Copy the SecureStorageBackup.exe and ManagementServerConfigTool.exe utilities to the Operations Manager installation folder on the other management server (*%ProgramFiles%*\System Center Operations Manager 2007). These files are available on the Operations Manager installation media in the \SupportTools folder.

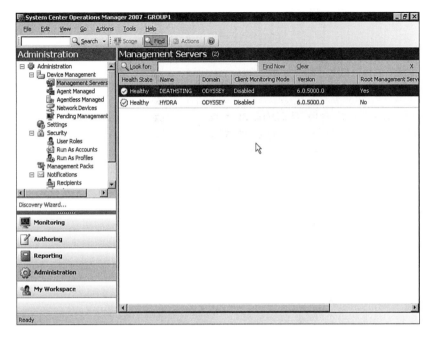

FIGURE 12.15   Initial Root Management Server and Management Server before changing roles.

7. From the command prompt in the *%ProgramFiles%*\System Center Operations Manager 2007 folder, run the SecureStorageBackup.exe tool to restore the key, using the following syntax:

```
SecureStorageBackup Restore <BackupFile>
```

where *<BackupFile>* is the shared path and filename of the previously backed up encryption key. Enter the password you entered when you created the keyfile.

8. At the command prompt, run the ManagementServerConfigTool.exe utility to promote the management server:

```
ManagementServerConfigTool.exe PromoteRMS /DeleteExistingRMS:true
```

You will receive a warning message:

```
Running this tool can cause irreversible damage to
your Operations Database.
Type Y to continue to promote the Management Server
to become the Root Management Server.
```

9. Type **Y** (yes) to continue. The utility completes and displays the information in Figure 12.16.

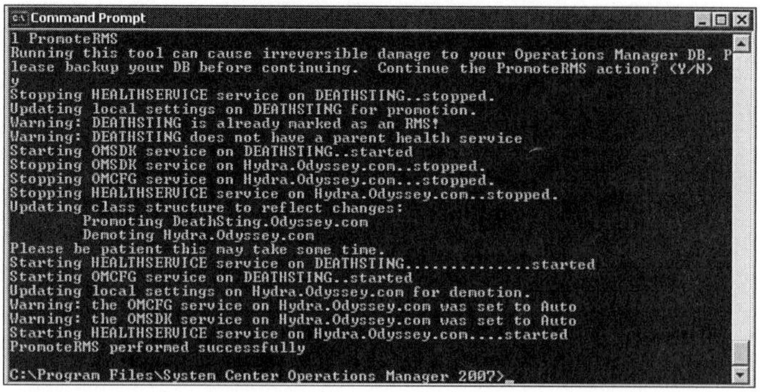

FIGURE 12.16   Changing the role of the Root Management Server to a management server.

10. Restart the Health Service on the original RMS. From the command prompt window in step 3, type the following commands:

```
Net Stop OpsMgr Health Service
Net Start OpsMgr Health Service
```

11. On the newly promoted RMS, open the Operations console. You are prompted for the name of the new Root Management Server to connect to.

Figure 12.17 shows the server roles reversed. The original RMS server is now a management server and the management server is now the RMS.

The full syntax for the ManagementServerConfigTool is included in Chapter 10.

TIP

Creating a New RMS Encryption Key with SP 1

With OpsMgr 2007 Service Pack 1, Microsoft includes a CREATE_NEWKEY command line switch that allows you to recover a lost RMS without a backed up encryption key. The switch is used when running MOM.msi on the management server that will become the new RMS.

J.C. Hornbeck of Microsoft provides preliminary documentation about this switch at http://blogs.technet.com/smsandmom/archive/2007/12/05/opsmgr-2007-what-if-i-lose-my-rms-encryption-key.aspx. You should still backup your encryption key, but this new capability gives you a way to recover without having to rebuild.

Other Components to Update After Moving the RMS

When you move the RMS to another management server, you will also need to update the Reporting Server and the Web Console Server with the new location of the RMS.

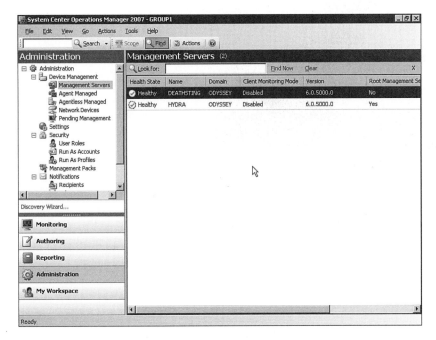

FIGURE 12.17   The Root Management Server and the management server after changing roles.

Perform the following steps on the Reporting Server:

1. On the Reporting Server, navigate to *%ProgramFiles%*\Microsoft SQL Server\MSSQL.2\Reporting Services\ReportServer.

2. Open the rsreportserver.config file using Notepad.

3. Find the two entries for *<ServerName>* and change it to the new RMS name.

Now perform the following steps on the Web Console Server:

1. On the Web Console Server, navigate to *%ProgramFiles%*\System Center Operations Manager 2007\Web Console.

2. Open the Web.config file using Notepad.

3. In the <configuration> section, find the following:

```
<!--This is internal connection between the web server and the MOM server .-->
<add key= "MOMServer" value="Hydra.Odyssey.com"/>
```

4. Change the contents of **value** from the old RMS name (using the Fully Qualified Domain Name) to the new RMS name (specify the Fully Qualified Domain Name)— for example, value= *"DeathSting.Odyssey.com"*.

See KB article 555950 for additional information, at http://support.microsoft.com/kb/555950.

The rsreportserver.config and web.config files will now contact the new RMS.

For pre-SP 1 OpsMgr 2007 environments, Microsoft confirms there are additional issues with promoting a management server to the RMS role, as the data warehouse processing is still on the old RMS after the promotion. The data warehouse operations code and promotion code have a "misunderstanding" such that the data warehouse operations are not moved to the new RMS. The synchronization process assumes the SDK is local, but it actually is not—as the RMS has moved and the SDK service is stopped on the old RMS. (The SDK service moves management pack information between the operational and data warehouse databases.)

There is no "easy" fix except for starting the SDK service on the old RMS, which takes care of the data transfer. Once SP 1 is in place, you can promote some other management server to be the RMS and then back to move your data warehouse processing to the real RMS.

Restoring a Clustered RMS

If your RMS is on a cluster, the disaster recovery process is a bit more interesting, as you will be reinstalling the RMS and the Operational database. The high-level recovery steps are as follows:

1. Back up the Operations Manager database to a separate system (disk or tape). See the "Database Backups" section of this chapter for specific steps.

2. Back up the RMS Encryption key, which we describe in the "Backing Up the RMS Encryption Keys" section.

3. Create a new clustered RMS configuration in the same fashion as the previous management group:

   ▶ Reinstall the Operations Database Server Component using the same management group name as was originally used.

   ▶ Reinstall management servers on all cluster nodes.

   ▶ Back up the new encryption key from the new RMS (this is the first cluster node on which a management server was installed), in order to create the new clustered RMS.

   ▶ Restore the new encryption key on all the other cluster nodes.

   ▶ Run the ManagementServerConfig.exe tool using the InstallCluster action (this tool is documented in Chapter 10).

   Specifying InstallCluster removes all the local changes on the cluster nodes that will compromise its recovery. Running this tool requires that all OpsMgr services are stopped on all management servers.

4. Drop the new Operational database and restore the original database (see the "Database Restores" section for additional information).

5. Restore the original encryption key on all cluster nodes using the SecureStorageBackup.exe tool.

6. Using the Cluster Administrator, bring the clustered RMS back online.

7. In SQL Server Management Studio, run the following query:

```
SELECT is_broker_enabled FROM sys.databases WHERE
name-'OperationsManager'
```

If the returned value is "0," you will need to reset the broker service, using these SQL queries:

```
ALTER DATABASE OperationsManager SET SINGLE_USER WITH ROLLBACK IMMEDIATE
ALTER DATABASE OperationsManager SET ENABLE_BROKER
```

Close SQL Management Studio and reopen it; then run this query:

```
ALERT DATABASE OperationsManager SET MULTI_USER
```

8. Restart the SQL services if they are stopped; then restart the SDK service.

Backing Up Management Packs

It is just as important to back up modifications to management packs as it is to back up the SQL Server databases used by Operations Manager. All overrides and custom rules in monitors are saved to a user-specified unsealed management pack stored in the Operational database. Backing up and maintaining management packs as separate objects gives you the granularity to restore a specific management pack rather than the entire database. You may want to create a separate management pack to store your overrides for each of the various management packs. Microsoft provides an unsealed management pack, named *Default*, where you may also be storing changes (although this is typically not recommended).

You can back up (export) unsealed management packs in an ad-hoc manner using the Operations console. We discuss this technique in Chapter 13, "Administering Management Packs." For purposes of regularly scheduled backup jobs, we suggest that you back up your unsealed management packs in a batch mode, using PowerShell cmdlets to export the management packs from the RMS.

> **NOTE**
>
> **Implementing a Full Change Control Process**
>
> A good change control process will include backing up management packs and storing them in a code repository solution.

Microsoft's PowerShell command-line shell is a new scripting language, allowing IT professionals to more easily control system administration. PowerShell is included with Windows Server 2008, Exchange Server 2007, and Operations Manager 2007. The Operations Manager Command Shell is a customized instance of PowerShell; it is a superset of PowerShell with cmdlets specific to OpsMgr functions. You can make OpsMgr SDK calls using the Command Shell.

Chapter 8, "Configuring and Using Operations Manager 2007," included a PowerShell example of importing management packs. In this chapter, we will export management packs using the export-managementpack PowerShell cmdlet.

Microsoft helps make the cmdlet easy to use by giving us a syntax example when you type **get-help** for this cmdlet. The example will export all unsealed management packs ($_ .Sealed –eq $false) to the root of the C:\ drive:

```
$mps = get-managementpack ¦ where-object {$_.Sealed -eq $false}
foreach($mp in $mps)
{
export-managementpack -managementpack $mp -path "C:\"
}
```

To put this syntax in a script, perform the following steps:

1. Open Windows Notepad and add code that initiates a connection to the RMS and loads the OpsMgr PowerShell extensions:

   ```
   param ($ServerName)
   add-pssnapin
   "Microsoft.EnterpriseManagement.OperationsManager.Client";
   set-location "OperationsManagerMonitoring::";
   new-managementGroupConnection -ConnectionString:$ServerName;
   set-location $ServerName;
   ```

   Because we are loading the OpsMgr extensions, we can run our script from the standard PowerShell environment, without having to run from inside the OpsMgr Command Shell. This is useful if you want to run scripts in a batch mode.

2. Now, add the original code from our get-help example, modified to export the management packs to C:\backups:

   ```
   $mps = get-managementpack ¦ where-object {$_.Sealed-eq $false}
   foreach($mp in $mps)
   {
   export-managementpack -managementpack $mp -path"C:\backups"
   }
   ```

3. Save the text file with a .ps1 extension for it to be executable by PowerShell. Figure 12.18 shows Notepad open to the ExportMP.ps1 PowerShell script we created to export all unsealed management packs.

To run the script shown in Figure 12.18 (saved as Z:\ExportMP.ps1), perform the following commands: Start -> Run > **CMD**, then type **PowerShell**. This opens a PowerShell instance.

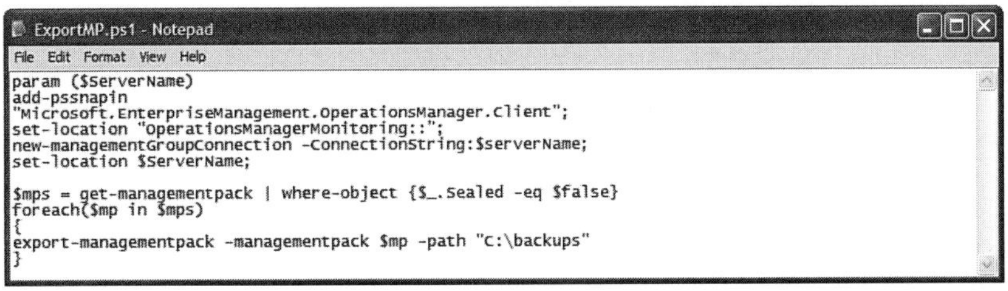

```
ExportMP.ps1 - Notepad
File  Edit  Format  View  Help
param ($ServerName)
add-pssnapin
"Microsoft.EnterpriseManagement.OperationsManager.Client";
set-location "OperationsManagerMonitoring::";
new-managementGroupConnection -ConnectionString:$serverName;
set-location $ServerName;

$mps = get-managementpack | where-object {$_.Sealed -eq $false}
foreach($mp in $mps)
{
export-managementpack -managementpack $mp -path "c:\backups"
}
```

FIGURE 12.18   A PowerShell script to export all unsealed management packs.

From the PowerShell prompt, type the following, specifying the RMS for the ServerName variable:

```
Z:\ExportMP.ps1 -ServerName:<rootmgmtserver>
```

How the ExportMP PowerShell Script Works

The script looks for the SDK service, which runs on the RMS only. If the RMS is not properly specified as the –ServerName value, you will receive the following error:

```
New-ManagementGroupConnection : The sdk service is either not running or not yet
initialized.
```

If you attempt to run the script from the same directory it is located, be sure to prepend the script name with a ".\" . For this particular example, the script name would be typed **.\ExportMP.ps1**.

Another Approach for Exporting Management Packs

If you want to back up management packs associated with a certain application or service, you can use the following PowerShell Script as a starting point. This example, which also uses the export-managementpack cmdlet, searches for management pack names that include the literal "AD" and then exports all management packs (sealed or unsealed) related to Active Directory:

```
param ($ServerName)
add-pssnapin "Microsoft.EnterpriseManagement.OperationsManager.Client";
set-location "OperationsManagerMonitoring::";
new-managementGroupConnection -ConnectionString:$ServerName;
```

```
set-location $ServerName;
$ mps = Get-ManagementPack ¦ where{$_.Name -match 'AD'}
=foreach($mp in $ad_mps)
{
export-managementpack -ManagementPack:$mp -Path:"c:\backups"
}
```

When you run this script, you will notice that all exported management packs have an extension of .xml—even the sealed ones. This is by design. Microsoft created sealed management packs (MPs) so you will not edit directly into the management pack; the vast majority of support calls for MOM 2005 were from problems with customers changing something inside of a management pack. With sealed MPs, you must use overrides to change rules and monitors, and those overrides are stored separately from the sealed MP.

Save the preceding code to a file with a .ps1 extension, open a PowerShell instance: Start -> Run > and type **CMD**, and then type **PowerShell**. Run the script by typing the following command:

Z:\mpexportAD.ps1 -ServerName:*<rootmgmtserver>*

You can build on this example to develop other customized export scripts.

Backing Up Management Packs from a Batch File

Now, let's take it one more step. We can create a batch file that invokes a PowerShell script, which can be part of a nightly backup routine. We will save our ExportMP.ps1 script to our c:\backups directory, and execute it from a batch file containing the following command:

```
%systemroot%\system32\windowspowershell\v1.0\powershell.exe
➥c:\Backups\exportMP.ps1-ServerName:<rootmanagmentserver>
```

The command invokes the PowerShell environment and runs our PowerShell export script. Running this nightly ensures that all customized management packs are extracted to the file system on a regular basis, where they can then be backed up to tape as part of your standard backup process.

Using the Operations Console

Chapter 13 discusses exporting and importing management packs. The functionality can also be used as part of your backup strategy. This chapter focuses on those steps of particular significance when backing up management packs.

The Operations console only allows you to export unsealed management packs. To use the Operations console to back up and restore management packs, perform the following steps:

1. In the Administration node of the Operations console, right-click on the specified management pack in the Details pane to bring up the option to Export Management

Pack, shown in Figure 12.19 (for sealed management packs, this option is grayed-out). This option is also available in the Actions pane, although it is grayed-out unless you have highlighted an unsealed management pack.

We will back up (export) the Default management pack, which is where all management pack changes are saved, by default.

2. You are asked to browse to the folder where the exported management pack will be saved. Figure 12.20 shows that we will export the Default management pack to the C:\backups folder. We are not given the option to specify a filename.

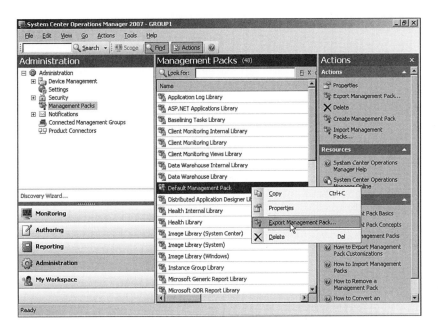

FIGURE 12.19   Specifying a management pack to export.

FIGURE 12.20   Specifying the folder to store the management pack.

3. If the management pack has already been exported to that folder, you are asked if you want to overwrite it (see Figure 12.21). If you choose No, the management pack is not exported and you are not given an option to save to another filename or folder.

4. Successfully exporting the management pack brings up the message displayed in Figure 12.22.

Restoring the management pack using the Operations console is accomplished using the Import function discussed in Chapter 13.

FIGURE 12.21   Prompt to replace previously exported management pack.

FIGURE 12.22   Management pack export complete.

Backing Up Reports

Before we discuss backing up reports, let's talk about how reports work. Similar to MOM 2005, Operations Manager 2007 uses SQL Reporting Services as its report engine, although the Operations console now front-ends and displays the reports. You can also access the OpsMgr reports from the SQL Reporting console, but that is not the recommended approach, as the report names display with their GUIDs (Globally Unique Identifiers) and the information (metadata) about the report is only displayed in the Operations console.

When you display the report hierarchy in the Operations console, you actually are seeing information from two places:

▶ SQL Reporting Services provides the list of reports.

▶ The management pack provides metadata such as the report display name and knowledge about the report.

The reports displayed in the Reporting node of the Operations console are actually those found in the SRS root folder. This means that any report is visible, whether or not it is part of a management pack—and is one reason why you want a dedicated SRS for Operations

Manager Reporting (a second reason is the Reporting Component installation changes security such that any existing reports are no longer accessible).

This model also means that you can create a directory in SRS, store a report under it, and have it appear in the OpsMgr console. That makes it easy to add reports, but it doesn't help if you want to deploy a new report to a new management group, deal with localization or dependencies, or easily back up any new reports you have created for Operations Manager. Out-of-the-box, reports are included with management packs, and OpsMgr expects that and deploys them to SQL Reporting Services for you.

There are two steps to backing up custom reports you develop. You can export the report as an RDL file, save it in XML format, and then optionally package it in a management pack. To keep things simple from an administrative standpoint, we recommend that you package your reports in management packs.

Backing Up OpsMgr Reports

To export the custom report as a RDL file, open it in Report Builder and choose File -> Save As File.... This creates the RDL file, which is in XML format. To package the RDL in a management pack, edit it in a text browser and paste its content in an unsealed MP under the `Reporting/Report/Definition` node in the management pack. As an example:

```
<Reporting>
    <Reports>
        <Report ID="Sample.Report1" Accessibility="Public" Visible="true">
            <Definition>
                [RDL XML file content here...]
            </Definition>
        </Report>
    </Reports>
</Reporting>
```

Where:

- ► ID is the name of your report in SRS. It must be a unique name within the management pack.

- ► Accessibility="Public" allows other management packs to reference this report. If the report is Public, the ID must be unique in your OpsMgr reporting environent.

- ► Visible="true" makes your report visible within the catalog.

Many other parameters can be specified within the node. See Chapter 23, "Developing Management Packs and Reports," for more information.

For purposes of backup, we will assume you have saved your RDL files and included them in unsealed management pack .XML files. These should be placed in a folder with your other customized and unsealed management packs to be backed up.

Backing Up ACS Reports

Microsoft does not support including ACS custom reports in management packs, as by default an OpsMgr administrator does not have access to ACS Reporting. Customized ACS reports should be extracted using the Report Builder and stored in a separate directory. By default, the Report Builder saves to your \My Documents folder; we suggest establishing a common location to save all customized ACS RDL files. You would later use the Report Builder to import RDL files back into the SRS environment.

The ReportingConfig.exe utility, found in the installation media under the \SupportTools folder, is used to reload Microsoft-supplied ACS reports. Chapter 15 provides additional information.

Backing Up SQL Reporting Services Encryption Keys

The SQL Server Reporting Services setup process creates encryption keys that are used to secure credentials, connection information, and accounts used with server operations. If you should need to rebuild or repair your SRS installation, you must apply the key to make the ReportServer database operational. If the key cannot be restored, database recovery will require deleting the encrypted data and respecifying any values that require encryption.

The RSKeyMgmt.exe utility can be used to extract a copy of the encryption key from the ReportServer database. The utility writes the key to a file you specify and scrambles that key using a password you provide. This file should be backed up as part of your backup and recovery procedures. You should also document the password used for the file. Table 12.6 lists the parameters used by RSKeyMgmt.

To create a backup of the encryption key, use the following syntax:

```
RSKeyMgmt -e -fC:\Backups\rsdbkey.txt -p<password>
```

You would run this locally on the computer hosting the report server. The SQL Server Reporting Services Books Online discusses managing the encryption keys under "Managing Encryption Keys." Michael Pearson has written an excellent article discussing SRS Recovery Planning, available online from the SQL Server Central community (SQLServerCentral.com) at http://www.sqlservercentral.com/columnists/mpearson/recoveryplanningforsqlreportingservices.asp. This article discusses SQL Reporting Services 2000, but it is also applicable to the 2005 version.

TABLE 12.6   RSKeyMgmt Parameters

Parameter	Value	Description
-e		Extract a key from a report server instance.
-a		Apply a key to a report server instance.
-d		Delete all encrypted content from a report server database.
-r	installation ID	Remove the key for the specified installation ID.
-f	file	Full path and filename to read/write key.
-i	instance	Server instance to which operation is applied; default is MSSQLSERVER.
-j	join	Join a remote instance of report server to the scale-out deployment of the local instance.
-l	list	Lists the report servers announced in the ReportServer database.
-p	password	Password used to encrypt or decrypt key.
-s	reencrypt	Generates a new key and reencrypts all encrypted content.
-t	trace	Include trace information in error message.
-u	user name	User name of an administrator on the machine to join to the scale-out deployment. If not supplied, current user is used.
-w	password	Password of an administrator on the machine to join to the scale-out deployment.

Automating the Backup Process

As an aid to backing up the files discussed in this chapter, we have created a simple batch file that automates the process from the command line. The backup scripts in the batch file are intended as an example and can be customized for your own environment.

The batch file (backup.bat) is on the CD included with this book. Running the batch file has the following requirements:

Prerequisites:

▶ Functional Operations Manager 2007 environment

▶ PowerShell installed on the RMS

Installation Steps:

1. Copy the full "\backups" folder on the CD accompanying this book to each OpsMgr 2007 server (including database servers). (This content should include backup.bat, exportmp.ps1, and savekey.exe.)

2. On the RMS, copy SecureStorageBackup.exe to the *%ProgramFiles%*\System Center Operations Manager folder from the installation media within the \SupportTools folder.

3. Customize the script to enable the installed components on the server for each OpsMgr 2007 server.

4. Schedule the backup.bat program to run according to your schedule (daily is recommended).

Disaster Recovery Planning

Although we hope you never need to restore Operations Manager from a catastrophic failure, you must be prepared for the possibility that this could happen. You should have a well-documented recovery plan that would work for every conceivable type of disaster that could occur, from hardware failures to a total datacenter loss. Essentially, you want to be able to get OpsMgr up and running with minimal data loss.

Your plan should assume the worst but be able to concisely and efficiently restore Operations Manager at a minimum to the last backup of your databases. You need to not only develop a detailed plan for the various contingencies, but should also practice the various scenarios in a development environment until you (and others on your staff for when you are not available) are comfortable with the process.

There are at two potential scenarios for disaster recovery, discussed in the next sections.

Recovering from a Total Loss

What would it take to recover OpsMgr assuming a "total loss?" Assume the following scenario:

▶ The Operational database is installed on the RMS.

▶ The management server is monitoring 200 agent-managed systems.

▶ There is only one management server in our management group.

▶ The Web console is installed.

▶ OpsMgr Reporting and ACS are not installed.

Although this is a very simple implementation of Operations Manager, it is intended to show you the steps necessary to recover OpsMgr from a complete hardware failure of the management server. We will assume that our server team has already built a new server using the same NetBIOS name in the same domain, installed SQL Server 2005, and enabled IIS because we will use the OpsMgr 2007 Web console. The appropriate level of service packs and security patches are applied—be sure to be at the same level of software maintenance that you had with your original system. We are ready to recover Operations Manager.

At a general level, here are the steps involved:

1. Install Operations Manager 2007 from the installation media—selecting the option for a typical installation and using the same management group name as the original install. Remember that the group name is case sensitive. Specify the same accounts (SDK and Config service, Management Server Action account) as used by your original installation.

   This type of information should be documented as part of your disaster recovery planning. Detailed steps on installing OpsMgr can be found in Chapter 6, "Installing Operations Manager 2007."

2. After Operations Manager is installed, immediately stop the SDK service to prevent the RMS from sending data to the Operational database. This prevents OpsMgr from writing data to this database, which you will be overlaying as part of your recovery process. Because any data written to this new database will be lost, immediately really means immediately!

3. Install any additional hotfixes previously installed with your original installation.

4. Delete the OperationsManager database created from your OpsMgr installation in step 1.

5. Restore the latest OperationsManager database created from your SQL backup.

6. Restore the RMS encryption keys.

7. Import any additional management packs that were loaded to your old management server or changed and backed up after your last Operational database backup.

8. Install the Web console.

9. Start the SDK service. Operations Manager will now be functional.

These steps constitute a high-level process for recovering Operations Manager. Your actual plan should contain greater detail, including specific hard drive configurations, the exact installation options, the SQL steps necessary to delete and restore the databases, and so forth.

Using Log Shipping

Another approach for disaster recovery is to implement log shipping. As we discuss in Chapter 10, log shipping automates the process of backing up database transaction logs and storing them on a standby server. This process keeps your production and standby SQL Server systems in synch. Figure 12.23 illustrates a sample disaster recovery solution that includes log shipping for the Operational and Data Warehouse databases.

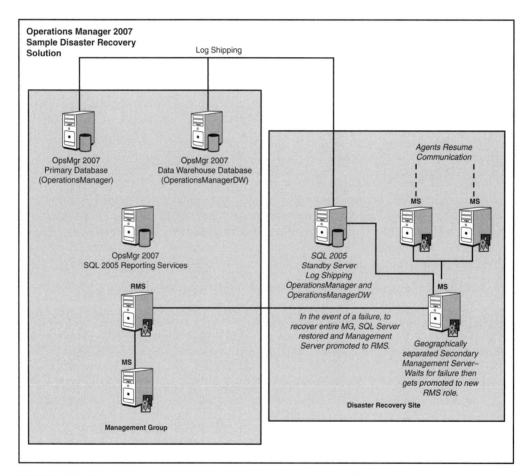

FIGURE 12.23   A sample disaster recovery solution using log shipping.

In addition to deploying log shipping, you will need the RMS and SRS encryption keys for a successful recovery. If you have the OperationsManager database without the RMS key, you will not be able to restore the management group (unless you have SP 1 installed and use the NEWKEY option previously introduced in the "Recovering from a RMS Loss" section of this chapter). The steps to recover from a downed RMS are discussed in the next section.

Recovering from a Downed RMS

Another potential scenario to discuss is if you only lose one of your OpsMgr servers. In this example, we will consider the steps to take if you lose the most important component, the RMS. If your RMS is not available, OpsMgr is not functional. If your RMS is down and you will not be available to meet your SLAs, you will want to promote an existing management server to become the RMS, as depicted in Figure 12.24.

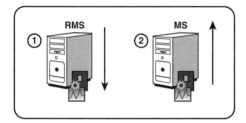

FIGURE 12.24   When the RMS goes down, you can promote an existing management server.

Recovering a downed RMS requires that you have previously backed up the RMS encryption keys, as we discuss in the "Backing Up the RMS Encryption Keys" section of this chapter. You would then promote a functional management server to become the RMS, using the steps we discuss in the "Recovering from a RMS Loss" section. Note that you cannot move from a non-clustered RMS to a clustered RMS, or vice-versa.

A Virtualization Plan for Disaster Recovery

An additional approach for disaster recovery planning is virtualizing your disaster recovery (D/R) environment. This concept would take backups of the physical drives you used when installing and configuring Operations Manager, and convert them to virtual drives.

The advantage of virtual drives is they are hardware independent of the physical environment they run on, making them easy to bring up in a D/R site. You could create a D/R management server in place, maintain a copy of the RMS encryption key, and establish an empty SQL Server(s). If you need to recover your systems, you would restore database backups, promote the management server to become the RMS, and connect the systems. This scenario would work in any software environment supporting virtualization.

Another approach to use virtualization to provide an off-site disaster recovery solution would be through sending regularly scheduled backups of the virtual hard drives to the disaster recovery location. In the event of a disaster, the backup copies of the virtual hard drives are activated and IP address changes made to reflect their new physical location.

Inventorying Your OpsMgr Configuration

Part of any successful disaster recovery plan includes understanding your current configuration. The Operations Manager 2007 Resource Kit includes a tool to assist in taking an inventory of the components changed on each computer where you install an OpsMgr component. This tool, Operations Manager Inventory, collects information about your installation and saves it to a XML-formatted .cab file. Data collected includes the following:

▶ Windows Installer logs for Operations Manager 2007

▶ Registry information for Operations Manager 2007

▶ Operations Manager 2007 configuration information

▶ Management packs

▶ All running processes

▶ All Windows NT event logs on that system

▶ The report produced by the Prerequisite Checker when you installed Operations Manager 2007

The inventory tool (MOMInventory.exe) must be run locally on each computer. The computer must have Microsoft .NET 3.0 installed. To run the inventory tool, perform the following steps:

1. Open a command prompt (Start -> Run -> and type **CMD**) and type **MOMInventory.exe**.

2. A dialog box will appear. You can click either Run Collection or Close. Click Run Collection.

3. In the Save As dialog box, enter a name and location for the .cab file the tool will create.

4. While the tool is running, a status window is open, showing information about the data that is collected. When the tool is finished, the status window provides the name and location of the .cab file (see Figure 12.25).

You can also run the tool in "silent" mode. At the command prompt, type the following:

```
mominventory.exe/silent/cabfile:<drive>:\<folder>\<filename>.cab
```

Figure 12.26 shows sample content of the .cab file created by executing MOMInventory.exe.

You can download the OpsMgr 2007 Resource Kit utilities from the System Center Operations Manager TechCenter at http://go.microsoft.com/fwlink/?LinkId=94593.

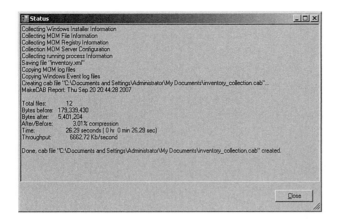

FIGURE 12.25   The MOMInventory tool status window.

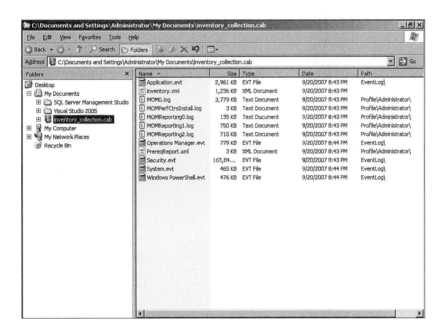

FIGURE 12.26   CAB file contents from running the MOMInventory tool.

Summary

This chapter discussed the need for backups, the components to back up regularly, and the tools available for performing backups. We also discussed an approach for backing up the data warehouse and overall disaster recovery planning for Operations Manager. The next chapter covers administering management packs, including best practices for implementing management packs, and Microsoft resources to help with management pack administration.

# CHAPTER 13

Administering Management Packs

This chapter discusses the underlying concepts and fundamental uses of management packs (MPs). We include the processes of importing and exporting management packs, and discuss best practices for incorporating management packs into your Operations Management (OpsMgr) environment. We also cover a number of utilities and resources developed by Microsoft to simplify management pack administration.

Any discussion of management packs invariably leads to questions about the information generated by those management packs. To that end, we include a brief discussion of some tuning and troubleshooting techniques that can help in your implementation of management packs.

Management Packs Defined

Management packs (MPs) make it possible to collect and utilize a wide range of information from various sources. An OpsMgr management pack is an eXtensible Markup Language (XML) document that provides the structure to monitor specific hardware or software. It contains the definitions of the different components and the information needed by an administrator who must operate that application, device, or service, which we will collectively refer to as *objects*. MPs operate by discovering and monitoring these objects. After an object is discovered, it is monitored according to the health model defined in the management pack.

MPs describe what data to examine and provide analysis of that data, giving a snapshot of the monitored component's health. Management packs are authored by Microsoft or by third parties. You may decide to write rules or monitors to augment or improve the functionality of an existing MP or choose to create a management pack from scratch, particularly if you need to manage a product where Microsoft or a third party has not released a corresponding management pack. In Chapter 23, "Developing Management Packs and Reports," we discuss the process of developing management packs.

One of the strengths of Operations Manager is that its management packs are typically produced by the same engineers who wrote the particular application or service. For instance, the management packs for Microsoft products are produced by the respective product teams. The management packs represent the best efforts of the developers to expose relevant and useful monitoring-related information, to determine what issues require attention, and to assess the level of product knowledge required for administrators to resolve a given situation.

NOTE

Management Packs Imported During Installation

As part of the Operations Manager 2007 RTM (Release to Manufacturing) installation, a number of management packs were imported by default, 32 of which are libraries. Libraries are MPs that provide a foundation of object types and settings that other management packs depend on. The management packs you import to monitor applications, services, and devices will require (have dependencies on) one or more of these libraries.

Model-Based Management

Operations Manager 2007 employs models as the basis for monitoring applications, devices, and services. Using models makes it possible to define the semantics of an object, discover the object, and observe the health of the object.

A *model* refers to a definition of the application, device, or service, and the components that make up that entity. It also describes the relationships between the components and how the application, device, or service relates to other applications, devices, and services. Model-based management requires that monitored applications, devices, or services are modeled in management packs.

Operations Manager provides a core model for management packs. This core model is used to declare common types of objects, and provides a starting point for management pack authors to refine the model and define particular monitoring logic. The model consists of a collection of classes, relationship types, modules, data types, and other building blocks. Monitoring capabilities are defined in an extensible way through management packs.

Management Pack Structure and Functionality

A management pack contains knowledge about an application, including the following:

- ▶ The structure of the application

- ▶ How to discover the application

- ▶ How to monitor the application

- ▶ What to do when the application breaks

The defined schema file used for management packs is MPSchema.xsd. XSD (XML Schema Definition) files define what elements and attributes may appear in an XML document, the relationship between the elements, and what data may be stored in those elements.

As we will discuss in Chapter 23, MPs can be built using the Operations Manager Operations console, the Authoring console, a XML editor, or even a vendor-provided tool such as Silect's MP Studio, which incorporates version control. MPs include collections of types, rules, monitors, tasks, views, overrides, and reports; these components are used to determine how an object collects, handles, and responds to data related to a specific monitored application, device, or service.

Those of you familiar with Microsoft Operations Manager (MOM) 2005 may remember that in MOM 2005, rules were targeted at a computer group. This is no longer the case; OpsMgr 2007 uses the object type to target rules and monitors. Let's see how these differ in functionality.

In MOM 2005, you would:

- ▶ Create a computer group.

- ▶ Create a rule group.

- ▶ Add rules to the rule group.

- ▶ Associate the rule group with the computer group.

For Operations Manager 2007, you:

- ▶ Create an object type.

- ▶ Create the discovery for that type.

- ▶ Create a rule or monitor targeted to that type.

This new approach represents a philosophical change in how management packs, rules, and monitors work, and demonstrates the object-oriented approach used by OpsMgr 2007. Rather than monitoring computers, OpsMgr monitors objects and focuses on the health of those managed objects. Several articles have been written about how targeting changes in OpsMgr 2007, including the following:

- ▶ **http://www.networkworld.com/community/node/21504**—Written by one of the authors of this book.

▶ **http://blogs.technet.com/momteam/archive/2007/10/31/targeting-series-part-1-differences-between-2005-and-2007.aspx**—Authored by Jonobie Ford, a technical writer for Operations Manager at Microsoft.

▶ **http://blogs.technet.com/ati/archive/2007/05/14/targeting-rules-and-monitors.aspx**—Written by Brian Wren, a principal consultant with Microsoft Consulting Services (MCS).

We also discuss this in some depth in Chapter 14, "Monitoring with Operations Manager."

Not only are management packs now written in XML, OpsMgr 2007 management packs can be sealed. A *sealed* management pack has an extension of .MP, while an *unsealed* MP has an extension of .XML. An unsealed management pack can reference other (sealed) MPs, but cannot be referenced by another management pack.

Sealed management packs are binary and read-only, and cannot be modified. They are digitally signed by the vendor. Sealed management packs provide the following benefits:

▶ Simplifies upgrading to a new version

▶ Easy to roll back to original version

▶ Simplifies troubleshooting for the vendor

By being read-only, the vendor knows that the objects in the MP cannot be modified, as the only changes allowed by OpsMgr are to disable and override rules and monitors. Most vendor-supplied management packs for OpsMgr are sealed, and are thus easier for the vendor to support.

Differing from MOM 2005 management packs, OpsMgr 2007 does not include the option to merge or update a management pack when you import a new version of that management pack; the MP is always replaced. As customizations are made to a separate, unsealed MP, the contents of the original management pack are not affected during the replacement process.

NOTE

How Read-Only MPs Make Maintenance Easier

In MOM 2000 and MOM 2005, it often was difficult to upgrade to a new version of a vendor-supplied management pack because many MOM administrators had modified rules and other objects in the existing MP. Implementing a newer version of the management pack often resulted in losing those changes even if the management pack was updated rather than replaced.

In addition, the merge option was very messy and not recommended by Microsoft!

Some of the more interesting features of OpsMgr 2007 management packs include the following:

▶ **Dependency checks**—Dependencies on other management packs are defined within each MP. You cannot import a management pack if you have not already imported all the management packs it depends on. Many management packs rely on libraries that include core definitions.

As an example, you cannot import the SQL Server 2005 (Monitoring) management pack unless you already have imported the SQL Server Core Library MP. Conversely, you cannot delete a management pack that other MPs depend on; so before deleting the SQL Server Core Library management pack, you must delete all SQL Server management packs that reference it. As an example, Figure 13.1 shows the SQL Server 2005 (Discovery) management pack having dependencies on a number of other management packs, and also being depended on by a management pack.

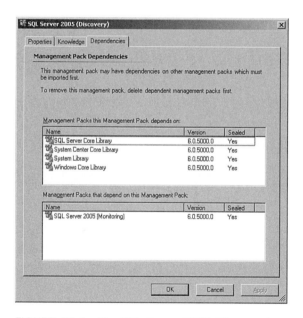

FIGURE 13.1   The SQL Server 2005 (Discovery) management pack both depends on other management packs and has management packs that depend on it.

▶ **Ability to upgrade to new versions of (sealed) management packs without losing overrides**—This capability is possible because overrides are saved in a separate management pack. As we discussed earlier in this section, overrides cannot be saved to a sealed vendor management pack.

▶ **Ability to export and store overrides**—This item is related to the previous bullet. Because overrides are saved separately, you can easily export your changes for backup purposes or in preparation for importing them to another management group.

▶ **Knowledge improvements**—This includes the ability to include inline views and tasks in the knowledge portion of the management pack, plus the ability to use Microsoft Word to edit knowledge. Actually, Word is required for customizing knowledge, and there are some who question whether having to license an additional copy of Word and install it on a management server is an improvement! The requirement for Word reinforces the idea that administrators should access the Operations console from their desktops when possible.

Real World—Editing Knowledge

The Operations console can be installed on a desktop operating system such as Windows XP or Windows Vista. If you use the console on your desktop to create knowledge, you can forgo the requirement for an additional Office license on a management server. Editing knowledge has two software prerequisites:

▶ Visual Studio 2005 Tools for Office Runtime (available at http://go.microsoft.com/fwlink?linkid=74969)

▶ Microsoft Office Word 2003

After installing the prerequisites, perform the following steps to edit company knowledge:

1. Click on the Company Knowledge tab; then click on Edit.

2. Within the Edit window, click on the Company Knowledge tab located here; then click the Edit button.

3. This launches Microsoft Word (see Figure 13.2). Type the desired information in the Word document.

4. Now select File -> Save. Do not close the Word document, or you will lose any information you have saved.

5. Alt-tab to the Company Knowledge screen within the Operations console and press the Save button there.

6. Close out the console screens. When you reopen them, the company knowledge should be there.

▶ **Extensible monitoring**—If you worked with MOM 2005, there were a set number of monitoring types that came with the product. With OpsMgr 2007, new types of monitoring can be plugged in at any time, and you can customize existing monitoring definitions to meet your needs. (The standard monitoring types are defined in system libraries imported during setup.)

▶ **Ability to uninstall a management pack**—In earlier versions of Operations Manager, management packs could not be easily (or officially) uninstalled. Now you can just do it through the Operations console. Notice the Delete capability in the Actions pane of the Administration space in Figure 13.3.

FIGURE 13.2   Launching Microsoft Word to edit management pack knowledge.

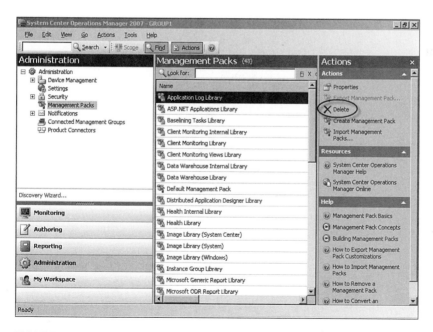

FIGURE 13.3   Delete action in the Operations console.

Objects

Management packs focus on discovering and monitoring applications, components, and devices—referred to as objects. Discovered objects are monitored according to the health model defined in the management pack. Every class, or object type, has a health model. Health models will represent the status (health) of even the simplest managed object.

Objects can have different levels of specialization. Chapter 3, "Looking Inside OpsMgr," uses the analogy of parts in a body to describe objects and relationships. You may recall the following diagram from Chapter 3. Figure 13.4 describes object types showing increasingly specialized objects, and relationships between objects.

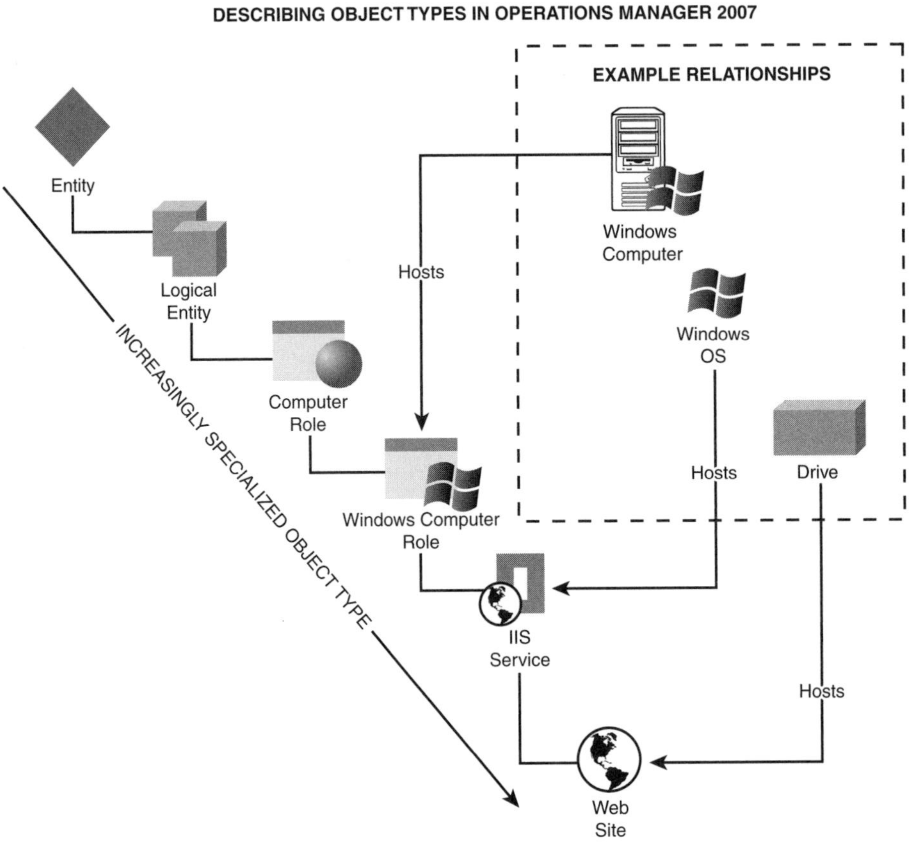

FIGURE 13.4   OpsMgr 2007 object types.

TIP

Objects and Classes

One of our co-workers offers a pearl of wisdom for those of you who are application developmentally-challenged engineers:

Management packs contain "monitoring classes." An instance of a monitoring class is called a monitoring object.

Another way to put this is to say that an *object is an instance of a class*.

Performing Diagnostics and Recovery

Management packs may contain diagnostic and recovery actions. These actions include tasks that can run automatically or on demand. A management pack can also contain common administrative tasks that you can launch from the Operations console or the Health Explorer. Console tasks can include loading management consoles or running utilities such as **ipconfig** or **ping** against a targeted computer. Figure 13.5 shows tasks loaded into OpsMgr as part of the Windows Server management pack. These tasks are listed under the Actions pane in the Operations console when the focus is on the Windows Server MP.

FIGURE 13.5   Tasks included with the Windows Server management pack.

For an example of running an inline task, see Figure 13.6. This figure shows restarting the Health Service as a recovery task being initiated from the Health Explorer.

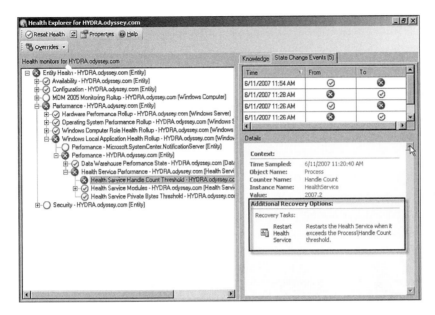

FIGURE 13.6   An inline task to run from the Health Explorer.

Workflows

Monitoring is based around the concept of *workflow*, which is shorthand for how information flows to support tasks. An Operations Manager agent and server will run many workflows simultaneously in order to discover and monitor applications, devices, and services. Some workflows are loaded by the Health service on the agent or server and run continuously, whereas others are loaded as they are required. A management pack may ship one workflow or thousands of workflows. As we discuss in Chapter 3, workflows are used in many ways—including collecting information and storing data in the operational and data warehouse databases, running timed scripts, creating alerts, and running tasks on demand.

Each workflow is targeted at a type of object or a class. The workflow only runs where an object of the specified type has been discovered and is managed by OpsMgr. A separate workflow executes for every object of that type. Workflow types include rules, discoveries, tasks, monitors, diagnostics, and recoveries. We discuss these different types of workflows in the next sections.

Rules

A *rule* uses three module types: data source, condition detection, and write action. The rule will include one or more data source modules, zero or one condition detection modules, and one or more write action modules. It is not enough to just say that a rule has a source, optionally detects a condition, and then performs an action; because OpsMgr

2007 is model-based, each of these modules is of a particular module type, with the type defining the behavior of the module.

Rules are loaded into memory when an object of the type the rule is targeting begins to be managed by the Health service. The rule stays in memory, waiting for data items to be generated from the specified data source(s). Rules end with at least one write action that changes the monitored system state or OpsMgr state (raises an alert), or stores data in the database.

A rule is a generic workflow that can do a number of things. Rules are generally used for one of the following purposes:

▶ Collecting and storing data in the Operational database or data warehouse (collection rules).

   Collection rules can be event, performance, or probe based. Event and performance rules collect data from various data providers; probe-based rules collect data from data sources based on a probe.

▶ Generating an alert (alert-generating rules).

   Alert-generating rules are event based. Alerts can be based on generic Comma Separated Value (CSV) text logs, generic text logs, Windows Event logs, Simple Network Management Protocol (SNMP) traps, Syslog information, or Windows Management Instrumentation (WMI) events.

▶ Running a timed action (timed command).

   Timed commands execute a command-line task or a script based on a recurring timed interval.

Rules are primarily used to collect data to show in the console or reports and to provide stateless alerting.

Discoveries

A *discovery* is a special type of workflow that discovers one or more objects of a particular type. It is used to "discover" instances of classes. A discovery can discover objects of multiple types at one time. A discovery uses a single module, which must be a data source module type.

Discovery is important because monitoring cannot occur for a class of object without prior discovery. Discovery usually uses a probing action to discover instances of a class. These probing actions include querying WMI, querying the Registry, or executing a script to discover instances of a class. Once instances of a class are discovered, these instances can be monitored.

Discoveries are actually a specialized type of rule. A discovery inserts discovery data into the Operations database. This data may be object or relationship instances. Unlike rules, discoveries do not include condition detection or write action modules. All discoveries have an implicit write action that OpsMgr handles internally; the write action inserts the discovery data into the database. For performance reasons, discovery data is cached and is only sent to the management server and database if it changes from the previous execution of the discovery.

Tasks

A *task* is a workflow, but it is not loaded by the Health service until it is requested by the user—either through the Operations console or a SDK call, and is typically initiated by a user using the Operations console. The user will execute the task for one or more objects. After a task is executed, it is unloaded from memory until it is called again. The default account used to run tasks is the Action account.

Tasks do not have data sources or condition detection modules.

Monitors

A *monitor* detects the state of an associated managed object. A monitor uses module types and will define workflows using those module types.

There are three types of monitors: aggregate, unit, and dependency:

▶ An *aggregate monitor* rolls up health from child monitors according to some algorithm. The current algorithms in OpsMgr 2007 for aggregate monitors are *Worst of* and *Best of*.

▶ A *unit monitor* monitors a particular aspect of an object, and is discussed further in the "UnitMonitorType" section of this chapter.

▶ A *dependency monitor* rolls up health of other objects across a containment or hosting relationship, based on an algorithm. Health cannot be rolled up across a reference relationship. The algorithms available in OpsMgr 2007 are *Worst of*, *Best of*, and *Percentage of*.

These types define the states the monitor can be in and the conditions causing each state. The monitor type can also define on-demand detection, which means that when a reset is called, the monitor can recalculate its current state without waiting for the next instrumentation to appear.

Monitors are used to determine the state of a monitored object, and they are the only thing that can affect the state of an instance. Each monitor is a state machine with a set number of states. A monitor can only be in a single state at any one time.

Diagnostics

A *diagnostic* is an on-demand workflow, attached to a specific monitor. Diagnostics are a specialized type of task. The workflow is either initiated automatically when a monitor enters a particular state or on-demand by a user when the monitor is in a particular state. Multiple diagnostics can be attached to a monitor as required. A diagnostic should not change an application state.

Recoveries

A *recovery* is also an on-demand workflow and a specialized type of task attached to a specific monitor or a specific diagnostic. The recovery workflow is automatically initiated whenever a monitor enters a particular state, a diagnostic runs, or on-demand by a user request. Multiple recoveries can be attached to a monitor if required. A recovery will change application state in some manner.

Data Types

To better understand module types and workflows, we can look at the concept of a data type.

OpsMgr passes data between modules. The format of that data varies depending on the module sending the data. A data source reading Windows performance counters will output a different type of data than a module reading and sending WMI data, or one that reads from the Windows Event log. Different module types expect different types of data— a threshold module type expects performance data, while a module type writing data to the OpsMgr database expects event data. What this means is that OpsMgr must define and use multiple data types.

These data types are defined in management packs. Because management packs are object-oriented, they follow an inheritance model—similar to class definitions. Whereas a class hierarchy will start with a base class of System.Entity, a data type module starts with a data type of System.BaseData. All data types will eventually inherit from the base data type.

When a module type is first defined, the definition includes the specification of input and output data types it will accept and provide. Each data type must be defined in the management pack containing the module or a referenced management pack. These data types must also be compatible with other modules used with the workflow.

Management Pack Elements

The following list includes XML elements contained in a management pack; these are also known as *management pack elements*. Each element has an ID attribute; the ID must be unique across all elements in that management pack.

- ▶ Workflows:
    - ▶ Discovery
    - ▶ Rule
    - ▶ Task
    - ▶ Monitor
    - ▶ Diagnostic
    - ▶ Recovery

▶ Class Type

▶ Relationship Type

▶ Data Type

▶ Schema Type

▶ Module Types:

   ▶ DataSource Module Type

   ▶ ProbeAction Module Type

   ▶ ConditionDetection Module Type

   ▶ WriteAction Module Type

▶ UnitMonitor Type

▶ Override

▶ Template

▶ ViewType

▶ Image

▶ UIPage

▶ UIPageSet

▶ Console Task

▶ View

▶ Folder

▶ Report

▶ ReportParameterControl

Note that some elements in a management pack have child elements called *sub-elements*; these are referenced by other objects in a management pack. An example of a sub-element is a property of a class. Using the analogy from Chapter 3, a class would be an eye, and the property is whether the eye color is blue or brown.

We previously discussed (in the "Workflows" section of this chapter) the Rule, Discovery, Task, Monitor, Diagnostic, and Recovery elements. We discuss the other elements in the next sections.

ClassType

The class type defines a type of object that is discovered and optionally monitored by OpsMgr.

RelationshipType

Objects (classes) can have relationships with other objects. A relationship type defines a relationship between two class types. It optionally defines properties that can be populated during discovery.

DataType

The data type defines types of data that OpsMgr modules can use and pass between each other. The data type is a pointer to a native or managed implementation. Data types are not extensible in OpsMgr 2007, except by Microsoft.

SchemaType

Any time you define a new monitor module, you must also define the schema for that type. When the type is used, the configuration provided must validate against the schema specified. If you plan to use schema elements across multiple modules, it is easiest to define the schema elements once, and then reference those in the multiple modules.

Module Types

Module types define the core monitoring capabilities of the OpsMgr product. OpsMgr 2007 module types come in four types: data source, condition detection, probe action, and write action, displayed in Figure 13.7. Each module type performs a distinct role.

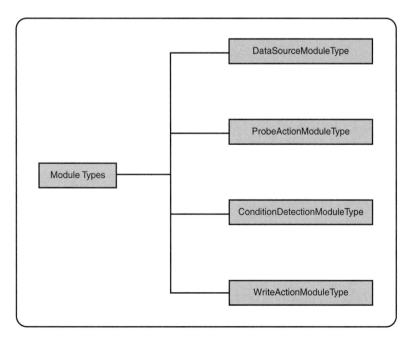

FIGURE 13.7   Module types in OpsMgr 2007.

DataSourceModuleType

The data source module type requires a single output type, which must be a valid data type defined in the management pack or a referenced MP. It does not define any additional attributes.

ProbeActionModuleType

The probe action type requires a single output type to be declared, similar to the data source module type. It also requires either a declared input type or that the trigger only flag is set.

Trigger only specifies that the input data item is only used to trigger execution of the module; the data is actually not used by the module.

ConditionDetectionModuleType

The condition detection module type has two additional attributes, which are the PassThrough and Stateful boolean attributes. These attributes are optional and default to a value of False.

The condition detection module type requires that one or more input types and a single output type are declared.

WriteActionModuleType

The write action module type does not define additional attributes. It requires that a single input type is declared, and optionally an output type.

UnitMonitorType

A unit monitor watches (monitors) a particular aspect of an object. This could be an application, device, or service. A unit monitor will use instrumentation or a probing action to determine the current state of the aspect (Windows Events, Performance data, log files, WMI information, SNMP information, scripts, OLEDB, LDAP, and so on).

A unit monitor is defined to be of a particular unit monitor type. OpsMgr ships with over 200 monitor types, which are predefined workflows that monitor for specific types of instrumentation.

Unit monitors will always roll up health to a parent aggregate monitor; the health is ultimately rolled up to the health of an object.

Overrides

Each management pack contains default settings and thresholds that are set by the vendor of the MP, and represent that vendor's definition of a health state for its products. As an administrator, you can use overrides to adjust these default settings and customize them for your organization. Figure 13.8 illustrates how overrides fit architecturally in OpsMgr 2007.

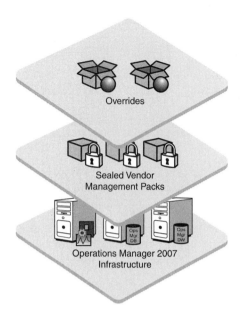

FIGURE 13.8   Structure of overrides in OpsMgr 2007.

Overrides are the only way to modify management pack behavior. You will store overrides separately from the vendor management pack either in a new management pack, or in the Default management pack (a new management pack is recommended over using the Default management pack). Because most management packs are sealed, if you want to change the behavior of the MP, you must create an override. The impact of this is as follows:

▶ Overrides will be used much more than they were in MOM 2005.

▶ Administrators are less likely to make a change that will impede the intended functionality of a management pack.

▶ Administrators should never lose changes made to a management pack when a newer version is imported, since changes are stored externally to the original management pack.

After testing your overrides, you can export the management pack containing the overrides and import it into your production management group.

Overrides can be applied to rules, monitors, discoveries, or tasks:

▶ Rule overrides change the frequency of a rule or a parameter such as a threshold.

▶ Monitor overrides change a parameter such as a threshold.

▶ Discovery overrides change the frequency of the discovery.

▶ Task overrides are used to change one of the parameters the MP author allowed for override.

Overrides can also be applied at several levels:

▶ **Type**—A *type* refers to the type of object that is being monitored. Examples of types would be all SQL Server databases, all Exchange mail servers, all DNS servers, and so on.

▶ **Group**—A *group* is a subset of a type. For example, instead of monitoring all Exchange mail servers, perhaps you want to apply the override to only the back-end mail servers in a particular domain, or the DNS servers in one of your branch offices.

▶ **Object**—An *object* would be a particular instance of a type. You may decide to apply an override to an individual database—perhaps the OperationsManagerDB on the Operations Database Server Component, or a specific DNS server.

If overrides conflict with each other, a hierarchy is applied. The Object override, which is the most granular, will win over a Group or Type override; a Group Override wins over a Type override.

Override types include the following:

▶ Category

▶ Monitoring

▶ Rule Configuration

▶ Rule Property

▶ Monitor Configuration

▶ Monitor Property

▶ Diagnostic Configuration

▶ Diagnostic Property

▶ Recovery Configuration

▶ Discovery Configuration

▶ Discovery Property

Each of these overrides will change monitoring behavior in some manner. You can view which overrides are affecting a managed object by viewing the override summary of the object, available on the Summary node of the Overrides menu in the Authoring workspace of the Operations console, displayed in Figure 13.9.

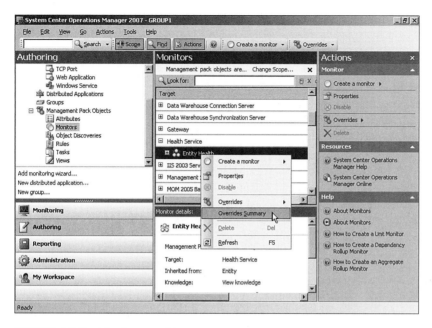

FIGURE 13.9   Viewing overrides.

Don't Store Overrides in the Default Management Pack

The Default management pack is the only unsealed MP imported during the OpsMgr 2007 installation. By default, any time you create an override or other monitoring setting, those changes are saved to the Default management pack.

This may not always be the best option, partly because the Default MP can become quite large and in part because you do not have any granularity if the Default MP stores all the objects you create. Saving overrides in the Default management pack also makes it difficult to later remove the management pack the override applies to, as you have created a dependency between the two that is not removed even when you remove the override.

Eliminating this dependency requires a number of steps:

1. Use the console to delete the overrides you've created.

2. Export the Default MP, and make a backup copy.

3. Delete the management pack you wish to remove.

4. Edit the exported Microsoft.SystemCenter.OperationsManager.DefaultUser.xml with the editor of your choice. (XML Notepad is nice; you can download it from the Microsoft Downloads site at www.microsoft.com/downloads.)

5. Find the Reference tags at the beginning of the XML (in XML Notepad, they are on the left side under ManagementPack -> Manifest -> References). Remove all Reference tags that point to the management pack you deleted.

6. Import the Default management pack back into Operations Manager.

Rather than using the Default MP, Microsoft recommends you create a separate management pack for each workload (Exchange, SQL Server, DNS, and so on), to simplify managing overrides. Select an existing (unsealed) management pack, or create a new one on the Override Properties page.

We suggest you use a naming convention that follows the management pack holding the original settings. As an example, if you are customizing settings defined in the Windows Core Library, create an unsealed MP named Windows Core Customizations. Your unsealed MP can be used to save overrides and any other customizations, such as new monitors, that will supersede the default settings in the Windows Core Library.

Template

A template is used in a manner similar to templates in other applications such as Microsoft Word. Users specify configuration information and run the template—the result is a new management pack or part of an MP—based on the information in the template.

Templates can be used to create classes, rules, monitors, tasks, and so on. Templates are intended to fulfill common monitoring scenarios such as monitoring a Windows service, monitoring a Transmission Control Protocol (TCP) port, or monitoring an Object Linking and Embedding Database (OLE DB) connection. Rather than OpsMgr administrators and authors creating the individual management pack objects, configuration information is provided using a wizard; OpsMgr runs the template, creating that portion of the MP.

Open the Operations console and select the Authoring button. Take a look at the left-hand pane in the Authoring space, shown in Figure 13.10. Under the Management Pack Templates section, you can see there are management pack templates to create ASP .NET Applications and Web Services, OLE DB Data Sources, TCP Ports, Web Applications, and Windows Services.

The Management Pack Objects section also includes several templates for management pack objects—monitors (Add Monitoring Wizard), rules (Create Rule Wizard), and tasks (create Task Wizard).

Presentation Types

Presentation types include view types, images, UI pages, and UI page sets. We discuss these in the following sections.

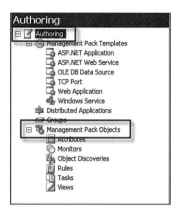

FIGURE 13.10   The Authoring section of the Operations console.

ViewType
Views are created in the Monitoring space of the Operations console. View types include alert, event, state, performance, diagram task status, web page, and dashboard views; when you create a new view, you can choose from one of these available types. OpsMgr 2007 view types are not extensible.

Image
An image element contains a binary blob of data. Images are assigned to classes or other management pack objects and rendered in the Operations console when instances of that targeted object are shown.

UIPage
A UI page references a managed code implementation of a WinForm page. The page is used to configure a module, monitor type, or template. You can share pages between different types.

UIPageSet
A UI page set defines a flow of UI pages that is shown when configuring a template, monitor type, or module type. This page set can define pages that show on creation, on edit, or both. The page set can define exact pieces of configuration that are passed to each page and optionally transform the configuration. The output configuration is a composite of all the output on each page.

ConsoleTask

Tasks were previously defined in the "Tasks" section of this chapter. A *console task* is a workflow that runs on demand, initiated through the Operations console.

View

A *view* is a customized subset of information available in the Operations console. As we discussed in the "ViewType" section, view types can include alert, event, state, performance, diagram task status, web page, and download views.

Folder

Folders organize information in the Operations console. Folders are used for views, the rule and task wizard, the unit monitor wizard, and management pack templates.

Report

Source definitions for reports are included in OpsMgr management packs, rather than as separate XML files as they were in MOM 2005.

ReportParameterControl

You can use parameters to control which data gets retrieved from a data source when a report is processed, and you can also use parameters to filter the data after it has been retrieved.

Sealing a Management Pack

Management packs are sealed with certificates. The certificate should be a valid public certificate from a certificate authority, such as Verisign. If you are developing MPs within your own company for internal use only, you can use a private certificate authority. Two utilities are used when sealing management packs: MPSeal and MPVerify.

Using MPSeal

The MPSeal utility is used to sign a management pack. MPSeal is located on the Operations installation media under the \SupportTools folder. The utility requires two DLLs on the machine used to seal the management pack:

▶ Microsoft.EnterpriseManagement.OperationsManager.dll

▶ Microsoft.EnterpriseManagement.OperationsManager.Common.dll

The syntax for MPSeal is as follows:

```
MPSeal.exe [<ManagementPack file.xml>] [/I <IncludePath>] /Keyfile <keyfilepath>
➥/Company <CompanyName> /Outdir <OutputDirectory> /DelaySign
➥/Copyright <CopyrightText>
```

All MPs referenced by the management pack must be available in the current directory, or specified as within an additional folder using the /I parameter.

The steps for using MPSeal are discussed in Chapter 23.

Checking Your Management Pack with MPVerify

After sealing a management pack, run MPVerify against the management pack to ensure it is correctly defined. A MP may be valid according to its schema, but may actually not be valid because not all validation rules can be defined within the XML schema. The Management Pack Verification tool is a command-line tool that performs verifications of a management pack file, validating the MP against the schema and then running through a set of rules to ensure that the MP is valid. MPVerify stops on the first error it finds, allowing the author to resolve each issue before any further tests are run.

Any time you import an MP into OpsMgr, the management pack must pass all verification tests prior to completing the import. Running MPVerify yourself on management packs you have developed helps to ensure a clean import into your management group.

When you run MPVerify, all referenced MPs must be available. By default, MPVerify looks for referenced management packs in the current directory; you can specify, however, an alternate directory with the /I parameter. The syntax for MPVerify is as follows:

```
MPVerify.exe [/I <IncludePath>] [/checkupgrade <OlderVersion
➡ManagementPackfile.mp>] [<ManagementPack file.xml>]
```

While authoring a management pack, you should run MPVerify against your MP regularly to catch and fix any mistakes early on. MPVerify is available on any OpsMgr server and can also be run on Windows XP or Windows Server 2003 systems. It requires that the .NET Framework 2.0 is installed and the following files exist in the same folder:

▶ MPVerify.exe

▶ Microsoft.EnterpriseManagement.OperationsManager.dll

▶ Microsoft.EnterpriseManagement.OperationsManager.Common.dll

These are the same DLLs used with MPSeal.

Finding Management Pack Information

Microsoft has written management pack guides giving in-depth information and deployment details for many of the management packs for Microsoft products. The guides for Microsoft's management packs are listed and available for download at http://go.microsoft.com/fwlink/?linkid=83259. Guides are also often distributed within the download package for a particular management pack.

Microsoft's System Center Pack Catalog provides one-stop shopping for management packs from Microsoft and third-party vendors. The catalog is located at http://go.microsoft.com/fwlink/?linkid=71124 and provides a central location for accessing Operations Manager management packs. The web page also includes access to management packs for earlier versions of Operations Manager and packs for System Center Configuration Manager. There are also individual links for each of the Operations Manager versions and Configuration Manager. You can access these pages at the following locations:

▶ **All packs for all products**—https://www.microsoft.com/technet/prodtechnol/scp/catalog.aspx.

▶ **Operations Manager 2007**—https://www.microsoft.com/technet/prodtechnol/scp/opsmgr07.aspx.

▶ **Operations Manager 2005**—https://www.microsoft.com/technet/prodtechnol/scp/opsmgr05.aspx.

▶ **Operations Manager 2000**—https://www.microsoft.com/technet/prodtechnol/scp/opsmgr00.aspx.

▶ **Configuration Manager 2007**—https://www.microsoft.com/technet/prodtechnol/scp/configmgr07.aspx.

For your convenience, we also include these as links in Appendix E, "Reference URLs," which are live on the CD accompanying this book.

Management Pack Updates

The System Center Pack Catalog site is updated regularly; it is a good idea to check it often for new management packs. However, that is a manual process.

If you worked with MOM 2005, you may remember Microsoft's MP Notifier management pack. This utility compared the versions of your installed Microsoft management packs with the current version at the Operations Manager 2005 Catalog. The MP Notifier is not available with OpsMgr 2007, and migrating the 2005 version of this management pack into OpsMgr does not provide the anticipated results.

The System Center Internal Library management pack includes a rule, *Check for Updated Management Packs*, which continues the functionality of the MP Notifier. The rule runs on the Root Management Server (RMS) and checks for new updated Microsoft management packs every 24 hours by default. This rule runs a PowerShell script.

A restriction on the use of this script is that the script requires the RMS Action account to be a member of the Operations Manager Administrators group. If you have configured this Action account to use Local System or a user not belonging to the OpsMgr Admins group, the script will not work.

Obtaining Management Packs for Earlier Versions of Operations Manager

The System Center Pack Catalog also lists management packs for MOM 2005 and earlier versions. MOM 2000 management packs are 100% compatible with MOM 2005, although they do not take advantage of newer functionality such as reports, State views, and a number of other features. MOM 2005 (and MOM 2000) management packs can be used in OpsMgr 2007 but must first be converted to OpsMgr 2007 management pack format, which we discuss in the "Converting MOM 2005 Management Packs" section of this chapter. This process does not convert MOM 2005 Reports, Operators, and Console Scopes.

Determining Management Pack Versions on Microsoft.com

For any particular management pack, the catalog listing includes a description of the management pack and a link to its vendor's website. The management pack description may or may not include its version. Figure 13.11 shows the catalog listing for the OpsMgr 2007 Windows Server 2000/2003 Operating System management pack.

Clicking on the link to the management pack (in this case, the Windows Server MP) takes you to the download center page for that management pack. Information at the download center includes the name and size of the downloaded file and its published date and version, an example of which is shown in Figure 13.12.

System Center Pack for	Vendor	Release Date Version	System Center Pack Name / Description / Languages	Provide Feedback
Windows Server 2000/2003 Operating System	Microsoft	11/8/2007 (6.0.5000.25)	Microsoft Windows Server 2000/2003 Operating System Management Pack Microsoft Windows Server 2000/2003 Operating System provides the fundamental monitoring basics for computers running the Windows Server 2000 and 20003 Operating System. 9/28/2007 - Updated release Version 6.0.5000.25	Provide Feedback

FIGURE 13.11   Management pack listing in the System Center Catalog.

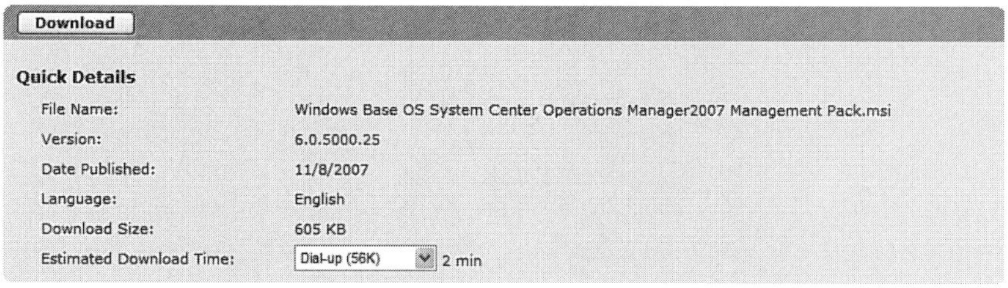

Download

Quick Details

File Name:	Windows Base OS System Center Operations Manager2007 Management Pack.msi
Version:	6.0.5000.25
Date Published:	11/8/2007
Language:	English
Download Size:	605 KB
Estimated Download Time:	Dial-up (56K) 2 min

FIGURE 13.12   Quick Details for a management pack at the Download Center.

TIP

Quick Details Information

Quick Details information is available for management packs developed by Microsoft; management packs from third-party vendors may not necessarily follow this convention.

The functionalities provided by the management packs covered in this book are based on the versions of those management packs available during mid-2007. Management packs are periodically revised, often more frequently than the corresponding product. It is best to keep up-to-date with the latest release of a management pack so that you will have the latest bug fixes and any improved monitoring routines.

Checking the Version of an Installed Management Pack

To determine the installed version of any management pack, open the Operations console and navigate to Administration -> Management Packs. In the Details pane, select the specific management pack you are interested in and right-click, displaying its property sheet. The version number is in the middle of the Properties tab, as shown in the example in Figure 13.13.

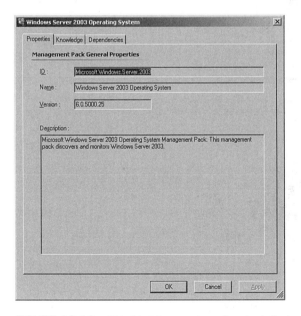

FIGURE 13.13   Checking the version of an installed management pack.

Management packs written for OpsMgr 2007 usually show a version of at least 6.0.5000.0. By comparison, MOM 2005 management packs start with version 05.0, and management packs written for MOM 2000 do not include version information and typically show a version of 00.0.0000.0000.

An Interesting Database Table

The OpsMgr 2007 operational database maintains information regarding each installed management pack. You can query this information, which is maintained in the ManagementPack table. The ManagementPack table contains a row for each management pack installed in the management group.

To find all installed management packs in the database, run the following query:

SELECT * FROM ManagementPack

Output from this query includes the Globally Unique Identifier (GUID) of the management pack, its name and "friendly name," whether the MP is sealed, and when it was last modified.

Converting MOM 2005 Management Packs

Implement the OpsMgr 2007 version of a management pack whenever one is available. If there is no OpsMgr 2007 management pack for the product you need to monitor, you can convert a MOM 2005 MP using the Migration Tool documented in Chapter 7, "Migrating to Operations Manager 2007." Security requirements for the Migration Tool include the following:

▶ Local administrator rights on the MOM 2005 management server

▶ Member of the Operations Manager 2007 Administrators group

▶ Both management groups in the same domain or have a one-way trust between the domains

You will also want to import the MOM 2005 Backwards Compatibility management pack into your OpsMgr 2007 management group. Be sure to download the most recent version from the System Center Pack Catalog.

If you want to convert multiple management packs at once, you may prefer to do your conversion in batch mode, although this process is not currently supported by Microsoft. Using batch mode requires two utilities, MP2XML and MPConvert:

▶ MP2XML is available in the MOM 2005 Resource Kit (http://go.microsoft.com/fwlink/?linkid=34629). This tool converts an AKM file to a XML file. Syntax for MP2XML is as follows:

```
MP2XML.exe [<Source Directory>\]<Source2005MPName>.akm
➥[<Destination Directory>\]<Destination2005MPName>.xml
```

MP2XML must be run on a MOM 2005 management server. It was initially designed to allow a MOM 2005 administrator to track changes to management packs by converting MPs from a binary AKM format to a more readable XML format.

▶ MPConvert is located in the OpsMgr installation media in the \SupportTools folder. MPConvert changes the XML file from the MP2XML utility to OpsMgr 2007 format. The syntax for MPConvert is as follows:

```
MPConvert.exe <Source Directory>\<OpsMgr2005XMLFile> <Destination
Directory>\<OpsMgr2007XMLFile>
```

You can run MPConvert on any workstation running Microsoft Windows XP or Microsoft Windows 2003 Server with the .NET Framework 2.0 installed. MPConvert does not require installing any MOM 2005 or OpsMgr 2007 components. The utility validates the input XML file against the MOM 2005 schema, so your input file must be a valid MOM 2005 XML file (from MP2XML.exe) for the conversion to be successful.

You would then import the converted management pack into Operations Manager 2007. You may want to take the additional step of sealing the management pack so the contents cannot be altered. This process is documented in the "Sealing a Management Pack" section of this chapter.

You can read more about the batch conversion process at http://technet.microsoft.com/en-us/library/bb309603.aspx. Additional documentation on syntax for these tools is available at http://technet.microsoft.com/en-us/library/bb309532.aspx.

TIP

On the CD

For convenience, we include the MP2XML utility and its documentation from the MOM 2005 Resource Kit on the CD accompanying this book.

Note that the conversion process is not foolproof. If you convert a management pack that includes a timed script, you may experience a memory leak in OpsMgr 2007. You can see the leak by checking the following performance monitors in Perfmon for the Process object:

▶ Private Bytes

▶ Virtual Bytes

The problem occurs because the MOMModules.dll module is not correctly managing allocated memory. The OpsMgr Health service will restart when the monitored threshold of the service is breached. Microsoft has released a hotfix for this; see http://support. microsoft.com/kb/935896 for additional information. The hotfix is incorporated in OpsMgr 2007 Service Pack 1.

Planning for Deployment

Deploying management packs involves planning, evaluating in a preproduction or limited production environment, and importing and exporting management packs. Just as you evaluate a new software program before deploying it into production, you should assess management packs before importing and deploying them across your production environment.

Testing gives you an idea of how the management pack operates, what monitoring features are important in your environment, and any additional configuration that may be needed for the management pack. Testing may also reveal possible adjustments you will want to make as overrides. After testing, tuning, and configuring a management pack, you will export it from your preproduction environment and import it into your production system.

> **TIP**
>
> **Only Install the Management Packs You Need**
>
> We suggest installing only those management packs you need. Extra rules impose a cost on your system resources: increased memory utilization of the agents targeted by the management pack and increased traffic between the managed computers and the management server.

Determine an Order to Implement Management Packs

When planning management pack deployments, a first consideration would be to decide which ones you want to deploy, and in what order. Some applications have dependencies on others, so you may want to implement the related management packs as you deploy those products. For example, say that you use Exchange Server. Exchange requires Active Directory, which in turn utilizes DNS. Another consideration is where you might get the most "bang for the buck"—which management packs will give you the most benefit for the least amount of cost measured either as time, resources, or effort. Typically this would be examined from a functional viewpoint. Let's look at two examples:

▶ You may decide that monitoring Active Directory is a high priority in your environment. Monitoring directory services would best be accomplished by using the Active Directory (AD), DNS, and Group Policy management packs. You might also consider implementing the Windows Server management pack as part of this, or perhaps prior to any of the other management packs.

▶ Alternatively, you may decide to focus first on monitoring your messaging environment. This would include using one or more of the Exchange-related management packs. As we mentioned, Exchange has dependencies on Active Directory, so monitoring Exchange could include monitoring AD.

The order in which you implement management packs really depends on the priorities of your organization and your goals for monitoring.

Implementing Management Packs

It is best to deploy a single management pack at a time. This practice makes it easier to deal with management pack issues as they occur. When you have more than one management pack involved, it may be difficult to determine what initially caused a problem.

Initial Tuning: Tuning by Function

Let's presume that you have determined your strategy and order for deploying management packs and have started importing selected management packs one at a time into your preproduction environment. As part of your approach, you should refer to that MP's management pack guide. Each management pack guide discusses particulars for installing, configuring, and tuning that particular management pack. The management pack guides (available at the System Center Operations Manager 2007 Product Documentation page at http://go.microsoft.com/fwlink/?linkid=83259) are often included in the download package with the management pack.

NOTE

Importing Management Packs

The process of importing management packs is described in the "Importing Management Packs" section later in this chapter.

You will want to do some initial tuning because testing and tuning in a non-production environment is always advisable prior to unleashing something new into production. Testing at this point also helps minimize the information load and unnecessary work for your production computer operators.

After evaluating a management pack's behavior, you may decide to tune one or more monitors or rules to meet your organization's needs. For example, you may find a performance monitor generating an alert at a threshold value inappropriate for your environment. You can tune that setting by overriding the default settings for that monitor.

13

TIP

Managing Alerts

As you implement a management pack, it will generate alerts that you will want to review and evaluate for tuning. Some rules and monitors may generate low severity alerts; depending on your environment, these may not be worth investigating or resolving, and you may consider disabling that rule or monitor.

For sealed management packs, the option to uncheck the enabled checkbox on the general properties sheet is grayed-out; go to the Overrides tab of the object and select the Disable button. You can choose if you want to disable the action for all objects of that type, a group, a specific object or type, or all objects of another type.

Any changes made are saved to an unsealed management pack (the Default management pack unless you specify otherwise). Remember that you can document your actions using the Company Knowledge section of the object.

A suggested approach for tuning a management pack is to work on a server-by-server or application-by-application basis, tuning from the highest severity alerts and dependencies to the lowest. There are several ways to approach this. A server-by-server approach addresses issues identified during while deploying servers into Operations Manager. After that is completed, the process should be an application-by-application/service-by-service basis, focusing on the overall health of the application or service. You can look at alerts first, and then open the Health Explorer to drill down specifically into the problem.

You will also want to consider dependencies. For example, if your plan is to monitor DNS, Active Directory, and Exchange, you would first implement and tune the DNS management pack because Active Directory and Exchange are dependent on DNS.

You can limit which object types display by using the Scope feature, which applies a temporary filter. Select the Scope button on the Operations console toolbar, and the Change View Scope dialog box displays, as shown in Figure 13.14.

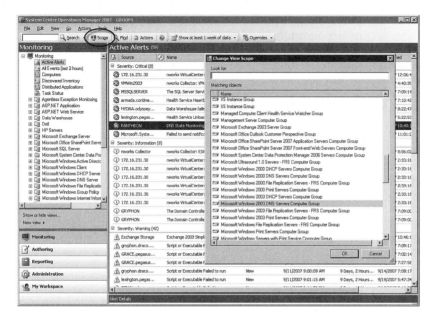

FIGURE 13.14   Changing the viewing scope.

This box displays a list of existing groups and distributed applications. If the list is long, you can find a specific group or application by entering a word or phrase in the Look for box. After making a selection, click OK; only the objects meeting your scope criteria are shown in the results pane. (To later remove the scope, click the X at the top-right corner of the scoping area at the top of the results pane.)

To troubleshoot DNS issues, open the Operations console, and in the Monitoring space, change the group scope at the top to either Microsoft Windows 2000 DNS Servers or Microsoft Windows 2003 DNS Servers, depending on which version of DNS is installed. (If both exist, start with one and then move onto the other.) Select the Active Alerts view (shown in Figure 13.15) to identify issues needing attention. Notice in Figure 13.15 that all alerts for computers in the DNS Server computer group are listed, not specifically alerts related to DNS.

Although the Active Alerts view provides detailed information, the State view and Health Explorer are better methods for monitoring and seeing the high-level health of the organization. From the Active Alerts view, you can right-click on an alert of interest, highlight Open, and select the State view or open the Health Explorer (other options include the Diagram, Event, and Performance views and the PowerShell Command Shell). Using the State view here (see Figure 13.16) exposes the servers running DNS, along with the monitored state areas with their health status.

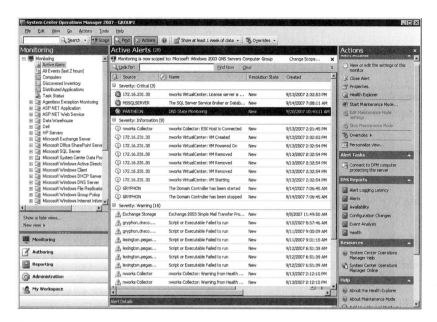

FIGURE 13.15   Checking DNS Server alerts.

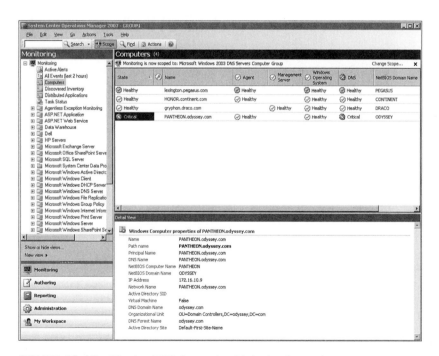

FIGURE 13.16   Viewing DNS Server health in the State view.

Right-click on each system you want to examine; then open the Health Explorer for that entity to view the various monitors associated with that rollup monitor. At each monitor, you can view associated alerts and check the properties for that monitor. Figure 13.17 shows the Health Explorer for Pantheon. Notice we are looking at the DNS monitor.

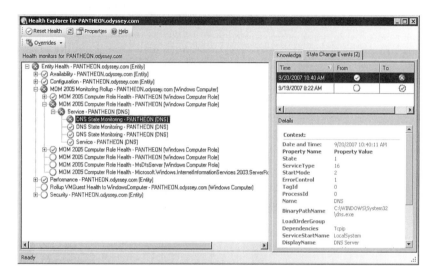

FIGURE 13.17   Using the health monitor to view DNS.

You should also investigate which events are sent to the management server. Perform the following steps to create a new view within the Monitoring space that displays events:

1. Open the Operations console and go to the top of the Monitoring space.

2. Right-click on Monitoring, and select New -> Event View.

3. Give the view a name and optional description, and choose under the criteria section if you want to limit the events returned.

   In Figure 13.18, we are selecting all events, which of course will return quite a bit of information.

Additional Configuration—Establishing Overrides for the Management Server Computer Group

There are several monitors for which you will want to set up overrides that affect the Management Server Computer Group. You may have already noticed that when you open the Health Explorer to query a management server, the entity health monitor will display Critical for one or both of the following threshold settings:

▶ Health Service Handle Count Threshold

▶ Health Service Private Bytes Threshold

This occurs because the default threshold values for these monitors may be too low. (In the case of the Health Service Handle count, the default threshold value was supposed to include an override for the Management Server Computer Group, but the override was not included in the OpsMgr 2007 RTM code; we expect it is addressed with SP 1.) Configure an override for these health monitors applying to the Management Server Computer Group. We suggest creating a separate management pack in which to store your overrides and not saving them in the Default management pack.

KB 938626 (http://support.microsoft.com/kb/938626) provides detailed information for configuring these overrides.

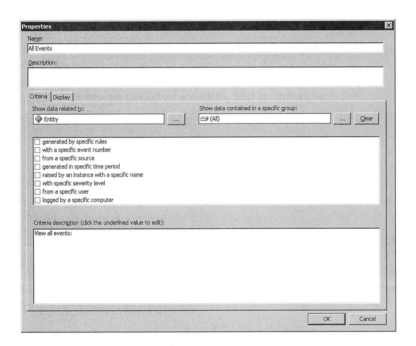

FIGURE 13.18   Creating a view for all open events.

Review the Operations console regularly to see whether events are captured that are unnecessary for your environment, as this could take up an excessive amount of storage within Operations Manager. Use the Monitoring section of the Operations console to disable or override unnecessary events. Using the Event view we just created, right-click on the specific event, and select disable or override rule, as shown in Figure 13.19.

Microsoft also provides several reports that you can use to identify your most common alerts and events. These are the Most Common Alerts and Most Common Events generic reports. See the later "Tuning Thoughts" section for additional information.

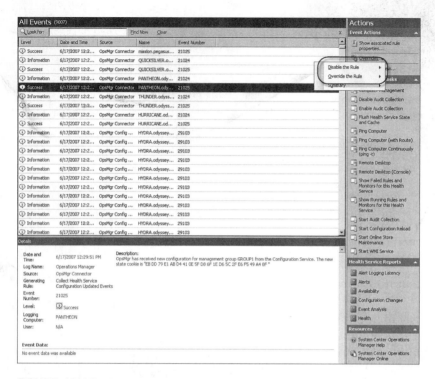

FIGURE 13.19   Disable or override a rule generating an event.

TIP

Where Does That Data Go?

Remember that everything seen here takes up space somewhere in the Operational database, so if the information is not relevant, you should adjust the underlying monitors, rules, or conditions so that it is no longer collected.

After you have resolved alerts and events in each function and management pack, implement the next management pack on your list. In our example, that would be Active Directory, and then finally Exchange. Import the management pack, and after it is functional, work through the Operations console, changing the viewing scope as discussed previously for the DNS servers.

After you reach a comfort level with each management pack, it is time to put it into production. Because you have already "tuned" the MP and want to keep your changes, export your customizations from the test environment and then import it into production along with the vendor-provided management pack. We discuss the processes of exporting and importing management packs in the "Exporting Management Packs" and "Importing Management Packs" sections later in this chapter.

TIP

Monitoring Database Space

Another aspect of monitoring OpsMgr is tracking space utilization of the Operational and Data Warehouse databases. You can use the SQL Management Studio to determine how much free space exists in each database on a regular basis.

If you are using the SQL Server management pack, you can have OpsMgr alert you when free space drops below a defined threshold. You will want to monitor space utilization in both your test and production environments. You may also want to adjust the grooming settings for these databases, following the procedures described in Chapter 12, "Backup and Recovery."

You may also want to investigate the OpsMgr Database Tracking management pack, which we discuss in Chapter 23.

Tuning Thoughts

Some general guidelines for testing and tuning management packs include the following:

▶ Review any new alerts reported for the servers monitored with the new management pack. Operations Manager Reporting includes the *Alerts* and *Most Common Alerts* reports to help you discover your most common alerts. These reports are in the Microsoft Generic Report Library under the Reporting space. If alerts are occurring, there are several actions to consider:

Resolve the issue generating the alert. View the product knowledge base information regarding the specific error occurring in your environment. Typically when a management pack is first installed, it discovers a multitude of previously unknown issues in your environment. Monitor the alerts to determine potential areas of concern.

Override the monitor or rule. Operations Manager allows you to override the configuration for all types, a particular object type, a group, or a specific object. As an example, you may want to override the default free space threshold value for specific databases when they are of significantly different sizes.

Disable the monitor or rule. Go to the specific object for that management pack in the Authoring space of the Operations console; open its properties sheet, and under the Overrides tab, disable the object. You should only disable a monitor or rule after concluding that the issue is not severe enough to warrant an alert and you do not need to be made aware of the specific situation monitored for that object type or group. Some rules are initially disabled when delivered in management packs because they may not apply in all situations. (An example of this is the SMS management pack where a number of the SQL Server monitoring rules are initially disabled because the SQL Server MP checks for similar events.)

Change the threshold of a monitor that is generating the alert when you want the underlying condition to be monitored, but the alert is generated before the condition is actually a problem for your particular environment. Consider this option if the monitor is not a good candidate for an override or disable/enable. An example of where this may occur would be free space thresholds for databases monitored by the SQL Server management pack. Note that OpsMgr incorporates self-tuning thresholds, so in many instances the software will do this for you.

TIP

Which Rule Is It?

You can identify the rule by opening the alert in the Monitoring space and looking in the Alert Details pane in the bottom section of the Active Alerts section. The Details pane gives you a hypertext link to the properties page of the rule. You can also find rules using PowerShell. The System Center Forum (www.systemcenterforum.org) provides a PowerShell script that searches a group for a specified rule using the display name of the rule. For your convenience, we include their script, FindRule.ps1, on the CD accompanying this book.

▶ If a new management pack generates many alerts, you may want to disable monitors or rules within that management pack. You can turn them on gradually, making the new management pack easier to tune and troubleshoot.

Real World—Troubleshooting Management Packs

If a management pack does not appear to function properly, refer to the management pack guide or included documentation for configuration requirements. For example, you will want to verify that the OpsMgr Agent Action account has the appropriate privileges needed for that management pack.

If logging is enabled, you may be able to determine from specific log entries what the problem is. The OpsMgr 2007 log files are stored in the *%Temp%* folder. (ACS log files are stored at *%SystemRoot%*/Temp.)

How Long to Tune?

There is no simple logic about how long to tune a management pack. Evaluate and tune each management pack until you are comfortable with its functionality and behavior. This may include resolving any outstanding alerts that are not actual problem indicators or adjusting underlying rules and alerts for issues that aren't significant in your environment. You probably will want to go through a full application production cycle for your applications in each area being examined:

▶ For example, if you are tuning the SQL Server management pack and you have heavy month-end processing activity, go through a month-end cycle to see whether OpsMgr turns up anything unexpected.

▶ Gauge the effect of any new application added to your environment. Are new alerts being generated?

▶ Tune and test the impact of any new management pack or new version of an existing management pack.

After completing initial tuning, you may want to further tune management packs after they are in production or when new applications are introduced into your server environment.

How Many Test Environments Should You Have?

The Operations Manager 2007 Operations Guide speaks of a pre-production management group that is multi-homed (for example, agents on the production network can belong to the pre-production management group). This gives you a testing bed, so to speak, of real "data" (or at least real-life monitoring). This is a good way to test some of the capabilities of new management packs before they go into production.

However, for a new management pack that has not been tested previously (including those written in-house!), you would want to first import it into an isolated environment. This is because there could be a rule or monitor that needs some serious tuning for your particular environment (or is just misconfigured), which produces a significant amount of network activity generating alerts or performance counters. If you are multi-homing the computers in your production network, you could generate more traffic on your production network segments than you might want!

You may want to consider the following for an approach:

1. Maintain an isolated test environment. Import your MP(s) and do initial testing and tuning.

2. Export out any customizations, and import those along with the sealed MP(s) into the pre-production environment. Test again, using the multi-homed agents.

3. When you have a comfort level (and have devised a backout plan if necessary), export customizations from your pre-production environment. Import those along with the sealed MP(s) into production.

This may seem onerous or hardware heavy, but you only need to "get bit" once to change your mind! Also, consider using virtual machines for your test environment, and potentially your pre-production servers as well. This can help save on hardware costs.

Troubleshooting Recap

To recap some of the key approaches to managing management packs:

▶ Introduce management packs one-by-one into your management group, to more easily isolate changes in performance and behavior.

▶ Only install management packs you need. Management packs increase the load on the management server(s); they also increase the size of the agent on any computers targeted by the management pack.

▶ Work with your in-house experts for each application to understand how the rules will function in your particular organization; you may decide to disable some monitors or modify threshold limits that would trigger an alert. (The structure of an alert is described in Chapter 14.)

▶ Identify rules and monitors that are generating the most activity and focus on understanding what is taking place. If the OpsMgr Reporting Component is installed and you are collecting data, Microsoft provides reports you can use to start investigating your most common events and issues, found in the Microsoft Generic Report Library. Figure 13.20 lists the Generic Report Library Reports available with OpsMgr 2007.

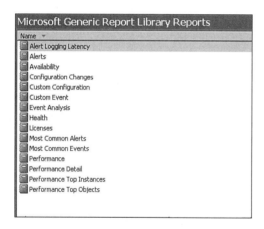

FIGURE 13.20   Operational Health Analysis reports in the Generic Report Library.

NOTE

Determine How Much Data You Are Collecting

A quick way to find out how many event and performance records are in the Operational database is by running these two SQL queries:

```
select count(*) as count from eventview
select count(*) as count from performancecounterview
```

For MOM 2005, similar views were documented in the MOM 2005 Software Development Kit. Microsoft no longer supports working directly with the database and does not plan to document these going forward; the managed assemblies in the System Center Operations Manager 2007 Software Development Kit are the only supported way of interacting with the product.

▶ The Agent Send Queue may be full. This may be noted by Event IDs of 21006, 21016, 2034, and 2024. You can modify the size of the send queue by modifying the following Registry value (see Figure 13.22) on the affected agent:

```
HKEY_LOCAL_MACHINE\SYSTEM\CurrentControlSet\Services\HealthService\
Parameters\Management Groups\<Management Group name>\MaximumQueueSizeKb
```

Where <*Management Group name*> is the name of the management group the agent is reporting to.

By default, the agent queue size is 15360KB. Restart the OpsMgr Health service on the agent-managed server for the changes to take effect.

You can use the Operations console to check the changes in the Health service queue size. Open the Monitoring space, and on the left side, navigate to the Operations Manager -> Agent performance folder and view the "Send queue % used" and the "Send queue size" for that specific agent to see your changes.

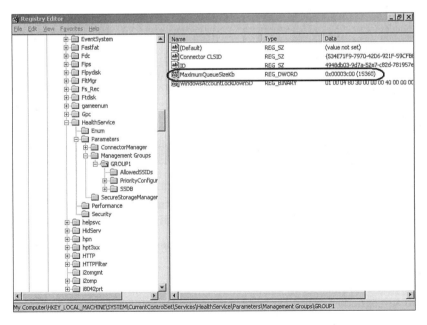

FIGURE 13.21   Agent send queue Registry settings.

After identifying the system that is generating the messages, you need to determine what is generating those events and how to resolve unnecessary events—which can include disabling rules or monitors, using overrides, changing thresholds, or utilizing consolidation rules.

Now that we have discussed some initial approaches for tuning your management packs, let's look at the process to move management packs with their changes from a preproduction environment to a production environment. Remember, the recommended approach for implementing management packs is to test them in a preproduction environment, make tuning changes as necessary, and then import your customized management packs to your production OpsMgr 2007 environment.

Exporting Management Packs

The Operations console allows you to export any unsealed management pack. Use the Export function to back up or to move management packs from one system to another (such as from your test environment to production). Perform the following steps:

1. Open the Operations console, and in the Administration space, highlight the management pack you want to export, right-click on it, and click Export Management Pack.... In our example, we are selecting the Windows Server 2003 Operating System Customizations management pack. You can also select the Export Management Pack option from the Actions pane. Both options are highlighted in Figure 13.22.
   Note that the export option is grayed-out except for unsealed management packs.

2. You are next asked to browse to or create the folder to export the management pack into. Select the folder, and the management pack is exported, with the success message displayed in Figure 13.23. You do not get to specify the name of the exported file.

   If you have previously exported that management pack to the same folder, you are asked if you want to overwrite it (if you do not specify the overwrite option, the management pack is not exported).

You can also export management packs in a batch mode, using PowerShell cmdlets. PowerShell export procedures were previously described in Chapter 12.

After exporting the management pack from your test environment, your next step is importing it to a production management server and integrating the management pack into the targeted management group.

Ways to View Sealed Management Packs

To unlock a sealed MP, look in the Health Service State\Management Packs folder on your agent. The sealed management packs are pushed down to the agent and stored in raw XML format, allowing you to look through them and glean what you can from them.

If you look in the %*ProgramFiles*%\System Center Operations Manager 2007\Health Service State\Management Packs folder on the management server, you will also find management packs in XML format.

Another technique, suggested by Boris Yanushpolsky of the MOM team, is to use PowerShell to export the management pack and then import it. His blog entry at http://blogs.msdn.com/boris_yanushpolsky/archive/2007/08/16/unsealing-a-management-pack.aspx explains this process. As he points out, it is best to still use the sealed version of an MP in your management group—Microsoft will maintain (upgrade) sealed versions of their management packs, and changes are implemented using overrides, which makes them easier to roll back.

For your convenience, we include his script for exporting management packs, MPtoXML.ps1, on the CD accompanying this book. Chapter 12 also includes utilities for exporting sealed management packs.

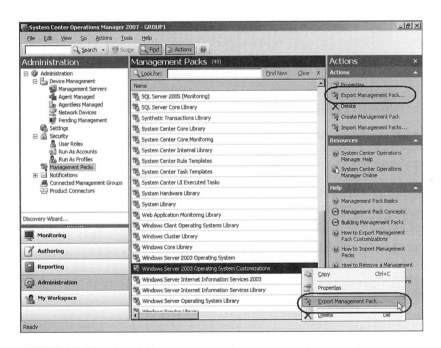

FIGURE 13.22   Select the management pack you want to export.

FIGURE 13.23   Successful export of unsealed management pack.

Importing Management Packs

The Administration space in the Operations console is used to import management packs. You can also use the `install-Managementpack` PowerShell cmdlet, described in Chapter 8, "Configuring and Using Operations Manager 2007," to bulk-import management packs.

Real World: Guidelines when Importing Management Packs

Remember Murphy's Law that if anything could go wrong, it might, where humans are involved! To minimize the impact of human error, keep these tips in mind:

- ▶ Only replace an existing production management pack with one you have checked out in your test or preproduction environment.

- ▶ If you are importing a newer version of a previously imported unsealed management pack, be sure you have backed up your production version, enabling you to return to your former management pack state by importing the backup should that become necessary.

- ▶ If you modify any of the original vendor rules, use an override to disable the original rule— you will be making your changes to a copy of the rule in an unsealed, custom management pack.

After downloading a management pack through Microsoft's System Center Pack Catalog, extract the contents of the package into files that can be utilized by Operations Manager. Copy the executable package to a system with the Operations console installed and run the package to extract the files to the file system.

Packages contain one or more management packs (with an extension of .MP, or .XML if the management packs are unsealed), and may include documentation such as a management pack guide or readme file.

TIP

Extracting Management Pack Packages

Extract to the same server and directory all management packs that you want to import in order to simplify the installation process later.

Using the Operations Console

To import a management pack, open the Operations console and perform the following steps:

1. Select the Administration space. In the Administration node, you can highlight Management Packs, right-click, and select the option to Import Management Packs....

   You can also select the import option from the Actions pane on the right-hand side of the console. Both options are highlighted in Figure 13.24.

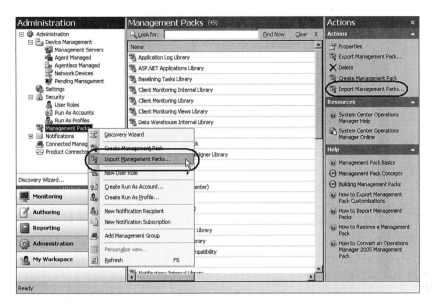

FIGURE 13.24   Begin the process to import a management pack.

2. Navigate to the folder containing the management pack(s) you wish to import. If you are importing customized management packs from a test environment, this would be the folder you previously exported to from your preproduction management server.

3. Select the management pack(s) to import by highlighting the file and pressing the Open button. This opens the Import Management Packs window displayed in Figure 13.25, where we have selected the Windows Server Operating System Customizations MP we exported in the "Exporting Management Packs" section of the chapter. The details section of the window tells us that this management pack has previously been imported and the new version will replace the one already in the system.

   We also can select additional management packs for import by pressing the Add button at this time.

4. Press Import to begin the process. If the management pack has dependencies on another management pack not already loaded to the management group or in the list to import, you will receive an error.

5. Click Close at the bottom of the window when the installation is complete.

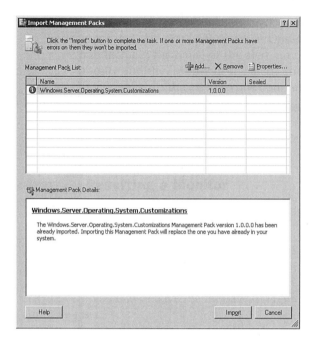

FIGURE 13.25   The import management packs window in the Operations console.

Receiving an "OutOfMemoryException" Error When Importing a Management Pack

You may receive an "OutOfMemoryException" error message when trying to import a management pack using the Operations console. The console also stops responding. KB article 933987 at http://support.microsoft.com/kb/933987 describes this issue. To resolve the problem, you need to install a Microsoft.NET Framework hotfix, described at http://support.microsoft.com/kb/921217.

Using PowerShell cmdlets

PowerShell gives OpsMgr administrators the capability to automate many actions using script files with cmdlets. You can create a text file with an editor such as Notepad, where each line contains an install-Managementpack PowerShell cmdlet to import a management pack into your management group in batch mode. This capability allows you to schedule maintenance activities during off-hours and have a record of your steps for change-control purposes.

As an example, the PowerShell syntax for importing the Windows Server Operating System Customizations management pack would be as follows:

```
install-Managementpack –filepath <filepath>Windows.Server.OperatingSystem.
➥Customizations.xml
```

Deploying Changes
The enabled settings in your imported management packs begin monitoring as soon as they are deployed to an agent; these updates occur as needed.

TIP

Information on Agents

OpsMgr Agents are discussed in Chapter 9, "Installing and Configuring Agents."

Verifying the Management Pack Installation
After installing a management pack, you will see changes in several areas of the Operations console, as follows:

▶ In the Administrator space, if you navigate to the Management Packs node, the detail section in the center of the console will show the name of your new management pack.

▶ In the Authoring space, under the Groups node, you will see any new groups related to the management pack. Under the Management Pack objects node, new attributes, monitors, object discoveries, rules, tasks, and views will be visible if those were included in your management pack.

NOTE

More About Attributes

An OpsMgr 2007 attribute can check the Registry or a WMI query; this is controlled by the Discovery Type. When creating an attribute, you must specify an object type as its target. The object type can include a number of attributes—for instance, a number of Registry values. You could then create a group with a dynamic inclusion rule for servers with only that object type.

▶ The Monitoring space displays the results of monitoring. It contains folders and views that are defined by each individual management pack that is imported.

On the left side under the Monitoring node, you should see a folder structure for your new management pack; it will have subfolders for any Alerts, Events, Tasks, and other objects defined by the new management pack.

▶ If you have installed OpsMgr reporting on your system and the management pack import included reports, the Reporting space lists reports for that management pack.

Managing Management Packs

Now that we have presented some information about how management packs work and the import/export process, we will look at several utilities and management packs that assist in managing management packs.

TIP

Configuring for a Firewall

If your organization has a firewall, make sure that the web browser settings on the server you will be using include appropriate proxy information. This information is discussed in Chapter 11, "Securing Operations Manager 2007."

System Center Internal Task Library

The System Center Internal Task Library MP helps analyze which rules and monitors are running for a server and which rules and monitors have failed. This is an optional management pack, and can be loaded from the Operations Manager 2007 installation media at \SupportTools\Microsoft.SystemCenter.Internal.Tasks.mp. The management pack adds two tasks to the Health Services Tasks pane:

▶ Show Failed Rules and Monitors for this Health Service

▶ Show Running Rules and Monitors for this Health Service

These tasks are displayed from the Monitoring console when you navigate to Operations Manager -> Agent -> Agent Health State in the Monitoring pane and select a monitored computer (see Figure 13.26).

The Operations Manager Automatic Agent Management Library

The Operation Manager Automatic Agent Management Library (Microsoft.SystemCenter.OperationsManager.AM.AutoDR.2007.mp) is a fully automated management pack used for agent remediation. It is loaded into OpsMgr during the initial install. If an alert or problem occurs on a monitored server, this MP can restart, restore, or even reinstall the agent on the monitored device, depending on the diagnostic conditions of the remote agent.

Before OpsMgr can automatically recover agents, you must add a Run As Account to the Automatic Agent Management account Run As Profile. This Run As Account must have administrator-level access on the target computers.

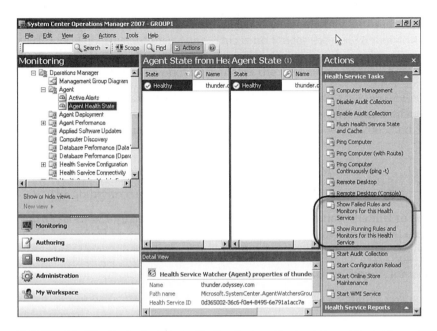

FIGURE 13.26   Tasks included with the System Center Internal Task Library MP.

Viewing Management Pack Content

Because a management pack is written in XML, trying to view and understand the content can be daunting. This is particularly the case with overrides. Boris Yanushpolsky of the MOM Team has developed several utilities to assist with viewing management pack content.

The MPViewer displays rules, monitors, views, tasks, console tasks, and reports. The utility also shows you the knowledge associated with that particular management pack object. You can get Boris's script to dump the contents of a management pack at http://blogs. msdn.com/boris_yanushpolsky/archive/2007/10/11/what-s-in-my-management-pack.aspx. To run the script, open the Operations Manager command shell and enter the following command:

```
C:\DumpMPContents.ps1 -mpDisplayName:'<management pack name>'
```

The MPViewer itself can be downloaded from http://blogs.msdn.com/boris_yanushpolsky/ archive/2007/10/11/what-s-in-my-management-pack-take-2.aspx.

Listing All Management Packs Associated with a Server

You can use PowerShell to list all management packs associated with a server with the get-rule cmdlet. Perform the following steps to extract the list to a CSV file:

1. Open the Command Shell (Start -> Programs -> System Center Operations Manager 2007 -> Command Shell).

2. In the command window, type the following:

```
get-rule ¦ select-object @{Name="MP";Expression={ foreach-object
➥{$_.GetManagementPack().DisplayName }}},DisplayName ¦ sort-object
➥-property MP ¦export-csv "c:\rules.csv"
```

You can open the c:\rules.csv file with Excel, and it will have two columns of information: the name of the management pack and a display name. This information is also documented at http://blogs.technet.com/momteam/archive/2007/08/01/get-a-list-of-management-pack-rules-with-powershell.aspx.

Exploring Overrides

Boris Yanushpolsky also wrote an Override Explorer. This utility provides two views, type-based and computer-based:

▶ The type-based view shows types for rules, monitors, and discoveries for which overrides were created.

▶ The computer-based view is basically a resultant set of overrides that apply to a computer. It also allows you to drill in and see what overrides are applied to various components such as the operating system, databases, and websites.

This is discussed further in Chapter 14.

Additional information and the zip file for the Override Explorer is available at http://blogs.msdn.com/boris_yanushpolsky/archive/2007/08/09/override-explorer-v3-3.aspx.

Resultant Set of Rules

Although the MOM 2005 Resource Kit included a utility that let you view the set of rules that were targeted to an agent, OpsMgr 2007 out-of-the-box does not include this functionality, and it is not currently part of the OpsMgr 2007 Resource Kit. However, Pete Zerger (http://www.it-jedi.net/ and www.systemcenterforum.org) has documented a procedure that allows you to view a resultant set of rules running on an agent-managed machine.

The first step is creating a custom State view targeted at the Agent class that exposes the Health Service Task menu with the appropriate task:

1. Open the Operations Console and navigate to the Monitoring pane.

2. Select Monitoring -> New -> State View.

3. In the Properties dialog, enter **Agent View** in the Name field.

4. At the Criteria tab and in the Show data related to: section, click the ... button.

5. From the Select a Target Type window, select Agent. Click OK twice to save the State view.

Now you can use the Agent view to return the resultant set of rules, as follows:

1. In the Navigation pane, select the Agent view you created.

2. At the top center of the view in the Results pane, right-click the agent you want to query.

3. Using the context menu, select Health Service Tasks -> Show running rules and monitors for this Health Service, as shown in Figure 13.27.

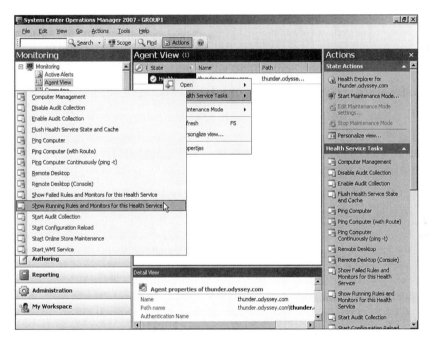

FIGURE 13.27   Creating a view to show running rules and monitors.

4. Click Run at the Run Task—Show Running Rules and Monitors for this Health Service window.

5. The results (see Figure 13.28) will be returned in XML format in the Task Status window.

FIGURE 13.28   Showing running rules and monitors for an agent.

MP2XMLDumper

The MP2XMLDumper is an SDK application provided by Clive Eastwood of Microsoft. The utility dumps your management packs in XML format to the folder of your choice. You can run this tool on a management server, or any other computer where the SDK assemblies for either OpsMgr or Essentials are installed. If run remotely, the assemblies Microsoft.EnterpriseManagement.OperationsManager.DLL and Microsoft.EnterpriseManagement.OperationsManager.Common.DLL must be present.

If running on a management server, the syntax is as follows:

```
MP2XMLDumper <path>
```

An example of this is MP2XMLDumper C:\MyMPs, where the destination folder will be created if it does not exist.

If run remotely (targeting a management server), use the following syntax:

```
MP2XMLDumper -s <managementserver> <userdomain\user> <path>
```

An example of this is `MP2XMLDumper -s Hydra Odyssey/OMAdmin C:\MyMPs`. You will be prompted for the connecting user's password, and the folder will be created if it does not exist.

The MP2XMLDumper can be downloaded from http://www.mediamax.com/opsmgr/Hosted/MP2XMLDumper.zip. It provides similar functionality to the ExportMP.ps1 PowerShell script we discussed in Chapter 12.

Diagnostic Tracing

Both OpsMgr 2007 and System Center Essentials 2007 implement a diagnostic tracing method. This new tracing method creates binary files in which to store tracing information. The utility is implemented at the Windows kernel level, and is able to log tens of thousands of trace methods per second.

Because the trace information is in binary, any traces must be sent to Microsoft CSS (Customer Service and Support) for conversion. Additional information about diagnostic tracing is available at http://support.microsoft.com/kb/942864.

Summary

In this chapter, you were introduced to management packs and tuning techniques. We discussed the process to implement management packs and best practices for deployment. In the next chapter, we will look at how OpsMgr monitors managed systems by using the various monitors and rule types you find in its management packs. We also discuss monitoring tips and techniques to use with OpsMgr 2007.

CHAPTER 14

Monitoring with Operations Manager

System Center Operations Manager 2007 (OpsMgr) facilitates monitoring and managing servers, clients, applications, operating systems, network devices, and business services, using a combination of built-in technology and third-party additions. The monitoring architecture of Operations Manager 2007 is significantly different from that of Microsoft Operations Manager (MOM) 2000 and 2005; in OpsMgr 2007, the focus moves from rule-based monitoring to the concept of monitors. Monitors can provide the real-time state of a component at a very granular level.

This chapter discusses rules, monitors, and alerts (defined in Table 14.1), including the process for locating them in a complex environment. We will also discuss *providers*, which dictate what data OpsMgr will collect. Additionally, we will look at the process for tuning rules in a typical environment.

Rules and monitors, together with everything else needed for monitoring, are assembled into *management packs*, which are grouped by application or operating system, such as the Windows Server 2003 and Exchange 2003 management packs. We discuss the structure of a management pack in Chapter 13, "Administering Management Packs."

This chapter discusses the different rule and monitor types in OpsMgr and the process of creating rules and monitors. We will also address alerts and adding knowledge information to alerts. We explain the concept of overrides as well as document the process for creating an override and locating a previously created override. Finally, we will look at approaches for monitoring and tuning alerts in OpsMgr.

TABLE 14.1   Primary Monitoring Objects Used by OpsMgr 2007

Object	Description
Rules	Rules define what you want to monitor. In MOM 2000 and 2005, rules formed the backbone of the business logic. Rules defined what data to collect, and they described how to process and respond to that data. Rules are still very important in OpsMgr 2007.
Monitors	Monitors represent the state of individual components of a system. They gather data from events, performance counters, scripts, and other sources such as Windows services. You can configure monitors to "roll up" their state; this allows for the creation of dependencies that assist in the accurate mapping and monitoring of complex and distributed systems. Monitors can generate changes in state and perform diagnostic and recovery tasks based on that change.
Alerts	Alerts are raised by either rules or monitors and call attention to issues that are occurring. Although monitors and states are more prevalent than alerts in Operations Manager 2007, using alerts provides additional information to an issue by interfacing with the Knowledge Base. Unlike in MOM 2000 and 2005, an alert generated by a monitor in OpsMgr 2007 can be automatically resolved when the monitor returns to normal, thus reflecting the fact that the issue no longer exists.

Why Is Monitoring Important?

As Information Technology (IT) systems continue to become more inclusive and versatile, the quantity and complexity of potential issues can proliferate. With businesses becoming more reliant on their IT systems, these issues are more noticeable and failures have a greater impact. Ensuring your systems are working correctly is a difficult and time-consuming task, particularly in a distributed environment. Traditional monitoring for IT systems tends to be reactive, with problems unidentified until they have a noticeable impact. Reactive response to issues is unacceptable in today's business and IT environments.

Operations Manager 2007 provides a means to consolidate and automate system monitoring and maintenance into a single user interface where you can identify potential issues early on. This capability enables you to address and resolve a large number of issues before they affect your production systems!

OpsMgr collects data from monitored systems about the operational health state of each computer and the applications and components that make up those systems, including hard drives and databases. This data enables an accurate and up-to-date overview of one's IT environment. In addition, OpsMgr is able to initiate scripts and responses based on a schedule or meeting a condition, such as a certain event appearing in a monitored system's Windows NT Event log.

In complex environments with a large number of installed management packs, the number of rules and monitors can run into the thousands, making the environment cumbersome to manage. With that in mind, it is critical to tune the alerts in OpsMgr to minimize the number of false alerts appearing in the monitoring console. With the introduction of monitors in OpsMgr 2007, this process is significantly less difficult than with earlier versions, but it is still an essential part of any OpsMgr deployment.

The process of tuning involves disabling rules and monitors when they are not required. It also includes altering threshold values to ensure that the configuration is appropriate to your specific environment. This chapter begins with focusing on the major types of rules available in Operations Manager 2007.

Rules

As with previous versions of Operations Manager, rules exist to perform various functions. Although OpsMgr 2007 now includes monitors, rules still form a key part of the product. You will use rules where it is not appropriate to create a monitor—and a large amount of OpsMgr monitoring still utilizes rules.

Rules exist primarily to collect performance data, execute timed tasks, and launch scripts. OpsMgr 2007 has three major rule types:

- ▶ Alert-generating rules
- ▶ Collection rules
- ▶ Timed commands

We will look at these in detail in the next three sections.

TIP

Viewing a Demo of Creating Rules

Microsoft provides step-by-step instructions on creating rules with a rule creation webcast, located at http://www.microsoft.com/winme/0701/28666/Rules_Demo.asx.

Alert-Generating Rules

To generate an alert for a condition that does not call for a monitor (such as a backup success event), you can use an *alert-generating rule*. A number of different providers are supported by alert-generating rules, similar to the providers used with monitors:

- ▶ Windows NT Event log
- ▶ Log file
- ▶ Windows Management Instrumentation (WMI)
- ▶ Simple Network Management Protocol (SNMP) events

This section explains the process for creating an alert rule by creating a basic Windows Event Log alert rule. The rule generates an alert if the Computer Browser service stops. Perform the following steps:

1. Open the Operations console and navigate to the Authoring space.

2. Expand Monitoring Objects and right-click Rules. Select Create New Rule....

3. The Create Rule Wizard displays the Select a Rule Type screen shown in Figure 14.1. From this screen, select Alert Generating Rules -> Event Based -> NT Event Log (Alert). You will also want to specify the destination management pack or target for the rule. We will use a management pack we created called Sample Management Pack. (If you need to create the management pack here, go ahead and click the New... button and then enter the name of your new management pack.) Click Next.

4. We need to name the rule and configure a target for it. In our example, we will call the rule **Computer Browser Stopped**. We will target the Windows Server class because we want the rule to apply to all Windows servers. We also have the option to enable (the default) or disable the rule.

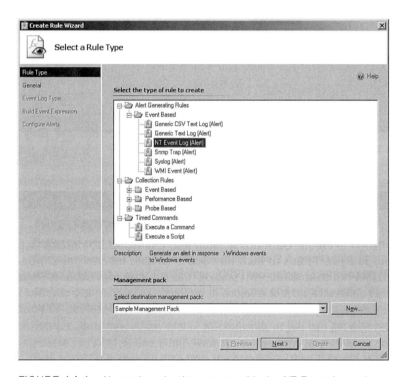

FIGURE 14.1   Alert rule selection screen with the NT Event Log rule type selected.

Figure 14.2 displays the completed Rule Name and Description screen. Click Next to continue.

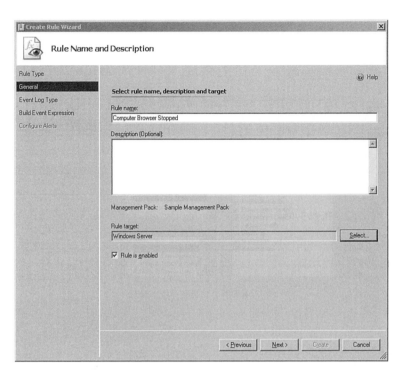

FIGURE 14.2   Defining the general properties of the rule.

5. On the following screen, we select the Event log in which we will look for the event. In this particular case, it is the System log. You can click the ... button to browse and select the log, or you can simply type in the name of the log. Click Next.

6. At the next screen, we configure the condition we want to match for the alert rule. The *condition* is those items we will check against to find the event when it appears in the event log. Figure 14.3 displays the event (Event ID 8033) in the System Event log on which we want to alert.

7. Because we now know what we want to match against, we can configure the Build Event Expression screen in the wizard. To match the event, we will use the Event ID and Event Source parameters. Configure the Event ID to be **Event ID Equals 8033** and the Event Source to be **Event Source Equals BROWSER.** This expression (known as a filter) is shown in Figure 14.4. Click Next to continue.

8. The final screen of the Create Rule Wizard configures the actual alert that OpsMgr will generate. We will leave the alert name as it is (Computer Browser Stopped) and add the description text **This indicates the Computer Browser service has stopped.** (see Figure 14.5). Notice this rule has a Priority of Medium and a Severity level of Critical. Click Create to create the new alert rule.

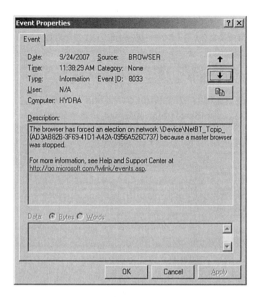

FIGURE 14.3   Computer browser event in the System Event log.

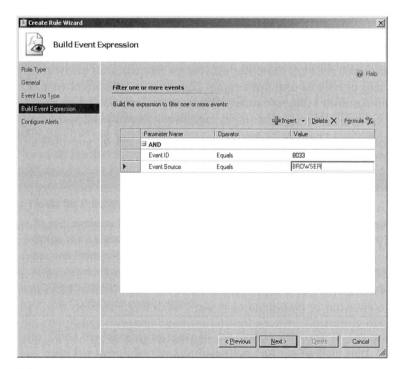

FIGURE 14.4   The Build Event Expression screen completed.

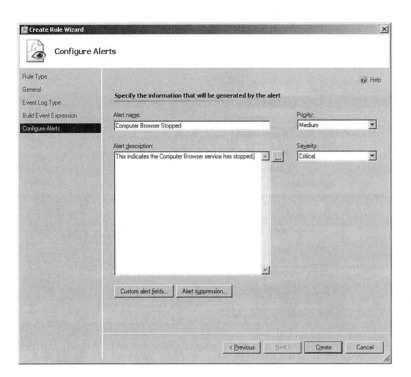

FIGURE 14.5   Configure Alerts screen in the Create Rule Wizard.

NOTE

Closing Alerts

When you configure an alert using an alert-generating rule, the resulting alert will *not* close automatically, as is the case with alerts generated by monitors. You will need to close these alerts manually.

Collection Rules

Collecting data is an important function of rules. Whereas you will use monitors to represent the health of a component based on an event or performance threshold, using rules provides the means to collect this data for trending and reporting purposes.

You can configure collection rules to collect event or performance data and can additionally configure them to launch a script, which generates an event for collection. This is referred to as a *probe*.

Because the most common type of collection rule is a performance collection rule, we will discuss the specific steps to create one. We will also describe the new Probe collection rule type. Configuring a performance collection rule is actually quite similar to configuring a monitor.

Creating a Performance Collection Rule

This process will show you how to create a performance collection rule. For our example, we will collect the % Processor Time counter for the print spooler (spoolsv) process. Perform the following steps:

1. Open the Operations console and navigate to the Authoring space.

2. Expand Monitoring Objects and right-click Rules. Select Create New Rule....

3. The Create Rule Wizard displays the Select a Rule Type screen shown in Figure 14.6. This is similar to the screen shown in Figure 14.1, but we are selecting Collection Rules -> Performance Based -> Windows Performance as the rule type. We also select the Sample Management Pack we previously created as a target for the rule. Click Next to continue.

4. On the Rule Name and Description screen, we name the rule and configure a target for it. We will call our rule **Print Spooler Process CPU Time** and target the Management Server class because we want the rule only to apply to management servers.

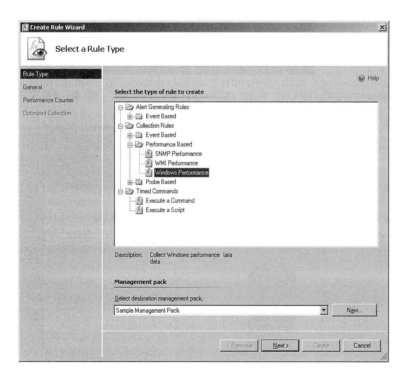

FIGURE 14.6   Rule selection screen with performance collection rule selected.

5. Now we select the performance counter we want to collect. You can type this manually. However, this is often confusing and time consuming. It is usually easier to browse and select the Process -> % Processor Time counter for the spoolsv process (Select instance from list). For this example, we will select the counter on Hydra (the counter actually exists on all servers; specifying Hydra simply means we are not browsing to another server to select the counter). Figure 14.7 shows the performance counter selected.

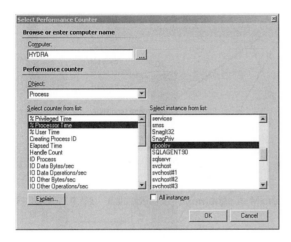

FIGURE 14.7   Selecting the performance counter for the spoolsv process.

6. At the Performance Object, Counter, and Instance screen (shown in Figure 14.8), we will leave the collection interval at the default of 15 minutes. Click Next to continue to the final screen of the wizard.

7. The last screen in the wizard allows you to configure optimized collections. OpsMgr uses optimized collections to reduce the amount of disk space a performance counter collection uses in the Data Warehouse. We explain this next in more detail. Click Create to create the performance collection rule.

Optimized Collections

In previous versions of Operations Manager, performance data constituted a large part of the reporting data warehouse, and it was very easy to (inadvertently) generate huge amounts of data with a small number of performance counters. Microsoft has addressed this issue in OpsMgr 2007 by introducing optimized collections. You configure this new feature on the final screen of the Create Rule Wizard screen when creating a new performance collection rule, which we show in Figure 14.9.

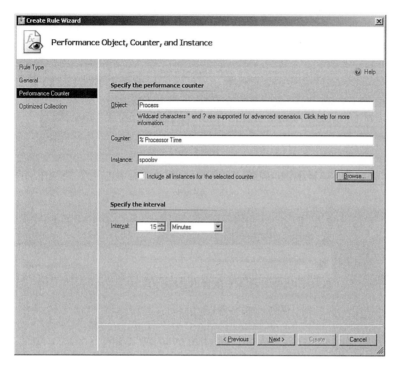

FIGURE 14.8   The counter collection screen with all settings specified.

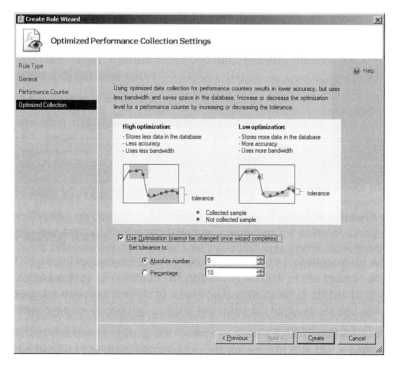

FIGURE 14.9   Optimizing performance collection settings for a counter.

Use the Optimized Performance Collection Settings screen to enable optimized collections and set the tolerance level for the performance data you are collecting. You can configure two options on this screen (shown in Figure 14.9):

- **Absolute number**—This is where you specify the top value for a collection, regardless of the collection schedule. For example, if the value is set to 90% for CPU, and the CPU hits 90%, a data collection takes place regardless of the collection schedule.

- **Percentage**—This is the percentage of change that must occur for a data collection to occur. For example, if the percentage were set to 10%, the performance counter would need to change by 10% (say, from 60% to 70%), for a data collection to occur.

We are not suggesting that you configure all performance collection rules to use optimized collection, but this may be appropriate for counters that typically generate a large amount of data.

Probe-Based Rules

The probe-based rule is a new type of rule in OpsMgr. In MOM 2005, it was possible to create a script and forward events and alerts into the MOM database using the VBScript `ScriptContext` object. This was a useful technique because it allowed you to output the results of a script such as a file size-monitoring script directly into MOM. The VBScript `ScriptContext` object does not exist in OpsMgr. In place of this feature, you can use a probe-based rule. In OpsMgr 2007, instances of using a probe-based rule include

- When you want a script to generate events for a condition but you do not want those events appearing in the log files on the computer.

- When you want to pass more information to OpsMgr than is possible in a basic Windows event.

With this new method, the script is inserted into the probe rule and the new VBScript object `objPropertyBag` is used. This object is a container for the information that OpsMgr understands.

Script Rules

In addition to probe-based rules, you can still launch scripts using rules, similar to MOM 2005. For instance, you could use a rule to launch a script that logs an event directly to the Operations Manager Event log.

One example of this would be a ping script. The script would generate events logged to the Operations Manager Event log for collection by OpsMgr.

The following steps document how to create an Execute a Script rule to run a ping script:

1. Open the Operations console and navigate to the Authoring space.
2. Expand Monitoring Objects and right-click Rules. Select Create New Rule....

3. The Select a Rule Type Screen appears. In Figure 14.10, select Collection Rules ->
   Timed Commands -> Execute a Script. Also, select the Sample Management Pack we
   used earlier in this chapter as a target for the rule. Click Next.

4. Next, we name the rule and configure a target for it. We will call this rule **Ping
   Script Rule** and will target the Management Server class because we want to launch
   the ping script from a management server. Alternatively, you could create a group
   and target the monitoring to the group.

   Set the rule category to AvailabilityHealth. Because we are targeting a class with a
   number of subclasses, you may want to disable the rule to prevent it running on all
   subclasses. (To run the script, you would create an override enabling the rule, and
   target the override to the agent where you want the script to run.) Click Next.

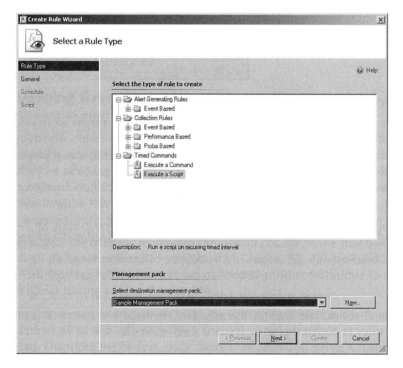

FIGURE 14.10   Rule type selection screen with Execute a Script rule selected.

5. Now, we select the schedule for running our script. In our example, we will accept
   the default of 15 minutes and click Next.

6. The Script screen is where the script itself is entered. The script we will use is shown
   here:

```
Option Explicit
On Error Resume Next

' -- Define variables
```

```
Dim wshShell
Dim objOpsMgrAPI
Dim oArgs
Dim objFileSystem
Dim strDeviceListName
Dim objDeviceList
Dim objResultsFile
Dim strDevice
Dim fOpenResults
Dim strResultsData
Dim objMOMEvent

Const ForReading=1

' -- Create a Shell object
Set wshShell = CreateObject("WScript.Shell")

' -- Create MOM Script API Object
Set objOpsMgrAPI = CreateObject("MOM.ScriptAPI")

' -- Create the object for Parameters
Set oArgs = WScript.Arguments

' -- Get the script values from parameters
strDeviceListName = oArgs.Item(0)

' -- Define results file location
objResultsFile = "C:\PingResults.txt"

' -- Create a FileSystemObject and open device list
Set objFileSystem = CreateObject("Scripting.FileSystemObject")
Set objDeviceList = objFileSystem.OpenTextFile(strDeviceListName,
➡ForReading)

' -- Run ping against each device one at a time'
➡ -- until all devices have been read from the file and pinged
Do Until objDeviceList.AtEndOfStream
  strDevice = objDeviceList.Readline

    ' -- Run the ping and pipe output to the results file
    wshShell.Run
➡"cmd.exe /c ping " & strDevice & " -n 2 > " & objResultsFile,,true

    ' -- Open log file and read line 4
    Set fOpenResults =
➡objFileSystem.OpenTextFile(objResultsFile, ForReading)
```

```
            fOpenResults.ReadLine
            fOpenResults.ReadLine
            fOpenResults.ReadLine
            strResultsData = fOpenResults.ReadLine

     ' -- Generate alert if the 4th line is Request timed out.
      Select Case strResultsData
        Case "Request timed out." & vbCR

          ' -- Create error event to be submitted to MOM server
          ' --(Ping Test failed)
              Call objOpsMgrAPI.LogScriptEvent
        ➥("PingTest.vbs", 101, 0, "Ping Failed for " & strDevice)
          Case Else

          End Select

 ' -- Close Results File
 objResultsFile.Close

 ' -- Clear ResultsData Variable
 Set strResultsData = Nothing


Loop

 ' -- Close Device List
 objDeviceList.Close

 ' -- Reset all variables
 Set wshShell = Nothing
 Set objFileSystem = Nothing
 Set objOpsMgrAPI = Nothing
 Set oArgs = Nothing
 Set objDeviceList = Nothing
 Set strDeviceListName = Nothing
 Set objResultsFile = Nothing
 Set strDevice = Nothing
 Set fOpenResults = Nothing
 Set strResultsData = Nothing
 Set objMOMEvent = Nothing
```

The script reads the name of the device list from the parameter that we will specify
in the rule. You must create the device list manually and copy it to all servers where
you want to run the ping script. List the devices you want to ping in a text file (we
named ours C:\DeviceList.txt), with one on each line, as shown here:

```
192.168.10.1
192.168.8.1
192.168.10.10
```

The IP addresses and devices listed may not apply to your environment and will most likely need to be changed. Using IP addresses and DNS names are both acceptable, providing the server you are launching the script from can resolve DNS names.

Also ensure that the device name can be resolved. In order for the script to work, the device must respond either as "Reply..." or "Request Timed Out."

7. We name the script PingTest.vbs and configure the timeout to 2 minutes, as shown in Figure 14.11.

8. After naming the script and copying it into the rule, you need to configure the parameters to be loaded into the script. Click the Parameters... button to display the Parameters screen. For the PingTest script, this screen should be configured as shown in Figure 14.12. Our script only requires specifying one parameter: the location of the device list. We have set it to **C:\DeviceList.txt**. Click OK and then Next to continue to the Event Mapper screen.

9. Finish the wizard by clicking Create to create the Execute a script rule.

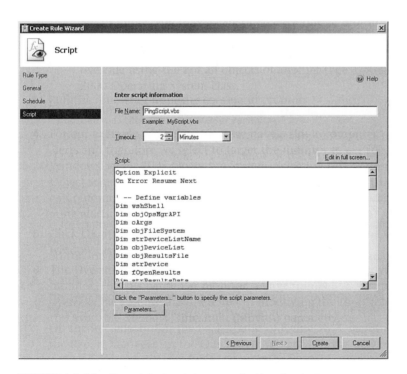

FIGURE 14.11   Completed script screen for the ping test.

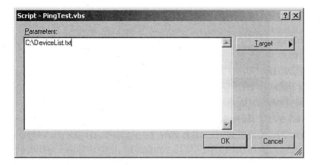

FIGURE 14.12   Completed Script Parameters screen specifying the C:\DeviceList.txt file.

Once the script runs on the appropriate server, the event logged by the script will look like the event displayed in Figure 14.13.

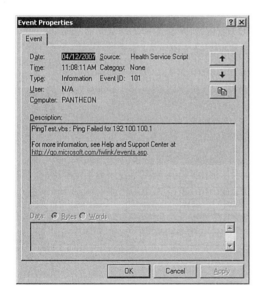

FIGURE 14.13   Event raised.

TIP

On the CD

The PingTest.vbs script is on the CD accompanying this book.

Timed Commands

The next rule type in OpsMgr we will discuss is the timed command. Timed command rules are very simple and can launch a script or execute a command based on a schedule. This capability is similar to using the scheduled provider in previous versions of MOM.

Timed commands are particularly useful for launching ping scripts, for example, as you can use OpsMgr to control the schedule and manage the script. OpsMgr also supports using a timed command for launching Windows commands and scripts.

In this section, we show you how to launch a batch file using a timed script. The batch file we will launch is a very simple one that restarts the print spooler service. The file has the following two lines of code and should be saved as **C:\SpoolerRestart.bat**:

```
@echo off
Net stop spooler & net start spooler
```

TIP

A Scripting Tip Using an Ampersand

You can use the ampersand (&), as in the preceding example, to allow two commands to exist on the same line.

The following process shows you how to create a timed command rule to launch a batch file:

1. Open the Operations console and navigate to the Authoring space.

2. Expand Monitoring Objects and right-click Rules. Select Create New Rule....

3. The Select a Rule Type screen is shown in Figure 14.14. From this screen, select Timed Commands -> Execute a Command. Once again, we will select our Sample Management Pack as a target for the rule. Click Next.

4. At the Rule Name and Description screen, we name the rule and configure a target for it. In our example, we will call the rule **Print Spooler Service Restart** and target the Management Server class, because we want the rule only to apply to management servers. Click Next to continue.

5. We will now create the schedule for running the batch file. We will configure our script to run daily at midnight. Click the Base on fixed weekly schedule radio button and select the Add button. Check the box for each day and specify the time range as being between 00:00 to 00:01, as shown in Figure 14.15. Click OK.

6. After creating the schedule, click Next to continue.

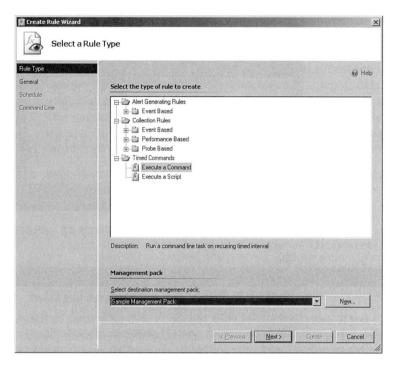

FIGURE 14.14   Specify creating a timed command in the Create Rule Wizard.

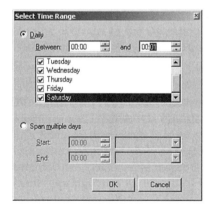

FIGURE 14.15   Specify the time range for the schedule.

7. The final screen of this wizard is where you configure the actual batch file to run. We will configure the timed command to run the C:\SpoolerRestart.bat file we created earlier in this section. We do not need to specify parameters in this example. The working directory can be set to **C:**. Click Create to create the timed command. Figure 14.16 displays this screen.

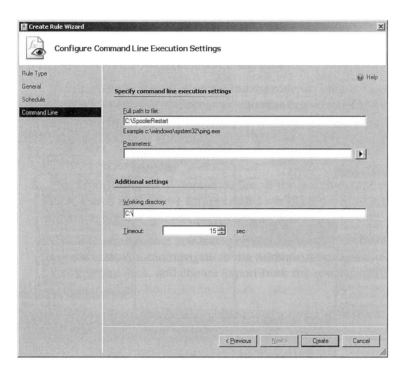

FIGURE 14.16   Select the batch file for the command-line execution.

Targeting Rules and Monitors

The following information is available on Brian Wren's blog at http://blogs.technet. com/ati/archive/2007/05/14/targeting-rules-and-monitors.aspx. We found it so useful we are paraphrasing it here.

You may have noticed several times in this discussion on rules the use of the word *target*. OpsMgr 2007 requires that you specify a target to use for a particular rule or monitor. If you are familiar with MOM 2005, this may be perplexing. In MOM 2005, rule groups are applied to computer groups. If a computer was in the computer group, it would get the rule. OpsMgr 2007 groups are not used to target rules or monitors. This really becomes confusing to the MOM 2005 administrator when they see that groups are available in the list of targets when creating a rule or target in the console!

With MOM 2005, we would think about which *computer* to use to retrieve to retrieve a piece of information from, and we targeted rules at groups that contained those computers. Formulas existed for the groups to identify which computers held different components, but ultimately we targeted groups of agents. In OpsMgr 2007, we think about the *component* that generates the information. OpsMgr will determine which agents hold instances of the component, deliver the rule or monitor to those agents, and execute that object for each instance.

OpsMgr 2007 also works against multiple instances of a class. Look at an example using SQL Server databases. The SQL scripts in MOM 2005 were enormous because they enumerated the entire list of databases and other SQL objects each time they executed. Now we just apply those rules to the SQL Database class, and OpsMgr executes the rule for each database instance it discovers. For each rule or monitor, OpsMgr enumerates all instances of the target class and applies the rule/monitor to each. If there are no instances of the target class on that agent, the rule does nothing.

Groups are classes just like any other object, although they are seldom targeted. If you apply a rule or monitor directly to a group, it executes against the group object itself and does *not* enumerate members of the group. (Since groups have no host, any rules targeted at groups operate on the RMS as the RMS manages unhosted objects.)

To target some groups of objects—e.g., get a particular rule or monitor to a subset of components—you have two available options. Let's consider a subset of websites we want to apply a particular rule to. You could target the rule at the IIS 2003 Web Site class, but then the rule would apply to all instances of that class, and probably to sites that you didn't want to include.

▶ Create a new class and target the rule at that class. For an IIS site, you would have to go to the Authoring console or raw XML to create a new class and discovery. That's a fairly advanced approach!

▶ Create a rule target at the whole class and disable it. Then create a group with the sites you want and create an override for that group to enable your rule.

The easiest method to validate you are using a target that actually has instances to use is with the Discovered Inventory view in the Operations console. Check here before you create your monitor. The Actions pane has an option called Change target type.... The option brings up the same Select a Target Type dialog box you see when selecting the target for a rule or monitor. This view lists all instances of the target class you are selecting. Use this technique to validate which agents have an instance of that class, and how many instances each have.

If no instances are listed in the view, the rule will not do anything. If there are instances, you will know that not only will the rule/monitor execute on the agents, but you can also view the properties of the instance that will be accessible to what you are targeting at it.

Jonobie Ford, a Microsoft technical writer for OpsMgr, discusses this topic as well at http://blogs.technet.com/momteam/archive/2007/10/31/targeting-series-part-1-differences-between-2005-and-2007.aspx. Microsoft has published a white paper titled "Key Concepts for Operations Manager 2007" that includes this topic; see Appendix E, "Reference URLs," for the live link at the Microsoft download site.

Monitors

In addition to using rules, OpsMgr 2007 introduces monitors. Although monitors perform the same functions as rules in MOM 2000 and 2005, they are representative of a specific component on a managed machine. This capability makes them very powerful. Monitors also update in near real time, meaning they accurately represent the current state of the managed computer.

Although the monitoring capability of OpsMgr 2007 is similar to the State feature in MOM 2005, OpsMgr has a large number of monitors that can observe every aspect of a managed machine down to the component level, whereas previously there were a limited number of levels you could monitor. You can appreciate the sheer volume of monitors when looking at the Health Monitor for a managed computer, shown in Figure 14.17.

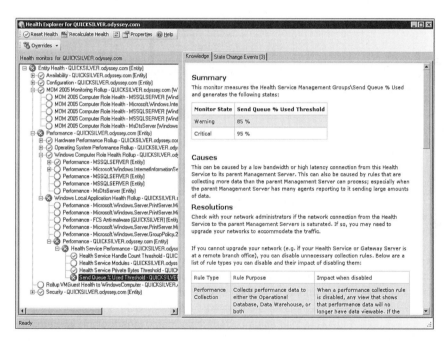

FIGURE 14.17   Viewing the Health Monitor on Quicksilver, our Odyssey data warehouse server.

It is worth mentioning that while we use monitors for monitoring, monitors are not responsible for collecting performance data or launching scripts. Use rules for this purpose. We discussed the functionality and capabilities of rules previously in the "Rules" sections of this chapter.

There are many different types of monitors in OpsMgr. This chapter discusses the main types. Figure 14.18 shows some of the different monitor types.

We discuss the major types of monitors in the following sections.

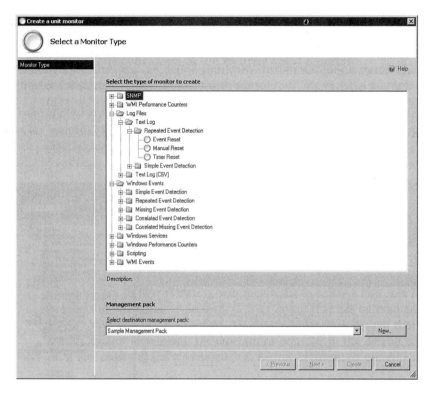

FIGURE 14.18   Types of monitors you can create.

Windows Events Monitor

One of the most basic types of monitor is the Windows Events monitor. This monitor detects Windows events and uses these events to update its status. These monitors can vary in complexity from simple, single-event detection to a complex correlation of events; even missing events can contribute to the status of a Windows Events monitor.

We will walk through the process to create a Windows Events monitor in the "Creating a Monitor" section later in this chapter.

Windows Performance Counters Monitor

The Windows Performance Counters monitor collects data from a Windows operating system or application performance counter and reacts to that data. There are two key types of Windows Performance Counters monitors, which we discuss in the following sections:

▶ Static Thresholds

▶ Self-Tuning Thresholds

The Static Thresholds Monitor

The Static Thresholds monitor is the simplest monitor type. It is used to monitor for changes in a static threshold, such as exceeding a threshold of 90% CPU utilization. With that said, you can still create five distinct types of Static Threshold monitors for additional granularity in the monitoring process:

▶ Average Threshold

▶ Consecutive Values over Threshold

▶ Delta Threshold

▶ Simple Threshold

▶ Double Threshold

The first four of these are of the Single Threshold type.

Average Threshold   The Average Threshold monitor takes the average value of a performance counter over a certain number of samples. The state changes if the average is above the specified threshold.

This monitor is particularly useful when you need to receive an alert when a performance counter is running near to or over a threshold for a defined period, rather than every time the performance exceeds a threshold.

Figure 14.19 displays the average threshold configuration screen.

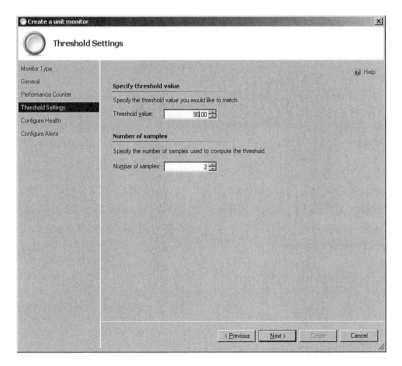

FIGURE 14.19   Specifying threshold settings for the average threshold configuration screen.

Consecutive Values over Threshold   Use the Consecutive Values over Threshold monitor when you need to reflect the state of a computer that consistently and repeatedly exceeds a threshold (so monitoring the average threshold is not appropriate). This capability is useful for systems that may occasionally have spikes on performance counters that do not indicate a problem, although it is an issue if a spike does not return to normal.

We have configured this monitor using the settings shown in Figure 14.20. We check for a value greater than or equal to 20 (the threshold), but collect four samples for comparison before defining it as a concern.

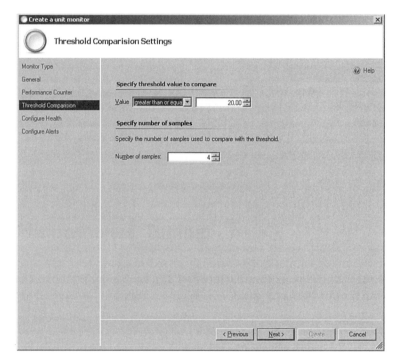

FIGURE 14.20   Specifying the threshold to compare in the Threshold Comparison Settings screen.

Delta Threshold   A Delta Threshold monitor does not measure the actual value of a performance counter but rather the change in value. For example, if you were measuring a change of 50, a performance counter change from 75 to 20 would be of interest, whereas a change from 75 to 30 would not. You can also configure the monitor to measure for a percentage drop rather than a physical value change.

Figure 14.21 shows the configuration screen for this monitor.

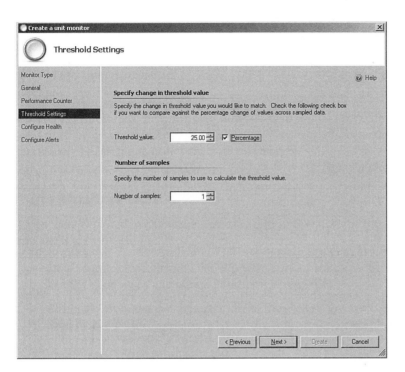

FIGURE 14.21   Configuring settings for a change in threshold value at the Delta threshold screen.

Simple Threshold   The Simple Threshold monitor does exactly what is says. It simply monitors a performance counter and changes the status of the monitor when the threshold is exceeded. This is the most basic and easiest to configure Performance Threshold monitor in OpsMgr 2007.

Figure 14.22 displays the Threshold Value screen for configuring the Simple Threshold monitor.

Double Threshold   OpsMgr allows you to configure a double threshold where a single monitor checks both a high and low threshold. For example, you can configure the health state of the monitor to be affected if a performance counter falls below a "low" value or exceeds a "high" value.

Self-Tuning Thresholds

The MOM 2000 and MOM 2005 products were somewhat static, reacting to performance issues only if the particular counters deviated outside of a predefined value. Although this method of monitoring is effective, it has its drawbacks. The main issue is the fact that not all servers perform equally, even servers that fulfill the same role (Exchange servers being a good example).

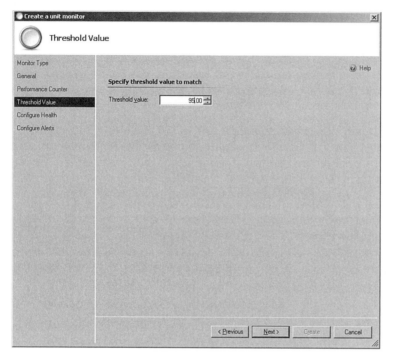

FIGURE 14.22   Simple Threshold monitor configuration screen.

When servers perform differently, a performance value appropriate for one server may not be applicable for another system, making it necessary to create separate performance thresholds for different servers. This can be very time consuming and difficult to manage in large and complex environments, especially when you consider previous versions of MOM did not have the luxury of sealed management packs! It was not uncommon for management packs to become very messy with changes often accidentally overwritten, especially when the vendor released a new version of its management pack.

With self-tuning thresholds, this is no longer the case. Self-tuning thresholds are a completely new feature in Operations Manager. Using self-tuning thresholds enables dynamic monitoring of performance counters, where OpsMgr adapts the thresholds as appropriate. As an example, if you monitor an Active Directory Domain Controller (DC) for CPU utilization using a self-tuning threshold, the threshold will "learn," noticing repeating CPU fluctuations on the server, such as the extra demand placed when users log in at the same time on a Monday morning. The monitor will then ignore these CPU fluctuations, and the state of the monitor will only change if the fluctuations are sufficient to move outside of the baseline that the monitor has learned.

A self-tuning threshold is also particularly useful to simply collect a baseline of a particular performance counter. When you view the associated performance graph, you can overlay the baseline, which gives you an overview of the trend of the counter in addition to the exact values.

Baselines

OpsMgr 2007 uses baselines to continually monitor and collect the usual running values for a performance counter. This allows it to automatically set and adjust alert thresholds to limit the amount of extraneous alerts that appear.

In addition, baselines are available in performance graphs to show the trend of a particular performance counter. To access a baseline from a performance view graph (where available), simply generate the graph, right-click, and select Show Baseline.

The process for configuring a self-tuning threshold is similar to that of configuring a normal threshold. The only real difference is in configuring the logic for the self-tuning threshold to "learn." You define this using the wizard when you initially create the threshold monitor, or by creating an override or editing the InnerSensitivity and OuterSensitivity values directly in the monitor.

Changing sensitivity using the wizard is straightforward. Perform the following steps:

1. After you select the performance counter you will use, the Baselining Configuration screen appears, shown in Figure 14.23.

2. From this screen, you can configure your business cycle, meaning what you consider a unit of time to monitor. A business cycle is defined in terms of days or weeks; the default is 1 week.

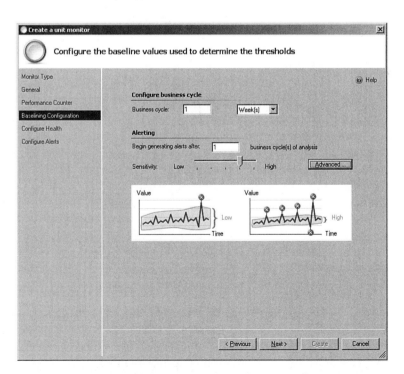

FIGURE 14.23   Self-tuning threshold Baselining Configuration screen.

The screen also allows you to configure how many business cycles should pass before generating alerts. This is useful because the monitor is able to learn efficiently before it starts generating alerts for exceeded thresholds.

3. You can also specify how sensitive (or insensitive) the threshold monitor will be. Moving the sensitivity slider automatically adjusts the sensitivity, or you can configure it in more detail by clicking the Advanced button. Selecting Advanced displays the screen shown in Figure 14.24.

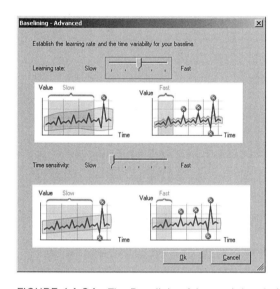

FIGURE 14.24   The Baselining Advanced threshold sensitivity configuration screen.

4. From the Baselining Advanced screen, you can configure the two settings for the sensitivity manually: the learning rate and time sensitivity settings. The *learning rate* is the rate at which the baseline is adjusted based on frequency of occurrences, and *time sensitivity* is the rate at which the baseline is adjusted based on a time interval.

There are a number of different self-tuning thresholds:

▶ **2-state Above**

The 2-state Above baseline is used to generate a status change and an alert when the performance counter strays above the learned baseline. When it is below the baseline, the status of the monitor is normal.

▶ **2-state Baselining**

This monitor is very much the same as the 2-state Above threshold monitor except that the baseline information is recorded for use in performance graphs.

▶ **2-state Below**

The 2-state Below baseline is the opposite of the 2-state Above baseline. If the counter strays below the learned baseline, the status is updated and an alert generated.

▶ **3-state Baselining**

The 3-state Baselining monitor collects the baselining information. It also allows the monitor to update the health state when the performance deviates both above and below the learned baseline.

Issues with Self-Tuning Thresholds

Despite the benefits of self-tuning thresholds, there are still drawbacks to using this new technology. Currently, self-tuning thresholds are unable to take into account periods of prolonged inactivity, such as weekends and holidays. As an example, OpsMgr may calculate a baseline for a server during the month of November. The baseline is automatically calculated over the period of a month, and is thus assumed relatively accurate.

However, during December many businesses close or run reduced operations over the Christmas period, which negatively affects the baseline. The monitored servers are less heavily utilized during the holiday period, and the baseline adjusts to reflect this. When everyone returns to work the server has a more typical load, and its new baseline is no longer accurate. When the server now becomes busy, it will have unnecessary alerts generated for performance counters outside the baseline, because OpsMgr still thinks the server should not have that much activity.

Currently, the only way to work around this issue is by temporarily disabling the baseline rule using an override for the periods of extended inactivity, or putting the machine or class object the performance counter applies to in maintenance mode. However, we do not recommend the latter method because it results in the computer or class object no longer being monitored.

Windows Service Monitor

A Windows service monitor does what the name suggests. It monitors a Windows service and updates the status of the monitor based on whether the service is running or not. You can also monitor a Windows service with a management pack template (explained in Chapter 18, "Using Synthetic Transactions") that creates a Windows service monitor.

Using the management pack template creates a class for the monitored service. This is useful when you want to monitor the service as an individual item and potentially add it to a distributed application (DA). We cover distributed applications in more detail in Chapter 19, "Managing a Distributed Environment."

14

Not All Services Show Up When Using the Monitor Wizard

When you use the Monitor Wizard to create a monitor for a Windows service, you can browse to see the services available for monitoring. However, you may notice that the list is shorter than the list of services in the Services MMC (Microsoft Management Console). The reason for this is that this version of OpsMgr only monitors services that are not shared. If a service is shared, it runs under svchost.exe and it is not picked up by the wizard.

This is a known problem. If you are developing your own services in house, ask your developers to create separate services for their applications so you will be able to monitor them.

We will step through the process of creating a Windows service monitor that monitors the Print Spooler service. Perform the following steps:

1. Open the Operations console and navigate to the Authoring space.

2. Expand Monitoring Objects and right-click Monitors. Select Create a Monitor -> Unit Monitor....

3. The Create a Unit Monitor Wizard displays the screen shown in Figure 14.25. From this screen, select Windows Services -> Basic Service Monitor. Also, select the Sample Management Pack as a target for the monitor. Click Next to continue.

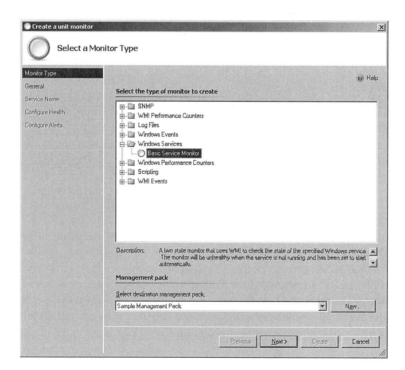

FIGURE 14.25   Select Basic Service Monitor.

4. On the next screen, we name the rule and configure a target for it. For our example, we will call the rule **Print Spooler Service Monitor** and we will target the Windows Server class, because we want the rule to apply to all Windows Servers. Notice here, unlike when we named rules, we are asked to specify the parent monitor. In this case, we will leave the setting at the default of Availability. Figure 14.26 shows the completed General Properties screen. Click Next to continue.

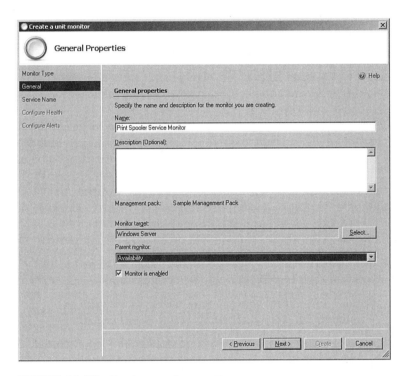

FIGURE 14.26   Service monitor creation name screen.

5. Now, we will configure the service we want to monitor. In this case, it is the Print Spooler (Spooler) service. You can either click the ... button to browse for the service or type **Spooler** into the service name box. Click Next.

6. The next screen is the Configure Health screen. This is where you define what the health of the monitor will be in relation to the state of the service. Because this is a basic service monitor, it is already correctly defined (see Figure 14.27).

7. The final screen of the wizard configures the actual alert OpsMgr will generate. We will tick the Generate alerts for this monitor check box, leave the alert name as it is, and add an alert description, as shown in Figure 14.28. We will also leave the check box enabled for Automatically resolve alert when.... This means that once the monitor returns to a Healthy state, any generated alerts are automatically resolved. Click Create to create the new service monitor.

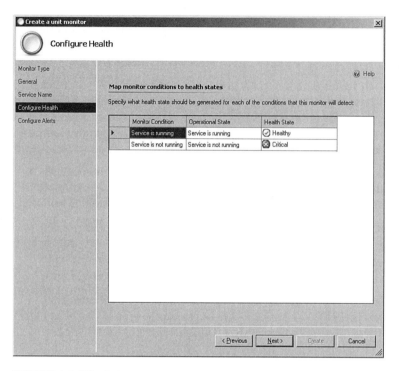

FIGURE 14.27   Select the health state for a service monitor.

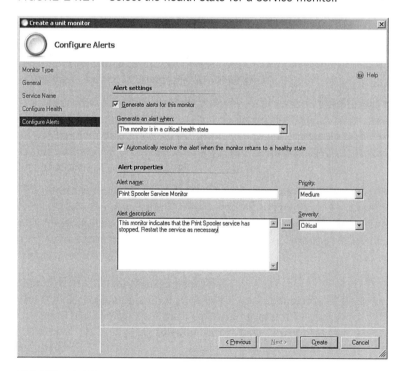

FIGURE 14.28   Generate alert screen for a basic service monitor.

Monitoring a Process with OpsMgr

Sometimes you may want to know if a process (not a service) is running on a server. This scenario is common for functions such as batch processes, which often run logged in to a console as a specific user and are launched using a shortcut on the desktop. We have created a custom management pack that provides alerts when a process is not running within an acceptable range of occurrences that you specify. That is, if MyBigApp.exe is not running at least once on the specified server, OpsMgr generates a critical alert; if it is running too many times, OpsMgr will create a warning alert.

We include the Process Monitor as part of the OpsMgr Unleashed management pack accompanying Chapter 23, "Developing Management Packs and Reports." Note that in the management pack, the monitor is disabled by default and is designed to be disabled. If you enable the monitor using the default configuration, it alerts on every server if either too few or too many svchost.exe processes are running on the system; therefore, do not enable the monitor. You will want to activate its functionality on a per-server basis through overrides. You can specify the acceptable number of processes and the name of the process on the parameters page for the monitor.

Log File Monitor

If the data you want to gather is located in a log file rather than an Event log, you can configure OpsMgr to monitor for a particular line or string appearing in a log file of your designation. As with other monitor types, multiple options are available, but the different monitor types will basically allow you to watch for a single event or text string, or watch for repeated events or text strings. Figure 14.29 shows the complete list of choices.

Here are some points to keep in mind:

▶ Watching for a single event is simple. OpsMgr looks for an event that appears in an Event log or a text string that appears in a log file.

▶ Looking for a repeated event is the same as looking for a single event, although the health state is not updated and no alerts are generated until an event has appeared a certain number of times within a certain time period.

SNMP Monitor

If you need to monitor a SNMP-enabled device, you can create a monitor. A couple of approaches are available:

▶ The monitor can react to a SNMP trap received by the server.

▶ You can configure a SNMP probe that will actively run a SNMP query based on a schedule you specify; the monitor will update depending on the results of the query.

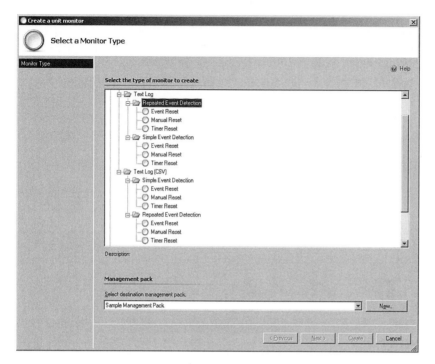

FIGURE 14.29   Log file monitor selection screen.

To configure SNMP monitoring, you must first add the network devices into OpsMgr; then you can create SNMP trap-based or performance-based rules, depending on your requirements. When creating these rules, you use the OIDs (Object Identifiers) of the SNMP objects. OIDs are unique labels for SNMP counters and traps.

To collect SNMP traps on the management server, you must first install the Windows SNMP trap provider (Control Panel -> Add/Remove Programs).

SNMP monitoring is particularly useful for those devices or servers you wish to monitor that run non-Windows operating systems, or for monitoring hardware appliances such as firewall nodes. Chapter 17, "Monitoring Network Devices," discusses SNMP monitoring in detail.

WMI Event and Performance Monitors

WMI event and performance monitors behave in a similar way to the normal event and performance monitors. The data, however, is not obtained using the operating system and application APIs (application programming interfaces) but is instead collected using WMI. Due to the nature of these performance counters, self-tuning thresholds are not available when you use WMI performance monitors.

These particular monitor types are typically configured for machines monitored using the Agentless monitoring mode.

Creating a Monitor

In this section, we will create a basic Windows event monitor. Perform the following steps:

1. Open the Operations console and navigate to the Authoring space. Highlight the Monitors object, as displayed in Figure 14.30.

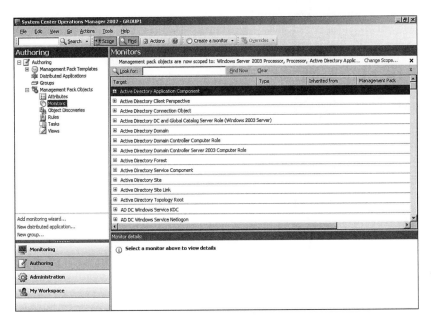

FIGURE 14.30   The Monitors space in the Operations console.

2. You can now begin to create a new monitor. Right-click Monitors in the right pane and then select Create a monitor. This displays three options (see Figure 14.31). You have the choice of the following monitors:

   ▸ **Unit Monitor**—The Unit monitor is the lowest level of monitor and charged with actually carrying out the monitoring of a particular component or aspect of a monitored machine. This is the most commonly used monitor.

     You can roll up Unit monitors to either Dependency or Aggregate Rollup monitors.

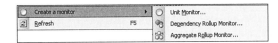

FIGURE 14.31   The different monitor types you can select.

▶ **Dependency Rollup Monitor**—The Dependency Rollup monitor is configured to roll up the health state of a particular monitor or component to the next level in the monitored computer's health state. For example, if a SQL Server database resides on a physical disk and the disk fails, a Dependency Rollup monitor is created to ensure that the state of the physical disk affects the state of the database that relies on it.

▶ **Aggregate Rollup Monitor**—An Aggregate Rollup monitor is designed to reflect the state of a collection of Unit monitors, Dependency Rollup monitors, or other Aggregate Rollup monitors. For example, the state of multiple SQL Servers can be grouped and rolled up to a SQL Servers group.

3. Generally, you will be creating simple monitors, so this example will create a Windows Event monitor, which is a Unit monitor.

   From the list in Figure 14.31, select Unit Monitor. The Create a unit monitor Wizard opens with the Select a Monitor Type screen displayed, similar to the screen shown in Figure 14.25.

4. We will create a monitor that updates its state based on Windows events. The monitor will fail based on a Windows event and return to a normal state based on a different Windows event. From the Select a Monitor Type screen, select Windows Events -> Simple Event Detection -> Windows Event Reset.

   You will also need to specify the management pack you want to add the monitor to (we will use the Sample Management Pack we previously created). Click Next.

5. Enter a name, description, monitor target, and parent monitor for the new monitor. Type a name for the monitor and a description if desired. We will call our monitor **Server Time out of Sync**.

   Set the target for the monitor to Windows Server by browsing to the object and selecting it. For this example, we will set the parent monitor (the monitor under which this one will reside) to Configuration. Click Next.

6. The next few screens of the wizard, we configure Windows events that alter the state of the monitor, both healthy and unhealthy.

   On the first of these screens, shown in Figure 14.32, we select the source of the Windows events for the event that will cause the monitor to register an unhealthy state. For this instance, set the log to System either by typing the name or clicking ... to select the log. The System log is where the events will appear. Click Next.

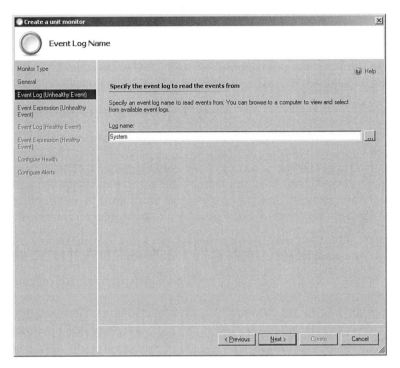

FIGURE 14.32   Input the source of the event that uses the monitor to register an unhealthy state.

7. At the next screen, we specify the formula by which OpsMgr will match the unhealthy state event. Figure 14.33 displays this screen.

   The Build Event Expression screen is where we specify the parameters of the event that enables OpsMgr to accurately detect and update the state to unhealthy when the event appears in the System Event log. By default, the wizard adds the Event ID and Event Source parameters. You can remove these parameters as required, and you can add different or additional parameters such as Event Description and Logging Computer Used. To add a new parameter, simply click the Insert button and then use the ... button on the newly created row to specify the parameter you want to add.

   For this example, we will look for an event with an Event ID of 50 and a source of W32Time. This event indicates that time synchronization is not working.

   Once you have specified the event information for the unhealthy event, repeat the processes illustrated in Figures 14.32 and 14.33. This will define the event that causes the monitor to return to a healthy state. For this monitor, we will use an event from the System log with an Event ID of 37 and a source of W32Time. Event 37 indicates that time synchronization is now working correctly.

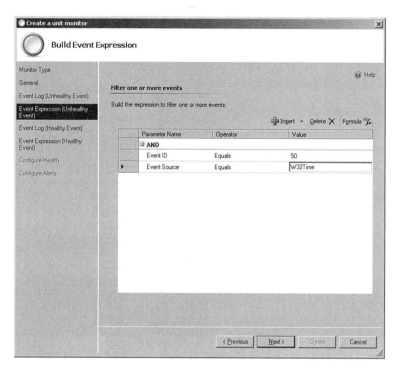

FIGURE 14.33   Configuring the formula for OpsMgr to use to match the unhealthy state event.

8. After you complete these steps and click Next, the Configure Health screen displays, shown in Figure 14.34.

   Here we can specify the severity of the different states of the monitor. For our example, we will change the First Event Raised option (unhealthy event) to Critical and leave the Second Event Raised option (healthy event) as Healthy. Click Next.

9. In the final screen of the Configure a unit monitor Wizard, you can specify if the monitor will generate an alert (explained in more detail in the "Alerts" section, later in this chapter). Figure 14.35 displays the Configure Alerts screen.

   For this monitor, we will choose to create an alert. Once you check the Generate alerts for this monitor check box, a number of options appear below. Although we will leave most of these at the default setting for our example, we will explain each option:

   ▶ You can configure at what level the monitor must be at before an alert is generated (Warning or Critical). In this case, we will keep the default setting of Critical. You can use the check box below this option to specify whether OpsMgr will automatically close the alert when the monitor returns to a healthy state. You will want to do this in most cases—by enabling monitors to resolve their own alerts, you minimize the number of excess alerts residing in the console at any one time.

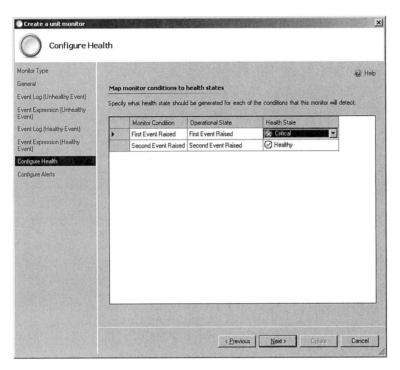

FIGURE 14.34   Configuring the health monitor.

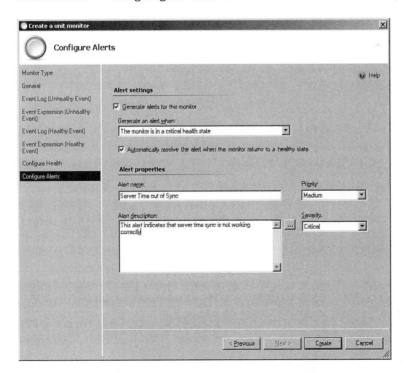

FIGURE 14.35   The Configure Alerts screen in the Create a unit monitor Wizard.

▶ In the bottom section of the screen, you can configure the details of the alert, which defines what appears when OpsMgr generates the alert. This information includes the name of the alert, any descriptive information, and the priority and the severity of the alert. The alert description field has similar functionality to the event expression builder we used earlier in step 7.

10. After you are satisfied with the alert details and the rest of the settings in the wizard, click Create. Creating the monitor will take several seconds; once it is complete, the monitor is visible and accessible in the console.

Manually Resetting a Monitor

You may have noticed that the Health Explorer includes the option Reset Health. Figure 14.36 displays the Reset Health button.

This feature's functionality is limited in the pre-Service Pack 1 (SP 1) version of OpsMgr. Although some of the monitors can manually reset, many monitors will not. In this case, when you click the button, you may not receive an error, but the monitor does not reset. Alternatively, you may receive the message in Figure 14.37 stating that the monitor cannot be reset.

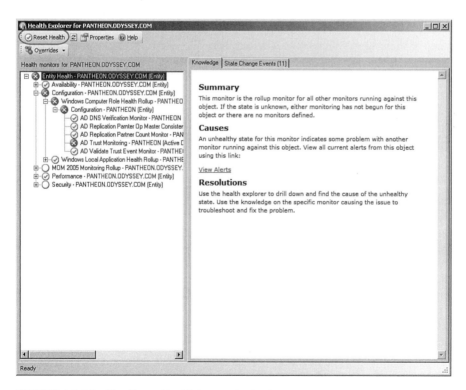

FIGURE 14.36   The Reset Health button in the Health Explorer.

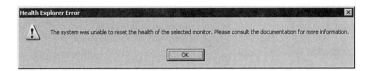

FIGURE 14.37   Warning that is displayed when trying to reset a monitor.

The ability to reset the health state is a good idea in principle, because sometimes monitors do not reset on their own. In extreme cases, it may be necessary to restart or even reinstall the agent to reset the monitor.

This issue occurs in the base version of OpsMgr 2007 because the button tries to spawn "on-demand detection." If the monitor you selected does not have on-demand detection defined on its monitor type, or if the monitor is a Dependency Rollup monitor, selecting Reset Health has no effect.

This means it is up to the monitor type to be able to do something with the Reset option. Most monitor types you build do not implement the required option for Reset Health to have any effect. The result—reset doesn't really mean reset at all, or at least for the vast majority of monitors!

With SP 1, Microsoft has announced that the reset monitor feature will be fully functional, and it will be possible to reset any monitor to a healthy state regardless of the actual status of the issue. SP 1 will also include a Recalculate button that allows you to initiate a recalculation of the state of any monitor in real time, rather than having to wait for the configured schedule. This is particularly useful with certain monitors such as the monitor that checks the age of the Exchange log files, which checks once every 24 hours. Now you will be able to check on demand as required!

Now that we have covered rules and discussed monitors, we will look at alerts in OpsMgr.

TIP

On the CD

Microsoft has released a poster with best practices for rule and monitor target monitoring. We include this information (Rule and Monitor Targeting Best Practices.pdf) with content for this chapter on the CD accompanying this book.

Alerts

As we mention in the "Rules" and "Monitors" sections of this chapter, both rules and monitors generate alerts. Alerts represent an overview of all active issues in the system. Alerts contain more information than monitors contain, and therefore are very useful for troubleshooting. In addition, alerts are not necessarily resolved when a monitor's status returns to normal. You can configure alerts to remain active, thus assisting in visibility and hopefully resolving the issue in question. You will find alerts in the Active Alerts view in the Monitoring space of the Operations console.

Alerts contain a number of pieces of information in the Alert Details pane in the Monitoring space of the console, an example of which is displayed in Figure 14.38.

This pane of the console contains specific information about the alert, such as the computer that raised it, the source of the alert (the application or operating system component generating the alert), and any additional knowledge included by the vendor or that you created yourself.

A neat feature of OpsMgr 2007 is that you can embed tasks within the Alert Details section. This allows the user who discovers the alert to carry out troubleshooting steps, such as restarting a service directly from the Alert Details section in the Operations console, which reduces administrative overhead. Figure 14.38 is an example of this capability, including an embedded task to start the SQL Agent service because the service has stopped.

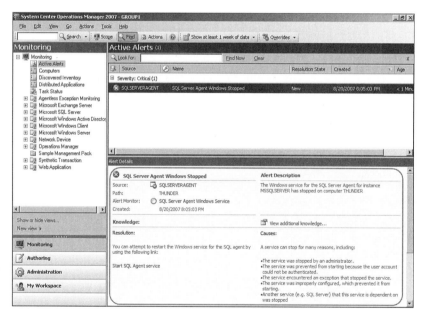

FIGURE 14.38   The Alert Details pane.

Generating Alerts

As just mentioned, rules and monitors generate alerts. Unlike with MOM 2000 and MOM 2005, monitors can now automatically resolve alerts when the state of the object returns to normal (although rules cannot). This helps minimize the number of inactive alerts resident in the console at any one time.

In MOM 200 and MOM 2005, alerts triggered email alerting and various other forms of alerting, such as instant messaging. This is no longer the case. A new feature of OpsMgr 2007 is the *notification workflow*, which is the engine that underpins all aspects of alert generation. Notification workflow manages the generation and resolution of alerts, and it includes the following capabilities:

▶ Creating and forwarding email messages and other external notifications such as instant messaging/SIP with Live Communications Server 2005 and Short Message Service (text messaging).

▶ Alert aging (previously referred to as *escalation* in MOM 2005).

▶ The ability to customize the messaging format at the user level.

   User-level formatting requires at least one notification channel to be previously configured by an OpsMgr administrator, and it allows individual users to configure their own recipient object and notification subscriptions.

▶ Multiple Simple Mail Transport Protocol (SMTP) server support for redundancy.

   It's not particularly useful to try to send emails via Exchange saying that Exchange is down!

Configuring Notification

Configuring notification requires the following steps:

1. **Establish a notification channel.**
   This can be via SMTP, instant messaging, or Short Message Service.

2. **Create notification recipient(s).**
   Defining notification recipients includes specifying the scheduled hours during which they will receive notifications, with the address information for each channel on which the notification is available.

   Recipients are defined in the Operations Console under Administration -> Notifications -> Recipients.

3. **Create notification subscription(s).**
   Each subscription defines those management groups and objects for which alert notifications are sent, the alert criteria (severity, priority, category), email format, and resolution state criteria for filtering out unnecessary alerts. You can even specify alert aging as notification criteria.

   You will establish subscriptions in the Operations console under Administration -> Notifications -> Subscriptions.

4. **Create a Notification Action account (previously defined in Chapter 11, "Securing Operations Manager 2007").**
   The email address associated with the Notification Action account is used as the email and instant message "From" address. Be sure to give this account the appropriate rights for the notification channel it will be using.

These steps are well documented in the white paper "Notification Setup Guide for Operations Manager 2007," developed by Anders Bengtsson and Pete Zerger. You can download this white paper from either http://systemcenterforum.org/wp-content/uploads/ SCOM_Notification1.pdf or http://contoso.se/blog/?p=132. For your convenience, we include these sites as live URLs in Appendix E.

Forwarding Alerts by Email

We have developed a small management pack that creates a task you can use to forward alerts. The Forward Alerts via Email MP provides a right-click capability for forwarding the alert name and description to someone via email. You are prompted for the email address. We include this utility on the CD accompanying this book as part of the OpsMgr Unleashed management pack with Chapter 23.

To configure the management pack, import it and then copy the email_alert.vbs script to the C:\scripts directory on the system you want this task to work on. You have to edit two values in the script:

▶ Change the value for OPSMGREMAIL to the name of the email address you are sending from (for example, OpsMgr@odyssey.com)

▶ Change the value associated with SMTPFQDN to the fully qualified name of your SMTP server (for example, SMTP.ODYSSEY.COM).

This is a very useful tool for forwarding alerts to individuals who don't have subscriptions but need to be aware of a specific alert.

TIP

Validating Email Format

There will be times when it is necessary to test whether SMTP mail is working and to validate the way the message looks before configuring OpsMgr to send emails to a mail server. A useful tool that enables testing emails from the command line is available at https://blogs.pointbridge.com/Blogs/morse_matt/Lists/Posts/ Post.aspx?ID=24.

Using the Notification Workflow Engine

Once notification is configured, administrators no longer have to create alert rules to generate email alerts; they simply need to subscribe to the alert using the notification workflow engine. We cover notification workflow and the creation of alert subscriptions in the following section.

The Life Cycle of an Alert

You configure alerting using the Notification Workflow capability of Operations Manager. In addition to managing the generation of alerts, you can configure subscriptions to alerts to ensure that only the appropriate alerts are forwarded via email, and only to the correct recipients. This also allows sending alerts and monitoring data to different recipients during off-hours. The Notification Workflow in OpsMgr is also used to configure which alerts are passed to connectors for forwarding to third-party systems. More information on integrating OpsMgr with other systems is in Chapter 22, "Interoperability."

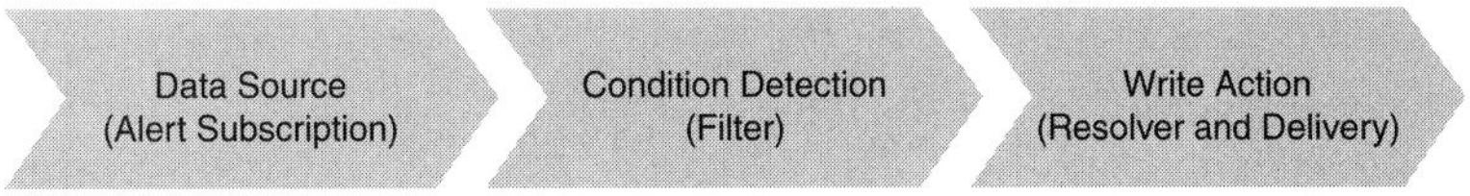

FIGURE 14.39   Notification workflow.

Figure 14.39 shows the structure of the notification workflow.

At a high level, the steps OpsMgr takes to create the workflow are as follows:

1. **Create the recipient and subscription.**

   This is where we configure the recipient to send the alerts to. This can be an email recipient, IM recipient, SMS message recipient, or based on a command (which is useful for sending notifications to a third-party message system, for example).

2. **Create a notification rule for generating notifications.**

   Here we create the actual notification rule to define which alerts to send and to which recipients.

3. **Generate an alert.**

   The alert is generated by OpsMgr.

4. **The AlertSubscription Data Source module periodically polls subscriptions.**

   Periodically, the OpsMgr notification workflow polls the subscriptions and enumerates the configuration to define whether the alert(s) that generated since the last poll need to be forwarded to a recipient.

5. **The Resolver module processes (filters) alerts that match.**

   Matching alerts are passed to the next stage of the notification workflow.

6. **The Resolver module enumerates the recipient list, addresses, and schedule for each notification.**

   At this point, the alert has been matched but OpsMgr carries out one final check, to ensure the subscription is configured to receive alerts during the specified time. In other words, if an alert is matched at 5 a.m. and the subscription is not configured to receive alerts between 1 a.m. and 6 a.m., the alert is not forwarded.

Real World—Problems with Subscriptions When Selecting Categories

During our work with Operations Manager 2007, we have found situations where subscriptions defined to specific categories do not appear to work correctly. As an example, we wanted to define a subscription where all alerts are sent via email, but when a subscription is no longer online, a notification is sent to a pager. This technique would provide an approach to notification where the majority of alerts are sent with email, and if systems are offline, a page is generated that is sent during off-hours.

However, if we limited the criteria, the notification does not work correctly—if the system was taken offline, no notification was sent to the pager. To re-create this test, we performed the following steps:

1. Install a functional OpsMgr 2007 environment.
2. Install hotfix 937470 (an existing fix for subscription functionality).
3. Test subscriptions to the recipient email address and validate the functionality.
4. Configure a subscription for the recipient and restrict the category to State Collection.
5. Create an alert that should be part of the state collection. To determine what the state collection information should be for the alert that was created, we reviewed the alert information in the Operations database. You can find the criteria information using the following SQL query from the database:

```
Select * from dbo.alert
```

From the SQL query, we determined the following important information:

▶ Severity: 2
▶ Priority: 2
▶ Resolution State: 255
▶ Category: State collection

We configured our subscription that provides pager notification for systems that became available during off-hours as follows:

▶ Severity: Error, Warning
▶ Priority: High, Medium
▶ Resolution State: New, Closed
▶ Category: State collection

However, no alerts were generated. If we select all available categories, the subscription successfully creates the notification, but it does not happen if any categories are specified. This information has been submitted to Microsoft (https://connect.microsoft.com/OpsMgrFeedback/feedback/ViewFeedback.aspx?FeedbackID=306577) and is currently under review.

7. **Notification subject and body is generated for each device per recipient.**
The notification message is created and generated, based on the default notification format and any additional changes to the default format configured in the rule or monitor that generated the alert.

8. **Delivery Action executes the delivery, with notification content included.**
The message is delivered. At this point, OpsMgr passes responsibility of the message to the notification delivery software (Microsoft Exchange, for example). OpsMgr does not monitor to verify that the message arrives. If the message does not arrive, you will need to attempt to locate it in the notification delivery device.

As OpsMgr monitors its own notification workflow, if no alerts are generated in the Operations console suggesting there is a problem with the workflow, we can safely assume that the message has left the OpsMgr notification workflow and has been passed to the configured notification device.

In the next sections, we describe the process to create a recipient and notification subscription, using email to forward the messages.

Creating a Recipient

Before you can configure alerts and monitors to send data via email, you must configure a recipient address for the emails to be sent to. Follow these steps:

1. Open the Administration space and locate the Notifications -> Recipients tree. Right-click and select New Notification Recipient. This displays the Notification Recipient Properties screen, shown in Figure 14.40.

FIGURE 14.40   The General tab on the Notification Recipient Properties screen.

2. Begin with giving the new recipient a name. The easiest way to do this is to search Active Directory (AD). (If the user does not exist in AD, you will have to enter the details manually.) Click the ... button to browse the directory. Type the user's name and click the Check Names button to validate your entry. Click OK.

3. The user's account name now displays in the top box. On this first screen, you can also choose to configure a schedule to send the emails. We will assume notifications will always be sent, so accept the defaults.

4. We must now choose which type of notifications to send to this address (in our case, email). Click the Notification Devices tab at the top of the window. Then click Add to start the Create Notification Device Wizard.

5. On the screen shown in Figure 14.41, select E-mail from the dropdown list. If the user is an AD user with a mailbox, his or her email address automatically appears in the delivery address box. If the user is not in AD, you can manually add the address.

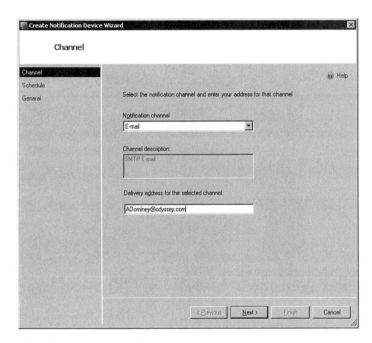

FIGURE 14.41   Specifying the notification channel and delivery address.

6. Click Next and accept the default on the schedule screen because we want emails to always be sent. Click Next.

7. You are prompted to give the notification channel a name. Something along the lines of **E-mail alerting for** *xxxx* (where *xxxx* is the user's name) is appropriate.

8. Click Finish, then click OK again to finish. The new recipient (ODYSSEY\ADominey) is displayed in Figure 14.42.

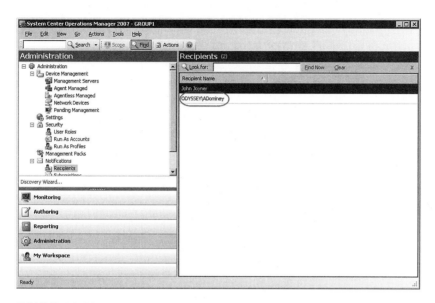

FIGURE 14.42   The new recipient defined.

Creating a Subscription

After creating a recipient, you must create a subscription for the recipient to get email alerts. Perform the following steps:

1. In the Administration space, locate the Notifications -> Subscriptions tree. Right-click and select New Notification Subscription to display the General properties screen. The General screen is where you give a name to the subscription and add the appropriate recipients. Click Next. We will name the subscription **Alerting to Andy Dominey**. Click the Add icon and then select the ODYSSEY\ADominey recipient. Figure 14.43 shows the completed screen.

2. The next screen is the User Role Filter screen. This screen is very useful if you have configured customized user roles (which we discuss in Chapter 11) because you can create a subscription based on the objects the user role has permissions to simply by checking the tick box and selecting the appropriate user role. Because we will be creating a subscription from scratch, we will not use this functionality for this example. Click Next.

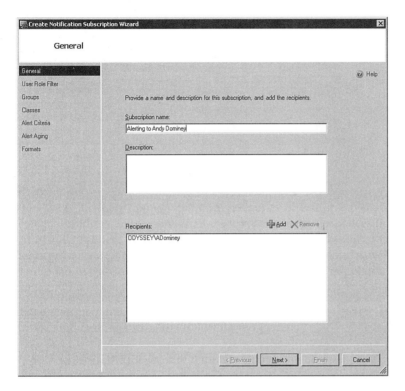

FIGURE 14.43   Naming the subscription and specifying a recipient.

3. The Groups screen is next. It allows configuring the groups this subscription will apply to. In this example, we are only interested in Windows Server alerts, so we will select the following groups:

▶ Windows Server 2000 Computer Group

▶ Windows Server 2003 Computer Group

▶ Windows Server Computer Group

▶ Windows Server Instances Group

Figure 14.44 displays the completed screen. Click Next to continue.

FIGURE 14.44   Specifying the groups we want to notify on alerts and alert updates.

4. The next screen is the Classes screen. This is where you can choose to limit your subscription to individual classes or simply to accept all classes. It is worth noting that if you choose to select individual classes and any new classes are added later, you will have to add them manually. We will choose the classes displayed in Figure 14.45. Click Next.

5. The Alert Criteria screen is a very important one. Here you choose the severity, type, priority, and resolution state of the alerts you want to email. We will configure our subscription as shown in Figure 14.46. Here we are choosing to receive only alerts of severity Error that are of high priority. We are only interested in new alerts but want to be notified for all alert categories. Click Next.

6. The Alert Aging screen allows you to configure additional emails for alerts that have not been updated for a specified period of time. In other words, if an alert has not been updated for a long period of time, this screen can be used to configure a "reminder" email that the alert is still unresolved. We will leave this option off for this example. Click Next to move on to the final screen of this wizard.

7. The Formats screen allows us to customize the format in which the email will be sent. We will leave this at the default (global) setting for this example. Click Finish to create the subscription.

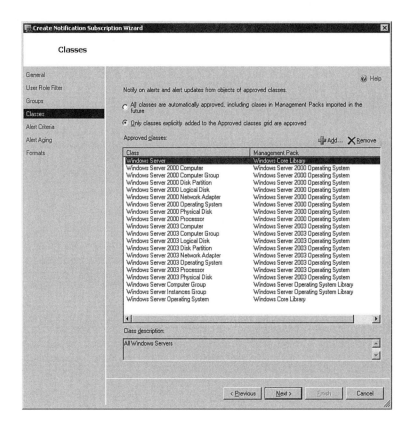

FIGURE 14.45   The notification class selection screen.

TIP

Screen Capture Alert Text

Have you ever wanted to capture—as text—the screen content of an alert in the Operations console (or anything/anywhere else)? A small utility named Kleptomania uses Optical Character Recognition (OCR) technology to let capture text from anywhere on the screen, including database lists, forms and reports, error messages, dialog boxes, status lines, folder trees, and file lists.

You can get a free 40-day trial of Kleptomania, or you can get a private single user license for $29.95. See http://www.structurise.com/kleptomania/ for future information. In addition, copying data from the console to the Clipboard is scheduled to be included in OpsMgr 2007 Service Pack 1.

.

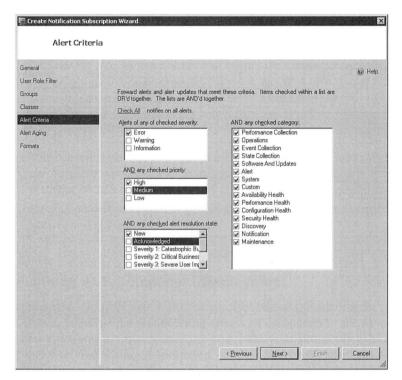

FIGURE 14.46   Specifying the criteria for forwarding alerts.

Adding Knowledge

Now that we have looked at the different types of rules and monitors in OpsMgr, we will highlight the methods to add knowledge and troubleshooting data to alerts.

Despite the fact that monitors are now the preferred method for monitoring servers and applications because they are "real time," alerts are still the primary source of information in OpsMgr. This is the reason a large number of monitors are configured to generate alerts.

A typical alert contains a large amount of knowledge and information about the problem that occurred and about how to troubleshoot the problem, and it often includes steps to assist in resolving the problem.

When you select an alert in the Monitoring pane of the Operations console, the bottom (Alert Details) pane displays additional information about an alert. We show an example in Figure 14.47.

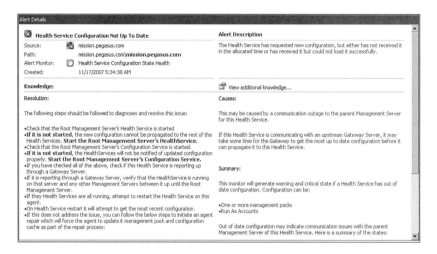

FIGURE 14.47   Viewing the Alert Details pane.

As shown in Figure 14.47, some alerts contain quite a bit of information. However, the information supplied by the management pack vendor may not necessarily be applicable for every environment, or there may be other specific information you want to include such as additional troubleshooting steps or the telephone numbers and names of the engineers who manage the system in question.

This is where the Company Knowledge section of the alert comes in. By incorporating company knowledge, you can add information into an alert so that every time that alert appears in the console, it appears with your customized information in addition to vendor-supplied product knowledge.

The following list documents the steps for adding company knowledge to an alert.

NOTE

Tools for Creating Company Knowledge

To add company knowledge to an alert or management pack, you must install Microsoft Office Word (version 2003 recommended) and the Visual Studio 2005 Tools for Office Second Edition Runtime. You can download the runtime tools from http://www.microsoft.com/downloads/details.aspx?FamilyID=F5539A90-DC41-4792-8EF8-F4DE62FF1E81&displaylang=en (we include this link in Appendix E as a live link on the CD for your convenience).

---

1. Open the Monitoring space in the Operations console. Select an alert. This example uses the Health Service Configuration Not Up To Date alert, but the specific alert really isn't important for this process.

2. You will notice that as you select the alert, the Alert Details pane fills with information. This includes a hyperlink to view additional knowledge, which we circled in Figure 14.48.

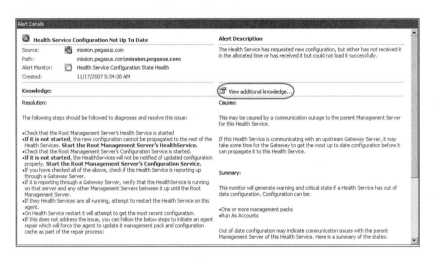

FIGURE 14.48   The hyperlink to view additional knowledge in the Alert Details section.

3. Selecting the hyperlink opens the Alert Properties dialog box with the Product Knowledge tab active. Select the Company Knowledge tab, as we have in Figure 14.49.

4. To add company knowledge, you need to click the Edit Monitor button. This displays the Properties window for the monitor. Select the Company Knowledge tab here, and you will see an Edit button, which we circled in Figure 14.50.

5. Also highlighted in Figure 14.50 is the Select destination management pack drop-down. Because we cannot edit sealed management packs, we need to select a management pack in which to store our customizations. Select the Sample Management Pack we created earlier and then click Edit.

   If you have not installed Microsoft Word and the Visual Studio Tools for Office Runtime, you will receive an error stating that the tools are not installed. It is necessary to install this software before editing company knowledge.

6. After Microsoft Word loads, you are presented with the screen shown in Figure 14.51.

7. Now edit the company knowledge and click the Save icon in Microsoft Word. After saving the knowledge, you can close Word. The knowledge is added to the monitor. Click OK to save your changes.

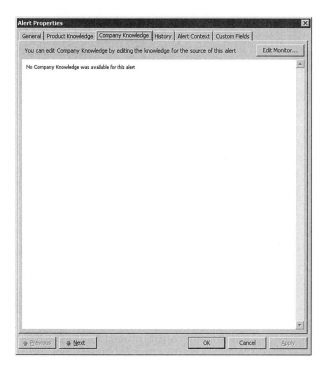

FIGURE 14.49   The Company Knowledge tab in the Alert Properties dialog box.

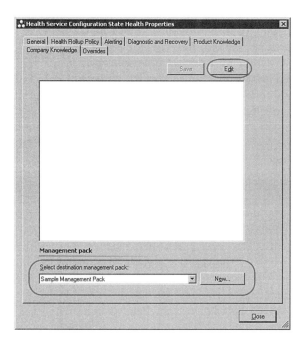

FIGURE 14.50   The Edit button for editing company knowledge.

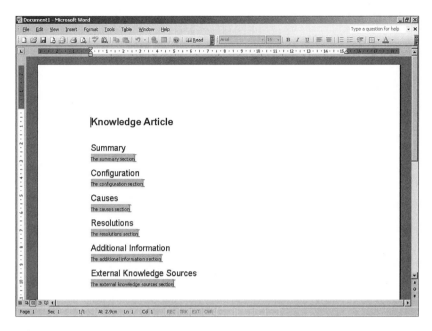

FIGURE 14.51   Edit company knowledge in Microsoft Word.

Locating Rules and Monitors in the Operations Console

Now that we have explained rules, monitors, and alerts, we will take you through the process of locating those rules, monitors, and other objects in the Operations console.

Search Options

Unlike MOM 2000 and MOM 2005 objects, OpsMgr 2007 objects are indexed within the product itself. This indexing allows searching to be far more accurate and speeds up the process for finding objects in OpsMgr.

With OpsMgr 2007, you can search in your current view using the search bar shown at the top in Figure 14.52.

You can also use the advanced search capability located in the Tools menu (Tools -> Advanced Search). This menu simply allows you to target your search at a particular type of object in OpsMgr, rather than searching just the view you are currently looking at in the Operations console. Figure 14.53 displays the Advanced Search window.

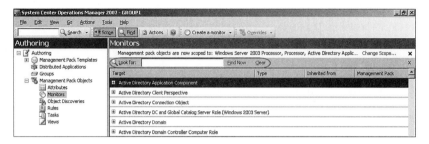

FIGURE 14.52   The search bar in the Operations console.

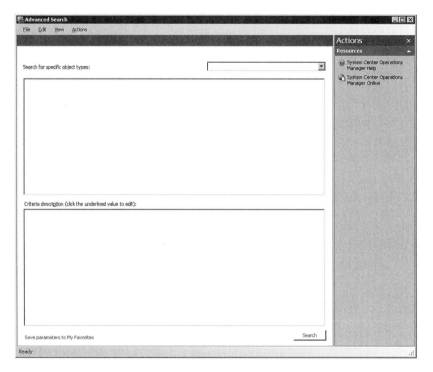

FIGURE 14.53   The Advanced Search window.

Finding Rules and Monitors

Due to the large number of classes and objects in OpsMgr, we do not recommend displaying objects for all classes in the Authoring section of the console at one time. Therefore, you can *scope* the console to a particular class or set of classes to minimize the number of items you are displaying, making searching for items easier and faster.

When you are navigating the Authoring space of the console, you will notice at the top of the pane on the right, just underneath the section title bar, a narrow yellow strip with a

Change Scope... option on the far-right side. This is the scoping bar, which we circled in Figure 14.54. We can use the scoping bar to rescope the console to a specific class or group of classes.

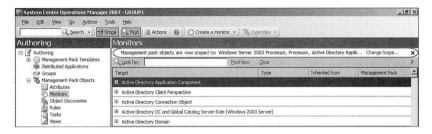

FIGURE 14.54   The scoping bar in the Operations console.

After you click Change Scope..., the Scope Management Pack Objects by target(s) screen appears (see Figure 14.55). From here, you can choose to view either common targets or all targets using the radio button near the top of the window.

To select the objects you wish to scope or filter by, you can scroll through the list of targets and select the appropriate objects, or you can narrow the search further by typing text in the Look For box. Once the list displays the objects you wish to select, tick the check boxes next to them and click OK. The console's right pane will then reload to display your selection, and the list of objects on the yellow scoping bar will include those items.

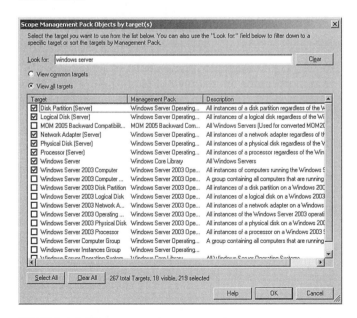

FIGURE 14.55   Selecting the scope of management pack objects you wish to view.

The scoping feature is particularly useful, not just for locating rules and monitors, but also when finding alerts and objects in the Monitoring space of the Operations console. The ability to select scope is invaluable in environments with a large number of objects and/or alerts present at any one time.

Overrides

In MOM 2005, overrides allowed you to enable and disable rules and alter (*override*) threshold values for particular monitored computers or groups of computers. You could also use overrides to target script parameters. The technique of using overrides significantly reduces the need for changing rules and therefore editing the rule base. Although in MOM 2005 using overrides was a recommended technique, that practice was limited—there were other ways to modify management packs. However, the mechanism is predominant in OpsMgr 2007 and therefore deserves special attention in this chapter. You cannot edit management packs directly in OpsMgr 2007, and all changes to management pack objects will incorporate overrides.

Defining Overrides

Overrides are the capability that enables you to modify settings in a rule or monitor for a particular object such as a managed computer, *without* actually editing the rule. As an example, you could use an override to disable a rule for a specific monitored computer without affecting the rule for all other monitored systems. Alternatively, you could specify a higher CPU threshold value for a heavily utilized server to prevent false alerts, without affecting the value used with other monitored computers.

MOM 2005 overrides were attached to the GUID of a rule; although the rule itself was not changed, the override represented an overall change to the rule base. Because management packs are now sealed (explained in Chapter 13), this method is no longer available. With OpsMgr 2007, Microsoft has developed another technique to utilize overrides, without having to alter the rule base.

In this version of Operations Manager, rule settings such as the Enabled flag (which defines whether a rule or monitor is enabled) are presented as values that can be overridden. Overrides themselves, once created, are stored in either a custom management pack of your choice or the Default MP. The overrides are grouped together, forming a set of policies to be applied to managed computers. When rules pass to OpsMgr-monitored computers, those policies are applied before the rules arrive. Because the clients have the overrides applied, the copy of rules on the client will differ from the rules on the management server(s). Figure 14.56 illustrates this process.

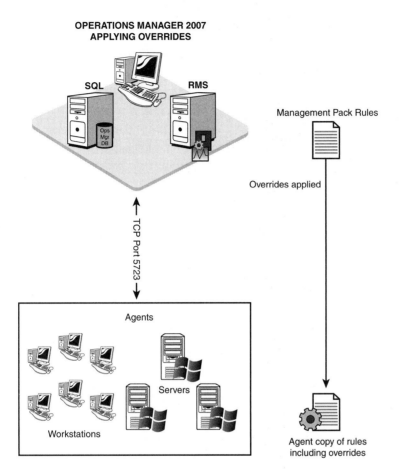

OPERATIONS MANAGER 2007
APPLYING OVERRIDES

SQL   RMS

Management Pack Rules

Overrides applied

TCP Port 5723

Agents

Servers

Workstations

Agent copy of rules
including overrides

FIGURE 14.56   How overrides are applied in OpsMgr 2007.

Creating an Override

This section looks at the process for creating an override against a monitor. Here are the steps to follow:

1. As in the previous examples in the "Monitors" section of this chapter, navigate to the Authoring space in the Operations console and select Monitors.

2. Using one of the search methods discussed in the "Search Options" section of this chapter, locate the monitor you wish to override. For our example, we will override the Available Megabytes of Memory monitor located under the Windows Server 2003 Operating System class. Using the scoping bar, scope the console to this class. You will find this monitor under the Performance aggregate monitor, as shown in Figure 14.57.

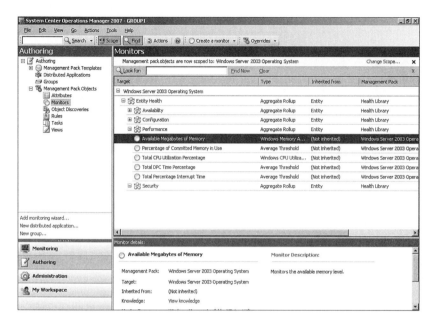

FIGURE 14.57   Locating the monitor.

3. After locating the monitor, right-click it and select Overrides. Next, choose Override the Monitor (there is also the option Disable the Monitor, which is a simple way to disable the monitor for an object, class, or group without going through the steps listed in this section). Choosing Override the Monitor opens a submenu with the following options:

   ▶ **For all objects of type:** *<Class the monitor is attached to>*

     The For all objects of type: option creates the override and targets it at all objects encompassed by the class to which the monitor is attached. For example, in our case the override is targeted to all objects that are members of the Windows Server 2003 Operating System class.

     An example of this configuration would be if you needed to update a threshold value for all occurrences of a performance counter. To change the threshold value for the Total CPU Percentage Utilization monitor for all Windows Server 2003 computers, you would create an override on that monitor using the For all objects of type: option.

   ▶ **For a group...**

     The For a group... option allows you to select a group instead of a class or object.

This is useful when you need to apply the override to a group rather than a class, such as a specific collection of computers. You can create a group, populate it with those computers, and then apply the override to that new group.

▶ **For a specific object of type:** *<Class the monitor is attached to>*

The For a specific object of type: option is similar to the For all objects of type: option, other than the fact that this option gives you the opportunity to select a specific object (perhaps the processor on a specific monitored computer) to target the override to.

This option is useful if you want to create an override for a specific object. Take the CPU Percentage Utilization monitor that we used in the For all objects of a type: example. The For a specific option of type: option would be useful if you want to update the performance threshold for a single instance of the counter, on a single computer.

▶ **For all objects of another type...**

The For all objects of another type... option allows you to apply the override to all objects of a type different from that of the rule or monitor you are overriding.

For example, you may locate or create a rule or monitor assigned to the Windows 2003 Operating System class that will also work against Windows 2000 servers. For the rule to apply to Windows 2000 servers as well, create an override using the For all objects of another type: option to select the Windows 2000 Operating System class.

These options define which object or group of objects the override will target.

4. For our example, we will assume we have a single computer that is causing excessive alerts and therefore we select to target the monitor to a ...specific object of type Windows Server 2003 Operating System. Selecting this option presents the Select Object screen, as shown in Figure 14.58. Here we will select Hydra, which is the computer in our environment that is experiencing heavy usage and therefore generating alerts.

5. Click OK after selecting the object you wish to override. The Override Properties window displays, as shown in Figure 14.59.

6. The Override Properties window displays all the parameters you can override for the monitor. For this particular monitor, a large number of parameters are available to override. Because we are interested in modifying the threshold values, we will alter the Available Memory Threshold (Mbytes) parameter.

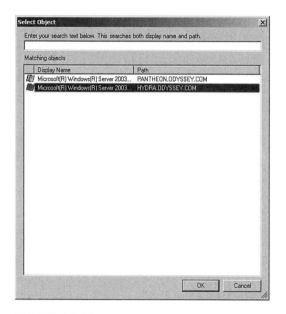

FIGURE 14.58   Select an object for override.

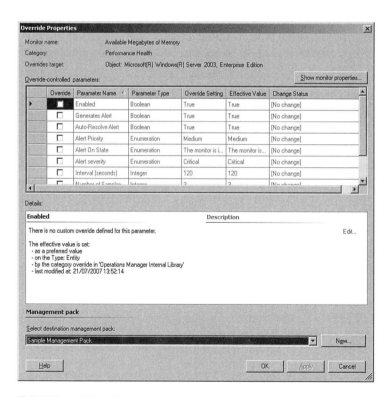

FIGURE 14.59   The Override Properties window.

To modify this parameter, scroll down to tick the check box next to the parameter and type the new value in the Override Setting column, which should highlight automatically when you put a tick in the check box. The default value is 2.5MB, but you can change this as necessary. For our example, we will change this to 6MB. Type **6.0** into the column and click Apply (see Figure 14.60).

The next column (Effective Value) will change to reflect the change you made. Click OK to apply the override.

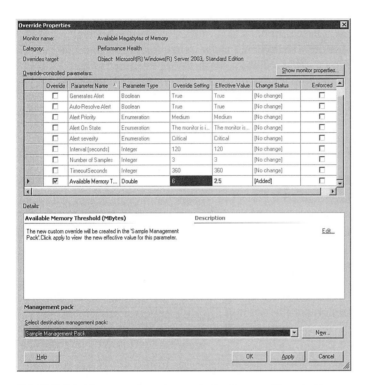

FIGURE 14.60   Changing the Available Memory Threshold parameter.

7. To verify the override, you can look in the Overrides Summary window. To locate this window, right-click the monitor and then choose Overrides Summary. You will see the override listed in the Overrides Summary screen shown in Figure 14.61. From here, you can delete or edit any overrides as required.

This section looked at overrides and stepped through configuring an override to a Windows performance monitor.

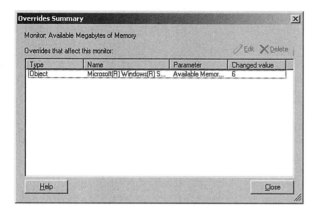

FIGURE 14.61   The Overrides Summary screen.

NOTE

Overriding Parameters

Not all parameters in monitors and rules can be overridden. If you cannot find the parameter you wish to override, it may be that it is not possible to override that parameter. If that is the case, it may be necessary to disable the rule/monitor using an override and create a custom rule or monitor to edit the values you require.

Using the Command Shell to Locate Overrides

Finding overrides in the Operations console is not difficult, but in large, complex implementations where there may be many hundreds and even thousands of overrides, it can become difficult and time consuming to locate them in the console. In this case, consider using the Operations Manager Command Shell.

The Command Shell builds on Windows PowerShell. It contains the Operations Manager functions and cmdlets you can use to manage Operations Manager from the command line. Some features, such as configuring connected management groups, are only possible using the Command Shell, so you will want to familiarize yourself with it. More information on the Operations Manager Command Shell can be found in Chapter 3, "Looking Inside OpsMgr."

In this section, we will look at one aspect of the Operations Manager Command Shell—managing overrides using the Command Shell. Follow these steps:

1. Load the Command Shell. Although you can do this manually through the PowerShell interface, the easiest way to load the Command Shell is to navigate to Start -> Programs -> System Center Operations Manager 2007 -> Command Shell. This opens a PowerShell interface with the OpsMgr functions and cmdlets already loaded.

2. Once the Command Shell window appears, you can use the following command structure to export a list of overrides to a .csv file:

```
Get-override –managementPack <MP name>.mp ¦ export-csv <csv file name>.csv
```

In this example, we will look for the override we created earlier in the "Creating an Override" section of this chapter. From the Command Shell, type the following command on a single line in the Command Shell:

```
Get-override –managementPack Sample.Management.Pack.mp ¦ export-csv
    "C:\orExport.csv"
```

3. This exports into a CSV-formatted file all the overrides for our Sample Management Pack, which is where we earlier created our override. After running this command, open the file and you will see the output displayed in Figure 14.62.

This step assumes that you have previously exported the management pack. If this is not the case, you can navigate to the Administration space, right-click the Sample Management Pack, and choose Export from the context menu.

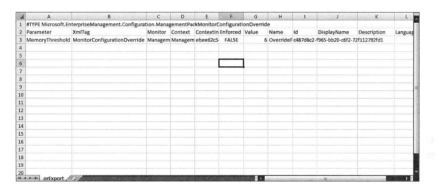

FIGURE 14.62   Output from the Override CSV file.

As you can see in Figure 14.62, the file output is rather raw. To get the most from the output, we suggest opening the file in a spreadsheet application (such as Microsoft Excel) that allows you to resize the columns to help with viewing the data.

Using this cmdlet is a very quick way to locate all overrides in a management pack.

TIP

Using Excel with CSV Files

Although you can view CSV files in a number of applications, we recommend Microsoft Excel because the data is automatically grouped into columns and can be manipulated as required.

After locating the appropriate override, you can modify it in the Authoring space of the Operations console, using the method described earlier in the "Monitors" section of this chapter.

More about Overrides

Several additional techniques are available for listing active overrides:

- ▶ You can simply use a Command Shell command to dump all the overrides out at one time. The following command will dump all overrides in descending order sorted by LastModified date to a CSV file. You can view the file as we did in the previous example in the "Using the Command Shell to Locate Overrides" section. The code is as follows on a single line in the Command Shell:

  ```
  get-ManagementPack ¦ where {$_.Name -like "*" } ¦ get-Override ¦sort-object
  LastModified -descending ¦ select-object name, displayname, xmltag, value,
  timeadded, lastmodified ¦ export-Csv -Path "c:\overrides.csv"
  ```

  More information on this technique is available from http://systemcenterforum.org/ tip-dumping-all-overrides-in-operations-manager-2007/.

- ▶ There also is a very useful tool written by Boris Yanushpolsky of the MOM Team that you can use to locate overrides. This is the Overrides Explorer graphical tool, which simply reads from the OpsMgr configuration. You can download the tool from http://blogs.msdn.com/boris_yanushpolsky/archive/2007/08/09/override-explorer-v3-3. aspx.

  When you run the tool, select File -> Connect and input the name of the Root Management Server. The tool reads the data, and the overrides are listed by group or by managed entity. We have found it most useful when searching by group. Figure 14.63 displays this utility.

  One of the neatest features of this tool is its ability to move overrides to a different unsealed management pack. Say, for example, you have created a custom management pack for overrides and a junior OpsMgr administrator creates a new override—but does not specify your custom management pack to store it. Typically, you would re-create the override to specify the correct management pack to save it. That is no longer necessary! Now you can simply locate the override in the tool, right-click, and select the Move to different MP option to move it to the correct management pack, without actually deleting and re-creating the override.

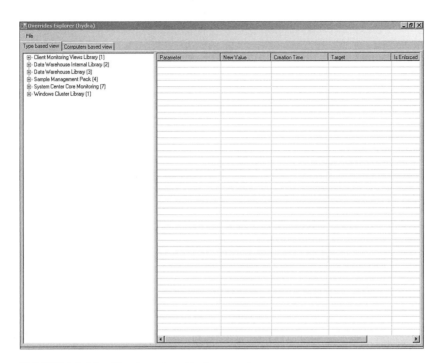

FIGURE 14.63   The Overrides Explorer tool.

Real World—Best Practices for Overrides

Microsoft has released information detailing its recommendations and best practices when creating overrides. This guide is available at http://support.microsoft.com/kb/ 943239.

This document recommends you create a separate Overrides management pack for each of your management packs. Although this approach is suitable for some environments, it will potentially create a large number of additional management packs and make managing the overall environment more challenging. Another option would be to create a single management pack that contains all overrides. Although some environments have reported problems from consolidating all overrides into a single management pack (due to the large number of dependencies for that management pack), for others this method is a valid way of managing overrides.

Other best practices for overrides include:

- ▶ Do not use the "Disable" command in the override menu.
- ▶ Make sure the parameter is overridden in all the rules and monitors.
- ▶ Configure overrides for groups instead of specific instances whenever possible.

In the next section of the chapter, we discuss creating custom resolution states.

Creating Custom Resolution States

OpsMgr 2007 ships with two defined resolution states: New and Closed. To provide additional granularity, you can define your own custom resolution states. The following is the process for creating a custom resolution state:

1. Open the Operations console and navigate to the Administration space.

2. Select Settings. You will see the Settings pane on the right. Notice that we have highlighted Alerts in Figure 14.64.

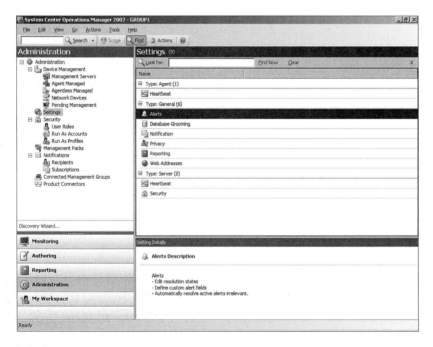

FIGURE 14.64   The Settings pane with Alert settings selected.

3. Double-click the Alerts option to open the Global Management Group Settings – Alerts window displayed in Figure 14.65.

4. Click the New icon.

5. The Add Alert Resolution State screen appears. Type a name for the new resolution state and select a unique ID for it. (The ID impacts where it appears in the context menu. The number 1 appears at the top, whereas 255 is at the bottom.) In our example, we will call the resolution state **Support** and give it an ID of **100**. Figure 14.66 displays the completed screen.

FIGURE 14.65   Alert Resolution States screen.

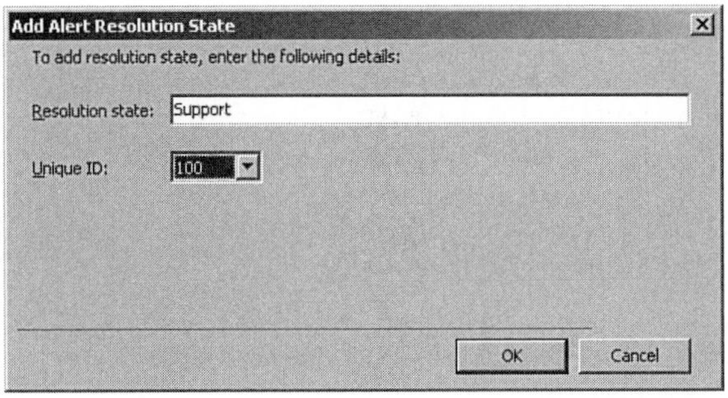

FIGURE 14.66   Add Alert Resolution State screen completed.

6. Click OK and OK again to finish creating the new alert resolution state.

7. To use the new state, navigate to the Active Alerts view in the Monitoring space, right-click an alert, and select Set Resolution State. The Support resolution state is now available. Figure 14.67 shows the context menu and an alert we placed in the Support resolution state.

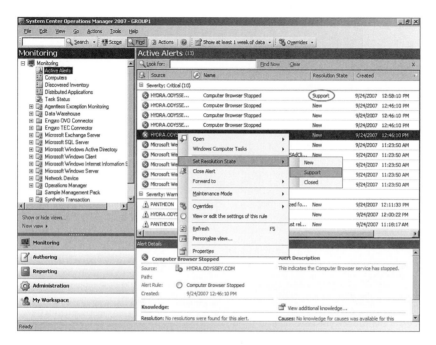

FIGURE 14.67   Using alert resolution states.

Maintenance Tuning

Now that we have looked at the different types of rules and monitors and have explained alerts in Operations Manager, let's look at some recommendations for tuning your OpsMgr environment.

NOTE

Using Overrides to Modify Thresholds and Disable Rules

As you modify thresholds and disable rules during the tuning process, keep in mind that you cannot directly modify the rules themselves in OpsMgr. To be able to make the necessary changes, you will need to use overrides. We discussed overrides in the "Overrides" section earlier in this chapter.

Tuning by Color

The easiest way to carry out alert tuning is using the status of a managed machine to prioritize the tuning. There are three main color states in OpsMgr, which should be self-explanatory:

▶ Critical/Error (Red)

▶ Warning (Yellow)

▶ OK/Success (Green)

Using these colors, you can focus your tuning and alert analysis on the systems that are marked as critical (red) first, working down to warning (yellow). Unless any specific overrides must be created for a managed machine, machines that are showing as OK (green) can usually be left alone unless their status changes.

State Monitors vs. Alerts

As we have explored in the "Rules" and "Monitors" sections of this chapter, state monitors and alerts are very different:

▶ State monitors are updated based on the current status of the system and return to a healthy state when the failure condition is resolved.

▶ Although monitors can generate alerts, these alerts are more often than not managed by the monitor, meaning that if the state monitor condition returns to normal, not only will the status return to Healthy but any alerts that have been raised by the monitor are automatically resolved.

Alerts raised by rules behave differently. These alerts will not resolve by themselves and require managing. In MOM 2000 and MOM 2005, these types of alerts were the only type available; this meant when large numbers of computers were being managed, the alerts in the console would require a huge amount of resources to manage. Large numbers of alerts were generated on a daily basis, and each alert had to be manually managed and resolved.

With monitor-managed alerts, the Operations console is less cluttered by alerts and therefore requires less human intervention, because the monitors resolve alerts automatically when the error condition is resolved. However, it will still require some degree of watching, and the number of alerts will continue to increase with the number of systems you are managing.

You should consider this difference in status monitors and alerts when you create custom rules and monitors, because creating a large number of alert-generating rules can affect the number of alerts that appear in the system and increase your management overhead for those alerts. Additional information on creating management pack objects is included in Chapter 23.

Managing Alerts

When you are managing issues, they might fall outside your knowledge, expertise, or responsibility. In those cases, you will want to reassign the issues to a more knowledgeable party. OpsMgr allows you to manage this escalation process using the Alerts view in the Operations console. OpsMgr (as did previous versions of MOM) supports creating custom resolution states.

Out of the box, OpsMgr 2007 has two resolution states: New and Closed. However, you may add additional alert resolution states as necessary to assign alerts to different support groups. We discussed this process in the "Creating Custom Resolution States" section of this chapter. After creating customized alert resolution states and using them, you may want to create custom views to view alerts from specific groups separately from the rest.

There are many different types of views, including Alert views, Performance views, and Event views. The process for creating each different view type is similar, so we will not cover each of them here. However, we will show you how to create a basic Alert view. To create an Alert view, follow this procedure:

1. Open the Operations console and navigate to the Monitoring space (or to My Workspace, depending on your access rights).

2. From the Navigation pane, right-click the subfolder where you will create the view. Now select New -> Alert View, as shown in Figure 14.68.

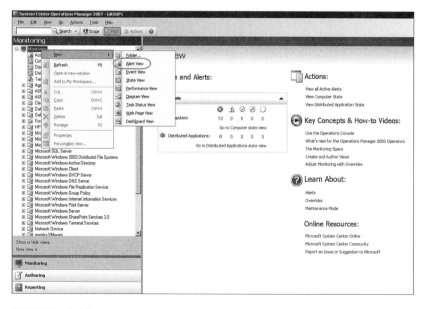

FIGURE 14.68   Selecting New, Alert View.

3. The Properties screen for the view opens, displayed in Figure 14.69. Input a name for the view. We will call ours **Windows Server Alert View**. Enter a description as appropriate.

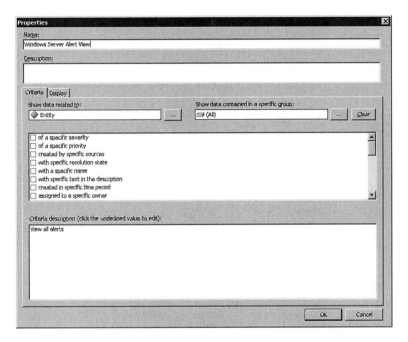

FIGURE 14.69   Viewing the Properties screen.

4. You can configure the view to display information from either a specific class or a group. We will be displaying critical alerts from the Windows Server class only. First, we must select the class we want to return data for. Click the ... button next to Show data related to. The familiar Select a Target Type dialog box will open. Type **Windows Server** into the Look For box and select the Windows Server class in the Windows Core Library management pack, as shown in Figure 14.70. Click OK.

5. Back at the Properties screen, we will filter the alerts so that only alerts with a severity of Critical are displayed. From the options that appear in the middle pane of the screen, check the box for a specific severity.

6. The information is now transferred to the bottom pane where the word *specific* is a hyperlink. Click this hyperlink to input the required filter.

7. Selecting the hyperlink presents the dialog box shown in Figure 14.71. Check the box for Critical and click OK.

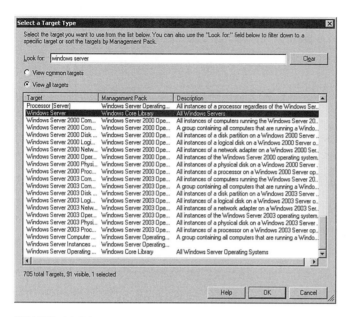

FIGURE 14.70   The Select a Target Type dialog box.

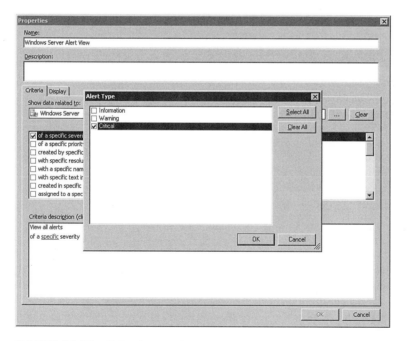

FIGURE 14.71   Selecting an alert severity.

8. The Properties dialog box should now look similar to the one shown in Figure 14.72. Click OK to create the view.

   To use this new view, select it as with any other view. The results will display in the right-side pane of the console.

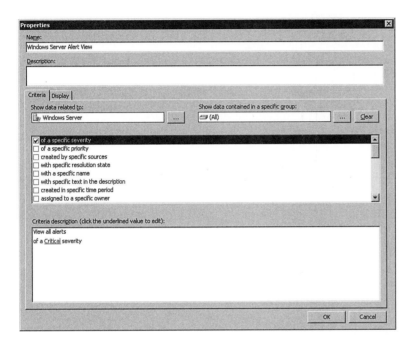

FIGURE 14.72   The completed alert view creation screen.

Typical Alerts for Tuning

We will now discuss some of the rules and monitors that are usual candidates for tuning and/or threshold changes.

We will break down the process of alert tuning by management pack, addressing the core Operating System and Application management packs. You can also look at Appendix A, "OpsMgr by Example: Tuning and Configuring Management Packs," for additional tuning tips.

Exchange Server 2003 Management Pack

When you're configuring the Exchange Server 2003 management pack, it is critical to use the Exchange Management Pack Configuration Wizard. You can download the Configuration Wizard from http://go.microsoft.com/fwlink/?LinkId=35942. Be sure to rerun the wizard whenever you add another Exchange 2003 server.

NOTE

Exchange Management Pack Configuration Wizard

This tool only applies when configuring the Exchange 2003 management pack. It does not apply to the Exchange 2007 management pack.

Alert Tuning for Exchange 2003   The Exchange management pack is one of the biggest and most complicated Operations Manager management packs and therefore may require heavy tuning. In this section, we discuss the most common alerts that require tuning in the Exchange management pack.

The following rules and monitors generate alerts that are not required in all environments (you may disable these rules/monitors using an override if necessary):

▸ **SSL should be enabled (Monitor)**—Detects whether or not HTTP access to the Exchange server is secured in IIS. If you are not using HTTPS to secure this and do not intend to, this monitor should be disabled.

▸ **Disabled user does not have a master account SID (Rule)**—This feature is by design in Exchange. Once an account has been disabled for x days, the Exchange mailbox SID is deleted. This rule should be disabled if you intend to keep user accounts for a period of time after the accounts are no longer required.

▸ **Outlook Web Access Logon Monitor (Monitor)**—This runs the script that performs a synthetic logon to OWA and verifies that OWA is working correctly. You should only disable this monitor if there is no requirement to monitor OWA.

Rule/Monitor Tuning for Exchange   There is an additional monitor in the Exchange management pack requiring further configuration that does not fall under the category of threshold modification. This monitor is the Log Files Truncated monitor.

The monitor detects if Exchange backups are not truncating the Exchange Transaction logs. The number of days set as the maximum is 2 by default. Depending on your Exchange backup schedule, the number of days may need to be increased. You can configure the number of days using an override by changing the Max Allowed Days Old parameter in the override.

Active Directory Management Pack
For the Active Directory management pack, you will first want to verify that it has been correctly configured, that the Active Directory management pack Helper Objects (oomads.msi) are installed on the DCs, and that the necessary MOMLatencyMonitors Active Directory container has been created and all required permissions applied. Instructions on carrying out this configuration are in the Active Directory Management Pack Deployment Guide, which you can download from http://technet.microsoft.com/en-us/opsmgr/bb498235.aspx.

Alert Tuning for Active Directory   Although the Active Directory management pack is not the largest management pack, it does require some level of alert tuning.

The following rules and monitors generate alerts that may not be required in your environment (you can disable these rules/monitors if necessary):

▶ **AD Trust Monitoring (Monitor)**—Used to launch the AD Monitor Trusts script. Unless you have a specific requirement to monitor Active Directory Trusts, this monitor should be disabled because the script is known to generate errors if no trusts are found.

▶ **The AD Machine Account Authentication Failures Report has data available (Rule)**—This rule can generally be disabled because it provides information that is not required, provided you correctly configure a subscription to the report.

Script Tuning for Active Directory   In addition to the rules and monitors listed in the previous section, you may need to modify the following values for them to function correctly in your environment:

▶ **The script AD Replication Monitoring**—The AD Replication Monitoring monitor launches the AD Replication Monitoring script, which monitors Active Directory replication both within the local site and in the enterprise. These settings are presented as overrides on the monitor and therefore can be changed via an override.

> ▶ **Intersite Expected Max Latency (min)**—The value for replication across all DCs in the enterprise. The default value is 15 minutes.

> ▶ **Intrasite Expected Max Latency (min)**—The value for replication across all DCs in the local site. The default value is 5 minutes.

Additional information on configuring these values is available in the Active Directory Management Deployment Guide, downloadable from http://technet.microsoft.com/en-us/opsmgr/bb498235.aspx.

▶ **The script AD Client GC Availability Performance Collection (rule)**—Checks the number of Global Catalog servers available and responding in the local site, generating an alert if the value of MinimumAvailableGCs is less than the default of 3. You can change this value with an override if necessary.

NOTE

Positioning Your Global Catalog Servers

Exchange requires at least one Global Catalog (GC) server to be available at all times in the local site. Exchange will fail over to a GC in a remote site in the event of a local GC failure, but this increases network traffic and affects Exchange performance with the overhead of making regular lookups to a remote GC.

We recommend *at least* two Global Catalog servers for fault tolerance, and additional servers as required depending on the size of the Exchange infrastructure and the number of Active Directory and Exchange users in the local site.

14

Microsoft Windows Server Operating System

The rules and monitors most likely to require threshold customization are those that monitor operating system performance.

By default, the Windows Server Operating System management pack requires very little alert tuning. Most of the changes required are threshold changes. The following rules/monitors may require threshold changes in your environment. Note that if a monitor is configured as a self-tuning threshold monitor, it may be necessary to modify the sensitivity of the baseline rather than changing a static threshold value.

▶ **Performance Threshold: Processor % DPC Time threshold exceeded (Rule)**—Monitors the Processor % DPC Time. A requirement to set a high threshold value may indicate processor performance issues on one or more of your servers.

▶ **Performance Threshold: Memory % Committed Bytes In Use threshold exceeded (Rule)**—Monitors the Memory % Committed bytes in use. A requirement to set a high threshold value here could indicate memory usage issues on one or more of your servers.

▶ **Performance Threshold: Physical Disk Average Disk Seconds per Write threshold exceeded (Rule)**—Monitors the Physical Disk Average Disk Seconds per Writes. A need to set a high threshold value here could indicate disk performance issues.

▶ **Performance Threshold: Processor % Interrupt Time threshold exceeded (Rule)**—Monitors the Processor % Interrupt Time. A requirement to set a high threshold value here could indicate performance issues on one or more of your servers.

▶ **Performance Threshold: Physical Disk Average Disk Seconds per Read threshold exceeded (Rule)**—Monitors the Physical Disk Average Disk Seconds per Reads. A requirement to set a high threshold value here could indicate processor performance issues on one or more of your servers.

▶ **Performance Threshold: Processor % Processor Time Total threshold exceeded (Rule)**—Monitors the Processor % Processor Time. A requirement to set a high threshold value here could indicate processor performance issues on one or more of your servers. It may also indicate that an application or process is utilizing a large amount of processor time.

▶ **Performance Threshold: Memory Available Megabytes threshold exceeded (Rule)**—Monitors the Memory Available Mbytes. A requirement to set a high threshold value here could indicate a requirement to upgrade memory on one or more of your servers.

Microsoft SQL Server Management Pack

The SQL Server management pack is the final management pack we will address in this chapter. This management pack contains several rules/monitors with thresholds to customize. The following rules/monitors have thresholds that you can configure as required:

▶ **Number of deadlocks (Monitor)**—Detects SQL deadlocks. A deadlock occurs when two users (or sessions) have locks on separate objects and each user wants a lock on the other's object. Each user waits for the other to release his or her lock. If this threshold needs to be increased, investigate the affected SQL Server database, because deadlocks can cause a significant performance impact to the database. This monitor only applies to SQL 2000 servers and is disabled by default. If you wish to use this rule, you will need to enable it using an override.

▶ **Collect Buffer Cache Hit Ratio < 90% for 15 minutes (Rule)**—Monitors the hits on the SQL cache. A cache hit occurs when the server requests data pages that are stored in a memory buffer pool. If the threshold for this rule needs to be increased, it may indicate that the memory in the SQL Server is not sufficient and needs to be increased.

▶ **SQL User Connections Performance/User Connection Baseline (Monitor)**—These monitors are the most likely to require changes because they monitor the number of SQL users concurrently connected to the database. Because they are self-tuning threshold monitors, they require sensitivity changes rather than static threshold changes. If you have a SQL Server configured to accept a large number of connections, you may need to change the sensitivity of these monitors to prevent extraneous alerts. These monitors are also disabled by default and will need to be enabled, if required, using an override.

Maintenance Mode in OpsMgr

After tuning your alerts and configuring overrides as required, you will want to keep new false alerts to a minimum. As we know, sometimes it is necessary to shut down or reboot computers when applying patches and performing essential maintenance; when you have planned outages, alerts and health status changes in OpsMgr are not particularly welcome.

With that in mind, you can use the *maintenance mode* feature to stop monitoring a monitored system during scheduled maintenance periods.

Although maintenance mode existed in MOM 2005, OpsMgr 2007 lets you target maintenance mode at any object, not just a managed computer. This means, as an example, you could put a single SQL Server database into maintenance mode to take it offline, while still monitoring all other databases on the server and all other components of that server such as hard disk and CPU. This granular level of applying maintenance mode mirrors the level of granularity found throughout OpsMgr 2007.

We will provide an example of applying maintenance mode to an object by putting the C: drive of the Hydra computer in maintenance mode for 30 minutes to carry out some essential maintenance.

The easiest way to put a component into maintenance mode is to use the Diagram view of the monitored computer to locate the component. Perform the following steps:

1. Navigate to the Computers view in the Monitoring space and right-click the Hydra computer. From the context menu, select Open -> Diagram View.

2. A Diagram view similar to the one shown in Figure 14.73 appears.

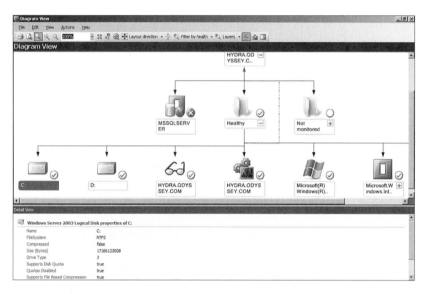

FIGURE 14.73   The OpsMgr Diagram view for Hydra.

3. From the Diagram view, right-click the C: drive object (highlighted in Figure 14.73) and from the context menu, select Maintenance Mode -> Start Maintenance Mode.... This opens the Maintenance Mode Settings window.

4. Check the Planned box on the right and the Selected objects only radio button. Now, select a category for planned maintenance, as displayed in Figure 14.74. We will select the Hardware: Maintenance (Planned) category from the dropdown list. Click OK, and add a comment if you like. Set the number of minutes to 30 and then click OK.

5. If you refresh the Diagram view, you will see that the object now has a small spanner icon (circled in the screenshot) to indicate it is in maintenance mode, as shown in Figure 14.75.

   You can edit maintenance mode and remove a managed machine/object from maintenance mode using the same context menu as we used in step 3.

   Of course, you can put higher-level objects in maintenance mode, including an entire managed computer.

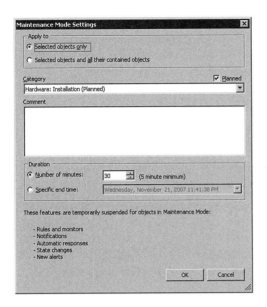

FIGURE 14.74   The Maintenance Mode Settings window.

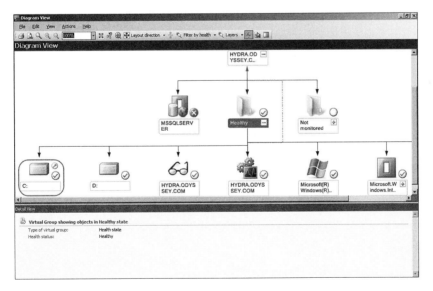

FIGURE 14.75   Looking at the Diagram view while in maintenance mode.

By default, maintenance mode automatically filters down to lower-level objects. As we just saw with the Maintenance Mode Settings window, you can change this by choosing Selected objects only.

You can also initiate maintenance mode using the Command Shell. This is useful when you want to script the adding of monitored objects into maintenance mode. You can find additional information on using the Command Shell to put a monitored object in maintenance mode in Chapter 8, "Configuring and Using Operations Manager 2007."

Resource Kit Utilities

In September 2007, Microsoft released the first wave of the Operations Manager 2007 resource kit. We discuss three of those utilities in the next sections:

- ▶ AD integration sample script
- ▶ Effective Configuration Viewer
- ▶ Vista gadget bar

You can download the resource kit from the OpsMgr 2007 TechCenter, located at http://go.microsoft.com/fwlink/?LinkId=94593.

AD Integration Sample Script

The AD integration sample script (SGPopulate.js) enables you to extract a list of computer names from your inventory database (System Center Configuration Manager, for example) or CMDB database and add them to an Active Directory security group.

The purpose of the tool is to assist in assigning machines to a management server when using OpsMgr Active Directory integration.

When you run the script, you must input a number of parameters to enable the script to carry out the following steps:

- ▶ Connect to the SQL Instance hosting your inventory or CMDB database.
- ▶ Connect to the inventory or CMDB database.
- ▶ Run a SQL query to return the NetBIOS or host name of a group of computers.

The script uses the returned computer names to populate the specified AD security group. You must specify the following parameters when running this script:

- ▶ **serverInstance**—The SQL Server Instance hosting the inventory database
- ▶ **database**—Inventory database name
- ▶ **query**—SQL query to return the list of computer names
- ▶ **sgName**—Active Directory security group name

The following is an example of how the script could be used:

```
SGPopulate.js CMDBServer01 MyCMDB
➥"SELECT ComputerName FROM Computers WHERE Location = US" OpsMgr-SG-01
```

Using this example, the AD security group OpsMgr-SG-01 is populated with the computer names returned from our SQL query. You can then use the Agent Assignment and Failover Wizard in OpsMgr to create a Lightweight Directory Access Protocol (LDAP) query to return all members of this group. Additional information on the Agent Assignment and Failover Wizard can be found in Chapter 9, "Installing and Configuring Agents."

Effective Configuration Viewer

The Effective Configuration Viewer returns the resultant set of monitors and rules running on a monitored object after all management packs and overrides are applied. This is particularly useful because it is often difficult to see this information—particularly given that the appearance of the rules and monitors in the Operations console can be significantly different from those on the agent, because the rules and monitors in the Operations console are displayed before the overrides are applied.

Download the tool and extract the executable from the zip file. When you execute the tool, click File -> Connect. Then input the RMS server name and click OK.

To view the resultant data for an object, click File -> Pick an Object and select the object you want to view the configuration for in the Object Picker, as we have in Figure 14.76. You can select computers or distributed applications, or you can specify Other to choose another OpsMgr object.

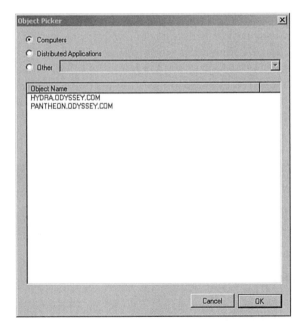

FIGURE 14.76   Selecting an object using the Object Picker.

After selecting the object, clicking OK displays rules, as shown in Figure 14.77.

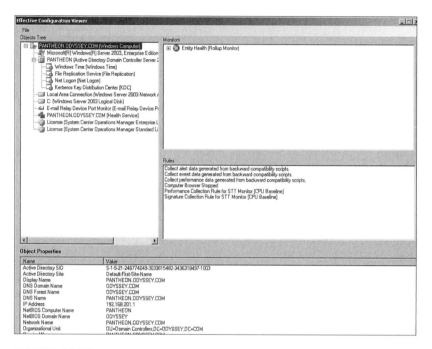

FIGURE 14.77   Effective configuration results.

The Objects Tree shows that you can view OpsMgr licensing information for that object as well (see Figure 14.78).

You can export data captured by the Viewer to XML by selecting the Export to XML option from the File menu.

In addition, you can execute this tool from the command line. Open a command prompt (select Start -> Run -> and then type **CMD**) and navigate to the folder where you extracted the tool. If you run it from the command line, it seems that nothing is happening because the prompt is still available, but the executable is doing its work in the background!

The following code syntax can be used to show the effective configuration of an agent. In this example, we will return the effective configuration of the Pantheon server object.

Use the following command-line example to create and save a file that lists the rules and monitors for a particular object:

```
effectiveconfigurationviewer Hydra.odyssey.com Pantheon.odyssey.com
➥c:\pantheonresults.xml
```

FIGURE 14.78 The Effective Configuration Viewer captures OpsMgr licensing information.

This sample line of code specifies three parameters:

- **Hydra.odyssey.com** as the RMS
- **Pantheon.odyssey.com** as the target
- **C:\pantheonresults.xml** as the output file

Note that the utility does not provide an option to enter credentials other than those with which you are currently logged on.

Vista Gadget Bar

If your Vista computer has the Operations console installed, you can attach a Vista gadget that is similar to the Red/Yellow/Green state counter toolbar in MOM 2005. This feature complements the Operations console significantly, so much that it makes Vista almost a preferred desktop platform for OpsMgr operators. Figure 14.79 displays the gadget.

The top section of Figure 14.79 lists active alerts from that target, and you can modify the sort order. Underneath that, we see the state of the objects in the target class or group.

FIGURE 14.79   The Vista gadget bar.

To use the gadget, you select the target class or group you are interested in, such as the Computer class or the All Computers group. As an example, Exchange administrators can run the gadget focused on the Exchange group, to keep a handle on Exchange server events and state.

If you hover over the gadget body and click the mini-wrench icon that appears to the upper right of the gadget in Figure 14.79, you open the OpsMgr Gadget Connection Settings dialog box (see Figure 14.80). Note at the bottom of Figure 14.80 that we selected the Computer object class for the Criteria setting.

We can also drill down into the alerts and state sections of the gadget bar. Figure 14.81 shows a fly-out view you get from clicking the Alerts section of the gadget.

FIGURE 14.80   Configuring the class and connection settings.

Source	Resolution State	Created
HURRICANE	New	9/28/2007 5:33:23 PM
SUSDB	New	9/10/2007 8:53:01 PM
Microsoft(R) Windows(R) Server 2003, Standard Edition	New	10/1/2007 4:01:43 PM
HURRICANE	New	9/28/2007 5:33:16 PM
Microsoft.SystemCenter.NotificationServer	New	9/20/2007 10:41:19 AM
AD Client Monitoring	New	9/24/2007 11:53:25 AM
Microsoft(R) Windows(R) Server 2003, Standard Edition	New	10/1/2007 3:56:48 PM
ambassador.continent.com	New	9/24/2007 7:59:32 PM
mission.pegasus.com	New	9/24/2007 3:36:41 AM
SCE	New	9/29/2007 8:25:23 AM
MS$DPMV2BETA2$	New	9/29/2007 8:25:50 AM
HYDRA.odyssey.com	New	10/1/2007 3:24:14 PM
lexington.pegasus.com	New	9/30/2007 6:25:39 AM
HONOR.continent.com	New	9/24/2007 6:36:45 PM
HONOR.continent.com	New	9/24/2007 6:36:45 PM
HONOR.continent.com	New	9/24/2007 6:36:45 PM
HONOR.continent.com	New	9/24/2007 6:36:45 PM
lexington.pegasus.com	New	9/30/2007 6:25:03 AM
lexington.pegasus.com	New	9/30/2007 6:25:03 AM
THUNDER.odyssey.com	New	9/30/2007 2:06:57 AM

FIGURE 14.81   Seeing alerts from the Vista gadget bar.

Figure 14.82 shows the fly-out view from clicking the State section of the Vista gadget.

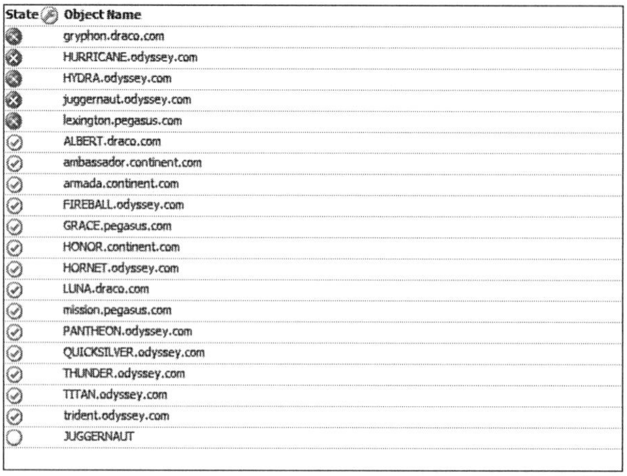

State	Object Name
✖	gryphon.draco.com
✖	HURRICANE.odyssey.com
✖	HYDRA.odyssey.com
✖	juggernaut.odyssey.com
✖	lexington.pegasus.com
✔	ALBERT.draco.com
✔	ambassador.continent.com
✔	armada.continent.com
✔	FIREBALL.odyssey.com
✔	GRACE.pegasus.com
✔	HONOR.continent.com
✔	HORNET.odyssey.com
✔	LUNA.draco.com
✔	mission.pegasus.com
✔	PANTHEON.odyssey.com
✔	QUICKSILVER.odyssey.com
✔	THUNDER.odyssey.com
✔	TITAN.odyssey.com
✔	trident.odyssey.com
○	JUGGERNAUT

FIGURE 14.82   The State view from the Vista gadget bar.

Summary

In this chapter, we explained the various rule and monitor types in OpsMgr 2007. We discussed alerts and defined the life cycle of an alert by explaining the notification work-flow. We also described overrides and the process for creating and locating an override, including the process for exporting overrides using the Command Shell.

We also looked at the process for tuning alerts, supplying you with information on typical rules and monitors that may need tuning in your environment. We provided advice on using maintenance node to minimize alerts and health status changes for objects that were subject to scheduled outages. Finally, we looked at some of the Resource Kit utilities that assist in the configuration, maintenance, and management of OpsMgr 2007.

The next chapter discusses Audit Collection Services, a new capability introduced with Operations Manager 2007.

PART V

Service-Oriented Monitoring

IN THIS PART

CHAPTER 15

Monitoring Audit Collection Services

I n today's Information Technology (IT) landscape, administrators must concern themselves with the following key issues:

- ▶ Achieving maximum availability and optimum performance from those systems they are responsible for monitoring

- ▶ Ensuring the organization complies with internal procedures and external regulations that facilitate auditing network security

The successful administrator not only keeps systems running, but also proves to regulators and business stakeholders that there is an appropriate and effective audit capability for those systems.

Many organizations today rely extensively or completely on Windows networking functions to get their business done, and a credible security auditing solution must focus on monitoring the Windows security infrastructure. To investigate potential security breaches, the auditing solution (the audit trail) must be able to provide sufficient information to establish what events occurred, when they occurred, and who (or what) caused them.

Microsoft has included the Windows NT Security Event log mechanism with Windows since the first versions of the operating system. Depending on the security audit policies enabled on the computer, the Security Event log can record a full spectrum of security-related events. Information captured can range from no security auditing to full auditing of every file and object access event that happens on the computer. Deciding what to audit is among the most

IN THIS CHAPTER

- ▶ Using ACS
- ▶ Administering ACS
- ▶ ACS Audit Policy and Reporting Scenarios

critical decisions to be made, because while capturing "everything" sounds great, it is rarely practical, desirable, or even possible to audit everything for everyone, all the time.

Audit events are stored on each computer in a local Security log, making analysis of each individual log extremely time-consuming. There are various Event log consolidation tools, but the huge volume of security events collected when auditing is enabled will overwhelm most operators and systems. In addition, simple Event log collection tools may not offer powerful search technologies to comb through the inevitable millions of security events for constructing that all-important audit trail. Given the clear business requirement to capture this information, many organizations have dedicated considerable effort to implementing their own tools for collecting, consolidating, and retaining audit-related data.

With Operations Manager (OpsMgr) 2007, Microsoft introduces Audit Collection Services (ACS) as an optional but integrated component of an OpsMgr management group. By deploying and using the ACS components of Operations Manager, the administrator fulfills a small but crucial part of an overall security compliance challenge for his organization. ACS overcomes the difficulties administrators have encountered in managing security and audit data by gathering, storing, and presenting security audit information. If you have invested in System Center Operations Manager 2007 for managing your network, additionally implementing ACS for security auditing is the logical choice.

TIP

Good Read: Regulatory Compliance Demystified

We found a very readable summary of Sarbanes-Oxley, HIPAA, and other security regulations at Microsoft—the link is http://msdn2.microsoft.com/en-us/library/aa480484. This document, written for the developer, takes a very practical approach to meeting the technical requirements of the various compliance requirements in a half-dozen industries.

Using ACS

This chapter walks though the primary activities that need to occur so you can take advantage of the new ACS features in OpsMgr 2007. To deploy ACS, we recommend following this sequence of procedures:

1. Plan an audit policy for your organization.
2. Plan your ACS component deployment. This includes making decisions about which management server(s) will be ACS collectors, provisioning each collector with a SQL Server database server, and identifying which managed computers will be ACS forwarders. Figure 15.1 illustrates the basic components of any ACS deployment.

   An ACS *collector* is a management server that receives and processes data from ACS forwarders and then sends this data to the ACS database.

   An *ACS forwarder* is a computer running the Audit Forwarder service and collecting security audit events. The service on ACS forwarders is included in the Operations Manager agent; it is installed but not enabled when the OpsMgr agent is installed.

FIGURE 15.1   The ACS Database Server, ACS Collector, and ACS Forwarder Components.

After this service is enabled, all security events are sent to the ACS collector in addition to the local Windows NT Security log.

3. Install and configure your ACS database(s) and collector(s).

4. Install the ACS reports into the management group.

5. Run the Enable Audit Collection task to start the ACS Forwarder service on computers selected to be forwarders (OpsMgr agents that participate in ACS).

6. Implement your audit policy. There are ongoing organizational (people) and technical components to administer.

The bottom-line measure of success for an ACS deployment is that you satisfy regulatory requirements for security audit record keeping without degrading the organizational efficiency of the network. In the following sections, we'll look at each of the primary activities involved in implementing ACS.

Planning an Audit Policy

To get audit data into the ACS database, you must enable auditing at the Windows operating system level on each ACS forwarder. You enable auditing through security policies. Security policy in Windows is found in three locations:

▶ **Local Security Policy**, accessed via Start-> Administrative Tools -> Local Security Policy.

Local Security Policy only exists on client computers and member servers; domain controllers do not have a Local Security Policy. Settings in the Local Security Policy are effective on the local computer unless they are overridden by Domain Security Policy.

▶ **Domain Security Policy**, accessed via Start -> Administrative Tools -> Domain Security Policy on domain controllers, or using the Group Policy Management Console (GPMC).

Settings in the Domain Security Policy are effective on all non-domain controller computers in the domain and override the settings in the Local Security Policy of domain members. Domain Security Policy has no effect on domain controllers. You can override the Domain Security Policy on non-domain controllers using custom

Group Policy Objects (GPOs); however, it is a best practice to use a standard security policy across your domain.

▶ **Domain Controller Security Policy**, accessed via Start -> Administrative Tools -> Domain Controller Security Policy on domain controllers, or using the Group Policy Management Console (GPMC).

Settings in the Domain Controller Security Policy are effective on all domain controller computers in the domain. This is the only security policy that has any effect on domain controllers.

Comparing the Different Windows Security Policies

Whereas the settings available in the Domain and the Domain Controller Security Policies are identical to each other, the settings available in the Local Security Policy are a subset of those available in the domain policies. Table 15.1 summarizes these security-critical settings and indicates which are available as domain versus local policies. (The items in bold are at the same hierarchy level in the Security Settings for the local, domain, or domain controller policy.)

TABLE 15.1   Windows Server 2003 Security Policies

Setting	Description	Location
Account Policies Password Policy	Password requirements (length, complexity, maximum age, history).	Local and domain
Account Lockout Policy	Lockout parameters (number of permitted logon attempts, duration of lockout).	Local and domain
Kerberos Policy	Kerberos key policies (how long the keys are valid).	Domain only
Local Policies Audit Policy	Defines the events logged (for example, failed/successful logon attempts, access to specific resources, and so on). *These are the key ACS settings; logged events are forwarded to the ACS collector. Table 15.2 provides the details.*	Local and domain
Event Log	Retention periods and parameters for event logging. *This is not a security policy but is involved in ACS functionality; the Security Event log must not be too small.*	Domain only
Public Key Policies Encrypting File System (EFS)	Allows you to define whether to use the Encrypting File System (EFS) to encrypt files and folders on NTFS partitions.	Local and domain
IP Security Policies	Configures the use of Internet Protocol Security (IPSec) to encrypt data in transit over the network.	Local and domain

Using the Local Security Policy

Any ACS forwarder not a member of a Windows domain must use Local Security Policy to enable auditing. Local Security Policy can be set manually at each computer using the Local Security Policy tool (Start -> Programs -> Administrative Tools -> Local Security Policy). Windows includes some built-in security templates (in particular SecureWS.inf) that you can import manually into the Local Security Policy on multiple computers.

You can import a built-in template using the Local Security Policy tool by right-clicking the Security Settings root and selecting Import Policy. The tool looks in the default location where security templates are stored, which is %*windir*%\Security\Templates.

Using the Domain and Domain Controller Security Policies

Generally, an ACS forwarder belongs to a Windows domain, making administration much simpler because we can concern ourselves only with the security settings in two locations in each domain—the Domain and the Domain Controller Security Policies (assuming you have not created GPOs to override the domain security settings on non-domain controllers). There is a double-edged sword effect however; the ease of configuring domain-based policies brings with it the ability to wreak havoc on the entire domain if there are incorrect policy settings.

Between the Domain and the Domain Controller Security Policy settings, every computer in the domain is equally and immediately impacted when it loads the security policy. If you inadvertently enable overly aggressive auditing, it can literally stop the network from functioning—due to the overhead of performing audit-related functions.

In a domain environment, you have the capability to enable auditing to a certain extent on some computers and in a different manner on others. Whereas all domain controllers will always implement the full Domain Controller Security Policy, non-domain controllers (workstations and member servers) can have one or more custom GPOs applied that override specific settings of the Domain Security Policy. In special circumstances, you can consider deploying custom security settings to subsets of non-domain controller computers; however, we recommend this be done very sparingly, if at all. The reasoning is the same as that behind the best practice of avoiding use of the Enforced and Block Inheritance settings on GPOs. The complexities of GPO inheritance can cause unintended results; in the security arena, standardization, consistency, and simplicity are of paramount importance.

You can choose which computers will be ACS forwarders, and the AdtAdmin.exe application on the ACS Collector Component has the ability to discard certain categories of security events without writing them to the ACS database (we cover how to do this later in the "Using AdtAdmin.exe" section of this chapter). However, every computer in the domain will begin auditing in accordance with the domain security policies regardless of whether that system participates in ACS or not.

15

> **TIP**
>
> **Verifying with the Group Policy Management Console**
>
> The Group Policy Management Console (GPMC) is quite useful to include as a management tool for ACS. Using GMPC, you can quickly edit and verify all GPOs in the organization. Significantly, GMPC includes the Group Policy Modeling Wizard, which lets you sight-verify what GPOs a specific computer is going to apply. This step verifies that the GPOs are correctly configured to enforce your security policies.

Windows Server 2003 Auditing Categories

Now we will closely examine the nine categories of auditing available in the Local Policy -> Audit Policy section of all three types of security polices (local, domain, and domain controller). Table 15.2 lists each category, a description of its effect, the audit settings (success or failure) in a default Windows installation, as well as the settings contained in the SecureDC.inf and SecureWS.inf security templates.

If your organization does not have more specific security needs (or if you just need a validated starting point to decide which auditing categories to enable and with what settings), we recommend importing the following templates:

▶ The SecureDC.inf security template to the Default Domain Controller Policy. Modify the Default Domain Controller Policy to enable success auditing for system events after importing the SecureDC.inf template.

▶ The SecureWS.inf security template to the Default Domain Security Policy.

The selection of category and audit settings shown in Table 15.2 is effective for collecting useful security audit data for most organizations.

TABLE 15.2   Window Server 2003 Audit Policies

Category	Description	Default Setting	"Secure" Templates
Account Logon Events	Audits each instance of a user logging on to or logging off from another computer in which this computer validates the account.	DC: Success Non-DC: None	Success, Failure
Account Management	Account management events including whether a user account or group is created, changed, or deleted; a user account is renamed, disabled, or enabled; and a password is set or changed.	DC: Success Non-DC: None	Success, Failure

TABLE 15.2 Continued

Category	Description	Default Setting	"Secure" Templates
Directory Service Access	Audits the event of a user accessing an Active Directory object that has its own system access control list (SACL) specified.	DC: Success Non-DC: N/A	Failure
Logon Events	Audits each instance of a user logging on to or logging off from a computer.	DC: Success Non-DC: None	Success, Failure
Object Access	Audits the event of a user accessing an object—for example, a file, folder, Registry key, printer, and so forth—that has its own system access control list (SACL) specified.	None	None
Policy Change	Audits every incident of a change to user rights assignment policies, audit policies, or trust policies.	DC: Success Non-DC: None	Success, Failure
Privilege Use	Audits each instance of a user exercising a user right, with the exception of Bypass traverse checking, Debug programs, Create a token object, Replace process level token, Generate security audits, and Back up or restore files and directories.	None	Failure
Process Tracking	Audits detailed tracking information for events such as program activation, process exit, handle duplication, and indirect object access	None	None
System Events	Audits when a user restarts or shuts down the computer or when an event occurs that affects either the system security or the security log, such as clearing the security log.	DC: Success Non-DC: None	None (Should be enabled for DCs)

In addition to deploying the appropriate audit settings through Domain Group Policy or Local Security Policy, we suggest you enforce minimum security log sizes for domain controllers and non-domain controllers. In a domain environment, you can easily configure the Security Settings -> Event Log -> Maximum security log size setting in the Domain and Domain Controller Security Policies. We recommend domain controllers have a maximum security log size of at least 163,840KB (160MB) and non-domain controllers at least 16,384KB. In a workgroup environment, apply these settings manually at each computer (Event Viewer -> Security -> Properties -> Log Size). Figure 15.2 shows the maximum security log size policy setting for domain controllers.

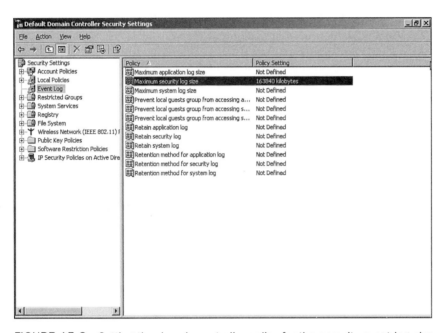

FIGURE 15.2   Setting the domain controller policy for the security event log size.

You may notice that the security auditing mechanisms of Windows are cleanly divided into domain controller and non-domain controller modes of operation. This is because most of the relevant security events you want to audit take place on the domain controller. Domain user accounts receive their authentication token from a domain controller and then use that token to access resources across the domain. Capturing the issue of that token on the domain controller is how any audit trail involving domain security will begin.

NOTE

Determining the Number of Security Events Generated

Joseph Chan has written a script that counts the number of security events generated per second on the local computer. (To run it against a remote computer, supply the computer name as an argument). The script will continue to run until you kill it using Ctrl+C. We suggest you pipe the output to a file. Here's an example:

```
SecurityEventPerSecond.vbs >> NumberOfEventsGeneratedPerSec.csv
```

This command sends the output to a CSV file that you can load with Excel. This utility can be useful when you want to measure the incoming event rate before or without installing an ACS collector.

For your convenience, we include this script, SecurityEventPerSecond.vbs, on the CD accompanying this book.

Planning ACS Component Deployment

Planning an audit policy in itself does not involve considering the ACS components of OpsMgr, because enabling auditing affects all computers in the domain, regardless of their potential status as forwarders. After you make your audit policy decisions and deploy audit policies to your managed computers, you are ready to prepare the ACS components that will forward, collect, and store the auditing events generated at each computer in accordance with the settings in the audit polices. Your deployment planning includes the following decision points for the ACS components:

▶ If you will host any of your ACS databases on clustered SQL Servers

▶ If you will be implementing a security partition between your principal OpsMgr environment and the ACS Database Component

▶ If you will integrate the ACS Reporting Component with the OpsMgr Reporting Component by sharing the same SQL Reporting Server, or if you will install ACS reports to a dedicated SQL Reporting Server

▶ The number of ACS collectors/database pairs to include in your management group(s)

▶ Whether to use SQL 2005 Standard or Enterprise Edition for your ACS database server(s)

15

Clustering ACS Database SQL Servers

The simplest of these decisions might be whether to cluster one or more of your ACS database servers. This is typically based on the following decision points:

▶ Cost of downtime and possible emergency system restore costs

▶ Loss of ability to collect or analyze security events while replacing a failed SQL Server hosting the ACS database

▶ Liability for possible loss of safeguarded auditing data

Because OpsMgr 2007 does not require an Agent Component on the ACS database server, the procedures for ACS database installation and configuration on a single SQL Server or on a multinode SQL cluster are virtually identical.

Creating a Security Boundary

Beyond the SQL cluster/no SQL cluster issue, the preferred configuration for larger environments is separating the Collector and Database Components on different servers. Separating the processing load of these dissimilar components increases the capacity of the Audit Collection Services in the management group and provides security separation between the Collector and Database Components. Because the collector is always a management server, it is subject to administrative control by the OpsMgr administrators.

Figure 15.3 illustrates the OpsMgr components delivering Audit Collection Services in Operations Manager 2007. On the left side, you can see OpsMgr Agent Components on managed clients and servers, with the ACS forwarder enabled. While normal OpsMgr client-server communication occurs with the agents' designated management server(s), ACS data is streamed directly from the forwarder to a collector, bypassing the regular OpsMgr management servers. On the right side of the diagram, you can see the ACS Audit Database Component and a representation of an external storage system (assuming long-term retention of audit data).

Notice in Figure 15.3 the vertical line labeled "Security Partition" separating the ACS database and archive storage system from the rest of the management group. This line represents a logical security boundary between the stored audit data and the audited management group.

It is not necessary, or in some environments even desirable, to install an OpsMgr Agent Component on the ACS database server in the same management group as the audited computers. For security considerations, you may decide to create a dedicated (even an "all in one server") OpsMgr management group that monitors the ACS database computers in your organization. Using a separate management group prevents a careless or criminal user with elevated access to an OpsMgr configuration to run tasks on managed computers that completely compromise organizational security. Separating the ACS database server(s) (and any servers hosting long-term archive data from the organizational group they are data repositories for) can avoid this potential vulnerability.

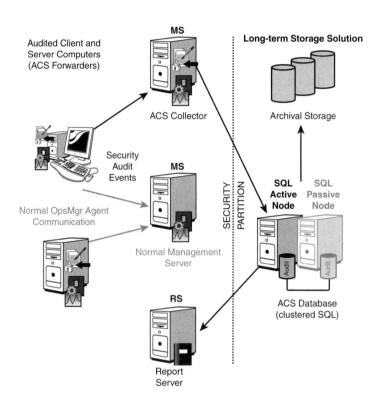

Audited Client and
Server Computers
(ACS Forwarders)

MS

ACS Collector

Long-term Storage Solution

Archival Storage

Security
Audit
Events

MS

Normal OpsMgr Agent
Communication

Normal Management
Server

SECURITY PARTITION

SQL
Active
Node

SQL
Passive
Node

RS

Report
Server

ACS Database
(clustered SQL)

FIGURE 15.3   ACS topology for an organization with separation of audit control.

Integrating ACS with OpsMgr Reporting

If you require a security boundary between network administrators and network auditors, you can achieve the most complete separation when the ACS and OpsMgr Reporting Components are not integrated. This is Microsoft's preferred deployment model and means that the SQL 2005 Reporting Services instance of the OpsMgr management group Reporting Server is not used for the audit reports. In this scenario, the audit reports are never visible in the Operations console.

You would enable this most secure scenario by installing the SQL Reporting Server Component of SQL 2005 on an additional SQL Server on the auditor's (external) side of the security boundary. As part of installation, upload the audit reports to the external reporting server(s) where auditing personnel will have exclusive access to ACS reports. We discuss this further in the "Installing the ACS Reports" section of this chapter.

How Many ACS Collectors Are Required and Their Placement

Another planning decision involves the number of ACS collector/database pairs to include in your OpsMgr deployment. Because each collector must have its own dedicated ACS database, there is always one ACS database (hosted on a standard or clustered SQL Server) for each collector. Whether you need more than one collector and database depends on the capacity of a single, given collector, as well as the bandwidth between the forwarder population(s) and their associated collector(s).

The maximum number of forwarders you can assign to the same collector will vary depending on the types of audit events selected in your audit policies. Assuming high-performance server hardware and sufficient database storage resources for the collectors and databases, here are estimated maximum loads of a single ACS collector/database pair:

▶ 150 domain controllers, or

▶ 3000 member servers, or

▶ 15,000 workstations

Most collectors have a mix of domain controller, member server, and workstation forwarders assigned to them. In that case, you can create weighted values for each type of ACS forwarder to estimate their aggregate load. We provide an example of creating weighted values later in this chapter, in the section "Managing ACS Database Size."

A large number of forwarders cannot effectively share a low-bandwidth connection to a remote collector—for that scenario you might want to deploy several collectors, with each located in proximity to the largest forwarder populations. Figure 15.4 shows a possible ACS deployment with three collector/database pairs. Each collector is in a different physical location, with good network connectivity to its respective connected groups of ACS forwarders.

To estimate the bandwidth a particular forwarder requires to communicate with its collector, multiply the average size of a security audit event compressed for transmission (140 bytes) by the average number of security audit events in the Event log of the forwarder during a given period. For example, a moderately busy domain controller, with the desired security policy enabled, might generate 500,000 events in a 24-hour period. That equates to 70MB of network throughput per day, or about 1KB per second sustained bandwidth consumption.

Figure 15.4 illustrates each collector requiring its own dedicated ACS database and hosting SQL Server. You can implement a combination of clustered or non-clustered ACS SQL database servers, based on the requirements for each collector. This particular topology also features a shared long-term archive solution, although you can also architect dedicated archive solutions for each ACS database.

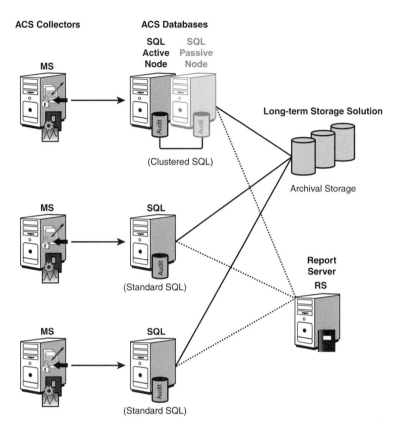

ACS Collectors

ACS Databases

SQL
**Active
Node**

SQL
Passive
Node

MS

Long-term Storage Solution

(Clustered SQL)

Archival Storage

MS   **SQL**

**Report
Server**

(Standard SQL)

RS

MS   **SQL**

(Standard SQL)

FIGURE 15.4   ACS topology with multiple collector-database pairs.

15

Sharing ACS Database Server Hardware

When you install ACS, you can select a named instance of SQL Server 2005 to connect to. To accommodate the one-to-one relationship between collectors and databases, you can use a single SQL Server 2005 box with named instances to create multiple ACS databases, provided it can support the additional load.

SQL 2005 Standard versus Enterprise Edition

A final design decision to make is the version of SQL Server 2005 to use for the ACS database. ACS supports the use of SQL Server 2005 Standard Edition and SQL Server 2005 Enterprise Edition. The version used impacts how the system behaves during the daily 2:00 a.m. database maintenance window while the ACS database is reindexed. During the maintenance window, any database partitions with timestamps outside the data-retention schedule (14 days in the default configuration) are dropped from the database. Keep the following points in mind:

▶ If SQL Server 2005 Standard Edition is used, security event insertion halts and events queue up on the collector until maintenance is completed. This is because SQL 2005 Standard Edition cannot perform online index operations, whereas the Enterprise Edition can.

▶ If SQL Server 2005 Enterprise Edition is used, insertion of processed security events continues during the daily database maintenance, but at only 30%–40% of the regular rate.

SQL 2005 Enterprise Edition is probably mandatory in high-volume environments because it reduces the chance of lost security events from filling the collector queue during the maintenance window.

Installing and Configuring the ACS Database and Collector

In Chapter 6, "Installing Operations Manager 2007," we discuss the prerequisites and basic installation steps for deploying the ACS Database and Collector Components. This chapter picks up at that point. We have installed the ACS database on a separate server from the ACS collector, in the same manner as illustrated earlier in Figure 15.3.

If your organization does not include a separate auditing team—for example, if your OpsMgr deployment is in a smaller organization with a single IT group (or single individual!) and no one outside IT will use ACS—then no additional initial configuration of the ACS database is required. If, however, you are separating audit control from the IT group (typical in larger organizations), you must perform the following critical steps during the initial ACS database setup:

▶ Creating a security group for the ACS auditors

▶ Granting read-only permissions on the ACS database to the ACS auditors' security group

TIP

About the ODBC Data Source

The ACS collector communicates with the SQL Server ACS database using an ODBC data source of the System DSN type, created on the collector during ACS installation. You can view this data source with the ODBC Data Source Administrator, launched from the Data Sources (ODBC) program in the Administrator Tools group on the Windows Start menu.

Select the System DSN tab to see the OpsMgrAC data source. Clicking the Configure button lets you change parameters of the ACS database connection, such as switching from Windows to SQL authentication, or moving the ACS database associated with the collector to another SQL Server.

Optionally Create ACS Auditors Security Group

Installing the ACS components does not create any security groups in the domain or on the ACS collector and database computers. If you need to create an ACS auditors security group, you can create a local or domain security group based on your particular conditions. This security group will contain the user accounts of those individuals who access and run reports on the data in the ACS database.

Base your choice of whether to use a domain or local security group on the following criteria:

▶ "Ownership" of the security group

▶ Ease of monitoring the membership of the group to ensure it continues to contain only the desired members

If your auditing team also owns the ACS database server, using a local group makes it easier for that team to control membership of the ACS auditors' security group, whereas a domain security group is easier for a central IT department to administer. Most likely, if you are not integrating ACS and OpsMgr reports, you will create a local security group on the SQL Reporting Server(s) dedicated to ACS. If you install ACS reports to the same instance of SQL Reporting Server used by the OpsMgr Reporting Component, a domain security group for ACS auditors is appropriate.

In our example, we will create a local security group on the ACS database computer (server name Fireball) and add domain user accounts as members to the group. If your ACS database is on a clustered SQL Server, create same-named local groups with the same memberships on each node of the cluster. We gave the local group on the ACS database server the name *ACS Auditors*. For our example, the ACS Auditors local group on Fireball has several user accounts from the Odyssey domain added as members. Figure 15.5 displays the local security group created on Fireball.

In Figure 15.5, the users who are members of the local ACS Auditors security group, Dennis Cooper and Janet Valenti, represent Odyssey Corp's employees charged with auditing the network. If those individuals are administrators of the ACS database server and the SQL Server application is running on it, they can guarantee unauthorized employees cannot access the ACS database—by verifying their user accounts remain the only members of the security group.

FIGURE 15.5 The ACS Auditors local group on the ACS database server contains domain user accounts as members.

Granting ACS Database Permissions

Now we need to grant our ACS Auditors security group read-only rights to the ACS database. Read-only rights let those users access and run reports on the data in the ACS database without risk of modifying or deleting the collected security audit events. Perform this procedure using the SQL Server Management Studio application on the ACS database server. Open the SQL Server Management Studio and perform the following steps:

1. Navigate to Security -> Logins. Right-click Logins and select New Login to start the New Login Wizard.

2. Next to the Login name field, click the Search button.

3. On the Select Users or Group dialog box, click the Object Types button and add the Groups type of object. Click OK.

4. The From this location field should already contain the name of the ACS database server (the local machine and instance). If it does not, click the Locations button and select the local ACS database computer name. Click OK.

5. Enter the name of your local group (for example, **ACS Auditors**) and click OK. This returns you to the New Login Wizard. You should see the Login name field populated with your local ACS Auditors security group on the ACS database server.

6. In the Default database dropdown list, select the OperationsManagerAC database (assuming you used the default name during the installation) and click OK.

7. Navigate to Databases -> OperationsManagerAC -> Security -> Users. Right-click Users and select New User.

8. In the User name field, type a meaningful name, such as *<Your Organization>* ACS **Auditors**. (We use Odyssey ACS Auditors in our example.)

9. Click the selector button to the right of the Login name field. In the Select Login dialog box, click the Browse button.

10. In the Browse for Objects dialog box, locate the SQL login for the ACS database computer's local ACS Auditors security group you just created. Check the box in the left column next to the local ACS Auditors security group and then click OK twice.

11. Back at the Database User – New dialog box, in the Database role membership area, check the box next to the db_datareader role and click OK.

Figure 15.6 shows the SQL Server Management Studio application after the described steps were used to create the ACS Auditors local group. We are viewing the properties of the Odyssey ACS Auditors database user. Notice the db_datareader role is the only selected role. Members of this role can run a SELECT statement against any table or view in the specified database.

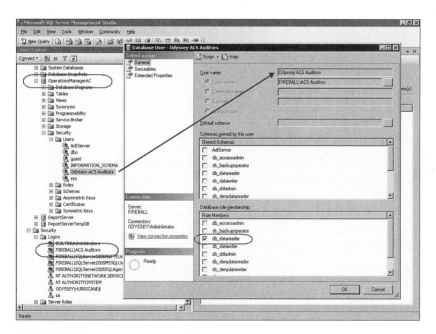

FIGURE 15.6   Granting the ACS Auditors local group read-only rights to the ACS database.

ACS Database Default Install Does Not Allow User Access

Let's examine the peculiar security settings of the OperationsManagerAC database. If you check the SQL user mapping performed during the ACS database installation on the SQL Server that hosts the database, you'll notice that no users are listed in the security node of the OperationsManagerAC database. The effect of not including any user accounts is that normally privileged OpsMgr administrator and service accounts cannot access the ACS database. Only the computer account of the ACS collector has a SQL user mapping. Contrast these permissions with those on the OpsMgr operational database (which include the Management Server Action and SDK accounts) or those on the OpsMgr data warehouse database (which include the SDK and the Data Warehouse Writer and Reader accounts). You can see that the normal security environment in a management group does not extend to the ACS database; in fact, you see the ACS database is isolated from OpsMgr security permissions by design.

The computer account of the ACS Collector Component is the only account with permissions on the ACS database, of which it is the owner and runs using the SQL user account AdtServer. This matches the name of the ACS Collector service executable, which is AdtServer. AdtServer.exe runs on the ACS collector as the Operations Manager Audit Collection service. The AdtServer.exe process receives audit events over the network and writes them to the SQL database OperationsManagerAC using the computer account of the ACS Collector Component.

Installing the ACS Reports

Audit Collection Service Reporting uses SQL 2005 Reporting Services. In the highest security scenario, which is Microsoft's designed environment for using ACS, audit reports run on dedicated SQL 2005 Reporting Server instances that are not part of the OpsMgr 2007 management group. Optionally and alternatively, you can integrate ACS reports with the Reporting Server Component of the OpsMgr 2007 management group. The OpsMgr installation media includes the report models and an installation utility. Follow these steps to upload the ACS reports to your management group:

1. Create a temporary staging folder on a server in the management group (for example, C:\ACS on the collector). Figure 15.7 is a composite screen capture showing the steps in this procedure. See the correct contents of this temporary staging folder on the upper-right side of Figure 15.7.

2. Copy the files and folders in the ReportModels\acs folder on the OpsMgr installation media to the staging folder. Copy the folder structure just as it is on the installation media to the staging folder.

3. Copy the ReportingConfig.exe file from the \SupportTools folder on the OpsMgr installation media to the staging folder.

4. Open a command prompt (click Start -> Run and then type **CMD**) on the server where the staging folder is located and change directory to that folder (C:\ACS).

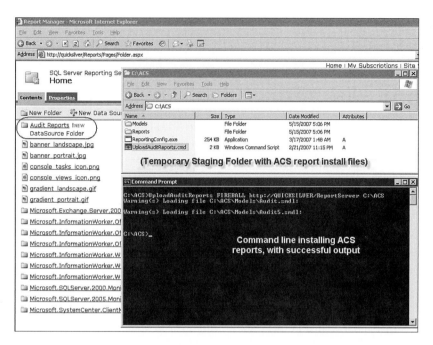

FIGURE 15.7 Staging the ACS Reporting install files, uploading the reports, and confirming a successful install.

5. Run the following from the command prompt:

```
UploadAuditReports <ACSDBServerName>
http://<ReportingServerName>/ReportServer <Drive:\StagingFolder>
```

Here, *<ReportingServerName>* is the name of the OpsMgr management group's Reporting Server only if you are integrating ACS reports with normal OpsMgr reports; otherwise, it is the name of the SQL 2005 Reporting Server instance used exclusively for audit reports.

If the report upload is successful, output from the UploadAuditReports command will have nothing listed after the Warning(s) message. See the command prompt output on the lower-right side of Figure 15.7 for a sample successful command-line output.

6. Confirm successful report loading by opening your browser and entering the web address of your management group's reporting server, such as http://<ReportServerName>/Reports. Note the presence of the Audit Reports folder. On the left side and in the background of Figure 15.7, see Internet Explorer open to the Report Manager on the Quicksilver server, with the new report folder circled.

ACS Reporting Server Integration Scenarios

A fundamental decision is whether you will integrate ACS reports with your OpsMgr Reporting Server or will keep the ACS Reporting components completely separate from the OpsMgr management group. Microsoft designed ACS Reporting primarily to function in the "completely separate" model. Using this model, OpsMgr administrators have no access whatsoever to the collected audit data, report models, or templates uploaded to the SQL Reporting Server used by ACS. Auditing staff have complete ownership of, and exclusive access to, all the resources and data associated with collected security audit events.

This model is designed for larger and more security-conscious organizations. There are two other modes to deploy ACS reports; these other scenarios integrate ACS Reporting components with OpsMgr Reporting components to differing extents. The first alternative model installs the ACS reports to the OpsMgr Reporting Server but retains a separation between auditors and administrators. The second alternative model provides complete integration of ACS reports with OpsMgr reports but eliminates the security boundary. We will walk through these three different scenarios and discuss the procedures to implement them:

▶ **Complete Separation Scenario**—OpsMgr administrators and ACS auditors use different SQL Reporting Servers (ACS as designed).

To implement this scenario, install the audit reports to an instance of SQL Reporting Services separate from the instance used by the OpsMgr Reporting Component. ACS auditors are local administrators or power users of the SQL Server hosting the SQL Reporting Services instance used for collected audit data. Audit reports do not appear in the OpsMgr Operations console, and auditors use the web-based SQL Report Manager exclusively to configure and run audit reports.

▶ **Integration with Security Boundary Scenario**—Use the same SQL Reporting Server for both systems with separation between administrators and auditors, and no audit report access by OpsMgr administrators (supported by Microsoft).

This scenario retains a security boundary and simply leverages the same SQL Reporting Server instance the OpsMgr management group uses, thereby conserving SQL asset deployment. Audit reports appear in the Operations console, but you cannot run them from the console. Instead, you must use the web-based SQL Report Manager.

To implement this scenario, create a domain-based security group for the ACS auditors. Add that domain security group to the Power Users built-in local security group of the OpsMgr Reporting Server (necessary because the auditors require interactive logon rights to access the web-based SQL Reporting Manager). Also, add the domain ACS Auditors security group to the OpsMgr Report Operators user role (in the Operations console, navigate to Administration -> Security -> User Roles -> Operations Manager Report Operators -> Properties -> Add).

Additionally, you must modify the default settings of the SQL data source for the audit reports for this scenario to work. To make this modification, follow these steps:

1. Open the web-based SQL Report Manager in your browser. The address is http://<*ReportServerName*>/Reports.

2. Click the Audit Reports folder to open it.

3. In the Audit Reports folder, click the Show Details button on the upper-right side of the page.

4. Click the Db Audit data source object to open it.

5. Under Connect using, select Credentials supplied by the user running the report and Use as Windows credentials when connecting to the data source. Figure 15.8 shows the Db Audit source modified for this scenario.

▶ **Complete Integration Scenario**—Full integration of audit reports with the Operations console, with no security boundary between administrators and auditors (not supported by Microsoft).

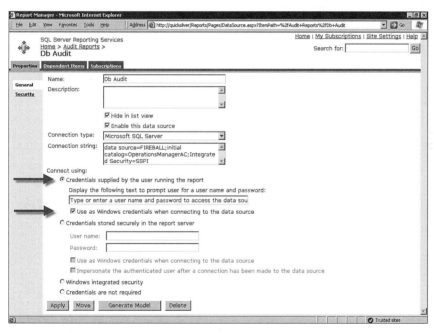

FIGURE 15.8   Modifying the Db Audit data source for integration of ACS and OpsMgr reporting.

This scenario is only appropriate where there is no concern over Operations console users having the ability to run audit reports. In a smaller OpsMgr deployment or an organization without dedicated auditing staff, implementing this scenario lets you run audit reports from the Operations console in almost the same manner as regular OpsMgr reports. Microsoft's design for ACS is that report data will only be accessed using SQL Report Manager and only by members of the ACS Auditors security group. This scenario implements the opposite of that design, namely that report data is accessed in the Operations console by any OpsMgr administrator or user who is a member of the OpsMgr Report Operators User or Administrator role.

In an integrated ACS reporting installation, if you attempt to run an audit report in the same fashion as other reports in the Operations console's Reporting space, you will see the following error message:

```
An error has occurred during report processing.
Cannot create a connection to data source 'datasource1'
```

Reviewing the Application Event log of the Reporting Server, you will see that at that moment, the OpsMgr Data Reader account attempted to make a connection to the ACS database but permission was denied.

Because this scenario is not a supported configuration for ACS, if you choose to implement it, there may be various ways to circumvent default ACS security to make it work as desired. A simple way we discovered was to create the ACS Auditors local security group on the Reporting Server and then add the domain's OpsMgr Data Reader Account to the ACS Auditors local security group. No changes to the default SQL data source are necessary when using this technique.

Running the Enable Audit Collection Task

The stage is now set to begin collecting audit data from the managed computers. The final task in launching your organization's audit collection components is to run the Enable Audit Collection task from the Operations console against the managed computers selected as ACS forwarders. By default, the service needed for an OpsMgr agent to be a forwarder (AdtAgent.exe) is installed but not enabled when the OpsMgr Agent Component is installed. Now that we have installed and configured the ACS collector and database, we must enable and configure the ACS Forwarder Component on those managed computers we identified in our audit policy to be ACS forwarders. Perform the following steps:

1. Open the Operations console and navigate to the Monitoring -> Operations Manager -> Agent -> Agent Health State view.
   This view has two panes in the center area, and the actions in this procedure take place using the pane on the right, Agent State.

2. Select the computers the task will run against. You can make multiple selections by pressing Ctrl or Shift as you click.

3. After selecting the computers in the Agent State pane, click the Enable Audit Collection task in the Health Service Tasks area of the Actions pane in the lower-right section of the console. Figure 15.9 highlights the console features involved in this step.

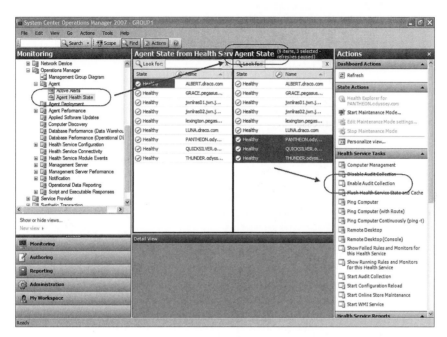

FIGURE 15.9   Selecting managed computers to become ACS forwarders.

4. Selecting the Enable Audit Collection task shown in Figure 15.9 opens a Run Task window. Specify the Fully Qualified Domain Name (FQDN) of the collector to assign to the selected forwarders, using the Override button in the Run Task window. Figure 15.10 shows the Enable Audit Collection task after specifying the FQDN of hurricane.odyssey.com as the collector.

   If you have planned for only one collector in your OpsMgr management group, you will always enter the same FQDN in this task. However, if there is more than one ACS collector in your organization, take care to specify the correct FQDN for the appropriate collector. You would also need to run the Enable Audit Collection task again to target other forwarders to other collectors, because you can only specify the FQDN for one collector with each run of the task.

5. Click the Run button at the bottom of Figure 15.10 and optionally observe the progress of the task in the status window. When the task completes on a managed computer, the Operations Manager Audit Forwarding service on that forwarder changes from disabled startup type to automatic startup type, and then the service starts. Event 4368 from source AdtAgent will appear in the Application Event log of that system confirming that the forwarder connected to the collector. At the same

time, event 4628 from source AdtServer will appear in the Application Event log of the collector. Figure 15.11 shows these two connection events from the perspectives of the Forwarder and Collector components.

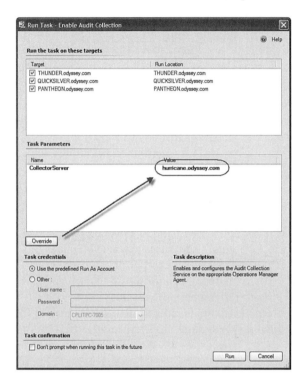

FIGURE 15.10   Using the Override button to specify the FQDN of the appropriate ACS Collector.

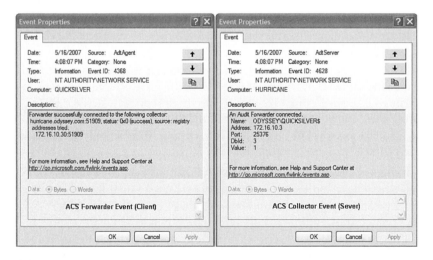

FIGURE 15.11   Application log connection events from the forwarder (left) and collector (right).

Enabling ACS in Bulk with PowerShell

During the beta-testing phase for Operations Manager 2007, Joseph Chan of Microsoft provided a PowerShell script that enables ACS on all agents to the provided ACS collector. Neal Browne from SystemCenterForum has modified the script to take the display name of the group as an added parameter, so you can control which agents are enabled.

Table 15.3 lists the parameters used by the scripts.

TABLE 15.3   PowerShell Script Parameters

Parameter	Usage
rmsServerName	FQDN of the RMS.
collectorServerName	FQDN of the ACS collector.
displayName	Display name of the group (for example, "Sample group"). Used with the ACSBulkEnableGroupDisplayName.ps1 script only.

For your convenience, we include these two scripts—ACSBulkEnableAllAgents.ps1 and ACSBulkEnableGroupDisplayName.ps1—on the CD accompanying this book. You can also view http://goteamshake.com/?p=34 for information on these scripts.

> **NOTE**
>
> **On the CD**
>
> The two scripts to enable ACS in bulk using PowerShell, ACSBulkEnableAllAgents.ps1 and ACSBulkEnableGroupDisplayName.ps1, can be found on the CD accompanying this book.

Implementing Your Audit Policy

Now that you have deployed, configured, and enabled ACS, your organization enters the long-term operating phase of the auditing solution. Your primary technical goal is to set in motion a perpetual process that keeps the ACS components secure and functioning as desired by the auditing stakeholders. You achieve your business goal when appropriate auditing reports are reviewed in a timely and recurring fashion by cognizant internal network security staff or external auditing personnel.

Here are some questions to answer regarding processes you must implement to sustain a production ACS deployment:

▶ **Who are the consumers of the security audit reports?**

If the primary constituents of the ACS solution are external auditors not part of the normal IT team, those individuals must be positively identified by the senior leadership of the organization. If the members of IT staff are not to concern themselves with the collected audit data, make sure they are informed so they do not raise suspicion by running ACS reports! If no one is looking at the ACS reports on a scheduled basis (that is, if you deployed ACS only for use in possible future forensic investigations), someone must still periodically run some audit reports to verify the integrity and operation of the auditing solution.

▶ **How will authorized viewers of security audit reports physically access the reporting data?**

If you extend access to ACS reports within the Operations console (by modifying the default security of an ACS installation), you can also provide console access to the ACS auditors. In that situation, you may want to create a user role for the auditors (under Administration -> Security -> User Roles) that has tailored and minimized access to console views and tasks. Microsoft designed ACS such that security audit reports are not viewable in the Operations console; in the default configuration of ACS, you must use the web-based SQL Report Manager to generate reports of audit data.

It may be incumbent on the IT staff to support and train the auditors in use of SQL Report Manager, even though the IT staff is subject to audit scrutiny. Another excellent alternative, if acceptable to the auditing team, is to export audit reports on an automatic scheduled basis to files posted or otherwise delivered to the auditors for their review and offline retention.

▶ **Must auditing data be preserved in archives beyond the ACS database retention period?**

Security audit data is automatically and permanently purged from the database after the specified retention period. To preserve data, you must create a mechanism or procedure to export data from the ACS database for longer-term retention. Because the security audit data exists in a regular SQL Server 2005 database, you can employ any standard method for SQL backup, export, log shipping, or external subscription of database data to create archival copies of records in the database. For some organizations, it is acceptable to permit grooming the ACS database records without archiving because exported audit report files provided to auditors remain available until deleted by the auditors themselves.

Chapter 12, "Backup and Recovery," discusses a methodology for archiving data from the OpsMgr data warehouse so the report data is available after the retention period. You can apply a similar technique to the ACS database. See Chapter 12 for additional information.

▶ **Is the ACS deployment in your organization secured to prevent circumvention?**

Put yourself in the shoes of the malicious user who wants to do something wrong without being caught. That user might have intimate knowledge of the ACS topology in your organization. A rogue administrator would likely focus on disabling the ACS forwarder process on the computer where the illegal activity is contemplated and then wipe the local security log of the computer after the deed was done. Knowing a determined individual with broad administrative access, time, and opportunity can probably defeat almost any security initiative, it is at least prudent to perform some due-diligence "what ifs." Implement as many reasonable countermeasures as you can envision.

A simple but critical proactive measure is to eliminate common or shared use of the BUILTIN\Administrator account. To audit individual administrator activity, each administrator must be required to use his own unique, named logins exclusively.

▶ **Have you provided for system-level management of the ACS database components?**

Because the ACS database server(s) in your organization may not participate in your primary OpsMgr management group, you need to make sure that "care and feeding" of the SQL Server(s) is taking place. This includes antivirus, backup, updates, and server hardware health monitoring. An individual with SQL Server experience should also be responsible for periodically inspecting the ACS database server(s) to confirm there are no emerging issues with performance or database size.

▶ **Is the default 14-day ACS data retention period sufficient for your organization?**

Once a day (by default 7 hours after midnight Greenwich Mean Time [GMT]), grooming removes ACS database records of security audit events if they are older than the retention period. If the 14-day window is satisfactory for your organization, and if your ACS database hardware has sufficient storage resources, you need not modify the default retention period.

However, you may not have enough storage for 14 days of data and you need to lower the number of days data is retained; alternatively, you may have plenty of storage and need to increase the number of days to satisfy your auditing goals. In these cases, you can modify the retention period by changing the number of partitions variable (ID 6) in the dtConfig table of the ACS database. Figure 15.12 is a view of the SQL Server Management Studio, open to the OperationsManagerAC database and showing the contents of the dtConfig table. Edit the value "n" such that "n×1" is equal to the number of days you desire to retain audit data in the ACS database.

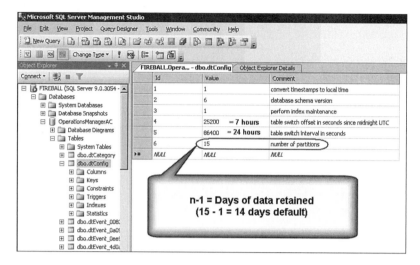

FIGURE 15.12   Configuration table in the ACS database, where the retention period is set.

Administering ACS

How you perform ongoing administration of ACS depends a great deal on whether you have implemented a security boundary between the primary management group and the ACS Database Component. It is not possible to operate an ACS deployment that is both convenient for OpsMgr administrators to access auditing data and strictly accountable to external auditing entities for integrity of the auditing solution.

ACS was designed primarily with the latter of these deployment models in mind, which makes the assumption that network administrative staff is not to be fully trusted. In this paradigm, administrators of systems are always assumed to be able to thwart security if that is their intention. The best auditing solution, therefore, is one that captures security events of interest in real time and speeds that information away from the sphere of influence of the administrator. Once the security audit events are safely stored in a location or manner that is inaccessible to your system administrators, that database of events retains its integrity as a record of the administrators' activities.

We can approach methods of accessing ACS information from two perspectives:

▶ An OpsMgr management group that opened up the ACS database permissions to allow access by users of the Operations console

▶ An external auditor who has no access to the Operations console and interacts with security audit data exclusively through the web-based SQL Report Manager

Common to both approaches is that using ACS requires running reports against the ACS database. Reporting is the only mechanism to examine the collected ACS security audit data; there is no other user interface.

Using the Operations Console to Access ACS Report Data

Importing the ACS reports into the management group using one of the integrated reporting scenarios creates a new folder in the Reporting space named Audit Reports. Inside the Audit Reports folder are 18 predefined reports and two report templates, included on the Operations Manager installation media. The audit report names are prefixed to sort alphabetically into six categories. The categories suggest scenarios in which specific predefined reports might be useful or applicable:

- ▶ Access Violation (unsuccessful login attempts)

- ▶ Account Management (password, group membership changes, user account created and deleted)

- ▶ Forensic (events for specific computers or users)

- ▶ Planning (event counts, hourly event distribution)

- ▶ System Integrity (audit failure and audit log cleared)

- ▶ Usage (object access, user logon, sensitive security group changes)

The two security audit report templates are cryptically named Audit and Audit5. The Audit template contains fields for up to 22 security audit event strings, basically 22 lines or elements of text that might appear in the Description area of a security audit event examined with the Windows Event Viewer. The Audit5 template provides for only the first five text elements (strings or lines of text) from the security audit event Description area. Use these criteria when selecting a template for the basis of a new custom report:

- ▶ Generally select the Audit5_Report_Template, because the great majority (over 90%) of possible security audit events has five or fewer description strings anyway, and reports based on the Audit5 template will index a little faster than those based in the Audit template.

- ▶ Select the Audit_Report_Template when you know that the type of security event you are creating the custom report for will contain more than five description strings.

There are several differences in the behavior of the audit reports compared to the other predefined reports available in the OpsMgr Reporting space (remember that the data for security audit reports is coming from the ACS database rather than the Data Warehouse database like the other historical data viewed in the Reporting space):

- ▶ An immediate visual difference is that audit reports open in a running state, with fully predefined report parameters.

  The date range and object selection are preset, the report parameters pane is not displayed, and the report window opens with the "Report is being generated" message appearing as soon as you click the Open button in the Action pane of the Reporting space. Other OpsMgr reports begin with a static windows waiting for the operator to input the desired data range and add groups or objects in the parameters pane of the report window.

▶ After generating the report, you can optionally view the report's parameters pane (View -> Parameters in the report window).

This is a mini-parameters pane compared to the parameters pane in the regular OpsMgr reports, with only the date range available to modify. There is no object or group selection area, although some audit reports (such as Event Counts by Computer) also include a parameter for a computer name. The default date range is from midnight the calendar day before the current time to midnight the day after. Depending on the time of day you run the report, the default view will include from 24 to 48 hours of data backward from the current time.

Figure 15.13 is a screenshot of the Reporting pane in the OpsMgr Operations console, listing the audit reports and templates imported from the OpsMgr 2007 installation media.

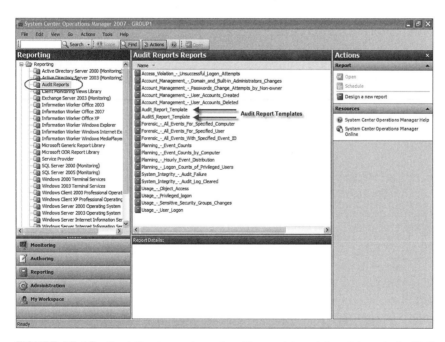

FIGURE 15.13   Predefined reports and audit report templates, integrated with the Operations console.

Like all OpsMgr reports, one can schedule audit reports for publication to file shares for offline viewing, rather than viewing them live in the Operations console or with the web-based SQL Report Manager. Audit reports lend themselves in particular to scheduled and published report generation in these scenarios:

▶ Providing an offline record of selected audit events before grooming them from the ACS database, mitigating the purging of data due to the enforcement of the ACS retention interval

▶ Furnishing to auditing staff for a permanent record of the state of select collected data, in lieu of auditors running the reports live themselves either from the Operations console or the SQL Report Manager

When scheduling publication of most security audit reports (also called *creating a subscription* in SQL Report Manager), you only need to specify the date range of the selected report. For those reports that also require the computer name parameter, there is a prompt for this when you schedule the report. Figure 5.14 shows the Report Parameters page while scheduling the Event Counts by Computer audit report. The scheduled report in this example will run against audit events from the computer Thunder (our Operational database server).

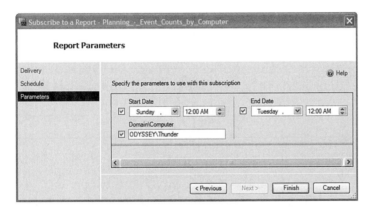

FIGURE 15.14   Scheduling an audit report to be generated and published for offline viewing.

Using SQL Report Manager with ACS

Microsoft intended that ACS reporting use the SQL Report Manager to view ACS security audit data. Unless you implement the completely integrated ACS reporting scenario, the SQL Report Manager is used exclusively for live interaction with security event data collected in the ACS database.

Even if you implement the completely integrated ACS reporting scenario and use the Operations console to run audit reports routinely, there are still several ACS-related functions that can only be performed using SQL Report Manager. For example, deleting either a predefined or a custom audit report from the Reporting Server is accomplished only through Report Manager (select Audit Reports -> Show Details and then select the report to delete and click Delete).

You can drill down into the properties of any predefined or custom audit report using SQL Report Manager. In the properties of each report, you can view and modify details such as the report's default parameters or security. After you have scheduled an audit report for automatic publishing to a file share, you can modify the settings of that subscription by returning to SQL Report Manager. Figure 15.15 shows the Subscriptions tab of the Unsuccessful Logon Attempts audit report. Selecting Edit here would allow you to modify the schedule, published file share location, and security credentials for generation of the report.

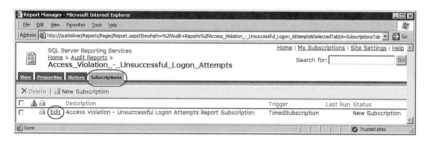

FIGURE 15.15   Modifying the properties of a previously scheduled audit report.

All new and custom ACS reports are created using SQL Report Builder, a component of the SQL Reporting Service. The first time you open an audit report for editing or start a custom report authoring session, the system downloads a 6.5MB Report Builder runtime module from the SQL Reporting Server to your computer. We will be taking a closer look at the Report Builder when we create a custom report in the "Policy Changes Scenario" section later in this chapter.

Using AdtAdmin.exe

The primary tool for administering ACS is a command-line tool, AdtAdmin.exe. This tool runs locally on the collector at the server console or in a Remote Desktop session. There are four categories of functions for using AdtAdmin.exe:

▶ To change the authentication method or credentials the ACS collector uses to access the ACS database.

▶ To use as a statistical and configuration tool for connected ACS forwarders.

▶ To create ACS forwarder groups and assign ACS forwarders to ACS forwarder groups.

  ACS forwarder groups are for convenience when updating or disconnecting large numbers of forwarders at one time.

▶ To create Windows Management Instrumentation-based queries that limit the events stored in the ACS database.

We grouped the 12 AdtAdmin.exe commands into these categories in Table 15.4.

TABLE 15.4   AdtAdmin.exe Command Syntax

Category	AdtAdmin.exe Switches	Usage
Authentication Method and Credentials	`/GetDBAuth` `/SetDBAuth`	Displays and sets the authentication method used by the ACS collector to access the ACS database. The two available authentication methods are Windows Authentication and SQL authentication.
ACS Forwarder Statistical and Configuration Tool	`/Stats`	Lists statistical information about ACS forwarders connected to the ACS collector. See Table 15.5 for a list of statistics displayed.
	`/ListForwarders`	Lists the forwarders that have ever connected to the collector, along with some statistics on each. The data that displays is a subset of the data that displays using the `/Stats` switch.
	`/UpdForwarder`	Changes the name and the priority value of an ACS forwarder. Also changes the group membership of a forwarder.
	`/Disconnect`	Disconnects a specified forwarder or group of forwarders from the collector.
Create and Manage ACS Groups	`/AddGroup` `/DelGroup`	Creates and deletes groups used to organize forwarders.
	`/UpdGroup`	Renames an existing group.
	`/ListGroups`	Outputs a comma-separated list of groups maintained by the collector.
WMI Queries to Limit Events Stored to ACS Database	`/GetQuery` `/SetQuery`	Lists and sets the Windows Management Instrumentation (WMI) Query Language (WQL) queries used as filters on the ACS collector.

Creating and using forwarder groups is an advanced task, only useful in very large and distributed environments where there are multiple collectors with weighted priority values or you wish to operate against large numbers of forwarders at once. Many environments use AdtAdmin.exe primarily to confirm lists of ACS forwarder populations, confirm forwarder-to-collector assignments, and manage WMI queries that filter out some events before writing to the ACS database. We exercise these common AdtAdmin.exe tasks at the command line, as shown in Figure 15.16.

FIGURE 15.16 Performing an ACS Forwarder census and setting a WMI query filter.

Four command-line runs of the AdtAdmin.exe utility are shown in Figure 15.16. Here is an explanation of what is happening on each line:

1. `AdtAdmin.exe /listforwarders`

   We see the names of the computers in the management group that are forwarders reporting to this collector. (The command AdtAdmin.exe /stats would list even more details about the state of each forwarder.) This is useful to confirm that the list of ACS forwarders we expect to be reporting to the ACS collector matches the forwarders actually reporting to the collector.

2. `AdtAdmin.exe /getquery`

   This query shows that the default WMI query is still effective. The default query state is `"select * from AdtsEvent"` without any modifiers (filters). The default state writes all received security events to the database without filtering out any of them.

3. `AdtAdmin /setquery /query:"SELECT * FROM AdtsEvent WHERE NOT (HeaderUser='SYSTEM' OR HeaderUser='LOCAL SERVICE' OR HeaderUser='NETWORK SERVICE')"`

   This particular query creates and enables a WMI query-based filter that will discard security events when the user account in the security event is the local computer account of the ACS forwarder. This is useful in a setting where you are interested in tracking only the activity of actual user accounts.

   Applying one or more WMI queries as filters is a way to reduce the size of the ACS database, possibly allowing you to retain more days of meaningful audit data in the ACS database and certainly reducing the overhead of the system because there are fewer events to write to the database. WMI query-based filters apply globally to the ACS collector; any targeting of queries to specific forwarders takes place in the context of the query.

4. `AdtAdmin.exe /getquery`

We run this command again (the same as command line 2) to confirm the WMI query that we created in command line 3 is now effective. Compared to the output of command line 2, command line 4 output includes the `WHERE NOT` condition after the default `"select * from AdtsEvent"`. This indicates that if one of those conditions is true (in this case, if the user account is the local computer [machine] account), that condition is filtered from the event stream and not written to the ACS database.

We also wanted to include a list of the statistics returned with the command `AdtAdmin.exe /stats`. The output of this command can be redirected to a file (`AdtAdmin.exe /stats > <filename>.csv`) and the file opened in Excel as a Comma-Separated Value (CSV) text file. Viewed as a spreadsheet, there are 17 columns of data, with a row for each forwarder including a header row. Table 15.5 is a list of the contents of the header row, numbered from left to right as they appear in the spreadsheet.

TABLE 15.5   AdtAdmin.exe /stats Output Column Headers

Number	Header
1.	Value (Priority)
2.	SID
3.	Name (Domain\Computer)
4.	GroupID (ACS Group)
5.	Version
6.	Connected (State)
7.	Total Transmitted Events
8.	Total Size of Transmitted Events
9.	Recv Packet Count
10.	Recv Packet Size
11.	Seconds Since Connection
12.	Average Event Rate
13.	Current Event Rate
14.	Average time to collector (in ms)
15.	Connect Time
16.	Last Action (Time)
17.	Disconnect Time

Managing ACS Collector Performance

From time to time, performance issues regarding the ACS collector may arise. These issues will manifest themselves in a lack of timeliness in writing security audit events to the ACS database or ceasing to collect events from forwarders. In an ideal ACS world, an unlimited number of forwarders could connect to a single ACS collector, and that collector would have limitless memory and network resources. In actuality, the capacity of a given collector is finite, and it is incumbent on the administrator of the ACS collector (the OpsMgr Administrator) to keep an eye on collector performance. Three Registry keys can be tuned to help performance. These keys work in conjunction with each other:

▶ `BackOffThreshold`

▶ `MaximumQueueLength`

▶ `DisconnectThreshold`

The first indication that a particular collector is nearing or exceeding its capacity limit is typically noticed when the ACS collector queue reaches the `BackOffThreshold` value. This is one of three parameters that control the behavior of the collector when it cannot write events to the database quickly enough. Memory on the collector is used for caching ACS events that need to be written to the ACS database. The `BackOffThreshold` value is a percent specifying how full the memory-based collector queue can become before the collector denies new connections from its forwarders. The default size of the collector queue is 262,144 events. With each event consuming an average 512 bytes, this means the collector queue occupies about 134MB of memory. Figure 15.17 shows the Registry Editor on the ACS collector open to the key where the threshold and queue levels are set (HKLM\System\CurrentControlSet\Services\AdtServer\Parameters).

As exposed in the Registry of the collector in Figure 15.17, we see the `BackOffThreshold` is set to 75% of the `MaximumQueueLength` value. An additional performance-sensitive Registry key is highlighted in the figure, which is the `DisconnectThreshold`, also stated as a percent and by default set to 90% of the `MaximumQueueLength`. The settings of these three parameters work together to manage event insertion to the ACS database during capacity overload periods. When ACS is operating normally, the queue length should rarely reach the `BackOffThreshold` value, and it should never exceed the `DisconnectThreshold` (except during periods when the ACS database server is known to be unavailable, such as when the server is restarted after operating system updates have been loaded).

When the capacity of a given collector is completely exhausted, the sequence of events illustrated in Figure 15.18 will occur. Following the events clockwise in the figure, we describe what is happening at each step:

1. (Upper-left corner of Figure 15.18, AdtServer Event ID 4615.) The ACS Collector queue status is reported at 100%, which is above the 90% `DisconnectThreshold`. All new ACS forwarder connections will be denied and some current connections will be disconnected.

2. (Upper-right corner, Event ID 4630.) A particular forwarder (the computer Pantheon, in this case) is disconnected due to the `DisconnectThreshold` being exceeded. The ACS collector will methodically disconnect ACS forwarders one by one until the queue is lower than the `DisconnectThreshold`. A separate Event ID 4630 will occur for each disconnected forwarder.

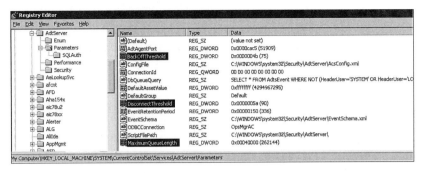

FIGURE 15.17   Performance-sensitive queue and threshold settings on the ACS Collector.

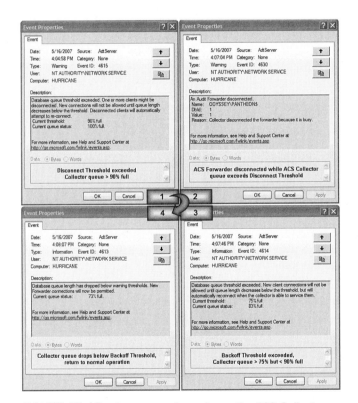

FIGURE 15.18   Sequence of events as the ACS Collector responds to overload.

3. (Lower-right corner, Event ID 4614.) The ACS Collector queue (now at 83%) has drawn down to below the DisconnectThreshold (90%), but is still above the BackOffThreshold (75%). In this mode, new ACS forwarder connections continue to be denied, but the ACS collector stops actively disconnecting forwarders.

4. (Lower-left corner, Event ID 4613.) The ACS Collector queue, at 73%, has now dropped below the `BackOffThreshold` and resumed normal operation. ACS forwarders that were disconnected or denied connections will automatically and rapidly reconnect.

If you observe this sequence of events occurring frequently on a collector, that collector's capacity has been exceeded and you need to modify the ACS environment to provide a credible and reliable audit collection service. To resolve collector performance issues, you can either reduce the volume of events written to the ACS database or add hardware to the ACS infrastructure.

To reduce the quantity of events, you can take one of the following approaches:

▶ Modifying your security policies to collect fewer events

▶ Applying WMI-based queries using AdtAdmin.exe on the collector to filter out unnecessary events

▶ Reducing the population of forwarders

Hardware solutions to capacity issues include the following:

▶ Adding one or more collectors to the management group to split the forwarder loads

▶ Adding memory or otherwise upgrading the collector

▶ Upgrading the SQL Server hosting the ACS database to provide faster disk writes

---

TIP

Detailed Logging on ACS Forwarders

If you are experiencing a performance issue with a particular forwarder, you might find it useful to temporarily enable detailed logging on the forwarder. To do so, create a new DWORD value named `TraceFlags` with a decimal value of `524420` in the Registry of the ACS forwarder at this location:

`HKLM\SYSTEM\CurrentControlSet\Services\AdtAgent\Parameters`

After you create the Registry key, restart the Operations Manager Audit Forwarding service (AdtAgent.exe) on the forwarder. A detailed log will be created at %*systemroot*%\Temp\AdtAgent.log.

A precursor condition, and one that may indicate collector performance issues, is increasing event latency—that is, an increase in the average time between event generation and collection. This is a measure of how quickly security audit events are captured to the ACS database after the events actually occur on the forwarder. A latency of between 1 and 2 seconds indicates a healthy forwarder-collector-database relationship. Although this latency may grow slightly as large numbers of forwarders are connected to a collector, if you keep an eye on this indicator, you will know when performance is beginning to degrade (hopefully in time to take corrective action before queue threshold events start to occur).

The Windows Performance Monitor is a great tool for observing ACS system health in real time. When you install the ACS Collector Component on an OpsMgr management server, two Performance Monitor objects are added: ACS Collector and ACS Collector Client. The ACS Collector object exposes 16 counters related to the functions of the ACS Collector server itself. The ACS Collector Client object adds just three counters—one of these is the average time between event generation and collection, a latency counter useful for assessing the health of a collector. Figure 15.19 shows the Performance Monitor running against the ACS collector.

In the Windows Performance Monitor chart view shown in Figure 15.19, we have loaded several ACS Collector counters related to the collector itself (the bottom two rows in the chart legend). Notice the Database Queue % Full counter, which can help you keep tabs on that important measure of the ACS Collector queue before it exceeds any thresholds.

We also loaded a pair of ACS Collector Client counters: the Average time between event generation and collection in milliseconds counter and the Incoming Audits/sec counter. An instance of each counter is running against three individual forwarders (computers Pantheon, Quicksilver, and Thunder). This information is also available in a snapshot format by running AdtAdmin.exe /stats, but it can be more convenient and useful to watch a live representation of the data in the Performance Monitor.

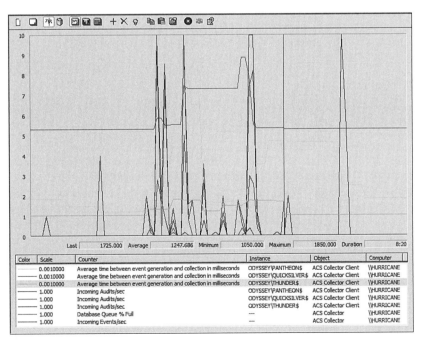

FIGURE 15.19   Windows Performance Monitor with some relevant ACS counters loaded.

Managing ACS Database Size

You must closely manage the ACS database size on the storage system of the SQL Server hosting it. Actively tracking database growth can avoid a possible database shutdown or system crash, which will occur if the database consumes all disk space. Once forwarders begin to send security events to the collector, the ACS database will grow in size.

Assuming a constant number of forwarders connect to the collector and you are collecting a uniform daily quantity of security events, the database will grow at a constant rate until it reaches the ACS database retention period, which is 14 days by default. If nothing changes after that, beginning at the 15th day, the ACS database would remain at about the same size indefinitely.

In the real world, of course, conditions are often constantly changing. It is difficult to precisely manage the size of the ACS database, due to the large number of variables that can rapidly affect the quantity and type of events collected by ACS. You can, however, make some informed estimates of how much disk space your ACS database is going to need—based on the number and composition of forwarders that are planned to connect to a particular collector.

From reviewing the ACS database, we determined that immediately after a fresh installation of OpsMgr 2007 ACS components, the database size on disk was 132MB, with the used portion of the total database size being 8MB. Microsoft has also published the capacity of a single collector based on weighted values that correspond to the volume of security audit events expected by different types of ACS forwarders. These maximum capacities are:

▶ 150 domain controllers, or

▶ 3000 member servers, or

▶ 15,000 workstations

This means we can assign a cost to each of these types of forwarders and interpolate mixes of the types of forwarders. We can assign workstations a value of 1 (15,000/15,000), member servers a value of 5 (15,000/3000), and domain controllers a value of 100 (15,000/150). We will use these weighted values in calculations that include all three types of forwarders.

Another key piece of data needed to create an ACS database size approximation is the average size (in MB) that a single forwarder contributes each day to database growth. We selected a base estimate of 8MB per day per workstation for this value, based on the data Microsoft published about its own experiences using ACS. We also have validated that member servers generate at least triple the quantity of events as workstations, and that domain controllers generate at least 100 times as many security events as workstations, so these weighted values appear reasonably accurate.

> **NOTE**
>
> **ACS Database Daily Growth**
>
> Although Microsoft's daily growth rate is approximately 8MB per day per workstation, you may consider this to be "heavy" usage (for example, growth in an environment with heavy logging). Your experience may vary based on daily activity.
>
> We have determined that an environment with light usage will likely see 2MB per day, and with an average load, 4MB. The formula and graphic in this chapter show the upper-bound sizing of 8MB per day, because it is best to scale for worst-case unless you know how large the volume of data will be. If you know you will have significantly less activity, you can adjust the formula accordingly.

From this exercise, we developed the following formula to estimate the size of the ACS database:

```
(8 MB/day x (Number of Workstations) x Retention Days) +
(8 MB/day x (Number of Servers * 5) x Retention Days) +
(8 MB/day x (Number of Domain Controllers * 100) x Retention Days) +
8 MB (original base DB size) = ACS Database Size
```

Figure 15.20 displays a chart representing possible ACS database growth for given mixes of ACS forwarder types. At the top of the scale in our estimate, for a large environment with 3000 workstations, 600 servers, and 14 domain controllers, we can project an ACS database of about 840GB with a 14-day retention period. A large-scale real-world statistic comes from Microsoft's own early use of ACS. Microsoft monitored the security of 5000 servers and 10,000 workstations, with a 30-day retention period, and it had about an 8TB (8000GB) ACS database. (We understand that Microsoft has since trimmed its retention period to 12 days.)

If you experience ACS database growth that is beyond what the SQL Server hosting your database can support, you can take one of several approaches:

▶ Increase the storage available for the database

▶ Reduce the amount of data going into the database

▶ Modify the number of days of data you are retaining

You can reduce the amount of data written to the database in the same manner as if you were experiencing overloading of a collector, namely collecting fewer events by changing audit policies or discarding unneeded events with WMI query filters. Reducing the number of days in the retention period is the primary way to quickly cut the size of the ACS database.

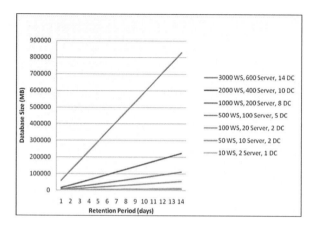

FIGURE 15.20   Estimated ACS database growth given different mixes of ACS Forwarder types.

Implementing Agent Failover Support

Earlier in the "Planning ACS Component Deployment" section of this chapter, we discussed the ability to cluster the SQL database server that hosts the ACS database. Doing so can provide uninterrupted audit collection services while one of the SQL cluster nodes is unavailable. However, the secondary management server that has the ACS Collector Component cannot be clustered, leaving a single point of failure in the audit collection architecture. If the collector is down temporarily, such as during a restart following the routine installation of updates, the forwarders remain in a disconnected state and audit collection is paused. If the ACS Collector component fails completely, such as a drive array crash, the organization stops collecting audit data while a new ACS Collector Component is installed and the ACS architecture realigned.

To avoid these situations involving downtime of the ACS Collector Component, install multiple ACS collector/database pairs in your organization and configure your ACS forwarders for failover operation. Figure 15.21 illustrates an organization that has deployed two ACS collector/database pairs and has enabled failover operation of its ACS forwarders.

The procedure to activate an ACS forwarder and assign that forwarder to a particular collector, covered previously in this chapter in the "Running the Enable Audit Collection Task" section, is not used when enabling failover operation. The forwarder locates collectors by checking the Registry on the local agent computer. A list of ACS collectors is maintained at this Registry key on each forwarder:

HKLM\SOFTWARE\Policies\Microsoft\AdtAgent\Parameters\AdtServers

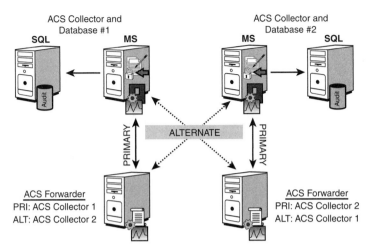

FIGURE 15.21   Achieving highly available ACS Collector Components with agent failover.

When the forwarder starts up, and when it is attempting to reconnect to a collector after being disconnected, it looks up the list of collector names at that Registry key and connects to the first one it can establish a connection with. The value at that key is of the REG_MULTI_SZ type, meaning that multiple string elements can exist, each on a different line of the value. When you invoke the Enable Audit Collection task in the Operations console, you can only enter a single collector name (a single string value), and the task running on the forwarder will overwrite whatever was at that Registry key with the single string value.

To implement ACS agent failover support in your organization, you must deploy one or more additional ACS collector/database pairs. You still run the Enable Audit Collection Task in the Operations console to enable an ACS forwarder initially—specify the name of that forwarder's assigned primary collector when you run the task. Then you return to each ACS forwarder and edit the Registry key, adding the alternate forwarder names on the second and subsequent lines of the REG_MULTI_SZ value.

The VBScript command shell.regwrite, often used to automate Registry changes, does not handle multistring values, so you will have to make the change manually on computers that are to participate in the ACS agent failover scheme. The AdtServer Registry key, configured on a given forwarder as desired for a particular set of primary and alternate collectors, could be exported to a .REG file using the Regedit utility, and that .REG file merged into forwarder registries.

Once the AdtServer Registry key is configured with multiple collector names for agent failover support, be careful not to run the Enable Audit Collection Task in the Operations console again, because doing so overwrites the multiple collector names with the one name specified when running the task!

To force failover of forwarders to their alternate ACS collector(s), you can stop the Operations Manager Audit Collection service (AdtServer.exe) on the primary collector.

Once a forwarder connects to an alternate collector, it will remain connected until disconnected for any reason (such as running `AdtAdmin.exe /disconnect` on the alternate
collector). After each disconnection event, the forwarder again processes the list of collectors found at the Registry key. If the primary collector is available, the forwarder will
connect to it and resume normal communication.

Implementing Agent Support with Certificates

There may be situations where you want to audit computers that are not in the domain of
the management group, or are not in domain(s) that trust the management group
domain. Specifically, you may have computers in workgroups and in untrusted domains
that need to participate in ACS.

To provide security auditing services to a computer that does not trust the collector, first
enable certificate-based mutual authentication of the OpsMgr Agent Component as
discussed in Chapter 11, "Securing Operations Manager 2007." Then follow these steps to
enable ACS:

1. One time only, on the ACS collector, stop the AdtServer service and run
   `AdtServer.exe -c` at the command prompt. Select to import the certificate already
   issued and in use for the OpsMgr Gateway Component communication. Restart the
   AdtServer service.

2. For each certificate-based ACS forwarder, use the Certificates MMC (Microsoft
   Management Console) to export the agent communication certificate in .CER file
   format (also known as an X.509 certificate).

3. Using the Active Domain (AD) Users and Computers MMC in the OpsMgr AD
   domain, create computer accounts with names that match the certificate-based
   forwarder computer names.

4. From the Name Mapping tab on the computer account object in AD Users and
   Computers, import the X.509 certificate exported in step 2 to the computer account
   created in step 3.

5. Run the Enable Audit Collection task against the agent in the Operations console.

6. On the forwarder, stop the AdtAgent service and run `AdtAgent.exe -c` at the command prompt. Select to import the certificate already issued and in use for the
   OpsMgr Agent Component communication. Restart the AdtAgent service.

ACS Audit Policy and Reporting Scenarios

We close this chapter with four real-world situations where you can use ACS. Each
scenario demonstrates the underlying audit plan and corresponding audit report that
together meet a particular auditing objective. Essentially, ACS exists to enable enforcement of audit plans by reporting on compliance with those plans. In these scenarios, we
describe a business-oriented situation that ACS can help with, and we clearly state the
objective of the auditors, who are the customers of the ACS reports.

A couple of categories of audit reports are not covered in the four scenarios, those being the Planning and the Forensic audit reports. There are four predefined reports in the Planning audit report category:

- ▶ **Event Counts**—What are most common events across all computers?

- ▶ **Event Counts by Computer**—What are the most common events on a particular computer?

- ▶ **Hourly Event Distribution**—Show me the ACS utilization pattern.

- ▶ **Logon Counts of Privileged Users**—Are privileged logon accounts being overused or abused?

The predefined Planning reports are very useful to the ACS administrator for assessing the ongoing health of ACS. The two event count reports are excellent baselines the administrator should be familiar with to be able to compare against future similar reports and establish trends. If you are experiencing a capacity or performance issue with your ACS database or collector components, the event count reports can help you make informed decisions about which events to stop collecting. The Hourly Event Distribution report provides another baseline and helps you in detecting spikes and troughs. Marked departures from average hourly event volume should be accounted for by expected user activity levels or investigated further to determine the origin of the anomalies. Figure 15.22 shows off the Hourly Event Distribution report, in this case a copy of the report exported as a PDF file.

15

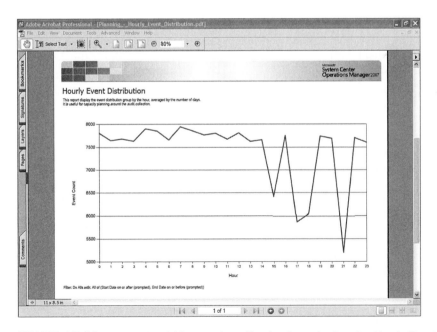

FIGURE 15.22   Assessing ACS capacity utilization by reviewing the Hourly Event Distribution report.

There are three predefined reports in the Forensic audit report category:

- **All Events for Specified User**—What computers did this person log on to?

- **All Events for Specified Computer**—Show me everyone that logged on to this computer.

- **All Events with Specified Event ID**—Show me every event of this type on any computer where it occurred.

Reports in the Forensic category are useful when investigating recent security-sensitive activity. These reports are broad nets cast across the entire ACS database, combing for and collecting specific events of interest. Although the reports in the scenarios that follow have specific focused objectives based on audit plans, the forensic reports can help auditors answer fundamental investigative questions. The following scenarios cover situations that lend themselves to routine and recurring generation of reports for enforcing ongoing audit objectives. The reports in the Forensic category are used "on demand" for live interactive queries to the database on an as-needed basis.

Account Management Scenario

Situation
The controlling authority of a network wants to keep a close eye on the membership of the powerful Domain Admin and Builtin (Local) Administrators groups. The membership of these groups is set by organizational policy and should never change without advance knowledge and permission of the controlling authority.

Without ACS, the authority must manually and periodically examine the membership of the groups using the Active Directory Users and Computers MMC snap-in for the domain, the local Computer Management MMC snap-in for member servers, or command-line utilities that retrieve group membership. Group membership must be compared to lists of authorized members to detect unauthorized changes.

Auditing Objective
Verify that the membership of the administrator groups remains the same. Auditors need to be aware that changes have taken place and validate discovered changes with the controlling authority. When there are authorized changes, auditors will expect positive confirmation that the expected changes occur.

Audit Plan

1. Audit success events in the account management category. Figure 15.23 shows the Default Domain Controller Security Settings, with the Audit account management policy and Success event auditing enabled.

2. Deploy this policy to the Default Domain Controllers Security Settings to monitor the membership of the Domain Admin and Builtin\Administrator groups.

3. Deploy this policy to the Default Domain Security Settings as well if you will be monitoring the membership of the administrators groups on member servers.

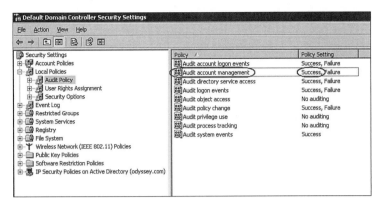

FIGURE 15.23   Enable Success events in the Audit account management policy.

Audit Report: Domain and Built-in Administrators Changes

The Domain and Built-in Administrators Changes report, shown in Figure 15.24, lists membership changes in the Domain Admin and BUILTIN\Administrators groups. It looks for events 632, 633, 636, and 637 (membership change event for local and global groups) when the target is an administrator group. Figure 15.24 shows the results of this report, revealing changes did occur to both the Domain Admins group and the BUILTIN\Administrators group of both the domain controller (Pantheon) and a domain member server (Thunder).

Auditors can review a report similar to that shown in Figure 15.24 on a scheduled basis, such as weekly, and confirm that membership additions and removals are expected and authorized. This report is a good candidate for scheduling publication to a file share for auditors to review offline. A blank or empty report indicates no changes occurring during the report period. Make sure the period of the report is equal to or greater than the interval between published reports (that is, if auditors receive a weekly scheduled report, the report period should cover at least 7 days).

FIGURE 15.24   Reporting on changes in the membership of domain and computer administrator groups.

Other reports in the Account Management Category include the following:

▶ **User Accounts Created and User Accounts Deleted**—These reports look for event 624, which tracks user account creation, and event 630, which tracks user account deletion. These reports serve as excellent offline records of user entry and exit from the organization's directory services.

▶ **Password Change Attempts by Non-Owner**—This report details any password change or reset attempts by someone other than the account owner. Event 627 indicates password change attempt, and event 628 indicates password reset. Only routine and expected events should appear in the report, such as administrators and account operators provisioning and maintaining user accounts for the organization. You want to investigate password change attempts by unauthorized users or against privileged accounts.

Access Violation Scenario

Situation

Highly sensitive files in the Human Resources (HR) department file share require close watch. Network administrators must comply with an organizational policy forbidding any access attempts or access to certain folders in the file system of the HR networked file server.

Examples of these types of highly sensitive files include employee compensation information and legal correspondence. When high dollar values and very personal information is involved, senior management has requested the most stringent object access logging is enabled.

Auditing Objective

Protect sensitive files by alerting on possible unauthorized access attempts, and show access by authorized users. Senior management and auditors need to verify that only authorized users have accessed the sensitive files, and they need to follow up on any instance of a network administrator violating the access policy.

The official warning to IT staff, combined with auditing enabled to detect violations, should create a self-enforcing and auditable file integrity solution. The goal is to prove to senior management that highly sensitive files do not have inappropriate access by anyone, including IT staff.

Audit Plan

1. Audit success and failure events in the system event and logon event categories, and audit success events in the object access category. Figure 15.25 shows the Default Domain Security Settings, with the Audit logon events and Audit system events policies set for Success and Failure event auditing. Also, the Audit object access policy is set for Success event auditing.

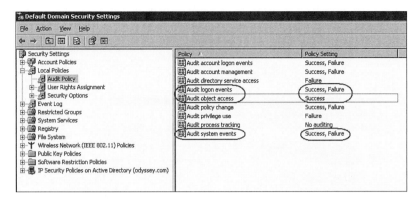

FIGURE 15.25   Audit Policy settings to monitor access to sensitive files or folders.

2. Deploy this policy to the Default Domain Controllers Security Settings only if the sensitive files reside on a domain controller.

3. Deploy this policy to the Default Domain Security Settings in order to monitor the sensitive files on member servers such as file servers.

4. Enable auditing on the sensitive files or folders. Enabling auditing of object access is a two-step procedure. First, you apply the Audit Object Access policy to the domain or domain controller security policy, then you specify what kind of object accesses are to be audited in the advanced security properties of the files, folders, or other objects of interest.

Enable Auditing on the Files, Folders, or Objects of Interest

After deploying security settings to computers that include any auditing of object access, you must then specify in the advanced security properties of the objects to be audited exactly what event(s) you want to audit. In our example, illustrated in Figure 15.26, we have enabled object access auditing of members of the IT Department Staff against the folder used by the Human Resources department for highly sensitive files. Only object accesses and attempted object access by members of the IT Department Staff security group generate audit events.

Notice that because we want to audit all the files and folders in this sensitive folder, we have selected the Replace auditing entries on all child objects setting before clicking the Apply button. We want to point out that this same method of auditing file and folder access can be used for other Active Directory objects such as GPOs and Organizational Units (OUs). Once object access auditing is enabled in the domain, any object in the Windows environment that includes advanced security properties can be enabled for audit.

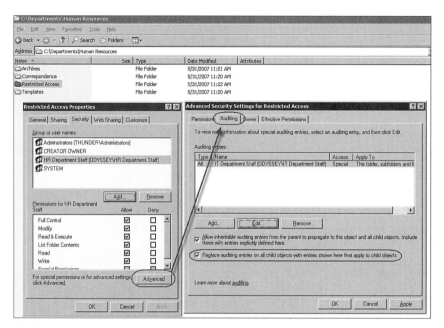

FIGURE 15.26   Enable auditing on the folder, including all child objects.

TIP

Be Specific when Enabling Object Auditing

To reduce the volume of events generated and maximize the effectiveness of each
event, only audit the actions that really interest you. For example, if you are interested in
users reading a file, do not audit Full Control. Also, for best system performance, minimize the number of auditing entries on the Security properties, Auditing tab through the
judicious use of Windows security groups. Avoid adding many individual auditing entries
for particular users and groups—it is better to create a group that contains all the users
and groups to be audited and specify just that group on the Auditing tab.

Audit Report: Usage Object Access

The Object Access report shows all object access-related audit events within the specified
time range. It uses the events 560 (permission requested) and 567 (permission exercised)
to track items with object access auditing enabled. Figure 15.27 shows the results of this
report, which did discover an attempted access violation. User CPrice, who is a member of
the IT Department Staff security group, attempted to access the Pending Legal Cases.xls
file, which is in the Legal subfolder of the Departments\Human Resources\Restricted
Access folder on server Thunder, which we are auditing.

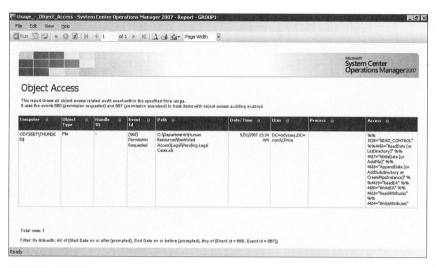

FIGURE 15.27   An organizational directive to not attempt access was violated.

Policy Changes Scenario

Situation

An organization has deployed ACS as its primary vehicle to track compliance with auditing objectives. We have seen in this chapter that audit settings, deployed via Active Directory group policy, underpins all of Audit Collection Services. If an administrator were to surreptitiously or inadvertently modify the audit settings in the group policy, entire categories of audit reports may no longer contain the data ACS was deployed to collect. The organization needs a positive means to catch changes in audit policy as they occur; in other words, a way to audit the auditing system.

Auditing Objective

Verify that no changes to audit policy occur without direction from the controlling authority of the network. As with the Domain and Administrator Group Changes report we looked at previously in the "Account Management Scenario" section, auditors need to review a report on a regular and scheduled basis. The objective is to both detect unauthorized changes to audit policy and validate implementation of authorized changes.

Audit Plan

1. Audit success events in the policy change event category. Figure 15.28 shows the Default Domain Controller Policy, Security Settings, with the Audit policy change policy set to audit Success events.

2. Deploy this policy to the Default Domain Controllers Security Settings to monitor changes to the domain controller audit policy.

3. Deploy this policy to the Default Domain Security Settings as well if you will be monitoring changes to the local audit policy of member servers. Note that if the setting for a particular policy in the domain security settings is undefined, local policy on a member server can be modified by any user with administrator rights on the member server.

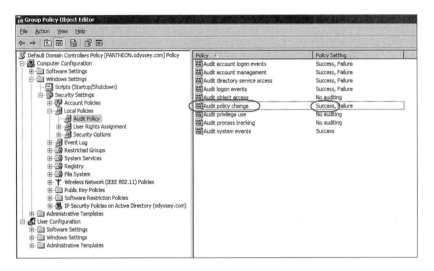

FIGURE 15.28   Enable Success events in the Audit policy change policy.

Audit Report: All Audit Policy Changes (Custom Report)

A predefined report to detect audit policy changes is not included with Operations Manager 2007, so we will create a custom report to detect audit policy changes as part of this scenario. The basis of this report is security event ID 612; an example of this event type is shown in Figure 15.29.

Security event ID 612 has an atypical construction; the description field of the event is actually a little chart with plus and minus symbols in columns lined up with audit policy names. The pluses indicate auditing was enabled; minuses indicate it was disabled. For example, in the Event ID 612 shown in Figure 15.29, circled to the left of the System policy row, notice the plus in the Success column and the minus in the Failure column. This corresponds to setting the Audit system events policy to audit success events and to not audit failure events.

Each of the plusses and minuses in the description of Event ID 612 is stored in the event as a separate string value. ACS reporting is able to extract those string values individually, and you can create a custom report with columns that match those in the event description field. We will now step through the creation of a custom report using the SQL 2005 Report Builder. Because this report focuses on a particular event ID, we will save time by copying the All Events With Specified Event ID report and modifying it, rather than starting with a generic report template. Perform the following steps:

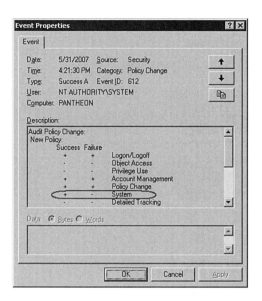

FIGURE 15.29   Security event ID 612 indicates a policy change occurred.

1. Open your browser and enter the address **http://<*ReportServerName*>/Reports**. The SQL Server Reporting Services page will open. Click the Audit Reports folder in the main window.

2. In the Audit Reports folder, click the Report Builder button in the menu bar of the window. The SQL Server 2005 Reporting Services Report Builder application will download and open.

3. In the lower-right corner of the Report Builder window, click the Open from Report Server link. Browse to the Audit Reports folder, select the Forensic_-_All_Events_With_Specified_Event_ID report, and click the Open button. The Report Builder will launch, with the All Events With Specified Event ID report open for editing.

4. First, we will change the report, from one that prompts you to input the event ID of interest at runtime, to one that is fixed on a particular event. Click the Filter button on the menu bar and change the setting of the event ID from prompt to specified, and select 612 as the value. Figure 15.30 shows the Filter Data window. Click the item Event ID next to the green question mark and unselect Prompt. Click OK to return to the main Report Builder window.

5. Because this report now only contains events with the same ID, you can delete the report column that displays the event ID. Right-click the Event ID column and select Delete.

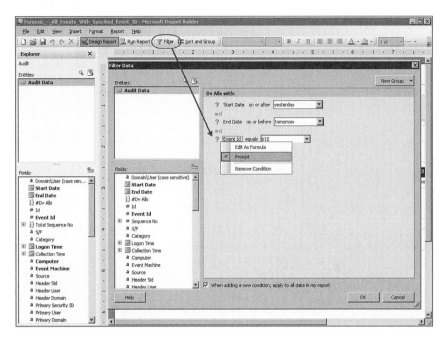

FIGURE 15.30   Modifying the predefined report to look for a fixed event ID rather than prompt for one when it runs.

6. The predefined report we are modifying only has columns for the first five string fields in the event. By counting the 18 plusses and misuses in the Event 612 description field, we know that our custom report will need 18 columns to display the 18 string fields. Beginning with String 06, select the 13 string fields from 06 to 18 in the Fields area in the lower left of the Report Builder, and drag them using the left mouse button to the right edge of String 05 in the main design window. Release the mouse button, and you should see your report now extend further to the right and contain String 01 to String 18 in 18 contiguous columns. Figure 15.31 illustrates this select, drag, and add action.

7. The foundation of our custom report is now built! The remaining steps are cosmetic and increase the readability and meaningfulness of the report. Begin by changing the report title and description to match the new custom purpose of the report. For example, change the All Events with Specified Event ID report title to **All Audit Policy Changes**. Optionally, add additional text boxes (Insert -> Text Box) with information that might be useful to readers of the report anywhere on the report that makes sense.

8. Because we added so many columns, the report now extends off the page to the right. Select File -> Page Setup from the Report Builder menu and set the report orientation to Landscape. We also selected a custom paper width of 15 inches (38 centimeters) to accommodate the wide format.

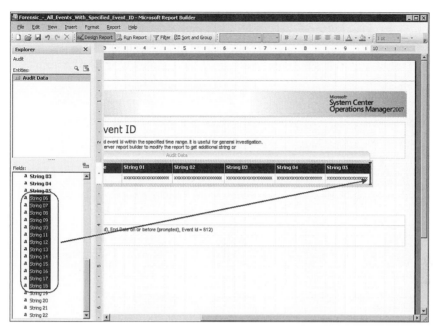

FIGURE 15.31   Adding more event string fields as columns in a custom report.

9. Now, we will modify the column headers from their generic text (String 01, String 02, and so on) to headers that match the meaning of the plus or minus signs that will appear in the columns. Double-click each string column header and type the new text, such as **Logon-Logoff Success** and **Logon-Logoff Failure** for the first two string columns.

10. Save the report with a new name to the Report Server (select File -> Save As). To maintain consistency with the predefined reports, we gave this custom report the name Policy_Changes_-_All_Audit_Policy_Changes.

11. Before you close the Report Builder, export a file-based copy of your custom report. Select File -> Save to File. The Report Builder saves your custom report to an RDPL (sometimes also called a RDL) file that can be backed up for archive purposes, as well as imported to other ACS report servers in your organization.

By default, RDPL files are saved to the My Documents folder. Because this folder is unique to each user, we suggest a centralized place to store your reports, such as c:\exports. This not only makes it easy to see all customized ACS reports in one place (because each person has a unique My Documents folder), but it also gives you a single location from which to collect them for backup purposes.

To import your custom report to another instance of ACS, open Report Builder from another SQL Reporting Server (as we did in step 2 of this procedure), but select Open from File rather than Open from Report Server as we did in step 3. Select the RDPL file exported from the original instance, and once it's loaded in Report Builder, save it to the additional Report Server (File -> Save).

Figure 15.32 displays the custom report after it has run against the ACS database. Each occurrence of Event ID 612 is listed with the plusses and minuses in columns that describe their significance. We circled the same System Success and System Failure policy status indicators on the custom report as we did in Figure 15.29, a sample Event ID 612 from an ACS forwarder.

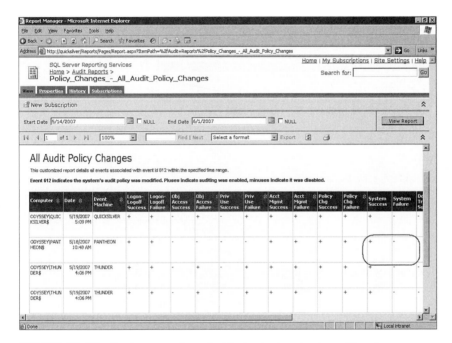

FIGURE 15.32   Custom report created to track changes in audit policy.

System Integrity Scenario

Situation

An organization acknowledges that an administrator wishing to destroy evidence of inappropriate activities will seek to disable the ACS forwarder before the unauthorized activity and then clear the security event logs of the involved computers afterward (covering his tracks). The controlling authority of the network has instructed network administrators that they are never to clear the security log on audited computers. The organization needs a way to detect when the security log is cleared on computers—which is always a violation of policy—so that an investigation can be initiated.

Auditing Objective

Verify that no occurrences of security event logs being cleared exist. Auditors need to review a report of any instances of the prohibited action on a regular and scheduled basis.

Audit Plan

It is not necessary to deploy any audit policy setting to enable the collection of Event ID 517, The audit log was cleared. This event is always written to a Windows computer's security event log when the log is cleared. To detect security event logs being cleared, it is sufficient to enable the forwarder on a computer and run this report at least as frequently as the retention period of events in the ACS database.

Audit Report: Audit Log Cleared

The Audit Log Cleared report, shown in Figure 15.33, shows which computers' audit logs were cleared and who cleared them. In this example, the domain Administrator account cleared the security event log on computer Thunder, then two minutes later it was cleared again by user IFong—definitely something suspicious that should be checked out.

If you run the Audit Log Cleared report and get a blank or empty report, it means there were no instances of the security audit log being cleared during the period of the report. This, of course, is the normal and desired result at most organizations! Be aware that if you implement the WMI query-based filter to discard events sourced from computers' system accounts, as we demonstrated in the "Using AdtAdmin.exe" section of this chapter, you will not get any data in the Audit Log Cleared report. That is because the user for Event ID 517 is the NT AUTHORITY\SYSTEM account.

There is one other report in the System Integrity category that is useful to run on a scheduled basis in tandem with the Audit Log Cleared report—the Audit Failures report. The Audit Failures report looks for Event ID 516 and indicates that the system failed to audit events due to a lack of resources. If any computers appear in the Audit Failures report, it indicates a serious problem that should be resolved as soon as possible to prevent further loss of audit data.

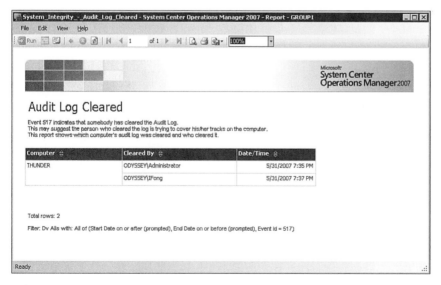

FIGURE 15.33   Detecting instances of the security audit log being cleared on computers.

Summary

Before the introduction of the Audit Collection Services (ACS) in Operations Manager 2007, organizations desiring to achieve a central view of all critical security-related events in their enterprise faced some daunting challenges. Microsoft's bundling of ACS with OpsMgr is a triumph that for some organizations will justify the deployment of OpsMgr just to get ACS!

In this chapter, we stepped through the process of deciding which audit polices we will deploy as well as how to deploy ACS components to enable enforcement of those policies. We covered how ACS is administered during routine operations and how to handle some special challenges related to the capacity and redundancy of the ACS infrastructure. We closed with four reporting scenarios that tied the selection of audit policies to deploy with the reports to be run, which together deliver the desired information to auditors. The next chapter discusses additional new capabilities in Operations Manager 2007, user workstation management, and client monitoring features.

CHAPTER 16

Client Monitoring

With its newest version of Operations Manager (OpsMgr), Microsoft broadens its monitoring scope to include user workstation management, and adds new client monitoring features not present in previous versions. Although in Microsoft Operations Manager (MOM) 2000 and MOM 2005 you could add user workstations to the management group just like servers, Microsoft did not design those products for workstation management:

▶ The monitoring features available for workstations were identical to those of servers. In other words, you could only manage a workstation as if it were a server.

▶ You had to purchase an Operations Management License (OML) for workstations at the same price as for servers. That was a relatively costly solution— overkill even—and explains MOM's low implementation rate for monitoring client workstations such as desktop and notebook computers.

New Client Monitoring Features

The three new client monitoring features in System Center Operations Manager 2007 are as follows:

▶ **Agentless Exception Monitoring (AEM)**—Collecting and reporting application errors and system crashes without installing an OpsMgr Agent component.

▶ **Customer Experience Improvement Program (CEIP)**—Centrally compiling and forwarding information about Microsoft product usage; requires AEM to be enabled.

▶ **Client-specific Management Packs**—Comprehensive, tailored monitoring of OpsMgr agent-managed workstations, with optional enhanced monitoring of selected business critical workstations.

The first half of this chapter covers AEM and the CEIP; the second part discusses the Client Operating System and Information Worker management packs. Together, these new features represent a significant investment by Microsoft to extend the ways in which you can get value from OpsMgr.

Monitoring any computer, server or client, incurs costs of various types. These expenditures start with licensing management agent(s) and include the reoccurring cost of technical staffing resources to evaluate and act on generated alerts. Historically, the sheer quantity of clients compared to servers restricted the implementation of monitoring those clients.

The resources for monitoring a server are justified by the lost productivity of many or all users in an organization when a server-based application malfunctions; yet the loss of productivity from a client workstation malfunction, typically used by a single individual, is seldom noticeable. Historically, the economies did not justify proactively managing large numbers of client computers other than some non-conventional clients not used as personal workstations, such as Point of Sale (POS) devices and critical kiosks.

A number of factors have led to the increased importance of client computers in today's business environment, including team collaboration and real-time presence applications that depend on peer-to-peer functionally between user workstations. In addition, no one can dispute that modern business practices have dramatically reduced the job functions a user can perform without using an operational workstation. Although simple disruptions, like the time spent waiting for an application to restart after a crash or the inability to connect to an email server, are a nuisance to a single user, when they occur frequently across many workstations, they can have a dramatic impact on productivity—similar or greater to that of a server outage.

Whatever Happened to Dr. Watson?

The short answer is that he lost his title, and became known just as "Watson," and now he is even losing his name and being replaced as *Windows Error Reporting*. In the process, the good doctor has become more useful to Microsoft and now to you.

Over fifteen years ago, Microsoft released a simple debugger application for the Windows NT 3.0 beta named Dr. Watson (drwatson.exe), taking its name from fictional medical doctor John Watson, sidekick of Sherlock Holmes, the detective created by the author Sir Arthur Conan Doyle. The icon for the Dr. Watson and Watson applications in Windows depicts a man carefully listening with a stethoscope. Like the icon representation, the point of Dr. Watson was to collect information, unobtrusively.

The initial drwatson.exe application created an on-command snapshot of the computer state when a user application hung (became non-responsive). The snapshot was stored in a user.dmp file on Windows NT systems, and sets of "WLG" and "TXT" files were created on Windows 95 or Windows 98/ME systems.

The drwtsn32.exe version of Dr. Watson replaced drwatson.exe in Windows 2000, creating a text file named Drwtsn32.log when it detected errors. This version, labeled by Microsoft as a "program error debugger," included crash dump support for kernel-mode crashes (blue screens), in addition to user-mode application crashes. Over time, Microsoft dropped the "Dr." title, and the term "Watson" came to describe the anonymous error collection process.

Early Watson versions wrote only crash state information such as stack traces to local files on the hard drive. This information was available to in-house developers or sent to Microsoft as part of a product support troubleshooting investigation. Later, with the release of Office XP, Microsoft added the Watson debugger, which with user permission, anonymously forwards crash information to Microsoft itself.

Something to remember about Watson data is that because the automatically forwarded information is anonymous, it has always been necessary to provide Microsoft with Watson information manually for a specific crash investigation. In other words, even when you are working with Microsoft product support personnel on a case, they do not have access to the Watson data forwarded automatically to Microsoft by your computer(s). Since 2001, Microsoft has collected, aggregated, and analyzed vast numbers of application error reports to identify problems that users experience with their Windows computers and applications. This information helps to prioritize development resources for bug fixes and service packs.

Corporate Error Reporting

In 2002, Microsoft started making Watson crash information available to network administrators, as well as to Microsoft, with the release of Corporate Error Reporting (CER) 1.0 as part of the Office XP Resource Kit. Naturally, once administrators learned that Microsoft was receiving this information, some wanted to see just what that information was, and possibly make use of it in-house. At that time, Office XP was the only application that was Watson-aware.

CER 1.1 included support for the Windows XP operating system, and required the Office XP Resource Kit as a prerequisite. CER 1.5, the first version of Corporate Error Reporting to include a stand-alone download, existed side-by-side with version 1.1. In late 2003, Microsoft made CER 2.0 available to Software Assurance customers through the Volume Licensing program. This newer version uninstalled and replaced the earlier versions.

Installing CER creates a shared folder structure to contain error report data on the server hosting the service. The error-reporting client (Watson) accesses the root of the CER shared folder through a Universal Naming Convention (UNC) path, specified in the local computer's policy for error reporting. CER 2.0 also provides a group policy template to help administrators deploy the CER settings to workstations.

CER 2.0 provides administrators with a console to view application error data collected in the shared folder and synchronize that data with Microsoft as appropriate. Using CER 2.0, the administrator can collect explicit data on problems with those products capable of reporting crash and error information to Microsoft, and evaluate the solutions reported back by Microsoft (returned in the form of a URL) before they reached the error reporting clients. CER 2.0 also gives administrators a reference of quantified data collected about crashes. Operations Manager 2007's Agentless Exception Monitoring feature retains and extends CER 2.0's functionality.

AEM is the successor and replacement for CER. Although CER was a free benefit for Microsoft customers with Software Assurance (SA), the AEM feature set is no longer free, even for SA customers. Microsoft SA customers looking for a CER replacement can either purchase OpsMgr 2007 (to deploy AEM along with monitoring their environment), or license the Microsoft Desktop Optimization Pack (MDOP) for their client workstations.

The MDOP includes the Microsoft System Center Desktop Error Monitoring (DEM) component. DEM is a modified OpsMgr 2007 management group, with only the AEM collection and reporting features enabled. DEM (a subset of the Operations console) is essentially an updated CER console for those SA customers who do not want to deploy the entire OpsMgr 2007 product. For more information about MDOP, see this link: http://www.microsoft.com/windows/products/windowsvista/enterprise/mdopoverview.mspx.

Monitoring Client Machines

One can consider the modern desktop or portable workstation as a platform service for a business or organization. The client is where the user experience happens. Looking at the client as a *platform* means you are envisioning the operating system and stack of interrelated applications on the client as a manageable service. Managing that platform as a discrete entity, rather than as many independent components, can improve the user experience as well as achieve a lower Total Cost of Ownership (TCO) for the platform.

The client monitoring features in OpsMgr 2007 actually construct this manageable platform entity. OpsMgr assembles monitoring tools for many constituent components involved in delivering the user experience and integrates them in the Operations console. We have seen this concept described with the phase "desktop as a service." The client monitoring features in OpsMgr 2007 allow you to measure the quality of your users' desktop experience.

Client Monitoring Challenges

An organization's success depends on the success of its people, and making employees more productive through communication is the main reasoning behind Information Technology (IT) investments. However, it is difficult to measure an IT organization's effectiveness in delivering the client experience to employees using traditional tools and methodologies. Compare this with server and infrastructure support teams that often have a variety of diagnostic and reporting tools to provide metrics on their performance. For example, availability of a server farm is a valid measure of the job performance of the farm's administrator or service provider. How do you measure the quality of the user experience on your organization's desktops?

Many IT organizations divide responsibility for server, network infrastructure, and desktop support between multiple staff teams. No one disputes the critical importance of desktop support to employee and organizational morale and business success, but the desktop support staff seldom has tools other than queues of end-user service tickets to measure their effectiveness and contribution. It is a paradox that client desktop support—where IT service delivery generally occurs—is historically in the low position on the totem pole when it comes to budgeting and staffing resources.

Fortunately, this less-glamorous side of the IT world is gaining attention. TCO savings in the arena of server and storage management has been dramatic in recent years, and we expect this trend to continue. However, a big slice of pie (the support portion of TCO for the desktop platform) remains ripe for innovation and investment, and small gains in improving the quality and usefulness of the desktop experience can have immediate and noticeable impact on bottom-line productivity.

Using Systems Management Server and System Center Configuration Manager

Client monitoring tools should provide insight into the quality of the desktop experience and the availability and performance of the users' applications. Traditionally, desktop management software such as Microsoft's Systems Management Server (SMS) and System Center Configuration Manager (ConfigMgr) focus on initial provisioning and configuration compliance of workstations. SMS and ConfigMgr are great at getting an application out there, and keeping it configured and updated as needed. However, these tools do not provide feedback regarding the health and use of the applications.

Using Network-level Monitoring

Network-level monitoring of workstations, such as ping monitors, is problematic. Although you expect mobile devices to be unavailable some or most of the time, a workstation that does not respond to a ping does not indicate a user does not have a functioning desktop! The user may be working just fine on a different network you are not pinging, or they could be offline while working on an airplane. More importantly, a workstation that is present and alive to respond to pings tells us nothing about the health or use of the operating system and user applications.

Doing the Math

A final consideration that has made client monitoring a difficult proposition is the numbers. A global organization might have 100,000 or more desktops. Even if you could effectively instrument all clients in an organization for monitoring, it would require a massive IT staff to evaluate every error that occurred. With the overhead of such a monitoring operation, few organizations have attempted to collect metrics on application usability.

End-User Problems Are Costly

When an application or the operating system hangs or crashes, the typical person just reboots their computer. This is a somewhat satisfying experience for users, as they remain in control of their workstation, they don't need to bother anyone else, and 90% of the time, they can continue work after the reboot. However, there are some steep downsides to this behavior:

▶ Employee productivity loss during the system restart, plus loss of employee confidence in using their workstation platform.

▶ Possible data loss, with lost time to re-create the data lost coincident with the crash or hang.

▶ No IT department awareness of the event, and no ability to correlate problems to enterprise infrastructure changes.

▶ Root cause remains unknown and unrepaired, with no association made between the problem and possibly available solutions.

For those users who do contact the IT help desk (when there is a help desk!), there are costs incurred by the help desk staff plus the additional productivity loss by the employee while interfacing with the help desk. The help desk will escalate issues they are unable to resolve (perhaps because they have not seen the problem before) to a desktop administrator, who often cannot devote much time to solving a one-off error—particularly if that error just disrupts or slows down the user, rather than derailing him completely.

Total work stoppages tend to get attention fast—a user or his supervisor quickly telephones the help desk when one or more people cannot do their job. What we're looking at here are those intermittent work interruptions that can actually go unnoticed, or perhaps even be accepted as a cost of doing modern business. However, think about the incremental and recurring nature of the little productivity losses that organizations suffer. All of us in the IT industry want to drive down those losses as low as they can go.

Occasional hangs and crashes of applications and desktop operating systems do occur with real-world users (although hopefully rarely). In an impossibly perfect infrastructure, crash and hang errors are randomly distributed across users, computers, applications, and data sources with no particular source of errors. Of course, real-world desktops do run imperfect applications, possibly encountering corrupt files or instructions. Users will execute unanticipated or disallowed procedures that produce crashes and hangs. Real-world analysis of crash and hang information does not indicate a random distribution of errors and crashes—leading causes of errors can be usually identified, indicating where first efforts at remediation should take place.

Yet without a way to capture the frequency and nature of the inevitable hangs and crashes, decisions regarding effectiveness of the desktop platform end up based on subjective opinion and anecdotal evidence. Meanwhile, a tremendous amount of effort goes into end user support. A 2005 Gartner Group study found that 50% of the TCO for a workstation in the enterprise went toward supporting end user operations.

Enormous sums can be at stake when making strategic decisions about the desktop. The Information Technology industry needs to provide metrics on the effectiveness of the desktop platform, enabling decision-making based on more than just employee satisfaction with the IT department. The graph shown in Figure 16.1 highlights the logarithmic distribution of the types of errors collected by Microsoft. Knowing which errors occur most often facilitates more effective targeting of resolution efforts.

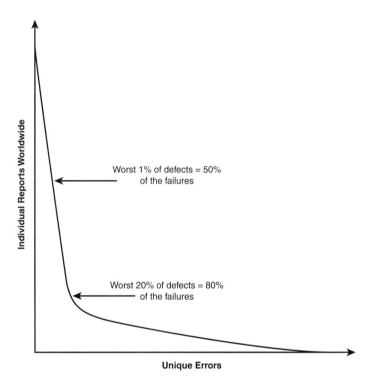

FIGURE 16.1   The shape of the error-reporting curve is what makes AEM so powerful.

New Set of Features in OpsMgr for Monitored Clients

Operations Manager 2007 combines existing technologies in new ways to create a very credible client monitoring package. As you will see, its client monitoring features effectively address the issues related to large-scale workstation populations.

Elevating client monitoring to the integrated enterprise view of the Operations console is a giant step for Microsoft and the industry. With independent options for a client monitoring solution, there is a lot of latitude in your deployment architecture for the "right" solution. Smaller organizations can certainly deploy an OpsMgr agent to every client workstation; however, for larger client populations (a rule of thumb might be above about 500 desktops), you will probably get better results with a mix of agentless and agent-installed monitoring types.

Microsoft believes that the most effective deployment of client monitoring involves identifying four classes of client computers, applying a specific monitoring model to each class:

▶ **Agentless Exception Monitoring-only**—This is going to be the bulk of your clients, perhaps 90% or more in very large organizations. These computers have no OpsMgr agent. AEM settings, pushed by Active Directory group policy, integrate with Windows Error Reporting (Watson). AEM provides visibility to aid resolution knowledge for client crashes.

   Using this model, all client computers in the enterprise, including those with OpsMgr agents, have group policies enabled to use AEM.

▶ **Aggregated Client Monitoring**—These computers are representative of the supported client populations. Some small percentage of distributed clients has an installed OpsMgr agent, leveraging the concept that a randomly selected subset of a larger population has statistical relevance to the entire population. The purpose of Aggregated Monitoring is to collect metrics, viewed in the Reporting space of the Operations console, that detect trends and top issues; Aggregated Client Monitoring does not raise individual alerts on clients. Alerts occur when a large number of client systems have the same problem; this is known as *aggregated alerting*.

> **NOTE**
>
> **Client Monitoring Terminology**
>
> Collective Client Monitoring and collective alerting are interchangeable terms with Aggregated Client Monitoring and aggregated alerting.

▶ **Business Critical Monitoring**—This deepest level of monitoring includes individual computer alerting for key events. These will be your most important client computers—typical candidates are VIP computers, Point of Sale, kiosk, and network administration workstations. You can optionally enable alerting on loss of heartbeat for these computers.

▶ **Synthetic Transaction Monitoring**—These selected client computers, known as *watcher nodes*, play a key role in managing larger enterprise applications. Any client with an OpsMgr agent can host instances of synthetic transaction monitors that will perform certain client functions, measuring the success of the operation from the user perspective. Use synthetic transactions to guarantee end-to-end service delivery.

Basically, your tasks are to deploy AEM for the enterprise, and then identify which client computers will have OpsMgr agents installed for either Aggregated, Business Critical, or Synthetic Transaction Monitoring. After installing those agents, designate selected agent-managed clients for Business Critical Monitoring and/or Synthetic Transaction Monitoring. The remainder of this chapter discusses and demonstrates the use of each of these client monitoring capabilities.

Monitoring Agentless Systems

Agentless Exception Monitoring does not use the OpsMgr agent. Implementing AEM involves just two steps: activating the AEM feature on an OpsMgr management server, and deploying a group policy object (GPO) with Active Directory (AD). We previously activated the AEM feature on a management server in Chapter 6 of this book, "Installing Operations Manager 2007;" now we will deploy the GPO and begin collecting crash and hang information from computers in our domain. Before starting to monitor agentless systems, we will introduce the architecture of AEM so you can understand what is happening under the hood.

AEM Architecture

To explain the architecture of AEM, we will look at the default behavior of the Watson and Windows Error Reporting (WER) clients without AEM deployed, and compare this with how things work after AEM is in the picture. Remember that Windows 2000 and Windows XP computers have the legacy Watson clients included with the operating system; Windows Vista computers have the new WER built-in.

These error reporting clients, by default, request user permission after a crash or hang to transmit the information to Microsoft's back-end error reporting services. Here are the events that take place after invoking Watson or WER, illustrated in Figure 16.2:

▶ If the user gives permission, the Watson or WER client makes direct Internet connection using Hyper Text Transfer Protocol (HTTP) to the Microsoft back-end servers. These back-end servers have the Uniform Resource Locators (URLs) of watson. microsoft.com and sqm.microsoft.com. The Watson back-end service receives error information, and the SQM (Software Quality Metrics component of the Microsoft Customer Experience Program) back-end receives CEIP information.

▶ During the initial HTTP connection, a check takes place to see if Microsoft is aware of this type of error. If Microsoft has not seen the type of error before, the interface asks the user for permission to upload additional information about the error.

▶ The connection is changed to secure mode (HTTPS), and the crash or hang error information is uploaded, along with the additional data if it was requested and permission was granted.

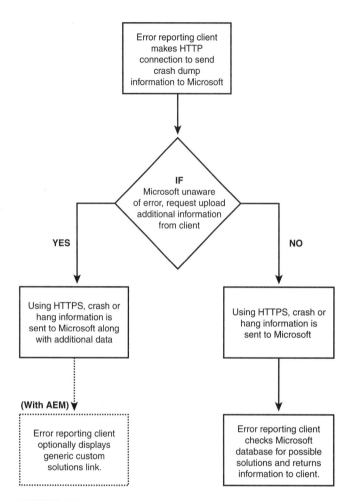

FIGURE 16.2   Error reporting client processing flow.

▶ The error reporting client checks a Microsoft database of possible solutions to known errors during the connection. If there is a known patch, update, or workaround for the reported error, the user gets a dialog box with a link marked More Information. If the user clicks on that link, a web page at microsoft.com will open on their desktop, hopefully providing helpful information. (Optionally, AEM returns a generic web link to the user when no possible solutions link is available.)

When you deploy AEM polices via a GPO, it configures registry keys on the client computer with values that change the behavior of Watson or WER. The error reporting clients look for these registry keys prior to sending any reports to Microsoft. If you have configured Watson or WER for AEM, it redirects the error reports to the organization's AEM server. Computers configured as AEM clients no longer attempt to connect directly to Microsoft over the Internet.

Activating AEM on an OpsMgr management server creates two avenues for collecting error data. One is for legacy Watson clients (Windows 2000 and Windows XP) and the other is for WER clients (Windows Vista). The Watson collection component is a shared folder on the AEM server accessible by all domain users and computers (but not anonymously). The WER collection component is an HTTPS listener endpoint, by default on port 51906.

When an error or crash occurs on a computer configured to use AEM, the report goes to the designated management server:

▶ The Watson client on Windows 2000 and Windows XP computers uses the Remote Procedure Call (RPC) protocol to create a folder structure, based on the error parameters, inside the expected shared folder on the management server.

▶ If the error or crash occurs on a Windows Vista computer, the WER client connects to the HTTPS listener to upload the information.

Advances in the WER client over Watson include extracting relevant information from the error report such as where the crash happened, what machine crashed, and which user experienced the crash. In addition, the WER client only requires access to the AEM management server (the management server enabled for AEM) on port 51906, making operation through firewalls much simpler than the RPC and file share method used by Watson.

Figure 16.3 ties it all together, showing how AEM sits between the error reporting clients and the Microsoft back-end error reporting services.

Crash and Hang Monitoring

After enabling AEM on a selected management server, the next step for the OpsMgr administrator is deploying the AEM Group Policy Object (GPO) with Active Directory. Running the Configure Client Monitoring wizard (launched in the Operations console from the Administration -> Device Management -> Management Servers node) creates an administrative template file, saved in the root of %*ProgramFiles*%\System Center Operations Manager folder. The file name is the Fully Qualified Domain Name (FQDN) of the server and has the .ADM file extension. In our Odyssey management group, the file name is hydra.odyssey.com.adm.

Deploying the AEM Policy

We recommend installing the Group Policy Management Console (GPMC) on the AEM management server, as you will need to import, link, and edit the GPO in the domain's Active Directory. Here are the recommended steps required to deploy the AEM policy to your domain(s) using the GMPC:

1. Open the GPMC and navigate to the Group Policy Objects node in the domain (Group Policy Management -> Forest: *forest* -> Domains -> *domain* -> Group Policy Objects). Select the node, right-click, and choose New.

2. Name the policy as desired. We used **Windows Error Reporting (Watson)** to distinguish this GPO.

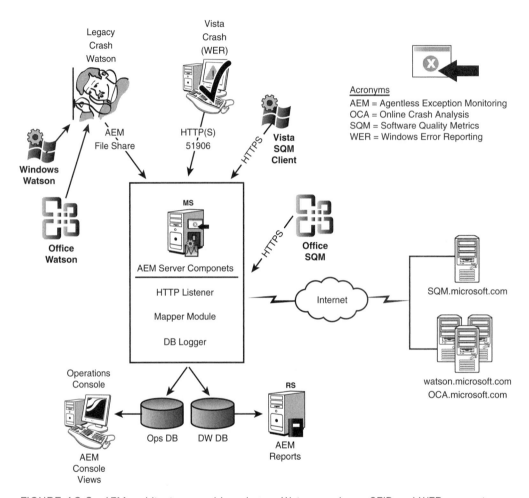

FIGURE 16.3   AEM architecture combines legacy Watson and new CEIP and WER support.

3. Locate the new policy in the tree below the Group Policy Objects node, select the policy, right-click, and choose Edit.

4. The Group Policy Object Editor opens. Navigate to the Computer Configuration -> Administrative Templates node, right-click, and select Add/Remove Templates.

5. The Add/Remove Templates dialog opens; push the Add button. Browse to the location of the template file saved by the Configure Client Monitoring wizard. In our case, the path was D:\Program Files\System Center Operations Manager 2007\hydra.odyssey.com.adm. Select the file and press the Open button.

6. Observe that the Current Policy Templates list now includes the imported template, and press the Close button.

7. Returning to the Group Policy Object Editor, notice there is now a Microsoft Applications node under the Computer Configuration -> Administrative Templates node.

8. Expand the Microsoft Applications -> System Center Operations Manager (SCOM) node to reveal the four subordinate nodes that begin with the words *SCOM Client Monitoring*.

9. Beginning with the first node, SCOM Client Monitoring CEIP Settings, select the node in the left side of the GPMC and then double-click to open each Settings item in the right side of the GPMC. With the individual Settings item open, push the Enabled radio button. This exposes the values for that setting that you selected when running the Configure Client Monitoring wizard.

10. Walk the tree of subordinate nodes in the System Center Operations Manager (SCOM) node, selecting and enabling each feature as desired. In all there are 11 Settings items that correspond to the questions and responses utilized by the Configure Client Monitoring wizard.

11. **IMPORTANT:** Now navigate to the Computer Configuration -> Administrative Templates -> System -> Internet Communications Management -> Internet Communications settings node. Double-click on the Turn Off Windows Error Reporting setting, select Enabled, and press OK. This step inhibits the Watson or WER client from attempting the default behavior of sending error information directly to Microsoft.

12. Optionally, disable the User Configuration portion of the GPO. In environments with many GPOs, user logon processing is faster when you disable the user portion of GPOs that contain no user settings.

    To disable the User Configuration portion of the GPO, right-click on the root of the policy in the Group Policy Object Editor, and select Properties. Tick the Disable User Configuration Settings item and press OK.

13. Select File -> Exit (or push the X button) to close the Group Policy Object Editor and return to the GPMC. Now select where to link the new GPO. Because there is only one AEM server per management group, and since you want to include all computers in the domain, we recommend linking the GPO at the root of the domain.

    To enable AEM on all computers in the domain, right-click on the domain object and choose Link an Existing GPO. Select the GPO—in our case, Windows Error Reporting (Watson)—and push OK.

14. Observe that the new GPO appears under the domain root with a shortcut (link) icon. Figure 16.4 illustrates the GPO linked at the domain root in the GPMC. If you have other domains in your Active Directory forest, you can expose them in the GPMC by right-clicking the Domains node and selecting Show Domains. Repeat the linking procedure from step 13 in this checklist for each domain as desired. Close the GPMC.

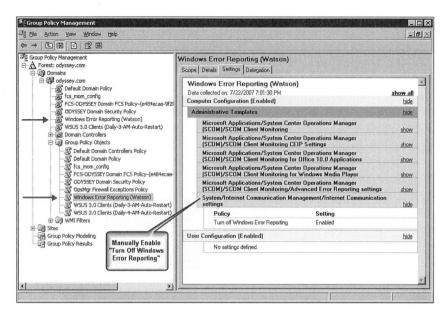

FIGURE 16.4   The Windows Error Reporting (Watson) GPO linked at the domain root.

You have now enabled centralized collection and forwarding of AEM and CEIP information in your organization. No other setup or maintenance of the AEM feature in OpsMgr is required to achieve full use of this capability. Regardless of how many client and server computers there are in your organization, as soon as they refresh their group policy (which can take up to a few hours in a larger domain with multiple sites), they will begin reporting crash and hang information to the management group. Likewise, domain computers will no longer attempt to send Watson/WER or CEIP information directly to Microsoft once they apply the GPO.

TIP

Utilities to Generate Crashes and Hangs

We used a pair of excellent crash test programs to exercise the error collection features of AEM—Accvio.exe (Access Violation) and NotMyFault.exe. You can download these utilities, written by the Microsoft SysInternals team, at http://www.microsoft. com/technet/sysinternals/information/windowsinternals.mspx. The Not My Fault driver crash test utility prompts the user to "Pick your poison" and offers such cyber-toxins as Buffer Overflow, Stack trash, and Deadlock.

As the OpsMgr administrator, you may want to verify that AEM is working, and familiarize yourself with the console and reporting options available to view crash and hang information. If you have a known misbehaving application or invalid procedure that invokes

Watson or WER, you can cause a crash or hang and observe the error reporting client in action, and then see the error in the Operations console appear shortly. If you don't deliberately initiate some crashes, in time, actual crash and hang information should appear in the Operations console.

Working with the AeDebug Registry Key

There are several occasions where OpsMgr administrators may be interested in the software registry key that controls launching the error reporting client. On Windows XP and 2003 computers, drwtsn32.exe is the default debugger, and launching Watson is what sets AEM functionality in motion. Installing other applications with debugging features such as Microsoft Visual Studio can modify the default debugger setting, resulting in a loss of AEM reporting functionality from that computer. To restore Watson as the default debugger and thereby enable AEM, you can run this .REG script on the Windows XP or 2003 computer (this does not apply to Windows Vista systems, which use WER and not drstsn32.exe):

```
Windows Registry Editor Version 5.00

[HKEY_LOCAL_MACHINE\SOFTWARE\Microsoft\WindowsNT\CurrentVersion\AeDebug]

"Auto"="1"

"Debugger"="drwtsn32.exe -p %ld e %ld"
```

A different purpose of this registry key on Windows Vista systems is to exclude processes from kicking off the debugger. This feature came from the need to exclude DWM.EXE from the "auto debug" mechanism. In Vista, DWM.exe is responsible for the display graphics; therefore, if it crashes, there is no way for DWM to display the dialog that debuggers show.

On Vista systems, you will find an AutoExclustionList subkey under AeDebug that includes DWM.EXE. Add additional DWORD values to that subkey to exclude other processes you do not want to invoke WER even if they crash.

Before we step through some crashes and demonstrate the resulting AEM behaviors, let's look at the shared folder structure created on the OpsMgr server hosting AEM. The AEM views in the Monitoring space of the Operations console are essentially windows into these folders. Under the root of the AEM file share, created when you ran the Configure Client Monitoring wizard, are four folders:

- **Cabs**—Contains subfolders based on the signature of the error report, where the last folder contains reporting data stored in a compressed archive .CAB file.

- **Counts**—Contains subfolders based on the error report where the last folders contain counts of .CAB files collected and total reports for the error signature.

▶ **Status**—Holds responses from Microsoft, to be relayed to the error reporting client on the next instance of a report with an existing signature.

▶ **PersistedCabs**—Contains .CAB files, previously sent to Microsoft, for historical reference. The AEM forwarding component on the management server clears the Cabs and Counts folders when the report to Microsoft is complete. Links in the Operations console to .CAB files in the PersistedCabs folder let the administrator browse details of past crashes.

TIP

File and Share Security on the AEM Server

The file shares created when enabling AEM on a management server have share permissions of Everyone\Full Control. Security is enforced at both the file and folder level. AEM setup creates two local computer security groups on the AEM server: AEMAgent and AEMUsers. The AEMAgent group membership consists of the local Administrators group with Full Control file and folder permissions. The AEMUsers group membership consists of all Authenticated Users, effectively all computer and user accounts in the domain, with special file and folder permissions.

These permissions allow error reports to be uploaded by client computers and processed by the management server. It should not be necessary to modify these permissions.

Figure 16.5 illustrates the AEM shared folder structure on the OpsMgr management server. We expanded the PersistedCabs folder to expose the error report of a particular problem application (in this case, the crash generator program from SysInternals). You can see that the contents of the .CAB file include some text files with information about the version of Windows the computer was running and details of the application causing the crash. There is also a file with the .MDMP extension; this is a mini-dump file and accessible to application developers using Microsoft Visual Studio to assist with debugging the error condition.

AEM Console Views

There are five pre-defined views in the Agentless Exception Monitoring view folder. When the AEM server receives crash and hang error information from client computers, it updates one or more AEM views with that information. The server processes collect reports on a timed basis—it can take up to two minutes from the moment the client transmits the error report until you see the error reflected in the console. Here is a description of each AEM view:

▶ **Application Error Events**—This is a conventional OpsMgr event view folder, containing an entry for each application error received. The other application error views list aggregated data by the application name, so if you are looking for the record of a specific instance of a computer uploading an application error report, you will see it here.

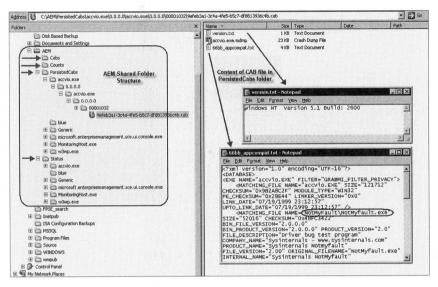

FIGURE 16.5   The AEM folder structure on the OpsMgr server stores crash histories.

▶ **Application Error Group View**—This is a dynamic view, created by reading the application names and contents of the shared folder structure where error reports are stored. The view includes an entry for each error signature reported. A single application name may appear several times if the same application reports different error signatures. If there are more than 50 instances of the same error signature, the error group shows as a Critical state.

From this view, you can select application errors and customize the error buckets, which are the settings that guide the behavior of the Watson or WER client. We will explore the bucket customization options later in this section. Figure 16.6 shows several application error groups present in a management group, with one group over the 50-count threshold.

▶ **Application View**—Also a dynamic view, listing application errors by application name. Each application name appears only once in this view, even if the application reports a variety of error conditions. The health monitor for an application error includes counters for computers, users, and applications—if any of these elements exceeds the threshold, that application has a Critical health state.

▶ **Crash Listener View**—This is a read-only view that confirms the settings of the AEM management server. The view will show only one entry, the AEM server. When you select the server, the Details pane confirms all the selections made when running the Enable Client Monitoring wizard.

16

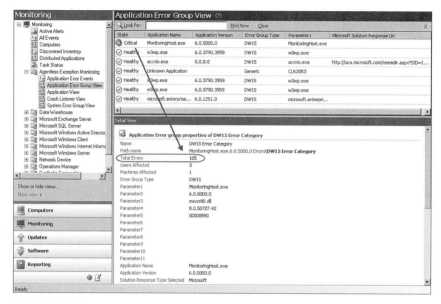

FIGURE 16.6   Each application error group represents a unique error signature.

To change one or more of these settings, you must disable AEM on the management server, then re-enable AEM by running the Enable Client Monitoring wizard again with the desired new setting(s). No data is lost during the re-enable sequence, when and if you change the settings.

▶ **System Error Group View**—This view functions like the Application Error Group View, only this view is for system crashes such as blue screens. This view treats each crash report like a separate object that will always have a Critical state. A link in the Details view of each crash shows the path of the .CAB file, located in the PersistedCabs folder of the AEM server corresponding to the crash report. Figure 16.7 shows the System Error Group View, with the contents of the sysdata.xml file in the linked .CAB file.

We will demonstrate viewing an application crash in the console and customize the error bucket for that particular crash signature. Using the Accvio.exe (Access Violation) utility, we generate an application crash on our Windows Vista desktop. Figure 16.8 shows the series of dialogs the user experiences after an application crash.

Something to notice in Figure 16.8 is that the values in the lines of the Problem signature (in the upper-left dialog box detail area) correspond to the folder structure created for this error report in the shared folder on the AEM server. In this case, the folder path, called the error bucket, is APPCRASH\accvio.EXE\0.0.0.0\379b0f9\accvio.EXE\0.0.0.0\3793b0f9\ c0000005\00001032. You can also observe the names of the files that will be uploaded as information to the shared folder location listed in the lower dialog box detail area, such as the mini-dump file (WEREFA3.tmp.mdmp, in this case).

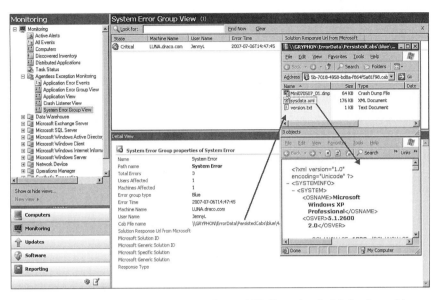

FIGURE 16.7   Viewing the contents of the .CAB file uploaded following a blue screen.

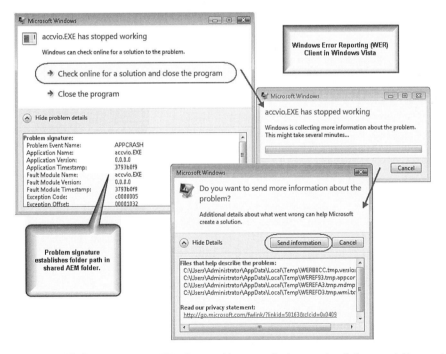

FIGURE 16.8   The Vista WER client asking permission to check for a solution and send additional details.

Shortly after the application error, we can see an error event appear in the Application Error Events View in the Operations console. Figure 16.9 gives us some information about the error event. We can see that the user Administrator has had two application errors. We selected an error in the top of the Results pane, and in the lower Details pane, we can see the name of the computer reporting the error (Titan). There is also a live link to the .CAB file in the AEM server's shared folder. We opened that link, and you can see the four files in the .CAB, matching those the user gave permission to send (see Figure 16.9).

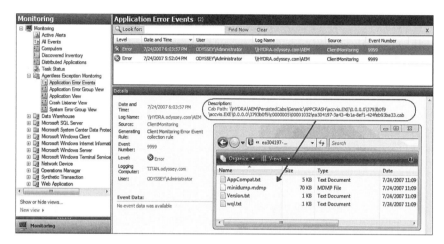

FIGURE 16.9   Viewing an application error and the contents of the .CAB file.

Customizing Error Buckets

In addition to identifying the top application errors in your organization, AEM can optionally collect additional, custom information and reach back to users with a custom solution link. When the AEM server receives an application error, a unique sequence of nested folders is created that match the characteristics of the error—creating an error bucket (the last folder created).

Subsequent Watson and WER clients discover an existing bucket, created by the first error report. The bucket contains an instruction text file, status.txt. The error reporting client reads the status.txt file in the bucket before performing the error upload. The error reporting process now executes, including any additional custom actions added to the file. Microsoft automatically modifies the status.txt file with updated information from its back-end WER servers, and an administrator using the Operations console can customize it manually.

To view and modify the error bucket settings, navigate to the Application Error Group View, select the application in the Results pane, and click the Show or Edit Error Group Properties task in the State Actions pane on the right.

The Error Bucket Reponses dialog box will open. Here you can customize the actions to take the next time the same error occurs. The options exposed by this feature include the following:

- ▶ Disable collection of diagnostic data.

- ▶ View the diagnostic data collection options Microsoft requests for this error (this option is not always present).

- ▶ Create a custom diagnostic data collection configuration to include a memory dump, specific files from the hard disk, Windows Management Instrumentation (WMI) queries of any type, and copies of registry keys you specify.

- ▶ Select to show no error information to the user, even if Microsoft has provided a solution link for that error.

- ▶ View and test a solution link if Microsoft has provided one.

- ▶ Specify your own custom solution link, rather than none, or one Microsoft may provide.

Figure 16.10 applies most of the custom features. Note that we selected collecting the WindowsUpdate.log file, running a WMI query that returns the computer domain, manufacturer name, and other data, and collecting a registry key with the current anti-malware signatures used by Windows Defender. We also created a demonstration web page as a custom error solution.

After applying these customizations to the error bucket for our ACCVIO.exe application error group, we can collect the custom diagnostic data and furnish users with a custom solution link each time they encounter this error. Additional options for customizing the handling and forwarding of crash and hang error information are located at the Settings node in the Administration space of the Operations console. We will cover these options later in this chapter in the "CEIP and the Microsoft Privacy Statement" section.

Next, we will again run our ACCVIO.exe error-generating utility. When the WER client asks permission to send more information, the list of files to upload now includes the WindowsUpdate.log file, as we expected. When we review the contents of the .CAB file, we will also find a registry.txt file with the custom registry data, and a wql.txt file with the WMI query information we wanted to collect.

Additionally, when the user clicks for more information about their error, they are directed to our custom error link on the corporate intranet—rather than the Microsoft online crash analysis link on the Internet. Figure 16.11 contrasts the Microsoft online response on the left with the custom in-house response on the right. Notice that we included a pair of voting buttons and an external web hyperlink to our custom response.

16

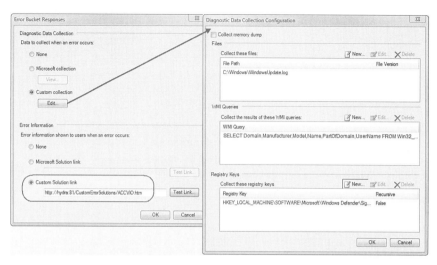

FIGURE 16.10   Specifying custom diagnostic data collection and solution link.

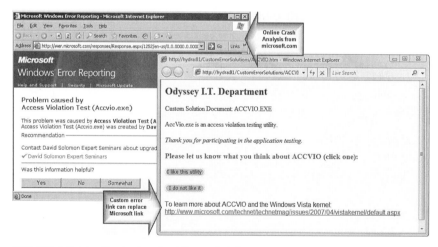

FIGURE 16.11   Replacing the Microsoft information link with a custom web-based form.

Incorporating Surveys

Consider employing a web-based survey technique to help solve particular errors in custom applications. You can stage a short automatic interview with the end user to gather targeted information. Some sample questions that might be helpful for a survey include the following:

1. What other applications (besides the one that crashed) were you running at the time of the crash?

2. What steps can the I.T. department take to reproduce the crash that occurred?

3. Will the application crash consistently if you follow the preceding steps? (Yes, Sometimes, or Never)

4. Are you running any macros, COM add-ins, or templates?

5. Does the crash occur for other people who log into this computer? (Yes, No, or Unknown)

TIP

Public Access to Microsoft WER Back-end Database

Microsoft's Winqual services enable software and hardware vendors to access reports to analyze and respond to problems caused by their applications. Vendors can use WER at no charge to view error reports.

You must register with Microsoft to participate in the Winqual program. You can use the Winqual website to view driver-specific, application-specific, or operating system-specific error reports associated with your organization, which are stored in error buckets in the Microsoft WER back-end. Each error report provides details related to that bucket, and you could then request a file of the associated data. For more information about Winqual, visit http://www.microsoft.com/whdc/maintain/StartWER.mspx.

Client Monitoring Reports

Beyond the five views available in the Agentless Exception Monitoring view folder in the Monitoring space, there are also four client monitoring reports in the Client Monitoring Views Library in the Reporting space of the Operations console. These reports aggregate the information in the monitoring views and perform data analysis. They also provide a historical record of the performance of applications in use on the network.

In addition to offering further ways to gain insight from collected AEM data, the reports provide a convenient way to extend access to this valuable data across a broader audience. Because you can schedule OpsMgr reports as Adobe .PDF files to network file shares or intranet sites, people do not need have direct interaction with the Operations console or OpsMgr report server to see which applications are causing the most trouble for users. As an example, you can have weekly or monthly reports automatically generated and posted to departmental servers for viewing by application developers and desktop administrators.

Using AEM Reporting to Track SLAs

Consider the scenario where an organization wants to hold a custom application contractor accountable for the solid performance of their custom code. AEM reports provide an objective and portable means to verify whether a particular application is crashing excessively or not. A Service Level Agreement (SLA) between the Application Service Provider (ASP) and the organization can specify that error rates will not exceed a certain threshold. The AEM reporting features can provide the metrics for compliance with such an SLA.

16

Top Applications Reports

The first of two application-related reports is the Top Applications report. This report displays a bar-graph chart showing the top applications reporting errors, a summary table, and a detailed table with the application name, version, crash count, and average daily crash count. Figure 16.12 shows this exported report, open in Adobe Viewer.

The Top Applications Report Summary table, in the center of the report, lists the average crash count per application and the average daily count per application. Knowing these average values helps you assess the statistical significance of the differences between the highest application(s) and the next few down the list in the detailed chart. The report defaults to including the top 25 applications. If you want to change this report setting, modify the N value in the parameters header of the report. For example, set the N value to five to report on the top five applications with errors.

The other application report is the Top Applications Growth and Resolution report. Like the Top Applications report, this report also defaults to N equals 25, where N is the number of top applications to include in the report. You can modify a second setting in the report parameters section, Interval Duration in Days, which defaults to seven. Because this report provides a measure of the percent of error increase over time, be careful not to specify a Previous Interval From value earlier than you have data for—this will result in an empty report. Figure 16.13 shows the graph portion of this report.

In the Top Applications Growth bar graph shown in Figure 16.13, the longer bars indicate a higher rate of error increase. The lower two listed applications, which show a 100% increase, increased in frequency more than the upper two applications from the first comparison period to the second. The significance of this graph, to us, is that even though we know (from the Top Applications report) that the second listed process has the highest quantity of errors, the other listed applications are getting worse at a faster rate than the top application.

This error-trending capability is a great way to detect a problem before it affects a large number of users. This may help you correlate an increase in errors with a recent configuration change, such as a patch or service pack deployment. You catch the new error because of its comparatively high rate of change, even though the raw number of reports for that particular error may be much less than the top applications.

Notice the unique construction of the Report Time field in the report header. The Report Current Interval and Report Previous Interval dates take their starting values from the Current Interval From and Previous Interval From values in the report parameters. Those are the start dates of the two comparison periods. The report construction then adds the Interval Duration in Days you specify to both dates, to arrive at the end dates of the two sampling periods. This report lends itself to comparing one week to the previous week, or to the same week in the previous month.

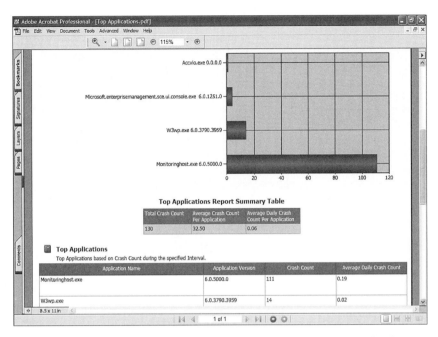

FIGURE 16.12   The Top Applications report quickly shows which applications are causing the most problems.

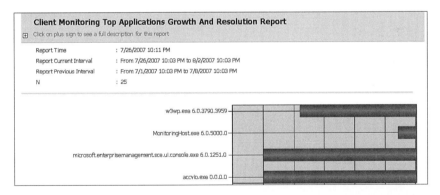

FIGURE 16.13   The Top Applications Growth report compares the error rates of two periods.

Top Error Groups Reports

A second pair of AEM reports focuses on error groups, rather than applications with errors. The main difference between the application error reports and the error group reports is that the application error reports list one instance of an application, summing up the errors associated with all error signatures received from that application. Compare this to the error group reports that include an entry for each error signature, regardless of what application it came from.

The error group reports display data about individual error buckets, while the application reports aggregate data from all error buckets of the same application. You can use the application-based reports to see what applications in general are causing problems, and then use the error group-based reports to identify exactly which unique errors are responsible for the most error events.

The first of two error group reports included with OpsMgr 2007 is the Top Error Groups report. This report displays a bar-graph chart with the top reported errors, a summary table, and a detailed table with the application name, application version, error group ID, bucket type, crash count, and average daily crash count. Figure 16.14 shows the detailed table portion of this report.

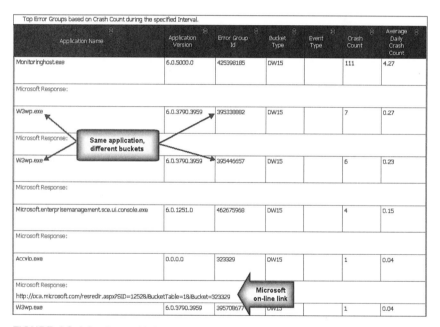

FIGURE 16.14   Spot which errors have Microsoft resolution links in the Top Error Groups report.

In the Top Error Groups report displayed in Figure 16.14, we highlighted two error buckets associated with the same application. We also placed an arrow next to an error group that has a Microsoft response available from online crash analysis. Periodically reviewing this report is a great way to find out which errors users are experiencing that Microsoft may already have a solution for.

A unique column in the Top Error Groups report lists the bucket type that the error group is based on. There are eight bucket types defined in the Operations Manager 2007 SDK (Software Development Kit); we list them in Table 16.1. The various bucket types are made available to developers to help them code WER support into their applications.

TABLE 16.1   AEM Bucket Types

Bucket Type	Description
AppCompat	Application-compatible bucket type
Blue	Blue screen
DW15	Watson 1.5 (legacy) error report
DW20	Watson 2.0 error report
Generic	Generic bucket type
Setup	Setup errors
Shutdown	Shutdown errors
Simple	Simple bucket type

The other error group report is the Top Error Groups Growth and Resolution report. This report shows the top error groups based on their growth and resolution rate during the specified period. Like the Top Applications Growth and Resolution report, this report compares the average daily crash count during one multi-day period (the Previous Interval), against a second multi-day period of equal length (the Current Interval). The resulting quotient, the Crash Count Percentile Increase, calls attention to error groups that are growing faster than others are.

CEIP and the Microsoft Privacy Statement

When you ran the Configure Client Monitoring wizard to enable AEM on a management server in your management group, you could elect to participate in the Customer Experience Improvement Program (CEIP). When CEIP is active on a client or server, it gathers information about Microsoft products used on that particular computer, processes it, and sends it to Microsoft, combining it with other CEIP data for further analysis. The transmission uses outbound TCP port 51907. The collected data is used to help Microsoft solve problems and to improve the products and features that customers use most often. Examples of collected data include the following:

▶ Configuration, such as the number of processors, the version of Windows used, and the number of network connections.

▶ Performance and reliability, such as program responsiveness and the speed of data transmission.

▶ Program use, such as the most frequently used features and Help and Support center usage.

Instead of having a large number of clients each reporting this data individually, you can have your clients send their CEIP data to the AEM server as a central collection point for the organization. The management server hosting AEM then forwards the data to Microsoft. This feature of OpsMgr helps minimize (or eliminate) direct access to the Internet by client workstations. In addition, some enterprise firewalls might not open port 51907 between internal networks and the Internet. Using the CEIP forwarding component of AEM means only the OpsMgr management server running AEM needs outbound port 51907 open to access the Internet.

A compelling reason to use the AEM features in OpsMgr is you can control how and when your organization forwards information to Microsoft. Let's explore the customization options available to the OpsMgr administrator for these features.

Navigate to the Settings node in the Administration space and open the properties page of the Privacy setting. There are four tabs controlling different aspects of CEIP and AEM as they relate to exchanging information over the Internet with Microsoft. The first three tabs (CEIP, Operational Data Reports, and Error Reporting) control your organization's level of participation in Microsoft's CEIP and WER programs as they relate to the function of OpsMgr itself. The fourth tab is Error Transmission and deals with handling crash and hang report forwarding for all applications in the management group, including OpsMgr. We will look at the functionality of these settings tabs, as follows:

▶ **CEIP**—On this tab, you can join the CEIP or select not to join the program.

This setting has a different function than the CEIP Forwarding screen of the Configure Client Monitoring wizard. When you enabled AEM by running that wizard, if you chose to collect and forward CEIP data, you redirected client computer CEIP transmissions from the Internet to the management server. You were not turning CEIP on or off for any particular user or application—that is still determined by the user, unless Group Policy or some other mechanism is in place to force enabling of CEIP features in an application.

The setting on this particular tab turns CEIP on or off for the Operations Manager 2007 software application in your management group. Enabling this setting facilitates CEIP data collection from the management group. Microsoft receives this data along with all the other CEIP data from other applications in your organization.

Specifically, CEIP collects information about computer hardware with an installed Operations console, and how all Operations console users in the management group use the product. The setting for this tab is initially set when you install the OpsMgr database component for your management group—the setup process asks if you want to participate in CEIP as part of the management group setup.

▶ **Operational Data Reports**—This is a unique feature for Operations Manager, a sort of super-CEIP. If you elect to send Operational Data Reports (ODR) to Microsoft, CEIP generates weekly reports to upload to Microsoft. ODR gathers information about OpsMgr's usage in the management group. Microsoft collects the configuration data to understand customer environments. In addition, these reports help Microsoft determine what extra rules, monitors, or management packs can help customers lower the total cost of monitoring their networks. CEIP for OpsMgr, enabled on the first tab of the Privacy settings, only looks at use of the Operations console. ODR looks beyond console usage patterns and assesses product usage in monitoring devices.

You must install the OpsMgr Reporting component for ODR to function. You can see the ODR reports used by this feature in the Reporting space of the Operations console. These reports are intended to be most useful to Microsoft, rather than the administrators of the management group. However, you can run the reports at any time yourself and see what data Microsoft is receiving, or would receive with ODR enabled. Here are the three reports contained in the Microsoft ODR Report Library:

▶ **Management Group**—Displays workload classes (enterprise vs. standard) performed by management servers, their operating systems, and the percentage of virtual and cluster nodes managed. This report helps Microsoft understand the infrastructure customers use to deploy OpsMgr and the amount of load on the management group. Figure 16.15 is a screenshot of the Management Group ODR Report.

▶ **Management Packs**—This is a very long report that contains three detailed tables—the tables report on the installed management packs and their versions, the overrides applied in the management group, and the rules created through the Operations console.

▶ **Most Common Alerts**—Shows an overview of the top 24 most common alerts across all management packs. This is the same report you see in the Microsoft Generic Report Library, just preconfigured with a seven-day date range. Microsoft uses this information to improve management pack quality and to reduce alerting noise levels.

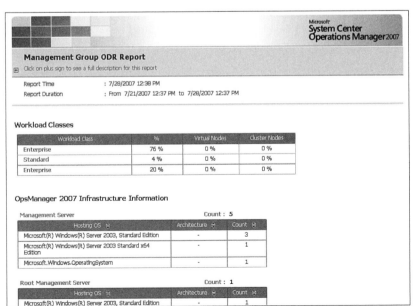

FIGURE 16.15   The Management Group ODR Report summarizes your infrastructure.

▶ **Error Reporting**—This tab allows you to control the participation of OpsMgr 2007 itself in the error reporting mechanism. You can select to not generate error reports, to prompt the user for approval before sending error reports, or to automatically send error reports without prompting the user.

If you enable error reporting on this tab, Watson and WER clients on OpsMgr component computers will initiate the error reporting process when crashes and hangs occur in the OpsMgr product. If AEM is also enabled, those error reports will be collected from the management group and forwarded to Microsoft along with all the other crash and hang reports from other applications in your organization.

The OpsMgr components using this setting are the management servers, gateway servers, and agents. Error reporting behavior for the OpsMgr database and data warehouse uses the settings specified for SQL Server 2005, rather than those specified on this tab for the OpsMgr components.

▶ **Error Transmission**—The error transmission tab is the location of some important configuration settings for the management group. Figure 16.16 displays this tab. There are three sections:

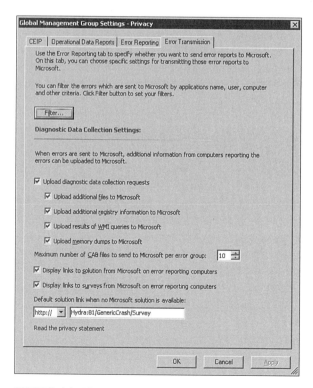

FIGURE 16.16   The Error Transmission tab in the Privacy settings controls many AEM functions.

▶ The top section with the Filter button

▶ The center section that involves uploading errors to Microsoft

▶ The bottom three items controlling what links users may see after an application error occurs

You can filter the errors sent to Microsoft by application name, user, computer, and other criteria. This lets you exempt your most sensitive users, computers, and applications from having their error reports forwarded to Microsoft. This filter capability lets the bulk of your organization contribute error information to Microsoft's back-end WER servers, while reserving specific confidential information to the organization's AEM servers only. Pressing the Filter button allows you to specify these exemption options:

▶ Specific users (from Active Directory)

▶ Specific computers (from Active Directory)

▶ Specific applications

▶ Specific modules

▶ Specific application error types (bucket types, such as DW15 or Blue)

▶ Specific event types (such as Appcrash or MPTelemetery)

In the central area of the Error Transmission tab shown in Figure 16.16, labeled Diagnostic Data Collection Settings, you can enable or disable uploading of data collection requests globally. Additionally, you can granularly enable or disable the type of data uploaded to Microsoft's back-end WER services. The types of data you can control are additional files, registry information, WMI queries, and memory dumps. You can also modify the maximum number of .CAB files uploaded to Microsoft per error group (bucket). The default is ten, which is probably sufficient to notify Microsoft that an organization is experiencing multiple reports with the same error signature!

At the bottom of the Error Transmission tab is a location to optionally specify a default solution link when no Microsoft or custom solution link is available. If you populate this field, every time a user's Watson or WER client completes the error reporting procedure, they will see an Error Reporting dialog box with a More Information link, even if neither you nor Microsoft specified a solution link for that error. If your default link points to a generic crash survey form, you can collect information from users about errors as they occur in your organization, even the first time they are reported.

We recommend that Operations Manager administrators enable some or all of the Microsoft forwarding features, particularly those that apply to OpsMgr itself. Having Microsoft receive such feedback on a large scale from the real world enables more rapid and accurate improvement of the products we all use for our livelihood. Just as Watson/WER collection shows Microsoft the top problems and allows them to target their

16

hotfix, update, and service pack development, CEIP and ODR show Microsoft what is working in their products and what features get used the most. That data provides input into development of add-ons, feature packs, and new versions of software that build on the features most in demand.

If you enable all the CEIP, ODR, and Watson/WER collection and forwarding features in your AEM deployment, Microsoft will receive a lot of information about your organization. There is naturally some discomfort at sharing some organizational data like server names and some user data such as file names. You can opt-out your most sensitive sources of information using the Privacy settings previously described in this section.

Error information uploaded to Microsoft is indexed by the nature of the error—i.e., the target error bucket—not the identity or location of the contributing organization. The only uniquely identifiable information associated with uploading error reports to Microsoft is the source IP address. Microsoft uses the IP address to generate aggregate statistics; it is not used to identify or contact you.

As for the safety and security of the Watson/WER back-end services themselves, Microsoft assures us they use a variety of security technologies and procedures to help protect personal information from unauthorized access, use, or disclosure. For example, Microsoft stores the information on computer servers with limited access, located in controlled facilities. We are not aware of any instances where Microsoft has been accused or suspected of misuse of error reporting data. Conversely, we are aware of numerous occasions where error and CEIP information have resulted in improvements in Microsoft software that directly benefitted us and other customers.

Microsoft publishes a simple and clear two-page Privacy Statement for the Microsoft Error Reporting Service, available at http://oca.microsoft.com/en/dcp20.asp. There is also a specific Microsoft System Center Operations Manager 2007 Privacy Statement at http://www.microsoft.com/systemcenter/privacy/opsmgr.mspx. The specific OpsMgr privacy statement includes sections that address the privacy issues of each component described in this chapter, including CEIP, ODR, and WER.

Monitoring Agent-Managed Systems

Although many or most client computers in your organization may participate in Agentless Exception Monitoring (AEM), some client computers should also have an OpsMgr agent installed on them. In this section, we will explore the three scenarios where it is a good idea to consider deploying agents on some client computers, as follows:

▶ Smaller organizations, perhaps those with 50 or fewer computers, may find it simplest to deploy an agent on every client computer, particularly if their client computer hardware can leverage hardware vendor management packs imported into the management group. This also lets all the computers participate in other OpsMgr features like Audit Collection Services (ACS).

▶ Mid-size organizations, between 50 and 500 client computers, can make the decision on whether to have all computers with agents—or implement a mix of AEM-only and agents on clients—based on economics of the licensing, and the hardware capacity of the computer(s) running the OpsMgr server and database components. A single-server OpsMgr management group can easily handle 50 client computers; however, somewhere on the road toward and above 500 computers, a single management server is going to start to slow down.

▶ Larger organizations—for example, those with above 500 client computers—will almost certainly employ a mix of AEM-only clients and clients with agents. This is because the large client populations let you leverage statistical techniques like the significance of random sampling and looking for rate of change.

The math and the economics make deploying a full monitoring agent to every client unnecessary and expensive. In addition, deploying an agent to any computer incurs acquisition costs for the agent license, an incremental cost of resources consumed in the Operations Manager management group, and an ongoing cost to support the agent in terms of licensing, maintaining, and upgrading.

Organizations of any size should consider deploying OpsMgr agents on client computers in these categories and scenarios:

▶ **Aggregated (Collective) Client Monitoring**—Scenario: Random, proportional sampling of client computers within each client population. The more homogeneous the client population, the smaller the sample can be and remain statistically significant. If you have a set of various desktop images for certain models of computers, try to monitor equally across each desktop model. You generally don't care if the individual computers are always on the network; computers can be powered off, or mobile.

▶ **Business Critical Monitoring**—Scenarios: VIP and high-impact workstations and application boxes such as IP Telephony, kiosk, POS, Supervisory Control And Data Acquisition (SCADA) instrumentation, and network administration workstations. We recommend you select at least one client computer at each branch or remote office for Business Critical Monitoring. You generally want to know if these computers go offline—you monitor them like servers for high availability.

▶ **Synthetic Transaction Monitoring**—Scenarios: Endpoint watcher nodes defined in the health model of a distributed application, remote/proxy agent to monitor another device, or third-party/external service from a local point of presence. We recommend you seek ways to exploit this feature in OpsMgr. You can easily deploy multiple, smart sets of watcher nodes to measure the end-to-end service delivery of distributed enterprise applications. Watcher nodes for Synthetic Transaction Monitoring are subject to Business Critical Monitoring as well.

16

TIP

Comparing Aggregated to Business Critical Monitoring

Aggregated (or Collective) Client Monitoring is the default client monitoring mode for all discovered client computers after you import the client monitoring management packs. Some Aggregated Client Monitoring client computers are also selected to be subject to Business Critical Monitoring. Business Critical Monitoring and Aggregated Client Monitoring both use the OpsMgr 2007 agent for collecting Aggregated Client Monitoring data; the management packs are just tuned differently. Specifically, the Business Critical management pack allows for individual alerting.

Client Monitoring Management Packs

If you have decided to include client monitoring as a mission of your management group (in addition to monitoring servers, network devices, and distributed applications), then you begin by importing the client monitoring management packs. The management packs for monitoring the Windows XP and Windows 2000 Professional client operating systems—as well as the Information Worker management packs covering Office XP, 2003, and 2007 and Internet Explorer 5, 6, and 7—are included with the initial Operations Manager 2007 software distribution, although you will want to check the System Center pack catalog for updates. You will download the Windows Vista Client Monitoring management pack from the Operations Manager 2007 online catalog.

Five operating system management packs need to be imported in order to use all the client operating system monitoring features, as follows:

▶ **Microsoft.Windows.Client.Library.mp**—Required for monitoring both Windows 2000 and XP client operating systems.

▶ **Microsoft.Windows.Client.2000.mp**—Enables collective monitoring of Windows 2000 Professional client computers.

▶ **Microsoft.Windows.Client.XP.mp**—Enables collective monitoring of Windows XP client computers.

▶ **Microsoft.Windows.Client.Vista.mp**—Enables collective monitoring of Windows Vista client computers. Only aggregated alerting is available on Vista clients; you cannot add Vista client computers to Business Critical Monitoring.

▶ **Microsoft.Windows.Client.BusinessCritical.xml**—Enables selected collective monitoring clients to also be Business Critical Monitoring clients. This management pack has a dependency on both the Windows 2000 and Windows XP operating system management packs, so even if you have no Windows 2000 clients to manage, you still need to import the Windows 2000 client management pack in order to import and use the Business Critical Monitoring management pack with Windows XP client computers.

Nine management packs are part of the Information Worker monitoring feature of OpsMgr. In addition to a Common Library management pack, there are management packs for the following products:

▶ Each version of Microsoft Office (XP, 2003, and 2007)

▶ Windows Explorer

▶ Internet Explorer

▶ Windows Media Player

▶ Outlook Express and Mail

▶ MSN Messenger

Figure 16.17 illustrates the matrix of client monitoring options available with OpsMgr 2007. Importing the client monitoring management packs enables the Collective (Aggregated) and Business Critical Monitoring features.

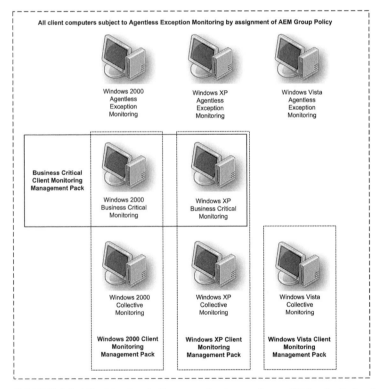

FIGURE 16.17   Matrix of client monitoring options: AEM-only, Collective, and Business Critical.

Import the client monitoring management packs in the conventional manner using the Operations console's Administration space. After the management packs are imported, you will notice a single top-level view folder—Microsoft Windows Client—listed in the Monitoring space. That folder contains all the views installed by the client operating system and Information Worker management packs. Now we will look at the new views, reports, and functionality you can expect after importing the client monitoring management packs.

Collective Health Monitoring Management Packs

Collective (or Aggregated) Client Monitoring is Microsoft's solution to effectively measure the quality of users' desktop experiences without overloading the management group and IT support staff. Microsoft's design goal with the client monitoring management packs was that they should require zero configuration to function in a useful way and that they would not be noisy—that is, not create a management burden to evaluate a lot of non-critical alerts.

Collective Client Monitoring gathers and stores information about client computers, but does not monitor individual computers or generate alerts about specific computers.

Collective Client Monitoring is the default configuration for the Windows Client and Information Worker management packs. In other words, when you discover and install OpsMgr agents on client computers after importing the client monitoring management packs, those client computers are automatically and immediately subject to Collective Client Monitoring. Usage scenarios for Collective Client Monitoring center around identifying when large numbers of client computers are experiencing the same problem (using the Monitoring views in the Operations console), and performing historical and trending analysis on collected data (using the Reporting views).

We will first look at the Enterprise Health Monitoring views in the Microsoft Windows Client view folder of the Monitoring space. Figure 16.18 highlights the three Enterprise Health Monitoring views and exposes the health model for the Outlook Client Mail Access State view.

The Outlook Client Mail Access collective monitoring feature enables the Information Worker management pack to flag when large volumes of Outlook clients are unable to send and receive mail. Specifically, the client mail access monitor changes state and generates an alert when 10% or more of the Outlook application instances managed by OpsMgr are unable to contact their respective Exchange server.

Other views you can see in the Enterprise Health Monitoring folder in Figure 16.18 are the Internet Explorer Services State and Windows Explorer Data Source Services State. Although the Outlook Client Mail Access view is enabled automatically, the other two Enterprise Health Monitoring views require configuration before any data will appear in the console:

  ▶ **Internet Explorer Services State**—Identifies the inability of client computers to access a specified web application, such as the order-taking process at an e-commerce website. To enable this feature, run the Add Monitoring wizard, creating a Web Application to detect a failure to connect to the specified website. Next use the Windows Internet Explorer Service template in the Distributed Application Designer to create a Distributed Application based on the Web Application. This populates the folder with an Internet Explorer Service whose health represents a client's ability to access the specific website.

▶ **Windows Explorer Data Source Services State**—Identifies the inability of client computers to access a specified OLE DB data source, such as an Excel spreadsheet that connects to a database. To use this view, run the Add Monitoring wizard to create an OLE DB Data Source that detects a failure to connect to the specified database. Next use the Windows Explorer Data Source Service template in the Distributed Application Designer to create a Distributed Application based on the OLEDB Data Source; that populates the folder with a Windows Explorer Data Source service whose health represents a client's ability to access the specific database.

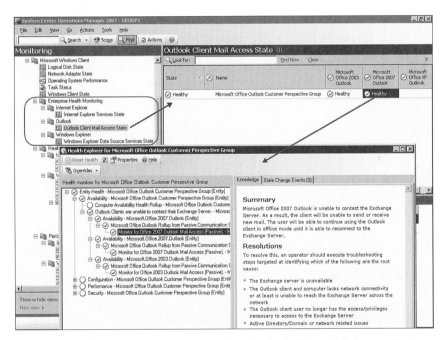

FIGURE 16.18   Collective Monitoring of the Outlook Client Mail Access State.

The report views added to the management group by the client monitoring management packs are probably more useful on an ongoing basis, as the Collective Monitoring views in the Monitoring space are most relevant when you have a major problem in progress. You can see the extensive list of Information Worker report folders and views in Figure 16.19.

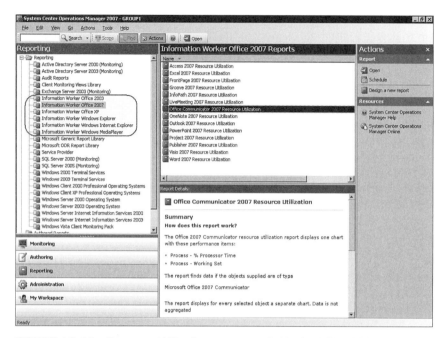

FIGURE 16.19   Resource Utilization reports available for Office 2007 products.

You can access the Information Worker reports from the Reporting space, as shown in Figure 16.19, and from the Information Worker Application Health Monitoring folder in the Monitoring space. In that folder are the Office Application Health and Windows Application Health dashboard views. For example, if you select an instance of an Office application on one or more client computers in the Office Application Health view folder, the appropriate Resource Utilization report becomes available in the Actions pane. Clicking the report link opens a report view with the selected computer(s) pre-defined as objects in the report parameters. Likewise, selecting a computer in the Windows Application Health view makes a pre-defined report link available for the version of Internet Explorer and/or Media Player installed on the selected computer.

TIP

CD Content—Client Monitoring Alert Thresholds

The Client and Information Worker Collective Monitoring management packs, as well as the Business Critical Monitoring management pack, utilize pre-defined thresholds that are not exposed in the Operations console. For example, Office application thresholds are greater than 90% CPU utilization or 500 MB memory utilization for any single Office application. Client OS thresholds are greater than 95% CPU utilization, less than 10 MB available memory, or greater than 80% committed memory. To see all the thresholds in your management group, run the PowerShell script get_thresholds.ps1 by Microsoft's Boris Yanushpolsky, included with the CD that accompanies this book.

The output from the script includes the type of objects the monitor is targeted to, the display name and threshold used by the monitor, whether the monitor generates an alert when its state changes, if the alert is autoresolved, and the severity of the alert.

Figure 16.20 shows the Internet Explorer 6.0 Resource Usage report for a specific Windows XP computer during a 24-hour period. Because this report focuses on just one computer, the sample count of 96 reflects exactly a 15-minute sample rate for this performance counter. We can also note that with an average processor time of .1%, Internet Explorer is not causing any problems on this computer. You can see how the reporting features let you zero in on the performance of particular Collective Monitoring client computers.

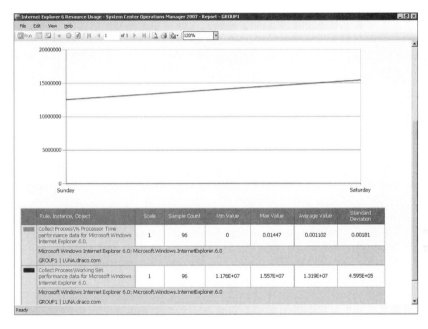

FIGURE 16.20   Resource Usage report for Internet Explorer 6.0 on a Windows XP computer.

Collective monitoring of Windows 2000 and Windows XP computers provides almost identical functionality for both operating systems. Collective monitoring of Windows Vista computers, in contrast, has a lot more features that result from the richer diagnostics infrastructure built into Vista. Look at the type of information that you can get from Collective Monitoring of Vista client computers in the boot performance report shown in Figure 16.21.

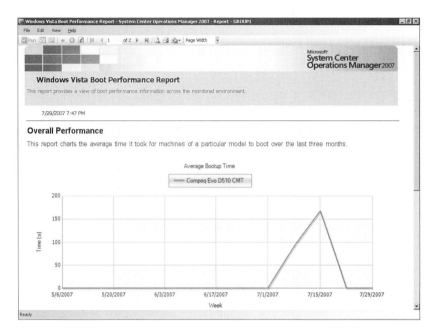

FIGURE 16.21   View trends and comparisons in boot time between client computer populations.

If you had multiple models of desktop computers in your organization, this report lets you compare how long each model took to reboot. That would quantify the speed improvement of newer, faster computers compared to older, slower ones—as well as allow you to spot an increasing boot time within the same model family, which would merit further investigation. There is similar analysis for Resume, Shutdown, and Standby performance of Windows Vista computers. There reports are tools that really help the IT department understand issues users may be facing in more detail than "my computer is slow!"

Using the data collected by the client monitoring management packs, administrators can objectively compare the performance of the same application on different client operating systems, or different versions of the same application on the same operating system. Figure 16.22 displays the Windows Application Performance view in the Information Worker Application Performance view folder.

Figure 16.22 compares the performance of Internet Explorer 7.0 on two different Vista client computers over a 24-hour period. The Vista Client Monitoring management pack integrates with the Windows 2000 and XP management packs to allow you to compare application performance across platforms. For example, you could compare the experience of Internet Explorer (IE) 7.0 on both Windows XP and Windows Vista computers to see what advantage users would experience by upgrading the operating system to Windows Vista. Alternatively, you could assess IE 6 versus IE 7 performance on your Windows XP computers to help make a decision about upgrading in-place to IE 7.

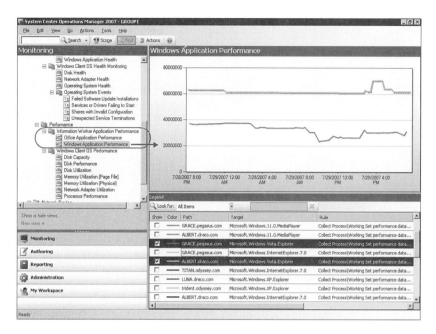

FIGURE 16.22   Compare the performance of information worker applications.

We think that once OpsMgr administrators become familiar with the significantly improved manageability of Windows Vista compared to Windows 2000 and XP, they will lean even more toward migration to the new client operating system. Take a look at the reports available for the Windows Vista operating system in Figure 16.23. There are 17 sophisticated, client-focused reports available to view that promise to improve the client experience for organizations running Windows Vista. (There are six generic reports available for Windows 2000 and XP clients: Logical Disk, Memory, Network Adapter, NTFS Quota, Physical Disk, and Processor.)

TIP

Give the Vista Reports Some Time

Initially, Windows Vista Client Monitoring reports may contain no information. This is normal, since reports built on aggregated data require at least 24 hours of collection. Many of the Vista reports are designed to trend data over large timeframes, such as three to six months, so there may not be much useful data for several weeks after installing the Vista Client Monitoring management pack. Also, consider that a lack of data for reports based on failures, such as disk failure, might mean none of those failures has occurred in your organization.

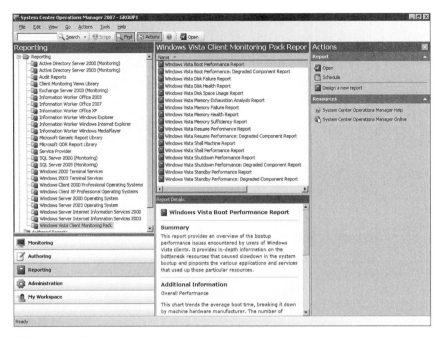

FIGURE 16.23   Reports for the Vista operating system focus on the client experience.

Business Critical Monitoring Management Pack

Business Critical Monitoring least one client computer at each is the most comprehensive client monitoring solution with OpsMgr. This is the only level of monitoring that can watch client computers individually and generate alerts. Adding client computers to Business Critical Monitoring requires more overhead than other types of client monitoring. You can only bring client computers into Business Critical Monitoring after discovery takes place and the clients have an agent installed on them. This means that client computers must first be made Collective Monitoring clients; then they can be promoted to Business Critical Monitoring status.

Here are the steps to perform to add client computers to Business Critical Monitoring:

1. Navigate to the Authoring space and select the Groups node.

2. Type **Business Critical** in the Look for box and press the Find Now control.

3. Select the appropriate group for the operating system of the client computers to add. For example, if you are adding Windows XP client computers, select the All Business Critical Windows XP Clients group. Right-click on the group and select Properties.

4. On the Explicit Members tab, press the Add/Remote Objects button.

5. In the Search for drop-down box, select Windows Client XP Computer and press the Search button. (If you are adding Windows 2000 clients, select Windows Client 2000 Computer.)

6. All the Windows XP computers with OpsMgr agents installed will appear in the Available items area.

7. Select one or more computers to be added to Business Critical Monitoring, and push the Add button. After confirming that the desired computers are in the Selected objects area, push the OK button, then OK again.

8. Repeat steps 3 through 7 for the other operating system—i.e., if you also have Windows 2000 client computers to be added to Business Critical Monitoring.

Figure 16.24 illustrates these steps to add Windows XP client computers to the All Business Critical Windows XP Clients group.

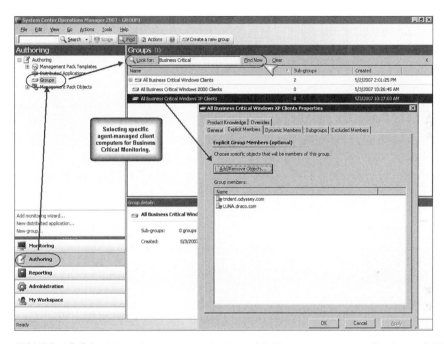

FIGURE 16.24   Manual step is required to add client computers to Business Critical Monitoring.

Populating either or both the All Business Critical Windows XP Clients and the All Business Critical Windows 2000 Clients groups will enable Business Critical Monitoring in your organization. Those groups are the target of an override that enables most of the monitors and alerts included in the client management packs, particularly those that raise individual alerts for disk health and operating system health events.

When you enable Business Critical Monitoring for one or more client computers, you can optionally enable Advanced Monitoring on selected client computer objects. A definition of Advanced Monitoring, in the context of Business Critical Monitoring clients, is a monitor setting that you must manually enable.

Advanced Monitoring is disabled out of the box with OpsMgr. The reasoning is that Microsoft wants to protect the performance and usability of the OpsMgr management group, at the expense of making you do a little extra work. Microsoft wanted to prevent hundreds or thousands of client computers from overwhelming a management group after they are discovered. Therefore, some monitors that are data-processing intensive are turned off, even for Business Critical Monitoring. It is up to you to identify any Advanced Monitoring features that you need, and then enable them on a case-by-case basis.

An example of Advanced Monitoring is the Network Adapter state and performance views. Some network adapter performance information is not collected by default, even from client computers subject to Business Critical Monitoring. Examining the Network Adapter State view in the root of the Microsoft Windows Client view folder, or the Network Adapter Health dashboard view in the Windows Client OS Health Monitoring, shows all unknown status icons for each computer's network interface(s). Those monitors are in the Advanced Monitoring category. To enable Advanced Monitoring on an object of interest, such as the network interface of a VIP or mission-critical client computer, follow these steps:

1. Select the Not monitored status indicator in the results pane of the monitor that you want to enable. Right-click and select Open -> Health Explorer.

2. Expand the branch of the health model that contains the monitor you want to enable. Click on the monitor to select it.

3. Press the Override button and select Override the Monitor -> For a Specific Object of Type.

4. The Select Object picker should appear; select the matching object that you want to monitor and press OK.

5. The Override Properties page should appear; tick the Override box in the top Enabled line and change the Override Setting from False to True. Be sure and save the override to a custom management pack (not the Default management pack) and press OK.

6. Push OK and close the Health Explorer. Within several minutes, the state icon for the object should change from Not Monitored to Healthy.

Although some business critical monitors fall into the Advanced Monitoring category (such as some network interface monitors), most of the monitoring views in the Operations console provide data on client computers added to Business Critical Monitoring without further configuration. This is referred to by Microsoft as *Standard Monitoring* for business critical clients (requiring no additional configuration), compared to Advanced Monitoring.

All the views in the Windows Client OS Performance view folder feature Standard Monitoring, and are populated for business critical Windows 2000 and Windows XP client computers. Figure 16.25 shows the Disk Utilization dashboard view in the Windows Client OS Performance view folder.

In Figure 16.25, all views in the left pane except the Microsoft Windows Client view are hidden, and the navigation buttons are collapsed, exposing the entire client monitoring view folder hierarchy. The Disk Utilization dashboard view is seen in the Results pane. Notice each logical disk of each business critical client is available for charting in the Results pane.

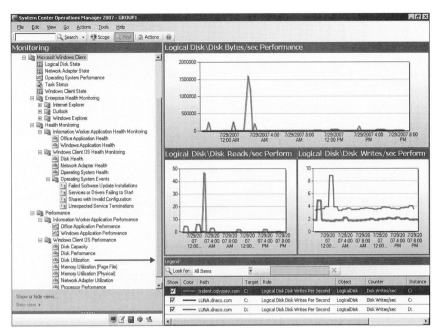

FIGURE 16.25   Standard monitoring for business critical client computers: disk, memory, network, and processor.

Likewise, each of the other dashboard views in the Windows Client OS Performance folder are populated with computer names of business critical Windows 2000 and Windows XP client computers: Disk Capacity, Disk Performance, Memory Utilization (Page File and Physical), Network Adapter Performance, and Processor Performance. Windows Vista client computers cannot take part in business critical client monitoring in this release of OpsMgr; remember that the Vista management pack is only for Collective Monitoring.

Further up the view hierarchy in Figure 16.25, notice the Windows Client OS Health Monitoring view folder. This is where you perform operational monitoring of your business critical client computers. Alerts raised by business critical clients appear here. There are the Disk, Network Adapter, and Operating System Health dashboard views, as well as the Operating System Events folder with four subfolders (Failed Software Update Installations, Services or Drivers Failing to Start, Shares with Invalid Configuration, and Unexpected Service Terminations).

Remember to look at the tasks area of the Action pane when you select particular business critical client monitors. Context-sensitive tasks are provided with most views, such as Run Chkdsk when logical disks are selected in the Results pane.

In addition to the views in the Monitoring space that are populated with data from business critical client computers, you can run reports to learn more details about client computer performance. In Figure 16.26, we show the Processor Report, targeted to the Windows XP computers that we placed in Business Critical Monitoring.

FIGURE 16.26   Selecting multiple clients to report on aggregates their data and performs statistical analysis.

Here are the steps to follow to produce the Processor Report seen in Figure 16.26:

1. Navigate to the Reporting space and select the Windows Client XP Professional Operating System report folder.

2. Select the Processor Report and press the Open button.

3. Change the From time from Today to Yesterday (this creates a 24-hour report window).

4. Press the Add Group button, and in the Contains field, type **Windows XP** and press the Search button.

5. Select the All Business Critical Windows XP Clients group name; then press the Add button and the OK button.

6. Press the Run button to generate the report.

In Figure 16.26, we circled the column headers and the values in the lower row for the % Processor Time Total. Notice that there is a population size of two (2) objects (the two Windows XP computers we placed into Business Critical Monitoring), and that the various columns present statistics using the aggregated data from all computers in the report's population.

This is a different kind of report view than you might be used to seeing, which typically is a chart of server-based performance. Most server-based reports call out the performance of individual servers, whereas the client-based reports, even for business critical clients, emphasize collective performance.

Preparing for Synthetic Transaction Monitoring

Chapters 18, "Using Synthetic Transactions," and 19, "Managing a Distributed Environment," of this book provide examples of employing client computers as watcher nodes for Synthetic Transaction Monitoring. However, we include this section in Chapter 16, "Client Monitoring," to remind you to plan to import the client management packs in order to use that feature. You can't select client computers to be watcher nodes for your distributed applications unless you have deployed an OpsMgr agent to them.

Often, strategically located client computers are the best platform to serve as watcher nodes for end-to-end monitoring of enterprise applications. You need a monitor "at the end" to capture service delivery in the context that matters, which is usually at the user desktop. This technique is also known as *User Perspective Monitoring*.

We recommend that all client computers selected as distributed application watcher nodes also are subject to Business Critical Monitoring. You need to be alerted when a watcher node for a distributed application is down or malfunctioning; otherwise, you may not be able to correlate the root cause of a distributed application failure alert to the watcher node itself being down.

Even if your organization does not intend to employ any of the client monitoring features we have talked about in this chapter, it is still a good idea to be familiar with the client operating system management packs, and to import them into your management group. That way, your monitoring infrastructure is staged to deploy watcher nodes in support of managing end-to-end enterprise applications.

16

> **NOTE**
>
> **AEM Resource Kit Utilities**
>
> Wave 1 of the OpsMgr 2007 Resource Kit includes two utilities pertaining to AEM: the AEM Toolkit and the AEM Test tool.
>
> The AEM Toolkit contains an unsealed mangement pack, which is documented as identifying generic errors sent from WER clients to AEM-enabled management servers. The AEM Test tool is intended to help you determine whether AEM is running correctly by crashing itself so you can check the results produced by OpsMgr.
>
> However, we were unable to produce any results (or crashed applications), after trying to test both utilities in multiple management groups running OpsMgr 2007 RTM as well as the SP1 Release Candidate, so we cannot discuss these tools. There also appears to be a dearth of knowledge in the newsgroups or elsewhere.

Summary

We started this chapter with an introduction to the roots of Microsoft's client monitoring initiatives, Dr. Watson and the Corporate Error Reporting program. We talked both about the historical challenges presented by client monitoring, and the enormous opportunity to improve the organizational bottom line by investing in this area. After explaining the architecture of Agentless Exception Monitoring, we gave examples of the value of collecting crash and hang information. We also described how to customize the AEM experience by collecting additional information from users and providing them with just-in-time solutions once errors occur. We introduced the concepts of Collective (or Aggregated) Client Monitoring and Business Critical Monitoring of client computers, and closed with a reminder of how client computers can play an important role in the end-to-end monitoring of distributed enterprise applications. Our next chapter, "Monitoring Network Devices," will help you connect all the dots between your clients and servers.

CHAPTER 17

Monitoring Network Devices

In this chapter, we discuss deploying Operations Manager 2007 (OpsMgr) to extend your monitoring reach to those computers and devices not running a Windows operating system. If you have a computer running a Windows operating system that you want to manage, of course you will deploy an OpsMgr agent to that system, or possibly set up that computer for agentless monitoring.

However, what if there are computers not running Windows operating systems? And how do you monitor devices that are not computers—devices that users depend on to get their work done, such as printers and network switches? You cannot deploy the OpsMgr agent to these non-Windows computers and devices, nor can you employ agentless monitoring. In both cases, the answer is to use the Simple Network Management Protocol (SNMP) monitoring features built into OpsMgr. In OpsMgr 2007, network devices are non-Windows computers and other devices managed with SNMP.

We strongly suggest that OpsMgr administrators monitor network devices alongside the computers in their organization. A fundamental concept of End-to-End (E2E) service monitoring is knowing the health of the devices between the major components delivering the service. Integrating network device status into health models of service delivery can tell a story and save hours of troubleshooting.

This chapter begins with a brief primer on the SNMP protocol itself, because the OpsMgr network device monitoring features are wrapped tightly around SNMP. We will then discover several SNMP-enabled devices on our managed networks and add those devices as objects to our management group. We will also spend some time on the basic network device monitoring features included with OpsMgr, receiving SNMP traps and viewing them in the Operations console. In addition, we will build-out our SNMP management capability by importing several hardware management packs and creating some custom SNMP-based rules and monitors.

SNMP Primer

In an electronic world that seems to always have competing standards—from longstanding Windows vs. Mac rivalries, to today's Blue-ray vs. HD-DVD media formats—there does exist a *lingua franca* among the intelligent machines of the world. That common language is SNMP, a protocol designed in the late 1980s to facilitate the exchange of management information between networked devices.

SNMP Architecture

The Simple Network Management Protocol is popular not only because it is truly simple in its operation, but because it is easy for manufacturers and vendors to use SNMP technology to add network management functions to their products. The SNMP architecture contains three entities:

- ▶ **Managed device**—Any piece of equipment connected to the data network that is SNMP compliant. These devices are also referred to as *network elements*.

- ▶ **SNMP agent**—A network management software module residing in a managed device. The agent collects data from the managed device, translating that information into a format you can pass over the network using SNMP.

- ▶ **Network Management System (NMS)**—An application that monitors and controls managed devices. The NMS issues requests, and devices return responses.

Communication channels in the SNMP architecture are narrowly defined. A network management system will exchange three primary types of messages:

- ▶ **SNMP Get**—Used by the NMS to retrieve one or more values from a SNMP agent by a read-only process. The get command is often used on a scheduled (synchronous) basis to verify the status of a managed device, in a process referred to as *polling*.

- ▶ **SNMP Set**—Used by the NMS to change the values of variables stored within the managed device, controlling the device by changing its settings.

- ▶ **SNMP Trap**—An unsolicited (or asynchronous) message sent from the agent to the NMS, often indicating a warning or error condition. When certain types of events occur, a managed device sends this immediate notification to the NMS.

Each of the primary SNMP message types (get, set, and trap) is associated with a *community name*, which is just a text string used like a password to authenticate the message sender. Figure 17.1 illustrates the interaction of the three components of the SNMP architecture and the three primary types of SNMP messages.

The left side of Figure 17.1 shows a NMS, and the right side has a managed device with a SNMP agent. In the case of most network hardware, the agent comes integrated into the firmware or Internetwork Operating System (IOS) of the managed device; you merely are able to enable and configure the agent, or disable it. Computers, including Windows computers, often have a separate SNMP agent software component you must install or add to the operating system.

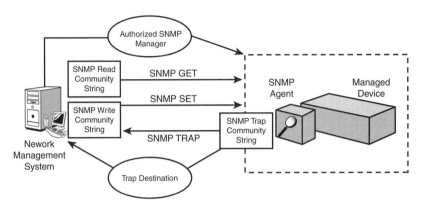

FIGURE 17.1   Basic architecture of the Simple Network Management Protocol (SNMP).

Notice in Figure 17.1 that the SNMP set and get messages originate with the NMS, and each message is authenticated by a unique community string. All SNMP trap messages originate with the agent and are authenticated by a community string. Several configuration steps are necessary on both the NMS and the agent to prepare the communication channels. Here are the fundamental concepts for making these SNMP communications work:

▶ **SNMP Get and Set**—The agent settings will define the NMS as an authorized SNMP manager. You can configure agents to respond to several specified managers. Read-only and Read/Write permissions are defined using two or more different community strings. The agent processes incoming SNMP get and set commands from the NMS when the source is an authorized manager and when the community string(s) match those the agent is set to allow.

▶ **SNMP Trap**—The agent is configured to send traps to one or more specified Network Management Systems, the NMS being the trap destination(s). The NMS is prepared to expect traps from a particular agent (this sometimes is referred to as creating a *trap receiver* on the NMS). Traps are sent by the agent using a specified community string. The traps are processed by the NMS if a trap receiver has been prepared for that device with that particular community string.

17

OpsMgr natively supports the SNMP get and trap mechanisms. As we proceed through this chapter, we will refer back to these SNMP architecture fundamentals as we cover the corresponding OpsMgr components.

About MIBs and OIDs

Effectively managing network devices via SNMP with OpsMgr also involves knowledge of MIBs and OIDs:

▶ A MIB (Management Information Base) is analogous to a mini-management pack for a network device. It is a collection of attributes and characteristics that describe the configuration and operation of a managed device. A MIB is organized in a hierarchical tree with a nameless root. MIBs are authored by equipment vendors and distributed as text files that a NMS can compile and import.

▶ An OID (Object Identifier) is a unique label within the MIB hierarchy. OIDs at the top of the MIB tree belong to different standards organizations, whereas different associated organizations such as hardware vendors assign lower levels. This means that a higher-order OID (with a smaller and shorter OID name) is more generic and applies to all or most managed devices, whereas a lower-level OID (with a longer name) is specific to a particular vendor's devices.

Figure 17.2 is a graphical representation of a MIB tree to help you understand how the OID for a particular object is derived. Notice the unnamed root at the top of Figure 17.2 represented by a tree symbol. Each MIB object in successively lower levels of the tree is represented by both a name and a number. To identify any particular MIB object, you describe the path through the MIB tree to arrive at the specific object. This is usually done by appending the numerical codes assigned to the objects at each preceding level in the MIB tree.

Flowing down from the MIB tree root in Figure 17.2, little stars have been added in the figure at each branch of the tree to help you trace two selected OIDs. On the lower left, notice the "mib-2" OID that is circled—the numerical OID is 1.3.6.1.2.1, which represents the path followed down the MIB tree from the root to arrive at that object. The MIB-2 OID is important because it is used by all SNMP-compliant devices, regardless of the vendor. The MIB-2 OID is like a universal passport for network devices that identifies the name and type of device, and provides some convenient location, contact, and networking information to enable basic management of any SNMP-compliant device.

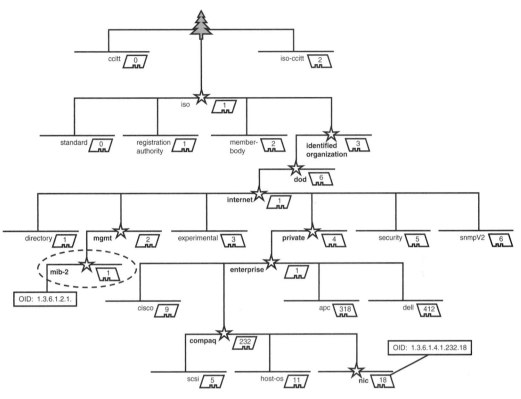

FIGURE 17.2   Tracing the MIB tree to the MIB-2 and the compaq.nic OIDs.

The second OID we call attention to in Figure 17.2 is the compaq.nic OID, which is in the lower right of the figure. The OID of 1.3.6.1.4.1.232.18 uniquely represents the collection of variables and data associated with the network interface card (NIC) in a HP/Compaq server. In Figure 17.2, we include a few other vendors' enterprise OIDs, such as Cisco (1.3.6.1.4.1.9), APC (1.3.6.1.4.1.318), and Dell (1.3.6.1.4.1.412). Each vendor has its own enterprise OID, and the vendors are pretty much free to create whatever subordinate levels of OIDs are appropriate for their products. You can enable OpsMgr 2007 to interact with OIDs other than MIB-2, such as the enterprise OIDs, by importing vendor-supplied hardware management packs or by creating custom SNMP rules and monitors.

OIDs are not always associated with hardware; software vendors often incorporate SNMP monitoring features with their products. This permits software applications to be monitored by any industry-standard SNMP Network Management System (NMS). Examples here include Microsoft, whose operating systems use the enterprise OID 1.3.6.1.4.1.311, and Symantec (Veritas), which is assigned enterprise OID 1.3.6.1.4.1.1302. That OID is used with the company's popular Backup Exec software products.

About the Compaq MIBs

You may be wondering about the reference to HP/Compaq MIBs. The enterprise name "Compaq" is still used by HP in the MIB line that supports ProLiant servers, including version 7.70—the current version of HP Insight Agents.

Since HP adopted Compaq's management solution (Insight Manager) and dropped its own (Top Tools), the company kept the MIBs from Compaq. Rather than trying to reissue all the Compaq MIBs (e-OID 232) with HP MIBs (e-OID 11), the company stuck with the "winner" and didn't sweat the name behind the curtain.

Network Device Discovery and Administration

The next sections discuss the basics of using OpsMgr network device management features. It is quite simple with OpsMgr 2007 to discover network devices running SNMP agents; all you need to know is a SNMP community string recognized by the devices. It is somewhat more time-consuming to prepare the devices for OpsMgr to discover them than to actually perform the discovery.

After you discover a device, administrative tasks that you can later perform include changing the proxy agent (watcher node) for the device and deleting the device from the management group.

Discovering Network Devices

Two activities are required to bring a network device into management with OpsMgr:

▶ Preparing the device for discovery

▶ Performing the discovery

You can discover devices with the Discovery Wizard in the Operations console, as well as via the command line using PowerShell.

Preparing Devices for Management

Network devices cannot be discovered by OpsMgr until they are prepared to be managed using SNMP. Here are the steps to perform before running the Discovery Wizard or using PowerShell to bring the devices into your management group:

1. **Enable the SNMP agent component.**

    For simple, common-use devices such as network printers, SNMP is often enabled by default. More complex equipment (for example, security-sensitive devices such as firewalls) usually have SNMP disabled by default. Non-Windows computers may require the installation of optional SNMP components to enable SNMP agent functionality.

2. **Permit SNMP community names.**

    As we described in the "SNMP Architecture" section of this chapter, the SNMP set, get, and trap communications are authenticated with a text string known as the *community name.* Many devices have their SNMP agent configuration prepopulated with the string *public* being authorized for read-only access. Unless you have a very small network without any devices exposed to the Internet, it is a best practice to change the *public* read-only SNMP community name to some other string. SNMP community names are always transmitted across the network in clear text, so they are quite easy to intercept. The SNMP protocol has primitive security; anyone who knows or guesses the SNMP community name can query your devices and get quite a lot of configuration information about them.

    OpsMgr 2007 natively only uses read-only SNMP functionality; however, if you will be importing third-party hardware management packs that use the SNMP set command, or plan to create custom tasks that use SNMP sets, you will also need to create write-access community names on your devices.

TIP

SNMP set Commands Are Not Secure

OpsMgr 2007 utilizes the SNMP V2(c) standard, or version 2 of the SNMP protocol based on community strings. (Service Pack 1 will include support for SNMP V1 as well.) SNMP V2(c) transmits community strings in the clear over the network; so if you send a SNMP set command, that write-capable community string can be easily intercepted by unauthorized parties using network monitoring tools. Although including SNMP set commands in OpsMgr tasks and responses offers great convenience and extensibility, there is also a security risk. Larger and very security-conscious environments should probably shy away from using SNMP set commands. SNMP V3 is a new standard that includes an authentication process, but OpsMgr 2007 does not support that version at this time.

---

3. **Enable permitted SNMP managers.**

    As a security feature, many SNMP-enabled devices allow you to modify the SNMP agent configuration to respond only to SNMP get and set commands from a list of particular network addresses, referred to as the permitted, or authorized, SNMP managers.

17

This may not be necessary for very small networks. The large enterprise probably will want to lock down the addresses your network devices accept SNMP communications from, certainly in the case of your high-value and security-sensitive devices. You would include the addresses of your Root Management Server (RMS) and the OpsMgr Agent Components that will be the proxy (watcher node) for the device(s).

4. **Populate useful MIB-2 OIDs.**
When OpsMgr discovers a network device, the object name you see in the Operations console is the IP address of the device, which is not particularly useful in determining what device it is! The values of these particular MIB-2 OIDs are important in helping you manage the devices with OpsMgr:

   ▶ Device Name

   ▶ Device Description

   ▶ Device Contact

   ▶ Device Location

Although the vendor sets the Device Description, you generally can change the Device Name to something more meaningful, and you can always populate the Device Contact and Device Location OIDs with local information that is useful to support staff. Using a network printer as an example, the Device Location could be an office or room number, and the Device Contact could be the name and telephone extension of the employee whose desk is closest to the printer.

5. **Enable the sending of traps.**
If you will be creating custom event rules that alert on receipt of traps from the network device, you can optionally enable sending traps. You should not enable sending traps from a device unless you are certain that OpsMgr has an alert rule for that device (called a *trap destination*). Otherwise, OpsMgr will receive traps it is not expecting, thus creating unnecessary overhead for the management group. Most network devices give you the option of entering one or more SNMP trap receivers.

If you plan to use this feature in your management group, configure the device's trap destination with the address of the proxy agent (watcher node) you are assigning to the device.

TIP

OpsMgr RTM Only Finds SNMP V2 Network Devices Using the Network Device Discovery Process

Although some network devices respond to the GET packets that SNMPUTIL sends, OpsMgr 2007 cannot discover the devices and therefore cannot manage them.

This occurs because the base or RTM version of OpsMgr 2007 only supports SNMP V2. Devices that do not support this version of SNMP ignore the GET packets sent by Operations Manager. Because SNMPUTIL supports SNMP V1 and V2, you may get a response using SNMPUTIL but not be able to discover the devices using OpsMgr.

See http://support.microsoft.com/kb/939364 for more information, as well as information regarding a hotfix. After the hotfix is applied, the Discovery Wizard will use SNMP V1 to detect those particular network devices.

Microsoft has announced support for SNMP V1 devices with Service Pack 1.

Adding Network Devices with the Discovery Wizard

After you have prepared network devices for discovery, perform the following procedure to add them to the management group using the Operations console:

1. Log on to the computer with an account that is an OpsMgr Administrator and open the Operations console.

2. Click the Administration button, and at the bottom of the navigation pane, click the Discovery Wizard link.

3. On the Auto or Advanced page of the Computer and Device Management Wizard, select Advanced Discovery.

4. In the Computer & Device Types list, select Network Devices.

5. In the Management Server list, take care to specify which management server (or gateway server) will perform the discovery. If you have more than one management server or any gateway servers in this management group, they will be available for selection in the list.
   Select a server that has direct network connectivity to the devices you want to discover. Figure 17.3 shows you can select from five servers in the management group to perform the discovery. We select a gateway server, gryphon.draco.com, because the network devices we want to discover are on the remote network, in the untrusted domain of draco.com.

6. On the Discovery Method page, enter the starting and ending addresses of the IP address range you want to scan. Note that the maximum number of IP addresses you can have in the range is 50,000, and the interface only returns a maximum of 1000 discovered devices. If you have more than 50,000 addresses to scan or more than 1000 devices to discover, you will need to subdivide the range and run the wizard several times.

7. In the Simple Network Management Protocol (SNMP) Community Strings box, type the read-only community string you have prepared your network devices to accept. In Figure 17.4, we show the wizard ready to scan the IP range of **172.16.231.94** to **172.16.231.99**, because we know that range contains the devices we want to bring into management. We have also changed the default community string from *public* to **umbrella**, a random codeword selected to use on that network as the SNMP read-only community string.

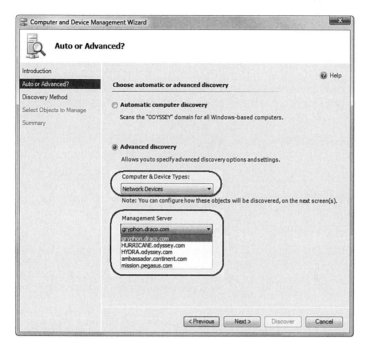

FIGURE 17.3   Selecting which management or gateway server will discover network devices.

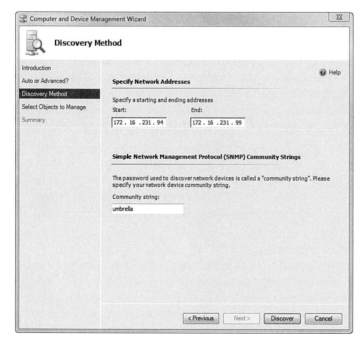

FIGURE 17.4   Entering the IP address range to scan and the SNMP community name.

8. Click the Discover button and wait several moments while the selected management server or gateway server performs the discovery task.

   Discovery runs for a maximum of 60 seconds. The time it takes for discovery to complete will depend on a number of factors, including the criteria you specified and your particular Information Technology (IT) environment and topology.

9. After the discovery task completes on the selected server, you are given a list of discovered devices. Any devices already managed by the management group are not included in the list.

10. Place a check mark next to the devices you want to manage, or click the Select All button. Figure 17.5 shows the results of our scan for network devices on the draco.com network. The scan discovered four devices, listed only by their IP addresses. We selected all four devices in Figure 17.5.

11. If the management server or gateway server that performed the discovery will be monitoring the devices, click Next to continue through the wizard.

   To specify a different computer to act as the watcher node, notice the circled Proxy Agent setting and Change button in Figure 17.5. Click Change, then select the computer you want to be the proxy agent for the selected objects. The proxy agent can be any agent-managed computer or management server in the management group. It must have SNMP (an optional component for Windows) installed, as well as direct network connectivity to the network objects it will manage.

12. Click Next, and you will get a final Summary page confirming the number of network devices that will be added to the management group. Click Finish.

Almost immediately, the new devices will appear in the Monitoring space of the Operations console. Because the Discovery Wizard does not provide any details other than the IP address of the devices we choose to manage, you should verify the device properties in the Monitoring space to confirm these devices are indeed the ones you intended to manage. Figure 17.6 shows the Network Devices State view in the Monitoring space. We selected one of the newly added devices (172.16.231.96) so that we could see its properties in the Detail View pane.

Notice in Figure 17.6 that the Device Name, Device Description, Device Contact, and Device Location settings (circled) are exposed in the view, making it easy to identify the device. This device is a Cisco switch, and it is one of the devices we expected to discover. Notice also that the Device OID begins with the Cisco enterprise OID 1.3.6.1.4.9 we included in the MIB tree in Figure 17.2. Below the Device OID, see the strange community string *YwBwAG8AcABzAA==*. We know we used the community string *umbrella* for this device! That strange community string is a security enhancement and is a mask added by the console to hide the actual community string.

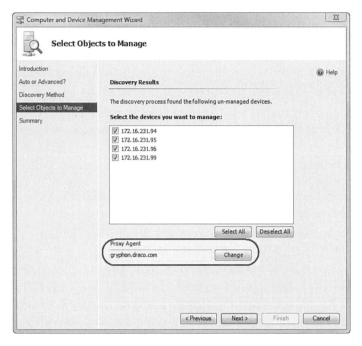

FIGURE 17.5   Selecting which discovered devices to manage and (optionally) changing the proxy agent.

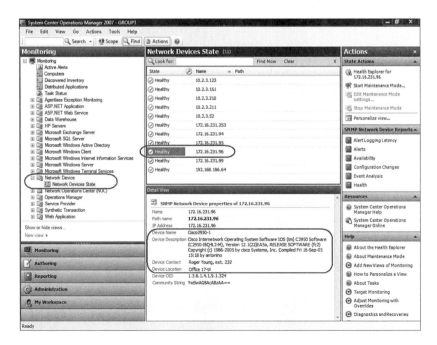

FIGURE 17.6   Confirming the identify of new network devices.

Adding Network Devices with PowerShell

As an alternative to using the Discovery Wizard in the Operations console, you can use a series of PowerShell commands to perform the same work. Here is a sequence of PowerShell cmdlets you could use to discover and add network devices to the management group from the command line. (We italicize the portions of the command lines that you would modify to fit your environment.)

1. Use the `get-MonitoringClass` cmdlet to create a monitoring class for network devices. Here we store the monitoring class in the $networkdeviceclass variable:

   ```
   $networkdeviceclass = get-monitoringclass -name 'System.NetworkDevice'
   ```

2. Next, use the `new-DeviceDiscoveryConfiguration` cmdlet to specify an IP address range with the monitoring class just created. The result is stored in the $dc variable, and will be used with `start-Discovery` to retrieve corresponding device information.

   In this case, we are scanning the IP address range 172.16.10.1 to 172.16.10.10.

   ```
   $dc = New-DeviceDiscoveryConfiguration -monitoringclass
   ➥$networkdeviceclass-fromipaddress 172.16.10.1 -toipaddress 172.16.10.10
   ```

3. Now, the `new-Object` cmdlet is used to set the `ReadOnlyCommunity` property to the community string accepted by the devices we want to manage. On this network, the SNMP read-only community string is *venti*.

   ```
   $encoding = new-object System.Text.UnicodeEncoding
   $encodedCommunityString = $encoding.GetBytes("venti")

   $dc.ReadOnlyCommunity = [System.Convert]::
   ➥ToBase64String($encodedCommunityString)
   ```

4. The `get-ManagementServer` cmdlet gets an object representing the RMS and stores a reference to it in the $managementServer variable.

   ```
   $managementServer = Get-ManagementServer -Root: $true
   ```

5. Next, we can perform discovery using the `start-Discovery` cmdlet. We provide it with the configuration objects $managementServer and $dc built using the previous commands. The results of the discovery are stored in the $discovery_results variable.

   ```
   $discovery_results = start-discovery -ManagementServer:
   ➥$managementServer-DeviceDiscoveryConfiguration: $dc
   ```

6. This command line pipes the discovery results to the `select-Object` cmdlet, which selects and expands the `CustomMonitoringObjects` property. Figure 17.7 shows the PowerShell window with the expected responses from steps 4 through 6 and indicates that four devices were discovered. (Steps 1 through 3 will not provide feedback at the command line if they are successful.)

   ```
   $discovery_results ¦ select-object -expand custommonitoringobjects
   ```

17

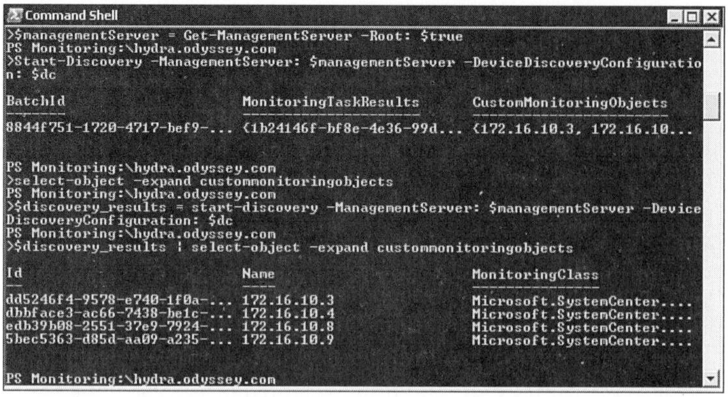

FIGURE 17.7   Network device discovery being performed at the command line with PowerShell.

7. We will now use the get-Agent cmdlet to retrieve a reference to the proxy agent that will monitor the network devices, and we store the reference in the $agent variable. We select the computer THUNDER.odyssey.com as our proxy agent for the new devices.

```
$agent = get-agent ¦ where-object {$_.Name -eq "THUNDER.odyssey.com"}
```

8. Last, we use the add-RemotelyManagedDevice cmdlet to add the network devices to the agent. We pass to the cmdlet the previously created variables for the proxyagent and the expanded list of custommonitoringobjects.

```
add-remotelymanageddevice -proxyagent $agent-device
➥$discovery_results.custommonitoringobjects
```

Figure 17.8 shows the expected success output of steps 7 and 8. Details on the first two of the four newly discovered devices are visible in the PowerShell screenshot. After these PowerShell commands have been executed, the new network devices will appear in the Operations console, just as if they were discovered with the Discovery Wizard.

You can combine these command lines into a PowerShell script if desired, running them as a single procedure.

TIP

On the CD

We have consolidated these commands into the PowerShell script Discover-and-Add-Network-Devices.ps1, which is on the CD accompanying this book. You will need to customize the cmdlets for your particular environment.

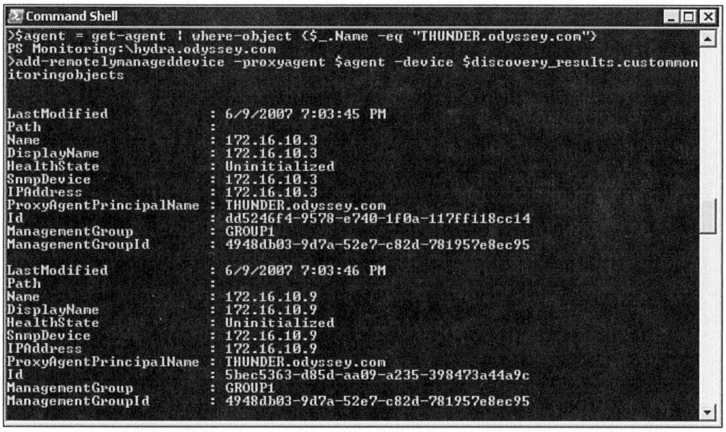

FIGURE 17.8   Newly discovered devices being added to the management group.

You can also enter the commands individually, but only in the same PowerShell instance—because the command lines pass variables from one to the next, and the temporary variables only exist while that PowerShell instance is open.

Why Use PowerShell for Network Device Discovery?

It may be obvious that it is a little more complicated to use the command line (PowerShell) than the graphical Discovery Wizard to bring network devices into management. So why consider using PowerShell? Here are a couple of reasons:

▶ One reason would be to avoid the possibility for human error while performing the operations in the GUI—multiple sets of eyes can review and approve a set of printed PowerShell commands; you can then schedule the script for execution without risk.

This capability is particularly true and useful if you are working out a fairly complex assignment matrix of proxy agents to network devices.

▶ A second reason would be to bring devices into management on a precise schedule; for example, if a Service Level Agreement (SLA) begins at midnight on a given day, you can stage a scheduled task to perform the work at the appointed time without human intervention.

Changing the Proxy Agent for a Network Device

After adding a network device to your management group, you can change the proxy agent for that device at any time. The proxy agent is the management group component that is the watcher node for the network device. You may assign the duty of a proxy agent to any existing Management Server, Gateway Server, or Agent Component in the management group. The proxy agent performs SNMP polling operations every few minutes to confirm the health of the network device. It also serves as the trap destination for unsolicited notification of events that originate from the device.

Consider changing the proxy agent for a network device in these circumstances:

▶ Distributing and load-balancing the monitoring duties for network devices across several components of the management group.

This is analogous to changing the primary management server for an agent-managed computer, or changing the proxy agent for an agentless-managed computer.

▶ Deliberately selecting the proxy agent as a watcher node that provides meaningful perspective.

As an example, if you are monitoring a printer in a branch office, you might select a client computer at that branch to serve as the proxy agent for the printer.

To change the proxy agent for a network device, navigate to the Administration -> Device Management -> Network Devices node in the Operations console and select one or more devices. As shown in Figure 17.9, right-click and select Change Proxy Agent. (This is the same area of the console where you can delete a managed device from the management group—see the Delete action available in the Actions pane in the upper right.)

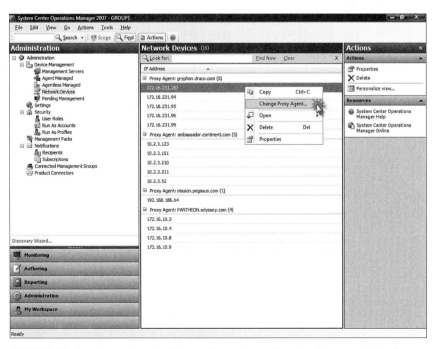

FIGURE 17.9   Accessing the Change Proxy Agent function for network devices.

After you click Change Proxy Agent on the pop-up menu, as shown in Figure 17.9, a list appears of all candidates eligible to become the new proxy agent for the network device. Figure 17.10 shows the Change Proxy Agent selection box. All management servers, gateway servers, and agent-managed computers in the management group are available for selection. Take care to select a proxy agent (or agents) that has direct network connectivity to the network device and has aggregated uptime equal to or greater than the SLA on the SNMP device being monitored. The console process does not verify that the network the device is on has connectivity to the network where the selected proxy agent is.

FIGURE 17.10   Selecting a new proxy agent for an existing network device.

If you select an agent-managed computer in the management group to be the new proxy agent for a network device, you must confirm that the computer has the Windows SNMP service installed and configured to perform the proxy agent function. The OpsMgr Agent Component alone is insufficient for a computer to serve as proxy agent for a network device; both the OpsMgr agent and the Windows SNMP service are required. Remember that SNMP is an optional Windows component, and it is manually installed or enabled on computers running any version of Windows. Here are some points to keep in mind:

▶ For computers running Windows XP, Windows 2000, and Windows 2003, add the SNMP service to the local computer using Control Panel -> Add/Remove Windows Components -> Management and Monitoring Tools -> Details -> Simple Network Management Protocol.

The Windows Management Instrumentation (WMI) SNMP Provider, another optional tool for installation, is not part of the proxy agent functionality. The WMI SNMP Provider enables the computer running it to be a SNMP agent of another

Network Management System. If you install the WMI SNMP Provider, an external NMS can manage the operating system using SNMP get commands, which will translate into WMI calls.

▶ Computers running Windows Vista have the SNMP service installed but not enabled. Activate the SNMP feature on Vista with Control Panel -> Programs -> Programs and Features -> Turn Windows features on or off -> SNMP feature.

Figure 17.11 points out the Windows Vista feature selection page with the SNMP feature selected.

FIGURE 17.11   Turning on the SNMP feature in the Windows Vista operating system.

After you install and run the SNMP feature on an agent-managed computer in the management group, that computer is eligible to serve as a proxy agent for network devices. However, additional configuration is necessary on the computer that will be the proxy agent. Figure 17.12 shows the Security tab of the SNMP service running on a Windows Vista computer. The accepted community names list must include the community string you configured the device to use; in this case, the community name is *venti*.

Notice in Figure 17.12 that we have restricted the SNMP service from responding to SNMP communications from sources other than localhost (address 127.0.0.1) and have limited the address of the network device that the computer will be a proxy agent for (only 172.16.231.10); this is an optional but recommended step in a security-conscious environment. Alternatively, you may select the less-secure option Accept SNMP packets from any host.

One final configuration step we will perform involves SNMP traps. If you have enabled sending SNMP traps on the network device, you need the agent proxy to be running the

SNMP Trap service in addition to the SNMP service. Figure 17.13 shows the Services MMC on a Windows Vista computer after the SNMP service has been turned on. Notice that the SNMP Trap service is set to Manual startup. In order for the management group to receive unsolicited SNMP traps from the network device, change the Startup Type setting of the SNMP Trap service to Automatic.

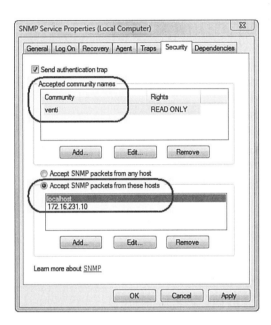

FIGURE 17.12   Configuring SNMP Service security on an agent proxy computer.

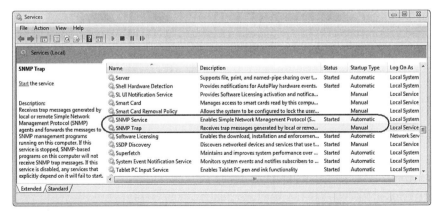

FIGURE 17.13   The default startup type for the SNMP Trap service is Manual.

17

Contents of the SNMP Polling Conversation

You may be interested in the SNMP device communication strings exchanged during the conversation between a SNMP proxy agent and the SNMP device. OpsMgr 2007 does a SNMP "read/walk" of the device. It collects attributes such as Location, Device type, and Model to associate as information for the instance during discovery.

There is a single monitor, called *Device status check*, that is a unit monitor from the Microsoft.SystemCenter.NetworkDevice.Library, and it has the following configuration:

```
<UnitMonitorID=
"Microsoft.SystemCenter.NetworkDevice.CheckDeviceStatus" Accessibility="Public"
➥Enabled="true" Target="Microsoft.SystemCenter.NetworkDevice"
➥ParentMonitorID="Health!System.Health.AvailabilityState" Remotable="true"
➥Priority="Normal"TypeID="Microsoft.SystemCenter.NetworkDevice.CheckDeviceState"
➥ConfirmDelivery="false">
        <Category>PerformanceHealth</Category>
        <OperationalStates>
          <OperationalState ID="Success" MonitorTypeStateID="DeviceUp"
          ➥HealthState="Success" />
          <OperationalState ID="Error" MonitorTypeStateID="DeviceDown"
          ➥HealthState="Error" />
        </OperationalStates>
        <Configuration>
          <Interval>120</Interval>
          <IsWriteAction>false</IsWriteAction>
          <IP>$Target/Property[Type=
          ➥"Microsoft.SystemCenter.NetworkDevice"]/IPAddress$</IP>
          <CommunityString>$Target/Property[Type=" Microsoft.SystemCenter.
          ➥NetworkDevice"]/CommunityString$</CommunityString>
          <SnmpVarBinds>
            <SnmpVarBind>
              <OID>.1.3.6.1.2.1.1.5.0</OID>
              <Syntax>1</Syntax>
              <Value VariantType="8" />
            </SnmpVarBind>
          </SnmpVarBinds>
        </Configuration>
      </UnitMonitor>
```

This XML extraction from the management pack shows that the monitor tries to read/bind to the specified OID during a SNMP read. If the action fails, the object assumes the Critical health state. The read-queries are issued to the device every 120 seconds.

Importing and Using Hardware Management Packs

The quickest way to begin getting practical output from Operations Manager 2007's network device management capabilities is by importing hardware management packs that someone else has already created. If you look again at the default Network Devices State view in the Monitoring space in Figure 17.6, you can observe that the Network Device node is rather Spartan. There is only one view, a very simple state view, and a few generic linked reports that are mainly useful to track the uptime of the device. That is the starting point we will use.

In the following two sections, we import two management packs that will significantly expand the usefulness of OpsMgr to manage hardware. One is from Microsoft—the network device management pack distributed with the System Center Essentials 2007 product. The second is from HP. We will be importing HP Server Management Pack version 1.0 for Microsoft System Center Operations Manager 2007.

System Center Essentials Network Device Monitoring Library

Those using the Microsoft System Center Essentials 2007 (Essentials) product will discover that Microsoft has bundled a network device monitoring management pack with Essentials; this management pack is not included with Microsoft System Center Operations Manager 2007. (We cover the System Center Essentials relationship with System Center Operations Manager in detail in Chapter 21, "Reading for the Service Provider: Remote Operations Manager.") In this chapter, we borrow some material on network device management using Essentials to show you what OpsMgr can do with its native SNMP device management features effectively configured.

The System Center Essentials–provided Microsoft System Center Network Device Monitoring Library management pack contains definitions for monitoring discovered SNMP-enabled network devices. We copied the management pack from the Essentials installation media and imported it into our OpsMgr 2007 management group using the Administration -> Management Packs -> Import Management Packs function.

Right away, we noticed in the Monitoring space that the Network Devices State view includes additional columns that summarize the health of the different interfaces a network device might have. In addition, the Network Devices node has three new views: a performance view, an alert view named Network Devices Problems, and a diagram view labeled Network Topology. A new SNMP Network Device Task action panel has six tasks.

Figure 17.14 shows our Operations console view of Network Devices State after we imported the Microsoft System Center Network Device Monitoring Library management pack from System Center Essentials.

17

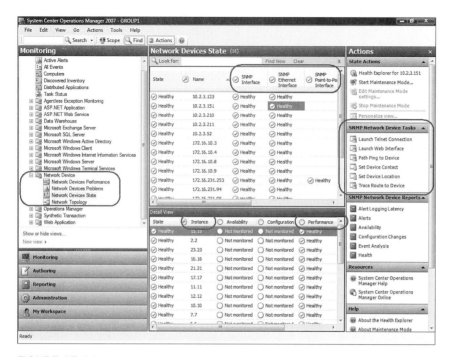

FIGURE 17.14   Views and tasks added by the Essentials Network Devices management pack.

We have circled some interesting features of the Essentials Network Device Monitoring management pack (MP) Network Devices State view in Figure 17.14. At the top center of the results pane, notice the new columns such as SNMP Interface, SNMP Ethernet Interface, and SNMP Point-to-Point interface. Columns not seen in the window include SNMP DS3/E3 interface, DS1/E1, Frame Relay, and ATM interfaces. All devices with interfaces will populate the SNMP Interface column, and most devices include Ethernet interfaces to populate that column. Only routers will most likely have the other interface types, so those columns are blank unless the device is a router.

We selected the SNMP Ethernet Interface status icon for device 10.2.3.151, which is a managed network switch with 24 interfaces. The lower-portion Detail View in Figure 17.14 lists each port of the switch as an instance, and we can see some performance data collected for each port on the switch. On the right side of the console, notice the SNMP Network Device Tasks in the Actions pane. Several of these tasks are really useful. We selected a network printer (172.16.231.99) and launched the Telnet and Web Interface tasks, shown in Figure 17.15.

Something we liked about launching the tasks in Figure 17.15 was the one-click access to those common functions. If you work often with network devices, you can shave many seconds from your chores by not having to open separately the command prompt or web browser and then type the address of the device.

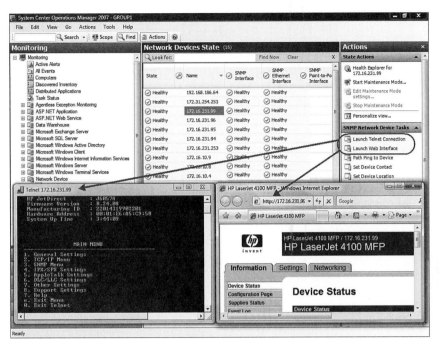

FIGURE 17.15   The Launch Telnet Connection and Launch Web Interface tasks.

We also want to demonstrate a couple other handy tasks available in the SNMP Network Device Tasks action pane, which are the Set Device Contact and Set Device Location tasks. If you elect to enable SNMP sets (write community strings) on your network devices, you can take advantage of several features in the Essentials Network Device Monitoring MP that utilize the SNMP set feature and are demonstrated in this section.

The Network Devices State view customized by the Essentials Network Device Monitoring MP that we saw in Figure 17.14 featured columns for each SNMP interface type with health status icons. We will leave that useful view the way it is and will create a new, custom folder and state view called Network Device Information, shown in Figure 17.16.

Notice in our custom Network Device Information view in Figure 17.16 that the columns at the top of the center results pane include the device name, OID, and description, making it much easier to identify and work with network devices in the Operations console. We selected the network printer NPIA5C958 (address 172.16.231.99). Notice in the lower detail view that the Device Contact and Device Location fields are not populated. That is the default state for most SNMP-enabled devices—it is incumbent on the device owner to populate those fields and keep them updated. (In practice, it is difficult to keep that information up to date.)

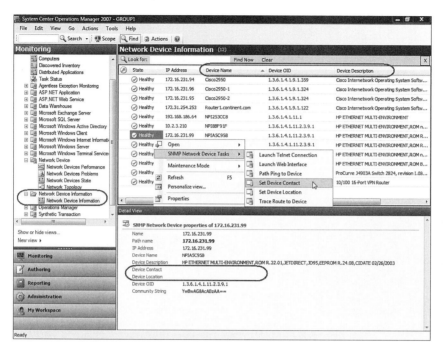

FIGURE 17.16   Launching the Set Device Contact task against a network printer.

TIP

Populating the Device Contact and Device Location Fields for Console Searches

Keeping these fields populated with current information can really help you locate particular objects when you are managing many network devices. The *Look for* search feature in the Results pane will find text in the additional device fields, such as the contact and location. So if you were able to consistently populate your device location fields with room numbers, and you created a custom view like we did that included those fields (as demonstrated in Figure 17.16), you could type the room number in the Look for box, click Find, and immediately filter the view for network devices in that room.

The Essentials Network Device Monitoring MP can make it simple to keep the Device Contact and Device Location fields on your network devices accurate and current. Launching the Set Device Contact task brings up the Run Task dialog box show in Figure 17.17. We clicked the Override button and entered the SNMP write string for this device (**trenta**), as well as the name and telephone extension of the employee closest to the printer. Running the task quickly updates the device's contact field. We can repeat the procedure with the Set Device Location task to update that field as well.

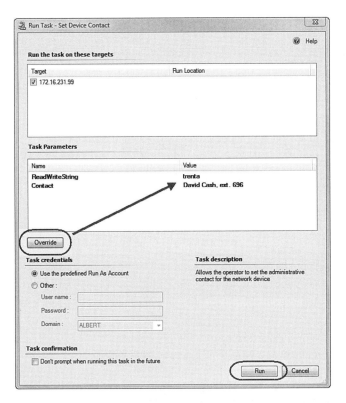

FIGURE 17.17   Updating the contact information using a SNMP set command.

You may be curious, as we were, to learn what performance parameters the Essentials Network Device Monitoring MP is watching. The quickest way to answer that question is to launch the Health Explorer against a network device. In Figure 17.18, we show the health model for a network device exposed in the Health Explorer.

The Health Explorer for a network device, shown in Figure 17.18, has many interesting elements defined in the Interface Performance Health Rollup, although only the Late Collisions OID monitor is enabled. In fact, we discovered that late collisions and a basic Device Status Check in the Availability aggregate monitor are the only two metrics the management pack uses to assess the health of network device Ethernet interfaces. (Some additional monitors are enabled on routers.) The Causes and Resolutions sections on the Knowledge tab on the right side of Figure 17.18 provide valuable and targeted information.

The last feature of the Essentials Network Device Monitoring MP we want to share comes into play in the diagram view of a router. We need to point out that the Network Topology diagram view in the Essentials Network Device Monitoring MP does not render objects in the OpsMgr Operations console the way it was designed to do in the Essentials console. However, it is possible to select the object of interest in the Network Topology diagram view and open a dedicated diagram view (right-click and select Open -> Diagram View). Figure 17.19 shows the diagram view of a router.

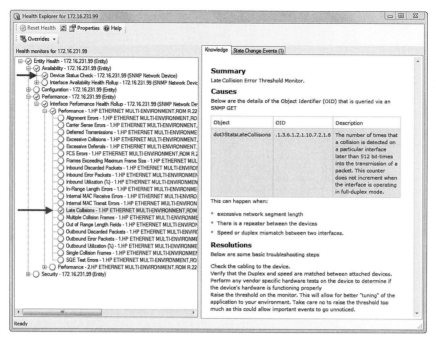

FIGURE 17.18   The health model for network devices only includes two indicators.

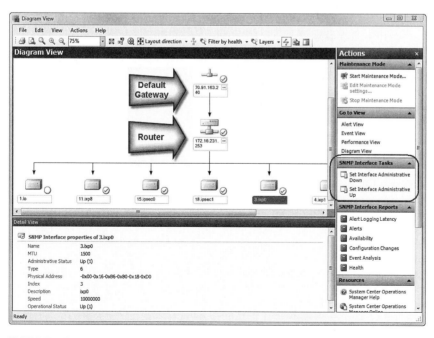

FIGURE 17.19   Setting interface administrative status from a router's diagram view.

The diagram view of a router, shown in Figure 17.19, is easy to understand. The default gateway of the router is clearly called out, as are the individual interfaces of the router. Selecting an interface as we have done (interface 3.ixp0) exposes information about the interface in the lower-center detail view as well as offers two context-specific tasks in the Actions pane. We circled these tasks on the right side: Set Interface Administrative Status Down and Up. These tasks allow the operator to control the router's interfaces very conveniently. Bringing those powerful network administrative tasks into the Operations console is a welcomed achievement.

System Center Essentials Network Device MP Is Not for Everyone

Microsoft did not include the Essentials Network Device management pack with OpsMgr on purpose. There are several reasons not to consider broadly deploying the Microsoft System Center Network Device Monitoring Library MP from Essentials into OpsMgr management groups:

▶ The MP is designed for the small to medium business space and not for large-scale environments; it may have undesirable effects on management group performance in the enterprise setting.

▶ The Network Topology view does not work properly in the Operations console.

▶ The relatively shallow performance monitoring (looking just for late collisions) can provide administrators with a false sense of security should they assume their network devices are more completely instrumented.

HP Server Management Pack for Operations Manager 2007

HP is heavily invested in its HP Systems Insight Manager (HP-SIM) systems management product, built on the successful Compaq Insight Manager (CIM) technology foundation. HP-SIM is an advanced and feature-rich product that is indispensible to an organization with many HP ProLiant or Integrity servers, particularly for managing firmware on HP servers and attached HP StorageWorks hardware. HP-SIM has its own alerting system based on SNMP traps and regular SNMP polling, and it facilitates a real-time, incident-based management capability for HP devices.

Dell has a similar product, OpenManage; IBM's product is IBM Director. HP-SIM, Dell OpenManage, and IBM Director are all members of the same class of management software designed for the midrange-sized organization with up to several hundred devices. The vendor provides these management products at no cost or low-cost to equipment owners.

HP and IBM also have high-end management platforms, HP OpenView and IBM Tivoli. These expensive and highly scalable products can manage tens of thousands of devices. If your organization uses one of those high-end enterprise management products, you might seek to deploy a connector solution that integrates alert management between Operations Manager and OpenView and/or Tivoli. We discuss external connector solutions for OpenView and Tivoli in Chapter 22, "Interoperability."

For the majority of HP, Dell, and IBM server customers, the manufacturers' midrange/low-cost management offerings (HP-SIM, OpenManage, and Director) are a great deal. Each of these dedicated server management platforms excels at working with the respective vendor's hardware. However, network administrators in any size of organization do not want to have to watch two consoles for alerts and status (such as OpsMgr and HP-SIM, or OpsMgr and OpenManage).

The solution is to deploy OpsMgr management packs provided by the hardware vendors that can leverage the Operations console for alerting and health status. With these hardware management packs in place, one need use the dedicated vendor product console only for particular hardware-specific tasks, such as uploading firmware to devices. The rest of the time, administrators can use the Operations console exclusively to manage their server hardware on a day-to-day basis without loss of fidelity or function, compared to using the vendors' dedicated consoles.

HP, Dell, and IBM have all published MOM 2005 management packs for their server hardware. HP was first out of the gate with a native OpsMgr 2007 management pack, and we are going to look at this MP in action now. (Dell's updated MP Version 3.0 and IBM's Director MP 5.20 now also include support for OpsMgr 2007 and are discussed in Chapter 22.) The HP Server Management Pack for Operations Manager 2007 contains predefined discoveries, views, monitors, event-processing rules, and tasks for HP ProLiant and Integrity servers.

HP strongly discourages the use of converted HP MPs for MOM 2005 with OpsMgr 2007, and in particular warns against having both converted HP MOM 2005 MPs and the native HP OpsMgr 2007 MP installed in the same management group. The company advises that you start fresh using the native OpsMgr 2007 MPs only. Another caution from HP is that its MPs will not function with agentless managed computers—to use the HP Servers MP for OpsMgr 2007, HP servers must have the OpsMgr 2007 Agent Component installed as well as the HP Insight Agents application, which along with SNMP is the client portion of the HP-SIM architecture.

The HP Servers Management Pack for Operations Manager 2007 uses the following underlying elements to collect data and process hardware events and state changes:

▶ **Discovery rules**—These rules use the Insight Agents, system BIOS data, and the information from WMI to identify HP ProLiant and Integrity servers and collate individual system configuration attributes.

▶ **State monitoring rules**—These rules use data from the Insight Agents MIB to monitor the condition of server hardware and to populate the state view in the Operations console. State monitoring includes the availability of the Insight Agents, which run as services in the servers' operating systems.

▶ **Event-processing rules**—These rules rely on the Insight Agents and data written to the server event logs to identify and process HP hardware events. When an Insight Agent generates an event, it writes a corresponding entry to the System Event log.

If this HP event has an associated event-processing rule defining the HP Server MP, OpsMgr generates an alert.

HP distributes its hardware MPs as four installation kits, one each for HP ProLiant and HP Integrity servers, with both types available for x86 and x64 processor–based computers. You install the appropriate kit(s) on an existing OpsMgr 2007 management server or client computer with the OpsMgr 2007 console installed. The installation program for the kits places a custom application tool on the local machine. It also automatically imports three MPs into the management group:

▶ **Hewlett-Packard Servers Core Library**—This library defines the basic HP Server Class structure to support ProLiant and Integrity server management.

▶ **Hewlett-Packard ProLiant Servers Base**—The base MP defines the HP ProLiant Server Class structure to process primary monitoring to ProLiant servers.

▶ **Hewlett-Packard ProLiant Servers SNMP Management Pack**—The SNMP management pack defines the HP Insight Agent–based management for states and events.

For full functionality of the HP Servers management packs, install the kit on each instance of the Operations console in the management group. When performing the successive installations of the kit on other console instances, select the Custom setup type and install only the Console Task Tools.

As part of importing the management packs and installing the kit, a new view folder named HP Servers appears in the Monitoring space, with eight included views, which consist of five targeted state views, and one each of an alerts, diagram, and task view. Figure 17.20 shows the OpsMgr Web Console -> HP Servers -> Server Diagram view, with the HP Servers views circled.

In our view of the OpsMgr Web console in Figure 17.20, we have navigated in the diagram view to highlight a particular HP server (Lexington). Expanding the diagram branch below the server exposes each of the hardware elements monitored by the HP Servers management pack. From this view, you could select a particular subcomponent and effect a granular management mode action. For example, if you were going to replace a power supply on a system with multiple redundant power supplies, you could put just the Power Supplies component in maintenance mode during the swap. That action would permit continued monitoring of the rest of the server's components, without unnecessarily alerting operations staff when the power supply replacement is taking place.

In the lower details pane we can see useful hardware information, such as the server's serial number, firmware revision, and the IP address of its Integrated Lights-Out (ILO) card. The HP ILO, like the Dell Remote Access Card (DRAC) and the Intel Out of Band Management NIC, provides administrators with a remote management capability to access and operate the server's video, keyboard, and mouse—even when the server is powered off.

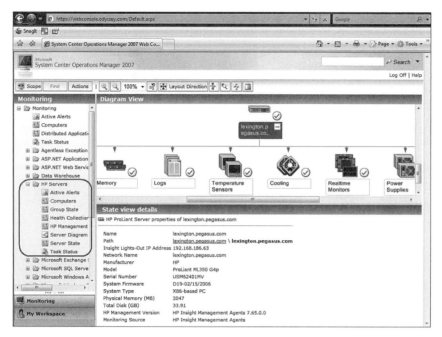

FIGURE 17.20   Hardware details for a HP server in a Web console diagram view.

Returning to the HP Servers -> Server State view in the Operations console, we will show you why you need to install that console task tool on each console in the management group (which is necessary to get full use out of the HP Servers MP). In Figure 17.21, for clarity we have filtered the server state list to show only the server Lexington. We now invoke the HP Custom Data Manager task from the HP ProLiant Server Tasks Actions pane in the upper-right corner. This task opens the Custom Data Manager in its own window, seen in the lower-right side of the screenshot. The Custom Data Manager is the console task tool installed on each computer in the management group running the Operations console.

The Custom Data Manager is an applet that lets the operator interact with 10 custom data fields added to the Operational database by the HP Servers management pack. The data fields provide a way to track five custom attributes, each with its own custom title. If you accept the default values for the custom data titles, they include useful elements such as the service contact name, email, and phone number and the warranty expiration date for the server.

After updating the values in the Custom Data Manager tool, click the Update Custom Data to Operations Manager toolbar button to update the Operational database. Once the custom data is in the database, you can customize your state view by adding columns for the custom data and then sort by item of interest, such as the warranty expiration date (01/15/2010 in the example in Figure 17.21).

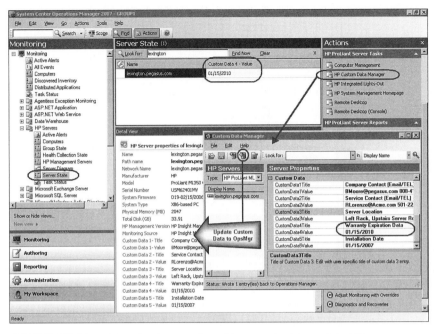

FIGURE 17.21   Using the Custom Data Manager tool to update HP server management information.

Suppose you really did have a power supply failure on one of your servers. How would you learn about that? In the case of an actual hardware event, the HP Insight Agents on the managed computer generate a SNMP trap, routed internally to the OpsMgr Agent Component on the computer. The agent transcribes the SNMP trap information into an OpsMgr alert and sends that to its assigned OpsMgr Management Server Component. Figure 17.22 displays an external notification of such an alert and a view of the Product Knowledge page from the alert.

The Outlook 2007 message open on the left side of Figure 17.22 is an external notification of a failed power supply in a HP server. The alert clearly lets us know which power supply failed (Bay 1 in Chassis 0); also, we see a note about trap 6050 in CPQHLTH.MIB. You may recall from the "About MIBs and OIDs" section of this chapter that HP uses enterprise OID 232, so it should not surprise you that the full OID of this trap is 1.3.6.1.4.1.232.6050 (cpqHe4FltTolPowerSupplyFailed).

On the right side of Figure 17.22 we show the Product Knowledge tab on the Alert Properties page (in the Operations console) for the corresponding alert we received the email notification on. Notice that the Causes and Resolutions sections include relevant tips to help you evaluate or further troubleshoot the alert condition. There are also two inline tasks in the Resolutions section:

▶ HP System Management Homepage

▶ HP Integrated Lights-Out (ILO)

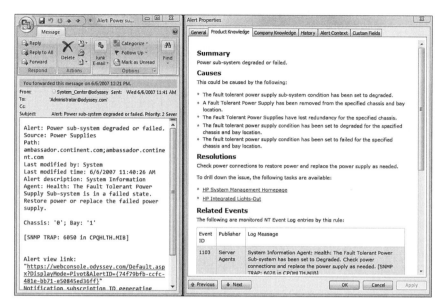

FIGURE 17.22   (Left) Email alert notification and (right) product knowledge for a HP hardware event.

These task links provide convenient one-click access to the respective HP server tools in a web browser.

A final feature of the HP Server MP we want to demonstrate is a task that retrieves the contents of the server's Integrated Management Log (IML). On HP servers, the IML is a hardware-based record of major server events, such as blue screens and hardware component failures. Normally you can examine the IML only using the ILO, running an IML log viewer utility on the server; or, with appropriate Windows security permissions, running the IML log viewer utility from another computer with network connectivity to the server. Figure 17.23 shows the IML contents being examined in a new way—without direct network connectivity—using OpsMgr 2007!

In Figure 17.23, we navigated in the Operations console to the HP Servers -> Health Collection State view and again filtered on just the server Lexington. We can see each of the hardware components monitored on that server, as we did in the Web console diagram view shown in Figure 17.20. When we highlight the Logs component in the Health Collection State view, two log-specific tasks appear in the Logs (ProLiant SNMP) Tasks pane: IML Clear and IML Export.

Running the HP ProLiant IML Export task, as we did, opens a Task Status window with the contents of the server's IML in the Task Output area. We can see there was a Network Adapter Link Down event on Port 1 of the NIC in PCI slot 5 on 6/13/2007 that is now repaired. If you manage HP servers that are located on remote, unconnected networks using an OpsMgr gateway server, this new way to view server IMLs is revolutionary and promises to be a great timesaver!

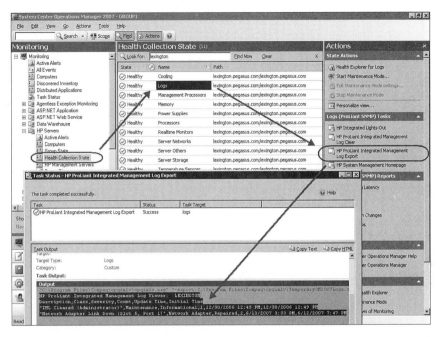

FIGURE 17.23   Examining the contents of the server's hardware management log.

Custom SNMP Rules and Monitors

After seeing how Operations Manager 2007 can shine using imported network device management packs, let's get started creating our own custom SNMP rules and monitors. You will need to create custom SNMP rules or monitors to extend your OpsMgr capability to manage network devices that do not have precreated or vendor-supplied management packs.

Here is a list of the types of devices that may support SNMP; consider adding these kinds of network devices to your management group:

▶ Core and edge network devices such as routers, switches, hubs, bridges, and wireless access points

▶ Operating systems of non-Windows computers, such as UNIX, AIX, RS/6000, Macintosh, Sun, and Linux systems

▶ Broadband network devices such as cable and DSL modems

▶ Consumer electronic devices such as cameras and image scanners

▶ Office equipment such as printers, copiers, and fax machines

▶ Network security equipment such as Intrusion Detection Systems (IDS) and firewalls

▶ Access control equipment such as standalone biometric scanners and door control systems

▶ Uninterruptable power supplies (UPS) and generator controls

▶ Manufacturing and process equipment, including Supervisory Control and Data Acquisition (SCADA) instrumentation

The first step when creating custom SNMP rules and monitors is to refer to a copy of the MIB for the device you want to manage, or at least a reference guide from the device vendor or another source including the OIDs supported by the device. All SNMP devices respond to the general MIB-2 OID of 1.3.6.1.2.1, which provides basic system name and networking information.

When creating a custom rule or monitor in OpsMgr, you will want specific information regarding the particular device you want to manage. For example, the percentage battery life remaining OID would only exist in a MIB written by an uninterruptable power supply vendor. Because custom rules and monitors in OpsMgr are created using OIDs, you need to know the OIDs in the enterprise MIB of the device you want to manage.

The device we will use to demonstrate the custom SNMP rules and monitors is a HP chassis switch, a ProCurve 4000M series with eighty (80) 10/100 Ethernet ports. This is an enterprise switch that is well supported and has lots of SNMP features built into it. Information on this device was easy to locate on the Internet. For your network devices, in your search for MIB information, use the vendor's website and your general-purpose search engines—search on MIB and your equipment model number. You will want to check the DVD, CD, or floppy disk that your equipment came with. UNIX and Linux distributions may include their MIB files in their local file systems. With a little detective work, you can generally discover the MIBs your device supports.

Using SNMPUTIL.exe

With the appropriate documentation for a device's OIDs and their meanings and values, you can proceed to create your custom SNMP rule or monitor. If you cannot locate an understandable reference on the MIBs for your device, you can alternatively interrogate the device about its OIDs. You can download or purchase a variety of tools and utilities, often called *MIB walkers*, to examine the MIB contents of network devices.

Microsoft provided a rudimentary tool called SNMPUTIL.exe with the Windows 2000 operating system; SNMPTUTIL can also be used with Windows Server 2003 (see http://support.microsoft.com/kb/323340 for information about this tool). Using SNMPUTIL.exe, you can interactively walk the OIDs and their values in the device's MIBs to discover the OIDs you want to monitor the values of. SNMPUTIL.exe is easy to use (see Figure 17.24 for output of the tool). The figure shows the first value in the MIB of the HP switch.

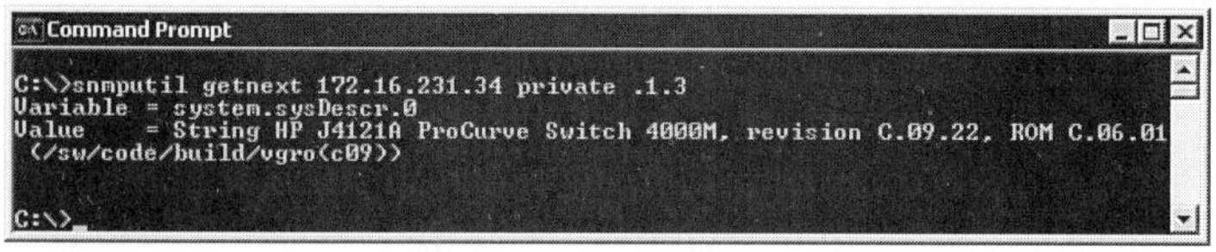

FIGURE 17.24   Using the SNMPUTIL.exe tool to get the next object after OID 1.3.

In Figure 17.24, we used the SNMP browsing command `getnext` to return the first value in the MIB tree after OID 1.3. The first OID that appears in the tree numerically after 1.3 is the first value in the mib2 MIB, which is the system description (OID .1.3.6.1.2.1.1.1). We would have received the same output using the SNMP browsing command `get` targeted directly at the system description OID .1.3.6.1.2.1.1.1, rather than the `getnext` command targeted high in the MIB tree at the identified organization OID 1.3. Using the `getnext` command is convenient for skipping forward in the MIB tree without knowing exactly what the next MIB branch might be.

A very useful SNMP browsing command is `walk`, which returns the OIDs and their values from the specified OID and forward, until the end of the subkey or MIB branch. In Figure 17.25, we walked (listed) the seven elements in the system branch of the MIB.

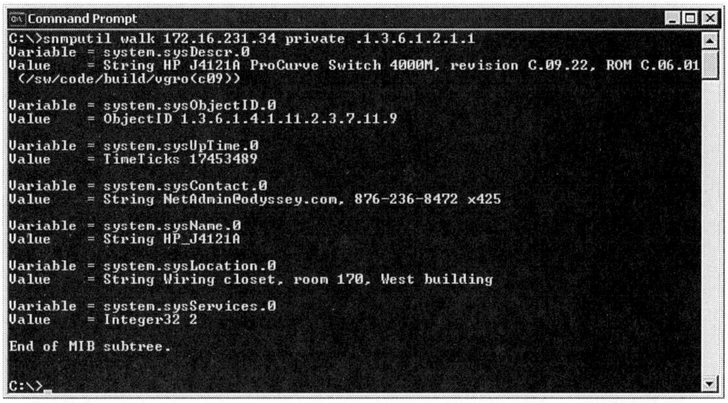

```
Command Prompt                                                    _ □ ×
C:\>snmputil walk 172.16.231.34 private .1.3.6.1.2.1.1
Variable = system.sysDescr.0
Value    = String HP J4121A ProCurve Switch 4000M, revision C.09.22, ROM C.06.01
(/sw/code/build/vgro(c09))

Variable = system.sysObjectID.0
Value    = ObjectID 1.3.6.1.4.1.11.2.3.7.11.9

Variable = system.sysUpTime.0
Value    = TimeTicks 17453489

Variable = system.sysContact.0
Value    = String NetAdmin@odyssey.com, 876-236-8472 x425

Variable = system.sysName.0
Value    = String HP_J4121A

Variable = system.sysLocation.0
Value    = String Wiring closet, room 170, West building

Variable = system.sysServices.0
Value    = Integer32 2

End of MIB subtree.

C:\>_
```

FIGURE 17.25   Walking the system subtree with the SNMPUTIL.exe tool returns all OIDs in that subtree.

In Figure 17.25, in addition to the system description OID, we see listed the Object OID 1.3.6.1.4.1.11.2.3.7.11.9. The first portion of OID 1.3.6.1.4.1 (not underlined) leads down the MIB tree to the enterprise OID; HP is assigned enterprise OID 11. The second (underlined) portion of the OID, from enterprise OID 11 and further down the MIB tree lists all HP-unique OIDs used by HP to identify and classify its equipment. OID 1.3.6.1.4.1.11.2.3.7.11.9 corresponds in the HP enterprise OID subtree to hpEtherSwitch-hpSwitch4000. This is the Device OID listed in the OpsMgr detail pane when you select the device in the Monitoring -> Network Device -> Network Device State view.

The other OIDs in the system OID you can see in Figure 17.25 include the system uptime in seconds, the familiar system name, contact and location information, and a services value that is an integer (2 in this case). The services value is an additive sum that represents the complexity of the device relative to the seven layers of the OSI (Open System Interconnection) network model. Our HP switch's services value of 2 indicates this device operates only at the datalink/subnetwork layer. The International Standards Organization (ISO) reference document RFC (Request for Comments) 1213 (the MIB-2 definition) lists the algorithm used to obtain the value of the system-services OID.

To list all the OIDs in all the MIB subtrees a device may support, you can use the SNMP browsing command walk and start from the top of the MIB tree, at OID 1.3. This will return every OID the device supports, and from that list, you can determine which OIDs you will configure Operations Manager to look for (in the case of custom probe action-based rules and monitors) or to expect (in the case of custom trap-based rules and monitors). Because this can result in a very long list of OIDs (in fact, too many to view at the command prompt), it is convenient to redirect the command-line output to a text file and then review the text file using Windows Notepad. Here is the command line we ran:

```
snmputil.exe walk 172.16.231.34 private .1.3 > 4000SNMP.TXT
```

The resultant text file (4000SNMP.TXT) listing every OID supported by the switch was 58,072 lines long! In addition to the universal MIB-2, the switch supports the Bridge (RFC 1493), Ethernet (RFC 1515), and Interfaces (RFC 1573) standard OID subtrees, as well as various proprietary HP enterprise subtrees. We are going to create some custom rules to monitor this device with, and we will be using our 4000SNMP.TXT file as a reference.

Creating Custom SNMP Rules

After you have discovered a network device and added it to your management group, basic features are operational—there is a state view that indicates whether or not the device is reachable. If the device cannot be reached, it will have a critical state. If you want more information about that network device, in lieu of importing precreated management packs, you can create custom SNMP rules and monitors. You can create four types of custom SNMP rules:

- **Event-based alert-generating rule**—Generates an alert in response to SNMP traps
- **Event-based event-generating rule**—Generates an event in response to SNMP traps
- **Event-based collection rule**—Collects a specified list of SNMP OIDs
- **Performance-based collection rule**—Collects SNMP performance data

The simplest types of custom SNMP rules you can create are event-based rules that can generate alerts or events in response to SNMP traps. The trap mechanism is a feature of the SNMP protocol that Operations Manager can easily leverage. To begin collecting traps from a network device, you would define the proxy agent computer as the trap destination in the device's SNMP settings, and then you would create a custom SNMP trap alert rule in the management group. You can create a rule that receives all traps (all OIDs) a device may send, or you can create focused alert rules that only operate against particular OIDs.

Creating a SNMP Trap (Alert) Rule

To create a SNMP trap-based alert rule that collects all traps sent by a device, follow these steps:

1. Navigate to the Authoring space -> Management Pack Objects -> Rules node and select the action Create a rule.

2. Select the type of rule to create at Alert Generating Rules -> Event Based -> Snmp Trap (Alert). We recommend that you select your own custom management pack as the destination for the new rule (do not use the Default management pack). If you have not created a custom management pack to contain your custom rules, you can do so at this time by clicking the New button. Figure 17.26 points out the correct rule type to create, and it highlights the New button to create a new custom management pack if you do not have one yet. In this case, we named the custom management pack **Network Operations Center (NOC)**. Click Next.

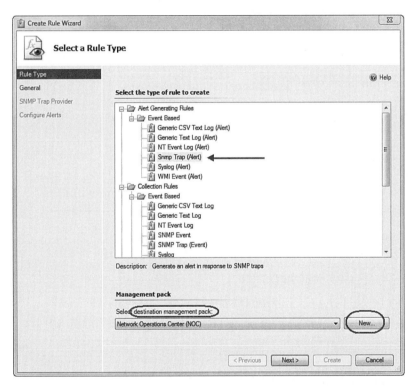

FIGURE 17.26   Authoring a custom alert-generating rule using SNMP traps and saving the rule to a custom management pack.

3. On the Rule and Description page, enter a meaningful rule name and description as desired. We used the rule name **An SNMP trap was received**. For the rule target, click the Select button. In the Select a Target Type box, click the View all targets radio button. Locate and select the SNMP Network Device target and click OK and Next.

4. Leave the Configure the trap OIDs to collect section empty and check only the All Traps box at the bottom of the wizard page.

If you are configuring the device to send traps with the same community name used by the management server during discovery of the device, click Next.

If the device is configured to send traps with a different community string than that used by the management server during discovery of the device, before clicking Next, click the Use custom community string radio button and enter the trap community string.

5. On the Configure Alerts page, you need to create some text that will appear in the alert; otherwise, any alerts you receive will only indicate the IP address of the device that sent the trap. In Figure 17.27, we have constructed an alert description that includes the device name, address, contact, and location from the MIB-2 system OID. Click the ... button (circled in the figure) to pop up the Alert Description builder. Click the Target button and select the desired variables to use in creating your custom alert description.

Because we targeted the custom rule at the SNMP Network Device class, the rule will apply to all network devices in the management group. OpsMgr will generate alerts for any managed network device configured to send traps to a designated proxy agent in the management group. You can view these alerts in the Active Alerts global view in the Monitoring space of the console.

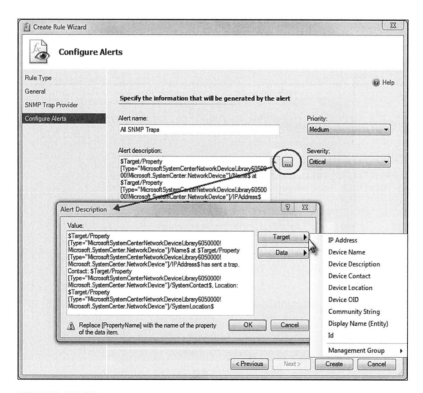

FIGURE 17.27   Creating a meaningful alert description using information from the MIB-2 system OID.

To create a custom view that only shows open alerts from network devices, follow these steps:

1. Select the folder to create the view in. Then right-click and select New -> Alert View.
2. Give the rule a name such as **Network Device Alerts**.
3. In the Show data related to field, select SNMP Network Device from the drop-down menu.
4. Tick the checkbox for a specific resolution state, and in the Criteria description area, click the underlined word *specific*.
5. Select all the states except the Closed state and click OK.

We created our Network Device Alerts view in the Network Device Information view folder we created earlier in the "System Center Essentials Network Device Monitoring Library" section of this chapter. You can see this view in Figure 17.28, already populated with some traps from the device.

Notice the customized alert description in the alert details shown in Figure 17.28—that information helps us quickly determine which device sent this trap. Looking at the list of alerts (traps) received, you notice they all have the same alert name: An SNMP trap was received. To learn details about source of the trap, you need to open the properties of an alert and examine the Context tab. In the context event data, you will see the OID and meaning of the trap.

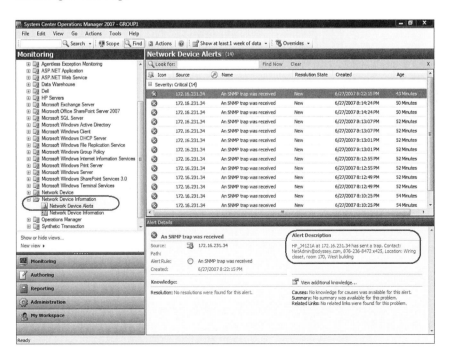

FIGURE 17.28   Viewing all SNMP trap alerts (notice the customized alert description).

We caused some SNMP trap-generating events to occur on our switch by removing a hot-swappable switch component and attempting a SNMP get operation with an invalid community string. Figure 17.29 shows the alert context of those traps.

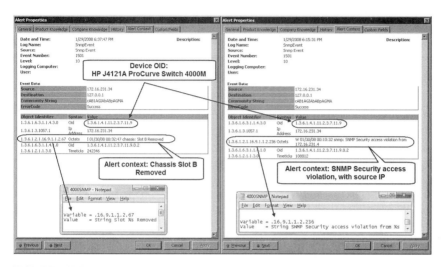

FIGURE 17.29   The Alert Context tab of the Alert Properties window lists the trap source OID and value.

The first OID value, in the event data of each alert from the device, is the device OID, seen in Figure 17.29 as 1.3.6.1.4.1.11.2.3.7.11.9. That device OID uniquely identifies alerts as coming from a HP J4121A ProCurve Switch 4000M. The most useful part of the alert context is the Octets line of the event data. On the left side of that line, we see the complete and unique OID of the alert; on the right side are the plain-language strings the MIB author selected to communicate the meaning of the trap. We can validate these OIDs and strings by examining the corresponding portions of the 4000SNMP.TXT output file of the SNMPUTIL.exe walk command that we created in the "Using SNMPUTIL.exe" section of this chapter. Figure 17.29 includes a small Notepad window with that portion of the 4000SNMP.TXT output file, visible in the bottom of each alert window.

Once you know the device OID associated with the traps you want alerts for, you are ready to create custom SNMP trap-based rules that include the trap source and other useful information in the rule name and alert. We have now demonstrated several ways to determine the device OIDs of interest so that you can create specific rules for them:

▶ Create an all-traps rule, as we did, and collect at least one trap from the device of interest, possibly by creating a condition that will cause sending a trap.

▶ Run the SNMPUTIL.exe walk command and locate the device OID in the output of the command. (See Figure 17.25 for an example.)

Of course, these manual methods of OID discovery are in addition to the MIB details you can learn by searching the Web and documentation provided by the device vendor. Once you have that information and know the OID that represents the device type you want to receive alerts about, you are ready to create a specific rule for that device type. To create a SNMP trap-based alert rule that collects traps sent by a specific device type, follow these steps:

1. Navigate to the Authoring space -> Management Pack Objects -> Rules node and select Create a rule from the Actions pane.

2. Select the type of rule to create at Alert Generating Rules -> Event Based -> Snmp Trap (Alert). Remember to select a custom management pack (that you previously created) as the destination management pack, rather than the Default management pack. Click Next.

3. Name the rule, provide a description, and select SNMP Network Device as the rule target. We are creating this alert to fire upon receipt of traps with the device OID for this particular model of switch, so we will name this rule **HP J4121A ProCurve Switch 4000M Alert**.

4. On the Configure the trap OIDs to collect page, click in the Object Identifier box and type the device OID the rule will look for. From the alert we previously received, we know in this case the device OID we are looking for is 1.3.6.1.4.1.11.2.3.7.11.9. (Remember to modify the community string if the trap community string is different from the read or write community string for the device.)

   You can add more device OIDs on this page if you want the same alert to fire regardless of the OID received. If you list multiple OIDs, the alert will fire if one or more device OIDs match the device OID in the received traps(s). Click Next.

5. Provide a detailed alert description. Because this alert applies only to a specific device type, you should make your description as meaningful as possible for future console operators and other recipients of the alert notification. You can also select your choice of appropriate priority and severity. Click OK when done.

You can review your newly created rule in the Authoring space to confirm the details. You can also return here to modify the rule configuration, add custom knowledge, and apply overrides. Figure 17.30 shows the SNMP Security Alert rule and its configuration page in the Authoring space. For this particular view, we scoped the rule list to show only objects in the SNMP Network Device class.

Notice that Figure 17.30 has an Add button in the Responses area. After you create the rule, you can return to the Authoring space, access the Add responses button, and instruct OpsMgr to run one or more command lines or Visual Basic scripts in response to receiving the alert. For example, you could create a command-line task that runs the SNMPTRAP.exe tool and sends another SNMP trap to a third-party SNMP NMS.

Another reason to return to the Authoring space and edit the custom rule is to add knowledge to the alert. Include knowledge that will be useful to recipients of the alert, particularly those receiving external notifications of events. Using the Resolution and Summary sections of the Knowledge feature, you can greatly increase the value of the alert by providing just-in-time information to recipients of the alert.

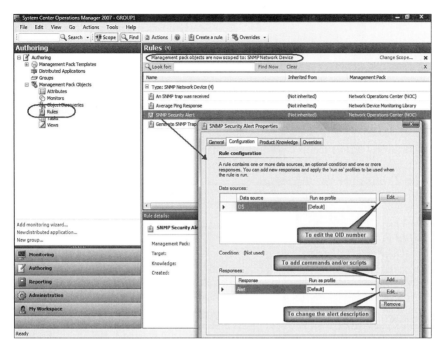

FIGURE 17.30   Modifying a custom rule's properties, such as adding response actions.

Look at the Network Device Alerts view in Figure 17.31. Notice the alert we received from the switch is now clearly part of the alert name, making the custom alert stand out from the generic "An SNMP trap was received" alert. Notice that we also used the Knowledge feature to add contact information in the Network Operations Center (NOC), as well as hyperlinks to the vendor's ftp and websites for the management and configuration guide and a FAQ (frequently asked questions) list.

Creating a SNMP Trap (Event) Rule

You can also create custom SNMP trap collection rules that only generate events, rather than alerts. Follow these procedures to create an event-generating SNMP trap collection rule:

1. Navigate to the Authoring space -> Management Pack Objects -> Rules node and select the action Create a rule.

2. Select the type of rule to create at Collection Rules -> Event Based -> Snmp Trap (Event). Remember to select your own custom management pack as the destination. Click Next.

3. On the Rule and Description page, enter a meaningful rule name and description as desired. We used the rule name **SNMP Trap (Event) Collection**. For the rule target, click the Select button. In the Select a Target Type box, click the View all targets radio button. Locate and select the SNMP Network Device target and then click OK and Next.

4. Leave the Configure the trap OIDs to collect section empty and check only the All Traps box at the bottom of the wizard page.

If you configured the device to send traps with the same community name used by the management server during discovery of the device, click Next.

If the device is configured to send traps with a different community string than that used by the management server during discovery of the device, before clicking Next, click the Use custom community string radio button and enter the trap community string.

5. Click Create when you are done.

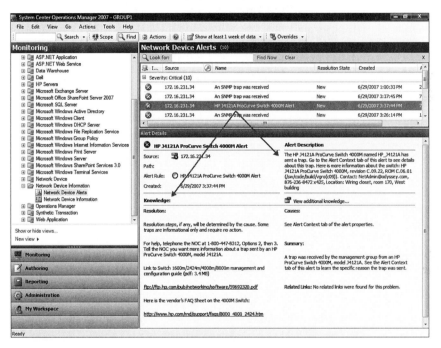

FIGURE 17.31   A custom device alert, with relevant knowledge and links to vendor documentation.

After you've created this rule, all traps received from all SNMP network devices will appear in the All Events global view in the Monitoring space. You can also create a custom view to observe only events from SNMP network devices. To create a custom view that only shows open alerts from network devices, follow these steps:

1. Select the folder to create the view in, right-click, and select New -> Event View.
2. Give the rule a name, such as **Network Device Events**.
3. In the Show data related to field, select SNMP Network Device and click OK.

We created our Network Device Events view in the Network Device Information view folder that we created earlier (in the "System Center Essentials Network Device Monitoring Library" section of this chapter). You can see this view in Figure 17.32, populated with a trap from a device.

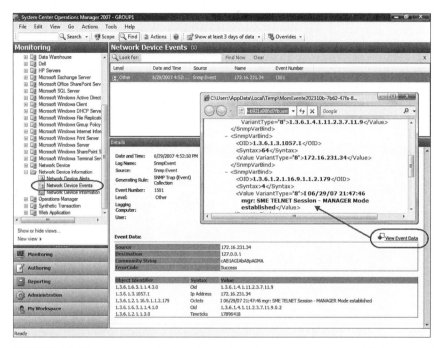

FIGURE 17.32   A custom device alert, with relevant knowledge and links to vendor documentation.

You can also add knowledge to custom event rules, as you can with alert rules. However, because events do not generate external notifications, knowledge tends to be more useful when applied to alert rules. Notice in Figure 17.32 that we circled the View Event Data link, and we show an arrow pointing to the Internet Explorer window that the link opens. The browser window exposes a raw XML view of the event data, which consists of the OIDs and values contained in the trap. This is the same set of SNMP OIDs appearing in the Event Data portion of SNMP alerts and events.

One advantage to viewing SNMP traps as events rather than as alerts is that the event data, where the Octets line and its device-specific meaning are located, is visible in the Details pane of the Monitoring console. In the case of SNMP alerts, that important information is only available on the Alert Context tab of the Alert Properties window.

Creating an Event-based Collection Rule

The two types of custom rules we just covered—the SNMP trap alert and SNMP trap event rules—use the SNMP trap technique to receive status information from the network device. The next two types of custom rules, the event-based and performance-based collection rules, use the SNMP get technique to poll the network device for status information. Whereas the trap-based rules require configuring the OpsMgr Proxy Agent Component as the trap destination in the device's SNMP settings, collection rules require that the OpsMgr proxy agent be an authorized SNMP manager in the device settings. In other words, the network device must respond to SNMP get commands issued by the proxy agent that it will receive on a recurring, timed basis.

Creating this type of rule brings information about device status into the OpsMgr Operations database and makes that information available to view in the event details. The Proxy Agent Component will poll the device for a particular OID value, recording an event with the value of the OID in its Details section.

The scenario we will step through involves monitoring a particular port on the switch, which we will call the VIP User port. We will poll the switch every 2 minutes and retrieve the state of the port. Here are the steps to create this custom event-based collection rule:

1. Navigate to the Authoring space -> Management Pack Objects -> Rules node and select the action Create a rule.

2. Select the type of rule to create at Collection Rules -> Event Based -> SNMP Event. Remember to select your own custom management pack as the destination. Click Next.

3. On the Rule and Description page, enter a meaningful rule name and description, as desired. We used the rule name **VIP User Port State**. For the rule target, click the Select button. In the Select a Target Type box, click the View all targets radio button. Locate and select the SNMP Network Device target and click OK.

   Unlike trap-based rules, where the proxy agent waits passively for traps to arrive, collection rules create activity for the proxy agent. If we enabled this rule at the time of its creation, every proxy agent in the management group would poll every SNMP network device it was responsible for. Accordingly, it is important to uncheck the Rule is enabled box—we want the rule disabled upon creation—and then click Next.

4. On the Configure the object identifier settings for SNMP probe module, we left the default frequency at 2 minutes, and we entered the OID that represents the operational status of the switch port of the VIP user. Normally you will use the discovery community string for the probe action; however, on this page you can specify an alternative SNMP community string.

   The OID we want to poll the switch for is 1.3.6.1.2.1.2.2.1.8.37. We learned this OID by running SNMPUTIL.exe with the walk option against the MIB-2 OID 1.3.6.1.2.1.2.2.1.8 (interfaces.iftable.ifentry.ifOperStatus). This returned the OIDs for each of the interfaces of the switch. The switch has 80 interfaces, and the port we are monitoring is port E5, which is interface number 37 on the device. Click Create when done.

5. Now, we need to enable the rule for the particular switch the VIP user connects to. Locate the new rule at the Authoring -> Management Pack Objects -> Rules node of

the console. Then right-click and select Overrides -> Override the rule -> For a specific object of type SNMP Network Device. A selection box will pop up listing all the network devices in the management group. Select the IP address of the network device the collection rule is applicable to and click OK.

6. On the Override Properties page, check the Override box, change the Override Setting to True, and click OK. Confirm that the override was successful by right-clicking again on the rule name and selecting Overrides Summary. The Overrides Summary box will pop up, as shown in Figure 17.33. Make sure the Enabled parameter is set to true.

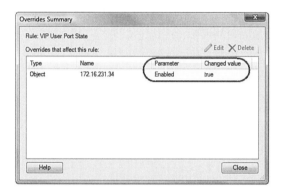

FIGURE 17.33   Enabling the SNMP event rule (probe) only for the switch with the VIP user port.

With the SNMP event collection (probe) rule created in a disabled state and then enabled for the correct target device, events will begin to appear in the Operations console. As you can see in Figure 17.34, SNMP polling events by the VIP User Port State rule occur every 2 minutes. In the Event Data portion of the Details pane, you can see the target OID and a value of 1, which means the switch port is operational (it has a link). If the value were 2, it would mean the port was not operational (no link).

We also inset a command-line window in Figure 17.34, showing the output of the SNMPUTIL.exe get command against the same switch port. You can see that a SNMP event collection (probe) rule is just like running the SNMPUTIL.exe get command on a scheduled basis and putting the results in the Operations console where all console operators can view them.

Creating a Performance-based Collection Rule

The last type of custom rule for monitoring network devices is the SNMP performance collection rule. This rule type collects numeric data for a specific OID. Once the numeric data is in the OpsMgr database, you can display the data by creating a performance view or by running a report.

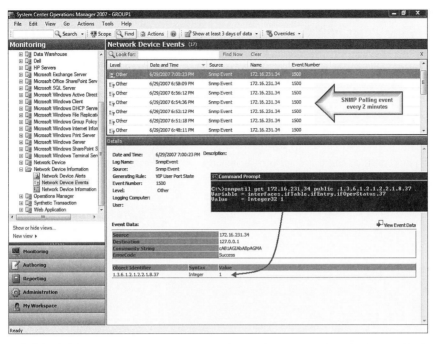

FIGURE 17.34   The operational status of the VIP user port is polled every 2 minutes.

To demonstrate the use of performance-based collection rules, we will create a rule that gathers the total number (counter) of SNMP network packets sent by each network device. This is a measure of the volume of network activity generated while using the SNMP protocol. We will poll our network devices every 2 minutes and retrieve the value of this counter. Here are the steps to create a custom SNMP performance collection rule:

1. Navigate to the Authoring space -> Management Pack Objects -> Rules node and select the action Create a rule.

2. Select the type of rule to create at Collection Rules -> Performance Based -> SNMP Performance. Remember to select your own custom management pack as the destination. Click Next.

3. On the Rule and Description page, enter a meaningful rule name and description as desired. We used the rule name **Network Device Received SNMP Packets Total**. For the rule target, click the Select button. In the Select a Target Type box, click the View all targets radio button. Locate and select the SNMP Network Device target and click OK.

4. On the Configure the object identifier settings for SNMP probe module, we left the default frequency at 2 minutes, entered the OID that represents the number of SNMP packets received over the device's network interface, and clicked Create. Normally you will use the discovery community string for the probe action; however, on this page you can specify an alternative SNMP community string.

The OID we want to poll our devices for is 1.3.6.1.2.11.1.0. We learned this OID by running SNMPUTIL.exe with the walk option against the MIB-2 OID 1.3.6.1.2.1.11 (snmp). This returned the OIDs for various counters related to the SNMP protocol—such as the number of times a bad SNMP community string was received (snmp.snmpInBadCommunityNames) and the number of SNMP traps sent (snmp.snmpOutTraps).

Figure 17.35 shows the output of the SNMPUTIL.exe get command for the OID we are creating our received packets rule for (snmp.snmpInPkts), as well as the corresponding sent packets OID (snmp.snmpOutPkts). Notice there are three more outbound packets than there are inbound packets. That difference is accounted for by the number of traps sent (snmp.snmpOutTraps). This means that since restarting the device, 30,272 packets associated with probe events (SNMP get commands) were received and replied to, and three SNMP traps were sent, for a total of 30,275 outbound SNMP packets.

FIGURE 17.35   Validating the OID to be used in the SNMP collection rule.

After you create a SNMP performance collection rule, the designated proxy agents for your network devices begin polling their devices and writing the OID values to the OpsMgr database. You can review collected SNMP performance data in two ways:

▶ Using a performance view in the Monitoring space

▶ Running a report

Running a report provides you with more detailed and configurable results, which are easier to read than using the performance views in the Monitoring space. Create a report on SNMP network device performance for a particular device using the following procedure:

1. Navigate to the Reporting Space -> Microsoft Generic Report Library -> Performance node and select Open in the Actions pane.

   If you expect to run this report on a regular basis, select Schedule, also in the Actions pane. Scheduled reports retain their custom report parameters, whereas the custom report parameters of a report only run once and cannot be saved.

2. In the report interval section in the upper-left corner of the report, change the From value from Today to Yesterday. This sets up the report for the previous 24 hours.

3. In the Objects section in the upper-right corner of the report, click the Change button.

4. The Settings box will appear. Click the New Chart button in the upper right and enter a name in the Chart title box in the Details area. We used the title **SNMP Packets Received**.

5. Click the New Series button in the upper right and then click the Add Object button in the center portion.

6. The Add Object box appears. Enter the IP address of the network device to report on in the Object name box and then click the Search button. The desired network device should appear in the Available items area. Select the device and click the Add button. The device should now appear in the Selected objects section in the lower portion of the Add Object box. Click OK.

7. Back at the Settings box, click the Browse button next to the Rule item on the lower-right side. The Select rule box will appear. Click the Search by Counter button at the top. In the Performance object dropdown selection list, pick Snmp Performance Object. In the Counter dropdown list, select the 1.3.6.1.2.1.11.1.0 OID (snmp.snmpInPkts). Click the Search button. The object should appear in the Available items list. Select it and click OK.

8. Repeat steps 5 though 7 for each additional counter you would like displayed on the report. (We are just going to show the one counter on this report.) Figure 17.36 shows the report's Settings page completed per this procedure.

9. Click the Run button, and a line-chart graph is generated that shows the selected OID values over the 24-hour period. Below the graph in the Rule, Instance, Object column, you will see a coded rule reference (similar to MomUIGeneratedRule90db33525...). Click that rule to open a detailed version of the graph that includes histogram features such as average and standard deviation. A second smaller chart details the number of performance counter samples making up the report.

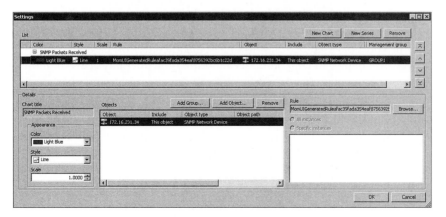

FIGURE 17.36   Setting up a report to graph SNMP network device performance.

Figure 17.37 shows this detailed chart view. Notice the most recent data values (on the right of the chart) are in the ~30,000 count range, as we expected after validating the current OID value with the SNMPUTIL.exe get command. The chart indicates that the switch was restarted at 11 p.m. the previous evening, which reset the OID value (counter) to zero.

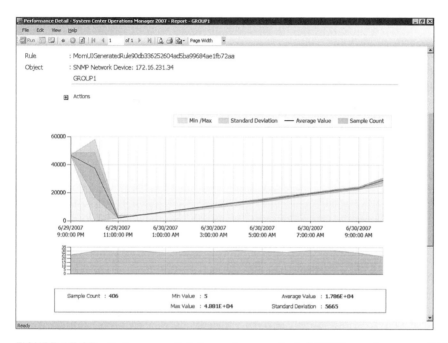

FIGURE 17.37   Performance Detail report on a selected SNMP counter over a 24-hour period.

Creating Custom SNMP Monitors

The rules created so far in the chapter that monitor SNMP network devices were mainly about collecting and displaying data. The hardest part about creating these rules was identifying and verifying the OID(s) that represent the value(s) we are interested in. SNMP monitors build on the concepts used by rules—trap based and collection based. Therefore, if you have followed this chapter so far, you understand the fundamentals of SNMP monitors already.

What SNMP monitors do is add some intelligence to the management group, to allow for traps and the output of probes to change the health state of a monitored network device, as well as optionally raise an alert. Using only a rule, you can just see an event, receive an alert, or view a report to learn the value of an OID of interest. Using a monitor, you can focus on the present health state of the device, without having to manually review the historical or real-time output of rules.

Figure 17.38 shows the monitor type selection screen, displayed when you begin to create a custom SNMP monitor. You can see that there are two choices:

▶ Probe Based Detection

▶ Trap Based Detection

Each type of monitor features Single Event and Single Event simple detection. Other classes of OpsMgr monitors (Windows Events as an example) include complex monitors such as repeated event and missing event detection. SNMP monitors only include the simple detection type.

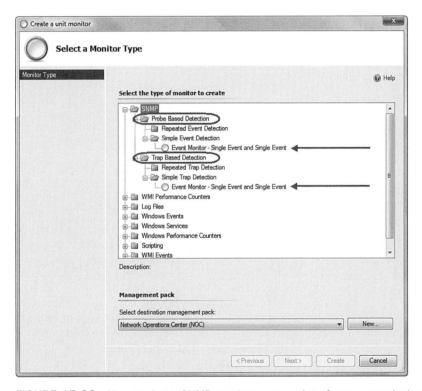

FIGURE 17.38   You can base SNMP monitors on receipt of traps or probe-based detection.

Creating a SNMP Probe-based Detection Monitor

We will demonstrate creating a SNMP probe-based detection monitor to watch the operational status of the switch port for our VIP user, the same scenario we used in the "Creating an Event-based Collection Rule" section of this chapter. Here are the steps we used to create the monitor:

1. Navigate to the Authoring space -> Management Pack Objects -> Monitors node and select the action Create a monitor -> Unit monitor.

2. Select the type of monitor to create at SNMP -> Probe Based Detection -> Simple Event Detection -> Event Monitor – Single Event and Single Event. Remember to select your own custom management pack as the destination. Click Next.

3. On the General Properties page, enter a meaningful monitor name and description as desired. We used the monitor name **VIP Switch Port Monitor**. For the monitor target, click the Select button. In the Select a Target Type box, click the View all targets radio button. Locate and select the SNMP Network Device target and click OK.

   In the Parent monitor dropdown selection list, select the appropriate type of parent monitor that this monitor's status should be rolled up with. There are four choices:

   ▶ Availability

   ▶ Configuration

   ▶ Performance

   ▶ Security

   We selected the Availability type because that category is appropriate for this monitor. Also, we unchecked the Monitor is enabled box (we want the monitor disabled upon creation). Click Next.

4. On the Configure the object identifier settings for SNMP probe module for the First SnmpProbe, we left the default frequency at 2 minutes and entered the OID that represents the operational status of the switch port of the VIP user. Normally you will use the discovery community string for the probe action, although here you can specify an alternative SNMP community string.

   The OID we want to poll the switch for is 1.3.6.1.2.1.2.2.1.8.37, which is the MIB-2 interfaces.iftable.ifentry.ifOperStatus OID for port E5, which is interface number 37 on the device. The VIP user's computer connects to that switch port. Click Next.

5. On the Build Event Expression page for the First Expression, click Insert -> Expression. In the Parameter Name field, enter **SnmpVarBinds/SnmpVarBind[x]/Value**, where x is the order of the OID/Value pair that is contained in the event context. We know from examining the event data for this OID in Figure 17.34 that there is only one OID/Value pair, so x=1 in the case of this monitor. We then selected Equals from the drop-down Operator selection list and typed a value of **2**, which will indicate that the interface is down. Click Next.

TIP

SNMP Monitors Needed for SNMP Granularity

A big difference between simple SNMP rules and more powerful SNMP monitors is that only monitors can filter one or more of the multiple OID values that may be associated with a SNMP trap or probe response. Only when creating a monitor can you specify **SnmpVarBinds/SnmpVarBind[x]/Value**, where x is the ordinal sequence of the additional OID in the event details.

Think of this as allowing the monitor to see inside the event details, and then perform an operation on a particular line number of the event details. That makes monitors much more attractive (and logical) to create than rules, which only operate at the device OID level. However, monitors do carry the requirement that you specify a compensating (or self-correcting) action, which can add undesired overhead to your monitoring operation.

---

6. Configure the object identifier settings for the SNMP probe module for the Second SnmpProbe, and the Build Event Expression page for the Second Expression, in the same manner as for the first probe and expression pair, except enter the expression value of **1**, which will indicate that the interface is back up. Click Next on each page.

7. On the Configure Health page, confirm that the Second Event Raised indicates a Healthy state, and the First Event Raised indicates a Warning (or Critical) state. Click Next.

8. On the Configure Alerts page, we selected Generate alerts for this monitor. In the Alert description area, we provided instructions to console operators and alert recipients on how to evaluate this alert. In the sample scenario of monitoring a VIP switch port, we include suggestions to rule out that the VIP computer has malfunctioned or been unplugged from the network. Click Create when done.

9. Now, we need to enable the monitor for the particular switch the VIP user is connected to. We located the new monitor at the Authoring -> Management Pack Objects -> Monitors node of the console, right-clicked, and selected Overrides -> Override the monitor -> For a specific object of type SNMP Network Device. A selection box popped up listing all the network devices in the management group. We selected the IP address of the network device the monitor is applicable to and clicked OK. On the Override Properties page, we checked the Override box, changed the Override Setting to True, and clicked OK.

Within a few minutes of enabling the monitor for the switch the VIP user computer connects to, the health model of the switch should update in the console to include the VIP Switch Port monitor in a Healthy state. Because it would be prudent to test the new monitor, we unplugged the VIP computer's network cable from switch port E5. This generated the First Event Raised state change event, properly generated an alert, and changed the health status of the switch to the warning state.

Figure 17.39 shows the switch's Health Explorer open to show the VIP Switch Port Monitor in a warning state. Plugging the computer back into switch port E5 will generate a Second Event Raised state change event at the next polling interval, automatically clear the alert, and restore the switch to a success health state.

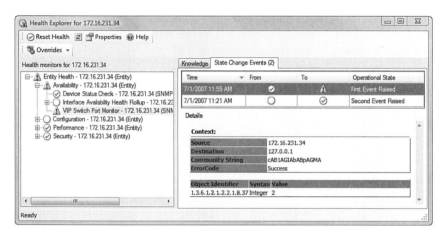

FIGURE 17.39   Custom probe-based monitor for operational status of a VIP switch port in the warning state.

Creating a SNMP Trap-based Detection Monitor

We will now demonstrate the last type of custom SNMP monitor that you can create, which is a SNMP trap-based detection monitor. SNMP trap-based detection monitors have the same features as SNMP probe-based detection monitors, except that received traps provoke the state change events, rather than polling results.

Our sample monitor will track security-related events on the switch. The scenario is that unauthorized attempts to access the switch will create a warning health state and that operators will follow a standard procedure to access the switch's management interface via Telnet to confirm the switch is secure, which returns the switch's security monitor to a healthy state. Here are the steps we used to create the monitor:

1. Navigate to the Authoring space -> Management Pack Objects -> Monitors node and select the action Create a monitor -> Unit monitor.

2. Select the type of monitor to create at SNMP -> Trap Based Detection -> Simple Event Detection -> Event Monitor – Single Event and Single Event.

   Remember to select your own custom management pack as the destination. Click Next.

3. On the General Properties page, enter a meaningful monitor name and description as desired. We used the monitor name **VIP Switch Security Monitor.** For the monitor target, click the Select button. In the Select a Target Type box, click the View all targets radio button. Locate and select the SNMP Network Device target and click OK.

In the Parent monitor dropdown selection list, select the appropriate type of parent monitor that this monitor's status should be rolled up with. Again, the choices are Availability, Configuration, Performance, and Security. We selected the Security type because that category is appropriate for this monitor. Also, we unchecked the Monitor is enabled box (we want the monitor disabled upon creation). Click Next.

4. On the Configure the trap OIDs to collect for the First SnmpTrapProvider, we left the default frequency at 2 minutes and selected the All Traps option. Normally you will use the discovery community string for the probe action, although here you can specify an alternative SNMP community string. Click Next.

5. On the Build Event Expression page for the First Expression, click Insert -> Expression. In the Parameter Name field, enter **SnmpVarBinds/SnmpVarBind[x]/Value**, where x is the order of the OID/Value pair that is contained in the event context. We know from examining the trap event data for this device in Figure 17.29 that the third OID/Value pair (circled) contains the information we are interested in, so x=3 in the case of this monitor. We then selected Contains from the dropdown Operator selection list and typed the string **SNMP Security access violation**, which will indicate that an unauthorized attempt to access the switch occurred. Click Next.

6. We configured the trap OIDs to collect for the Second SnmpTrapProvider, as well as the Build Event Expression page for the Second Expression, in the same manner as for the first trap provider and expression pair, except we entered the expression string **TELNET Session – MANAGER Mode**, which will indicate that the desired operator action has taken place. We learned that this was the correct text string to filter on by examining the details of a trap received from that device for that event. Click Next on each page.

7. On the Configure Health page, confirm that the Second Event Raised indicates a Healthy state and that the First Event Raised indicates a Warning (or Critical) state. Click Next.

8. On the Configure Alerts page, we selected Generate alerts for this monitor. In the Alert description area, we provided instructions to console operators and alert recipients on how to evaluate this alert. In the sample scenario of monitoring the switch security, we included directions to the operator to open a Telnet session with the device and confirm that device integrity is not compromised, which can be accomplished by reviewing the device's internal log of events. Click Create when done.

9. Now, we need to enable the monitor for the particular switch the VIP user connects to. We located the new monitor at the Authoring -> Management Pack Objects -> Monitors node of the console, right-clicked, and selected Overrides -> Override the monitor -> For a specific object of type SNMP Network Device. A selection box popped up listing all the network devices in the management group. We selected the IP address of the network device the monitor is applicable to and clicked OK. On the Override Properties page, we checked the Override box, changed the Override Setting to True, and clicked OK.

17

Figure 17.40 points out the location of the custom monitors we have created in the Authoring space of the console. Notice that the monitors we have created are disabled by default and are saved to a custom management pack—both best practices for network device monitors.

Remember that when you extend the health model of an object class, as we did to the Network Device class, all objects sharing that health model (that is, all network devices) will incorporate the custom monitor and make the monitor visible in the Health Explorer view. It is important to enable custom monitors only for those devices or device groups the monitors were created for.

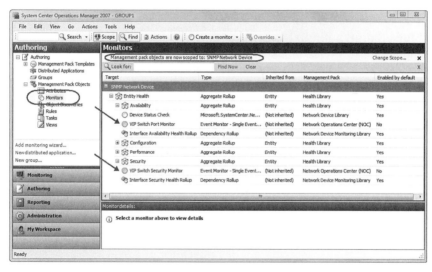

FIGURE 17.40   Custom monitors are disabled by default and saved to a custom management pack.

Within several minutes after enabling the monitor for the switch that the VIP user computer connects to, the health model of the switch should update in the console to include the VIP Switch Security monitor in a Healthy state. To test the new monitor, we attempted to access the switch with an unauthorized community string. This properly generated an alert and changed the health status of the switch to Warning. Then we opened a Telnet session to the switch, which cleared the alert condition and restored the switch to Healthy status. See the switch's Health Explorer open in Figure 17.41 to show the VIP Switch Security Monitor in a success state, after self-correcting from the warning state.

Perhaps you can see that SNMP monitors of both the probe type and the trap type are the stuff hardware management packs are made of. By knowing all the contents of a device's MIB, you can create a parallel health model of SNMP monitors in OpsMgr. You could apply smart thresholds as additional criteria in the filter expressions of the probe and trap events, and you can add lots of relevant content in the alert descriptions and knowledge pages. You can optionally export the management pack the custom monitors are saved to for backup, sharing, or licensing of the management pack.

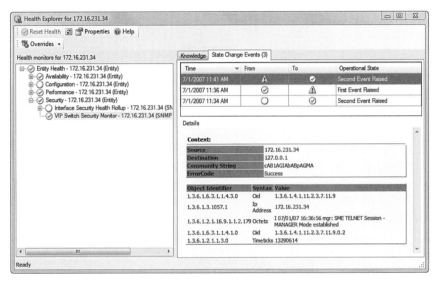

FIGURE 17.41   Security monitor returns to healthy state after complying with security policy.

Summary

We left the comfort zone of the Windows operating system in this chapter, as we extended the scope of our management group to include network devices. We started with a dive into MIBs and OIDs, because the OpsMgr network device monitoring features are wrapped tightly around OIDs. We discovered several SNMP-enabled devices on our managed networks, and added those devices as objects to our management group using the Discovery Wizard and PowerShell. We configured our devices and management group components to receive SNMP traps and view them in the Operations console. We imported some hardware management packs and explored the kinds of features you can add to OpsMgr's native SNMP monitoring capability. Finally, we created a pair of SNMP monitors that showed how you could extend the health model of network devices.

In the next chapter, we discuss various types of synthetic transactions you can use to monitor your environment.

17

Using Synthetic Transactions

Microsoft System Center Operations Manager (OpsMgr) 2007 can monitor Windows events, services, and performance thresholds, in addition to providing availability monitoring for servers, components, and distributed applications, capabilities that we covered in detail in Chapter 14, "Monitoring with Operations Manager." With this detailed level of monitoring, OpsMgr facilitates alerting and reporting the availability status and health of servers and applications. However, just because an application has not generated errors, it does not necessarily mean that the application is working correctly. The application could be running slowly or simply not responding to user requests, but without errors, one may have an artificial comfort level regarding the application's health. Often, these sorts of problems are undetected until someone accesses the application, and compares their experience against the results that are expected.

As part of OpsMgr 2007, Microsoft provides synthetic transactions. *Synthetic transactions* allow you to configure and simulate a connection into an application. You run these actions in real time, against monitored objects. You can use synthetic transactions to measure the performance of a monitored object and to see how the object reacts when (synthetic) stress is placed on it. You create synthetic transactions by recording a website, or by manually creating requests.

Using synthetic transactions means that in addition to monitoring an application or server to ensure that it is online and working correctly, you can also simulate a connection or login to an application to validate that it is actually responding to user requests. This additional aspect of monitoring helps proactively identify potential issues with an application, typically long before an issue is identified using traditional methods such as Windows events or seeing services fail.

Synthetic transactions are particularly useful in monitoring High Availability (HA) architectures, where a single or multiple components may be taken offline without the overall service being significantly affected. When monitoring HA configurations, you can use synthetic transactions to augment the SLA (Service Level Agreement) and availability data gathered from OpsMgr for the components by actually monitoring to ensure the system is responding as expected, regardless of the status of the individual components.

As an example, consider a large web farm where multiple servers can fail before users are affected—OpsMgr may show the failure of servers, and this will affect the SLA data for the farm. In reality, however, the farm is not adversely affected by the fact that servers are down. Configuring a synthetic transaction to monitor the websites hosted by the farm is a way of validating the availability of the farm and the websites it hosts as a whole rather than as individual servers. If a server is offline, the SLA information for this server will show a failure, but the synthetic transaction SLA that is testing the website will still show as healthy, giving us more accurate availability information.

Synthetic transactions are able to monitor response times, in addition to monitoring to ensure something is online. This means that you are not simply limited to validating that an application or website is responding; you can also track and alert against response time. This capability allows you to monitor the end user experience, as you are able to trend the response time of an application from an agent-managed end user system.

Synthetic transactions can also be configured to monitor specific components of an application (especially web applications), allowing you to pinpoint problems to a specific sub-component of the application. As an example, you can configure a web application synthetic transaction to monitor the login process to a web-based system and the process for creating a record in the system, separately from one another. That way, if the login succeeds but creating the record fails, you are able to identify this and take the appropriate troubleshooting steps based on which sub-component has generated the errors.

Synthetic transactions utilize the OpsMgr class-based architecture; this means that you can target and use these transactions just like a server object or role. When you create a distributed application, you can add the synthetic transaction as an object in that distributed application. From a monitoring and reporting perspective, this capability allows the synthetic transaction to affect the status of the distributed application, with any failure of the transaction then reflected in availability reporting. (We cover distributed applications in depth in Chapter 19, appropriately named "Managing a Distributed Environment.")

This chapter looks at the different types of synthetic transactions provided in Operations Manager 2007 and the process for creating synthetic transactions.

Predicting Behavior by Simulation

The most reliable way to ensure an application or server is working is to actually log into it, perform a typical process, and then observe the results. If the results are what you expected, chances are that the application or server is working correctly. If not, those results will often indicate where the problem is located, or at least provide a starting point to troubleshoot the problem. OpsMgr's ability to simulate a transaction and mimic the user experience makes its simulation capabilities quite valuable.

OpsMgr provides the ability to synthetically monitor a number of different applications out of the box, and the capability is included in several of the key management packs available for download at Microsoft's System Center Pack Catalog (http:// go.microsoft.com/fwlink/?linkid=71124). A number of management pack templates to create synthetic transactions are included with the OpsMgr product, and we anticipate that we will see additional templates included as Microsoft releases new management packs. The current templates include the following:

- ▶ Web application monitoring

- ▶ Transmission Control Protocol (TCP) port monitoring

- ▶ ASP.NET application monitoring

- ▶ Windows Service monitoring

You could also create a VBScript to carry out synthetic monitoring of a particular application and launch the script using a rule. This is useful when monitoring proprietary applications that you may not be able to monitor using the out of the box management pack templates. An example of this would be creating a script to send a SOAP message to a SOAP-enabled application and validating the response. You could configure this script to generate an alert as required.

Note that this chapter will not look at the Windows Service management pack template, as it is not strictly a synthetic transaction.

The management pack templates are a set of wizards that walk you through the steps to create all the necessary rules, monitors, classes, and so on, to carry out a simulated connection to the monitored object. Using the templates makes configuring these synthetic transactions very simple and straightforward, without manually needing to create large numbers of rules or monitors to achieve the same results.

In the following sections, we will discuss the processes to create the different synthetic transactions using the management pack template wizards. We will start with explaining the terms we will be using. The term *synthetic transaction* refers generally to any transaction that simulates user activity. A *management pack template* refers to the object in the Operations console used to create the necessary rules, monitors, and so on that enable the synthetic transaction to occur.

18

Watcher Nodes

When simulating connections to the application, you want to do more than ensure that the connection is accurate and reflective of what users would do. You also want to initiate the connection from different locations, as this simulates the user experience. You should initiate the connection from a server close to what you are connecting to, in addition to initiating the connection from a computer in the same location(s) as the users that are making the connections. You can then compare the results from each location to see whether the user experience is the same.

The agents performing synthetic transactions are known as *watcher nodes*. These watcher nodes actually perform the actions of a synthetic transaction, such as connecting to a website or querying the specified database. Placing these watcher nodes where the users are located is particularly important when those servers hosting the applications are located in geographically remote locations from the users, which often is the case with Information Technology (IT) systems today.

You configure the watcher nodes (the client computers designated to run these transactions) as part of creating the synthetic transaction. Watcher nodes allow you to specify the computer(s) that will launch the simulation. The only prerequisite is that the computer you want to run the simulation from has an installed OpsMgr agent. The computer can be running a Windows server or client operating system and can be located anywhere, provided it can communicate with the OpsMgr environment and the application it is configured to "watch."

The information collected from one or more watcher nodes can assist you with locating the source of a problem. As an example, let's say you have configured two watcher nodes, with one on the same network segment as the server you are connecting to and one located elsewhere on the client network. If your (remote) client network watcher fails to connect, this would indicate a network problem because the application is still responding, yet the client network is not able to connect. We illustrate this scenario in Figure 18.1.

As Figure 18.1 shows, using watcher nodes properly can help to not only detect when an application is failing, but can additionally be used to assist in locating the source of other problems—such as network connectivity problems when the application itself is responding correctly.

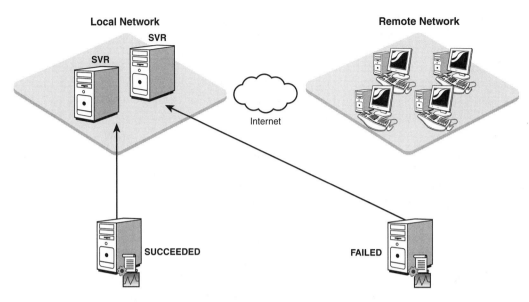

FIGURE 18.1   Remote watcher node failed.

An additional way to use synthetic transactions is by using Operations Manager to assist with monitoring network devices. You can use these transactions to highlight potential network problems, and to simulate connections to network devices. You can connect to network devices using the TCP port monitor monitoring template that we discuss in the "Monitoring LOB Applications Through Port Activity" section of this chapter.

You can monitor other issues external to the application with any type of synthetic trans-actions, since physical connectivity is always required from the client to the server, regard-less of the connection type.

Using OpsMgr 2007's capability to monitor network devices means the location of network-related problems can also be determined and resolved. For additional information on network device monitoring in OpsMgr, see Chapter 17, "Monitoring Network Devices."

Monitoring Web Applications

Businesses utilize the Internet in many different ways, and websites continue to become increasingly popular as a way to access information. Companies use websites to display and share information within their company as well as externally. This high level of inter-est in the Internet and web technologies brings with it a requirement to monitor these technologies, ensuring they are working correctly and within required parameters. Out of the box, OpsMgr monitors not only the core Microsoft technologies behind the Internet, that being the Internet Information Services (IIS) application and services, but also allows you to configure synthetic transactions to simulate a connection to a website. Using synthetic transactions offers an additional level of monitoring, alerting you to errors in the web application and simulating user access to the site. These transactions lets you validate that the site loads correctly, displays as expected, and loads within an acceptable amount of time.

The level of monitoring provided by the web application monitor in OpsMgr goes beyond loading a page and validating that the page loads correctly and does not produce any errors. The monitor also allows you to configure navigating through different pages within the website and provides the ability to input information into the web pages. For instance, you may browse a site, navigate to the search page, input some search terms, and then use the results to validate that the website is working correctly. This capability is particularly useful for identifying issues that affect the website but may not be linked directly to the site itself.

As an example, consider a website with a backend database containing data you are able to search against. Although the page may display correctly, an error may be generated if the database is offline when you are running a search. Using the Web application management pack template allows you to detect this condition.

You can also utilize the Web application management pack template to collect performance data from the website, including DNS response time and total response time. The level of performance data you can collect is very impressive; Figure 18.2 shows an example of the counters you can collect using an application created with the template.

As Figure 18.2 illustrates, a huge number of counters can be collected. After collecting the information, you can display it in a performance graph in the Monitoring space in the Operations console, or perhaps generate a report to show the trend in website performance over time.

Creating a Web Application Synthetic Transaction

This section looks at the process to monitor a web application using the Web application management pack template. Configuring a web application synthetic transaction is quite straightforward; a wizard allows you to configure basic monitoring, and OpsMgr includes a Web Application Designer that allows you to configure advanced settings such as login information for the website. The designer also makes it easy to configure the website for monitoring, providing a web recorder you can use to record the synthetic transaction you will create using Internet Explorer.

FIGURE 18.2   Website performance counters.

> **NOTE**
>
> **Recording SSL (Secure Sockets Layer) Sites**
>
> Currently, there is no way to record an SSL-enabled (HTTPS) site using the web recorder. To add a site of this type, it is necessary to use the Insert Request button in the web application designer. When you click the button, the Create New Request dialog launches. This dialog is very similar to the Web Application Properties dialog, which we cover in more detail in the "Configuring Advanced Monitoring for a Website" section of this chapter. Therefore, we will not look at this dialog in detail in this section.

The following steps look at the process for creating a web application synthetic transaction:

1. Launch the Operations console and navigate to the Authoring space.

2. Right-click on the Management Pack Templates sub-tree and select Add monitoring wizard..., as shown in Figure 18.3.

3. The wizard displays the screen shown in Figure 18.4. From this screen, select Web Application as the monitoring type, and then click Next.

18

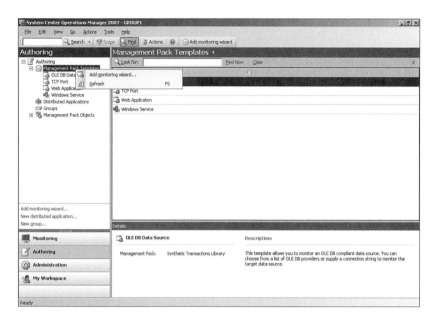

FIGURE 18.3   The Add Monitoring wizard.

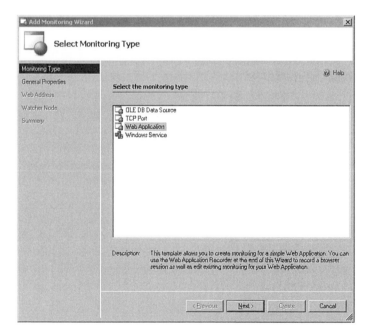

FIGURE 18.4   Select Web Application as the monitoring type.

4. On the following screen, input the name and a description for the synthetic transaction, and select the management pack to create the transaction rules in. We will call the transaction **Microsoft Website Monitor** and select the Sample management pack we have used elsewhere in this book. Click Next to continue.

5. The next screen is the Enter and Test Web Address screen. Here you will enter the basic URL you wish to monitor. We will enter **www.microsoft.com** (although, as you will see later in this process, the information you enter here is irrelevant—we will change it using the Web Application Editor in the "Configuring Advanced Monitoring for a Website" section of this chapter). After entering the URL, click the Test button to validate you can contact that URL. Figure 18.5 displays this completed screen. Click Next.

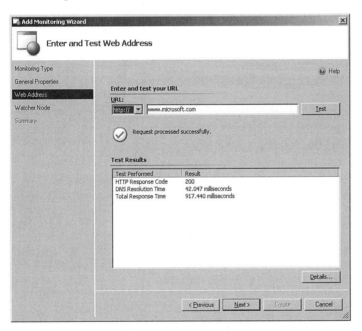

FIGURE 18.5   The Enter and Test Web Address screen.

6. We now are at the Choose Watcher Nodes screen, where you will identify and configure the computer initiating the test. The screen lists all machines running OpsMgr agents; you simply tick the checkboxes to carry out the test on the machines you choose. In our example, we will run the test from PANTHEON.ODYSSEY.COM. We will also configure the test to run every five (5) minutes instead of the default setting of two (2) minutes. Figure 18.6 shows the completed Watcher Node screen. Click Next to continue.

7. The final screen displays a summary of the information you have inputted throughout the wizard. The screen also allows you to Configure Advanced Monitoring or Record a browser session. If you do not check this option, the wizard completes and the web application synthetic transaction is saved to the management pack you specified.

18

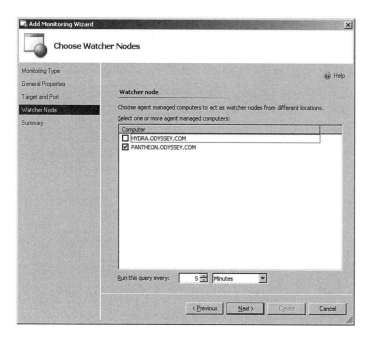

FIGURE 18.6   The Choose Watcher Nodes screen in the Add Monitoring wizard.

For our example, we want to configure more advanced monitoring of the website, so we will tick the checkbox at the bottom of the screen, as we show in Figure 18.7.

In the next section, we cover the steps for advanced website monitoring.

Configuring Advanced Monitoring for a Website

Now that we have stepped through the Add Monitoring wizard, we will look at the process to configure advanced monitoring of a website or web application:

1. When you click Create in the Add Monitoring wizard with the Configure Advanced Monitoring option checked, the wizard closes and the Web Application Editor will open, as shown in Figure 18.8.

2. Using the Web Application Editor, we will record a web session and look at the extra options available when creating a web application synthetic transaction. The first step is to delete any web addresses present in the editor in preparation for recording a web session. Select the website we configured in the wizard earlier and click the Delete option on the right-hand side in the Actions pane under the Web Request section. Click OK when prompted.

3. With the editor cleared, we record a web session where we will browse a number of pages on the Microsoft website and enter a search term, demonstrating OpsMgr's ability to simulate entries in a website.

FIGURE 18.7   The Web Application Monitoring Settings Summary screen.

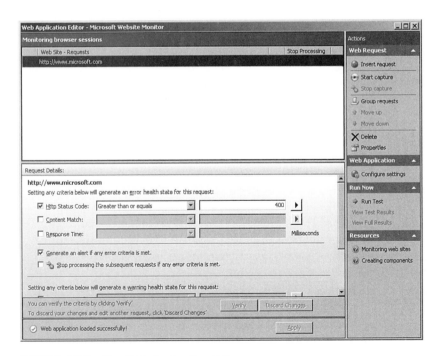

FIGURE 18.8   The Web Application Editor.

Click the Start Capture button. This opens an Internet Explorer browser window with a Web Recorder pane on the left-hand side, displayed in Figure 18.9.

4. For our example, we will visit the main Microsoft website (http://www.microsoft. com). Once we visit the page, we will enter the search parameter **SQL Server** in the Live Search bar as shown in Figure 18.10. We click the search button, and allow the results page to load.

FIGURE 18.9   Starting a website capture session.

5. When the search results page loads, you will notice the Web Recorder pane has the search information added, as displayed in Figure 18.11.

6. After you complete recording the web session, click the Stop button in the Web Recorder pane. This closes Internet Explorer, bringing you back to the editor with the web addresses displayed in the console.

7. We will now configure the performance counters we wish to collect for the entire web application monitor. Click the Configure Settings link, which opens the Web Application Properties window shown in Figure 18.12.

8. From the screen shown in Figure 18.12, you can configure a number of options that affect the entire web application, including performance counters to collect, and any logon information required to access the website (the logon information is specified using Run As Accounts, which we explain in Chapter 11, "Securing Operations Manager 2007"). You can also add or remove watcher nodes from this screen.

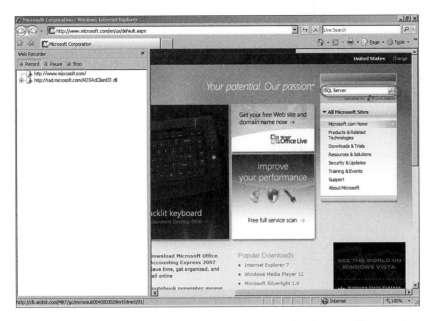

FIGURE 18.10   Enter search criteria of SQL Server for the recording session.

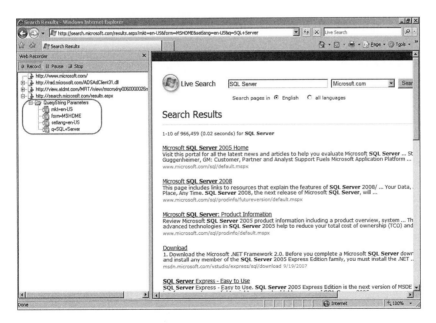

FIGURE 18.11   Viewing search results.

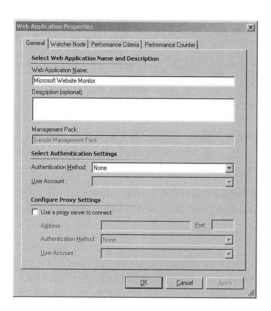

FIGURE 18.12   The screen for configuring Web Application Properties.

Using the Performance Criteria tab, you can also configure additional alerts to generate when the total response time for the entire website takes longer than an amount of time you specify.

9. We will next configure the performance counters we want to collect. Navigate to the Performance Counter tab and tick the checkbox next to the following counters:

   ▶ Total—DNS Resolution Time

   ▶ Total—Time To First Byte

   ▶ Total—Time To Last Byte

   ▶ Total—Total Response Time

10. Click OK to save the options and close the options window.

   This example configured performance counters for an entire web application. Note that a large number of the options we configured globally are also available to each individual website. You can also configure extra options such as custom conditions for generating alerts. Figure 18.13 shows the options we configured.

11. The last setting we need to apply will limit the number of alerts generated in the event of a failure. Although this option is not required, we recommend you use this functionality to prevent an alert storm. To prevent the transactions continuing to process when the previous transaction fails (and limit the number of alerts generated), select all web addresses in the editor and select the Stop processing the subsequent requests if any error criteria is met checkbox, circled in Figure 18.14.

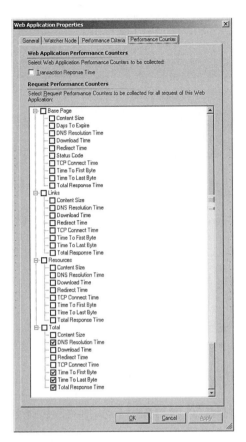

Web Application Properties

General | Watcher Node | Performance Criteria | Performance Counters |

Web Application Performance Counters

Select Web Application Performance Counters to be collected:

☐ Transaction Response Time

Request Performance Counters

Select Request Performance Counters to be collected for all request of this Web Application:

- ☐ Base Page
  - ☐ Content Size
  - ☐ Days To Expire
  - ☐ DNS Resolution Time
  - ☐ Download Time
  - ☐ Redirect Time
  - ☐ Status Code
  - ☐ TCP Connect Time
  - ☐ Time To First Byte
  - ☐ Time To Last Byte
  - ☐ Total Response Time
- ☐ Links
  - ☐ Content Size
  - ☐ DNS Resolution Time
  - ☐ Download Time
  - ☐ Redirect Time
  - ☐ TCP Connect Time
  - ☐ Time To First Byte
  - ☐ Time To Last Byte
  - ☐ Total Response Time
- ☐ Resources
  - ☐ Content Size
  - ☐ DNS Resolution Time
  - ☐ Download Time
  - ☐ Redirect Time
  - ☐ TCP Connect Time
  - ☐ Time To First Byte
  - ☐ Time To Last Byte
  - ☐ Total Response Time
- ☐ Total
  - ☐ Content Size
  - ☑ DNS Resolution Time
  - ☐ Download Time
  - ☐ Redirect Time
  - ☐ TCP Connect Time
  - ☑ Time To First Byte
  - ☑ Time To Last Byte
  - ☑ Total Response Time

[OK] [Cancel] [Apply]

FIGURE 18.13   Performance counters selected for the website.

Additional Options for Individual Web Addresses

When you select individual web addresses from the Web Application Editor, you can use the Properties button to configure additional options that are not available when configuring the options globally.

Properties for individual web addresses include custom HTTP header information and additional monitoring settings; you can also configure additional performance counters to collect for individual web addresses. We will not document these individual settings in any detail as they are beyond the scope of the example in this chapter.

12. After selecting the Stop processing the subsequent requests option, verify the settings you have applied. Click the Verify button, also displayed in Figure 18.14.

13. Finally, click the Apply button to save the settings. This creates all of the monitoring components automatically (this button is grayed out until you verify your criteria). You can then close the editor.

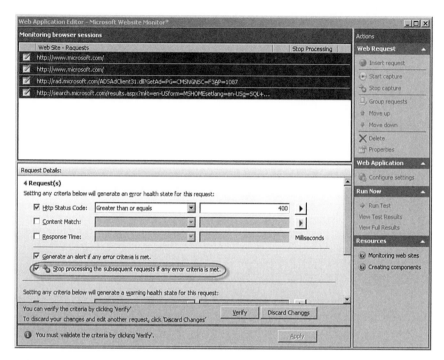

FIGURE 18.14   Stop processing option.

Configuring Advanced Monitoring for a Secure Website

You may want to monitor websites that require authentication. In this case, you can configure authentication options from the Web Application Editor using the following process:

1. Open the Web Application Editor by navigating to the Authoring Pane and the Web Application sub-tree. From there, left-click the web application we created earlier in the "Creating a Web Application Synthetic Transaction" section of this chapter. From the Actions Pane, select Edit web application settings, as shown in Figure 18.15. This reopens the Web Application Editor.

2. Click the Configure settings link, which opens the Web Application Properties screen shown previously in Figure 18.12.

3. Using the Authentication drop-down (in the middle of the screen), select the Authentication Method for the website.

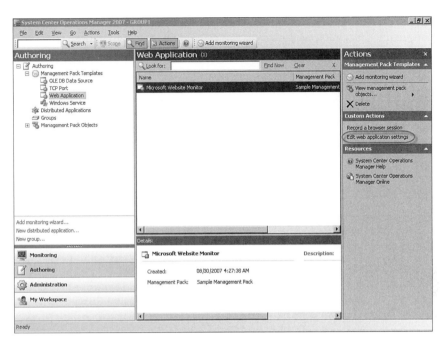

FIGURE 18.15   Choosing the Edit web application settings action.

TIP

Setting the Authentication Method

The authentication method should match the type used in IIS for that website. If you are using another Internet technology such as Apache, you will want to match the authentication type with that application. For reference, with IIS, the NTLM (NT LAN Manager) authentication type is the same as Integrated Authentication.

18

4. After selecting the authentication method, you need to specify a user account. This account needs to be created as a Run As Account before you can use it. More information on creating Run As Accounts can be found in Chapter 11.

NOTE

Testing the Connection

When you configure a website that requires authentication, you will not be able to test the connection from the Web Application Editor. If you attempt to test the settings, you are presented with the following pop-up warning:

Running a test of this web application may fail. While running the test, credentials that have been configured for this web application will not be used. If the site you are testing does not explicitly require authentication, the test may still succeed.

To test sites that are using authentication, you will need to use the monitor state and alerts generated in the Operations console.

Viewing the Website Performance Data

Now that we have a web application to monitor the Microsoft website, we will look at the performance counters we specified for collection.

TIP

Leave Time Before Viewing Performance Data

Be aware that it can take some time to collect the performance data. The amount of time depends on the frequency of the specific test; we recommend waiting up to 24 hours before viewing the data. This time allows enough data to be collected to generate a report with sufficient performance data.

To view the performance counters, perform the following steps:

1. Navigate to the monitoring space of the Operations console; expand the Web Application folder in the navigation tree, and right-click the Web Application State view. In the right-hand pane, we see the web application monitor displayed that we created earlier. Right-click on the object, then select Open -> Performance View, as shown in Figure 18.16.

2. You now see the Performance view for the web application, and you will notice that the available performance counters are the ones that we selected in our example. To demonstrate the performance graph, we will select the Total Response Time and the Total DNS Resolution Time counters, displayed in Figure 18.17.

This section discussed the web application synthetic transaction and documented the procedures to create a web application synthetic transaction using the Web application management pack template. We looked at the Web Application Designer and the process for recording web sessions to enable advanced monitoring of websites and web applications. We also covered the process for creating synthetic transactions to connect to sites that require authentication.

In addition, we highlighted the large amount of performance information you can collect with the web application synthetic transaction, and the steps to display the data using the Performance view in the Operations console.

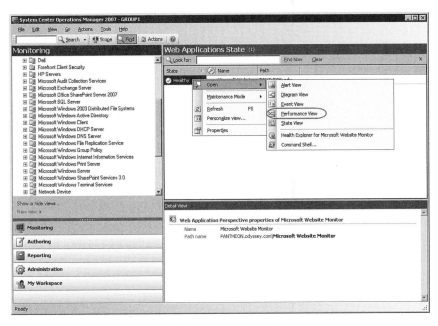

FIGURE 18.16   Opening the Performance View submenu.

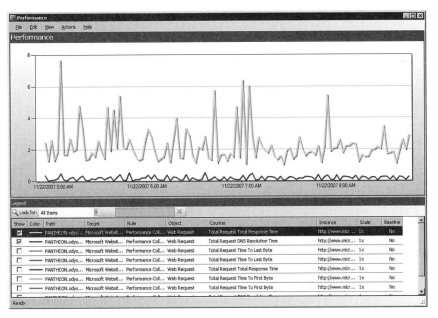

FIGURE 18.17   Viewing web application performance results.

Using OLE DB to Monitor Databases

Operations Manager can monitor SQL Server databases, including availability, performance, and size monitoring. This is in addition to its capability for monitoring the SQL Server platform that hosts the databases. But what about verifying that the database is responding, or monitoring the databases that underpin your business critical application and are not hosted by SQL Server? This is where OLE DB synthetic transactions come in. The OLE DB (Object Linking and Embedding Database) management pack template allows you to create a synthetic connection to any database that supports OLE DB.

OLE DB is an Application Programming Interface (API) designed by Microsoft for accessing different types of data stores in a uniform manner. OLE DB is implemented using the Component Object Model (COM) and was designed as a replacement for ODBC (Open Database Connectivity). OLE DB enables supporting connections to a much wider range of non-relational databases than possible with ODBC, such as object databases and spreadsheets that do not necessarily implement SQL technology or Microsoft SQL Server.

This support for non-Microsoft SQL Server databases using OLE DB makes the management pack template in OpsMgr much more powerful, enabling it to accurately monitor databases hosted in other non-Microsoft SQL enterprise database systems such as Oracle.

Creating an OLE DB Synthetic Transaction

We will now look at the process for creating an OLE DB synthetic transaction, as follows:

1. Open the Operations console and navigate to the Authoring space.
2. Right-click on the Management Pack Templates sub-tree and select Add monitoring wizard....
3. The screen shown in Figure 18.18 is displayed. From this screen, select OLE DB Data Source and click Next.
4. On the next screen, input the name and a description for the synthetic transaction and select the management pack in which you want to create the transaction rules. We will call our transaction **Operations Manager Database Monitor** and select the Sample management pack we have used elsewhere in this book. Click Next to continue.
5. The next screen is the Enter and Test OLE DB Data Source Settings screen. Here you will enter the connection information for the database you wish to test. On this screen, you have two options:

    ▶ You can use the Simple Configuration option, which allows you to input the server, database, and connection provider using a drop-down list.

    ▶ If you are an accomplished database administrator, you may wish to use the Advanced Configuration option and input the connection string manually.

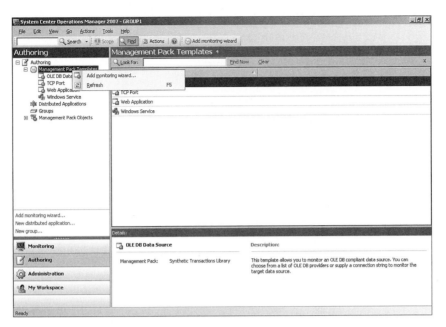

FIGURE 18.18   Selecting the Add monitoring wizard.

For this example, we will use the Simple Configuration option and configure the connection, as shown in Figure 18.19:

▶ The Provider is specified in the drop-down list as Microsoft OLE DB Provider for SQL Server.

▶ For the IP address or device name, we entered **THUNDER.ODYSSEY.COM**.

▶ The Database is **OperationsManager**.

Note that as you are entering the information, the connector string is formed in the grayed-out box under the Advanced Configuration option. After configuring the database connection, click the Test button to validate the configuration. Figure 18.19 shows the completed screen. Click Next to continue.

6. The following screen is the Choose Watcher Nodes screen, where you specify the computer(s) initiating the test. The list displays all computers running OpsMgr agents, and you can tick the checkboxes to perform the test on the machines you choose. In our example, we will simply run the test from the HYDRA.ODYSSEY.COM machine. We will also configure the test to run every five (5) minutes instead of the default setting of two (2) minutes. Figure 18.20 shows the completed screen, which is similar to what we saw earlier as Figure 18.6, except that in Figure 18.6, we specified the watcher node as PANTHEON. Click Next.

18

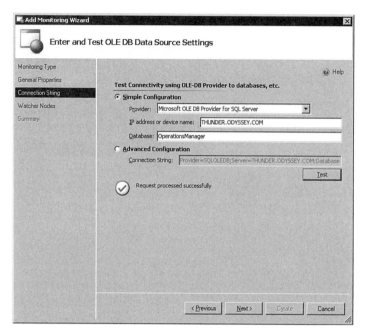

FIGURE 18.19   Entering and testing the OLE DB Data Source Settings.

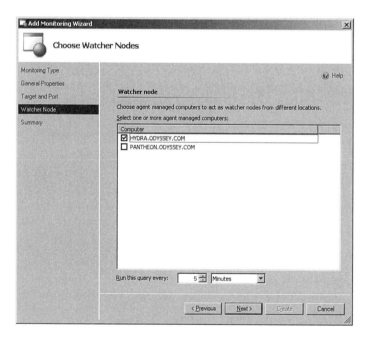

FIGURE 18.20   Configuring the Choose Watcher Nodes screen.

7. The final screen displays a summary of the information you have entered through-out the wizard. Click Create to complete creating the OLEDB synthetic transaction. Figure 18.21 shows the summary screen for this monitoring template.

By default, the OLE DB management pack template allows you to configure a synthetic transaction to connect to a database and verify that the database is online. Although this level of monitoring is adequate for a large number of environments, there may be instances where an additional level of monitoring is required.

The OLEDB module defined within the System Library management pack supports an additional level of monitoring. This module allows you to configure custom queries to run against the monitored database, meaning not only can you verify that the database is online, but you can also verify that the database is responding to queries. In addition, you can output the results of the query, allowing validation of data in the database. As an example, you can configure a SELECT statement to run against the database and then have the results of the query appear in an alert to validate the data that is returned. We discuss this capability in the next section.

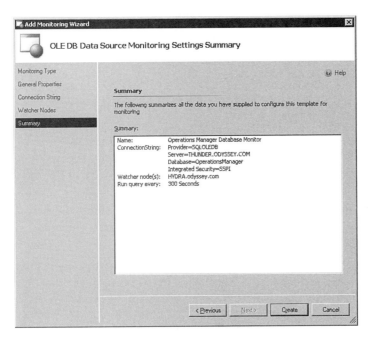

FIGURE 18.21   The OLE DB Data Source Monitoring Settings Summary screen.

Using Queries in an OLE DB Synthetic Transaction

There is a downside to using the additional options available in the System Library—you cannot configure these options using the Operations console graphical interface. To use this synthetic transaction, you would create it using the Operations console, and then use

Visual Studio to edit the XML file for the management pack that contains the synthetic transaction to configure the other options.

In this section, we walk through the steps to accomplish this. Before you can perform this process, you must create the OLE DB synthetic transaction using the Operations console, and export the management pack containing the transaction. We will assume here that the management pack has been exported to the Sample.Management.Pack.xml file on the desktop:

1. Open the management pack file using Visual Studio 2005 and search for "System.OleDbProbe." The search locates the section of the management pack containing the XML that makes up the OLE DB synthetic transaction. The section will look something like this:

   ```
   <ProbeAction ID="Probe" TypeID="System!System.OleDbProbe">
   <ConnectionString>Provider=SQLOLEDB;Server=THUNDER.ODYSSEY.COM;
   ➥Database=OperationsManager;Integrated Security=SSPI</ConnectionString>
   </ProbeAction>
   ```

2. After locating the section in the XML document, add the following additional options before the </ProbeAction> line:

   ▶ **Query**—Used to run a query against the database defined in the connection string (example: `Select * FROM Table1`).

   ▶ **GetValue**—Sets whether or not the query defined in the previous option is outputted or not (possible values are "true" or "false").

   ▶ **IncludeOriginalItem**—Because the Oledb.Probe module is a probe-action module, it will need a trigger in most cases. However, in some scenarios, the input item data needs to be preserved, and this element allows you to set this (values are "true" or "false").

   ▶ **OneRowPerItem**—If multiple rows are returned by the query string, then setting this causes multiple items to have a separate row for each (values are "true" or "false").

   ▶ **DatabaseNameRegLocation**—In your environment, the database name might not be available to you and must be read from a Registry location. In other words, you would use this option if the DatabaseName is not provided in the ConnectionString and you can provide the Registry location information here (example: SOFTWARE\Microsoft\Microsoft Operations Manager\3.0\Setup\DatabaseName, which is stored in the Registry on the management server).

   ▶ **DatabaseServerNameRegLocation**—As with the previous option, this allows you to read the database server name from a Registry key in place of entering it in the connection string (example: SOFTWARE\Microsoft\Microsoft Operations Manager\3.0\Setup\DatabaseServerName, also stored in the Registry on the management server).

3. For this example, we will simply configure a query to run against the OperationsManager database. Therefore, the updated section of the XML should look something like this:

```
<ProbeAction ID="Probe" TypeID="System!System.OleDbProbe">
<ConnectionString>Provider=SQLOLEDB;Server=THUNDER.ODYSSEY.COM;
➥Database=OperationsManager;Integrated Security=SSPI</ConnectionString>
<Query>SELECT MPName FROM dbo.ManagementPack</Query>
<GetValue>true</GetValue>
</ProbeAction>
```

This code will run the "`SELECT MPName from dbo.ManagementPack`" query against the Operational database, and display the management packs imported into OpsMgr. We will know by seeing output that the database is online and responding.

Be aware that this test does not output the query results. If you need to display the output in an alert, the best approach is to create a monitor and use the Oledb.Probe write action (which is a standard OpsMgr write action) to generate the data for the monitor. Chapter 23, "Developing Management Packs and Reports," includes additional information on creating management packs using XML.

TIP

More Information on Write Actions

More information about write actions and other components of the OpsMgr workflow can be found on Steve Wilson's AuthorMPs site at http://www.authormps.com/dnn/Concepts/WorkflowBasics/ModuleTypes/tabid/115/Default.aspx.

To read data in from the Registry (if the database information cannot be provided in the connection string for some reason), you can use the DatabaseNameRegLocation and DatabaseServerNameRegLocation options. The following is an example of code that would read these values from the Registry. For our example, we will assume that we have stored the database name in the HKLM\Software\Microsoft\Microsoft Operations Manager\3.0\Setup\DatabaseName key, and the server information in the HKLM\Software\Microsoft\Microsoft Operations Manager\3.0\Setup\DataBaseServerName key by default. (These are the locations used to store the location of the Operational database.) You may need to create these keys as required. The code sample is shown here:

```
<ProbeAction ID="Probe" TypeID="System!System.OleDbProbe">
<ConnectionString>Provider=SQLOLEDB;Integrated Security=SSPI</ConnectionString>
<Query>SELECT MPName FROM dbo.ManagementPack</Query>
<GetValue>true</GetValue>
<DatabaseNameRegLocation>
SOFTWARE\Microsoft\Microsoft Operations Manager\3.0\Setup\
➥DatabaseName</DatabaseNameRegLocation>
```

18

```
<DatabaseServerNameRegLocation>
SOFTWARE\Microsoft\Microsoft Operations Manager\3.0\Setup\DatabaseServerName
</DatabaseServerNameRegLocation>
</ProbeAction>
```

This code runs the SELECT MPName from dbo.ManagementPack query again, but the server and database information is not included in the connection string. This time, we read the information from the Registry on the management server. This may be for security reasons, where it is not acceptable to show server and database information in clear text in a connection string.

Viewing the OLE DB Transaction Performance Data

After creating the OLE DB data source monitor and allowing sufficient time to pass to enable data to populate the reports, we are able to look at the performance data related to the OLE DB data source monitor we created. Perform the following steps:

1. Navigate to the Monitoring space and expand the Synthetic Transaction folder in the navigation tree to open the OLE DB Data Source State view. You can see the OLE DB data source monitor we configured displayed on the right-hand side. Right-click the object; then select Open -> Performance View, as we previously showed in Figure 18.16.

2. You can see the performance view for the OLE DB data source. The available performance counters are Open Time and Connection Time. Select one or both of these counters and view the graph. Figure 18.22 shows the graph from our Odyssey environment, where the watcher node is Hydra. If you configured additional watcher nodes, these will appear as separate counters, so you can compare the open time and connection time from different watcher nodes.

This section looked at the process for creating a synthetic transaction to monitor a database using an OLE DB connection. Although we monitored the OperationsManager database hosted by SQL Server, you can monitor any database that supports OLE DB as long as the OLE DB driver is installed where required. As an example, if you will be monitoring Oracle databases, you will need to install the Oracle client to use either the Microsoft or Oracle OLE DB driver.

We also showed the performance data you could generate using the OLE DB data source synthetic transaction.

Monitoring LOB Applications Through Port Activity

Although Operations Manager makes it straightforward to monitor applications, the level of monitoring you ultimately achieve depends on how well the application integrates with the operating system. Factors that play into this include the following:

▶ Whether the application logs events to the Windows NT Event logs

▶ If the application runs using Windows services

▶ Whether there are Windows performance counters associated with the application

Even if an application is well integrated with the operating system, it still may be necessary to validate that the application is actually responding. This is where the TCP port synthetic transaction comes in.

A large number of applications use a particular TCP port to send data. Some examples include port 25, used by email applications, and port 5723, used by the OpsMgr agent. The level of integration between the application and the operating system will affect the amount and type of monitoring data that may be collected. For those applications that are not integrated, TCP port monitoring may be the only way to verify whether an application is online and responding.

It is important to note that just because an application's TCP port is responding, this does not necessarily indicate that the application is working correctly. Monitoring a TCP port does help build a picture of application availability and response, but preferably it is not the only method used for testing an application. This is particularly true for non-Microsoft applications that run on the Windows platform, such as Oracle and Siebel, for example.

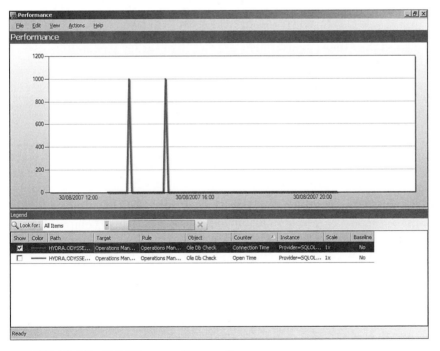

FIGURE 18.22   OLE DB connection results.

The TCP port management pack template allows you to create the necessary monitoring objects to test connectivity to a specified TCP port. The template also collects the performance and response information of that port, allowing you to analyze the response time of the TCP port.

In addition to monitoring applications using the TCP port synthetic transaction, you can also monitor hardware devices such as Simple Mail Transfer Protocol (SMTP) relay hardware devices that respond on port 25, as an example. We do not address the SMTP relay aspect of TCP port monitoring in this chapter; you can find that information in Chapter 22, "Interoperability."

Creating a TCP Port Monitor

This section looks at the process for creating a TCP port monitor. Perform the following steps:

1. Launch the Operations console and navigate to the Authoring space.

2. Right-click on the Management Pack Templates sub-tree and select Add monitoring wizard..., as we previously showed in Figure 18.3.

3. The screen shown in Figure 18.23 is displayed. From this screen, select TCP Port and click Next.

4. On the following screen, input the name and a description for the synthetic transaction and select the management pack you will save the transaction rules to. For this example, we will call the transaction **OpsMgr Management Server Port Monitor** and we will select the Sample management pack we have already used in this book. Click Next to continue.

5. The next screen is the Enter and Test Port Settings screen. Enter the TCP Port and IP Address or device name for the object and port you wish to test. Because we are monitoring the OpsMgr port on the management server, we will configure the device to be **HYDRA.ODYSSEY.COM** and configure the port as **5723**. Type these values into the boxes.

   Of course, in your environment you would input any server or network device's IP address or DNS name, and the appropriate port to monitor. Click the Test button to validate the port. Figure 18.24 shows the completed screen. Click Next to continue.

6. The following screen is the Choose Watcher Nodes screen, where the computer initiating the test is selected and configured. The screen lists all computers running OpsMgr agents, and you can tick the checkboxes to carry out the test on the computers you choose. In our example, we will run the test from the PANTHEON.ODYSSEY.COM machine. We will also configure the test to run every five (5) minutes instead of the default setting of two (2) minutes. You can refer to Figure 18.6 for an example of the Watcher Node screen. Click Next, and you will continue to the final screen of the Add Monitoring wizard.

7. The final screen summarizes the information you have inputted throughout the wizard. Click Create to complete creating the TCP port synthetic transaction. Figure 18.25 displays the summary screen.

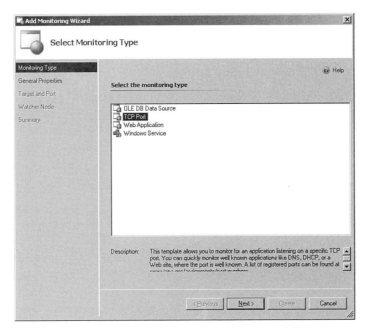

FIGURE 18.23   Selecting the TCP port in the Add Monitoring wizard.

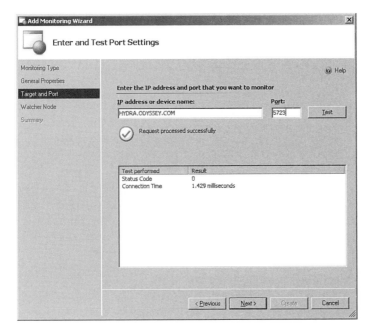

FIGURE 18.24   Entering and testing settings for the TCP port.

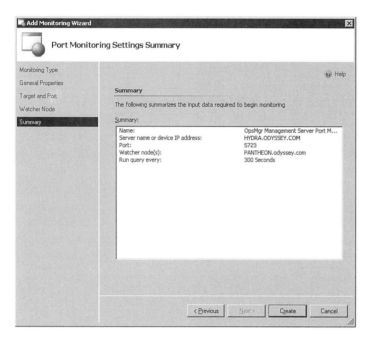

FIGURE 18.25   TCP Port wizard summary screen.

Viewing the TCP Port Performance Data

Similar to the other synthetic transactions we have discussed in this chapter, the TCP port monitor synthetic transaction collects performance data. You can view this information using the process described next:

1. Navigate to the Monitoring space; expand the Synthetic Transaction folder in the navigation tree, then open the TCP Port Checks State view. Displayed on the right-hand side is the web application monitor we configured earlier. Right-click the object, then select Open Performance View, similar to what we did earlier in Figure 18.16.

2. The Performance view opens, with the only performance counter available being the Connection Time counter for the TCP port we are monitoring. Of course, if we configured additional watcher nodes, these nodes would appear as separate counters, allowing us to compare the connection time from different watcher nodes. Figure 18.26 shows this Performance view.

We have discussed the basics of monitoring LOB applications using TCP ports, documenting the process for creating a TCP port monitor, and monitoring the OpsMgr management server port of 5723. Although we chose to focus on monitoring an application port, it is very useful to use the TCP port monitor to test ports used by network devices and SMTP relay devices as well. Chapter 22 discusses the process for creating a TCP monitor.

We also looked at the performance data available from the TCP port monitor synthetic transaction, and we showed you where to view this information in the Operations console.

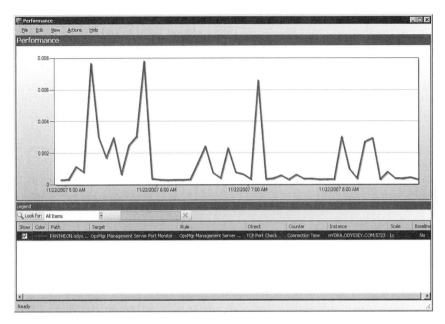

FIGURE 18.26   Viewing TCP port performance.

Managing Exchange

In addition to the synthetic transaction management pack templates available out of the box with OpsMgr, a number of individual product management packs provide synthetic transaction monitoring of their own.

The Microsoft Exchange management pack is one of the major management packs to use synthetic transactions for validating application response and availability.

NOTE

Clarifying the Exchange Management Pack Version

In this section of the chapter, all references to the Microsoft Exchange management pack reference the Microsoft Exchange 2003 management pack for Operations Manager 2007, unless otherwise specified.

The Exchange management pack performs in-depth monitoring of Exchange, including monitoring for Windows events, monitoring the status of the services, and checking for performance thresholds that are exceeded. The management pack also contains a number of scripts that perform Exchange simulations. We will look at these simulations or synthetic transactions in more detail.

The Exchange management pack includes scripts, rules, and monitors to carry out simulations on the key Exchange components. It contains synthetic transactions for MAPI (Messaging Application Programming Interface) logon, Mail Flow, Outlook Web Access (OWA), Outlook Mobile Access (OMA), and Exchange ActiveSync (EAS). These synthetic transactions are performed using an Active Directory user account and Exchange mailboxes, which typically are configured when you deploy the management pack.

We will examine some of these different transactions in more detail in the next sections, and look at the process for configuring the Exchange environment prior to deploying the management pack, which uses the Exchange Management Pack Configuration Wizard.

Preparing to Monitor Exchange

In order for the Exchange management pack to fully monitor Exchange, you must configure your Exchange environment for Operations Manager.

The configuration includes creating of a number of disabled user accounts and associated mailboxes and assigning a number of security permissions throughout the Exchange environment. You can perform these configurations manually as documented in the Exchange Management Pack Guide (which you can download from http://technet.microsoft.com/en-us/opsmgr/bb498235.aspx#EFG) or use the Exchange Management Pack Configuration Wizard, which is by far the easiest (and recommended) method. You can find the specific details of the changes to make in the Exchange Management Pack Guide.

The Exchange Management Pack Configuration Wizard is available for download at http://go.microsoft.com/fwlink/?LinkId=35942.

After downloading the configuration wizard, extract the downloaded files and install the utility. The utility requires that you have .NET Framework 2.0 and the Exchange System Manager tools installed on the computer on which you run the wizard. Therefore, unless you have these client tools on a workstation, we advise installing the tool on an Exchange front-end server.

Creating an Exchange Access Account

Before running the Configuration Wizard, we recommend you create an Active Directory user account. The Wizard and Exchange management pack use this account in the following manner:

- ▶ The mailboxes created by the wizard will use this account to access Exchange.
- ▶ The scripts in the Exchange management pack will use this account.

The account should belong to the Domain Users security group and have a mailbox created.

After meeting the prerequisites and installing the tool, execute it using an account with Exchange Administrator rights to the entire Exchange Organization. Perform the following steps:

1. When you launch the tool, the wizard presents a welcome screen that we show in Figure 18.27.

2. Click Next, and select the Administrative group to apply the changes to. We will select the <All> option from the drop-down list. Figure 18.28 shows the Administrative Group screen. Click Next to continue.

3. The following screen displays the Exchange servers in your environment. Select those computers with OpsMgr agents installed that you wish to monitor. The server selection screen is shown in Figure 18.29. Click Next.

4. At the next screen, you can choose to select the default configuration or customize your options. We will select Custom configuration so that we can choose our own settings throughout the wizard.

5. The first screen of the custom configuration option allows us to choose the properties we want to configure. Select all options, as shown in Figure 18.30, and click Next to continue.

6. The screen shown in Figure 18.30 allows you to enable or disable Message Tracking and Front-End monitoring. We will choose to enable both and continue.

FIGURE 18.27   The Welcome to the Exchange Management Pack Configuration Wizard screen.

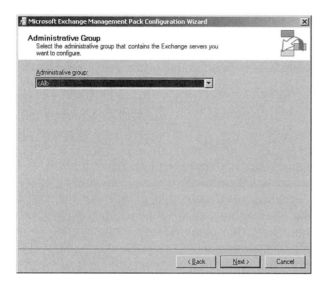

FIGURE 18.28   Choosing the Administrative Group in the Exchange Management Pack
Configuration Wizard.

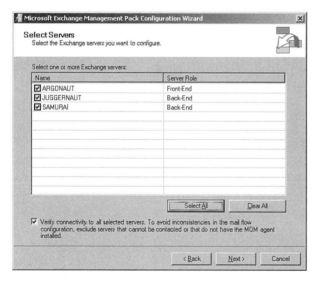

FIGURE 18.29   Exchange servers displayed in the Exchange Management Pack Configuration
Wizard.

Figure 18.31 allows you to specify the Exchange services to monitor. Unless you
have a requirement to monitor a specific service, click the Default button and click
Next to continue.

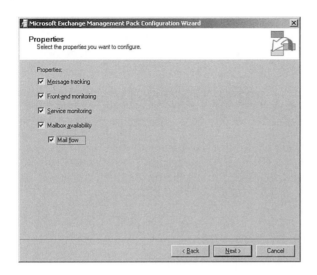

FIGURE 18.30   Select the properties you want to configure.

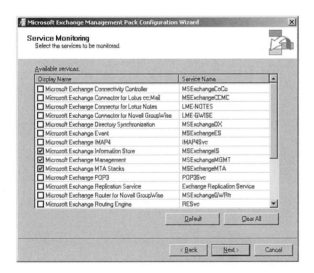

FIGURE 18.31   Select the Exchange services you want to monitor.

7. The next screen is an important one. It allows you to choose whether to have an Exchange mailbox created and therefore whether to monitor servers or individual stores. We will choose to monitor servers. Click Next to continue.

8. In the following screen, we configure the mail flow options. We are indicating which email servers send mail to which other email servers. The configuration here will depend entirely on your environment. We have configured our environment as shown in Figure 18.32.

9. The final screen of the Exchange Management Pack Configuration Wizard is where you specify the Exchange Access user account that we mentioned earlier. Input the account, click Next to continue, and finally click Next on the summary screen.

The wizard will apply the changes to the Exchange environment; once that is complete and Active Directory has sufficient time to replicate the changes, the Exchange environment is ready for monitoring by Operations Manager. You will need to rerun the wizard if you add additional Exchange servers.

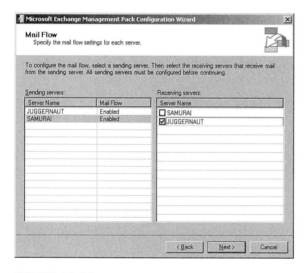

FIGURE 18.32   Configuring mail flow in the Exchange Management Pack Configuration Wizard.

NOTE

Importing the Exchange MP Prior to Running the Configuration Wizard

Before running the wizard, it is essential to import the Exchange management pack into OpsMgr and verify that the Exchange servers are already discovered. The discovery process can take up to 24 hours, particularly if you have Exchange hosted in a clustered environment. If you have not imported the management pack and discovered the servers before running the wizard, you may receive errors.

Monitoring Mail Flow

Now that we have configured Exchange for Operations Manager, let's look at what we want to accomplish with monitoring Exchange. The bottom line when it comes to Exchange functionality is that Exchange needs to route mail between mailboxes and between different Exchange servers in the environment and beyond. If this functionality is not working, Exchange's functionality is severely hindered.

For this reason, monitoring Exchange mail flow is critical to ensure your Exchange environment is working correctly. The Exchange management pack provides a number of scripts that work out of the box after preparing the Exchange environment (discussed in the "Preparing to Monitor Exchange" section of this chapter), monitoring mail flow in your environment and beyond.

These scripts use Exchange mailboxes configured specifically for OpsMgr to use to send emails and verify they arrive at their destination within an acceptable timeframe. The data is used to determine the health of the Exchange system, generating alerts and altering the status of the relevant monitors if mail messages are not received as expected. This level of monitoring helps identify mail flow problems before they seriously affect the Exchange infrastructure by filling up mail queues and such.

Monitoring MAPI Logons

After mail flow, the next most important capability in an Exchange infrastructure is to login to mailboxes from Microsoft Outlook or another MAPI-compatible application. This process is known as *establishing a MAPI logon*.

MAPI is a messaging architecture and a Component Object Model-based API for Microsoft Windows. MAPI allows client programs to become email-enabled or aware by calling MAPI subsystem routines that interface with certain messaging systems and message stores. A typical example of a MAPI-enabled server product is Microsoft Exchange, and an example of a MAPI-enabled client program is Microsoft Outlook.

The scripts in the Exchange management pack perform synthetic MAPI logons, using the mailboxes created by the Exchange Management Pack Configuration Wizard. These scripts behave as if they were a connection coming from a MAPI-enabled application; as far as Exchange is concerned, these connections *are* coming from such an application. Exchange thus responds as it would to a true MAPI logon, allowing OpsMgr to verify whether MAPI logons are working and if the logon performance time is acceptable.

As with mail flow monitoring, Operations Manager will generate alerts and change monitor states if the script fails to perform a MAPI logon to a particular Exchange server or mailbox store.

18

Monitoring OWA/OMA and EAS

In addition to using MAPI-enabled applications such as Outlook to log into Exchange, many companies use OWA, OMA, and EAS to access mail across the Internet. If these systems are unavailable, remote users are often not able to access their emails or synchronize their smartphones.

To assist with checking availability, the Exchange management pack includes rules that monitor these Internet-based components of Exchange. The Exchange management pack contains scripts, rules, and monitors that simulate a login to the OWA, OMA, and EAS websites and validate that the sites respond correctly and within an acceptable time. These scripts also use the Exchange mailboxes created specifically with the Configuration Wizard to monitor Exchange using OpsMgr.

OpsMgr will generate alerts if OWA, OMA, or EAS do not respond. It is also possible to specify custom URLs to monitor if you have customized the OWA, OMA, or EAS sites in your particular environment. You will specify the URLs in the Registry on the front-end Exchange servers, in the HKLM\Software\Microsoft\ExchangeMOM\ *<FrontEndServerName>* key. You will create the following string values to store OWW, OMA, and EAS URLs:

▶ CustomUrls

▶ CustomOMAUrls

▶ CustomEASUrls

These processes are documented in the Exchange Management Pack Guide.

The Exchange sections of this chapter looked at the synthetic transactions provided in the Exchange management pack and the additional monitoring capabilities this adds to OpsMgr. We also discussed the process for preparing the Exchange environment for monitoring with OpsMgr by using the Exchange Management Pack Configuration Wizard.

Using Synthetic Transactions in Application Monitoring

After creating your synthetic transactions, you will want to utilize the monitoring provided by these transactions to the maximum. You will also want to create and configure distributed applications (DAs) using the designer tool (more information on the Distributed Application Designer is found in Chapter 19).

One very nice feature of OpsMgr is the ability to take the synthetic transaction objects you created and use them in your own distributed applications. This capability enables the results of the simulations to affect the status of the application, and therefore affects your availability reports. The synthetic transaction functionality allows the status and availability of the applications to not only be based on Windows events, service status, and performance thresholds, but also on whether or not the application is actually responding as you expect. By measuring response time, synthetic transactions can assist you in meeting your SLAs.

The additional depth of monitoring utilized with DAs means that the monitoring information obtained from a DA you configure can be very accurate when comprised of a combination of service information, Windows events, performance data, and simulated connections into the application.

When you create a synthetic transaction, Operations Manager adds that transaction to the Perspective class. This is true for all synthetic transactions and allows them to be easily located and added to DAs as required. We will use the Perspective class in our example to add the synthetic transaction we have created to a new DA.

We will now look at the process to add a synthetic transaction to a DA. In this example, we will create a basic DA to monitor Operations Manager using the TCP port and OLE DB synthetic transactions we created earlier in this chapter (in the "Using OLE DB to Monitor Databases" and "Monitoring LOB Applications Through Port Activity" sections). Please be aware that the process for creating a DA is also included in Chapter 19. There may be a level of duplication with the material in this chapter, but this duplication is necessary to enable us to demonstrate the example in this chapter.

To reiterate, in this section, we will:

- ▶ Create a distributed application
- ▶ Add component groups
- ▶ Associate components with component groups
- ▶ Establish relationships between component groups

We illustrate this in the flowchart in Figure 18.33.

To configure the new DA, perform the following steps:

1. Open the Operations console and navigate to the Authoring space.
2. Right-click Distributed Applications and select Create a new Distributed Application.... The first screen in the Distributed Application Designer opens. You will provide a name and optional description for the DA, and select a template to use and a management pack for saving the DA. In our example, we will name our distributed application **OpsMgr Environment**, and we will select the Line of Business Web Application template. We will use the drop-down box to save the DA to the Sample management pack we have previously used in this book. We show the completed screen in Figure 18.34.

   Click OK, which loads the template and enters the Distributed Application Designer.

18

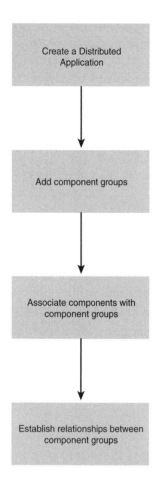

FIGURE 18.33   DA Design process flowchart.

3. The screen shown in Figure 18.35 is displayed. From here, you can build out the DA.

4. We will start by populating our application with the database and website components we created earlier in the "Using OLE DB to Monitor Databases" and "Monitoring Web Applications" sections of this chapter. Drag the OperationsManager database from the database object type on the left into the database component. We show this in Figure 18.36.

5. Next, repeat the procedure to add the Operations Manager 2007 web console site to the website's component, dragging it from the bottom-left side of the screen up into the website's component.

6. Now that we have the default components populated, we need to create a custom component that will contain our transactions.

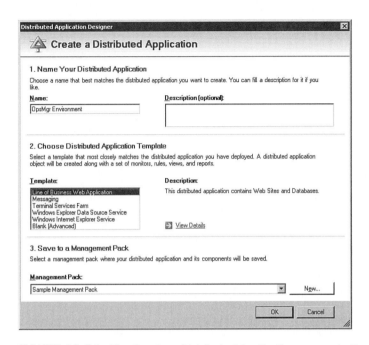

FIGURE 18.34   The Create a Distributed Application screen in the Distributed Application Designer.

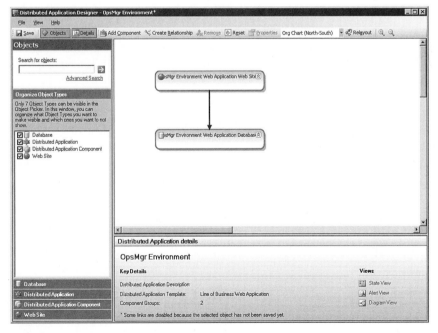

FIGURE 18.35   The main screen of the Distributed Application Designer.

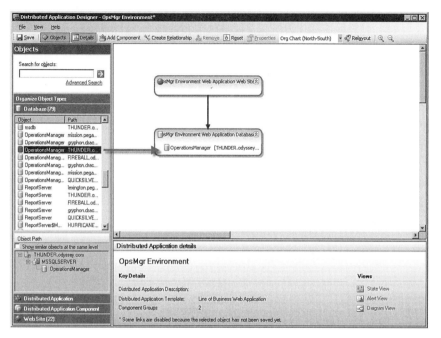

FIGURE 18.36   Adding a database to the distributed application.

7. Click the Add Component button, highlighted in Figure 18.37.

8. After a short delay during which the designer collects information about all the classes present in OpsMgr, the Create New Component Group dialog appears. We will name our component **OpsMgr Live Tests**, select the objects of the following type(s): radio button, and tick the classes shown in Figure 18.38. This screen allows us to add the transactions we created earlier. As you can see, we have ticked the checkbox next to the Perspective class, which is the class all synthetic transactions are added to automatically.

9. After selecting the relevant classes, click OK and the class appears in the object organizer on the left. Under Perspective, you can locate the two synthetic transactions we created—Operations Manager database monitor and OpsMgr Management Server Port Monitor—and drag them into the new component we have just created. Figure 18.39 shows the result.

10. We know that if the Operations database is offline, the management server cannot work correctly, which means that one or both of the synthetic transactions will fail. We will want to create a relationship to ensure that if the Operations database is offline, the transaction's state will update to reflect this.

In Figure 18.39, click the Create Relationship, and drag the cursor from the OpsMgr Live Tests component to the database component since the transactions use the database (e.g., are dependent on it). Figure 18.40 shows the results.

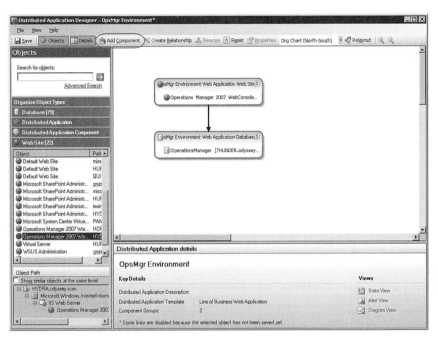

FIGURE 18.37   Select the Add Component button.

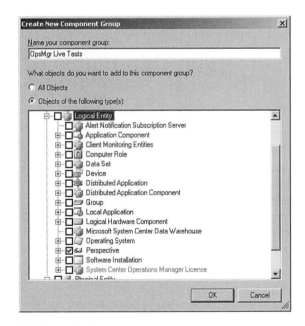

FIGURE 18.38   Add objects (classes) to the new component group.

18

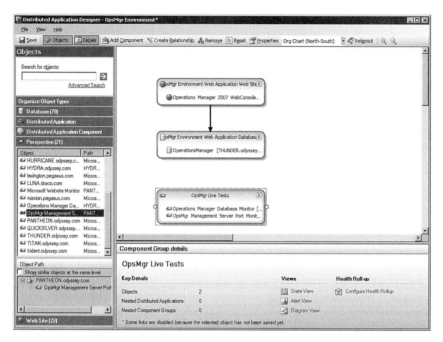

FIGURE 18.39   All components configured in the Distributed Application Designer.

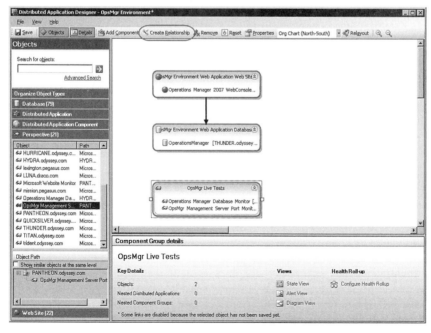

FIGURE 18.40   Creating a relationship between the OpsMgr Live Tests component and the OpsMgr Environment Web Application Database.

11. For this particular example, we will assume that we do not want to customize the DA any further; therefore, we will click Save and close the DA designer. Chapter 19 includes more information on the Distributed Application Designer and additional options.

12. After creating the DA, we can look at the diagram view to validate that it is configured correctly. Open the diagram view for the DA (by right-clicking on it and selecting Open -> Diagram view), and you will be presented with a view similar to that shown in Figure 18.41.

In this section, we looked at the functionality included in OpsMgr that makes it possible to add synthetic transactions to new and existing DAs for monitoring and reporting purposes. We also summarized the process for adding a previously created synthetic transaction to a new DA that we created in this section.

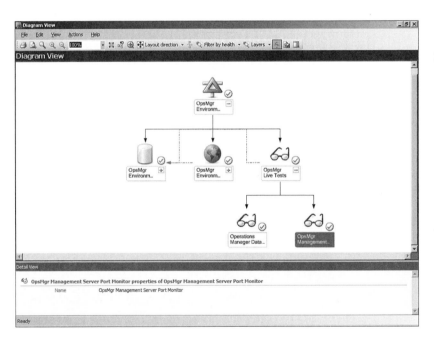

FIGURE 18.41   The Distributed Application Diagram view.

Summary

In this chapter, we looked at the different synthetic transactions offered by OpsMgr out of the box. These include the Web Application, TCP Port, ASP.NET Application, ASP.NET Web Application, and Windows Service management pack templates.

We explained the role of watcher nodes in monitoring applications using simulation, and covered the process for selecting watcher nodes. We also looked at the different types of synthetic transactions including web application, TCP port monitors, and OLE DB data source synthetic transactions and the processes for creating them and configuring advanced options.

In addition, we covered the role synthetic transactions play in monitoring Exchange using the Exchange management pack and the different types of synthetic transactions that are included with the management pack. Finally, we looked at the ability to add synthetic transactions to distributed applications created using the Distributed Application Designer, and we included the process for adding synthetic transactions to distributed applications.

The next chapter discusses managing a distributed environment. It covers the built-in distributed applications provided by OpsMgr and discusses using the Distributed Application features of OpsMgr to create your own custom management solutions.

CHAPTER 19

Managing a Distributed Environment

If you review Microsoft's marketing materials and the white papers released about the System Center Operations Manager (OpsMgr) 2007 product, you will notice one of the three design pillars is *end-to-end service management*. OpsMgr achieves end-to-end (E2E) service management primarily with the Distributed Application feature, the subject of this chapter. Other E2E service management components of OpsMgr are the following:

▶ Synthetic transactions (covered in Chapter 18, "Using Synthetic Transactions").

▶ Client monitoring and Agentless Exception Monitoring (see Chapter 16, "Client Monitoring").

▶ The Service Modeling Language (SML)-based system and health models (covered in Chapter 3, "Looking Inside OpsMgr").

The first part of this chapter discusses and defines distributed applications in the systems management arena, and then covers in detail the built-in distributed applications provided by OpsMgr with the management packs that are included with OpsMgr. The second half of the chapter explores how you can leverage the Distributed Application features of OpsMgr to create custom management solutions that are a perfect fit for your organization's business goals.

What Is a Distributed Application?

This question is particularly appropriate for our discussion. As Operations Manager 2007 basically reinvents the term, we must cover some new definitions. The term *distributed application* originated in the software development community; with OpsMgr 2007, it migrates to the systems management community with added meaning. In the following sections, we briefly explain the programming origins of the term, and then show how OpsMgr stretches out that concept to the next dimension.

Background

The existence of distributed applications became possible with the invention of client/server computing. The capability for a single application to process and store data on both a central server and a client desktop led to the two-tiered distributed application. The earliest two-tiered distributed application, still enormously popular, is the database client, where the client application on the user desktop interacts directly with the database application on the network server.

However, for the larger enterprise, there emerged almost immediately a market for middleware, also known as business object applications or business logic. *Middleware* acts as the data-processing intermediary between the client and the back-end service. Implementing middleware created the classic three-tier distributed application, often used as a model for intranet-based enterprise applications. A distributed application has three logical tiers—data, business logic, and the user interface—which are described here:

▶ The data tier is a database such as Microsoft SQL Server.

▶ The business logic tier handles accessing the data and distributing it to the clients; it is the brain of the three-tier application.

▶ The user-interface tier (or presentation tier) often consists of both a web browser-based application and/or a traditional Windows application.

Figure 19.1 illustrates the classic three-tiered distributed application familiar to software developers.

Stratifying and segmenting a complex distributed application into defined tiers essentially creates software containers. Developing standardized software containers to host application components helps considerably in shortening development lifecycles for large applications. This approach allows optimizing subordinate functions within the tiers, yet keeps the focus of the development effort on the overall distributed application.

With distributed applications, it is not unusual to see release cycles of six months or fewer for major enhancements, and three months or fewer for minor feature additions. The application development industry has thus experienced great success by adopting the distributed application model. Using the distributed application model has markedly increased the agility of organizations, facilitating rapid roll out of major features to enterprise applications in response to changing demands and opportunities.

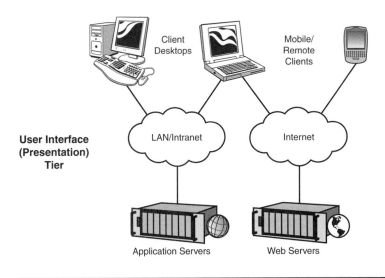

User Interface
(Presentation)
Tier

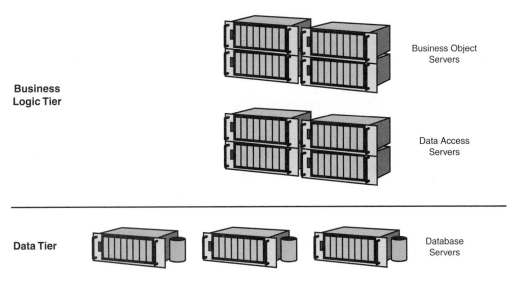

Business
Logic Tier

Data Tier

FIGURE 19.1 The classic three-tiered distributed application model used by developers.

This leads to an emerging paradigm, however: Because programmer-facing component models that simplify development have enjoyed such success, complexity is shifting to the operations side of managing these applications! The professional development community got their act together when it comes to rapid response to changing business goals; the widespread adoption of the distributed application development methodology has had a greatly beneficial effect on the opportunities, professionalism, and increased business value of the software development community.

Now, the systems management community is under similar scrutiny to seek efficiencies and apply holistic methodologies to their areas of responsibility. In particular, there is a clear systems management responsibility to keep up with the rapid pace of release updates to business-critical enterprise applications. Although the development side of the house may have a streamlined and efficient change management solution, the systems management team maintains responsibility for monitoring application performance and availability in production—even with a high and increased rate of application change.

As an application transitions from development to production (the release management stage), gaps in management control can occur unless the management system is prepared at that time to begin delivering service delivery metrics on the application. For pre-packaged applications, one hopes that the software vendor releases an OpsMgr management pack supporting whatever new features are in the application. However, for custom enterprise distributed applications, the burden for designing a monitoring solution falls on the Information Technology (IT) staff in that organization.

IT needs to identify whether distributed application problems stem from a failed host, application process, network component, or other infrastructure failure. Even with a perfect monitoring infrastructure in place, it is beyond most humans' capability to *synthesize* the raw state of hundreds or thousands of component monitors and determine the root cause of distributed application failures. The system administrator needs a holistic way of viewing and managing the complex distributed application, processes that are also capable of rapid revision to keep in step with application change releases.

Enter the OpsMgr Distributed Application

A holistic approach to managing complex systems results in better results than trying to manage many sub-systems independently. (Aristotle's observation that "The whole is more than the sum of its parts" rings true as an early proof statement of this concept.) An OpsMgr Distributed Application (DA) is the framework for integrating meaningful metrics of the usability of a complex system composed of many subordinate components, such as the software containers (and the hardware hosts) of that application.

Integration and *synthesis* are pursuits related to holism, that being the intellectual processes our brains use to create the whole from the parts. Synthesis is one of the higher functions in our human brains, and appeals to the seeker of a holistic approach to IT management. Using OpsMgr, a new paradigm emerges—systems management professionals are being provided with a tool we can use to encapsulate the problem-solving processes in our heads.

Let's take a real-world example: A system administrator gets a phone call in the middle of the night—a critical e-commerce application is down. What starts going through his (or her) mind? What does he check first, what are the things to look at, what is the decision tree? You can capture those diagnostic decision trees, apply your collective event integration and synthesis knowledge, and transfer that information to an OpsMgr 2007 Distributed Application.

The OpsMgr DA represents your best bet for defining what you really need to monitor for delivering your business-critical services. See the contrast between these problem-resolution techniques:

▶ Without a holistic means to view the health of the e-commerce application, the administrator must pour over the status of disk arrays, network devices, firewalls, server processes, and many more components.

Sometimes, the administrator can spot an obvious failure point. However, it is just as likely that a cascading series of less-obvious failures has occurred in one or more distributed application components. This can lead to a time-consuming troubleshooting chase involving a lot of people!

▶ Using a previously created OpsMgr DA that clearly defines the components involved in delivering the e-commerce application, a quick look at the Health Monitor for the application reveals the source of the outage. The effective design of the OpsMgr DA has already done the troubleshooting work. Targeted recovery operations can begin immediately to get the e-commerce application running.

How far can we take this concept? An ambitious but achievable goal of an advanced network management system is to enable a synthesis function in the monitoring engine, a step along the road toward Artificial Intelligence (AI) in back-end support systems. If the management software can synthesize large amounts of highly diverse time-disparate data, it can do some front-line thinking for us, employing techniques that determine how application environments can configure and heal themselves when there are problems.

It has been postulated that increased operational complexity has reached a point where it is no longer feasible for humans to manage the applications required for running an enterprise. OpsMgr Distributed Applications are an early tool to facilitate self-managing applications—a paradigm known as "autonomic computing," the ultimate expression of zero-touch and lights-out network management principles.

Learning how to leverage the DA feature in OpsMgr not only equips you to deal with the middle-of-the-night phone calls; it is a foundation for a new approach—one that foreshadows eliminating those midnight calls.

Predefined Distributed Applications

Distributed applications run on many different physical tiers and often scale out over the Internet, or over disparate and different networks. In the Microsoft world, there are three such applications that most OpsMgr administrators will encounter, and that Microsoft has provided predefined services for monitoring:

19

▶ **Operations Manager Management Group**—Installed by default.

▶ **Active Directory Topology Root**—Installed by the Active Directory management pack.

▶ **Exchange Service**—Installed by the Exchange management pack.

Figure 19.2 highlights these three services at the Distributed Applications global view in the Operations console. In the next sections of this chapter, we will describe how you can use each of these services effectively.

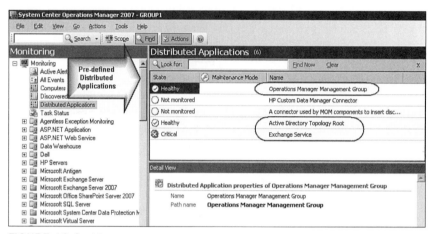

FIGURE 19.2   Most management groups will include these Distributed Applications.

Operations Manager Management Group

The action of installing an OpsMgr 2007 management group automatically creates this DA, so you will find it in every Operations Manager 2007 management group. Even before importing any management packs, this service is visible in the Distributed Applications view. We encourage you to become familiar with the features available in the Operations Manager Management Group DA, as that is where Microsoft has tried to make data relevant to the functioning of the OpsMgr product easy to access.

Using the Health Explorer

As you review the health of your management group, a great technique is to flip (or pivot) through the different views that are available by right-clicking on the Operations Manager Management Group DA, starting with the Health Explorer. The "master view" for any DA is the Health Explorer; this is what you will open first after that middle-of-the-night phone call.

Figure 19.3 shows the Health Explorer for the Operations Manager Management Group DA, focused on a low free space alert in the Operations database.

Also in Figure 19.3, we highlight some branches of the health model to point out the many different functions that can be bundled into a DA. In the upper portion of the view, notice that each gateway server is watched as part of the Gateway Management Server Group Availability Health Rollup. Lower down in the view, notice that three aspects of the SDK service are watched: database connectivity, port availability, and the Windows service. These features highlight the broad scope of monitoring that a DA can perform.

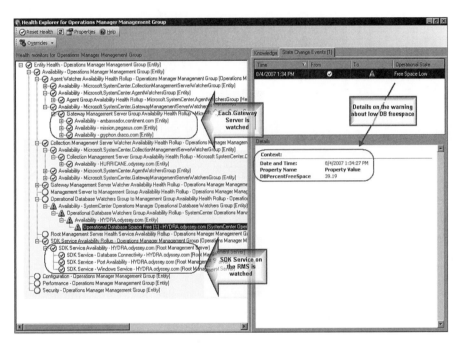

FIGURE 19.3   Management group Health Explorer exposes and organizes monitors.

Alerts and Performance Views

There is an Alerts view for the Operations Manager Management Group DA, shown in Figure 19.4. We customized our view to include the Last Modified time and the Repeat Count of the alert, as this helps triage the alerts listed.

The Alerts view of the Operations Manager Management Group DA, displayed in Figure 19.4, is a convenient feature since it segregates alerts dealing just with the health of the OpsMgr management group. Similarly, a Performance view is available that contains just the monitors Microsoft believes are relevant to assessing the health of the management group. Figure 19.5 shows the Performance view of the Operations Manager Management Group DA.

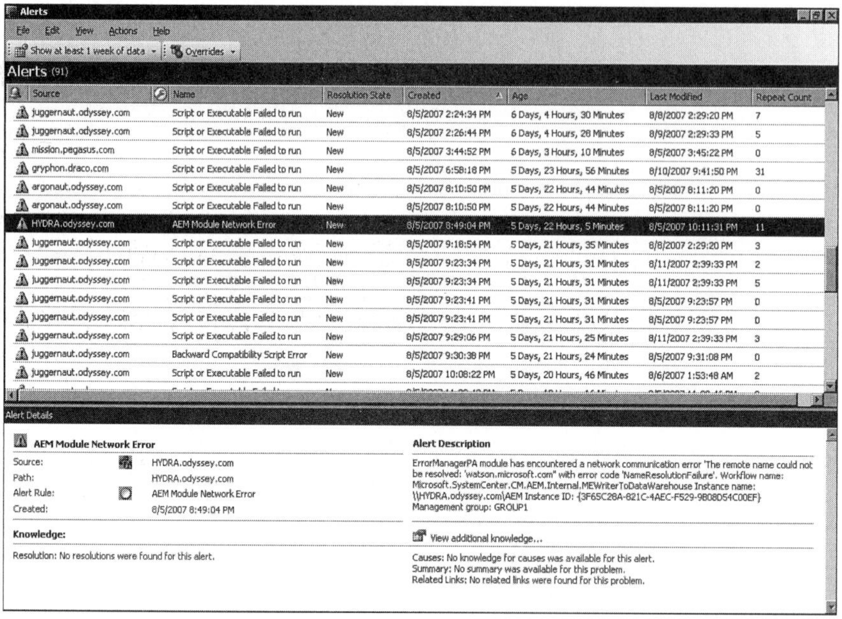

FIGURE 19.4   Examining just the alerts that are relevant to management group health.

In Figure 19.5, we selected the Send Queue % Used performance counter of a sample agent population to verify there are no unexpected connectivity issues between agents and management servers. If any send queue exceeds what is normally a near-to-zero quantity, it indicates a problem with agent communication. Microsoft makes available a variety of pre-selected counters from both agents and management server components to add to the Performance view. An intelligence feature of the DA is the pre-selection of the counters available in the console.

The Diagram View

The most advanced view available for a DA is the Diagram view. This view allows you to discover containment and dependency relationships between application components that you cannot observe in the other views. Figure 19.6 shows the Diagram view of the Operations Manager Management Group DA.

Notice in the Diagram view in Figure 19.6 (on the left side), we circled the processes that are watching the file share and HTTP listener components of the Agentless Exception Monitoring (AEM) service. That is just one small section of the DA Diagram view we selected to expand—when using the Diagram view, you can expose just the portions of the application you want to look at.

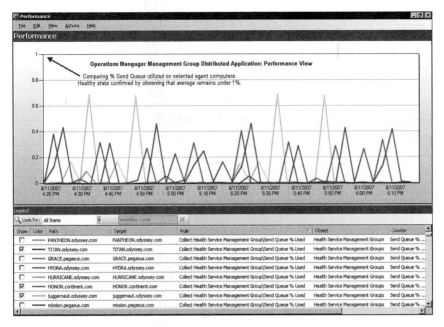

FIGURE 19.5   The DA contains pre-selected performance counters.

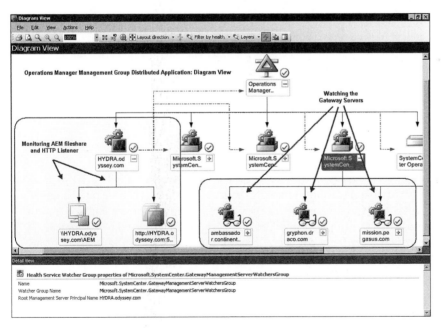

FIGURE 19.6   The diagram view of the Operations Manager Management Group.

Comparing the DA Diagram View and the Health Explorer

In some ways, the Diagram view of a DA presents the same information as the Health Explorer. For example, in the Diagram view shown in Figure 19.6, we highlighted (on the right side) the watcher processes for the gateway servers. These correspond to the availability monitors circled in the top portion of the Health Explorer shown in Figure 19.3.

The main difference in presentation between the Health Explorer and the Diagram views is that you can interact with objects in the Diagram view by clicking and dragging them, rearranging the objects in the view. Doing so causes the solid (containment) and the dotted (non-containment) lines to move with the object. This capability lets you spot relationships between components that you might not otherwise detect. We will drill down into all the advanced features of the diagram view later in the "Creating a Distributed Application Health Model" section of this chapter.

A take-away from reviewing the Operations Manager Management Group DA is that a well-authored DA can save you a lot of time when it comes to assessing the health state of the application. By identifying the classes of objects that are involved in delivering the application (and their relationships), and then collecting sets of targeted views that focus on the service delivery of the application, knowledge is encapsulated, preserved, and made portable.

> **TIP**
>
> **Forests and Predefined Distributed Applications**
>
> The three predefined applications have different behaviors in a forest environment. The Operations Manager Management Group DA is forest-neutral. All Active Directory forests that have computers with management group components installed will participate in the DA. The Active Directory Topology Root is specific for the forest of the management group; it does not monitor other forests' Active Directories. The Exchange Service DA does cross forest boundaries, and recognizes the managed Exchange Organization of any forest.

Active Directory Topology Root

Microsoft's Active Directory (AD) Service, so integrated with Windows networking, itself is an archetypal distributed application. Active Directory components can be on a single physical server for a small business, or distributed across hundreds of domain controllers for a global enterprise. In its simplest, small business implementation, all that matters is the local authentication experience for user workstations; whereas for the larger enterprise, you want to monitor Active Directory processes such as inter-site replication.

Microsoft provides management packs to monitor both the client experience and the server-side components of Active Directory. Appendix A, "OpsMgr by Example: Configuring and Tuning Management Packs," includes instructions for installing the Active Directory management packs. After importing the AD-related management packs, enabling the agent proxy setting on all domain controllers, and configuring an account for replication monitoring, you will want to perform the following steps to enable the client monitoring perspective:

1. In the Authoring space of the Operations console, navigate to Management Pack Objects -> Object Discoveries.

2. Locate the AD Client Monitoring Discovery rule. This rule is disabled by default. Use overrides to enable this rule on desired AD client monitoring systems.

   Do not enable client monitoring on all your member servers or desktop client computers. Too many clients running the synthetic transactions of these monitors can degrade your AD deployment. Either create a new group with explicit members, or decide to use an existing group that is already a subset of your AD client computer population. We will select an existing subset of client computers, those already identified as Business Critical.

3. Right-click on the rule and select Overrides -> For a group. Select your group; in our case, we selected the All Business Critical Windows Clients.

4. On the Override Properties page, tick the Override box and change the Override Setting drop-down value to True. Select your custom management pack (not the Default management pack) as the destination and press OK.

Within several minutes, state views and performance data from the selected AD client monitoring computers will begin appearing in the console. The left-hand side of Figure 19.7 exposes the majority of the Monitoring view folder tree added to the console when importing the client and server AD management packs.

In Figure 19.7, we circled the View folders for the server, client, and replication monitoring aspects of the AD management packs. In the Results pane, we have populated the dashboard view with metrics from business critical client computers related to the client AD experience, such as Client GC (Global Catalog) Search Time. You can see in the left-side Navigation pane that there are a number of very specific dashboard and performance views covering each aspect of AD health.

Using Monitors to View AD Health

What procedure should you follow to assess the overall health of AD? It's not actually necessary to open every AD view node in the Monitoring space, as Microsoft has included a DA with the AD management packs named Active Directory Topology Root. By examining the Health Explorer of the Active Directory Topology Root DA, you know that you are looking at a meaningful and accurate representation of your overall AD health. To illustrate the power of this DA, we extracted the principal monitors that constitute the health model for the Active Directory Topology Root DA and show those in Figure 19.8.

The monitors listed in Figure 19.8 exist for each domain controller in each AD site, from the AD Database Free Space Monitor to the AD Processor Overload Monitor. Regardless of how distributed or compact your AD deployment is, Operations Manager looks at all those listed health factors. Consolidating these many different kinds of monitors, all relating to AD performance and availability, into a single view is an example of how OpsMgr helps you perform synthesis and integration to solve problems.

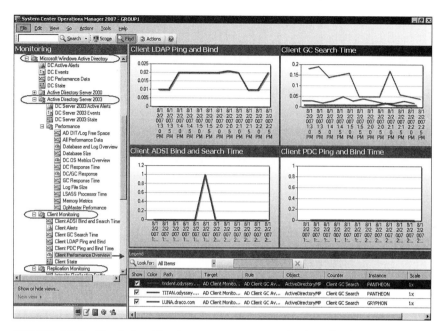

FIGURE 19.7   The Active Directory management packs install client and server views.

TIP

Install an Agent on Your DCs First

If you import the Active Directory management packs before installing OpsMgr agents on your domain controllers (DCs), the DCs appear as Not Monitored objects in the Operations console Computers global view. This occurs because the Active Directory Topology Root DA discovers the DCs in the management group's domain, and makes them objects in the management group. However, without OpsMgr agents, the DCs, now identified as objects, show up as unmonitored. To keep this from occurring, install an OpsMgr agent on your DCs before importing the Active Directory management packs.

Of course, the Active Directory Topology Root DA includes many other monitors than the principal ones listed in Figure 19.8. For example, physical dependencies of Active Directory are also included in the health model of the DA. Figure 19.9 shows the Health Explorer of the Active Directory Topology Root DA; in the upper portion, we highlighted the Logical Disk Availability and Free Space monitors of a domain controller.

In the lower portion of Figure 19.9, we highlighted the selected monitor (the AD General Response Monitor), and circled the in-line tasks available in the lower-right corner. Using these in-line tasks, when investigating a problem with general AD responsiveness, you have one-click access to the following features:

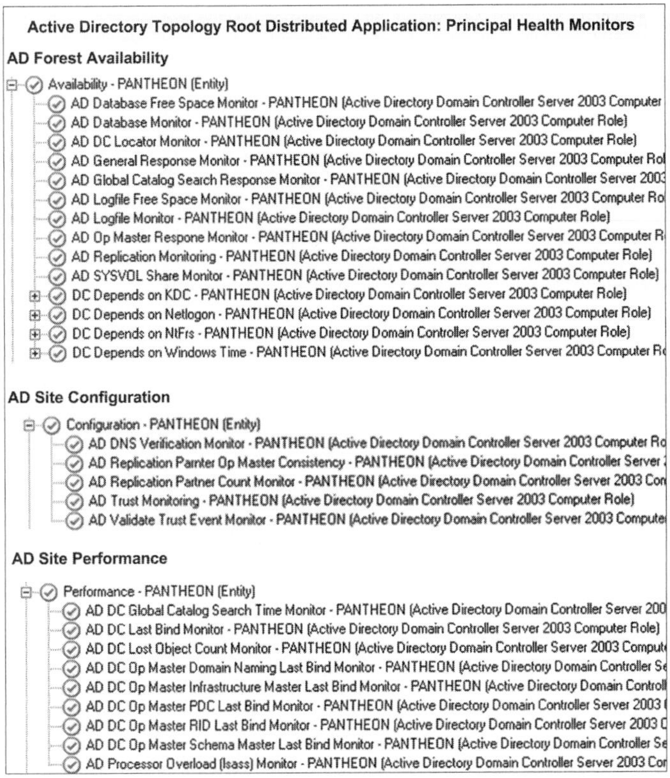

FIGURE 19.8   Principal health monitors of the Active Directory Topology Root DA.

▶ **Check current LDAP response time**—Verifying what the actual Lightweight Directory Access Protocol (LDAP) responsiveness is at this moment.

▶ **Check top processes currently using the processor**—If response is slow, perhaps a process is monopolizing the processor.

▶ **AD DC General Response Performance View**—Quickly look at the trending of LDAP responsiveness over the last few hours or days.

In-line Tasks

In-line tasks are another location for capturing knowledge in the DA model. The goal is that after using the Health Explorer to zero in on the cause of a problem, the tools for your troubleshooting decision tree are there where you need them. Tactical placement of in-line tasks can help accelerate your systems management workflow.

19

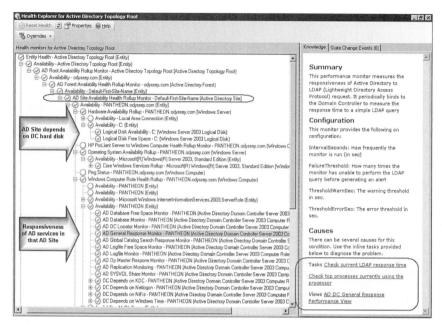

FIGURE 19.9   The Distributed Application includes hardware and service dependencies.

Other Diagram Views

Finally, there is a very useful Diagram view available when working with the Active Directory Topology Root DA, shown in Figure 19.10. We used annotated arrows to point out each main feature of the diagram, and in the lower left, we circled the same Logical Drive monitor highlighted in Figure 19.9.

There are dedicated diagram views installed by the AD management packs at the Monitoring -> Microsoft Windows Active Directory -> Topology Views folder. These diagram views are AD Domains, AD Sites, Connection Objects, and Topology. Each view focuses on a particular aspect of AD health. The Diagram view of the Active Directory Topology Root DA shown in Figure 19.10 is a superset view that includes all the information you can see in the dedicated diagram views.

Exchange Service

Microsoft Exchange Server is the world's most popular groupware application, providing email, calendaring, and collaboration services to organizations around the globe. Due to its many features, highly scalable design, mission-critical status, and constant high-volume usage, Exchange is also perhaps the most demanding application to manage. Outages in Exchange-related services often have an immediate impact on possibly hundreds or even thousands of employees, customers, and business partners. There is no faster way to get the phone ringing in the IT department than to mess with people's email access.

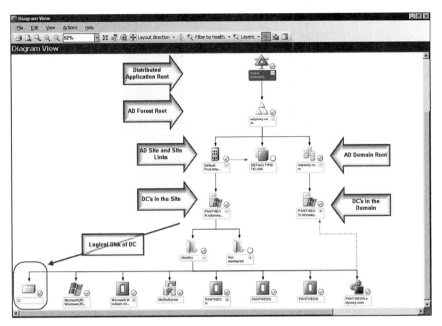

FIGURE 19.10   The Distributed Application diagram illustrates your AD topology.

Exchange is a challenging application to manage, in part because it is also a highly distributed application. Within a single Exchange server, there are many interdependent components, such as the Mail Transfer Agent (MTA), the Exchange routing engine, and the Simple Mail Transfer Protocol (SMTP) service. These components (among other processes) work together to move a single message between the Internet and your mailbox. As an organization increases in size and adds additional Exchange servers, particularly as it creates other Exchange sites and installs front-end servers dedicated to Internet-facing communication, the complexity of your management challenge increases exponentially.

Traditional approaches to managing Exchange focus on server-level monitoring. Focusing at the server-level has scaling limitations; an administrator of a large Exchange organization trying to track down a problem can have a "needle in a haystack" situation when trying to discover the root cause. For example, if all the Exchange administrator is presented with is a server-centric health view, he or she must evaluate the health of each server in a critical or warning state (for any reason!) to locate which Exchange-impacting components might be involved on each computer. Meanwhile, the timeliness of problem resolution in a demanding Exchange environment is very important—thousands of people might be unable to work while waiting for the administrator to locate and fix the problem with their email.

Microsoft provides management packs to monitor all aspects of Exchange. Appendix A includes instructions for installing the Exchange 2003 management packs. This particular chapter discusses Exchange 2003, not all versions of Exchange. Mainstream lifecycle support for Microsoft Exchange 2000 ended on January 10, 2006, so anyone still running Exchange 2000 should primarily be concerned about upgrading to Exchange 2003 or Exchange 2007.

Availability of Exchange 2007 Management Pack for Operations Manager 2007

Although Microsoft released a MOM 2005 version of the Exchange 2007 management pack in June 2007, the OpsMgr 2007 version was not available until after we completed this chapter. Our discussion of Exchange functionality in this chapter focuses on Exchange 2003, unless otherwise specified.

After importing the Exchange management packs into your OpsMgr Management group, you must perform the following actions:

▶ Run the Exchange Management Pack Configuration Wizard in each managed Exchange organization.

▶ Enable the agent proxy feature on each managed Exchange server.

▶ Add each server to an override of the Exchange 2003 Topology Discovery object discovery rule.

You must perform those minimum configuration steps after importing the Exchange management packs.

Exchange Views

The Exchange management packs add a large number of views to the monitoring space in the Microsoft Exchange Server folder, as well as eighteen reports in an Exchange Server 2003 (Monitoring) reports view folder. Figure 19.11 shows the monitoring folder expanded to show the more interesting views.

The Exchange management pack provides a rich management environment for focusing on a particular area of Exchange performance. In Figure 19.11, in the navigation pane on the left, we expand the Components, Mail Queues, and Overview folders. Most of the other View folders in the figure contain alerts and performance views; for example, the IMAP4 folder has an IMAP4 Active Alerts view and an IMAP4 Performance Data view. Here's a quick drill-down on what's in the View folders we expanded in Figure 19.11:

▶ The *Components* folder has Directory Service (DS) Access Performance Data and Information Store (IS) Performance Data views. The counters in these views are mainly about LDAP search times and server loading; they are useful to track down the source of Exchange performance bottlenecks.

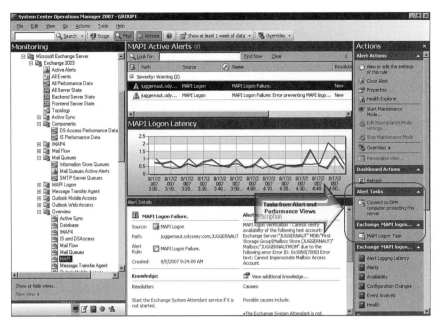

FIGURE 19.11   Overview dashboards in the Exchange 2003 monitoring View folder.

▶ The *Mail Queues* folder lets you follow up on mail queue issues by quickly checking mail queue active alerts and charting recent metrics of SMTP and IS queues.

▶ The *Overview* folder holds a dozen dashboard views, like the MAPI dashboard view seen in Figure 19.11. These dashboard views powerfully combine alerts and performance views, along with workflow-accelerating in-line tasks that create a true information fusion and synthesis center.

▶ The *Storage* folder (not seen in Figure 19.11) contains an active alerts view and nine performance views to chart such metrics as Mailbox Average Size in MB and Public Folder Average Message Count.

Although you could spend all day wandering around the nearly 60 views installed by the Exchange management pack and learn a lot about each component of your Exchange organization(s), would this help you confidently and accurately assess the overall health of your Exchange services? To assist, Microsoft provides a tool that lets you perform high-level yet targeted health analysis on Exchange in real-time: the Exchange Service DA. Figure 19.12 shows the Health Explorer for the Exchange Service DA.

The Exchange Service DA
The Exchange Service DA has a richly detailed Availability rollup and a very simple Performance rollup monitor. Both health model rollups operate against multiple Exchange organizations; you can see in the top of Figure 19.12 that we are monitoring two Exchange organizations, and that the Pegasus Exchange organization is healthy and the Odyssey Exchange organization is in a critical state.

19

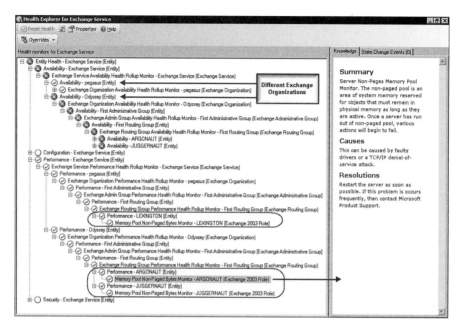

FIGURE 19.12   The Health Explorer for the Exchange Service DA.

This multi-organization feature is a boon to hosted Exchange operators, Exchange Application Service Providers (ASPs), and Managed Service Providers (MSPs) responsible for the Exchange service of multiple customer or tenant organizations. Following the Exchange organization hierarchy, the health model rollups proceed to the Exchange Administrative Group, then the Exchange Routing Group, and finally the individual Exchange servers and their respective functions.

The lower portion of Figure 19.12 displays the Performance rollup. Notice that there are two branches, one for each of the Exchange organizations we are managing: Pegasus and Odyssey. Each organization's branch continues through the Administrative and Routing Group structure, arriving at performance counters for the individual Exchange servers. We circled the individual server performance monitors. You can see that there is only one performance monitor per server in the health model: the Memory Pool Non-Paged Bytes Monitor.

The Memory Pool Non-Paged Bytes Monitor

Microsoft selected the Memory Pool Non-Paged Bytes Monitor as a singularly important measure of Exchange server health because of a longstanding and well-known Exchange service issue that has the same effect as a memory leak. Over time, and depending on server memory configuration, an Exchange server can fail to release memory after it is finished using it. This reduces the system memory area reserved for objects that must remain in memory as long as they are active.

Accordingly, Microsoft knows that if you watch that memory performance counter, you are watching the most important metric of Exchange performance health.

Using the Availability Monitor

As we noted, the Pegasus Exchange organization is healthy at this time—we expanded the Availability monitor for Pegasus in Figure 19.13. You can see the health monitor consists of nineteen subordinate monitors and rollups. There are three "checks," where the management pack verifies the following:

▶ The health of the Exchange services

▶ The health of the Exchange front-end services

▶ Whether SSL is enabled on the Exchange virtual web directories

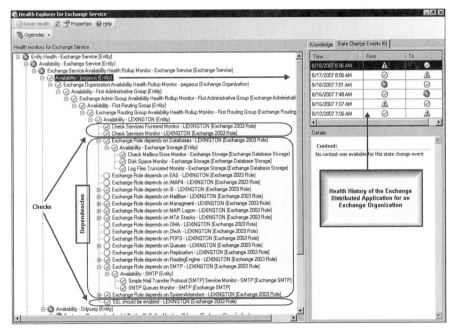

FIGURE 19.13   The Availability Rollup Monitor of a healthy Exchange organization.

These are the first two and the last of the listed monitors, which we circled in Figure 19.13. The other monitors (which we labeled Dependencies) gauge the status of the objects that Exchange availability is dependent on, such as Exchange Storage, MAPI Logon, MTA Stacks, Routing Engine, SMTP, and System Attendant.

Notice on the right side of Figure 19.13, there is a record of state change events for the Pegasus Exchange organization. Although we know the service is healthy now, we can see that in the last week there have been problems. In fact, the state change record of the Exchange DA is a very meaningful history of the availability of Exchange, and one on which you can base a Service Level Agreement (SLA). For example, see that at 7:48 AM on 8/16/2007, Exchange in the Pegasus organization went into a critical state, recovering to the healthy state at 7:51 AM. That three-minute lapse in Exchange service could be accounted for by a server restarting; however, for a customer with a "five nines" (99.999%) availability expectation, this might represent an SLA violation.

Now let's look at the other Exchange organization in our DA, the unhealthy one named Odyssey. Figure 19.14 shows the Availability monitor for Odyssey. We can see that there are two Exchange servers in this organization, front-end Argonaut and back-end Juggernaut, and both are in the critical state. We expanded the availability health rollup monitor for the back-end Exchange server Juggernaut.

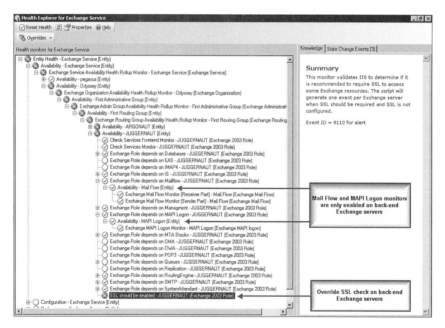

FIGURE 19.14   The Availability health rollup monitor for a back-end Exchange server.

We can tell that Juggernaut is a back-end Exchange server because the Mail Flow and MAPI Logon monitors are enabled (see the arrows in the central part of the Health Explorer in Figure 19.14). Those particular monitors are only enabled on back-end servers. At the bottom of the Health Explorer, we see why this server is in the critical state—the SSL should be enabled monitor. Unlike front-end Exchange servers, back-end Exchange servers do not require SSL on their Exchange web directories. So all we need to do to make Juggernaut healthy in the OpsMgr Exchange Service DA is to create an override for the SSL should be enabled monitor. We followed these steps to create the override:

1. In the Health Monitor for Exchange Service, select the SSL should be enabled monitor for the particular back-end server.

2. Right-click on the monitor and select Override the Monitor -> For a specific object of type: *<servername>*.

3. On the Override Properties page, tick the Override box and change the Override Setting drop-down value to False. Select your custom management pack (not the Default management pack) as the destination and press OK.

Within several minutes, the Availability state of the back-end server will change to healthy. Now we will look at the condition of the front-end server Argonaut, using the diagram view of the Exchange DA. The complete diagram for both our managed Exchange organizations (Odyssey and Pegasus) is far too large to present in this book in a readable form. For Figure 19.15, we arranged a continuous topology diagram with two diagram views side-by-side.

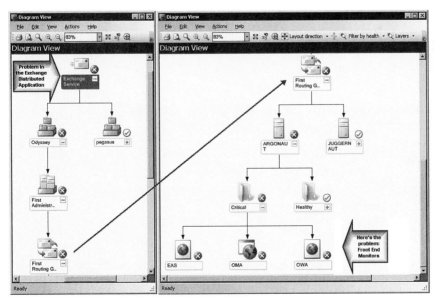

FIGURE 19.15 The Exchange Service diagram view clearly identifies the problem.

When we open the Exchange Service diagram seen in Figure 19.15, we see the two
Exchange organizations: Odyssey in a critical state and Pegasus in a healthy state. By
expanding the Odyssey organization through the Administrative and Routing Groups, to
the involved servers, we can "follow the red" (X symbol) to track the problem. Arriving at
the server with the problem (Argonaut), and expanding the diagram to the next level, it
becomes very obvious that the problem was with the front-end monitors (EAS, OMA, and
OWA). These front-end monitors perform synthetic logon to the Exchange Active Sync
(EAS), Outlook Mobile Access (OMA), and Outlook Web Access (OWA) services on the
front-end Exchange server.

A nice thing about the Diagram view, compared to the Health Explorer view, is that it
segregates the unhealthy monitors, making problem identification much simpler than
wading through hundreds of nested health model monitors.

Configuring the Front-End Monitors

Getting the front-end monitors to work in your Exchange environment will probably take
some manual configuration. By default, the monitors will attempt to make an SSL connection to the "localhost" hostname and to the IP address hostname of the server. For
example, the OWA monitor will perform a synthetic logon attempt using the URLs
https://localhost/Exchange and https://<*ServerIPAddress*>/Exchange. Because your front-end
Exchange server will generally have an SSL certificate issued in the server name of the
front-end server, or in the name of the public-facing URL used on the Internet, the default
URLs will fail.

To help the Exchange front-end monitors do their job, you need to create and populate
some Registry values on the front-end server itself. These Registry values will contain the
custom URLs that match your environment. Basically, the custom URLs need to match the
name of the SSL certificate installed on the front-end server. Figure 19.16 shows the piece
of the Registry with the custom URLs.

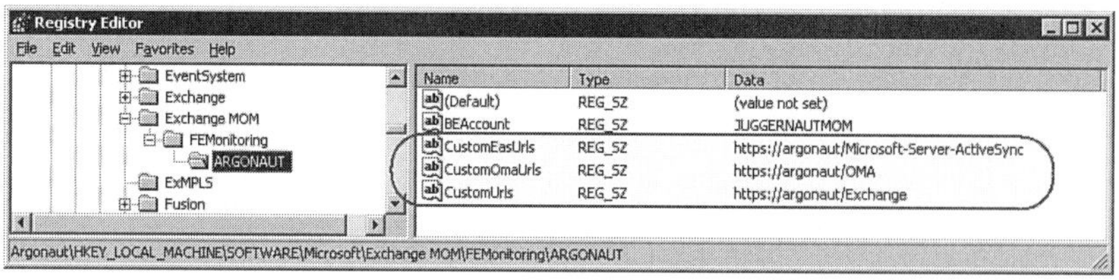

FIGURE 19.16   Specifying the custom URLs to be used by the front-end monitors.

The Registry key highlighted in Figure 19.16, HKLM\SOFTWARE\Microsoft\Exchange
MOM\FEMonitoring\<*servername*>, is automatically created when you run the Exchange
Server Management Pack Configuration Wizard. However, the only value expected to be
present is the BEAccount (back-end account). The BEAccount value represents the name of

the mailbox test account on the back-end server. You need to manually add the three custom URL values in the manner shown in Figure 19.16.

TIP

Exchange Tuning Tips

Additional tuning tips for the Exchange management pack are found in Chapter 14, "Monitoring with Operations Manager," and in Appendix A, "OpsMgr by Example: Configuring and Tuning Management Packs."

Another thing to watch for regarding the front-end monitors is to require SSL on these Exchange virtual web directories:

▶ Exchange

▶ Public

▶ OMA

▶ Microsoft-Server-ActiveSync

Specifically, in the Internet Information Services (IIS) Manager of the front-end server (for those Exchange virtual web directories), you should verify that the Require secure channel (SSL) option on the Directory Security tab is selected.

Enterprise Health Monitoring

Microsoft gave Operations Manager administrators a jump-start in making use of the Distributed Application feature by including several DA templates in the Information Worker management pack. We first saw the Enterprise Health Monitoring view (seen in Figure 19.17) in Chapter 16, "Client Monitoring."

In Figure 19.17, we circled the Enterprise Health Monitoring folder; observe that it contains three View folders:

▶ Internet Explorer

▶ Outlook

▶ Windows Explorer

As we discussed in Chapter 16, the Outlook Client Mail Access State view generates an alert when 10% or more client computers running Microsoft Outlook cannot contact their Exchange server(s). The Outlook Client Mail Access State view automatically populates as the management pack discovers client computers running Outlook.

19

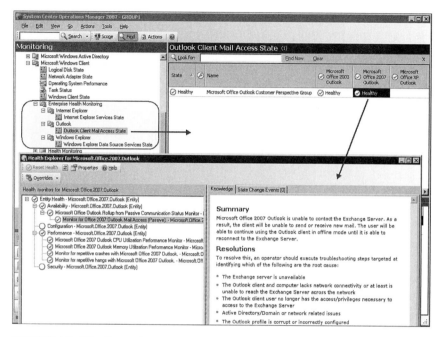

FIGURE 19.17   Enterprise Health Monitoring views of information worker services.

The other two Enterprise Health Monitoring views, Internet Explorer Services and Windows Explorer Data Source Services, are not populated until you create Distributed Applications (DAs) based on specific pre-defined templates. Importing the Information Worker management pack adds two DA templates to the Distributed Application Designer—you can choose one of these templates when creating a DA.

These are the views added in the Monitoring -> Microsoft Windows Client -> Enterprise Health Monitoring folder and the scenarios they support:

▶ *View:* Internet Explorer -> Internet Explorer Services State.

  Scenario: Internet Explorer Clients utilize Proxy Services and Network Services, and depend on a Physical Network.

▶ *View:* Windows Explorer -> Windows Explorer Data Source Services State.

  Scenario: Data Source Clients utilize Directory Services and Network Services, and depend on a Physical Network.

The monitoring views will be empty until you create custom monitoring services (using the Distributed Application Designer) based on the pre-defined templates. The names of the templates correspond to the two views. As we continue through the sections on Enterprise Health Monitoring, we will step though creating each of these two types of DAs, and discuss effective means to employ these Enterprise Health Monitoring features of OpsMgr.

Internet Explorer Service Template

Also known as the Client Web Access feature of the Information Worker management pack, you use the Internet Explorer Service template to create a DA to let you know when web browser clients are unable to access critical web application resources. The websites and web-based applications you monitor can either be internal to your network or on the Internet. If your organization depends on information workers accessing a web-based application for a critical business function, consider using the Internet Explorer Service template to author a DA that models that web access. Monitoring the DA will provide visibility into the ability of client computers to use the critical web-based application.

Creating the Web Application

The first step to enabling the Client Web Access (Internet Explorer Service) DA is to create one or more web applications using the Add Monitoring Wizard in the Authoring space. Then you will use the Distributed Application Designer, specifying the Windows Internet Explorer Service template, and then adding the web application as an object to monitor. The scenario we will use to demonstrate the Internet Explorer Service DA is employees accessing a business-critical website. We want to detect problems in getting to that website.

Define the website you will monitor by creating a web application in the authoring space. After you create the web application, the health of that application will be viewable in the Monitoring -> Web Application -> Web Applications State view. More importantly, it will make the web application selectable in the Object Picker later in the Distributed Application Designer. Follow these steps to define the critical website:

1. In the Authoring space, navigate to the Management Packs node and run the Add monitoring wizard.

2. Select Web Application as the monitoring type and press Next.

3. On the Web Application Name and Description page, enter a name and description of the critical website. The name entered here will appear as a component of the DA, so name it something that makes the most sense in that context. We named ours **Critical Website Access**. Select (or create) a custom management pack (not the Default management pack) to save the changes to and press Next.

4. Enter and test the URL you will be monitoring. This test is performed from the Root Management Server (RMS) and does not necessarily validate that the URL is reachable from the watcher node that you select in the next step. After a moment, the results of the test are displayed along with a Details button.

   Figure 19.18 shows how you can expose the actual Hyper Text Markup Language (HTML) returned from the monitored web server. You can later use details from the HTML reply to further validate proper response from the critical website.

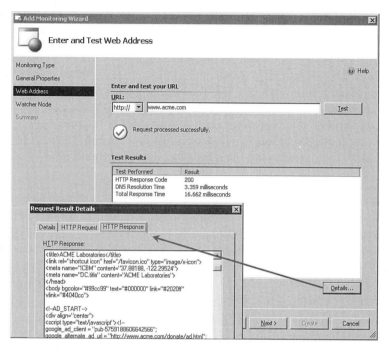

FIGURE 19.18   Viewing the detailed results of the web address test.

5. On the Choose Watcher Nodes page, select one or more managed computers to act as watcher nodes, preferably from multiple and different locations. Monitoring an external web server through different outbound Internet Service Providers (ISPs) is a good idea. Also, consider monitoring an internal web server from watcher nodes at each branch office or outlying building.

It is generally best to select at least two watcher nodes for each web address. This way when you are alerted to a problem accessing the critical website, you can more easily rule out individual watcher node failure. Each instance of a watcher node monitoring a URL creates a new object in the Web Applications State view, which becomes usable by the DA.

The default interval to run the web query is every two minutes. This might be too short an interval if you have a larger number of watcher nodes or a complex set of web application tests. Adjust the query interval as appropriate and press Next.

6. Press Create and wait several moments. You should then be able to locate the new web application monitor(s) in the Monitoring -> Web Application -> Web Applications State View folder. There will be a separate monitor for each watcher node.

You can return at any time to view or modify the characteristics of the web application you created. Perform this task using the Web Application Editor, launched from the Authoring -> Management Pack Templates -> Web Application node. There are many advanced features of the web application accessed through the Web Application Editor. You can modify and fine-tune the web application to fit many business needs.

In Figure 19.19, we have opened our Critical Website Access Web Application in the Web Application Editor. We launched the Web Application Editor by selecting the Critical Website Access Web Application at the Authoring -> Management Pack -> Web Application node and selected the Edit web application settings Custom Action.

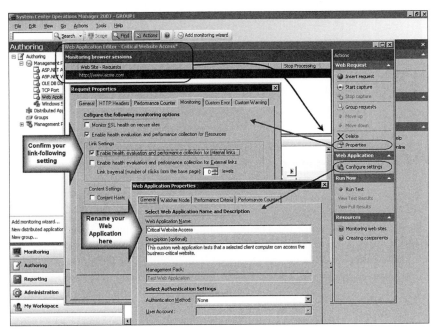

FIGURE 19.19   Advanced options for monitoring websites in the Web Application Editor.

If you select the Properties action in the Web Application Editor, it exposes a particularly important setting. This is the Link Settings on the Monitoring tab of the Request Properties box (see the large upper-left arrow in Figure 19.19). The Enable health evaluation and performance collection for Internal links setting is enabled by default. This setting causes the web application to follow all links on the monitoring website that are part of the same domain as the main URL. A failure state will occur if any of the internal links are down. This may or may not be your desire, so consider disabling that feature if you only want to monitor the default page of the website.

The large, lower arrow in Figure 19.19 points to the Web Application Properties box exposed by selecting the Configure settings action. Here you can rename your web application, enable authentication for intranet sites, and modify the assignment of watcher nodes for the web application.

Creating the Windows Internet Explorer Service DA

With our web application configured and our watcher nodes appearing in the healthy state at the Monitoring -> Web Application -> Web Applications State View folder, we are ready to create the Critical Website Access DA, in which the watcher nodes will participate.

Follow these steps to create the Critical Website Access DA:

1. Navigate to and select the Authoring -> Distributed Applications node. Click the Create a new distributed application action.

TIP

Distributed Application Designer Is x86 Only

If you attempt to open the Distributed Application Designer from a 64-bit version of the Operations console, you will receive a console error message. The DAD runs as a 32-bit application only.

Suggestions offered by Microsoft are to dual-boot to a 32-bit (x86) version of Windows, install a 32-bit version of Windows in a Virtual PC, or run the Distributed Application Designer from another computer that is running a 32-bit version of Windows.

---

2. Enter a name and description for the DA. The name you enter here is what you will see in the Monitoring -> Distributed Applications global view, so use a name that communicates its purpose. We selected the same name **Critical Website Access** that we used in defining the web application.

3. Choose the Windows Internet Explorer Service template.

4. Select a custom management pack to save the DA to, or create a new one just for this DA (our recommendation!), and press OK.

After opening the Distributed Application Designer and choosing to use the Internet Explorer Service template, you have a logical view of four components (with relationships), as follows:

▶ Windows Internet Explorer Clients, which depend on Proxy Services, Network Services, and a Physical Network.

▶ Windows Internet Explorer Proxy Services, which depend on a Physical Network.

▶ Windows Internet Explorer Network Services, which depend on a Physical Network.

▶ A Physical Network.

What this arrangement suggests is that client computers depend on several components, such as proxy services and network services, to access the critical website in addition to the interconnecting physical network. Defining your DA with these components and relationships will help you identify root causes when there are problems accessing the critical website. Components in the DA are containers that hold one or more managed objects.

To adapt the template to your environment, decide what network services you want to associate with this DA—specifically, what services the web browser client depends on using in order to access the critical website. In our example, we will use the Dynamic Host Configuration Protocol (DHCP) Services on one server, and the Windows Proxy Automatic Detection (WPAD) Services, hosted by Internet Information Service (IIS) on another server, as our client computer dependencies.

We will also identify the network devices, such as routers or switches, which the web browser client, DHCP, and WPAD servers depend on to provide outbound access to the critical website. A failure in DHCP or WPAD services, as well as a failure of the interconnecting network devices, can result with the web browser client unable to access the critical website. Our DA will rapidly disclose the failure origin if it is related to DHCP or WPAD services or the network devices.

It is a good idea to rename the components created by the Internet Explorer Service template, so they make sense to operators in your environment. Here is how we renamed the DA components in our demonstration (to rename the components, right-click each in turn, then select Properties):

▶ Windows Internet Explorer Clients (renamed to) -> Client computer watcher node

▶ Windows Internet Explorer Proxy Services -> DHCP Services

▶ Windows Internet Explorer Network Services -> WPAD Services

▶ Physical Network -> Edge Switches

Now we are ready to add the components. Here are the steps we followed to populate our DA components with managed objects (clockwise from the top component, seen in Figure 19.20):

1. On the left side of the Distributed Application Designer, under Objects, double-click the Perspective object type tile.

2. Click the Object tile at the top of the object list to sort the perspectives by object name.

3. Locate and select both Critical Website Access watcher nodes, the ones created as web applications.

4. Right-click and select Add To -> Client computer watcher node. Observe that the Client computer watcher node component now contains two Critical Website Access watcher nodes.

5. Double-click the Computer Role object type tile.

6. Click the Path tile at the top of the object list to sort the computer roles by object path.

7. Locate the server name hosting the WPAD services in the path column; then select the Microsoft.Windows.InternetInformationServices.2003.Server.Role object for that server name.

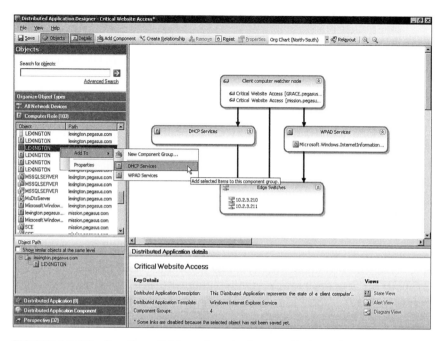

FIGURE 19.20   Creating a DA based on the Internet Explorer Service template.

8. Right-click and select Add To -> WPAD Services. Observe that the WPAD Services component now contains the IIS Services of the WPAD server.

9. Double-click the All Network Devices object type tile.

10. Click the Object tile at the top of the object list to sort the network devices by object name (IP address).

11. Locate and select one or more network devices. We selected two network devices that are the edge switches the client and server computers depend on for outbound access.

12. Right-click and select Add To -> Edge Switches. Observe that the Edge Switches component now contains the network devices.

13. Double-click the Computer Role object type tile.

14. Click the Object tile at the top of the object list to sort the computer roles by object name.

15. Locate the server name hosting the DHCP Services in the Object column. Move the cursor slowly over the server names (hover) to view a floating tip describing each object. Do so until you locate the DHCP services object and select it.

16. Right-click and select Add To -> DHCP Services. Observe that the DHCP Services component now contains the DHCP service object of the selected server. Figure 19.20 illustrates this step.

17. Press the Save button (or File -> Save).

18. Exit the Distributed Application Designer (File -> Close or push the X button).

After several minutes, you can view the health status of the new DA in the Monitoring -> Distributed Applications view and the Monitoring -> Microsoft Windows Client -> Enterprise Health Monitoring -> Internet Explorer Services State view.

Access to the DA object itself remains at the Authoring -> Distributed Applications node. You can return to that node at any time to modify the components, objects, relationships, and other settings in the DA. From that location, you can also launch the diagram view for the DA, as shown in Figure 19.21.

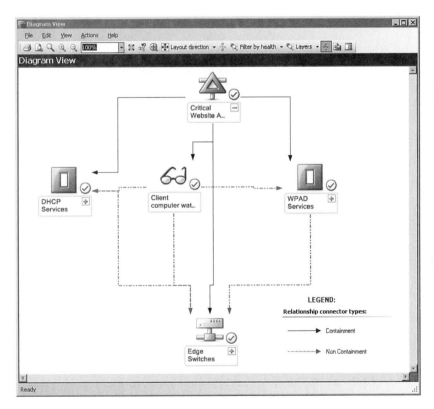

FIGURE 19.21   The diagram view of a DA communicates containment information.

In the diagram view of our Critical Web Access DA, seen in Figure 19.21, we have manually moved the icons around so they appear in the same topology as in the Distributed Application Designer. We also added the legend for the containment vs. non-containment connector types in the lower right of the figure. Solid (black) relationship connector lines identify containment, while dotted (blue) lines identify non-containment dependency.

This view discloses that the Client computer watcher node is dependent on (but not contained by) the DHCP Services and the WPAD Services. Likewise, the Client computer watcher node, the DHCP Services, and the WPAD Services are all dependent on the Edge Switches, even though they are not objects contained within the Edge Switches.

In creating the Critical Website Access DA, we have instrumented several infrastructure components in a way that will help us quickly evaluate problems detected in client computers accessing a business critical website. Next, we will use the Windows Explorer Data Source Service template to create a similar DA, this time where the client accesses an important data source, rather than a business-critical website.

Windows Explorer Data Source Service Template

Also known as the Client Data Source Access feature of the Information Worker management pack, you use the Windows Explorer Data Source Service template to create a DA that lets you know when data source clients are unable to access important data source providers. The data source providers you monitor can be any of the 20 types supported by the OLE DB Data Source. These include Microsoft Jet sources (such as Microsoft Access legacy applications), and Open Database Connectivity (ODBC) to database sources like Microsoft SQL Server and Oracle.

If your organization requires information workers to access a data source for a critical business function, consider using the Windows Explorer Data Source Service template to author a DA modeling that data source access. Monitoring the DA provides visibility into the ability of client computers to use the essential data source.

Creating the OLE DB Data Source

The first step to enabling the Client Data Source Access (Windows Explorer Data Source Service) DA is creating one or more OLE DB Data Sources with the Add Monitoring Wizard in the Authoring space. You then use the Distributed Application Designer, specifying the Windows Explorer Data Source Service template, and add the OLE DB Data Source as an object to monitor.

The scenario we will use to demonstrate the Windows Explorer Data Source Service DA is access to the Audit Collection Services (ACS) database. We want to detect problems with network access to the ACS database SQL data source. This demonstration of the DA using the ACS database is applicable to any two-tier (Client/Server) distributed application.

Define the data source you will monitor by creating an OLE DB Data Source in the authoring space. After you create the OLE DB Data Source, the health of that application will be viewable in the Monitoring -> Synthetic Transaction -> OLE DB Data Source State view. The OLE DB Data Source will also be selectable in the Object Picker later in the Distributed Application Designer.

Follow these steps to define the OLE DB Data Source:

1. In the Authoring space, navigate to the Management Packs node and start the Add monitoring wizard.

2. Select OLE DB Data Source as the monitoring type and press Next.

3. On the OLE DB Data Source Name and Description page, enter a name and description of the data source. The name entered here will appear as a component of the DA, so name it something that makes the most sense in that context. We named ours **ACS Database SQL Connectivity**. Select (or create) a custom management pack (not the Default management pack) to save the changes to and press Next.

4. On the Enter and Test OLE DB Data Source Settings page, select the Simple Configuration option.

5. Select the appropriate Provider in the drop-down list. Because the ACS database is a Microsoft SQL database data source, we selected the Microsoft OLE DB Provider for SQL Server.

6. Enter the database server's name in the IP address or device name box and the database name in the Database box. We entered the name of the ACS database server (**FIREBALL**) and the name of the ACS database, **OperationsManagerAC**. Press the Test button.

   This test is performed from the RMS and does not necessarily validate that the OLE DB Data Source is reachable from the watcher node selected in the subsequent step. After a moment, you should see a green checkmark icon and the notice Request processed successfully, as seen in Figure 19.22.

7. On the Choose Watcher Nodes page, select one or more managed computers to act as watcher nodes, ideally from several different locations. Because the ACS database can only be accessed from inside the private network, it would be appropriate to select watcher nodes physically in separate physical portions of the network, such as different floors or wings.

   It is generally best to select at least two watcher nodes for each OLE DB data source. This way, when you are alerted to a problem accessing the data source, you can more easily rule out individual watcher node failure. Each instance of a watcher node monitoring an OLE DB data source creates a new object in the OLE DB Data Source State view, which becomes usable by the DA.

   The default interval to run the OLE DB data source query is every two minutes. Adjust the query interval as appropriate and press Next.

8. Press Create and wait several moments. You should then be able to locate the new OLE DB data source monitor(s) in the Monitoring -> Synthetic Transaction -> OLE DB Data Source State View folder. There will be one monitor for each watcher node.

You can return at any time to view or modify the characteristics of the OLE DB Data Source you created. Perform this task using the Authoring -> Management Pack Templates -> OLE DB Data Source node. Select the data source and press Properties. You can rename the data source, modify the data source connection string, and change the watcher node assignments.

19

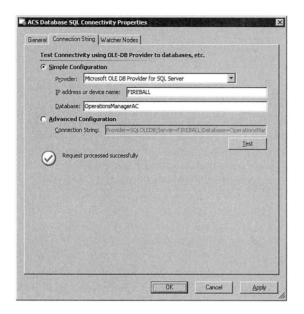

FIGURE 19.22   Successful test of OLE DB connection to the SQL database data source.

Creating the Windows Explorer Data Source Service DA

With our OLE DB data sources configured and our watcher nodes appearing in a healthy state at the Monitoring -> Synthetic Transaction -> OLE DB Data Source State View folder, we are ready to create the ACS Database Connectivity DA. Perform the following steps:

1. Navigate to and select the Authoring -> Distributed Applications node. Click the Create a new distributed application action.

2. Enter a name and description for the DA. The name you enter here is what you will see in the Monitoring -> Distributed Applications global view, so use a name that communicates its purpose. We selected the name **ACS Database Connectivity**, similar to how we named the OLE DB Data Source.

3. Choose the Windows Explorer Data Source Service template.

4. Select a custom management pack to save the DA to, or create a new one just for this DA (recommended), and press OK.

After opening the Distributed Application Designer and choosing to use the Windows Explorer Data Source Service template, you have a logical view of four components and some dependencies, as follows:

▶ Windows Explorer Data Source Clients, depending on Directory Services, Network Services, and a Physical Network

▶ Windows Explorer Data Source Directory Services, depending on a Physical Network

> ▶ Windows Explorer Data Source Network Services, depending on a Physical Network

> ▶ A Physical Network

This configuration suggests client computers depend on several components, such as directory services and network services, as well as the interconnecting physical network, to access the important data source. To adapt the template to your environment, decide what network services you want to associate with this DA—specifically, what services the data source client depends on using in order to access the data source.

For our example, we will use the Active Directory Domain Controller Server 2003 Computer Role for our directory services component and the MSSQLSERVER –SQL DB Engine on the ACS database server, as our client computer dependencies. We know there is a router that some watcher nodes use to reach the ACS database server, so we will add that router for our physical network component. Our DA will rapidly disclose the failure origin if it is related to Active Directory, the SQL Server database service itself, or the router.

Using the Object Picker in the Distributed Application Designer, we proceeded to populate the components suggested by the template (following our plan of how we will utilize them), with the objects appropriate for those tasks. Figure 19.23 shows what the DA looks like at this stage in its creation.

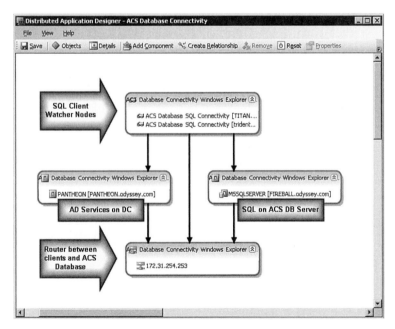

FIGURE 19.23   Initial view of the DA after assigning objects to components.

19

The next task is to rename the DA components (which have long names that include the string Windows Explorer Data Source) with shorter, meaningful names. Here were the reassignments we made:

▶ Windows Explorer Data Source Clients (renamed to) -> ACS Database Watcher Nodes

▶ Windows Explorer Data Source Directory Services -> Domain Controller

▶ Windows Explorer Data Source Network Services -> ACS SQL Server

▶ Physical Network -> ACS DB Router

Customizing the Data Source Service DA

Now we have the option to continue to customize the DA with more information about the environment we are managing. You can add more components to your custom DA and increase the fidelity of the health model as desired. In this case, we will add the network switch layer to the health model. Here are the steps we took to add a network switch to the DA to promote failure point recognition:

1. In the Distributed Application Designer, press the Add Component toolbar button.

2. Name the component with a meaningful group name, and select the Objects of the following host type(s) radio button. We used the name **Network Switches (Server Room)**, because this component is going to contain Network Device objects for the network switches that the Active Directory and SQL Server use to connect through in the server room.

3. Select the Device -> All Network Devices class type. Press OK.

4. In the Objects area on the left, double-click on All Network Devices to expose the list of network devices in the management group. Select the switches used by the servers.

5. Add the switches to the Network Switches (Server Room) component by either clicking and dragging, or by right-clicking and selecting Add to -> Network Switches (Server Room).

6. Press the Create Relationship toolbar button.

7. Click first on the Domain Controller component, and then click on the Network Switches (Server Room) component. This creates a component relationship named literally, Domain Controller uses Network Switches (Server Room). You can see that component relationship name in the Details pane when you select the relationship in the Distributed Application Designer.

8. Repeat step 7 for the ACS SQL Server component, then for the ACS DB Router component. Each of these components uses the Network Switches (Server Room) component.

9. Disengage the Create Relationship tool (click the toolbar button again).

10. Push the Relayout toolbar button.

11. Select the connecting (relationship) line between the domain controller and the ACS DB Router and press the Remove toolbar button. Also remove the connection between the ACS SQL Server and the ACS DB Router.

12. Push the Relayout toolbar button. Figure 19.24 illustrates the DA topology after this step.

 The value in this topology is that should a problem occur, it will be easier to detect if the network switches in the server room are involved. Likewise, failure of a server room switch can be more quickly ruled out when troubleshooting data source connectivity problems.

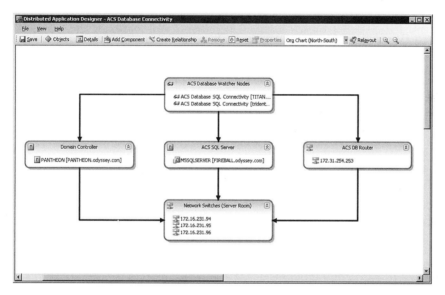

FIGURE 19.24   After adding network switches in the server room as a component.

13. Press the Save button (or File -> Save).

14. Exit the Distributed Application Designer (File -> Close or push the X button).

After several minutes, you can view the health status of the new DA in the Monitoring -> Distributed Applications view and the Monitoring -> Microsoft Windows Client -> Enterprise Health Monitoring -> Windows Explorer Data Source Services State view.

We will close this section on Enterprise Health Monitoring with a demonstration of the power of the Operations console and OpsMgr DAs feature to deliver an information fusion center. We have created a new View folder, **ACS Database Connectivity**, to contain different views of our DA. After creating a performance, alert, and state view for the DA, we created a dashboard view that contained all three of them. See it all at Figure 19.25, where we circled the View folder created for this DA.

The dashboard view of a DA is a place where you can synthesize data across all component groups and objects. For example, ACS database connectivity issues may correspond to domain controller outages in the same timeframe. The side-by-side presentation of the dashboard view greatly facilitates the ability to compare the alert times with the performance events. Creating the DA assembles the meaningful dashboard elements used in the data fusion.

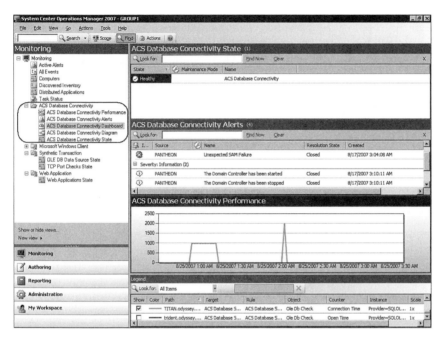

FIGURE 19.25   Correlating events across components of the DA with a dashboard view.

Creating a Distributed Application Health Model

This last portion of the chapter looks at monitoring custom applications. A primary purpose of the Distributed Application Designer is to help you create health models for custom applications. A DA is really just a health model—a hierarchical representation of the health of an object, where the object is the subject of the DA.

The most fundamental way to create a health model is by authoring a management pack with the OpsMgr Software Development Kit (SDK). However, in addition to using the SDK to author the health model for an object, you can also use the Distributed Application Designer to create a health model. The Distributed Application Designer is almost like a "layman's SDK," allowing you to transfer knowledge, about how the health of an IT service should be assessed, from your mind to the DA.

To create a custom DA, you need to model the end-to-end service you will be monitoring. This means that you must identify all the components that make up the service, and determine the relationships between components. E2E service modeling—done right—is the process of instrumenting and monitoring every application layer and component, in such a way that the appropriate level of visibility and information is provided at the right time. Remember, a potent characteristic of DAs is that they do not monitor everything—they monitor specific, key objects. Monitoring key objects reduces management burden and speeds problem resolution. Selecting those key objects is the critical task in E2E service modeling.

Real World—Using the SDK Versus a DA

We recommend that, if your organization is critically dependent on a complex custom application, sometimes known as a Line of Business (LoB) application, to consider creating a health model programmatically using the SDK for the long term. Health models authored with the SDK can include advanced monitoring, diagnostic, and recovery features that you cannot include in a DA. However, it is relatively easy and quick to create and deploy a DA using the graphical Distributed Application Designer, compared to authoring a management pack in eXtensible Markup Language (XML) using the SDK. You might also deploy a DA as a first step toward authoring a custom health model in the SDK, gathering initial performance data and piloting component relationships.

The tool for graphically building E2E service models is the Distributed Application Designer. We have already used the Distributed Application Designer a few times in the "Enterprise Health Monitoring" sections of this chapter. We also used the Windows Explorer Data Source Service and the Windows Internet Explorer Service DA templates to create and customize DAs that monitor connectivity to a SQL database, and access to a critical website. There are four other templates available in the Distributed Application Designer:

▶ Line of Business Web Application

▶ Messaging

▶ Terminal Services Farm

▶ Blank

We previously looked (in the "Windows Explorer Data Source Service Template" and "Internet Explorer Service Template" sections) at the Windows Explorer Data Source Service and the Windows Internet Explorer Service DA templates. These two templates are integrated with the Information Worker management pack, and both feature watcher node perspective components. Because they are part of a complete management pack solution, those two Enterprise Health Monitoring templates have some enhanced predefined views and alerting features.

The other four templates exist to help speed up the deployment of DAs in your organization, and we will look at the characteristics of each one. The idea is that you start by selecting a template that most closely matches the DA you want to monitor.

19

> **TIP**
>
> **Getting a Quick Start with Service Modeling**
>
> Selecting a template that matches the DA you want to monitor gives you a head start in your service modeling task. After creating the DA, you add views in the Monitoring space and create custom reports as desired.

Figure 19.26 shows the Create a Distributed Application dialog, with the template selected to create a Line of Business Web Application.

Line of Business Web Application Template

A Line of Business application is a "big" application that businesses bet their company on. LoB applications automate "big" processes such as financials, customer support, marketing, sales, and commerce. Most large organizations have one or more LoB applications, which may be purchased or leased from a single LoB application vendor, or may be a patchwork assemblage of applications from various vendors that together constitute the LoB application.

Many modern LoB applications utilize a web browser as a user interface, and almost all LoB applications include one or more back-end databases. The components of the Line of Business Web Application DA template represent these common features of LoB applications. After creating our LoB DA as shown in Figure 19.26, the Distributed Application Designer will open with a very simple view: a Web Sites component that uses a Databases component. Figure 19.27 is the initial view of the LoB DA in the Distributed Application Designer (with the Objects pane hidden).

In Figure 19.27, we selected the connector between the Web Sites component and the Databases component. This causes the header of the Details pane to change to read Reference details and the contents of the Details pane to spell out the relationship between the components the connection references, that being the Web Application Web Sites uses Web Application Databases. The Diagram view of the DA represents the connector as a non-containment relationship.

> **TIP**
>
> **Save Custom DAs to Unique Management Packs**
>
> Consider a policy of always saving new, custom DAs to their own dedicated management packs. This will make it easier to create custom views in the Monitoring space that target information about the DA. In addition, this makes the DA a portable solution by causing its configuration to be stored in the unique XML file of the custom management pack. Also, remember to make saving your DA the first action you take in the Distributed Application Designer (press the Save button in the left side of the toolbar). The dynamic view shortcuts in the object details area only become available after the first time you save the DA.

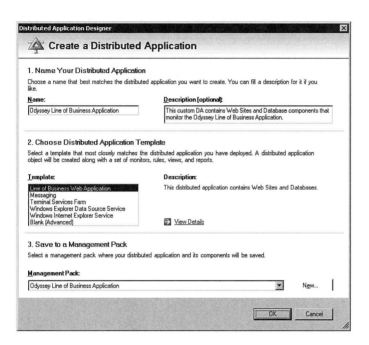

FIGURE 19.26   Creating a distributed application based on the LoB template.

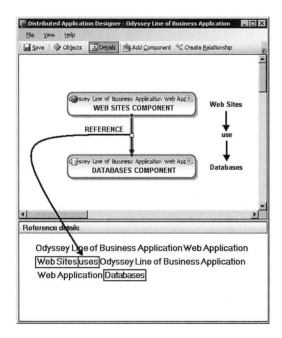

FIGURE 19.27   The core of a LoB application is websites using databases.

The default custom LoB DA has two components with a single relationship. The Line of Business Web Application template pre-defines those components as Web Sites and Databases.

Before monitoring a service, you must add objects to components. Every entity in your Operations Manager management group is an object you can add to a component in a DA. If you have discovered the entity already via any other management pack, it will be an object available to select for adding to a DA component.

To utilize the function of Line of Business Web Application template, you need to add one or more websites that use (depend on) one or more databases. Once you add a monitored object of the Web Sites class (a website) to the Web Sites component, that component begins to report the rolled-up health status of the objects. To add objects to the Web Sites component, you must locate suitable objects in the Web Sites object class. You will find the Web Sites object(s) of interest in the Object Picker.

Working with the Object Picker

The *Object Picker* is the name of the navigation and multi-purpose panel on the left side of the Distributed Application Designer. Using the Object Picker, you expose the objects available to select from the Organize Object Types portion of the Object Picker. Figure 19.28 is a composite illustration of the same instance of the Object Picker, where we present three kinds of information.

The Object Picker has a top-level organizer window that lists all the object classes available to select objects from for adding them to components in the DA. Seen in the left side of Figure 19.28, the new DA opens with this organizer window active. Here is a description of the purpose and usage of the organizer window:

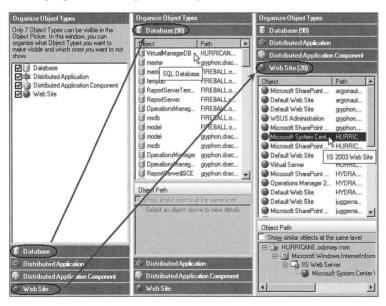

FIGURE 19.28   The Object Picker organizer (left), and object type views (center, right).

▶ All eligible classes (those classes that have components of the type that can be added to components in the DA) appear in the organizer window list.

▶ Only up to seven object types (classes) can be visible in the Object Picker—for example, made available to select from.

▶ It is possible that many more classes will be associated with the components in the DA than these seven, in which case there will be too many to be visible for selection in the Object Picker.

▶ You use the checkmarks in the organizer window to select which seven classes you are working currently with; you can change these selections on the fly as you use the Object Picker.

Object types that have a checkmark in the organizer window will then also appear as navigation tiles to select in the lower portion of the Object Picker. These object types can be seen in the lower-left corner of Figure 19.28; they are as follows:

▶ Database

▶ Distributed Application

▶ Distributed Application Component

▶ Web Site

The Distributed Application and Distributed Application Component object types are always available in the organizer. The Database and Web Site object types are available because the components in the DA based on the LoB template are associated with the Database and Web Sites object classes.

Clicking on the Database navigation tile exposes the objects in the management group that are in the Database class. These are all the instances of databases on managed computers in your management group. See the center portion of Figure 19.28, with the Database object type selected in the Object Picker. In the center of the window is a scrolling list of monitored databases. There are columns for the database name and the computer hosting the database.

Hovering over the object names exposes the third dimension of the Object Picker, the object type tip, which confirms the object class. In the top center portion of Figure 19.28, hovering over the VirtualManagerDB object causes the tip SQL Database to appear for a few seconds. We added the VirtualManagerDB object to the Database component of our DA. That database is associated with the Microsoft System Center Virtual Machine Manager (SCVMM) application, the subject of our LoB DA. The SCVMM self-service website depends on the SQL database of the SCVMM service—this application compactly demonstrates the model of the LoB DA template.

The Web Site object type is selected in the Object Picker on the right side of Figure 19.28. When selected, all the websites of all the monitored computers in the management group are exposed. If you hover over the Microsoft System Center Virtual Machine Manager

2007 Self-Service Portal object in the center-right portion of this figure, the tip IIS 2003 website appears for a few seconds. Selecting the object populates the Object Path panel in the bottom of the Object Picker. The Object Path panel exposes the Service Modeling Language of the object. The tip and the Object Path are there to assist you in selecting the correct and desired object. We added that website to the Web Sites component of our DA.

A Distributed Application Concept: Monitoring Specific Objects

The action of adding a specific website demonstrates a powerful concept of the DA. We are not monitoring the IIS services on the web server; we are watching the particular website of interest. Likewise, we are not watching the SQL services on the system running SQL Server; rather, we are monitoring just the database the website depends on. In conventional server-based monitoring, if anything were amiss on either the web or the database servers, the state rollup would be unhealthy. In the E2E model, some unrelated problem can exist on either server—but as long as the components in the DA remain healthy, administrators responsible for the DA are not unnecessarily alerted to those unrelated infrastructure issues. Also, SLAs written against the health of the DA are not penalized due to non-impacting IT issues.

Customizing the LoB DA

The DA is now ready to run in a valid minimum configuration. One website in the Web Sites component depends on one database in the Databases component. You can add additional SCVMM websites and additional SCVMM databases in the organization to the same two components now or in the future. You can also add other components and relationships to increase the fidelity of the health model. One customization we did perform was to rename the components to just **Odyssey VMM Web Sites** and **Odyssey VMM Databases**, and we renamed the whole custom DA to **Odyssey VMM**. (Rename the DA by selecting File -> Properties.)

The initial design of the Odyssey SCVMM DA is complete. Figure 19.29 shows the finished DA in the Distributed Application Designer.

In the center of Figure 19.29, you can see the Odyssey VMM Web Sites component (above), using the Odyssey VMM Databases component (below) in the main window of the Distributed Application Designer. We clicked the Diagram View shortcut in the lower-right corner of the Details pane (circled). The Distributed Application Dynamic Diagram View opens in a new window.

The Distributed Application Dynamic view feature of the Distributed Application Designer lets you preview the appearance of your DA in the State, Alert, and Diagram views. These handy shortcuts let you see those views before creating associated View folders in the Monitoring space. Notice in the Diagram view of the Odyssey VMM DA, the relationship *Web Sites uses Databases* is reflected in the non-containment arrow (light blue and dotted) pointing from the Odyssey VMM Web Sites icon to the Odyssey VMM Databases icon.

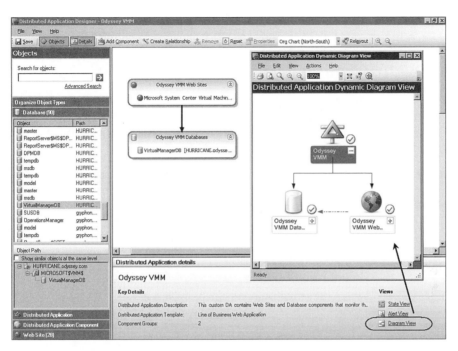

FIGURE 19.29   The Dynamic Diagram View lets you preview monitoring views.

After closing the Distributed Application Designer, a final task in deploying the LoB DA (that monitors the Odyssey VMM application) is to create views in the Monitoring space. When we saved our Odyssey VMM management pack for the first time, it created an empty View folder in the Monitoring space. (This is the case with all custom-created management packs, not only those associated with the Distributed Application Designer.) To make it easy to create monitoring views focused on the DA, you can make the DA the target of custom views created in the view folder. The next procedure shows you how to do this.

In the Monitoring space, we created an Odyssey VMM Performance view and an Odyssey VMM State view in the Odyssey VMM View folder. Now we will add an Alert view. To add an Alert view, perform the following steps:

1. In the Monitoring space, locate the View folder with the name of the DA.
   If you renamed the DA in the Distributed Application Designer, you will see the View folder with the original DA name. Right-click and select Rename to make the View folder name match the new name of the DA.

2. Right-click on the View folder and select New -> Event View.

3. Enter the name and description of the View folder. This name will appear in the navigation pane of the Monitoring space. We used the Name **Odyssey VMM Alert View** to match our naming scheme for this View folder.

4. Next to the Show data related to Entity item, push the "..." button.

5. Locate the name of the DA in the list of targets, or type the DA name in the Look for field. If you can't locate the DA, make sure you have selected the View all targets radio button. Figure 19.30 illustrates this step.

6. Select the name of the DA and press OK twice.

You could create additional custom views of the DA and combine the custom views in a custom dashboard. You could also enable particular notification features for alerts from the DA, such as email or instant message notification. Finally, remember you can target the generic Alerts and Availability reports in OpsMgr against the DA.

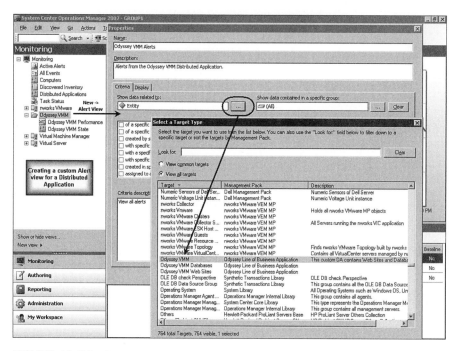

FIGURE 19.30   Creating a custom Alert view for a Distributed Application.

Messaging Template

As we covered in the "Predefined Distributed Applications" section of this chapter, you install the Exchange Service DA as part of importing the Exchange management packs. However, regardless of whether you imported the Exchange management packs, or even if you don't use Exchange server, Microsoft has provided a template for creating a DA that represents an enterprise messaging system.

If your organization uses Exchange, the Exchange Service DA may fit your requirements just fine. However, the Exchange Service DA is part of the sealed Exchange management packs and cannot be edited—for example, you cannot define new components and relationships in the Exchange Service DA. A custom DA based on the Messaging template can be edited as needed. If your organization does not use Exchange, you can create a custom DA based on the Messaging template that exactly models whatever messaging services and components you do have.

We created a custom DA named **Odyssey Enterprise Messaging** to demonstrate how you can augment the monitoring of your Exchange organization. Figure 19.31 presents our completed DA based on the Messaging template.

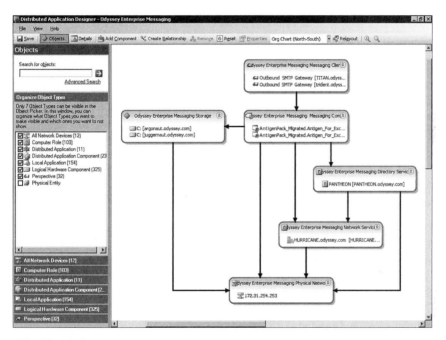

FIGURE 19.31   A custom enterprise messaging DA based on the Messaging template.

Table 19.1 lists the components of the Messaging template, as well as the object type each component accepts, and suggestions on what objects to include in your custom DA.

Our Odyssey Enterprise Messaging DA (shown in Figure 19.31) has eight object types listed in the organizer section of the Object Picker. Seven of the eight have checkmarks next to them, indicating that those object types are visible for selection. If you try to check an eighth object type, you will see the message: "You will have to unselect a selected Object Type first in order to select a new one and make it visible." Remember, you can have only seven visible object types on the Object Picker!

19

TABLE 19.1   Components Included in the Messaging DA Template

Component	Object Type	Suggested Uses
Messaging Client	Perspective	Create TCP Port or web application synthetic transactions to model your client messaging application; assign watcher nodes
Messaging Components	Local Application	Server applications that are core to messaging functions
Messaging Storage	Logical Hardware Component	Physical location(s) of the messaging database(s)
Messaging Directory Services	Computer Role	Active Directory Domain Controller(s)
Messaging Network Services	Computer Role	Other network services such as IIS or DHCP
Messaging Physical Network	All Network Devices	Routers, switches used by the components in the DA

Terminal Services Farm Template

Many organizations support groups of identical servers, known as *farms*, which work together to provide load balancing and failover for client connections. A web farm is a common scenario, where multiple web servers are load balanced either by round-robin or Network Load Balancing (NLB) techniques. Another very common farm application is terminal services, either using the native Windows Terminal Services, or using the popular Citrix Metaframe application (a Citrix farm). Farm applications are by definition also distributed applications, with the same service extended across multiple computers.

The OpsMgr software distribution media includes Microsoft Windows Terminal Services management packs available for import. Importing these management packs creates views and adds reports, and also adds a Terminal Services Farm DA template. The views and reports present an aggregate listing of all terminal servers and related services that exist in the management group—they do not include any diagram views or topology generation features as do the Active Directory and Exchange management packs.

Microsoft provides a template for specifying the architecture and dependencies of a Terminal Services Farm. Creating a DA based on the Terminal Services Farm template gives you a topology-based tool to monitor and troubleshoot your farm. You can create a DA for each terminal services or Citrix farm in your organization. Table 19.2 lists the components in the Terminal Services Farm DA template.

Figure 19.32 illustrates a new custom DA named Odyssey Terminal Services Farm in the process of being created. We have already added the Terminal Server Session Directory object (top left) and a network device object (bottom center). We are adding a domain controller (DC), by selecting the DC object in the Object Picker, and then dragging and dropping it on the DC component.

TABLE 19.2   Terminal Services Farm Template Components

Component	Object Type	Suggested Uses
Terminal Server	Terminal Server Role	All terminal servers in the farm
Terminal Services Session Directory	Terminal Services Session Directory Role	The server specified as the session directory server in the farm configuration
Terminal Services Licensing Server	Terminal Services Licensing Server Role	The Terminal Services Licensing Server for your domain
Windows Domain Controller	Windows Domain Controller	Active Directory Domain Controller(s) used by the farm members, session directory, and licensing servers
Network Devices	All Network Devices	Routers, switches used by the involved servers

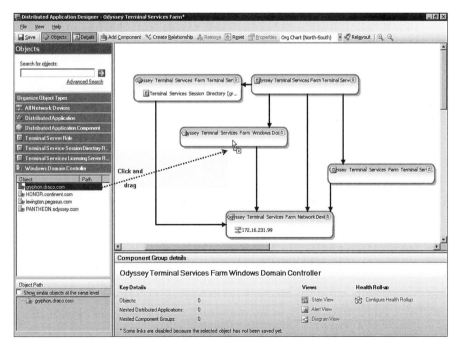

FIGURE 19.32   Adding a domain controller to the Terminal Services Farm DA.

The Terminal Server Session Directory component is a feature allowing users to automatically reconnect to disconnected sessions in a load balanced Terminal Services Farm. The session directory keeps a list of sessions, indexed by user name and server name. A Terminal Services Farm will not function correctly if there are problems with the Terminal Server Session Directory. Likewise, the farm will fail if connectivity to the Terminal Server Licensing server is lost or if the licensing service fails.

DAs based on the Terminal Services Farm template will help you keep track of the vital services that are specific to the Terminal Services application. If you support more than one farm, having multiple DAs will be especially helpful for segregating views of the terminal servers and the session directory server (for a particular farm) from the licensing server and domain controllers that may be shared by multiple farms.

Blank Template

Building a new custom DA based on the Blank template in the Distributed Application Designer is about as unleashed as you can be in the Operations console. You have available as your palette every object that has been discovered in your management group. The only constraint you have with the Blank template is that you can only add objects to components that match the type (or class) the component was created for. However, because you can also create a custom component for every class in the management group, the possibilities are infinite.

When you begin creating a DA based on the Blank template, the Object Picker only contains the Distributed Application and Distributed Application Component object types. OpsMgr efficiently allows custom DA and DA component reuse across all DAs. In our final demonstration of the capabilities of Distributed Application Designer, we will build out the monitoring of our enterprise messaging system.

We named the DA **External Messaging Components**. This is going to be an outside-in, high-level view of our messaging architecture. The first component we added was an existing DA—the Odyssey Enterprise Messaging DA we created in the "Messaging Template" section of this chapter.

The primary purpose of this DA is to monitor external services that the in-house messaging systems depend on. The scenario is that in-house messaging is still dependant on off-site hosted DNS, and an off-site hosted anti-spam service, such as Microsoft Exchange Hosted Services (MEHS), is used for the receipt of inbound Internet email. Part of the MEHS offering that we will monitor includes an off-site hosted anti-spam quarantine web service, where users can optionally review spam intercepted by MEHS. We will also add monitoring for a messaging compliance appliance that performs archiving and content inspection on all messages. Although the actual delivery of email would continue should the quarantine service website or the compliance appliance fail, we want our DA to holistically report on the high-level view of everything involved with our enterprise messaging system.

To monitor external services, create synthetic transactions or web applications that run on watcher nodes and look outside the management group. We created two pairs of TCP Port

Synthetic Transaction monitors and a pair of Web Application monitors for this purpose. We selected a pair of watcher nodes for each monitor, since it is a best practice to always assign at least two watcher nodes to each synthetic transaction or web application.

TIP

Monitoring External Sites Requires OML

Microsoft Licensing says that an Operations Management License (OML) is required for each device managed by Operations Manager 2007, except for those functioning only as network infrastructure devices (OSI layer 3 or below). Microsoft has officially stated that the Synthetic Transaction and Web Application features of OpsMgr require an OML for the target. If the target is an internal server that already has an OpsMgr agent and OML, there is no additional license required. However, an OML is required for external servers and services that you monitor. That makes using OpsMgr too expensive to use as a general-purpose service-based ping monitor. You will probably only purchase OMLs on external targets for applications that are really business critical, in which case the OMLs are not expensive at all.

We named each of these six monitors using the prefix "Off-site." To add monitors to a custom DA based on the Blank template, you must use the Search for objects and Advanced Search features of the Object Picker. Figure 19.33 illustrates using the Search for objects feature. We typed the string **Off-site** in the Search for objects field and pushed the green arrow button to the right of the data entry field. This action made visible the Results for: Off-site panel in the Object Picker, where we can see some of the custom monitors we created for this DA.

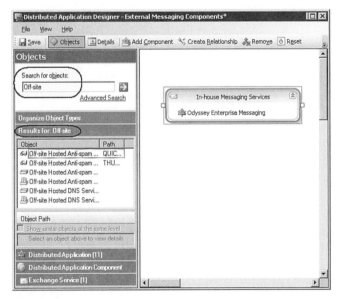

FIGURE 19.33   Use the Search for objects to locate monitors to add to the DA.

We selected and right-clicked the first pair of objects, performing the Add to -> New Component Group task. This placed the second component in the display area, joining the In-house Messaging Service component we created for the Odyssey Enterprise Messaging DA. We used the Advanced Search feature of the Distributed Application Designer to add the remaining objects to the DA. In Figure 19.34, notice that the Search for drop-down box at the top lists all the object classes in the management group, including custom transaction monitors and web applications.

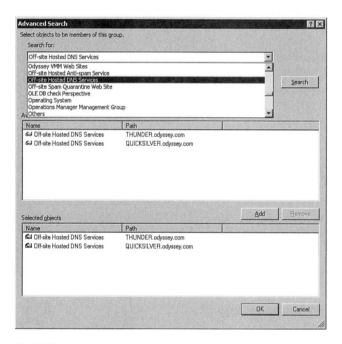

FIGURE 19.34   Adding custom transaction monitors to the DA using the Advanced Search.

In Figure 19.34, we are creating the Off-site Hosted DNS Services component. We press the Search button when selecting the Off-site Hosted DNS Services TCP Port Synthetic Transaction in the Search for drop-down list. The search returns the watcher nodes for that TCP Port Synthetic Transaction. The results are in the central Available objects section of the Advanced Search dialog. Next, we select both watcher nodes from the search results area, press the Add button, and then the OK button.

After creating the component, you define the relationship between the new component and the central component and/or other components. You can also define reciprocal relationships, by creating a relationship in both directions between the same two components. For this DA, the In-house Messaging Services uses the Off-site Hosted DNS Services. While the Create Relationship toolbar button was pressed, we clicked first on the In-house Messaging Services, then on the Off-site Hosted DNS Services component. This created the non-containment relationship between the components.

In sum, the External Messaging Components DA features the In-house Messaging Services as the central component. Of course, that component is the Odyssey Enterprise Messaging DA, which as a DA is already an abstraction of carefully selected monitoring objects. The central component depends on three external components:

- ► Off-site Hosted DNS Service, watched by two nodes running TCP Port 53 monitors targeted at the DNS servers of the DNS hosting service.

- ► Off-site Hosted Anti-spam Service, watched by two nodes running TCP Port 25 monitors targeted at the SMTP server of the anti-spam hosting service.

- ► Off-site Spam Quarantine Web Service, watched by two nodes running Web Application monitors targeted at the self-service spam quarantine website of the anti-spam hosting service.

Additionally, we wanted this DA to include monitoring for an appliance administered by another department. The appliance performs corporate compliance functions like archiving and checking for keywords or content. Although we don't manage the appliance, it is business critical and we need to include its online status in our enterprise health model. We discovered the appliance as an SMTP Network Device and put that in an Email Compliance Appliance component. We created a relationship where the Email Compliance Appliance uses the In-house Messaging Services. Figure 19.35 displays the completed External Messaging Components DA.

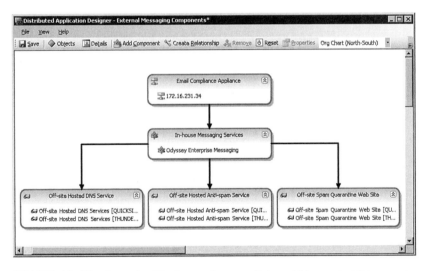

FIGURE 19.35   From the Blank template, an External Messaging DA emerges.

As we mentioned, the Off-site Hosted DNS Service and the Off-site Hosted Anti-spam Service are mission critical (highest priority), while the Off-site Spam Quarantine Web Service and the Email Compliance Appliance are business critical (but still important). We can incorporate this distinction in the DA.

19

You can modify the level of the alert generated by individual DA components. Using the Configure Health Rollup tool in the Distributed Application Designer (with the component selected), you can override the default alerting behavior that is to send a critical alert. In our scenario, you might reduce the alert level for the business-critical components from critical to warning.

Summary

We made it through the whole chapter without monitoring even a single server! The focus was on the dispersed net of components that deliver a service to users and customers, achieving End-to-End monitoring in many applications. We started with the roots of the distributed application in the programming world, and explained what a Distributed Application means in OpsMgr. We took a close look at three pre-defined DAs for OpsMgr, Active Directory, and Exchange. We learned about client perspective and watcher nodes in the Enterprise Health Monitoring scenarios. Finally, we started building DAs like a Line of Business application and a Terminal Services Farm. In Chapter 20, "Automatically Adapting Your Environment," we discuss ideas on how to take OpsMgr beyond monitoring to automatically adapt to changes in your environment.

PART VI

Beyond Operations Manager

IN THIS PART

CHAPTER 20

Automatically Adapting Your Environment

In this last part of the book, we move from more quotidian or mundane discussions of how Microsoft presents using Operations Manager 2007 to thinking "outside of the box." Whereas earlier chapters covered topics such as planning, installing, configuring, administering, and monitoring, this chapter will look at some more out-of-the-ordinary approaches for using the product, perhaps stretching your horizon to look at Operations Manager in new and different ways.

As we have discussed throughout this book, Operations Manager 2007 (OpsMgr) is most commonly used to identify conditions that occur, providing notification if these conditions take place. Generically speaking, the concept of monitoring is, "Watch my back (uh, environment) and let me know what's going on." Monitoring with OpsMgr allows us to react more quickly than we would otherwise. Once we are aware of an issue, OpsMgr can provide product knowledge to help us more quickly resolve the problem. The user community also assists with problem solving—there are numerous articles and blogs discussing the use of the product.

A recent development in the user community is a new resource called the *ReSearch This! Management Pack* (RTMP). The RTMP provides a shared community-based knowledge repository for OpsMgr, System Center Essentials, and MOM 2005. You can download the Ops2007 version of the RTMP at http://systemcenterforum.org/wp-content/uploads/ReSearchThisOpsMgr.zip. A version for MOM 2005 is available as well (http://systemcenterforum.org/wp-content/uploads/ReSearchThisMOM.zip). These links are also available as live links in Appendix E, "Reference URLs." The

RTMP includes tasks that search the SystemCenterForum repository for the alert you specify and link to the SystemCenterForum repository so you can share your resolutions with the community.

Using the RTMP, we can choose an action from the Alert Tasks pane (shown in Figure 20.1), which will search for the alert in the SystemCenterForum shared repository.

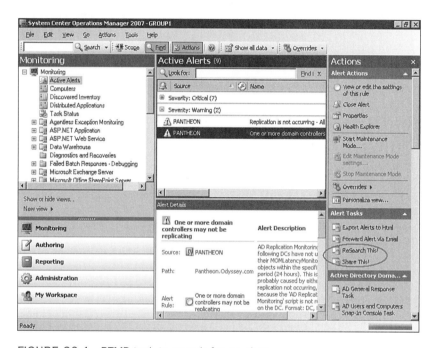

FIGURE 20.1   RTMP task to search for an alert.

Known resolutions for the alert, if available, will display using the format shown in Figure 20.2.

After an issue is resolved, information on its resolution can be stored in company knowledge and/or shared with the community using the RTMP with the screen shown in Figure 20.3. These two approaches work together to allow an administrator running OpsMgr the means to resolve issues more quickly than would be possible without using a monitoring solution.

In addition to identifying conditions that have occurred, OpsMgr provides functionality to help proactively monitor your environment—a better approach to operations management than just resolving problems in reactive mode. Here are two examples:

▶ As a simple example, it is far easier to fix a drive that is low on free space by freeing up additional space than it is to recover from a crash of the system caused by running out of free space.

FIGURE 20.2   Results of the RTMP task to search for an alert.

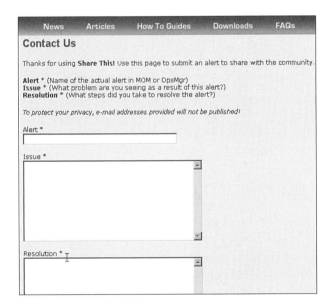

FIGURE 20.3   RTMP task results for sharing an alert resolution.

▶ A more complex illustration is trending system usage to predict when systems may become bottlenecked. To illustrate, if a server is at 50% of memory utilization in January, trends to 60% utilization by March, and 70% utilization in June, it is likely that memory utilization will become the bottleneck prior to September.

Utilizing trending with OpsMgr allows us to be proactive by identifying bottlenecks and resolving them before they affect performance or functionality provided to end users.

OpsMgr enables you to more quickly identify and resolve problems, becoming more proactive in monitoring issues; yet this only scratches the surface of the functionality available with the product. This chapter will tie it all together, discussing what you can accomplish above and beyond the monitoring aspects of OpsMgr.

We will examine how you can use OpsMgr to automatically adapt to your environment. We will also discuss how OpsMgr can integrate with other products and provide examples of an environment that can automatically adapt by using Operations Manager 2007. Consider what we are emphasizing throughout as the *art of adapting*.

Operations Manager Functionality

Operations Manager 2007 provides many different capabilities for automatically adapting your environment. These functions include diagnostics, recoveries, notifications, and console and agent tasks. OpsMgr also provides functionality that is used dynamically. An example of this is through computer groups, which also lend themselves toward the ability to adapt automatically to changes in the IT environment.

We will first look at two commonly overlooked functions available within OpsMgr: diagnostics and recoveries.

Diagnostics and Recoveries

As we discussed in Chapter 14, "Monitoring with Operations Manager," Operations Manager 2007 uses monitors. Differing from rules, monitors present the state of objects within OpsMgr. When a monitor changes from a healthy state to a nonhealthy state, such as a warning or error state, OpsMgr can activate diagnostic and recovery tasks.

A *diagnostic task* assists with determining why the change in state occurred. As an example, if there was an issue with Active Directory replication, you could configure a diagnostic task to run that would automatically perform an analysis on replication, such as the `repadmin.exe /replsum` command. You can configure diagnostic tasks to run automatically or on demand, depending on your requirements:

▶ Make use of *automatically run* diagnostic tasks when you want to gather information from the system at the time when the change in state occurred (such as the `repadmin` example in the preceding paragraph).

▶ Utilize *on-demand* diagnostic tasks when there are common tasks that will occur when the system is in an error state. Different diagnostic tasks can be defined for the different states (such as warning or critical), and multiple diagnostic tasks can be defined on a per-state level. A simple example of an on-demand diagnostic task would be a ping test, which would validate that the system can at least be reached via ping (in the case of a web server, a send or get command test could be used).

A *recovery task* performs an action that should reverse the state change that occurred. As an example, if there was an issue with the print server spooler service, you could configure a recovery task to restart the service automatically. A more in-depth example of this would gather the job information currently in the queue (to assist in debugging why the queue failed or to know the print jobs affected) and then restart the service. As with diagnostic tasks, you can define multiple recovery tasks for each state level. You can also configure recovery tasks that automatically reset the monitor to a healthy state.

> **TIP**
>
> **Diagnostics and Recoveries Online**
>
> Microsoft provides a series of webcasts to assist with learning the key features within OpsMgr. These videos are available at http://technet.microsoft.com/en-us/opsmgr/bb498237.aspx.
>
> A video that Microsoft created specifically about diagnostics and recoveries is available at http://www.microsoft.com/winme/0701/28666/Diagnostics_and_Recoveries_Demo.asx.

Diagnostic and recovery tasks are available only within monitors, and they are configured within the monitor properties on the Diagnostic and Recovery tab. Figure 20.4 shows an example of this tab on a monitor (this particular case uses the Active Directory Availability Health Rollup monitor). You will find monitor properties either through the Health Explorer or in the Authoring space of the Operations console.

Diagnostic and recovery tasks are available when there is a state change for the monitor. The tasks are accessed by opening the Health Explorer for the generated alert (or you can navigate to Authoring -> Management Pack Objects -> Monitors). Next, click the monitor, click the State Change Events tab, and then scroll down on the right-side panel to find any available diagnostic and recovery information, including the results of any diagnostic or recovery tasks configured to run automatically. Figure 20.5 illustrates an example of this information in the Health Explorer for a Health Service Heartbeat Failure.

Notice the Details pane (bottom right) shows a diagnostic task called Check If Health Service Is Running and a recovery task called Reinstall Health Service Manually.

Creating diagnostic and recovery tasks is fairly simple. Open the monitor where you want to define the action to occur (shown in Figure 20.4); on the Diagnostic and Recovery tab, click the appropriate Add... button to configure either diagnostic or recovery tasks.

Creating Diagnostic Tasks

Perform the following steps to create a diagnostic task:

1. Click the Add... button under Configure diagnostic tasks and then choose which state you will create the diagnostic for (shown in Figure 20.6).

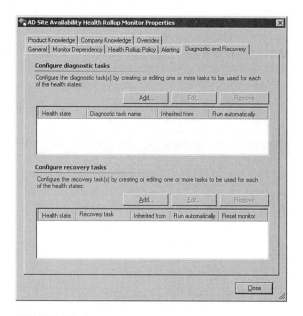

FIGURE 20.4   The Active Directory Availability Health Rollup monitor's Diagnostic and Recovery tab.

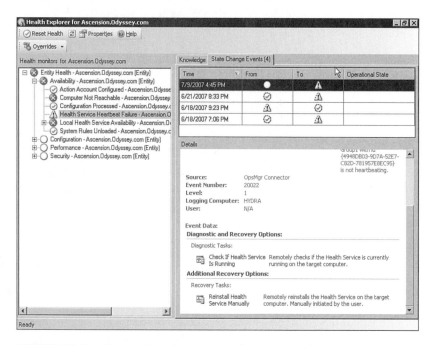

FIGURE 20.5   Diagnostic and recovery tasks shown within the Health Explorer.

2. After you identify the criticality level for the diagnostic (critical or warning), the only type of diagnostic task available is Run Command. You will also specify the management pack to store the diagnostic in (as with storing overrides, we do not recommend using the Default management pack!).

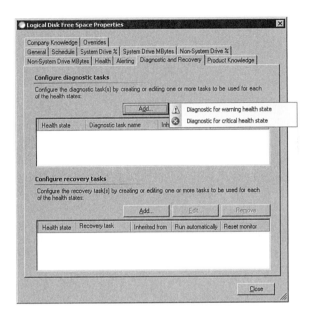

FIGURE 20.6   Determining the criticality level for the diagnostic being created.

3. Next, the Create Diagnostic Task Wizard asks you to define the name, description, and the target of the diagnostic task, and whether the task will start automatically when the state changes to the criticality level you defined.

Figure 20.7 shows an example of creating a diagnostic task to determine top disk space usage.

4. On the Command Line page, specify the command-line execution settings. In Figure 20.8, we show a diagnostic task with a script that reports on the top space usage on the drive (`diskuse /s` does a great job, and it's free for download as part of the Windows Server 2003 Resource Kit at http://technet.microsoft.com/bb693323.aspx; the full link to the Microsoft download site is available in Appendix E). The script specified here provides information to help with a faster problem resolution for the lack of disk space on the system.

20

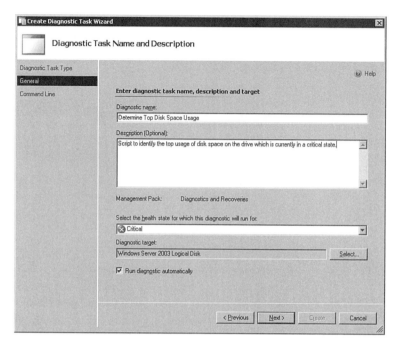

FIGURE 20.7   Defining the name, description, and target for the diagnostic task.

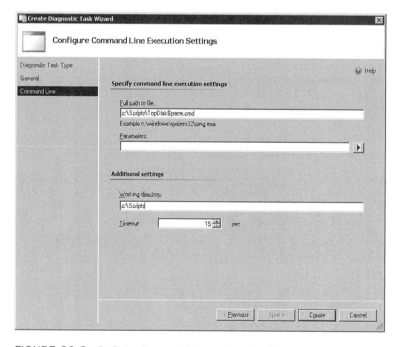

FIGURE 20.8   Defining the script to run for the diagnostic task.

Creating Recovery Tasks

The process for creating a recovery task is similar to the process of creating a diagnostic task. Create the recovery task on the monitor where you want to define the action to occur (shown in Figure 20.4). Perform the following steps:

1. On the Diagnostic and Recovery tab, click the Add... button under Configure recovery tasks and then choose the state to create the recovery task for. You can define recovery tasks to run either a command line or a script. In Figure 20.9, we show a recovery task defined to clear additional disk space on a drive. This recovery task is set to run automatically and to reset the monitor after the recovery is complete.

    This configuration means that when the (critical) condition occurs, the script will run and reset the monitor to a healthy state. The state will update again the next time the monitor is scheduled to run; for the Windows 2003 Logical Free Space monitor, it will run once an hour.

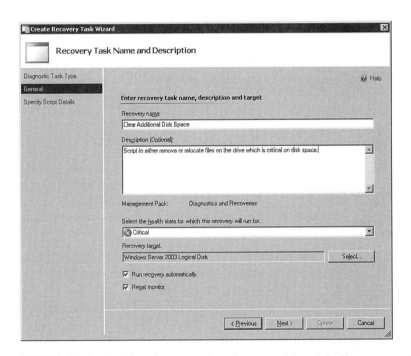

FIGURE 20.9   Defining the name, description, and target for the recovery task.

2. Figure 20.10 shows a recovery task with a script defined to either remove or relocate files on the drive (with an increased value for the timeout from 15 seconds to 120 seconds). This example of a recovery task runs a script that removes or relocates temporary files to help resolve the free disk space issue on the drive that is in a critical state.

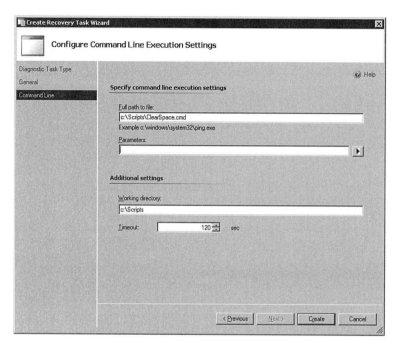

FIGURE 20.10   Defining the script to run for the recovery task.

Diagnostic and recovery tasks provide Operations Manager with the capability to perform automated actions based on the change of the state of objects that OpsMgr is monitoring. They also provide a core capability for creating an environment that can automatically adapt to changes.

Auto-restarting the Health Service

When Operations Manager 2007 was first released, there was a common situation where agents stopped functioning and went to a gray state because the OpsMgr Health service failed. This situation regularly occurred on a large number of systems over time. If this occurs, you may choose to manually recover using a recovery task (you could also open the Computer Management MMC [Microsoft Management Console] and restart the service, but that doesn't fit our example, so we will disregard that).

If you prefer to have the service auto-start itself, you can configure an override. Open the Health Service Heartbeat Failure monitor in the Operations console (select Authoring -> Management Pack Objects -> Monitors and then find the monitor by name). On the Diagnostics and Recovery tab, highlight the Restart Health Service recovery task and select Edit. Create an override that selects the Enabled option and sets the Override Setting to True.

A quick way to determine whether this is functional is to stop the OpsMgr Health service on a system, wait several minutes (by default this is three heartbeat intervals of 60 seconds and the time it takes to activate the recovery task, or about 5 minutes in our test case example). See if the Health service restarts as part of the OpsMgr recovery functionality.

To actually stop the Health service on a system, you would either remove this override or stop and then disable the service.

Notification

In Chapter 14, we discussed the improvements in how notification workflow occurs in this version of Operations Manager. Notification can be performed using a variety of methods, with the most common being email. Other available techniques include instant messaging, Short Message Service, and command notification. These different formats are *notification channels*. The command notification provides an important capability to consider in an adaptable OpsMgr.

The configuration for command notification is available in the Operations console in the Administration space, under Settings -> Notification. Select the Command tab, as shown in Figure 20.11.

FIGURE 20.11   The Command Notification screen.

20

You can define multiple notification channels, which perform custom actions. In general, notifications provide information that will require human intervention, using a format such as email or instant messaging.

Command notification opens up a set of more complex potential functions that you might use. A command channel can run a script or an executable file. For example, a notification could be defined that causes a file to be created, which could become part of a workflow. Alternatively, a portal could be updated, with its content reflecting a list of users whose accounts are currently disabled. The limits to this are restricted only to what you can script!

As an extreme example, Figure 20.12 shows how you could create a notification that would cause an audible alert to occur when the notification channel is used. As an example, we imagine the robot from *Lost in Space* saying "Danger, Will Robinson" for the audible alert, but hey that could just be us.

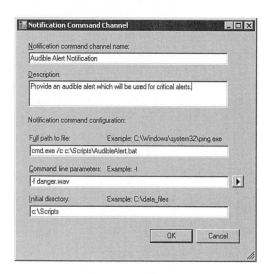

FIGURE 20.12   Creating an audible alert command.

Notification not only provides a method to present information for human intervention, but can be used as part of a workflow to integrate more automated interactions. Notifications (particularly command notification) are a key piece of functionality required to adapt automatically to changes in your environment.

Computer groups in Operations Manager 2007 gather computers into logical units that can be used for a variety of reasons, including scoping the Operations console and providing criteria for notifications.

Computer Groups

Operations Manager 2007 computer groups are defined with either static membership or through dynamic membership:

- *Static membership* is when a system is added by name to the computer group.

- *Dynamic membership* is when a computer is determined to be part of a computer group, based on some property of the computer (such as an Exchange server having Exchange services installed).

Computer groups within OpsMgr are very flexible, and you can use them to provide a variety of functions. These functions include the ability to logically group together disperse systems based on specified criteria. As an example, you might define a computer group based on the Active Directory (AD) site it belongs to. Creating custom groups based on AD sites provides an easy method to scope the OpsMgr console based on the sites that specific administrators are responsible for, or to mass resolve any alerts created by the loss of a link between sites. To create computer groups based on AD sites, perform the following steps:

1. First, get a list of your AD sites by using the Active Directory Sites and Services tool (we will use Plano as a sample site name for this example). Next, open the Operations console under Authoring -> Groups. Right-click and create a new group. Enter a friendly name (for example, **Odyssey Plano Computers**) and a description.

2. Choose the management pack to store this in (preferably create a separate management pack versus using the Default management pack). Click Next to continue.

3. Click Next to continue on the Explicit Group Members page.

4. Click Create/Edit rules on the Dynamic Inclusion Rules page.

5. Select the class Windows Computer and click the Add button.

6. Select Active Directory Site, Equals, and the AD Site Name (for example, Active Directory Site, Equals, Plano). Click OK.

NOTE

Custom Computer Group Options for the Windows Computer

The Windows Computer group type has properties that include Principal Name, DNS Name, NetBIOS Computer Name, NetBIOS Domain Name, IP Address, Network Name, Active Directory SID, Virtual Machine, DNS Domain Name, Organizational Unit, DNS Forest Name, Active Directory Site, and Display Name. Therefore, a lot of cool things can be done here, such as easily identifying systems in Organizational Units (OUs), forests, and even virtual machines!

---

7. Click Next to continue on the Dynamic Inclusion Rules page.

8. Click Next to continue on the Add Subgroups page.

9. Click Create to create the computer group on the Exclude Objects from this group page.

10. In the Monitoring space, you can now use the Scope button to choose the new group. In addition, if you prefix the computer names with the name of your company (in our example, we would start the computer group names with Odyssey), you can easily choose from the list of AD sites.

Computer groups are extremely flexible within OpsMgr 2007 and are important in an adaptable environment. The fact that OpsMgr groups can automatically identify their appropriate management packs brings OpsMgr another step closer to meeting the requirements of a changing information technology environment.

TIP

Populate Dynamic Computer Groups with Health Service Watchers

The Watchanator is a management pack developed by Timothy McFadden to populate dynamic computer groups with the associated Health Service (Agent) watchers. This is useful because you would then receive heartbeat (up/down) alerts for your systems!

You can download the Watchanator from http://timothymcfadden.googlepages.com/Watchanator2.zip. Timothy's write-up is at http://scom2k7.blogspot.com/2007/10/watchanator-20-heart-beat-alert-tool.html.

Console Tasks

OpsMgr uses console tasks to automate the process of performing commonly executed functions from the Operations console. Tasks make it easier to complete these functions, and they also provide us with a basis to extend the capabilities available with the diagnostic and recovery tasks we discussed in the "Diagnostics and Recoveries" section earlier in this chapter.

Console tasks exist within management packs and are context specific—meaning that they are only available when the object you are working with allows that particular console task to occur. As an example, if you highlight an Active Directory–related alert, you would not want to see SharePoint-related console tasks. A number of console tasks are delivered within the management packs from Microsoft, and you can use them to automate various functions. You can create tasks to run a command line or a script, running them from the console (alternatively, you can run *agent tasks* on a managed system).

Enhancing Diagnostics and Recoveries

At first glance, console tasks would appear to be irrelevant to automatically adapting an environment, because they require activation by someone using the Operations console. Yet while the console tasks themselves require interaction, they can provide functionality to incorporate into diagnostics and recoveries.

There is no easy way to include an existing console task in a diagnostic or recovery task (because you are not able to choose console tasks or scripts from the drop-down box when creating a recovery task). However, the commands and scripts used by console tasks can easily be re-created using Windows Notepad and then copied and pasted between the console task and the diagnostic or recovery task.

Figure 20.13 shows a script used by a console task (the List Top Processes on DC task in this case). You can transfer the script from the console task to a diagnostic or recovery task by copying the script from the console task, pasting it into Notepad temporarily, and then copying and pasting it from Notepad into the diagnostic or recovery task.

FIGURE 20.13   Top CPU script within the List Top Processes script.

Transferring command-line tasks is a little more difficult because the configuration for the task displays in XML. However, the important information is easy enough to interpret. Figure 20.14 shows the configuration from the Repadmin /replsum task.

20

FIGURE 20.14   Configuration for the Repadmin /replsum task.

In Figure 20.15, we show creating a diagnostic task with the following information from the Repadmin command-line task added to it:

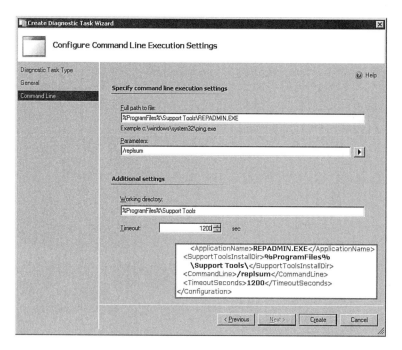

FIGURE 20.15   Creating a diagnostic from the repadmin task.

- ▶ `ApplicationName` provides the name of the command line to run.
- ▶ `SupportToolsInstallDir` is the path to the executable.
- ▶ `CommandLine` provides the information for the parameters.
- ▶ `TimeoutSeconds` provides the value for the timeout value.

The information in the box below the timeout is the information copied from the script in Figure 20.14.

Console tasks provide a wealth of scripts and command-line options that increase the capabilities of diagnostics and recoveries. There are not many predefined diagnostics and recovery tasks, but there are quite a few predefined console tasks to use for providing additional functionality with diagnostics and recoveries.

Identifying Conditions

OpsMgr has the capability to identify conditions based on a variety of different sources of information, including the Windows Event log, generic log files, Windows Services, Windows Management Instrumentation (WMI), performance counters, and Simple Network Management Protocol (SNMP) events (see Chapter 14 for additional information). After identifying a condition, OpsMgr can perform an action using the notification and/or diagnostic and recovery functions, which provide a method to react to the condition. As we discussed, notifications, diagnostics, and recoveries all provide the ability to run a script (among other actions).

All of this reduces to a core concept: Can you identify it, and can you script it? If so, you can do it using OpsMgr. This concept is the foundation we will build on for the remainder of this chapter.

TIP

On the CD

Microsoft's *TechNet* magazine includes a column where the "Scripting Guys" address commonly asked questions about system administration scripting. These questions are also available on the Microsoft website, at http://www.microsoft.com/technet/scriptcenter/resources/qanda/default.mspx. The Scripting Guys have created a downloadable archive of these scripts from August 2004 to June 2006 in CHM format. For your convenience, we include this archive on the CD accompanying this book.

Operations Manager Integration

20

Although Operations Manager is an important piece of the puzzle in automatically adapting to a changing environment, you can significantly increase its capabilities by interacting with products both within the System Center family and with other Microsoft products. In the next sections, we will discuss a variety of products that can work together with OpsMgr to provide a foundation for automatically adapting to changes.

Configuration Manager

System Center Configuration Manager (formerly named *Microsoft Systems Management Server*, or *SMS*) provides hardware and software inventory, software distribution, patch management, remote control, software metering, Operating System Deployment (OSD), and device management for Windows-based environments. There is built-in integration with Operations Manager. This integration includes

▶ Putting a monitored system into maintenance mode prior to rebooting it with ConfigMgr through software deployment

▶ Generating alerts on application (or OSD) deployments

▶ Deploying agents using ConfigMgr

This section focuses on ways to increase the functionality or automation of OpsMgr through integration with ConfigMgr.

Using Collections

ConfigMgr uses collections to target software or operating systems for deployment. You define collections using either static or dynamic membership (similar to defining computer groups in OpsMgr 2007). As we discussed in Chapter 9, "Installing and Configuring Agents," you can use ConfigMgr to deploy the Operations Manager 2007 agent. However, this is only the beginning of how these two products can complement each other.

Using ConfigMgr, you can create collections that will identify systems requiring service packs prior to deploying the Operations Manager agent (the same collections can also be the target of the service pack and deployed via ConfigMgr/SMS). As an example, the following query identifies systems running Windows Server 2003 that do not have Service Pack 1 (SP 1) applied. We are interested in this query because SP 1 is a prerequisite to installing the OpsMgr agent on Windows Server 2003 systems.

```
select SMS_R_System.Name, o.CSDVersion, o.Version from SMS_R_System inner join
SMS_G_System_OPERATING_SYSTEM as o on o.ResourceID = SMS_R_System.ResourceId
where o.Version = "5.2.3790" and o.CSDVersion not in ( "Service Pack 1",
"Service Pack 2" )
```

At first glance, this query looks pretty complex, but the query was created using the ConfigMgr graphical user interface (GUI), and it's just shown here to provide a quick way to reuse any queries that are created. The following query identifies systems running Windows Server 2000 that do not have SP 4 applied, a requirement for installing the OpsMgr agent on Windows 2000 systems:

```
select SMS_R_System.Name, SMS_R_System.NetbiosName, o.CSDVersion, o.Version from
SMS_R_System inner join SMS_G_System_OPERATING_SYSTEM as o on o.ResourceID =
SMS_R_System.ResourceId where o.Version = "5.0.2195" and o.CSDVersion not in
( "Service Pack 4" )
```

Another example of where the two products complement each other is creating a collection to identify the systems with the ConfigMgr agent deployed. You could then target this collection to deploy additional support tools used by the management packs. Here's an example of a query defining a collection that identifies systems with the OpsMgr agent:

```
select Name from SMS_R_System where ResourceId in (select SMS_R_System.ResourceId
from SMS_R_System inner join SMS_G_System_ADD_REMOVE_PROGRAMS on
SMS_G_System_ADD_REMOVE_PROGRAMS.ResourceID = SMS_R_System.ResourceId where
SMS_G_System_ADD_REMOVE_PROGRAMS.DisplayName in ( "System Center Operations Manager
2007 Agent")) order by Name
```

> **TIP**
>
> **On the CD**
>
> The queries shown here are on the CD accompanying the book, and you can copy/paste them into your ConfigMgr environment.

This query states that to be a member of the System Center Operations Manager 2007 Agent collection, the agent application must be listed in the Control Panel Add/Remove programs applet. After defining this collection, you can configure a package to push out to that collection that will automate installing additional support tools for the system.

ConfigMgr, coupled with OpsMgr's Active Directory Integration capability (see Chapter 9), lets you automatically deploy OpsMgr agents and then automate additional supplemental software deployments.

Using ConfigMgr to Install the Operations Console

You can use ConfigMgr to automate deploying the Operations console, perhaps to a collection of OpsMgr administrator workstations. The installation requires creating four packages (the package installing the Operations console requires that the other three are installed first).

▶ The first package installs .NET Framework 2.0 with this command:

`Microsoft.NET Framework 2.0.exe /Q`

▶ The second installs .NET Framework 3.0:

`dotnetfx3.exe /q`

▶ The third installs PowerShell:

`powershell2003sp1.exe /quiet`

▶ The fourth package installs the Operations console only (substitute *RMSServer* with your environment's RMS server).

20

```
%WinDir%\System32\msiexec.exe /i <path>\MOM.msi /qn /l*v
%Temp%\MOMUI_install.log ADDLOCAL=MOMUI
ROOT_MANAGEMENT_SERVER_DNS=<RMSServer>
```

Thanks to Tarek Ismail (http://tarek-online.blogspot.com/) for writing this one up!

Integrating with Agentless Exception Monitoring

Configuration Manager also integrates with the Agentless Exception Monitoring (AEM) capability of Operations Manager. AEM identifies applications that have crashes. You can use Configuration Manager to patch the application that is crashing, and then use AEM again to determine whether the patch had an impact on the number of crashes occurring within that application.

Extending Functionality with Scripting

Some of the functionality available within ConfigMgr is executable from the command line, and various scripts are available from locations such as www.myitforum.com and www.faqshop.com. We include scripts that provide the ability to perform a software or hardware inventory, or to add a computer to a static collection. These scripts are on the CD accompanying this book.

The synergy between the OpsMgr and ConfigMgr products provides new capabilities for Operations Manager 2007 that are of use for automatically adapting with OpsMgr.

Capacity Planner

System Center Capacity Planner (SCCP) provides the ability to develop architectures for Exchange 2003/2007 and eventually OpsMgr 2007 to test various "what if" scenarios and to identify potential bottlenecks. Although the new version of SCCP 2007 does not currently support OpsMgr 2007, we expect it to provide similar functionality for OpsMgr 2007 in 2008. SCCP is currently a standalone product, but it has the potential for integration with OpsMgr 2007.

SCCP asks a variety of questions that assist with describing a model for a recommended architecture. When Exchange is being modeled, for example, the information gathered includes the number of sites and Outlook client usage, network connectivity between sites, and potential hardware configurations.

Looking at the information SCCP uses for its capacity model, you may notice that the majority of this data could be drawn from existing sources. Drawing from these sources would automate the integration of the Capacity Planner. Examples include the following:

▶ Site information from Active Directory sites and services.

▶ Hardware configurations from ConfigMgr hardware inventory.

▶ Outlook and client usage from ConfigMgr software metering.

▶ Network connectivity information may be available from OpsMgr; the product includes integration with network devices, and that functionality is enhanced in the next version.

Why does it matter that we already have this information in the System Center product line? Using information already available gives us the ability to proactively plan changes (such adding sites to the network), changes in the usage of Exchange, and changes in user counts. Let's work with this idea, using Exchange as an example.

Your boss walks into your office and tells you that your company is thinking about acquiring another company (hey, it would be nice if they actually told you that in advance for a change). He wants you to migrate the new user base into your current Exchange environment (the other company has 1000 users with 400GB of mail that will need to be transferred if the company is acquired). With an integrated OpsMgr/ConfigMgr/SCCP, you could build a projection that would indicate potential bottlenecks from adding the users into the current environment, as well as display any upgrades required to make it possible.

We can take another more common Exchange scenario. Your mailbox store is increasing at a rate of 30GB per month. You use OpsMgr to run a scheduled SCCP plan based on current growth rates, getting bottleneck information in advance. This allows you to make changes and resolve issues before they occur.

The further integration of the System Center product line, including SCCP with OpsMgr, holds some exciting potential capabilities that will work toward providing a more proactive monitoring and management solution.

Virtual Machine Manager and Virtual Server 2005 R2

The System Center Virtual Machine Manager (SCVMM) provides a centralized product for deploying and managing virtual machines in a virtual server environment. It includes the ability to determine servers that are good candidates for virtualization, and it provides an easy-to-use Physical to Virtual (PtoV) conversion process. SCVMM also provides a self-service provisioning capability and the ability to perform automated processes with PowerShell. Figure 20.16 shows the SCVMM interface, running on a host system called Hurricane with a guest operating system named Honor.

The user interface on SCVMM is very similar to the OpsMgr 2007 Operations console. The left side shows the different host systems available, with different views for virtual machine statuses such as running, paused, and saved. The bottom-left panel provides a list of options, including the Hosts, Virtual Machines (shown), Library, Jobs, and Administration. The Actions pane shows a variety of items that perform tasks such as creating a new virtual machine, adding a library server, adding hosts, and changing the state of a guest operating system (Start, Stop, Pause, Save State, Discard saved state, Shut down).

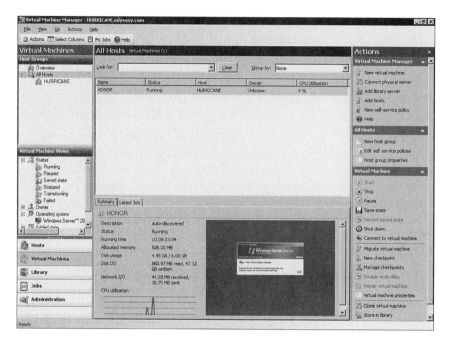

FIGURE 20.16   The System Center Virtual Machine Manager interface.

TIP

SCVMM Scripting Guide

Microsoft has released a scripting guide for SCVMM, which contains nearly 150 pages of information (including sample scripts) on how to script for System Center Virtual Machine Manager 2007. The scripting guide is available for download at http://go.microsoft.com/fwlink/?LinkId=104290.

You can also clone virtual machines and store them in a library for reuse. SCVMM provides some capabilities that greatly enhance the functionality currently available in Virtual Server R2. There are a lot of very exciting possibilities for automatically adapting your environment, which we will discuss later in this chapter in the "Automatically Adapting with Operations Manager" section.

PowerShell/Command Shell

In our opinion, PowerShell is one of the more exciting concepts to come out of Microsoft in a long time. One of the true strengths of UNIX-based systems is the ability to script just about anything, automating any process. Whereas UNIX started as a command-line user interface, Windows began as a graphical user interface. Although a GUI is much more intuitive and oftentimes more easy to use, it can lack the power of a command-line environment, where you can script and automate processes. Microsoft designed PowerShell (previously called Monad) to provide the best of both worlds, bringing an extremely powerful command-line interface to the Windows platform. The Operations Manager Command Shell is the OpsMgr-specific version of the PowerShell interface.

PowerShell is integrated into several Microsoft products, including Exchange 2007, OpsMgr 2007, System Center Data Protection Manager V2, SCVMM, and all versions of Windows Server 2008 except for the Server Core. There are even extensions to add PowerShell functionality into non-PowerShell-integrated products such as SMS 2003 (for details see http://www.microsoft.com/technet/technetmag/issues/2007/11/ UtilitySpotlight/, which discusses adding the management of SMS clients from the command line).

> **TIP**
>
> **PowerShell cmdlets and Additional Functionality**
>
> PowerShell is really catching on; even third-party organizations are providing free down-loadable cmdlets. As an example, Quest Software provides a free set of PowerShell commands for Active Directory, available at http://www.quest.com/activeroles-server/ arms.aspx. PowerGUI, an extensible console based on PowerShell, is also available for download at http://www.powergui.org/downloads.jspa.

The PowerShell syntax is straightforward and works using the following format:

```
Verb-Noun Parameter
```

As an example, to get the status of a service, we would use get-service and then the name of the service. The syntax to get the status for the OpsMgr HealthService would be

```
get-service HealthService
```

The results of this command present the status of the service as shown next (shown when the service is running):

```
Status    Name            DisplayName
Running   HealthService   OpsMgr Health Service
```

You can run get-service HealthService ¦ fl for a more detailed description of the HealthService. Using this syntax gives us the following output:

```
Name                  : HealthService
DisplayName           : OpsMgr Health Service
Status                : Running
DependentServices     : {}
ServicesDependedOn    : {rpcss}
CanPauseAndContinue   : True
```

20

```
CanShutdown        : True
CanStop            : True
ServiceType        : Win32ShareProcess
```

PowerShell for Beginners

When we were starting out with PowerShell, we wanted a quick way to find out what custom-built collections existed within an SMS site and to save that information to a file for review. We started by installing PowerShell and checking into what functionality was available. (PowerShell requires installation of .NET 2.0).

Not knowing what command (known as a *cmdlet* in PowerShell) we needed, we opened PowerShell (available on the Start menu, in the Windows PowerShell 1.0 folder -> Windows PowerShell). We started, logically enough, with the following command:

```
help
```

Help provided us with a list of all cmdlets available. There were quite a few, so we did the following:

```
help *wmi*
```

This gave us a list limited to the cmdlets with *wmi* in them. This led us to find out that get-wmiobject likely was what we were looking for. To get additional information on this cmdlet, we typed the following:

```
help get-wmiobject -detailed
```

```
help get-wmiobject -full
```

The help information provided us with what we needed, because we already had the query to use with WMI. Here's the resultant command:

```
get-wmiobject -query "select * from sms_collection where collectionid like
'DAL%'" -namespace root\sms\site_DAL -computername monarch >
collections.txt
```

This resulted in creating a collections.txt file with the detail for custom collections available within our SMS site (which is DAL, and for the computer we specified "monarch").

Additional documentation and versions of PowerShell for Windows XP and Windows 2003 Server (and 2003 x64) are available for download if you go to http://download.microsoft.com and search on "PowerShell." Microsoft also has developed webcasts on PowerShell, available at http://www.microsoft.com/technet/scriptcenter/webcasts/ps.mspx. In addition, we provide a PowerShell Cheat Sheet created by Microsoft, available on the CD accompanying this book.

There is also a PowerShell cmdlet named Start-Transcript. You can use this to record your PowerShell session in a text file. This is useful to help remember what you did!

From an OpsMgr functionality perspective, we anticipate PowerShell will be indispensable, because it will provide command-line control of tasks previously performed with the GUI. This also provides direct benefits to OpsMgr, because new functions should be available to use as tasks or diagnostics and recoveries through integration with PowerShell.

Service Manager

Although the System Center Service Manager (ServiceMgr) product is currently in beta, the functionality currently planned integrates with Active Directory, Operations Manager, and SMS/ConfigMgr. ServiceMgr is a new product in the System Center product line, designed to provide incident management, change management, knowledge sharing, and self-service provisioning capabilities. ServiceMgr builds on multiple technologies, including Windows 2003 SP 1, the .NET 2.0 and 3.0 Frameworks, SQL 2005 SP 2 with Reporting Services, and SharePoint 2007.

ServiceMgr uses connectors that integrate information from other sources:

▶ The Active Directory connector gathers user information into ServiceMgr, so you do not need to configure the same information in both locations.

▶ The connector for SMS/ConfigMgr integrates the hardware and software asset information available within that product into ServiceMgr.

▶ The connector for OpsMgr provides the ability to create incidents from alerts or to view Operations Manager knowledge.

ServiceMgr also includes a self-service portal function, which you can use to file incidents and request software for deployment. The software request functionality includes the ability to provide a workflow and approval for the requests. After a request is approved, SMS/ConfigMgr deploys the software to the resource specified by the user.

We believe the direction for Service Manager is one that will continue to integrate the System Center product line and leverage benefits from the existing products. We will discuss implications of the self-service portal function within the "Automatically Adapting with Operations Manager" section of this chapter.

In addition to the System Center family, other products outside of the System Center product line can also be integrated with OpsMgr, which we will look at in the next sections of this chapter. These products provide pieces of functionality needed to create an environment that automatically adapts.

SharePoint

In Microsoft Operations Manager (MOM) 2005, Microsoft provided a SharePoint 2003 WebPart that integrated the state of computers monitored by MOM 2005 into a SharePoint site. This functionality provided a dashboard-level view of the state of the MOM environment for non-MOM administrators.

20

NOTE

MOM 2005 SP 1 and the SharePoint WebPart

With the release of MOM 2005 SP 1, the MOM 2005 SharePoint WebPart stopped working correctly. The first issue we ran into was getting it installed. The installation failed unless we included the correct SharePoint Virtual Server information, which we show next. The virtual server's physical location defaulted correctly, but the SharePoint virtual server defaulted incorrectly.

```
SharePoint Virtual Server (including port)
http://monarch:81
Virtual Server Physical Location:
C:\inetpub\wwwroot
```

Next, we had to change the config.web file for SharePoint (for us located under C:\Inetpub\SharePoint) from

```
<trust level="Full" originUrl="" />
```

to

```
<trust level="WSS_Minimal" originUrl="" />
```

And then we had to perform an IISreset.

Now we could add the WebPart to the SharePoint (or WSS) site, but it would error out when we attempted to configure it by clicking the Show MOM 2005 Property ToolPane button. With significant help from Microsoft, we made the change detailed next.

Edit the config.web file for SharePoint (for us located under C:\Inetpub\SharePoint) to add the following information just after the `</configSections>` tag:

```
<runtime>
    <assemblyBinding xmlns="urn:schemas-microsoft-com:asm.v1">
     <dependentAssembly>
      <assemblyIdentity name="microsoft.web.ui.webcontrols"
                       publicKeyToken="31BF3856AD364E35"
                       culture="neutral" />
      <!-- Redirecting to version 5.0.2749.5 of the assembly. -->
      <bindingRedirect oldVersion="5.0.2749.0"
                       newVersion="5.0.2911.0"/>
     </dependentAssembly>
    </assemblyBinding>
</runtime>
```

Next, we did an IISreset. Finally, we had to copy the microsoft.web.ui.webcontrols.dll file to the SharePoint bin directory (for us it was C:\inetpub\SharePoint\bin). After this, we were able to configure the WebPart.

Although there is not currently a WebPart available for OpsMgr 2007, the existence of a WebPart for the MOM 2005 version implies that the same functionality could exist with OpsMgr 2007.

The same concepts that applied to the previous versions of Microsoft Operations Manager (MOM) and SharePoint should apply to the current versions. WebParts can be developed to integrate the two products, providing server status information for the servers monitored with OpsMgr. With OpsMgr, the potential capabilities of integration between these two products may be even more exciting. Instead of only reporting on the state of the computers monitored by OpsMgr, you can also report the state of a distributed application. OpsMgr provides the capabilities to schedule reports and to publish them. You can then link to these reports through SharePoint.

SharePoint could also provide a storage area for items that are not scheduled reports but provide good general information to have available on a website. One could publish information gathered from various sources such as console tasks, diagnostics, and recoveries. You could send that information to the SharePoint site, providing a centralized repository for non-OpsMgr administrators to check on the state of recent technical tasks performed. As an example, if your organization created a script to report periodically on the status of key pieces of the infrastructure (dcdiag, netdiag, replmon, netdom query fsmo, and so on), you could publish those results to SharePoint.

SharePoint provides both the potential for a dashboard view of the environment as well as a web-based repository of information, which is not available through OpsMgr's Reporting services.

Exchange 2007

Microsoft Exchange 2007's integration with PowerShell is a significant change when compared with Exchange 2003. This integration significantly increases the potential of scripting actions that previously were not possible. As we increase what we can script, we also increase our options for automating processes.

Exchange 2003 incorporated two roles: frontend server and backend server. In Exchange 2007, there are now five roles: Edge Transport, Hub Transport, Mailbox, Client Access, and Unified Messaging.

▶ The Edge Transport is installed on a standalone server on the edge of the network and provides functions such as antivirus and antispam protection. This is the only role that can't be installed with other roles.

▶ The Hub Transport provides functions similar to message-routing functionality.

▶ The Mailbox server holds mailbox data.

▶ The Client Access server is the connection point for Outlook clients (among others), ActiveSync, and Outlook Web Access.

▶ The Unified Messaging server merges VoIP infrastructures with the Exchange organization.

20

Mass-creating User Accounts in Exchange 2007/Active Directory

One of our clients had a requirement to create a large number of email-enabled users. Although they did not have current accounts to use for a migration, they provided a phone list we could use to generate the user information. Because the client required Exchange 2007 accounts, we decided to use PowerShell to create the accounts. There is plenty of good documentation on how to use the new-mailbox cmdlet, but we are including this information here to show how Excel can be used to format data that you can save to a .csv format and then integrate into a cmdlet.

To create the user accounts, we took the phone list and formatted it into the structure shown in Table 20.1 with Excel (to simplify the import process, we named each of the fields with the same naming conventions used to import mailboxes with the new-mailbox cmdlet).

Next, we used the following PowerShell script to add the users:

```
import-csv create_users.csv ¦ foreach {new-mailbox -alias $_.alias -name
$_.name -userPrincipalName $_.UserPrincipalName -database $_.database
-organizationalunit $_.organizationalunit -firstname $_.firstname -lastname
$_.lastname }
```

After the users were added and replication occurred, the user accounts appeared within the Exchange Management console. There was only one downside with this approach; we had to type the password for each account.

TABLE 20.1   User Account Fields

Alias	Name	UserPrincipalName	OrganizationalUnit	Database	FirstName	LastName
John. Smith	Smith, John	John.Smith@ odyssey.com	Import	First Storage Group\ Mailbox Database	John	Smith

Microsoft released the Exchange 2007 management pack for OpsMgr 2007 in October 2007. Based on the Exchange 2003 management pack, we anticipated the Exchange 2007 management pack to provide the following information:

▶ Up/down status of the Exchange services.

▶ Dynamic thresholds on common performance counters.

▶ Mail-flow testing between Exchange servers.

▶ Reporting on common items (such as top mailbox sizes, SMTP usage).

▶ Identifying best-practice antivirus configurations. (Exclude Exchange programs, databases, and log files from antivirus scanning because scanning is a common cause of data corruption.)

▶ Synthetic transactions to test Outlook Web Access and ActiveSync.

The area that is exciting to consider here is how well the new PowerShell functionality will integrate with the Exchange 2007 management pack. Based on the current Exchange 2003 management pack, common tasks would include the stopping/restarting of Exchange-related services, querying of queue state, and executing the best practices analyzer functions.

There are many interesting possibilities for tasks or features of the management pack, such as the following:

▶ Performing configuration changes identified by the Exchange Best Practices Analyzer (a Do-IT button).

▶ Mailbox migration between Exchange servers.

▶ Execution of a script to fix alias names that include spaces. (Exchange 2007 does not allow spaces or special characters in the alias names field.)

▶ Automating load balancing between Exchange servers using PowerShell scripts, which would migrate mailboxes between the servers and keep track of the changes through alerts. (For client mailbox recovery, you need to know where the mailbox was located.)

▶ Testing to validate the certificates on servers to verify that they exist in the trusted store, the date is valid, and when they will expire. You can pull the cert information using PowerShell with the following command on the Hub Transport server:

```
Get-ExchangeCertificate ¦ fl
```

▶ Using SMS/ConfigMgr to gather an inventory of PST information (users' personal mail folders) on the network and integrate it into reports, which will assist with capacity planning for Exchange and potential archive solutions.

▶ A health check for the existence of Recovery Storage Groups (RSG). The RSG should be deleted if it is not currently in use.

The Exchange 2007 management pack has the potential to provide a significant increase in functionality within OpsMgr, especially with the integration of PowerShell into the core functionality of Exchange 2007.

Active Directory

Active Directory maintains and provides information such as users, groups, passwords, security, and other information required within a directory service. As we discussed in the "Exchange 2007" section of this chapter when we talked about creating user accounts in Exchange 2007/Active Directory, we can see the level of integration between those two products.

The Active Directory management pack enables OpsMgr to gather information on Active Directory to identify issues in your domain environment. Looking at the integration between the System Center family of products leads to another series of potential capabilities for making an environment more capable of being automatically adapted.

If the System Center Capacity Planner can be integrated with OpsMgr (see the "Capacity Planner" section of this chapter), and if Active Directory can be designed using a future version of SCCP, it introduces the ability to make capacity decisions based on how the current environment is designed.

This type of functionality has significant potential implications. As an example, if remote users are continuously experiencing long delays logging in to the environment, you could run SCCP to simulate a domain controller installed at the remote user location, thus validating whether it would be beneficial to add a domain controller at that location.

VMWare MP

Multiple vendors, including eXc (http://www.excsoftware.com/version3/version3/Products. aspx), Jalasoft (http://www.jalasoft.com/jalasoftweb/jsp/products/xianio/), and nworks (http://www.nworks.com/vmware/index.php), offer management packs providing monitoring capabilities for the VMWare product line. The ability to monitor VMWare in a capacity similar to the Virtual Server and SCVMM products opens up the potential to provide a dynamically changing virtual environment that will adjust based on changes in the environment, similar to those discussed within the "Virtual Machine Manager and Virtual Server 2005 R2" section of this chapter.

Custom Management Packs

For the purposes of building the foundation for an environment that can automatically adapt, an important insight is developing custom management packs, which allows us to add functions not currently available in OpsMgr. In Chapter 23, "Developing Management Packs and Reports," we discuss the process used to create custom management packs for OpsMgr 2007.

Some examples of adding functionality would include management packs with capabilities such as the following:

▶ Notifying the help desk when a user account locks out (so they can contact the user instead of the user contacting the help desk)

▶ Monitoring for files placed in a particular folder and performing a specified action when they are found

▶ Providing database sizing trending information for the OpsMgr databases in your environment

Each of these different technologies provides a piece of the landscape required to develop an environment where OpsMgr 2007 can automatically adapt to changes. In the next section, we will discuss a variety of possible concepts and scenarios for applying these technologies with Operations Manager 2007.

Automatically Adapting with Operations Manager

We have discussed the inherent capabilities of OpsMgr 2007 and ways to integrate it with other products to increase its functionality. Using these concepts, we created a foundation we can build on for OpsMgr (combined with other products) to automatically adapt to changes in your environment. This section of the chapter provides a vision of how you could configure systems to automatically adapt to changing conditions.

Many organizations prefer an environment where manual alterations are performed, because this minimizes the number of changes, the potential for unexpected changes, and the potential for errors resulting from automated changes. The common response here against automating the responses to particular errors is, "What if something goes wrong?"

In numerous situations, automatically adapting an environment is extremely useful. Examples include changes that are time critical and cannot wait on manual intervention, commonly executed tasks, and tasks that are often overlooked. We will review several of these scenarios, in addition to concepts to consider about how you might automatically change systems based on circumstances as they occur.

Maintaining Systems

When life as an administrator gets really busy, the first thing typically dropped is standard maintenance procedures. Administrators generally focus on the higher priority issues that occur, and do not have the time to spare to work on lower priorities. This is an area where OpsMgr automation can assist us.

Operations Manager 2007 gathers information on systems, including when they have high and low utilization. This puts Operations Manager 2007 in a unique situation—it has the information required to determine when to schedule maintenance based on when it would have the least impact on the system.

Using Operations Manager, we can create a script that executes daily, weekly, or monthly, performing checks of commonly missed maintenance tasks such as defragmentation, patch management, antivirus updates, and even determining whether files on the system have been backed up within a specified period of time. This script is assigned to a computer group. This can be an existing computer group, or we can create our own main-tenance computer group.

The script tests for each condition. If there is an action that needs to be performed, it writes an event to the event log on the local system. We configure OpsMgr with a rule that checks for each condition and acts accordingly.

Disk Defragmentation

Let's walk through an example of this. We create a computer group called Maintenance in OpsMgr that has a timed rule that executes a script on the target computers on a weekly basis. The script checks the level of disk fragmentation; if it is determined necessary to "defrag" the disk (defined as higher than 30% total fragmentation), the script writes an event to the Windows Application log on that system that includes specific information:

- ▶ A source of OpsMgr Maintenance

- ▶ An event number of 1001

- ▶ An event category that indicates the drive letter that is heavily fragmented

If multiple drives are fragmented, there will be multiple events. If the drive is not fragmented, the script returns a value of 1000.

We create a monitor that has a state for Logical Disk Fragmentation that is in a healthy state if the event number is 1000 and warning state if it is 1001. We define a recovery for the warning state, running a command to perform a defragmentation on the system and reset the monitor state.

At the weekly timed interval, the members of the computer group (in this case, Hurricane) run the maintenance script. The script detects that the C: drive is highly fragmented, and it writes event 1001 to the Windows NT Application log from the OpsMgr Maintenance source, with an event category of C (C being the drive letter that is highly fragmented). The monitor finds event 1001 and it changes to a warning state, causing the recovery to fire. The recovery runs the defragmentation process on the system for the drive specified and resets the monitor to a healthy state.

As an interesting positive for this type of approach to system maintenance, OpsMgr could also place the system into maintenance mode during the time when any or all of the maintenance tasks were performed. (We discuss a script to automate maintenance mode in Chapter 8, "Configuring and Using Operations Manager 2007.")

Patch Management

Patch management is another aspect of maintenance often overlooked. Organizations can either deploy a product to manage patches in their environment (such as Configuration Manager, WSUS [Windows Server Update Services], or third-party vendor software), or they can manually patch their systems. Manually patching is very labor intensive but quite common.

MOM 2005 included a Baseline Security Analyzer management pack that would check for a variety of conditions, including the current patch state. Currently there is no equivalent functionality available for OpsMgr 2007.

If we look into how we would integrate checking patch management status into our maintenance script, it might look like this:

- ▶ When the maintenance script runs, the script would check the current state of patching. If it is out of compliance, the script writes the event 1011 from the OpsMgr Maintenance source (and if it is in compliance, event 1010 is written).

- There would be a monitor to check for this, which would have a healthy state for the 1010 condition and a warning state for 1011.

- A recovery would either call a script to patch the system or add the system to the patch management collection (see the script AddComputerToCollection.vbs [included on the CD with this book] for an example).

- If there is no automated method available to patch the system, we could configure an alert to notify the appropriate personnel that the system is not being patched.

- The alert could be integrated with a workflow that asks for approval from an administrator (or user) and then causes the system to be patched during the next maintenance window.

Disk Backups

Backups are another aspect of maintenance to consider as part of a maintenance script. If it were discovered the drive has not been backed up within a configured threshold (30 days, for example), an event would write for a warning state; if the drive was backed up within that period, an event would write for the healthy state. Based on the events, another monitor would be configured with a recovery defined to run a backup on the system and to store the data out to a defined network share. This network share would need to have a large amount of storage available. You would also want to monitor it (with OpsMgr!) to prevent it from filling up completely.

TIP

Backing Up Running VMs

You can even integrate backup automation with running virtual machines. Redmondmag.com provides a script that backs up Virtual Server 2005 SP 1 virtual machines while they are running, using the Volume Shadow Copy Service (VSS). Information on the script and the article are available at http://redmondmag.com/columns/print.asp?EditorialsID=2324.

Antivirus

Antivirus configurations are generally handled through scheduled updates, but the same concepts discussed for defragmentation, patch management, and backups apply to antivirus software as well. If a system were determined not current in its antivirus data files, a script to update the data file would run as part of a recovery.

Additional Maintenance Functions

As part of the same set of monitors, you can apply the same concepts to additional maintenance functions. As another example of this, in the "Diagnostics and Recoveries" section of this chapter, we discussed a recovery that would run a script to free up disk space by either removing unnecessary files or relocating them to network temporary storage.

20

The ability to automate routine maintenance tasks such as defragmentation, patch management, backups, antivirus, and drive space checks within Operations Manager 2007 provides a method to gain additional benefits from deploying OpsMgr, thus freeing up administrators to focus on other aspects of the environment. (Remember the 10 reasons for deploying Operations Manager discussed in Chapter 1, "Operations Management Basics"?)

It is important to provide a log of what automatic changes occur from your OpsMgr automation. A log provides both the information required to roll back from a change, if required, and a way to report on what OpsMgr has accomplished (for example, in the month of December how many systems were defragmented, how many disks were backed up, and so on).

Distributed Application Provisioning

As we discussed in previous chapters, OpsMgr focuses on health, and as a major part of this it includes the ability to monitor distributed applications (such as Active Directory, Exchange, custom-built applications, and even Operations Manager itself). As part of automatically adapting with OpsMgr 2007, we will discuss several options available for distributed applications to adapt to changes detected in the environment.

The Operations Manager Management Group

We will start with the concept of OpsMgr as a distributed application. OpsMgr does many things very well, but one thing it does not do well is correlate events. As an example, within our Odyssey organization we have a site in Plano and a site in Carrollton. We have servers in both locations, monitored by a centralized OpsMgr environment located in Plano. We monitor the site links with a TCP port test so we can identify when the link goes down. When the link goes down, we receive our alert from the TCP port test but we also receive health alerts that each server on the other side of the link is down as well. When the link comes back online, we receive a set of alerts from the remote servers indicating that they had problems while the link was down.

Although this is logical, it really is not that helpful. We don't really care if we can't talk to the servers or that the result is a lack of connectivity. We care that the link is down because it affects how (or if) servers and workstations can communicate with each other, and we understand the ramifications of that situation. So maybe we could adapt to the loss of the link within OpsMgr?

As an example, if the TCP port test fails, OpsMgr could put all remote servers into maintenance mode, close the alerts found by the servers in the remote site, and alert that the link is down. Then, when the link comes back up, it could bring the servers back out of maintenance mode. We like this approach because we now receive only the alert telling us that the link is down (the root cause), not the various side effects that resulted from the link going down. This is really an awesome capability—it prevents generating alerts based on one event causing a snowball of other events!

Custom Distributed Applications

Custom developed applications also need to be able to adapt to changes in the environment. For Odyssey, we have a distributed application called OdysseySimpleApp. A recovery can perform an action such as restarting the application, running a script, or restarting a service. Our custom application uses a Windows service that often stops responding. To resolve the issue, we restart the service, which we can now automate via a recovery.

Distributed applications can often have a tie into the world of Service Oriented Architectures (SOA). SOA, looked at from a high level, isolates the core business functions into independent services. These services work like functions that are called.

As an example of this, we can look at the OdysseyWeb application. OdysseyWeb is a web-based application that runs on multiple IIS 6.0 servers for the frontend, running in a load-balanced configuration (WebServer1 through WebServer50). They communicate to a service that runs on a series of load-balanced processing systems that perform the required transactions (Processing1 through Processing50). The data required for the application is stored in a SQL 2005 cluster (Data1 through Data4). From an SOA perspective, we have a frontend service, a processing service, and database services.

For monitoring distributed applications, we perform tests at each level of the application to validate functionality. Starting with the web services, we test for connectivity to each web server to validate that they are responding to port 80/443 calls. If they are not responding, a recovery task is fired, resetting the web-based application. On the processing systems, we check via a TCP port test and performance counters to validate that transactions are actively being accepted by the services. If the transactions are not being accepted, the service is restarted as part of a recovery task. On the database cluster, we perform an OLE DB Data Source check to validate that it is functional. If it is not, the cluster is moved to the second node and retested.

For an overall test of the application, we configure a synthetic test, using the Web Application Management Pack Template. If the synthetic test fails, we perform a recovery based on the error, provided within the test. With this example we see some of the range of tests and recovery tasks that can be accomplished with OpsMgr, specifically related to how distributed applications function. Later in the "Server Provisioning" section of this chapter, we will discuss server adaptation and addressing changes in application performance with changes to the servers themselves.

Workflow and Application Provisioning

Applications and their provisioning is another area where OpsMgr can adapt to changes. Although OpsMgr is not a workflow product, it can respond to events that occur in the monitored environment. As an example, we could create a SharePoint website to provide an area for users to request applications. As part of the workflow, the requests could be accepted or denied, based on manager approval. If a change was accepted to install an application for the user, an event can be written on the SharePoint server indicating the application and the workstation it should be deployed to.

20

OpsMgr can have a rule to check for this condition, which would then update the collection to include the new user or workstation (see the AddComputerToCollection.vbs script on the accompanying CD for an example of how to add computers to collections). Through this, OpsMgr provides a part of the workflow required to deploy (or potentially uninstall) an application in the environment.

If we consider the concept of application provisioning, by adding Service Manager we can now take the concepts above where OpsMgr provides the workflow and replace that with the capabilities of ServiceMgr, using the self-provisioning functionality discussed in the "Service Manager" section of this chapter. The self-provisioning capabilities of ServiceMgr offer a more seamless method to integrate the System Center product line and automatically adapt to changes such as when application deployments are required.

We could also automatically deprovision applications. SMS and ConfigMgr provide the ability to meter application usage. If a metered application is not used within a specific timeframe (such as 13 months), an event could be fired that causes SMS/ConfigMgr to remove the application from the system not using the application. Automated application deprovisioning provides an effective method to decrease the software licensing requirements of an organization, only allowing the application to be on systems where it is actually used. If we wanted a check-and-balance on application deprovisioning, OpsMgr could send a notification to the users, requesting they authorize that the application remain on their systems. If they approve its removal, SMS/ConfigMgr can deinstall the software; if they deny the approval, they would be notified again if the application were not used within a defined timeframe.

You could configure this deprovisioning as part of a scheduled process, where one month prior to reviewing existing product licenses (called *TrueUP* in Microsoft Enterprise Agreements), an automatic deprovision of applications would occur, based on applications that have not been used in the specified period of time. By running this a month before TrueUP, there is time for the users to determine whether they actually require the application and reprovision it to their systems. This approach provides a method for organizations to truly pay only for the software they are using.

User and Computer Provisioning

OpsMgr can also assist with the process of adding users to a domain or automating the process for deprovisioning user and computer accounts.

When you add a user account in the Active Directory domain, it generates an event that OpsMgr can respond to. When OpsMgr finds the event, it adds information to SharePoint, which would add the user automatically to a user provisioning workflow. Applications could also be provisioned to the user, as discussed in the "Distributed Application Provisioning" section of this chapter. A simpler interaction would be to create a help desk ticket when the user-creation event occurs. As we discussed in the "Service Manager" section of this chapter, Service Manager can automatically generate tickets based on alerts from OpsMgr.

We can also use OpsMgr to automatically deprovision unused users, computers, and computer accounts. Computer accounts that are inactive for a defined time period can be moved to an Active Directory Organizational Unit where they are stored for an additional retention period. If the computer accounts are still inactive at that time, they can be deleted.

These same concepts apply to user accounts. A user inactive for a defined time period can be moved to an OU where the account is stored for an additional retention period (you would want to identify a set of accounts not to disable or delete). If the user account is still inactive after the additional retention period, the user account is deleted. As an example, if user account Joe.Smith is not in use after 60 days, it is placed in the DISABLED OU. If the same user does not access his account for another 90 days, the account is automatically deleted from Active Directory.

The timings of when accounts are disabled or deleted could be customized to the requirements of the specific environment, and exclusions can be made for user or computer accounts that should not be subject to automatic deprovisioning. These processes can be automated, and we provide a set of scripts with this book. You would want to log all items and publish them on a SharePoint website, or send them to a manager for auditing purposes.

TIP

On the CD

Sample scripts for automatic deprovisioning user and computer accounts are included on the CD accompanying this book.

Security Adaptation

OpsMgr can also automatically adapt to changes that result from security modifications that may occur. With a strong auditing policy in place and Audit Collection Services (ACS) integrated (see Chapter 15, "Monitoring Audit Collection Services," for details), Operations Manager is capable of immediately being aware of changes in the security environment. Once a change is detected, we can respond to the change in security using the concepts discussed throughout this chapter.

As an example of how OpsMgr can automatically adapt to a security change, we will take a situation where a user has attempted to log in to the network multiple times but mistyped his password and ended up locking out his user account. Normally, the user would call the help desk, and the help desk would work with him to unlock the account. Alternatively, OpsMgr could detect the account lockout and notify the help desk via email so that they could contact the user instead of the user contacting them! This allows the help desk to be more proactive in nature, which directly affects the user's satisfaction in his experience with the help desk. If the user did not mistype his password (as in a case where someone else is attempting to access the account), the help desk can now identify this situation more quickly as well.

20

We can also proactively gather information that will assist in determining whether a user lockout is actually an attempt to breach security or is just a case of a mistyped password. If multiple failed logon attempts occur, we could configure a diagnostic to activate a NetMon capture to collect network information at the time of the user lockout. Reviewing the network information could generate additional information about the attempts to log in to the systems. A good example of creative uses of NetMon traces is available at http://marcusoh.blogspot.com/2007/07/os-capturing-netmon-traces-in-such.html, where a NetMon trace starts based on an event and stops based on a specified condition.

Security attacks or changes in security can occur very quickly, and OpsMgr can help by responding to the conditions more quickly than manual intervention can take place. Automatically adapting to security situations in real time is one of the key benefits to embracing this concept!

Server Provisioning

We saved the best for last here, because the potential benefits for server provisioning are among the most striking areas where OpsMgr can automatically adapt. Before we can discuss the OpsMgr capabilities from a server provisioning perspective, however, we need to review the concepts of scaling servers.

Scaling an application can provide the ability to increase the number of individuals who can use the application, or the ability to adapt to changes in business requirements. An application that can only run on a single server in a single-processor configuration is an example of an application that does not scale well. In a well-designed enterprise application, all components of the application need to support scaling to be able to provide continuous growth to meet user demand and business requirements. Scaling occurs either through vertical or horizontal scaling.

Vertical scaling (often referred to as *scaling up*) increases scalability through adding capacity to existing resources. Examples of this include adding more processors/memory/network adapters or faster disks. Vertical scaling depends on the application or service being able to leverage the new resources. As an example, a single-threaded application will not scale well to multiple processors.

Horizontal scaling (often referred to as *scaling out*) increases scalability through adding different systems that work together as one logical unit. A good example of horizontal scaling is web farms, which can have their scalability increased through the addition of more servers to the web farms.

Scaling Out

Let's examine a situation where we have multiple web servers that provide a component of a web-based application. There are three available web servers, with each web server running as a guest operating system on a different host operating system. Normally, two of the web servers are sufficient to meet the requirements of the web piece of the application.

Suppose that OpsMgr detects a bottleneck both on the application and on the operating system level. From this, we can determine that the web servers in the environment are each reporting high processor levels, and the application response time is not within acceptable performance levels. OpsMgr performs a recovery based on this condition and activates the web server on the third system. This action splits the load between the three web servers instead of the two web servers. If the load on the websites then declines for a long period of time, the third web server is set to no longer accept connections by OpsMgr. Once there are no longer any remaining connections, that virtual server is put back into a saved state.

This process may sound like a far-fetched concept, but this is a technically viable solution using components currently available: OpsMgr 2007 combined with the SCVMM management pack, using Virtual Server R2. Figure 20.17 shows the SCCVMM management pack in OpsMgr, with a guest operating system (Honor). Available tasks for the guest operating system include Create Checkpoint, Pause, Save State, Shutdown, Start, and Stop. As we discussed in the "Console Tasks" section of this chapter, we can integrate console tasks into diagnostics and recoveries, which in turn activate based on conditions found in the environment.

Using the Virtual Machine Manager management pack shows how OpsMgr can automatically adapt to changes in the environment based on application performance, and that it can horizontally scale up and down based on the requirements of the application.

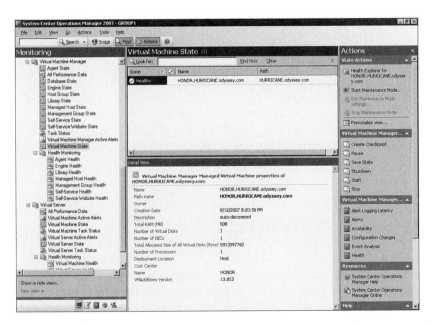

FIGURE 20.17   The System Center Virtual Machine Manager management pack.

20

Scaling Up

Vertical scaling can also occur with OpsMgr 2007, but capabilities are currently limited. If OpsMgr identifies a bottleneck condition in a guest operating system running within Virtual Server 2005 R2, the system can be shut down at a scheduled interval, additional memory or disk resources can be added, and the system then be brought back online. These same functions can be performed using the VMWare product line (which also requires the system be shut down to add resources). We will discuss updates to the Microsoft virtualization functionality at the end of this chapter.

Provisioning Techniques

OpsMgr can also automate the process of provisioning servers. You can provision server resources automatically, either through SMS/ConfigMgr using Operating System Deployment (OSD) or through SCVMM. With a pool of available servers, OpsMgr could automatically provision as required, using the OSD functionality. This, however, would represent a large investment in hardware that would not be efficiently used until it was required.

The usage of virtualization technologies to provision servers provides a method that dramatically increases the efficiency of resource utilization. The SCVMM interface provides self-service server-provisioning functionality that can be integrated with OpsMgr. The same processes used to provide the functionality within the self-service server provisioning could be automated based on conditions identified by OpsMgr.

For the Odyssey Corporation, each remote location has a server that provides Virtual Server 2005 R2 to use for various server functions. By monitoring Active Directory, Odyssey can determine whether user logon times are within an acceptable range. OpsMgr can provision the server in the remote location to provide domain controller functionality and can automate the process of performing a dcpromo of the system into a domain controller. This shows an extreme example of how one can automate the provisioning of servers to address issues identified by OpsMgr. Most organizations would not want to automate the process of promoting a domain controller (it could be disconcerting to come to work and have a few new DCs online), so this could be done through different tasks that would first provision the server and then perform a dcpromo of the server.

OpsMgr can also use the capabilities of SCVMM to determine which servers are good candidates for virtualization, and provide tasks to automate the process to convert the system from a physical server to a virtual server. Providing the capability to consolidate physical servers onto virtual servers decreases the hardware requirements for an organization and increases the usage of the server resources that are available.

In the "Capacity Planner" section, we discussed how to integrate SCCP with OpsMgr to identify potential bottlenecks and configuration changes, thus addressing them proactively. Applying these capabilities to virtualize servers, automatically provision servers, and proactively plan for potential hardware changes together opens up a completely new level of concepts to consider.

As an example, we will discuss an Exchange 2007 environment with two mailbox servers and one Client Access Server. The SCVMM recommended virtualizing the Client Access Server, so it was changed from a physical to a virtual system. If the Capacity Planner identified a potential bottleneck on the Client Access Server, an additional server could be provisioned, and the new Client Access Server can now share the load with the original one. This is an example of how these various technologies could all work together to provide an environment that continues to evolve and adapt to changes in the environment around it.

Servers provide functionality to an organization and normally have a life cycle. New servers are typically added to provide new functionality as required. Applications and functions are replaced over time, but often the server providing the functionality is not identified for removal or reprovisioning. OpsMgr can call scripts to identify whether or not the system is actively being used. If a system is identified as not in use for a long enough period of time, the server can be deprovisioned and then can either be removed (if it is obsolete) or reprovisioned for usage elsewhere in the organization.

When OpsMgr is combined with other technologies, there is potential to provide both increased scalability and performance for the applications used in an organization.

Virtualization: Windows Server 2008 and Beyond

During the early beta versions of Windows Server 2008, functionality was available that allowed for the addition and removal of resources to the operating system while the system was running. Although this functionality was removed from the product, it indicates a direction where Microsoft may be moving beyond the Windows Server 2008 timeframe. Microsoft is also introducing new virtualization technologies within Windows Server 2008 that will increase the scalability of guest operating systems so that they can use more than one processor and more than 3.6GB of memory. It is not known at this time whether this functionality will be included with the release version of Windows Server 2008 or with the hypervisor technology currently scheduled for release approximately 6 months after Windows Server 2008 is released.

These enhancements have significant impacts on the ability to automatically adapt an environment. Increasing the amount of resources available within a guest operating system and adding the capability to add and remove resources while the operating system is running allow us to greatly increase the ability to vertically scale our servers.

As a last example, let's take an application that cannot be configured to horizontally scale. Due to limits in the application, it can only run on a single server, but it is a multi-threaded application. OpsMgr detects a bottleneck on the application and the guest operating system. OpsMgr adds resources to the guest operating system to address the bottleneck. Once the resources are no longer required, they are removed and added back to the pool of available resources. This floating resource pool is available to provide horizontal scaling of each of the business-critical applications in the environment.

Summary

Although Operations Manager 2007 provides for solid monitoring and notification of issues in an environment, this is not the limit of its capabilities. OpsMgr's ability to automatically adapt can be summarized as follows: Can you identify it? Can you script it? If so, you can do it with OpsMgr.

This chapter not only explained how OpsMgr can adapt, but also discussed some of the capabilities you have with OpsMgr. With Microsoft's creation of the PowerShell functionality and its integration into products, we expect those things we can automate today to be only the tip of the iceberg.

In the next chapter, we will discuss how you can integrate Operations Manager 2007 and System Center Essentials using Microsoft's Remote Operations Manager, thus increasing the functionality of both applications.

CHAPTER 21

Reading for the Service Provider: Remote Operations Manager

This chapter shows how you can use System Center Operations Manager (OpsMgr) 2007 in combination with System Center Essentials 2007 to create a hybrid application with its own name: *Remote Operations Manager (ROM)*. The audience for this chapter is the service provider—a Microsoft partner that can use these System Center technologies to help deliver a managed services solution to its customers.

If you are the administrator of a conventional non–Information Technology (IT) business or organization, large or small, Remote Operations Manager is *not* for you. ROM is specific for IT service providers, because Microsoft designed it to deliver management services to remote, untrusted customer networks without a Virtual Private Network (VPN) or other direct network access. The Remote Operations Manager solution integrates System Center components installed on both the ROM service provider network (the Operations Manager management group) and the customer network (the Essentials server). ROM is only available for license to service providers that are Microsoft partners; you cannot purchase it through retail or volume license channels.

System Center Essentials is a new product from Microsoft, and it is far removed from the Microsoft Operations Manager 2005 Workgroup Edition originally perceived as its predecessor. Essentials combines the systems management features of Operations Manager with a strong desktop support component that includes software distribution and update management. You can only install one Essentials server per domain, and Essentials is hard-coded for a maximum of 30 servers (31 servers including itself) and

500 client computers. Microsoft designed Essentials for the small or medium-sized network in a single organization, to function as a central administration console for all server and client computer management.

NOTE

System Center Essentials

The Essentials console combines subsets of features from Microsoft Operations Manager (MOM)/OpsMgr, System Management Server (SMS)/Configuration Manager (SCCM or ConfigMgr), and Windows Server Update Services (WSUS) that are relevant to the administrators of small and medium-sized networks. These network administrators can purchase Essentials as their primary network management tool, rather than deploying the Operations Manager product (the topic of this book). However, that would be the subject of another book—on Essentials!

In this chapter, we focus on how Essentials integrates with the Operations Manager management group at the service provider to create the Remote Operations Manager solution.

The Challenge and Opportunity

Economies of scale regulate most production systems—the more of something that you make or do, the lower the average cost to make the thing or perform the service. Of course, some activities, such as home cooking, do not have the economies of scale that others might, such as distributing electric power.

The discipline of network management in the enterprise space can leverage economies of scale in a dramatic fashion; witness the large organizations, such as Microsoft itself, that manage hundreds of thousands of computers and devices with just a few control centers. These efficiencies become possible with platform standardization and management tools that present a common view of physically distributed systems. With proper network automation, you can perform a maintenance action against thousands of identically managed computers all over the world in just minutes.

Smaller-Sized Organizations

Small and medium-size organizations (those with about 500 employees or less) have historically been less able to take advantage of scaling economies because they are small "islands" of technology. The smaller organization usually has a higher average Total Cost of Ownership (TCO) for its IT assets; this is from the increased manual work involved in maintaining the network and the friction and mistakes that happen from reinventing the wheel, over and over.

> **NOTE**
>
> **Small and Medium Business Acronym**
>
> The acronym *small and medium business (SMB)* is often applied to the sector of the IT market with fewer than 500 employees.

The challenge in extending large organization-style IT efficiencies to the smaller network is rooted in the difficulty SMBs face in adopting enterprise IT management techniques. For example, using the Information Technology Infrastructure Library (ITIL), the internationally accepted framework of best practice approaches to IT service delivery, is not something that a SMB network administrator is typically familiar with. The smaller organization rarely has long-range strategic technology plans, including those of IT asset life cycle management. Without a mature management approach such as ITIL and lacking multiyear IT planning, the SMB is unable to make dramatic advances in increasing IT efficiency and lowering the TCO of its IT assets.

A common characteristic of IT departments of both traditional organizations and IT businesses is that the larger the IT department, the more likely that the individual members are specialists, rather than IT generalists. Microsoft has identified this demographic as a key ingredient in the planning behind its ROM offering. It is the nature of the larger organization, including teams of specialized experts, that allows the large network to adopt strategies such as ITIL that have a dramatic impact on TCO. Because the SMB IT staff usually consists of IT generalists, operations management approaches and strategies do not play well in that space. This phenomenon produces a natural divide between the enterprise approach and the SMB approach to managing IT, and it pervades every aspect of the IT industry.

Tools for Measuring Service

Enterprise IT management approaches outsourcing IT services using the vehicle of the Service Level Agreement (SLA). A *SLA* is a contract between a customer and a service provider specifying the terms for delivering an IT service. SLAs generally focus on the application needed by the customer. For example, a SLA for Exchange services might specify that employees can log into their mailboxes and use Exchange 99.99% of the time, equating to allowing less than 4 minutes of mailbox unavailability per month. If the service provider fails to deliver that level of service uptime, a SLA violation occurs. Depending on the wording of the SLA, SLA violations can result in the service provider paying the customer a penalty, and can even lead to automatic cancellation of the contract.

A primary benefit of the SLA mechanism is that it aligns the business goals of the customer and the service provider. Both parties have incentive to achieve the uptime metrics specified in the SLA. When things break, the burden is on the service provider to fix the problem, rather than the customer. This self-enforcing, shared-goals arrangement permits the customer to focus its IT department on strategic goals specific to that industry and business, and frees the customer from worrying about supporting the hardware and software platforms used to deliver the service. If one service provider cannot deliver the service properly, the customer finds another service provider. Just as importantly, the customer enjoys fixed costs to use the delivered service for the period of the SLA, regardless of how often the service provider has to perform preventative or corrective maintenance on the involved hardware and software platforms.

SLAs, with their many attendant business benefits, have been a staple in the enterprise space for over a decade. Large organizations (such as airlines and credit card companies) outsource some portions of their infrastructure to other large organizations such as IBM or EDS. Because the customers and the service providers both are large organizations, employing enterprise methodologies for service delivery is natural and straightforward.

SMB Service Providers

Characteristics of the enterprise space include centralized datacenters, uniformity in supported technologies and devices, and secure private connectivity between Network Operations Centers (NOCs) and managed computers and devices. Those characteristics of the enterprise space contrast sharply with the SMB networked landscape. SMB networks (in aggregate) are extremely decentralized, do not feature uniform technology sets, and are not equipped for secure remote access by service providers. From the disjointed, patchwork nature of the IT business in the SMB space, a paradigm sometimes called "break-fix" has emerged as a primary business model for many SMB service providers. Quite simply, the service provider waits for things to break, is called by the customer, dispatches the technical staff to fix the problem, and bills the customer for the repair costs. This upside-down model actually incents the service provider when the customer has problems! The model is diametrically different from the planned and preventive approach espoused by ITIL.

Of course, many SMB service providers also have a consulting component and assist customers with designing and deploying new hardware and software. This work is often contracted for via a Statement of Work or similar document, defining that a project is completed within a certain timeframe. Customers may retain a legitimate suspicion that there may be a conflict of interest where the service provider (not necessarily consciously) will deploy solutions that will break and require periodic fixing (by that service provider of course).

The combination of project-based and break-fix revenue is how the service provider stays in business. There are numerous downsides to this model:

▶ Customer dissatisfaction when downtime occurs

▶ Inefficient human resource utilization while service provider staffs wait on the bench for service calls

▶ Unpredictable and irregular monthly revenue for the service provider

In particular, the inability to forecast accurate future revenue hampers the SMB service provider's ability to attract investment and grow to the point where it could start specializing staff members and introducing enterprise management techniques!

The challenge is for IT service companies to transition their businesses from those that depend on project-based and break-fix revenue, to subscription-based business models based on SLAs. In recent years, a new sector of the IT industry known as "managed services" has emerged as a transformative vehicle for the IT service provider. A September 12, 2007 *New York Times* article titled "Outsourcing I.T. To Unlikely Places, Like America" identifies four trends as contributing to the success of the rising managed services industry:

▶ Internet connectivity is getting cheaper; this provides a cost-effective avenue for the Managed Services Provider (MSP) to remotely maintain its customers' networks.

▶ The Internet is playing a larger, integral role in the day-to-day operations of businesses; similar to electric power, companies cannot function without it.

▶ Software tools (such as ROM!) performing the remote IT management functions of the MSP are cheaper and more reliable than in the past.

▶ Regulatory pressures such as Sarbanes-Oxley are forcing even small businesses to deploy sophisticated audit, compliance, and disaster recovery solutions; the expertise and resources of the MSP fill this gap.

For individual IT service providers that transition to becoming MSPs and joining the managed services industry, the opportunity for growth and stabilization is enormous. The economics are also overpowering for the SMB customers, because they pay less in managed services fees than they did with traditional IT service delivery models such as break-fix, while enjoying dramatically increased availability of the IT services they use to conduct their primary business.

Microsoft has published a number of statistics that validate the large and growing market for managed services in the SMB space, including the following:

▶ **More Microsoft partners are providing remote IT management services.** Between 2004 and 2005, the number of partners providing remote management of desktop and network devices grew by 10%, according to a 2006 AMI Partners study.

▶ **Customers say they will increase the use of external service providers.** Twenty-three percent of SMB customers intended to increase their company's use of external/outsourced resources in a 2006 Data Overview survey of 665 SMB decision makers.

▶ **Almost half of customers express interest in remote IT management.** Forty-five percent of SMB customers said they were interested in remote monitoring and management services in a 2005 Forester survey of 869 SMB decision makers.

▶ **Customer demand for remote IT management is expected to surge.** Gartner predicts SMB spending on remote monitoring and management services will more than double between 2005 and 2009, from $4.6 billion to $10 billion annually.

Remote Operations Manager is Microsoft's solution to help its partners that are SMB service partners transform their business models. This transformation is a win-win-win circumstance:

▶ Microsoft sells more software and penetrates yet another market.

▶ The partner benefits from a dependable revenue stream, efficient staff utilization, and achieves (via the alignment of customer and partner business goals) the role of trusted IT advisor to its customers.

▶ Most importantly, the customer ends up paying less money for IT services, enjoys higher application uptime, and is free to focus on running its primary business without IT friction.

Architecture

How does Operations Manager become Remote Operations Manager? There are three phases involved in deploying ROM. The transition from a conventional OpsMgr instance to a ROM instance takes place as follows:

▶ By implementing architectural changes to the management group

▶ By importing the Service Provider management pack

▶ By converting a customer Essentials server to Service Provider Mode (which connects Essentials to the service provider)

An OpsMgr instance with the additional ROM features does not look any different in the Operations console, other than the new views added by the Service Provider management pack. However, using ROM enables the service provider to integrate the health views of dozens or hundreds of subsequently connected customer networks into the ROM OpsMgr management group.

Essentials Everywhere

Although Essentials has its roots in OpsMgr and uses the same Agent Component, understand that the primary deployment scenario for Essentials does not involve OpsMgr or ROM. Essentials is marketed primarily to the SMB network administrator as a standalone, comprehensive management solution for his or her environment. Essentials will be bundled with the new multiserver Microsoft offering for the mid-market (code name "Centro"). Intel, which has built its System Management Software 2.0 solution around Essentials 2007, is distributing Essentials as well.

These offerings mean there is going to be a lot of Essentials installations out there! Many administrators of smaller Microsoft networks will use Essentials to manage their networks; for a good percentage of them, Essentials may be their first experience with network management tools. Let's look at the Essentials console. At first glance, this console is very similar to the OpsMgr Operations console, but look more closely! Figure 21.1 displays the Essentials console, focusing on the Computers navigation space.

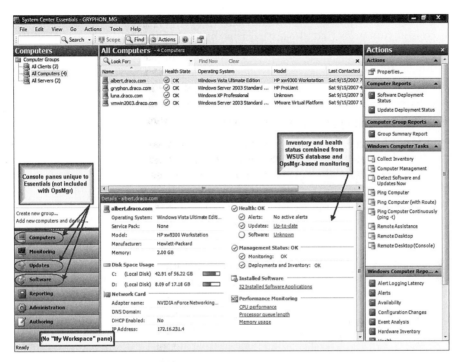

FIGURE 21.1   The Computers pane includes WSUS status; this is unique to Essentials.

OpsMgr administrators may be jealous of their Essentials counterparts when they see the
attractive presentation of computer details in the Essentials console—the Computers space
shown in Figure 21.1 is unique to Essentials, and it allows the administrator to browse the
status of his or her managed computers. The Essentials Computers view combines inventory data provided by WSUS and health status from the Agent Component. Notice in
Figure 21.1 we highlighted the Updates and Software console spaces (these are also unique
to Essentials):

- The Updates space is an extension and display vehicle for WSUS server functionality,
  so that the Essentials administrator does not have to leave the Essentials console to
  approve WSUS updates and review updating status.

- The Software space contains functionality to package Microsoft or third-party software installation files and publish the package to managed computers as if it were
  another WSUS update (a Configuration Manager/SMS-lite!).

Although the Updates and Software components are wonderful features for the Essentials
administrator, the ROM solution actually does not offer a collective access mechanism
into these two Essentials functions.

In the first release of ROM, the service provider running ROM only has a central view of the Essentials console functions that already exist in the OpsMgr Operations console. Data from managed customer computers appear in the ROM Monitoring, Administration, Authoring, and Reporting spaces—the same navigation spaces shared between the OpsMgr and Essentials consoles. The ROM service provider cannot centrally view or interact with the Computers, Updates, or Software spaces of its customers.

In one sense, Essentials features are a subset of those in OpsMgr, because OpsMgr features such as the Audit Control System (ACS) and My Workspace pane are not present in Essentials. Yet, in another sense, Essentials features are also a superset that includes most OpsMgr features and adds functionality not present in OpsMgr. Chapter 2, "What's New," includes two tables that display the differences between Essentials and other Microsoft System Center products:

▶ Table 2.5 compares System Center Operations Manager 2007 features to those of System Center Essentials 2007.

▶ Table 2.6 compares System Center Configuration Manager 2007 features to those of System Center Essentials 2007.

Some of these differences deal with market positioning and licensing schemes and may not immediately make sense. Technically, the composition of the Essentials server is more cut and dried. An Essentials 2007 server in the Remote Operations Manager solution consists of three entities:

▶ A Windows Server Updates Service (WSUS) 3.0 server, which is not directly involved in the centralized ROM solution.

▶ An Operations Manager 2007 management group instance that is preconfigured and hard-coded to be an all-in-one management group server, but excludes Audit Collection Services (ACS) and a small number of other features only available in OpsMgr.

  The OpsMgr management group components installed on the Essentials server are the Management Server, Reporting Server, Operational Database, and Data Warehouse Database. (The Operational Database Component can optionally be located on a dedicated, separate SQL Server for larger Essentials customers with between 250 and 500 computers managed by the local Essentials server.)

▶ An Operations Manager 2007 Gateway Server Component. This is the key component in the ROM solution. The Gateway Server Component on the Essentials server is only active when the Essentials server is attached to a ROM service provider.

The Hidden Gateway

The ROM solution performs a bit of a magic trick. Here we are pulling the covers off the essence of Remote Operations Manager: the sleeping OpsMgr Gateway Server Component hidden in every Essentials server. Microsoft created the Gateway Server Component, new with OpsMgr 2007, for customers that need to monitor computers in untrusted domains, possibly at remote sites without a direct network or VPN connection. Both MOM 2000 and 2005 required a one-way domain trust and routed network connection between management servers and managed computers to accomplish a similar feat. This configuration had significant overhead and imposed scaling limitations on those service providers that used a multitenant MOM solution to deliver managed services.

We cover using the Gateway Server Component in management group architecture in Chapter 5, "Planning Complex Configurations," and Chapter 10, "Complex Configurations." The ROM solution transplants that identical gateway functionality—the Gateway Server Component of OpsMgr links the customer's Essentials server to the ROM instance at the service provider.

The Gateway Server Component is not a separate piece of software; it is an additional functionality of the Health service available on every Essentials Server Component in any management group. Here's the magic: The ROM solution leverages the flexibility of a management server in one management group (the Essentials management group) to also be a gateway server for another management group (the ROM management group), in a sense dual-homing the management server!

When a customer Essentials server is converted to Service Provider mode, the gateway server functionality is activated and the Essentials server is permitted to proxy OpsMgr Agent Component connections between other computers on the customer network and ROM. The Essentials server becomes a gateway server in the Remote Operations Manager management group while remaining a fully functional Essentials server.

However, as far as the ROM service provider is concerned, the customer's (Essentials) server is technically an OpsMgr gateway server. For this reason, the ROM solution differentiates little between an Essentials server and a gateway server configuration at the customer network. Although some features of the Service Provider management pack only function when the customer gateway server is an Essentials server, native OpsMgr gateway servers and Essentials servers in Service Provider mode are generally interchangeable.

A Certificate to Bind Us

The native behavior for the OpsMgr Agent and Management Server Components in authenticating with one another is through Kerberos, the default Windows Active Directory authentication process. Managing computers in other domains seamlessly with OpsMgr, including features such as automatic and push installation of agents, requires a trust relationship and the routing of many Windows domain protocols, such as private DNS and Lightweight Directory Access Protocol (LDAP), as well as NetBIOS over TCP/IP (NBT). Because those networking elements cannot traverse Internet firewalls, we use private networks or VPNs to route the native OpsMgr agent/server communications between remote computers and the OpsMgr management group core components.

Microsoft needed a way to extend its System Center–based management to remote computers in untrusted domains and even workgroups, and in a more seamless manner than the model required with native Kerberos authentication (which involves Active Directory forests, domains, and trusts). Microsoft selected a Public Key Infrastructure (PKI) approach. This takes place by issuing the gateway servers of the ROM service provider and the Gateway Server Component of the customer Essentials server digital certificates from the same trusted Certificate Authority (CA). Fundamentally, the organizations are federated by virtue of their mutual trust of the same CA, a mutual authentication system that extends beyond any one organization's Active Directory (AD).

In addition to furnishing a means of authentication, the digital certificates are dual-purposed for encrypting communications between the gateway servers. The Secure Sockets Layer (SSL) connection on TCP port 5723 is encrypted with the digital certificate issued for authentication purposes. This means that in order for a validated SSL connection to be established, the host name on the certificate (issued by the mutually trusted CA) must match the expected DNS host name of the remote server.

This is a PKI scenario where you do *not* want to use a publicly trusted root CA certificate provider. The ROM service provider must utilize a private CA, because possessing the specific private trusted root certificate is part of the ROM security mechanism. Using a public CA such as VeriSign compromises a portion of the ROM security, because it would be easy to obtain the trusted root certificate. You can utilize either a standalone or an enterprise CA infrastructure for this purpose.

Minimum Requirements

The ROM solution is Internet-centric. You can begin to sketch the minimum implementation of ROM using an Internet cloud and a pair of firewalls on each end of a communication channel:

▶ The communication channel is a TCP port 5723 outbound connection from the customer Essentials server to an Internet-based destination.

▶ The target is an Internet IP permitted by a firewall of the ROM service provider, which in turn publishes that Internet IP to the private IP of an OpsMgr gateway server in a DMZ or other protected network.

▶ The SSL connection across the Internet is created between the Essentials server at the customer and the gateway server of the ROM provider.

The ROM solution does not support any direct communication between a remote customer Essentials server and the OpsMgr management server. Although it is technically feasible, Microsoft believes there are security mandates for supporting communication only between a remote customer Essentials server and an OpsMgr gateway server. For example, there is the security tier isolation created by the fact that gateway servers (that might be Internet-facing) do not have direct write access to the OpsMgr Operational database, as do management servers.

For this security reason, the ROM provider must minimally provision at least one gateway server in addition to the minimal all-in-one deployment scenario of an OpsMgr management group. In other words, the minimal installation would include all OpsMgr components on a single server and one Gateway Server Component on an additional server. Your gateway server can be a virtual server, provided there is appropriate network-level security—for example by associating the network adapter of the gateway server virtual machines (VMs) with a DMZ, perimeter network, or other network-isolation scheme such as virtual LANs (VLANs).

For security reasons, the gateway server should be in a separate secure domain from that of the OpsMgr management group, or in a hardened workgroup configuration. An inbound firewall publishing rule is created on the firewall of the ROM provider, mapping an Internet IP to the private IP of the gateway server. Figure 21.2 illustrates the minimum architecture for deploying the ROM solution.

Figure 21.2 highlights the central importance of the Certificate Authority in the ROM solution. Notice the management server, the gateway server, and the Essentials server are each issued digital certificates by the same mutually trusted CA. The certificates are issued using the Fully Qualified Domain Names (FQDNs) that match the DNS records or the hosts file name records each server uses to locate the other server with. Each server is issued one certificate that is used for all encrypted gateway server traffic on that server, and each server is configured to use only one certificate at a time.

REMOTE OPERATIONS MANAGER (ROM): MINIMUM IMPLEMENTATION

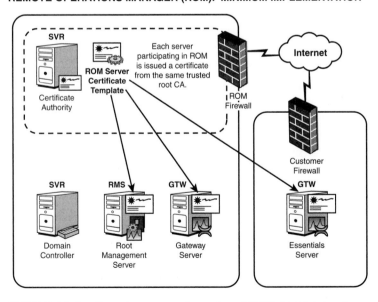

FIGURE 21.2   The minimum configuration of ROM, highlighting the mutually trusted CA.

The minimum configuration of Remote Operations Manager shown in Figure 21.2 is suitable for the Lab, Pilot, and Proof of Concept phases. The capacity of such a configuration on adequate hardware could support perhaps 10 customers (with Essentials) and 100 managed computers (average 10 per customer). However, this minimal configuration has a big single point of failure: the all-in-one management server at the ROM provider. Risk analysis shows that the economic value of a ROM instance increases rapidly as customers are added. It just doesn't make business sense to deploy ROM in this minimal configuration when SLAs and contracts are involved.

Of course, it is not mandatory to employ the ROM solution as part of a SLA-based offering. Service providers can use ROM technology to achieve a central view of their customers' network health, perhaps only for the service provider's convenience, or to leverage the Web console or Mobile console features of ROM (which are not available with Essentials). However, because the service provider is paying a per-computer, per-month license fee (SPLA) for each customer computer in the ROM instance, ROM is by no means free. Most likely, you will see ROM employed as a value-add to a managed services offering that delivers applications of a stated availability and capacity. ROM itself is the centerpiece of the solution, providing sensors to detect problems, built-in Microsoft best-practice response to events, and reports to verify compliance with SLAs.

The ROM instance becomes a business-critical service for every managed services customer network, requiring accommodations for fault tolerance and redundancy in architecture of the ROM management group. At the least, a pair of gateway servers, a pair of management servers, a clustered Root Management Server (RMS), and a clustered Operational database will remove the single points of failure in maintaining continuity of monitoring operations.

Remote Web Workplace

In addition to the minimum configuration of the OpsMgr ROM instance (such as the Certificate Authority and gateway server), there is a big piece of the Remote Operations Manager solution optionally installed on the customer network. *Remote Web Workplace (RWW)* is a web-based Remote Desktop Protocol (RDP) proxy application. When the service provider does not have a VPN or other access to the customer's private network, RWW provides a secure means for support engineers to remotely control managed customer computers over the Internet.

Service provider staff periodically require RDP access to managed customer computers. RDP allows them to assist with customer service requests and perform routine and unscheduled maintenance. By installing RWW on the customer's Essentials server and making two changes on the customer's firewall, you create a secure portal between the ROM service provider network and the customer network. The key feature of RWW is to actively proxy Internet-facing proprietary TCP port 4125 to the inside-facing standard port used by Terminal Services on client computers, TCP port 3389. RWW securely routes the RDP application across those ports and is a single-purpose application gateway.

Communicating with managed customer computers in the RWW scenario takes place differently than the normal OpsMgr gateway server-to-gateway server traffic on TCP port 5723. By using the RWW web portal, the connection is between the service provider's browser and the customer's Essentials server website over the Internet. You first establish an inbound browser-based connection to the RWW web portal on SSL port 443 with conventional HTTPS. After authenticating with the server and selecting the computer to connect to, the workstation sends a second inbound connection on port 4125. The RWW translates this to port 3389, creating an application-layer (RDP) bridge to the computer you selected. Look at Figure 21.3, where the top-center section highlights that the customer firewall must permit inbound TCP ports 443 and 4125 for RWW to function.

Publishing and using RWW is more secure than direct Remote Desktop Protocol via a VPN, because removing the VPN removes any opportunity for undesired traffic to come over a VPN connection into the protected customer network. You can safely use RWW from public, kiosk-type computers, which is not an option when VPN is in the picture. In addition, there is nothing left on the remote computer (such as a VPN connection definition) to be exploited to gain access to the customer network. More than one simultaneous user of RWW is supported, so multiple IT employees can work independently with the same customer network. You can work on multiple customer computer desktops at the same time by opening new Remote Web Workplace sessions from your workstation.

REMOTE OPERATIONS MANAGER (ROM): REMOTE WEB WORKPLACE (RWW)

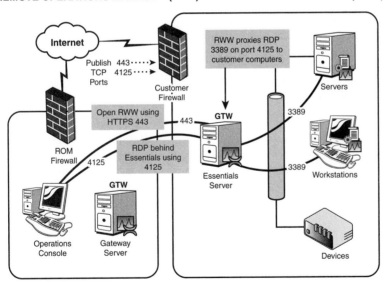

FIGURE 21.3   The web browser on a workstation uses the reason for RWW: RDP proxy.

Of course, there is always the option to publish the customer Essentials server RDP port 3389 and establish the terminal server connection directly to the desktop of the server. That is a less secure solution compared to the multilayer security added by using the RDP proxy features of RWW. There are several security benefits to employing RWW compared to directly publishing the RDP port 3389 of the Essentials server:

▶ Before RWW opens up TCP port 4125 (used by the proxy RDP process), the secure RWW portal must authenticate the user. RWW thus improves the security of the RDP application by adding an SSL-based authentication tier. Additionally, the source IP address of the RDP proxy connection must match the source IP address of the SSL connection made to RWW by the remote computer. These checkpoints provide two more levels of security before any remote desktop access occurs.

▶ Port 3389 is a well-known port often included in port scan attacks from the Internet. Because an open RDP session basically gives anyone access to the logon screen of the computer, a dictionary password attack against the Administrator account is quite possible. In the RDP implementation, port 3389 is a live port (actually a Terminal Services port) that cannot be obfuscated, because the service must always be listening for inbound connections. The Remote Web Workplace uses the less-well-known port 4125, which is only activated when an authorized RWW session is in progress.

Enterprise Implementation: The Master Hoster

The Remote Operations Manager product is licensed only to Microsoft partners that are service providers, by definition those partners who license ROM components under the Service Provider License Agreement (SPLA). Yet, many Microsoft partners with customers in the SMB space can leverage ROM to participate in the delivery of managed services without becoming traditional service providers. The *Master Hoster* concept recognizes a new partner-to-partner opportunity created by ROM.

In this solution, Microsoft partners have the option of attaching their SMB customer networks to a backend Network Operations Center (NOC) running ROM, the Master Hoster. The partner retains the customer relationship and optionally uses Essentials independently for workstation management. The servers and network devices are under SLA with the ROM service provider; essentially the partner is outsourcing the continuous eyes-on of the NOC (and the enterprise OpsMgr infrastructure) of the Master Hoster. Deploying the OpsMgr Web console with role-based security is key to sharing managed computer health information between customer contacts, partner contacts, and NOC staff.

Figure 21.4 illustrates the relationship between the Microsoft System Center products in the ROM Master Hoster scenario, with the Master Hoster, the partners, and the customer. Notice the Master Hoster handles the per-computer, per-month Service Provider Access License (SAL) payment to Microsoft under the terms of a Service Provider License Agreement (SPLA). The Master Hoster will deliver the remote NOC services for the partner.

To deliver software as a service to customers, which is what ROM facilitates, you have to invest in infrastructure. The operator of the ROM instance(s) at the Master Hoster is a larger Microsoft partner. This partner can staff the NOC with Level 1 engineers 24×7×365 and have additional specialized staff and support partners available to immediately escalate unresolved events to Level 2 and 3 engineers and necessary Subject Matter Experts (SMEs), thus supporting SLAs on applications and services.

The Master Hoster runs scalable and highly redundant instance(s) of ROM, installing OpsMgr in similar configurations to those used by large enterprise OpsMgr customers. The Master Hoster NOC hardware and staff may exist in different locations, with the hardware located in an Internet datacenter and the staff in a secure NOC with emergency generator power that has redundant remote access paths to the datacenter. Figure 21.5 shows the core components of the OpsMgr management group, optimized for supporting the ROM scenario.

MASTER HOSTER SCENARIO

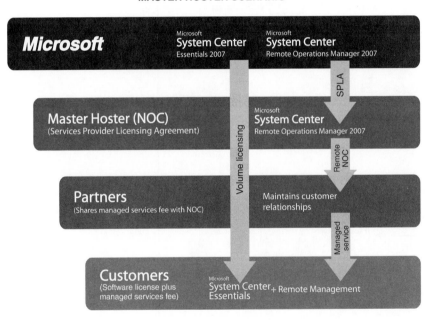

FIGURE 21.4   The Managed Services Provider (MSP) partner leverages the ROM NOC.

Other Servers in the ROM Solution

Figure 21.5 illustrates the core components of the ROM management group. Noted at the bottom is a number of server roles not shown, including DCs, email, and backup servers. We do not recommend that the ROM NOC share any IT resources with the service provider's corporate networks; you should treat the corporate network of the service provider as a customer in the ROM solution.

The ROM service provider will end up fielding as many as 30 servers to cover all the necessary bases in a maximum-capacity ROM management group and NOC. Gateway servers and those management servers that are not the RMS are good candidates for virtualization.

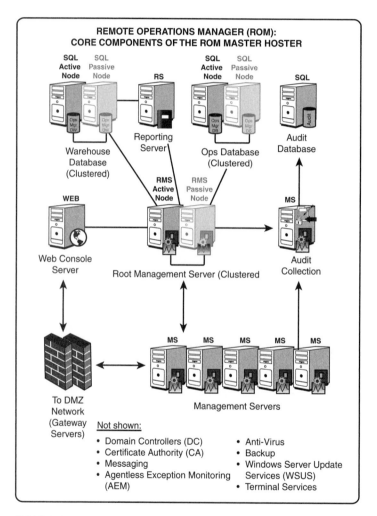

FIGURE 21.5   ROM management group core components, includes clustered servers.

Redundant Configurations

Figure 21.5 (ROM-management group core components) includes three clustered servers:

- ▶ The RMS
- ▶ The Operations Database Component
- ▶ The Data Warehouse Database Component

Clustering these servers allows their production loads (that is, the OpsMgr components) to roll between cluster nodes during maintenance actions such as operating system, application, and firmware upgrades. Also, multiple management servers are present (five in this configuration); these servers provide primary and secondary management server assignments for failover by agents and gateways. These measures provide for end-to-end redundancy for collecting monitoring data. Gaps in monitoring can penalize the service provider by inaccurately flagging server unavailability, when it actually is due to failure of a component in the ROM management group.

Audit Collection Services

Another key architecture component of the ROM management group is deploying Audit Collection Services. This is not mandatory, but highly recommended for the indemnity it provides the ROM service provider. Regulatory pressures on many organizations, especially in the banking and finance industries and in publicly traded companies, are creating audit requirements involving IT data networks. The ROM service provider needs to be ready to present evidence of internal compliance with security best practices to inspectors of its customers' networks. ACS provides the foundation for an inspection-ready NOC, increasing the ROM solution's value to customers in regulatory-sensitive industries.

Customers-per-Gateway Capacity

The five management servers shown in Figure 21.5 can comfortably support 2000–4000 or more direct-attached agent computers with n+1 redundancy, meaning that even if one management server is not operating, there is still enough capacity to support the production load. However, in the ROM solution, the only computers agent-managed by the ROM management servers are the server components and possibly the workstations of the NOC. All customer computers and devices are managed via a gateway-to-gateway server connection. Figure 21.6 shows the DMZ side of the ROM Master Hoster infrastructure and illustrates the five management servers in the NOC core from Figure 21.5 communicating with 10 gateway servers in a DMZ network.

The 10 gateway servers in the DMZ shown in Figure 21.6 offer a secure communications interface for at least 100 (and as many as 200 or more) customer networks. Microsoft recommends a baseline of 10 remote customer networks (Essentials or gateway servers) assigned per ROM service provider gateway server. This recommendation is more due to a desire to create a firebreak, or security bulkhead, between certain quantities of customer networks than it is for capacity reasons.

Connecting up to 20 customer networks to each of the 10 gateway servers puts the capacity of the ROM instance pictured at about 2000 to 4000 managed computers. The NOC physical plant for the Master Hoster should be carefully designed to scale, including the actual room(s) where the monitoring staff will work. As an example, the NOC of Master Hoster ClearPointe (shown in Figure 21.7) is designed to support over 4000 managed servers on a 24×7 engineer shift rotation. A "Mission Control" design with tiered platforms and big-screen projectors can create a purposeful atmosphere.

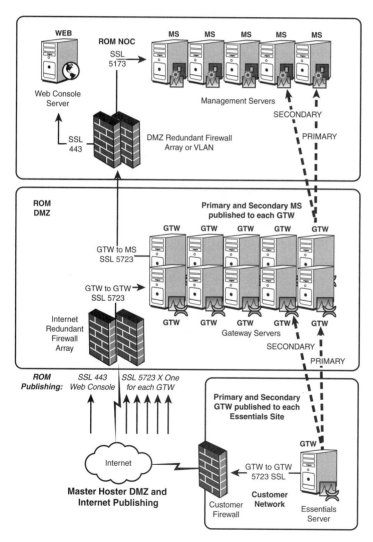

FIGURE 21.6   Gateway servers and the Web Console server are published from the DMZ.

FIGURE 21.7   The NOC at ClearPointe, a large-scale ROM Master Hoster.

Preparing Operations Manager for ROM

Before the ROM service provider's OpsMgr instance can accept inbound connections from customer Essentials and gateway servers, it is necessary to make a number of modifications to the service provider's network environment. This section covers what the service provider needs to do to prepare to operate with Remote Operations Manager. The Microsoft reference for preparing both the ROM service provider and the Essentials customer networks is the 25-page document "Remote Operations Manager Deployment Guide." The Deployment Guide is included with the ROM distribution media and is also available for download from the public Microsoft website at http://www.microsoft.com/downloads/details.aspx?FamilyId=4B621EB7-01BB-45F5-9A77-52853F06EEC9%20&displaylang=en (the URL is also listed in Appendix E, "Reference URLs," and on the CD accompanying this book).

Active Directory and DNS

Remote Operations Manager integrates tightly with the Active Directory of the service provider, because the service provider needs to provision AD user accounts and distribution groups for customers and partners participating in ROM. Because there is no trust relationship between customer and partner domains and the ROM domain, the AD in the ROM domain becomes the directory service and security provider for user-level activities involving customer and partner staff.

In particular, one will specify user accounts from the ROM service provider's AD when creating user roles for customer and partner staff, and those credentials are used to access the OpsMgr Web console. The ROM service provider will customize group scopes, console tasks, and views to apply to user roles, thus limiting customer access to only their managed objects. Likewise, partner staff has access only to the managed objects of its customers.

You will also want to leverage user accounts in the ROM AD for creating email distribution groups targeted at each customer and partner. You can mail-enable the AD user accounts of customers and partner staff, specifying their external SMTP email addresses. As an example, if a customer has three points of contact, and each customer contact has a mail-enabled user account defined in the ROM AD, you can create a distribution list with those three user accounts as members. Emailing to the distribution list automatically emails each of the customer contacts. This saves time when contacting customers and facilitates customer communication.

The ROM service provider should prepare its AD for creating these user account and distribution list objects. We recommend an Organizational Unit (OU) structure that segregates these external objects from the rest of the ROM AD. For example, a top-level OU named ROM contains a child OU named Partner, which contains OUs for each ROM partner. You would create user accounts and distribution groups for partner staff here. Within each ROM partner OU, there are child OUs for each customer associated with that partner, where you would create user accounts and distribution groups for customer staff. Back at the higher level Partner OU, there are distribution groups such as All Customers and All Partners that include appropriate customer and partner distribution lists as members. You should also consider using Access Control Lists (ACLs) to restrict who can send email to these distribution lists, to guard against embarrassing unintended broadcast emails. Figure 21.8 shows the service provider's AD hosting two partners, each with one customer.

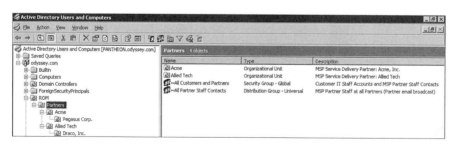

FIGURE 21.8   OUs in the ROM service provider's AD host partner and customer objects.

21

> **NOTE**
>
> **Security Least Privilege Considerations for Email**
>
> A security best practice is to extend a user the least privileged access needed to per-
> form the business mission. If a customer or partner contact will never require or desire
> access to the ROM Web console, you can create an AD contact object with the appro-
> priate external email address—rather than a mail-enabled AD user account. A mail-
> enabled contact can still participate in ROM AD distribution groups, but does not have
> the ability to log in to the Web console using credentials in the ROM AD.

You can also use the ROM service provider's DNS for name resolution of customer Essentials servers. In order to use Remote Web Workplace from the ROM network, the service provider workstation initiating the RWW session needs to resolve the FQDN of the customer server to the Internet IP address of the customer firewall that is publishing RWW.

Although name resolution of the FQDN can occur using a local hosts file on each ROM workstation, we recommend using the private DNS of the ROM AD. Each customer will have a standard primary DNS zone established in the private DNS of the ROM AD, with an address (A) record created in the zone with the host name of the customer Essentials server. To utilize RWW effectively, the customer firewall publishing RWW must have a static IP address on the Internet (preferred); alternatively, the customer can participate with the ROM service provider in a reliable Dynamic DNS (DDNS) service.

Certificate Authority

The Certificate Authority service is a critical and required component in a ROM solution. The ROM service provider can utilize an existing CA on its network (an enterprise or standalone CA) or establish a CA just for the ROM solution. A 26-page document titled, "Obtaining Certificates for Service Providers Scenario," is included with the ROM distribution media. This document includes detailed procedures, with a screenshot at each step, for deploying a standalone CA for ROM. If the ROM service provider does not yet have a CA, following the procedures in the document is the simplest method of deployment.

We recommend you publish your CA with a publicly resolvable DNS name, to avoid having to create host file entries with private DNS names on customer servers for the one-
time purpose of certificate issue.

Standalone versus Enterprise CA

There is quite a bit of difference in the feature set of standalone CAs compared to enter-
prise CAs. The standalone CA can be essentially independent of the ROM service provider's AD; you can take a standalone root CA offline, whereas a single-tier enterprise CA must remain online. You can use a new or existing enterprise CA for the ROM

scenario. Advantages to the enterprise CA over the standalone CA include the flexibility to use the automatic certificate issue feature with computers in the ROM domain, automatic approval of certificate requests, and integrated support for smart-card login.

The fundamental decision-making component is probably whether the ROM service provider uses, or intends to use, certificates for additional purposes besides ROM gateways:

▶ When the only planned use for certificates is issuing them to customer Essentials and gateway servers and to ROM gateway and management servers, a standalone CA is the easier choice.

▶ If the ROM service provider wants to expand use of certificates to include such features as email encryption and smartcard logon, use an enterprise CA.

The ROM implementation requires a certificate for each customer Essentials or gateway server, and also for each ROM gateway and management server. The certificate has the same enhanced keys as the default Computer Certificate template from a Windows CA (client authentication 1.3.6.1.5.5.7.3.2, and server authentication 1.3.6.1.5.5.7.3.1). The subject name of the certificate contains the FQDN of the server where you are installing the certificate. You can obtain certificates by using the web-based certificate issue feature of Microsoft's CA.

TIP

Copy the Computer Template If Using Enterprise CA

If the ROM service provider is already using an enterprise CA in its environment, and that CA is running on the Windows 2003 Enterprise operating system, you can leverage the existing Computer Certificate template. Open the Certificate Templates Microsoft Management Console (MMC), select the Computer template, and choose Duplicate Template. Name the new template something meaningful, such as **Managed SCE Server**, and optionally extend the certificate lifetime from the default 1 year to 2 years (the maximum period allowed by the MMC).

The certificate must exist in the Personal store of the computer account on each Essentials, gateway, and management server. Also, you must import the certificate of the CA that issued the ROM certificates into the Trusted Root Certification Authorities store of each of those computers. System engineers who have worked with Microsoft CAs in the past will be familiar with those certificate store locations and procedures. What is different in the ROM scenario is that once the certificates are in the certificate stores, they are then exported to files, and subsequently imported into the OpsMgr gateway process on each participating server.

On the OpsMgr management servers and gateway servers of the ROM service provider, and on customer gateway servers, the exported certificate files are imported using the MOMCertImport.exe tool. You will find that tool in the SupportTools folder of the OpsMgr 2007 software media. You copy the tool to the %*ProgramFiles%*\System Center Operations Manager 2007 folder in order to use it. (MOMCertImport is discussed in length in Chapter 10.)

On customer Essentials servers, the exported certificate files are imported using the Configure Service Provider Mode tool, which is located on the Start menu in the All Programs -> System Center Essentials 2007 program group.

Importing the Certificate on ROM Servers

Here are the steps to enable certificate-based communication on an OpsMgr management server or gateway server (this procedure assumes the ROM service provider is operating an enterprise CA with automatic certificate request approval enabled):

1. From the desktop of the management server or gateway server, open Internet Explorer and browse to the published URL of the ROM service provider's web-based certificate issue, such as https://ca.odyssey.com/CertSrv.

2. Select the Request a Certificate option and then specify an advanced certificate request.

3. Select the option Create and submit a request to this CA.

4. In the Type of Certificate Needed drop-down list, select the certificate the ROM service provider has provisioned for this purpose, such as Managed SCE Server.

5. In the Name field, enter the FQDN of the management server or gateway server.

6. Click the Mark keys as exportable and Store certificate in the local computer certificate store check boxes.

7. Click Submit and then Yes. When the Certificate Issued page appears, click the Install this certificate link.

8. Return to the Home page of the certificate issue website. Select the Download a CA certificate, certificate chain, or CRL link.

9. Click the install this CA certificate chain link. Click Yes to each of several security warnings. Close the web browser.

10. Open the Certificates MMC (Current User account) on the management server or gateway server. Expand the Certificates (Current User) node, navigating to the Trusted Root Certificates -> Certificates folder.

11. Locate the root certificate issued by the ROM service provider. Right-click and select Copy. Navigate to and select the Local Computer -> Trusted Root Certificates -> Certificates folder. Then right-click and select Paste.

12. Open the Certificates MMC (Computer account) on the management server or gateway server. Expand the Certificates (Local computer) node, navigating to the Personal -> Certificates folder.

21

13. Locate the certificate issued by the ROM service provider. Right-click and select All Tasks -> Export.

14. Follow the prompts of the Certificate Export Wizard, specifying Yes, and then export the private key. Take note of the password you assign to the exported key. This creates a certificate file with the extension .PFX in the location you specify (for example, hydra.odyssey.com.pfx).

15. Open a command prompt on the management server or gateway server and change the directory to the System Center Operations Manager 2007 folder.

16. Import the certificate with the MOMCertImport tool, using this command-line syntax (in this example, the exported PFX file is located at the root of the C: drive):

```
MOMCertImport.exe C:\hydra.odyssey.com.pfx /Password password
```

17. Stop and restart the OpsMgr Health service on the management server or gateway server.

Firewall and DMZ

The ROM service provider requires a robust firewall solution on the Internet edge. Optionally (and recommended), ROM gateway servers are also isolated to their own DMZ. The ideal architecture includes a separate highly available firewall solution to segregate the gateway servers from the management servers and the ROM core components. If you are not using a separate firewall, consider employing VLANs or IPSec to isolate traffic from the Internet-facing gateway servers. The gateway servers only need to communicate with their assigned management servers on TCP port 5723. TCP port 3389 (Remote Desktop Protocol) is also useful for remote management of the gateway servers from the NOC core network.

If there is only one gateway server, a best practice is to install the gateway component on a server in hardened workgroup mode (that is, on a computer that is not a domain member and that passes the Microsoft Baseline Security Analyzer test). If there are to be two or more gateway servers in a DMZ (required for gateway redundancy), consider installing DCs in the DMZ for a dedicated domain. Utilizing a dedicated DMZ domain lets you use domain-based Group Policy to enforce uniform security policies on gateway servers. Gateway servers remain fully and seamlessly monitored by the ROM management group in a DMZ.

Using Microsoft Internet Security and Acceleration Server

Our best practice for publishing ROM to the Internet is to use the Microsoft Internet Security and Acceleration (ISA) Server 2006 firewall. Utilize ISA 2006 Standard Edition (SE) for SMB Remote Operations Manager service providers and use ISA 2006 Enterprise Edition (EE) for Master Hoster implementations. The justification for ISA is the requirement to publish the OpsMgr Web console to the Internet using a public-facing SSL certificate. A public-facing SSL certificate allows partners and customers to click an Internet URL hyperlink in notification emails and connect to the OpsMgr Web console to view or update alert status. This public URL may change to reflect the name of the service provider, and it usually does not match the private FQDN of the Web Console Component.

ISA Server performs the following security functions:

▶ Listens on the Internet with a public-facing SSL certificate

▶ Decrypts the SSL connection

▶ Performs security checks on the HTML

▶ Reencrypts the inspected HTML in a separate SSL connection, directly to the Web Console Component using a private-facing SSL certificate

To operate over the Internet, the OpsMgr Web console must use Forms Authentication mode, which in turn requires enabling basic authentication. A certificate-based SSL session is required to avoid sending passwords in the clear during basic authentication. Configuring an array of fault-tolerant (n+1) ISA 2006 EE firewalls lets you share the same public certificate for highly available publishing of the Web console.

You could also utilize a different firewall solution than ISA Server, if that firewall is capable of bridging public-to-private SSL-certificate connections. In other words, what is crucial is the ability to listen on the Internet with a public-facing SSL certification using a different FQDN and CA than the private-facing SSL certificate on the Web Console Component.

You will also want to avoid supporting a management server in the DMZ hosting the Web console. The SSL traffic inspection feature of ISA Server is equivalent to an application firewall; this distinction lets you safely keep the Web Console Component in the ROM core network. With no management servers in the DMZ, you can maintain simpler (and thereby more secure) DMZ security.

Firewall Publishing Rules

Figure 21.9 shows the firewall publishing rules created for publishing ROM to the Internet using ISA Server 2006. (This screenshot is from the ISA Server Management console.)

The firewall policies in Figure 21.9 are explained as follows:

▶ The first two firewall rules shown in Figure 21.9 (rules 7 and 8) support the Internet publishing requirement to map TCP port 5723 from Internet-facing TCP/IP addresses to the private TCP/IP addresses of the gateway servers in the DMZ.

Two gateway servers are published in this example, so there is one server publishing rule for each gateway server. Each gateway server has an associated Internet-facing TCP/IP address, which is the address the customer Essentials server or gateway server will resolve from the FQDN of the gateway server.

▶ Rule 9 in Figure 21.9 shows publishing the Web console on port 443 from the Internet to the Web Console server.

Order ▲	Policy	Name	Action	Protocols	From / Listener	To
7	Array	Server Publish OpsMgr GW 1 to Customers	Allow	OM Server	External	172.16.10.35
8	Array	Server Publish OpsMgr GW 2 to Customers	Allow	OM Server	External	172.16.10.36
9	Array	SSL Web Publish OpsMgr Web Console	Allow	HTTPS	Odyssey OM Web Console	hydra.odyssey.com
10	Array	SSL Web Publish CA (Issue) to Customers	Allow	HTTPS	CA Certificate Issue Website	ca.odyssey.com

FIGURE 21.9   Firewall array policies used to publish Remote Operations Manager with Microsoft ISA Server 2006.

▶ An additional web publishing rule (number 10) directs port 443 requests to the web certificate issue page on the CA used by the ROM service provider. The rule that publishes the CA to the Internet should be disabled during normal operations and only enabled when a new customer Essentials or gateway server is actually performing a certificate request.

Installing the Service Provider Management Pack

Installing the centerpiece of the ROM solution, the Service Provider management pack, is probably the easiest part of an OpsMgr-to-ROM transformation. The Remote Operations Manager software distribution media contains the Microsoft System Center Service Provider Management Pack 2007.msi file. This package installs the management pack on a computer, but does not import the management pack into the management group. After running the installer, if you accept the default installation location, the management pack is placed in the C:\Management Packs\Microsoft System Center Service Provider Management Pack 2007 folder. Import the Microsoft.SystemCenter.ServiceProvider.2007.mp management pack file in the conventional manner, using the Operations console or PowerShell.

Here are the changes made to the management group when the Service Provider management pack is imported:

▶ The Microsoft.SystemCenter.ServiceProvider.CustomerSite object class (part of the System Center Core Library) is created. This is the type of object that represents customer Essentials and gateway servers.

▶ The AllCustomers system group is created, representing the collection of customer sites.

▶ Two discovery rules are created:

   ▶ One rule discovers customer Essentials and gateway servers.

   ▶ The second discovers customer sites to add them to the All Customers system group.

▶ The SSIDRegSyncRule rule is created. This rule synchronizes identification keys between the Registries of the Essentials or gateway server and the ROM gateway server.

▶ A new Reporting view folder Service Provider is created containing one predefined report: Alerts generated in last 24 hours.

▶ A new Monitoring view folder Service Provider is created, which contains five predefined views:

  ▶ Customer Alerts

  ▶ Customer Computers

  ▶ Customer Health

  ▶ Customers (diagram)

  ▶ System Center Essentials Servers

▶ A number of console tasks are made available in the System Center Essentials Servers view folder. One of these tasks is used to configure customer site details.

Hotfixes (sometimes called QFEs) might need to be applied to the OpsMgr management servers and/or gateway servers of the ROM service provider before Service Provider Mode is enabled on any customer Essentials server. The QFE folder on the ROM software distribution media will contain any such hotfixes. Install those QFEs following the instructions included with each hotfix.

No additional configuration is needed after importing the Service Provider management pack and applying any QFEs; the ROM functionality is ready to use. The next task for the ROM service provider, bringing a customer into management, occurs after installing Essentials on the customer network.

TIP

Monitoring Customer Network Devices with ROM

The Essentials 2007 Network Device Monitoring Library includes an unpublished feature for ROM service providers. We have confirmed with Microsoft that you can legally import the Network Device Monitoring management pack, distributed with Essentials 2007, into the ROM OpsMgr 2007 management group. This management pack extends the features available with Essentials to monitor SNMP network devices.

If you deploy the management pack in this manner, use it with caution. The "smart defaults" in the Essentials management pack prudently disable all SNMP performance counters except one. Because of the heavy load SNMP polling can place on a management server and database server, override the smart defaults (to collect more performance data) very selectively. We do not recommend that the ROM service provider use this management pack on a large scale.

Installing Essentials at the Customer

System Center Essentials servers are the eyes and ears of ROM on managed customer networks. The ROM service provider uses the Gateway Server Component of the Essentials server to communicate over the Internet with the customer network. This gateway feature is what enables ROM to work without needing a VPN or other private network connection to a customer network. In addition to being a communications gateway, the Essentials server discovers customer computers and network devices for ROM to manage. When ROM discovers a customer computer that is already managed by Essentials, the Essentials (OpsMgr) Agent Component on the computer becomes dual-homed to the Essentials management group and the ROM management group.

Installing Essentials automatically installs Windows Server Update Services (WSUS) 3.0 on the customer server, if not already installed. If you plan to use Essentials-specific features, Essentials requires itself to be the designated Automatic Updates source for all managed computers. Using the local WSUS server is necessary to render the details display of the Computers space and populate the information in the daily health report. In addition, you cannot employ the local WSUS server in an upstream/downstream (distributed) WSUS server hierarchy—manually modifying the WSUS server properties to do so renders most Essentials console views inoperative.

Real World—Keeping Essentials and OpsMgr Separate

Microsoft includes another avenue for the ROM service provider to interact directly with customer Essentials servers. This feature involves publishing customer Essentials servers (TCP port 5124) to the Internet in the same manner as ROM gateway servers. TCP port 8531 must also be published, which exposes the customer's WSUS component.

These firewall publishing rules allow the ROM service provider to launch the customer Essentials console over the Internet using the inline tasks in the ROM Operations console (with attendant DNS name resolution and importing of customer Essentials and WSUS certificates in the ROM NOC). This overly complex method depends on the Windows Stored User Names and Passwords feature of a selected workstation or server in the service provider's network to host a unique administrative credential for each customer. This methodology does not scale well, and installing the Operations Manager console and the Essentials console on the same computer often results in the incorrect console being launched.

Even when this feature is implemented and working, refreshing views and executing tasks over the Internet is very slow. There is not enough in labor savings versus just establishing a Remote Desktop (or RWW) session to the customer server and opening the Essentials console locally. This is a part of the ROM solution we do not recommend including in your production architecture.

Essentials and ROM Are OpsMgr Management Groups

It is important to understand that an Essentials server is an all-in-one OpsMgr management server group, capable of importing management packs and monitoring computers and devices just like a native OpsMgr management group. Without ROM, Essentials is the primary and only monitoring engine involved on the customer network. In the ROM scenario, the primary monitoring engine is the remote instance of OpsMgr the ROM service provider runs, so some features of the local Essentials instance become redundant. That does not mean Essentials is no longer useful, but for performance reasons you want to prevent the Essentials and the ROM instances of OpsMgr from running the same application management packs against the same computers. Here are the possible modes of operation for a managed services partner considering Essentials:

▶ **Essentials only**—No ROM involvement; Essentials functions as all-in-one management group server on the customer network. The customer uses Essentials for monitoring, like a mini-OpsMgr, as they see fit. SMB partners may attempt to manage multiple customers' Essentials installations manually, without the central view of ROM. For example, you could configure each customer's Essentials instance to email every alert to a single mailbox at the SMB partner. There are obvious scaling limitations to this scenario, but for the very small IT service company, Essentials alone can provide value.

▶ **Essentials + ROM, Essentials engaged**—In this scenario, some Essentials features remain actively utilized, such as update management, workstation management, and the daily health report. The ROM service provider monitors the critical infrastructure, such as servers and network devices, whereas Essentials manages workstations and software updates.

This model is preferred for the Master Hoster implementation, allowing an easy division of duties between the Master Hoster service provider and the customer's managed services partner. Using this solution, the customer's managed services partner provides desktop support and maintains the customer relationship, and the Master Hoster manages customer servers and network devices with a Service Level Agreement from a 24×7 NOC. The customer workstations have Essentials agents, and they are not dual-homed; they only report to Essentials. (Dual-homing only is applicable when customer workstations are managed by both the ROM NOC and the local Essentials instance. If you are paying the SPLA for the clients, normally you will manage them only from ROM.)

▶ **ROM only, Essentials dormant**—This model does not use any of the System Center features unique to Essentials. This headless Essentials implementation uses only the gateway component of the Essentials server, and all other features of Essentials are turned off. Customer computers (other than the Essentials server itself) are not dual-homed and are discovered only by the ROM instance of OpsMgr.

Because this scenario will not use Essentials features such as the daily health report and the Essentials console, you can employ WSUS in whatever manner you like, including the upstream/downstream server functionality of WSUS 3.0. This scenario is functionally similar to installing the Gateway Server Component of an OpsMgr management group.

The reference procedures to install Essentials are available online at http://go.microsoft.com/fwlink/?LinkId=94444, which is an online document discussing System Center Essentials deployment planning and installation. All else being equal, an Essentials server–based connection is more useful to the service provider than an OpsMgr gateway server–based connection to an SMB customer network. (When customers have Essentials servers, you can use all the features of the Service Provider management pack.) However, the hardware requirements and software footprint for Essentials are larger than for a gateway server. In particular, a 64-bit Essentials server requires a full instance of 64-bit SQL Server 2005 for a local database, whereas the 64-bit OpsMgr Gateway Server Component has no database overhead.

Essentials Configuration Options

If the customer has an existing Essentials 2007 server, the ROM service provider can evaluate the capacity of that server to handle the load of the added Gateway Server Component. Remember that the Remote Web Workplace goes on the customer Essentials server as well. If Essentials does not exist in the customer environment, the service provider either selects an existing server to install Essentials on or installs a new server hosting Essentials. We do not recommend deploying Essentials in production environments on a virtual machine. Because Essentials (and its SQL Server database) can be memory-intensive, we recommend allocating 2GB RAM for 32-bit Essentials server and 3GB RAM for 64-bit Essentials server processes.

Essentials as ROM Grooming Tool

Regardless of how you plan to utilize the local Essentials instance after converting the Essentials server to Service Provider Mode, the Master Hoster service provider can consider using Essentials as a grooming tool/staging area for ROM. Here is a possible protocol to employ for customer network discovery:

▶ Prior to admitting new managed customer computers to the larger population of existing computers in the ROM NOC, let Essentials first discover customer networks.

▶ ROM and MSP partner staffs employ the local Essentials instance to groom customer computers and achieve a healthy state in the Essentials console, prior to discovering those computers from the ROM instance.

▶ After the healthy computers are under the management of ROM, uninstall their Essentials agents (removing dual-homing) and/or uninstall redundant management packs from the Essentials management group.

The service provider will want to leverage some features of the Essentials Feature Configuration Wizard, which is the post-setup configuration tool launched from the Essentials Administration space. For example, you will need the same Windows firewall exceptions that enable remote administration from the Essentials server for employing the Gateway Server Component in the ROM scenario. The wizard will add the firewall exception to the System Center Essentials All Computers Policy Group Policy Object (GPO). In other words, what would normally be a manual procedure if you were only employing a gateway server (creating the GPO) becomes automated with the Feature Configuration Wizard on an Essentials server.

Figure 21.10 shows the Introduction page of the Feature Configuration Wizard. We indicated which portions are always useful in the ROM scenario and which are optional, depending on the proposed use of the Essentials instance after placing the server in Service Provider Mode.

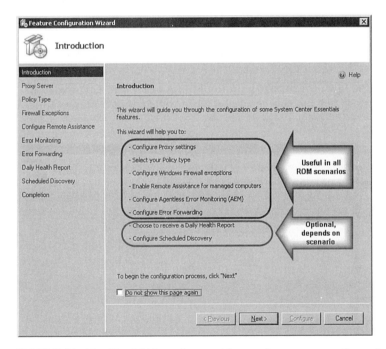

FIGURE 21.10   The ROM service provider can leverage many Essentials features.

Essentials Minimum Installations

You can convert an existing Essentials installation to a minimum configuration by deleting management packs. An occasion for this might be after you are finished using the default installation of Essentials as a grooming tool. An Essentials minimum installation consists of a management group with only system-level management packs installed.

By uninstalling management packs not necessary for the core Essentials functionality, you significantly reduce the resource load on the Essentials server. This is appropriate when the ROM service provider exclusively manages all customer computers.

Delete the following management packs from a default installation of Essentials to convert it into a minimum installation:

▶ Microsoft Exchange Server.

▶ Microsoft SQL Server.

▶ Microsoft Windows Active Directory.

▶ Microsoft Windows Client. (Do not delete libraries; only delete management packs without the word *library* in their name.)

▶ Microsoft Windows Internet Information Services.

▶ Microsoft Windows Server. (Do not delete libraries.)

You can install Essentials in a minimum configuration using the command-line switch /ImportSystemMPsOnly. Installing Essentials from the command line with this switch disables the import of all management packs except those needed for its core functionality. There are two commands to use when installing Essentials in minimum configuration:

```
<Essentials Path>\Setup\SetupSCE.EXE /Path: <Essentials Path> /SQLExpressPath
<Path> /User: <UserName> /Password: <Password> /Domain: <Domain> /UpdateLocation:
<location to store local WSUS files> /ImportSystemMPsOnly /Silent
Msiexec /i <Essentials Path>\helperobjects\SCECertPolicyConfig.msi /qn
```

Enabling Service Provider Mode in Essentials

Converting a customer Essentials server from the default, standalone mode to Service Provider Mode has three mandatory steps and an optional step (we will cover each step in detail):

1. Enable name resolution and, if needed, configure an outbound firewall rule.
2. Obtain certificates from the ROM service provider's CA using the web-based certificate issue process.
3. Run the Configure Service Provider Mode tool.
4. (Optional) Install the Remote Web Workplace.

As was the case when preparing the ROM gateway and management servers, you might need to apply hotfixes (or QFEs) to the Essentials server at the customer site before enabling Service Provider Mode. The QFE folder on the ROM software distribution media will contain any such hotfixes; install those QFEs following the instructions included with each hotfix.

NOTE

First Step Is to Create Customer Site in ROM

Before enabling Service Provider Mode on a customer Essentials server, create the customer site using the gateway approval tool in the ROM service provider's instance of Operations Manager. This procedure is covered later in this chapter in the section "Customer Site Creation."

Name Resolution and Outbound Firewall Rule

You need to enable name resolution of the ROM gateway server FQDN(s) from the Essentials server. The simplest way to accomplish this is by adding the FQDN(s) of the ROM gateway server(s) to the local hosts file of the Essentials server—the Essentials server is the only customer server that requires name resolution of the ROM gateway server(s).

Additionally, if the customer firewall is locked down to allow only certain ports or protocols to the Internet, you must permit outbound communication on port 5723 from the Essentials server to the ROM gateway server(s). If the customer firewall permits all outbound ports to the Internet, which is common, no outbound rule firewall changes are necessary.

Obtaining Certificates for Essentials Server

The customer Essentials server needs to be issued a digital certificate by the mutually trusted CA in the same manner as the ROM management servers and gateway servers. Follow steps 1 through 14 from the "Importing the Certificate on ROM Servers" section earlier in this chapter and then add these two steps:

1. Return to the Certificates (Local computer) node of the Certificates MMC, navigating to the Personal -> Certificates folder. Locate the certificate issued by the ROM service provider, right-click, and select All Tasks -> Export.

2. Follow the prompts of the Certificate Export Wizard, accepting the defaults. This creates a certificate file with the extension .CER in the location you specify (for example, odyssey.com-CA.cer).

So really, creating the exported CER file is the only difference between obtaining certificates for customer Essentials servers and ROM management and gateway servers.

Configuring Service Provider Mode

After issuing the certificates and staging the certificate files, launch the Configure Service Provider Mode tool from the Windows Start menu -> All Programs -> System Center Essentials 2007 program group. There are just five information fields to populate, as you can see in Figure 21.11.

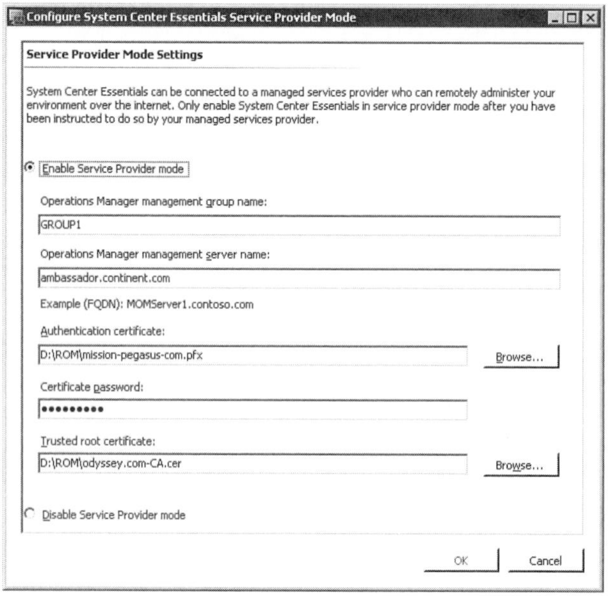

FIGURE 21.11   Enabling Essentials Service Provider Mode on the customer server.

Notice in Figure 21.11 that the FQDN entered in the Operations Manager management server name field is **ambassador.continent.com**, which is the FQDN of the primary gateway server for this customer in the DMZ of the ROM service provider. The DMZ domain for this ROM service provider is continent.com, whereas the core domain for the ROM service provider is odyssey.com. The customer Essentials server needs DNS name resolution only for the gateway server(s) in the ROM service provider's DMZ domain.

After entering the correct information in the five fields and clicking the OK button, the message "Successfully enabled service provider mode" appears. Communication with the ROM management group begins immediately, assuming you previously created the customer site in the ROM service provider's OpsMgr management group.

Installing Remote Web Workplace

In most cases, because using RWW offers a more secure remote access solution than RDP alone, we recommend that the ROM service provider install Remote Web Workplace on the customer Essentials server. The RWW feature in the ROM solution is derived from the same-named RWW that is a component of Microsoft Small Business Server 2003 (SBS). If the customer network already is running an instance of RWW on its SBS server, that instance suffices for the ROM solution and you do not need to install the RWW that is distributed with Remote Operations Manager.

Key characteristics of the RWW solution include

▶ An existing IIS website that can be enabled for SSL.

▶ The RWW server's inbound TCP ports 433 and 4125 are published to the Internet by the customer firewall.

Because the Essentials server already requires IIS, and because web server certificates are easily available from the same ROM CA furnishing the computer certificates for the gateway components, deploying RWW on the Essentials server is usually a simple matter. Here are the steps to follow to install RWW in the ROM solution on the customer server:

1. From the Remote Web Workplace folder on the ROM installation media, run the appropriate installer package (MSI file). There are i386 and x64 versions of the RemoteWW.msi package.

   The installer package creates a Remote virtual directory in the default IIS website on the Essentials server. The virtual directory maps to the Inetpub\Remote folder created in the System Center Essentials 2007 program folder. Figure 21.12 shows the RWW login page in the browse window of IIS Manager before we enable SSL.

2. Require an SSL connection on the Remote virtual directory of the default website in IIS Manager. Specifically, select the Require secure channel (SSL) check box in the Secure Communications settings (right-click the Remote virtual directory and select Properties -> Directory Security -> Secure Communications -> Edit).

3. Download and install the latest Remote Desktop Web Connection software (tsweb-setup.exe) available from Microsoft at http://go.microsoft.com/fwlink/?LinkId=86340.

4. Install the application, and afterwards navigate to the \Inetpub\wwwroot\TSWeb folder. Copy the msrdp.cab file and paste it into the *%ProgramFiles%*\System Center Essentials 2007\Inetpub\Remote folder.

5. Optionally brand the customer RWW login page with the ROM service provider's logo and/or help desk telephone number. Edit the RwwOEMLogo.gif file located in the *%ProgramFiles%*\System Center Essentials 2007\InetPub\Remote\Images folder to enable branding.

6. Configure the customer firewall to map an Internet IP address to the private IP of the Essentials server on TCP ports 443 and 4125 inbound.

To use RWW, you must possess a username and password that is a member of the Administrators local security group on the Essentials server. Service providers must stage administrative user credentials on the customer server or in the customer domain for using RWW.

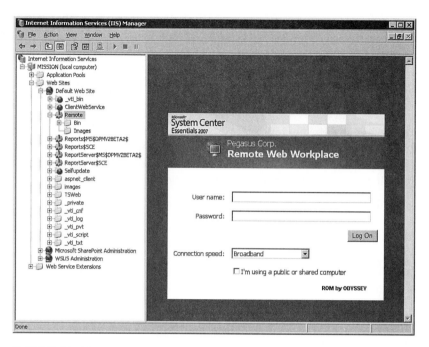

FIGURE 21.12   RWW login page in the Remote virtual directory of the default website.

Real World—Piggyback on the OWA Certificate

The ROM RWW solution can leverage an existing public-facing SSL certificate at customers that are already publishing Outlook Web Access (OWA) with Microsoft ISA Server. Because ISA can route inbound web requests to different internal servers depending on the URL path, you can use the same SSL listener currently employed for OWA publishing. Just create a secure web server publishing rule using the OWA web listener for the path /Remote, and map it to the Essentials server. If the customer Essentials server is already an OWA server, just add the path /Remote to the existing paths (such as /Exchange and /Public) in the OWA secure web server publishing rule.

Provisioning Customer Networks

Finally all the preparatory work is about to pay off, and the ROM service provider is now ready to accept customer networks into management. Technically, this is not difficult to accomplish, and we will cover those steps in detail in the following sections. Administratively, there is a good deal of information about the customer network to collect, some of which is very sensitive. Although some of this information can be stored in the Operations database, other data must be collected and made available separately from the OpsMgr Operations console to support teams for reference.

We recommend using a high security private intranet at the ROM service provider for storing sensitive customer configuration information. Administrative access to the Essentials console, ROM Operations console, or ROM PowerShell equals administrative access to customer networks—any location where passwords of administrator accounts are available requires the maximum security protection possible! Using two-factor security such as smartcards, tokens, or biometrics with PIN codes that enforce the "something you have + something you know" security policy is recommended to minimize the ROM service provider liability. Employing the Audit Collection Services component in the ROM NOC is crucial in creating an audit trail of accesses of shared credentials, such as a customer Essentials administrator accounts. You will want to compartmentalize each customer's sensitive data, with granular security access and audit controls.

Here are some examples of the information necessary for supporting a customer Essentials site:

▶ Warranty information or uplifted hardware service contract, such as HP Care Pack, Dell Gold Support, or Cisco SMARTNet contract

▶ Expiration date of warranty or service contract

▶ Customer (and partner) points of contact and preferred means of contact

▶ Internet IP address that the ROM service provider will see coming from the customer (usually the default gateway of the customer network, such as its firewall)

▶ Customer time zone, hours of operation, and desired escalation and notification procedures

▶ In the ROM Master Hoster scenario, the partner information associated with the customer network

▶ Expiration date of Managed SCE Server certificate

If you configured the ROM service provider firewall in the most secure configuration possible, inbound connection to the Internet-facing ROM gateway servers will be restricted to the Internet IP-based addresses that correspond to each customer Essentials server. In this scenario, add the Internet IP address of a new customer firewall to the set of customer sites (in the firewall publishing rule) that are permitted to make inbound connections on port 5123.

Creating and Approving the Customer Site

There is a two-step procedure required to enable management of customer networks by the ROM service provider. We will step through each of these procedures:

▶ Create the customer site at the command line, using the gateway approval tool on a management server in the ROM management group. This is the very first step in bringing a customer into management, and it should occur *before* converting Essentials into Service Provider mode.

▶ After installing Essentials at the customer site and it is communicating with the ROM management group, approve the customer site using a task in the Monitoring space.

Customer Site Creation

The ROM service provider should create the customer site (and add the customer Internet IP to the ROM firewall rule) as soon as the Essentials server name and customer site name are known. This ensures the ROM management group is prepared to communicate at the gateway-to-gateway level when you convert the customer Essentials server to Service Provider Mode. After creating the customer site in ROM, the ROM service provider notifies the customer and/or managed services partner that the Essentials server is ready for conversion to Service Provider Mode.

You might wonder what happens if the conversion of a customer Essentials server to Service Provider Mode takes place before the ROM service provider creates the site. In that case the Essentials server appears as a manually installed agent awaiting approval in the Administration space, rather than as a gateway server.

You can easily delete customer sites using the same OpsMgr gateway approval tool, in the event there is an error or for some reason the Essentials server does not successfully end up being converted to Service Provider mode. Copy the Microsoft.EnterpriseManagement.GatewayApprovalTool.exe tool from the SupportTools folder on the OpsMgr installation media to the *%ProgramFiles%*\System Center Operations Manager 2007 folder.

Run the tool at the command prompt in the *%ProgramFiles%*\System Center Operations Manager 2007 folder. The following code is the command-line syntax of the gateway approval tool, used to create the customer site for Pegasus Corp. (the Essentials server name is mission.pegasus.com), using the ROM gateway server ambassador.continent.com:

```
Microsoft.EnterpriseManagement.GatewayApprovalTool.exe /ManagementServerName=
ambassador.continent.com /GatewayName=mission.pegasus.com /SiteName="Customer
Pegasus Corp."
```

It is important to supply a site name for the Essentials customer, even though the /SiteName switch is optional. The Service Provider management pack uses the site name to populate the System Center Essentials Servers view in the Monitoring space.

You may want to consider prefacing each customer name with the word *Customer* to create the site name. Using a common prefix makes managing customer networks easier by sorting them together whenever an alphabetical list of management group objects is presented in the Operations console.

Almost immediately after the gateway approval tool that creates the customer site is run, the name of the customer Essentials server and the customer site name appear in the System Center Essentials Servers view in the Monitoring space. The state of the new site will be unmonitored (gray) until Essentials is successfully converted into Service Provider Mode.

Customer Site Approval

After a customer Essentials server is successfully converted into Service Provider Mode, the customer Essentials server will appear healthy in the System Center Essentials Servers view in the Operations console Monitoring space. Simultaneously, key Event ID 1210 appears in the Operations Manager event log of the customer Essentials server, as shown in Figure 21.13. The gateway-to-gateway connection to the service provider is operational when that event appears with the name of the ROM service provider management group (GROUP1 in this example).

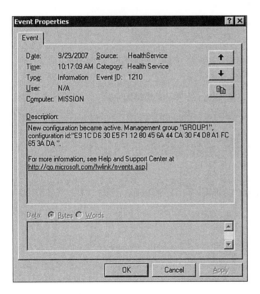

FIGURE 21.13   Event ID 1210 in the customer Essentials Operations Manager log signals success.

You will want to wait about 10 minutes after observing Event ID 1210 on the customer Essentials server and confirming the healthy status of the customer Essentials server in the System Center Essentials Servers view in the Monitoring space. This is necessary for the Service Provider management pack discovery rule to discover the customer Essentials server, and this discovery occurs every 5 minutes.

When the customer site is ready for approval, it appears healthy (green) as the Customer Pegasus Corp. customer site does, seen in Figure 21.14. Notice the Health Service Task area on the right (the cursor is highlighting the Create/Edit Customer Site). Select the new customer site you want to approve and then click that shortcut to launch the Create/Edit Customer Site Health Service Task.

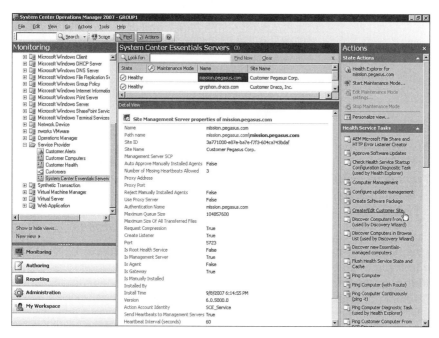

FIGURE 21.14   Essentials servers represent gateways to customer sites.

Running the Create/Edit Customer Site task against a healthy customer Essentials server (gateway) accomplishes two things:

▶ The gateway is validated to be an Essentials server. This one-time invisible action makes a change to the Operations database that indicates this is an Essentials server. After this task is run one time, the other Service Provider views, such as the Customer Health state view, will populate with data from that customer site.

▶ A remote task is run on the Essentials server, optionally populating Registry keys on the Essentials server with information useful for performing customer service. Customer information entered here includes the customer time zone, point of contact, and three customizable fields to track other management information.

Figure 21.15 shows the Create/Edit Customer Site task dialog box after we have populated the overrides in the task parameters. In the ROM Master Hoster scenario, you can use one of the custom fields to track the managed services partner associated with the customer. In this example, see a partner named Acme in CustomerCustomField3.

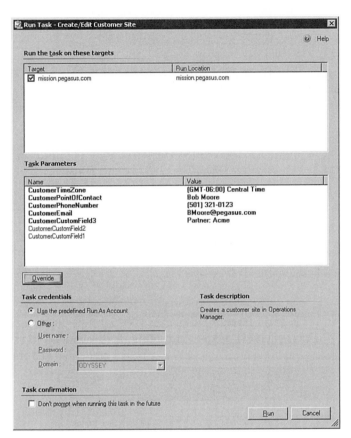

FIGURE 21.15   The Create/Edit Customer Site task enables features of the Service Provider management pack.

Within 5 minutes of running the Create/Edit Customer Site task (Figure 21.15), a rule from the Service Provider management pack reads the information from the customer server's Registry and writes it to the Operational database. The override data entered in the Create/Edit Customer Site task then becomes visible in the details pane of the Customer Health view. Figure 21.16 shows the Customer Health view of the Pegasus Corp. site after successful customer site approval.

FIGURE 21.16   Customer service details are exposed in the Customer Health view.

Discovering Customer Computers and Network Devices

Until this point, only the customer's Essentials server is involved in the ROM scenario. This Essentials server is fully monitored and manageable by the ROM management group due to its gateway server role. If the Essentials server is the only computer that the ROM service provider will manage, no additional discovery is necessary. However, usually and hopefully, there are other customer computers and/or network devices, such as routers and switches, that will be also be managed by the ROM service provider.

To begin managing other computers or devices, the ROM service provider must run one or more discovery tasks against the customer network, using the standard Discovery Wizard in the Administration space. When running an advanced discovery task, select the management server in the drop-down list that is the customer Essentials server. Figure 21.17 shows the mission.pegasus.com management server selected to perform the discovery.

The remote computer and network device discovery function in the ROM solution works exactly like the same-named function in the OpsMgr gateway server solution. Using the Discovery Wizard, scan for and select customer objects to manage in the same manner as if Essentials servers were just OpsMgr gateway servers. Microsoft designed both Essentials servers in Service Provider Mode and OpsMgr gateway servers to operate in a remote, untrusted domain, without direct network connectivity to the ROM management group.

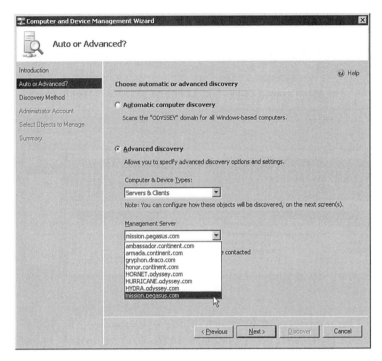

FIGURE 21.17   Using the Discovery Wizard to discover computers on the customer network.

After the ROM management group discovers the customer objects, data begins to appear in the Customer Alerts, Computers, and Customers (diagram) views in the Service Provider view folder. If the Essentials management group was already managing a customer computer, the Agent Component will be dual-homed. Monitoring of customer SNMP network devices is proxied by the Essentials server or another designated customer watcher node. Figure 21.18 demonstrates using the Find Now filter in the Customer Alerts view folder to look for Exchange server alerts from customer computers.

Configuring Custom and Value-Add Features

There likely will be some post-configuration tasks you will want to perform in the ROM management group after discovering customer computers and devices. These will be customizations to the management group that provide value to the customer. The next sections cover setting up each of these features:

▶ Creating user roles for customer and/or partner staff in order to securely access the Web console and see only objects in their site(s)

▶ Enabling Notification actions for ROM Subject Matter Experts (SMEs) and customer and/or partner contacts

▶ Assigning failover gateways to customer Essentials servers

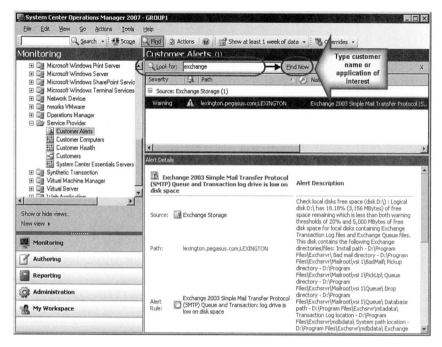

FIGURE 21.18   Filter on customer name or application of interest in the Customer Alerts view.

User Roles for Customers and Partners

A big value-add to the ROM solution is the Web console, which in the System Center family is only available with the Operations Manager product. The Essentials product lacks a Web console equivalent, much less one that can aggregate the views of many Essentials servers. The role-based security in OpsMgr 2007 is a perfect framework to create profiles that easily and securely offer up a customer or partner view of its share of the ROM solution. Figure 21.19 shows the ROM Web console as viewed by a partner with two customer networks in management (in our case Draco and Pegasus).

Figure 21.20 shows a user role being created for the Customer Pegasus Corp. Essentials customer site. The Read-Only Operator Role or the Operator Role might be appropriate for both customers and partners. On the Group Scope tab of the User Role Properties, select the customer group that is a subgroup of the All Customers group. Click the View group members link (circled in upper right) to confirm the identity of the objects the user role will have access to.

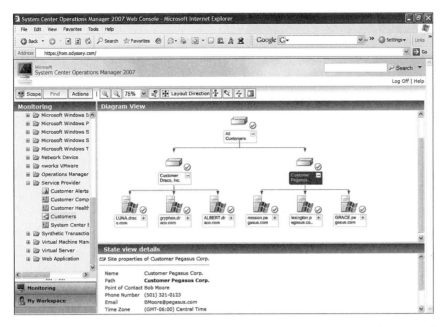

FIGURE 21.19   The ROM Web console presents an aggregate view of a partner's customers.

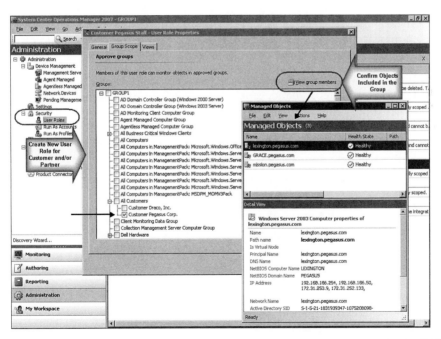

FIGURE 21.20   Creating a user role for a customer or partner to use with the Web console.

Real World—No Customer Names in Management Packs

The ROM service provider must take care in naming management packs created in the ROM instance of OpsMgr. When managed customer computers join the ROM management group, the names of all management packs in the management group may appear in the Operations Manager event log of the customer computer. To avoid one customer seeing the name of another customer in the name of a management pack, use a customer-neutral naming scheme for ROM management packs.

Notifications for SMEs and Customer and Partner Contacts

To expedite staff workflow, the ROM service provider may want to enable custom notification actions to designated Subject Matter Experts (SMEs) on particular advanced aspects of managed customer environments. As an example, if you know a predicted condition will be beyond the capability of engineers staffing the NOC to resolve, you can speed issue resolution by prenotifying SMEs before the NOC staff contacts them.

Each customer's Essentials server has its own notification actions that can originate from alerts occurring in the Essentials management group. The ROM scenario does not utilize the local notification features of Essentials, and any notifications arising from managing a customer (such as an email, instant message, SMS text message, or a command-line process) are launched from the ROM service provider instance of OpsMgr. An exception is if the customer or managed services partner actively uses Essentials for workstation management. In that case, alerts from the Client OS and Information Worker management packs, which may not be under management by ROM, can be enabled to send notifications directly from the Essentials server.

Customers or partners may want the opportunity to leverage the notification features of OpsMgr. In the ROM Master Hoster scenario, generally neither the customer nor the partner will desire an automatic notification feature, because freedom from such alerts is a reason for engaging the Master Hoster! However, there may be situations where a notification action is appropriate for one or more customer site groups. OpsMgr Notification Subscriptions make this is easy to implement.

Figure 21.21 shows two steps in the Notification Subscription Properties Wizard. Configure the wizard's User Role Filter to limit the groups and classes available for approval to those already granted to the user role for the customer. Doing so makes only the customer site group available for selection on the Groups page of the wizard. This linkage efficiently associates the Notification Subscription to the scope of the user role already created for access to the Web console.

Failover for Customer Gateways

If the ROM service provider has more than one Internet-facing gateway server, assign each customer Essentials server a failover gateway server. Having a failover gateway server specified for a customer Essentials server permits the primary gateway server for that customer to be restarted, or be otherwise down for maintenance, without affecting monitoring uptime for the customer.

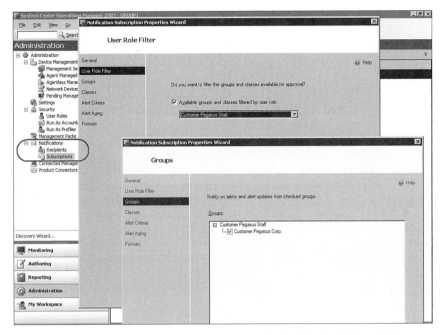

FIGURE 21.21   The User Role Filter property of a Notification Subscription.

You cannot make failover assignments for customer Essentials servers in the Operations console or on the customer Essentials server. Rather, you will run a small PowerShell script to make these failover assignments. Run the script on a management server in the ROM management group. We include this PowerShell script on the CD accompanying this book, with the name of GW-Assign-Failover-MS.ps1. Customize the script with the gateway servers and Essentials server appropriate for the environment.

The following example of the GW-Assign-Failover-MS.ps1 script targets customer Essentials server mission.pegasus.com, sets ROM gateway server ambassador.continent.com as the primary gateway server, and the ROM gateway server armada.continent.com as the failover gateway server:

```
$primaryMS = Get-ManagementServer | where {$_.Name –eq 'ambassador.continent.com' }
$failoverMS = Get-ManagementServer | where {$_.Name –eq 'armada.continent.com' }
$agent = Get-Agent | where {$_.Name –eq 'mission.pegasus.com' }
Set-ManagementServer -AgentManagedComputer: $agent -ManagementServer: $primaryMS
-FailoverServer: $failoverMS
```

Summary

Microsoft created Essentials for small and medium business (SMB) customers that have fewer than 500 clients and fewer than 30 servers. Essentials will also be widely used when it becomes bundled with other systems management products and with next-generation "Centro" offerings. Some Essentials owners will seek to outsource some or all server and network device infrastructure management to service providers as part of managed service agreements.

Remote Operations Manager is a solution that leverages the Gateway Server Component of OpsMgr that is present on every Essentials server. ROM can be employed as a central view of customer networks for SMB partners, and also in a Master Hoster mode that further outsources the ROM backend to a multitenant enterprise NOC. A series of procedures is used to securely link up customer networks to the ROM service provider using a mutually trusted CA.

In the next chapter, we go beyond Operations Manager and discuss interoperability with other technologies.

CHAPTER 22

Interoperability

This book has discussed a variety of ways that Operations Manager 2007 (OpsMgr) provides solutions to various business challenges. One of these challenges is effectively monitoring and managing disparate computing and network systems. Although OpsMgr is primarily designed for monitoring Windows-based computers and Microsoft applications and services, many businesses possess dissimilar systems in addition to having Windows servers and desktops. There are also network devices, which form a key part of any Information Technology (IT) infrastructure and should be monitored and maintained as well.

OpsMgr meets this challenge with a variety of methods to monitor and connect to non-Windows systems and network devices as well as to monitor non-Microsoft applications. These capabilities extend monitoring beyond the Windows environment, enabling OpsMgr to perform a much broader role in systems monitoring and management. Here are some points to keep in mind:

▶ Operations Manager uses management packs and connectors as tools to enhance its native capabilities in managing dissimilar systems and devices. This interoperability employs a combination of vendor-created management packs enabling OpsMgr to monitor third-party applications, as well as product connectors that allow OpsMgr to connect to other software systems—including other systems' management products and help desk applications. Additionally, Operations Manager 2007 supports connecting to other OpsMgr management groups, allowing information exchange across very large and possibly geographically remote OpsMgr implementations.

▶ Network device monitoring in OpsMgr is available out of the box, although the monitoring capabilities are somewhat limited in this version. You can enhance the native monitoring capabilities by using Simple Network Management Protocol (SNMP) trap monitoring (discussed in Chapter 17, "Monitoring Network Devices") or by incorporating third-party products to further augment network device monitoring.

▶ Third-party OpsMgr-compatible agents facilitate monitoring non-Windows operating systems such as HP-UX, Linux, and UNIX, to name a few. These agents extend the capability of OpsMgr 2007, enabling effective monitoring of non-Microsoft operating systems and applications, with their status reflected in the OpsMgr Operations console. The data collected using these third-party agents is also available to write to the data warehouse, for reporting purposes.

In this chapter, we examine the processes to connect two OpsMgr management groups together using the Connected Management Group architecture, which is a new feature in OpsMgr. We will also discuss the various product connectors that allow OpsMgr to connect to other systems management applications and help desk systems, highlighting the process one should take to configure one of these product connectors.

We will examine the third-party application management packs available at the time of writing this book. We will also look at the methods to monitor non-Windows systems and network devices, using some of the available third-party solutions to enhance the monitoring available with OpsMgr.

Talking to the Rest of the World

Although Microsoft designed OpsMgr primarily for monitoring and maintaining Windows-based systems and Microsoft applications, it did not limit the product just to these systems. Microsoft intended that OpsMgr be able to communicate with disparate systems and monitor devices that do not support an OpsMgr agent.

Many businesses use a variety of operating systems to provide IT services. These systems may include Windows, Linux, UNIX, and HP-UX, among others, and the operating systems may be installed on a variety of hardware, including Intel-based systems, IBM AS400, and Sun machines. Not only are there heterogeneous systems, but network devices such as switches and routers also play a critical part in any network infrastructure. With that in mind, a robust monitoring solution should provide the ability to monitor and connect to many different types of systems, minimizing the need to maintain multiple monitoring solutions and processes for monitoring all these systems.

Comparing Operations Manager 2007 to Other Enterprise Monitoring Solutions

Although it is beyond the scope of this book to compare each enterprise console to OpsMgr 2007's functionality, it is relevant to position the advantages of Operations Manager versus other enterprise solutions. Why should you use OpsMgr instead of another management tool? Here are the primary areas where OpsMgr excels:

▶ Product knowledge created by the Microsoft product groups and Microsoft Consulting Services (MCS) is included in each of the Microsoft management packs.

▶ The Operations Manager Connector Framework allows OpsMgr to connect to other systems for integration with other enterprise monitoring solutions.

▶ OpsMgr integrates with no-cost hardware management packs from Dell, Hewlett Packard, IBM, and other hardware vendors.

▶ OpsMgr supports customized management packs, which further extend its capabilities. We discuss this further in Chapter 23, "Developing Management Packs and Reports."

▶ Third-party organizations provide management packs, which increase OpsMgr's monitoring capabilities.

Although OpsMgr is able to act as the "manager of managers," Microsoft understands that in many situations other management systems are already in place. Therefore, OpsMgr offers the ability to connect to third-party management systems such as IBM Tivoli and HP OpenView Operations (HP-OVO) using connectors written by Microsoft or third parties. These connectors use a Web service–based architecture and enable OpsMgr (or earlier versions of Microsoft Operations Manager [MOM]) to connect to third-party applications.

Using this design allows full alert forwarding and synchronization between OpsMgr and any third-party system. Therefore, alerts generated in OpsMgr can be raised in the connected system, and vice versa. Once an alert is raised, it can be updated automatically from either system and the update will synchronize with the connected system.

With previous versions of MOM, organizations implementing multiple management groups could create tiered management group infrastructures, enabling the creation of a structured monitoring and management solution in very large and complex environments.

This functionality differs in OpsMgr, and the idea of a tiered infrastructure no longer exists. Instead, we have the concept of *connected management groups*, which is a logical relationship defined using the Operations console. The following section looks at the changes in multiple management group structure in OpsMgr, and the methods to configure management group connections.

Operations Manager–Connected Management Groups

In large or complex environments, it may be necessary to utilize more than one OpsMgr management group to perform effective monitoring. Earlier versions of Operations Manager implemented a tiered architecture, where alert and status data rolled up the tiers, enabling presentation of data from multiple management groups in a single MOM Operators console. We show an example of a tiered management group in Figure 22.1.

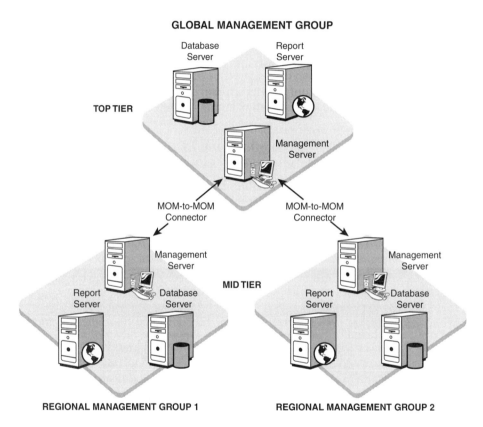

FIGURE 22.1   A MOM 2005 tiered management group.

Although the tiered configuration model was very useful, it had its limitations:

▶ One aspect of the tiered architecture is the alert data itself was copied from the source management group to the destination management group.

In addition to the network impact, copying the data meant duplicate data would appear in the console and reports. To prevent this data from appearing in the console and the reporting data warehouse, you needed to create a dedicated management group that acted as a top level for the tiered infrastructure.

▶ Adding a top-level management group increases cost and complexity to a MOM infrastructure; this is yet another management group, which itself must then be monitored and maintained.

With OpsMgr 2007, these tiered management groups no longer exist. Microsoft has replaced tiered management groups with the concept of connected management groups. The title itself suggests its function—a method by which you can connect management groups without the need to physically copy data from one management group to another. Using connected management groups eliminates the requirement to dedicate a separate management group to act as a top-level management group; this saves time, expense, and future management overhead. We should note, however, that you still have the capability to configure a tiered structure if required in OpsMgr 2007, using the PowerShell Command Shell. However, this configuration is not common, and we will not cover it in this chapter.

You can view an example of a connected management group infrastructure in Figure 22.2.

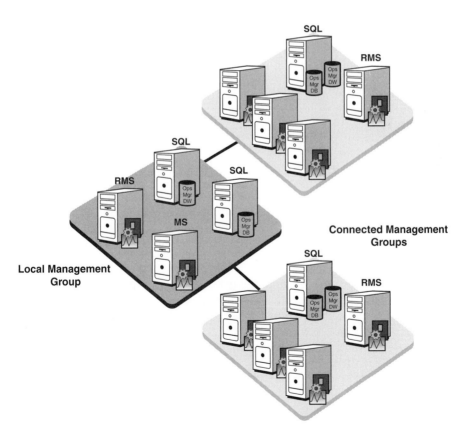

FIGURE 22.2   Connected management groups.

Using connected management groups in this manner, the Operations console is configured to display alert and status data from other connected management groups. After you
configure the console this way, each time it is loaded or refreshed it makes a web request
to the Root Management Server (RMS) of the selected connected management group. Alert
data is identified and sent back to the RMS of the requesting management group, and can
be viewed in the Operations console. No alert or status data is permanently stored in the
requesting management group; it is simply presented for viewing in the console.

In earlier versions of Operations Manager, you configured tiered management group infrastructures using a graphical user interface (GUI), the Administrator console. With OpsMgr
2007, you establish a connected management group connection using the Operations
console, and you use the Command Shell to define configurations that are more complex.
After establishing a connected management group connection, you can configure the
Operations console to request data from the connected management group.

Advantages of Connected Management Groups Versus a Tiered Configuration

Viewing the data rather than storing it not only removes the need to replicate data across
management groups, but it also means that the data is much more accurate. With a tiered
configuration, it is easy for alert data to become out of date. We can illustrate this by
looking at a problem occurring in a low-level management group that rolls up through
the tiers. By the time it reaches the top, the issue may have been resolved, yet it could
take some time for that resolution to synchronize throughout the infrastructure.

With OpsMgr connected management groups, outdated information is no longer of
concern. The Operations console issues a new web query each time it is loaded or
refreshed, so only the most current information appears. We not only have less overhead,
we have information that is up to date!

Security Implications

Data viewed in the Operations console is also subject to a user's role scope in the
connected management group (we discuss security and user roles in Chapter 11, "Securing
Operations Manager 2007"). Having user roles means the user running the Operations
console that is requesting data can only see the data for which he or she is scoped in the
source management group.

We can illustrate how roles work across connected management groups with an example.
We have a user connected to the GROUP1 management group (located in the ODYSSEY
domain in Plano) that requests all alerts from the GROUP2 management group in the
ECLIPSE domain, located in Frisco. If the user role in GROUP2 is scoped to Exchange
Servers only, that user sees the Exchange Server data from GROUP2, regardless of his or
her user role scope in GROUP1.

Establishing a Connection

In this section, we will look at the process of creating an OpsMgr management group connection using the Operations console.

We will view the data using the Operations console in the GROUP2 management group located in the ECLIPSE Active Directory domain, and we will connect to the GROUP1 management group located in the ODYSSEY domain. Here are the steps to follow:

1. The first stage to connecting to a management group is to validate both the local (connecting) and the connected management groups. In this case, the GROUP2 management group is the local management group because it is initiating the connection; therefore, GROUP1 is the connected management group.

    We will open the Operations console in each management group in turn and validate there are managed agents and that there are no critical alerts active before we attempt to connect. This ensures that any major issues are resolved before we connect the two management groups.

    This process is not essential, but we recommend it as a best practice because it ensures no significant issues exist in either management group that may be ignored or missed.

    We will start with the Operations console in the GROUP1 management group. You can see the status of this management group in Figure 22.3.

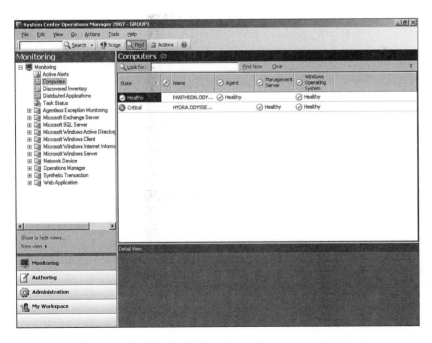

FIGURE 22.3   The GROUP1 Operations console.

2. As you can see, currently Hydra (the RMS) is in a critical state. If we look at the Health Explorer, shown in Figure 22.4, we can see that the SQL Server Reporting service on Hydra is stopped.

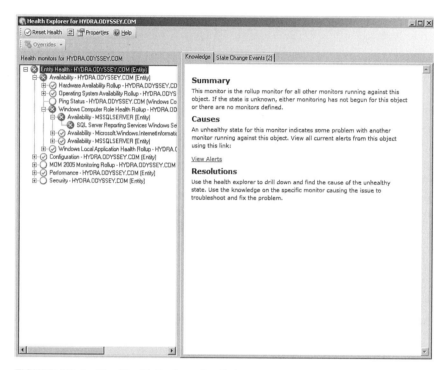

FIGURE 22.4   The Health Explorer for Hydra.

Before we continue, we should resolve this issue. In this case, we simply start the service to resolve the issue.

3. Now that we have resolved the issues with the GROUP1 management group, we can look at the GROUP2 Operations console. Figure 22.5 displays the status of the GROUP2 management group.

You can see that GROUP2 is working correctly and is healthy. It therefore does not need any action.

NOTE

Determining Health Is More Complex with Larger Environments

The process of checking management group health becomes more difficult as you deploy more agents. In the event that not all monitored machines can be brought to a healthy state, particular attention should be paid to resolving issues on OpsMgr management servers and the RMS in particular.

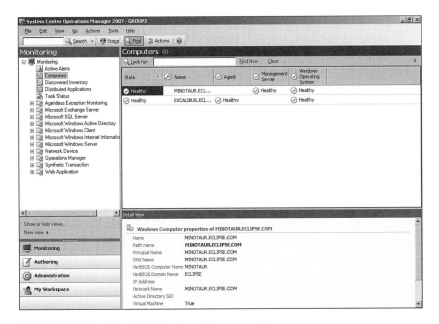

FIGURE 22.5   The GROUP2 Operations console.

After we validate the two management groups and resolve all issues, we connect the management groups. You will connect the management groups using the Operations console in the local management group. In our case, we will carry out the tasks in this example using the Minotaur server in the ECLIPSE domain, because this RMS (GROUP2) is initiating the management group connection.

Prerequisite Tasks

Before connecting management groups, it is important to carry out several prerequisite tasks to ensure that the process of establishing the connection is successful:

▶ Ensure that you can resolve the Fully Qualified Domain Name (FQDN) of the RMS in the connected management group (in this case, HYDRA.ODYSSEY.COM). This FQDN should be able to be resolved from the RMS in the local domain.

In our example, we need to ensure that MINOTAUR.ECLIPSE.COM can resolve this FQDN. To ensure this is successful in our environment, we will need to create a secondary DNS zone for the ODYSSEY.COM domain.

TIP

Installing and Configuring DNS

You can find information on installing and configuring Domain Name Services (DNS) at http://technet2.microsoft.com/windowsserver/en/technologies/featured/dns/default.mspx.

▶ Once DNS resolution is working, add the SDK and Config accounts to the Operations Manager Administrators role in Operations Manager. Use the Operations console to add the accounts to this role.

We recommend you create a global security group in each domain. Add the SDK and Config accounts to this group, and then add the other domain's security group to the local domain you are in. For our environment, we will add the ODYSSEY group to the Operations Manager Administrators user role in GROUP2, and vice versa. If you are dealing with domains that do not have a trust established, you will need to create an account in the connected management group to use to connect.

Now perform the following steps to update the user role:

1. Open the Operations console and navigate to the Administration space.
2. Click Security -> User Roles and then open the Properties window for the Operations Manager Administrators user role. Figure 22.6 shows the Properties window.

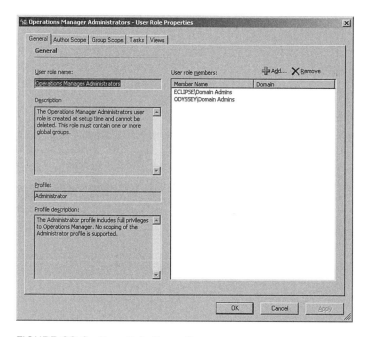

FIGURE 22.6   User Role Properties.

3. Click the Add... button and locate the domain security group containing the accounts for the SDK and Config services and then select them (you must use a domain security group because this user role does not support adding single accounts). Click OK, and then click OK again.

Because we are connecting to a management group in a separate domain, we need to iden-tify the SDK and Config service accounts for the connected management group. In this case, the account ODYSSEY\OM_SDK is running both services and is the one we need to specify.

Establishing a Connection

Now that we have carried out the prerequisites, we can establish the connection.

1. Open the Operations console, if it is not already running, and then open the Administration space.

2. Click the Connected Management Groups node. The right pane currently is empty, because there are no connected management groups.

3. Right-click in the right-side pane and select Add Management Group. This displays the Add Management Group window.

4. At the Add Management Group window, we will add the name of the management group, which in this case is **GROUP1**. We will also add the FQDN of the RMS of this management group, **HYDRA.ODYSSEY.COM**.

5. We will select the radio button Other user account to establish the connection. Once this radio button is selected, the User name, Password, and Domain boxes will appear. Here, we will enter the SDK service account information from the ODYSSEY domain (**ODYSSEY\OM_SDK**).

   Figure 22.7 shows the completed Add Management Group window.

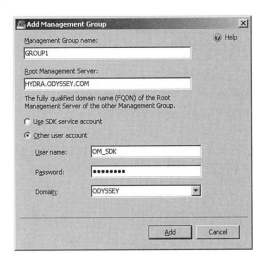

FIGURE 22.7   The completed Add Management Group window.

6. Once the connection is established, it will appear in the right-side pane. We show the connection in Figure 22.8.

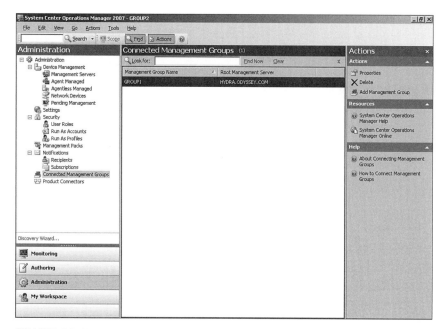

FIGURE 22.8   Connection established.

Viewing Connected Data

To view alerts, you must scope the user account in the local management group to data in the connected management group. If the two management groups are in separate domains with no trust relationship, you will need to create separate accounts in the connected management group for the local management group to use. In our environment, a trust is in place, so we must simply scope the account we are running the Operations console as in the local management group (GROUP2) to data in the connected management group (GROUP1).

You will accomplish this using the User Roles node in the Administration space in the Operations console. We discussed user role scoping in Chapter 11. For our example, we will scope the account in the ECLIPSE domain (GROUP2 management group) to see all data in the GROUP1 management group, so we will simply add the account to the Operations Manager Operators user role in GROUP1. Of course, you could limit the data accessed by the account by creating a new user role scope.

After you correctly configure the user scoping, the Show Connected Alerts button becomes visible on the toolbar at the top of the Operations console window.

When you click the Show Connected Alerts button, you are prompted to enter a user account to connect to the connected management group and retrieve alerts. Once you enter the details and click OK, relevant alerts from the connected management group are displayed.

Figure 22.9 shows the Show Connected Alerts button and an example of a connected management group alert.

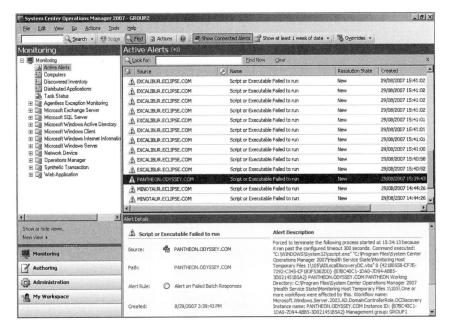

FIGURE 22.9   A connected management group alert.

TIP

The OpsMgr 2007 Deployment Guide

The Operations Manager 2007 Deployment Guide documents the process of implementing connected management groups. You can download the Deployment Guide from the System Center Operations Manager 2007 Product Documentation center at http://go.microsoft.com/fwlink/?LinkId=85414.

Product Connectors

In addition to connecting to other OpsMgr management groups and requesting data, the capability to connect to third-party management suites and help desk systems is critical to ensuring OpsMgr can fit into an existing management infrastructure.

Product connectors pass alert data between OpsMgr and the third-party management or help desk systems, allowing the alerts that appear in the OpsMgr Operations console to display in a different management system or be used to log calls in a help desk system. Most connectors support bidirectional communication, which means that alerts and alert updates are passed both to and from OpsMgr and the third-party system.

In MOM 2000 and MOM 2005, product connectors used the MOM Connector Framework (MCF) to exchange data. The Operations Manager Connector Framework (OMCF) replaces the MCF in OpsMgr 2007.

The process for selecting which alerts are transferred has been improved in OpsMgr 2007; it now utilizes the extremely powerful Notification Workflow process (explained in detail in Chapter 14, "Monitoring with Operations Manager"). The Notification Workflow allows you to configure the subscriptions linked to the product connector, using the Product Connectors node in the Administration space in the Operations console. The Product Connectors node is where you subscribe to alerts, which marks them to be forwarded to the product connector and beyond to the third-party system.

The significance of this is that unless you specifically add an alert to the subscription, the alert is not forwarded! This functionality was far less granular in MOM 2000 and MOM 2005. Figure 22.10 shows the Product Connector Properties window. You can click the Add... button to create a subscription, configuring the subscription in a manner similar to how you create email subscriptions.

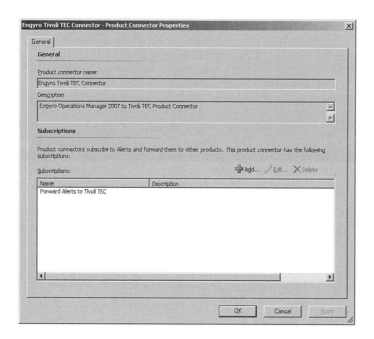

FIGURE 22.10   Product Connector Properties window.

These new capabilities allow OpsMgr product connectors to be more configurable and precise than in MOM 2000 and MOM 2005; when properly configured, product connectors should reduce the number of false and unnecessary alerts passed to the connected system, thus reducing network traffic and storage requirements.

We will look at connectors for two of the most popular management appliances seen in the field: HP-OVO and IBM Tivoli. We will use the connectors developed by Engyro for the examples in this chapter, because in our opinion they offer the best balance between supportability, ease of configuration, and value for the money. We will, however, also provide information on other product connectors that are available.

TIP

Microsoft Purchase of Engyro

Microsoft acquired Engyro, a privately held company, in June 2007. As a Microsoft subsidiary, Engyro will continue to sell the Engyro product connectors. Microsoft's acquisition furthers its commitment to its customers' long-term need for interoperable solutions.

Although Microsoft will continue to support the existing Engyro MOM 2005 solutions, it will no longer sell MOM 2005–related connectors, agents, or management packs. Microsoft will support existing Engyro MOM 2005 Connector customers with rights to upgrade to the Operations Manager 2007 Connectors.

Connecting to HP-OVO

The Microsoft Engyro product connector for HP-OVO is very simple to configure. It supports a number of advanced features, such as deployment into a redundant configuration and automatic failover capability. The connector consists of two major components:

- A product connector, which runs on a Windows system with network connectivity to the Operations Manager RMS.

- A web services daemon (EXD), installed on the HP-OVO server. The daemon runs in either Windows Server/Workstation 2000/2003 or HP-UX (a version of the web services daemon is supplied for both).

In addition to the two main components, there is also the Connector Management console, which you access from within the OpsMgr Operations console, and a management pack that helps OpsMgr manage and monitor the connector. Finally, there is a set of OVO templates for the transmission and management of data between OpsMgr and OVO.

After the product connector is installed, it is managed through the OpsMgr Operations console. Figure 22.11 shows Engyro as a node in the Monitoring space of the Operations console.

The screen displayed in Figure 22.11 is the initial screen you see when opening the EngyroOVOConfig screen. This screen shows you the overall status of the connector.

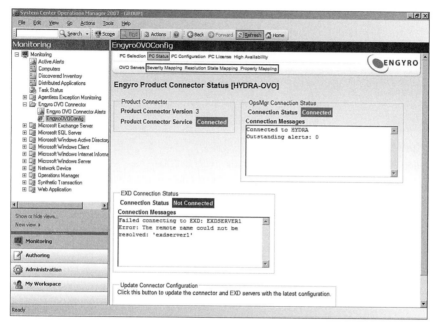

FIGURE 22.11   OVO connector management.

Along the top of this initial screen are a number of tabs used to configure the connector. The most important tabs to consider are the Severity Mapping, Resolution State Mapping, and Property Mapping tabs. These tabs configure how the alert fields from OpsMgr map to alerts in OVO.

Selecting Severity Mapping in Figure 22.11 opens the Severity Mapping tab screen shown in Figure 22.12. You can see three preconfigured severity mappings displayed here, which help in mapping OpsMgr severities to ones recognized by OVO. Using this screen, you can create additional mappings as required by selecting the Add Mapping button. HP-OVO and OpsMgr query the mapping information directly, so if you update any information in these systems, the connector configuration screens will reflect those changes shortly.

To summarize, the Engyro HP-OVO connector provides bidirectional communication for transmission of alert data from OpsMgr to HP-OVO. This functionality facilitates integrating OpsMgr with an existing HP management infrastructure.

Connecting to Tivoli TEC

Connecting to Tivoli using the Engyro connector is very similar to the process of using the OVO connector. The components of the product connector are the same as those of the OVO connector, except that this connector comes packaged with Tivoli TEC classes and rules to assist in passing data between the two systems.

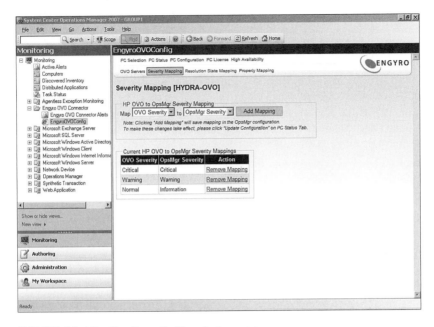

FIGURE 22.12   The Severity Mapping screen.

Again, once you install the connector, it is managed using the OpsMgr Operations console with the EngyroTECConfig screen, as shown in Figure 22.13.

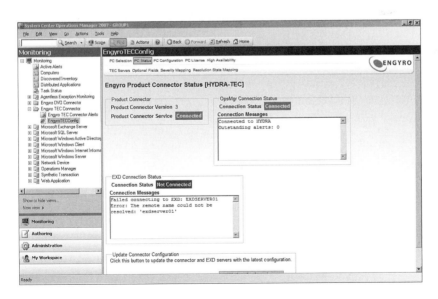

FIGURE 22.13   TEC connector management.

Using the OVO and TEC Connectors with Different Versions of Operations Manager

It is important to be aware of the following when using the Engyro OVO or Tivoli TEC connectors:

▶ MOM 2005 allowed you to specify data in the alert rules, such as OVO and TEC queue information, using custom alert fields.

▶ Using custom alert fields is not possible in OpsMgr 2007, because management packs are sealed and these alert fields are not currently presented as an override.

We expect Microsoft to address this in a future product update or version release.

Similar to the Engyro HP-OVO connector, the Engyro Tivoli connector provides bidirectional communication and allows you to integrate OpsMgr within an existing management infrastructure using Tivoli TEC.

Overview of Third-Party Connectors

The product connectors we have covered here are by no means the only product connectors available; they are simply the ones we have chosen to look at in detail in this chapter. This section looks at other connectors available and specifies the versions of Operations Manager these connectors support. Table 22.1 lists the connectors currently available for MOM 2000/2005 and OpsMgr 2007. Appendix E, "Reference URLs," includes live links to these connectors.

TABLE 22.1   Connector Compatibility with Versions of Operations Manager

Connector	MOM 2000/2005	OpsMgr 2007
Engyro OpsMgr to BMC Remedy ARS Product Connector	X	X
Engyro OpsMgr to HP OpenView Operations Product Connector	X	X
Engyro OpsMgr to Tivoli TEC Product Connector	X	X
Zenprise BlackBerry Connector for OpsMgr 2007		X
Zenprise Exchange Connector for OpsMgr 2007		X
message master® Enterprise Alert 2007	X	X
CA SPECTRUM Connector for MOM	X	
eXc Software BMC Patrol	X	X
eXc Software IBM Tivoli	X	X
eXc Software CA UniCenter	X	X
eXc Software HP Open-View Connector	X	X
Micromuse NetCool Connector—connectors available from IBM and eXc Software	X	

TABLE 22.1   Continued

Connector	MOM 2000/2005	OpsMgr 2007
eXc Nagios Connector	X	X
Remedy ARS Connector—connectors available from Engyro and eXc Software	X	X
MOM-CRM Connector for Microsoft Dynamics 3.0	X	
AppManager Connector for MOM	X	
NetIQ Extended Management Pack (XMP) AppManager Connector for MOM	X	
OpalisRobot	X	
InTrust Connector for Microsoft MOM	X	
BMC Impact Integration for MOM	X	X
MOM Integration for BMC Patrol	X	X
EMC Smarts InCharge Connector	X	
iWave Integrator OpsMgr to Amdocs Clarify Integration	X	X
iWave Integrator MOM 2005 to CA Solve for z/OS Integration	X	
iWave Integrator MOM 2005 to CA Unicenter Integration	X	
iWave Integrator OpsMgr 2007 to CA NSM		X
iWave Integrator OpsMgr 2007 to CA UniCenter Service Desk		X
iWave Integrator MOM 2005 to HP OpenView Network Node Manager (NNM) Integration	X	
iWave Integrator OpsMgr to HP OpenView Operations (OVO) Integration	X	X
iWave Integrator OpsMgr to Peregrine Service Center Integration	X	X
iWave Integrator OpsMgr to Remedy ARS Integration	X	X
iWave Integrator OpsMgr to Tivoli Enterprise Console (TEC) Integration	X	X
iWave Integrator OpsMgr to Tivoli Information/Management for z/OS Integration	X	X
iWave Integrator MOM 2005 to Tivoli Net View Integration	X	
iWave Integrator MOM 2005 to Tivoli Net View for OS/390 Integration	X	
iWave Integrator MOM 2005 to Tivoli Service Desk Integration	X	
iWave Integrator MOM 2005 to Vantive Integration	X	
iWave Integrator OpsMgr 2007 to Microsoft Operations Manager		X

As you can see from Table 22.1, currently there is a larger selection of connectors available for MOM 2000/2005 than there are for OpsMgr. This is not a surprise, because the product is relatively new. Because Microsoft redesigned the connector framework components in this version Operations Manager, third-party vendors will have to alter their connectors to function correctly in OpsMgr 2007. As the OpsMgr product matures, more connectors will become available.

As we mention in the "Managing Non-Windows Systems" section later in this chapter, eXc Software already has developed a large number of management packs and virtual agents available for OpsMgr 2007. Table 22.1 shows that the company also has developed connectors for BMC, Tivoli, UniCenter, and OpenView. Additionally, all of the eXc MOM 2005 management packs and virtual agents are now available in OpsMgr 2007 versions, including a variety of different network device manufacturers such as Cisco and 3Com, non-Windows operating systems, and enterprise applications such as Oracle. eXc has redesigned its base framework (which hosts all of the virtual agents) with a goal of seamless integration with OpsMgr 2007.

The other provider of a wide variety of third-party options is iWave. iWave provides a large number of different connectors for MOM 2000 and 2005 and has recently released connectors for OpsMgr 2007. The iWave Integrator product was created in 1993, and the iWave Integrator team is well versed in enterprise management applications and is able to implement fully bidirectional, real-time integrations in as little as 3 to 5 days.

Monitoring Using Third-Party Management Packs

In addition to the multitude of Microsoft application and operating system management packs listed in the System Center Pack Catalog (available at http://go.microsoft.com/fwlink/?linkid=71124), third-party hardware and software vendors have created a variety of no-cost management packs for monitoring their hardware and Windows-based software. The next sections highlight some of these management packs.

HP Server Management Packs for OpsMgr 2007

Hewlett-Packard (HP) has always been on the forefront of new technology, particularly in the business server arena in recent years with the release of the HP ProLiant and Integrity server lines.

HP provides its own software for monitoring hardware (HP Systems Insight Manager or HP SIM), but the company also recognizes the value offered by OpsMgr in integrating monitoring into a single console.

With that in mind, HP has released the HP Server management packs for OpsMgr 2007. There are two distinct management packs: one to monitor HP's ProLiant range of servers, and the other to monitor HP's Integrity servers.

The monitoring utilizes HP's System Management Agents, which are installed when building an HP server using their SmartStart deployment software (the HP management packs support SmartStart server agent versions 7.5 and above).

After installing the HP management packs, you can view the status of your HP servers in the Operations console. The management packs also offer a number of HP server–specific tasks to make managing HP systems easier. These tasks include the ability to access the HP Systems Management Homepage (web-based server hardware information) from the Operations console and the ability to discover information about an iLO (Integrated Lights-Out board) in a server and then connect to it—also from the Operations console.

Providing visibility of server hardware further enhances the monitoring performed by OpsMgr, extending its capabilities beyond the operating system and application layers to the physical hardware layer.

HP also offers a separate management pack for monitoring its StorageWorks line, further extending Operations Manager monitoring to SAN hardware and external storage and backup devices.

Figure 22.14 displays an example of monitoring using the State view of the HP Server Hardware management pack. Chapter 17 includes several other examples of using the HP management packs.

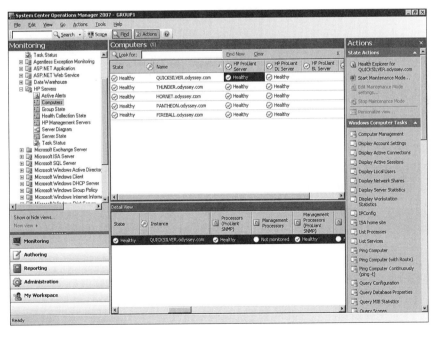

FIGURE 22.14   HP State view.

The HP management packs are available from the HP Global website at http://h18004. www1.hp.com/products/servers/management/mom2007/index.html.

Dell Server Management Pack

Similar to HP, Dell has made its server hardware information available through OpsMgr to enable better visibility of your IT environment.

The Dell management pack works by using the Windows Management Instrumentation (WMI) information published by its own OpenManage systems management agents to populate OpsMgr. The management pack collects this information from monitored machines and reflects their statuses based on the information collected. To utilize this management pack, the agents must be running version 5.2 or greater of the Dell OpenManage software. Using an earlier version could result in script errors and a failure of hardware monitoring on the affected machines.

TIP

Early Versions of OpenManage Generate Errors

We have seen situations where Dell servers create a large number of "Script or Executable has failed to run..." errors on the Dell management pack when the version of OpenManage is not at least 5.2. Specifically we have had this error with versions 1.8 and 1.9.

The Dell management pack enables integrating Dell PowerEdge server hardware information into the OpsMgr Operations console. The management pack comes with a variety of Dell-specific views you can use to quickly locate server hardware problems and assist in resolving these problems.

Figure 22.15 displays an example of monitoring using the State view of the Dell management pack.

Because the Dell management pack is fully integrated into Operations Manager, other standard views are available. Figure 22.16 shows Health Explorer monitoring information captured using the Dell management pack.

The Dell management pack is available at http://support.dell.com/support/downloads/ download.aspx?c=us&l=en&s=gen&releaseid=R158716&formatcnt=1&libid=0&fileid= 212055.

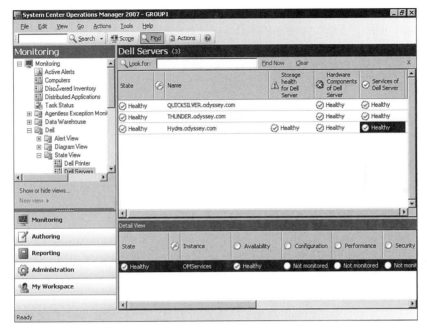

FIGURE 22.15   Dell State view.

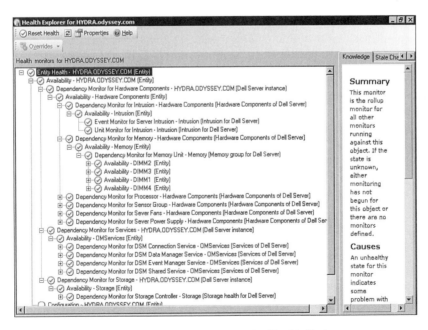

FIGURE 22.16   Dell Hardware monitored in the Health Explorer.

IBM Director Management Pack

As with both HP and Dell, IBM also provides a hardware monitoring management pack for its xSeries Windows servers.

This management pack utilizes the Director agents deployed when installing a server with IBM's Server deployment software.

NOTE

Recommended Director Agent Version

We recommend that you install version 5.20 or above of the Director agent on all managed servers prior to importing the IBM Director management pack.

The IBM Director management pack (which is sometimes referred to as the IBM Upward Integration Management Pack) provides server hardware status information via the Operations console. Similar to other hardware management packs, it enables monitoring to be extended beyond the software level.

IBM also provides a management pack for monitoring its BladeCenter chassis.

More information on the two management packs is available at http://publib. boulder.ibm.com/infocenter/eserver/v1r2/index.jsp?topic=/einfo/icmain.htm.

Unisys ES7000 Management Pack

The Unisys management pack for its ES7000 hardware enables you to monitor the Service Processors on your ES7000 systems for information about system hardware alerts and status, including partition hardware health information.

You must install the OpsMgr agent software on the Unisys system, and the Service Processor must be running either Server Sentinel 2.0 or higher, or Unisys Server Management Services 1.0 or higher. Remember that there can be a delay of up to 20 minutes after you import and configure the management pack before the Operations console will display the new components. Available views include Active Alerts, Diagram, Partition Health, and Partition State. Figure 22.17 shows alerts running on a ES7000 system.

You will need to register with Unisys to get access for the download. You can download the management pack from https://www.support.unisys.com/pcproducts/ InterfaceProducts/home.htm.

Citrix Presentation Server Management Pack

Since MOM 2005, Citrix has provided management packs for its MetaFrame and Presentation Server range of products.

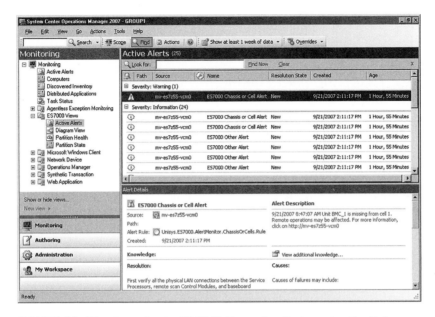

FIGURE 22.17   Alerts for the ES7000 Enterprise Series using the Unisys management pack.

The new Citrix management pack for OpsMgr 2007 facilitates the monitoring of Citrix Presentation Server 4.0 and above for Windows servers. The management pack consists of a variety of rules, scripts, and monitors used to detect potential issues, configuration points, and faults with the Citrix Presentation Server platform. Similar to most of the Microsoft-provided management packs, the Citrix management pack includes best-practice and configuration information and an excellent knowledge base along with the monitoring content.

You can download the Citrix management pack from MyCitrix. You must have an account with Citrix to download the management pack.

Using Notifications to Communicate with Other Applications

If you are interested in integrating OpsMgr with your help desk solution to create tickets based on OpsMgr alerts, we developed a technique that may lead you in the right direction. In our particular case, we wanted to create tickets in the Altiris help desk product (Altiris Helpdesk) based on specific alerts that occurred in OpsMgr.

Doing some web searches, we found a command-line tool to create help desk tickets for the Altiris Helpdesk product at http://juice.altiris.com/download/612/create-an-incident-using-a-command-line-tool. We downloaded this tool and determined the following as the required syntax:

```
CreateWorkitem -u:user -p:password -d:domain -h:host -w:workerGUID
➥-o:objectGUID -t:title -c:comment -x:URLtext -l:URLlink
```

We then started down a path to use OpsMgr's notification capabilities to create a command-line notification. We created a notification and recipient for an alert as described in the following steps:

1. The notification calls the script passing the required information to create the ticket. We used only the required parameters, so the actual syntax was as follows:

```
CreateWorkitem -h:<AltirisServerName> -t:<Alert Name> -c:"Created by OpsMgr
and <Alert Description>" -l:<WebConsole Link>
```

The items in brackets ("<>") are parameters that can be pulled via the dropdown arrow on the screen.

2. Next, we define a recipient using OpsMgr's notification device, and we define a subscription that specifies what alerts the recipients receive. Be sure to install hotfix #937470 (see http://support.microsoft.com/kb/937470) prior to attempting to define subscriptions that will not include all alert criteria.

3. When the alert occurs, it finds the subscription and sends a notification via the command-line script to create the ticket for the alert.

As a potentially simpler approach to this situation, the Altiris product appears to be able to generate help desk tickets based on email sent to a specified email address. The subject of the email provides the ticket name; the body of the email is the body of the ticket. This type of approach would not require command-line notification. The rest of the process would be the same (create a recipient and a subscription to send to this email address).

Managing Non-Windows Systems

In addition to connecting to different management systems such as HP-OVO and Tivoli, as discussed earlier in this chapter, OpsMgr can monitor non-Windows systems (such as machines running Linux, UNIX, other non-Windows operating systems, and network devices) using third-party products.

Out of the box, OpsMgr is able to carry out limited monitoring of non-Windows systems (after all, it is primarily a Windows management suite). You can collect and monitor UNIX Syslogs, and you can add network devices to monitor for them up/down status.

Similar to MOM 2000 and MOM 2005, OpsMgr 2007 supports receiving of SNMP traps, allowing you to monitor devices capable of sending SNMP messages such as network devices, firewall appliances, and so on. We discuss SNMP-level monitoring in Chapter 17. You can also monitor TCP ports in OpsMgr 2007 using the TCP Port management pack template, which we explain in the "TCP Port Monitoring with OpsMgr" section later in this chapter.

In addition to the out-of-the-box functionality mentioned so far, a number of scripts are available that enable OpsMgr to ping devices and generate alerts should the devices not respond. A good example of these scripts is on the SystemCenterForum website at http://systemcenterforum.org/wp-content/uploads/MultiHostPing.zip.

Although this basic level of monitoring is adequate for many companies, it will not be sufficient for everyone. A number of third-party software vendors have developed products augmenting the monitoring capabilities of OpsMgr. The following sections look at four of these products and highlight others that are available. In addition, we will look in more detail at the TCP Port management pack template that is available out of the box in OpsMgr. The products we will discuss are as follows:

▶ eXc Software's management packs and virtual agents

▶ Jalasoft's Xian Network Manager IO

▶ Quest's Management Xtensions

▶ nworks VMware Management

eXc Software

The eXc software and virtual agents provide the ability to monitor non-Windows and network devices from within the OpsMgr console. eXc Software has been developing custom management packs and virtual agents since the early days of MOM 2005. The eXc products provide seamless integration with the OpsMgr console and collect all aspects of health, such as performance information, availability, and system health.

The software supports monitoring of UNIX, Linux, SNMP devices, mainframe systems, applications, and databases (this is by no means an exhaustive list). In addition, eXc is very quick to assist in writing custom management packs and virtual agents for systems it does not currently support.

The eXc Software virtual agents are independent of the OpsMgr infrastructure. They can run on any management server or server hosting an OpsMgr agent. These virtual agents connect to the systems being monitored, but do not actually require any software to be installed on those systems. This means that there is very little impact on the monitored machines, and there is no need to install software onto a critical system such as a UNIX mainframe.

Another attractive feature of the eXc Software solution is that it is written in Jscript, and the user is not restricted from viewing the code. This allows competent developers to write their own code, further customizing the product as required.

Figure 22.18 shows the eXc Software Administration console with the Cisco monitoring agents installed.

The eXc Software solution offers a cost-effective way to monitor non-Windows devices with OpsMgr and has a wide variety of virtual agents. We have found eXc to be very accommodating in developing additional virtual agents, should that be required.

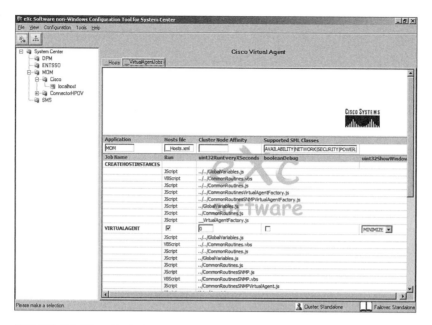

FIGURE 22.18   eXc Software Administration console.

Real World: Using eXc

One area that could be better with the eXc Software solution is the user interface. Although technically minded people will have no problems configuring the software, it can be confusing and a little cluttered for the less technical individual.

Overall, the eXc solution comes highly recommended for its broad level of monitoring and the level of data it collects.

An additional no-charge management pack from eXc is a dynamic map feature that works with OpsMgr. This is a topical and drilldown view of your device alerts, enabling you to see what is happening across your infrastructure throughout the globe. Each alert presents itself on the map relative to the latitude/longitude coordinates defined, and contains the device name and alert count extracted from Operations Manager as it occurs. You can use this virtual earth dynamic to drill down closer to the street, city, state, or county level to get more drawn-out or focused views. You can also create additional maps that call out individual locations and display multiple maps for various areas.

Figure 22.19 shows a dynamic map alert for our Odyssey environment.

eXc Software was recently acquired by Quest Software. Moving forward, you will see the eXc products included within the System Center offerings from Quest, although we understand support will stay within the eXc group. You may recall Quest previously bought Vintella.

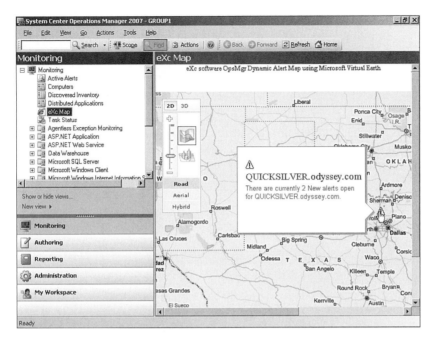

FIGURE 22.19   Viewing two new alerts on Quicksilver using eXc's dynamic mapping technology.

Another Mapping Technology

eXc is not the only one developing mapping software. Savision's Live Maps product, launched in November 2007, allows you to create your own fully configurable maps and place OpsMgr objects in them. You can even turn an existing Visio diagram into a live monitoring map! Live Maps lets you put alerts and the state view into a single view, as well as create your own dashboard showing the state of your business process.

Live Maps comes with over 300 geographical maps and provides the ability to drop maps on each other to create nested maps. It is also integrated with the Operations console. Savision provides a Live Maps demo at http://www.savision.com/demo.

Jalasoft Xian IO

Jalasoft developed the Xian Network Manager IO product specifically for use with OpsMgr. The software is primarily designed to allow full monitoring of network devices through the OpsMgr Operations console.

Unlike product connectors, which simply run as a service and are typically administrated through the Operations console, Xian IO is actually a standalone application that runs alongside OpsMgr. Network devices are discovered and administered using the Xian IO console, and status, alerts, and performance data is passed to the Operations console for monitoring and reporting. This type of architecture is well suited to its purpose—large companies typically have many network devices, and this type of architecture does not put unnecessary strain on the OpsMgr environment.

Xian IO is designed from the ground-up to monitor and maintain network devices, but it can also monitor non-Windows operating systems such as Solaris and other flavors of UNIX.

In Figure 22.20, we display the Xian IO console. Although you will perform installation and configuration with this console, remember the OpsMgr Operations console is used for monitoring. Notice the standard views available for a number of third-party servers and devices.

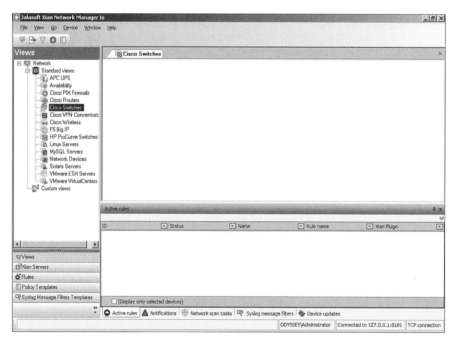

FIGURE 22.20   The Xian IO console.

The software uses policies, which define exactly what information to collect from a device and what the performance thresholds should be. You define these policies in the Xian IO console, and they are applied to devices according to device type. To configure a policy, navigate to the Policy Templates node shown in Figure 22.21 (on the left side of the screen).

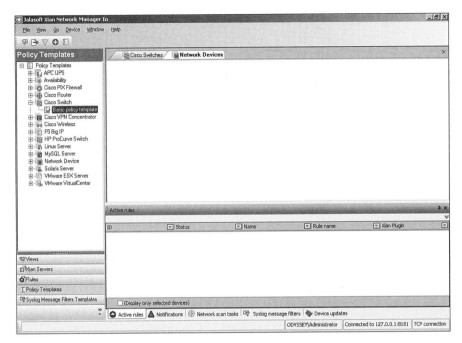

FIGURE 22.21   The Policy Templates node in the Xian IO console.

You can create your own policy templates or use the default policies. Policies are applied either to devices already discovered, or to single devices or groups of devices as they are discovered. Right-click the object type (in this case we will select the Cisco switch). You can select New to display the policy options screen in Figure 22.22. There is a large number of different policy items, which you can apply to a single policy.

This is an example of just one of the devices you can monitor using Jalasoft. Currently, Jalasoft provides management packs for the following devices:

- ► Availability (ICMP only)
- ► APC UPS
- ► Cisco Switches
- ► Cisco VPN Concentrators
- ► Cisco Routers
- ► Cisco PIX/ASA
- ► Cisco Wireless
- ► F5 Big Ip
- ► Generic Network Device

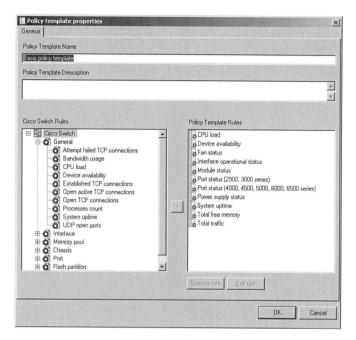

FIGURE 22.22   Policy options for Cisco switches.

▶ HP Procurve Switches

▶ Linux MySQL

▶ Linux Servers

▶ Solaris Servers

▶ VMware ESX

▶ VMware VirtualCenter

Figure 22.23 shows the Xian Monitored Network Devices State in the Operations Manager Operations console. Other views available include discovery diagrams and performance views.

Real World—Installing Xian IO

You can install Xian IO on an OpsMgr management server. However, as a best practice for environments where there is a large number of network devices or when you have a requirement to collect a large amount of performance information from discovered devices, we recommend provisioning additional physical or virtual servers to host the Xian IO product.

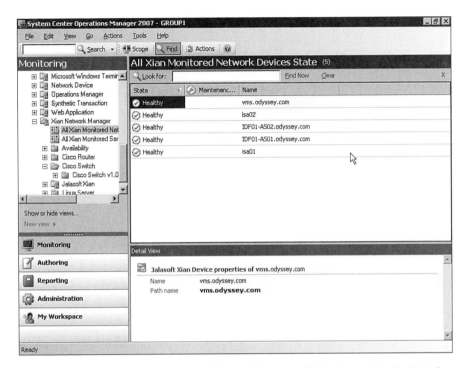

FIGURE 22.23   The Xian Monitored Network Devices State view in the OpsMgr Operations console.

Another key feature of Xian IO is the powerful Smart Management Pack Generator tool, which enables creating custom management packs for the Xian IO tool. Provided you have access to the .mib file for the device (usually obtainable from the hardware/software manufacturer), you can use the tool to create a Xian IO management pack for your device. This enables the Xian tool to be more dynamic, and it reduces the demand on the Jalasoft development team to develop management packs for uncommon devices.

In conclusion, the Jalasoft software is to be commended for its excellent user interface and ease of configuration. Its integration into OpsMgr is very impressive and appears nearly seamless. Providing the Management Pack Generator tool to create custom management packs offers increased flexibility, although you should not expect the level of monitoring you see with Jalasoft management packs in the ones you create yourself.

However, due to the product's complexity, it has a limited selection of monitored devices and may not be adequate for all environments. This is a small complaint though, and overall the Jalasoft Xian software is excellent.

Quest Management Xtensions

The Quest Management Xtensions software, originally designed for MOM 2005, was formerly known as Vintella Systems Monitor. Unlike eXc Software and Jalasoft, Quest Management Xtensions uses an agent that you install on the monitored system.

Quest Management Xtensions are designed to monitor UNIX and Linux systems. They accomplish monitoring by means of a specially designed agent and a set of rules and scripts managed by the product, deployed to the managed systems as required.

One of the defining features of the Quest Management Xtensions is the ability to author rules and scripts similar to how you would in OpsMgr for a Windows agent. These custom rules are distributed to the appropriate managed machines alongside the default set of rules supplied with the product.

The Quest Management Xtensions software is also designed to be secure, including mutual authentication support to ensure that the UNIX/Linux agent you are communicating with is a trusted machine. We discuss mutual authentication and how it relates to OpsMgr in Chapter 11.

The Quest software is more difficult to configure than eXc or Jalasoft, but it's unique because it has a dedicated agent that resides on the monitored machine. It allows custom rules to be created and deployed to the monitored machines as if they were Windows devices, which is an excellent feature.

nworks VMware Management

Many businesses now are beginning to realize that, thanks to virtualization, server hardware in many cases is an unnecessary expense. Server virtualization is the idea of hosting multiple "logical" servers on one piece of "physical" hardware. These logical machines are each a server (or workstation) in themselves, and they are managed and segregated through virtualization software. Two main software companies are offering operating system virtualization products: Microsoft and VMware.

The Microsoft offering for managing large enterprises is System Center Virtual Machine Manager (SCVMM). SCVMM extends the basic capabilities of Virtual Server management into a more scalable solution. It offers centralized virtual machine management across hundreds or even thousands of physical machines, and it can handle thousands or even hundreds of thousands of virtual machines. We discuss Virtual Machine Manager integration with OpsMgr in the "Integrating OpsMgr 2007 with Other System Center Applications" section of this chapter.

VMware has been working in this arena longer than Microsoft, and it is somewhat better established. Its software comes in a number of flavors, but the most commonly seen in the enterprise space is GSX and ESX server.

Although you can manage a virtual machine by simply deploying the OpsMgr agent as if it were a physical server, the layer that manages the virtualization is more difficult to monitor. This is particularly true when using the VMWare ESX product. This product is hosted on a modified Linux kernel and thus does not even provide an environment where an OpsMgr agent can exist.

This is where nworks comes in. The nworks management pack and collector software allows data collection and monitoring of the VMware virtualization environment. Using this management pack, you can obtain information about the VMware environment, the virtual machines, and the health of the VMware server itself.

This solution further enhances OpsMgr by allowing it to integrate with VMware GSX and ESX servers, and with the VMware VirtualCenter application that manages all VMware servers and virtual machines in your environment. The information collected by the nworks software integrates into the Operations console, giving you a holistic view of your virtualized environment in addition to your physical systems. In Figure 22.24, we see the health of two (agentless) host machines monitored by the nworks management pack. The add-on application converts VMware instrumentation into WMI for Operations Manager.

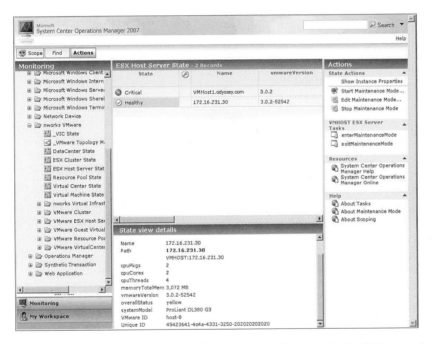

FIGURE 22.24   Viewing ESX Host Server state with nworks in the Web console.

Monitoring VMware installations are becoming more important as virtualization becomes more popular. The nworks software offers an excellent level of monitoring for a VMware environment. Not only can we monitor the health of hosts, as shown in Figure 22.24, but we can monitor the virtual resources of the guest machines, as in Figure 22.25, which displays a group diagram for three monitored VMware guest machines running on the hosts shown in Figure 22.24.

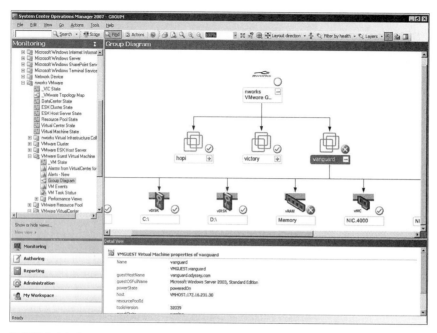

FIGURE 22.25   An nworks-provided diagram view of virtual machines.

The only drawback is for those organizations that are not heavily using virtualization, because the product is a little pricey when a basic level of monitoring can be achieved by using OpsMgr agents on the virtual guests. Event and service monitoring can also be carried out when using VMware GSX Server, which is hosted on a Windows Server.

TIP

Monitoring VM ESX Using SNMP and Telnet

VMware ESX 3.x/VI3 includes a variety of methods for collecting critical performance and configuration data including SNMP, Syslog, ESXTOP utility (using ssh), the SDK Web Service, and the ESX COM API, which is now deprecated.

For those of you without the budget to license nworks, Jonathan Hambrook has created a 60-page how-to guide taking users through the configuration of basic ESX monitoring using SNMP and Telnet. You can download his guide at http://www.mediamax.com/opsmgr/Hosted/Monitoring%20ESX%20on%20SCOM%202007%20v2.2.pdf (we also include this link in Appendix E as a live link).

TCP Port Monitoring with OpsMgr

In addition to the Microsoft-created management packs for OpsMgr 2007, Microsoft provides a number of management pack templates. These templates enable you to create all the items necessary to carry out synthetic monitoring of TCP ports, database connections, websites, and ASP.NET applications.

Creating items using these templates is very simple and wizard based, with OpsMgr automatically creating all the complex items required to carry out the actual monitoring. In this section, we will create a monitoring object to monitor a TCP port. The TCP Port template is one of the most appropriate monitoring templates to use when configuring monitoring for systems without agents, because it has no dependency on an agent.

You can use this template to monitor ports on network devices. As an example, consider an SMTP relay device, where you can test port 25 to ensure the device is responding and that the email port that services the primary function of the device is working.

For this example, we will create a TCP port monitor that monitors port 25 on an email device that is not running Windows and therefore cannot host an agent. Perform the following steps:

1. In the Operations console, navigate to Authoring -> Management Pack Templates.

2. Right-click and select Add Monitoring Wizard. You will be presented with the screen shown in Figure 22.26.

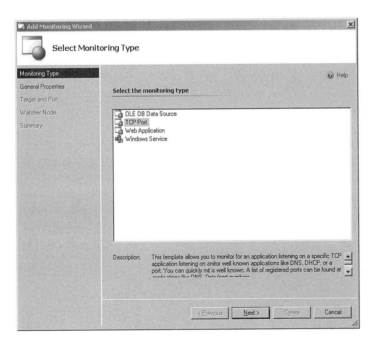

FIGURE 22.26   Select the TCP Port monitoring type in the Add Monitoring Wizard.

3. Click Next and give the monitor a name. We will call our monitor **E-mail Relay Device Port Monitor**. You can enter a description if you like. We will save the new object to our Sample Management Pack, as shown in Figure 22.27. Click Next.

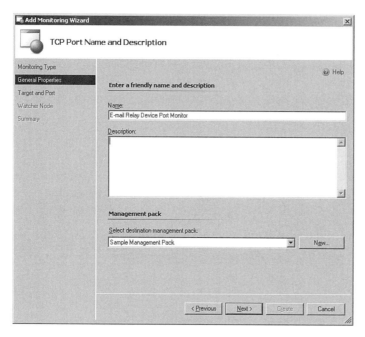

FIGURE 22.27   General properties for the Add Monitoring Wizard.

4. You are now prompted to enter the IP address or device name of the device to be monitored and the TCP port.

   The device name is only appropriate if you have DNS configured correctly; otherwise, you should enter the IP address. We will use a device called **RELAY1** and a Port setting of **25** (which is the default port for SMTP mail). You can click the Test button to verify that the port is working. Figure 22.28 displays this screen.

5. Click Next to proceed to the Choose Watchers Node screen of the wizard. Here, you have the option to configure the machine that should run the test. This machine is a watcher node. You will notice that the computers listed here all have the OpsMgr agent deployed because the agent is required to initiate the test. We will select the PANTHEON.ODYSSEY.COM server and leave the frequency of the test at the default setting of 2 minutes. See Figure 22.29 for the Choose Watcher Nodes screen.

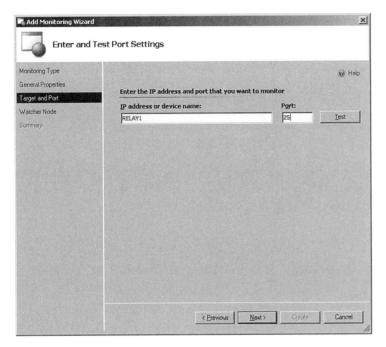

FIGURE 22.28   Target and port information.

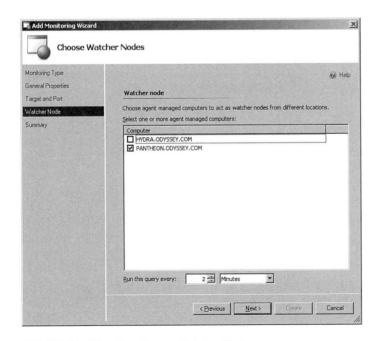

FIGURE 22.29   The Choose Watcher Nodes screen.

6. Click Next to review the summary information; then click Create to create the monitoring object. Figure 22.30 shows the object we created.

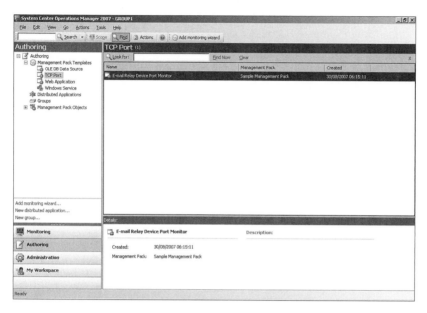

FIGURE 22.30   Created object.

7. The individual objects created automatically by OpsMgr are shown in Figure 22.31.

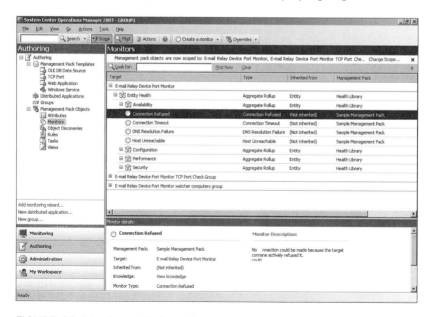

FIGURE 22.31   Associated monitors.

8. Notice in Figure 22.32 that we have a class object. This means you can add this TCP Port test to other management packs—for example, a distributed application (DA).

Creating a TCP Port enables synthetic tests to be carried out in addition to standard monitoring. State is reflected in a distributed application created to monitor the platform for which this device is a member.

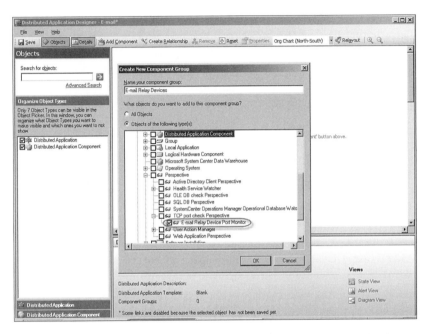

FIGURE 22.32   Using TCP port monitor to create a distributed application.

Capturing Syslog Messages

You can collect Syslog messages based on certain criteria, such as a collection rule. You can also respond to a Syslog message by using an alert-generating rule to generate an alert, run a script, or run a command. To utilize either of these rule types requires the following:

▶ Identifying OpsMgr agents that will listen for Syslog messages. These agents will be the targets (destination) for deploying collection rules or alert-generating rules.

▶ The agents the Syslog monitoring rules are deployed to will listen on UDP port 514. This requires that your UNIX hosts are configured to forward Syslog messages to the appropriate agent. Note that OpsMgr can only use the default Syslog listening port of UDP 514.

To configure a rule, perform the following steps:

1. In the Operations console, select the Authoring space and then navigate to Management Packs -> Rules.

2. In the Actions pane, select Create a Rule. The Create Rule Wizard will appear. Click a management pack in the Select a destination management pack list (preferably not the Default management pack).

3. In the Select a type of rule to create box, expand Event Based and then click Syslog (Alert). Click Next.

4. In the Rule name box, type the name you want to use for this rule and then select a rule target such as Agent.

5. Click Next. Then define the criteria under which the alert response will be generated using the Filter one or move events option. To create an alert for the Cron daemon that generates a Critical severity condition, enter the following values and then click Next:

   ▶ Parameter Name: **Facility**

   ▶ Operator: **Equals**

   ▶ Value: **9**

6. In the Alert name box, type the name you want to use for an alert, click an alert priority in the Priority list, and then select a severity level in the Severity list. If you want to configure alert suppression, select Alert Suppression, configure how you want to handle duplicate alerts, and then click OK.

7. In the Alert description box, you can configure the display of the Syslog message by using an Alert string. Displaying the Syslog message would use the `$Data/EventData/DataItem/Message$` Alert string.

8. Click Create to create the rule when you are finished defining the alert information.

Table 22.2 displays a list of facility values, whereas Table 22.3 lists severity values. This information is also available at http://support.microsoft.com/kb/942863.

The list of alert strings includes the following:

▶ `$Data/EventData/DataItem/Facility$`

▶ `$Data/EventData/DataItem/Severity$`

▶ `$Data/EventData/DataItem/Priority$`

▶ `$Data/EventData/DataItem/PriorityName$`

▶ `$Data/EventData/DataItem/TimeStamp$`

▶ `$Data/EventData/DataItem/HostName$`

▶ `$Data/EventData/DataItem/Message$`

TABLE 22.2   Table of Facility Values

Facility	Description	Value
Kernel	Kernel messages	0
User	User-level messages	1
Mail	Mail system	2
Daemons	System daemons	3
Auth	Security and authorization	4
Syslog	Syslog internal messages	5
LPR	Line printer subsystem	6
News	Network news	7
UUCP	UNIX-to-UNIX Copy Program	8
Cron	Cron daemon	9
Auth2	Security and authorization	10
FTP	FTP daemon	11
NNTP	Network Time subsystem	12
LogAudit		13
LogAlert		14
Cron2	Cron daemon	15
Local0	Local use 0	16
Local1	Local use 1	17
Local2	Local use 2	18
Local3	Local use 3	19
Local4	Local use 4	20
Local5	Local use 5	21
Local6	Local use 6	22
Local7	Local use 7	23

22

TABLE 22.3   Table of Severity Values

Severity	Description	Value
Emergency	System is unusable.	0
Alert	Immediate action required.	1
Critical	Critical condition.	2
Error	Error condition.	3
Warning	Warning condition.	4
Notice	Normal, but significant.	5
Info	Informational message.	6
Debug	Debug level.	7

Integrating OpsMgr 2007 with Other System Center Applications

In this chapter, we have looked at approaches you can take to integrate OpsMgr into an existing management infrastructure utilizing product connectors to connect OpsMgr to other management suites. We also looked at no-cost third-party–created hardware management packs available from the hardware vendors, and we discussed monitoring non-Windows systems using additional third-party applications.

Although these capabilities are very important, it is also important for OpsMgr to integrate with existing and future products, in particular other System Center products such as System Center Service Manager and System Center Virtual Machine Manager. This section looks at what integration is currently available and the integration planned during the life cycle of OpsMgr 2007.

Microsoft is committed to systems management and therefore it has and will continue to invest heavily in the System Center suite of tools. Currently, the Systems Management area of the System Center family consists of the following tools:

- ▶ Operations Manager
- ▶ Configuration Manager
- ▶ Data Protection Manager
- ▶ Virtual Machine Manager
- ▶ Essentials
- ▶ Capacity Planner
- ▶ Service Manager

Although this list does not document the entire suite of System Center tools, it does represent the major tools in the Systems Management area, which is where OpsMgr is firmly focused.

In terms of integration with OpsMgr, unfortunately, the majority of the integration is planned for future releases, although we see great potential as we discussed in Chapter 20, "Automatically Adapting Your Environment." That is not to say that OpsMgr cannot monitor the aforementioned products, because it can. Some of these management packs, such as the Virtual Machine Manager (SCVVM) management pack, have been released, although not all management packs are currently available.

Management pack integration varies greatly depending on the product and management pack in question. Take, for example, the old SMS 2003 management pack (and the Configuration Manager management pack). The SMS management pack provides the ability to monitor individual packages and advertisements from within the Operations console. It includes a number of tasks that makes it easier and quicker to manage SMS, and it enables a large number of SMS tools and features to be accessible through the OpsMgr Operations console.

The Virtual Machine Manager management pack provides some impressive levels of management pack integration. The level of monitoring provided by the SCVMM management pack includes the following capabilities:

- Health and availability of the Virtual Machine Manager service and database
- Health and availability of Virtual Machine Manager agents
- Health and availability of self-service Web servers supporting virtual machine self-service in VMM
- Significant status changes for virtual machines in Virtual Machine Manager
- Monitoring virtual machine health and availability through warnings, errors, and critical errors raised by Virtual Server
- Reports showing virtualization candidates, virtual machine allocation, virtual machine utilization, host utilization, and host utilization growth

True integration, however, is something altogether different. The sort of integration we hope for is the type of bidirectional communication intended between OpsMgr and Service Manager, as an example. Although this level of integration does not appear to be in the first release of the SCVMM management pack, it certainly is the direction in which Microsoft is heading.

Summary

This chapter discussed a variety of ways to integrate Operations Manager 2007 with diverse platforms and technologies. We looked at the OpsMgr connected management group architecture and the process for connecting two management groups together. We examined the concept of OpsMgr product connectors and looked in detail at the Engyro OpsMgr to OVO and Tivoli connectors in particular, because these connectors appear to be the most widely utilized.

We highlighted some of the no-cost third-party management packs that are available to further enhance monitoring in OpsMgr and extend monitoring to physical server and storage hardware. We also looked at the products that are available to monitor non-Windows systems and network devices using OpsMgr, including products offered by Jalasoft, eXc Software, Quest, and nworks.

Finally, we discussed integration with OpsMgr and the current role management packs play in integrating software applications with OpsMgr. We also looked at Microsoft's recent release of System Center Virtual Machine Manager and the associated management pack for OpsMgr 2007, and we discussed some of the integration we hope to see in future versions of these products and other Microsoft products such as Service Manager.

The next chapter discusses extending OpsMgr in a different direction, by creating your own management packs and reports.

# CHAPTER 23

Developing Management Packs and Reports

The previous chapter discussed various methods available to extend the functionality of Operations Manager 2007 (OpsMgr) through interoperability with various technologies. In this chapter, we will discuss another way you can extend OpsMgr—by creating your own management packs and reports. As an early warning, this chapter gets pretty deep into the details of how to create management packs and reports, including several sections that dissect eXtensible Markup Language (XML). We believe that this level of depth is required to equip you with what you need to know to create management packs and reports in OpsMgr.

You can create OpsMgr 2007 management packs using a variety of methods discussed in this chapter. These methods include the following:

▶ The Authoring pane of the Operations console

▶ The Authoring console

▶ Third-party products such as Silect MP Studio

▶ XML (eXtensible Markup Language)

Additionally, we will discuss different ways you can create reports. This includes the Operations console, using linked reports, and with Visual Studio.

Developing Management Packs

Operations Manager 2007 functionality is contained in its management packs. These management packs consist of a variety of objects. Management packs can contain rules, monitors, tasks, views, and product knowledge. Management packs can be imported into your management group (discussed in Chapter 8, "Configuring and Using Operations Manager 2007") and exported (discussed in Chapter 12, "Backup and Recovery") using the Operations console or the PowerShell Command Shell. Management pack development can occur using a variety of different interfaces, including the Operations console, the Authoring console, Silect MP Studio, and editing XML. Using the Operations console is the simplest method, but XML allows more functionality and flexibility, although it is far more intricate and complex.

Before delving into how to create management packs, it is important to make a distinction between what a management pack can be versus what it has to be:

▶ A management pack can be a very large and complex development effort that includes the health state and provides monitors, rules, alerting, views, and tasks.

▶ A management pack can also be a single useful rule, monitor, or task that provides benefit.

It is easy to become locked into the perspective that to create a management pack you need to include all the functionality available, but as we will show in the "Using the Operations Console" section of this chapter, a beneficial management pack can often be created with only a single component such as a monitor, rule, or a task.

Using the Operations Console

You can create management packs and the objects within them using the Operations console, utilizing a variety of approaches. The next sections describe these approaches.

Creating and Deleting Management Packs

Before adding objects to a management pack, we must first create the management pack. Create the management pack object in the Administration space of the Operations console. To create the management pack, right-click Administration and choose Create Management Pack.

For those clients we work with, our practice is to create a management pack incorporating the company name to store that company's overrides. In general, each organization will want to create multiple override management packs, with one for each application or service it is managing overrides for.

You will want to create other management packs based on the functionality they will be providing. In this case, we will be creating the "OpsMgr Unleashed" management pack, where we will be storing many of the various management pack objects we create as we progress through this chapter. You can also create management packs as part of the process of creating objects such as monitors, tasks, and rules, which we will discuss in the next sections of this chapter.

Management Packs Defined

As we discussed in Chapter 13, "Administering Management Packs," management packs (MPs) provide a snapshot of product health and are the mechanism OpsMgr 2007 uses to manage and monitor specific applications and services. Management packs make it possible to collect and utilize a wide range of information from various sources. They describe what data to examine and provide analysis of that data.

As an OpsMgr administrator, you can utilize customized management packs in a variety of ways:

- Storing overrides
- Monitoring single-functional components
- Developing in-house monitoring applications

Although these have different purposes, each is a customized management pack.

You can delete management packs in the Administration space, from the same location where you create them. Right-click the management pack and choose Delete. If other management packs are dependent on the management pack you are attempting to delete, the interface will not allow you to delete the management pack until you remove those that are dependent on it. As an example, if you create overrides from the Exchange management pack and store them in the Default management pack, you cannot delete the Exchange management pack until you delete the Default management pack. This is a major reason why you do not want to store customizations in the Default management pack!

Creating Monitors

As a starting point for developing a management pack, we will discuss each of the different objects (Monitors, Tasks, Rules, Views, and Knowledge) and how to create them in the Operations console. For information on each of these different objects and their usage, see Chapter 14, "Monitoring with Operations Manager." As we discuss in that chapter, there are a variety of different monitors:

- Windows Event monitors
- Windows Service monitor
- Windows Performance Counter monitor (static or self-tuning)
- Log File monitor
- SNMP monitor
- Scripting (timed script two-state and three-state monitors)
- WMI Event and Performance monitors

In this chapter, we will first focus on providing examples of how to create the objects, and then we will discuss how to put them all together. Because Chapter 14 discussed creating a

Windows Event monitor, in this chapter we will start with creating a simple monitor. This monitor will be an example of how to create a Windows Service monitor, which we will use as part of our OpsMgr Unleashed management pack.

For this particular case, we will add our monitor to the existing Windows Server 2003 Operating System target as part of the Availability monitor. In the "Using the Operations Manager Authoring Console" section of this chapter, we will show how you can create your own self-contained management pack, including monitors.

The default configuration of Operations Manager 2007 monitors a core set of services, invoking alerts if any of these services stops running. These services include the following:

- Computer Browser
- DHCP Client
- DNS Client
- Logical Disk Manager
- Messenger Service
- Plug and Play
- RPC
- Server
- TCP/IP NetBIOS
- Windows Event Log
- Workstation

Services not on this list are monitored by the management packs that specifically support them (such as the DNS management pack, which monitors the availability of the Microsoft DNS server service). So what can we do to notify (alert) if some other service is down that we want to know about?

Let's say we have McAfee software deployed to provide antivirus functionality. Multiple McAfee services are running on our servers (McAfee Framework Service, McAfee McShield, and McAfee TaskManager), and we want to generate alerts if they are not running. Perform the following steps:

1. Open the Operations console and browse to Authoring -> Management Pack Objects -> Monitors.
2. Set the scope to Windows Server 2003 Operating System (or Windows 2000 Operating System, depending on your specific requirements) and check the Windows Server 2003 Operating System check box, as shown in Figure 23.1.
3. Next, browse in the console to Windows Server 2003 Operating System -> Entity Health -> Availability -> Core Windows Services Rollup. Right-click and choose to create a new Unit monitor (see Figure 23.2).

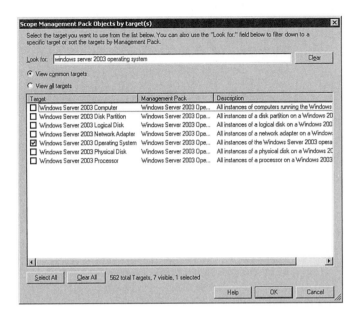

FIGURE 23.1   Limiting the scope within the authoring section of the Operations console.

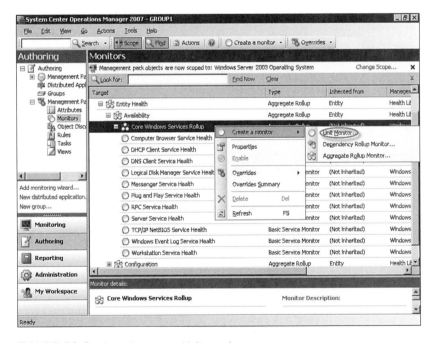

FIGURE 23.2   Creating a new Unit monitor.

4. Now, we must specify the type of monitor we will create. Select the Windows Services -> Basic Service Monitor type (see Figure 23.3). Choose a destination management pack (preferably something other than the default one) and click Next to continue.

5. Enter the service name for the name of the monitor (**McAfee Anti-Virus** in our example). Verify that the monitor target is correct (Windows Server 2003 Operating System) and that the parent monitor is correct (Core Windows Services Rollup). See Figure 23.4 for an example.

6. To find the service on the server, select the ellipsis (...) on the Service Name screen, use the wizard to browse the computer's services, and then click the service. Click Next to continue.

TIP

Connecting to Services Not in the Forest

When browsing for a Windows service, you can connect to those computers where you have permissions to browse for the services. If you need to browse to a system you do not have permissions for (such as a computer in a workgroup), first map a drive to that computer and then browse for the services on the system.

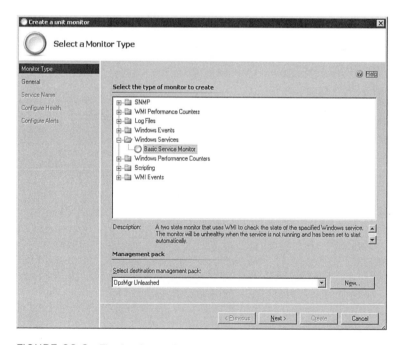

FIGURE 23.3   The basic services monitor.

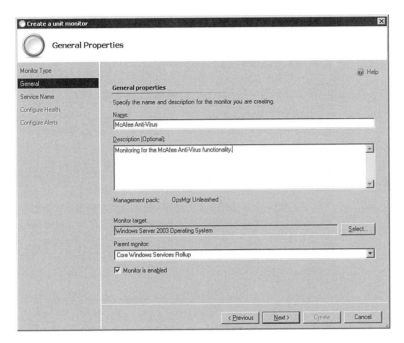

FIGURE 23.4   Setting the general properties of the monitor.

7. The default configurations for Health work well for services. These configurations set the monitoring condition as Healthy if the service is running and Critical if the service is not running. Click Next to continue.

8. At the Configure Alerts screen, check the box to generate alerts for this monitor. Accept the defaults for Automatically resolve the alert when the monitor returns to a healthy state, Alert name, Priority, and Severity, as shown in Figure 23.5. Click the Create button to create the completed monitor.

Once you have created the monitor, you can see it under the list of monitors for the Windows Server 2003 operating system, displayed in Figure 23.6.

NOTE

Creating Additional Monitors for Different Targets

In our example, we defined the target as Windows Server 2003 Operating System. To monitor the service on both Windows 2000 and Windows 2003 servers, you will need to create a monitor for each target.

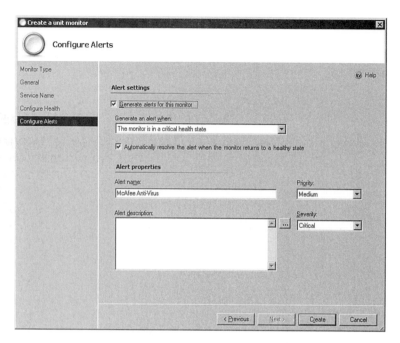

FIGURE 23.5   Configuring the alert for the monitor and creating it.

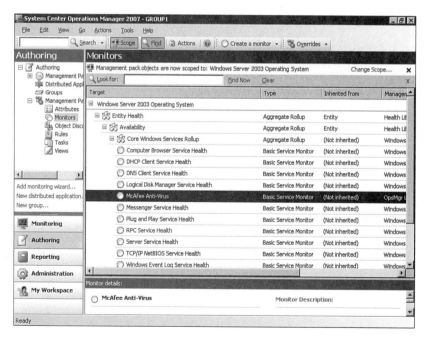

FIGURE 23.6   The new monitor displayed under the Windows Server 2003 Operating System target.

For another example of how to use service monitoring functionality, you could create a monitor that checks the state of the services providing backup functionality. CommVault, for instance, installs services on the servers for which it provides backup functionality. You can use a monitor to watch the backup services, and you can configure that monitor to monitor whatever backup program you run in your environment (CA ARCserve, CommVault Galaxy, EMC Networker, Tivoli Storage Manager, Symantec NetBackup, and so on), as long as it runs a local service on the system you want to monitor.

Creating Console Tasks

You can create Console or Agent tasks, which run on the console or agent, respectively. The different types of tasks include the following:

- ▶ Agent Task -> Command line
- ▶ Agent Task -> Run a script
- ▶ Console Task -> Alert command line
- ▶ Console Task -> Command line
- ▶ Console Task -> Event command line

We previously discussed the concepts behind tasks in Chapter 20, "Automatically Adapting your Environment," where our discussion focused on using existing tasks as part of diagnostics and recoveries. In this chapter, we will focus on using tasks to simplify managing OpsMgr 2007. We will create a console task to resolve alerts that have not been incremented or updated in a specified timeframe. This is useful for cleaning out old alerts that have not recurred. Perform the following steps to create the task:

1. Open the Operations console. Navigate to Authoring -> Management Pack Objects -> Tasks. Right-click and choose Create a new task....

   For our example, we will create a task that will run on the console through the command line (see Figure 23.7). We will store the task in the OpsMgr Unleashed management pack we previously created.

2. Next, we define the task's general properties, such as Task Name (Resolve Alerts), Description, and Task Target (Management Server), as shown in the General Properties screen displayed in Figure 23.8. Click Next to continue.

3. On the Command Line screen, specify the Application, Parameters, and Working directory settings, as well as whether to display output when this task is run. Click Create to finish creating the task.

   The command will run a PowerShell script (included on the CD for the book) named resolve_alerts.ps1. The script is a variation of one written in the newsgroups by Neale Brown, which we altered to run with parameters that we pass as part of the task. The following are the parameters for the Command Line screen in our example, displayed in Figure 23.9:

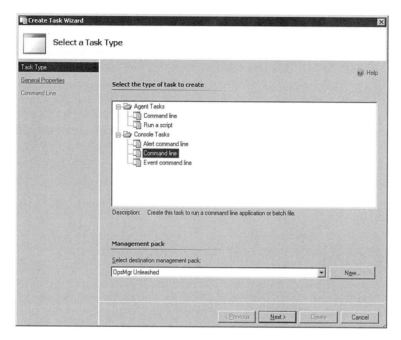

FIGURE 23.7   Creating a console command-line task.

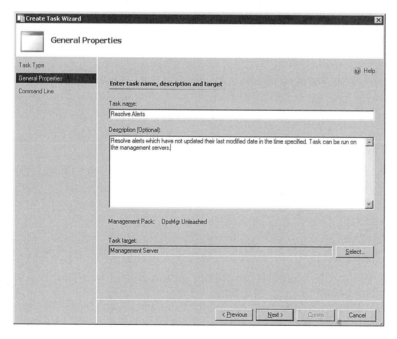

FIGURE 23.8   Specifying the general properties of the task.

▶ Application:
   `%windir%\system32\windowspowershell\v1.0\powershell.exe`

We start with specifying the location and name of the PowerShell application.

▶ Parameters:
   ```
   c:\scripts\resolve_alerts.ps1 -
   rootMS:$Target/Property[Type="SystemLibrary6050000!System.Entity"]
   /DisplayName$ -Minutes:1440
   ```

The full parameter line is too long to display within the parameters field on the screen, so we expanded this into the text shown in the box at the bottom of Figure 23.9.

▶ Working directory:
   `%windir%\system32\windowspowershell\v1.0\`

▶ Display output when this task is run: Not checked

To summarize, the application we are launching is PowerShell, and the parameters specify a PowerShell script (resolve_alerts.ps1) stored in the c:\scripts folder.

4. Within the parameters section of Figure 23.9, we next need to define the parameters the PowerShell script will use.

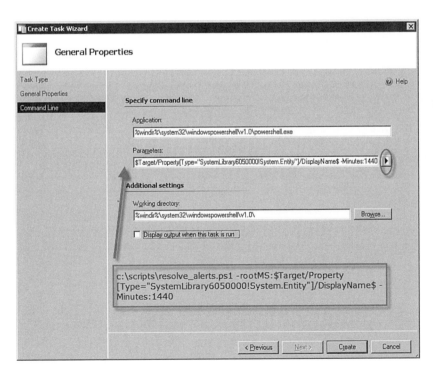

FIGURE 23.9   Specifying the command-line properties of the task.

The section following -rootMS on the parameters is defined by browsing through the available variables (the arrow circled on Figure 23.9 is the button that displays the available variables that can be added).

Figure 23.10 gives an example of the options available. The information is added as command-line variables; when the script runs, the variables are substituted with the appropriate value. In our example, we could have typed in the name of our Root Management Server (RMS) on the parameters line after where it says rootMS:, but instead we will pass a variable that uses the DisplayName of the system where the task runs.

Because we have set the task target to Management Server (shown in Figure 23.8), this substitutes correctly when the script runs.

Finally, we add the -Minutes parameter; this indicates the number of minutes an alert would have not been updated prior to its being resolved (1440 is the number of minutes in a day, or 60 times 24). You can change this parameter to the value you prefer for your environment, such as a value of 360 to resolve alerts that have not updated or had activity in 6 hours.

We are not selecting the check box to display the output. However, when you are debugging your scripts, it is a good idea to have this checked so that you can validate if the script fails to run.

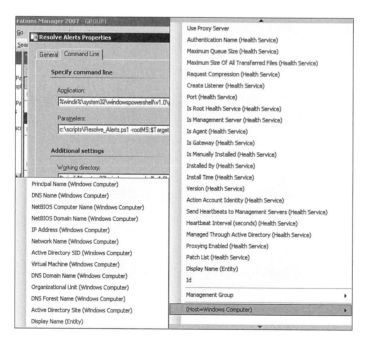

FIGURE 23.10   Sample of variables available within the parameters of a task.

The PowerShell script used by the task is stored in the c:\scripts folder with a name of scriptresolve_alerts.ps1. The content of this script follows:

```
param ($rootMS,$Minutes)


#Initializing the Ops Mgr 2007 Powershell provider
    add-pssnapin "Microsoft.EnterpriseManagement.OperationsManager.Client"
    ➥-ErrorVariable errSnapin;
    set-location "OperationsManagerMonitoring::" -ErrorVariable errSnapin;
    new-managementGroupConnection -ConnectionString:$rootMS -ErrorVariable
    ➥errSnapin;
    set-location $rootMS -ErrorVariable errSnapin;


#Checks to see if it failed or succeeded in loading the provider
    if ($errSnapin.count -eq 0){
    Write-host "'nOpsMgr 2007 PSSnapin initialized!'n";
    }
    else{
            Write-host "'nOpsMgr 2007 PSSnapin failed initialize!'
            ➥nPlease verify you are running this script on a
            ➥Ops Mgr 2007 Management Server";
    Write-Host;
    }


$alerts = get-alert


foreach($alert in $alerts)
{
$timespan = new-timespan (get-date $alert.LastModified)
if ($timespan.totalMinutes -gt $Minutes)
{
Write-Host "id: " $alert.id
Write-Host "Total Minutes: " $timespan.TotalMinutes
Write-Host "Alert Resolved!"
$alert ¦ resolve-alert -comment "Auto-Resolved Alert"
}
}
```

The first line of the script identifies the parameters we defined with the task. Our example passes two parameters, rootMS and Minutes. The names should exactly match the parameter name specified on the command-line task.

23

Creating Views

Now that we created a task to resolve alerts, we want to make it easy to find and use this task. We can do this by creating a State view in the OpsMgr Unleashed management pack. Perform the following steps:

1. Open the Operations console and navigate to Monitoring -> OpsMgr Unleashed (this folder exists from creating the management pack in the "Creating and Deleting Management Packs" section of this chapter). Right-click and select New; you will see a variety of options available, as shown in Figure 23.11.

2. For our alert resolution example, we will create a State view that shows us the RMS. To do this, choose the New -> State View option.

3. We specify the name of the view, the description, and what this view will show data related to. In our example, we name the view **Resolve Alerts** and choose to show data related to the Root Management Server, as shown in Figure 23.12.

4. After creating this view, we open the Actions pane and click the State view at the top of the middle pane. Within the Actions pane, under Health Service Tasks, we now have a Resolve Alerts option available, circled at the bottom right in Figure 23.13.

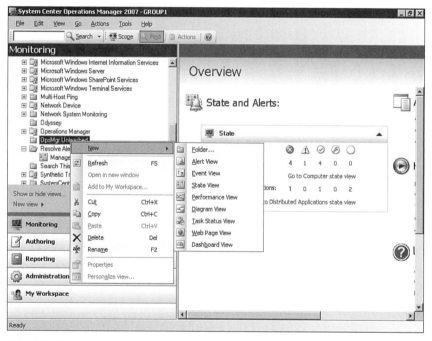

FIGURE 23.11   Options available when creating a view in the Operations console.

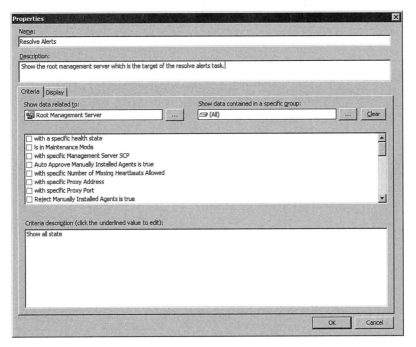

FIGURE 23.12   Creating the State view to use the Resolve Alerts task.

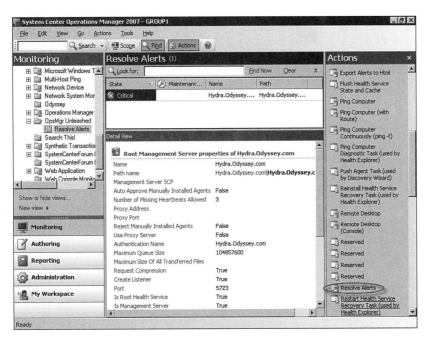

FIGURE 23.13   Showing the Resolve Alerts task in the State view.

The Resolve Alerts task provides us with a quick process to use for resolving alerts that have not been updated in a specified time period. There is also the Console task (Event command line), which performs a lookup on Eventid.net based on the event view of Operations Manager. Eventid.net is a website that provides information on events found within the various Windows Event logs. This task assists with debugging issues identified by OpsMgr. The Resolve Alerts and Console tasks are included on the CD for this book as part of the OpsMgr Unleashed management pack.

Creating Rules

Chapter 14 introduced the different types of rules that are available. These are alert-generating rules, collection rules, and timed commands. Alert-generating and collection rules may be event based, performance based, or probe based. The different types of alert-generating rules include the following:

- Event Based: Generic CSV Text Log (Alert)
- Event Based: Generic Text Log (Alert)
- Event Based: NT Event Log (Alert)
- Event Based: Snmp Trap (Alert)
- Event Based: Syslog (Alert)
- Event Based: WMI Event (Alert)

Here are the different types of collection rules:

- Event Based: Generic CSV Text Log (Alert)
- Event Based: Generic Text Log (Alert)
- Event Based: NT Event Log (Alert)
- Event Based: Snmp Trap (Alert)
- Event Based: Syslog (Alert)
- Event Based: WMI Event (Alert)
- Performance Based: SNMP Performance
- Performance Based: WMI Performance
- Performance Based: Windows Performance
- Probe Based: Script (Event)
- Probe Based: Script (Performance)

Finally, here are the different types of timed commands available:

- Execute a Command
- Execute a Script

As we discuss in Chapter 14, the process for creating rules is very similar to the process for creating monitors. As an example, we will create a timed command rule that executes the resolve_alerts.ps1 PowerShell script we built in the "Creating Console Tasks" section of this chapter. To create a new rule, perform the following steps:

1. Open the Operations console and navigate to Authoring -> Management Pack Objects -> Rules. Right-click and choose Create a new rule....

2. Select the Timed Commands -> Execute a Command option and OpsMgr Unleashed as the destination management pack, as shown in Figure 23.14. Click Next to continue.

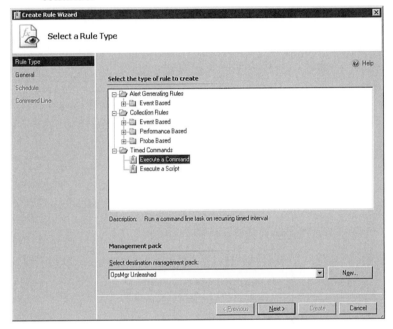

FIGURE 23.14   Creating a timed command that will execute a command to resolve alerts.

3. Enter a rule name (**Execute Resolve Alerts script**, in our example) and description (optional). Then choose a rule target (the Root Management Server) and validate that the Rule is enabled check box is checked, as we show in Figure 23.15. Click Next.

4. We now need to specify the schedule settings for our timed rule. Two options are available:

   ▶ **Based on fixed simple recurring schedule**—With this option, you can special a number of days, hours, minutes, or seconds.

   ▶ **Base on fixed weekly schedule**—Using this option, you can specify a specific time and day(s) of the week.

   We want our task to run Monday morning at 4:00 a.m. (see Figure 23.16). We specify this configuration and click Next to continue.

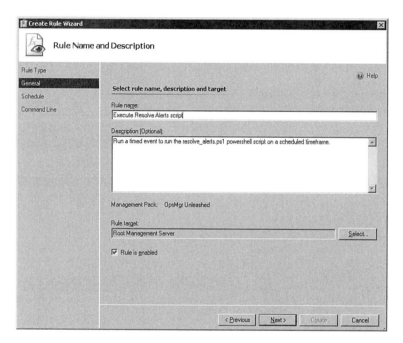

FIGURE 23.15   Specifying the rule name, description, and target.

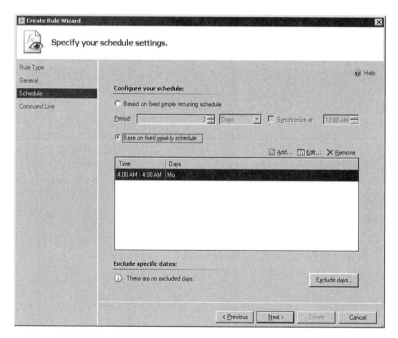

FIGURE 23.16   Specifying when the rule will run.

5. To finish creating the rule, we complete the Configure Command Line Execution Settings screen, where we specify settings for Full path to file, Parameters, Working directory, and Timeout (in seconds). Figure 23.17 shows our settings, which are very similar to the configuration we used when creating the Console task command-line properties shown in Figure 23.9. (The Application specification in Figure 23.9 is the same as the Full path to file setting in Figure 23.17, and the Working directory setting is the same.)

We changed the Minutes parameter to a value of 5760 (a 4-day period) so we will only resolve alerts that have not updated in 4 days. We also set a 300-second time-frame for the script (5 minutes). This parameter determines how long alerts have to have gone without an update to their modification date. As mentioned in step 4, the script itself runs every Monday at 4:00 a.m.

We finish specifying the settings by selecting the Create button to create the rule, thus completing the process.

This example shows how you can use the Operations console to create rules that will perform a variety of actions, including the requirement of running tasks at a scheduled time.

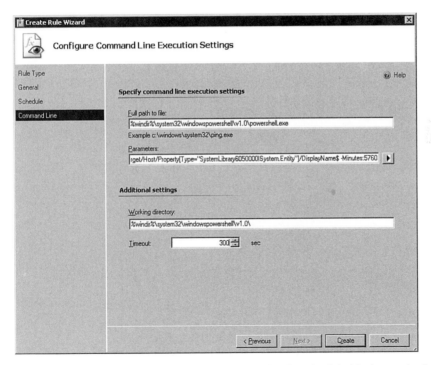

FIGURE 23.17   Configuring the command line that is scheduled to be run by the rule.

Other Management Pack Objects

These sections discussed the steps required and provided examples of management pack objects you can create with the Operations console. These objects included monitors, alerts (within the monitor), console tasks, views, and rules. You can create other components using the Operations console; these include diagnostic and recovery tasks, which we discussed in Chapter 20, and company knowledge, discussed in Chapter 14.

Options for Creating Management Packs

Although you can perform many of the tasks required to create management packs using the Operations console, a number of objects cannot be created with this console at this time. Table 23.1 shows the list of different management pack objects and the options currently available for their creation. The table reflects the options to create management packs that were available with the RTM version of Operations Manager.

These options will continue to evolve as new tools become available (such as Microsoft's Operations Manager Authoring console, which will be released with OpsMgr Service Pack 1) and new functionality is added (for example, Silect's MP Studio). We will discuss both of these tools later in this chapter in the "Using the Operations Manager Authoring Console" and "Using Silect MP Studio" sections, respectively.

As you can see from Table 23.1, some objects must be created using XML and cannot be created with the Operations console.

There is some debate whether XML is a reasonable solution for management pack development. Some consider XML to be HTML with a bad-hair day, meaning it is one thing to write HTML, but XML looks like HTML written in an obscure dialect. The following sections of this chapter discuss XML and offer a perspective of what XML is and how it works.

TABLE 23.1   Management Pack Objects and Creation Methods

Management Pack Object	Creation Methods Available
Management Pack file	Operations console, XML
Class	XML only
Relationship	XML only
Object Discovery	XML only
Monitor	Operations console, XML
Rule	Operations console, XML
Task	Operations console, XML
Diagnostics	Operations console (with XML editing), XML
Recoveries	Operations console (with XML editing), XML
View	Operations console, XML
Console Task	Operations console, XML
Folders	XML only

Using XML

In these next sections, we help you gain a general understanding of the XML document format. We will discuss how Operations Manager 2007 management packs use XML, and how to use XML editing when creating management packs.

You may have noticed that many new applications can read and write XML documents. As an example, XML documents are used in various aspects of OpsMgr 2007, such as when working with unsealed management packs or viewing event log information.

XML usage extends beyond OpsMgr with Microsoft products. For example, while Microsoft Office 2007 can read and write documents based on the Office file types we are familiar with (*filename*.XLS for Microsoft Excel spreadsheets, *filename*.DOC for Microsoft Word documents, and so on), Office 2007 can also read and write Office data files as XML documents. This may make you think that XML is a new technology, but that actually is not the case. XML was first established as a recommendation by the World Wide Web Consortium (W3C) in 1998, just one year after a relatively better-known markup language, HTML (HyperText Markup Language), became a W3C recommendation.

So, we know that XML is not new, and we know that many new applications are capable of interpreting documents that utilize the XML language. But just what is XML, and why it is so important in Operations Manager?

The XML acronym stands for eXtensible Markup Language. *A markup language* provides a way to combine text and extra information about it. The extra information is described using markup and is typically intermingled with the primary text. XML is a markup language, as is HTML, but there is one key difference between the two:

▶ XML describes a set of data and identifies what the data is.

▶ HTML displays data and specifies how the data looks.

Put another way, XML deals with defining data whereas HTML handles displaying data. This is an important distinction.

As markup languages, both XML and HTML documents combine text and additional information about the text. The additional information in the document defines the structure and presentation of the text by using the markup language, which consists of tags and elements within the document. In HTML, an element may be a paragraph of text displayed in the user's web browser. For a simple example, consider the following HTML syntax:

```
<p><b>I think Operations Manager is cool.</b></p>
```

Remember that HTML deals with displaying information, so if you executed this HTML statement in a web browser, the result on the screen would be a bold-faced paragraph:

I think Operations Manager is cool.

This example uses the "bold" HTML tag (the <b> and </b> entries) to define that the statement should be in bold face, and the "paragraph" HTML tag (the <p> and </p> entries) to define the start and end points of the paragraph element. All HTML tags are predefined, and one can only use those tags previously defined.

NOTE

The HTML Connection

Because HTML is the closest thing to XML that many OpsMgr administrators may be familiar with, we use it here for comparison as we introduce the capabilities of XML.

To execute our sample statement using XML, we would revise it slightly. The XML language deals with describing the data, not with how to display the data. In the HTML example, the bold tags defined that the sample text should appear in bold face, so those commands affect what the web browser displays. In XML, that type of information is irrelevant, because XML defines what the information is, not how it looks.

This actually is why XML is so useful in OpsMgr. When we are building a new management pack, we want to define exactly what type of information to monitor and gather, and the XML programming language will provide the structure we need to define the data. Going back to our sample code, in XML the sample statement might be something like this:

```
<mycomment>I think Operations Manager is cool.</mycomment>
```

This example defines an element called "mycomment," and the data for that element is "I think Operations Manager is cool." Unlike the predefined tags in HTML, XML allows us to create any elements that are needed in order to define a set (or sets) of data. Here we defined the "mycomment" element, and the information contained within that element ("I think Operations Manager is cool") is the data we are interested in gathering (rather than data we are interested in formatting).

An XML parser (like OpsMgr) can read our XML command and take whatever action was previously defined for the "mycomment" element. (The action might even include making it a bold-faced paragraph!) The element structure will become a little more obvious in the next section, "XML Management Pack Structure," where we look at an OpsMgr management pack—which is an XML document.

What Happened to the AKM Format for Management Packs?

If you worked with earlier versions of Microsoft Operations Manager (MOM), you may be wondering what happened to the AKM files. Both MOM 2000 and 2005 used the AKM file format to store management pack files. For a MOM administrator, drawbacks of the AKM file format included its proprietary format and that the AKM files were binary files and not readable by humans. If you wanted to view the contents or commands in a given management pack, you would use the AKM2XML resource kit utility to convert the AKM file to an XML document, and then you could view the XML document. However, you did not have the ability to modify the XML document and then import it back into MOM, because MOM only supported the AKM file format when importing management packs. The only way to modify the AKM file was within the MOM environment itself.

There were obvious limitations of this approach. Perhaps the most important one is that this process made it hard to create or modify your own (or utilize someone else's) customized management packs. As you may have already learned from Chapter 13, the ability to import XML-based, unsealed management packs is a powerful new feature of Operations Manager 2007. XML is an open format, and you can use a variety of tools to create XML documents. This openness provides the ability for anyone to author customized management packs using the XML document format and then import them into OpsMgr.

XML Management Pack Structure

As with any computer language, an XML document must follow a prescribed format in order for a parser to be able to read and execute the commands in that document. In the case of Operations Manager, the XML document must follow the OpsMgr management pack schema, which in turn complies with the standard XML document format adopted by the W3C. If you would like to review the XML document standard format, the W3C website, www.w3.org, discusses it in extensive detail.

The Operations Manager management pack schema is divided into sections or elements, with each section used to define a certain aspect of the management pack. The following list includes the available sections and a brief description:

▶ **Manifest**—The manifest defines the identity of the management pack and contains information about any other management packs referenced in the management pack. This section is mandatory, and all other sections are optional.

▶ **TypeDefinitions**—Several different type definitions are available (entity, data, schema, and so on). You can use these to define the information that is gathered.

▶ **Monitoring**—After the type definitions are defined, the monitoring section establishes the monitoring to perform. Several different monitoring types are available (rules, tasks, and so on).

> ▶ **Templates**—Templates provide a wizard a user can follow to define how to configure the monitoring in a management pack.

> ▶ **PresentationTypes**—Presentation types define the types that will appear in the Operations console. These can be views (State view, Event view, and so on) or images if the management pack provides a Diagram view.

> ▶ **Presentation**—Presentation defines what an administrator will see in the Operations console. This could be tasks, views, or other objects.

> ▶ **Reporting**—Reporting is used to define the reports included in the management pack. It also contains information on linked reports.

> ▶ **Language Types**—The language types section is available for creating a single management pack that would work in multiple languages.

Although the sections utilized will vary between different management packs, every management pack must have a *manifest*. The manifest is the only required section in an OpsMgr management pack.

Digging Deeper into XML

Now that you have a general idea of how the management pack schema is broken down into different elements, we will dig a bit deeper into the management pack schema and take a closer look at the elements, discussing how the management pack schema relates to an XML document. Although we can accomplish this several ways, perhaps the most interesting method would be to create an unsealed management pack with the Operations console and then view the resultant XML document and discuss its sections, and how those sections relate to the management pack.

To that end, we used the Operations console to create a simple management pack that monitors the status of the print spooler service. If the print spooler service stops, it triggers an alert that appears in the Active Alerts section of the Monitoring node in the console, as displayed in Figure 23.18.

When the print spooler service starts, the alert is auto-resolved and the alert is removed from the Active Alerts view. Again, this is a very simple management pack—but we can use it to illustrate the various elements contained in a management pack XML document.

As we discuss in Chapter 13, filenames for sealed management packs have an .MP extension. Most of the management packs that you download from the System Center Pack Catalog (http://go.microsoft.com/fwlink/?LinkId=71124) are sealed. Because we created this management pack, it is currently unsealed and therefore will be an XML document. When we use the Operations console to create a management pack, OpsMgr does the work for us and automatically creates the XML document containing the structure of our management pack. We can find the XML documents on disk in the Health Service

State\Management Packs folder, under the folder used to store the OpsMgr binary files. The default location for the binary files is *%ProgramFiles%\System Center Operations Manager 2007*. We could also use the Export Management Pack feature in the Operations console to export our management pack to a different XML file, but for this example, we will use the XML file OpsMgr has already created.

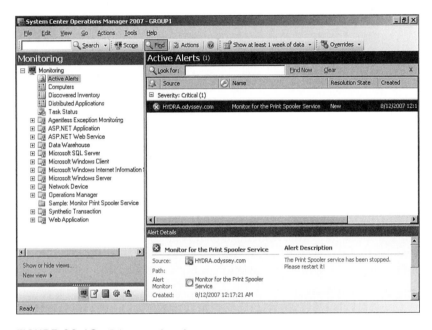

FIGURE 23.18   Print spooler alert.

When you create or import a management pack, OpsMgr creates a unique identifier for the management pack and assigns it to the management pack. Operations Manager appends this unique identifier to the filename of the management pack. In our example, the friendly name of the management pack is *Sample: Monitor Print Spooler Service* but the actual .XML filename in the \HealthServiceState\Management Packs folder is *Sample.Monitor.Print.Spooler.Service.{F16AD92A-81DA-4586-95DE-F0E3D37E1E11}.{843447D6-DB8D-AB9E-3FA5-5F09A09F69F2}.xml*.

Now let's look at our management pack XML document. You can use a variety of tools to view and edit XML documents. If we open our XML file in Windows Notepad, it would look something like what you see in Figure 23.19.

```
File  Edit  Format  View  Help
<?xml version="1.0" encoding="utf-16"?><ManagementPack xmlns:xsd="http://www.w3.org/2001/XMLSchema"
xmlns:xsl="http://www.w3.org/1999/XSL/Transform" ContentReadable="false" RevisionId="f16ad92a-81da-4586-95de-
f0e3d37e1e11"><Manifest><Identity><ID>Sample.Monitor.Print.Spooler.Service</ID><Version>1.0.0.0</Version></Identi
ty><Name>Sample: Monitor Print Spooler Service</Name><References><Reference
Alias="MicrosoftWindowsLibrary6050000"><ID>Microsoft.Windows.Library</ID><Version>6.0.5000.0</Version><PublicKeyT
oken>31bf3856ad364e35</PublicKeyToken></Reference><Reference
Alias="SystemCenter"><ID>Microsoft.SystemCenter.Library</ID><Version>6.0.5000.0</Version><PublicKeyToken>31bf3856
ad364e35</PublicKeyToken></Reference><Reference
Alias="Health"><ID>System.Health.Library</ID><Version>6.0.5000.0</Version><PublicKeyToken>31bf3856ad364e35</Publi
cKeyToken></Reference></References></Manifest><Monitoring><Monitors><UnitMonitor
ID="UIGeneratedMonitor27b238bfd49842e5a49a1fd79b556cc4" Accessibility="Public" Enabled="true"
Target="MicrosoftWindowsLibrary6050000!Microsoft.Windows.Computer" ParentMonitorID="Health!
System.Health.AvailabilityState" Remotable="true" Priority="Normal" TypeID="MicrosoftWindowsLibrary6050000!
Microsoft.Windows.CheckNTServiceStateMonitorType"
ConfirmDelivery="false"><Category>Custom</Category><AlertSettings
AlertMessage="UIGeneratedMonitor27b238bfd49842e5a49a1fd79b556cc4_AlertMessageResourceID"><AlertOnState>Error</Ale
rtOnState><AutoResolve>true</AutoResolve><AlertPriority>Normal</AlertPriority><AlertSeverity>Error</AlertSeverity
></AlertSettings><OperationalStates><OperationalState ID="UIGeneratedOpStateIde44b646cc2ee4542854e3430a95b592c"
MonitorTypeStateID="Running" HealthState="Success" /><OperationalState
ID="UIGeneratedOpStateId993a982f7aca4b8ea0d05c64f92d563c" MonitorTypeStateID="NotRunning" HealthState="Error"
/></OperationalStates><Configuration><ComputerName>$Target/Property[Type="MicrosoftWindowsLibrary6050000!
Microsoft.Windows.Computer"]/NetworkName$</ComputerName><ServiceName>Spooler</ServiceName></Configuration></UnitM
onitor></Monitors></Monitoring></ManagementPack>
```

FIGURE 23.19   A management pack XML file in Windows Notepad.

If we were experienced XML programmers, we might be able to view an XML document like the one in Windows Notepad and make perfect sense out of the commands and the element structure that is defined. In fact, if we were highly skilled XML programmers and if we had extensive experience with the management pack XML format, we could create the entire management pack using Windows Notepad!

However, for most of us, using Windows Notepad to view the contents of an XML document is not especially helpful—Windows Notepad is not an XML parser, and the element structure inherent in a properly formatted XML document is not particularly obvious to us as we view it in Windows Notepad. The element structure is there because this is a valid XML document, but it is hard to identify that structure using this particular tool.

Microsoft's Internet Explorer has been able to parse XML documents since version 4.0, released in 1997. Viewing our sample XML document with Internet Explorer (see Figure 23.20) we should get a view of the management pack that is easier to understand.

Using Internet Explorer, we are able to view the data in a more structured format than we saw when we used Windows Notepad. We can see the various elements that are defined and some of the management pack schema sections we discussed previously (Manifest, Monitoring, and so on), which you may notice we circled in Figure 23.20.

Internet Explorer is useful if we want to view the structure of the elements in an XML document, but is not very helpful if we want to make changes directly to the XML document. To easily edit a XML document, we need an XML editor (or there is always Notepad). An XML editor can obviously parse XML documents, and it also provides the ability to edit directly the document as needed.

Although several different XML editors are available, we will use XML Notepad. XML Notepad 2007 provides great functionality and is available at no cost from Microsoft at http://www.microsoft.com/downloads/details.aspx?familyid=72d6aa49-787d-4118-ba5f-4f30fe913628&displaylang=en. (This location is included on the CD accompanying this book in Appendix E, "Reference URLs.")

Using XML Notepad 2007 to open our sample XML document, we get a vastly different view of our document, as shown in Figure 23.21.

```xml
<?xml version="1.0" encoding="utf-16" ?>
<ManagementPack xmlns:xsd="http://www.w3.org/2001/XMLSchema" xmlns:xsl="http://www.w3.org/1999/XSL/Transform" ContentReadable="false"
  RevisionId="f16ad92a-81da-4586-95de-f0e3d37e1e11">
  <Manifest>
    <Identity>
      <ID>Sample.Monitor.Print.Spooler.Service</ID>
      <Version>1.0.0.0</Version>
    </Identity>
    <Name>Sample: Monitor Print Spooler Service</Name>
    <References>
      <Reference Alias="MicrosoftWindowsLibrary6050000">
        <ID>Microsoft.Windows.Library</ID>
        <Version>6.0.5000.0</Version>
        <PublicKeyToken>31bf3856ad364e35</PublicKeyToken>
      </Reference>
      <Reference Alias="SystemCenter">
        <ID>Microsoft.SystemCenter.Library</ID>
        <Version>6.0.5000.0</Version>
        <PublicKeyToken>31bf3856ad364e35</PublicKeyToken>
      </Reference>
      <Reference Alias="Health">
        <ID>System.Health.Library</ID>
        <Version>6.0.5000.0</Version>
        <PublicKeyToken>31bf3856ad364e35</PublicKeyToken>
      </Reference>
    </References>
  </Manifest>
  <Monitoring>
    <Monitors>
      <UnitMonitor ID="UIGeneratedMonitor27b238bfd49842e5a49a1fd79b556cc4" Accessibility="Public" Enabled="true" Target="MicrosoftWindowsLibrary6050000!
        Microsoft.Windows.Computer" ParentMonitorID="Health!System.Health.AvailabilityState" Remotable="true" Priority="Normal"
        TypeID="MicrosoftWindowsLibrary6050000!Microsoft.Windows.CheckNTServiceStateMonitorType" ConfirmDelivery="false">
        <Category>Custom</Category>
        <AlertSettings AlertMessage="UIGeneratedMonitor27b238bfd49842e5a49a1fd79b556cc4_AlertMessageResourceID">
          <AlertOnState>Error</AlertOnState>
          <AutoResolve>true</AutoResolve>
          <AlertPriority>Normal</AlertPriority>
          <AlertSeverity>Error</AlertSeverity>
        </AlertSettings>
        <OperationalStates>
          <OperationalState ID="UIGeneratedOpStateIde44b646cc2ee4542854e3430a95b592c" MonitorTypeStateID="Running" HealthState="Success" />
          <OperationalState ID="UIGeneratedOpStateId993a982f7aca4b8ea0d05c64f92d563c" MonitorTypeStateID="NotRunning" HealthState="Error" />
        </OperationalStates>
        <Configuration>
          <ComputerName>$Target/Property[Type="MicrosoftWindowsLibrary6050000!Microsoft.Windows.Computer"]/NetworkName$</ComputerName>
          <ServiceName>Spooler</ServiceName>
        </Configuration>
      </UnitMonitor>
    </Monitors>
  </Monitoring>
</ManagementPack>
```

FIGURE 23.20   Viewing an XML file in Internet Explorer.

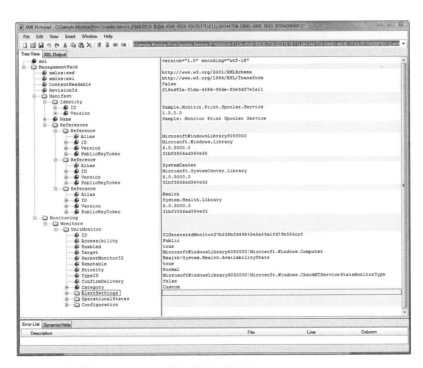

FIGURE 23.21   Viewing an XML file in XML Notepad.

23

In Figure 23.21, we can clearly see the structure of the XML document, and we have the ability to expand (or collapse) specific sections if we want to view additional data in those sections. We also have the ability to edit the contents of the document if necessary.

We will now dig a bit deeper into our sample XML document and discuss some of the elements.

Digging Even Deeper

If we look at the top section of this XML document, we can see some standard preamble information for an XML document, including links to the XML schema and the XSL (eXtensible Stylesheet Language) transform. We also see a revision ID, which is the unique identifier that OpsMgr assigned to the management pack when it was created. We can see this same unique identifier appended to the filename of the management pack XML file at the top of Figure 23.22.

FIGURE 23.22   The revision identifier.

If we continue in XML Notepad, we see the manifest, which as you may recall is the only mandatory element in the management pack. In the manifest, we see a variety of information. First, we see the converted name of the management pack. The friendly name of the management pack is provided in the Name attribute, which is just below the Identity attribute. The friendly name for our management pack is *Sample: Monitor Print Spooler Service*. OpsMgr will always take the friendly name and convert it into a "dotted" name, which in this case is *Sample.Monitor.Print.Spooler.Service*. Operations Manager uses the dotted management pack name during internal processing, not the friendly name. When we created the management pack, we provided a version number (1.0.0.0), and this information is recorded in the Version element, under the Identity element. Figure 23.23 highlights the version number.

The reference element is the next section of the manifest element we will look at. The *reference element* in a management pack is important because it contains information about the other management packs referenced in the management pack. It is worth noting that an unsealed management pack can reference only sealed management packs, and an unsealed management pack cannot be referenced by any other management pack. Whereas most management packs will reference multiple sealed management packs or libraries, every OpsMgr management pack, regardless of the purpose of the management pack, will reference Microsoft.SystemCenter.Library. This is the core library for Operations Manager, and you will always see a reference to it in a management pack.

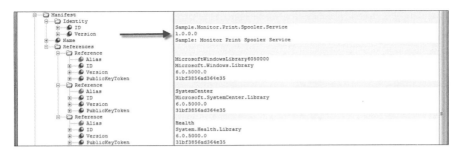

FIGURE 23.23   The version number.

Our sample management pack refers to three libraries, which you can also see in Figure 23.23, under the References section:

▶ Microsoft.Windows.Library

▶ Microsoft.SystemCenter.Library

▶ System.Health.Library

The logic for including these three libraries is as follows:

▶ Microsoft.SystemCenter.Library is there by default.

▶ Microsoft.Windows.Library is there because the management pack is monitoring a Windows service.

▶ System.Health.Library is there because the management pack determines the health of our computer based on the status of the print spooler service.

The purpose of this management pack is to monitor the print spooler service and generate an alert when the service stops. To accomplish this, we created a Unit monitor and configured it to monitor the Windows Print Server service. If we look at the Monitoring element of our XML document in Figure 23.24, we can clearly see that there is a UnitMonitor element defined and highlighted, and this element includes some additional elements related to the Unit monitor. From this information, we can determine a number of things:

▶ We know that the target for this event is Microsoft.Windows.Computer.

▶ We also know that the management pack is enabled and active because the Enabled element under UnitMonitor has a value of "true."

▶ We can look at the AlertSettings element and see that the event is configured to auto-resolve (defined as "true"). Also, the alert severity is configured to report an error.

▶ If we look at the OperationalStates element, we can see the criteria used to determine the health state of the computer: Running is a success event, and NotRunning is an error.

▶ The last element displayed is ServiceName, and this obviously is used to identify the Windows service that is being monitored, which is Spooler.

This very simple management pack only has a few elements defined. Larger, more complex management packs could contain hundreds of different elements.

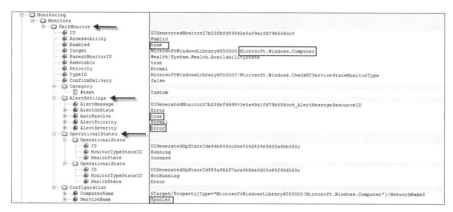

FIGURE 23.24 Viewing the Monitoring element in XML Notepad.

XML and Management Pack Creation

Now that we have discussed various methods to view and dig into XML, we will now look at a simple management pack created in XML. We can use this example to provide the framework we will use to build out a management pack that extends the existing functionality provided with the SQL Server management pack provided by Microsoft. This management pack includes the object discovery information, classes, and relationships we will use within this chapter. Figure 23.25 shows this management pack within the Operations console.

The XML we used to create this management pack follows, including an explanation of the various sections:

```
<?xml version="1.0" encoding="utf-8"?>
<ManagementPack xmlns:xsd="http://www.w3.org/2001/XMLSchema"
                xmlns:xsl="http://www.w3.org/1999/XSL/Transform"
                ContentReadable="true">
```

The code above is the Schema Definition section of XML. It defines the XML schema that will be used. The management pack file uses the standard public XML schema.

```
  <Manifest>
   <Identity>
     <ID>OpsMgr.SQL.Extension</ID>
     <Version>1.0.0.0</Version>
   </Identity>
```

```xml
<Name>OpsMgr SQL Extension</Name>
<References>
  <Reference Alias="MicrosoftSystemCenterServiceDesignerLibrary60500028">
    <ID>Microsoft.SystemCenter.ServiceDesigner.Library</ID>
    <Version>6.0.5000.0</Version>
    <PublicKeyToken>31bf3856ad364e35</PublicKeyToken>
  </Reference>
  <Reference Alias="Windows">
    <ID>Microsoft.Windows.Library</ID>
    <Version>6.0.5000.0</Version>
    <PublicKeyToken>31bf3856ad364e35</PublicKeyToken>
  </Reference>
  <Reference Alias="Performance">
    <ID>System.Performance.Library</ID>
    <Version>6.0.5000.0</Version>
    <PublicKeyToken>31bf3856ad364e35</PublicKeyToken>
  </Reference>
  <Reference Alias="Image">
    <ID>System.Image.Library</ID>
    <Version>6.0.5000.0</Version>
    <PublicKeyToken>31bf3856ad364e35</PublicKeyToken>
  </Reference>
  <Reference Alias="MicrosoftSQLServerLibrary6050000">
    <ID>Microsoft.SQLServer.Library</ID>
    <Version>6.0.5000.0</Version>
    <PublicKeyToken>31bf3856ad364e35</PublicKeyToken>
  </Reference>
  <Reference Alias="Reporting">
    <ID>Microsoft.SystemCenter.DataWarehouse.Report.Library</ID>
    <Version>6.0.5000.0</Version>
    <PublicKeyToken>31bf3856ad364e35</PublicKeyToken>
  </Reference>
  <Reference Alias="System">
    <ID>System.Library</ID>
    <Version>6.0.5000.0</Version>
    <PublicKeyToken>31bf3856ad364e35</PublicKeyToken>
  </Reference>
  <Reference Alias="SC">
    <ID>Microsoft.SystemCenter.Library</ID>
    <Version>6.0.5000.0</Version>
    <PublicKeyToken>31bf3856ad364e35</PublicKeyToken>
  </Reference>
  <Reference Alias="Health">
    <ID>System.Health.Library</ID>
    <Version>6.0.5000.0</Version>
```

23

```
        <PublicKeyToken>31bf3856ad364e35</PublicKeyToken>
      </Reference>
    </References>
  </Manifest>
```

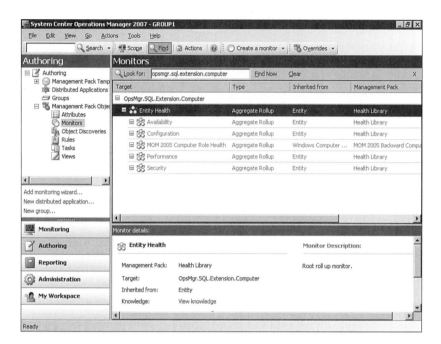

FIGURE 23.25   The monitor information available from the OpsMgr SQL Extension created with XML.

This is the Manifest section, where the management pack name is defined as well as the version (the version number should be modified when updates are made for consistency). The section also contains the references to other management packs that this management pack will use. The minimum references we recommend for all management packs are as follows:

▶ Health

▶ SC (System Center)

▶ System

▶ Performance

▶ Windows

```
<TypeDefinitions>
  <EntityTypes>
    <ClassTypes>
      <ClassType ID="OpsMgr.SQL.Extension.Computer"
                 Accessibility="Public"
                 Abstract="false"
                 Base="Windows!Microsoft.Windows.ComputerRole"
                 Hosted="true"
                 Singleton="false">
      </ClassType>
    </ClassTypes>
  </EntityTypes>
</TypeDefinitions>
```

The TypeDefinitions section is the part of the XML code where we define and create classes. This particular example creates the OpsMgr.SQL.Extension.Computer class object, which we are basing on the Windows!Microsoft.Windows.ComputerRole role. Because we base it on that role, the class will appear under the Windows Computer role in the class list in OpsMgr.

```
<Monitoring>
  <Discoveries>
    <Discovery ID="OpsMgr.SQL.Extension.Discovery"
               Enabled="true"
               Target="Windows!Microsoft.Windows.Server.Computer"
               ConfirmDelivery="false"
               Remotable="true"
               Priority="Normal">
      <Category>Discovery</Category>
      <DiscoveryTypes>
        <DiscoveryClass TypeID="OpsMgr.SQL.Extension.Computer">
          <Property TypeID="System!System.Entity"
                    PropertyID="DisplayName" />
        </DiscoveryClass>
        <DiscoveryRelationship TypeID="Windows!Microsoft.Windows.
        ➥ComputerHostsComputerRole" />
      </DiscoveryTypes>
      <DataSource ID="DS" TypeID="Windows!Microsoft.Windows.
      ➥FilteredRegistryDiscoveryProvider">
      <ComputerName>$Target/Property
      ➥[Type="Windows!Microsoft.Windows.Computer"]/NetworkName$</ComputerName>
        <RegistryAttributeDefinitions>
          <RegistryAttributeDefinition>
            <AttributeName>SQLInstalled</AttributeName>
            <Path>SOFTWARE\Microsoft\Microsoft SQL Server</Path>
            <PathType>0</PathType>
```

```
            <AttributeType>0</AttributeType>
          </RegistryAttributeDefinition>
        </RegistryAttributeDefinitions>
        <Frequency>300</Frequency>
        <ClassId>$MPElement[Name="OpsMgr.SQL.Extension.Computer"]$</ClassId>
        <InstanceSettings>
          <Settings>
            <Setting>
            <Name>$MPElement[Name="Windows!Microsoft.Windows.
            ➥Computer"]/PrincipalName$</Name>
              <Value>$Target/Property[Type="Windows!Microsoft.
              ➥Windows.Computer"/PrincipalName$</Value>
            </Setting>
            <Setting>
              <Name>$MPElement[Name="System!System.Entity"]/DisplayName$</Name>
               <Value>SQL Server ($Target/Property[Type="Windows!Microsoft.
               ➥Windows.Computer"]/NetbiosComputerName$)</Value>
            </Setting>
          </Settings>
        </InstanceSettings>
        <Expression>
          <SimpleExpression>
            <ValueExpression>
              <XPathQuery Type="Boolean">Values/SQLInstalled</XPathQuery>
            </ValueExpression>
            <Operator>Equal</Operator>
            <ValueExpression>
              <Value Type="Boolean">true</Value>
            </ValueExpression>
          </SimpleExpression>
        </Expression>
      </DataSource>
    </Discovery>
  </Discoveries>
</Monitoring>
```

The Monitoring section of the management pack file contains the rules, the monitors, and all the monitoring objects in the management pack. Typically, it is a large section! In this example, we simply created a discovery rule that finds computers with SQL Server installed and adds them to our newly created class. Although the section can look rather intimidating, all we are doing here is using the XML beneath TypeID="Windows! Microsoft.Windows.FilteredRegistryDiscoveryProvider"> to locate the HKLM\ SOFTWARE\Microsoft\Microsoft SQL Server Registry path. If the path is found, we add the computer to the class; then we discover and populate the PrincipleName and DisplayName attributes so that the object displays correctly in the Operations console.

```
<LanguagePacks>
  <LanguagePack ID="ENG"
                IsDefault="false">
    <DisplayStrings>
      <DisplayString ElementID="OpsMgr.SQL.Extension">
        <Name>OpsMgr SQL Extension</Name>
        <Description>Provides Advanced monitoring of SQL</Description>
      </DisplayString>
      <DisplayString ElementID="OpsMgr.SQL.Extension.Computer">
        <Name>OpsMgr SQL Extension Computer</Name>
      </DisplayString>
      <DisplayString ElementID="OpsMgr.SQL.Extension.Discovery">
        <Name>OpsMgr SQL Extension Computer Discovery</Name>
      </DisplayString>
      <DisplayString ElementID="OpsMgr.SQL.Extension.Discovery"
                     SubElementID="DS">
        <Name>Registry Probe</Name>
      </DisplayString>
    </DisplayStrings>
  </LanguagePack>
</LanguagePacks>
</ManagementPack>
```

The LanguagePacks section is extremely important and affects all objects created in the management pack file. When you create an object, it is given an ID within the management pack, such as our class `OpsMgr.SQL.Extension.Computer`. This is an appropriate ID to be called from within the management pack, but it is not very readable to the end user. The LanguagePacks section resolves this by mapping a user friendly DisplayString for every object in the management pack. Remember, whenever you create an object in the management pack, whether it be a monitor, a rule, or a class, it will need a corresponding entry in the LanguagePacks section. This section also contains all product knowledge—although we recommend you add this level of detail using the Operations console, not directly in XML, as this is easier to do in the Operations console.

Now that you have seen an example of how the internals of XML are used within Operations Manager 2007, we will discuss additional options that are either currently available or will soon be available for creating management packs in Operations Manager 2007.

Using the Operations Manager Authoring Console

Microsoft has developed a separate Authoring console, which is in release candidate (RC) status as we are finishing this book. The RC version of the Authoring console is available for download on the Microsoft Connect website (http://connect.microsoft.com).

After its release, the Authoring console should be available for download at http://technet.microsoft.com/en-us/opsmgr/bb498232.aspx. The Authoring console will require Operations Manager 2007 Service Pack (SP) 1.

The Operations Manager Authoring console will provide easier-to-use functionality than XML to write management packs, and it will extend the ability to write management packs without creating them using XML. The Authoring console is a separate program from the Operations console (which is available on the Start menu -> Programs -> System Center Operations Manager 2007 folder).

Functionality

The Authoring console has a similar look and feel to the Operations console, and provides visibility into areas not accessible from the Operations console. We will look at three of these:

▶ Figure 23.26 shows the ability to add to the classes included with the Windows Server 2003 management pack.

▶ The Authoring console also provides the ability to display and add relationship information within the management pack (see Figure 23.27).

▶ A third area in the console, which otherwise can only be manipulated using XML, is object discoveries. Although you can review object discoveries with the Operations console, you are not able to create them. As you see in Figure 23.28, the ability to create discoveries is functionality available with the RC version of the Authoring console.

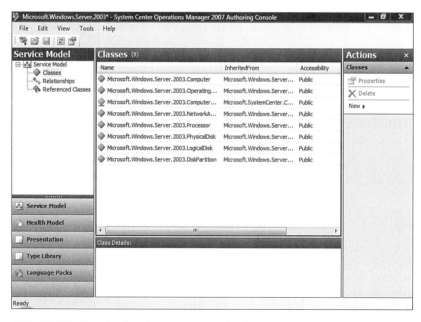

FIGURE 23.26   OpsMgr Authoring console classes.

Based on the current capabilities of the Operations Manager Authoring console, it appears that the majority of the requirements for using XML to create management packs will no longer be necessary once Microsoft fully supports this utility.

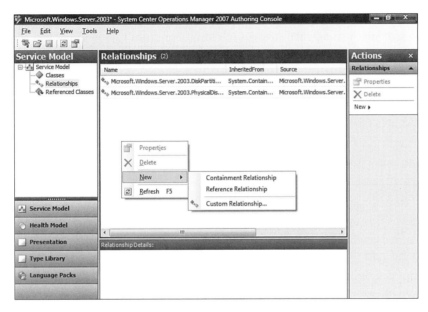

FIGURE 23.27   OpsMgr Authoring console relationships.

FIGURE 23.28   OpsMgr Authoring consoled discoveries.

Creating a Class

We will now use the Authoring console to create a custom management pack. The management pack's functionality includes defining a new OpsMgr class, based on discovering computers with a certain Registry key. The Authoring console includes a wizard that will help us create the basic building blocks of the management pack.

The subject of this particular management pack is Microsoft Forefront Client Security (FCS). We can discover computers running FCS by examining their Registry. Therefore, before we begin, we determine what Registry key we will use to discover the presence of the FCS anti-malware (AM) application on a computer. We have determined we will look for the following key:

HKEY_LOCAL_MACHINE\SOFTWARE\Microsoft\Microsoft Forefront\Client Security\1.0\AM

Now we launch the wizard by selecting File -> New. Here are the steps we followed to create the management pack:

1. At the Select a management pack template page, you can select either Empty Management Pack or Windows Application (Registry). We selected the Registry type and typed the management pack name **Microsoft.Forefront.ClientSecurity**. Management pack dotted names cannot contain spaces. Click Next.

2. At the General page, enter the (friendly) display name and description. The display name can contain spaces. We entered the name **Forefront Client Security**. Click Next.

3. On the Windows Application page, enter in the ID field of the class name that you assign to this management pack. We used the name **Microsoft.Forefront. ClientSecurity.Custom** for the ID and the name used in step 2 for the Display Name field. Click Next to continue.

4. At the Registry Probe Configuration page, click the Add button. We selected the key attribute type and used **FcsExists** for the attribute name. (The attribute name is a label you select to represent a true or false value, which indicates whether or not the Registry key exists.)

   We are looking for the presence of the key at this path: SOFTWARE\Microsoft\ Microsoft Forefront\Client Security\1.0\AM (omit the leading HKEY_LOCAL_ MACHINE part of the Registry path). This is the Boolean attribute type (the value will be true or false). Figure 23.29 shows the properties of the attribute on the Registry Probe Configuration page of the wizard. Click Next.

5. Build the expression to filter the Parameter name setting Values/FCSExists, the Operator setting Equals, and the Value setting true. The format of the expression will always be the string Value/ followed by the attribute name. This parameter lets OpsMgr know how to map discovered data to a class instance. Now click Create.

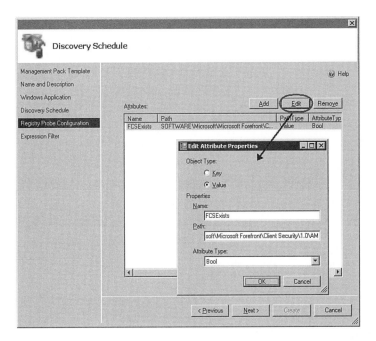

FIGURE 23.29   The Authoring console includes a wizard that helps create discoveries.

6. Next, populate the DiscoveryTypes section with a DiscoveryClass section to define the classes and relationships that cay be discovered by the Discovery. Open the Properties of the discovery rule in the Authoring -> Management Pack Objects -> Object Discoveries node. On the Discovery Types tab, associate the Forefront.Client.Security.Custom class with this discovery, and specify that a hosting relationship exists with the Microsoft Windows Computer HostsLocalApplication type ID. Press OK.

7. Save the management pack as an XML file in the Authoring console. Import the management pack into the OpsMgr management group using the Operations console; navigate to Administration -> Management Packs and run the Import Management Pack task.

8. Now, check to see if the management pack correctly discovered computers in the management group with FCS installed. Wait a few minutes and then navigate to the Monitoring -> Discovered Inventory view.

9. Click the Change target type... action in the State Actions pane. Find the new class listed in the Target and Management Pack columns. In our case, this is Forefront Client Security. Click OK.

10. Within a few minutes, you should see listed in the Results pane all the instances of the new class discovered in the management group. We correctly observed that all the computers with FCS installed appear in the console. They appear unmonitored because we have not yet defined any monitors. Figure 23.30 is our view of the newly discovered objects, also known as *class instances*, and in this case they represent computers where FCS AM is installed.

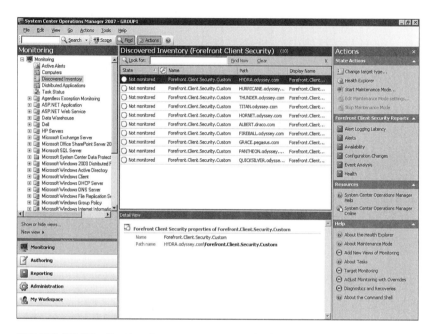

FIGURE 23.30   Testing the management pack: Expected new objects are discovered.

We have now created and tested a basic custom management pack. After importing the unsealed management pack into the management group, you can create views, rules, monitors, and other OpsMgr features in the Authoring space of the Operations console. A big value-add for the Authoring console is that it created valid manifest, language pack, class definition, display strings, and discovery logic. Most critically, we have also defined a new class that we can target rules and monitors against throughout the Operations console.

Which Console to Use?

You can create views, rules, and monitors in the Authoring console. So why are we proposing that you import a management pack you started from the Authoring console to the Operations console to continue working on it?

We suggest using the Authoring console to create the framework for the management pack (or you could use native XML) because the Operations console does not support creating that basic framework. However, the Operations console is easier for development work because you can see the results of your work immediately, without having to export from the Authoring console, version increment, and then import into your management group and the Operations console.

We recommend that vendors use the Authoring console and an XML editor in combination, and that OpsMgr customers create the base framework in the Authoring console or XML and then augment additional functionality using the Operations console.

We performed one additional customization to the management pack (in XML) that is not yet possible in the RC version of the Authoring console. A manual XML addition appears in the Non-Key properties (optional) section of the Discovery Mapper tab in the configuration of the discovery. See this entry highlighted in Figure 23.31. We added another setting to the InstanceSettings that defines the display name to use for objects discovered in the class. Our setting is **FCS Anti-malware (*<NetBIOS Computer Name>*)**.

After each time you save the XML file in the Authoring console, manually open the XML file in Notepad or your XML editor and increment the version number. This lets you quickly import (slipstream) the updated management pack into your test management group. Because the management pack is unsealed, you can also use the Authoring space of the Operations console to edit the XML directly, although this does not preserve a versioning trail for rollback purposes.

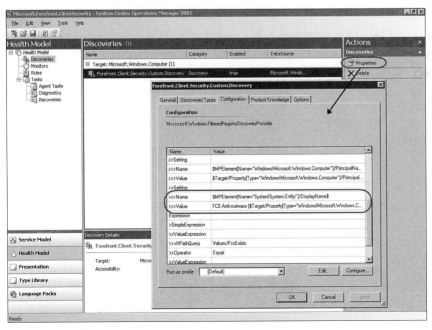

FIGURE 23.31   Discovery configuration: Custom XML added to set the display name.

Creating a Unit Monitor

To deliver a simple but functional management pack, we used the Authoring console to create a new Unit monitor, of the Basic Service Monitor type (the same monitor type we previously created to monitor McAfee), targeting the Forefront Client Security class. This monitor will allow the management pack to display a meaningful health state in the Monitoring space. The monitor will confirm that the FCSAM service is running on customer computers with FCS client software installed. If the service is running, the state of the monitor is healthy. The monitor will generate alerts when the service is not running.

To add that functionality, we created a new view folder in the Monitoring space named **Forefront Client Security** and saved the folder to our new custom management pack. Then we created new State and Alert view folders targeted to the Forefront Client Security class. The State view populated with the computers as expected. Stop and start tests of the service confirmed the health monitor and alerting action were working. See the State view and Health Explorer for the monitor in Figure 23.32.

The resultant custom management pack we created in this section is on the CD accompanying this book; the filename is Microsoft.Forefront.ClientSecurity.xml. It would be instructive to open that file in Notepad, Internet Explorer, or with an XML editor, after having read this section of the chapter to observe the XML components we discussed.

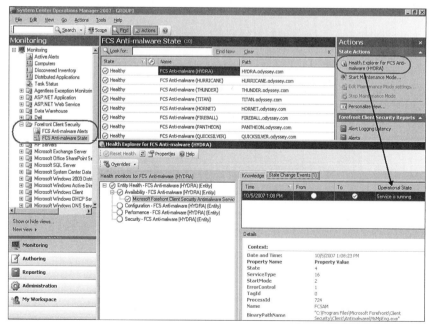

FIGURE 23.32   Anti-malware service health on computers where the software is installed.

> **TIP**
>
> **On the CD**
>
> The Microsoft.Forefront.ClientSecurity.xml management pack is on the CD accompanying this book.

Using Silect MP Studio

Silect Software's MP Studio product provides a third-party solution to assist with management packs in Operations Manager 2007. MP Studio provides version control (check-in, check-out), backup, and auditing capabilities. MP Studio requires a system running Windows XP, Windows Vista, or Windows Server 2003, and a backend database of either SQL Server 2000 or SQL Server 2005 (MSDE or SQL Server 2005 Express Edition will work as well).

One of the features of MP Studio is a graphically driven layout for the management packs. We show this in Figure 23.33, displaying the layout for the Windows Server 2003 management pack (to see this view, right-click the management pack on the left side of this screen and choose View Reference Tree).

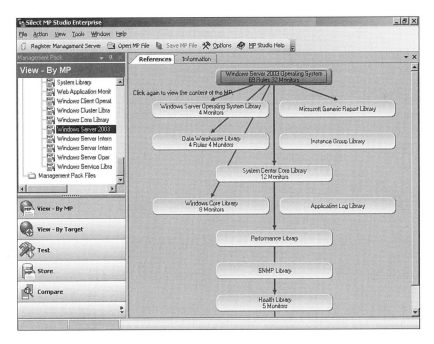

FIGURE 23.33   MP Studio view by management pack.

Some very nice features of the MP Studio include its ability to compare multiple copies of a management pack to a single standard or master copy, as well as its ability to list out the rules in a management pack, test a management pack, and to document management packs (shown in Figure 23.34). To document a management pack, right-click the management pack on the left side of the screen and choose Document Management Pack.

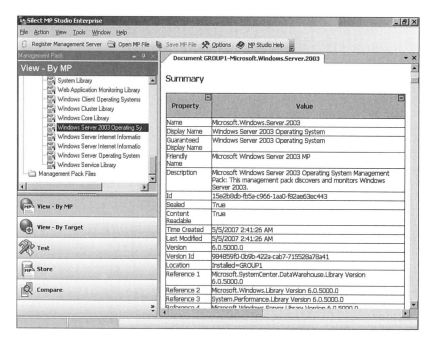

FIGURE 23.34   MP Studio document management pack.

The screenshots shown in this chapter are from MP Studio 2007 SP 1 and Beta 1 for MP Studio 2007 R2. Silect's MP Studio 2007 R2 adds more capabilities around testing management packs and includes a wizard-driven approach for creating simple management packs. Silect released the production version of MP Studio 2007 R2 in mid-November 2007.

Using the wizard allows you to easily gather performance and event information and generate alerts based on the information gathered. To create a management pack using the wizard, open MP Studio under the View by Management Pack section. Now perform the following steps:

1. Create a management pack folder (point it to the directory where Operations Manager is installed). Then right-click this folder and choose the Create New Management Pack option. This starts the wizard with a typical welcome screen, and then continues to the dialog box titled Specify the manifest information for your new MP. Here you can configure the manifest as shown in Figure 23.35.

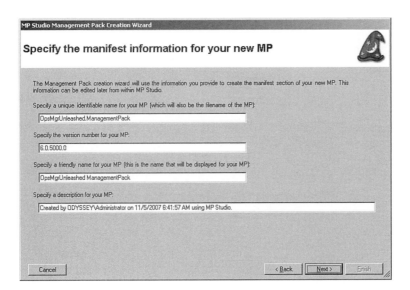

FIGURE 23.35   Specifying manifest information in the wizard.

2. On the Manifest screen (shown in Figure 23.35), we specify the name of the management pack, the version number, the friendly name, and the description for the management pack. Click Next to continue.

3. Next, we specify where we will target the management pack (see Figure 23.36).

    Targets are added using the Add Target(s) button visible in Figure 23.36. For our example, we have chosen Microsoft.Windows.OperatingSystem to be the target of our management pack. After choosing the target(s), click Next to continue.

4. We now specify performance information that we want to gather as part of the management pack. This is added by choosing the target, object, counter, and instance of the performance counter we want to gather (shown in Figure 23.37 in the Counter column, using % Processor as our sample counter).

    Then we specify the name, display name, and description for the counter. Multiple counters can be added and performance data can be found through browsing to different monitored computers. Click Next to continue.

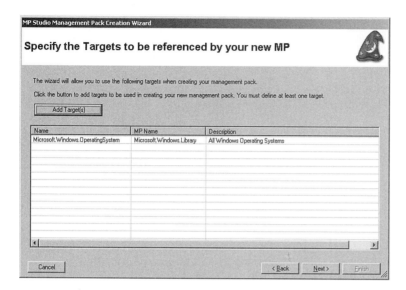

FIGURE 23.36   Management Pack Creation Wizard targeting.

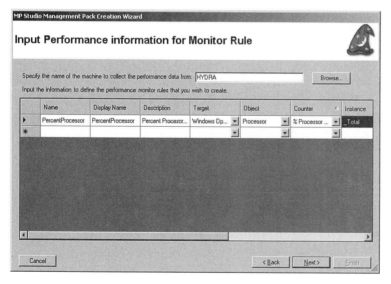

FIGURE 23.37   Management Pack Creation Wizard performance information.

5. Event information can also be gathered using the screen we show in Figure 23.38, which specifies an event from the System Event log related to system startup. Different event logs can be chosen, and events can be found by browsing to different systems. Click Next to continue.

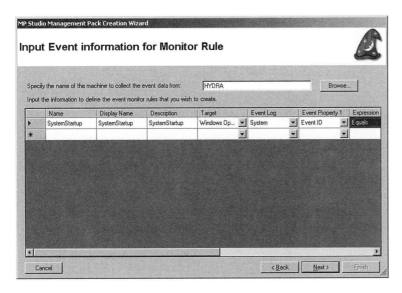

FIGURE 23.38   Management Pack Creation Wizard event information.

6. Now that we have specified the performance and event information, we can configure any alerts that need to be generated based on what we discover with this information. For our example (shown in Figure 23.39), restarting a system creates an
   event that is logged to the System Event log; when this event is found, the management pack will create an information alert in OpsMgr. Click Next to continue.

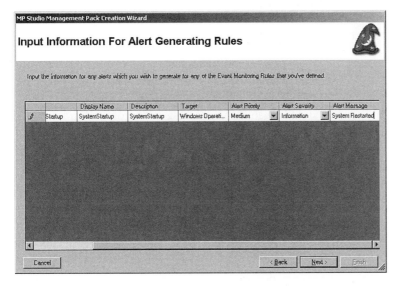

FIGURE 23.39   Management Pack Creation Wizard alert generation.

7. Once we have finished configuring the management pack, we are asked to confirm and finish the process. This creates the management pack in MP Studio.

Information on Silect and MP Studio is available on Silect's website at http://www.silect.com. The MP Studio product is also available as a trial version, which is available for download at http://www.silect.com/products/product_info.php.

So far, this chapter has investigated the steps required to create management pack objects and bring them together into simple management packs. We have explored technologies to create management packs and their objects and have shown different options planned to be available for management pack development. A major part of a management pack is its reports. The next part of this chapter discusses report development with Operations Manager 2007.

Developing Reports

Operations Manager 2007 includes a variety of options for creating reports. These approaches include the following:

- Building reports for My Workspace in the Operations console
- Publishing reports (new with SP 1)
- Creating linked reports
- Using Visual Studio to create reports

Before we discuss how to develop a report, we should mention that sometimes it is often quicker and easier to view results by using the Monitoring section of the Operations console! If the information you are looking for is available as a performance counter and the time in which you need to track it is less than the grooming interval of your Operations Manager environment (7 days by default), then a performance-monitoring view will work well.

Let's take an example where we want to provide a view of the free disk space on systems over a 2-day period of time. Perform the following steps to create a simple view of the data:

1. Open the Operations console and navigate to Monitoring -> Microsoft Windows Server -> Performance -> Disk Capacity.

2. On the Actions pane under Performance Actions is the option Select time range.... Selecting a time range provides the ability to change the view to show data from a specific start and end time, or you can select a time range in minute, hours, or days.

3. For this example, we configured the view to show data over a 2-day period for the Hurricane and Quicksilver servers. Alternatively, we could specify how long the graph should show data by clicking the Select Time Range option, shown in Figure 23.40.

Figure 23.41 displays Logical Disk performance graphs for the two servers, using the time range of 9/23/2007 through 9/24/2007.

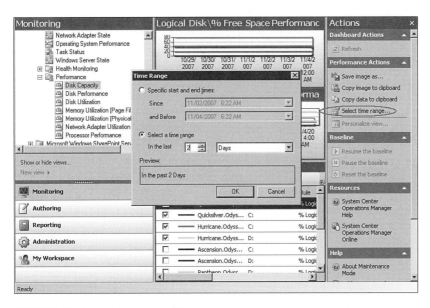

FIGURE 23.40   Selecting the time range for the performance view.

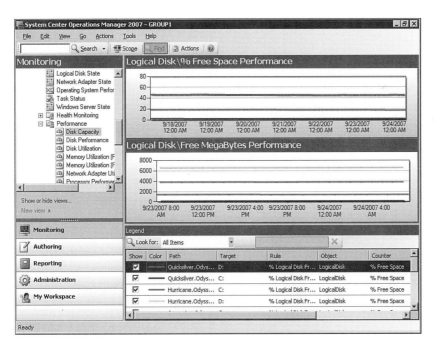

FIGURE 23.41   Performance view showing free disk space.

> **NOTE**
>
> **Viewing Older Data in the Operations Console**
>
> Remember, your capability to set a date range for viewing data older than 7 days depends on the grooming thresholds set for the Operational database. We discuss database grooming in Chapter 12.

Operations Console Favorite Reports

Although we can create a graph showing free space over the short term, we also want to be able to see trending of available free disk space over a longer period than available with the Monitoring space of the Operations console. Our next step is to create a report that will provide this information. The Reporting space in the Operations console draws its data from the Data Warehouse database, which by default retains the majority of its data for 400 days (13 months, so that trending can be done over a 1-year period). To create this report, we will take the following steps:

1. Open the Operations console. Navigate to Reports -> Microsoft Generic Report Library -> Performance. Then double-click to open the Performance report.

2. Set the date to Yesterday as a starting date.

3. Click Change to configure the report.

4. Click the New Chart button and add the chart title.

5. On the Settings screen, click the New Series button (highlighted in Figure 23.42) and then click the Add Object button.

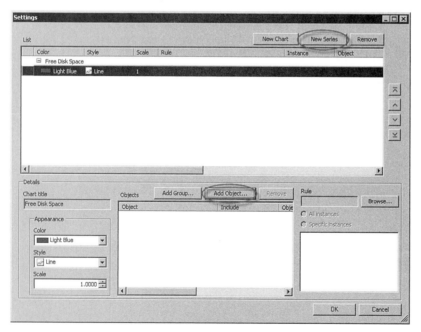

FIGURE 23.42   Creating a new chart and a new series.

6. At the Add Object screen, type **C:** in the field next to Object Name with the Contains dropdown box.

7. Select the first server on the list that you want to report on (shown in Figure 23.43) and click OK.

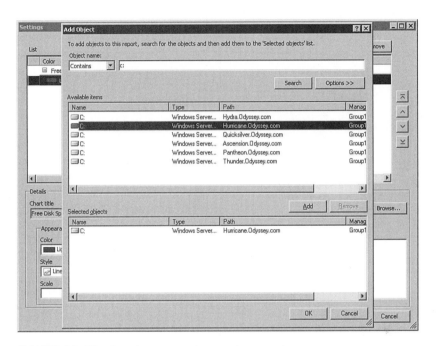

FIGURE 23.43   Creating a new chart and new series.

8. Back at the Settings screen, click New Series and then click Add Object....

9. Specify the drive to include for the object. We selected **D:** because we will be reporting on the D: drive's free space on the server.

10. Add the next server on the list and click OK.

11. Repeat steps 8–10 until all servers and drives required for the report are added, as shown in Figure 23.44.

12. Now, click the first of the series shown in the chart and click the Browse button at the right side of Figure 23.44, to the left of the Rule selection.

13. At the Select rule screen, choose Search by Counter.

14. Choose the Performance object LogicalDisk and set Counter to % Free Space. Then click Search.

15. Add % Logical Disk Free Space, as shown in Figure 23.45, and click OK.

16. Choose the specific instance for the rule to match the drive on which you are reporting.

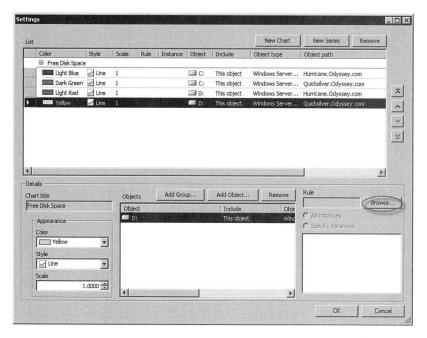

FIGURE 23.44 Creating a new chart and setting the first server.

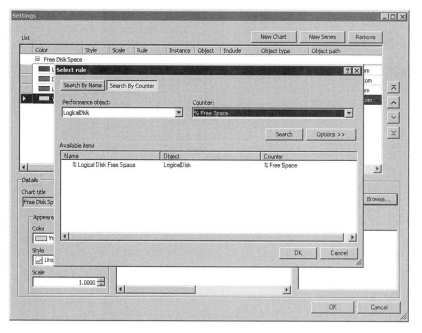

FIGURE 23.45 Matching the performance object to the series.

17. Perform the same action for the remaining counters. The objects should now be matched to the appropriate instances, as shown in Figure 23.46. Click OK when complete.

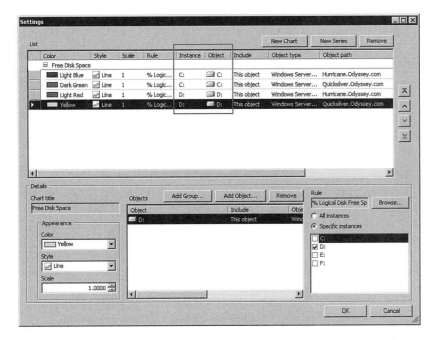

FIGURE 23.46   Completed matching of objects and rules.

18. Now click the Run button to run the report and validate that it runs correctly. Once it runs correctly, update the start date of the report (go to View -> Parameters to change this setting).

19. Select File -> Save to Favorites to make the report accessible after it is configured.

Figure 23.47 shows the output from the report.

Publishing Reports

With the release of Operations Manager 2007 SP 1, Microsoft provides new functionality allowing you to publish reports. Published reports are prerendered reports with preselected parameters. These parameters allow the reports to run without requiring input. When this type of report is created, it first appears in the Operations console -> Reporting -> Authored Reports section.

To publish a report, run the report and then choose the File -> Publish option, as shown in Figure 23.48 (if you do not see the Publish option listed, your environment most likely does not have OpsMgr 2007 SP 1 installed).

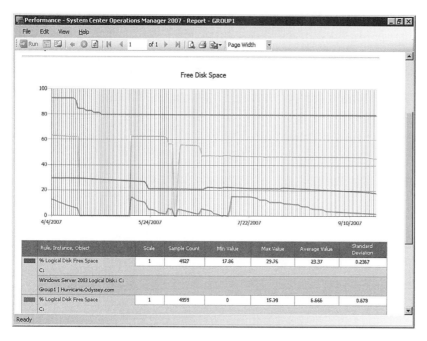

FIGURE 23.47   Trending report for free disk space on Hurricane and Quicksilver.

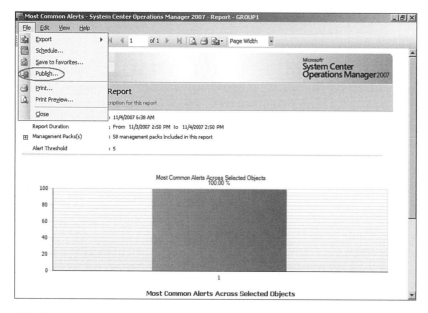

FIGURE 23.48   The Publish Report option.

Although this report is now published, only the user who created the report can see it. To make this report available to all users, we will create a new folder for the report and add the RPDL file (also known as a RDL file) created when we published our report. Perform the following steps:

1. Browse to the Reporting Server (http://localhost/reports on the local system or http://<servername>/reports if it is a remote system) and create a new folder (see Figure 23.49), which we will name **Published Reports**.

   The report that we published is initially stored under the My Reports folder (circled in Figure 23.50).

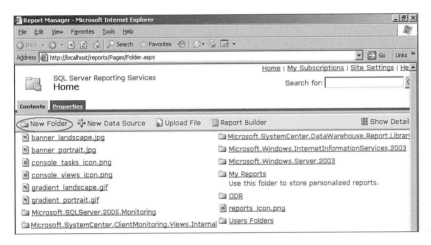

FIGURE 23.49   Creating a new folder in SQL Server Reporting Services.

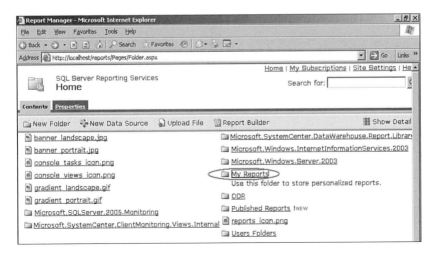

FIGURE 23.50   My Reports folder.

2. We want to move this report to the Published Reports folder. To do this, open the My Reports Folder, open the report, and select the Properties tab, as shown in Figure 23.51. Click the Move button (circled in Figure 23.51).

3. Now, we need to select the folder we created earlier (Published Reports), as high-lighted in Figure 23.52. Click OK to continue.

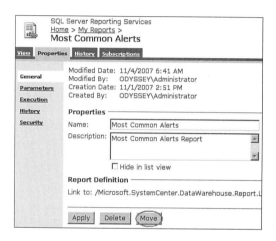

FIGURE 23.51   The Move button under Report Properties.

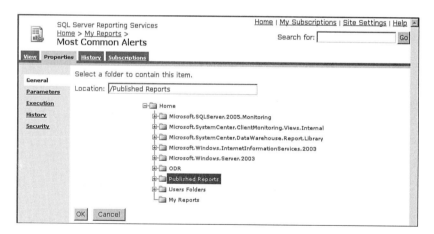

FIGURE 23.52   Specifying where to move the report to.

4. We now need to move the RPDL file to the correct location. Go back to the My Reports folder and click Show Details (see Figure 23.53).

5. Once the details are visible, you can see the Most Common Alerts.rpdl file, which we need to move. To do this, check the box on the first column of that line and select the Move icon, as shown in Figure 23.54.

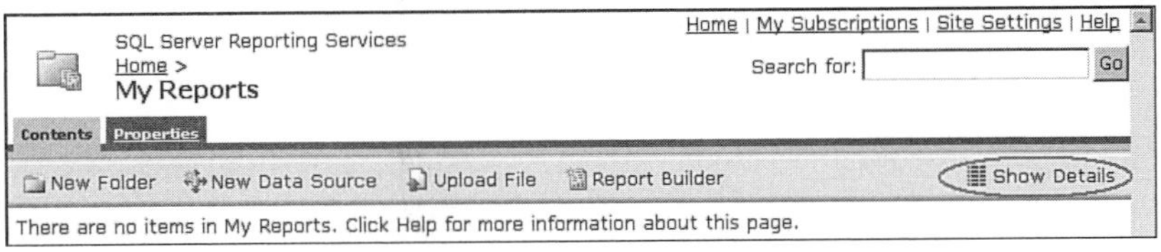

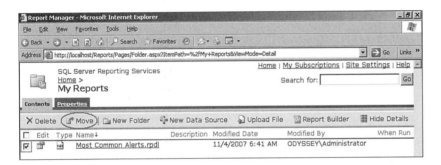

FIGURE 23.53   The Show Details icon.

FIGURE 23.54   Moving the RPDL file.

6. Select the Published Reports folder, as we did when we moved the report in Figure 23.52. Click OK to continue. The new folder (Published Reports) that we created is visible within the Operations console in the Reporting space under Reporting -> Published Reports (see Figure 23.55). Because our folder and report are under the Reporting structure in the console (not Authored Reports or Favorite Reports), they are now visible to other users of Operations Manager!

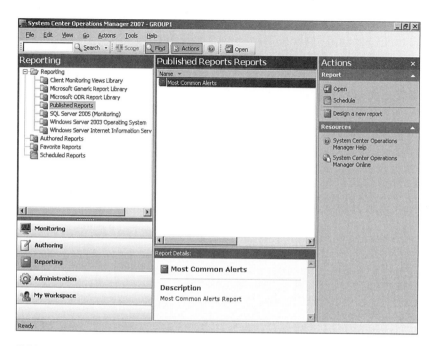

FIGURE 23.55   Viewing the Most Common Alerts published report in the Operations console.

Creating Linked Reports

The linked report capability allows you to create a linked copy of a report and then customize the parameters to suit a particular function. You can use linked reports to provide a custom report for any performance counter OpsMgr collects. A linked report is only a pointer to an existing report, but it can pass different parameters and results for each user in a separate report with its own name. Linked reports are shortcuts to existing reports.

OpsMgr 2007 uses linked reports extensively. You can generate linked reports quickly (without affecting the original report) and integrate them into Operations Manager, just like other customized reports. However, there are several restrictions when using linked reports:

▶ A linked report cannot provide reports on non-performance-counter-related information.

▶ You cannot export and import a linked report into another OpsMgr management group; it has to be manually re-created.

▶ Linked reports do not have the flexibility often required when building custom reports in OpsMgr.

Linked reports are created using SQL Reporting Services or XML. To best understand how linked reports work, this chapter will look at the XML. Of course, many OpsMgr administrators are not XML coders, so we include this information primarily for reference.

Another reason for discussing the XML is if you include the report information in the XML, you can import the report as part of a management pack into another management group or environment!

In an XML document, you first define linked reports in the Reporting section. The XML for a linked report definition would look something like this:

```
<Reporting>
  <LinkedReports>
    <Linked Report ID="Custom.Linked.Report" Accessibility="Public"Visible="true"
                <Base="Reporting!Microsoft.SystemCenter.
                ➡DataWarehouse.Report.Availability">
      <ParameterBlock columns="4" xmins=http://schema.microsoft.com/mom/
      ➡reporting/2007/ReportParameterSettings">
        <Controls>...
      </ParameterBlock>
    </Linked Report>
  </LinkedReports>
</Reporting>
```

Notice the <base> tag, which is specific to a linked report. Base tells us which report this is a shortcut to. In this case, it is a generic availability report, although you can use any publicly defined report from any management pack.

The XML also includes a reference to the management pack including the original generic report. You may recall that the "XML and Management Pack Creation" section of this chapter introduced the References section of an XML document. That particular example included the Microsoft.SystemCenter.DataWarehouse.Report.Library section. We need that library (management pack) referenced to include reports in our management pack because it contains the original report. We are referencing version 6.0.6246 of this MP, which is the version current with the RC 0 version of OpsMgr 2007 SP 1.

```
    </Reference>
     <Reference Alias="Reporting">
      <ID>Microsoft.SystemCenter.DataWarehouse.Report.Library<ID>
      <Version>6.0.6246.0</Version>
      <PublicKeyToken>...</PublicKeyToken>
     </Reference>
    </References>
```

We use the <LanguagePacks> section to specify the management pack and report display name.

```
<LanguagePacks>
  <LanguagePack ID="ENG" IsDefault="false">
    <DisplayStrings>
      <DisplayString ElementID="Custom.CustomLinkedReport">
```

```
      <Name>Custom Linked Report</Name>
      <Description>Example of a Custom Linked Report</Description>
    </DisplayString>
    <DisplayString ElementID="Custom Reporting">
      <Name>Custom Linked Reports</Name>
    </DisplayString>
    </DisplayStrings>
  </LanguagePack>
</LanguagePacks>
```

This XML code is just to establish the environment for the report itself. Because our linked report is based on the Availability Report, we are going to define a linked report based on the existing report.

The report will preselect data aggregation, the time range, and the required downtime values. We are defining Availability using the System.State.EntityHealth monitor, with states of Warning (2) and UnMonitored (3) as downtime. We will aggregate daily, and we will calculate based on availability during business hours.

We suggest you use an XML editor such as XML Notepad to view and edit your code, which we introduced in the "Digging Deeper into XML" section of this chapter. An editor designed for XML makes it much easier to see the sections of the document.

In the Parameters section of the XML file, you will want to add the following information (using an editor tailored for XML will make this much easier to locate and edit):

▶ Default the `DataAggregation` parameter to Daily:

```
<Parameter Name="DataAggregation"><Value>1</Value></Parameter>
```

▶ Update the `DownTime` parameter for values of 2 or 3:

```
<Parameter Name="DownTime"><Value>2</Value><Value>3</Value></Parameter>
```

▶ Enable reporting during business hours only by adding the `TimeType` parameter:

```
<Parameter Name="TimeType"><Value>Business</Value></Parameter>
```

▶ Add the System.Health.EntityState monitor to calculate availability:

```
<Parameter Name="MonitorName"><Value>System.Health.EntityState
➥</Value></Parameter>
```

▶ You will also want to define the business hours as being between 8 a.m. and 5 p.m., Monday through Friday, with a default report range from Friday of the previous week to today. The following XML code accomplishes this:

```
<Parameter Name="StartDate_BaseType"><Value>Friday</Value></Parameter>
<Parameter Name="StartDate_OffsetType"><Value>Week</Value></Parameter>
<Parameter Name="StartDate_OffsetValue"><Value>-1</Value></Parameter>
<Parameter Name="EndDate_BaseType"><Value>Today</Value></Parameter>
<Parameter Name="EndDate_OffsetType"><Value>None</Value></Parameter>
<Parameter Name="EndDate_OffsetValue"><Value>0</Value></Parameter>
<Parameter Name="TimeType"><Value>Business</Value></Parameter>
<Parameter Name="StartDate_BaseValue"><Value>11/13/2007 08:00:00 AM
➥</Value></Parameter>
<Parameter Name="EndDate_BaseValue"><Value>11/13/2007 5:00:00 PM
➥</Value></Parameter>
<Parameter
Name="TimeWeekMap"><Value>Monday</Value><Value>Tuesday</Value><Value>
➥Wednesday</Value><Value>Thursday</Value><Value>Friday</Value></Parameter>
```

That's it! It did seem like a lot of effort. You can now save the XML file and import it into OpsMgr. If you open the Reporting space of the Operations console, the imported folder and report should be visible.

Creating Linked Reports from Your Favorites

In the "Operations Console Favorite Reports" section of this chapter, we created a favorite report of free disk space trending information. Now that we have this report, it would be great if we could share this with others (report favorites are stored on a per-user basis). Unfortunately, there is no built-in way to publish your favorite reports within the Reporting Server, but there is a process to accomplish this goal manually. We can use a linked report to share a favorite report.

As we discussed in the "Creating Linked Reports" section, linked reports are shortcuts to reports that has a different set of parameters, and they are available only to the user who created them. Favorite reports are also shortcuts to reports with a different set of parameters, but they are not user specific. Whereas linked reports are stored on the Reporting Server, favorite reports are not. To find a list of your favorite reports, you can use the PowerShell Command Shell with the following command:

```
$userSettings = (get-item .).ManagementGroup.GetUserSettings()

$userSettings.GetFavoriteMonitoringReports()
```

If you want to get only a specific report, you can specify the report by adding a parameter to the command, as shown next (the example shows our Logical Disk Free Space report created earlier in this chapter):

```
$userSettings = (get-item .).ManagementGroup.GetUserSettings()

$userSettings.GetFavoriteMonitoringReport("Logical Disk Free Space")
```

From the output of the Command Shell script, several fields are displayed. We are interested in Name (the name shown in the console), the list of parameters (ReportParameters) that are in XML format, and MonitoringReportPath, which is the path to the original report in SQL Reporting Services.

To create a linked report, open SQL Reporting Services Manager. Find the report that corresponds to MonitoringReportPath, select Properties tab -> General, and click the Create Linked Report option. Name the report. On the Parameters tab, paste the parameters value shown in the XML ReportParameters into the appropriate fields within the report's parameters. If you need help on translating these from XML to the more friendly report parameters, refer back to the "Using XML" section of this chapter.

After creating the linked report, copy the corresponding RPDL file to the same location where you put the linked report. Once the linked report is created, copy the corresponding RPDL file to the same location where the linked report was stored; then name it the same as the linked report, but with an .rpdl extension.

Creating Reports in Visual Studio

Now that you are becoming an expert at navigating through the Reporting space of the Operations console, you probably have noticed the Authored Reports section, which we referred to in the "Publishing Reports" section of this chapter. This is where you can add your own custom reports, augment reports supplied out of the box, and store any management packs you may have imported.

For MOM 2005, which used SQL Server 2000 Reporting Services technology, creating new reports was a completely manual process using Visual Studio. One of the best (and certainly easiest) ways to create a report was to copy an existing report and simply modify the areas you needed to change.

With OpsMgr 2007, this is no longer the case. OpsMgr 2007 uses the newer SQL Server Reporting Services 2005. This updated version of Reporting Services allows you to use report models, which are metadata descriptions of a data source and contain all the relationships that exist within that data source. In real terms, this means that a report model contains the information you need to help you select the correct items to add to a report.

Using a report model along with the Report Builder (another SQL Reporting Services 2005 and Visual Studio feature) makes the process for creating a custom report painless, simple, and fast. To make the process even easier, OpsMgr comes packaged with a number of predefined report models. The report models already contain the most commonly used objects.

This section will discuss the process for creating a basic report using the OpsMgr report models and the Report Builder.

The first process in authoring a report is to ensure you have Visual Studio installed. For ease of use, we recommend that you create the reports from an OpsMgr management server, because the required tools are installed with the OpsMgr product. If this is not appropriate, you will need to install Visual Studio 2005 (Service Pack 1 is recommended) and the Business Intelligence components. These components install with the client components of SQL Server 2005 Reporting Services; install them by running SQL 2005 Setup (or the SQL Server Express edition with advanced services, available at http://msdn2. microsoft.com/en-us/express/aa718379.aspx) and selecting the Client Components installation.

Creating a Report Model

To create a report model, perform the following steps:

1. Open Visual Studio by selecting Start -> Programs –> Microsoft Visual Studio 2005 –> Microsoft Visual Studio 2005.

2. Select File –> New –> Project to create a new Visual Studio Project file.

3. From the dialog box, select Report Model Project, input a name and a location for the file, and click OK. We will save the file in \My Documents and we will call the project **Example OpsMgr Report Model**. Figure 23.56 shows the dialog box.

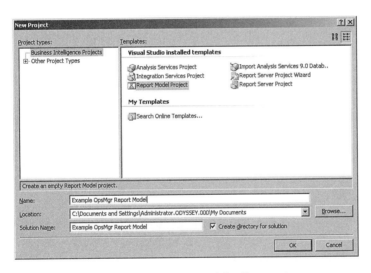

FIGURE 23.56   Creating a new Visual Studio report.

Creating a Data Source

The next part of this process is to create a data source. Perform the following steps:

1. In the Solution Explorer pane, right-click Data Sources and select Add New Data Source. This starts the wizard. Click Next on the welcome screen.

2. On the next screen, click New. You will see the screen shown in Figure 23.57. Here you need to enter the connection information for SQL Server, which is the Fully Qualified Domain Name of your SQL Server and the database you will use. In our example, the server name is Quicksilver.Odyssey.com and our database is the Data Warehouse database, which is OperationsManagerDW by default.

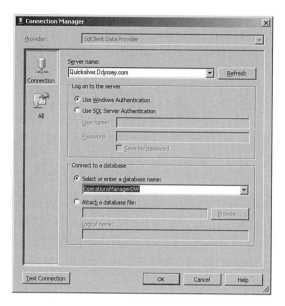

FIGURE 23.57   The completed SQL Database connection screen.

You can click the Test Connection button at this point to verify the information you entered is correct.

3. Click OK and then Finish, which completes creating the data source.

Creating a Data Source View

Now that we have a data source, which is a connection to the database, we need to create a data source view. The data source view is where we choose what data we will view from the database. Follow these steps:

1. From the Visual Studio Solution Explorer pane on the left side of Figure 23.58, right-click Data Source Views and then select Add New Data Source View.

2. Selecting the option to create a new data source view opens the Data Source View Wizard. Start by clicking Next at the Welcome screen.

3. The following screen is where we select the data source to use to connect to the database. Because we have only created one data source, this selection will not be difficult. Select the data source you created earlier in the "Creating a Data Source" section of this chapter. Click Next to continue.

4. You will proceed to the Select Tables and Views screen shown in Figure 23.59. From here, you need to select the tables and/or views you want to include in the report model. For this example, we will choose Alert.Alert_<GUID> table, which is the table that contains all alert data.

5. Click Next and then click Finish to complete the wizard and create the data source view.

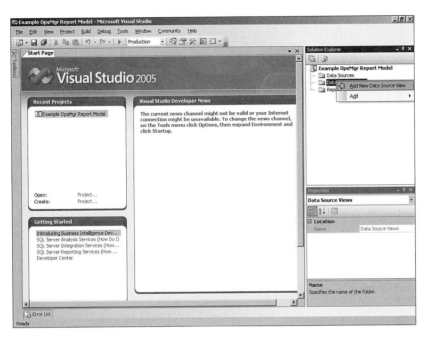

FIGURE 23.58   Selecting the option to create a new data source view in the Visual Studio Solution Explorer.

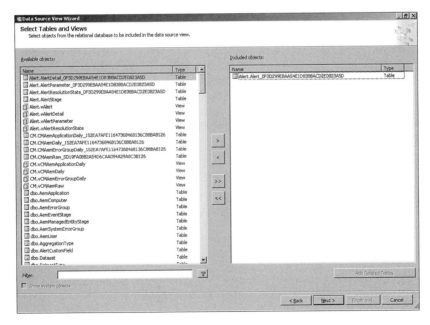

FIGURE 23.59   Selecting the data for the data source view.

Creating the Report Model

Now that we have created the data sources, we will create the actual model itself with the following steps:

1. Right-click Report Models from the Solution Explorer and then select Add New Report Model. Click Next to advance past the Welcome screen.

2. On the next screen, select the data source view we previously created and click Next to continue.

3. The subsequent screen is where you configure the report model generation rules. Leave the settings at the default and click Next to continue.

4. On the next screen, click Update model statistics before generating and then click Next.

5. Click Finish on the Completing the Wizard screen to generate the report model. This screen is shown in Figure 23.60.

FIGURE 23.60   Creating the report model.

Deploying the Report Model

Finally, we must deploy the report model to the Reporting Server. Right-click the model file we just created from the Solution Explorer and select Deploy. Check for errors and look for the status message at the bottom of the screen for verification that the deployment was successful. The status is in the bottom left corner and is circled in Figure 23.61.

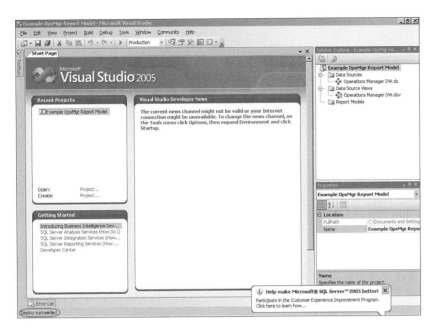

FIGURE 23.61   Deploy deployment status.

Creating the Report

After creating the report model, we can create a report to display the data. The next steps document the creation of a basic alert report:

1. Open the Operations console and navigate to the Reporting space.

2. Highlight Authored Reports on the left side of the screen, and under the Actions section, select Design a new report (circled in Figure 23.62).

   If this is the first time you have selected this action, you may get a security warning, generated by the Report Builder. It is safe to click Run. The Report Builder will then download and run.

3. After the Report Builder loads, you will see the Report Builder model we just created displayed on the right side of the screen. We will use the radio buttons circled at the bottom right of Figure 23.63 to select the display method for the report we will be creating. For this example, we will select Table. Click OK to create the empty report.

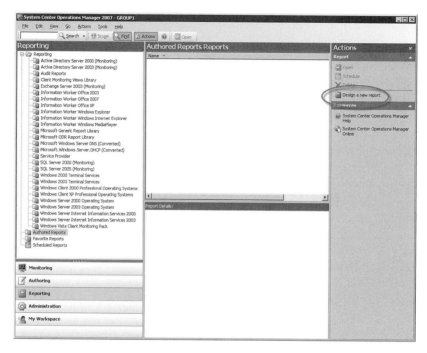

FIGURE 23.62   The Design a new report action.

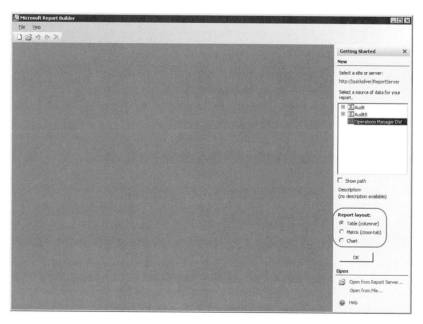

FIGURE 23.63   The Create a New Report screen in the Report Builder.

4. Once you select the report model and display type and click OK, the screen shown in Figure 23.64 is displayed. This is where we actually create the report.

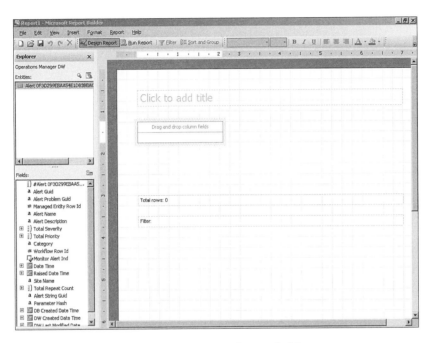

FIGURE 23.64   Edit report screen in the Report Builder.

5. We will create a basic report that returns all alerts that indicated a HealthService failure. First, we will select the Click to add title box and enter **HealthService Failure Alerts** as the title.

6. Next, we need to add some data. First, we will add the Alert Name column. Locate it in the Fields section on the left side and drag it into the empty table on the right side. Your screen should now look like the one shown in Figure 23.65.

7. In Figure 23.65, we have also decreased the size of the column. This allows us to add some more columns without moving off the page.

8. Now, we will add more columns: Alert Description, and Raised Date and Time. Resize as necessary. You should see something similar to the image displayed in Figure 23.66.

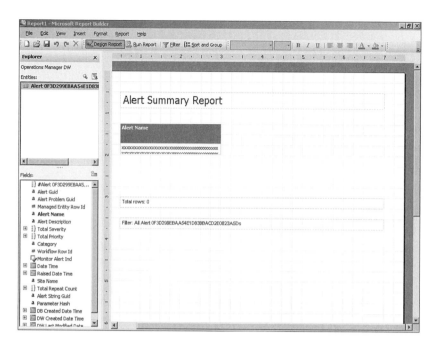

FIGURE 23.65   Report Builder with the first column added.

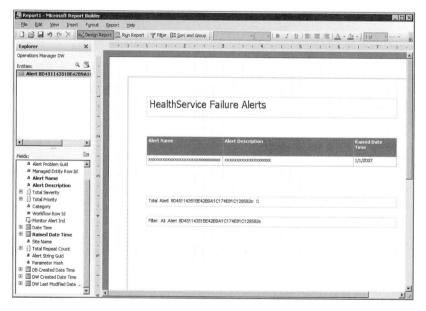

FIGURE 23.66   Report edited with additional columns.

9. Our next step is to limit the report to display the Health Service failure alerts. To do this, click the Filter button located on the toolbar at the top Figure 23.66 (and circled in Figure 23.67) to proceed to the screen shown in Figure 23.68.

FIGURE 23.67   The Filter button.

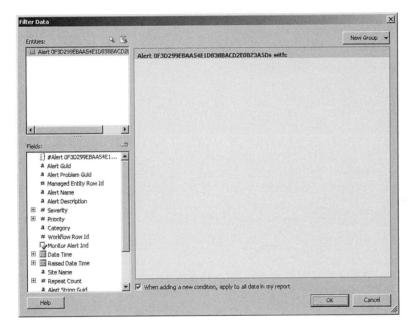

FIGURE 23.68   Creating a filter.

10. From the Filter Data screen, find the Alert Name field and drag it to the main pane in the middle of the screen. This adds the filter and allows you to specify the settings for the filter.

    We will select Alert Name, equals, Health Service Heartbeat Failure. Click OK to apply the filter.

11. We now need to verify that the report runs properly. Click the Run Report button and wait to see if the report runs correctly. In our example, we also removed the two fields at the bottom of the report displaying the totals. This makes the report appear

cleaner, but it's a matter of choice. We also added a new text box with **Odyssey Example Report** in it, again for cosmetic reasons.

12. If the report runs correctly and you have valid alert data in your system, you should see a report similar to the one shown in Figure 23.69.

13. Save the report so you can access it later. Click the Save button and browse to a location to save the report in the local Reporting Services report store. We recommend saving it in the My Reports folder. We named our report **HealthService Failure Report**.

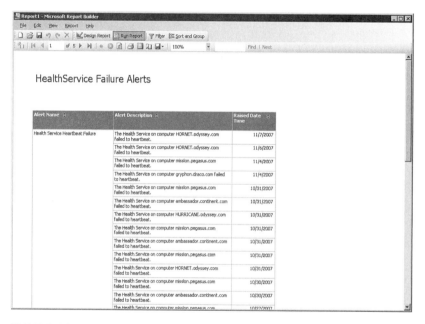

FIGURE 23.69   The created report.

14. After saving the report, you can run it from the Reporting pane in the Operations console in the Authored Reports folder! Figure 23.70 shows the report listed in that folder.

15. Running the report should give output such as displayed in Figure 23.71.

You could make this report available to other users by following the procedure we discussed in the "Publishing Reports" section of this chapter.

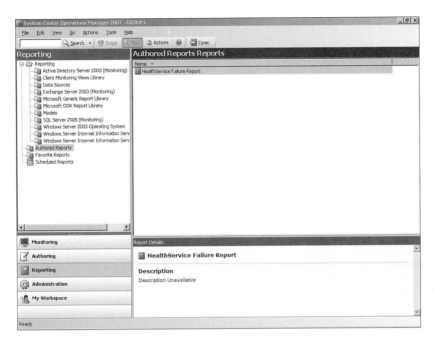

FIGURE 23.70   Running the report from the Operations console.

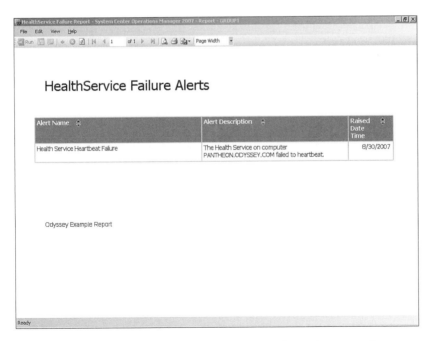

FIGURE 23.71   Viewing the finished report in the Operations console.

Scheduling Reports

How do you schedule reports for delivery in OpsMgr? Let's start with a simple built-in report—the Most Common Alerts report. This report is available under Reporting -> Microsoft ODR Report Library -> Most Common Alerts. (There is also a report with this name in the Microsoft Generic Report Library. The version in the ODR folder is preconfigured with a 7-day date range.) We will start by generating report output to a file share, and we will follow that process by sending the report via email.

Creating the Report Output

Perform the following steps to deliver the report to a file share:

1. Before running the report, create a share (preferably on the Reporting Server) with permissions that allow the user to create files on it and other users to read the contents of the directory. For our Odyssey environment, this is \\Quicksilver\reports.

2. Right-click the report in the Reporting space and select Schedule to bring up the Subscribe to a Report dialog box.

3. For the description, we will give the name of the report and the parameter information that is important to the report. For this example, we will name it **Most Common Alerts per Week**.

4. Under the Delivery Method dropdown menu, there should be at least two options available:

   ▶ Report Server File Share

   ▶ Null Delivery Provider

   Choose the Report Server File Share option.

5. Choosing to deliver to a share expands the Delivery Settings screen by adding a Settings section. Specify the settings for File name (including its extension), File Extension (check box), Path, Render Format, User name (Domain\Username format), Password, and Write mode (Autoincrement or Overwrite) to write to the share.

Now that we have created the schedule, what actually makes the report run? In the background, the SQL Server Agent now lists a new job (with a GUID for a name, lots of fun to track those down!) that runs the scheduled report we created. By default, notifications are written to the Application Event log if the job fails.

To determine what subscriptions we have, you can look in the Reporting space of the Operations console. Select Scheduled Reports on the Reporting pane on the left side for the list and status of scheduled reports in the middle section of the console. The Actions section allows you to open, edit, or cancel the various schedules. If any issues occurred when the subscription ran, they will appear on this page.

Once the job runs, there should be a file in the directory specified in step 1 of the preceding list (\\Quicksilver\reports in our example).

Delivering a Report Using Email

Now that we have delivered a report to a file share, we also want to send it using email. Perform the following steps:

TIP

Configuring the Report Server to Send Reports via Email

If you want to deliver reports by email but this is not a listed delivery method (in the Subscribe to a Report -> Delivery Settings section), the problem may be that the Sender Address and SMTP Server are not specified in the Reporting Services Configuration tool. Duncan McAllyn points this out at http://www.mcalynn.com/2007/08/email-not-an-option-in-your-opsmgr-reporting-delivery-methods-read-this/.

---

1. For this example, we will configure a daily email on the Most Common Alerts report. With the E-Mail option available on the list (Report Server E-Mail), we can now configure it with a description and an email delivery method.

2. The settings for the delivery method include to whom we are going to email it, how often to generate the report (once, hourly, daily, weekly, monthly), and when the subscription is effective.

   You will also specify how to render the report. We recommend using the PDF format when send the report via email because this is the most readable format.

3. We now specify the parameters to use with our subscription. In our example, we will update the Start Date to be Yesterday, and select Finish. Let the report run and validate that it works.

4. The resultant email includes a link to the report, allowing direct access to the report via the Reporting Server.

Real World—Problems Sending Reports via Email

If nothing happens when you try to send a report via email, you can look at the report definition in the Operations console under Reporting -> Scheduled Reports (or look under Scheduled Reports on the Report server, which is http://quicksilver/reports for us).

Reports of problems are common when configuring the Reporting Server to send email between domains. In our case, we were unable to send email to outside email accounts, but internal email worked without any issues. If an address is considered invalid, the message shown is "The e-mail address of one or more recipients is not valid." The Report Server will not attempt to send the report to the account configured on the schedule (even though both the schedule and the external email address are valid).

You can find a good article on sending mail with Reporting Services at http://blogs. msdn.com/ketaanhs/archive/2005/09/05/461055.aspx. This article shows how to change the PermittedHosts entry in the RSReportServer.config file in the \Reporting Services\ReportServer folder. You would want to change this entry for each permitted domain. In our Odyssey environment, the entries would look like this:

```
<PermittedHosts>
  <HostName>Odyssey.com</HostName>
  <HostName>ExternalDomain.com</HostName>
</PermittedHosts>
```

Because we did not have a requirement to send our report to multiple domains, we did not make any changes other than to configure RSReportServer.config only for the valid email address (on our internal network).

The ability to schedule the delivery of reports is a definite benefit of deploying OpsMgr 2007.

We have discussed the concept of custom reports and report models. We covered the steps to create a custom report model and deploy it to the Reporting Server. We also covered the process for creating a new custom report using Visual Studio 2005 and the new Report Builder installed with OpsMgr, and we wrapped up with a discussion on how to schedule reports in OpsMgr.

We will now tie together many of the concepts discussed in this chapter to create a sample management pack.

Creating a Sample Management Pack

Because MOM 2005 did not include counters to track the size of the MOM databases (and logs), there was no trending information for proactively planning the size of the databases. Operations Manager 2007 includes three of the four major counters required to do this (DB Size, DB Free Space %, Log Free Space %), but without the actual log file size the ability to trend off of this information is incomplete.

The OpsMgr GetSQL2005DBSpace.js script gathers the first three performance counters. We reviewed this script and found that as it was part of a sealed management pack, so our ability to alter it was limited; therefore, we thought about this from the perspective of what we created with our *Microsoft Operations Manager 2005 Unleashed* book.

In that book, we developed scripts to generate database tables to store the information we wanted to gather. We next created a script that updated the data in those tables and pulled the information into performance counters in MOM 2005. The end result was a series of custom performance counters available in MOM, actually generated from values stored in a SQL database.

Creating the Management Pack and Rules

To provide similar functionality for Operations Manager 2007, we created a management pack called OpsMgr Database Tracking using the steps we discussed earlier in the "Creating and Deleting Management Packs" section. Within the management pack, we created four rules based on the information discussed in the "Creating Rules" section of this chapter. These four rules are part of the SQL DB Engine class, as shown in Figure 23.72.

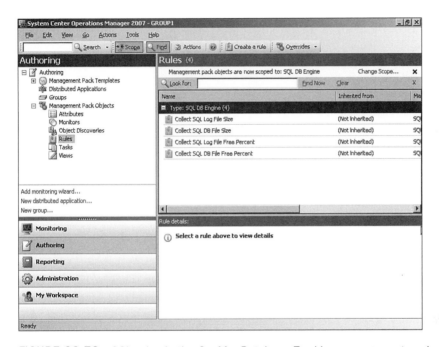

FIGURE 23.72   SQL rules in the OpsMgr Database Tracking management pack.

We also created four VBScripts, named scriptSQLLogSize.vbs, SQLDBSize.vbs script, SQLLogUsedPercent.vbs script, and SQLDBUsedPercent.vbs script. These scripts are used by the rules we defined. Figure 23.73 shows a portion of the SQLLogSize.vbs script in the Script tab of the Collect SQL Log File Size rule.

Each script gathers information from customized SQL tables, translating that information into performance counters defined on the Performance Mapper tab of the rule, as displayed in Figure 23.74.

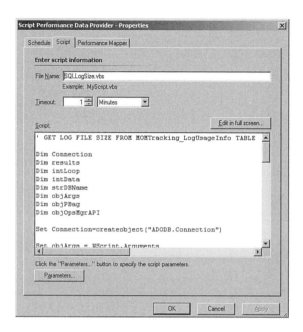

FIGURE 23.73   Example of the VBScripts created for each rule.

FIGURE 23.74   Performance mapping.

The Performance Mapper tab defines the object, counters, instance, and value for the counter that will be created. To understand how this works, we need to see the code that is actually sending information back to the Performance Mapper tab. The following code is what is included within the Collect SQL Log File Size rule's Script tab. The Performance Mapper tab defines the name of the object (SQLLogData), defines the name of the counter within the object (TotalSize), maps the instance to the DatabaseName (shown in bold), and maps the value to the LogSizeData (also displayed in bold).

```
' GET LOG FILE SIZE FROM MOMTracking_LogUsageInfo TABLE
Dim Connection
Dim results
Dim intLoop
Dim intData
Dim strDBName
Dim objArgs
Dim objPBag
Dim objOpsMgrAPI
Set Connection=createobject("ADODB.Connection")
Set objArgs = WScript.Arguments
Connection.Open "Provider=sqloledb;Data Source=localhost;Integrated
➥Security=SSPI;Initial Catalog=Master"
'Get script parameter values from OpsMgr
strDBName = objArgs.Item(0)
Set results=Connection.execute("SELECT CONVERT(int, log_size) FROM
➥master.dbo.MOMTracking_LogUsageInfo Where DB_Name = '" & strDBName & "'")
 If results.BOF then
   Set objOpsMgrAPI = CreateObject("MOM.ScriptAPI")
   Set objPBag = objOpsMgrAPI.CreateTypedPropertyBag(2)
   objPBag.AddValue "DatabaseName", strDBName
   objPBag.AddValue "LogSizeData", 0
   objOpsMgrAPI.AddItem(objPBag)
   objOpsMgrAPI.ReturnItems
 else
 do until results.EOF
   For intLoop = 0 To results.Fields.Count -1
     intData = intData & results.fields(intLoop).value
   Next
  results.MoveNext
   loop
     Set objOpsMgrAPI = CreateObject("MOM.ScriptAPI")
     Set objPBag = objOpsMgrAPI.CreateTypedPropertyBag(2)
     objPBag.AddValue "DatabaseName", strDBName
     objPBag.AddValue "LogSizeData", intData
     objOpsMgrAPI.AddItem(objPBag)
     objOpsMgrAPI.ReturnItems
 end if
```

```
' -- Reset Variables
Set Connection = Nothing
Set results = Nothing
Set intLoop = Nothing
Set intData = Nothing
Set strDBName = Nothing
Set objArgs = Nothing
Set objPBag = Nothing
Set objOpsMgrAPI = Nothing
```

The information on the Performance Mapper tab is returned via a property bag.

When the rule runs the script, the information is passed back using the property bag and is available as a performance counter. We display examples of these performance counters in the Performance view shown Figure 23.75.

Installing and Configuring the Management Pack

To install and configure our management pack, we performed the following steps:

1. To create the tables we would gather information from, we ran two SQL scripts (MonitorDatasize.sql and Monitor Logfile Size.sql). These scripts generated two stored procedures (DBAMOMLogStats and MonitorDataSize) used to gather sizing information and store the data in tables in the database.

2. After creating and populating these tables, we imported the XML file (named OpsMgr Database Tracking.xml before we sealed the management pack) within the Operations console in the Administration space, under Administration -> Management Packs -> Import Management Pack.

3. Next, we added an account with SQL rights to the Run As Profile. Navigate in the Operations console to Administration -> Security -> Run As Accounts, right-click, and choose Create Run As Account. Then add the account to the SQL Data File Collection Account. This action gives the required rights to the rules so that they have permission to run.

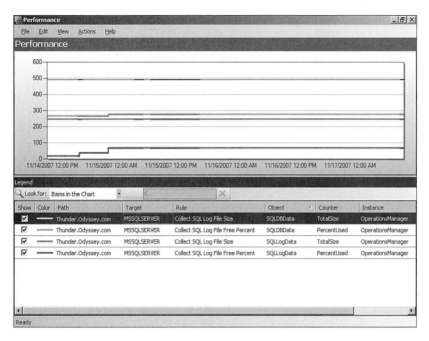

FIGURE 23.75   SQL performance counters.

4. To activate the rules, we created overrides, which enabled each rule for a specific server on a specific database.

To do this, open the Operations console -> Authoring -> Management Pack Objects -> Rules. Then scope the Operations console to the SQL DB Engine and find the rules. Right-click each rule (one at a time) and create an override for a specific object of type SQL DB Engine. Set the enabled parameter to True, and the script arguments to the database you want to monitor (in Figure 23.76, we are targeting the OperationsManager database, although you can create another override for the OperationsManagerDW as well).

5. With the rules now activated, we need to schedule the information in the SQL tables to update periodically. To do this, we can create rules that run SQL scripts to call the stored procedures, or we can use the built-in SQL Server Agent job functionality. Figure 23.77 shows a SQL Server Agent job to update the information for this management pack on a daily basis. Jobs are created using SQL Server Management Studio. See Chapter 12 for the specific steps to create SQL Agent jobs.

Figure 23.78 is an example of how a stored procedure runs within the SQL Agent job.

The result of this configuration is a nightly job that updates the contents of the tables we query using the rules we previously defined.

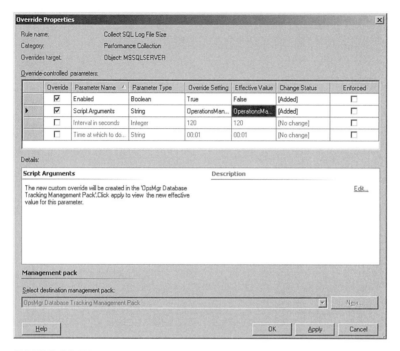

FIGURE 23.76 Activating the rules with an override.

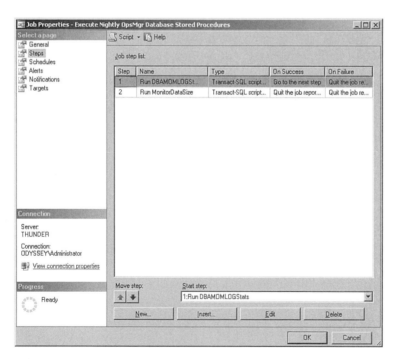

FIGURE 23.77 Creating a SQL Server Agent job.

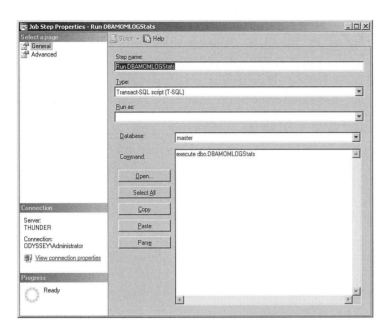

FIGURE 23.78   Configuring a SQL job step.

6. Our final step is to set the configuration for the rules. Select the Configuration tab of the rule, edit the data source, and configure the job to run at a timeframe that will be in sync with when the data is updated in the database. Figure 23.79 shows a daily run of this rule that matches the timing we defined for running our SQL Agent job.

Sealing a Management Pack

As we have discussed in previous chapters, OpsMgr is able to seal a management pack. The management pack we have just discussed is included on the CD accompanying this book as a sealed MP. Sealing management packs is a new feature added to Operations Manager 2007. So when you are developing your own management packs, how do you seal them?

MPSeal.exe (in the \SupportTools directory on the OpsMgr installation media) is the utility that seals management packs. The syntax for MPSeal is as follows (using our Odyssey corporation as an example):

```
MPSeal.exe <ManagementPack File.xml> [/I <IncludePath>] /Keyfile <keyfilepath>
➡/Company <CompanyName> [/Outdir <OutputDirectory>] [/DelaySign] /Copyright
➡<CopyrightText>

MPSeal.exe Microsoft.SQLServer.xml /I c:\mps /keyfile Odyssey.snk
➡/Company "Odyssey"
```

To seal a management pack, perform the following steps.

1. Log in to a system that has .NET Framework 2.0 installed.

2. Copy a client certificate and the MPSeal tool to a folder.

3. Copy your Operations Manager 2007 management pack to this same folder.

4. From the command prompt in the folder where you copied the MPSeal utility, run the MPSeal tool.

The MPSeal tool converts the XML-formatted management pack into a new binary file. The management pack will have the same name with an .MP extension after it is sealed.

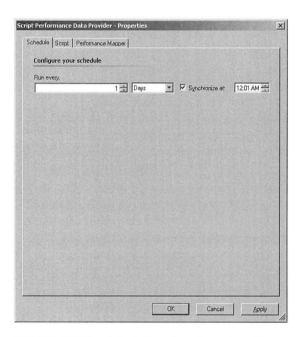

FIGURE 23.79   Scheduling when the script will run.

This sample management pack illustrated how we can use a variety of different techniques to develop management packs. Although this particular type of functionality is just the tip of the iceberg of what one can do using custom management packs, it shows that you can even integrate information stored in SQL Server databases with OpsMgr to provide additional functionality. In the case of the OpsMgr Database Tracking management pack, we could take the information it collects to generate regular reports showing database growth. We could also choose to generate alerts when the size, remaining free space, or rate of growth hits a specified level. Although we are now only tracking statistics for the Operational database, we can create another override to target the data warehouse.

> **TIP**
>
> **On the CD**
>
> The OpsMgr Database Tracking management pack is included on the CD accompanying this book.

Bringing It All Together

This chapter has discussed a variety of different concepts, all with a central focus on how to develop management packs and reports for Operations Manager 2007. We discussed how to use the Operations console, XML editing, the Authoring console, and Silect MP Studio in the development process; for each we reviewed the options available and provided examples of how to use them. We discussed the four major options available when creating management packs: favorites, published reports, linked reports, and Visual Studio. Having discussed these concepts has hopefully helped you understand the capabilities of each option and sparked ideas for how to use them.

The question may remain, Which method should you use when you are writing a management pack? Like many questions in IT (Information Technology), the answer is, *It depends*, based on what you want to accomplish and the technique(s) you are most proficient with. Here are some examples:

- ▶ You may want to create a simple management pack, in which case you could use the Operations console, the Authoring console, or the MP Studio Wizard.

- ▶ You may be an ace with XML and decide to write your MP in XML and create your reports with Visual Studio.

- ▶ Perhaps your requirements are best met using a variety of the different methods discussed in this chapter.

Your approach will vary based on what you are most comfortable working with and what you need to accomplish.

This chapter has shown you the available options so you can decide what makes the most sense for your own particular skill set and the requirements you are attempting to meet.

Summary

This chapter discussed the approaches you can use to create management packs and management pack objects. We discussed different methods for creating management packs. We have discussed options available for the development of reports, and we provided an example using what you have learned in the chapter to create a management pack using many of the objects and technologies discussed in this chapter. As we discussed in Chapter 20, the capabilities of Operations Manager 2007 are extremely diverse and extensive. By creating custom management packs, we can further extend the capabilities of Operations Manager and provide capabilities that may have not even been considered yet.

The remainder of this book provides supplemental material to assist in using Operations Manager 2007. Appendixes include information on implementing and tuning management packs, Registry settings, performance counters, database views, and reference URLs.

PART VII

Appendixes

IN THIS PART

OpsMgr by Example: Configuring and Tuning Management Packs

This appendix is a compilation of the "OpsMgr by example" articles published in our Operations Manager (OpsMgr) blog (http://ops-mgr.spaces.live.com) that discuss configuration and tuning tips for several of the OpsMgr 2007 management packs. The intent is to provide a 5000-foot/meter perspective as well as show the details for a particular type of tuning performed in a sample deployment.

For new "by example" information and updates to existing articles, be sure to check http://ops-mgr.spaces.live.com. We expect to continue adding to the "by example" series on the blog.

The Active Directory Management Pack

Because so much of Windows hinges on a successful implementation of the Active Directory (AD), we will begin by looking at installation, configuration, and tuning tips for the AD management pack.

Installing the Active Directory Management Pack

Perform the following steps to install the AD MP:

1. Download the Active Directory management pack (http://www.microsoft.com/downloads/details. aspx?FamilyId=008F58A6-DC67-4E59-95C6-D7C7C34A1447&displaylang=en) and the Active

Directory Management Pack Guide (http://www.microsoft.com/downloads/details.aspx?FamilyID=4b945737-e77f-4851-a11c-c4f79c36c360&DisplayLang=en).

2. Read the Management Pack Guide from cover to cover. This document spells out in detail some important pieces of information you will need to know.

3. Import the AD management pack, using either the Operations console or PowerShell.

4. Deploy the OpsMgr agent to all domain controllers (DCs). The agent *must* be deployed to all DCs. Agentless configurations will *not* work for the AD management pack.

5. Get a list of your domain controllers from the Operations console. In the Authoring space, navigate to Authoring -> Groups -> Domain Controllers. Right-click the group(s) and select View Group Members.

6. Enable Agent Proxy configuration on all DCs identified from the groups. This is in the Administration space, under Administration -> Device Management -> Agent Managed. Right-click each domain controller, select Properties, click the Security tab, and then check the box labeled Allow this agent to act as a proxy and discover managed objects on other computers. Perform this for *every* domain controller, even if the DC is added after your initial configuration of OpsMgr.

7. Configure the Replication account in the Operations console, under Administration -> Security (full details for this are in the AD MP Guide). This also has to be done for every domain controller, even if a DC is added after your initial OpsMgr configuration.

8. Validate the existence of the MOMLatencyMonitors container. Within this container, subfolders should be created for each DC, with the name of each domain controller. If the container does not exist, it is often due to insufficient permissions. (See information on configuring the Replication account within the AD MP Guide for details.)

9. Open the Operations console. Go to the Monitoring space and navigate to Monitoring -> Microsoft Windows Active Directory -> Topology Views. You may have to set the scope to the AD Domain Controllers Group to get these views to populate.

10. Check to make sure Active Directory shows up under Monitoring -> Distributed Applications as a distributed application that is in the Healthy, Warning, or Critical state. If it is in the Not Monitored state, check for domain controllers that are not properly installed or are in a "gray" state.

AD Management Pack Tuning and Alerts to Look For

We encountered and resolved the following alerts while tuning the Active Directory management pack:

▶ **Alert:** AD Replication Monitoring – Access denied.

Issue: This occurred on one domain controller. There was also an alert telling us the MOMLatencyMonitors container could not be created. We validated the container by logging in to the domain controller and opening up Active Directory Users and Computers. We specified View/Advanced Features and verified the container (and the two existing domain controllers as subcontainers) did exist, per Figure A.1.

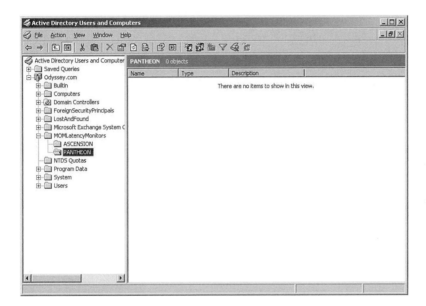

FIGURE A.1   Viewing the Latency Monitors container in Active Directory Users and Computers.

Resolution: The issue was already resolved because the Management Server Action account (MSAA) had the permissions required to create this container. We validated the MOMLatencyMonitors container existed and that the container included subfolders matching the name of each domain controller. (If the container does not exist, it is often due to insufficient permissions; see the AD MP Guide for configuration information for the Replication account.)

▶ **Alert:** The Op Master PDC Last Bind latency is above the configured threshold.

Issue: The bind from the domain controller identified in the alert to the PDC emulator is slower than 5 seconds for a warning, and slower than 15 seconds for an error. This occurred in a remote site connecting to a central site with the PDC emulator role.

Resolution: The alert is caused by a slow link between the two locations, or by a condition where one of the two servers identified may have been overloaded. In this particular case, it was caused by a domain controller that was overloaded due to insufficient hardware and had to be decommissioned.

▶ **Alert:** Session setup failed because no trust account exists: Script – AD Validate Server Trust Event.

Issue: Specific computer accounts were identified multiple times as not containing a trust account.

Resolution: This is caused by systems that believe they are part of the domain but no longer are, or by imaged systems. Resolve this by dropping and rejoining the system to the domain, or closing the alert if the system is no longer online.

▶ **Alert:** KCC cannot compute a replication path.

Issue: KCC detected problems on multiple domain controllers.

Resolution: Connectivity was lost from the central site to a remote site for a period of several hours. The remote site was down due to a power outage, and errors were logged every 15 minutes from when it was down until when the site was back online.

This also occurred when a domain controller was shut off, but still existed from the perspective of Active Directory. This can also occur in environments where the site topology automatically generates the site links, but the network is configured such that some sites cannot see other sites. (As an example, consider a configuration with a hub in Dallas and sites in Frisco and Plano, where both sites can see Dallas but cannot see each other.)

▶ **Alert:** A problem was detected with the trust relationship between two domains.

Issue: The domain controllers (DCs) could not connect to the domain controller in the other domain. This was due to a routing issue between the specific domain controllers and the domain controller in the remote domain. Remote sites were connected via VPN and could not route to that subnet.

Resolution: Provide routing from the domain controllers to the domain controller in the other domain.

▶ **Alert:** AD Replication is slower than the configured threshold.

Intersite Expected Max Latency (min) default 15.

Intrasite Expected Max Latency (min) default 5.

Issue: This alert will also occur if connectivity is lost between sites for a long enough period of time.

Resolution: If the alert is not current and not repeating, and if replication is occurring and the Repadmin Replsum task comes up clean, this alert can be noted (to see if there is a consistent day of the week or time at which it occurs) and closed. We added a diagnostic to the AD Replication Monitoring monitor for the critical state, taking the information from the Repadmin Replsum task (you must have the admin utilities installed on the DC for this to work):

```
<Configuration>
<ApplicationName>REPADMIN.EXE</ApplicationName>
<SupportToolsInstallDir>%ProgramFiles%\Support Tools\
➥</SupportToolsInstallDir>
<CommandLine>/replsum</CommandLine>
<TimeoutSeconds>1200</TimeoutSeconds>
</Configuration>
```

We created the diagnostic to run automatically using the following:

▶ **Program**—REPADMIN.EXE

▶ **Working Directory**—*%ProgramFiles%*\Support Tools

▶ **Parameters**—/replsum

Available options included changing the replication topology to replicate every 15 minutes and configuring overrides. To resolve the issue, we tried creating a custom group for the servers in the location (see the article "Creating Computer Groups Based on AD Site in OpsMgr" at http://cameronfuller.spaces.live.com/blog/cns!A231E4EB0417CB76!950.entry for additional information). We created an override for the new group, changing the Intersite Expected Max Latency to 120, making it double the configuration in AD Sites and Services.

We performed this configuration for each remote location that did not have a 15-minute replication interval. You can also do this for all domain controllers, using the domain controller computer group(s). This did not function as expected but is being used as an example for how overrides can be creatively configured, in this case based on sites!

▶ **Alert:** AD Replication is slower than the configured threshold.

Intersite Expected Max Latency (min) default 15.

Intrasite Expected Max Latency (min) default 5.

Issue: The remote location replication topology was defined to be 60 minutes, not the standard of 15.

Resolution: Currently there is no good workaround to change these configurations and maintain a Microsoft-supported configuration after the change is made. There are discussions in the newsgroups about changing these configurations through exporting the MP, changing the XML, and reimporting it as unsealed, but Microsoft will not support the AD MP if it is changed in this way. If your environment does not use the 15-minute latency, the recommendation right now is to disable both this alert and the AD Replication is occurring slowly alert.

▶ **Alert:** AD Replication is occurring slowly.

Issue: This is the same issue identified in the AD Replication is slower than the configured threshold alert. This rule does not provide the ability to override the default configuration of 15 minutes. The AD environment is not configured with the default of 15 minutes, so these rules do not apply because they are still replicating within a successful timeframe.

Resolution: We disabled this rule (AD Replication is occurring slowly) for group AD Domain Controller Group (Windows 2003 Server). You could alternatively do this for individual servers if there were a limited number of these where the AD replication was not configured with default replication time of 15 minutes. We then closed the alerts.

▶ **Alert:** Script Based Test Failed to Complete.

Issue: AD Database and Log: The script 'AD Database and Log' failed to create object 'McActiveDir.ActiveDirectory.' The error returned was ActiveX component can't create object (0x1AD).

Resolution: This occurred on a 64-bit system. Uninstall OOMADS using Add/Remove Programs -> Active Directory Management Pack Helper Object (the original version was .05MB in size). Then reinstall the 64-bit equivalent (AMD64 in this case). To do this, we had to copy the MSI locally to the system to install it; after installation, the size was .07MB within Add/Remove programs.

▶ **Alert:** Script or executable failed to run.

Issue: On the domain controllers, a failure on ADLocalDiscoverDC.vbs occurred on each domain controller prior to OpsMgr 2007 SP 1.

Resolution: Based on a thread on the Microsoft TechNet website (http://forums.microsoft.com/technet/showpost.aspx?postid=1628491&siteid=17&sb =0&d=1&at=7&ft=11&tf=0&pageid=1), this appears to be a pre-SP 1 issue, so we disabled the rule until SP 1 is available. To disable it, navigate to Authoring -> Management Pack Objects -> Object Discoveries. Then perform a Find operation on AD DC Local Discovery. You may have two of these rules (Windows 2000 Server and Windows Server 2003), depending on the versions of the management pack that were imported into your management group. Create an override to disable both rules for all objects of Windows Domain Controller. Remove these overrides when you implement Service Pack 1 for OpsMgr 2007.

Problem: You cannot disable this until *all* domain controllers are already in OpsMgr. If you disable the rule before adding domain controllers, those domain controllers are never added.

AD Tuning: Other Issues

We encountered a number of other issues while tuning the AD MP.

▶ **Issue:** Domain controllers in the DMZ would not install, even though they are in a domain within the forest.

Resolution: We copied over the files and manually installed the agents. We then opened up port 5723 on the firewall between these systems and the OpsMgr server and removed port 1270, which had been used for MOM 2005. (This issue should only occur if you previously used MOM 2005.)

▶ **Issue:** One DC showed extremely high CPU usage/cscript errors.

Resolution: The server was running with 256MB of memory and using significantly more than that even before the OpsMgr agent was deployed to the server. After we deployed the agent, memory usage went significantly higher and resulted in cscript errors that timed out, due to the slowness of alerts.

▶ **Alert:** One or more domain controllers may not be replicating.

Issue: The AD MP will report replication issues across all DCs if only one is down (and thus not able to replicate its monitor objects).

Resolution: Ensure all domain controllers are monitored by OpsMgr. Validate replication in the environment.

▶ **Tuning concept:** On a weekly basis, close out any unresolved alerts older than 5 days if they represent issues that may have self-resolved.

TIP

Installing the Windows Support Tools

We recommend installing the support tools on the domain controllers so you can take advantage of the tasks and use the tools as part of the diagnostics and recoveries.

The Exchange 2003 Management Pack

With Active Directory now under control, we will move to the Exchange 2003 management pack. The Exchange MP is probably the most complex OpsMgr management pack.

NOTE

Version of the Exchange Management Pack

Unless noted otherwise, all references to Exchange refer to Exchange 2003, because this material was developed prior to the release of the Exchange 2007 management pack for Operations Manager 2007.

Installing the Exchange 2003 Management Pack

Perform the following steps to install the Exchange MP:

1. Download the Exchange 2003 management pack (http://www.microsoft.com/
   downloads/details.aspx?FamilyId=9FF454F4-6D34-4FB9-9E0B-F5B68C6EDC4F&
   displaylang=en) and the Exchange Management Pack Guide (http://download.
   microsoft.com/download/7/4/d/74deff5e-449f-4a6b-91dd-ffbc117869a2/om2007_
   mp_exsrvr2003.doc).

2. Read the Management Pack Guide from cover to cover. This document spells out in
   detail important pieces of information you need to know.

3. Import the Exchange management pack (using either the Operations console or
   PowerShell).

4. Deploy the OpsMgr agent to all Exchange servers. The agent must be deployed to all
   Exchange servers. Agentless configurations will *not* work for the Exchange management pack.

5. Get a list of all Exchange servers from the Operations console. In the Authoring
   space, navigate to Authoring -> Groups -> Microsoft Exchange 2003 Server Group.
   Right-click the group(s) and select View Group Members.

6. Enable Agent Proxy configuration on all Exchange servers identified from the
   groups. This is in the Administration space, under Administration -> Device
   Management -> Agent Managed. Right-click each domain controller, select
   Properties, click the Security tab, and then check the box labeled Allow this agent to
   act as a proxy and discover managed objects on other computers. This has to be
   done for *every* Exchange server, even if the server is added after your initial configuration of OpsMgr.

7. Download and run the Exchange 2003 MP Wizard (http://go.microsoft.com/fwlink/
   ?LinkId=82103) on one of the Exchange servers. Run the wizard using the credentials of an Exchange Full Administrator and take the default configurations.

8. Enable the Exchange Topology View in the Operations console -> Authoring ->
   Management Pack Objects -> Object Discoveries. Find the Exchange 2003 Topology
   Discovery and override it for a specific object, choosing the Exchange server that
   you want to perform this role (set it to True).

9. Enable the mailbox and mailflow rules. To enable these rules, go to Authoring ->
   Rules and search on **message tracking**. Sort the results by the Enabled by Default
   field and then find the following two rules:

   ▶ Performance Collection Rule to Collect Message Tracking Log Statistics – Top
     Destinations by Message Count

   ▶ Performance Collection Rule to Collect Message Tracking Log Statistics – Top
     Destinations by Size

   Eight reports are based on these two rules. Because the rules are not enabled by
   default, they are set to be not visible in the Exchange management pack, so they do

not show up on the reporting server. Using an override will make them visible.

There is also an error in the collect message tracking statistic VBScript that generates an error in the OpsMgr event log.

10. Configure overrides to Enable these rules for all objects of Type: Exchange Database Storage.

11. Verify that Exchange shows up under Monitoring -> Distributed Applications as a distributed application that is in the Healthy, Warning, or Critical state. If it is in the Not Monitored state, check for Exchange servers that are not installed or are in a gray state. This may take some time to populate after all the preceding tasks have been completed.

Exchange Management Pack Issues

A management group with an Exchange server may intermittently stop receiving alerts, and Event ID 2114 is logged in the Operations Manager event log on the RMS (Root Management Server). Alerts will again be received if you take one of the following actions:

▶ Restart the Health service on agents in that management group.

▶ Restart the RMS.

The problem occurs because OpsMgr 2007 does not correctly handle data submitted from the Exchange management point. You can work around this by disabling the Exchange Server Topology Discovery. Further information is available at http://support.microsoft.com/kb/941985.

Exchange Management Pack Tuning and Alerts to Look For

The following alerts were encountered and resolved while tuning the Exchange 2003 management pack:

▶ **Alert:** Multiple or any alert with Baseline in the title.

Issue: Default sensitivity levels within the Exchange management pack.

Resolution: See the "Configuring Baselines" section of this appendix.

▶ **Alert:** The Internet Information Service NNTP virtual server named NNTPSVC/1 is unavailable as the virtual server has been stopped.

Issue: On Exchange servers, this service is required to install, but it is not required after it is installed.

Resolution: If this service is disabled/not in use, you can remove it. To remove service, log in to the server and from the command line, enter `sc delete NNT`. Otherwise, create an override to ignore this on the Microsoft Exchange 2003 Group. NNTP was required for the installation, but can be disabled after the lation is complete.

▶ **Alert:** Verify Test Mailboxes: This Exchange Server does not have any MOM test mailboxes.

Issue: Test mailboxes are created by the Exchange MP Configuration Wizard.

Resolution: Run the Configuration Wizard to create the mailboxes.

▶ **Alert:** No MOM test mailbox account for some mailbox databases.

Issue: Test mailboxes are created by the Exchange Configuration Wizard.

Resolution: Run the Configuration Wizard and create test mailboxes on each database or disable the rule.

▶ **Alert:** Replication is not occurring – All replication partners have failed to synchronize.

Issue: The Alert Description is the key on this alert.

Resolution: Alert Description of AD Replication Monitoring: All replication partners are now replicating successfully is a success condition; it does not require any intervention other than closing the alert.

▶ **Alert:** Some replication partners have failed to synchronize.

Issue: A domain controller was offline and unable to be synchronized with.

Resolution: Bring the domain controller back online.

▶ **Alert:** Outlook Web Access logon failure: Unexpected error during synthetic Outlook Web Access logon.

Issue: OWA logon failure: You can only configure OWA (Outlook Web Access) to be monitored if the site runs on HTTPS.

Resolution: Disable the rule (For all objects of type: Exchange OWA) because this particular environment is running with HTTP on the OWA configuration.

lert: Exchange ActiveSync logon failure: Unexpected Error.

ue: Exchange EAS is not required in this environment.

olution: We disabled the rule for all objects of type Exchange EAS because we not using this functionality.

: The 3GB virtual address space option is not enabled.

The 3GB configuration should be used for Exchange servers, except for those ning as bridgeheads or frontend servers (per the Exchange Best Practices r [BPA]).

on: Disabled this rule for frontend and bridgehead servers.

led to probe the state of monitored services.

Issue: This was occurring on the SMTP services on an Exchange server the administrators have manually restarted.

Resolution: The alert was notifying on a true business-impacted situation. We requested that the administrators put the server into maintenance mode prior to making changes like this, unless it is an emergency.

▶ **Alert:** Data Publisher object is not installed.

Issue: This is a system misidentified as an Exchange server using a third-party product to provide Exchange restoration functionality.

Resolution: We disabled the rule for this system using an override.

▶ **Alert:** Microsoft Windows Internet Information Server 2003 NNTP Virtual Server is Unavailable.

Issue: NNTP Service Down on non-active cluster node.

Resolution: The NNTP service is supposed to be down because it is running on a cluster and the system showing this error is not the active node in the cluster. We created a group for the servers running Exchange and part of the cluster, and disabled the rules for the group. NNTP was not used on Exchange, and optionally we could have removed it as a service from the systems.

▶ **Alert:** Microsoft Windows Internet Information Server 2003 SMTP Virtual Server is Unavailable.

Issue: SMTP Service Down on non-active cluster node.

Resolution: The SMTP service is supposed to be down because it is running on a cluster and the system showing this error is not the active node in the cluster. We created a group for the servers running Exchange and part of the cluster, and disabled the rules for the group.

▶ **Alert:** Microsoft Windows Internet Information Server 2003 Web Site is Unavailable.

Issue: Web Service Down on non-active cluster node.

Resolution: The Web service is supposed to be down because it is running on a cluster and the system showing this error is not the active node in the cluster. We created a group for the servers running Exchange and part of the cluster, and disabled the rules for the group.

▶ **Alert:** Check Services FE Monitor reported a problem.

Issue: Microsoft product knowledge on this: Services State monitoring with this Registry key is a legacy from the MOM 2005 Exchange 2003 MP. This monitor is included since configuration is possible from within the Exchange MP Configu Wizard. OpsMgr 2007 provides a dedicated health model for monitoring Wind Service Health.

Resolution: Right-click and choose Overrides -> Disable the Monitor for all objects of type: Exchange 2003 Role.

▶ **Alert:** Exchange EAS monitor reported a problem.

Issue: Synthetic Exchange ActiveSync requires SSL.

Resolution: Closed the alert because it had not reoccurred/repeated for 2 days and the script checking for the condition runs on a 15-minute schedule. Issue repeated. EAS logon verification: Cannot measure EAS availability for the following URL: 0x80131537(-214233033) Invalid URI: The format of the URI could not be determined. We found the following information at MyItForum:

This script problem is caused by OMA and EAS virtual directories not being SSL-enabled. So in order to correct it, simply enable SSL:

▶ Open Internet Information Services (IIS Manager).

▶ Connect to the server name of your frontend Exchange server.

▶ Drill down to Web Sites, then to the website.

▶ Locate the two virtual directories named OMA and Microsoft-Server-ActiveSync.

▶ Open the properties of the virtual directories. Choose the Directory Security tab.

▶ Under Secure communications, click Edit.

▶ Check the box labeled Require security channel (SSL).

▶ **Alert:** No MOM test mailbox account for some mailbox databases.

Issue: No MOM mailboxes were created on a per-storage group when the Configuration Wizard was run. The alert is being created expecting that per-store monitoring will be configured, which is not the case in this particular environment.

Resolution: We disabled this rule for all objects (of type Exchange 2003 role) because this rule is monitoring on a per-store basis, but we are monitoring on a per-server basis. We then closed the alerts.

Alert: SSL is not configured on this Exchange server.

Issue: This occurs on servers that have SSL enabled if they do not require usage of SSL within IIS. Backend servers communicate with frontend servers via HTTP, not HTTPS, so SSL should not be required on the backend Exchange servers. We found the following information at Notes from the Underground:

Front-End/Back-End Scenario

While it's possible to implement SSL on a front-end (FE) server, resulting in all passed data between the FE and your client browsers being encrypted, you must be aware that you can't use SSL between any FE and back-end (BE) servers—it simply doesn't work. This means that if your FE server is placed in a perimeter network (also known as a demilitarized zone, or DMZ), all traffic between the FE and BE would be unencrypted. So if you are planning such a scenario, consider using IPSec between the FEs and BEs. More and more organizations place their FEs directly on their private networks (and instead place an ISA server or similar in the DMZ), which eliminates this security risk.

Resolution: Disabled the alert on Exchange backend servers.

▶ **Alert:** Calendaring agent failed with error while saving appointment.

Issue: Calendaring agent failed with error code 0x8004010f while saving appointment.

Resolution: Good links on this at http://www.eventid.net/display.asp?eventid=8206&eventno=1103&source=EXCDO&phase=1. Lots of product knowledge on this related to virus scanners, Registry settings, and so on. This is a result of an event ID of 8206 on the Exchange server.

▶ **Alert:** Disabled user does not have a master account SID.

Issue: The user does not have the Associated external account permission, and the Exchange server does not have the hotfix available to resolve this issue.

Resolution: To resolve this, open the user account in Active Directory Users and Computers and then go to Properties -> Exchange Advanced -> Mailbox Rights. For the Self account, we added the Associated external account permission, which resolves the error. The error itself does reappear, but it appears with the next user identified that had the issue. If there are a large number of these, you can also locate them by going to each Exchange backend server and doing a Filter operation on event number 9548 within the application event log. An Exchange hotfix for this issue is available at http://support.microsoft.com/kb/916783. (This information is a subset of what was originally posted at http://cameronfuller.spaces.live.com/blog/cns!A231E4EB0417CB76!835.entry.)

▶ **Alert:** Low Free Disk Space.

Issue: Part of the Exchange management pack checks free space on all drives, including those drives that do not have Exchange directories or files on them. This activates a warning at less than 5% free disk space and less than 1000MB of free disk space on Exchange server drives that do *not* have the transaction logs or queue files on them.

Resolution: Free up disk space on the drive. See the "Logical Disk Free Space is L bullet for potential approaches to free up disk space on the drive.

▶ **Alert:** Very low free disk space.

Issue: Part of the Exchange management pack checks for free space on all dri including those drives that do not have Exchange directories or files on ther activates an error at less than 2% free disk space and less than 400MB of fre space on Exchange server drives that do *not* have the transaction logs or queue files on them.

Resolution: Free up disk space on the drive. See the "Logical Disk Free Space is Low" bullet for potential approaches to free up disk space on the drive.

▶ **Alert:** Logical Disk Free Space is Low.

Issue: Low disk space on a drive on a server monitored by OpsMgr.

Resolution: You can either free up disk space on the drive or configure an override for the drive to change the monitoring configurations for the drive (see http:/ /cameronfuller.spaces.live.com/blog/cns!A231E4EB0417CB76!1001.entry for details on how to do this override). Here are some other items to consider:

▶ If the page file is currently on the drive that is critical on drive space, move it to another drive.

▶ The Windows Disk Cleanup Wizard can also be used to provide methods to free up disk space (right-click the drive, select Properties, and click the Disk Cleanup button).

▶ If the drive is critically low on available free disk space, automatic updates can be turned off in the Control Panel and the *%windir%*\softwaredistribution\ download folder can be removed. (Of course, automatic updates will not occur after this change is made.)

▶ The default IIS configuration puts the IIS log files under *%windir%*\system32\ LogFiles\W3SVC1. The files can be moved within the Internet Information Services (IIS) Manager by clicking the properties of the websites, under the properties of the log files. The log files can either be moved or disabled if required.

▶ Exchange log files can take up a large amount of disk space on a drive if the Exchange server is not backed up regularly. When the Exchange server has a full backup completed, the log files are removed. If an Exchange server is critical on space on the log drive, determine if backups are occurring. If they are not, perform an ntbackup of the Exchange files to truncate the logs. Circular logging (which removes this type of a situation) can also be enabled in some configurations, but is not recommended if there is any mailbox data on the system.

MAPI Logon Failure.

This occurred almost immediately after running the Exchange 2003 ᵐment Pack Configuration Wizard.

on: The issue was resolved when the wizard completed its configurations only repeated once. We ran the MAPI Logon task to validate that the issue resolved and confirmed there were no errors. Then we closed the alert.

▶ **Alert:** MAPI session closed due to excessive number of store objects in use.

Issue: Exceeded the maximum of 250 objects of type objtMessage (1 repeat), or exceeded the maximum of 32 objects of type session (0 repeats), or exceeded the maximum of 500 objects of type objtFolder.

Resolution: Microsoft resolution is provided with the Product Knowledge for the alert. Eventid.net provides the following on this: http://www.eventid.net/display. asp?eventid=9646&eventno=3449&source=MSExchangeIS&phase=1. You can also view the Microsoft KB article on this issue at http://support.microsoft.com/kb/ 830836.

▶ **Alert:** Outlook Web Access logon failure: Unexpected error during synthetic Outlook Web Access logon.

Issue: OWA Logon failed. Cannot measure OWA availability. Unexpected error. No Exchange virtual servers and virtual directory (SSL enabled) can be found on this server to form a valid URL. Try providing the URL in the CustomUrls Registry key.

If the name in the URL matches the name in the certificate, we learned that when SSL is enabled, the MP reports an error like this when the Require SSL check box is not checked on the Directory Security tab of the website. See Andy Dominey's blog write-up on this at http://myitforum.com/cs2/blogs/adominey/archive/2007/04/10/ mom-2005-and-om-2007-exchange-2003-management-pack-issue.aspx.

This rule requires OWA to be installed with SSL and requires SSL to be checked on the system. It will *not* work without both of these configured. This also requires the name to match the name on the certificate.

Resolution: Enable SSL and require SSL on the OWA server. If the name of the URL does not match the certificate, this rule will not work. You may also want to see the "Synthetic OWA Testing" section of this appendix for an alternative approach.

▶ **Alert:** The MAD Monitoring thread was unable to read the CPU usage information.

Issue: This had repeated eight times in 5 days and 16 hours. The MAD Monitoring thread was unable to read the CPU usage information, error 0x800706be. From the knowledge summary, if this happens occasionally, it can be safely ignored. If it happens every 5 minutes, there is an issue.

Resolution: Closed the alert because it was not occurring frequently.

▶ **Alert:** The Offline Address List (OAL) Generator could not generate full details for some entries in the OAL. To see which entries are affected, event logging for the OAL must be set to at least medium.

Issue: MSExchangeSA Event ID 9320.

Resolution: Refer to the event ID link on this: http://www.eventid.net/display.asp?eventid=9320&eventno=3692&source=MSExchangeSA&phase=1. The Microsoft article on this issue is located at http://support.microsoft.com/kb/908496.

▶ **Alert:** The Offline Address List Generator could not generate full details because the total size of the details information is greater than 64 kilobytes.

  Issue: See the Microsoft support article.

  Resolution: The Microsoft article on this issue is available at http://support.microsoft.com/kb/908496.

Synthetic OWA Testing

If you have already tried everything that you can do to get rid of the OWA logon failure (other than disabling it) in Exchange 2003, this may be of assistance. We would like to give a huge thanks to Tony Greco who pointed out the issue and found this creative approach to resolving it!

▶ **Alert:** OWA: Outlook Web Access logon failure: Authentication error.

  Issue: The OpsMgr script in the Exchange 2003 management pack will not work if you are using a custom URL and HTTPS with certificates. If you're not already familiar with this problem, Andy Dominey discusses it at http://myitforum.com/cs2/blogs/adominey/archive/2007/04/10/mom-2005-and-om-2007-exchange-2003-management-pack-issue.aspx). For example, if you have a server named JUGGERNAUT in the ODYSSEY domain and your webmail address is https://webmail.odyssey.com on SERVER1, the current MP cannot perform the check on this web location correctly because the server name (juggernaut.odyssey.com) does not match the certificate name of webmail.odyssey.com.

  Resolution: Create a custom simple monitor with two views to monitor the OWA frontend functionality. Perform the following steps:

  1. Open the Operations console. Navigate to Authoring -> Web Applications. Right-click and choose Add monitoring wizard.

  2. Choose the Web Application monitoring type.

  3. Enter a name (**OWA Web Test**, in our case) and description and then select a management pack for your changes (preferably not the default management pack; we created our own called OWA Web Test).

  4. Enter the URL to test. For our sample company ODYSSEY.com, we will use **https://juggernaut.odyssey.com** to match the organization's existing external name assigned to the SSL certificate.

5. Choose a watcher node (a management server or your RMS does well on this if it's not too busy) and the frequency (the default is 2 minutes).

6. Create the web application.

7. Highlight the new web application and choose Edit web application settings under Actions.

8. Start a capture and go through the following process (we actually were not able to select and preview messages because it caused too many issues with the monitor):

    ▶ Log in to the OWA server using appropriate credentials.

    ▶ Create and send a new message to the email of the specified credentials.

    ▶ Delete the message that was sent.

    ▶ Log out of the OWA browse session.

9. Remove any failed responses that are not required. As an example, we removed the links section on ours. We removed this by going to the Properties -> Monitoring tab and then unchecking Enable health evaluation and performance collection for Internal links. We also needed to remove other conditions that failed regularly. You can do this by highlighting the URL that failed and deleting it under the Actions selection.

10. Now that the web application is monitoring the OWA site, we can see the state of the monitor either under the management pack we specified (Administration -> OWA Web Test, in our case) or under Administration -> Web Application -> Web Applications State.

11. We can also right-click the particular state view and choose to open the Alerts view or the Performance view. The Performance view is especially useful, and it is a good idea to go ahead and create a customized Performance view so that you can easily access these counters. Be sure to limit the performance counters shown to the name you created (such as our OWA Web Test example); otherwise, there are a lot of counters. Figure A.2 shows an example of the Performance view.

12. Because we are now effectively monitoring OWA functionality, we can disable the original OWA: Outlook Web Access logon failure: Authentication error alert.

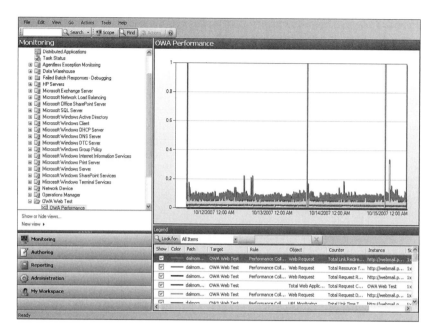

FIGURE A.2   Viewing OWA performance.

Configuring Baselines

As we were tuning the Exchange 2003 MP, we discovered the majority of alerts generated were a result of the calculated baseline rules. This section includes detailed steps to configure the sensitivity of these rules to decrease the alert volume. First, a huge thanks to a thread at EggheadCafe.com with an explanation of this issue, as that started us down the path on how to perform the tuning: http://www.eggheadcafe.com/software/aspnet/29844092/tuning-baselining-monitor.aspx.

The following were the primary alerts causing large amounts of volume:

▶ Information Store Transport Temp Table is outside the calculated baseline.

▶ Mailbox Store Send Queue is outside the calculated baseline.

▶ SMTP Local queue is outside the calculated baseline.

▶ SMTP Messages in the Queue Directory is outside the calculated baseline.

▶ SMTP Remote Queue is outside the calculated baseline.

▶ SMTP Remote Retry Queue is outside the calculated baseline.

▶ IS Virtual Bytes is outside the calculated baseline.

▶ Number of RPC requests is outside the calculated baseline.

Perform the following steps for all alerts causing significant volume that need to be tuned. It is best to implement these one at a time.

We recommend following the order listed in Table A.1, because it groups together the types of rules to make them easier to find. The steps that refer to the Exchange Queue will vary depending on the rule and monitor changed. The first six alerts in the preceding list are all part of the Exchange Queue; the last two are part of Exchange IS Service. Change each on both the monitor and rule level.

We also strongly recommend you save your changes to an unsealed MP *other* than the Default management pack.

TABLE A.1   Mapping for Alerts, Rules, and Monitors

Alert	Rule	Monitor
Information Store Transport Temp Table is outside the calculated baseline	Baseline Collection Rule for Information Store temp table number of entries (Rules, of type Exchange Queue)	IS Transport Temp Table Monitor (Exchange Queue, Entity Health, Performance)
Mailbox Store Send Queue is outside the calculated baseline	Baseline Collection Rule for Mailbox Store Send Queue Length (Rules, of type Exchange Queue)	MB Store Send Queue Monitor (Exchange Queue, Entity Health, Performance)
SMTP Local queue is outside the calculated baseline	Baseline Collection Rule for SMTP Server Local Queue (Rules, of type Exchange Queue)	SMTP Local Queue Monitor (Exchange Queue, Entity Health, Performance)
SMTP Messages in the Queue Directory is outside the calculated baseline	Baseline Collection for SMTP Message Queue Directory (Rules, of type Exchange Queue)	SMTP Message Queue Directory Monitor (Exchange Queue, Entity Health, Performance)
SMTP Remote Queue is outside the calculated baseline	Baseline Collection Rule for SMTP Server Remote Queue Length (Rules, of type Exchange Queue)	SMTP Remote Queue Monitor (Exchange Queue, Entity Health, Performance)
SMTP Remote Retry Queue is outside the calculated baseline	Baseline Collection Rule for SMTP Server Remote Retry Queue Length (Rules, of type Exchange Queue)	SMTP Remote Retry Queue Monitor (Exchange Queue, Entity Health, Performance)
IS Virtual Bytes is outside the calculated baseline	Baseline Collection Rule for IS Virtual Bytes (Rules, of type Exchange IS Service)	IS Virtual Bytes Monitor (Exchange IS Service, Entity Health, Performance)

A

TABLE A.1   Continued

Alert	Rule	Monitor
Number of RPC requests is outside the calculated baseline	Baseline Collection Rule for IS RPC Requests (Rules, of type Exchange IS Service)	MONITOR=IS RPC Requests Monitor (Exchange IS Service, Entity Health, Performance)

1. **Find the rule that applies to the alert.** To find the rules, it is easiest to change the scope to filter by the two areas we need—the Exchange Queue and Exchange IS Service. Both of these are available when you click Scope and choose the option to view all targets. Then find rules starting with Baseline Collection. This scopes the list down to about 17 rules versus over 6000.

    Details on the names of each of these rules are listed in Table A.1. Disable the rule (right-click the rule and select Overrides -> Disable the Rule -> For all objects of type: Exchange Queue, and then click Yes to accept).

2. **Change the rule sensitivity to 2.81.** Right-click the rule, select Overrides -> Override the Rule -> For all Objects of type: Exchange Queue, and then check the Sensitivity parameter and set it to **2.81** if it is not already set to that value. Click OK.

3. **Find the monitor that applies to the alert.** This can be located by searching for or scoping to the type of object identified for the monitor. Disable the monitor by right-clicking the monitor, selecting Overrides -> Disable the Monitor -> For all objects of type: Exchange Queue, and then clicking Yes to accept.

4. **Change the monitor inner sensitivity to 2.81.** Right-click the monitor, select Overrides -> Override the Monitor -> For all Objects of type: Exchange Queue, and then check the Inner Sensitivity parameter and set it to **2.81** if it's not already set to that value. Click OK.

5. **Change the monitor outer sensitivity to 3.31.** Right-click the monitor, select Overrides -> Override the Monitor -> For all Objects of type: Exchange Queue, and then check the Outer Sensitivity parameter and set it to **3.31** if it's not already set to that value. Click OK.

6. **Reenable the monitor.** Right-click the monitor, click Overrides Summary, and delete the override that reads Type, Exchange Queue, Enabled, False.

7. **Go back to the rule identified in step 1 and reenable it.** Right-click the rule, click Overrides Summary, and delete the override that reads Type, Exchange Queue, Enabled, False.

After we configured the inner and outer sensitivities (steps 4 and 5 in this section), several of the rules were still generating large volumes of alerts, including the following:

▶ IS Virtual Bytes is outside the calculated baseline

▶ Number of RPC requests is outside the calculated baseline

The alerts were identified as Above Inner Envelope. To minimize their frequency, we had previously changed both the rule and the monitor's sensitivity from 2.81 to 3.31 on the overrides.

After reading up on this sensitivity concept, it appears that *increases* to this value *decrease* the frequency of the alerts, because this decreases the sensitivity to the difference from the calculated baseline.

In theory, if the 3.31 override is not sufficient, you should next try 3.81 because the increase from 2.81 to 3.31 is an increase of .5; therefore, another .5 increase seems logical if another value change is required. This is an extrapolation based on what we have seen so far because we do not know the internal workings of the algorithm!

The feedback we have seen indicates that 3.81 works quite well.

The SQL Server Management Pack

Next, we will look at installing and configuring the SQL Server management pack.

Installing the SQL Server Management Pack

Perform the following steps to install the SQL Server MP:

1. Download the SQL Server management pack (http://www.microsoft.com/downloads/details.aspx?FamilyID=8c0f970e-c653-4c15-9e51-6a6cadfca363&DisplayLang=en), and the SQL Server Management Pack Guide (http://download.microsoft.com/download/7/4/d/74deff5e-449f-4a6b-91dd-ffbc117869a2/OM2007_MP_SQLSrvr.doc).

2. Read the Management Pack Guide from cover to cover. This document spells out in detail some important pieces of information that you need to know.

3. Import the SQL Server management pack. The management pack for each monitored version of SQL Server (2000 and 2005) consists of two .mp files. These files provide logic for discovery and monitoring, meaning you can use a smaller management pack to discover the existence of SQL Server and deploy the monitoring MP to the

agent after OpsMgr has discovered SQL Server there. There is also a SQL Server Library MP, which is a prerequisite for the other management packs.
Be sure to download the most recent version of the SQL Server management pack. Versions 6.0.4247.5 and above, for example, solve an issue discovered in the OpsMgr 2007 Service Pack 1 Release Candidate with the SQL 2005 discovery script GETSQL2005DBSpace.js failing.

4. We recommend you also import the appropriate version of the Windows Server management pack for your operating system (Windows 2000 or 2003). The Windows Server management packs monitor various aspects of the OS that can influence the performance of those computers running SQL Server! This includes disk capacity, disk performance, memory utilization, network adapter utilization, and processor performance.

5. Install the SQL Management Studio and Profiler if you will be running the associated tasks from the Operations console; otherwise, you will receive an error message telling you the system cannot find the file specified. Installing the Management Studio and Profiler is not required unless you want to run those tasks.

The SQL Server MP supports agentless monitoring with the exception of tasks that start and stop SQL Server services and SQL Server mail.

The management pack installs two Run As Profiles: the SQL Server Discovery account and the SQL Server Monitoring account. By default, the management pack uses the Default Action account.

Optional Configuration

The SQL Server MP does not automatically discover all object types. Go to the Authoring pane of the Operations console to enable discovering additional components. Components not discovered include the following:

▶ SQL Server 2005 Publisher

▶ SQL Server 2005 Subscriber

▶ SQL Server 2005 Subscription

▶ SQL Server 2005 Agent Job

▶ SQL Server 2000 Agent Job

▶ SQL Server 2005 DB File Group

▶ SQL Server 2005 DB File

> **TIP**
>
> **The Impact of Undiscovered Components**
>
> Because OpsMgr does not discover the components listed previously unless you tell it to, you will not receive alerts if there is a failure because OpsMgr is not monitoring them! If, for example, you have scheduled SQL database backups using the SQL Agent and the job fails, OpsMgr won't tell you about it. If an agent job failed in MOM 2005, the SQL MP generated an alert. In MOM 2005, the alert was enabled, but in OpsMgr 2007, the component isn't even monitored (by default). So these behaviors are not necessarily the same between MOM 2005 and OpsMgr 2007.

You can use overrides to change the settings for automatic discovery to enable these object types. Be sure to change your settings in an unsealed MP other than the Default management pack.

SQL Server Management Pack Tuning and Alerts to Look For

The following alerts were encountered and resolved while tuning the SQL Server management pack:

▶ **Alert:** The SQL Server Service Broker or Database Mirroring transport is disabled or not configured. (Event ID 9666)

▶ **Issue:** This alert may occur even if the broker *is* enabled.

▶ **Resolution:** Verify the broker is enabled by running the following query in SQL Management Studio while connected to the Master database:

```
SELECT is_broker_enabled FROM sys.databases WHERE name =
➥'OperationsManager'
```

If the result is 1, the broker is enabled. If the result is 0, you can enable the broker as follows:

1. Stop the SDK, Config, and Health services on the RMS as well as the Heath service on any secondary management servers.

2. Execute the following statement from SQL Management Studio:

```
ALTER DATABASE OperationsManager SET ENABLE_BROKER
```

3. Restart the services.

If the alert continues to occur, disable the rule using an override.

For SP 1, Microsoft added some instrumentation around the SQL Service Broker not enabled message by adding checks to determine if the service was running or not.

In test environments, often there are issues where the database is too busy and SQL Server is unable to process the query to determine if the Broker is actually running.

▶ **Issue:** Clustered virtual servers are discovered and display as agentless managed, but the SQL Server database engine on the cluster does not appear to be monitored.

Resolution: Only the virtual SQL Servers are discovered (the cluster and not the individual cluster nodes). In the Monitoring tab under Windows Server, check that each virtual server shows up as a Windows Server with the property Is Virtual Server set to True. Restart the Health service on the RMS and any other management servers after adding the cluster. You may need to restart the Health service on the cluster as well, which will re-run the discovery.

It is also possible that you are having RPC issues. For additional information, see KB article 306985 (http://support.microsoft.com/kb/306985).

▶ **Alert:** 8957 Monitor Name: DBCC executed found and repaired errors – but found 0 errors and repaired 0.

Issue: When DBCC runs, it generates this event log message with the same event ID regardless of whether any problems were found.

Resolution: Disable the rule and create your own. For the new rule, copy all the same settings from the original but set the description to not contain "found 0 errors." For all other events with this ID, an alert will be generated to indicate a problem was found.

▶ **Alert:** Health Monitor Description: Service Pack Compliance – MSSQLSERVER (SQL 2005 DB Engine) Warning (against ACS database).

Issue: SQL Server 2005 Service Pack 2 is installed, which is acceptable for the ACS database server. SP 2 has been approved for all OpsMgr database components.

Resolution: We created an override (for a specific object of type SQL Engine DB) to allow this configuration for the server, and we set the enabled parameter to False for the server. We also reset the health for the health monitor on this server and refreshed the Health Explorer, and the state updated to green from yellow.

▶ **Issue:** The Management Server Action account is used as the Default Data Warehouse Action account, rather than the DW Action account you specified during setup.

Resolution: This will be fixed in SP 1. In the interim, create a Run As account, type **Simple**, and set the username and password to a single space. In the same-name profile, associate this account to all management servers, including the RMS. Also, be sure that the Data Warehouse Action account profile is correctly associated with an account for all management servers where it will be used as the Windows authentication account. This information was obtained from the newsgroups (nntp://msnews.microsoft.com/microsoft.public.opsmgr.setup/7363632A-A650-4367-9DCE-27CC2887B786@microsoft.com).

▶ **Issue:** SQL Server 2000 database engine health is not monitored. This is an aggregate monitor that includes the SQL Service State terminated unexpected monitor and the SQL Service terminated unexpectedly monitor. (If you have SQL Server 2000 databases, you will want to turn on monitoring!)

Resolution: The SQL DB Engine Service Health Rollup monitor is not enabled by default. Use the Authoring pane of the Operations console to enable the Aggregate Rollup monitor.

Under Management Pack objects, select Monitors, change the scope to SQL 2000 DB Engine, search, then expand the SQL 2000 DB Engine, expand Entity Health, expand Availability, select SQL DB Engine Serve Health Rollup, and create an override to override the monitor for all objects of type SQL 2000 DB Engine. KB article 938991 (http://support.microsoft.com/kb/938991) has additional information.

The following issues are related to specific applications you may have installed:

▶ **Issue:** Alert Rule or Alert Monitor: Auto Shrink Flag Alert Description: The auto shrink flag for database SUSDB in SQL instance MSSQL SERVER on computer 123.abc.com is not set according to best practice.

Resolution: This is a standard Microsoft application (WSUS) and a default configuration. Create an override to exclude this database.

▶ **Issue:** Alert Rule or Alert Monitor: Auto Shrink Flag Alert Description: The auto shrink flag for database BEDB in SQL instance MSSQL SERVER on computer endeavor.odyssey.com is not set according to best practice.

Resolution: This is the standard configuration for Backup Exec's database.

▶ **Issue:** Alert Rule or Alert Monitor: Auto Shrink Flag Alert Description: The auto shrink flag for database MSCUPTDB in SQL instance MSSQL SERVER on computer endeavor.odyssey.com is not set according to best practice.

Resolution: This is a standard Microsoft application (patch management for SMS and Configuration Manager) and a default configuration. Create an override to exclude this database.

▶ **Issue:** Alert Rule or Alert Monitor: Auto Close Flag Alert Description: The auto close flag for database MSCUPTDB in SQL instance MSSQL SERVER on computer endeavor.odyssey.com is not set according to best practice.

Resolution: This is a standard Microsoft application (patch management for SMS and Configuration Manager) and a default configuration. Create an override to exclude this database.

A

The IIS Management Pack

The IIS management pack enables OpsMgr 2007 to monitor the following IIS object types:

- ▶ IIS Server Role
- ▶ IIS Web, FTP, NNTP, and SMTP servers
- ▶ IIS Web and FTP sites
- ▶ IIS NNTP and SMTP virtual servers

Installing the IIS Management Pack

Perform the following steps to install the IIS MP:

1. Download the IIS management pack (http://www.microsoft.com/downloads/
   details.aspx?FamilyId=D351BCA8-182B-4223-8C9E-627E184BA02B&displaylang=en)
   and the IIS Management Pack Guide (http://download.microsoft.com/download/7/4/
   d/74deff5e-449f-4a6b-91dd-ffbc117869a2/OM2007_MP_IIS.doc).

2. Read the Management Pack Guide from cover to cover. This document spells out in
   detail some important pieces of information you need to know.

3. Import the IIS management pack. The components include the Windows Server
   Internet Information Services Library and individual management packs for IIS 5
   (Internet Information Services 2000 with Windows 2000) and IIS 6 (Internet
   Information Services 2003 with Windows Server 2003). Import the library, which is a
   prerequisite, plus the appropriate management pack for the version of IIS you will be
   monitoring.

4. We recommend you also import the appropriate version of the Windows Server
   management pack for your operating system (Windows 2000 or 2003). Some of the
   views provided with the IIS MP require the MPs for the appropriate level of operating systems to have data to display.

5. Even if you do not have any custom web applications using IIS, remember that
   Exchange, SQL Server Reporting Services, and Operations Manager itself have
   components that use IIS; you will want to implement the IIS MP as part of rolling
   out and monitoring those applications.

6. The IIS management pack does not support agentless monitoring. Verify you have
   installed the OpsMgr agent on your IIS servers.

7. The IIS MP collects data from the IIS logs. If logging is not enabled, the MP will only
   collect and analyze service data. The IIS logs must be set to the W3C Extended Log
   File format. Enable logging for each type of site and virtual server for which you
   want to collect monitoring data. This can include FTP sites, websites, SMTP virtual
   servers, and NNTP virtual servers.

   Enable logging for a virtual server in the IIS Services Manager by double-clicking the
   local computer, right-clicking the SMTP or NNTP Virtual Server folder you want to

enable logging for, and selecting Properties. Then, on the General tab, select Enable logging. Be sure to select W3C Extended Log File format on the Active log format dropdown list.

Rolling Up Health

The IIS MP for OpsMgr 2007 has the ability to tell you whether a specific website is healthy, in addition to being able to tell you whether the web server is healthy.

The health of the IIS server is dependent on the health of the objects at the next lower level—the IIS Web, FTP, NNTP, and SMTP servers. If any of these servers is in a critical health state, the IIS server will display in a critical health state. By default, the health of the IIS FTP, NNTP, SMTP, and Web servers are not dependent on the health of the objects at the next lower level. If one or more websites is in a critical state, the Web Server object will not change state.

IIS Management Pack Tuning and Alerts to Look for

We encountered and resolved the following alerts while tuning the IIS management pack:

▶ **Alert:** An unknown token name (s-event) was encountered.

Issue: IIS logging is configured by default on Windows Server 2000 to include Process Accounting extensions for websites.

Resolution: Disable logging Process Accounting Extensions. (In IIS Service Manager, select Default Web Site -> Properties and then select Enable logging on the Web Site tab. From the Active log format dropdown list, select W3C Extended Log File Format. Select Properties -> Extended Properties, and clear Process Accounting from the Extended Logging Options list box.)

Issue: IISReset causes a ton of alerts.

Resolution: Put the IIS object in maintenance mode before doing the IISReset. You could use PowerShell (use the command New-MaintenanceWindow to put the server into maintenance mode and then start the IISReset cmd operation) to automate this.

Issue: IIS MP does not work well with clusters. This can be a real issue if you are monitoring Exchange.

Resolution: None currently available. We anticipate this will be addressed in Service Pack 1 or the next release of the IIS MP.

If you are using the Exchange management pack, you will encounter a number of IIS-related issues. See the "Exchange Management Pack Tuning and Alerts to Look For" section of this appendix for a detailed list.

The Web Application Management Pack Template

Operations Manager 2007 includes built-in website monitoring functionality (similar to that provided by MOM 2005's Web Sites and Web Services MP), using the Web Application Management Pack Template. This functionality is quite useful for monitoring websites. The template records where you go with your browser. To use this functionality, you need to configure your browser. In Internet Explorer, select Tools -> Internet Options -> Advanced -> Enable third-party browser extensions (requires restart) in both IE 6 and IE 7. Web applications are created in the Operations console under Authoring -> Management Pack Templates -> Web Application.

We decided to start simple, and then move into more complex monitoring configurations.

Starting Simple

We began with developing a web application that monitors a single web page (such as www.google.com or www.microsoft.com) without requiring authentication. There is a great write-up available at http://www.technotesblog.com/?p=432 that provides a detailed process to create monitoring for a single web page. For our example, we use www.google.com, and as in the TechNotes blog example (which uses the Microsoft website), we disabled link tracking.

Getting More Complex

After our application was in a working state, we went to the next step that we wanted to test—monitoring the OpsMgr Operations Web console. Because the Operations Web console requires authentication, the monitoring setup is more difficult.

We created a new web application called Operations Web console (and stored it in a new, nondefault management pack), and we had the application browse to http://<*servername*>:51908/default.aspx for the Operations Web console. We created the web application using the default configurations and ran it on Windows 2003, Windows XP, and Windows Vista workstation systems (one of each for testing purposes). Each of these systems went to a critical status due to an "access is denied" error message.

You can check the status of the monitored websites by navigating in the Operations console to Monitoring -> Web Application -> Web Applications State. You can also right-click and open the Performance view for any system you are monitoring to receive a large number of collected performance information (check out Figure A.3 for an example).

Resolving the security issue required creating a Run As Account of type Windows (under Administration -> Security -> Run As Accounts), using an account with permissions to access the Operations Web console. We then configured this account to be used by the web application in the Authoring section under Authoring -> Management Pack Templates -> Web Application:

▶ Edit the web application settings for the Operations Web console just created.

▶ Select the General tab to configure its settings, select the authentication method of NLTM, and specify the account created to monitor the website.

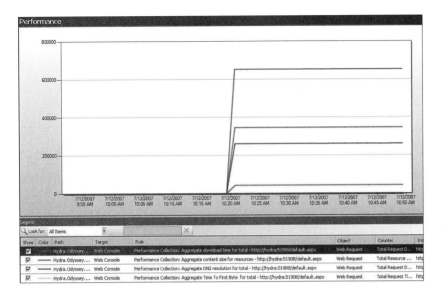

FIGURE A.3   Viewing the website performance counters.

After going back to monitoring section (Operations Console -> Monitoring -> Web Application -> Web Application State) and waiting a little bit, the Operations Web console monitor went to green.

To get even more complex, we created a web test that used the recorder. The Reporting Server Component was a good test for this. The URL for this server is located under Administration -> Settings -> Reporting. In our environment, this has a value of http://QUICKSILVER:80/ReportServer. To record, we started with http://QUICKSILVER/Reports and worked from that point. We opened up a graphic, a folder, and a report during the capture process. Running a report would also be an option, but because this would run on a regular basis (every few minutes), we did not want to create that level of overhead with our monitoring. We configured the authentication method (NTLM and the account we previously created) and the watcher node. We checked its status in the Health Explorer (see Figure A.4); everything was green.

Lessons Learned Using the Web Application Management Pack Template

The systems performing the watcher function did not have any customizations made to their web browsers, such as adding the browser location to the trusted sites. Some servers would work well as watchers and other would not (in our case, the RMS). We were unable to identify a specific reason for this.

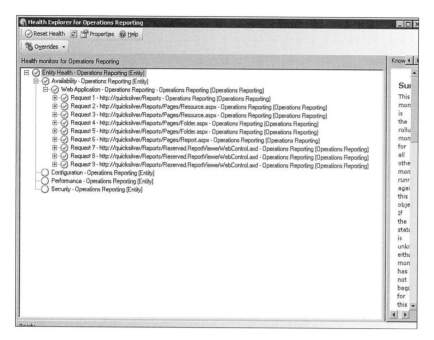

FIGURE A.4   Viewing entity health for our web application.

Do not test authentication items within the Web Application creator. It brings up a pop-up warning that running a test of this web application may fail. While the test is run, credentials that have been configured for this web application will not be used. If the site you are testing does not explicitly require authentication, the test may still succeed.

The best way to test authentication items is by actually checking their alerts and status in the Monitoring space.

If the site requires authentication to get to it, you need to configure authentication for the web tests. Check IIS to see what type it allows and provide a match (NTLM = Integrated Authentication in this particular case).

Some SSL Monitoring Monitors Display an Incorrect Status or Name

If you are using the Web Application management pack template to monitor a website secured with SSL, the following monitors may display improperly:

▶ The SSL Certificate Expired monitor status may display a healthy status, even if the certificate used by the website has expired.

▶ The Certificate CN Invalid monitor displays a healthy state even if a common name for the certificate is invalid.

▶ In the Health Explorer, Certificate CN Invalid appears incorrectly as the display name for the Untrusted CA monitor, and two Certificate CN Invalid monitors appear under the SSL Monitoring node, with one of the monitors displaying a description for the Untrusted CA monitor.

A hotfix is available. See KB article 939585 (http://support.microsoft.com/kb/939585) for additional information. The hotfix is incorporated into Service Pack 1.

Lessons Learned with the Dell Hardware Management Pack

The Dell Management Pack Guide is part of the Dell management pack download, available at http://support.dell.com/FileLib/Format.aspx?c=us&l=en&ReleaseID=R158716. The OpsMgr Dell management pack actually only takes the information provided by the Dell OpenManage agent and integrates that with OpsMgr. As a result, the alerts raised are directly related to hardware issues shown in the logs available through the OpenManage interface.

Prerequisites

Before you install the Dell MP, you must install the updated Microsoft Operations Manager 2005 Backward Compatibility management pack. You can download the Backward Compatibility MP at http://go.microsoft.com/fwlink/?LinkId=98874. Without the updated Backward Compatibility MP, you may experience CPU spikes!

Using the Dell Management Pack

Make sure all the systems in your environment that have the Dell OpenManage software installed are at least version 5.2. A variety of errors will occur if you try to monitor using the OpsMgr management pack and an older version of Dell OpenManage (including a lot of Script or Executable Failed to run alerts). You can check the version either by running the Dell Server Administrator and checking the version it lists or by checking the Registry key available under HKLM\SOFTWARE\Dell Computer Corporation\OpenManage\Applications\SystemsManagement, in the Version field.

Dell Management Pack Tuning and Alerts to Look For

The following alerts were encountered and resolved while tuning the Dell management pack:

▶ **Alert:** Dell.Connections.ServerAdministrator.Alert.1306.Critical.

Issue: Redundancy lost Redundancy unit: System Power Unit Chassis location: Main System Chassis Previous redundancy state was Normal Number of devices required for full redundancy: 2.

We checked with the Launch Server Administrator task and did not find any current issues on the server. The actual issue was in the alert log, not the hardware log.

Resolution: Found the issue through the alert log on Dell OpenManage. This appears to be an issue with a sensor or a power supply on the system. Entered company knowledge on the time and server on which the alert occurred to determine if this is a component that may be failing.

▶ **Alert:** Dell.Connections.ServerAdministrator.Alert.1104.

Issue: Fan sensor detected a failure Sensor location: ESM MB Fan7 RPM Chassis location: Main System Chassis Previous state was: OK (Normal) Fan sensor value (in RPM): 0.

We checked with the Launch Server Administrator task and did not find any current issues on the server. The actual issue was in the alert log, not the hardware log.

Resolution: We found the issue through the alert log on Dell OpenManage. This appears to be an issue with a sensor or a power supply on the system.

Issue: DellStorageDiscovery.vbs failing on an Exchange 2003 server, process exited with 0. Searched the XML files to validate that this is part of the Dell management pack. Checked the Dell Server Administrator on the system, and it was running version 1.9 (5.2 is required).

Resolution: Upgrade the version of the Dell Server Administrator software or disable the alert on this system.

▶ **Alert:** Script or Executable Failed to run.

Issue: DellServerFansUnitUnitMonitor.vbs failing on a Windows 2003 server. We checked the Dell Server Administrator on the system, and it was running version 1.8 (5.2 is required).

Resolution: Upgrade the version of the Dell Server Administrator software or disable the alert on this system.

▶ **Alert:** Dell.Connections.ServerAdministrator.Alert.1554.

Issue: Log size is full Log type: ESM.

Resolution: We validated that the log was full (used the Launch Server Administrator task) and then we used the Clear ESM Logs task to clear out the logs because the items were not current but were historical. Finally, we closed the alert.

▶ **Alert:** Dell.Connections.ServerAdministrator.Alert.1553.

Issue: Log size is near or at capacity Log type: ESM.

Resolution: We used the Clear ESM Logs task after reviewing them with the Launch Server Administrator task. We closed the alert.

Performance Counters

Operations Manager (OpsMgr) 2007 collects a number of performance counters for the agent (monitored computer), management server, and Audit Collection System (ACS) collector. These counters are created when the corresponding component is installed on a computer.

Counters Maintained by the Monitored Computer

Each managed agent maintains two sets of performance counters. Management servers maintain these counters as well.

▸ **Health Service counters**—These are performance counters for the Health Service running on that computer (see Table B.1).

▸ **Health Service Management Group counters**—These are performance counters relating to activity for the management group associated with that agent (see Table B.2). If the agent reports to multiple management groups (multihomed), there will be multiple instances of the Health Service Management Group counters.

TABLE B.1   Health Service Counters

Counter*	Description
Malformed Data Items Dropped	The total number of malformed data items that have been dropped
Malformed Data Items Dropped Rate	The rate at which malformed data items are being dropped
Module Count	The number of modules running in the Health Service
Task Count	The number of tasks running in the Health Service
Workflow Count	The number of workflows running in the Health Service

*There will be an instance of each of these per management group.

TABLE B.2   Health Service Management Group Counters

Counter*	Description
Active File Downloads	The number of file downloads to this management group that are currently active.
Active File Uploads	The number of file uploads from this management group that are currently active.
Active Batch Processing Time	The average amount of time in milliseconds it takes to process a batch of data.
Average Bind Write Action Batch Size	The average amount of time in milliseconds it takes to process a batch of data.
Batch Processing Rate	The rate at which batches of data are being processed.
Bind Data Source Average Batch Size	The average number of items inserted per batch into the workflow which originated from a remote Health Service.
Bind Data Source Batch Post Rate	The rate at which batches that originated from a remote Health Service inserted into the workflow.
Bind Data Source Item Drop Rate	The rate at which items are dropped by the bind data source because the workflow cannot process them quickly enough.
Bind Data Source Item Incoming Rate	The rate at which items are received from another Health Service.
Bind Data Source Item Post Rate	The rate at which items received from another Health Service are inserted into the workflow.
Bind Write Action Batch Insertion Rate	The rate at which batches are sent through the workflow destined for a remote Health Service.

TABLE B.2   Continued

Counter*	Description
Bind Write Action Multiple Item Batches	The number of batches sent through the workflow destined for a remote Health Service with more than one item in them.
Bind Write Action Single Item Batches	The number of batches sent through the workflow destined for a remote Health Service that have exactly one item in them.
Bind Write Action Zero Item Batches	The number of batches sent through the workflow destined for a remote Health Service that have zero items in them (NULL Sets).
Incoming Management Data Rate	The rate at which management data is received by the Health Service.
Item Incoming Rate	The rate at which items are being received by the Health Service.
Maximum Send Queue Size	The maximum size of the Send Queue.
Send Queue % Used	The percentage of the Send Queue in use.
Send Queue Ack Timeout Rate (>4 send attempt)	The number of Ack timeouts for items that have been sent more than four times.
Send Queue Ack Timeout Rate (1 send attempt)	The number of Ack timeouts for items that have been sent only once.
Send Queue Ack Timeout Rate (2 send attempts)	The number of Ack timeouts for items that have been sent twice.
Send Queue Ack Timeout Rate (3 send attempts)	The number of Ack timeouts for items that have been sent three times.
Send Queue Ack Timeout Rate (all send attempts)	The rate of items scheduled to re-send because they have not been acknowledged and are marked as requiring guaranteed delivery.
Send Queue Incoming Acknowledgement Rate	The rate of incoming acknowledgements for items sent with guaranteed delivery.
Send Queue Insertion Rate	The number of items inserted into the queue.
Send Queue Insertion Rate (Guaranteed Delivery)	The number of items marked as guaranteed delivery inserted into the queue.
Send Queue Insertion Rate (Non-Guaranteed Delivery)	The number of items marked as nonguaranteed delivery inserted into the queue.
Send Queue Item Expiration Rate	The rate at which items are being purged from the queue because they have not been sent within the queue expiration time.
Send Queue Send Rate	The number of items sent from the queue.

B

TABLE B.2   Continued

Counter*	Description
Send Queue Send Rate (Guaranteed Delivery)	The number of items sent that are marked for guaranteed delivery. This only records items sent; it does not account for whether or not the items are acknowledged.
Send Queue Send Rate (Non-Guaranteed Delivery)	The number of items sent that are not marked for guaranteed delivery.
Send Queue Size	The size of the send queue in bytes, not including any journaled data.

There will be an instance of each of these per management group.

Counters Maintained by the Management Server

In addition to the counters referenced in Tables B.1 and B.2, all management servers maintain performance counters for a number of items.

The first three groups of performance counters are located on each management server, but the associated service only runs when that management server is a Root Management Server (RMS). When the server is not acting as the RMS, these counters do not collect data.

▶ OpsMgr Config Service (see Table B.3)

▶ OpsMgr Config Service per Agent (see Table B.4)

▶ OpsMgr SDK Service (see Table B.5)

The next sets of counters are maintained on each management server.

▶ OpsMgr DB Write Action Cache (see Table B.6)

▶ OpsMgr DB Write Action Modules (see Table B.7)

▶ OpsMgr DW Synchronization Module (see Table B.8)

▶ OpsMgr DW Write Module (see Table B.9)

TABLE B.3   OpsMgr Config Service

Counter*	Description
Avg Management Pack Request	Average time to service a management pack (MP) request
Avg Request Queue Length	Average length of the request queue
Avg Request Queue Wait Time	Average wait time of requests in the queue
Change Notifications Failed	Number of change notifications that failed
Dirty State Notifications Failed	Number of dirty state notifications that could not be sent
Management Pack Requests Failed	Number of MP requests that could not be processed
Number of Active Requests	Number of requests being processed
Number of Queued Requests	Number of requests waiting in the queue
Number of Requests per Sec	Requests competed per second

These are active on the RMS and are per management group.

TABLE B.4   OpsMgr Config Service per Agent

Counter*	Description
Avg. State Sync Request (sec)	Average time to service a State Sync Request from this agent
State Sync Requests Failed	Number of State Sync Requests received from this agent that could not be processed
State Sync Requests Received	Number of State Sync Requests received from this agent

These are active on the RMS and are per management group.

TABLE B.5   OpsMgr SDK Service

Counter*	Description
Client Connections	Number of current clients connected to the OpsMgr SDK service
Client Connections Using Cache	Number of current clients connected to the OpsMgr SDK service that are using the cache
Pending Client Type Cache Refresh	Number of currently executing type cache refresh threads in the OpsMgr SDK service

These are active on the RMS and are per management group.

TABLE B.6   OpsMgr DB Write Action Cache

Counter*	Description
Cache Hit Ratio	Hit ratio for the cache
Cache Hit Size	Number of entries in the cache

*These are active on each management server.

TABLE B.7   OpsMgr Write Action Modules

Counter*	Description
Avg. Batch Size	Average number of entries processed by the module
Avg. Processing Time	Amount of time it takes to process an incoming batch on average

*These occur on each management server for the following instances: Alert Write Module, Discover Write Module, Event Write Module, Performance Signature Write Module, Performance Write Module, SQLobj Write Module, and State Change Module.

TABLE B.8   OpsMgr DW Synchronization Module

Counter*	Description
Avg Batch Processing Time, ms.	Average batch processing time in milliseconds
Avg Batch Size	Average batch size
Batch Age/sec	Batch age in seconds
Batch Size	Batch size
Batches/sec	Batches per second
Data Items/sec	Data items per second
Errors/sec	Errors per second
Total Error Count	Total error count

*These occur on each management server for the following instances: Configuration, Domain Snapshot, Health Service Outage, Maintenance Mode, Managed Identity, Relationship, and Type Managed Entity.

TABLE B.9   OpsMgr DW Writer Module

Counter*	Description
Avg. Batch Processing Time, ms	Average batch processing time in milliseconds
Avg Batch Size	Average batch size
Batches/sec	Batches per second
Data Items/sec	Data items per second
Dropped Batch Count	Dropped batch count
Dropped Data Item Count	Dropped data item count
Errors/sec	Errors per second
Total Error Count	Total error count

These occur on each management server for the Alert, Event, Performance, and State instances.

Counters Maintained by the OpsMgr Connector

The OpsMgr Connector is located on management servers and database servers. The Connector is an interface to the OpsMgr SDK Service that allows applications to communicate synchronously with the RMS. Counters used by the OpsMgr Connector are listed in Table B.10.

TABLE B.10   OpsMgr Connector Counters

Counter	Description
Bytes Decrypted	The number of bytes decrypted by the connector per second. This may be more or less than the number of data bytes received by the connector due to compression.
Bytes Encrypted	The number of bytes encrypted by the connector per second. This may be more or less than the number of data bytes submitted for transmission due to compression.
Bytes Received	The total number of network bytes received by the OpsMgr connector per second. This may be more or less than the number of data bytes received due to compression and encryption.
Bytes Transmitted	The total number of network bytes transmitted by the OpsMgr connector per second. This may be more or less than the number of data bytes submitted for transmission due to compression and encryption.

TABLE B.10 Continued

Counter	Description
Fragmented Compression Packets	The number of compression packets that were received by the connector and had to be reassembled per second. This can be caused by a number of factors, including the size of the packet, the Maximum Transmission Unit (MTU) of the network interface, the quantity of traffic on the network, and/or the amount of load on the connector. Packet reassembly can hurt performance and the ability of the server to scale.
Fragmented Data Packets	The number of data packets that were received by the connector and had to be reassembled per second. This can be caused by a number of factors, including the size of the packet, the MTU of the network interface, the quantity of traffic on the network, and/or the amount of load on the connector. Packet reassembly can hurt performance and the ability of the server to scale.
Fragmented Encryption Packets	The number of encrypted packets that were received by the connector and had to be reassembled per second. This can be caused by factors including the size of the packet, the MTU of the network interface, the quantity of traffic on the network, the encryption algorithm used, and/or the amount of load on the connector. Packet reassembly can hurt performance and the ability of the server to scale.
Fragmented Session Packets	The number of session packets that were received by the connector and had to be reassembled per second. This can be caused by a number of factors, including the size of the packet, the MTU of the network interface, the quantity of traffic on the network, and/or the amount of load on the connector. Packet reassembly can hurt performance and the ability of the server to scale.
Fragmented SSPI Packets	The number of Security Support Provider Interface (SSPI) negotiation packets that were received by the connector and had to be reassembled per second. This can be caused by a number of factors, including the size of the packet, the MTU of the network interface, the quantity of traffic on the network, and/or the amount of load on the connector. Packet reassembly can hurt performance and the ability of the server to scale.
I/O Errors	The number of I/O errors encountered by the connector per second.
I/O Operations Timed Out	The number of I/O operations on the connector that were timed out due to inactivity per second.
Open Connections	The number of TCP/IP (Transmission Control Protocol/Internet Protocol) connections currently open in the connector.
Server Listen Queue Length	The number of outstanding listen requests that are queued. If this drops to zero, the connector will not be able to accept incoming connections.

Counters Maintained by the OpsMgr Web Console

Table B.11 lists the counters used the OpsMgr Web Console application.

TABLE B.11   OpsMgr Web Console Counters

Counter	Description
CacheItems	Number of items that have been cached
Connect	Number of connects
ConnectErrors	Connection errors
PrepareView Time	Amount of time it takes to prepare a view
Reconnect	Number of reconnects
Session	Number of sessions
Threads	Number of threads

Counters Maintained by the ACS Collector

On the ACS Collector, we find two specific performance objects:

▶ ACS Collector (see Table B.12)

▶ ACS Collector Client (see Table B.13)

TABLE B.12   ACS Collector Counters

Counter	Description
Connected Clients	Number of clients currently connected.
Database Queue % Full	This is the ratio of the number of events currently in the database loader queue divided by the size of the database loader queue, expressed as a percentage.
Database Queue Backoff Threshold	The collector will not allow new connections while the database queue length is greater than this threshold.
Database Queue Disconnect Threshold	The collector will disconnect existing connections while the database queue length is greater than this threshold.
Database Queue Length	This is the number of events currently in the database loader queue.
DB Loader Event Inserts/sec	This is the number of records per second inserted into the dtEvent database table.
DB Loaded Principal Inserts/sec	This is the number of records per second inserted into the dtPrincipal database table.

TABLE B.12   Continued

Counter	Description
DB Loader String Inserts/sec	This is the number of records per second inserted into the dtString database table.
DB Principal Cache Hit %	This is the percentage of all principal handling requests handled by the string cache, avoiding a principal insert or lookup in the database.
DB Request Queue Length	This is the number of requests from the collector currently waiting to be serviced by the ACS database. These requests are used during forwarder handshake and database maintenance and are not part of normal event handling.
DB String Cache Hit %	This is the percentage of all string-handling requests handled by the string cache, avoiding a string insert or lookup in the database.
Event time in collector in milliseconds	This is the current time between event arrival at the collector and insertion in the database queues in milliseconds.
Incoming Events/sec	This is the current time between event arrival at the collector and insertion in the database queues in milliseconds.
Interface Audit Insertions/sec	Number of interface audit insertions per second.
Interface Queue Length	Length of the internal queue to the subscriber interface.
Registered Queries	Number of queries currently registered.

TABLE B.13   ACS Collector Client Counters

Counter*	Description
Average Time between event generation and collection and seconds	This is the average time between event generation time (creation timestamp) and collection time in milliseconds.
Incoming Audit Size	This is the total size of events per second arriving at the collector from a specific forwarder.
Incoming Audits/sec	This is the total number of events per second arriving at the collector from a specific forwarder.

These occur for each collector/client pair.

Registry Settings

The Windows Registry is a hierarchical "database" that stores information about the operating system and applications on the local computer. The Registry is organized in a tree format and can be viewed using the Registry Editor program, regedit.exe.

About the Registry

Folders seen in the regedit utility represent keys. These folders are displayed in the left side or Navigation area in the Registry Editor window. There are five folders, or predefined keys:

▶ **HKEY_CURRENT USER (HKCU)**—Contains the root of configuration information for the currently logged-on user. This information is referred to as a user's *profile.*

▶ **HKEY_USERS (HKU)**—Contains the root of all user profiles on the computer. The HKEY_CURRENT_USER folder is actually a subkey of HKEY_USERS.

▶ **HKEY_LOCAL_MACHINE (HKLM)**—Contains configuration information specific to the computer. This information can be used by any user.

▶ **HKEY_CLASSES_ROOT (HKCR)**—A subset of information stored in HKEY_LOCAL_MACHINE. Information stored here ensures the correct program starts when you open a file using the Windows Explorer. It contains the linking between executable programs and the program extension used by data files on the system.

▶ **HKEY_CURRENT_CONFIG (HKCC)**—Contains configuration data for the current hardware profile. The HKCC\SYSTEM subkey contains a subset of the information (the CurrentControlSet) that is a subkey of HKEY_LOCAL_MACHINE\SYSTEM.

Every database has physical files stored on disk that hold the data you view using regedit. The physical files used by the Registry are called *hives* and are loaded by Windows at system startup. The hive files are stored in the *%systemroot%*\system32\config folder of your system. Table C.1 shows the relationship between the hive files and their corresponding Registry keys.

As shown in Table C.1, most of the hives are logical subkeys of HKEY_LOCAL_MACHINE. The exception is the Default hive, which is the default user profile.

TABLE C.1   Hive Files and Corresponding Registry Keys

Hive File Name	Registry Key
Default	HKEY_USERS\Default
SAM	HKEY_LOCAL_MACHINE\SAM
Security	HKEY_LOCAL_MACHINE\Security
Software	HKEY_LOCAL_MACHINE\Software
System	HKEY_LOCAL_MACHINE\System

The hive for the current logged on user profile, HKEY_CURRENT_USER, is the ntuser.dat file stored within *%systemdrive%*\documents and settings*<user name>*. (The location of this file may vary based on the version of the Windows operating system installed on your system.)

HKEY_LOCAL_MACHINE also has a Hardware subkey. This hardware "hive" is dynamically built at system startup and is not stored on disk.

Other files stored at *%systemroot%*\system32\config include

▶ Pristine versions of the five Registry hive files, which have an extension of .SAV. These are never-modified hive files for the corresponding keys, created when Windows was installed on the computer.

▶ A transaction log of changes to the keys and value entries in the hive, with a .LOG extension.

▶ The Windows event log files, with an extension of .EVT. The number of .EVT files on any particular system will vary based on the computer's role. For example, domain controllers, DNS (Domain Name Server), and FRS (File Replication Service) servers will have additional event logs.

Operations Manager 2007 also maintains an event log, named MOMLog.evt; you will find this file on any system with an installed OpsMgr component.

Additional information about the Registry is available at http://support.microsoft.com/kb/256986 ("Windows registry information for advanced users"). For steps on backing up and restoring the Registry for the different versions of Windows supported by OpsMgr 2007, see the following:

▶ http://support.microsoft.com/kb/322756 ("How to back up, edit, and restore the registry in Windows XP and Windows Vista") provides information applicable to Windows XP and Vista

▶ http://support.microsoft.com/kb/322755 ("How to back up, edit, and restore the registry in Windows 2000") includes the steps for Windows 2000

▶ http://support.microsoft.com/kb/326216 ("How to use the backup feature to back up and restore data in Windows Server 2003") discusses backing up the System State in Windows Server 2003

Incorrectly modifying the Registry may render your system unusable, so you should always make a backup of the Registry or its subkeys prior to making changes—because results may be unpredictable.

Operations Manager–Related Registry Keys

Keys used by Operations Manager 2007 are located in quite a few places in both the software and system areas of the Registry. The presence and content of these keys will vary based on the computer's role. The information we will look at is located in the following areas:

▶ HKLM\Software\Microsoft\Microsoft Operations Manager\3.0

▶ HKLM\Software\Microsoft\PowerShell

▶ HKLM\System\CurrentControlSet\Services\AdtServer

▶ HKLM\Software\ODBC\ODBC.INI\ODBC

▶ HKLM\Software\Policies\Microsoft\AdtAgent\Parameters\

▶ HKLM\System\CurrentControlSet\Services\Eventlog\Operations Manager

▶ HKLM\System\CurrentControlSet\Services\HealthService

▶ HKLM\System\CurrentControlSet\Services\MOMConnector

▶ HKLM\System\CurrentControlSet\Services\OpsMgr Config Service

▶ HKLM\System\CurrentControlSet\Services\OMCFG

▶ HKLM\System\CurrentControlSet\Services\OMSDK

▶ HKLM\System\CurrentControlSet\Services\OpsMgr SDK Service

▶ HKCU\Software\Microsoft\Microsoft Operations Manager\3.0

▶ HKLM\Software\Microsoft\SystemCertificates

▶ HKLM\Software\Policies\Microsoft\SystemCertificates\Operations Manager

We discuss these Registry keys in the following sections of this appendix. Values and keys are as of the OpsMgr 2007 RTM (Released to Manufacturing) version 6.0.50000.0.

TIP

Values "0" and "1" in the Registry

Unless other indicated, for all Registry values, a setting of "0" designates no (or off) and a setting of "1" is yes.

Agent Settings

In Operations Manager 2007, managed computers can be agent-managed or agentless managed. There are no Registry settings for agentless managed systems (on the management server *or* the agentless system). The Operations Manager database maintains information on agentless monitored systems; this data is stored in the BaseManagedEntity table. Table C.2 lists Registry settings for a managed agent. Remember that OpsMgr Server components are also agents, so you will find these Registry keys on every agent-managed server, including the Root Management Server (RMS).

TABLE C.2   Settings for a Managed Agent

Key Name	Name	Type	Data	Description
HKLM\Software\Microsoft\ Microsoft Operations Manager\ 3.0\Agent Management Groups\<ManagementGroup-Name>	AcceptIncoming Connections	REG_ DWORD	0x0	Indicates if incoming connections are accepted. 0 unless agent is configured as a proxy; otherwise 1.
	IsRootHealthService	REG_ DWORD	0x0	Indicates if system is RMS.
	IsSCEAgent	REG_ DWORD	0x0	Indicates if system is System Center Essentials agent.
	IsServer	REG_ DWORD	0x0	Indicates if system is management server. 0 on agent.

TABLE C.2   Continued

Key Name	Name	Type	Data	Description
	Request Compresion	REG_ DWORD	0x1	Indicates if compression is required. Default=1.
	Require Authentication	REG_ DWORD	0x1	Indicates if authentication is required.
	RequireEncryption	REG_ DWORD	0x1	Indicates if encryption is required.
	RequireValidation	REG_ DWORD	0x1	Indicates if validation is required.
	UseActive Directory	REG_ DWORD	0x0	Indicates if Active Directory is used for agent assignment. Default=0.
HKLM\Software\Microsoft\ Microsoft Operations Manager\ 3.0\Agent Management Groups\ <ManagementGroupName>\	Authentication Name	REG_SZ	RMS name	Fully Qualified Domain Name of RMS (example: "hydra. odyssey.com").
Parent Health Service\0	CanEstablish ConnectionTo	REG_ DWORD	0x1	
	MaxSendBytesPer Second	REG_ DWORD	0xf4240 (1000000)	Upper limit of the number of bytes sent per second (1,000,000 bytes by default from the agent).
	NetworkName	REG_SZ	RMS name	Fully Qualified Domain Name (example: "hydra.odyssey.com").
	Networktimeout Milliseconds	REG_ DWORD	0x3a98 (15000)	Networking timeout, in milliseconds (15,000).
	Port	REG_ DWORD	0x165b (5723)	Port used by agent to communicate with management server (5723 by default).
	RetryAttempts	REG_ DWORD	3	Number of retry attempts.
	RetryDelayMs	REG_ DWORD	0x3e8 (1000)	Amount of time for retry delay (in milliseconds).

TABLE C.2   Continued

Key Name	Name	Type	Data	Description
HKLM\Software\Microsoft\ Microsoft Operations Manager\ 3.0\Registration	Company	REG_SZ		Company name entered when running OMSetup.exe.
	RegisteredOwner	REG_SZ		Name of registered owner, entered when running OMSetup.exe.
HKLM\Software\Microsoft\ Microsoft Operations Manager\ 3.0\Setup	AgentVersion	REG_SZ	6.0.5000.0	Version of Operations Manager software installed on the agent. OpsMgr 2007 RTM is 6.0.5000.0.
	CurrentVersion	REG_SZ	6.0.5000.0	Current installed version.
	Install Directory	REG_SZ	%Program Files%\ System Center Operations Manager 2007\	Installation directory.
	InstalledOn	REG_SZ	MM/DD/YY-HH:MM:SS	Date and time of installation (example: 6/27/2007-9:52:46).
	InstalledOnLocal TimeStamp	REG_SZ	MM/DD/YY-HH:MM:SS	Example: 6/27/2007-9:52:46.
	Product	REG_SZ	System Center Operations Manager 2007	Name of product.
	SKU	REG_SZ		Product SKU (example:"Select"). May be blank on an agent.

Management Server Settings

An Operations Manager management group can have multiple management servers, but only one RMS. Table C.3 includes settings for these servers.

TABLE C.3   Management Server Settings

Key Name	Name	Type	Data	Description
HKLM\Software\Microsoft\ Microsoft Operations Manager\3.0\Config Service	Config Service State	REG_SZ	*%ProgramFiles%*\ System Center Operations Manager 2007\Config Service State\	
HKLM\Software\Microsoft\ Microsoft Operations Manager\3.0\Machine Settings	DefaultSDK ServiceMachine	REG_SZ	RMS Name	Fully Qualified Domain Name of system running SDK (example: "hydra.odyssey.com").
	Channel- CertificateSerial Number	REG_ BINARY	Example: 4D 00 00 00 00 00 4E 7E 6D 4D	Certificate information from MOMCertImport. Certificates are used as an alternative to Kerberos for mutual authentication and are found where there is a firewall, workgroup, or untrusted domain with agents you want to monitor. The Channel Certificate Serial Number is in the Registry on any machine that has a certificate. This can include a gateway server, management server, or RMS, as well as the agent if the agent is in a work-group. To remove a certificate, delete the binary data.
HKLM\Software\Microsoft\ Microsoft Operations Manager\3.0\Registration	Company	REG_SZ	Company name	Company name entered when running OMSetup.exe.
	ProductID	REG_SZ	Product ID	Product key.
	Registered Owner	REG_SZ	Owner Name	Name of registered owner.

C

TABLE C.3   Continued

Key Name	Name	Type	Data	Description
HKLM\Software\Microsoft\ Microsoft Operations Manager\3.0\SDK Service	SDK Service State	REG_SZ	%ProgramFiles%\ System Center Operations Manager 2007\SDK Service State\	
HKLM\Software\Microsoft\ Microsoft Operations Manager\3.0\Server Management Groups\	AcceptIncoming Connections	REG_ DWORD	0x1	Indicates if incoming connections are accepted.
<ManagementGroupName>	IsGateway	REG_ DWORD	0x0	0x1 for gateway server; otherwise, 0x0.
	IsRootHealth Service	REG_ DWORD	0x0	0x1 for RMS; 0x0 for management server.
	IsServer	REG_ DWORD	0x1	0x1 indicates a management server (including RMS).
	Port	REG_ DWORD	0x165b(5723)	Port number used (5723 by default).
	Request Compression	REG_ DWORD	0x1	Indicates if compression is required.
	Require Authentication	REG_ DWORD	0x1	Indicates if authentication is required.
	Require Encryption	REG_ DWORD	0x1	Indicates if encryption is required.
	Require Validation	REG_ DWORD	0x1	Indicates if validation is required.
HKLM\Software\Microsoft\ Microsoft Operations Manager\3.0\Server Management Groups\	Authentication Name	REG_SZ	RMS name	Fully Qualified Domain Name (example: "hydra. odyssey.com").
<Management Group Name>Parent Health Services\0	CanEstablish ConnectionTo	REG_ DWORD	0x1	
	MaxSendBytes PerSecond	REG_ DWORD	0xf4240(1000000)	Maximum number of bytes sent per second.
	NetworkName	REG_SZ	RMS name	Fully Qualified Domain Name (example: "hydra.odyssey.com").

TABLE C.3   Continued

Key Name	Name	Type	Data	Description
	Networktimeout Milliseconds	REG_ DWORD	0x3a98(15000)	Number of milliseconds for networking timeout.
	Port	REG_ DWORD	0x165b(5723)	Port used.
	RetryAttempts	REG_ DWORD	3	Number of retry attempts.
	RetryDelay Ms	REG_ DWORD	0x3e8(1000)	Amount of time for retry delay (in milliseconds).
HKLM\Software\Microsoft\ Microsoft Operations Manager\3.0\Setup	UIVersion	REG_SZ	6.0.5000.0	Version of Operations Manager console. (This setting appears on any machine with an installed Operations console.)

SDK Service Settings

Settings for the SDK service are found on all management servers, although the service is only enabled on the RMS. These settings are listed in Table C.4.

TABLE C.4   SDK Service Settings

Key Name	Name	Type	Data	Description
HKLM\System\ CurrentControlSet\ Services\OpsMgr Config Service\Performance	Counter Names	REG_ MULTI_SZ	Dirty State Notifications Failed	
			Management Pack Requests Failed	
			Avg. Management Pack Request (sec)	
			Avg. Management Pack Request Base	
			Change Notifications Failed	
			Avg. Change Notification (sec)	
			Avg. Change Notification Base	
			Number of Requests per Sec	
			Number of Active Requests	
			Number of Queued Requests	
			Avg. Request Queue Length	
			Avg. Request Queue Wait Time (sec)	
			Avg. Request Queue Wait Time (sec) Base	

TABLE C.4   Continued

Key Name	Name	Type	Data	Description
HKLM\System\ CurrentControlSet\	Description	REG_SZ	Microsoft Operations Manager SDK service	
Services\OMSDK	Display Name	REG_SZ	OpsMgr SDK Service	
	ImagePath	REG_ EXPAND_SZ	"%ProgramFiles%\System Center Operations Manager 2007\ Microsoft.Mom.SDKServiceHost. exe" -start	
	ObjectName	REG_SZ	ODYSSEY\OM_SDK	Credentials used
	Start	REG_ DWORD	0x4	Start type when not on the RMS
	Type	REG_ DWORD	0x10	

Config Service Settings

Table C.5 lists settings for the Operations Manager Configuration service. These settings are on all management servers.

TABLE C.5   Settings for the Configuration Service

Key Name	Name	Type	Data	Description
HKLM\System\CurrentControlSet\ Services\OpsMgr Config Service				
HKLM\System\CurrentControlSet\ Services\OMCFG	Description	REG_SZ	Microsoft Operations Manager Configuration service	
	Display Name	REG_SZ	OpsMgr Config Service	
	ImagePath	REG_EXP AND_SZ	"%Program Files%\System Center Operations Manager 2007\Microsoft.Mom.C onfigServiceHost.exe" -start	

TABLE C.5   Continued

Key Name	Name	Type	Data	Description
	Object Name	REG_SZ	Example: ODYSSEY\ OM_SDK	Credentials used
	Start	REG_ DWORD	0x4	Start type when not on the RMS
	Type	REG_ DWORD	0x10	

Operations Database Server Settings

There are no Registry settings specific to the Operations Database Server itself. Each management server has a Registry entry pointing to the database server, at HKLM\Software\Microsoft\Microsoft Operations Manager\3.0\Setup\ DatabaseServerName. If you move the operational database to another server, you will need to modify this value on each management server.

Data Warehouse Server Settings

The Data Warehouse server is also known as the Reporting Data Warehouse server. This server, which runs SQL Server 2005, contains the Data Warehouse database, with a default name of OperationsManagerDW. Table C.6 lists Registry settings that are unique for this OpsMgr server component.

TABLE C.6   Data Warehouse Server Settings

Key Name	Name	Type	Data	Description
HKLM\Software\Microsoft\ Microsoft Operations Manager\3.0\Reporting\	DWDBInstance	REG_SZ	Name of database server running Data Warehouse database	Example: Quicksilver
	DWDBName	REG_SZ	Name of Data Warehouse database	Example: Operations ManagerDW (default)
	DWDBVersion	REG_SZ	Version	6.0.5000.0 for RTM version

Report Server Settings

The Report Server Component is part of the SQL Server 2005 Reporting Services installation, and it is customized during Operations Manager setup. Operations Manager 2007 requires its own report server because it changes the security settings. This server component contains the ReportServer and ReportServerTempDB databases. Table C.7 lists Registry settings unique to this server.

TABLE C.7   Report Server Settings

Key Name	Name	Type	Data	Description
HKLM\Software\Microsoft\ Microsoft Operations Manager\3.0\Reporting\	Default SDKService Machine	REG_ SZ	Location of RMS, which runs the SDK service	Example: Hydra
	Reporting ServerUrl	REG_ SZ	URL and port for Reporting server	Example: http://Quicksilver:80/ ReportServer
	ReportRootFolder Name	REG_ SZ	Subfolder under ReportingSerUrl that is used as the Report Root folder	/
	SRSInstance	REG_ SZ	Name of database server running SQL Reporting Services	Example: Quicksilver
	Using86SQLOnx64	REG_ SZ	Whether SQL Server is running 32 bit on a 64-bit machine	

PowerShell Settings

Table C.8 shows the Registry settings for machines with PowerShell installed.

TABLE C.8   PowerShell Settings

Key Name	Name	Type	Data	Description
HKLM\Software\ Microsoft\PowerShell\ 1\PowerShellSnapIns\ Microsoft.Enterprise Management.Operations Manager.Client	ApplicationBase	REG_SZ	%ProgramFiles%\ System Center Operations Manager 2007\	Example: C:\Program Files\System Center Operations Manager 2007\

TABLE C.8   Continued

Key Name	Name	Type	Data	Description
	AssemblyName	REG_SZ	Name of assembly	Example: Microsoft.Enterprise Management.Operations Manager.ClientShell, Version=6.0.4900.0, Culture=neutral, PublicKeyToken=31bf3856 ad364e35
	ModuleName	REG_SZ	*%Program Files%*\ System Center Operations Manager 2007\Microsoft. Enterprise Management. OperationsManager. ClientShell.dll	Example: C:\Program Files\System Center Operations Manager 2007\Microsoft.Enterprise Management.Operations Manager.ClientShell.dll
	PowerShellVersion	REG_SZ	1.0	Version of PowerShell installed
	Types	REG_SZ	*%ProgramFiles%*\ System Center Operations Manager 2007\Microsoft. Enterprise Management. OperationsManager. ClientShell.Types. ps1xml	Location of Program type Example: C:\Program Files\System Center Operations Manager 2007\Microsoft.Enterprise Management.Operations Manager.ClientShell.Types. ps1xml
	Vendor	REG_SZ	Microsoft Corporation	
	Version	REG_SZ	6.0.4900.0	Version of PowerShell SnapIn installed
HKLM\Software\ Microsoft\PowerShell\ 1\ShellIds\Microsoft.	ExecutionPolicy	REG_SZ	RemoteSigned	
PowerShell	Path	REG_SZ	*%SystemRoot%*\ system32\Windows PowerShell\v1.0\ powershell.exe	Path to PowerShell executable. Example: C:\WINDOWS\system32\ WindowsPowerShell\v1.0\ powershell.exe

Audit Collection Services (ACS) Settings

Table C.9 includes the parameters stored in the Registry for the ACS server, including the size of the ACS collector queue. Table C.10 lists the Registry settings for the ACS forwarder.

TABLE C.9   Audit Collection Services—Server

Key Name	Name	Type	Data	Description
HKLM\System\Current ControlSet\Services\ AdtServer	DependOnService	REG_ MULTI_SZ	Eventlog	
	Description	REG_SZ	Service for receiving audit events over the network and writing them to a database	
	DisplayName	REG_SZ	Operations Manager Audit Collection Service	
	ErrorControl	REG_ DWORD	0x1	If the driver fails, produce a warning but let startup continue.
	ImagePath	REG_ EXPAND_ SZ	%SystemRoot%\ system32\Security\ AdtServer\AdtServer .exe	Location of executable. Example: C:\WINDOWS\system32\ Security\AdtServer\ AdtServer.exe
	ObjectName	REG_SZ	Credentials service is using	NT AUTHORITY\ NetworkService
	Start	REG_ DWORD	0x2	When in the boot sequence, the service should start. x2 indicates Autoload, meaning the service is always loaded and run.
	Type	REG_SZ	0x10	Defines the kind of service or driver. x10 indicates a Win32 service that should be run as a standalone process.
HKLM\System\Current ControlSet\Services\ AdtServer\Parameters	AdtAgentPort	REG_ DWORD	0xcac5 (51909)	Port used by AdtAgent.

TABLE C.9   Continued

Key Name	Name	Type	Data	Description
	BackOffThreshold	REG_ DWORD	0x4b	The percentage full the ACS collector queue can become before it denies new connections from the ACS forwarders.
	ConfigFile	REG_SZ	%SystemRoot%\ system32\Security\ AdtServer\ AcsConfig.xml	Configuration file. Example: C:\WINDOWS\system32\ Security\AdtServer\ AcsConfig.xml
	DBQueueQuery	REG_SZ	SELECT * FROM AdtsEvent	
	DefaultAssetValue	REG_ DWORD	0xffffffff	
	DefaultGroup	REG_SZ	Default	
	Disconnect Threshold	REG_ DWORD	0x5a	The percentage full the ACS collector queue becomes before the ACS collector begins discon-necting ACS forwarders (90% is the default).
	EventRetention Period	REG_ DWORD	0x150	Retention period (336 days by default).
	EventSchema	REG_ DWORD	%SystemRoot%\ system32\Security\ AdtServer\ EventSchema.xml	Location of Event Schema XML file.
	Maximum QueueLength	REG_ DWORD	0x40000	The maximum number of events that can queue in memory while waiting for the database (262144 by default).
	ODBC Connection	REG_ SZ	OpsMgrAC	Name of ODBC connection for Audit Collector data-base.
	ScriptFilePath	REG_SZ	%SystemRoot%\ System32\Security\ AdtServer\	Path to ACS script files.

TABLE C.9   Continued

Key Name	Name	Type	Data	Description
HKLM\Software\ODBC\ ODBC.INI\ODBC Data Sources	OpsMgrAC	REG_SZ	SQL Server	Type of ODBC data source used for Audit Collection database.
HKLM\Software\ODBC\ ODBC.INI\OpsMgrAC	Database	REG_SZ	OperationsManager AC	Name of Audit Collection database, used with ODBC.
	Description	REG_SZ	Audit Collection Services	Database description for ODBC.
	Driver	REG_SZ	%SystemRoot%/ System32\ SQLSRV32.dll	Location of ODBC driver.
	Server	REG_SZ	Example: Fireball	NetBIOS name of ACS database server.
	Trusted_ Connection	REG_SZ	Yes	Indicates if a trusted connection is used.

TABLE C.10   Audit Collection Services—Forwarder

Key Name	Name	Type	Data	Description
HKLM\Software\ Policies\Microsoft\ AdtAgent\ Parameters\	AdtServers	REG_ MULTI_ SZ	Example: hurricane.odyssey.com	List of collectors that the forwarder should attempt to connect to. Format: *<collector fqdn>*[: *<port>*[,*<priority>*[,*<asset value>*]]]
	EventLog Logging Level	REG_ DWORD	0	The level of logging that the forwarder performs when logging events to the Application log. 0=errors 1=warnings+errors 2=informational+warnings+errors
	Instance	REG_SZ	_adtserver. instancename._tcp. sitename._sites. *<domain>*	If present, allows the forwarder to be associated with a named deployment instance when an organization deploys multiple instances of ACS. Instance name is used to query for SRV resource records.

TABLE C.10   Continued

Key Name	Name	Type	Data	Description
	Local Config	REG_ DWORD	x01	If present and value is not 0, the forwarder does not use SRV resource records for locating collectors.
	NoCache	REG_ DWORD	x01	If present and value is not 0, the forwarder does not cache the last connector it used. Also does not use cache to preferentially connect to the collector.

There are no ACS-specific Registry settings for the server hosting the ACS database (unless it is on the ACS server (collector) itself); the ODBC settings on the ACS server identify the database server and the name of the database.

Operations Manager Event Log Settings

Every monitored system has an Operations Manager Event log. Table C.11 documents the related Registry settings.

TABLE C.11   Operations Manager Event Log

Key Name	Name	Type	Data	Description
HKLM\System\ CurrentControlSet\ Services\Eventlog\ Operations Manager\	AutoBackup LogFiles	REG_DWORD	0x0	
	File	REG_SZ	%SystemRoot%\ system32\Config\ MOMLog.evt	Name of OpsMgr Event log.
	MaxSize	REG_DWORD	15728640	
	RestrictGuest Access	REG_DWORD	0x1	
	Retention	REG_DWORD	0x0	

TABLE C.11   Operations Manager Event Log

Key Name	Name	Type	Data	Description
	Sources	REG_MULTI_SZ	OpsMgr SDK Service	Sources that write to the OpsMgr Event log.
			OpsMgr SDK Client	
			OpsMgr Root Connector	Each of these sources has a subkey located under HKLM\System\CurrentControlSet\Services\Eventlog\Operations Manager\ with information specific to that data source. This includes the specific DLL(s) for the EventMessageFile.
			OpsMgr Connector	
			OpsMgr Config Service	
			HealthService	
			Health Service Script	
			Health Service Modules	
			Health Service ESE Store	
			DataAccessLayer	
			Operations Manager	

Operations Manager Health Service

Settings for the Health Service are found on all systems other than those that are agentless monitored. We list the settings in Table C.12.

MOM Connector

Settings associated with the MOM Connector can be found at HKLM\System\CurrentControlSet\Services\MOMConnector\Performance\Library. This is string data (REG_SZ) describing the location of the Connector Performance Library. The data found at this key is %*ProgramFiles*%\System Center Operations Manager 2007\MOMConnectorPerformance.dll.

TABLE C.12   Health Service Settings

Key Name	Name	Type	Data	Description
HKLM\System\Current ControlSet\Services\ HealthService	DependOn Group	REG_ MULTI_SZ		Groups depended on.
	DependOn Service	REG_MULTI _SZ	rpcss	Service depended on to be able to start.
	Description	REG_SZ	Monitors health of the computer. The service may be configured to monitor the health of other computers in addition to this computer. If this service is stopped, detection of failures may not occur. If this service is disabled, any services that explicitly depend on it will fail to start.	Text describing the service.
	Display Name	REG_SZ	OpsMgr Health Service	
	Error Control	REG_ DWORD	0x0	
	ImagePath	REG_ EXPAND_ SZ	"%ProgramFiles%\System Center Operations Manager 2007\HealthService.exe"	Location of executable. Example: "C:\Program Files\System Center Operations Manager 2007\HealthService.exe"
	Object Name	REG_SZ	LocalSystem	Credentials used.
	Start	REG_ DWORD	0x2	Service Start type (x2 indicates autoload)
	Type	REG_ DWORD	0x20	Defines the kind of service or driver. x20 indicates a Win32 service that can share address space with other services of the same type.
HKLM\System\Current ControlSet\Services\ HealthService\ Parameters	Error Reports Enabled	REG_ DWORD	0x1	

TABLE C.12   Continued

Key Name	Name	Type	Data	Description
	Managed EnginePath	REG_SZ	%ProgramFiles%\System Center Operations Manager 2007\HealthServiceManaged .dll	
	Persistence Cache Maximum	REG_ DWORD	Management Server: 0x6400 Agent:0x1900	Maximum cache size. Management Server:25600 decimal Agent:6400
	Persistence Checkpoint Depth Maximum	REG_ DWORD	Management Server:0x1400000 Agent:0xa00000	Management Server:20971520 decimal Agent:10485760 decimal
	Persistence Initial Database Page Count	REG_ DWORD	Management Server:0x9600 Agent:0x3200	Management Server:38400 decimal Agent:12800
	Persistence Maximum Sessions	REG_ DWORD	Management Server:0x20 Agent:0x10	Management Server:32 decimal Agent:16 decimal
	Persistence Page Hint Cache Size	RE_DWORD	Management Server:0x40000 Agent:0x8000	Management Server:262144 decimal Agent:32768 decimal
	Persistence Version Store Maximum	REG_ DWORD	Management Server:0x1400 Agent:0x789	Management Server:5120 decimal Agent:1920 decimal
	Queue Error Reports	REG_ DWORD	0x0	0 or 1
	Service Sizing	REG_ DWORD	0x1	0 or 1
	State Directory	REG_SZ	%ProgramFiles%\System Center Operations Manager 2007\Health Service State	
	Use Backgroud Priority	REG_ DWORD	0x0	

TABLE C.12   Continued

Key Name	Name	Type	Data	Description
HKLM\System \CurrentControlSet\ Services\Health Service\Parameters\ ConnectorManager\ Approved AD Management groups				No values by default.
HKLM\System \CurrentControlSet\ Services\Health Service\Parameters\ Management Groups *<ManagementGroup Name>*	IsSourced fromAD	REG_ DWORD	0x1	If value is 1, indicates the agent is AD-integrated and gathers settings from the Service Connection Point. This is only present if the agent is AD-inte-grated.
	Maximum QueueSize Kb	REG_ DWORD	0x19000	102400 decimal. Agent maximum queue size.
HKLM\System\Current ControlSet\Services\ HealthService\ Parameters\ Management Groups*<Management GroupName>*\ AllowedSSIDs	Restrict SSIDs	REG_ DWORD	0x0	
HKLM\System\Current ControlSet\Services\ HealthService\ Parameters\Secure StorageManager	(Default)	REG_ BINARY	Private/private key pair	

Current Logged-on User

Operations console settings for the current logged-on user are listed in Table C.13.

TABLE C.13 Settings for the Current Logged-on User

Key Name	Name	Type	Data	Description
HKCU\Software\ Microsoft\Microsoft Operations Manager\ 3.0\Console	Various			Operations console settings that only affect the console for that user on that computer include the following: Connection history with the names of management groups the console has connected to. Show or Hide Views selections. Whether the console is in a window or full screen (if in a window, the size and position of the window). The last navigation pane the console was open to when it was closed.
HKCU\Software\ Microsoft\Microsoft Operations Manager\3.0\ Console\ CacheParameters	Polling Interval	REG_D WORD	1	Controls how often the Operations console polls. The default value (normal interval) is 1. 0 turns off polling. 2 doubles the interval, meaning polling occurs half as often. Maximum value is 10; any number larger is treated as 10. Add this key to the Registry to lessen polling occurrence.
HKCU\Software\ Microsoft\Microsoft Operations Manager\ 3.0\User Settings	SDK Service Machine	REG_SZ	RMS name	Fully Qualified Domain name of RMS (example: hydra.odyssey.com).

> **TIP**
>
> **Lost in Service Pack (SP) 1**
>
> In the RTM version of OpsMgr, you could right-click an alert and choose associated tasks from the context menu. This disappeared with SP 1, although the capability is still available on the Actions pane of the Operations console.
>
> Microsoft removed this functionality to improve interactive responsiveness of the context menu. You can turn it back on if you want via a Registry entry—set EnableContextMenuTasks to **1** under HKCU\Software\Microsoft\Microsoft Operations Manager\3.0\Console. If this key does not already exist, create it with type REG_SZ. Because this is under HKCU, you would want to script this change for all users.
>
> This information is current as of Release Candidate (RC) 0.

Certificate Information

You can find information regarding certificates used by Operations Manager in two places:

▶ HKLM\Software\Microsoft\SystemCertificates\Operations Manager

▶ HKLM\Software\Policies\Microsoft\SystemCertificates\Operations Manager

This is binary data, which varies on each system.

Active Directory and Exchange 2003 Management Pack Parameters

You can tune management packs by overriding parameters. This appendix lists parameters for shared scripts in the Active Directory (AD) and Exchange 2003 management packs. One of the enhancements we hope to see in the next version of Operations Manager (OpsMgr) is an easy way to find scripts used by the various rules and monitors. This was available with the Microsoft Operations Manager (MOM) 2005 interface, but is not included with OpsMgr 2007.

Contents of This Appendix

This appendix contains tables mapping rules and monitors used by Active Directory and Exchange to scripts with customizable parameters. The Exchange information is not specific to Exchange 2007 because the Exchange 2007 management pack for OpsMgr 2007 was not available when this material was compiled.

Parameters for Active Directory

Tables D.1 through D.9 document Active Directory rules, monitors, and script parameters.

Table D.1 documents Active Directory Replication Monitoring.

TABLE D.1   AD Replication (AD_Replication_Monitoring Script)

Rule/Monitor	Targeted Object	Customizable Parameters
AD Replication Monitoring	Active Directory Domain Controller Server 200X Computer Role	Interval Seconds
AD Replication Performance Collection – Metric Replication Latency	Active Directory Domain Controller Server 200X Computer Role	Log Success Event
AD Replication Performance Collection - Metric Replication Latency:Minimum	Active Directory Domain Controller Server 200X Computer Role	ObjectUpdateThreshold
AD Replication Performance Collection - Metric Replication Latency:Maximum	Active Directory Domain Controller Server 200X Computer Role	IntersiteExpectedMaxLatency
AD Replication Performance Collection - Metric Replication Latency:Average	Active Directory Domain Controller Server 200X Computer Role	MonitorDomainNC MonitorConfigNC MonitorApplicationPartitions FirstReplicationPeriod ChangeInjectionFrequency TimeoutSeconds

Table D.2 documents parameters for the Active Directory Database and Log.

TABLE D.2   AD Database and Log Monitors (AD_Database_and_Log Script)

Rule/Monitor	Targeted Object	Customizable Parameters
AD Logfile Free Space Monitor	Active Directory Domain Controller Server 200X Computer Role	IntervalSeconds
AD Logfile Monitor	Active Directory Domain Controller Server 200X Computer Role	LogSuccessEvent (Threshold values are hard-coded into scripts—although Microsoft plans to change this in the SP 1 timeframe)
AD Database Free Space Monitor	Microsoft.Windows.Server.200X.AD. DomainControllerRole	TimeoutSeconds
AD Logfile Free Space Monitor	Active Directory Domain Controller Server 200X Computer Role	

TABLE D.2   Continued

Rule/Monitor	Targeted Object	Customizable Parameters
AD Database Drive Free Collection	Active Directory Domain Controller Server 200X Computer Role	
AD Database Size Collection	Active Directory Domain Controller Server 200X Computer Role	
AD Log File Drive Free Space Collection	Active Directory Domain Controller Server 200X Computer Role	
AD Log File Size Collection	Active Directory Domain Controller Server 200X Computer Role	

Table D.3 documents parameters for Active Directory General Responses.

TABLE D.3   AD General Responses (AD_General_Response Script)

Rule/Monitor	Targeted Object	Customizable Parameters
AD General Response Monitor	Active Directory Domain Controller Server 200X Computer Role	IntervalSeconds
AD DC Last Bind Monitor	Active Directory Domain Controller Server 200X Computer Role	LogSuccessEvent
AD General Response Last Bind Performance Collection	Active Directory Domain Controller Server 200X Computer Role	FailureThreshold TimeoutSeconds

Table D.4 documents parameters for Active Directory Search Responses.

TABLE D.4   AD Search Responses (AD_Global_Catalog_Search_Response Script)

Rule/Monitor	Targeted Object	Customizable Parameters
AD Global Catalog Search Response Monitor	Active Directory Domain Controller Server 200X Computer Role	IntervalSeconds
AD DC Global Catalog Search Time Monitor	Active Directory Domain Controller Server 200X Computer Role	LogSuccessEvent
AD Global Catalog Search Response Performance Collection	Active Directory Domain Controller Server 200X Computer Role	Failure Threshold TimeoutSeconds

Table D.5 lists parameters for AD Op Master Responses.

TABLE D.5   AD Op Master Responses (AD_Op_Master_Response Script)

Rule/Monitor	Targeted Object	Customizable Parameters
AD Op Master Response Monitor	Active Directory Domain Controller Server 200X Computer Role	IntervalSeconds
AD DC Op Master Domain Naming Last Bind Monitor	Active Directory Domain Controller Server 200X Computer Role	LogSuccessEvent
AD DC Op Master Infrastructure Master Last Bind Monitor	Active Directory Domain Controller Server 200X Computer Role	FailureThreshold
AD DC Op Master PDC Last Bind Monitor	Active Directory Domain Controller Server 200X Computer Role	SuccessCount
AD DC Op Master RID Last Bind Monitor	Active Directory Domain Controller Server 200X Computer Role	TimeoutSeconds
AD DC Op Master Schema Master Last Bind Monitor	Active Directory Domain Controller Server 200X Computer Role	
AD Op Master PDC Last Ping Performance Collection	Active Directory Domain Controller Server 200X Computer Role	
AD Op Master PDC Last Bind Performance Collection	Active Directory Domain Controller Server 200X Computer Role	
AD Op Master Domain Naming Last Ping Performance Collection	Active Directory Domain Controller Server 200X Computer Role	
AD Op Master Domain Naming Last Bind Performance Collection	Active Directory Domain Controller Server 200X Computer Role	
AD Op Master Infrastructure Last Ping Performance Collection	Active Directory Domain Controller Server 200X Computer Role	
AD Op Master Infrastructure Last Bind Performance Collection	Active Directory Domain Controller Server 200X Computer Role	

TABLE D.5   Continued

Rule/Monitor	Targeted Object	Customizable Parameters
AD Op Master Infrastructure Last RID Performance Collection	Active Directory Domain Controller Server 200X Computer Role	
AD Op Master Infrastructure Last RID Bind Collection	Active Directory Domain Controller Server 200X Computer Role	
AD Op Master Infrastructure Last Ping Performance Collection	Active Directory Domain Controller Server 200X Computer Role	
AD Op Master Infrastructure Last Bind Performance Collection	Active Directory Domain Controller Server 200X Computer Role	

Table D.6 lists parameters for AD Essential Services.

TABLE D.6   AD Essential Services (AD_Essential_Services_Running Script)

Rule/Monitor	Targeted Object	Customizable Parameters
AD SYSVOL Share Monitor	Active Directory Domain Controller Server 200X Computer Role	IntervalSeconds
AD DC Locator Monitor	Active Directory Domain Controller Server 200X Computer Role	TimeoutSeconds

Table D.7 lists parameters for AD Client Connectivity.

TABLE D.7   AD Client Monitoring and Connectivity (AD_Client_Connectivity Script)

Rule/Monitor	Targeted Object	Customizable Parameters
AD Client Connectivity Monitor	Active Directory Client Perspective	IntervalSeconds
AD Client ADSI Client Search Time Collection	Active Directory Client Perspective	LogSuccessEvent
AD Client AD Client LDAP Ping Time Collection	Active Directory Client Perspective	BindThreshold
AD Client AD Client LDAP Bind Time Collection	Active Directory Client Perspective	PingThreshold FailureThreshold SearchThreshold TimeoutSeconds

Table D.8 lists parameters for AD Client Monitoring.

TABLE D.8   AD Client Monitoring (AD_Client_GC_Availability Script)

Rule/Monitor	Targeted Object	Customizable Parameters
AD Client Global Catalog Availability Monitor	Active Directory Client Perspective	IntervalSeconds
AD Client GC Availability Performance Collection	Active Directory Client Perspective	LogSuccessEvent MinimumAvailableGCs TimeoutSeconds

Table D.9 lists parameters for AD Client PDC Responses.

TABLE D.9   AD Client PDC Responses (AD_Client_PDC_Response Script)

Rule/Monitor	Targeted Object	Customizable Parameters
AD Client Global PDC Response Monitor	Active Directory Client Perspective	IntervalSeconds
AD Client PDC Response Bind Perf Performance Collection	Active Directory Client Perspective	LogSuccessEvent
AD Client PDC Response Ping Perf Performance Collection	Active Directory Client Perspective	FailureThreshold SuccessCount TimeoutSeconds

Parameters for Exchange

Tables D.10 through D.17 document Exchange rules, monitors, and script parameters.

Table D.10 shows parameters for Exchange related to synthetic transaction workflow.

TABLE D.10   Synthetic Transactions Workflow (VerifyMFR Script)

Rule/Monitor	Targeted Object	Customizable Parameters
Exchange Mail Flow Monitor (Receiver Part)	Exchange Mail Flow	IntervalSeconds
Mail_flow_receiver.PerformanceCollection	Exchange Mail Flow	SyncTime MaxSafeMissedRuns LatenchThreshold MaxNegativeLatency TimeoutSeconds

Table D.11 lists parameters for Exchange related to synthetic transaction MAPI logons.

TABLE D.11   Synthetic Transactions for MAPI Logons (VerifyMAPI Script)

Rule/Monitor	Targeted Object	Customizable Parameters
Exchange MAPI Logon Monitor	Exchange MAPI Logon	IntervalSeconds
Performance Collection Rule for MAPI logon latency	Exchange MAPI Logon	SyncTime MaxSafeMissedRuns LatenchThreshold MaxNegativeLatency TimeoutSeconds

Table D.12 lists parameters related to the Exchange Active Synch protocol.

TABLE D.12   Active Synch Protocol (VerifyEAS Script)

Rule/Monitor	Targeted Object	Customizable Parameters
Exchange Active Synch Monitor	Exchange EAS	IntervalSeconds
Performance Collection Rule for Exchange Active Synch logon latency	Exchange EAS	LogPerfData TimeoutSeconds

Table D.13 lists parameters related to the Outlook Web Access protocol.

TABLE D.13   Outlook Web Access (VerifyOWA Script)

Rule/Monitor	Targeted Object	Customizable Parameters
Outlook Web Access Logon Monitor	Exchange OWA	IntervalSeconds
Performance Collection Rule for Outlook Web Access logon latency	Exchange OWA	LogPerfData TimeoutSeconds

Table D.14 lists parameters related to the Outlook Mobile Access protocol.

TABLE D.14   Outlook Mobile Access Protocol (VerifyOMA Script)

Rule/Monitor	Targeted Object	Customizable Parameters
Outlook Mobile Access Logon Monitor	Exchange OMA	IntervalSeconds
Performance Collection Rule for Outlook Mobile Access logon latency	Exchange OMA	LogPerfData TimeoutSeconds

D

Table D.15 lists parameters related to Mailbox Statistics Collection.

TABLE D.15   Mailbox Statistics Collection (Collect_Mailbox_Statistics Script)

Rule/Monitor	Targeted Object	Customizable Parameters
Performance Collection Rule to Collect Mailbox Statistics-Top Mailbox by Size	Exchange Database Storage	IntervalSeconds
Performance Collection Rule to Collect Mailbox Statistics-Top Mailbox by Message Count	Exchange Database Storage	MaxEntries
Performance Collection Rule to Collect Mailbox Statistics-Average Mailbox Message Size	Exchange Database Storage	TimeoutSeconds
Performance Collection Rule to Collect Mailbox Statistics-Average Mailbox Message Count	Exchange Database Storage	
Performance Collection Rule to Collect Mailbox Statistics-Median Mailbox Size	Exchange Database Storage	
Performance Collection Rule to Collect Mailbox Statistics-Median Mailbox Message Count	Exchange Database Storage	

Table D.16 lists parameters related to Public Folder Statistics.

TABLE D.16   Public Folder Statistics (Collect_Public_Folder_Statistics)

Rule/Monitor	Targeted Object	Customizable Parameters
Performance Collection Rule to Collect Public Folder Statistics-Public Folder by Size	Exchange Database Storage	IntervalSeconds
Performance Collection Rule to Collect Public Folder Statistics-Public Folder by Message Count	Exchange Database Storage	MaxEntries TimeoutSeconds
Performance Collection Rule to Collect Public Folder Statistics-Average Public Folder Size	Exchange Database Storage	
Performance Collection Rule to Collect Public Folder Statistics-Average Public Folder Message Count	Exchange Database Storage	

TABLE D.16   Continued

Rule/Monitor	Targeted Object	Customizable Parameters
Performance Collection Rule to Collect Public Folder Statistics-Median Public Folder Size	Exchange Database Storage	
Performance Collection Rule to Collect Public Folder Statistics-Median Public Folder Message Count	Exchange Database Storage	

Table D.17 lists parameters related to Message Logging Statistics.

TABLE D.17   Message Logging Statistics (Collect_Message_Tracking_Log_Statistics Script)

Rule/Monitor	Targeted Object	Customizable Parameters
Collect_Message_Tracking_Log_Statistics.PerformanceCollection	Exchange Database Storage	IntervalSeconds
Collect_Message_Tracking_Log_Statistics.E2KMessageCount.PerformanceCollection	Exchange Database Storage	MaxEntries TimeoutSeconds

Although the message tracking log collection works, it cannot be reported on this data, because Reports needs a "single counter" per collection rule. These rules will need to be rewritten and split into 10 dedicated rules (status for 5000.0 and 500.11 of the Exchange 2003 management pack).

D

Reference URLs

This appendix includes a number of reference URLs associated with Operations Manager. These links are also available "live" on the CD included with this book. URLs do change—although the authors have made every effort to verify the references here as working links, we cannot guarantee they will remain current.

General Resources

A number of websites provide excellent resources for System Center Operations Manager 2007 (OpsMgr).

▶ Several articles are available on Operations Manager 2007 Audit Collection Services (ACS):

An early article on ACS is at MCPMag.com (September 2004) at http://mcpmag.com/columns/article.asp? EditorialsID=772. Obviously a bit dated, but it's a good overview of what Microsoft intended with the product.

An additional discussion is available at http:// opsmgr2007.wikidot.com/system:audit-collection-services.

You can read Microsoft's ACS white paper at http:// download.microsoft.com/download/E/E/7/EE797D69-02B2-420D-B0F2-196906CCE063/Whitepaper-Audit_ Collection_with_System_Center_Operations_Manager_ 2007_final.pdf.

For information on configuring ACS to use certificate-based authentication, a good place to start is Clive Eastwood's article at http://blogs.technet.com/cliveeastwood/ archive/2007/05/11/how-to-configure-audit-collection-system-acs-to-use-certificate-based-authenication.aspx.

While OpsMgr Service Pack 1 lets you enable the ACS forwarder on a management server or the RMS (Root Management Server), Jeff Skelton of Rede Consulting documents doing it in the base version of OpsMgr 2007 at http://helpmemanage. blogspot.com/2008/01/install-acs-forwarder-on-rms-or.html.

▶ Resources are also available regarding the Gateway Server Component:

You will find a great article by Marteen Goet on the gateway server approval process at http://www.techlog.org/archive/2007/02/14/operations_manager_2007_gateway.

Also, look at http://momresources.org/scom/how-to/Certificates%20in%20OM2007. pdf for Ondrej Vysek's article on gateway server setup. (Momresources.org has been replaced by SystemCenterForum.org, although the content previously posted is still available.)

System Center Forum has an excellent write-up on the gateway server and scenarios for it, available at http://systemcenterforum.org/wp-content/uploads/ OpsMgr2007_Gateway_Config_v1.2.zip. (They update the PDF file within the zip from time to time, so be sure you have the most recent version!)

Walter Eikenboom has written a guide on untrusted domain monitoring with the gateway server, at http://weblog.stranger.nl/files/guides/Un-trusted%20domain %20monitoring%20with%20SCOM%202007%20Gateway%20server_v0.1.pdf.

▶ Installing certificates? Check http://weblog.stranger.nl/files/DMZ_server_ monitoring_with_SCOM_2007.pdf by Walter Eikenboom for details.

Microsoft's Certificate Services overview is at http://technet2.microsoft.com/ windowsserver/en/library/7d30a7ec-438f-41f8-a33a-f2e89d358b121033.mspx.

▶ An excellent discussion on client monitoring by Andy Dominey is at http://www.server-management.co.uk/index.php?option=com_content&task= view&id=445&Itemid=62.

Andy also has a TechNet webcast discussing client monitoring, which you can access from http://msevents.microsoft.com/cui/WebCastEventDetails.aspx?culture=en-US&EventID=1032340080&CountryCode=US.

▶ If you install additional management servers after installing OpsMgr reporting, the new management servers will not be able to write to the data warehouse until you create profiles. The MOM team has documented this problem at http://blogs. technet.com/momteam/archive/2007/08/29/if-you-install-opsmgr-2007-reporting-and-then-install-secondary-ms-then-it-will-not-be-able-to-write-dw-data-as-profiles-are-not-created.aspx. (This bug is fixed in OpsMr 2007 Service Pack 1.)

▶ Walter Chomak of Microsoft has done some research on OpsMgr 2007 I/O considerations. Read about his results at http://wchomak.spaces.live.com/blog/cns!F56EFE25599555EC!610.entry.

▶ A great article by Satya Vel of the MOM team on network bandwidth utilization for the OpsMgr roles (components) is at http://blogs.technet.com/momteam/archive/2007/10/22/network-bandwidth-utilization-for-the-various-opsmgr-2007-roles.aspx.

▶ Satya also gives us steps (totally unsupported!) to install the Operations database and Reporting on Windows Server 2008, without waiting for SQL Server 2008. Check out his self-described "hack" at http://blogs.technet.com/momteam/archive/2007/12/17/steps-to-install-opsmgr-2007-db-and-reporting-on-windows-server-2008-longhorn.aspx.

▶ You will also want to check http://blogs.technet.com/momteam/archive/2008/01/09/support-plans-for-opsmgr-2007-sce-and-mom-2005-running-on-windows-server-2008.aspx for Microsoft's support plans for OpsMgr, System Center Essentials, and MOM 2005 running on Windows Server 2008..

▶ Looking for training? This is not an exhaustive list, but we have found several places that offer courses on OpsMgr 2007:

Check out the InFront Consulting Group's training at www.systemcentertraining.com.

JCA Academy (Telindus) also has material, described at http://www.jcacademy.be/_media/pdf_cursus/_en/MOC138%20-%20Opsmgr%202007%20training.pdf and taught by Rory McCaw of InFront Consulting, a MOM MVP. The main web page is http://www.jcacademy.be/.

There is also https://www.learnitstuff.com/c-7-ms-operations-manager.aspx.

▶ An interesting article by Ian Blyth on OpsMgr 2007 architecture appears at http://ianblythmanagement.wordpress.com/2006/08/01/scom-2007-architecture/.

▶ Also architecture-related is an article by Brian Wren at http://blogs.technet.com/ati/archive/2007/05/14/targeting-rules-and-monitors.aspx. The article talks about how to target rules and monitors, and the difference between groups in MOM 2005 and OpsMgr 2007.

You may also want to check Jonobie Ford's article at http://blogs.technet.com/momteam/archive/2007/10/31/targeting-series-part-1-differences-between-2005-and-2007.aspx.

▶ Satya Vel and one of his coworkers have adapted the MOM 2005 Resource Kit MOMNetCheck utility for command-line use in OpsMgr 2007. The tool can be used to remotely check installation prerequisites. Information and a download are available at http://blogs.technet.com/momteam/archive/2007/11/20/remote-agent-prerequisite-checker-tool-for-opsmgr-2007.aspx.

▶ Do you want to move the OpsMgr databases to another server? The authors of this book have researched the requirements and documented the steps in Chapter 12, "Backup and Recovery." Blog articles discussing this are also available at http://ops-mgr.spaces.live.com/blog/cns!3D3B8489FCAA9B51!177.entry and http://ops-mgr.spaces.live.com/blog/cns!3D3B8489FCAA9B51!225.entry for information on moving the Operational database; and http://ops-mgr.spaces.live.com/Blog/cns!3D3B8489FCAA9B51!235.entry for the steps to move the OpsMgr data warehouse.

▶ An article by Microsoft on using SQL Server 2005 in a virtual environment can be found at http://download.microsoft.com/download/a/c/d/acd8e043-d69b-4f09-bc9e-4168b65aaa71/SQLVirtualization.doc.

▶ A new troubleshooting tool, the ReSearch This! management pack, hosted by the System Center Forum. The more people that contribute knowledge to this tool, the better it becomes!

The OpsMgr 2007 version of ReSearch This! can be downloaded from http://systemcenterforum.org/wp-content/uploads/ReSearchThisOpsMgr.zip.

A version for MOM 2005 is also available, at http://systemcenterforum.org/wp-content/uploads/ReSearchThisMOM.zip.

▶ Several articles are available as early discussions of Operations Manager 2007:

http://www.eweek.com/article2/0,1895,1998763,00.asp is an early review by eWeek on OpsMgr 2007 (August 7, 2006). It is somewhat dated, but a good first look.

Justin Incarnato blogs about what's new in Operations Manager at http://blogs.msdn.com/incarnato/archive/2006/06/06/619420.aspx.

An overview of OpsMgr 2007 with a discussion during the Beta 2 timeframe by Stewart Cawthray, MOM Product Manager, is available at http://www.microsoft.com/technet/technetmag/issues/2006/09/BetaBox/.

▶ Trying to set up a virtual server cluster? An excellent two-part write-up providing step-by-step processes is available at http://www.roudybob.net/?p=118 and http://www.roudybob.net/?p=119.

The information is also available in PDF format at http://www.roudybob.net/downloads/Setting-Up-A-Windows-Server-2003-Cluster-in-VS2005-Part1.pdf and http://www.roudybob.net/downloads/Setting-Up-A-Windows-Server-2003-Cluster-in-VS2005-Part2.pdf.

▶ Have an interesting experience when trying to delete an agentless system? This happens if you first install agentless, then install as a managed agent without first deleting the agentless configuration. This information is discussed in Chapter 9, "Installing and Configuring Agents," but full details are available at http://ops-mgr. spaces.live.com/default.aspx?_c01_BlogPart=blogentry&_c=BlogPart&handle= cns!3D3B8489FCAA9B51!163.

▶ For information on debugging the infamous alert that the "Script or Executable Failed to Run," see http://cameronfuller.spaces.live.com/blog/ cns!A231E4EB0417CB76!1006.entry.

▶ Did you know you can back up a running virtual machine? See http://redmondmag.com/columns/print.asp?EditorialsID=2324 for information.

▶ The System Center Virtual Machine Manager (SCVMM) 2007 scripting guide is available for download at http://go.microsoft.com/fwlink/?LinkId=104290. Similar to OpsMgr (and Exchange 2007), SCVMM includes a command shell built on PowerShell.

▶ Boris Yanushpolsky's Override Explorer can be downloaded from http://blogs.msdn. com/boris_yanushpolsky/attachment/4301837.ashx.

▶ Several people have done some work on helping you put computers into mainte- nance mode in batch.

  This includes Clive Eastwood, who has a command-line tool, documented at http://blogs.technet.com/cliveeastwood/archive/2007/09/18/agentmm-a- command-line-tool-to-place-opsmgr-agents-into-maintenance-mode.aspx.

  Andrzej Lipka enhances Clive's approach using the PsExec Tool. See http://blogs. technet.com/alipka/archive/2007/12/20/opsmgr-2007-putting-computers-in-mainte- nance-mode-remotely.aspx. PsExec is available at http://technet.microsoft.com/en- us/sysinternals/bb897553.aspx.

▶ http://opsmgr2007.wikidot.com/ is a "wiki" dedicated to Operations Manager 2007, run of course by Maarten Goet!

▶ Want to mass-create computer groups? You can use XML to do this easily. See http://cameronfuller.spaces.live.com/blog/cns!A231E4EB0417CB76!982.entry.

▶ If you can't get OpsMgr reporting to send email subscriptions, check out http: //blogs.msdn.com/ketaanhs/archive/2005/09/05/461055.aspx for information on configuring the PermittedHosts entry in the RSReportServer.config file.

▶ You can download a tool that allows you to test emails from the command line; this lets you see how the message will look prior to configuring a mail server. The tool is available at https://blogs.pointbridge.com/Blogs/morse_matt/Pages/Post.aspx?_ ID=24.

▶ If you do a Help -> About in the Operations console, it displays a version number. The MOM team provides a cross-reference of version numbers to "common names" at http://blogs.technet.com/momteam/archive/2008/01/10/versioning-in-opsmgr. aspx.

▶ A nice white paper on configuring notifications written by Anders Bengtsson and Pete Zerger is available at the System Center Forum at http://systemcenterforum.org/ wp-content/uploads/SCOM_Notification1.pdf. Anders also posts this white paper at http://contoso.se/blog/?p=132.

▶ Wondering how to use a property bag? See http://www.systemcenterforum.org/ using-property-bags-with-custom-scripting-in-operations-manager-2007/ to download an article written by Neale Brown and Pete Zerger.

▶ A list of the top KB articles published for Operations Manager 2007 is available at http://kbalertz.com/Technology.aspx?tec=533.

▶ If you're not already receiving email notifications of new articles in the Microsoft Knowledge Base from kbAlertz, you can sign up at http://kbalertz.com/ for them! You just need to create an account and select the technologies you want to be alerted about.

Microsoft's OpsMgr Resources

The following list includes some general Microsoft resources available for OpsMgr 2007:

▶ **Microsoft's Operations Manager website**—http://go.microsoft.com/fwlink/ ?LinkId=86432.

▶ **Microsoft's System Center website**—http://www.microsoft.com/systemcenter/.

▶ **Management Pack website**—http://go.microsoft.com/fwlink/?LinkId=82105. Known for years as the Management Pack Catalog, this website was renamed in 2007 to the System Center Operations Manager 2007 Catalog, with an alternate link to the System Center Pack Catalog at http://go.microsoft.com/fwlink/?Linkid=71124.

▶ Microsoft's System Center Pack Catalog has multiple pages for all things OpsMgr and ConfigMgr. The catalog incorporates the following pages:

   ▶ **All packs for all products**—https://www.microsoft.com/technet/prodtechnol/ scp/catalog.aspx (http://go.microsoft.com/fwlink/?Linkid=71124).

   ▶ **Operations Manager 2007**— https://www.microsoft.com/technet/ prodtechnol/scp/opsmgr07.aspx (http://go.microsoft.com/fwlink/ ?LinkId=82105).

> ► Operations Manager 2005—https://www.microsoft.com/technet/
>   prodtechnol/scp/opsmgr05.aspx.
>
> ► Operations Manager 2000—https://www.microsoft.com/technet/
>   prodtechnol/scp/opsmgr00.aspx.
>
> ► Configuration Manager 2007—https://www.microsoft.com/technet/
>   prodtechnol/scp/configmgr07.aspx.

► **System Center Operations Manager 2007 Product Documentation site**—
  http://go.microsoft.com/fwlink/?LinkId=85414.

► **Microsoft download site for documentation for Operations Manager 2007**—
  http://www.microsoft.com/downloads/details.aspx?familyid=d826b836-59e5-
  4628-939e-2b852ed79859&displaylang=en&tm.

► What's OpsMgr all about, anyway? Microsoft has published "Key Concepts
  for Operations Manager 2007." You can download the document at http://
  www.microsoft.com/downloads/details.aspx?FamilyID=3a633532-1dde-49b6-
  930f-7df50b69b77b&DisplayLang=en.

  The document describes modeling in OpsMgr 2007 and key changes between MOM
  2005 and OpsMgr 2007.

► **OpsMgr Deployment Guide**—Available online at http://go.microsoft.com/fwlink/
  ?linkid=93785, or you can download it from the OpsMgr product documentation site
  at http://technet.microsoft.com/en-us/opsmgr/bb498235.aspx.

► **Operations Manager 2007 Online Help**—http://technet.microsoft.com/en-us/
  library/bb381409.aspx.

► You can find the Operations Manager 2007 Technical Library at http://technet.
  microsoft.com/library/bb310604.aspx.

► The Operations Manager 2007 Performance and Scalability white paper is at http://
  technet.microsoft.com/en-us/library/bb735308.aspx, or you can download the white
  paper at http://download.microsoft.com/download/d/3/6/d3633fa3-ce15-4071-
  be51-5e036a36f965/om2007_perfscal.doc.

► The Operations Manager 2007 Rule and Monitor Targeting Poster is available for
  download from the product documentation site at http://technet.microsoft.com/en-
  us/opsmgr/bb498235.aspx.

► **TechNet Manageability Center**—Links to resources and *TechNet* magazine articles at
  http://go.microsoft.com/?linkid=7280963.

► **Virtual Hands On Labs**—Virtual labs for System Center products including
  Operations Manager, Essentials, and Configuration Manager at http://technet.
  microsoft.com/en-us/bb539977.aspx.

▶ **Operations Manager 2007 management pack guides**—Available at the System Center Operations Manager 2007 Product Documentation site, http://go.microsoft.com/fwlink/?linkid=83259.

▶ **All about OpsMgr licensing for customers with Software Assurance (SA)**— The volume licensing brief for OpsMgr 2007 is at http://go.microsoft.com/ fwlink/?linkid=87480.

▶ **Operations Manager 2007 SDK (Software Development Kit)**—http://msdn2. microsoft.com/en-us/library/bb437575.aspx.

▶ XML Notepad 2007 is an intuitive tool for browsing and editing XML documents. Read about it at http://msdn2.microsoft.com/en-us/library/aa905339.aspx, and download the tool from http://www.microsoft.com/downloads/details.aspx? familyid=72d6aa49-787d-4118-ba5f-4f30fe913628&displaylang=en.

▶ A great website on management pack authoring, maintained by Steve Wilson, an OpsMgr team program manager, can be found at http://www.authormps.com/dnn/.

▶ **System Center Operations Manager 2007 Tools and Utilities**—http://technet. microsoft.com/en-us/opsmgr/bb625978.aspx.

▶ A collection of short training videos on OpsMgr 2007 is available online from http:// technet.microsoft.com/en-us/opsmgr/bb498237.aspx.

If you are interested in downloading the videos (webcasts), go to http://www.microsoft.com/downloads/details.aspx?FamilyID=1276a840-671f-4452- 98c7-5599c0d3ff9c&DisplayLang=en.

▶ You may also want to invest a couple of hours viewing the TechNet Support Webcast by Brian Wren, *Troubleshooting Microsoft Operations Manager Top Issues*, found online at http://support.microsoft.com/kb/828936.

▶ Other training videos and demos are available at http://www.microsoft.com/events/ series/technetmms.aspx?tab=webcasts&id=42365.

▶ Thanks to Justin Incarnato for putting together training videos for OpsMgr 2007 Service Pack 1. See http://technet.microsoft.com/en-us/opsmgr/bb986763.aspx.

▶ The SharePoint Monitoring Toolkit for OpsMgr is available for download at http://www.microsoft.com/downloads/details.aspx?FamilyID=e4600fd9-f53d-4ded- 88bf-6bb1932794f9&DisplayLang=en.

▶ Interested in learning more about the Microsoft Operations Framework? Check out the MOF at http://go.microsoft.com/fwlink/?LinkId=50015.

▶ Information on the IO (Infrastructure Optimization) model is available at http:// www.microsoft.com/technet/infrastructure.

▶ Details about the Microsoft Solutions Framework (MSF) are located at http://www. microsoft.com/technet/solutionaccelerators/msf.

▶ To create company knowledge, one of the required pieces of software is the Visual Studio 2005 Tools for Office Second Edition Runtime. This is available at http://www.microsoft.com/downloads/details.aspx?FamilyID=F5539A90-DC41-4792-8EF8-F4DE62FF1E81&displaylang=en. (Microsoft Word is also required.)

▶ View a TechNet webcast on Microsoft IT's implementation of OpsMgr 2007 at http://msevents.microsoft.com/CUI/WebCastEventDetails.aspx?culture=en-US&EventID=1032322478&CountryCode=US.

The related white paper is available for download at http://download.microsoft.com/download/6/8/4/6848d1c4-227c-4831-936b-98c10fec6c55/implementingscopsmgr2007twp.doc, or you can read it online at http://technet.microsoft.com/en-us/library/bb735238.aspx.

There is also an accompanying PowerPoint presentation, available for download at http://download.microsoft.com/download/6/8/4/6848d1c4-227c-4831-936b-98c10fec6c55/ImplementingSCOpsMgr2007TWP.ppt.

▶ You can download a 180-day evaluation copy of Operations Manager 2007 from http://www.microsoft.com/technet/prodtechnol/eval/scom/default.mspx.

▶ The Exchange Server Management Pack Configuration Wizard is located at http://go.microsoft.com/fwlink/?LinkId=35942. No longer required with Exchange 2007!

▶ Resource Kits for the various versions of Operations Manager:

OpsMgr 2007 ResKit is at the System Center Operations Manager TechCenter (http://go.microsoft.com/fwlink/?LinkId=94593).

The MOM 2005 Resource Kit is available at http://go.microsoft.com/fwlink/?LinkId=34629 and http://technet.microsoft.com/en-us/opsmgr/bb498240.aspx.

The MOM 2000 Resource Kit was pulled from the Microsoft website in late 2007 and is no longer available.

▶ You may want to implement the Windows Server 2003 Resource Kit tools if you have not already done so. You can download the tools from http://go.microsoft.com/fwlink/?linkid=4544.

The individual utilities can be found at http://technet.microsoft.com/en-us/windowsserver/bb405955.aspx.

E

Blogs

There has been an explosion of blogs with information regarding OpsMgr. Where previously we might direct you to websites and papers, now most information seems to appear on the blogs. Here are some blogs we have used. Some are more active than others, and new blogs seem to spring up overnight!

- ▶ A great source of information is available at Pete Zerger's (MOM MVP) System Center Forum (http://www.systemcenterforum.org).

- ▶ You won't want to miss the "bug blog" (http://blogs.technet.com/smsandmom/ archive/2007/12/19/new-knowledge-base-articles-for-12-2-through-12-8.aspx). This is hosted by the Microsoft System Center SMS and MOM teams, which publish new KB articles from the prior week (or longer if it's a slow period). This particular link shows new KB articles for 12-2-2007 through 12-8-2007.

- ▶ The bug blog is a subset of the Microsoft System Center MOM and SMS Team blog, located at http://blogs.technet.com/smsandmom/default.aspx.

- ▶ http://www.contoso.se/blog/ is the Operations Manager blog by Anders Bengtsson, a MOM MVP.

- ▶ See a blog by Stephan Stranger (former MOM MVP) at http://www.weblog. stranger.nl/operations_management/scom_2007.

- ▶ http://blogs.msdn.com/incarnato is a blog by Justin Incarnato, a Program Manager on the MOM team.

- ▶ http://blogs.technet.com/cliveeastwood is an OpsMgr, SCE, and MOM blog by Clive Eastwood, a Microsoft OpsMgr Supportability Program Manager.

- ▶ Kevin Sullivan's Management blog can be found at https://blogs.technet.com/ kevinsul_blog/. (Kevin is a Technology Specialist at Microsoft focusing on management products.)

- ▶ http://blogs.msdn.com/boris_yanushpolsky is a blog by Boris Yanushpolsky, a Program Manager for Operations Manager and Service Manager. Boris blogs quite often; this blog is one worth keeping up with!

- ▶ http://blogs.msdn.com/mariussutara contains notes on Operations Manager including troubleshooting, development information, and comments.

- ▶ http://blogs.technet.com/kevinholman is Kevin Holman's OpsMgr blog.

- ▶ http://blogs.technet.com/alipka is a blog by Andrzej Lipka on IT management and operations.

- ▶ http://blogs.msdn.com/rslaten is a blog by Russ Slaten, a Microsoft Escalation Engineer supporting management products.

- ▶ http://blogs.msdn.com/steverac is Steve Rachui's manageability blog. Steve is a Support Escalation Engineer at Microsoft.

- http://blogs.msdn.com/sampatton is a blog by Steve Patton, an OpsMgr developer.

- http://www.systemcentercommunity.com/ is an OpsMgr 2007 forum with questions and answers about OpsMgr. You will need to create a user ID to reply to the posts.

- http://blogs.msdn.com/jakuboleksy is a blog on programming with System Center Operations Manager by Jakub Oleksy, an OpsMgr developer.

- http://blogs.technet.com/mgoedtel/ is a blog by Matt Goedtel, a Microsoft MCS consultant focusing on Operations Manager.

- http://discussitnow.spaces.live.com/ is by Blake Mengotto, a MOM MVP and self-described "MOM dude."

- http://blogs.msdn.com/eugenebykov/ is great source of information on authoring OpsMgr reports by Eugene Bykov, an OpsMgr developer responsible for the reporting user interface.

- http://www.technotesblog.com/?cat=32 is Dustin Hannifin's Tech Notes blog, which has a section dedicated to OpsMgr 2007.

- http://scom2k7.blogspot.com/, by Timothy McFadden, is titled "Everything System Center Operations Manager 2007."

- System Center Operations Manager in Australia, by Jonathan Hambrook, can be found at http://opsmgr.wordpress.com/.

- http://www.techlog.org/ is all about everything Microsoft, by Maarten Goet (MOM MVP), Kenneth van Surksum, Steven van Loef, and Sander Klaassen in the Netherlands.

- http://advisec.wordpress.com/ by Bjorn Axell, a MOM MVP and senior consultant focusing on Microsoft infrastructure products.

- http://www.mcalynn.com is a blog by Duncan McAlynn that includes articles on OpsMgr, Configuration Manager, and SMS.

  Duncan recently decided to concentrate his blogging activity at systemcenterguide.com. He has transferred the articles from McAlynn.com to www.systemcenterguide.com.

- Gordon McKenna's blog is available at http://wmug.co.uk/blogs/gordons_blog/default.aspx. Gordon describes himself as a "nut" about OpsMgr. Gordon is a MOM MVP, and has worked with the software since its Mission Critical Software days, and is extremely knowledgeable on the product.

- http://blogs.technet.com/momteam/default.aspx, a blog by the MOM team, has information on OpsMgr 2007.

- Walter Chomak's blog on OpsMgr design and capacity planning is at http://wchomak.spaces.live.com/. Walter is a Senior Consultant with Microsoft MCS.

▶ Ian Blyth, previously a Lead Technical Specialist for MOM in Microsoft UK, blogs at http://ianblythmanagement.wordpress.com/.

▶ http://blogs.technet.com/monitoringmicrosoft/ is a blog by Chris Carlson and Cory Delamarter of Microsoft.

▶ Always interesting to look at is the PSS Manageability Official Blog at http://blogs. technet.com/pssmanageability/default.aspx.

And our own blogs:

▶ Kerrie and Cameron's Operations Manager and MOM blog is located at http://ops-mgr.spaces.live.com.

▶ http://cameronfuller.spaces.live.com is where Cameron discusses his technical theories, ramblings, and rants.

▶ http://www.networkworld.com/community/meyler is a new blog by Kerrie, with more general discussion topics, but concentrating on OpsMgr.

▶ And finally, the OpsMgr/MOM blog by our contributing author, Andy Dominey (http://myitforum.com/cs2/blogs/adominey/).

Command Shell

An extension to PowerShell, the Operations Manager Command Shell, allows you to do most everything you would ever want to for OpsMgr in a batch or scripted mode.

▶ http://blogs.msdn.com/scshell/ is about getting started with the OpsMgr Command Shell. This site is maintained by Robert Sprague, a PowerShell guru on the MOM team.

▶ A video introduction to the Command Shell can be found at http://www.microsoft. com/winme/0703/28666/Command_Shell_Intro_Edited.asx.

▶ SystemCenterForum.org provides a tutorial on using PowerShell scripts in custom console tasks at http://systemcenterforum.org/wp-content/uploads/ PowershellTasks_v1.0.pdf.

PowerShell Information

Information on PowerShell itself can be found at the following sites:

▶ http://www.redmondmag.com/columns/article.asp?editorialsid=1516 is the *Redmond Magazine* review of PowerShell Beta version.

▶ Read more about PowerShell in *TechNet* magazine at http://www.microsoft.com/ technet/technetmag/issues/2006/12/PowerShell/default.aspx.

▶ Check http://go.microsoft.com/?linkid=5637033 for a PowerShell webcast in Live Meeting.

▶ You may want to check all the PowerShell webcasts at http://www.microsoft.com/technet/scriptcenter/webcasts/ps.mspx.

▶ Find a PowerShell cheat sheet at http://blogs.msdn.com/powershell/archive/2007/01/25/powershell-cheat-sheet-redux-the-pdf-version.aspx. We include this with the CD content for Chapter 20, "Automatically Adapting Your Environment."

▶ The Windows PowerShell team has its blog at http://blogs.msdn.com/powershell/.

▶ PowerShell script examples can be found at http://www.microsoft.com/technet/scriptcenter/hubs/msh.mspx.

▶ Direct from the PowerShell guy himself (Marc van Orsouw, PowerShell MVP), is located at http://thepowershellguy.com/blogs/posh/default.aspx.

▶ PowerShell+ is a free PowerShell editing and debugging environment. You can get a free personal copy at http://www.powershell.com/downloads/psp1.zip.

▶ Even more about PowerShell and examples of some of the constructs are available at http://www.microsoft.com/technet/technetmag/issues/2007/01/PowerShell/default.aspx.

▶ Did you know you could add PowerShell management to SMS clients? See http://www.microsoft.com/technet/technetmag/issues/2007/11/UtilitySpotlight/ for information.

The System Center Family

Here are some references and articles regarding other components of Microsoft's System Center family:

▶ In 2006, Microsoft rebranded MOM and SMS under the System Center line. Read about the System Center Roadmap (which is always subject to change, and probably already has!) at MMS 2006 at http://www.entmag.com/news/article.asp?EditorialsID=7382.

  Related is Microsoft System Center announcements and DSI information as of May, 2006 (http://www.computerworld.com.au/index.php/id;83644086;relcomp;1).

▶ For System Center Essentials deployment planning and installation, see http://go.microsoft.com/fwlink/?LinkId=94444.

▶ Here are some blogs on System Center Essentials (Essentials) and Remote Operations Manager (ROM):

  Simplifying IT Management—http://blogs.technet.com/caseymck/

  Managed Services blog—http://blogs.technet.com/dustinj/

> **The System Center Essentials Team Blog (by the product group)**—http://
> blogs.technet.com/systemcenteressentials/
>
> **SCE Setup, Policy, and Reporting**—http://blogs.technet.com/rtammana/
>
> **Essentials 2007 Wiki site**—http://sce.editme.com/

- ▶ The System Center Essentials TechCenter can be found at http://technet.microsoft.
  com/en-us/sce/bb677155.aspx.

- ▶ Microsoft has a 30-day evaluation version of System Center Essentials available as a
  virtual machine. You can download it from http://www.microsoft.com/downloads/
  details.aspx?FamilyID=27342759-e9d6-4073-918c-e9dff77d0206&DisplayLang=en.

- ▶ Can't talk about Essentials without thinking about WSUS. See the WSUS 3.0 blog at
  http://msmvps.com/blogs/athif/.

- ▶ One scenario for System Center Essentials is as a means for managing and monitoring assets of small organizations, tied to a centralized Operations Manager server.
  Read our coauthor John Joyner's take on Microsoft's direction for management tools
  in the midsized market at http://www.thechannelinsider.com/article/Partners+
  Picture+SMB+Uses+for+Microsofts+SCE/167994_1.aspx and http://www.eweek.com/
  article2/0,1895,1905780,00.asp.

- ▶ Is it System Essentials or is it Operations Manager? It's both—the Remote
  Operations Manager! You can download the Deployment Guide from http://
  www.microsoft.com/downloads/details.aspx?FamilyId=4B621EB7-01BB-45F5-9A77-
  52853F06EEC9%20&displaylang=en.

- ▶ An interesting *New York Times* article about the Remote Operations Manager product
  ("Outsourcing I.T. To Unlikely Places, Like America") is available online at
  http://www.nytimes.com/2007/09/12/technology/techspecial/12OUT.html?_
  r=1&oref=slogin. (You may need to login or create an account to access this.)

- ▶ Introducing System Center's Service Manager at http://searchwinit.techtarget.com/
  originalContent/0,289142,sid1_gci1184995,00.html and http://www.eweek.com/
  article2/0,1759,1954020,00.asp?kc=EWRSS03119TX1K0000594.

> Pete Zerger includes an early review of Service Manager Beta 1 at http://
> systemcenterforum.org/wp-content/uploads/SvcMgrBeta1.pdf.

Connectors

Chapter 22, "Interoperability," includes a list of connectors and the version of Operations
Manager to which each applies. For your convenience, we include these connectors here
with the URLs where you can access them.

Please be aware that the available connectors as well as these links are constantly changing; your best bet is to check Microsoft's catalog at https://www.microsoft.com/technet/ prodtechnol/scp/opsmgr07.aspx, searching on the keyword *Connector*.

▶ **Engyro OpsMgr to BMC Remedy ARS Product Connector**—http://www.engyro. com/products/mom_interoperability/ars.html (MOM 2005, OpsMgr 2007).

▶ **Engyro OpsMgr to HP OpenView Operations Product Connector**—http:// www.engyro.com/products/mom_interoperability/hp-ovo.html (MOM 2005, OpsMgr 2007).

▶ **Engyro OpsMgr to Tivoli TEC Product Connector**—http://www.engyro.com/ products/mom_interoperability/tivoli.html (MOM 2005, OpsMgr 2007).

▶ **Zenprise BlackBerry Connector for OpsMgr 2007**—http://www.zenprise.com/ products/blackberry-monitoring.aspx (OpsMgr 2007).

▶ **Zenprise Exchange Connector for OpsMgr 2007**—http://www.zenprise.com/ products/exchange.aspx (OpsMgr 2007).

▶ **message master® Enterprise Alert 2007**—http://www.derdack.com/products/ea.htm (MOM 2005, OpsMgr 2007).

▶ **CA SPECTRUM Connector for MOM**—http://ca.com/files/DataSheets/ network_connector_for_microsoft_ops_manager.pdf (MOM 2005).

▶ **eXc Software BMC Patrol**—http://www.excsoftware.com/version3/version3/ Product.aspx?ID=1a37ab02-3310-4ed4-ab9e-12524997f3d6 (MOM 2005, OpsMgr 2007).

▶ **eXc Software IBM Tivoli**—http://www.excsoftware.com/version3/version3/ Product.aspx?ID=a7b00a9c-fe09-43b4-ae5e-c74ca9a21d0d (MOM 2005, OpsMgr 2007).

▶ **eXc Software CA UniCenter**—http://www.excsoftware.com/version3/version3/ Product.aspx?ID=3c114c05-d2f4-416d-a2df-96007e96a5e4 (MOM 2005, OpsMgr 2007).

▶ **eXc Software HP Open-View Connector**—http://www.excsoftware.com/version3/ version3/Product.aspx?ID=09439f74-f9e5-4a5c-a7fa-bc2480efb8f6 (MOM 2005, OpsMgr 2007).

▶ **Micromuse NetCool Connector**—Connectors available from IBM (http://www-1. ibm.com/support/docview.wss?rs=3120&context=SSSHTQ&dc=D400&uid=swg24015 869&loc=en_US&cs=UTF-8&lang=en) and eXc Software (http://www.excsoftware. com/version3/version3/Product.aspx?ID=e41976d3-70cf-4a63-a84a-42959ece0fe5) (MOM 2005).

▶ **Nagios**—http://www.excsoftware.com/version3/version3/Product.aspx?ID=4ac70518- 60b8-448a-812d-ad1f2553fc2d (MOM 2005).

E

▶ **Microsoft Remedy ARS Connector**—Connectors available from Engyro (http://www.engyro.com/products/product-sheets/Help_Connector_Overview.pdf) and eXc Software (http://www.excsoftware.com/version3/version3/Product.aspx?ID=aef28088-315c-42ac-8410-8d0236996eab) (MOM 2005, OpsMgr 2007).

▶ **MOM-CRM Connector for Microsoft Dynamics 3.0**—http://www.lambertconsulting.ch/EN/Competence_and_solutions/MOM-CRM_Connector/MOM-CRM_Connector/ (MOM 2005).

▶ **AppManager Connector for MOM**—http://www.netiq.com/products/am/connectors/mom.asp (MOM 2005).

▶ **NetIQ Extended Management Pack (XMP) AppManager Connector for MOM**—http://www.netiq.com/products/am/connectors/mom.asp (MOM 2005).

▶ **OpalisRobot**—http://www.opalis.com/Products_Opalis_Integration_Pack_for_MOM.asp (MOM 2005).

▶ **InTrust Connector for Microsoft MOM**—http://www.quest.com/intrust/momconnector.aspx (MOM 2005).

▶ **BMC Impact Integration for MOM**—http://www.seamlessti.com/products/momsim_integ.html (MOM 2005, OpsMgr 2007).

▶ **MOM Integration for BMC Patrol**—http://www.seamlessti.com/products/mompat_integ.html (MOM 2005, OpsMgr 2007).

▶ **EMC Smarts InCharge Connector**—http://www.emc.com/products/software/smarts/smarts_family/index.jsp (MOM 2005).

▶ **iWave Integrator**—http://www.iwaveintegrator.com/. Contact iWave directly for information on specific integrators. Available integrators include the following:

iWave Integrator OpsMgr to Amdocs Clarify Integration (MOM 2005, OpsMgr 2007)

iWave Integrator MOM 2005 to CA Solve for z/OS Integration (MOM 2005)

iWave Integrator MOM 2005 to CA Unicenter Integration (MOM 2005)

iWave Integrator OpsMgr 2007 to CA NSM (OpsMgr 2007)

iWave Integrator OpsMgr 2007 to CA UniCenter Service Desk (OpsMgr 2007)

iWave Integrator MOM 2005 to HP OpenView Network Node Manager (NNM) Integration (MOM 2005)

iWave Integrator OpsMgr to HP OpenView Operations (OVO) Integration (MOM 2005, OpsMgr 2007)

iWave Integrator OpsMgr to Peregrine Service Center Integration (MOM 2005, OpsMgr 2007)

iWave Integrator OpsMgr to Remedy ARS Integration (MOM 2005, OpsMgr 2007) iWave Integrator OpsMgr to Tivoli Enterprise Console (TEC) Integration (MOM 2005, OpsMgr 2007)

iWave Integrator OpsMgr to Tivoli Information/Management for z/OS Integration (MOM 2005, OpsMgr 2007)

iWave Integrator MOM 2005 to Tivoli Net View Integration (MOM 2005)

iWave Integrator MOM 2005 to Tivoli Net View for OS/390 Integration (MOM 2005)

iWave Integrator MOM 2005 to Tivoli Service Desk Integration (MOM 2005)

iWave Integrator MOM 2005 to Vantive Integration (MOM 2005)

iWave Integrator OpsMgr 2007 to Microsoft Operations Manager (OpsMgr 2007)

iWave's Adapter Guide for MOM 2005 is available at http://www.iwaveintegrator. com/images/library/iWaveIntegrator_Microsoft_Ops_Mgr_2005_Adapter_Guide.pdf.

You can also download their OpsMgr 2007 Adapter Guide at http://www. iwaveintegrator.com/images/library/iWaveIntegrator_Microsoft_Ops_Mgr_2007_ Adapter_Guide.pdf.

Public Newsgroups

If you need an answer to a question, the first place to check is the Microsoft public newsgroups. It is best to see if your question has already been posted before you ask it yourself! Microsoft's online link for its newsgroups is http://www.microsoft.com/communities/ newsgroups/default.mspx.

Operations Manager

Here's a list of the current OpsMgr newsgroups:

- ▶ microsoft.public.opsmgr.acs
- ▶ microsoft.public.opsmgr.ad
- ▶ microsoft.public.opsmgr.aem
- ▶ microsoft.public.opsmgr.authoring
- ▶ microsoft.public.opsmgr.connectors
- ▶ microsoft.public.opsmgr.docs
- ▶ microsoft.public.opsgmr.exchange
- ▶ microsoft.public.opsmgr.general
- ▶ microsoft.public.opsmgr.iis
- ▶ microsoft.public.opsmgr.managementpacks

- ▶ microsoft.public.opsmgr.powershell
- ▶ microsoft.public.opsmgr.reporting
- ▶ microsoft.public.opsmgr.sdk
- ▶ microsoft.public.opsmgr.setup
- ▶ microsort.public.opsmgr.sp1
- ▶ microsoft.public.opsmgr.sql
- ▶ microsoft.public.opsmgr.ui

Capacity Planner

As we complete this book, the OpsMgr portion of Capacity Planner is at Release Candidate (RC) status. A newsgroup dedicated to discussions of the beta / RC version is microsoft.beta.sccp07.opsmgr newsgroup.

This newsgroup is for questions when testing the unreleased capabilities of System Center Capacity Planner. (You can download the release candidate software at http://connect. microsoft.com/.)

On the CD

A CD is included with this book to provide add-on value to readers of *System Center Operations Manager 2007 Unleashed*. Note that the authors and publisher do not guarantee or provide technical support for its contents.

Available Elsewhere

The following content can be accessed from sources other than this CD:

▶ The file ProxyCFG.zip contains the executable tool by Microsoft's Clive Eastwood for configuring and viewing agent proxying. This is quite useful for configuring OpsMgr 2007, and is discussed in Chapter 8, "Configuring and Using Operations Manager 2007."

Chapter 8 also includes EnumberateGroups-andMembers.ps1, a PowerShell script by Boris Yanushpolsky of Microsoft that lists groups and the contents of each group.

▶ If you have clustered your RMS, you know the process at present is far from perfect. We discuss RMS clustering in Chapter 10, "Complex Configurations." The CD includes Microsoft's update to the ManagementServerConfigTool utility. Microsoft asks that you only use this utility in a test environment. RMSClusterDR.zip also includes instructions to promote back the clustered RMS after you have promoted another Management Server to this role while the clustered server was not available. The good news is this is all supposed to get better with Service Pack 1!

▶ Eugene Bykov (Microsoft) has made a PowerShell script available that creates a Report Operator role. SystemCenterForum took that script and customized it to be parameter driven. We include the customized version, AddReportingUserRole.ps1. As we discuss in Chapter 11, "Securing Operations Manager 2007," you cannot create a Report Operator role from the Operations console.

▶ If you move your Operational database to another database server, the error messages do not move because they are actually stored in the Master database. We include a script developed by Matt Goedtel of Microsoft (Fix_OpsMgrDb_ErrorMsgs.SQL.sql) to reapply the messages to the new server, which we discuss in Chapter 12, "Backup and Recovery."

▶ Part of the Microsoft Operations Manager (MOM 2005) Resource Kit, the MP2XML utility can be used as part of a batch process to convert your AKM-formatted management packs to the XML format used by OpsMgr 2007, as discussed in Chapter 13, "Administering Management Packs." We include MP2XML.exe and its Readme file.

Finding a rule in the Operations console can sometimes be a daunting task. SystemCenterForum provides a PowerShell script (FindRule.ps1), also discussed in Chapter 13. The script searches a group for a specified rule using the display name of the rule.

▶ Microsoft's best practices for rule and monitor targeting document (Rule and Monitor Targeting Best Practices.pdf) was released in November 2007. It discusses the right and wrong ways to target, and it fits in well with our monitoring discussion in Chapter 14, "Monitoring with Operations Manager."

▶ The first release of the Operations Manager (OpsMgr) 2007 Resource Kit is referred to as "Wave 1." The implication is that there will be future "waves." We include the tools in a zip file, OpsMgr 2007 ResKit.zip, with the Chapter 14 content.

▶ Two scripts (ACSBulkEnableAllAgents.ps1 and ACSBulkEnableGroupDisplay-Name.ps1) enable ACS in bulk using PowerShell. Microsoft's Joseph Chan provided the first script during the OpsMgr 2007 beta test cycle. SystemCenterForum later modified the script, producing ACSBulkEnableGroupDisplayName.ps1, which takes the display name of the group as an added parameter. We discuss these scripts in Chapter 15, "Monitoring Audit Collection Services."

The script SecurityEventPerSecond.vbs, also by Joseph Chan, counts the number of security events generated per second on the local computer. It's included for your convenience with our Audit Collection discussion in Chapter 15.

- The get_thresholds.ps1 PowerShell script, by Boris Yanushpolsky, shows all the thresholds in your management group. The output includes the type of objects the monitor is targeted to, the display name and threshold used by the monitor, whether the monitor generates an alert when its state changes, whether the alert is auto-resolved, and the severity of the alert. We discuss this script in Chapter 16, "Client Monitoring."

- The PowerShell Cheat Sheet, developed by Microsoft, provides tips for using PowerShell to make your environment more flexible and adaptable, which is the topic of Chapter 20, "Automatically Adapting Your Environment."

  Chapter 20 also includes a help file from the Microsoft Scripting Guys. This file (Hey_Scripting_Guy.chm) is a compilation of scripts released by the Scripting Guys over several years. Microsoft does not provide support for these scripts.

Only with This Book

We also include an extensive list of management packs, scripts, and references, available only with the book:

- Visio Stencils can be used to draw shapes you can use with Microsoft Visio in documenting your OpsMgr installation. We use the OpsMgr2007 (Workflow).vss stencil ourselves throughout the book, beginning in Chapter 3, "Looking Inside OpsMgr."

- The OpsMgr databases sizing spreadsheet is first used in Chapter 4, "Planning Your Operations Manager Deployment." (We presented the information used by this Excel spreadsheet at TechEd 2007.) OpsMgr Sizing.xls provides sizing information for the three databases used by OpsMgr and the ACS component. We have validated the accuracy of these numbers at various installations and fine-tuned the information discussed at TechEd.

- The OpsMgr Pre-installation Checklist assists you with your installation (see Chapter 6, "Installing Operations Manager 2007"). We developed the OpsMgr Pre-Installation Checklist.xls spreadsheet as a quick reference for your use. The spreadsheet includes the major components you will be installing and information you will need to have ready before starting your installation.

- PowerShell scripts for bulk-importing management packs (ImportMP.ps1) and for starting and stopping maintenance mode (maintenance mode.ps1 and stop maintenance mode.ps1) are introduced in Chapter 8.

- From the Microsoft Operations Manager 2000 Resource Kit, the Configurelogs.exe utility automates the process of setting Event log configurations by using an input file that lists the server names. It is discussed as part of Chapter 9, "Installing and Configuring Agents." The MOM 2000 Resource Kit is no longer available on the Microsoft website.

OpsMgr_x86.sms is an SMS/SCCM package for pushing out the Operations Manager agent. We include this as a tool to help the process of agent installation, also discussed in Chapter 9.

▶ Backup.bat, a backup script for files used by OpsMgr 2007, automates the process of backing up databases, management pack and report source files, and other customized files used by OpsMgr. Also included in the backups.exe self-extracting zip file is ExportMP.ps1 (a PowerShell script to export unsealed management packs) and SaveKey.exe (which saves the RMS encryption key). These two utilities are required by the batch file. We also include a readme file (Readme for Backup Scripts.doc). We describe the philosophy behind the batch script in Chapter 12. You can customize the batch file as necessary for your particular environment.

▶ PingTest.vbs, a Visual Basic Ping script, can be launched by a rule. An example of this is provided in Chapter 14.

▶ The All Audit Policy Changes audit report (Policy_Changes_-_All_Audit_Policy_Changes.rdl) is a custom report we created to track changes in audit policy. This is discussed in Chapter 15.

▶ Discover-and-Add-Network-Devices.ps1 is a PowerShell script for discovering and adding network devices. It was developed in conjunction with Chapter 17, "Monitoring Network Devices."

▶ Sample scripts for Configuration Manager and Active Directory are included in ConfigMgr Scripts.zip and Sample AD scripts.zip, respectively. These are useful for automatically adapting your environment. See Chapter 20 for additional information.

▶ GW-Assign-Failover-MS.ps1 is a PowerShell script used to assign a failover Gateway Server for an System Center Essentials configuration. The script is a very helpful utility when implementing Remote Operations Manager, discussed in Chapter 21, "Reading for the Service Provider: Remote Operations Manager." We used the information at http://technet.microsoft.com/en-us/library/bb381392.aspx to create the script.

▶ For Chapter 23, "Developing Management Packs and Reports," we developed several management packs that we include on the CD. These include the Microsoft Forefront Security management pack, which defines a new OpsMgr class (Forefront Client Security) based on discovering computers with a certain Registry key, the OpsMgr Unleashed management pack, and the OpsMgr Database Tracking management pack. With this last management pack (which we sealed), we also use two Transact SQL scripts to establish the required tracking tables and load the scripts that update these tables.

The Database Tracking management pack requires SP 1 of OpsMgr 2007; the other management packs can run with the RTM version (with the System Center Operations Manager 2007 Management Pack Update applied) or SP 1.

The OpsMgr Unleashed management pack is a collection of tools we have written for OpsMgr. This includes several PowerShell scripts we created tasks for so you can execute them from the Operations console:

▶ Resolve_alerts.ps1 was altered from a script written in the newsgroups by Neale Brown of SystemCenterForum. This PowerShell script is used by the Resolve Alerts task to close old alerts, as we discuss in Chapter 23. The task is visible as an action in the Resolve Alerts view.

▶ AlertstoHTML.ps1 converts alerts as a HTML-formatted table, saving them in a file named alerts.html in the root of the C:\ drive (you certainly can change that location, which is specified in the last line of the PowerShell script). It is invoked by the Export Alerts to Html task.

▶ The script email_alert.vbs is used by the Forward Alerts via Email tasks (there are two versions of this task because the syntax of the task changed with SP 1). The version of the task that works with the OpsMgr RTM is Forward Alerts via Email (RTM), whereas the version for SP 1 is named Forward Alerts via Email (SP 1).

▶ Another tool is the Event ID lookup task. Right-click a given alert and open the Event view, where you will see a task on the Actions pane for EventID Lookup. Selecting this task takes you to EventID.NET, which gives you information about that Event ID.

▶ MonitorProcess monitors the number of processes running for a specific process name. The monitor is activated through an override for the System Center Managed Computer (any OS) to enable the rule for a computer and define the name and range of the acceptable number of process for that computer.

The CD also includes the OpsMgr.Unleashed.zip file, which has the two PowerShell scripts, email_alert.vbs, and the OpsMgr.Unleashed.xml management pack. EventID lookup and MonitorProcess are included in the management pack.

▶ Reference URLs (see Appendix E, "Reference URLs") are provided as live links. These include more than 200 (clickable) hypertext links and references to materials and sites related to Operations Manager.

A disclaimer and unpleasant fact regarding live links: URLs change! Companies are subject to mergers and acquisitions, pages move and change on websites, and so on. Although these links were accurate in late 2007, it is possible some will change or be "dead" by the time you read this book. Sometimes the Wayback Machine (http://www.archive.org/index.php) can rescue you from dead or broken links. This site is an Internet archive, and it will take you back to an archived version of a site...sometimes.

Symbols

A

embedding tasks in, 688

Exchange 2003 management pack, 1237-1249

forwarding by email, 690

generating, 688-690

IIS management pack, 1255

knowledge, adding, 699-703

notification workflow, 691-699

reports, 627-630

resolution states, 358, 716-718

resolving, 317-319

SQL Server management pack, 1251-1253

state monitors versus, 719

transitory alerts, 315

tuning, 718, 723

   Active Directory management pack, 724-725

   by color, 718-719

   Exchange Server 2003 management pack, 723-724

   SQL Server management pack, 726-727

   Windows Server Operating System management pack, 726

viewing, 41-43

   creating views, 720-723

   product knowledge, 49-50

Alerts view (Operations Manager Management Group), 955-956

All Events for Specified Computer report, 784

All Events for Specified User report, 784

All Events with Specified Event ID report, 784, 790

ampersand (&), in scripts, 663

antivirus software, 1037

API (Application Programming Interface), 472

appending backups, 556

Application Error Group view, 813

Application Log Library, 374

Application Programming Interface (API), 472

Application Service Providers (ASPs), 966

Application view, 813

applications

   design stage (deployment planning), 164

   distributed applications, 1038-1040

errors, events, 812

LOB, monitoring, 928-933

monitoring, 940-941, 944, 947

Top Applications report, 820

watcher nodes, 906-907

Web, monitoring, 907-909, 912-920

Web Application Editor, 912

applying

   AeDebug, 811

   enterprise CA, 513-515

   standalone CA, 515-517

approving

   agents, modifying, 373-374

   customer sites (customer networks), 1085-1087

   gateway servers, 435-436

architecture

   AEM, 805-808

   management group design, 146-148

   online information, 1307

   of OpsMgr 2007, 98

      management groups, 98-100

      server components, 100-105

   of SNMP, 846-848

archiving audit reports, 764

ASP.NET, installation, 249

ASPs (Application Service Providers), 966

assessment documents, 141

assessment stage (deployment planning), 139-141, 425

assignments, roles, 474

attributes, 354-355, 639

audible alerts, creating, 1016

Audit Collection Services. See ACS

Audit Collector Component, 103

Audit Database Server Component, 103

Audit Failures report, 795

Audit Forwarding service, 79, 107

Audit Log Cleared report, 795

audit policies, 740

   categories, 744-746

   implementation, 763-766

   need for, 739-740

F

Q–R

SecureStorageBackup tool, 254, 570-575
security, 739
   accounts, 164-165, 239
   ACS, 526-527, 765
      enabling certificate support, 528
      encryption, 529
      installing certificates, 527-528
   agents, proxying, 511-512
   connected management groups, 1100
   for consoles, 75
   databases, 502-503
   firewalls, 529
      agents, 532-533
      configuring proxy settings, 534
      ports, 530-532
   Forefront, 1140
   for Health service, 106
   Health service lockdown tool, 525-526
   least privilege, email, 1067
   logs, 410
   migration, management packs, 289
   monitoring, 480
   multiple domains, 218
   mutual authentication, 503-507, 511
   for RMS clusters, 460-461
   role-based, 77-78, 471-474, 477
      Agent Installation account, 499
      Computer Discovery account, 499
      Config Service/SDK accounts, 496-499
      creating user roles, 477-478, 480-483
      Data Reader account, 500
      Data Warehouse Write Action
         account, 499
      Gateway Action account, 501-502
      Health Service account, 501
      low-privileged accounts, 493-494
      Management Server Action account, 493
      modifying credentials, 496
      MonitoringHost.exe process, 492
      Notification Action account, 499
      required accounts, 490-492
      resetting Administrator roles, 483-485
      Run As Accounts, 488-490

      Run As Profiles, 487-488
      troubleshooting user roles, 483
      Windows 2000/XP, 495
      Windows Server 2003/Vista, 495
   of set commands (SNMP), 851
   SSL, configuring, 525
security adaptations, 1041-1042
security boundary in ACS, creating, 748-749
Security Event log, 739
security events
   determining number of, 747
   network bandwidth utilization, 145
security groups, creating ACS auditors security
   group, 753-754
security health monitors, 121
security model, management group design
   planning, 143
Security node (Administration space), 360-361
security policies, 741-742
security policy enforcement, OpsMgr 2007
   solutions to, 43-44
security regulations, online information on, 740
security settings
   on ACS database, 756
   agents, 359
selecting
   authentication, 253
   management packs, 326
self-tuning thresholds, 46, 83, 671-675
sending error reports to Microsoft, 247
server components, 81-82
   design stage (deployment planning),
      148-156
      ACS Collector, 155
      ACS database servers, 155
      ACS Forwarder, 155
      agents, 156
      data warehouse servers, 155
      gateway servers, 152-153
      management servers, 151-152
      Operations console, 155
      Operations database, 152-154
      reporting servers, 154

How can we make this index more useful? Email us at indexes@samspublishing.com

U

1382   unsealed management packs

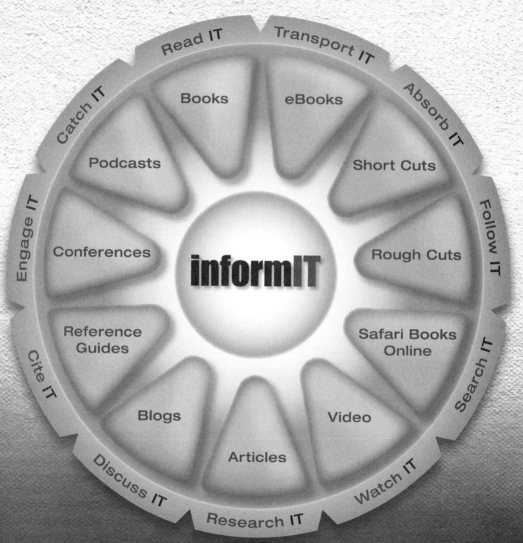

THIS BOOK IS SAFARI ENABLED

INCLUDES FREE 45-DAY ACCESS TO THE ONLINE EDITION

The Safari® Enabled icon on the cover of your favorite technology book means the book is available through Safari Bookshelf. When you buy this book, you get free access to the online edition for 45 days.

Safari Bookshelf is an electronic reference library that lets you easily search thousands of technical books, find code samples, download chapters, and access technical information whenever and wherever you need it.

TO GAIN 45-DAY SAFARI ENABLED ACCESS TO THIS BOOK:

- Go to **informit.com/safarienabled**
- Complete the brief registration form
- Enter the coupon code found in the front of this book on the "Copyright" page

If you have difficulty registering on Safari Bookshelf or accessing the online edition, please e-mail customer-service@safaribooksonline.com.

UNLEASHED

Unleashed takes you beyond the basics, providing an exhaustive, technically sophisticated reference for professionals who need to exploit a technology to its fullest potential. It's the best resource for practical advice from the experts, and the most in-depth coverage of the latest technologies.

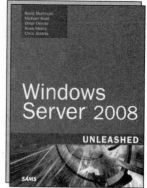

Windows Server 2008 Unleashed
ISBN: 0672329301

OTHER UNLEASHED TITLES

ASP.NET 3.5 Unleashed
ISBN: 0672330113

Microsoft Dynamics CRM 4.0 Unleashed
ISBN: 0672329700

Microsoft ISA Server 2006 Unleashed
ISBN: 0672329190

Microsoft Office Project Server 2007 Unleashed
ISBN: 0672329212

Microsoft SharePoint 2007 Development Unleashed
ISBN: 0672329034

Microsoft SQL Server 2005 Unleashed
ISBN: 0672328240

Microsoft Visual C# 2005 Unleashed
ISBN: 0672327767

Microsoft Visual Studio 2005 Unleashed
ISBN: 0672328194

Microsoft XNA Unleashed
ISBN: 0672329646

Silverlight 1.0 Unleashed
ISBN: 0672330075

VBScript, WMI and ADSI Unleashed
ISBN: 0321501713

Windows PowerShell Unleashed
ISBN: 0672329530

Windows Presentation Foundation Unleashed
ISBN: 0672328917

Windows Communication Foundation Unleashed
ISBN: 0672329484

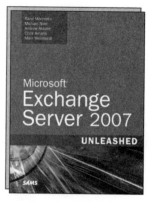

Microsoft Exchange Server 2007 Unleashed
ISBN: 0672329204

Microsoft SharePoint 2007 Unleashed
ISBN: 0672329476

SAMS

informit.com/sams